CW01522784

THE
POETICAL WORKS
OF
THOMAS MOORE

THE

POETICAL WORKS

OF

THOMAS MOORE.

PRINTED BY AD. BLONDEAU, 7, RUE RAMEAU.

Thomas Moore

THE

POETICAL WORKS

OF

THOMAS MOORE.

A NEW EDITION,

COLLECTED AND ARRANGED BY HIMSELF.

COMPLETE IN ONE VOLUME.

PARIS;

PUBLISHED BY A. AND W. GALIGNANI AND C⁰.,

N° 18, RUE VIVIENNE.

1842.

NOTICE OF THE PUBLISHERS.

In offering to the Public the present Edition of Mr. Moore's Works, reprinted from the London one, just published under the eye and with the latest corrections of the author, Messrs. Galignani and Co. beg leave to point out some advantages which it possesses, that render it superior to the London edition. In the first place, the various changes and improvements made by Mr. Moore have been scrupulously followed in the text, but every passage which has been altered is placed, as originally written, in a note beneath, thus enabling the reader at once to perceive and to judge of the value of the emendation. Another and more important advantage is that, in the London Edition, several of the lighter pieces among the well-known earlier productions of the poet having been altogether omitted, it has been thought right here to preserve them, and they are accordingly given as addenda. Though now rejected by the matured taste of the illustrious writer, these are gems far too precious to be cast away; besides which, it has been felt that their exclusion would be incompatible with the COMPLETENESS which, it is the aim of the publishers, should distinguish this FINAL EDITION of the most celebrated Lyric Poet of his age.

CONTENTS.

—◦◦◦◦◦—

	PAGE
BIOGRAPHICAL SKETCH OF THOMAS MOORE . . .	xvii

ODES OF ANACREON.

	PAGE
Preface	1
Dedication.	5
Index	5
Ode by the Translator.	6
Corrections of the preceding Ode . . .	6
Remarks on Anacreon	7
I. I saw the smiling bard of pleasure . . .	12
II. Give me the harp of epic song . . .	13
III. Listen to the Muse's lyre	13
IV. Vulcan! hear your glorious task . . .	13
V. Sculptor, wouldst thou glad my soul . .	13
VI. As late I sought the spangled bower . .	14
VII. The women tell me every day . . .	14
VIII. I care not for the idle state	15
IX. I pray thee, by the gods above . . .	15
X. How can I punish thee	15
XI. Tell me, gentle youth, I pray thee . .	16
XII. They tell how Atys, wild with love . .	16
XIII. I will, I will ; the conflict's past . . .	16
XIV. Count me, on the summer trees . . .	17
XV. Tell me, why, my sweetest dove . . .	18
XVI. Thou, whose soft and rosy hues . . .	19
XVII. And now with all thy pencil's truth . .	20
XVIII. Now the star of day is high	21
XIX. Here recline you, gentle maid . . .	22
XX. One day the Muses twined the hands . .	22
XXI. Observe when mother earth is dry . .	23
XXII. The Phrygian rock that braves the storm .	23
XXIII. I often wish this languid lyre	24
XXIV. To all that breathe the air of heaven . .	25
XXV. Once in each revolving year	25
XXVI. Thy harp may sing of Troy's alarms . .	26
XXVII. We read the flying courser's name . . .	26
XXVIII. As, by his Lemnian forge's flame . . .	26
XXIX. Yes—loving is a painful thrill . . .	27
XXX. 'Twas in a mocking dream of night . . .	28
XXXI. Arm'd with hyacinthine rod	28
XXXII. Strew me a fragrant bed of leaves . . .	28
XXXIII. 'T was noon of night, when round the pole	29
XXXIV. Oh thou, of all creation blest	29
XXXV. Cupid once upon a bed	30
XXXVI. If hoarded gold possess'd the power . .	31
XXXVII. 'T was night and many a circling bowl .	31
XXXVIII. Let us drain the nectar'd bowl	32
XXXIX. How I love the festive boy	32
XL. I know that heaven hath sent me here . .	32
XLI. When Spring adorns the dewy scene . .	33
XLII. Yes, in this glorious revel mine	33
XLIII. While our rosy fillets shed	33
XLIV. Buds of roses, virgin flowers	34
XLV. Within this goblet, rich and deep . . .	34
XLVI. Behold, the young, the rosy Spring . .	35
XLVII. 'T is true my fading years decline . . .	35
XLVIII. When my thirsty soul I sleep	35
XLIX. When Bacchus, Jove's immortal boy . .	36

	PAGE
L. When wine I quaff before my eyes . . .	36
LI. Fly not thus my brow of snow	37
LII. Away, away, ye men of rules	37
LIII. When I behold the festive train	38
LIV. Methinks the pictured bull we see . . .	38
LV. While we invoke the wreathed Spring . .	38
LVI. He, who instructs the youthful crew . .	40
LVII. Whose was the artist's hand that spread .	40
LVIII. When Gold, as fleet as zephyr's pinion . .	41
LIX. Ripen'd by the solar beam	42
LX. Awake to life, my sleeping shell. . . .	42
LXI. Youth's endearing charms are fled . . .	43
LXII. Fill me, boy, as deep a draught	44
LXIII. To Love, the soft and blooming child . .	44
LXIV. Haste thee, nymph, whose well-aim'd spear	44
LXV. Like some wanton filly sporting	44
LXVI. To thee, the Queen of nymphs divine . .	45
LXVII. Rich in bliss, I proudly scorn . . .	45
LXVIII. Now Neptune's mouth our sky deforms . .	46
LXIX. They wove the lotus band to deck . . .	46
LXX. A broken cake, with honey sweet . . .	46
LXXI. With twenty chords my lyre is hung . .	46
LXXII. Fare thee well, perfidious maid	46
LXXIII. Awhile I bloom'd, a happy flower . . .	46
LXXIV. Monarch Love, resistless boy	46
LXXV. Spirit of Love, whose locks unroll'd . .	47
LXXVI. Hither, gentle Muse of mine	47
LXXVII. Would that I were a tuneful lyre . . .	47
LXXVIII. When Cupid sees how thickly now . . .	47
Cupid whose lamp has lent the ray . .	47
Let me resign this wretched breath . .	47
I know thou lovest a brimming measure .	47
I fear that love disturbs my rest	48
From dread Leucadia's frowning steep . .	48
Mix me, child, a cup divine	48

PANEGYRICS ON ANACREON.

	PAGE
Around the tomb, oh, bard divine . . .	48
Here sleeps Anacreon, in this ivied shade .	49
Oh stranger! if Anacreon's shell . . .	49
When Harmony pursued my ways . . .	50
At length thy golden hours have wing'd their flight	50

JUVENILE POEMS.

	PAGE
Preface	51
Dedication	52
Fragments of College Exercises.	52
Is there no call, no consecrating cause . .	52
Variety. Ask what prevailing pleasing power .	53
To a boy with a watch	53
Song. If I swear by that eye, you'll allow . .	53
To . . . . Remember him thou leavest behind	54
Song. When Time, who steals our years away.	54
Song. Have you not seen the timid tear . . .	54
Reuben and Rose	54
Did not	55
To . . . . That wrinkle, when first I espied it	55

PAGE

To Mrs. ...., on some calumnies against her
   character 55
Anacreontic. Press the grape, and let it pour . 56
To . . . . When I loved you, I can't
   but allow 56
To Julia. In allusion to some illiberal criticisms 56
To Julia. Mock me no more with Love's beguil-
   ing 56
The Shrine 56
To a Lady, with some manuscript poems . . . 57
To Julia. Though Fate, my girl, may bid us part 57
To . . . . Sweet lady, look not thus again . 57
Nature's Labels; a fragment 57
To Julia, on her birthday 58
A Reflection at Sea 58
Cloris and Fanny 58
The Shield 58
To Julia, weeping 58
Dreams. To 59
To Rosa. Written during illness 59
Song. The wreath you wove, the wreath you
   wove 59
The Sale of Loves 60
To . . . . The world had just begun to
   steal 60
To . . . . Never mind how the pedagogue
   proses 60
On the Death of a Lady 61
Inconstancy 61
The Natal Genius; a Dream 61
Elegiac Stanzas, supposed to be written by Julia. 62
To the large and beautiful Miss 62
A Dream 62
To . . . . With all my soul, then, let us part . 62
Anacreontic. She never look'd so kind before . 63
To Julia. I saw the peasant's hand unkind . . 63
Hymn of a Virgin of Delphi 63
Sympathy. To Julia 64
The Tear 64
The Snake 64
To Rosa. Is the song of Rosa mute 64
Elegiac Stanzas 65
Love and Marriage 65
Anacreontic. I fill'd to thee, to thee I drank . 65
The Surprise 65
To Miss . . . . . ., on her asking the Author why
   she had sleepless nights 65
The Wonder 66
Lying. I do confess in many a sigh 66
Anacreontic. Friend of my soul, this goblet
   sip 66
The Philosopher Aristippus 66
To Mrs. ——, on her beautiful translation of Voi-
   ture's kiss 68
Rondeau. Good night! good night! and is it so . 68
Song. Why does azure deck the sky? . . . 68
To Rosa. Like one who trusts to summer skies. 69
Written in a Commonplace Book called "the
   Book of Follies" 69
To Rosa. Say, why should the girl of my soul be
   in tears 69
Light sounds the harp 69
From the Greek of Meleager 69
Song. Fly from the world, O Bessy! to me . . 70
The Resemblance 70
Fanny, dearest 70

PAGE

The Ring 71
To the Invisible Girl 71
The Ring, a tale 72
To . . . ., on seeing her with a white veil
   and a rich girdle 75
Written in the blank leaf of a Lady's Commonplace
   Book 75
To Mrs Bl——, written in her Album 75
To Cara, after an interval of absence 76
To Cara, on the dawning of a New Year's Day. . 76
To . . . ., 1801. To be the theme of every
   hour 76
The Genius of Harmony, an irregular ode . . 77
To Mrs. Henry Tighe, on reading her Psyche . . 79
From the High Priest of Apollo, to a Virgin of
   Delphi 80
Fragment. Pity me, love! I'll pity thee . . . 82
A Night Thought 82
The Kiss 82
Song. Think on that look whose melting ray . 82
The Catalogue 82
To . . . . Die when you will, you need
   not wear 83
Imitation of Catullus 83
Oh woman, if through sinful wile 83
Nonsense. Good reader, if you e'er have seen . 83
Epigram, from the French. I never give a kiss
   (says Prue) 83
On a squinting Poetess 83
To Rosa. And are you then a thing of art . . 84
To Phillis. Phillis, you little rosy rake . . . 84
To a Lady, on her singing 84
Song. On the Birth-day of Mrs. —— 84
Song. Mary, I believed thee true 84
Morality, a familiar Epistle 85
The Tell-tale Lyre 86
Peace and Glory, written on the approach of war. 86
Song. Take back the sigh thy lips of art . . . 87
Love and Reason 87
Nay, do not weep, my Fanny, dear 88
Aspasia. 'Twas in the fair Aspasia's bower . . 88
The Grecian Girl's Dream of the Blessed Islands . 88
To Cloe. Imitated from Martial 91
The Wreath and the Chain 91
To . . . . And hast thou mark'd the pen-
   sive shade 91
To . . . . . .'s Picture 92
Fragment of a Mythological Hymn to Love . . 92
To his Serene Highness the Duke of Montpensier 93
The Fall of Hebe, a dithyrambic ode 93
Rings and Seals 96
To Miss Susan B—ckf—d, on her singing . . . 96
Impromptu, on leaving some friends 97
A Warning, to 97
To . . . . 'T is time, I feel, to leave
   thee now 97
Woman. Away, away—you're all the same . . 97
To . . . . Come, take thy harp—'t is
   vain to muse 98
A Vision of Philosophy 98
To Mrs. . . . . . . To see thee every day that came. 101
The Devil among the Scholars, a fragment . . 101
To Lady Heathcote, on an old Ring found at Tun-
   bridge Wells 104
To Mrs. ——. If, in the dream that hovers . . 105
To Julia. Well, Julia, if to love and live . . . 105

PAGE

Epigram. Your mother says, my little Venus . 105
Song. Sweet seducer! blandly smiling . . . 105
Song. Why, the world are all thinking about it . 105
Impromptu. Look in my eyes, my blushing fair! 106
To Mrs. ——. Yes, I think I once heard of an
  amorous youth 106
To Julia. Sweet is the dream, divinely sweet . 106
To ——. Can I again that form caress . . . 106
Song. Away with this pouting and sadness . . 106
An Argument, to any Phillis or Cloe 107
The Kiss. Give me, my love, that billing kiss . 107
Elegiac Stanzas. How sweetly could I lay my
  head 107
Love in a Storm 107
Song. Jessy on a bank was sleeping 107
To a Sleeping Maid 107
Song. When the heart's feeling 107
The Ballad. Thou hast sent me a flowery band. 107
Written in a Commonplace Book 108
Song. Dear, in pity do not speak 108
To ——. So! Rosa turns her back on me . . 108
To Mrs. ——. Yes, heaven can witness how I
  strove 108
Fanny of Timmol, a mail-coach adventure . . 109
An Invitation to Supper. To Mrs. ——. . . 109
An Ode upon Morning 110
Song. Oh! nothing in life can sadden us . . 110
Julia's Kiss. When infant Bliss in roses slept . 110
A Fragment. To ——. 111
Song. A captive thus to thee, my girl . . . 111
Song. Sweetest love! I'll not forget thee . . 111
Song. Where is the nymph, whose azure eye . 111

POEMS RELATING TO AMERICA.

Preface 112
Dedication 115
Original Preface 116
To Lord Viscount Strangford 117
To the Flying-Fish 118
To Miss Moore, from Norfolk, in Virginia . . 118
A Ballad. The Lake of the Dismal Swamp . . 120
To the Marchioness Dowager of Donegal . . 120
Stanzas. A beam of tranquillity smiled in the
  West 121
To George Morgan, Esq. of Norfolk, Virginia . 122
Lines, written in a Storm at Sea 123

ODES TO NEA, WRITTEN AT BERMUDA.

Nay tempt me not to love again 124
I pray you, let us roam no more 124
You read it in these spell-bound eyes . . . 125
A Dream of Antiquity 125
Well—peace to thy heart, though another's it be 127
The Snow Spirit. 128
I stole along the flowery bank 128
A Study from the Antique 129
There 's not a look, a word of thine . . . 129
To Joseph Atkinson, Esq., from Bermuda . . 129
The Steersman's Song 131
To the Fire-Fly 131
To the Lord Viscount Forbes 131
Lines written on leaving Philadelphia . . . 133
To Thomas Hume, Esq. M.D. 134
Lines written at the Cohos, or Falls of the Mo-
  hawk River 135
Song of the Evil Spirit of the Woods . . . 136
To the Hon. W. R. Spencer 137

PAGE

Ballad Stanzas. I knew by the smoke that so
  gracefully curl'd 138
A Canadian Boat Song. Faintly as tolls the even-
  ing chime 138
To the Lady Charlotte Rawdon 139
Impromptu, after a visit to Mrs. —, of Montreal. 141
Written on passing Deadman's Island 141
To the Boston Frigate, on leaving Halifax for Eng-
  land 141
To Miss ——. With woman's form and woman's
  tricks 142
The Senses, a Dream 142
The Vase 143
To —, on her asking me to address a Poem to her. 144
On Seeing an Infant in Nea's arms 144
Fragments of a Journal to G. M., Esq. . . . 145
On the Loss of a Letter for Nea 146
Fanny, my love, we ne'er were sages . . . 147
To a Friend. When next you see the black-eyed
  Caty 147
Song. I ne'er on that lip for a moment have gazed 147
On a beautiful East Indian 147
To —. I know that none can smile like thee . . 147
From the Greek. I've press'd her bosom oft and
  oft 148
At night when all is still around 148
To —. I often wish that thou wert dead . . . 148

CORRUPTION AND INTOLERANCE.

Preface 148
Original Preface 149
Corruption, an Epistle 150
Intolerance, a Satire 157

THE SCEPTIC, A PHILOSOPHICAL SATIRE.

Preface 161
The Sceptic 162

INTERCEPTED LETTERS; OR, THE TWOPENNY POST-
  BAG.

Preface 166
Dedication 168
Original Preface 168
Preface to Fourteenth Edition 169
I. From the Pr—nc—ss Ch—l—e of W—l—s to
    the Lady B—rb—a Ashl—y. 170
II. From Colonel M' M—h—n to G—ld Fr—nc—s
    L—ckie, Esq. 170
III. From G—ge Pr—ce R—g—t to the E— of Y—r-
    m—h 171
IV. From the Right Hon. P—tr—k D—gen—n to
    to the Right Hon. Sir J—hn N—cb—l . . . 172
V. From the Countess Dowager of C—rk to Lady — 173
VI. From Abdallah, in London, to Mohassan, in Is-
    pahan 174
VII. From Messrs. L—ck—gt—n and Co. to ——,
    Esq. 175
VIII. From Colonel Th—m—s to — Sk—ff—ngt—n,
    Esq. 175
Appendix 177

SATIRICAL AND HUMOROUS POEMS.

The Insurrection of the Papers, a Dream . . . 179
Parody of a celebrated Letter 180
Anacreontic. To a Plumassier 181
Epigram. What news to-day? 182

b

	PAGE
Extracts from the Diary of a Politician	182
King Crack and his Idols	182
What's my thought like?	183
Epigram. Dialogue between a Catholic Delegate and his R—y—l H—ghn—ss the Du—e of C—b—l—d	183
Wreaths for the Ministers	183
Epigram. Dialogue between a Dowager and her maid on the night of Lord Y—rm—th's fête	183
Horace, Ode XI., lib. ii. Freely translated by the Pr—ce R—g—t	183
Horace, Ode XXII., lib. i. Freely translated by Lord Eld—n	184
The New Costume of the Ministers	185
Correspondence between a Lady and Gentleman.	185
Occasional Address for the opening of the new Theatre of St. St—ph—n	186
Little Man and Little Soul, a ballad	186
The Sale of the Tools	187
Reinforcements for Lord Wellington	187
Horace, Ode I., lib. iii., a fragment	188
Horace, Ode XXXVIII., lib. i., a fragment	188
Impromptu, on being obliged to leave a pleasant party for the want of a pair of breeches to dress for dinner in	188
Lord Wellington and the Ministers	188

IRISH MELODIES.

Preface	189
Dedication	194
Original Preface	195
Go where glory waits thee	195
War Song. Remember the glories of Brien the Brave	195
The harp that once through Tara's halls	196
Oh! breathe not his name	196
When he who adores thee	196
Erin! the tear and the smile in thine eyes	196
Fly not yet	196
Oh! think not my spirits are always as light	196
Though the last glimpse of Erin with sorrow I see	197
Rich and rare were the gems she wore	197
As a beam o'er the face of the waters may glow	197
The Meeting of the Waters	198
How dear to me the hour	198
Take back the Virgin Page	198
St. Senanus and the Lady	198
The Legacy	199
How oft has the Benshee cried	199
We may roam through this world	199
Eveleen's Bower	200
Let Erin remember the days of old	200
The Song of Fionnuala	200
Come, send round the wine	200
Sublime was the warning	201
Believe me, if all those endearing young charms.	201
Erin, oh Erin	201
Drink to her	201
Oh! blame not the bard	202
While gazing on the moon's light	202
Ill Omens	203
Before the Battle	203
After the Battle	203
'Tis sweet to think	203
It is not the tear at this moment shed	204
The Irish Peasant to his Mistress	204

	PAGE
On Music	204
The Origin of the Harp	205
Love's Young Dream	205
The Prince's Day	205
Weep on, weep on	206
Lesbia hath a beaming eye	206
I saw thy form in youthful prime	206
By that lake, whose gloomy shore	206
She is far from the land	207
Nay, tell me not, dear	207
Avenging and bright	207
What the bee is to the floweret	208
Love and the Novice	208
This life is all chequer'd with pleasures and woes	208
Oh, the shamrock	208
At the mid hour of night	209
One bumper at parting	209
'T is the last rose of Summer	210
The young May moon	210
The Minstrel-boy	210
The Song of O'Ruark	210
Oh! had we some bright little isle of our own	211
Farewell! but whenever you welcome the hour	211
Oh! doubt me not	211
You remember Ellen	211
I'd mourn the hopes	212
Come o'er the sea	212
Has sorrow thy young days shaded	212
No, not more welcome	213
When first I met thee	213
While History's Muse	213
The time I've lost in wooing	214
Where is the slave	214
Come rest in this bosom	214
'Tis gone, and for ever	214
Fill the bumper fair	215
In the morning of life	215
I saw from the beach	216
Dear harp of my country	216
My gentle harp	216
As slow our ship	216
When cold in the earth	217
Remember thee!	217
Wreath the bowl	217
Where'er I see those smiling eyes	218
If thou'lt be mine	218
To ladies' eyes	218
Forget not the field	218
Sail on, sail on	219
Ne'er ask the hour	219
They may rail at this life	219
Oh for the swords of former time	219
The Parallel	220
Drink of this cup	220
The Fortune-teller	220
Oh! ye dead!	221
O'Donohue's Mistress	221
Echo. How sweet the answer Echo makes	221
Oh, the sight entrancing	222
Thee, thee, only thee	222
Shall the harp then be silent	222
Sweet Innisfallen	223
'T was one of those dreams	223
Oh, banquet not	224
Fairest! put on awhile	224
Quick! we have but a second	224

CONTENTS. xi

	PAGE
And doth not a meeting like this	225
The Mountain Sprite	225
As vanquish'd Erin	225
Desmond's Song	226
They know not my heart	226
I wish I was by that dim lake	226
She sung of love	227
Sing—sing—music was given	227
Though humble the banquet	227
Sing, sweet harp	227
Song of the battle eve	228
The Wandering Bard	228
Alone in crowds to wander on	228
I've a secret to tell thee	229
Song of Innisfail	229
The Night Dance	229
There are sounds of mirth	229
Oh! Arranmore, loved Arranmore	230
Lay his sword by his side	230
The wine-cup is circling	230
Oh could we do with this world of ours	231
From this hour the pledge is given	231
The dream of those days	231
Silence is in our festal halls	231
Appendix. Advertisement to first and second numbers	232
Advertisement to the third number	232
Letter to the Marchioness Dowager of Donegal	233
Advertisement to the fourth number	236
Advertisement to the fifth number	237
Advertisement to the sixth number	237
Advertisement to the seventh number	237
Dedication to the Marchioness of Headfort	238

NATIONAL AIRS.

Advertisement	238
A temple to friendship	238
Flow on, thou shining river	238
All that's bright must fade	239
So warmly we met	239
Those evening bells	239
Should those fond hopes	239
Reason, Folly, and Beauty	239
Fare thee well, thou lovely one	240
Dost thou remember	240
Oh, come to me when daylight sets	240
Oft, in the stilly night	240
Hark! the vesper hymn is stealing	241
There comes a time	241
Love and Hope	241
My harp has one unchanging theme	241
Oh, no—not even when first we loved	242
Peace be around thee	242
Common Sense and Genius	242
Then, fare thee well	242
Gaily sounds the castanet	243
Joys of youth, how fleeting	243
Come, chase that starting tear away	243
Love is a hunter boy	243
Hear me but once	243
When Love was a child	244
Say, what shall be our sport to-day?	244
Bright be thy dreams	244
Go, then—'t is vain	244
The Crystal-hunters	244
Row gently here	245

	PAGE
Oh, days of youth	245
When first that smile	245
Peace to the slumberers	245
When thou shalt wander	245
Who'll buy my love-knots	245
See, the dawn from Heaven	246
Nets and Cages	246
When through the piazzetta	246
Go, now, and dream	247
Take hence the bowl	247
Farewell, Theresa	247
Oft, when the watching stars	247
When the first summer bee	247
Though 't is all but a dream	247
When the wine-cup is smiling	248
Where shall we bury our shame?	248
Ne'er talk of Wisdom's gloomy schools	248
Do not say that life is waning	248
The Gazelle	248
No—leave my heart to rest	249
Wind thy horn, my hunter boy	249
Where are the visions	249
Oh, guard our affection	249
Slumber, oh slumber	249
Bring the bright garlands hither	250
If in loving, singing	250
When abroad in the world	250
Thou lovest no more	250
Keep those eyes still purely mine	250
Hope comes again	250
O say, thou best and brightest	251
When night brings the hour	251
I would tell her I love her	251
Like one who, doom'd	251
Fear not that, while around thee	252
When love is kind	252
The garland I send thee	252
Spring and Autumn	252
How shall I woo?	252
Love alone	253
Hark! I hear a spirit sing	253

SACRED SONGS.

Dedication	253
Thou art, O God	253
The bird, let loose	254
Fallen is thy throne	254
Who is the maid?	254
This world is all a fleeting show	255
Weep not for those	255
The turf shall be my fragrant shrine	255
Oh thou who dry'd the mourner's tear	255
Sound the loud timbrel	256
Were not the sinful Mary's tears	256
Go, let me weep	256
As down in the sunless retreats	256
Come not, oh Lord	256
But who shall see	257
Almighty God!	257
Oh fair! oh purest!	257
Angel of charity	258
Lord, who shall bear that day	258
Behold the Sun	258
Oh, teach me to love thee	258
Like morning, when her early breeze	258
Weep, children of Israel	259

PAGE

Come, ye disconsolate 259
Awake, arise, thy light is come 259
There is a bleak desert 260
Since first thy word 260
Hark! 't is the breeze 260
Where is your dwelling, ye sainted . . . 261
How lightly mounts the muse's wing . . . 261
Go forth to the mount 261
Is it not sweet to think, hereafter 261
War against Babylon 262

LEGENDARY BALLADS.

Preface 262
Dedication 265
The Voice 265
Cupid and Psyche 265
Hero and Leander 265
The Leaf and the Fountain 266
Cephalis and Procris 266
Youth and Age 266
The Dying Warrior 267
The Magic Mirror 267
The Pilgrim 267
The High-born Ladye 268
The Indian Boat 268
The Stranger 268

SET OF GLEES.

Dedication 269
The Meeting of the Ships 269
Hip, hip, hurrah! 269
Hush, hush! 269
The Evening Gun 270
The Watchman 270
Say, what shall we dance? 270
The Parting before the Battle 270

BALLADS, SONGS, ETC.

To-day, dearest, is ours 271
When on the lip the sigh delays 271
Here, take my heart 271
Oh, call it by some better name 271
Poor wounded heart 271
The East Indian 272
Poor broken flower 272
The Pretty Rose-tree 272
Shine out, stars! 272
The young Muleteers of Grenada 272
Tell her, oh tell her 273
Nights of music 273
Our First Young Love 273
Black and Blue Eyes 273
Dear Fanny 273
From life without freedom 273
Here's the bower 274
Love and the Sun-dial 274
I saw the moon rise clear 274
Love and Time 274
Love's Light Summer-cloud 274
Love, wandering through the golden maze . . 275
Merrily every bosom boundeth 275
Remember the time 275
Love thee 275
Oh, soon return 275
One dear smile 276
Yes, yes, when the bloom 276

PAGE

When 'midst the gay I meet 276
The day of love 276
Lusitanian War Song 276
The Young Rose 277
When twilight dews 277
Young Jessica 277
How happy, once 277
I love but thee 277
Let joy alone be remember'd now 277
Love thee dearest? love thee? 278
My heart and lute 278
Peace, peace to him that's gone 278
Rose of the Desert 278
'T is all for thee 278
Wake thee, my dear 279
The Song of the Olden Time 279
The Boy of the Alps 279
For thee alone 279
Her last words at parting 280
Let's take the world as some wide scene . . . 280
Love's Victory 280
Song of Hercules to his Daughter 280
The Dream of Home 281
The Young Indian Maid 281
They tell me thou'rt the favour'd guest . . 281
The Homeward March 281
Wake up, sweet melody 282
Calm be thy sleep 282
The Fancy Fair 282
The Exile 282
If thou wouldst have me sing and play . . . 282
Still when daylight 283
The Summer Webs 283
Mind not though daylight 283
They met but once 283
Child's Song, from a Masque 283
With moonlight beaming 284
The halcyon hangs o'er ocean 284
The world was hush'd 284
The two Loves 284
The Legend of Puck the Fairy 285
Beauty and Song 285
Song of a Hyperborean 285
When thou art nigh 285
Cupid Arm'd 286
Round the world goes 286
Thou bidst me sing 286
Oh do not look so bright and blest 286
The Musical Box 286
When to sad music silent you listen . . . 287
The dawn is breaking o'er us 287
The Language of Flowers 287

UNPUBLISHED SONGS, ETC.

Ask not if still I love 288
Dear? Yes 288
Unbind thee, love 288
There's something strange 288
Not from thee 288
Guess, guess 289
When Love, who ruled 289
Still thou fliest 289
Then first from love 289
Hush, sweet lute 290
Bright Moon 290
Long years have pass'd 290

	PAGE
Dreaming for ever	290
The Russian Lover	290
Though lightly sounds the song I sing	291

SONGS FROM THE GREEK ANTHOLOGY.

Here at thy tomb	291
Sale of Cupid	291
To weave a garland for the rose	291
Why does she so long delay?	292
Twinest thou with lofty wreath thy brow	292
When the sad word	292
My Mopsa is little	292
Still like dew in silence falling	293
Up, sailor boy, 'tis day	293
In myrtle wreaths	293

EVENINGS IN GREECE.

Dedication	293
Advertisement	293
FIRST EVENING.—The sky is bright	293
As o'er her loom the Lesbian maid	295
Weeping for thee, my love	296
When the Balaika	296
Raise the buckler—poise the lance	297
As by the shore at break of day	297
I saw, from yonder silent cave	298
O Memory, how coldly	298
Ah! where are they, who heard, in former hours	299
Here, while the moonlight dim	299
SECOND EVENING.—Song. When evening shades are falling	300
As once a Grecian maiden wove	301
Up and march! the timbrel's sound	302
No life is like the mountaineer's	303
Thou art not dead—thou art not dead	304
Calm as beneath its mother's eyes	304
As Love, one summer eve, was straying	305
Who comes so gracefully	305
Welcome, sweet bird, through the sunny air winging	306
Up with the sparkling brimmer	307
March! nor heed those arms that hold thee	307
'Tis the Vine! 'tis the Vine! said the cup-loving boy	308

THE SUMMER FÊTE.

Preface	308
Dedication	309
Where are ye now, ye summer days	309
Song. Array thee, love, array thee, love	311
Song. Some mortals there may be, so wise, or so fine	312
Trio. Our home is on the sea, boy	313
Song. Smoothly flowing through verdant vales	313
Waltz Duet. Long as I waltz'd with only thee	314
Song. Bring hither, bring thy lute, while day is dying	315
Song and Trio. On one of those sweet nights that oft	315
Song. Oh, where art thou dreaming	316
Song. Who'll buy?—'t is Folly's shop, who'll buy	316
Song and Trio. The Levee and Couchee	316
Song. If to see thee be to love thee	317

LALLA ROOKH.

Preface	318
Dedication	321

	PAGE
Introduction	321
The Veiled Prophet of Khorassan	324
Paradise and the Peri	351
The Fire-Worshippers	360
The Light of the Haram	386

THE FUDGE FAMILY IN PARIS.

Preface	397
Original Preface	399
Letter I. Miss Biddy Fudge to Miss Dorothy ——.	399
II. Phil. Fudge, Esq. to Lord C—stl—r—gh	400
III. Mr. Bob Fudge to Richard ——, Esq.	402
IV. Phelim Connor to ——.	403
V. Miss Biddy Fudge to Dorothy ——	405
VI. Phil. Fudge, Esq., to his brother Tim Fudge, Barrister at Law	407
VII. Phelim Connor to ——	409
VIII. Mr. Bob Fudge to Richard ——, Esq.	411
IX. Phil. Fudge to the Lord Viscount C—stl—r—gh	413
X. Miss Biddy Fudge to Dorothy ——	416
XI. Phelim Connor to ——	418
XII. Miss Biddy Fudge to Miss Dorothy ——.	419

FABLES FOR THE HOLY ALLIANCE.

Dedication	421
Preface	421
Fable I. The Dissolution of the Holy Alliance.	421
II. The Looking-glasses	423
III. The Torch of Liberty	424
IV. The Fly and the Bullock	425
V. Church and State	425
VI. The Little Grand Lama	427
VII. The Extinguishers	428
VIII. Louis the Fourteenth's Wig	429

RHYMES ON THE ROAD.

Preface	431
Original Preface	433
Introductory Rhymes	433
Extract I. View of the Lake of Geneva, etc.	434
II. Fate of Geneva in the year 1782	435
III. Fancy and Truth, etc.	435
IV. The Picture Gallery, etc.	436
V. Fancy and Reality, etc.	436
VI. The Fall of Venice not to be lamented, etc.	437
VII. Lord Byron's Memoirs, etc.	438
VIII. Female Beauty at Venice, etc.	439
IX. The English to be met with every where, etc.	440
X. Verses of Hippolyta to her husband	440
XI. Florence	441
XII. Music in Italy, etc.	442
XIII. Reflections on reading Du Cerceau, etc.	442
XIV. Fragment of a Dream, etc.	444
XV. Mary Magdalen, her Story, etc.	445
XVI. A Visit to the House where Rousseau lived, etc.	446

THE LOVES OF THE ANGELS.

Prefatory Observations	448
Preface	450
Introduction	452
First Angel's Story	453
Second Angel's Story	468
Third Angel's Story	471

CONTENTS.

PAGE

THE FUDGES IN ENGLAND.

Preface 474
Letter I. Patrick Magan, Esq., to Rev. Richard — 475
  II. Miss Biddy Fudge to Mrs. Elizabeth ——. 476
  III. Miss Fanny Fudge to her Cousin, Miss
    Kitty —— 478
  IV. Patrick Magan, Esq. to Rev. Richard —— 479
  V. Larry O'Branigan to his wife Judy . . 481
  VI. Miss Biddy Fudge to Mrs. Elizabeth —— 482
  VII. Miss Fanny Fudge to her Cousin, Miss
    Kitty —— 484
  VIII. Bob Fudge, Esq., to Rev. Mortimer O'-
    Mulligan 486
  IX. Larry O'Branigan to his wife Judy . . 487
  X. Rev. Mortimer O'Mulligan to the Rev. —. 489
  XI. Patrick Magan, Esq., to the Rev. Richard— 490

TOM CRIB'S MEMORIAL TO CONGRESS.

Preface 494
The Memorial 495
Account of the Grand Set-to between Long Sandy
  and Georgy the Porpus 496
APPENDIX. No. I. Account of a grand Pugilistic
  Meeting 501
No. II. Account of the Milling-match between En-
  tellus and Dares 503
No. III. Bob Gregson, Poet Laureate of the Fan-
  cy 504
Lines to Miss Grace Maddox, the fair Pugilist . . 505
Ya-hip, my Hearties! 506

SATIRICAL AND HUMOROUS POEMS.

Preface 506
Epistle from Tom Crib to Big Ben 508
Fum and Hum, the two Birds of Royalty . . 509
Lines on the Departure of Lords C—stl—r—gh
  and St.—w—rt for the Continent 509
To the Ship in which Lord C—stl—r—gh sailed
  for the Continent 510
The Annual Pill 510
To Sir Hudson Lowe 511
Amatory Colloquy between Bank and Govern-
  ment 511
Dialogue between a Sovereign and a One Pound
  Note 512
An Expostulation to Lord King 512
The Sinking Fund cried 513
Ode to the Goddess Ceres 513
A Hymn of Welcome after the Recess . . . 514
Memorabilia of Last Week 515
All in the Family Way 515
Ballad for the Cambridge Election 516
Mr. Roger Dodsworth 516
Copy of an Intercepted Despatch 516
The Millenium 517
The Three Doctors 518
Epitaph on a Tuft-hunter 518
Ode to a Hat 518
News for Country Cousins 519
A Vision 519
The Petition of the Orangemen of Ireland . . 520
Cotton and Corn 521
The Canonization of Saint B—tt—rw—rth . . 521
An Incantation 522
A Dream of Turtle 523
The Donky and his Panniers 523

PAGE

Ode to the Sublime Porte 524
Corn and Catholics 524
A Case of Libel 524
Literary Advertisement 525
The Irish Slave 526
Ode to Ferdinand 526
Hat versus Wig 527
New Creation of Peers 528
The Periwinkles and the Locusts 528
Speech on the Umbrella Question 529
A Pastoral Ballad 529
A late Scene at Swanage 530
Wo! wo! 530
Tout pour la Tripe 531
Enigma 531
Dog-day Reflections 532
The "Living Dog" and "The Dead Lion" . . 532
Ode to Don Miguel 533
Thoughts on the Present Government of Ire-
  land 533
The Limbo of Lost Reputations 534
How to write by Proxy 534
Imitation of the Inferno of Dante 535
Lament for the loss of Lord B—th—st's Tail . 536
The Cherries 536
Stanzas written in anticipation of Defeat . . 537
Ode to the Woods and Forests 537
Stanzas from the Banks of the Shannon . . 538
"If" and "Perhaps" 538
Write on, write on 539
Song of the Departing Spirit of Tithe . . . 539
The Euthanasia of Van 540
To the Rev. —. On the Sixteen Requisitionists of
  Nottingham 540
Irish Antiquities 541
A Curious Fact 541
New-fashioned Echoes 542
Incantation, from the new tragedy of the Bruns-
  wickers 542
How to make a good Politician 543
Epistle of Condolence from a Slave-Lord to a Cot-
  ton-Lord 544
The Ghost of Miltiades 544
Alarming Intelligence—Revolution in the Diction-
  ary—one Galt at the head of it 544
Resolutions passed at a late Meeting of Reverends
  and Right Reverends 545
Sir Andrew's Dream 546
A Love Song 546
Sunday Ethics, a Scotch Ode 547
Awful Event 547
The Numbering of the Clergy 547
A Sad Case 548
A Dream of Hindostan 548
The Brunswick Club 549
Proposals for a Gynæcocracy 549
Lord H—nl—y and St. Cecilia 550
Advertisement. Missing or lost, last Sunday night 550
Missing. Whereas Lord ***** of ****** . . . 551
The Dance of Bishops, or the Episcopal Quadrille 551
Dick ****, a Character 552
A Corrected Report of some late Speeches . . 552
Moral Positions, a Dream 553
The Mad Tory and the Comet 554
From the Hon. Henry — to Lady Emma — . 554
Triumph of Bigotry 555

CONTENTS.

PAGE

Translation from the Gull Language, by Dr. Bow-
ring 555
Notions of Reform, by a Modern Reformer . . 556
Tory Pledges 557
St. Jerome on Earth, First Visit. 557
St. Jerome on Earth, Second Visit 558
Thoughts on Tar Barrels 558
The Consultation 559
To the Rev. Ch—rl—s Ov—rt—n, Curate of Ro-
maldkirk 559
Scene from a Play acted at Oxford, called "Matri-
culation." 560
Late Tithe Case. 560
Fool's Paradise. 561
The Rector and his Curate, or One Pound Two . 561
Paddy's Metamorphosis 562
Cocker on Church Reform 562
Les Hommes Automates 562
How to make One's self a Peer 563
The Duke is the Lad 564
Epistle from Erasmus on Earth to Cicero in the
Shades. 564
Sketch of the First Act of a new Romantic Drama 565
Animal Magnetism. 565
The Song of the Box 566
Announcement of a new Thalaba 566
Letter from Larry O'Branigan to the Rev. Murtagh
O'Mulligan 567
The Boy Statesman, by a Tory 568
Musings of an Unreformed Peer 568
Rival Topics, an Extravaganza 568
The Reverend Pamphleteer, a Romantic Ballad . 569
A recent Dialogue 569
The Wellington Spa 570
A Character 570
A Ghost Story 571
Thoughts on the late destructive Propositions of
the Tories. 571
Anticipated Meeting of the British Association in
the year 2836. 572
Leave me alone, a pastoral Ballad 573
Epistle from Henry of Ex—t—r to John of Tuam. 573
Song of Old Puck 574
Police Reports; Case of Imposture 574
Reflections, addressed to the Author of the Article
of the Church, in the last Number of the Quar-
terly Review. 575
New Grand Exhibition of Models of the Two Houses
of Parliament. 575
Announcement of a new Grand Acceleration Com-
pany for the Promotion of the Speed of Lite-
rature. 576
Some Account of the late Dinner to Dan . . . 577
New Hospital for Sick Literati 577
Religion and Trade 578
Musings suggested by the late Promotion of Mrs.
Nethercoat 578
Intended Tribute to the Author of an Article in
the last Number of the Quarterly Review, en-
titled Romanism in Ireland. 579
Grand Dinner of Type and Co 580
Church Extension 580
Latest Accounts from Olympus. 581
The Triumphs of Farce 581
Thoughts on Patrons, Puffs, and other Matters . 582
Thoughts on Mischief, by Lord Stanley. . . . 583

PAGE

Epistle from Captain Rock to Lord L—ndh—t. . 584
Captain Rock in London 584

MISCELLANEOUS POEMS.

Preface 585
Lines on the Death of Mr. P—rc—v—l. . . . 586
Lines on the Death of Sh—r—d—n. 586
A Melologue upon National Music 587
SONGS FROM M. P., OR THE BLUE STOCKING.
Young Love lived once in a humble shed . . 588
This is Love 588
Spirit of Joy 588
When Leila touch'd the lute 589
Boat Glee. The Song that lightens our languid
way. 589
Oh think when a Hero is sighing 589
Cupid's Lottery 589
Liberty. Though sacred the tie that our country
entwineth 589
Occasional Epilogue, spoken by Mr. Corry, in the
character of Vapid 590
Extract from a Prologue written and spoken by
the Author at the opening of the Kilkenny
Theatre 590
The Sylph's Ball. 590
Remonstrance, after a Conversation with Lord
John Russell 591
My Birth-day 592
Fancy. The more I've view'd this world . . . 592
TRANSLATIONS FROM CATULLUS.
To Lesbia. 592
Comrades and friends, with whom where'er . 593
Sweet Sirmio! thou the very eye. 593
Tibullus to Sulpicia 593
Invitation to Dinner 593
Verses to the Poet Crabbe's Inkstand 594
To Caroline, Viscountess Valletort 595
A Speculation 595
To my Mother 595
Love and Hymen 595
Lines on the entry of the Austrians into Naples . 595
Scepticism. Ere Psyche drank the cup, that shed. 596
A Joke versified 596
On the Death of a Friend 596
To James Corry, Esq. 596
Fragment of a Character 597
Imitation, from the French 597
What shall I sing thee? 597
Country Dance and Quadrille 598
Gazel. Haste Maami, the Spring is nigh . . . 599
Lines on the Death of Joseph Atkinson, Esq., of
Dublin. 599
Genius and Criticism 600
To Lady J'r''y 600
To the same, on looking through her Album . . 601
To Lady Holland, on Napoleon's Legacy of a
Snuff-box 601
Epilogue, written for Lady Dacre's Tragedy of
"Ina". 601
The Day-dream 601
Song. Where is the heart that would not give . 602
Song of the Poco-Curante Society 602
Anne Boleyn 603
The Dream of the Two Sisters 603
Sovereign Woman, a ballad 603
Come, play me that simple air again 603

                                                    PAGE
SONGS AND PIECES OMITTED IN LAST LONDON EDITION.
    Cease, oh cease to tempt 604
    Fanny was in the grove 604
    Holy be the Pilgrim's sleep 604
    I can no longer stifle 605
    Joys that pass away 605
    Little Mary's Eye 605
    Love, my Mary, dwells with thee 605
    Now let the warrior   605
    Oh, Lady fair! 606
    Oh, see those Cherries 606
    Poh, Dermot! go along with your goster . . . 606
    Send the bowl round merrily 606
    The Probability 607
    The Tablet of Love 607
    When in languor sleeps the heart 607
    Will you come to the bower ' . .   ' . . 607
    The Rabbinical Origin of Women 607
    Farewell, Bessy ! 608
    Song. I've roam'd through many a weary round 608
    Epitaph on a well-known Poet 608
    Epitaph on a Lawyer 608

                                                    PAGE
    Illustration of a Bore 609
    From the French. Of all the men one meets
        about 609
    Romance. I have a story of two lovers, fill'd . . 609
    On —. Like a snuffers, this old loving dame . . 609
    The Witch's Sabbath, a fragment 609
    Extempore. When they shall tell in future times 610
    A Voice from Marathon 610
    The two Bondsmen 611
    Crockfordiana. Epigrams 611
    Lines written in St. Stephen's Chapel after the
        Dissolution 611

ALCIPHRON, A FRAGMENT.
    Preface 612
    Letter I From Alciphron at Alexandria to Cleon
            at Athens 613
        II. From the same to the same 615
        III. From the same to the same 617
        IV. From the same to the same 622
        V. From Orcus, High Priest of Memphis, to
            Decius the Prætorian Prefect . . . 626

------▶▶▶▶▷▟▝◖◗▚▞◗◖◀◀◀◀------ --

A BIOGRAPHICAL SKETCH

OF

THOMAS MOORE.

NOTWITHSTANDING the number of literary men to whom Ireland has given birth, there is little connected with their names which conveys any thing of a national association. Congreve was an apostate, and Swift only by accident a patriot; whilst Goldsmith was weak enough to affect an air of contempt for a people whose accent was indelibly stamped on his tongue. We could protract the list of her ungrateful "men of mind" even to our own day; but the task would be invidious, and we gladly turn to one who forms a splendid exception—one who is not ashamed of Ireland, and of whom Ireland is justly proud.

Mr. Moore is every way an Irishman, in heart, in feelings, and in principles. For Ireland he has indeed done much; he has associated her name, her wrongs, and her music, with poetry which can never die while taste and patriotism subsist. It will be understood that we here allude to his beautiful *Irish Melodies*. Had Mr. Moore written nothing else, he would be entitled to the gratitude of his countrymen. In *Lalla Rookh* he has given his fire-worshippers the wrongs and feelings of Irishmen; while, in the *Memoirs of Captain Rock*, he has accomplished a most difficult task—written a history of Ireland that has been read.

In the present complete edition of his poetical works Mr. Moore has introduced in the prefatory notices several anecdotes of his life connected with the production of many of the poems, which give them the tone of the pleasantest of all memoir reading—an auto-biography. These have very materially abridged our present task; the poet having in fact left little but mere gleanings for the humble labourer who has undertaken the present sketch.

Mr. Moore is the only son of the late Mr. Garret Moore, a respectable tradesman in Dublin, where our poet was born on the 28th of May, 1780. He has two sisters; and his infantine days seem to have left the most agreeable impressions on his memory. Some of the most interesting passages of his life will be found, in the following pages, described by Mr. Moore as occurring at this early period. His home, though comparatively humble, was essentially a home of love, and his tastes and friendships formed almost in boyhood seem to have coloured his principles and feelings throughout life.—In an epistle to his eldest sister, dated November, 1803, and written from Norfolk in Virginia, he retraces with delight their childhood, and describes the endearments of home, with a sensibility as exquisite as that which breathes through the lines of Cowper on receiving his mother's picture.

Mr. Moore's school and college days are described by himself so fully as to warrant our only noticing them here to direct the attention of the reader to his own interesting account, merely remarking that he was distinguished, while at the University, by an enthusiastic attachment to his country, his classical attainments, and the sociability of his disposition. On the 19th November, 1799, Mr. Moore entered himself a member of the honourable Society of the Middle Temple, and in the course of the year 1800, before he had completed the 20th year of his age, he published his translation of the *Odes of Anacreon* into English verse with notes, from whence, in the vocabulary of fashion, he has ever since been designated by the appellation of Anacreon Moore. The work is introduced by a Greek ode from the pen of the Translator, and is dedicated, with permission, to his Royal Highness the Prince of Wales, afterwards George IV. When Mr. Moore first came to London, his youthful appearance was such, that being at a large dinner-party, and getting up to escort the ladies to the drawing-room, a French gentleman observed, "Ah! le petit bon homme qui s'en va!" Mr. Moore's subsequent brilliant conversation, however, soon proved him to be, though little of stature, yet, like Gay, "in wit a man." Assuming the appropriate name of Little, our author published, in 1801, a volume of original poems, chiefly amatory. Of the contents of this volume it is impossible to speak in terms of unqualified commendation. In the same year, his *Philosophy of Pleasure* was advertised, but never published.

Towards the autumn of 1803, Mr. Moore embarked for Bermuda, where he had obtained the appointment of Registrar to the Admiralty. This was a patent place, and of a description so unsuitable to his temper of mind, that he soon found it expedient to fulfil the duties of it by a deputy, with whom, in consideration of circumstances, he consented to divide the profits accruing from it. From this situation, however, he never derived any emolument; though he suffered severe pecuniary loss owing to the misconduct of his deputy, from which he relieved himself by the most brilliant production of his pen, *Lalla Rookh.* In October, 1804, he quitted America, on his return to England, in the Boston frigate, commanded by Capt. Douglas, whom he has highly eulogised for his attention during the voyage. In 1806, he published his remarks on the manners and society of America, in a work entitled *Odes and Epistles.*

The fate of Addison with his Countess Dowager holding out no encouragement for the ambitious love of Mr. Moore, he wisely and happily allowed his good taste to regulate his choice in a wife, and married Miss Dyke, a lady of great personal beauty, most amiable disposition, and accomplished manners, with whom and his children he has enjoyed a life of enviable domestic happiness.

Mr. Moore has cultivated a taste for music as well as for poesy, and the late celebrated Dr. Burney was perfectly astonished at his talent, which he emphatically called "peculiarly his own." Nor has he neglected those more solid attainments which should ever distinguish the well-bred gentleman, for he is an excellent general scholar, and particularly well read in the literature of the middle ages. His conversational powers are great, and his modest and unassuming manners have placed him in the highest rank of cultivated society.

The celebrated poem of *Lalla Rookh* appeared in 1817; in the summer of which year our poet visited the French capital, where he collected the materials for that humorous production, *The Fudge Family in Paris.* In the following year, he went to Ireland, on which occasion a public dinner was given to him, on the 8th of June, 1818, at Morrison's Hotel in Dublin, which was graced by a large assemblage of the most distinguished literary and political characters, the Earl of Charlemont taking the chair.

In 1822, our author made a second visit to Paris, where he resided for a considerable time, with his amiable wife and family. The fame of his genius, his social yet unpretending manners, and his musical talents and conversation, acquired him much esteem with the most eminent literary and literary-loving characters of the French capital.

Previous to Mr. Moore leaving Paris, the British nobility and gentry resident in that capital gave him a most splendid dinner at Roberts's. About sixty persons were present ; Lord Trimblestown was in the chair, supported on his right by Mr. Moore, and on his left by the Earl of Granard, and the proceedings at this farewell festival, which lasted till "soberkerchifeed morn " warned the company to depart, proved how well the poet had endeared himself to an extended circle, not less by his private worth and social qualities, than the brilliancy of his talents.

In 1823, Mr. Moore published *The Loves of the Angels,* of which two French translations soon after appeared in Paris. While Mr. Moore was composing this poem, Lord Byron, who then resided in Italy, was, by a singular coincidence, writing a similar poem, with the title of *Heaven and Earth,* both of them having taken the subject from the second verse of the sixth chapter of Genesis : " And it came to pass, that the sons of God saw the daughters of men that they were fair; and they took them wives of all which they chose."

We have already alluded to our author's *Memoirs of Captain Rock,* the celebrated " Rinaldo Rinaldini" of Ireland ; or rather the designation adopted by the "Rob Roys" of that unfortunately divided country. Mr. Moore afterwards published a *Life of Sheridan,* which, from the sources of information open to him, is, in a literary point of view at least, a valuable acquisition to the lovers of biography. But the vigorous and, alas ! " ower true" stanzas which he wrote on the death of that singularly-gifted man, and the treatment he experienced at the hands of the little great, are so brilliant that, brief as they are, they somewhat blind the reader to the more sober merits of the prose memoir. Perhaps the strong sympathy expressed by the poet, led the public to expect too much from the biographer. It is certain however, that the *Life* has been severely criticised ; even royalty, it is said, did not disdain to direct a not unpointed jest against the work. A gentleman, in the presence of the late King George IV, speaking of the work in question, declared that Moore had murdered his friend. " You are too severe," said his Majesty; "I cannot admit that Mr. Moore has *murdered* Sheridan, but he has certainly *attempted his life.*"

We here annex a list of Mr. Moore's works, with their respective dates of publication, as far as we have been able to verify them.

The Odes of Anacreon translated into English verse, with notes, dedicated by permission to his Royal Highness the Prince of Wales. 4to, 1800.

A Candid Appeal to Public Confidence, or, Considerations on the Dangers of the Present Crisis. 1803.

Corruption and Intolerance, two poems.

Poems, under the assumed name of the late Thomas Little, Esq. 8vo, 1803.

Epistles, Odes, and other Poems. 1806.

Letter to the Roman Catholics of Dublin. 8vo, 1810.

M. P., or the Blue Stocking, a comic opera, in three acts, performed at the Lyceum. 1811.

Intercepted Letters, or the Twopenny-Post Bag (in verse), by Thomas Brown the Younger. 8vo, 1812.—Of this upwards of fourteen editions have appeared in England.

A Selection of Irish Melodies, nine numbers.

Mr. Moore completed the translation of Sallust, which had been left unfinished by Mr. Arthur Murphy, and he superintended the printing of the work for the purchaser, Mr. Carpenter.

The Sceptic, a philosophical satire.

Lalla Rookh, an oriental romance. 1817.
The Fudge Family in Paris, letters in verse. 1818.
National Airs, six numbers.
Sacred Songs, two numbers.
Ballads, Songs, etc.
Tom Crib's Memorial to Congress, in verse. 1819.
Trifles, Reprinted, in verse.
Loves of the Angels. 1823.
Rhymes on the Road, extracted from the journal of a travelling member of the Pococurante Society. 1823.
Miscellaneous Poems, by different members of the Pococurante Society.
Fables for the Holy Alliance, in verse. 1823.
Ballads, Songs, Miscellaneous Poems, etc.
Memoirs of Captain Rock. 1824.
The Life of Richard Brinsley Sheridan. 1825.
The Epicurean. 1827.
Odes on Cash, Corn, Catholics, etc. 1829.
Evenings in Greece. 1829.
Life and Death of Lord Edward Fitzgerald. 1831.
Life of Lord Byron. 1831.
The Summer Fête. 1832.
Travels of an Irish Gentleman in search of a Religion. 1833.
The Fudges in England. 1835.
History of Ireland. 1835.
Alciphron. 1840.

For *Lalla Rookh* Mr. Moore received 3,000 guineas of Messrs. Longman and Co. For the *Life of Sheridan* he was paid 2,000 guineas by the same house. —Mr. Moore for many years enjoyed an annuity of 500*l.* from Power, the music-seller, for the *Irish Melodies* and other lyrical pieces; and he was, in the Whiggish days of that journal, engaged to write for the *Times* at a salary of 500*l.* a-year.

It is well known that the Memoirs of Lord Byron, written by himself, had been deposited in the keeping of Mr. Moore, and designed as a legacy for his benefit. It is also known that the latter, with the consent and at the desire of his lordship, had sold the manuscript to Mr. Murray, the bookseller, for the sum of two thousand guineas. These memoirs being however lost to the world, it may be worth while even at this distance of time to revert to the particulars of their destruction. Indeed in no sketch, however slight, of the life of Moore could these details be properly omitted, showing, as we think they do, the sensitive delicacy and chivalrous generosity of his character. The leading facts were related in the following letter addressed by Mr. Moore to the English journals:—

"Without entering into the respective claims of Mr. Murray and myself to the property in these memoirs (a question which, now that they are destroyed, can be but of little moment to any one), it is sufficient to say that, believing the manuscript still to be mine, I placed it at the disposal of Lord Byron's sister, Mrs. Leigh, with the sole reservation of a protest against its total destruction—at least without previous perusal and consultation among the parties.

The majority of the persons present disagreed with this opinion, *and it was the only point upon which there did exist any difference between us.* The manuscript was, accordingly, torn and burnt before our eyes; and I immediately paid to Mr. Murray, in the presence of the gentlemen assembled, two thousand guineas, with interest, etc., being the amount of what I owed him upon the security of my bond, and for which I now stand indebted to my publishers, Messrs. Longman and Co.

"Since then the family of Lord Byron have, in a manner highly honourable to themselves, proposed an arrangement, by which the sum thus paid to Mr. Murray might be reimbursed to me; but, from feelings and considerations which it is unnecessary here to explain, I have respectfully, but peremptorily, declined their offer."

We deem it proper to lay before our readers the various opinions, *pro et contra,* to which this letter of Mr. Moore gave rise. It is but justice, however, to Mr. Moore to premise, that neither by those who regretted the burning of Byron's Memoirs, as a public loss, nor by those who condemned it as a dereliction of the most important duty he owed to the memory and fame of his noble-minded friend, have Mr. Moore's honour, disinterestedness, or delicacy—extreme delicacy—ever been in the slightest degree impeached. The enemies of "The Burning" said, that Mr. Moore's *explanatory* letter was an ingenious but not an ingenuous one—for that, at any rate, it threw no light on the subject. They cavilled at the words "and it was the *only* point on which there did exist any difference between us," professing to wonder what other "point" of any consequence could possibly have been in discussion, save that of preserving or destroying the manuscript. They could not see, or were incapable of feeling, what paramount sense of delicacy or duty could operate upon a mind like Mr. Moore's to counterbalance the delicacy and duty due to his dead friend's fame, which, according to them, he had thus abandoned to a sea of idle speculation. Moreover they were unable to comprehend what business Mr. Murray the bookseller, or any of the gentlemen present, had with the business, when Mr. Moore had redeemed the MS., "with interest, etc.," and with his own money (that is, the sum he borrowed for the purpose). Finally, it was past their understanding to conceive, how any person could allow his own fair, just, and honourably-acquired property to be burnt and destroyed before his eyes, and against his own protested opinion, even if, from an honest but too sensitive deference for others, he had conceded so far as to withhold its publication to "a more convenient season ," or simply to preserve it as a precious relic in his family.

To this, the firm supporters of church and state—the pure sticklers for public morals—the friends of decorum and decency—the respecters of the inviolability of domestic privacy—the foes to unlicensed wit and poetic licence—the disinterested and tender regarders of Lords Byron's character itself—one and all, proudly replied, that Mr. Moore had performed one of the most difficult and most delicate duties that ever fell to the lot of man, friend, citizen, or christian to perform, in the most manly, friendly, patriotic, and christian-like manner. As a man, he had nobly sacrificed his private interest and opinion, out of respect to Lord Byron's living connections; as a friend, he had ev iced a real and rare friendship by with-holding, at his own personal loss, those self-and-thoughtlessly-intruded specks and deformities of a great character from the popular gaze, which delights too much to feast on the infirmities of noble minds.

The private and particular friends of Mr. Moore briefly and triumphantly referred to his unspotted character,

which never yet the breath of calumny had tainted, and they properly condemned uncharitable conjecture on a subject of which the most that could be said was

—— causa latet, vis est notissima.

The *Examiner* newspaper gave the subjoined statement, which, if properly authenticated, would at once set the matter at rest, to the entire justification of Mr. Moore:

"We were going to allude again this week to the question between Mr. Moore and the public, respecting the destruction of Lord Byron's Memoirs. We have received several letters, expressing the extreme mortification of the writers on learning the fact, and venting their indignation in no very measured terms against the perpetrators; and we should not have concealed our own opinion that, however nobly Mr. Thomas Moore may have acted as regards his own interest, his *published letters* make out no justification either in regard to his late illustrious friend, whose reputation was thus abandoned without that defence, which probably his own pen could alone furnish, of many misrepresented passages in his conduct; or in regard to the world, which is thus robbed of a treasure that can never be replaced. But we have learnt one fact, which puts a different face upon the whole matter. It is, that *Lord Byron himself did not wish the Memoirs published*. How they came into the hands of Mr. Moore and the bookseller —for what purpose and under what reservations— we shall probably be at liberty to explain at a future time, for the present, we can only say that such is the fact, as the noble poet's intimate friends can testify."

The explanation here hinted at has, however, never (to our knowledge at least) been given, and looking to the years which have since elapsed, in all probability never will.

Such were the conflicting opinions of the time relative to this painfully delicate subject, in which, though we confess that all the rights of the public, and also the legitimate interest which will be felt by ages yet to come, in the character and mind of the great poet of our age seem to have been sacrificed to the prudery of Lord Byron's connections, Mr. Moore's conduct seems irreproachable, except on the score of a too fastidious delicacy. It has been stated on reputable authority that Byron was desirous for the posthumous publication of his Memoirs, and to have intrusted them to Mr. Moore, as a safeguard against that very accident into which his deference to the relations and friends of the illustrious deceased actually betrayed them. If this be correct, the sacrifice is the more to be regretted, though it is still impossible to discommend the feeling which actuated Mr. Moore.

The extempore song, addressed by Lord Byron to Mr. Moore, on the latter's visit to Italy, proves the familiar intercourse and friendship that subsisted between them. The following stanzas are very expressive:—

Were 't the last drop in the well,
As I gasp'd upon the brink,
Ere my fainting spirit fell,
'T is to *thee* that I would drink.

In that water, as this wine,
The libation I would pour
Should be—Peace to thine and mine,
And a health to *thee*, Tom Moore.

When Lord Byron had published his celebrated satire of *English Bards and Scotch Reviewers*, in which our poet, in common with most of his distinguished contemporaries was visited rather "too roughly" by the noble modern Juvenal, his lordship expected to be "called out," as the fashionable phrase is, but no one had courage to try his prowess in the field, save Mr. Moore, who did not relish the joke about "Little's leadless pistols," and sent a letter to his lordship in the nature of a challenge, but which he, by his leaving the country, did not receive. On Byron's return, Mr. Moore made inquiry if he had received the epistle, and stated that, on account of certain changes in his circumstances, he wished to recall it, and become the friend of Byron, through Rogers, the author of *The Pleasures of Memory*, and who was intimate with both the distinguished bards. The letter, addressed to the care of Mr. Hanson, had been mislaid; search was made for it, and Byron, who at first did not like this offer, of one hand with a pistol, and the other to shake in fellowship, felt very awkward. On the letter being recovered, however, he delivered it unopened to Mr. Moore, and they afterwards continued to the last most particular friends.

It is but justice to the unquestionable courage of Moore to observe here, that though Byron had stated the truth about the said "leadless pistols," he had not stated the whole truth. The facts were these: Mr. Jeffrey, the celebrated critic, and editor of the *Edinburgh Review*, had, in "good set phrase," abused the Poems of Thomas Little, Esq., *alias* Thomas Moore, Esq.; and the latter, not choosing to put up with the flagellation of the *then* modern Aristarchus, challenged him. When they arrived at Chalk Farm, the place fixed on for the duel, the police were ready, and deprived them of their fire-arms. On drawing their contents, the compound of "villanous saltpetre" was found, but the cold lead,

> The pious metal most in requisition
> On such occasions,

had somehow disappeared. The cause was this: One of the balls had fallen out in the carriage, and the seconds, with a laudable anxiety to preserve the public peace, to save the shedding of such valuable blood, and to make both equal, drew the other ball.

Concluding here our slight biographical notice, we proceed to hazard a few—very few remarks upon the merits and blemishes of Mr. Moore's poetical style. The grand and pervading defect is the absence of plainness, simplicity, repose. Its unvarying brilliancy and never-ending glitter at once dazzles and fatigues the reader's attention; in his longer poems injuriously interfering with the interest of the narrative. In the author's smaller pieces this defect is less perceptible, and in many of them does not exist. Some of his lighter poems, among which we would be understood to quote a portion of his Epistles and other pieces written during his visit to America, are models of tenderness, warmth, and passion, without a tinge of grossness to sully their brilliancy. Others of Mr. Moore's minor productions are chiefly remarkable for the inordinate length of the notes appended to them. These, though creditable evidences of his college studies, add little to the enjoyment of the reader.

Turning to the greatest and most elaborate of our author's works, Lalla Rookh, we find it singularly faithful in what we would call its oriental costume; the colouring, imagery, gorgeousness of the poem, are all richly Asiatic. The beauteous forms, the dazzling splendours, the breathing odours of the East, have found in Moore a kindred poet. But while it is more splendid in imagery, and more rich in sparkling thoughts and original conceptions, and more fall indeed of exquisite pictures both of all sorts of beauties and virtues, and all sorts of sufferings and crimes, than any other poem we know of, we rather think we speak the sense of all classes of readers, when we add, that the effect of the whole is to excite admiration rather than any warmer sentiment of delight. It has been observed by some very zealous admirers of Mr. Moore's genius, that you cannot open his book without finding a cluster of beauties in every page. Now, this is only another way of expressing what we think its greatest defect. Mr. Moore is, in fact, too lavish of his gems and sweets; and it may truly be said, that he would be richer with half his wealth. His works are not only of rich materials and graceful design, but they are everywhere glistening with small beauties and transitory inspirations—sudden flashes of fancy that blaze out and perish; like earthborn meteors that crackle in the lower sky, and unseasonably divert our eyes

from the great and lofty bodies which pursue their harmonious courses in a serener region.

We have thought it right to point out the faults of our author's poetry, particularly in respect to Lalla Rookh; but it would be quite unjust to characterise that splendid poem by its faults, which are infinitely less conspicuous than its beauties. There are passages over which poetry seems to have breathed its richest enchantment. And though it is certainly to be regretted that he should occasionally have broken the measure with more frivolous strains, or filled up its intervals with a sort of brilliant falsetto, it should never be forgotten, that his excellencies are as peculiar to himself as his faults, and, on the whole, we may assert, more characteristic of his genius.

The Fire-Worshippers appears to us to be indisputably the finest and most powerful poem in Lalla Rookh. With all the richness and beauty of diction that belong to the best parts of Mokanna, it has a far more interesting story, and is not liable to the objections that arise against the contrivance and structure of the leading poem.

The Fudge Family in Paris, a humorous work, written partly in the style of The Twopenny-Post Bag, is another of the author's highly popular productions. Even those who disapprove of the author's politics must admire his wit; though every impartial reader must perceive that his satires are directed with far more regard to party than to impartial justice.

Mr. Moore, in his preface to the Loves of the Angels, states, that he had somewhat hastened his publication, to avoid the disadvantage of having his work appear after his friend Lord Byron's Heaven and Earth; or, as he ingeniously expresses it, "by an earlier appearance in the literary horizon, to give myself the chance of what astronomers call a heliacal rising, before the luminary in whose light I was to be lost should appear." This was an amiable, but, by no means, a reasonable modesty. The light that plays round Mr. Moore's verses, tender, exquisite, and brilliant, was in no danger of being extinguished even in the splendour of Lord Byron's genius.

However great the popularity Mr. Moore may have acquired as the author of Lalla Rookh, etc., it is probably as the author of the Irish Melodies that he will descend to posterity unrivalled and alone. Lord Byron justly and prophetically observed, that "Moore is one of the few writers who will survive the age in which he so deservedly flourishes. He will live in his Irish Melodies; they will go down to posterity with the music; both will last as long as Ireland, or as music and poetry."

With this splendid compliment from the greatest poet of modern times, we terminate our brief memoir—a mere outline, which the reader will find graphically filled up in the following pages, by the vivid and delightful pen of Mr. Moore himself.

THE

POETICAL WORKS

OF

THOMAS MOORE.

TO THE

MARQUIS OF LANSDOWNE,

IN GRATEFUL REMEMBRANCE OF NEARLY FORTY YEARS OF MUTUAL ACQUAINTANCE AND FRIENDSHIP.

THIS EDITION IS INSCRIBED,

WITH THE SINCEREST FEELINGS OF AFFECTION AND RESPECT,

BY

THOMAS MOORE.

PREFACE.

FINDING it to be the wish of my Publishers that this collection should be accompanied by some prefatory matter, illustrating, by a few biographical memoranda, the progress of my humble literary career, I have consented, though not, I confess, without some scruple and hesitation, to comply with their request. In no country is there so much curiosity felt respecting the interior of the lives of public men as in England; but, on the other hand, in no country is he who ventures to tell his own story so little safe from the imputation of vanity and self-display.

The whole of the "Odes of Anacreon," as well as the greater part of the "Juvenile Poems," were written between the sixteenth and the twenty-third year of the author's age. But I had begun still earlier, not only to rhyme but to publish. A sonnet to my schoolmaster, Mr. Samuel Whyte, written in my fourteenth year, appeared at the time in a Dublin magazine, called the "Anthologia,"—the first, and, I fear, almost only, creditable attempt in periodical literature of which Ireland has to boast. I had even at an earlier period (1793) sent to this magazine two short pieces of verse, prefaced by a note to the editor, requesting the insertion of the "following attempts of a youthful muse;" and the fear and trembling with which I ventured upon this step were agreeably dispelled, not only by the appearance of the contributions, but still more by

(1) Some confused notion of this fact has led the writer of a Memoir prefixed to my poems, printed at Zwickau, to

my finding myself, a few months after, hailed as "Our esteemed correspondent, T. M."

It was in the pages of this publication, — where the whole of the poem was extracted,—that I first met with the "Pleasures of Memory;" and to this day, when I open the volume of the "Anthologia" which contains it, the very form of the type and colour of the paper brings back vividly to my mind the delight with which I first read that poem.

My schoolmaster, Mr. Whyte, though amusingly vain, was a good and kind-hearted man; and, as a teacher of public reading and elocution, had long enjoyed considerable reputation. Nearly thirty years before I became his pupil, Richard Brinsley Sheridan, then about eight or nine years of age, had been placed by Mrs. Sheridan under his care; (1) and, strange to say, was, after about a year's trial, pronounced, both by tutor and parent, to be "an incorrigible dunce." Among those who took lessons from him as private pupils were several young ladies of rank, belonging to those great Irish families who still continued to lend to Ireland the enlivening influence of their presence, and made their country-seats, through a great part of the year, the scenes of refined as well as hospitable festivity. The Miss Montgomerys, to whose rare beauty the pencil of Sir Joshua has given immortality, were among those whom my worthy preceptor most boasted of as

state that Brinsley Sheridan was my tutor!—"Great attention was paid to his education by his tutor, Sheridan."

pupils; and, I remember, his description of them long haunted my boyish imagination, as though they were not earthly women, but some spiritual "creatures of the element."

About thirty or forty years before the period of which I am speaking, an eager taste for private theatrical performances had sprung up among the higher ranks of society in Ireland; and at Carton, the seat of the Duke of Leinster, at Castletown, Marley, and other great houses, private plays were got up, of which, in most instances, the superintendence was entrusted to Mr. Whyte, and in general the prologue or the epilogue contributed by his pen. At Marley, the seat of the Latouches, where the "Masque of Comus" was performed in the year 1776, while my old master supplied the prologue, no less distinguished a hand than that of our "ever-glorious Grattan" (1) furnished the epilogue. This relic of his pen, too, is the more memorable, as being, I believe, the only poetical composition he was ever known to produce.

At the time when I first began to attend his school, Mr. Whyte still continued, to the no small alarm of many parents, to encourage a taste for acting among his pupils. In this line I was long his favourite *show*-scholar; and among the play-bills introduced in his volume, to illustrate the occasions of his own prologues and epilogues, there is one of a play got up in the year 1790, at Lady Borrowes's private theatre in Dublin, where, among the items of the evening's entertainment, is "An Epilogue, *A Squeeze to St. Paul's*, Master Moore."

With acting, indeed, is associated the very first attempt at verse-making to which my memory enables me to plead guilty. It was at a period, I think, even earlier than the date last mentioned, that, while passing the summer holidays, with a number of other young people, at one of those bathing-places, in the neighbourhood of Dublin, which afford such fresh and healthful retreats to its inhabitants, it was proposed among us that we should combine together in some theatrical performance; and the "Poor Soldier" and a Harlequin Pantomime being the entertainments agreed upon, the parts of Patrick and the motley hero fell to my share. I was also encouraged to write and recite an appropriate epilogue on the occasion; and the following lines, alluding to our speedy return to school, and remarkable only for their having lived so long in my memory, formed part of this juvenile effort : —

Our Pantaloon, who did so aged look,
Must now resume his youth, his task, his book :
Our Harlequin, who skipp'd, laugh'd, danced, and died,
Must now stand trembling by his master's side.

I have thus been led back, step by step, from an early date to one still earlier, with the view of ascertaining, for those who take any interest in literary biography, at what period I first showed an

(1) Byron

aptitude for the now common craft of verse-making; and the result is—so far back in childhood lies the epoch—that I am really unable to say at what age I first began to act, sing, and rhyme.

To these different talents, such as they were, the gay and social habits prevailing in Dublin afforded frequent opportunities of display; while, at home, a most amiable father, and a mother such as in heart and head has rarely been equalled, furnished me with that purest stimulus to exertion—the desire to please those whom we, at once, most love and most respect. It was, I think, a year or two after my entrance into college, that a masque written by myself, and of which I had adapted one of the songs to the air of Haydn's Spirit-Song, was acted, under our own humble roof in Aungier Street, by my elder sister, myself, and one or two other young persons. The little drawing-room over the shop was our grand place of representation, and young——, now an eminent professor of music in Dublin, enacted for us the part of orchestra at the piano-forte.

It will be seen from all this, that, however imprudent and premature was my first appearance in the London world as an author, it is only lucky that I had not much earlier assumed that responsible character; in which case the public would probably have treated my nursery productions in much the same manner in which that sensible critic, my Uncle Toby, would have disposed of the "work which the great Lipsius produced on the day he was born."

While thus the turn I had so early shown for rhyme and song was, by the gay and sociable circle in which I lived, called so encouragingly into play, a far deeper feeling—and, I should hope, power—was at the same time awakened in me by the mighty change then working in the political aspect of Europe, and the stirring influence it had begun to exercise on the spirit and hopes of Ireland. Born of Catholic parents, I had come into the world with the slave's yoke around my neck; and it was all in vain that the fond ambition of a mother looked forward to the Bar as opening a career that might lead her son to affluence and honour. Against the young Papist all such avenues to distinction were closed; and even the University, the professed source of public education, was to him "a fountain sealed." Can any one now wonder that a people thus trampled upon should have hailed the first dazzling outbreak of the French Revolution as a signal to the slave, wherever suffering, that the day of his deliverance was near at hand. I remember being taken by my father (1792) to one of the dinners given in honour of that great event, and sitting upon the knee of the chairman while the following toast was enthusiastically sent round :—"May the breezes from France fan our Irish Oak into verdure."

In a few months after, was passed the memorable Act of 1793, sweeping away some of the most monstrous of the remaining sanctions of the penal code; and I was myself among the first of the young

Helots of the land who hastened to avail themselves of the new privilege of being educated in their country's university,—though still excluded from all share in those college honours and emoluments by which the ambition of the youths of the ascendant class was stimulated and rewarded. As I well knew that, next to my attaining some of these distinctions, my showing that I *deserved* to attain them would most gratify my anxious mother, I entered as candidate for a scholarship, and (as far as the result of the examination went) successfully. But, of course, the mere barren credit of the effort was all I enjoyed for my pains.

It was in this year (1794), or about the beginning of the next, that I remember having, for the first time, tried my hand at political satire. In their very worst times of slavery and suffering, the happy disposition of my countrymen had kept their cheerfulness still unbroken and buoyant; and, at the period of which I am speaking, the hope of a brighter day dawning upon Ireland had given to the society of the middle classes in Dublin a more than usual flow of hilarity and life. Among other gay results of this festive spirit, a club, or society, was instituted by some of our most convivial citizens, one of whose objects was to burlesque, good-humouredly, the forms and pomps of royalty. With this view they established a sort of mock kingdom, of which Dalkey, a small island near Dublin, was made the seat, and an eminent pawnbroker, named Stephen Armitage, much renowned for his agreeable singing, was the chosen and popular monarch.

Before public affairs had become too serious for such pastime, it was usual to celebrate yearly, at Dalkey, the day of this sovereign's accession; and, among the gay scenes that still live in my memory, there are few it recalls with more freshness than the celebration, on a fine Sunday in summer, of one of these anniversaries of King Stephen's coronation. The picturesque sea-views from that spot, the gay crowds along the shores, the innumerable boats, full of life, floating about, and, above all, that true spirit of mirth which the Irish temperament never fails to lend to such meetings, rendered the whole a scene not easily forgotten. The state ceremonies of the day were performed, with all due gravity, within the ruins of an ancient church that stands on the island, where his mock majesty bestowed the order of knighthood upon certain favoured personages, and among others, I recollect, upon Incledon, the celebrated singer, who arose from under the touch of the royal sword with the appropriate title of Sir Charles Melody. There was also selected, for the favours of the crown on that day, a lady of no ordinary poetic talent, Mrs. Battier, who had gained much fame by some spirited satires in the manner of Churchill, and whose kind encouragement of my early attempts in versification were to me a source of much pride. This lady, as was officially announced, in the course of the day, had been appointed his majesty's poetess

laureate, under the style and title of Henrietta Countess of Laurel.

There could hardly be devised a more apt vehicle for lively political satire than this gay travesty of monarchical power, and its showy appurtenances, so temptingly supplied. The very day, indeed, after this commemoration, there appeared, in the usual record of Dalkey state intelligence, an amusing proclamation from the king, offering a large reward in *cronebanes* (1) to the finder or finders of his majesty's crown, which, owing to his "having measured both sides of the road" in his pedestrian progress from Dalkey on the preceding night, had unluckily fallen from the royal brow.

It is not to be wondered at, that whatever natural turn I may have possessed for the lighter skirmishing of satire should have been called into play by so pleasant a field for its exercise as the state affairs of the Dalkey kingdom afforded; and, accordingly, my first attempt in this line was an Ode to his Majesty, King Stephen, contrasting the happy state of security in which he lived among his merry lieges, with the "metal coach," and other such precautions against mob violence, said to have been adopted at that time by his royal brother of England. Some portions of this juvenile squib still live in my memory; but they fall far too short of the lively demands of the subject to be worth preserving, even as juvenilia.

In college, the first circumstance that drew any attention to my rhyming powers was my giving in a theme, in English verse, at one of the quarterly examinations. As the sort of short essays required on those occasions were considered, in general, as a mere matter of form, and were written, at that time, I believe, invariably, in Latin prose, the appearance of a theme in English verse could hardly fail to attract some notice. It was, therefore, with no small anxiety that, when the moment for judging of the themes arrived, I saw the examiners of the different divisions assemble, as usual, at the bottom of the hall for that purpose. Still more trying was it, when I perceived that the reverend inquisitor, in whose hands was my fate, had left the rest of the awful group, and was bending his steps towards the table where I was seated. Leaning across to me, he asked suspiciously whether the verses which I had just given in were my own; and, on my answering in the affirmative, added these cheering words, " They do you great credit ; and I shall not fail to recommend them to the notice of the Board." This result of a step, ventured upon with some little fear and scruple, was of course very gratifying to me; and the premium I received from the Board was a well-bound copy of the "Travels of Anacharsis," together with a certificate, stating, in not very lofty Latin, that this reward had been conferred upon me, " propter laudabilem in versibus componendis pregressum."

(1) Irish half-pence, so called.

The idea of attempting a version of some of the "Songs or Odes of Anacreon" had very early occurred to me; and a specimen of my first ventures in this undertaking may be found in the "Dublin Magazine" already referred to, where, in the number of that work for February, 1794, appeared a "Paraphrase of Anacreon's Fifth Ode, by T. Moore." As it may not be uninteresting to future and better translators of the poet to compare this schoolboy experiment with my later and more laboured version of the same ode, I shall here extract the specimen found in the "Anthologia:"—

> "Let us, with the clustering vine,
> The rose, Love's blushing flower, entwine.
> Fancy's hand our chaplets wreathing,
> Vernal sweets around us breathing,
> We'll gaily drink, full goblets quaffing,
> At frighted Care securely laughing.

> "Rose! thou balmy-scented flower,
> Rear'd by Spring's most fostering power,
> Thy dewy blossoms, opening bright,
> To gods themselves can give delight;
> And Cypria's child, with roses crown'd,
> Trips with each Grace the mazy round.

> "Bind my brows,—I'll tune the lyre;
> Love my rapturous strains shall fire.
> Near Bacchus' grape-encircled shrine,
> While roses fresh my brows entwine,
> Led by the winged train of Pleasures,
> I'll dance with nymphs to sportive measures."

In pursuing further this light task, the only object I had for some time in view was to lay before the Board a select number of the odes I had then translated, with a hope,—suggested by the kind encouragement I had already received,—that they might consider them as deserving of some honour or reward. Having experienced much hospitable attention from Doctor Kearney, one of the senior fellows, (1) a man of most amiable character, as well as of refined scholarship, I submitted to his perusal the manuscript of my translation as far as it had then proceeded, and requested his advice respecting my intention of laying it before the Board. On this latter point his opinion was such as, with a little more thought, I might have anticipated, namely, that he did not see how the Board of the University could lend their sanction, by any public reward, to writings of so convivial and amatory a nature as were almost all those of Anacreon. He very good-naturedly, however, lauded my translation, and advised me to complete and publish it. I was also

(1) Appointed Provost of the University in the year 1799, and made afterwards Bishop of Ossory.

(2) When the monument to Provost Baldwin, which stands in the hall of the College of Dublin, arrived from Italy, there came in the same packing-case with it two copies of this work of Spaletti, one of which was presented by Dr. Troy, the Roman Catholic archbishop, as a gift from the Pope to the Library of the University, and the other (of which I was subsequently favoured with the use,) he

indebted to him for the use, during my task, of Spaletti's curious publication, giving a fac-simile of those pages of a MS. in the Vatican Library which contain the Odes, or "Symposiacs," attributed to Anacreon. (2) And here I shall venture to add a few passing words on a point which I once should have thought it profanation to question,—the authenticity of these poems. The cry raised against their genuineness by Robertellus and other enemies of Henry Stephen, when that eminent scholar first introduced them to the learned world, may be thought to have long since entirely subsided, leaving their claim to so ancient a paternity safe and unquestioned. But I am forced to confess, however reluctantly, that there appear to me strong grounds for pronouncing these light and beautiful lyrics to be merely modern fabrications. Some of the reasons that incline me to adopt this unwelcome conclusion are thus clearly stated by the same able scholar, to whom I am indebted for the emendations of my own juvenile Greek ode: — "I do not see how it is possible, if Anacreon had written chiefly in Iambic dimeter verse, that Horace should have wholly neglected that metre. I may add that, of those fragments of Anacreon, of whose genuineness, from internal evidence, there can be no doubt, almost all are written in one or other of the lighter Horatian metres, and scarcely one in Iambic dimeter verse. This may be seen by looking through the list in Fischer."

The unskilful attempt at Greek verse from my own pen, which is found prefixed to the Translation, was intended originally to illustrate a picture, representing Anacreon conversing with the Goddess of Wisdom, from which the frontispiece to the first edition of the work was taken. Had I been brought up with a due fear of the laws of prosody before my eyes, I certainly should not have dared to submit so untutored a production to the criticism of the trained prosodians of the English schools. At the same time, I cannot help adding that, as far as music, distinct from metre, is concerned, I am much inclined to prefer the ode as originally written to its present corrected shape; and that, at all events, I entertain but very little doubt as to which of the two a composer would most willingly set to music.

For the means of collecting the materials of the notes appended to the Translation, I was chiefly indebted to an old library adjoining St. Patrick's Cathedral, called, from the name of the archbishop who founded it, Marsh's Library. Through my

presented, in like manner, to my friend, Dr. Kearney. Thus, curiously enough, while Anacreon in English was considered—and, I grant, on no unreasonable grounds—as a work to which grave collegiate authorities could not openly lend their sanction, Anacreon in Greek was thought no unfitting present to be received by a Protestant bishop, through the medium of a Catholic archbishop, from the hands of his holiness the Pope.

acquaintance with the deputy librarian, the Rev. Mr. Cradock, I enjoyed the privilege of constant access to this collection, even at that period of the year when it is always closed to the public. On these occasions I used to be locked in there alone; and to the many solitary hours which, both at the time I am now speaking of and subsequently, I passed in hunting through the dusty tomes of this old library, I owe much of that odd and out-of-the-way sort of reading which may be found scattered through some of my earlier writings.

Early in the year 1799, while yet in my nineteenth year, I left Ireland for the first time, and proceeded to London, with the two not very congenial objects, of keeping my terms at the Middle Temple, and publishing, by subscription, my Translation of Anacreon. One of those persons to whom, through the active zeal of friends, some part of my manuscript had been submitted before it went to press, was Doctor Laurence, the able friend of Burke; and, as an instance, however slight, of that ready variety of learning, as well the lightest as the most solid, for which Laurence was so remarkable, the following extract from the letter written by him, in returning the manuscript to my friend Doctor Hume, may not be without some interest: —

"Dec. 20. 1799.

"I return you the four odes which you were so kind to communicate for my poor opinion. They are, in many parts, very elegant and poetical; and, in some passages, Mr. Moore has added a pretty turn not to be found in the original. To confess the truth, however, they are, in not a few places, rather more paraphrastical than suits my notion (perhaps an incorrect notion) of translation.

"In the fifty-third ode there is, in my judgment, a no less sound than beautiful emendation suggested—would you suppose it?—by a Dutch lawyer. Mr. M. possibly may not be aware of it. I have endeavoured to express the sense of it in a couplet interlined with pencil. Will you allow me to add, that I am not certain whether the translation has not missed the meaning, too, in the former part of that passage which seems to me to intend a distinction and climax of pleasure:—'It is sweet even to prove it among the briery paths; it is sweet again, plucking, to cherish with tender hands, and carry to the fair, the flower of love.' This is nearly literal, including the conjectural correction of Mynheer Medenbach. If this be right, instead of

' 'T is sweet to dare the tangled fence.'

I would propose something to this effect : —

'T is sweet the rich perfume to prove,
As by the dewy bush you rove;
'T is sweet to dare the tangled fence,
To cull the timid beauty thence,
To wipe with tender hands away
The tears that on its blushes lay, (1)
Then, to the bosom of the fair,
The flower of love in triumph bear.

"I would drop altogether the image of the stems ' dropping with gems.' I believe it is a confused and false metaphor, unless the painter should take the figure of Aurora from Mrs. Hastings.

"There is another emendation of the same critic in the following line, which Mr. M. may seem, by accident, to have sufficiently expressed in the phrase of 'roses shed their light.'

"I scribble this in very great haste, but fear that you and Mr. Moore will find me too long, minute, and impertinent. Believe me to be, very sincerely,

"Your obedient, humble servant,

"F. LAURENCE."

(1) "Query, if it ought not to be lie? The line might run,
With tender hand the tears to brush,
That give new softness to its blush (or, its flush).

ODES OF ANACREON,

TRANSLATED INTO ENGLISH VERSE, WITH NOTES.

DEDICATION.

TO HIS ROYAL HIGHNESS THE PRINCE OF WALES.

SIR,

IN allowing me to dedicate this Work to Your Royal Highness, you have conferred upon me an honour which I feel very sensibly : and I have only to regret that the pages which you have thus distinguished are not more deserving of such illustrious patronage.

Believe me, SIR, with every sentiment of respect,

Your Royal Highness's
Very grateful and devoted Servant,

THOMAS MOORE.

ADVERTISEMENT.

IT may be necessary to mention, that, in arranging the Odes, the Translator has adopted the order of the Vatican MS. For those who wish to refer to the original, he has prefixed an Index, which marks the number of each Ode in Barnes and the other editions.

INDEX.

ODE.		BARNES.
1. ΑΝΑΚΡΕΩΝ ιδων με		63
2. Δοτε μοι λυρην' Ομηρου.		48
3. Αγε, ζωγραφων αριστε		49
4. Τον αργυρον τορευων		17

ODE.	BARNES.
5. Καλλιτεχνα μοι τορευσον.	18
6. Στερος πλεκων ποτ' ευρον	59
7. Λεγουσιν αἱ γυναικες	11
8. Ου μοι μελει τα Γυγου	15
9. Αρες με τους ϑεους σοι	31
10. Τι σοι ϑελεις ποιησω	12
11. Ερωτα κηριναν τις	10
12. Οἱ μεν καλην Κυθηβην	13
13. Θελω, ϑελω φιλησαι.	14
14. Ει φυλλα παντα δενδρων	32
15. Ερασμιη πελεια	9
16. Αγε, ζωγραφων αριστε	28
17. Γραφε μοι Βαθυλλον οὑτω.	29
18. Δοτε μοι, δοτε, γυναικες	21
19. Παρα την σκιην, Βαθυλλου.	22
20. Αἱ Μουσαι τον Ερωτα	30
21. Ἡ γη μελαινα πινει.	19
22. Ἡ Ταντολου ποτ' εστη	20
23. Θελω λεγειν Ατρειδας	1
24. Φυσις κερατα ταυροις	2
25. Συ μεν φιλη χελιδων.	33
26. Συ μεν λεγεις τα Θηβης	16
27. Εν ισχιοις μεν ἱπποι.	53
28. Ὁ ακηρ ὁ της Κυθηρης	45
29. Χαλεπον το μη φιλησαι	46
30. Εδοκουν οναρ τροχαζειν.	44
31. Ὑακινθινα με ραβδω.	7
32. Επι μυρσιναις τερειναις	4
33. Μεσονυκτιοις ποθ' ὡραις.	3
34. Μακαριζομεν σε, τεττιξ	43
35. Ερως ποτ' εν ροδοισι	40
36. Ὁ πλουτος ειγε χρυσου	23
37. Δια νυκτος εγκαθευδων	8
38. Ἱλαροι πιωμεν οινον.	41
39. Φιλω γεροντα τερπνον	47
40. Επειδη βροτος ετυχθην	24
41. Τι καλον εστι βαδιζειν	66
42. Ποθεω μεν Διονυσου.	42
43. Στερανους μεν κροταροισι	6
44. Το ροδον το των ερωτων.	5
45. Ὁταν πινω τον οινον.	25
46. Ιδε, πως εαρος ρανεντος.	37
47. Εγω γερων μεν ειμι.	38
48. Ὁταν ὁ Βαχχος εισελθη.	26
49. Του Διος ὁ παις Βαχχος	27
50. Ὁτ' εγω πιω τον οινον.	39
51. Μη με φυγης ορωσα.	34
52. Τι με τους νομους διδασκεις.	36
53. Ὁτ' εγω νεων ὁμιλον.	54
54. Ὁ ταυρος οὑτος, ω παι	35
55. Στεραινηρρου μετ' Ηρος.	51
56. Ὁ τον εν πονοις ατειρη.	50
57. Αρα τις τορευσε ποντον.	49
58. Ὁ δραπετης ὁ χρυσος.	66
59. Τον μελανοχρωτα βοτρυν.	52
60. Ανα βαρβιτον δοησω	64
61. Πολιοι μεν ἡμιν ηδη.	56
62. Αγε δη, φερ' ἡμιν, ω παι.	57
63. Τον Ερωτα γαρ τον ἁβρον	58

ODE.	BARNES.
64. Γουνουμαι σ' ελαφηβολε	60
65. Πωλε Θρηκιη, τι δη με.	61
66. Θεαων ανασσα, Κυπρι	62
67. Ω παι παρθενιον βλεπων	67
68. Εγω δ' ουτ' αν Αμαλθειης.	68

For the order of the rest, see the Notes.

----◦❊◦❊◦----

ODE

BY THE TRANSLATOR.

ΕΠΙ ῥοδινοις ταπησι,
Τηϊος ποτ' ὁ μελιςης
Ἱλαρος γελων εκειτο,
Μεθυων τε και λυριζων·
Αμφι αυτον οἱ δ' ερωτες
Ἁπαλοι συνεχορευσαν·
Ὁ βελη τα της Κυθηρης
Εποιει, ψυχης ὀἰστους·
Ὁ δε λευκα πορφυροισι
Κρινα συν ῥοδοισι πλεξας,
Εφιλει στερων γεροντα·
Ἡ δε ϑεαων ανασσα,
ΣΟΦΙΗ ποτ' εξ Ολυμπου
Εσορωσ' Ανακρεοντα,
Εσορωσα τους ερωτας,
Ὑπομειδιασασας ειπε·
Σοφε, δ' ὡς Ανακρεοντα
Τον σοφωτατον ἁπαντων,
Καλεουσιν οἱ σοφισται·
Τι, γερων, τεον βιον μεν
Τοις ερωσι, τω Λυαιω,
Κ' ουκ εμοι κρατειν εδωκας;
Τι φιλημα της Κυθηρης;
Τι κυπελλα του Λυαιου,
Αιει γ' ετρυφησας αδων,
Ουκ εμους νομους διδασκων,
Ουκ εμοι λαχων αωτον;
Ὁ δε Τηϊος μελιςης
Μητε δυσχεραινε, φησι,
Ὁτι, ϑεα, σου γ' ανευ μεν,
Ὁ σοφωτατος ἁπαντων
Παρα των σοφων κελουμαι·
Φιλεω, πιω, λυριζω,
Μετα των καλων γυναικων·
Αρελως δε τερπνα παιζω,
Ὡς λυρη γαρ, εμον ητορ
Ανακνει μουνως ερωτας·
Ὡδε βιοτου γαληνην
Φιλεων μαλιςα παντων,
Ου σοφος μελωδος ειμι;
Τις σοφωτερος μεν εστι;

CORRECTIONS OF THE PRECEDING ODE,

SUGGESTED BY AN EMINENT GREEK SCHOLAR.

Ἐπὶ πορφυρέοις τάπησι	Επι ῥοδινοις ταπητι
Τήϊός ποτ' ῳ'δοποιὸς	Τηϊος ποτ' ὁ μελιςης
ἱλαρὸς γελῶν ἔκειτο,	
μεθύων τε καὶ λυρίζων· 4	

περὶ δ᾿ αὐτὸν ἀμφ᾿ Ἔρωτες   Ἀμφι αυτον οἱ δ᾿ Ἐρωτες
τρομεροῖς ποσὶν χόρευον·   Ἀπαλοι συνεχορευσαν
τὰ βέλεμν ὁ μὲν Κυθήρης
ἐποίει καλῆς, δίστοὺς   Εποιει, ψυχης οιστους
πυρόεντας, ἐκ κεραυνοῦ·   9
ὁ δὲ λευκὰ καλλιφύλλοις
κρίνα σὺν ῥόδοισι πλέξας,
ἐρίλει στέφων γέροντα.
Κατὰ δ᾿ εὐθὺς ἐξ Ὀλύμπου   } Ἡ δὲ Θεκων ανασσα
Σοφὴ Θέαινα βᾶσα,   }
ἐτορῶτ᾿ Ἀνακρέοντα,   15
ἐτορῶσι τοὺς Ἔρωτας,
ὑπομειδιῶσά φησι·   Ὑπομειδιασσας ειπε
Σόφ᾿, —ἐπεὶ βροτῶν σὲ τοῦτο   Τον σοφωτατον απαντων
καλέουσι φῦλα πάντα,   19
καλέουσιν οἱ σοφισταί, —
τί, γέρων, μάτην ὀδεύεις
βιότου τρίβον τεοῦ μὲν
μετὰ τῶν καλῶν Ἐρώτων,   Τοις Ερωσι, τῳ Λυαιῳ
μετὰ τοῦ καλοῦ Λυαίου,   Κ᾿ ουκ εμοι κρατειν εδωκας
ἐμὲ δ᾿ ὧδε λὰξ ἀτίζεις;   25
τί φίλημα τῆς Κυθήρης,
τι κύπελλα τοῦ Λυαίου,   Αιει γ᾿ ετρυφησας αδων
ἐταεὶ τρυφῶν ἀείδεις,   Ουκ εμους νομευς διδασκων
ἐμὰ Θέσμι᾿ οὐ διδάσκων,   Ουκ εμον λαχων αωτον
ἐμὸν οὐ λαχὼν ἄωτον;   30
ὁ δὲ Τήϊος μελῳδὸς   } Μητε δυσχεραινε, φησι
Σὺ παρέκ νόου γε μή μοι   }
χαλέπαινε, φῆς᾿, ἄνευθε
ὅτι σεῦ σοφὸς καλοῦμαι   Ὅτι, Θεα, σου γ᾿ ανευ μεν
παρὰ τῶν σοφῶν ἁπάντων.   Ὁ σοφωτατος απαντων
Φιλέω, πίω, λυρίζω,   36
μετὰ τῶν καλῶν γυναικῶν,
ἀρελῶς δὲ τερπνὰ παίδων·

κιθάρη γὰρ, ὡς κέαρ μεῦ,   Ὡς λυρη γαρ, εμον ητορ
ἀναπνεῖ μόνους Ἔρωτας.
βιότου δὲ τὴν γαλήνην   41   Ὡδε βιοτου γαληνην
φιλέω μάλιςα πάντων,
σοφὸς οὐ μελῳδός εἰμι ;   Ου σοφος μελῳδος ειμι
τί σοφώτερον γένοιτ᾿ ἄν ;
ἰμέθεν σοφώτερος τίς ;   45   Τις σοφωτερος μεν εστι

REMARKS ON ANACREON.

THERE is but little known with certainty of the life of Anacreon. Chamæleon Heracleotes, (1) who wrote upon the subject, has been lost in the general wreck of ancient literature.

The editors of the poet have collected the few trifling anecdotes which are scattered through the extant authors of antiquity, and supplying the deficiency of materials by fictions of their own imagination, have arranged, what they call, a life of Anacreon. These specious fabrications are intended to indulge that interest which we naturally feel in the biography of illustrious men ; but it is rather a dangerous kind of illusion, as it confounds the limits of history and romance, (2) and is too often supported by unfaithful citation. (3)

Our poet was born in the city of Téos, (4) in the delicious region of Ionia, and the time of his birth appears to have been in the sixth century before Christ. (5) He flourished at that remarkable period, when, under the polished tyrants Hipparchus and Polycrates, Athens and Samos were become the rival asylums of genius. There is nothing certain known about his family, and those who pretend to

1. πορφυρέοις vox trisyllabica. Anacr. Fragm. xxix.
3. ed. Fischer. πορφυρέητ᾿ Ἀφροδίτη. Id. Fragm.
xxxvi. 1. σφαίρῃ δεῦτέ με πορφυρέῃ, ut legendum planc ex Athenæo. Ἀλιπορφύροις τάπητσι dixit Pseud-Anacreon, Od. viii. 2. Theocr. Id. xv. 125. πορφύρεοι δὲ τάπητες ἄνω, μαλαχώτεροι ὕπνω.

5. Tmesis pro ἀμφεχόρευσαν. Theocr. Id. vii. 142, πωτῶντο ξουθαὶ περι πίδακας ἀμφὶ μέλισσαι, h. e. ἀμφεπωτῶντο.

6. Pseud-Anacr. Od. lii. 12. τρομεροῖς ποσὶν χορεύει.

7. 10. ὁ μέν, hic—ὁ δὲ, ille, Bion. Id. 1. 82. χὼ μὲν οἰστοὺς, | ὃς δ᾿ ἐπὶ τόξον ἔβαινε, x. τ. λ. itidem de Amoribus.

8, 9. ἐποίει—ἐκ κεραυνοῦ. Pseud-Anacr. Od. xxviii. 18. τὸ δὲ βλέμμα νῦν ἀληθῶς | ἀπὸ τοῦ πυρὸς ποίησον.

10, 11. καλλιφύλλοις—ῥόδοισι. Pseud-Anacr. Od. v. 3. τὸ ῥόδον τὸ καλλίφυλλον.

13. Tmesis pro καταβᾶσα. Pseud-Anacr. Od, iii. 15. ἀνὰ δ᾿ εὐθὺ λύχνον ἅψας, h. e. ἀνάψας.

18. Supple ὄνομα, quo τοῦτο referatur. Eurip. Phœn. 12. τοῦτο γὰρ πατὴρ | ἔθετο. h. e. τοῦτο ὄνομα. Βροτῶν φῦλα πάντα adumbratur ex Pseud-Anacr. Od. iii. 4. μερόπων δὲ φῦλα πάντα.

21. Pseud-Anacr. Od. xxiv. 2. βιότου τρίβον ὀδεύειν.
25. Æsch. Eumen. 538. μηδὲ νιν, | χέρδος ἰδὼν, ἀθέῳ ποδὶ λὰξ ἄτι- | σῃς.

32. παρὲκ νόου γε μή μοι χαλέπαινε, ne præter ratio-nem in me sævi. Il.Υ. 133. Ἥρη, μὴ χαλέπαινε παρὲκ

νόον. Similem positionem particularum μή μοι exhibet Pseud-Anacr. Od. xxviii. 13.

(1) He is quoted by Athenæus εν τῳ περι του Ανα-κρεοντος·

(2) The History of Anacreon, by Gacon (le Poète sans fard, as he styles himself), is professedly a romance ; nor does Mademoiselle Scuderi, from whom he borrowed the idea, pretend to historical veracity in her account of Anacreon and Sappho. These, then, are allowable. But how can Barnes be forgiven, who, with all the confidence of a biographer, traces every wandering of the poet, and settles him at last, in his old age, at a country villa near Téos ?

(3) The learned Bayle has detected some infidelities of quotation in Le Fèvre (Dictionnaire Historique, etc.) Madame Dacier is not more accurate than her father : they have almost made Anacreon prime minister to the monarch of Samos.

(4) The Asiatics were as remarkable for genius as for luxury. "Ingenia Asiatica inclyta per gentes fecêre Poetæ, Anacreon, inde Mimnermus et Antimachus, etc." —Solinus.

(5) I have not attempted to define the particular Olympiad, but have adopted the idea of Bayle, who says, "Je n'ai point marqué d'Olympiade ; car pour un homme qui a vécu 85 ans, il me semble que l'on ne doit point s'enfermer dans les bornes si étroites."

discover in Plato that he was a descendant of the monarch Codrus, show much more of zeal than of either accuracy or judgment. (1)

The disposition and talents of Anacreon recommended him to the monarch of Samos, and he was formed to be the friend of such a prince as Polycrates. Susceptible only to the pleasures, he felt not the corruptions of the court; and while Pythagoras fled from the tyrant, Anacreon was celebrating his praises on the lyre. We are told, too, by Maximus Tyrius, that, by the influence of his amatory songs, he softened the mind of Polycrates into a spirit of benevolence towards his subjects. (2)

The amours of the poet, and the rivalship of the tyrant, (3) I shall pass over in silence; and there are few, I presume, who will regret the omission of most of those anecdotes, which the industry of some editors has not only promulged, but discussed. Whatever is repugnant to modesty and virtue is considered in ethical science, by a supposition very favourable to humanity, as impossible; and this amiable persuasion should be much more strongly entertained, where the transgression wars with nature as well as virtue. But why are we not allowed to indulge in the presumption? Why are we allowed to be reminded that there have been really such instances of depravity?

Hipparchus, who now maintained at Athens the power which his father Pisistratus had usurped, was one of those princes who may be said to have polished the fetters of their subjects. He was the first, according to Plato, who edited the poems of Homer, and commanded them to be sung by the rhapsodists at the celebration of the Panathenæa. From his court, which was a sort of galaxy of genius, Anacreon could not long be absent. Hipparchus sent a

barge for him; the poet readily embraced the invitation, and the Muses and the Loves were wafted with him to Athens. (4)

The manner of Anacreon's death was singular. We are told that in the eighty-fifth year of his age he was choked by a grape-stone; (5) and, however we may smile at their enthusiastic partiality, who see in this easy and characteristic death a peculiar indulgence of Heaven, we cannot help admiring that his fate should have been so emblematic of his disposition. Cælius Calcagninus alludes to this catastrophe in the following epitaph on our poet. (6)—

> Those lips, then, hallow'd sage, which pour'd along
> A music sweet as any cygnet's song,
>   The grape hath closed for ever !
> Here let the ivy kiss the poet's tomb,
> Here let the rose he loved with laurels bloom,
>   In bands that ne'er shall sever.
>
> But far be thou, oh! far, unholy vine,
> By whom the favourite minstrel of the Nine
>   Lost his sweet vital breath;
> Thy God himself now blushes to confess,
> Once hallow'd vine! he feels he loves thee less,
>   Since poor Anacreon's death.

It has been supposed by some writers that Anacreon and Sappho were contemporaries; and the very thought of an intercourse between persons so congenial, both in warmth of passion and delicacy of genius, gives such play to the imagination, that the mind loves to indulge in it. But the vision dissolves before historical truth; and Chamæleon and Hermeslanax, who are the source of the supposition, are considered as having merely indulged in a poetical anachronism. (7)

To infer the moral dispositions of a poet from the tone of sentiment which pervades his works, is

(1) This mistake is founded on a false interpretation of a very obvious passage in Plato's Dialogue on Temperance ; it originated with Madame Dacier, and has been received implicitly by many. Gail, a late editor of Anacreon, seems to claim to himself the merit of detecting this error ; but Bayle had observed it before him.

(2) Ανακρεων Σαμιοις Πολυκρατην ημερωσε. Maxim. Tyr. ʃ 21. Maximus Tyrius mentions this among other instances of the influence of poetry. If Gail had read Maximus Tyrius, how could he ridicule this idea in Moutonnet, as unauthenticated?

(3) In the romance of Clelia, the anecdote to which I allude is told of a young girl, with whom Anacreon fell in love while she personated the god Apollo in a mask. But here Mademoiselle Scuderi consulted nature more than truth.

(4) There is a very interesting French poem founded upon this anecdote, imputed to Desyvetaux, and called "Anacréon Citoyen."

(5) Fabricius appears not to trust very implicitly in this story. "Uvæ passæ acino tandem suffocatus, si credimus Suidæ in οινοποτης; alii enim hoc mortis genere periisse tradunt Sophoclem."—Fabricii Bibliothec. Græc. lib. II. cap. 15. It must be confessed that Lucian, who tells us that Sophocles was choked by a grape-stone, in the very same treatise mentions the longevity of Ana-

creon, and yet is silent on the manner of his death. Could he have been ignorant of such a remarkable coincidence, or, knowing, could he have neglected to remark it? See Regnier's introduction to his Anacreon.

(6) At te, sancte senex, acinus sub Tartara misit,
  Cygneæ clausit qui tibi vocis iter.
Vos, hederæ, tumulum, tumulum vos, cingite lauri,
  Hoc rosa perpetuo vernet odora loco;
At vitis procul hinc, procul hinc odiosa facessat,
  Quæ causam diræ protulit, uva, necis.
Creditur ipse minus vitem jam Bacchus amare,
  In vatem tantum quæ fuit ausa nefas.

The author of this epitaph, Cælius Calcagninus, has translated or imitated the epigrams εις την Μυρωνος βουν, which are given under the name of Anacreon.

(7) Barnes is convinced (but very gratuitously,) of the synchronism of Anacreon and Sappho. In citing his authorities, he has strangely neglected the line quote. by Fulvius Ursinus, as from Anacreon, among the testimonies to Sappho: —

Ειμι λαβων εισαρας Σαπφω πκρθενον αδυφωνον.

Fabricius thinks that they might have been contemporary. but considers their amour as a tale of imagination. Vossius rejects the idea entirely: as do also Olaus Borrichius and others.

sometimes a very fallacious analogy; but the soul of Anacreon speaks so unequivocally through his odes, that we may safely consult them as the faithful mirrors of his heart. (1) We find him there the elegant voluptuary, diffusing the seductive charm of sentiment over passions and propensities at which rigid morality must frown. His heart, devoted to indolence, seems to have thought that there is wealth enough in happiness, but seldom happiness in mere wealth. The cheerfulness, indeed, with which he brightens his old age is interesting and endearing : like his own rose, he is fragrant even in decay. But the most peculiar feature of his mind is that love of simplicity, which he attributes to himself so feelingly, and which breathes characteristically throughout all that he has sung. In truth, if we omit those few vices in our estimate which religion, at that time, not only connived at, but consecrated, we shall be inclined to say that the disposition of our poet was amiable; that his morality was relaxed, but not abandoned ; and that Virtue, with her zone loosened,

may be an apt emblem of the character of Anacreon. (2)

Of his person, and physiognomy time has preserved such uncertain memorials, that it were better, perhaps, to leave the pencil to fancy ; and few can read the Odes of Anacreon without imagining to themselves the form of the animated old bard, crowned with roses, and singing cheerfully to his lyre. The head of Anacreon, prefixed to the first edition of this work, (3) and which has been considered as authentic, was even thought by some as by no means deficient in that benevolent suavity of expression which should characterise the countenance of such a poet.

After the very enthusiastic eulogiums bestowed both by ancients and moderns upon the poems of Anacreon, (4) we need not be diffident in expressing our raptures at their beauty, nor hesitate to pronounce them the most polished remains of antiquity. (5) They are, indeed, all beauty, all enchantment. (6) He steals us so insensibly along

(1) An Italian poet, in some verses on Belleau's translation of Anacreon, pretends to imagine that our bard did not feel as he wrote :—

Lyæum, Venerem, Cupidinemque
Senex lusit Anacreon poeta :
Sed quo tempore nec capaciores
Rogabat cyathos, nec inquietis
Urebatur amoribus, sed ipsis
Tantum versibus et jocis amabat,
Nullum præ se habitum gerens amantis.

To Love and Bacchus ever young
While sage Anacreon touch'd the lyre,
He neither felt the loves he sung,
Nor fill'd his bowl to Bacchus higher.
Those flowery days had faded long,
When youth could act the lover's part ;
And passion trembled in his song,
But never, never, reach'd his heart.

(2) Anacreon's character has been variously coloured. Barnes lingers on it with enthusiastic admiration ; but he is always extravagant, if not sometimes also a little profane. Baillet runs too much into the opposite extreme, exaggerating also the testimonies which he has consulted ; and we cannot surely agree with him when he cites such a compiler as Athenæus, as " un des plus savans critiques de l'antiquité."—Jugemens des Savans, M. CV.

Barnes could hardly have read the passage to which he refers, when he accuses Le Fevre of having censured our poet's character in a note on Longinus ; the note in question being manifest irony, in allusion to some censure passed upon Le Fevre for his Anacreon. It is clear, indeed, that praise rather than censure is intimated. See Johannes Vulpius (de Utilitate Poëtices), who vindicates our poet's reputation.

(3) It was taken from the Bibliotheca of Fulvius Ursinus. Bellori has copied the same head into his Imagines. Johannes Faber, in his description of the coin of Ursinus, mentions another head on a very beautiful cornelian, which he supposes was worn in a ring by some admirer of the poet. In the Iconographia of Canini there is a youthful head of Anacreon from a Grecian medal, with the letters ΤΕΙΟΣ around it; on the reverse there is a

Neptune, holding a spear in his right hand, and a dolphin, with the word ΤΙΑΝΩΝ inscribed, in the left ; "volendoci denotare (says Canini) che quelli cittadini la coniassero in honore del suo compatriota poeta." There is also among the coins of De Wilde one which, though it bears no effigy, was probably struck to the memory of Anacreon. It has the word ΤΗΙΩΝ, encircled with an ivy crown. " At quidni respicit hæc corona Anacreontem, nobilem lyricum ?"—De Wilde.

(4) Besides those which are extant, he wrote hymns, elegies, epigrams, etc. Some of the epigrams still exist. Horace, in addition to the mention of him (lib. iv. od.9.), alludes also to a poem of his upon the rivalry of Circe and Penelope in the affections of Ulysses, lib. i. od. 17.; and the scholiast upon Nicander cites a fragment from a poem upon Sleep by Anacreon, and attributes to him likewise a medicinal treatise. Fulgentius mentions a work of his upon the war between Jupiter and the Titans, and the origin of the consecration of the eagle.

(5) See Horace, Maximus Tyrius, etc. "His style (says Scaliger) is sweeter than the juice of the Indian reed." —Poet. lib. i. cap. 44. "From the softness of his verses (says Olaus Borrichius), the ancients bestowed on him the epithets sweet, delicate, graceful, etc."—Dissertationes Academicæ, de Poetis, diss. 2. Scaliger again praises him thus in a pun; speaking of the μελος, or ode, "Anacreon autem non solum dedit hæc μελη, sed etiam in ipsis mella." See the passage of Rapin, quoted by all the editors. I cannot omit citing also the following very spirited apostrophe of the author of the Commentary prefixed to the Parma edition: " O vos sublimes animæ, vos Apollinis alumni, qui post unum Alcmanem in totâ Hellade lyricam poesim exsuscitastis, coluistis, amplificastis, quæso vos an ullus unquam fuerit vates qui Teio cantori vel naturæ candore vel metri suavitate palmam præripuerit." See likewise Vincenzo Gravini della Rag. Poetic. libro primo, p. 97. Among the Ritratti of Marino, there is one of Anacreon beginning " Cin getemi la fronte," etc., etc.

(6) "We may perceive," says Vossius, "that the iteration of his words conduces very much to the sweetness of his style." Henry Stephen remarks the same beauty in a note on the forty-fourth ode. This figure of itera-

                                                                  2

with him, that we sympathise even in his excesses. In his amatory odes there is a delicacy of compliment not to be found in any other ancient poet. Love at that period was rather an unrefined emotion, and the intercourse of the sexes was animated more by passion than by sentiment. They knew not those little tendernesses which form the spiritual part of affection; their expression of feeling was, therefore, rude and unvaried, and the poetry of love deprived it of its most captivating graces. Anacreon, however, attained some ideas of this purer gallantry; and the same delicacy of mind which led him to this refinement prevented him also from yielding to the freedom of language which has sullied the pages of all the other poets. His descriptions are warm; but the warmth is in the ideas, not the words. He is sportive without being wanton, and ardent without being licentious. His poetic invention is always most brilliantly displayed in those allegorical fictions which so many have endeavoured to imitate, though all have confessed them to be inimitable. Simplicity is the distinguishing feature of these odes, and they interest by their innocence, as much as they fascinate by their beauty. They may be said, indeed, to be the very infants of the Muses, and to lisp in numbers.

I shall not be accused of enthusiastic partiality by those who have read and felt the original; but, to others, I am conscious, this should not be the language of a translator, whose faint reflection of such beauties can but ill justify his admiration of them.

In the age of Anacreon music and poetry were inseparable. These kindred talents were for a long time associated, and the poet always sung his own compositions to the lyre. It is probable that they were not set to any regular air, but rather a kind of musical recitation, which was varied according to the fancy and feelings of the moment. (1) The poems of Anacreon were sung at banquets as late as the time of Aulus Gellius, who tells us that he heard one of the odes performed at a birth-day entertainment. (2)

tion is his most appropriate grace :—but the modern writers of Juvenilia and Basia have adopted it to an excess which destroys the effect.

(1) In the Paris edition there are four of the original odes set to music, by Le Sueur, Gossec, Mehul, and Cherubini. "On chante du Latin et de l'Italien," says Gail, "quelquefois même sans les entendre : qui empêche que nous ne chantions des odes Grecques?" The chromatic learning of these composers is very unlike what we are told of the simple melody of the ancients ; and they have all, as it appears to me, mistaken the accentuation of the words.

(2) The Parma commentator is rather careless in referring to this passage of Aulus Gellius (lib. xix. cap. 9.). The ode was not sung by the rhetorician Julianus, as he says, but by the minstrels of both sexes, who were introduced at the entertainment.

(3) See what Colomesius, in his "Literary Treasures,"

The singular beauty of our poet's style, and the apparent facility, perhaps, of his metre have attracted, as I have already remarked, a crowd of imitators. Some of these have succeeded with wonderful felicity, as may be discerned in the few odes which are attributed to writers of a later period. But none of his emulators have been half so dangerous to his fame as those Greek ecclesiastics of the early ages, who, being conscious of their own inferiority to their great prototypes, determined on removing all possibility of comparison, and, under a semblance of moral zeal, deprived the world of some of the most exquisite treasures of ancient times. (3) The works of Sappho and Alcæus were among those flowers of Grecian literature which thus fell beneath the rude hand of ecclesiastical presumption. It is true they pretended that this sacrifice of genius was hallowed by the interests of religion; but I have already assigned the most probable motive; (4) and if Gregorius Nazianzenus had not written Anacreontics, we might now perhaps have the works of the Teian unmutilated, and be empowered to say exultingly with Horace,

> Nec, si quid olim lusit Anacreon,
> Delevit ætas.

The zeal by which these bishops professed to be actuated gave birth more innocently, indeed, to an absurd species of parody, as repugnant to piety as it is to taste, where the poet of voluptuousness was made a preacher of the gospel, and his muse, like the Venus in armour at Lacedæmon, was arrayed in all the severities of priestly instruction. Such was the "Anacreon Recantatus," by Carolus de Aquino, a Jesuit, published 1701, which consisted of a series of palinodes to the several songs of our poet. Such, too, was the Christian Anacreon of Patrignanus, another Jesuit, (5) who preposterously transferred to a most sacred subject all that the Grecian poet had dedicated to festivity and love.

His metre has frequently been adopted by the modern Latin poets; and Scaliger, Taubman, Barthius, (6) and others, have shown that it is by no

has quoted from Alcyonius de Exilio; it may be found in Baxter. Colomesius, after citing the passage, adds, "Hæc auro contra cara non potui non apponere."

(4) We may perceive by the beginning of the first hymn of Bishop Synesius, that he made Anacreon and Sappho his models of composition.

> Αγε μοι, λιγεια φορμιγξ,
> Μετα Τηιαν αοιδαν,
> Μετα Λεσβιαν τε μολπαν.

Margunius and Damascenus were likewise authors of pious Anacreontics.

(5) This, perhaps, is the "Jesuita quidam Græculus" alluded to by Barnes, who has himself composed an Ανακρεων Χριςιανος, as absurd as the rest, but somewhat more skilfully executed.

(6) I have seen somewhere an account of the MSS. of Barthius, written just after his death, which mentions

means uncongenial with that language. (1) The Anacreontics of Scaliger, however, scarcely deserve the name; as they glitter all over with conceits, and, though often elegant, are always laboured. The beautiful fictions of Angerianus (2) preserve more happily than any others the delicate turn of those allegorical fables, which, passing so frequently through the mediums of version and imitation, have generally lost their finest rays in the transmission. Many of the Italian poets have indulged their fancies upon the subjects, and in the manner of Anacreon, Bernardo Tasso first introduced the metre, which was afterwards polished and enriched by Chabriera and others. (3)

To judge by the references of Degen, the German language abounds in Anacreontic imitations; and Hagedorn (4) is one among many who have assumed him as a model. La Farre, Chaulieu, and the other light poets of France, have also professed to cultivate the muse of Téos; but they have attained all her negligence with little of the simple grace that embellishes it. In the delicate bard of Schiras (5) we find the kindred spirit of Anacreon; some of his gazelles, or songs, possess all the character of our poet.

We come now to a retrospect of the editions of Anacreon. To Henry Stephen we are indebted for having first recovered his remains from the obscurity in which, so singularly, they had for many ages reposed. He found the seventh ode, as we are told, on the cover of an old book, and communicated it to Victorius, who mentions the circumstance in his "Various Readings." Stephen was then very young; and this discovery was considered by some critics of that day as a literary imposition. (6) In 1554, however, he gave Anacreon to the world, (7) accompanied with annotations and a Latin version

of the greater part of the odes. The learned still hesitated to receive them as the relics of the Teian bard, and suspected them to be the fabrication of some monks of the sixteenth century. This was an idea from which the classic muse recoiled; and the Vatican manuscript, consulted by Scaliger and Salmasius, confirmed the antiquity of most of the poems. A very inaccurate copy of this MS. was taken by Isaac Vossius, and this is the authority which Barnes has followed in his collation. Accordingly he misrepresents almost as often as he quotes; and the subsequent editors, relying upon his authority, have spoken of the manuscript with not less confidence than ignorance. The literary world, however, has at length been gratified with this curious memorial of the poet, by the industry of the Abbé Spaletti, who published at Rome, in 1781, a fac-simile of those pages of the Vatican manuscript which contained the odes of Anacreon. (8)

A catalogue has been given by Gail of all the different editions and translations of Anacreon. Finding their number to be much greater than I could possibly have had an opportunity of consulting, I shall here content myself with enumerating only those editions and versions which it has been in my power to collect; and which, though very few, are, I believe, the most important.

The edition by Henry Stephen, 1554, at Paris—the Latin version is attributed by Colomesius to John Dorat. (9)

The old French translations, by Ronsard and Belleau—the former published in 1555, the latter in 1556. It appears from a note of Muretus upon one of the sonnets of Ronsard, that Henry Stephen communicated to this poet his manuscript of Anacreon, before he promulgated it to the world. (10)

The edition by Le Fevre, 1660.

---

many more Anacreontics of his than I believe have ever been published.

(1) Thus too Albertus, a Danish poet:—

> Fidii tui minister
> Gaudebo semper esse,
> Gaudebo semper illi
> Litare thure, mulso;
> Gaudebo semper illum
> Laudare pusillulis
> Anacreonticillis.
>
> *See the Danish Poets collected by Rostgaard.*

These pretty littlenesses defy translation. A beautiful Anacreontic by Hugo Grotius may be found Lib. i. Farraginis.

(2) To Angerianus Prior is indebted for some of his happiest mythological subjects.

(3) See Crescimbeni, Historia della Volg. Poes.

(4) "L'aimable Hagedorn vaut quelquefois Anacréon." —*Dorat, Idée de la Poésie Allemande.*

(5) See Toderini on the learning of the Turks, as translated by de Cournand. Prince Cantemir has made the Russians acquainted with Anacreon. See his Life, prefixed to a translation of his Satires, by the Abbé de Guasco.

(6) Robortellus, in his work "De Ratione corrigendi,"

pronounces these verses to be the triflings of some insipid Græcist.

(7) Ronsard commemorates this event:—

> Je vay boire à Henry Estienne
> Qui des enfers nous a rendu,
> Du vieil Anacreon perdu,
> La douce lyre Teienne.—Ode xv., book 5.
>
> I fill the bowl to Stephen's name,
> Who rescued from the gloom of night
> The Teian bard of festive fame,
> And brought his living lyre to light.

(8) This manuscript, which Spaletti thinks as old as the tenth century, was brought from the Palatine into the Vatican library; it is a kind of anthology of Greek epigrams, and in the 676th page of it are found the Ἡμιαμβεια συμποσιακα of Anacreon.

(9) "Le même (M. Vossius) m'a dit qu'il avoit possédé un Anacréon, où Scaliger avoit marqué, de sa main, que Henri Etienne n'etoit pas l'auteur de la version Latine des odes de ce poëte, mais Jean Dorat."—*Paulus Colomesius, Particularités.*

Colomesius, however, seems to have relied too implicitly on Vossius;—almost all these Particularités begin with "M. Vossius m'a dit."

(10) "La fiction de ce sonnet, comme l'autheur mesme

The edition by Madame Dacier, 1681, with a prose translation. (1)

The edition by Longepierre, 1684, with a translation in verse.

The edition by Baxter; London, 1695.

A French translation by La Fosse, 1704.

"L'Histoire des Odes d'Anacreon," by Gacon; Rotterdam, 1712.

A translation in English verse, by several hands, 1713, in which the odes by Cowley are inserted.

The edition by Barnes; London, 1721.

The edition by Dr. Trapp, 1733, with a Latin version in elegiac metre.

A translation in English verse, by John Addison, 1735.

A collection of Italian translations of Anacreon, published at Venice, 1736, consisting of those by Corsini, Regnier, (2) Salvini, Marchetti, and one by several anonymous authors. (3)

A translation in English verse, by Fawkes and Doctor Broome, 1760. (4)

Another, anonymous, 1768.

The edition by Spaletti, at Rome, 1781; with the fac-simile of the Vatican MS.

The edition by Degen, 1786, who published also a German translation of Anacreon, esteemed the best.

A translation in English verse, by Urquhart, 1787.

The edition by Gail, at Paris, 1799, with a prose translation.

m'a dit, est prinse d'une ode d'Anacréon, encores non imprimee, qu'il a depuis traduite, Συ μεν φιλη χελιδων."

(1) The author of Nouvelles de la Républ. des Lettr. bestows on this translation much more praise than its merits appear to me to justify.

(2) The notes of Regnier are not inserted in this edition; but they must be interesting, as they were for the most part communicated by the ingenious Menage, who, we may perceive, from a passage in the Menagiana, bestowed some research on the subject. "C'est aussi lui (M. Bigot) qui s'est donné la peine de conférer des manuscrits en Italie dans le temps que je travaillois sur Anacréon." —*Menagiana*, seconde partie.

(3) I find in Haym's Notizia de' Libri rari, Venice, 1670, an Italian translation by Cappone mentioned.

(4) This is the most complete of the English translations.

(5) This ode is the first of the series in the Vatican manuscript, which attributes it to no other poet than Anacreon. They who assert that the manuscript imputes it to Basilius have been misled by the words Του αυτου Βασιλεως in the margin, which are merely intended as a title to the following ode. Whether it be the production of Anacreon or not, it has all the features of ancient simplicity, and is a beautiful imitation of the poet's happiest manner.

(6) "How could he know at the first look (says Baxter) that the poet was φιλευνος?" There are surely many tell-tales of this propensity; and the following are the indices, which the physiognomist gives, describing a disposition perhaps not unlike that of Anacreon : Οφθαλμοι κλυδομενοι, κυμαινοντες εν ἑαυτοις, εις αφροδισια και ευπαθειαν επτοηται· ουτε δε αδικοι, ουτε κακουργοι,

ODES OF ANACREON.

ODE I. (5)

I saw the smiling bard of pleasure,
The minstrel of the Teian measure;
'T was in a vision of the night,
He beam'd upon my wondering sight.
I heard his voice, and warmly prest
The dear enthusiast to my breast.
His tresses wore a silvery dye,
But beauty sparkled in his eye;
Sparkled in his eyes of fire, (6)
Through the mist of soft desire.
His lip exhaled, whene'er he sigh'd,
The fragrance of the racy tide;
And, as with weak and reeling feet
He came my cordial kiss to meet,
An infant, of the Cyprian band,
Guided him on with tender hand.
Quick from his glowing brows he drew
His braid, of many a wanton hue;
I took the wreath, whose inmost twine. (7)
Breathed of him and blush'd with wine.
I hung it o'er my thoughtless brow,
And ah ! I feel its magic now : (8)
I feel that even his garland's touch
Can make the bosom love too much.

ουτε φυσεως φαυλης, ουτε αμουσοι.—*Adamantius.* "The eyes that are humid and fluctuating show a propensity to pleasure and love; they bespeak too a mind of integrity and beneficence, a generosity of disposition, and a genius for poetry."

Baptista Porta tells us some strange opinions of the ancient physiognomists on this subject, their reasons for which were curious, and perhaps not altogether fanciful. Vide Physiognom. Johan. Baptist. Portæ.

(7) Philostratus has the same thought in one of his Ερωτικα, where he speaks of the garland which he had sent to his mistress. Ει δε βουλει τι φιλω χαριζεσθαι, τα λειψανα αντιπεμψον, μηκετι πνεοντα ροδων μονον, αλλα και σου. "If thou art inclined to gratify thy lover, send him back the remains of the garland, no longer breathing of roses only, but of thee:" Which pretty conceit is borrowed (as the author of the Observer remarks,) in a well-known little song of Ben Jonson's :—

> " But thou thereon didst only breathe,
>   And sent it back to me;
> Since when thy fingers slily stole
>   Not of itself, but thee !"

(8) This idea, as Longepierre remarks, occurs in an epigram of the seventh book of the Anthologia.

> Εξοτε μοι πινοντι συνεςκουσα Χαρικλω
>   Λαθρη τους ιδιους αμφεβαλε ςεφανους,
> Πυρ ολοον δαπτει με.

> While I unconscious quaff'd my wine,
>   'T was then thy fingers slily stole
> Upon my brow that wreath of thine,
>   Which since has madden'd all my soul.

ODE II.

GIVE me the harp of epic song,
Which Homer's finger thrill'd along;
But tear away the sanguine string,
For war is not the theme I sing.
Proclaim the laws of festal rite, (1)
I 'm monarch of the board to-night;
And all around shall brim as high,
And quaff the tide as deep as I.
And when the cluster's mellowing dews
Their warm enchanting balm infuse,
Our feet shall catch the elastic bound,
And reel us through the dance's round.
Great Bacchus! we shall sing to thee,
In wild but sweet ebriety;
Flashing around such sparks of thought,
As Bacchus could alone have taught.
    Then, give the harp of epic song,
Which Homer's finger thrill'd along;
But tear away the sanguine string,
For war is not the theme I sing.

—o♦o—

ODE III. (2)

LISTEN to the Muse's lyre,
Master of the pencil's fire!
Sketch'd in painting's bold display,
Many a city first portray;
Many a city, revelling free,
Full of loose festivity.
Picture then a rosy train,
Bacchants straying o'er the plain;
Piping, as they roam along,
Roundelay or shepherd-song.
Paint me next, if painting may
Such a theme as this portray,
All the earthly heaven of love
These delighted mortals prove.

(1) The ancients prescribed certain laws of drinking at their festivals, for an account of which see the commentators. Anacreon here acts the symposiarch, or master of the festival. I have translated according to those who consider κυπελλα θεσμων as an inversion of θεσμους κυπελλων.

(2) La Fosse has thought proper to lengthen this poem by considerable interpolations of his own, which he thinks are indispensably necessary to the completion of the description.

(3) This ode, Aulus Gellius tells us, was performed at an entertainment where he was present.

(4) I have availed myself here of the additional lines given in the Vatican manuscript, which have not been accurately inserted in any of the ordinary editions :—

Ποιησον αμπελους μοι
Και βοτρυας κατ' αυτων
Και μαιναδας τρυγωσας.
Ποιει δε ληνον οινου,
Δηνοβατας πατουντας,
Τους σατυρους γελωντας,
Και χρυσους τους ερωτας,

ODE IV. (3)

VULCAN! hear your glorious task;
I do not from your labours ask
In gorgeous panoply to shine,
For war was ne'er a sport of mine.
No—let me have a silver bowl,
Where I may cradle all my soul:
But mind that o'er its simple frame
No mimic constellations flame;
Nor grave upon the swelling side
Orion, scowling o'er the tide.
I care not for the glittering wain,
Nor yet the weeping sister train.
But let the vine luxuriant roll
Its blushing tendrils round the bowl,
While many a rose-lipp'd bacchant maid (4)
Is culling clusters in their shade.
Let sylvan gods, in antic shapes,
Wildly press the gushing grapes,
And flights of Loves, in wanton play,
Wing through the air their winding way;
While Venus, from her arbour green,
Looks laughing at the joyous scene, (5)
And young Lyæus by her side
Sits, worthy of so bright a bride.

—o♦o—

ODE V. (6)

SCULPTOR, wouldst thou glad my soul,
Grave for me an ample bowl,
Worthy to shine in hall or bower,
When spring-time brings the reveller's hour. (7)
Grave it with themes of chaste design,
Fit for a simple board like mine.
Display not there the barbarous rites
In which religious zeal delights;
Nor any tale of tragic fate
Which History shudders to relate.

Και Κυθηρην γελωσαν,
'Ομου καλω Λυαιω,
Ερωτα χ' Αφροδιτην.

(5) This and the preceding line were originally rendered by Mr. Moore,

    While Venus, to her mystic bower,
    Beckons the rosy vintage-power.—P. E.

(6) Degen thinks that this ode is a more modern imitation of the preceding. There is a poem by Cælius Calcagninus, in the manner of both, where he gives instructions about the making of a ring.

    Torna bis annulum mihi
    Et fabre, et apte, et commode, etc., etc.

(7) The opening lines of this ode bear but a faint resemblance to those with which Mr. Moore formerly commenced it :—

    Grave me a cup with brilliant grace,
    Deep as the rich and holy vase,
    Which on the shrine of spring reposes,
    When shepherds hail that hour of roses.—P. E.

No—cull thy fancies from above,
Themes of heaven and themes of love.
Let Bacchus, Jove's ambrosial boy,
Distil the grape in drops of joy,
And while he smiles at every tear,
Let warm-eyed Venus, dancing near,
With spirits of the genial bed,
The dewy herbage deftly tread.
Let Love be there, without his arms, (1)
In timid nakedness of charms ;
And all the Graces, link'd with Love,
Stray, laughing, through the shadowy grove ;
While rosy boys disporting round,
In circlets trip the velvet ground.
But ah ! if there Apollo toys, (2)
I tremble for the rosy boys.

ODE VI. (3)

As late I sought the spangled bowers,
To cull a wreath of matin flowers,
Where many an early rose was weeping, (4)
I found the urchin Cupid sleeping.

(1) Thus Sannazaro in the eclogue of Gallicio nell'
Arcadia :—

> Vengan li vaghi Amori
> Senza fiammelle, o strali,
> Scherzando insieme pargoletti e nudi.

> Flattering on the busy wing,
> A train of naked Cupids came,
> Sporting around in harmless ring,
> Without a dart, without a flame.

And thus in the Pervigilium Veneris :—

> Ite, nymphæ, posuit arma, feriatus est Amor.

> Love is disarm'd — ye nymphs, in safety stray,
> Your bosoms now may boast a holiday !

(2) An allusion to the fable, that Apollo had killed his
beloved Hyacinth, while playing with him at quoits.
" This (says M. La Fosse) is assuredly the sense of the
text, and it cannot admit of any other."
The Italian translators, to save themselves the trouble
of a note, have taken the liberty of making Anacreon
himself explain this fable. Thus Salvini, the most literal
of any of them :—

> Ma con lor non giuochi Apollo ;
> Che in fiero risco
> Col duro disco
> A Giacinto flaccò il collo.

(3) This beautiful fiction, which the commentators have
attributed to Julian, a royal poet, the Vatican MS. pro-
nounces to be the genuine offspring of Anacreon. It has,
indeed, all the features of the parent :—

> et facile inscis
> Noscitetur ab omnibus.

(4) This idea is prettily imitated in the following epi-
gram by Andreas Naugerius :—

> Florentes dum forte vagans mea Hyella per hortos
> Texit odoratis lilia cana rosis,
> Ecce rosas inter latitantem invenit Amorem
> Et simul enneris floribus implicuit.
> Luctatur primo, et contra nitentibus alis
> Indomitus tentat solvere vincla puer :
> Mox ubi lacteolas et dignas matre papillas
> Vidit et ora ipsos nata movere Deos,

I caught the boy, a goblet's tide
Was richly mantling by my side,
I caught him by his downy wing,
And whelm'd him in the racy spring.
Then drank I down the poison'd bowl,
And Love now nestles in my soul.
Oh yes, my soul is Cupid's nest,
I feel him fluttering in my breast.

ODE VII. (5)

The women tell me every day
That all my bloom has past away.
" Behold," the pretty wantons cry,
" Behold this mirror with a sigh ;
The locks upon thy brow are few,
And, like the rest, they 're withering too ! "
Whether decline has thinn'd my hair, (6)
I 'm sure I neither know nor care ;
But this I know, and this I feel,
As onward to the tomb I steal,
That still as death approaches nearer, (7)
The joys of life are sweeter, dearer ;

> Impositosque comæ ambrosios ut sentit odores
> Quosque legit diti messe beatus Arabs :
> " I (dixit) mea, quære novum tibi, mater, Amorem,
> Imperio sedes hæc erit apta meo."

As fair Hyella, through the bloomy grove,
A wreath of many mingled flowerets wove,
Within a rose a sleeping Love she found,
And in the twisted wreaths the baby bound.
Awhile he struggled, and impatient tried
To break the rosy bonds the virgin tied ;
But when he saw her bosom's radiant swell,
Her features, where the eye of Jove might dwell ;
And caught the ambrosial odours of her hair,
Rich as the breathings of Arabian air ;
" Oh ! mother Venus," (said the raptured child,
By charms, of more than mortal bloom, beguiled,)
" Go, seek another boy, thou 'st lost thine own,
Hyella's arms shall now be Cupid's throne ! "

This epigram of Naugerius is imitated by Lodovico Dolce
in a poem, beginning, .

> Mentre raccoglie hor uno, hor l'altro fiore
> Vicina a un rio di chiare et lucid' onde,
> Lidia, etc., etc.

(5) Alberti has imitated this ode in a poem, beginning,

> Nisa mi dice e Clori :
> Tirsi, tu se' pur veglio.

(6) Henry Stephen very justly remarks the elegant
negligence of expression in the original here :—

> Εγω δε τας κομας μεν,
> Ειτ' εισιν, ειτ' απηλθον,
> Ουκ οιδα.

And Longepierre has adduced from Catullus what he thinks
a similar instance of this simplicity of manner :—

> Ipse quis sit, utrum sit, an non sit, id quoque nescit.

Longepierre was a good critic ; but perhaps the line
which he has selected is a specimen of a carelessness not
very commendable. At the same time I confess that
none of the Latin poets have ever appeared to me so capa
ble of imitating the graces of Anacreon as Catullus, if he
had not allowed a depraved imagination to hurry him so
often into mere vulgar licentiousness.

(7) Pontanus has a very delicate thought upon the sub-
ject of old age :

And had I but an hour to live,
That little hour to bliss I'd give.

————◦◦◦◦————

ODE VIII. (1)

I CARE not for the idle state (2)
Of Persia's king, the rich, the great :
I envy not the monarch's throne,
Nor wish the treasured gold my own.
But oh ! be mine the rosy wreath,
Its freshness o'er my brow to breathe ;
Be mine the rich perfumes that flow, (3)
To cool and scent my locks of snow.
To-day I'll haste to quaff my wine,
As if to-morrow ne'er would shine ;
But if to-morrow comes, why then—
I'll haste to quaff my wine again.
And thus while all our days are bright,
Nor time has dimm'd their bloomy light,
Let us the festal hours beguile
With mantling cup and cordial smile ;
And shed from each new bowl of wine
The richest drop on Bacchus' shrine.
For Death may come, with brow unpleasant,
May come, when least we wish him present,
And beckon to the sable shore,
And grimly bid us—drink no more !

————◦◦◦◦————

ODE IX. (4)

I PRAY thee, by the gods above,
Give me the mighty bowl I love,

Quid rides, Matrona ? senem quid temnis amantem ?
Quisquis amat nulla est conditione senex.
Why do you scorn my want of youth,
And with a smile my brow behold ?
Lady dear ! believe this truth,
That he who loves cannot be old.

(1) " The German poet Lessing has imitated this ode. Vol. i. p. 24." Degen. Gail de Editionibus.
Baxter conjectures that this was written upon the occasion of our poet's refusing the money to Polycrates, according to the anecdote in Stobæus.
(2) There is a fragment of Archilochus in Plutarch, "De tranquillitate animi," which our poet has very closely imitated here ; it begins,
Ου μοι τα Γυγεω του πολυχρυσου μελει."—Barnes.
In one of the monkish imitators of Anacreon we find the same thought :—
Ψυχην εμην ερωτω,
Τι σοι θελεις γενεσθαι;
Θελεις Γυγεω τα και τα ;
(3) In the original, μυροισι καταβρεχειν ὑπηνην. On account of this idea of perfuming the beard, Cornelius de Pauw pronounces the whole ode to be the spurious production of some lascivious monk, who was nursing his beard with unguents. But he should have known, that this was an ancient eastern custom, which, if we may believe Savary, still exists : " Vous voyez, Monsieur (says this traveller), que l'usage antique de se parfumer la tête et la barbe," célébré par le prophète roi, subsiste encore de
*"Sicut unguentum in capite quod descendit in barbam Aaronis. Psaume 133."

And let me sing, in wild delight,
" I will—I will be mad to-night ! "
Alcmæon once, as legends tell,
Was frenzied by the fiends of hell ;
Orestes too, with naked tread,
Frantic paced the mountain-head ;
And why ? a murder'd mother's shade
Haunted them still where'er they stray'd.
But ne'er could I a murderer be,
The grape alone shall bleed by me ;
Yet can I shout, with wild delight,
" I will—I will be mad to-night ! "
Alcides' self, in days of yore,
Imbrued his hands in youthful gore,
And brandish'd, with a maniac joy,
The quiver of the expiring boy :
And Ajax, with tremendous shield,
Infuriate scour'd the guiltless field.
But I, whose hands no weapon ask,
No armour but this joyous flask ;
The trophy of whose frantic hours
Is but a scatter'd wreath of flowers,
Even I can sing with wild delight,
" I will—I will be mad to-night ! "

————◦◦◦◦————

ODE X. (5)

How am I to punish thee,
For the wrong thou 'st done to me,
Silly swallow, prating thing— (6)
Shall I clip that wheeling wing ?

nos jours."—Lettre 12. Savary likewise cites this very ode of Anacreon. Angerianus has not thought the idea inconsistent, having introduced it in the following lines :
Hæc mihi cura, rosis et cingere tempora myrto,
Et curas multo delapidare mero.
Hæc mihi cura, comas et barbam tingere succo
Assyrio et dulces continuare jocos.
This be my care, to wreathe my brow with flowers,
To drench my sorrows in the ample bowl ;
To pour rich perfumes o'er my beard in showers,
And give full loose to mirth and joy of soul !
(4) The poet is here in a frenzy of enjoyment, and it is, indeed, " amabilis insania;"—
Furor di poesia,
Di lascivia, e di vino,
Triplicato furore,
Bacco, Apollo, ed Amore.
Ritratti del Cavalier Marino.
This is truly, as Scaliger expresses it,
————Insanire dulce
Et sapidum furere furorem.
(5) This ode is addressed to a swallow. I find from Degen and from Gail's index, that the German poet Weiss has imitated it, Scherz. Lieder. lib. II., carm. 5; that Ramler also has imitated it, Lir. Blumenlese, lib. IV., p. 335. ; and some others. See Gail de Editionibus.
We are here referred by Degen to that dull book, the Epistles of Alciphron, tenth epistle, third book, where Iophon complains to Eraston of being wakened by the crowing of a cock, from his vision of riches.
(6) The loquacity of the swallow was proverbialised; thus Nicostratus :—

Or, as Tereus did, of old, (1)
(So the fabled tale is told,)
Shall I tear that tongue away,
Tongue that utter'd such a lay?
Ah, how thoughtless hast thou been!
Long before the dawn was seen,
When a dream came o'er my mind,
Picturing her I worship, kind,
Just when I was nearly blest,
Loud thy matins broke my rest!

—o♦♦o—

ODE XI. (2)

"Tell me, gentle youth, I pray thee,
What in purchase shall I pay thee
For this little waxen toy,
Image of the Paphian boy?"
Thus I said, the other day,
To a youth who pass'd my way:
"Sir," (he answer'd, and the while
Answer'd all in Doric style,)
"Take it, for a trifle take it;
'T was not I who dared to make it;
No, believe me, 't was not I;
Oh, it has cost me many a sigh,
And I can no longer keep (3)
Little gods who murder sleep!"
"Here, then, here," (I said with joy,)
"Here is silver for the boy:
He shall be my bosom guest,
Idol of my pious breast!"
Now, young Love, I have thee mine,
Warm me with that torch of thine;
Make me feel as I have felt,
Or thy waxen frame shall melt:
I must burn with warm desire, (4)
Or thou, my boy—in yonder fire.

Ει το συνεχως και πολλα και ταχεως λαλειν
Ην του φρονειν παρασημον, αι χελιδονες
Ελεγοντ αν ημων σωφρονεστεραι πολυ.

> If in prating from morning till night,
> A sign of our wisdom there be,
> The swallows are wiser by right,
> For they prattle much faster than we.

(1) Modern poetry has confirmed the name of Philomel upon the nightingale; but many respectable authorities among the ancients assigned this metamorphose to Progne, and made Philomel the swallow, as Anacreon does here.

(2) It is difficult to preserve with any grace the narrative simplicity of this ode, and the humour of the turn with which it concludes. I feel, indeed, that the translation must appear vapid, if not ludicrous, to an English reader.

(3) I have not literally rendered the epithet παντορεκτα; if it has any meaning here, it is one, perhaps, better omitted.

(4) From this Longepierre conjectures, that, whatever Anacreon might say, he felt sometimes the inconveniences of old age, and here solicits from the power of Love a warmth which he could no longer expect from Nature.

(5) There are many contradictory stories of the loves of Cybele and Atys. It is certain that he was mutilated, but

ODE XII.

They tell how Atys, wild with love, (5)
Roams the mount and haunted grove,
Cybele's name he howls around, (6)
The gloomy blast returns the sound!
Oft too, by Claros' hallow'd spring, (7)
The votaries of the laurell'd king
Quaff the inspiring magic stream,
And rave in wild prophetic dream.
But frenzied dreams are not for me,
Great Bacchus is my deity!
Full of mirth, and full of him,
While floating odours round me swim, (8)
While mantling bowls are full supplied,
And you sit blushing by my side,
I will be mad and raving too—
Mad, my girl, with love for you!

—o♦♦o—

ODE XIII.

I will, I will; the conflict 's past,
And I 'll consent to love at last.
Cupid has long, with smiling art,
Invited me to yield my heart;
And I have thought that peace of mind
Should not be for a smile resign'd;
And so repell'd the tender lure,
And hoped my heart would sleep secure.

But, slighted in his boasted charms,
The angry infant flew to arms;
He slung his quiver's golden frame,
He took his bow, his shafts of flame,
And proudly summon'd me to yield,
Or meet him on the martial field.
And what did I unthinking do? (9)
I took to arms, undaunted, too;

whether by his own fury, or Cybele's jealousy, is a point upon which authors are not agreed.

(6) I have here adopted the accentuation which Elias Andreas gives to Cybele:—

> In montibus Cybelen
> Magno sonans boatu.

(7) This fountain was in a grove, consecrated to Apollo, and situated between Colophon and Lebedos, in Ionia. The god had an oracle there. Scaliger thus alludes to it in his Anacreontica:—

> Semel ut concitus œstro,
> Veluti qui Clarias aquas
> Ebibere loquaces,
> Quo plus canunt, plura volunt.

(8) Spaletti was quite mistaken the import of χορεσθεις, as applied to the poet's mistress—"Meâ fatigatus amicâ;" —thus interpreting it in a sense which must want either delicacy or gallantry; if not, perhaps, both.

(9) Longepierre has here quoted an epigram from the Anthologia, in which the poet assumes Reason as the armour against Love.

Ὡπλισμαι προς ερωτα περι στερνοισι λογισμον,
Ουδε με νικησει, μονος εων προς ενα·
Θνατος δ' αθανατω συνελευσομαι· ην δε βοηθον
Βαγχον εχη, τι μονος προς δυ' εγω δυναμαι;

Assumed the corslet, shield, and spear,
And, like Pelides, smiled at fear.
Then (hear it, all ye powers above!)
I fought with Love! I fought with Love!
And now his arrows all were shed,
And I had just in terror fled —
When, heaving an indignant sigh,
To see me thus unwounded fly,
And, having now no other dart, (1)
He shot himself into my heart!
My heart — alas the luckless day!
Received the God, and died away.
Farewell, farewell, my faithless shield!
Thy lord at length is forced to yield.

> With Reason I cover my breast as a shield,
> And fearlessly meet little Love in the field;
> Thus fighting his godship, I'll ne'er be dismay'd;
> But if Bacchus should ever advance to his aid,
> Alas! then, unable to combat the two,
> Unfortunate warrior, what should I do?

This idea of the irresistibility of Cupid and Bacchus united is delicately expressed in an Italian poem, which is so truly Anacreontic, that its introduction here may be pardoned. It is an imitation, indeed, of our poet's sixth ode.

> Lavossi Amore in quel vicino fiume
> Ove giuro (Pastor) che bevend' io,
> Bevei le fiamme, anzi l'istesso Dio,
> Ch'or con l'humide piume
> Lascivetto mi scherza al cor intorno.
> Ma che sarei s' io lo bevessi un giorno,
> Bacco, nel tuo liquore?
> Sarei, più che non sono ebro d' Amore.

> The urchin of the bow and quiver
> Was bathing in a neighbouring river,
> Where, as I drank on yester-eve,
> (Shepherd-youth, the tale believe,)
> 'T was not a cooling crystal draught,
> 'T was liquid flame I madly quaff'd;
> For love was in the rippling tide,
> I felt him to my bosom glide;
> And now the wily wanton minion
> Plays round my heart with restless pinion.
> A day it was of fatal star,
> But ah, 't were even more fatal far,
> If, Bacchus, in thy cup of fire,
> I found this fluttering young desire:
> Then, then indeed, my soul would prove,
> Even more than ever, drunk with love!

(1) Dryden has parodied this thought in the following extravagant lines :—

> ————I 'm all o'er Love;
> Nay, I am Love; Love shot, and shot so fast,
> He shot himself into my breast at last.

(2) The poet, in this catalogue of his mistresses, means nothing more than, by a lively hyperbole, to inform us, that his heart, unfettered by any one object, was warm with devotion towards the sex in general. Cowley is indebted to this ode for the hint of his ballad, called "The Chronicle;" and the learned Menage has imitated it in a Greek Anacreontic, which has so much ease and spirit, that the reader may not be displeased at seeing it here :—

ΠΡΟΣ ΒΙΩΝΑ.

Ει αλσεων τα φυλλα,
Δειμηνιους τε ποιας,
Ει νυκτος αερα παντα,
Παρακτιους τε ψαμμους,

Vain, vain, is every outward care,
The foe 's within, and triumphs there.

————————

ODE XIV. (2)

Count me, on the summer trees,
Every leaf that courts the breeze;
Count me, on the foamy deep,
Every wave that sinks to sleep;
Then, when you have number'd these
Billowy tides and leafy trees,
Count me all the flames I prove, (3)
All the gentle nymphs I love.

'Αλος τε κυματωδη,
Δυνη, Βιων, αριθμειν,
Και τους εμους ερωτας
Δυνη, Βιων, αριθμειν.
Κορην, γυναικα, χηραν,
Σμικρην, μετην, μεγιστην,
Λευκην τε και μελαιναν,
Ορειαδας, Ναπαιας,
Νηρειδας τε πασας
'Ο σος φιλος φιλησε.
Παντων χορος μεν εστιν.
Αυτην νεων Ερωτων
Δεσποιναν Αφροδετην,
Χρυσην, καλην, γλυκειαν,
Ερασμιαν, ποθεινην,
Αει μονην φιλησαι
Εγωγε μη δυναιμην.

Tell the foliage of the woods,
Tell the billows of the floods,
Number midnight's starry store,
And the sands that crowd the shore,
Then, my Bion, thou mayst count
Of my loves the vast amount.
I've been loving, all my days,
Many nymphs, in many ways;
Virgin, widow, maid, and wife—
I've been doting all my life.
Naiads, Nereids, nymphs of fountains,
Goddesses of groves and mountains,
Fair and sable, great and small,
Yes, I swear, I've loved them all!
Soon was every passion over,
I was but the moment's lover;
Oh ! I 'm such a roving elf,
That the Queen of Love herself,
Though she practised all her wiles,
Rosy blushes, wreathed smiles,
All her beauty's proud endeavour
Could not chain my heart for ever.

(3) This figure is called by rhetoricians the Impossible (αδυνατον), and is very frequently made use of in poetry. The amatory writers have exhausted a world of imagery by it, to express the infinite number of kisses which they require from the lips of their mistresses: in this Catullus led the way.

> —Quam sidera multa, cum tacet nox,
> Furtivos hominum vident amores;
> Tam te basia multa basiare
> Vesano satis, et super, Catullo est:
> Quæ nec pernumerare curiosi
> Possint, nec mala fascinare lingua.—Carm. 7

As many stellar eyes of light,
As through the silent waste of night,

3

First, of pure Athenian maids
Sporting in their olive shades,
You may reckon just a score,
Nay, I'll grant you fifteen more.
In the famed Corinthian grove, (1)
Where such countless wantons rove,
Chains of beauties may be found,
Chains, by which my heart is bound;
There, indeed, are nymphs divine, (2)
Dangerous to a soul like mine.
Many bloom in Lesbos' isle;
Many in Iona smile;
Rhodes a pretty swarm can boast;
Caria too contains a host.
Sum them all—of brown and fair
You may count two thousand there.
What, you stare? I pray you, peace!
More I 'll find before I cease.
Have I told you all my flames,
'Mong the amorous Syrian dames?
Have I number'd every one,
Glowing under Egypt's sun?
Or the nymphs, who blushing sweet
Deck the shrine of Love in Crete;
Where the God, with festal play,
Holds eternal holiday?

> Gazing upon this world of shade,
> Witness some secret youth and maid,
> Who fair as thou, and fond as I,
> In stolen joys enamour'd lie,—
> So many kisses, ere I slumber,
> Upon those dew-bright lips I 'll number;
> So many kisses we shall count,
> Envy can never tell the' amount.
> No tongue shall blab the sum, but mine;
> No lips shall fascinate, but thine!

(1) Corinth was very famous for the beauty and number of its courtezans. Venus was the deity principally worshipped by the people, and their constant prayer was, that the gods should increase the number of her worshippers. We may perceive from the application of the verb κορινθιαζειν, in Aristophanes, that the lubricity of the Corinthians had become proverbial.

(2) "With justice has the poet attributed beauty to the women of Greece."—*Degen.*

M. de Pauw, the author of Dissertations upon the Greeks, is of a different opinion; he thinks that, by a capricious partiality of nature, the other sex had all the beauty; and by this supposition endeavours to account for a very singular depravation of instinct among that people.

(3) The Gaditanian girls were like the Baladières of India, whose dances are thus described by a French author: "Les danses sont presque toutes des pantomimes d'amour: le plan, le dessin, les attitudes, les mesures, les sons et les cadences de ces ballets, tout respire cette passion et en exprime les voluptés et les fureurs."—*Histoire du Commerce des Europ. dans les deux Indes.*—*Raynal*

The music of the Gaditanian females had all the voluptuous character of their dancing, as appears from Martial :—

> Cantica qui Xili, qui Gaditana susurrat.
>   Lib. iii. epigr. 63.

Lodovico Ariosto had this ode of our bard in his mind, when he wrote his poem "De diversis amoribus." See the Anthologia Italorum.

Still in clusters, still remain
Gades' warm desiring train ; (3)
Still there lies a myriad more
On the sable India's shore ;
These, and many far removed,
All are loving—all are loved!

———◦◦◦———

ODE XV.

TELL me, why, my sweetest dove, (4)
Thus your humid pinions move,
Shedding through the air in showers
Essence of the balmiest flowers?
Tell me whither, whence you rove,
Tell me all, my sweetest dove.
   Curious stranger, I belong
To the bard of Teian song;
With his mandate now I fly
To the nymph of azure eye ; —
She, whose eye has madden'd many, (5)
But the poet more than any.
Venus, for a hymn of love, (6)
Warbled in her votive grove,
('T was in sooth a gentle lay,)
Gave me to the bard away.

(4) The dove of Anacreon, bearing a letter from the poet to his mistress, is met by a stranger, with whom this dialogue is imagined.

The ancients made use of letter-carrying pigeons, when they went any distance from home, as the most certain means of conveying intelligence back. That tender domestic attachment, which attracts this delicate little bird through every danger and difficulty, till it settles in its native nest, affords to the author of "The Pleasures of Memory" a fine and interesting exemplification of his subject.

> Led by what chart, transports the timid dove
> The wreaths of conquest, or the vows of love?

See the poem. Daniel Heinsius, in speaking of Dousa, who adopted this method at the siege of Leyden, expresses a similar sentiment.

> Quo patriæ non tendit amor? Mandata referre
> Postquam hominem nequiit mittere, misit avem.

Fuller tells us that, at the siege of Jerusalem, the Christians intercepted a letter, tied to the legs of a dove, in which the Persian Emperor promised assistance to the besieged.—*Holy War,* cap. 24. book i.

(5) For τυραννον, in the original, Zeune and Schneider conjecture that we should read τυραννου, in allusion to the strong influence which this object of his love held over the mind of Polycrates. See Degen.

(6) "This passage is invaluable, and I do not think that any thing so beautiful or so delicate has ever been said. What an idea does it give of the poetry of the man, from whom Venus herself, the mother of the Graces and the Pleasures, purchases a little hymn with one of her favourite doves!"—*Longepierre.*

De Pauw objects to the authenticity of this ode, because it makes Anacreon his own panegyrist; but poets have a licence for praising themselves, which, with some indeed, may be considered as comprised under their general privilege of fiction.

See me now his faithful minion,—
Thus with softly-gliding pinion,
To his lovely girl I bear
Songs of passion through the air.
Oft he blandly whispers me,
"Soon, my bird, I 'll set you free."
But in vain he 'll bid me fly,
I shall serve him till I die.
Never could my plumes sustain
Ruffling winds and chilling rain,
O'er the plains, or in the dell,
On the mountain's savage swell,
Seeking in the desert wood
Gloomy shelter, rustic food.
Now I lead a life of ease,
Far from rugged haunts like these.
From Anacreon's hand I eat
Food delicious, viands sweet;
Flutter o'er his goblet's brim,
Sip the foamy wine with him.
Then, when I have wanton'd round
To his lyre's beguiling sound;
Or with gently-moving wings
Fann'd the minstrel while he sings :
On his harp I sink in slumbers,
Dreaming still of dulcet numbers!
    This is all—away—away—
You have made me waste the day.
How I 've chatter'd! prating crow
Never yet did chatter so.

(1) This ode and the next may be called companion-pictures; they are highly finished, and give us an excellent idea of the taste of the ancients in beauty. Franciscus Junius quotes them in his third book "De Pictura Veterum."

This ode has been imitated by Ronsard, Giuliano Goselini, etc., etc. Scaliger alludes to it thus in his Anacreontica:—

> Olim lepore blando,
> Litis versibus
> Candidus Anacreon
> Quam pingeret amicus
> Descripsit Venerem suam.

> The Teian bard, of former days,
> Attuned his sweet descriptive lays,
> And taught the painter's hand to trace
> His fair beloved's every grace.

In the dialogue of Caspar Barlæus, entitled "An formosa sit ducenda," the reader will find many curious ideas and descriptions of womanly beauty.

(2) I have followed here the reading of the Vatican MS. ῥοδέης. Painting is called "the rosy art," either in reference to colouring, or as an indefinite epithet of excellence, from the association of beauty with that flower. Salvini has adopted this reading in his literal translation:—

> Della rosea arte signore.

(3) If this portrait of the poet's mistress be not merely ideal, the omission of her name is much to be regretted. Meleager, in his epigram on Anacreon, mentions " the golden Eurypyle" as his mistress.

Βεβληκως χρυσεην χειρας επ' Ευρυπυλην.

(4) The ancients have been very enthusiastic in their

ODE XVI. (1)

Thou, whose soft and rosy hues (2)
Mimic form and soul infuse,
Best of painters, come portray
The lovely maid that 's far away. (3)
Far away, my soul! thou art,
But I 've thy beauties all by heart.
Paint her jetty ringlets playing, (4)
Silky locks, like tendrils straying;
And, if painting hath the skill (5)
To make the spicy balm distil,
Let every little lock exhale
A sigh of perfume on the gale.
Where her tresses' curly flow
Darkles o'er the brow of snow,
Let her forehead beam to light,
Burnish'd as the ivory bright.
Let her eyebrows smoothly rise
In jetty arches o'er her eyes,
Each, a crescent gently gliding,
Just commingling, just dividing.
    But, hast thou any sparkles warm,
The lightning of her eyes to form?
Let them effuse the azure rays
That in Minerva's glances blaze,
Mix'd with the liquid light that lies (6)
In Cytherea's languid eyes.
O'er her nose and cheek be shed
Flushing white and soften'd red;

praises of the beauty of hair. Apuleius, in the second book of his Melesiacs, says, that Venus herself, if she were bald, though surrounded by the Graces and the Loves, could not be pleasing even to her husband Vulcan.

Stesichorus gave the epithet καλλιπλοκαμος to the Graces, and Simonides bestowed the same upon the Muses. See Hadrian Junius's Dissertation upon Hair.

To this passage of our poet, Selden alluded in a note on the Polyolbion of Drayton, Song the Second, where, observing that the epithet "black-haired" was given by some of the ancients to the goddess Isis, he says, "Nor will I swear, but that Anacreon (a man very judicious in the provoking motives of wanton love), intending to bestow on his sweet mistress that one of the titles of woman's special ornament, well-haired (καλλιπλοκαμος), thought of this when he gave his painter direction to make her black-haired."

(5) Thus Philostratus, speaking of a picture : Επαινω και τον ενδροσον των ῥοδων, και φημι γεγραφθαι αυτα μετα της οσμης. "I admire the dewiness of these roses, and could say that their very smell was painted."

(6) Marchetti explains thus the ὑγρον of the original:—

> Dipingili umidetti,
> Tremuli e lascivetti,
> Quai gli ha Ciprigna l'alma Dea d'Amore

Tasso has painted in the same manner the eyes of Armida :—

> Qual raggio in onda le scintilla un riso
> Negli umidi occhi tremulo e lascivo.
> Within her humid, melting eyes
> A brilliant ray of laughter lies,
> Soft as the broken solar beam,
> That trembles in the azure stream

Mingling tints, as when there glows (1)
In snowy milk the bashful rose.
Then her lip, so rich in blisses, (2)
Sweet petitioner for kisses,
Rosy nest, where lurks Persuasion,
Mutely courting Love's invasion.
Next, beneath the velvet chin, (3)
Whose dimple hides a Love within,
Mould her neck with grace descending,
In a heaven of beauty ending;
While countless charms, above, below,
Sport and flutter round its snow.
Now let a floating lucid veil (4)
Shadow her form, but not conceal;
A charm may peep, a hue may beam,
And leave the rest to Fancy's dream.
Enough—'t is she! 'T is all I seek;
It glows, it lives, it soon will speak!

———◦◖◦———

ODE XVII. (5)

AND now with all thy pencil's truth,
Portray Bathyllus, lovely youth!

The mingled expression of dignity and tenderness, which Anacreon requires the painter to infuse into the eyes of his mistress, is more amply described in the subsequent ode. Both descriptions are so exquisitely touched, that the artist must have been great indeed, if he did not yield in painting to the poet.

(1) Thus Propertius, eleg. 3. lib. ii.

> Utque rosæ puro lacte natant folia.

And Davenant, in a little poem called "The Mistress,"

> Catch as it falls the Scythian snow,
> Bring blushing roses steep'd in milk.

Thus too Taygetus :—

> Quæ lac atque rosas vincis candore rubenti.

These last words may perhaps defend the "flushing white" of the translation.

(2) The "lip, provoking kisses," in the original, is a strong and beautiful expression. Achilles Tatius speaks of χειλη μαλθακα προς τα φιληματα, " Lips soft and delicate for kissing." A grave old commentator, Dionysius Lambinus, in his notes upon Lucretius, tells us, with the apparent authority of experience, that "Suavius viros osculantur puellæ labiosæ, quam quæ sunt brevibus labris." And Æneas Sylvius, in his tedious uninteresting story of the loves of Euryalus and Lucretia, where he particularises the beauties of the heroine (in a very false and laboured style of latinity), describes her lips thus :— "Os parvum decensque, labia corallini coloris, ad morsum aptissima."—Epist. 114. lib. i.

(3) Madame Dacier has quoted here two pretty lines of Varro :—

> Sigilla in mento impressa Amoris digitulo
> Vestigio demonstrant mollitudinem.

> In her chin is a delicate dimple,
> By Cupid's own finger imprest;
> There Beauty, bewitchingly simple,
> Has chosen her innocent nest.

(4) This delicate art of description, which leaves imagination to complete the picture, has been seldom adopted in the imitations of this beautiful poem. Ronsard is exceptionably minute; and Politianus, in his charming por-

Let his hair, in masses bright, (6)
Fall like floating rays of light;
And there the raven's dye confuse
With the golden sunbeam's hues.
Let no wreath, with artful twine, (7)
The flowing of his locks confine;
But leave them loose to every breeze,
To take what shape and course they please.
Beneath the forehead, fair as snow,
But flush'd with manhood's early glow, (8)
And guileless as the dews of dawn,
Let the majestic brows be drawn,
Of ebon hue, enrich'd by gold,
Such as dark shining snakes unfold.
Mix in his eyes the power alike, (9)
With love to win, with awe to strike;
Borrow from Mars his look of ire,
From Venus her soft glance of fire;
Blend them in such expression here,
That we by turns may hope and fear!
  Now from the sunny apple seek
The velvet down that spreads his cheek;
And there, if art so far can go,
The ingenuous blush of boyhood show.

trait of a girl, full of rich and exquisite diction, has lifted the veil rather too much. The "questo che tu m' intendi" should be always left to fancy.

(5) The reader, who wishes to acquire an accurate idea of the judgment of the ancients in beauty, will be indulged by consulting Junius de Pictura Veterum, lib. 3. cap. 9. where he will find a very curious selection of descriptions and epithets of personal perfections. Junius compares this ode with a description of Theodoric, king of the Goths, in the second epistle, first book, of Sidonius Apollinaris.

(6) He here describes the sunny hair, the "flava coma," which the ancients so much admired. The Romans gave this colour artificially to their hair. See Stanisl. Kobienzick. de Luxu Romanorum.

(7) If the original here, which is particularly beautiful, can admit of any additional value, that value is conferred by Gray's admiration of it. See his letters to West.

Some annotators have quoted on this passage the description of Photis's hair in Apuleius; but nothing can be more distant from the simplicity of our poet's manner, than that affectation of richness which distinguishes the style of Apuleius.

(8) Torentius, upon the words "insignem tenui fronte," in Horace, Od. 33, lib. i., is of opinion, incorrectly, I think, that "tenui" here bears the same meaning as the word ἁπαλον.

(9) Tasso gives a similar character to the eyes of Clorinda :—

> Lampeggiar gli occhi, folgorar gli sguardi
>   Dolci ne l'ira.

> Her eyes were flashing with a heavenly heat,
> A fire that, even in anger, still was sweet.

The poetess Veronica Gambara is more diffuse upon this variety of expression :—

> Occhi lucenti e belli,
> Come esser può ch' in un medesmo istante
> Nascon da voi sì nuove forme e tante?
> Lieti, mesti, superbi, bumili, altieri,
> Vi mostrate in un punto, onde di speme,
> E di timor ne empiete, etc., etc.

While, for his mouth—but no,—in vain
Would words its witching charm explain.
Make it the very seat, the throne,
That Eloquence would claim her own; (1)
And let the lips, though silent, wear (2)
A life-look, as if words were there. (3)
    Next thou his ivory neck must trace,
Moulded with soft but manly grace;
Fair as the neck of Paphia's boy,
Where Paphin's arms have hung in joy.
Give him the winged Hermes' hand, (4)
With which he waves his snaky wand;
Let Bacchus the broad chest supply,
And Leda's son the sinewy thigh;
While, through his whole transparent frame,
Thou show'st the stirrings of that flame,
Which kindles, when the first love-sigh
Steals from the heart, unconscious why. (5)
    But sure thy pencil, though so bright,
Is envious of the eye's delight,

> Oh! tell me, brightly-beaming eye,
> Whence in your little orbit lie
> So many different traits of fire,
> Expressing each a new desire.
> Now with pride or scorn you darkle,
> Now with love, with gladness, sparkle,
> While we, who view the varying mirror,
> Feel by turns both hope and terror.

Chevreau, citing the lines of our poet, in his critique on the poems of Malherbe, produces a Latin version of them from a manuscript which he had seen, entitled "Joann. Falconis Anacreontici Lusus."

(1) In the original, as in the preceding ode, Pitho, the goddess of persuasion, or eloquence. It was worthy of the delicate imagination of the Greeks to deify Persuasion, and give her the lips for her throne. We are here reminded of a very interesting fragment of Anacreon, preserved by the scholiast upon Pindar, and supposed to belong to a poem reflecting with some severity on Simonides, who was the first, we are told, that ever made a hireling of his muse :—

> Ουδ' αργυρεη ποτ' ελαμψε Πειθω.
>
> Nor yet had fair Persuasion shone
> In silver splendours, not her own.

(2) In the original λαλον σιωπη. The mistress of Petrarch "parla con silenzio," which is perhaps the best method of female eloquence.

(3) This ode has undergone considerable changes since its first publication; among others the place of the eight preceding lines was originally occupied by the following :—

> And there let beauty's rosy ray
> In flying blushes richly play—
> Blushes of that celestial flame
> Which lights the cheek of virgin shame.
> Then for his lips, that ripely gem—
> But let thy mind imagine them!
> Paint, where the ruby cell uncloses,
> Persuasion sleeping upon roses;
> And give his lip that speaking air,
> As if a word was hovering there.—P. E.

(4) In Shakspeare's Cymbeline there is a similar method of description :—

> ———— this is his hand,
> His foot mercurial, his martial thigh,
> The brawns of Hercules.

Or its enamour'd touch would show
The shoulder, fair as sunless snow,
Which now in veiling shadow lies,
Removed from all but Fancy's eyes.
Now, for his feet—but hold—forbear—(6)
I see the sun-god's portrait there;
Why paint Bathyllus? when, in truth,
There, in that god, thou 'st sketch'd the youth.
Enough—let this bright form be mine,
And send the boy to Samos' shrine;
Phœbus shall then Bathyllus be,
Bathyllus then the deity!

————o•o————

ODE XVIII. (7)

Now the star of day is high,
Fly, my girls, in pity fly,
Bring me wine in brimming urns, (8)
Cool my lip, it burns, it burns!

We find it likewise in Hamlet. Longepierre thinks that the hands of Mercury are selected by Anacreon, on account of the graceful gestures which were supposed to characterise the god of eloquence; but Mercury was also the patron of thieves, and may perhaps be praised as a light fingered deity.

(5) These last four lines, as they appeared in former editions, were—

> But oh! suffuse his limbs of fire
> With all that glow of young desire
> Which kindles when the wishful sigh
> Steals from the heart, unconscious why.

To which Mr. Moore appended the following note:—

"I have taken the liberty here of somewhat veiling the original. Madame Dacier, in her translation, has hung out lights (as Sterne would call it,) at this passage. It is very much to be regretted that this substitution of asterisks has been so much adopted in the popular interpretations of the Classics; it serves but to bring whatever is exceptionable into notice, 'claramque facem præferre pudendis.'—P. E.

(6) The abrupt turn here is spirited, but requires some explanation. While the artist is pursuing the portrait of Bathyllus, Anacreon, we must suppose, turns round and sees a picture of Apollo, which was intended for an altar at Samos. He then instantly tells the painter to cease his work; that this picture will serve for Bathyllus; and that, when he goes to Samos, he may make an Apollo of the portrait of the boy which he had begun.

"Bathyllus (says Madame Dacier,) could not be more elegantly praised, and this one passage does him more honour than the statue, however beautiful it might be, which Polycrates raised to him."

(7) An elegant translation of this ode, says Degen, may be found in Ramler's Lyr. Blumenlese, lib. v. p. 405.

(8) Orig. πιειν αμυςι. The amystis was a method of drinking used among the Thracians. Thus Horace, "Threicia vincat amystide." Mad. Dacier, Longepierre, etc., etc.

Parrhasius, in his twenty-sixth epistle (Thesaur. Critic. vol. i.), explains the amystis as a draught to be exhausted without drawing breath, "uno haustu." A note in the margin of this epistle of Parrhasius says, "Politianus vestem esse putabat," but adds no reference.

Sunn'd by the meridian fire,
Panting, languid I expire.
Give me all those humid flowers, (1)
Drop them o'er my brow in showers.
Scarce a breathing chaplet now
Lives upon my feverish brow ;
Every dewy rose I wear (2)
Sheds its tears, and withers there.
But to you, my burning heart, (3)
What can now relief impart ?
Can brimming bowl, or floweret's dew,
Cool the flame that scorches you ?

——◦◦◦——

ODE XIX. (4)

HERE recline you, gentle maid, (5)
Sweet is this embowering shade ;

(1) According to the original reading of this line, the poet says, "Give me the flower of wine."—Date flosculos Lyæi, as it is in the version of Elias Andreas ; and,

Deb ! porgetemi del fiore
Di quell' almo e buon liquore,

as Regnier has it, who supports the reading. The word ανθος would undoubtedly bear this application, which is somewhat similar to its import in the epigram of Simonides upon Sophocles :—

Εσβεσθης, γεραιε Σοφοκλεες, ανθος αοιδων.

and flos in the Latin is frequently applied in the same manner—thus Cethegus is called by Ennius, Flos inlibatus populi, suadæque medulla, "The immaculate flower of the people, and the very marrow of persuasion." See these verses cited by Aulus Gellius, lib. xii., which Cicero praised, and Seneca thought ridiculous.

But in the passage before us, if we admit εκεινων, according to Faber's conjecture, the sense is sufficiently clear, without having recourse to such refinements.

(2) There are some beautiful lines, by Angerianus, upon a garland, which I cannot resist quoting here :—

Ante fores madidæ sic sic pendete corollæ,
Mane orto imponet Celia vos capiti ;
At quum per niveam cervicem influxerit humor,
Dicite, non roris sed pluvia hæc lacrymæ.

By Celia's arbour all the night
Hang, humid wreath, the lover's vow ;
And haply, at the morning light,
My love shall twine thee round her brow.

Then, if upon her bosom bright
Some drops of dew shall fall from thee,
Tell her, they are not drops of night,
But tears of sorrow shed by me !

In the poem of Mr. Sheridan's, "Uncouth is this moss-covered grotto of stone," there is an idea very singularly coincident with this of Angerianus :—

And thou, stony grot, in thy arch may'st preserve
Some lingering drops of the night-fallen dew ;
Let them fall on her bosom of snow, and they 'll serve
As tears of my sorrow entrusted to you.

(3) The transition here is peculiarly delicate and impassioned ; but the commentators have perplexed the sentiment by a variety of readings and conjectures.

(4) The description of this bower is so natural and animated, that we almost feel a degree of coolness and freshness while we peruse it. Longepierre has quoted, from the first book of the Anthologia, the following epigram, as somewhat resembling this ode :—

Sweet the young, the modest trees,
Ruffled by the kissing breeze ;
Sweet the little founts that weep,
Lulling soft the mind to sleep ;
Hark ! they whisper as they roll,
Calm persuasion to the soul.
Tell me, tell me, is not this
All a stilly scene of bliss ?
Who, my girl, would pass it by ? (6)
Surely neither you nor I.

——◦◦◦——

ODE XX.

ONE day the Muses (7) twined the hands
Of infant Love with flowery bands ;
And to celestial Beauty gave
The captive infant for her slave.

Ερχεο και κατ᾽ εμαν ιζευ πιτυν, ἁ το μελιχρον
Προς μαλακους ηχει κεκλιμενα ϛεφυρους.
Ηνιδε και κρουνισμα μελιϛαγες, ενθα μελισδων
Ἡδυν ερημαιοις ὑπνον αγω καλαμοις.

Come, sit by the shadowy pine
That covers my sylvan retreat ;
And see how the branches incline
The breathing of zephyr to meet.
See the fountain that, flowing, diffuses
Around me a splendid spray ;
By its brink, as the traveller muses,
I soothe him to sleep with my lay.

(5) The Vatican MS. reads Βαθυλλου, which renders the whole poem metaphorical. Some commentator suggests the reading of Βαθυλλον, which makes a pun upon the name ; a grace that Plato himself has condescended to in writing of his boy Αϛηρ. See the epigram of this philosopher, which I quote on the twenty-second ode.

There is another epigram by this philosopher, preserved in Laertius, which turns upon the same word.

Αϛηρ πριν μεν ελαμπες ενι ϛωοισιν εωοις,
Νυν δε θανων λαμπεις εσπερος εν φθιμενοις.

In life thou wert my morning star,
But now that death has stolen thy light,
Alas ! thou shinest dim and far,
Like the pale beam that weeps at night.

In the Veneres Blyenburgicæ, under the head of "Allusiones," we find a number of such frigid conceits upon names selected from the poets of the middle ages.

(6) The finish given to the picture by this simple exclamation τις αν ουν ὁραν παρελθοι, is inimitable. Yet a French translator says on the passage, "This conclusion appeared to me too trifling after such a description, and I thought proper to add somewhat to the strength of the original."

(7) The poet appears, in this graceful allegory, to describe the softening influence which poetry holds over the mind, in making it peculiarly susceptible to the impressions of beauty. In the following epigram, however, by the philosopher Plato (Diog. Laert. lib 3.), the Muses are represented as disavowing the influence of Love.

Ἁ Κυπρις Μουσαισι᾽ Κορασια, ταν Αφροδιταν
Τιματ᾽, η τον Ερωτα ὑμμιν εφοπλισομαι.
Αἱ Μουσαι ποτι Κυπριν᾽ Αρει τα στωμυλα ταυτα᾽
Ἡμιν ου πεταται τουτο το παιδαριον.

" Yield to my gentle power, Parnassian maids ;"
Thus to the Muses spoke the Queen of Charms—

His mother comes, with many a toy, (1)
To ransom her beloved boy;
His mother sues, but all in vain,—
He ne'er will leave his chains again.
Even should they take his chains away.
The little captive still would stay.
"If this," he cries, "a bondage be,
Oh, who could wish for liberty?"

———◦◊◊◦———

ODE XXI. (2)

Observe when mother earth is dry,
She drinks the droppings of the sky;
And then the dewy cordial gives
To every thirsty plant that lives.

" Or Love shall flutter through your classic shades,
    And make your grove the camp of Paphian arms!"
" No," said the virgins of the tuneful bower,
    " We scorn thine own and all thy urchin's art;
Though Mars has trembled at the infant's power,
    His shaft is pointless o'er a Muse's heart!"

There is a sonnet by Benedetto Guidi, the thought of which was suggested by this ode.

Scherzava dentro all' auree chiome Amore
    Dell' alma donna della vita mia :
E tanto era il piacer ch' ei ne sentia,
    Che non sapea, nè volea uscirne fore.

Quand' ecco ivi annodar si sente il core,
    Si, che per forza ancor convien che stia :
Tai lacci alta beltate orditi avia
    Del crespo crin, per farsi eterno onore.

Onde offre infin dal ciel degna mercede,
    A chi scioglie il fuliuol la bella Dea
    Da tanti nodi in ch' ella stretto il vede.

Ma ei vinto a due occhi l' arme cede :
    Eh ! l' affatichi indarno, Citerea ;
    Che s' altri 'l scioglie, egli a legar si riede.

Love, wandering through the golden maze
    Of my beloved's hair,
Found, at each step, such sweet delays,
    That rapt he linger'd there.

And how, indeed, was Love to fly,
    Or how his freedom find,
When every ringlet was a tie,
    A chain, by Beauty twined.

In vain to seek her boy's release,
    Comes Venus from above :
Fond mother, let thy efforts cease,
    Love 's now the slave of Love.
And, should we loose his golden chain,
    The prisoner would return again !

(1) In the first idyl of Moschus, Venus thus proclaims the reward for her fugitive child :—

'Ο μανυτας γερας εξει,
Μισθος τοι, το φιλαμα το Κυπριδος· ην δ' αγκγης νιν,
Ου γυμνον το φιλαμα, το δ', ω ξενε, και πλεον εξεις.

On him, who the haunts of my Cupid can show,
A kiss of the tenderest stamp I'll bestow ;
But he, who can bring back the urchin in chains,
Shall receive even something more sweet for his pains.

Subjoined to this ode, we find in the Vatican MS. the following lines, which appear to me to boast as little sense as metre, and which are most probably the interpolation of the transcriber : —

Ήδυμελης Ανακρεων,
Ήδυμελης δε Σαπφω·

The vapours, which at evening weep,
Are beverage to the swelling deep;
And when the rosy sun appears,
He drinks the ocean's misty tears.
The moon too quaffs her paly stream
Of lustre, from the solar beam.
Then, hence with all your sober thinking !
Since Nature's holy law is drinking ;
I 'll make the laws of nature mine,
And pledge the universe in wine.

———◦◊◦———

ODE XXII.

The Phrygian rock, that braves the storm,
Was once a weeping matron's form ; (3)

Πινδαρικον τοδε μοι μελος
Συγκερασας τις εγχεοι.
Τα τρια ταυτα μοι δοκει·
Και Διονυσος εισελθων,
Και Παφη παραχροος,
Και αυτος Ερως και επιειν.

(2) Those critics who have endeavoured to throw the chains of precision over the spirit of this beautiful trifle, require too much from Anacreontic philosophy. Among others, Gail very sapiently thinks that the poet uses the epithet μελαινη, because black earth absorbs moisture more quickly than any other ; and accordingly he indulges us with an experimental disquisition on the subject. See Gail's notes.

One of the Capilupi has imitated this ode, in an epitaph on a drunkard :—

Dum vixi sine fine bibi, sic imbrifer arcus,
    Sic tellus pluvias sole perusta bibit.
Sic bibit assiduè fontes et flumina pontus,
    Sic semper sitiens sol maris haurit aquas.
Ne te igitur jactes plus me, Silene, bibisse ;
    Et mihi da victas tu quoque, Bacche, manus.
                        HIPPOLYTUS CAPILUPUS.

While life was mine, the little hour
    In drinking still unvaried flew ;
I drank as earth imbibes the shower,
    Or as the rainbow drinks the dew ;
As ocean quaffs the rivers up,
    Or flushing sun inhales the sea :
Silenus trembled at my cup,
    And Bacchus was outdone by me!

I cannot omit citing those remarkable lines of Shakspeare, where the thoughts of the ode before us are preserved with such striking similitude :—

I 'll example you with thievery.
The sun 's a thief, and with his great attraction
Robs the vast sea. The moon 's an arrant thief,
And her pale fire she snatches from the sun.
The sea 's a thief, whose liquid surge resolves
The mounds into salt tears.   The earth 's a thief,
That feeds, and breeds by a composture stolen
From general excrements.
                        Timon of Athens, act. iv. sc. 3.

(3) Niobe.—Ogilvie, in his Essay on the Lyric Poetry of the Ancients, in remarking upon the Odes of Anacreon, says, "In some of his pieces there is exuberance and even wildness of imagination ; in that particularly, which is addressed to a young girl, where he wishes alternately to be transformed to a mirror, a coat, a stream, a bracelet, and a pair of shoes, for the different purposes which he recites ; this is mere sport and wantonness."

And Progne, hapless, frantic maid,
Is now a swallow in the shade.
Oh! that a mirror's form were mine,
That I might catch that smile divine;
And like my own fond fancy be,
Reflecting thee, and only thee;
Or could I be the robe which holds
That graceful form within its folds;
Or, turn'd into a fountain, lave
Thy beauties in my circling wave.
Would I were perfume for thy hair,
To breathe my soul in fragrance there; (1)
Or, better still, the zone, that lies (2)
Close to thy breast, and feels its sighs.

It is the wantonness, however, of a very graceful Muse; "ludit amabiliter." The compliment of this ode is exquisitely delicate, and so singular for the period in which Anacreon lived, when the scale of love had not yet been graduated into all its little progressive refinements, that if we were inclined to question the authenticity of the poem, we should find a much more plausible argument in the features of modern gallantry which it bears, than in any of those fastidious conjectures upon which some commentators have presumed so far. Degen thinks it spurious, and De Pauw pronounces it to be miserable. Longepierre and Barnes refer us to several imitations of this ode, from which I shall only select the following epigram of Dionysius :—

Ειθ' ανεμος γενομην, συ δε γε ςειχουσα παρ αυγας,
Στηθεα γυμνωσαις, και με πνεοντα λαβοις.
Ειθε ροδον γενοιμην ὑποπορφυρον, οφρα με χερσιν
Αραμενη, κομισαις ςεθετι χιονεοις.
Ειθε κρινον γενοιμην λευκοχροον, οφρα με χερσιν
Αραμενη, μαλλον σης χροτιης κορεσης.

> I wish I could like zephyr steal
> To wanton o'er thy mazy vest;
> And thou wouldst ope thy bosom-veil,
> And take me panting to thy breast!
>
> I wish I might a rose-bud grow,
> And thou wouldst cull me from the bower,
> To place me on that breast of snow,
> Where I should bloom, a wintry flower.
>
> I wish I were the lily's leaf,
> To fade upon that bosom warm;
> Content to wither, pale and brief,
> The trophy of thy fairer form!

I may add, that Plato has expressed as fanciful a wish in a distich preserved by Laertius :

Αςερας εισαθρεις, Αςηρ εμος· ειθε γενοιμην
Ουρανος, ὡς πολλοις ομμασιν εις σε βλεπω.

TO STELLA.

> Why dost thou gaze upon the sky?
> Oh! that I were that spangled sphere,
> And every star should be an eye,
> To wonder on thy beauties here!

Apuleius quotes this epigram of the divine philosopher, to justify himself for his verses on Critias and Charinus. See his Apology, where he also adduces the example of Anacreon; "Fecere tamen et alii talia, et si vos ignoratis, apud Græcos Teius quidam," etc., etc.

(1) The following lines, which were given in the original translation of this ode by Mr. Moore, scarcely appear less worthy a place here, than those substituted for them :—

Or even those envious pearls that show
So faintly round that neck of snow—
Yes, I would be a happy gem,
Like them to hang, to fade like them.
What more would thy Anacreon be?
Oh, any thing that touches thee;
Nay, sandals for those airy feet — (3)
Even to be trod by them were sweet!

—◦◦◦◦—

ODE XXIII. (4)

I OFTEN wish this languid lyre,
This warbler of my soul's desire,

> Or were I, love, the robe which flows
> O'er every charm that secret glows,
> In many a lucid fold to swim,
> And cling and grow to every limb!
> Oh! could I, as the streamlet's wave,
> Thy warmly-mellowing beauties lave,
> Or float as perfume on thine hair,
> And breathe my soul in fragrance there.—P. E.

(2) This ταινη was a riband, or band, called by the Romans fascia and strophium, which the women wore for the purpose of restraining the exuberance of the bosom. Vide Polluc. Onomast. Thus Martial :—

> Fascia, crescentes dominæ compesce papillas.

The women of Greece not only wore this zone, but condemned themselves to fasting, and made use of certain drugs and powders for the same purpose. To these expedients they were compelled, in consequence of their inelegant fashion of compressing the waist into a very narrow compass, which necessarily caused an excessive tumidity in the bosom. See Dioscorides, lib. v.

(3) The sophist Philostratus, in one of his love-letters, has borrowed this thought; ω αδετοι ποδες, ω καλλος ελευθερον, ω τρισευδαιμων εγω και μακαριος εαν πατησετε με.—"Oh lovely feet! oh excellent beauty! oh! thrice happy and blessed should I be, if you would but tread on me!" In Shakspeare, Romeo desires to be a glove :—

> Oh! that I were a glove upon that hand,
> That I might kiss that cheek!

And in his Passionate Pilgrim, we meet with an idea somewhat like that of the thirteenth line :—

> He, spying her, bounced in, where as he stood,
> "O Jove!" quoth she, "why was not I a flood?"

In Burton's Anatomy of Melancholy, that whimsical farrago of "all such reading as was never read," we find a translation of this ode made before 1632.—"Englished by Mr. B. Holiday, in his Techmog., act i., scene 7."

(4) According to the order in which the odes are usually placed, this (Θελω λεγειν Ατρειδας) forms the first of the series; and is thought to be peculiarly designed as an introduction to the rest. It, however, characterises the genius of the Teian but very inadequately, as wine, the burden of his lays, is not even mentioned in it :

> —— cum multo Venerem confundere mero
> Præcepit Lyrici Teia Musa senis.—OVID.

The twenty-sixth Ode, Συ μεν λεγεις τα Θηδης, might, with just as much propriety, be placed at the head of his songs.

We find the sentiments of the ode before us expressed by Bion with much simplicity in his fourth idyl. The above

Could raise the breath of song sublime,
To men of fame in former time.
But when the soaring theme I try,
Along the chords my numbers die,
And whisper, with dissolving tone,
" Our sighs are given to love alone !"
Indignant at the feeble lay,
I tore the panting chords away,
Attuned them to a nobler swell,
And struck again the breathing shell ;
In all the glow of epic fire,(1)
To Hercules I wake the lyre.
But still its fainting sighs repeat,(2)
" The tale of love alone is sweet !"
Then fare thee well, seductive dream,
That madest me follow Glory's theme;
For thou, my lyre, and thou, my heart,
Shall never more in spirit part ;
And all that one has felt so well
The other shall as sweetly tell !

---◦◦◦◦---

ODE XXIV. (3)

To all that breathe the air of heaven,
Some boon of strength has Nature given.
In forming the majestic bull,
She fenced with wreathed horns his skull ;
A hoof of strength she lent the steed,
And wing'd the timorous hare with speed. (4)

translation is, perhaps, too paraphrastical ; but the ode has been so frequently translated, that I could not otherwise avoid triteness and repetition.

(1) Madame Dacier generally translates λυρη into a lute, which, I believe, is inaccurate. " D'expliquer la lyre des anciens (says M. Sorel,) par un luth, c'est ignorer la difference qu'il y a entre ces deux instruments de musique."—*Bibliothèque Françoise.*

(2) The word αντερωνει in the original, may imply that kind of musical dialogue practised by the ancients, in which the lyre was made to respond to the questions proposed by the singer. This was a method which Sappho used, as we are told by Hermogenes ; " ὁταν την λυραν ερωτα Σαπφω, και ὁταν αυτη αποκρινηται."—Περι Ιδεων, τομ. δευτ.

(3) Henry Stephen has imitated the idea of this ode in the following lines of one of his poems :—

Provida dat cunctis Natura animantibus arma,
Et sua fœmineum possidet arma genus,
Ungulaque ut defendit equum, atque ut cornua taurum,
Armata est formâ fœmina pulchra suâ.

And the same thought occurs in those lines, spoken by Corisca in Pastor Fido :—

Così noi la bellezza
Ch' è vertù nostra così propria, come
La forza del leone,
E l'ingegno de l' uomo.

The lion boasts his savage powers,
And lordly man his strength of mind ;
But Beauty's charm is solely ours,
Peculiar boon, by Heaven assign'd.

"An elegant explication of the beauties of this ode (says Degen,) may be found in Grimm an den Anmerk. über einige Oden des Anakr."

She gave the lion fangs of terror,
And, o'er the ocean's crystal mirror,
Taught the unnumber'd scaly throng
To trace their liquid path along;
While for the umbrage of the grove,
She plumed the warbling world of love.
To man she gave, in that proud hour,(5)
The boon of intellectual power.
Then, what, oh woman, what, for thee,
Was left in Nature's treasury ?
She gave thee beauty—mightier far (6)
Than all the pomp and power of war.
Nor steel, nor fire itself, hath power
Like woman in her conquering hour.
Be thou but fair, mankind adore thee; (7)
Smile, and a world is weak before thee !

---◦◦◦◦---

ODE XXV. (8)

ONCE in each revolving year,
Gentle bird ! we find thee here.
When Nature wears her summer-vest,
Thou comest to weave thy simple nest ;
But when the chilling winter lowers,
Again thou seek'st the genial bowers
Of Memphis, or the shores of Nile,
Where sunny hours for ever smile.
And thus thy pinion rests and roves,—
Alas ! unlike the swarm of Loves,

(4) The four preceding lines originally appeared thus :
When the majestic bull was born,
She fenced his brow with wreathed horn :
She arm'd the courser's foot of air,
And wing'd with speed the panting hare.—P. E.

(5) In my first attempt to translate this ode, I had interpreted φρονημα, with Baxter and Barnes, as implying courage and military virtue; but I do not think that the gallantry of the idea suffers by the import which I have now given to it. For, why need we consider this possession of wisdom as exclusive? and in truth, as the design of Anacreon is to estimate the treasure of beauty above all the rest which Nature has distributed, it is perhaps even refining upon the delicacy of the compliment, to prefer the radiance of female charms to the cold illumination of wisdom and prudence ; and to think that women's eyes are,

———the books, the academies,
From whence doth spring the true Promethean fire.

(6) Thus Achilles Tatius :—Καλλος οξυτερον τιτρωσκει βελους, και δια των οφθαλμων εις την ψυχην καταρδει. Οφθαλμος γαρ ὁδος ερωτικω τραυματι. " Beauty wounds more swiftly than the arrow, and passes through the eye to the very soul ; for the eye is the inlet to the wounds of love."

(7) Longepierre's remark here is ingenious :—"The Romans," says he, " were so convinced of the power of beauty, that they used a word implying strength in the place of the epithet beautiful. Thus Plautus, act ii., scene 2., Bacchid.

Sed Bacchis etiam fortis tibi visa.

' Fortis, id est formosa,' say Servius and Nonius.'"

(8) We have here another ode addressed to the swallow. Alberti has imitated both in one poem, beginning,

4

That brood within this hapless breast,
And never, never change their nest!(1)
Still every year, and all the year,
They fix their fated dwelling here ;
And some their infant plumage try,
And on a tender winglet fly ;
While in the shell, impregn'd with fires,
Still lurk a thousand more desires ;
Some from their tiny prisons peeping,
And some in formless embryo sleeping.
Thus peopled, like the vernal groves,
My breast resounds with warbling Loves;
One urchin imps the other's feather,
Then twin-desires they wing together,
And fast as they thus take their flight,
Still other urchins spring to light.
But is there then no kindly art,
To chase these Cupids from my heart ;
Ah, no ! I fear, in sadness fear,
They will for ever nestle here !

———o❦❦o———

ODE XXVI.(2)

THY harp may sing of Troy's alarms,
Or tell the tale of Theban arms ;
With other wars my song shall burn,
For other wounds my harp shall mourn.

Perch' io pianga al tuo canto,
Rondinella importuna, etc.

(1) Thus Love is represented as a bird, in an epigram cited by Longepierre from the Anthologia :—

Διει μοι δυνει μεν εν ουασιν ηχος ερωτος,
Ομμα δε εγια ποθοις το γλυκυ δακρυ φερει.
Ουδ᾽ ἡ νυξ, ου φεγγος εκοιμισεν, αλλ᾽ ὑπο φιλτρων
Ηδε που κραδιη γνωςος εΝεςι τυπος.
Ω πταιοι, μη και ποτ εφιπταισθαι μεν, ερωτες,
Οιδατ᾽, αποπτηναι δ᾽ ουθ᾽ ὁσον ισχυετε.

'T is Love that murmurs in my breast,
And makes me shed the secret tear;
Nor day nor night my soul hath rest,
For night and day his voice I hear.

A wound within my heart I find,
And oh ! 't is plain where Love has been; .
For still he leaves a wound behind,
Such as within my heart is seen.

Oh, bird of Love! with song so drear,
Make not my soul the nest of pain;
But let the wing which brought thee here,
In pity waft thee hence again !

(2) "The German poet Uz has imitated this ode. Compare also Weisse Scherz. Lieder, lib. iii. der Soldat."—Gail, Degen.

(3) Longepierre has quoted part of an epigram from the seventh book of the Anthologia, which has a fancy something like this.

Ου με λεληθας,
Τοξοτα, Ζηνοφιλας ομμασι κρυπτομενος.

Archer Love! though slily creeping,
Well I know where thou dost lie;

'T was not the crested warrior's dart,
That drank the current of my heart;
Nor naval arms, nor mailed steed,
Have made this vanquish'd bosom bleed;
No—'t was from eyes of liquid blue,(3)
A host of quiver'd Cupids flew ;
And now my heart all bleeding lies
Beneath that army of the eyes!

———o❦❦o———

ODE XXVII.(4)

WE read the flying courser's name
Upon his side, in marks of flame ;
And, by their turban'd brows alone,
The warriors of the East are known.
But in the lover's glowing eyes,(5)
The inlet to his bosom lies ;
Through them we see the small faint mark,
Where Love has dropp'd his burning spark!

———o❦❦o———

ODE XXVIII.(6)

As, by his Lemnian forge's flame,
The husband of the Paphian dame
Moulded the glowing steel, to form
Arrows for Cupid, thrilling warm ;
And Venus, as he plied his art,
Shed honey round each new-made dart,

I saw thee through the curtain peeping,
That fringes Zenophelia's eye.

The poets abound with conceits on the archery of the eyes, but few have turned the thought so naturally as Anacreon. Ronsard gives to the eyes of his mistress "un petit camp d'amour."

(4) This ode forms a part of the preceding in the Vatican MS., but I have conformed to the editions in translating them separately.

"Compare with this (says Degen,) the poem of Ramler Wahrzeichen der Liebe, in Lyr. Blumenlese, lib. iv., p. 313."

(5) "We cannot see into the heart," says Madame Dacier. But the lover answers,—

Il cor ne gli occhi et ne la fronte ho scrito.

M. La Fosse has given the following lines, as enlarging on the thought of Anacreon :—

Lorsque je vois un amant,
Il cache en vain son tourment,
A le trahir tout conspire:
Sa langueur, son embarras,
Tout ce qu'il peut faire ou dire,
Même ce qu'il ne dit pas.

In vain the lover tries to veil
The flame that in his bosom lies;
His cheeks' confusion tells the tale,
We read it in his languid eyes :
And while his words the heart betray,
His silence speaks even more than they.

(6) This ode is referred to by La Mothe le Vayer, who, I believe, was the author of that curious little work, called "Hexameron Rustique." He makes use of this, as well as the thirty-fifth, in his ingenious but indelicate explanation of Homer's Cave of the Nymphs.—Journée quatrième.

While Love, at hand, to finish all,(1)
Tipp'd every arrow's point with gall;
It chanced the Lord of Battles came
To visit that deep cave of flame.
'T was from the ranks of war he rush'd,
His spear with many a life-drop blush'd;
He saw the fiery darts, and smiled
Contemptuous at the archer-child.
"What!" said the urchin, "dost thou smile?
Here, hold this little dart awhile,
And thou wilt find, though swift of flight,
My bolts are not so feathery light."
    Mars took the shaft—and, oh, thy look,
Sweet Venus, when the shaft he took!
Sighing, he felt the urchin's art,
And cried, in agony of heart,
"It is not light—I sink with pain!
Take—take thy arrow back again."
"No," said the child, "it must not be;
That little dart was made for thee!"

(1) Thus Claudian:—

Labuntur gemini fontes, hic dulcis, amarus
Alter, et infusis corrumpit mella venenis,
Unde Cupidineas armavit fama sagittas.

In Cyprus' isle two rippling fountains fall,
And one with honey flows, and one with gall;
In these, if we may take the tale from fame,
The son of Venus dips his darts of flame.

See Alciatus, emblem 91, on the close connection which subsists between sweets and bitterness. "Apes ideo pungunt (says Petronius), quia ubi dulce, ibi et acidum invenies."

The allegorical description of Cupid's employment, in Horace, may vie with this before us in fancy, though not in delicacy:—

    ——ferus et Cupido
Semper ardentes acuens sagittas
    Cote cruentâ.

And Cupid, sharpening all his fiery darts,
Upon a whetstone stain'd with blood of hearts.

Secundus has borrowed this, but has somewhat softened the image by the omission of the epithet "cruentâ."

Fallor, an ardentes acuebat cote sagittas?—Eleg. 1.

(2) The following Anacreontic, addressed by Menage to Daniel Huet, enforces, with much grace, the "necessity of loving:"—

Περι του δειν φιλησαι.
Προς Πετρον Δανιηλα Ὑεττον.

Μεγα θαυμα των αοιδων,
Χαριτων θαλος, Ὑεττε,
Φιλεωμεν, ω έταιρε.
Φιλησαν οἱ σοφισται.
Φιλησε σεμνος ανηρ,
Το τεκνον του Σωφρονισκου,
Σοφης πατηρ ἁπασης.
Τι δ' ανευ γενοιτ' Ερωτος;
Ακουη μεν εςι ψυχης.*

*This line is borrowed from an epigram by Alpheus of Mitylene, which Menage, I think, says somewhere, he was himself the first to produce to the world:—

Ψυχης εςιν Ερως ακουη.

ODE XXIX. (2)

Yes—loving is a painful thrill,(2)
And not to love more painful still;
But oh, it is the worst of pain,
To love and not be loved again!
Affection now has fled from earth,
Nor fire of genius, noble birth,
Nor heavenly virtue, can beguile
From beauty's cheek one favouring smile.
Gold is the woman's only theme,
Gold is the woman's only dream.
Oh! never be that wretch forgiven—
Forgive him not, indignant heaven!
Whose grovelling eyes could first adore,
Whose heart could pant for sordid ore.
Since that devoted thirst began,
Man has forgot to feel for man;
The pulse of social life is dead,
And all its fonder feelings fled!

Πτεουγεσσιν εις Ολυμπον
Καταχειμενους αναιρει.
Βραδεας τετηγμενοισι
Βελεεσι εξαγειρει.
Πυρι λαμπαδος φαεινω
Ρυπαρωτερους καθαιρει.
Φιλεωμεν ουν, Ὑεττε,
Φιλεωμεν, ω έταιρε.
Αδικως δε λοιδορουντι
Αγιους ερωτας ἡμων
Κακον ευξομαι το μουνον,
Ἱνα μη δυναιτ' εκεινος
Φιλεειν τε και φιλεισθαι.

Thou! of tuneful bards the first,
Thou! by all the Graces nurst;
Friend! each other friend above,
Come with me, and learn to love.
Loving is a simple lore,
Graver men have learn'd before;
Nay, the boast of former ages,
Wisest of the wisest sages,
Sophroniscus' prudent son,
Was by love's illusion won.
Oh! how heavy life would move,
If we knew not how to love!
Love 's a whetstone to the mind;
Thus 't is pointed, thus refined.
When the soul dejected lies,
Love can waft it to the skies;
When in languor sleeps the heart,
Love can wake it with his dart;
When the mind is dull and dark,
Love can light it with his spark!
Come, oh! come then, let us haste,
All the bliss of love to taste;
Let us love both night and day,
Let us love our lives away!
And when hearts, from loving free,
(If indeed such hearts there be,)
Frown upon our gentle flame,
And the sweet delusion blame;
This shall be my only curse,
(Could I, could I wish them worse?)
May they ne'er the rapture prove
Of the smile from lips we love!

War too has sullied Nature's charms,
For gold provokes the world to arms :
And oh ! the worst of all its arts,
It rends asunder loving hearts.

———o••o———

ODE XXX. (1)

'T was in a mocking dream of night—
I fancied I had wings as light
As a young bird's, and flew as fleet;
While Love, around whose beauteous feet,
I knew not why, hung chains of lead,
Pursued me, as I trembling fled ;
And, strange to say, as swift as thought,
Spite of my pinions, I was caught !
What does the wanton Fancy mean
By such a strange illusive scene ?
I fear she whispers to my breast,
That you, sweet maid, have stolen its rest ;
That though my fancy, for a while,
Hath hung on many a woman's smile,
I soon dissolved each passing vow,
And ne'er was caught by love till now !

(1) Barnes imagines from this allegory, that our poet married very late in life. But I see nothing in the ode which alludes to matrimony, except it be the lead upon the feet of Cupid ; and I agree in the opinion of Madame Dacier, in her life of the poet, that he was always too fond of pleasure to marry.

(2) The design of this little fiction is to intimate, that much greater pain attends insensibility than can ever result from the tenderest impressions of love. Longepierre has quoted an ancient epigram which bears some similitude to this ode :—

Lecto compositus, vix prima silentia noctis
Carpebam, et somno lumina victa dabam ;
Cum me sævus Amor prensam, sursumque capillis
Excitat, et lacerum pervigilare jubet.
Tu famulus meus, inquit, æoes cum mille puellas,
Solus Io, solus, dure, jacere potes ?
Exsilio et pedibus nudis, tunicâque solutâ,
Omne iter impedio, nullum iter expedio.
Nunc propero, nunc ire piget ; rursumque redire
Pœnitet ; et pudor est stare viâ mediâ.
Ecce tacent voces hominum, strepitusque ferarum,
Et volucrum cantus, turbaque fida canum.
Solus ego ex cunctis paveo somnumque torumque,
Et sequor imperium, sæve Cupido, tuum.

Upon my couch I lay, at night profound,
My languid eyes in magic slumber bound,
When Cupid came and snatch'd me from my bed,
And forced me many a weary way to tread.
" What ! (said the god) shall you, whose vows are known,
Who love so many nymphs, thus sleep alone?"
I rise and follow ; all the night I stray,
Unshelter'd, trembling, doubtful of my way ;
Tracing with naked foot the painful track,
Loth to proceed, yet fearful to go back.
Yes, at that hour, when Nature seems interr'd,
Nor warbling birds, nor lowing flocks are heard,
I, I alone, a fugitive from rest,
Passion my guide, and madness in my breast,
Wander the world around, unknowing where,
The slave of love, the victim of despair !

(3) I have followed those who read τειρεν ιδρως for πειρεν υδρος ; the former is partly authorised by the MS., which reads πειρεν ιδρως.

ODE XXXI. (2)

Arm'd with hyacinthine rod,
(Arms enough for such a god,)
Cupid bade me wing my pace,
And try with him the rapid race.
O'er many a torrent, wild and deep,
By tangled brake and pendent steep,
With weary foot I panting flew,
Till my brow dropp'd with chilly dew. (3)
And now my soul, exhausted, dying, (4)
To my lip was faintly flying ;
And now I thought the spark had fled,
When Cupid hover'd o'er my head,
And fanning light his breezy pinion, (5)
Rescued my soul from death's dominion ;
Then said, in accents half-reproving,
" Why hast thou been a foe to loving ? "

———o••o———

ODE XXXII. (6)

Strew me a fragrant bed of leaves,
Where lotus with the myrtle weaves,
And while in luxury's dream I sink,
Let me the balm of Bacchus drink !

(4) In the original, he says, his heart flew to his nose ; but our manner more naturally transfers it to the lips. Such is the effect that Plato tells us he felt from a kiss, in a distich quoted by Aulus Gellius :—

Την ψυχην, Αγαθωνα φιλων, επι χειλεσιν εσχον.
Ηλθε γαρ ἡ τλημων ὡς διαβησομενη.

Whene'er thy nectar'd kiss I sip,
And drink thy breath, in trance divine,
My soul then flutters to my lip,
Ready to fly and mix with thine.

Aulus Gellius subjoins a paraphrase of this epigram, in which we find a number of those mignardises of expression, which mark the effemination of the Latin language.

(5) " The facility with which Cupid recovers him signifies, that the sweets of love make us easily forget any solicitudes which he may occasion."—La Fosse.

(6) We here have the poet, in his true attributes, reclining upon myrtles, with Cupid for his cup-bearer. Some interpreters have ruined the picture, by making Ερως the name of his slave. None but Love should fill the goblet of Anacreon. Sappho, in one of her fragments, has assigned this office to Venus. Ελθε, Κυπρι, χρυσειαισιν εν κυλικεσσιν ἁβροις συμμεμιγμενον Θαλιαισι νεκταρ οινοχουσα τουτοισι τοις ἑταιροις εμοις γε και σοις.

Which may be thus paraphrased :—

Hither, Venus, queen of kisses,
This shall be the night of blisses ;
This the night, to friendship dear,
Thou shalt be our Hebe here.
Fill the golden brimmer high,
Let it sparkle like thine eye ;
Bid the rosy current gush,
Let it mantle like thy blush.

Goddess, hast thou e'er above
Seen a feast so rich in love ?
Not a soul that is not mine !
Not a soul that is not thine !

" Compare with this ode (says the German commentator,) the beautiful poem in Ramler's Lyr. Blumenlese, lib. iv., p. 296, 'Amor als Diener.'"

In this sweet hour of revelry
Young Love shall my attendant be—
Drest for the task, with tunic round
His snowy neck, and shoulders bound,
Himself shall hover by my side,
And minister the racy tide !
   Oh, swift as wheels that kindling roll,
Our life is hurrying to the goal :
A scanty dust to feed the wind,
Is all the trace 't will leave behind.
Then wherefore waste the rose's bloom
Upon the cold insensate tomb ?
Can flowery breeze or odour's breath,
Affect the still cold sense of death ?
Oh no ; I ask no balm to steep
With fragrant tears my bed of sleep :
But now while every pulse is glowing,
Now let me breathe the balsam flowing ;
Now let the rose, with blush of fire,
Upon my brow in sweets expire ;
And bring the nymph whose eye hath power
To brighten even death's cold hour.
Yes, Cupid ! ere my shade retire,
To join the blest elysian choir,
With wine, and love, and social cheer,
I 'll make my own elysium here !

———o◎◎o———

ODE XXXIII. (1)

'T was noon of night, when round the pole
The sullen Bear is seen to roll ;
And mortals, wearied with the day,
Are slumbering all their cares away :
An infant, at that dreary hour,
Came weeping to my silent bower,
And waked me with a piteous prayer,
To shield him from the midnight air.
" And who art thou," I waking cry,(2)
" That bid'st my blissful visions fly ?"
" Ah, gentle sire ! " the infant said,
" In pity take me to thy shed ;
Nor fear deceit : a lonely child,
I wander o'er the gloomy wild.

(1) M. Bernard, the author of " L'Art d'aimer," has
written a ballet called " Les Surprises de l'Amour," in
which the subject of the third entrée is Anacreon, and the
story of this ode suggests one of the scenes.—Œuvres de
Bernard, Anac., scene 4th.
   The German annotator refers us here to an imitation by
Uz, lib. iii., " Amor und sein Bruder ; " and a poem of
Kleist, " die Heilung." La Fontaine has translated, or
rather imitated, this ode.
   (2) Anacreon appears to have been a voluptuary even in
dreaming, by the lively regret which he expresses at being
disturbed from his visionary enjoyments. See the odes x.
and xxxvii.
   (3) See the beautiful description of Cupid, by Moschus,
in his first idyl.
   (4) In a Latin ode addressed to the grasshopper, Rapin
has preserved some of the thoughts of our author :—

Chill drops the rain, and not a ray
Illumes the drear and misty way !"
   I heard the baby's tale of woe,
I heard the bitter night-winds blow ;
And, sighing for his piteous fate,
I trimm'd my lamp and oped the gate.
'T was Love ! the little wandering sprite,(3)
His pinion sparkled through the night.
I knew him by his bow and dart ;
I knew him by my fluttering heart.
Fondly I take him in, and raise
The dying embers' cheering blaze ;
Press from his dank and clinging hair
The crystals of the freezing air,
And in my hand and bosom hold
His little fingers thrilling cold.
   And now the embers' genial ray
Had warm'd his anxious fears away ;
" I pray thee," said the wanton child,
(My bosom trembled as he smiled,)
" I pray thee let me try my bow,
For through the rain I 've wander'd so,
That much I fear the midnight shower
Has injured its elastic power."
The fatal bow the urchin drew ;
Swift from the string the arrow flew ;
As swiftly flew as glancing flame,
And to my inmost spirit came !
" Fare thee well," I heard him say,
As laughing wild he wing'd away ;
" Fare thee well, for now I know
The rain has not relax'd my bow ;
It still can send a thrilling dart,
As thou shalt own with all thy heart !"

———o◎◎o———

ODE XXXIV. (4)

Oh thou, of all creation blest,
Sweet insect that delight'st to rest
Upon the wild wood's leafy tops,
To drink the dew that morning drops,
And chirp thy song with such a glee, (5)
That happiest kings may envy thee.

   O quæ virenti graminis in toro,
   Cicada, blande sidis, et herbidos
      Saltus oberras, otiosos
         Ingeniosa ciere cantus.
   Seu forte adultis floribus incubas,
   Cœli caducis ebria fletibus, etc.

   Oh thou, that on the grassy bed
   Which Nature's vernal hand has spread,
   Reclinest soft, and tunest thy song,
   The dewy herbs and leaves among !
   Whether thou ly'st on springing flowers,
   Drunk with the balmy morning-showers,
      Or, etc.

   See what Licetus says about grasshoppers, cap. 93
and 185.
   (5) " Some authors have affirmed (says Madame Dacier,)
that it is only male grasshoppers which sing, and that the
females are silent ; and on this circumstance is founded a

Whatever decks the velvet field,
Whate'er the circling seasons yield,
Whatever buds, whatever blows,
For thee it buds, for thee it grows.
Nor yet art thou the peasant's fear,
To him thy friendly notes are dear;
For thou art mild as matin dew;
And still, when summer's flowery hue
Begins to paint the bloomy plain,
We hear thy sweet prophetic strain;
Thy sweet prophetic strain we hear,
And bless the notes and thee revere!
The Muses love thy shrilly tone; (1)
Apollo calls thee all his own;
'T was he who gave that voice to thee,
'T is he who tunes thy minstrelsy.
   Unworn by age's dim decline,
The fadeless blooms of youth are thine.
Melodious insect, child of earth, (2)
In wisdom mirthful, wise in mirth;

bon-mot of Xenarchus, the comic poet, who says, εἰτ' εἰσιν
οἱ τεττιγες ουκ ευδαιμονες, ὡν ταις γυναιξιν ουδ' ὁτιουν
φωνης ενι; 'are not the grasshoppers happy in having
dumb wives?'" This note is originally Henry Stephen's;
but I chose rather to make a lady my authority for it.

(1) Phile, de Animal. Proprietat., calls this insect Μου-
σαις φιλος, the darling of the Muses; and Μουσων ορνιν,
the bird of the Muses; and we find Plato compared for
his eloquence to the grasshopper, in the following pun-
ning lines of Timon, preserved by Diogenes Laertius:—

Των παντων δ᾽ ηγειτο πλατυγατος, αλλ᾽ αγορητης
Ἡδυεπης τεττιξιν ισογραφος, οἱ θ᾽ Ἑκαδημου
Δενδρει ερεζομενοι οπα λειριοεσσαν ἱεισι.

This last line is borrowed from Homer's Iliad, γ, where
there occurs the very same simile.

(2) Longepierre has quoted the two first lines of an
epigram of Antipater, from the first book of the Anthologia,
where he prefers the grasshopper to the swan:—

Αρχει τεττιγας μεθυσαι δροσος, αλλα πιοντες
Αειδειν κυκνων εισι γεγωνοτεροι.

     In dew, that drops from morning's wings,
       The gay Cicada sipping floats;
     And, drunk with dew, his matin sings,
       Sweeter than any cygnet's notes.

(3) Theocritus has imitated this beautiful ode in his nine-
teenth idyl; but is very inferior, I think, to his original, in
delicacy of point and naïveté of expression. Spenser, in
one of his smaller compositions, has sported more diffusely
on the same subject. The poem to which I allude begins
thus:—

     Upon a day, as Love lay sweetly slumbering
       All in his mother's lap;
     A gentle bee, with his loud trumpet murmuring,
       About him flew by hap, etc., etc.

In Almeloveen's collection of epigrams, there is one by
Luxorius, correspondent somewhat with the turn of Ana-
creon, where Love complains to his mother of being
wounded by a rose.

The ode before us is the very flower of simplicity. The
infantine complainings of the little god, and the natural
and impressive reflections which they draw from Venus,
are beauties of inimitable grace. I may be pardoned,

Exempt from every weak decay,
That withers vulgar frames away;
With not a drop of blood to stain
The current of thy purer vein;
So blest an age is past by thee,
Thou seem'st—a little deity!

————⋄⊙⊗⋄————

ODE XXXV. (3)

Cupid once upon a bed
Of roses laid his weary head;
Luckless urchin not to see
Within the leaves a slumbering bee;
The bee awaked—with anger wild
The bee awaked, and stung the child.
Loud and piteous are his cries;
To Venus quick he runs, he flies;
"Oh mother!—I am wounded through—
I die with pain—in sooth I do!

perhaps, for introducing here another of Menage's Ana-
creontics, not for its similitude to the subject of this ode,
but for some faint traces of the same natural simplicity,
which it appears to me to have preserved:—

Ερως ποτ᾽ εν χορειαις
Των παρθενων αωτον,
Την μοι φιλην Κορινναν,
Ὡς ειδεν, ὡς προς αυτην
Προσεδραμε· τραχηλω
Διδυμας τε χειρας ἁπτων·
Φιλει με, μητερ, ειπε.
Καλουμενη Κοριννα,
Μητηρ, ερυθριαϚει,
Ὡς παρθενος μεν ουσα.
Κ᾽ αυτος δε δυσχεραινων,
Ὡς ομμασι πλανηθεις,
Ερως ερυθριαϚει,
Εγω δε, οἱ παρασκας,
Μη δυσχεραινε, φημι.
Κυπριν τε και Κορινναν
Διαγνωσαι ουκ εχουσι
Και οἱ βλεποντες οξυ.

    As dancing o'er the enamell'd plain,
    The floweret of the virgin train,
    My soul's Corinna lightly play'd,
    Young Cupid saw the graceful maid;
    He saw, and in a moment flew,
    And round her neck his arms he threw;
    Saying, with smiles of infant joy,
    "Oh! kiss me, mother, kiss thy boy!"
    Unconscious of a mother's name,
    The modest virgin blush'd with shame :
    And angry Cupid, scarce believing
    That vision could be so deceiving—
    Thus to mistake his Cyprian dame!
    It made even Cupid blush with shame.
    "Be not ashamed, my boy," I cried,
    For I was lingering by his side;
    "Corinna and thy lovely mother,
    Believe me, are so like each other,
    That clearest eyes are oft betray'd,
    And take thy Venus for the maid."

Zitto, in his Capricciosi Pensieri, has given a translation
of this ode of Anacreon.

Stung by some little angry thing,
Some serpent on a tiny wing—
A bee it was—for once I know,
I heard a rustic call it so."
Thus he spoke, and she the while,
Heard him with a soothing smile ;
Then said, " My infant, if so much
Thou feel the little wild-bee's touch,
How must the heart, ah, Cupid ! be,
The hapless heart that 's stung by thee ? "

—————o☉o—————

ODE XXXVI. (1)

IF hoarded gold possess'd the power
To lengthen life's too fleeting hour,·
And purchase from the hand of death
A little span, a moment's breath,
How I would love the precious ore !
And every hour should swell my store ; (2)
That when death came with shadowy pinion,(3)
To waft me to his bleak dominion,
I might by bribes my doom delay,
And bid him call some distant day.
But since not all earth's golden store
Can buy for us one bright hour more,
Why should we vainly mourn our fate,
Or sigh at life's uncertain date ?
Nor wealth nor grandeur can illume
The silent midnight of the tomb.

(1) Fontenelle has translated this ode in his dialogue between Anacreon and Aristotle in the shades, where, on weighing the merits of both these personages, he bestows the prize of wisdom upon the poet.
"The German imitators of this ode are, Lessing, in his poem 'Gestern Brüder,' etc. ; Gleim, in the ode 'An den Tod ;' and Schmidt in der Poet. Blumenl., Gotting. 1783, p. 7."—*Degen.*
(2) From this line to the end of the ode, and more especially in the concluding lines, such considerable changes have been made by the author in his original translation, that the reproduction of it, with the exception of the first six lines, which remain as at first written, cannot fail to be agreeable to the lover of *variorum* readings. *Tempora mutantur* :—

That when the Fates would send their minion,
To waft me off on shadowy pinion,
· I might some hours of life obtain,
And bribe him back to hell again.
But, since we ne'er can charm away
The mandate of that awful day,
Why do we vainly weep at fate,
And sigh for life's uncertain date?
The light of gold can ne'er illume
The dreary midnight of the tomb !
And why should I then pant for treasures ?
Mine be the brilliant round of pleasures;
The goblet rich, the board of friends,
Whose flowing souls the goblet blends !
Mine be the nymph whose form reposes
Seductive on that bed of roses ;
And oh! be mine the soul's excess,
Expiring in her warm caress !—P. E.

(3) The commentators, who are so fond of disputing "de lanâ caprinâ," have been very busy on the authority of he phra se ἰν̓ ἀν Θανειν επελθη. The reading of ἰν̓ ἀν

No—give to others hoarded treasures—
Mine be the brilliant round of pleasures ;
The goblet rich, the board of friends,(4)
Whose social souls the goblet blends ;
And mine, while yet I 've life to live,
Those joys that love alone can give.

—————o☉o—————

ODE XXXVII. (5)

'T WAS night, and many a circling bowl
Had deeply warm'd my thirsty soul ;
As lull'd in slumber I was laid,
Bright visions o'er my fancy play'd.
With maidens, blooming as the dawn,
I seem'd to skim the opening lawn ;
Light, on tiptoe bathed in dew,
We flew, and sported as we flew !
Some ruddy striplings, who look'd on—
With cheeks, that like the wine-god's shone,
Saw me chasing, free and wild,
These blooming maids, and slyly smiled ;
Smiled indeed with wanton glee,
Though none could doubt they envied me.
And still I flew—and now had caught
The panting nymphs, and fondly thought
To gather from each rosy lip
A kiss that Jove himself might sip—
When sudden all my dream of joys, (6)
Blushing nymphs and laughing boys,

Θανατος επελθη, which De Medenbach proposes in his Amœnitates Literariæ, was already hinted by Le Fevre, who seldom suggests any thing worth notice.
(4) This communion of friendship, which sweetened the bowl of Anacreon, has not been forgotten by the author of the following scholium, where the blessings of life are enumerated with proverbial simplicity. Ὑγιαινειν μεν αριϛον ανδρι ϑνητω. Δευτερον δε, καλον φυην γενεϑαι. Το τριτον δε, πλουτειν αδολως. Και το τεταρτον, συνεβαν μετα των φιλων.

Of mortal blessings here the first is health,
And next those charms by which the eye we move ;
The third is wealth, unwounding guiltless wealth,
And then, sweet intercourse with those we love !

(5) "Compare with this ode the beautiful poem 'der Traum' of Uz."—*Degen.*
Le Fevre, in a note upon this ode, enters into an elaborate and learned justification of drunkenness ; and this is probably the cause of the severe reprehension which he appears to have suffered for his Anacreon. "Fuit olim fateor (says he in a note upon Longinus), cum Sapphonem amabam. Sed ex quo illa me perditissima fœmina pene miserum perdidit cum sceleratissimo suo congerrone, (Anacreontem dico, si nescis, lector,) noli sperare," etc., etc. He adduces on this ode the authority of Plato, who allowed ebriety, at the Dionysian festivals, to men arrived at their fortieth year. He likewise quotes the following line from Alexis, which he says no one, who is not totally ignorant of the world, can hesitate to confess the truth of:—

Ουδεις φιλοποτης εϛιν ανθρωπος κακος.

" No lover of drinking was ever a vicious man."

(6) "Nonnus says of Bacchus, almost in the same words that Anacreon uses,—

All were gone!—"Alas!" I said,
Sighing for the illusion fled,
" Again, sweet sleep, that scene restore, (1)
Oh! let me dream it o'er and o'er!"

————o❦o————

ODE XXXVIII. (2)

LET us drain the nectar'd bowl,
Let us raise the song of soul
To him, the god who loves so well
The nectar'd bowl, the choral swell;
The god who taught the sons of earth
To thrid the tangled dance of mirth;
Him, who was nursed with infant Love,
And cradled in the Paphian grove;
Him, that the snowy Queen of Charms (3)
So oft has fondled in her arms.
Oh 't is from him the transport flows,
Which sweet intoxication knows;
With him the brow forgets its gloom,
And brilliant graces learn to bloom.
Behold!—my boys a goblet bear,
Whose sparkling foam lights up the air.
Where are now the tear, the sigh?
To the winds they fly, they fly!
Grasp the bowl; in nectar sinking,
Man of sorrow, drown thy thinking!
Say, can the tears we lend to thought
In life's account avail us aught?
Can we discern with all our lore,
The path we 've yet to journey o'er?
Alas, alas, in ways so dark, (4)
'T is only wine can strike a spark.

Εγρομενος δε
Παρθενον ουκ ετιχησε, και ηθελεν αυθις ιαυειν."

Waking, he lost the phantom's charms,
The nymph had faded from his arms;
Again to slumber he essay'd,
Again to clasp the shadowy maid.—*Longepierre.*

(1) Doctor Johnson, in his preface to Shakspeare, animadverting upon the commentators of that poet, who pretended, in every little coincidence of thought, to detect an imitation of some ancient poet, alludes in the following words to the ode of Anacreon before us:—"I have been told that when Caliban, after a pleasing dream, says, 'I tried to sleep again,' the author imitates Anacreon, who had, like any other man, the same wish on the same occasion."

(2) "Compare with this beautiful ode to Bacchus, the verses of Hagedorn, lib. v., 'das Gesellschaftliche;' and of Bürger, p. 51," etc., etc. — *Degen.*

(3) Robortellus, upon the epithalamium of Catullus, mentions an ingenious derivation of Cytheræa, the name of Venus, παρα του κευθειν τους ερωτας, which seems to hint that "Love's fairy favours are lost, when not concealed."

(4) The brevity of life allows arguments for the voluptuary as well as the moralist. Among many parallel passages which Longepierre has adduced, I shall content myself with this epigram from the Anthologia.

Δουσαμενοι, Προδιχη, πυκασωμεθα, και τον ακρατον
'Ελχωμεν, κυλικας μειζονας αραμενοι.

Then let me quaff the foamy tide,
And through the dance meandering glide;
Let me imbibe the spicy breath
Of odours chafed to fragrant death;
Or from the lips of love inhale
A more ambrosial, richer gale!
To hearts that court the phantom Care,
Let him retire and shroud him there;
While we exhaust the nectar'd bowl,
And swell the choral song of soul
To him, the god who loves so well
The nectar'd bowl, the choral swell!

————❦ ❦ ❦————

ODE XXXIX.

How I love the festive boy,
Tripping through the dance of joy!
How I love the mellow sage,
Smiling through the veil of age!
And whene'er this man of years
In the dance of joy appears,
Snows may o'er his head be flung, (5)
But his heart—his heart is young.

————o❦o————

ODE XL.

I KNOW that Heaven hath sent me here,
To run this moral life's career;
The scenes which I have journeyed o'er,
Return no more—alas! no more,
And all the path I 've yet to go,
I neither know nor ask to know.

'Ραιος ὁ χαιροντων ες͙ι βιος· ειτα τα λοιπα
Γηρας χωλυσει, και το τελος θανατος.

Of which the following is a paraphrase :—

Let's fly, my love, from noonday's beam,
To plunge us in yon cooling stream;
Then, hastening to the festal bower,
We 'll pass in mirth the evening hour;
'T is thus our age of bliss shall fly,
As sweet, though passing as that sigh,
Which seems to whisper o'er your lip,
" Come, while you may, of rapture sip."
For age will steal the graceful form,
Will chill the pulse, while throbbing warm;
And death—alas! that hearts, which thrill
Like yours and mine, should e'er be still!

(5) Saint-Pavin makes the same distinction in a sonnet to a young girl.

Je sais bien que les destinées
Ont mal compassé nos années;
Ne regardez que mon amour:
Peut-être un serez-vous émue:
Il est jeune, et n'est que du jour,
Belle Iris, que je vous ai vue.

Fair and young thou bloomest now,
And I full many a year have told;
But read the heart and not the brow,
Thou shalt not find my love is old.
My love 's a child; and thou canst say
How much his little age may be,
For he was born the very day
When first I set my eyes on thee!

Away, then, wizard Care, nor think
Thy fetters round this soul to link ;
Never can heart that feels with me(1)
Descend to be a slave to thee !
And oh ! before the vital thrill,
Which trembles at my heart, is still,
I 'll gather Joy's luxuriant flowers,
And gild with bliss my fading hours;
Bacchus shall bid my winter bloom,(2)
And Venus dance me to the tomb !

—o◦◦o—

ODE XLI.

WHEN Spring adorns the dewy scene,
How sweet to walk the velvet green,
And hear the west wind's gentle sighs,
As o'er the scented mead it flies !
How sweet to mark the pouting vine,
Ready to burst in tears of wine ;
And with some maid, who breathes but love, (3)
To walk, at noontide, through the grove,
Or sit in some cool green recess—
Oh, is not this true happiness ? (4)

—o◦◦o—

ODE XLII. (5)

YES, be the glorious revel mine,
Where humour sparkles from the wine.

(1) Longepierre quotes here an epigram from the An-
thologia, on account of the similarity of a particular
phrase. Though by no means anacreontic, it is marked
by an interesting simplicity, which has induced me to pa-
raphrase it, and may atone for its intrusion.

Ελπις, και συ τυχη, μεγα χαιρετε, τον λιμεν ευρον.
Ουδεν εμοι χ ' υμιν, παιδετε τους μετ' εμε.

    At length to Fortune, and to you,
      Delusive Hope ! a last adieu.
    The charm that once beguiled is o'er,
    And I have reach'd my destined shore.
    Away, away, your flattering arts
    May now betray some simpler hearts,
    And you will smile at their believing,
    And they shall weep at your deceiving !

(2) The same commentator has quoted an epitaph,
written upon our poet by Julian, in which he makes him
promulgate the precepts of good fellowship even from the
tomb.

Πολλακι μεν τοδ' αεισα, και εκ τυμβου δε βοησω·
Πινετε, πριν ταυτην αμφιβαλησθε κονιν.

    This lesson oft in life I sung,
    And from my grave I still shall cry,
    " Drink, mortal, drink, while time is young,
    Ere death has made thee cold as I."

(3) Thus Horace :—

    Quid habes illius, illius
    Quæ spirabat amores,
    Quæ me surpuerat mihi.—Lib. iv. Carm. 13.
And does there then remain but this,
    And hast thou lost each rosy ray
Of her, who breathed the soul of bliss,
    And stole me from myself away ?

(4) The last four lines do not convey precisely the same
signification as in former editions ; they were,
    And with the maid whose every sigh
    Is love and bliss, entranced to lie
    Where the embowering branches meet,—
    Oh ! is not this divinely sweet !—P. E.

Around me, let the youthful choir
Respond to my enlivening lyre ;
And while the red cup foams along,
Mingle in soul as well as song.
Then, while I sit, with flowerets crown'd,
To regulate the goblet's round,
Let but the nymph, our banquet's pride,
Be seated smiling by my side,
And earth has not a gift or power
That I would envy in that hour.
Envy !—oh never let its blight
Touch the gay hearts met here to-night.
Far hence be slander's sidelong wounds,
Nor harsh dispute, nor discord's sounds
Disturb a scene, where all should be
Attuned to peace and harmony. (6)
    Come, let us hear the harp's gay note
Upon the breeze inspiring float,
While round us, kindling into love,
Young maidens through the light dance move.
Thus blest with mirth, and love, and peace,
Sure such a life should never cease !

—o◦◦o—

ODE XLIII.

WHILE our rosy fillets shed
Freshness o'er each fervid head,

(5) The character of Anacreon is here very strikingly
depicted. His love of social harmonised pleasures is ex-
pressed with a warmth, amiable and endearing. Among
the epigrams imputed to Anacreon is the following ; it is
the only one worth translation, and it breathes the same
sentiments with this ode :—

Ου φιλος, ὁς κρητηρι παρα πλεω οινοποταζων,
    Νεικεα και πολεμον δακρυοεντα λεγει.
Αλλ' ὁϛις Μουσεων τε, και αγλαα δωρ' Αφροδιτης
    Συμμισγων, ερατης μνησκεται ευφροσυνης.

    When to the lip the brimming cup is prest,
    And hearts are all afloat upon its stream,
    Then banish from my board the unpolish'd guest,
    Who makes the feats of war his barbarous theme.

    But bring the man who o'er his goblet wreathes
    The Muse's laurel with the Cyprian flower ;
    Oh ! give me him, whose soul expansive breathes
    And blends refinement with the social hour.

(6) The lines beginning "Then while I sit," and ending
" Attuned to peace and harmony," were formerly ren-
dered by Mr. Moore as follows :—

    Let the bright nymph, with trembling eye,
    Beside me all in blushes lie ;
    And, while she weaves a frontlet fair
    Of hyacinth to deck my hair,
    Oh ! let me snatch her sidelong kisses,
    And that shall be my bliss of blisses !
    My soul, to festive feeling true,
    One pang of envy never knew ;
    And little has it learn'd to dread
    The gall that Envy's tongue can shed.
    Away—I hate the slanderous dart
    Which steals to wound the unwary heart ;
    And oh ! I hate, with all my soul,
    Discordant clamours o'er the bowl,
    Where every cordial heart should be
    Attuned to peace and harmony.—P. E

5

With many a cup and many a smile
The festal moments we beguile.
And while the harp, impassion'd, flings (1)
Tuneful rapture from its strings,
Some airy nymph, with graceful bound,
Keeps measure to the music's sound ;
Waving, in her snowy hand,
The leafy Bacchanalian wand,
Which, as the tripping wanton flies,
Trembles all over to her sighs.
A youth the while, with loosen'd hair,
Floating on the listless air,
Sings, to the wild harp's tender tone,
A tale of woes, alas, his own ;
And oh, the sadness in his sigh, (2)
As o'er his lip the accents die!
Never sure on earth has been
Half so bright, so blest a scene.
It seems as Love himself had come (3)
To make this spot his chosen home ;—
And Venus, too, with all her wiles,
And Bacchus, shedding rosy smiles,
All, all are here, to hail with me(4)
The Genius of Festivity!

————◦◦◦————

ODE XLIV. (5)

Buds of roses, virgin flowers,
Cull'd from Cupid's balmy bowers,
In the bowl of Bacchus steep,
Till with crimson drops they weep.

Twine the rose, the garland twine,
Every leaf distilling wine ;
Drink and smile, and learn to think
That we were born to smile and drink.
Rose, thou art the sweetest flower
That ever drank the amber shower ;
Rose, thou art the fondest child
Of dimpled Spring, the wood-nymph wild.
Even the Gods, who walk the sky,
Are amorous of thy scented sigh.
Cupid, too, in Paphian shades,
His hair with rosy fillet braids,
When with the blushing sister Graces, (6)
The wanton winding dance he traces.
Then bring me showers of roses, bring,
And shed them o'er me while I sing,
Or while, great Bacchus, round thy shrine,
Wreathing my brow with rose and vine,
I lead some bright nymph through the dance,(7)
Commingling soul with every glance!(8)

————◦◦◦————

ODE XLV.

Within this goblet, rich and deep,
I cradle all my woes to sleep.
Why should we breathe the sigh of fear,
Or pour the unavailing tear ?
For death will never heed the sigh,
Nor soften at the tearful eye ;
And eyes that sparkle, eyes that weep,
Must all alike be seal'd in sleep.

(1) Respecting the barbiton a host of authorities may be collected, which, after all, leave us ignorant of the nature of the instrument. There is scarcely any point upon which we are so totally uninformed as the music of the ancients. The authors* extant upon the subject are, I imagine, little understood ; and certainly if one of their moods was a progression by quarter-tones, which we are told was the nature of the enharmonic scale, simplicity was by no means the characteristic of their melody ; for this is a nicety of progression, of which modern music is not susceptible.

The invention of the barbiton is, by Athenæus, attributed to Anacreon. See his fourth book, where it is called το εὑρημα του Ἀνακρεοντος. Neanthes of Cyzicus, as quoted by Gyraldus, asserts the same. Vide Chabot, in Horat., on the words "Lesboum barbiton," in the first ode.

(2) Longepierre has quoted here an epigram from the Anthologia :—

Κουρη τις μ᾽ εφιλησε ποθεσπερα χειλεσιν υγρος.

Νεκταρ εην το φιλημα᾽ το γαρ ϛομα νεκταρος επνει.

Νυν μεθυω το φιλημα, πολυν τον ερωτα πεπωκως.

Of which the following paraphrase may give some idea :—

The kiss that she left on my lip,
    Like a dew-drop shall lingering lie ;
'T was nectar she gave me to sip,
    'T was nectar I drank in her sigh.
From the moment she printed that kiss,
    Nor reason, nor rest has been mine ;
My whole soul has been drunk with the bliss,
    And feels a delirium divine !

     * Collected by Meibomius.

(3) The introduction of these deities to the festival is merely allegorical. Madame Dacier thinks that the poet describes a masquerade, where these deities were personated by the company in masks. The translation will conform with either idea.

(4) Κωμος, the deity or genius of mirth. Philostratus, in the third of his pictures, gives a very lively description of this god.

(5) This spirited poem is a eulogy on the rose ; and again, in the fifty-fifth ode, we shall find our author rich in the praises of that flower. In a fragment of Sappho, in the romance of Achilles Tatius, to which Barnes refers us, the rose is fancifully styled "the eye of flowers ;" and the same poetess, in another fragment, calls the favours of the Muse "the roses of Pieria." See the notes on the fifty-fifth ode.

"Compare with this ode (says the German annotator,) the beautiful ode of Uz, 'die Rose.'"

(6) "This sweet idea of Love dancing with the Graces is almost peculiar to Anacreon."—Degen.

(7) The epithet βαθυχολπος, which he gives to the nymph, is literally "full-bosomed."

(8) Mr. Moore originally gave the conclusion of this ode thus:—

Great Bacchus ! in thy hallow'd shade,
With some celestial glowing maid,
While gales of roses round me rise,
In perfume sweeten'd by her sighs,
I 'll bill and twine in every dance,
Commingling soul with every glance !—P. E.

Then let us never vainly stray, (1)
In search of thorns, from pleasure's way;
But wisely quaff the rosy wave,
Which Bacchus loves, which Bacchus gave;
And in the goblet, rich and deep,
Cradle our crying woes to sleep.

ODE XLVI. (2)

BEHOLD, the young, the rosy Spring,
Gives to the breeze her scented wing;
While virgin Graces, warm with May, (3)
Fling roses o'er her dewy way.
The murmuring billows of the deep (4)
Have languish'd into silent sleep;
And mark! the flitting sea-birds lave
Their plumes in the reflecting wave;
While cranes from hoary winter fly
To flutter in a kinder sky.
Now the genial star of day
Dissolves the murky clouds away;
And cultured field, and winding stream, (5)
Are freshly glittering in his beam.
  Now the earth prolific swells
With leafy buds and flowery bells;
Gemming shoots the olive twine,
Clusters ripe festoon the vine;
All along the branches creeping,
Through the velvet foliage peeping,
Little infant fruits we see,
Nursing into luxury.

(1) I have thus endeavoured to convey the meaning of τι δε του βιου πλανωμαι; according to Regnier's paraphrase of the line :—

> E che val, fuor della strada
> Del piacere alma e gradita,
> Vaneggiare in questa vita?

(2) The fastidious affectation of some commentators has denounced this ode as spurious. Degen pronounces the four last lines to be the patch-work of some miserable versificator, and Brunck condemns the whole ode. It appears to me, on the contrary, to be elegantly graphical; full of delicate expressions and luxuriant imagery. The abruptness of Ιδε πως εαρος φανεντος is striking and spirited, and has been imitated rather languidly by Horace:—

> Vides ut alta stet nive candidum
> Soracte———

The imperative ιδε is infinitely more impressive;—as in Shakspeare,

> But look, the morn, in russet mantle clad,
> Walks o'er the dew of yon high eastern hill.

There is a simple and poetical description of Spring, in Catullus's beautiful farewell to Bithynia. Carm. 44.
  Barnes conjectures, in his life of our poet, that this ode was written after he had returned from Athens, to settle in his paternal estate at Téos; where, in a little villa at some distance from the city, commanding a view of the Ægean Sea and the islands, he contemplated the beauties of nature, and enjoyed the felicities of retirement. Vide

ODE XLVII.

'T is true, my fading years decline,
Yet can I quaff the brimming wine,
As deep as any stripling fair,
Whose cheeks the flush of morning wear;
And if, amidst the wanton crew,
I 'm call'd to wind the dance's clue,
Then shalt thou see this vigorous hand,
Not faltering on the Bacchant's wand,
But brandishing a rosy flask, (6)
The only thyrsus e'er I 'll ask ! (7)
  Let those who pant for Glory's charms,
Embrace her in the field of arms;
While my inglorious placid soul
Breathes not a wish beyond this bowl.
Then fill it high, my ruddy slave,
And bathe me in its brimming wave.
For though my fading years decay,
Though manhood's prime hath pass'd away,
Like old Silenus, sire divine,
With blushes borrow'd from my wine,
I 'll wanton 'mid the dancing train,
And live my follies o'er again!

ODE XLVIII.

WHEN my thirsty soul I steep,
Every sorrow 's lull'd to sleep.
Talk of monarchs! I am then,
Richest, happiest, first of men;

Barnes, in Anacr. Vita, §xxxv. This supposition, however unauthenticated, forms a pleasing association, which renders the poem the more interesting.

Chevreau says that Gregory Nazianzenus has paraphrased somewhere this description of Spring; but I cannot meet with it. See Chevreau, OEuvres mêlées.

"Compare with this ode (says Degen,) the verses of Hagedorn, book fourth, 'der Frühling,' and book fifth, 'der Mai.'"

(3) De Pauw reads, Χαριτας ροδα βρυουσιν, "the roses display their graces." This is not uningenious; but we lose by it the beauty of the personification, to the boldness of which Regnier has rather frivolously objected.

(4) It has been justly remarked, that the liquid flow of the line απαλυνεται γαληνη, is perfectly expressive of the tranquillity which it describes.

(5) By βροτων εργα, "the works of men" (says Baxter), he means cities, temples, and towns, which are then illuminated by the beams of the sun.

(6) Ασκος was a kind of leathern vessel for wine, very much in use, as should seem by the proverb ασκος και θυλακος, which was applied to those who were intemperate in eating and drinking. This proverb is mentioned in some verses quoted by Athenæus, from the Hesione of Alexis.

(7) Phornutus assigns as a reason for the consecration of the thyrsus to Bacchus, that inebriety often renders the support of a stick very necessary.

Careless o'er my cup I sing,
Fancy makes me more than king;
Gives me wealthy Crœsus' store,
Can I, can I wish for more?
On my velvet couch reclining,
Ivy leaves my brow entwining, (1)
While my soul expands with glee,
What are kings and crowns to me?
If before my feet they lay,
I would spurn them all away!
Arm ye, arm ye, men of might, (2)
Hasten to the sanguine fight;
But let *me*, my budding vine!
Spill no other blood than thine.
Yonder brimming goblet see,
That alone shall vanquish me—
Who think it better, wiser far,
To fall in banquet than in war.

———o♦♦o———

ODE XLIX. (3)

WHEN Bacchus Jove's immortal boy,
The rosy harbinger of joy,
Who, with the sunshine of the bowl (4)
Thaws the winter of our houl—
When to my inmost core he glides,
And bathes it with his ruby tides,
A flow of joy, a lively heat,
Fires my brain, and wings my feet,

Calling up round me visions known
To lovers of the bowl alone.
Sing, sing of love; let music's sound
In melting cadence float around,
While, my young Venus, thou and I
Responsive to its murmurs sigh. (5)
Then waking from our blissful trance,
Again we 'll sport, again we 'll dance.

———o♦♦o———

ODE L. (6)

WHEN wine I quaff, before my eyes
Dreams of poetic glory rise; (7)
And, freshen'd by the goblet's dews,
My soul invokes the heavenly Muse, (8)
When wine I drink, all sorrow 's o'er;
I think of doubts and fears no more;
But scatter to the railing wind
Each gloomy phantom of the mind.
When I drink wine, the ethereal boy,
Bacchus himself, partakes my joy;
And while we dance through vernal bowers, (9)
Whose every breath comes fresh from flowers,
In wine he makes my senses swim,
Till the gale breathes of nought but him!
Again I drink,—and, lo, there seems
A calmer light to fill my dreams;
The lately ruffled wreath I spread
With steadier hand around my head;

(1) "The ivy was consecrated to Bacchus (says Montfaucon), because he formerly lay hid under that tree, or, as others will have it, because its leaves resemble those of the vine." Other reasons for its consecration, and the use of it in garlands at banquets, may be found in Longepierre, Barnes, etc., etc.

(2) I have adopted the interpretation of Regnier and others :—

> Altri segua Marte fero;
> Che sol Bacco è 'l mio conforto.

(3) This, the preceding ode, and a few more of the same character, are merely chansons à boire;—the effusions probably of the moment of conviviality, and afterwards sung, we may imagine, with rapture throughout Greece. But that interesting association, by which they always recalled the convivial emotions that produced them, can now be little felt even by the most enthusiastic reader; and much less by a phlegmatic grammarian, who sees nothing in them but dialects and particles.

(4) Λυαιος is the title which he gives to Bacchus in the original. It is a curious circumstance, that Plutarch mistook the name of Levi among the Jews for Λευι;one of the bacchanal cries, and accordingly supposed that they worshipped Bacchus.

(5) The preceding four lines have undergone some verbal changes since their first publication; they originally stood thus :—

> Sing, sing of love; let music's breath
> Softly beguile our rapturous death,
> While, my young Venus, thou and I
> To the voluptuous cadence die!—P. E.

(6) Faber thinks this Ode spurious; but, I believe, he is singular in his opinion. It has all the spirit of our au-

thor. Like the wreath which he presented in the dream, "It smells of Anacreon."

The form of the original is remarkable. It is a kind of song of seven quatrain stanzas, each beginning with the line

> 'Οτ' εγω πιω τον οινον.

The first stanza alone is incomplete, consisting but of three lines.

"Compare with this poem (says Degen) the verses of Hagedorn, lib. v., ' der Wein,' where that divine poet has wantoned in the praises of wine."

(7) "Anacreon is not the only one (says Longepierre,) whom wine has inspired with poetry. We find an epigram in the first book of the Anthologia, which begins thus :—

> Οινος τοι χαριεντι μεγας πελει ιππος αοιδῳ,
> 'Υδωρ δε πινων, καλον ου τεκοις επος.
> If with water you fill up your glasses,
> You 'll never write any thing wise;
> For wine 's the true horse of Parnassus,
> Which carries a bard to the skies!

(8) Without varying the ideas, Mr. Moore has given a new appearance to the opening lines of this ode, which formerly were,

> When I drink, I feel, I feel
> Visions of poetic zeal,
> Warm with the goblet's freshening dews,
> My heart invokes the heavenly Muse.—P. E.

(9) If some of the translators had observed Doctor Trapp's caution with regard to πολυανθεσιν μ εν αυραις, "Cave ne cœlum intelligas," they would not have spoiled the simplicity of Anacreon's fancy by such extravagant conceptions as the following :—

> Quand je bois, mon œil s'imagine
> Que, dans un tourbillon plein de parfums divers,

Then take the lyre, and sing "how blest
The life of him who lives at rest!"
But then comes witching wine again,
With glorious woman in its train;
And while rich perfumes round me rise,
That seem the breath of woman's sighs,
Bright shapes of every hue and form
Upon my kindling fancy swarm,
Till the whole world of beauty seems
To crowd into my dazzled dreams! (1)
When thus I drink, my heart refines,
And rises as the cup declines;
Rises in the genial flow
That none but social spirits know,
When, with young revellers, round the bowl, (2)
The old themselves grow young in soul!
Oh, when I drink, true joy is mine,
There 's bliss in every drop of wine.
All other blessings I have known,
I scarcely dared to call my own;
But this the Fates can ne'er destroy,
Till death o'ershadows all my joy.

—o●o—

ODE LI. (3)

FLY not thus my brow of snow,
Lovely wanton! fly not so.

Bacchus m'emporte dans les airs,
Rempli de sa liqueur divine.

Or this :—

    Indi mi mena
    Mentre lieto, ebro, deliro,
    Bacco in giro
    Per la vaga aura serena.

(1) The passage commencing "again I drink," has replaced the following lines in this ode, as originally published :—

    When I drink, I deftly twine
    Flowers, begemm'd with tears of wine;
    And, while with festive hand I spread
    The smiling garland round my head,
    Something whispers in my breast,
    How sweet it is to live at rest!
    When I drink, and perfume stills
    Around me all in balmy rills,
    Then as some beauty, smiling roses,
    In languor on my breast reposes,
    Venus! I breathe my vows to thee
    In many a sigh of luxury!—P. E.

(2) Subjoined to Gail's edition of Anacreon, we find some curious letters upon the Θιασοι of the ancients, which appeared in the French Journals. At the opening of the Odéon in Paris, the managers of that spectacle requested Professor Gail to give them some uncommon name for their fêtes. He suggested the word "Thiase," which was adopted; but the literati of Paris questioned the propriety of the term, and addressed their criticisms to Gail through the medium of the public prints.

(3) Alberti has imitated this ode; and Capilupus, in the following epigram, has given a version of it :—

    Cur, Lalage, mea vita, meos contemnis amores?
    Cur fugis e nostro, pulchra puella, sinu?
    Ne fugias, sint sparsa licet mea tempora canis,
    Inque tuo roseus fulgeat ore color.
    Aspice ut intexta deceant quoque flore corollas
    Candida purpureis lilia mista rosis.

Though the wane of age is mine,
Though youth's brilliant flush be thine,
Still I 'm doom'd to sigh for thee,
Blest, if thou couldst sigh for me!
See, in yonder flowery braid, (4)
Cull'd for thee, my blushing maid,
How the rose, of orient glow,
Mingles with the lily's snow;
Mark, how sweet their tints agree,
Just, my girl, like thee and me!

—o●o—

ODE LII. (5)

AWAY, away, ye men of rules,
What have I to do with schools?
They 'd make me learn, they 'd make me think,
But would they make me love and drink?
Teach me this, and let me swim
My soul upon the goblet's brim;
Teach me this, and let me twine
Some fond responsive heart to mine, (6)
For age begins to blanch my brow,—
I 've time for nought but pleasure now.
Fly, and cool my goblet's glow
At yonder fountain's gelid flow;
I 'll quaff, my boy, and calmly sink
This soul to slumber as I drink.

    Oh! why repel my soul's impassion'd vow,
    And fly, beloved maid, these longing arms?
    Is it, that wintry time has strew'd my brow,
    While thine are all the summer's roseate charms?
    See the rich garland cull'd in vernal weather,
    Where the young rosebud with the lily glows;
    So, in Love's wreath we both may twine together,
    And I the lily be, and thou the rose.

(4) "In the same manner that Anacreon pleads for the whiteness of his locks, from the beauty of the colour in garlands, a shepherd, in Theocritus, endeavours to recommend his black hair :—

    Και το ιον μελαν εςι, και α γραπτα υακινθος,
    Αλλ' εμπας εν τοις ςεφανοις τα πρωτα λεγονται."
    Longepierre, Barnes, etc.

(5) This is doubtless the work of a more modern poet than Anacreon; for at the period when he lived rhetoricians were not known."—Degen.

Though this ode is found in the Vatican manuscript, I am much inclined to agree in this argument against its authenticity; for though the dawnings of the art of rhetoric might already have appeared, the first who gave it any celebrity was Corax of Syracuse, and he flourished in the century after Anacreon.

Our poet anticipated the ideas of Epicurus in his aversion to the labours of learning, as well as his devotion to voluptuousness. Πασαν παιδειαν μακαριοι φευγετε, said the philosopher of the garden in a letter to Pythocles.

(6) By χρυσης Αφροδιτης here, I understand some beautiful girl, in the same manner that Λυαιος is often used for wine. "Golden" is frequently an epithet of beauty. Thus in Virgil, "Venus aurea;" and in Propertius, "Cynthia aurea." Tibullus, however, calls an old woman "golden."

The translation d'Autori Anonimi, as usual, wantons on this passage of Anacreon :—

Soon, too soon, my jocund slave,
You 'll deck your master's grassy grave;
And there 's an end—for ah, you know
They drink but little wine below ! (1)

————o❀❀o————

ODE LIII.

When I behold the festive train
Of dancing youth, I 'm young again !
Memory wakes her magic trance,
And wings me lightly through the dance.
Come, Cybeba, smiling maid !
Cull the flower and twine the braid ;
Bid the blush of summer's rose
Burn upon my forehead's snows ; (2)
And let me, while the wild and young
Trip the mazy dance along,
Fling my heap of years away,
And be as wild, as young, as they.
Hither haste, some cordial soul !
Help to my lips the brimming bowl ;
And you shall see this hoary sage
Forget at once his locks and age.

E m' insegni con più rare
Forme accorte d'involare
Ad amabile beltade
Il bel cinto d'onestade.

(1) Thus Mainard :—
La mort nous guette ; et quand ses lois
Nous ont enfermés une fois
Au sein d'une fosse profonde,
Adieu bons vins et bons repas ;
Ma science ne trouve pas
Des cabarets en l'autre monde.

From Mainard, Gombauld, and De Cailly, old French
poets, some of the best epigrams of the English language
have been borrowed.

(2) Lictus, in his Hieroglyphica, quoting two of our
poet's odes, where he calls to his attendants for garlands,
remarks, "Constat igitur floreas coronas poetis et potan-
tibus in symposio convenire, non autem sapientibus et
philosophiam affectantibus."—"It appears that wreaths of
flowers were adapted for poets and revellers at banquets,
but by no means became those who had pretensions to
wisdom and philosophy." On this principle, in his 152nd
chapter, he discovers a refinement in Virgil, describing the
garland of the poet Silenus as fallen off ; which distin-
guishes, he thinks, the divine intoxication of Silenus from
that of common drunkards, who always wear their crowns
while they drink. Such is the "labor ineptiarum" of
commentators !

(3) Wine is prescribed by Galen, as an excellent medi-
cine for old men : "Quod frigidos et humoribus expletos
calefaciat," etc.; but Nature was Anacreon's physician.

There is a proverb in Eriphus, as quoted by Athenæus,
which says, "that wine makes an old man dance, whether
he will or not."

Λογος ες᾽ αρχαιος, ου κακως εχων,
Οινον λεγουσι τους γερσντας, ω πατερ,
Πειθειν χορεειν ου θελοντας.

(4) This ode is written upon a picture which represented
the rape of Europa."—Madame Dacier.

It may probably have been a description of one of those
coins, which the Sidonians struck off in honour of Europa,
representing a woman carried across the sea by a bull.

He still can chant the festive hymn,
He still can kiss the goblet's brim ; (3)
As deeply quaff, as largely fill,
And play the fool right nobly still.

————o❀❀o————

ODE LIV.(4)

Methinks, the pictured bull we see
Is amorous Jove—it must be he !
How fondly blest he seems to bear
That fairest of Phoenician fair !
How proud he breasts the foamy tide,
And spurns the billowy surge aside !
Could any beast of vulgar vein
Undaunted thus defy the main ?
No : he descends from climes above,
He looks the God, he breathes of Jove ! (5)

————o❀❀o————

ODE LV. (6)

While we invoke the wreathed spring,
Resplendent rose ! to thee we'll sing : (7)

Thus Natalis Comes, lib. viii. cap. 23. "Sidonii numis-
mata cum fœminâ tauri dorso insidente ac mare transfre-
tante cuderunt in ejus honorem." In the little treatise
upon the goddess of Syria, attributed very falsely to Lucian,
there is mention of this coin, and of a temple dedicated
by the Sidonians to Astarté, whom some, it appears, con-
founded with Europa.

The poet Moschus has left a very beautiful idyl on the
story of Europa.

(5) Thus Moschus :—
Κρυψε θεον και τρεψε δεμας᾽ και γινετο ταυρος.
The God forgot himself, his heaven, for love,
And a bull's form belied the almighty Jove.

(6) This ode is a brilliant panegyric on the rose. "All
antiquity (says Barnes) has produced nothing more beau-
tiful."

From the idea of peculiar excellence, which the ancients
attached to this flower, arose a pretty proverbial expres-
sion, used by Aristophanes, according to Suidas, ῥοδα μ᾽
ειρηκας, "You have spoken roses," a phrase somewhat
similar to the "dire des fleurettes" of the French. In the
same idea of excellence originated, I doubt not, a very
curious application of the word ῥοδον, for which the inqui-
sitive reader may consult Gaulminus upon the epithala-
mium of our poet, where it is introduced in the romance
of Theodorus. Muretus, in one of his elegies, calls his
mistress his rose :—

Jam te igitur rursus teneo, formosula, jam te
(Quid trepidas ?) teneo ; jam, rosa, te teneo.—Eleg. 8.
Now I again may clasp thee, dearest,
What is there now, on earth, thou fearest ?
Again these longing arms infold thee,
Again, my rose, again I hold thee.

This, like most of the terms of endearment in the modern
Latin poets, is taken from Plautus ; they were vulgar and
colloquial in his time, but are among the elegancies of the
modern Latinists.

Passeratius alludes to the ode before us, in the begin-
ning of his poem on the rose :—
Carmine digna rosa est ; vellem canoretur ut illam
Teius arguta cecinit testudine vates.
(7) I have passed over the line συν εταιρει αυξει μελπην,

Resplendent rose, the flower of flowers,
Whose breath perfumes the Olympian bowers ;
Whose virgin blush, of chasten'd dye,
Enchants so much our mortal eye.
When pleasure's spring-tide season glows,
The Graces love to wreathe the rose ;
And Venus, in its fresh-blown leaves, (1)
An emblem of herself perceives.
Oft hath the poet's magic tongue (2)
The rose's fair luxuriance sung ;
And long the Muses, heavenly maids,
Have rear'd it in their tuneful shades.
When, at the early glance of morn,
It sleeps upon the glittering thorn,
'T is sweet to dare the tangled fence,
To cull the timid floweret thence,
And wipe with tender hand away
The tear that on its blushes lay!
'T is sweet to hold the infant stems,
Yet dropping with Aurora's gems,
And fresh inhale the spicy sighs
That from the weeping buds arise.
When revel reigns, when mirth is high,
And Bacchus beams in every eye,
Our rosy fillets scent exhale,
And fill with balm the fainting gale.
There 's nought in nature bright or gay,
Where roses do not shed their ray.

When morning paints the orient skies,
Her fingers burn with roseate dyes ;(3)
Young nymphs betray the rose's hue,
O'er whitest arms it kindles through.
In Cytherea's form it glows,
And mingles with the living snows.
The rose distils a healing balm,
The beating pulse of pain to calm ;
Preserves the cold inurned clay, (4)
And mocks the vestige of decay: (5)
And when at length, in pale decline,
Its florid beauties fade and pine,
Sweet as in youth, its balmy breath
Diffuses odour even in death !(6)
Oh! whence could such a plant have sprung?
Listen,—for thus the tale is sung.
When, humid, from the silvery stream,
Effusing beauty's warmest beam,
Venus appear'd, in flushing hues,
Mellow'd by ocean's briny dews ;
When, in the starry courts above,
The pregnant brain of mighty Jove,
Disclosed the nymph of azure glance,
The nymph who shakes the martial lance ;—
Then, then, in strange eventful hour,
The earth produced an infant flower,
Which sprung, in blushing glories drest,
And wanton'd o'er its parent breast.

which is corrupt in this original reading, and has been very little improved by the annotators. I should suppose it to be an interpolation, if it were not for a line which occurs afterwards : φερε δη φυσιν λεγωμεν.

(1) Belleau, in a note upon an old French poet, quoting the original here, αφροδιτων τ'αθυρμα, translates it, "comme les delices et mignardises de Venus."

(2) The following is a fragment of the Lesbian poetess. It is cited in the romance of Achilles Tatius, who appears to have resolved the numbers into prose. Ει τοις ανθεσιν ηθελεν ὁ Ζευς επιθεναι βασιλεα, το ῥοδον αν των ανθεων εβασιλευε· γης εςι κοσμος, φυτων αγλαισμα, οφθαλμος ανθεων, λειμωνος ερυθημα, καλλος αςραπτον. Ερωτος πνει, Αφροδιτην προξενει, ευειδεσι φυλλοις κομᾷ, ευκινητοις πεταλοις τρυφᾷ, το πεταλον τῳ Ζεφυρῳ γελᾷ.

> If Jove would give the leafy bowers
> A queen for all their world of flowers,
> The rose would be the choice of Jove,
> And blush, the queen of every grove.
> Sweetest child of weeping morning,
> Gem, the vest of earth adorning,
> Eye of gardens, light of lawns,
> Nursling of soft summer dawns ;
> Love's own earliest sigh it breathes,
> Beauty's brow with lustre wreathes,
> And, to young Zephyr's warm caresses,
> Spreads abroad its verdant tresses,
> Till, blushing with the wanton's play,
> Its cheek wears even a richer ray!

(3) In the original here, he enumerates the many epithets of beauty, borrowed from roses, which were used by the poets, παρα των σοφων. We see that poets were dignified in Greece with the title of sages ; even the careless Anacreon, who lived but for love and voluptuousness,

was called by Plato the wise Anacreon—"fuit hæc sapientia quondam."

(4) He here alludes to the use of the rose in embalming, and, perhaps (as Barnes thinks), to the rosy unguent with which Venus anointed the corpse of Hector.—Homer's Iliad, ψ. It may likewise regard the ancient practice of putting garlands of roses on the dead, as in Statius, Theb., lib. x., 782.

> — — — hi sertis, hi veris honore soluto
> Accumulant artus, patriâque in sede reponunt
> Corpus adoratum.

Where "veris honor," though it mean every kind of flowers, may seem more particularly to refer to the rose, which our poet in another ode calls εαρος μελημα. We read, in the Hieroglyphics of Pierius, lib. lv., that some of the ancients used to order in their wills that roses should be annually scattered on their tombs, and Pierius has adduced some sepulchral inscriptions to this purpose.

(5) When he says that this flower prevails over time itself, he still alludes to its efficacy in embalment (tenerâ poneret ossa rosâ, Propert., lib. i., eleg. 17), or, perhaps, to the subsequent idea of its fragrance surviving its beauty ; for he can scarcely mean to praise for duration the "nimium breves flores" of the rose. Philostratus compares this flower with love, and says, that they both defy the influence of time ; χρονον δε ουτε Ερως, ουτε ῥοδα. Unfortunately the similitude lies not in their duration, but their transcience :—

(6) Thus Casper Barlæus, in his Ritus Nuptiarum:

> Ambrosium late rosa tunc quoque spergit odorem,
> Cum fluit, aut multo languida suole jacet.
>
> Nor then the rose its odour loses,
> When all its flushing beauties die ;
> Nor less ambrosial balm diffuses,
> When wither'd by the solar eye.

The gods beheld this brilliant birth,
And hail'd the Rose, the boon of earth !
With nectar drops, a ruby tide, (1)
The sweetly orient buds they dyed,
And bade them bloom, the flowers divine
Of him who gave the glorious vine ;
And bade them on the splangled thorn
Expand their bosoms to the morn.

————o♦♦o————

ODE LVI. (2)

He, who instructs the youthful crew
To bathe them in the brimmer's dew,
And taste, uncloy'd by rich excesses,
All the bliss that wine possesses;
He , who inspires the youth to bound
Elastic through the dance's round,—
Bacchus, the god again is here,
And leads along the blushing year ;
The blushing year with vintage teems,
Ready to shed those cordial streams,
Which, sparkling in the cup of mirth,
Illuminate the sons of earth ! (3)
   Then, when the ripe and vermil wine,—
Blest infant of the pregnant vine,
Which now in mellow clusters swells,—
Oh ! when it bursts its roseate cells,

(1) The author of the "Pervigilium Veneris," (a poem attributed to Catullus, the style of which appears to me to have all the laboured luxuriance of a much later period,) ascribes the tincture of the rose to the blood from the wound of Adonis,—

    —— rosæ
    Fuscæ aprino de cruore—

according to the emendation of Lipsius. In the following epigram this hue is differently accounted for:—

    Illa quidem studiosa suum defendere Adonim,
    Gradivus stricto quem petit ense ferox,
    Affixit duris vestigia cæca roselis,
    Albæque divino picta cruore rosa est.

While the enamour'd queen of joy
   Flies to protect her lovely boy,
     On whom the jealous war-god rushes ;
She treads upon a thorned rose,
   And while the wound with crimson flows,
     The snowy floweret feels her blood, and blushes !

(2) "Compare with this elegant ode the verses of Uz, lib. i., ' die Weinlese.'"—*Degen.*

This appears to be one of the hymns which were sung at the anniversary festival of the vintage; one of the ἐπιληνιοι ὑμνοι, as our poet himself terms them in the fifty-ninth ode. We cannot help feeling a sort of reverence for these classic relics of the religion of antiquity. Horace may be supposed to have written the nineteenth ode of his second book, and the twenty-fifth of the third, for some bacchanalian celebration of this kind.

(3) In the original, ποτον αρονον κομιδων. Madame Dacier thinks that the poet here had the nepenthé of Homer in his mind. Odyssey, lib. iv. This nepenthé was a something of exquisite charm, infused by Helen into the wine of her guests, which had the power of dispelling every anxiety. A French writer, De Meré, conjectures that this spell, which made the bowl so beguiling, was the charm of Helen's conversation. See Bayle, art. Helène.

Brightly the joyous stream shall flow,
To balsam every mortal woe !
None shall be then cast down or weak,
For health and joy shall light each cheek ;
No heart will then desponding sigh,
For wine shall bid despondence fly.
Thus—till another autumn's glow
Shall bid another vintage flow.

————o♦♦o————

ODE LVII. (4)

Whose was the artist's hand that spread
Upon this disk the ocean's bed? (5)
And, in a flight of fancy, high
As aught on earthly wing can fly, (6)
Depicted thus, in semblance warm,
The Queen of Love's voluptuous form,
Floating along the silvery sea
In beauty's naked majesty !
Oh ! he hath given the enamour'd sight
A witching banquet of delight,
Where gleaming through the waters clear,
Glimpses of undreamt charms appear,
And all that mystery loves to screen, (7)
Fancy, like Faith, adores unseen. (8)
   Light as a leaf, that on the breeze
Of summer skims the glassy seas,

(4) This ode is a very animated description of a picture of Venus on a discus, which represented the goddess in her first emergence from the waves. About two centuries after our poet wrote, the pencil of the artist Apelles embellished this subject, in his famous painting of the Venus Anadyomené, the model of which, as Pliny informs us, was the beautiful Campaspe, given to him by Alexander; though, according to Natalis Comes, lib. vii. cap. 16, it was Phryne who sat to Apelles for the face and breast of this Venus.

There are a few blemishes in the reading of the ode before us, which have influenced Faber, Heyne, Brunck, etc., to denounce the whole poem as spurious. But, "non ego paucis offendar maculis." I think it is quite beautiful enough to be authentic.

(5) The abruptness of αρα τις ετορευσε ποντον, is finely expressive of sudden admiration, and is one of those beauties, which we cannot but admire in their source, though, by frequent imitation, they are now become familiar and unimpressive.

(6) This ode in former editions commenced thus :—

    And whose immortal hand could shed
    Upon this disk the ocean's bed ?
    And, in a frenzied flight of soul,
    Sublime as heaven's eternal pole, etc.—P. E.

(7) The picture here has all the delicate character of the semi-reducta Venus, and affords a happy specimen of what the poetry of passion *ought* to be—glowing but through a veil, and stealing upon the heart from concealment. Few of the ancients have attained this modesty of description, which, like the golden cloud that hung over Jupiter and Juno, is impervious to every beam but that of fancy.

(8) The four preceding lines, in former editions, were,
    And all those sacred scenes of love,
    Where only hallow'd eyes may rove,
    Lie faintly glowing, half conceal'd,
    Within the lucid billows veil'd.—P. E.

She floats along the ocean's breast,
Which undulates in sleepy rest ;
While stealing on, she gently pillows
Her bosom on the heaving billows.
Her bosom, like the dew-wash'd rose, (1)
Her neck, like April's sparkling snows,
Illume the liquid path she traces,
And burn within the stream's embraces.
Thus on she moves, in languid pride, (2)
Encircled by the azure tide,
As some fair lily o'er a bed
Of violets bends its graceful head.

Beneath their queen's inspiring glance,
The dolphins o'er the green sea dance,
Bearing in triumph young Desire, (3)
And infant Love with smiles of fire !
While, glittering through the silver waves,
The tenants of the briny caves
Around the pomp their gambols play,
And gleam along the watery way.

────o⊕o────

ODE LVIII. (4)

WHEN Gold, as fleet as zephyr's pinion,
Escapes like any faithless minion, (5)
And flies me (as he flies me ever), (6)
Do I pursue him ? never, never !
No, let the false deserter go,
For who would court his direst foe ?
But, when I feel my lighten'd mind
No more by grovelling gold confined,

(1) "'Ροδεων (says an anonymous annotator) is a whim
sical epithet for the bosom." Neither Catullus nor Gray
have been of his opinion. The former has the expression,
En hic in roseis latet papillis.
And the latter,
Lo ! where the rosy-bosom'd hours, etc.
Crottus, a modern Latinist, might indeed be censured
for too vague a use of the epithet "rosy," when he ap-
plies it to the eyes :—"e roseis oculis."
(2) In former editions :—
In languid luxury soft she glides,
Encircled by the azure tides.—P. E.
(3) In the original, 'Ιμερος, who was the same deity with
Jocus among the Romans. Aurelius Augurellus has a
poem beginning,—
Invitat olim Bacchus ad cœnam suos,
Comon, Jocum, Cupidinem.
Which Parnell has closely imitated:—
Gay Bacchus, liking Estcourt's wine,
A noble meal bespoke us ;
And for the guests that were to dine,
Brought Comus, Love, and Jocus, etc.
(4) I have followed Barnes's arrangement of this ode,
which, though deviating somewhat from the Vatican MS.,
appears to me the more natural order.
(5) In the original,'Ο δρακετης ὁ χρυσος. There is a
kind of pun in these words, as Madame Dacier has already
remarked; for Chrysos, which signifies gold, was also a
frequent name for a slave. In one of Lucian's dialogues,
there is, I think, a similar play upon the word, where the

Then loose I all such clinging cares,
And cast them to the vagrant airs.
Then feel I, too, the Muse's spell,
And wake to life the dulcet shell,
Which, roused once more, to beauty sings,
While, love dissolves along the strings !

But, scarcely has my heart been taught
How little Gold deserves a thought,
When, lo ! the slave returns once more,
And with him wafts delicious store
Of racy wine, whose genial art
In slumber seals the anxious heart.
Again he tries my soul to sever
From love and song, perhaps for ever !
Away, deceiver ! why pursuing
Ceaseless thus my heart's undoing?
Sweet is the song of amorous fire,
Sweet the sighs that thrill the lyre ;
Oh ! sweeter far than all the gold
Thy wings can waft, thy mines can hold.
Well do I know thy arts, thy wiles—
They wither'd Love's young wreathed smiles ;
And o'er his lyre such darkness shed,
I thought its soul of song was fled !
They dash'd the wine-cup, that, by him,
Was fill'd with kisses to the brim. (7)
Go—fly to haunts of sordid men,
But come not near the bard again.
They glitter in the Muse's shade,
Scares from her bower the tuneful maid ;
And not for worlds would I forego
That moment of poetic glow,

followers of Chrysippus are called golden fishes. The puns
of the ancients are, in general, even more vapid than our
own ; some of the best are those recorded of Diogenes.
(6) Αει δ', αει με φευγει. This grace of iteration has
already been taken notice of. Though sometimes merely
a playful beauty, it is peculiarly expressive of impassioned
sentiment, and we may easily believe, that it was one of
the many sources of that energetic sensibility which
breathed through the style of Sappho. See Gyrald. Vet.
Poet., Dial. 9. It will not be said that this is a mechanical
ornament by any one who can feel its charm in those
lines of Catullus, where he complains of the infidelity of
his mistress, Lesbia :—
Cœli, Lesbia nostra, Lesbia illa,
Illa Lesbia, quam Catullus unam,
Plus quam se atque suos amavit omnes,
Nunc, etc.
Si sic omnia dixisset!—but the rest does not bear citation.
(7) Original:—
Φιλημματων δε κεδνων,
Ποθων κυπελλα κιρνης.
Horace has "Desiderique temperare poculum," not
figuratively, however, like Anacreon, but importing the
love-philtres of the witches. By "cups of kisses" our poet
may allude to a favourite gallantry among the ancients,
of drinking when the lips of their mistresses had touched
the brim :—
" Or leave a kiss within the cup,
And I'll not ask for wine."
As in Ben Jonson's translation from Philostratus; and

6

When my full soul, in Fancy's stream,
Pours o'er the lyre its swelling theme.
Away, away ! to worldlings hence,
Who feel not this diviner sense ;
Give gold to those who love that pest,—
But leave the poet poor and blest.

——○○○○——

ODE LIX. (1)

Ripen'd by the solar beam,
Now the ruddy clusters teem,
In osier baskets borne along
By all the festal vintage throng
Of rosy youths and virgins fair,
Ripe as the melting fruits they bear.
Now, now they press the pregnant grapes,
And now the captive stream 'escapes,
In fervid tide of nectar gushing,
And for its bondage proudly blushing !
While, round the vat's impurpled brim,
The choral song, the vintage hymn
Of rosy youths and virgins fair,
Steals on the charm'd and echoing air.
Mark, how they drink, with all their eyes,
The orient tide that sparkling flies,
The infant Bacchus born in mirth,
While Love stands by, to hail the birth.
 When he, whose verging years decline (2)
As deep into the vale as mine,
When he inhales the vintage-cup,
His feet, new-wing'd, from earth spring up,

Lucian has a conceit upon the same idea, "῾Ινα και πινης ἁμα και φιλης," "that you may at once both drink and kiss."

(1) The title Επιληνιος ὑμνος, which Barnes has given to this ode, is by no means appropriate. We have already had one of those hymns (ode 56), but this is a description of the vintage; and the title εις οινον, which it bears in the Vatican MS., is more correct than any that have been suggested.

Degen, in the true spirit of literary scepticism, doubts that this ode is genuine, without assigning any reason for such a suspicion ;—"non amo te, Sabidi, nec possum dicere quare." But this is far from satisfactory criticism.

(2) The original translation of this ode by Mr. Moore terminated thus :—

> When he, whose verging years decline
> As deep into the vale as mine,
> When he inhales the vintage-spring,
> His heart is fire, his foot 's a wing ;
> And, as he flies, his hoary hair
> Plays truant with the wanton air !
> While the warm youth, whose wishing soul
> Has kindled o'er the inspiring bowl,
> Impassion'd seeks the shadowy grove,
> Where, in the tempting guise of love,
> Reclining sleeps some witching maid,
> Whose sunny charms, but half display'd,
> Blush through the bower, that, closely twined,
> Excludes the kisses of the wind !

* The original here has been variously interpreted. Some, in their zeal for our author's purity, have supposed that the youth only persuades her to a premature marriage ; others understand from the words προδοτιν γαμων γενεσθαι, that he seduces her to a violation of the nuptial vow. The turn which I have given it

And as he dances, the fresh air
Plays whispering through his silvery hair.
Meanwhile young groups whom love invites,
To joys ev'n rivalling wine's delights,
Seek, arm in arm, the shadowy grove,
And there, in words and looks of love,
Such as fond lovers look and say,
Pass the sweet moonlight hours away. (3)

——○○○○——

ODE LX. (4)

Awake to life, my sleeping shell,
To Phœbus let thy numbers swell ;
And though no glorious prize be thine,
No Pythean wreath around thee twine,
Yet every hour is glory's hour
To him who gathers wisdom's flower.
Then wake thee from thy voiceless slumbers,
And to the soft and Phrygian numbers,
Which, tremblingly, my lips repeat,
Send echoes from thy chord as sweet.
'T is thus the swan, with fading notes,
Down the Cayster's current floats,
While amorous breezes linger round,
And sigh responsive sound for sound.

Muse of the Lyre ! illume my dream,
Thy Phœbus is my fancy's theme ;
And hallow'd is the harp I bear,
And hallow'd is the wreath I wear,
Hallow'd by him, the god of lays,
Who modulates the choral maze.

> The virgin wakes, the glowing boy
> Allures her to the embrace of joy ;
> Swears that the herbage Heaven had spread
> Was sacred as the nuptial bed ; *
> That laws should never bind desire,
> And love was nature's holiest fire !
> The virgin weeps, the virgin sighs ;
> He kiss'd her lips, he kiss'd her eyes ;
> The sigh was balm, the tear was dew,
> They only raised his flame anew.
> And, oh ! he stole the sweetest flower
> That ever bloom'd in any bower !
> Such is the madness wine imparts,
> Whene'er it steals on youthful hearts.—P. E.

(3) Those well acquainted with the original, need hardly be reminded that, in these few concluding verses, I have thought right to give only the general meaning of my author, leaving the details untouched.

(4) This hymn to Apollo is supposed not to have been written by Anacreon ; and it is undoubtedly rather a sublimer flight than the Teian wing is accustomed to soar. But, in a poet of whose works so small a proportion has reached us, diversity of style is by no means a safe criterion. If we knew Horace but as a satirist, should we easily believe there could dwell such animation in his lyre ? Suidas says that our poet wrote hymns, and this, perhaps, is one of them. We can perceive in what an altered and imperfect state his works are at present, when

is somewhat like the sentiment of Heloisa, " amorem conjugio, libertatem vinculo præferre." (See her original Letters.) The Italian translations have almost all wantoned upon this description : but that of Marchetti is indeed " nimium lubricus aspici."
—P. E.

I sing the love which Daphne twined
Around the godhead's yielding mind ;
I sing the blushing Daphne's flight
From this ethereal son of Light ;
And how the tender timid maid
Flew trembling to the kindly shade, (1)
Resign'd a form, alas, too fair,
And grew a verdant laurel there ;
Whose leaves, with sympathetic thrill,
In terror seem'd to tremble still !
The god pursued, with wing'd desire ;
And when his hopes were all on fire,
And when to clasp the nymph he thought,
A lifeless tree was all he caught ;
And, 'stead of sighs that pleasure heaves,
Heard but the west-wind in the leaves!(2)
    But, pause, my soul, no more, no more—
Enthusiast, whither do I soar?
This sweetly maddening dream of soul
Hath hurried me beyond the goal.
Why should I sing the mighty darts
Which fly to wound celestial hearts,
When, ah, the song, with sweeter tone,
Can tell the darts that wound my own?

Still be Anacreon, still inspire
The descant of the Teian lyre : (3)
Still let the nectar'd numbers float,
Distilling love in every note !
And when some youth, whose glowing soul
Has felt the Paphian star's control,
When he the liquid lays shall hear,
His heart will flutter to his ear,
And drinking there of song divine,
Banquet on intellectual wine ! (4)

——>⚬⚭⚬<——

ODE LXI. (5)

Youth's endearing charms are fled ;
Hoary locks deform my head ;
Bloomy graces, dalliance gay,
All the flowers of life decay. (6)
Withering age begins to trace
Sad memorials o'er my face ;
Time has shed its sweetest bloom,
All the future must be gloom.
This it is that sets me sighing ;
Dreary is the thought of dying ! (7)

---

we find a scholiast upon Horace citing an ode from the third book of Anacreon.

.1) Original :—

> Το μεν εκπεφευγε κεντρον,
> Φυσεως δ' αμειψε μορφην.

I find the word κεντρον here has a double force, as it also signifies, that "omnium parentem, quam sanctus Numa," etc., etc. (See Martial.) In order to confirm this import of the word here, those who are curious in new readings may place the stop after φυσεως, thus :—

> Το μεν εκπεφευγε κεντρον
> Φυσεως, δ' αμειψε μορφην.

(2) In former editions the four preceding lines read,—

> And when he thought to hear the sigh
> With which enamour'd virgins die,
> He only heard the pensive air,
> Whispering amid her leafy hair.—P. E

(3) The original is Τον Ανακρεοντα μιμου. I have translated it under the supposition that the hymn is by Anacreon ; though, I fear, from this very line, that his claim to it can scarcely be supported. Τον Ανακρεοντα μιμου, "Imitate Anacreon." Such is the lesson given us by the lyrist ; and if, in poetry, a simple elegance of sentiment, enriched by the most playful felicities of fancy, be a charm which invites or deserves imitation, where shall we find such a guide as Anacreon' In morality, too, with some little reserve, we need not blush, I think, to follow in his footsteps. For if his song be the language of his heart, though luxurious and relaxed, he was artless and benevolent ; and who would not forgive a few irregularities, when atoned for by virtues so rare and so endearing? When we think of the sentiment in those lines :—

> Away! I hate the slanderous dart,
> Which steals to wound the unwary heart,

how many are there in the world, to whom we would wish to say, Τον Ανακρεοντα μιμου!

(4) Here ends the last of the odes in the Vatican MS., whose authority helps to confirm the genuine antiquity of them all, though a few have have stolen among the number which we may hesitate in attributing to Anacreon. In the little essay prefixed to this translation, I observed that Barnes has quoted this manuscript incorrectly, relying upon an imperfect copy of it, which Isaac Vossius had taken. I shall just mention two or three instances of this inaccuracy—the first which occur to me. In the ode of the Dove, on the words Πτεροισι συγκαλυψω, he says, "Vatican MS. συσκιαζων, etiam Prisciano invito :" but the MS. reads συγκαλυψω, with συσκιαζω interlined. Degen too, on the same line, is somewhat in error. In the twenty-second ode of this series, line thirteenth, the MS. has τενση with αι interlined, and Barnes imputes to it the reading of τενδη. In the fifty-seventh, line twelfth, he professes to have preserved the reading of the MS. Αλαλημενη δ' επ' αχτη, while the latter has αλαλημενος δ' επ' αυτα. Almost all the other annotators have transplanted these errors from Barnes.

(5) The intrusion of this melancholy ode, among the careless levities of our poet, reminds us of the skeletons which the Egyptians used to hang up in their banquet-rooms, to inculcate a thought of mortality even amidst the dissipations of mirth. If it were not for the beauty of its numbers, the Teian Muse should disown this ode. "Quid habet illius, illius quæ spirabat amores?" To Stobæus we are indebted for it.

(6) Horace often, with feeling and elegance, deplores the fugacity of human enjoyments. See book ii. ode 2. : and thus in the second epistle, book ii. :—

> Singula de nobis anni prædantur euntes ;
> Eripuere jocos, venerem, convivia, ludum.
> The wing of every passing day
> Withers some blooming joy away ;
> And wafts from our enamour'd arms
> The banquet's mirth, the virgin's charms.

(7) Regnier, a libertine French poet, has written some sonnets on the approach of death, full of gloomy and trem-

Lone and dismal is the road
Down to Pluto's dark abode;
And, when once the journey 's o'er,
Ah! we can return no more!(1)

———o••o———

ODE LXII. (2)

FILL me, boy, as deep a draught
As e'er was fill'd, as e'er was quaff'd;
But let the water amply flow,
To cool the grape's intemperate glow; (3)
Let not the fiery god be single,
But with the nymphs in union mingle.
For though the bowl 's the grave of sadness,
Ne'er let it be the birth of madness.
No, banish from our board to-night
The revelries of rude delight;
To Scythians leave these wild excesses,
Ours be the joy that soothes and blesses!
And while the temperate bowl we wreathe,
In concert let our voices breathe,
Beguiling every hour along
With harmony of soul and song.

———o••o———

ODE LXIII. (4)

To Love, the soft and blooming child,
I touch the harp in descant wild;
To Love, the babe of Cyprian bowers,
The boy, who breathes and blushes flowers;

To Love, for heaven and earth adore him,
And gods and mortals bow before him!

———o••o———

ODE LXIV. (5)

HASTE thee, nymph, whose well-aim'd spear
Wounds the fleeting mountain-deer!
Dian, Jove's immortal child,
Huntress of the savage wild!
Goddess with the sun-bright hair!
Listen to a people's prayer.
Turn, to Lethe's river turn,
There thy vanquish'd people mourn!(6)
Come to Lethe's wavy shore,
Tell them they shall mourn no more.
Thine their hearts, their altars thine;
Must they, Dian—must they pine?

———o••o———

ODE LXV. (7)

LIKE some wanton filly sporting,
Maid of Thrace thou fly'st my courting.
Wanton filly! tell me why
Thou trip'st away, with scornful eye,
And seem'st to think my doating heart
Is novice in the bridling art?
Believe me, girl, it is not so;
Thou 'lt find this skilful hand can throw
The reins around that tender form,
However wild, however warm.

bling repentance. Chaulieu, however, supports more consistently the spirit of the Epicurean philosopher. See his poem, addressed to the Marquis de Lafare,—
    Plus j'approche du terme, et moins je le redoute, etc.

(1) Scaliger, upon Catullus's well-known lines, "Qui nunc it per iter," etc., remarks, that Acheron, with the same idea, is called ανεξοδος by Theocritus, and δυσεκ-δρομος by Nicander.

(2) This ode consists of two fragments, which are to be found in Athenæus, book x., and which Barnes, from the similarity of their tendency, has combined into one. I think this a very justifiable liberty, and have adopted it in some other fragments of our poet.
Degen refers us here to verses of Uz, lib. iv., "der Trinker."

(3) It was Amphictyon who first taught the Greeks to mix water with their wine; in commemoration of which circumstance they erected altars to Bacchus and the nymphs. On this mythological allegory the following epigram is founded:—
    Ardentem ex utero Semeles lavêre Lyæum
    Naiades, extincto fulminis igne sacri;
    Cum nymphis igitur tractabilis, at sine nymphis
    Candenti rursus fulmine corripitur.
                    Pierius Valerianus.
Which is, non verbum verbo,—
    While heavenly fire consumed his Theban dame,
    A Naiad caught young Bacchus from the flame,
    And dipp'd him burning in her purest lymph;
    Hence, still he loves the Naiad's crystal urn,
    And when his native fires too fiercely burn,
    Seeks the cool waters of the fountain-nymph.

(4) "This fragment is preserved in Clemens Alexandrinus, Strom. lib. vi, and in Arsenius, Collect. Græc."—*Barnes.*

It appears to have been the opening of a hymn in praise of Love.

(5) This hymn to Diana is extant in Hephæstion. There is an anecdote of our poet, which has led some to doubt whether he ever wrote any odes of this kind. It is related by the Scholiast upon Pindar (Isthmionic. od. ii., v. 1, as cited by Barnes), that Anacreon being asked, why he addressed all his hymns to women, and none to the deities? answered, " Because women are my deities."

I have assumed, it will be seen, in reporting this anecdote, the same liberty which I have thought it right to take in translating some of the odes; and it were to be wished that these little infidelities were always allowable in interpreting the writings of the ancients; thus, when nature is forgotten in the original, in the translation "tamen usque recurret."

(6) Lethe, a river of Ionia, according to Strabo, falling into the Meander. In its neighbourhood was the city called Magnesia, in favour of whose inhabitants our poet is supposed to have addressed this supplication to Diana. It was written (as Madame Dacier conjectures,) on the occasion of some battle, in which the Magnesians had been defeated.

(7) This ode, which is addressed to some Thracian girl, exists in Heraclides, and has been imitated very frequently by Horace, as all the annotators have remarked. Madame Dacier rejects the allegory, which runs so obviously through the poem, and supposes it to have been addressed to a young mare belonging to Polycrates.

Pierius, in the fourth book of his Hieroglyphics, cites this ode, and informs us that the horse was the hieroglyphical emblem of pride.

Yes—trust me, I can tame thy force,
And turn and wind thee in the course.
Though, wasting now thy careless hours,
Thou sport amid the herbs and flowers,
Soon shalt thou feel the rein's control,
And tremble at the wish'd-for goal!

——o♦♦o——

ODE LXVI. (1)

To thee, the Queen of nymphs divine,
Fairest of all that fairest shine;
To thee, who rulest with darts of fire
This world of mortals, young Desire!
And oh! thou nuptial Power, to thee
Who bear'st of life the guardian key,
Breathing my soul in fervent praise,
And weaving wild my votive lays,
For thee, O Queen! I wake the lyre,
For thee, thou blushing young Desire,
And oh! for thee, thou nuptial Power,
Come, and illume this genial hour.

Look on thy bride, too happy boy,
And while thy lambent glance of joy
Plays over all her blushing charms,
Delay not, snatch her to thine arms,
Before the lovely trembling prey,
Like a young birdling wing away!

(1) This ode is introduced in the Romance of Theodorus Prodromus, and is that kind of epithalamium which was sung like a scolium at the nuptial banquet.

Among the many works of the impassioned Sappho, of which time and ignorant superstition have deprived us, the loss of her epithalamiums is not one of the least that we deplore. The following lines are cited as a relic of one of those poems :—

Ολβιε γαμβρε· σοι μεν δη γαμος ὡς αραο,
Εκτετελες', εχεις δε παρθενον αν αραο.

See Scaliger, in his Poetics, on the Epithalamium.

(2) Original Κυπαριττος δε πεφυκοι σευ ενι κηπω. Passeratius, upon the words "cum castum amisit florem," in the Nuptial Song of Catullus, after explaining "flos" in somewhat a similar sense to that which Gaulminus attributes to ρόδον, says, "Hortum quoque vocant in quo flos ille carpitur, et Græcis κηπος εςι το ερηβαιον γυναικων."

I may remark, in passing, that the author of the Greek version of this charming ode of Catullus has neglected a most striking and anacreontic beauty in those verses "Ut flos in septis," etc., which is the repetition of the line, "Multi illum pueri, multæ optavêre puellæ," with the slight alteration of nulli and nullæ. Catullus himself, however, has been equally injudicious in his version of the famous ode of Sappho; having translated γελωσας; ἱμεροεν, but omitted all notice of the accompanying charm, ἁδυ φωνουσας. Horace has caught the spirit of it more faithfully:—

Dulce ridentem Lalagen amabo,
Dulce loquentem.

(3) This fragment is preserved in the third book of Strabo.

(4) He here alludes to Arganthonius, who lived, accord-

Turn, Stratocles, too happy youth,
Dear to the Queen of amorous truth,
And dear to her, whose yielding zone
Will soon resign her all thine own.
Turn to Myrilla, turn thine eye,
Breathe to Myrilla, breathe thy sigh.
To those bewitching beauties turn ;
For thee they blush, for thee they burn.

Not more the rose, the queen of flowers,
Outblushes all the bloom of bowers,
Than she unrivall'd grace discloses,
The sweetest rose, where all are roses.
Oh! may the sun, benignant, shed
His blandest influence o'er thy bed;
And foster there an infant tree,
To bloom like her, and tower like thee! (2)

——o♦♦o——

ODE LXVII. (3)

RICH in bliss, I proudly scorn
The wealth of Amalthea's horn ;
Nor should I ask to call the throne
Of the Tartessian prince my own; (4)
To totter through his train of years,
The victim of declining fears.
One little hour of joy to me
Is worth a dull eternity! (5)

ing to Lucian, an hundred and fifty years; and reigned, according to Herodotus, eighty. See Barnes.

(5) This ode in preceding editions bore the number 68, the 67th being the following, which Mr. Moore has now suppressed, but which he formerly thus introduced to the reader :—

"I have formed this poem of three or four different fragments, which is a liberty that perhaps may be justified by the example of Barnes, who has thus compiled the fifty-seventh of his edition, and the little ode beginning φερ' ὑδωρ, φερ' οινον, ω παι, which he has subjoined to the epigrams.

"The fragments combined in this ode, are the sixty-seventh, ninety-sixth, ninety-seventh, and hundredth of Barnes's edition, to which I refer the reader for the names of the authors by whom they are preserved."

Gentle youth! whose looks assume
Such a soft and girlish bloom,
Why repulsive, why refuse
The friendship which my heart pursues!
Thou little know'st the fond control
With which thy virtue reins my soul !
Then smile not on my locks of grey,
Believe me, oft with converse gay
I 've chain'd the years of tender age,
And boys have loved the prattling sage ! *
For mine is many a soothing pleasure,
And mine is many a soothing measure;
And much I hate the beamless mind,
Whose earthly vision, unrefined,
Nature has never form'd to see
The beauties of simplicity !
Simplicity, the flower of heaven,
To souls elect, by Nature given !—P. E.

* Monsieur Chaulieu has given a very amiable idea of an old man's intercourse with youth :—

Que, cherché par les jeunes gens,
Pour leurs erreurs plein d'indulgence,
Je tolère leur imprudence
En faveur de leurs agréments.—P. E.

ODE LXVIII. (1)

Now Neptune's month our sky deforms,
  The angry night-cloud teems with storms,
And savage winds, infuriate driven,
  Fly howling in the face of heaven!
Now, now, my friends, the gathering gloom
  With roseate rays of wine illume:
And while our wreaths of parsley spread
  Their fadeless foliage round our head,
Let 's hymn the almighty power of wine,
  And shed libations on his shrine!

——————

ODE LXIX. (2)

THEY wove the lotus band to deck
  And fan with pensile wreath each neck;
And every guest, to shade his head,
  Three little fragrant chaplets spread: (3)
And one was of the Egyptian leaf,
  The rest were roses, fair and brief:
While from a golden vase profound,
  To all on flowery beds around,
A Hebe, of celestial shape,
  Pour'd the rich droppings of the grape!

——————

ODE LXX. (4)

A BROKEN cake, with honey sweet,
  Is all my spare and simple treat;
And, while a generous bowl I crown,
  To float my little banquet down,
I take the soft, the amorous lyre,
  And, sing of love's delicious fire:
In mirthful measures warm and free,
  I sing, dear maid, and sing for thee!

(1) This is composed of two fragments; the seventieth and eighty-first in Barnes. They are both found in Eustathius.

(2) Three fragments form this little ode, all of which are preserved in Athenæus. They are the eighty-second, seventy-fifth, and eighty-third, in Barnes.

(3) Longepierre, to give an idea of the luxurious estimation in which garlands were held by the ancients, relates an anecdote of a courtezan, who in order to gratify three lovers, without leaving cause for jealousy with any of them, gave a kiss to one, let the other drink after her, and put a garland on the brow of the third; so that each was satisfied with his favour, and flattered himself with the preference.

This circumstance resembles very much the subject of one of the *tensons* of Savari de Mauléon, a troubadour. See L'Histoire littéraire des Troubadours. The recital is a curious picture of the puerile gallantries of chivalry.

(4) Compiled by Barnes, from Athenæus, Hephæstion, and Arsenius. See Barnes, 80th.

(5) This I have formed from the eighty-fourth and eighty-fifth of Barnes's edition. The two fragments are found in Athenæus.

ODE LXXI. (5)

WITH twenty chords my lyre is hung,
  And while I wake them all for thee,
Thou, O maiden, wild and young,
  Disport'st in airy levity.

The nursling fawn, that in some shade
  Its antler'd mother leaves behind, (6)
Is not more wantonly afraid,
  More timid of the rustling wind!

——————

ODE LXXII. (7)

FARE thee well, perfidious maid,
  My soul, too long on earth delay'd,
Delay'd, perfidious girl, by thee,
  Is on the wing for liberty.
I fly to seek a kindlier sphere,
  Since thou hast ceased to love me here!

——————

ODE LXXIII. (8)

AWHILE I bloom'd, a happy flower,
  Till Love approach'd one fatal hour,
And made my tender branches feel
  The wounds of his avenging steel.
Then lost I fell, like some poor willow
  That falls across the wintry billow!

——————

ODE LXXIV. (9)

MONARCH Love, resistless boy,
  With whom the rosy Queen of Joy,
And nymphs, whose eyes have Heaven's hue,
  Disporting tread the mountain-dew;

(6) In the original :—

    ῝Ος εν ὑλῃ κεροεσσης
    Απολειφθεις ὑπο μητρος.

" Horned " here, undoubtedly, seems a strange epithet; Madame Dacier, however, observes, that Sophocles, Callimachus, etc. have all applied it in the very same manner, and she seems to agree in the conjecture of the scholiast upon Pindar, that perhaps horns are not always peculiar to the males. I think we may with more ease conclude it to be a license of the poet, "jussit habere puellam cornua."

(7) This fragment is preserved by the scholiast upon Aristophanes, and is the eighty-seventh in Barnes.

(8) This is to be found in Hephæstion, and is the eighty-ninth of Barnes's edition.

I have omitted, from among these scraps, a very considerable fragment imputed to our poet, Ξανθη δ᾽ Ευρυπυλη μελει, etc., which is preserved in the twelfth book of Athenæus, and is the ninety-first in Barnes. If it was really Anacreon who wrote it, " nil fuit unquam sic impar sibi." It is in a style of gross satire, and abounds with expressions that never could be gracefully translated.

(9) A fragment preserved by Dion Chrysostom. Orat. ii. de Regno. See Barnes, 93d.

Propitious, oh! receive my sighs,
Which, glowing with entreaty, rise,
That thou wilt whisper to the breast
Of her I love thy soft behest;
And counsel her to learn from thee,
That lesson thou hast taught to me.
Ah! if my heart no flattery tell,
Thou 'lt own I 've learn'd that lesson well!

———o•◊•o———

ODE LXXV. (1)

Spirit of Love, whose locks unroll'd,
Stream on the breeze like floating gold;
Come, within a fragrant cloud
Blushing with light, thy votary shroud;
And, on those wings that sparkling play,
Waft, oh, waft me hence away!
Love! my soul is full of thee,
Alive to all thy luxury.
But she, the nymph for whom I glow,
The lovely Lesbian mocks my woe;
Smiles at the chill and hoary hues,
That time upon my forehead strews.
Alas! I fear she keeps her charms,
In store for younger, happier arms!

———o⚬o———

ODE LXXVI. (2)

Hither, gentle Muse of mine,
Come and teach thy votary old
Many a golden hymn divine,
For the nymph with vest of gold.

Pretty nymph, of tender age,
Fair thy silky locks unfold;
Listen to a hoary sage,
Sweetest maid with vest of gold!

(1) This fragment, which is extant in Athenæus (Barnes, 101), is supposed, on the authority of Chamæleon, to have been addressed to Sappho. We have also a stanza attributed to her, which some romancers have supposed to be her answer to Anacreon."—*Nouvelles de la Rép. des Lettr.*, tom. ii. de Novembre, 1684. The following is her fragment, the compliment of which is finely imagined; she supposes that the Muse has dictated the verses of Anacreon.—

Κεινον, ω χρυσοθρονε Μουσ' ενισπες
'Υμνον, εκ της καλλιγυναικος εσθλας
Τηιος χωρας ὁν αειδε τερπνως
Πρεσβυς αγαυος.

Oh Muse! who sit'st on golden throne,
Full many a hymn of witching tone
The Teian sage is taught by thee;
But, Goddess, from thy throne of gold,
The sweetest hymn thou 'st ever told,
He lately learn'd and sung for me.

ODE LXXVII. (3)

Would that I were a tuneful lyre,
Of burnish'd ivory fair,
Which, in the Dionysian choir,
Some blooming boy should bear!

Would that I were a golden vase,
That some bright nymph might hold
My spotless frame, with blushing grace,
Herself as pure as gold!

———o•◊•o———

ODE LXXVIII. (4)

When Cupid sees how thickly now
The snows of Time fall o'er my brow,
Upon his wing of golden light
He passes with an eaglet's flight,
And flitting onward seems to say,
"Fare thee well, thou 'st had thy day!"

———o•◊•o———

Cupid, whose lamp has lent the ray, (5)
That lights our life's meandering way,
That God, within this bosom stealing,
Hath waken'd a strange mingled feeling,
Which pleases, though so sadly teasing,
And teases, though so sweetly pleasing!

———o•◊•o———

Let me resign this wretched breath, (6)
Since now remains to me
No other balm than kindly death,
To soothe my misery!

———o•◊•o———

I know thou lovest a brimming measure, (7)
And art a kindly cordial host;

(2) Formed of the 124th and 119th fragments in Barnes, both of which are to be found in Scaliger's Poetics.

De Pauw thinks that those detached lines and couplets, which Scaliger has adduced as examples in his Poetics, are by no means authentic, but of his own fabrication.

(3) This is generally inserted among the remains of Alcæus. Some, however, have attributed it to Anacreon. See our poet's twenty-second ode, and the notes.

(4) See Barnes, 173rd. This fragment, to which I have taken the liberty of adding a turn not to be found in the original, is cited by Lucian in his short essay on the Gallic Hercules.

(5) Barnes, 125th. This is in Scaliger's Poetics. Gail has omitted it in his collection of fragments.

(6) This fragment is extant in Arsenius and Hephæstion. See Barnes (69th), who has arranged the metre of it very skilfully.

(7) Barnes, 72d. This fragment, which is found in Athenæus, contains an excellent lesson for the votaries of Jupiter Hospitalis.

But let me fill and drink at pleasure—
Thus I enjoy the goblet most.

————

I FEAR that love disturbs my rest, (1)
Yet feel not love's impassion'd care ;
I think there 's madness in my breast,
Yet cannot find that madness there !

————

FROM dread Leucadia's frowning steep, (2)
I 'll plunge into the whitening deep;
And there lie cold, to death resign'd,
Since Love intoxicates my mind!

————

MIX me, child, a cup divine, (3)
Crystal water, ruby wine :
Weave the frontlet, richly flushing,
O'er my wintry temples blushing.
Mix the brimmer—Love and I
Shall no more the contest try.
Here—upon this holy bowl,
I surrender all my soul !

————

AMONG the Epigrams of the Anthologia are found
some panegyrics on Anacreon, which I had trans-
lated, and originally intended as a sort of Coronis to
this work. But I found, upon consideration, that
they wanted variety ; and that a frequent recurrence
in them of the same thought would render a col-
lection of such poems uninteresting. I shall take
the liberty, however, of subjoining a few, selected
from the number, that I may not appear to have to-
tally neglected those ancient tributes to the fame of
Anacreon. The four epigrams which I give are

(1) Found in Hephæstion (see Barnes, 95th), and reminds
one somewhat of the following :—

    Odi et amo ; quare id faciam fortasse requiris ;
    Nescio : sed fieri sentio, et excrucior.—*Carm.* 53.

    I love thee and hate thee, but if I can tell
      The cause of my love and my hate, may I die.
    I can feel it, alas ! I can feel it too well,
      That I love thee and hate thee, but cannot tell why.

(2) This is also in Hephæstion, and perhaps is a fragment
of some poem, in which Anacreon had commemorated
the fate of Sappho. It is the 123rd of Barnes.

(3) Collected by Barnes, from Demetrius Phalareus and
Eustathius, and subjoined in his edition to the epigrams
attributed to our poet. And here is the last of those little
scattered flowers, which I thought I might venture with
any grace to transplant ;—happy if it could be said of the
garland which they form, Το δ' ως' Ανακρεοντος.

(4) Antipater Sidonius, the author of this epigram, lived,
according to Vossius, de Poetis Græcis, in the second
year of the 169th Olympiad. He appears, from what Cicero
and Quintilian have said of him, to have been a kind o
improvisatore. See Institut. Orat. lib. x., cap. 7. There
is nothing more known respecting this poet, except some
particulars about his illness and death, which are men-

imputed to Antipater Sidonius. They are rendered,
perhaps, with too much freedom ; but, designing ori-
ginally a translation of all that are extant on the
subject, I endeavoured to enliven their uniformity
by sometimes indulging in the liberties of para-
phrase.

————

ΑΝΤΙΠΑΤΡΟΥ ΣΙΔΩΝΙΟΥ, ΕΙΣ ΑΝΑΚΡΕΟΝΤΑ.

ΘΑΛΛΟΙ τετρακορυμβος, Ανακρεον, αμφι σε κισσος,
    ἀβρα τε λειμωνων πορφυρεων πεταλα·
πηγαι δ' αργινοεντος αναθλιβοιντο γαλακτος,
    ευωδες δ' απο γης ἡδυ χεοιτο μεθυ,
οφρα κε τοι σποδιη τε και οςεα τερψιν αρηται,
    ει δε τις φθιμενοις χριμπτεται ευφροσυνα,
ω το φιλον ςερξας, φιλε, βαρβιτον, ω συν αοιδα
    παντα διαπλωσας και συν ερωτι βιον.

AROUND the tomb, oh, bard divine ! (4)
  Where soft thy hallow'd brow reposes,
Long may the deathless ivy twine,
  And summer spread her waste of roses !

And there shall many a fount distil,
  And many a rill refresh the flowers ;
But wine shall be each purple rill,
  And every fount be milky showers.

Thus, shade of him, whom Nature taught
  To tune his lyre and soul to pleasure,
Who gave to love his tenderest thought,
  Who gave to love his fondest measure,—

Thus, after death, if shades can feel,
  Thou may'st, from odours round thee streaming,
A pulse of past enjoyment steal,
  And live again in blissful dreaming !

tioned as curious by Pliny and others ;—and there re-
main of his works but a few epigrams in the Anthologia,
among which are found these inscriptions upon Ana-
creon. These remains have been sometimes imputed to
another poet * of the same name, of whom Vossius gives
us the following account :—"Antipater Thessalonicensis
vixit tempore Augusti Cæsaris, ut qui saltantem viderit
Pyladem, sicut constat ex quodam ejus epigrammate
Ανθολογιας, lib. iv., tit. εις ορχεςριδας. At eum ac Ba-
thyllum primos fuisse pantomimos ac sub Augusto
claruisse, satis notum ex Dione," etc., etc.

The reader, who thinks it worth observing, may find
a strange oversight in Hoffman's quotation of this article
from Vossius, Lexic. Univers. By the omission of a sen-
tence he has made Vossius assert, that the poet Antipater
was one of the first pantomime dancers in Rome.

Barnes, upon the epigram before us, mentions a version
of it by Brodæus, which is not to be found in that com-
mentator ; but he more than once confounds Brodæus
with another annotator on the Anthologia, Vincentius
Obsopœus, who has given a translation of the epigram.

* Pleraque tamen Thessalonicensi tribuenda videntur.—*Brunck,
Lectiones et Emendat.*

ΤΟΥ ΑΥΤΟΥ, ΕΙΣ ΤΟΝ ΑΥΤΟΝ.

ΤΥΜΒΟΣ Ἀνακρειοντος· ὁ Τηϊος ενθαδε κυκνος
Εὑδει, χἠ παιδων ζωροτατη μανιη.
Ακμην λειριοεντι μελιδεται αμφι Βαθυλλω
Ἱμερα· και κισσου λευκος οδωδε λιθος.
Ουδ᾽ Ἀϊδης σοι ερωτας απεσβεσεν, εν δ᾽ Αχεροντος
Ὡν, ὁλος ωδινεις Κυπριδι θερμοτερη.

Here sleeps Anacreon, in this ivied shade;
Here mute in death the Teian swan is laid.(1)
Cold, cold that heart, which, while on earth it dwelt,
All the sweet frenzy of love's passion felt.
And yet, oh Bard! thou art not mute in death,
Still do we catch thy lyre's luxurious breath ;(2)
And still thy songs of soft Bathylla bloom,
Green as the ivy round thy mouldering tomb.
Nor yet has death obscured thy fire of love,
For still it lights thee through the Elysian grove ;
Where dreams are thine, that bless the elect alone,
And Venus calls thee even in death her own!

(1) Thus Horace of Pindar :—

Multa Dircæum levat aura cycuoum.

A swan was the hieroglyphical emblem of a poet. Ana-
creon has been called the swan of Téos by another of his
eulogists.

Εν τοις μελιχροις Ἱμεροισι συντροφον
Λυκιος Ανακρεοντα, Τηϊον κυκνον,
Εσφηλας ὑγρη νεκταρος μελιηδονη.

Ευγενους, Ανθολ.

God of the grape! thou hast betray'd,
In wine's bewildering dream,
The fairest swan that ever play'd
Along the Muse's stream !—
The Teian, nursed with all those honey'd boys,
The young desires, light Loves, and rose-lipp'd Joys!

(2) Thus Simonides, speaking of our poet :—

Μολπης δ᾽ ου ληθη μελιτερπεος αλλ᾽ ετι κεινο
Βαρβιτον ουδε θανων ευνασεν εν αιδη.

Σιμωνιδου, Ανθολ.

Nor yet are all his numbers mute,
Though dark within the tomb he lies;
But living still, his amorous lute
With sleepless animation sighs !

This is the famous Simonides, whom Plato styled "divine,"
though Le Fevre, in his Poëtes Grecs, supposes that the
epigrams under his name are all falsely imputed. The
most considerable of his remains is a satirical poem upon
women, preserved by Stobæus, ψογος γυναικων.

We may judge from the lines I have just quoted, and
the import of the epigram before us, that the works of
Anacreon were perfect in the times of Simonides and Anti-
pater. Obsopœus, the commentator here, appears to
exult in their destruction, and telling us they were
burned by the bishops and patriarchs, he adds, "nec sane
id necquicquam fecerunt," attributing to this outrage an
effect which it could not possibly have produced.

(3) The spirit of Anacreon is supposed to utter these
verses from the tomb,—somewhat "mutatus ab illo," at
least in simplicity of expression.

(4) We may guess from the words εκ βιβλιων εμων, that

ΤΟΥ ΑΥΤΟΥ, ΕΙΣ ΤΟΝ ΑΥΤΟΝ.

ΞΕΙΝΕ, ταφον παρα λιτον Ανακρειοντος αμειβων,
Ει τι τοι εκ βιβλιων ἠλθεν εμων οφελος,
Σπεισον εμη σποδιη, σπεισον γανος, οφρα κεν οινω
Οστεα γηθησε ταμα νοτιζομενα,
Ὡς ὁ Διονυσου μεμελημενος ουασι κωμος,
Ὡς ὁ φιλακρητου συντροφος ἁρμονιης,
Μηδε καταφθιμενος Βακχου διχα τουτον ὑποισω
Τον γενεη μεροπων χωρον οφειλομενον.

On stranger! if Anacreon's shell (3)
Has ever taught thy heart to swell (4)
With passion's throb or pleasure's sigh,
In pity turn, as wandering nigh,
And drop thy goblet's richest tear (5)
In tenderest libation here!
So shall my sleeping ashes thrill
With visions of enjoyment still.
Not even in death can I resign
The festal joys that once were mine,

Anacreon was not merely a writer of billets doux, as some
French critics have called him. Amongst these M. Le
Fevre, with all his professed admiration, has given our
poet a character by no means of an elevated cast :—

Aussi c'est pour cela que la posterité
L'a toujours justement d'age en age chanté
Comme un franc goguenard, ami de goinfrerie,
Ami de billets doux et de badinerie.

See the verses prefixed to his Poëtes Grecs. This is unlike
the language of Theocritus, to whom Anacreon is indebted
for the following simple eulogium :—

ΕΙΣ ΑΝΑΚΡΕΟΝΤΟΣ ΑΝΔΡΙΑΝΤΑ.

Θασαι τον ανδριαντα τουτον, ω ξενε,
σπουδα, και λεγ᾽, επαν ες οικον ενθης·
Ανακρεοντος εικον᾽ ειδον εν Τεω,
των πρωσθ᾽ ει τι περισσον ωδοποιων.
προσθεις δε χωτι τοις νεοισιν ἁδετο,
ερεις κτρακεως ὁλον τον ανδρα.

UPON THE STATUE OF ANACREON.

Stranger! who near this statue chance to roam,
Let it awhile your studious eyes engage;
That you may say, returning to your home,
"I've seen the image of the Teian sage,
Best of the bards who deck the Muse's page."
Then, if you add, "That striplings loved him well,"
You tell them all he was, and aptly tell.

I have endeavoured to do justice to the simplicity of this
inscription by rendering it as literally, I believe, as a verse
translation will allow.

(5) Thus Simonides, in another of his epitaphs on our
poet :—

Και μιν αει τεγγει νοτερη δροσος, ἡς ὁ γεραιος
Λαροτερον μαλακων επνεεν εκ στοματων.

Let vines, in clustering beauty wreathed,
Drop all their treasures on his head,
Whose lips a dew of sweetness breathed,
Richer than vine bath ever shed !

7

When Harmony pursued my ways,
And Bacchus wanton'd to my lays.(1)
Oh! if delight could charm no more,
If all the goblet's bliss were o'er,
When fate had once our doom decreed,
Then dying would be death indeed ;
Nor could I think, unblest by wine,
Divinity itself divine!

————❦————

ΤΟΥ ΑΥΤΟΥ, ΕΙΣ ΤΟΝ ΑΥΤΟΝ.

ΕΥΔΕΙΣ εν φθιμενοισιν, Αναχρεον, εσθλα πονησας;
εὑδει δ᾽ ἡ γλυκερη νυκτιλαλος κιθαρα,
εὑδει και Σμαρδις, το Ποθων εαρ, ὡ συ μελισδων,
βαρβιτ᾽, ανεκρουου νεκταρ εναρμονιον.

(1) The original here is corrupted, the line ὡς ὁ Δισ-
νυσου, etc., is unintelligible.
Brunck's emendation improves the sense, but I doubt
if it can be commended for elegance. He reads the line
thus :—

ὡς ὁ Διωνυσοιο λελασμενος ουποτε κωμων.

See Brunck, Analecta Veter. Poet. Græc., vol. ii.

(2) In another of these poems, "the nightly-speaking
lyre" of the bard is represented as not yet silent even
after his death.

ὡς ὁ φιλακρητος τε και οινοβαρης φιλοκωμος
πανυυχιος κρουοι * την φιλοπαιδα χελυν.
Σιμωνιδου, εις Αναχρεοντα.

To beauty's smile and wine's delight,
To joys he loved on earth so well,
Still shall his spirit, all the night,
Attune the wild aërial shell !

(3) The original, το Ποθων εαρ, is beautiful. We regret
that such praise should be lavished so preposterously, and
feel that the poet's mistress Eurypyle would have deserved
it better. Her name has been told us by Meleager, as
already quoted, and in another epigram by Antipater.

ὑγρα δε δερκομενοισιν εν ομματιν ουλον αειδοις,
αιθυσσων λιπαρης ανθος ὑπερθε κομης,
ης προς Ευρυπυλην τετραμμενος, ...

Long may the nymph around thee play,
Eurypyle, thy soul's desire,
Basking her beauties in the ray
That lights thine eyes' dissolving fire!
Sing of her smile's bewitching power,
Her every grace that warms and blesses ;
Sing of her brows' luxurient flower,
The beaming glory of her tresses.

* Brunck has κρουων ; but κρουοι, the common reading, better
suits a detached quotation.

τιθεων γαρ Ερωτος ερυς σκοπος᾽ ες δε σε μουνον
τοξα τε και σκολιας ειχεν εκηβολιας.

At length thy golden hours have wing'd their flight,
And drowsy death that eyelid steepeth ;
Thy harp, that whisper'd through each lingering
night,(2)
Now mutely in oblivion sleepeth !
She too, for whom that harp profusely shed
The purest nectar of its numbers,(3)
She, the young spring of thy desires, hath fled,(4)
And with her blest Anacreon slumbers !
Farewell ! thou had'st a pulse for every dart (5)
That mighty Love could scatter from his quiver ;
And each new beauty found in thee a heart,(6)
Which thou, with all thy heart and soul, didst
give her !

The expression here, ανθος κομης, "the flower of the
hair," is borrowed from Anacreon himself, as appears by
a fragment of the poet preserved in Stobæus : Απεχειρα;
δ᾽ ἁπαλης αμομον ανθος.

(4) Thus, says Brunck, in the prologue to the Satires
of Persius :—

Cantare credas Pegaseium nectar.

"Melos" is the usual reading in this line, and Casaubon
has defended it; but "nectar" is, I think, much more
spirited.

(5) ερυς σκοπος, "scopus eras naturâ," not "specu-
lator," as Barnes very falsely interprets it.

Vincentius Obsopœus, upon this passage, contrives to
indulge us with a little astrological wisdom, and talks in a
style of learned scandal about Venus, "male posita cum
Marte in domo Saturni."

(6 This couplet is not otherwise warranted by the
original, than as it dilates the thought which Antipater has
figuratively expressed.

Critias, of Athens, pays a tribute to the legitimate gal-
lantry of Anacreon, calling him, with elegant conciseness,
γυναικων ηπεροπευμα.

Του δε γυναικειων μελεων πλεξαντα ποτ᾽ ωδας
Ἡδυν Αναχρειοντα᾽, Τεως εις Ἑλλαδ᾽ ανηγεν,
Συμποσιων ερεθισμα, γυναικων ηπεροπευμα.

Téos gave to Greece her treasure,
Sage Anacreon, rage in loving ;
Fondly weaving lays of pleasure
For the maids who blush'd approving.
When in nightly banquets sporting,
Where's the guest could ever fly him ?
When with love's seduction courting,
Where's the nymph could e'er deny him ?

* Thus Scaliger, in his dedicatory verses to Ronsard :—
Blandus, suaviloquus, dulcis Anacreon.

————◦✸❀◦————

JUVENILE POEMS.

PREFACE

BY THE EDITOR. (1)

THE Poems which I take the liberty of publishing were never intended by the author to pass beyond the circle of his friends. He thought, with some justice, that what are called Occasional Poems must be always insipid and uninteresting to the greater part of their readers. The particular situations in which they were written, the character of the author and of his associates, all these peculiarities must be known and felt before we can enter into the spirit of such compositions. This consideration would have always, I believe, prevented the author himself from submitting these trifles to the eye of dispassionate criticism: and if their posthumous introduction to the world be injustice to his memory, or intrusion on the public, the error must be imputed to the injudicious partiality of friendship.

Mr. LITTLE died in his one and twentieth year; and most of these Poems were written at so early a period that their errors may lay claim to some indulgence from the critic. Their author, as unambitious as indolent, scarce ever looked beyond the moment of composition; but, in general, wrote as he pleased, careless whether he pleased as he wrote. It may likewise be remembered, that they were all the productions of an age when the passions very often give a colouring too warm to the imagination; and this may palliate, if it cannot excuse, that air of levity which pervades so many of them. The "aurea legge, s'ei piace ei lice," he too much pursued, and too much inculcates. Few can regret this more sincerely than myself; and if my friend had lived, the judgment of riper years would have chastened his mind, and tempered the luxuriance of his fancy.

Mr. LITTLE gave much of his time to the study of the amatory writers. If ever he expected to find in the ancients that delicacy of sentiment, and variety of fancy, which are so necessary to refine and animate the poetry of love, he was much disappointed. I know not any one of them who can be regarded as a model in that style; Ovid made love like a rake, and Propertius like a schoolmaster. The mythological allusions of the latter are called erudition by his commentators; but such ostentatious display, upon a subject so simple as love,

would be now esteemed vague and puerile, and was even in his own times pedantic. It is astonishing that so many critics should nave preferred him to the gentle and touching Tibullus; but those defects, I believe, which a common reader condemns, have been regarded rather as beauties by those erudite men, the commentators; who find a field for their ingenuity and research, in his Grecian learning and quaint obscurities.

Tibullus abounds with touches of fine and natura feeling. The idea of his unexpected return to Delia, "Tunc veniam subito," etc.,(2) is imagined with all the delicate ardour of a lover; and the sentiment of " nec te posse carere velim," however colloquial the expression may have been, is natural, and from the heart. But the poet of Verona, in my opinion, possessed more genuine feeling than any of them. His life was, I believe, unfortunate; his associates were wild and abandoned; and the warmth of his nature took too much advantage of the latitude which the morals of those times so criminally allowed to the passions. All this depraved his imagination, and made it the slave of his senses But still a native sensibility is often very warmly perceptible; and when he touches the chord of pathos, he reaches immediately the heart. They who have felt the sweets of return to a home from which they have long been absent, will confess the beauty of those simple unaffected lines:—

> O quid solutis est beatius curis!
> Cum mens onus reponit, ac peregrino
> Labore fessi venimus Larem ad nostrum
> Desideratoque acquiescimus lecto.—*Carm.* xxix.

His sorrows on the death of his brother are the very tears of poesy; and when he complains of the ingratitude of mankind, even the inexperienced cannot but sympathise with him. I wish I were a poet; I should then endeavour to catch, by translation, the spirit of those beauties which I have always so warmly admired.(3)

It seems to have been peculiarly the fate of Catullus, that the better and more valuable part of his poetry has not reached us; for there is confessedly nothing in his extant works to authorise the epithet " doctus," so universally bestowed upon him by the ancients. If time had suffered his other writings to escape, we perhaps should have found among them some more purely amatory; but of those we possess,

---

(1) A portion of the following poems were published originally as the works of "the late Thomas Little," with the Preface here given prefixed to them.

The following motto was prefixed to the original edition of "Little's Poems:"—

LUSISSE PUDET.—*Horace.*

Ταδ' ες' ονειρων νεοτερων φαντασματα, οιον ληρος.
Metroc. ap. DIOG. LAERT., lib. vi., cap. 6.

(2) Lib. i., eleg. 3.

(3) In the following Poems will be found a translation of one of his finest Carmina: but I fancy it is only a mere schoolboy's essay, and deserves to be praised for little more than the attempt.

can there be a sweeter specimen of warm yet chastened description than his loves of Acme and Septimius? and the few little songs of dalliance to Lesbia are distinguished by such an exquisite playfulness, that they have always been assumed as models by the most elegant modern Latinists. Still, it must be confessed, in the midst of all these beauties,

—— Medio de fonte leporum
Surgit amari aliquid, quod in ipsis floribus angat.(1)

It has often been remarked, that the ancients knew nothing of gallantry; and we are sometimes told there was too much sincerity in their love to allow them to trifle thus with the semblance of passion. But I cannot perceive that they were any thing more constant than the moderns: they felt all the same dissipation of the heart, though they knew not those seductive graces by which gallantry almost teaches it to be amiable. Wotton, the learned advocate for the moderns, deserts them in considering this point of comparison, and praises the ancients for their ignorance of such refinements. But he seems to have collected his notions of gallantry from the insipid *fadeurs* of the French romances, which have nothing congenial with the graceful levity, the " grata protervitas," of a Rochester or a Sedley.

As far as I can judge, the early poets of our own language were the models which Mr. Little selected for imitation. To attain their simplicity (" ævo rarissima nostro simplicitas ") was his fondest ambition. He could not have aimed at a grace more difficult of attainment;(2) and his life was of too short a date to allow him to perfect such a taste; but how far he was likely to have succeed—d, the critic may judge from his productions.

I have found among his papers a novel, in rather an imperfect state, which, as soon as I have arranged and collected it, shall be submitted to the public eye.

Where Mr. Little was born, or what is the genealogy of his parents, are points in which very few readers can be interested. His life was one of those humble streams which have scarcely a name in the map of life, and the traveller may pass it by without inquiring its source or direction. His character was well known to all who were acquainted with him; for he had too much vanity to hide its virtues, and not enough of art to conceal its defects. The lighter traits of his mind may be traced perhaps in his writings; but the few for which he was valued live only in the remembrance of his friends.

T. M.

(1) Lucretius.

(2) It is a curious illustration of the labour which simplicity requires, that the Ramblers of Johnson, elaborate as they appear, were written with fluency, and seldom required revision; while the simple language of Rousseau, which seems to come flowing from the heart, was the slow

DEDICATION.

TO JOSEPH ATKINSON, ESQ.

My dear Sir,

I feel a very sincere pleasure in dedicating to you the Second Edition of our friend Little's Poems. I am not unconscious that there are many in the collection which perhaps it would be prudent to have altered or omitted; and, to say the truth, I more than once revised them for that purpose; but, I know not why, I distrusted either my heart or my judgment; and the consequence is, you have them in their original form:

Non possunt nostros multæ, Faustine, lituræ,
Emendare jocos; una litura potest.

I am convinced, however, that, though not quite a *casuiste relâché*, you have charity enough to forgive such inoffensive follies: you know that the pious Beza was not he less revered for those sportive *Juvenilia* which he published under a fictitious name; nor did the levity of Bembo's poems prevent him from making a very good cardinal.

Believe me, my dear friend, with the truest esteem,

Yours,

April 19, 1802.   T. M.

JUVENILE POEMS.

FRAGMENTS OF COLLEGE EXERCISES.

Nobilitas sola est atque unica virtus.—*Juv.*

Mark those proud boasters of a splendid line,
Like gilded ruins, mouldering while they shine,
How heavy sits that weight of alien show,
Like martial helm upon an infant's brow;
Those borrow'd splendours, whose contrasting light
Throws back the native shades in deeper night.

Ask the proud train who glory's shade pursue,
Where are the arts by which that glory grew?
The genuine virtues that with eagle-gaze
Sought young Renown in all her orient blaze!
Where is the heart by chymic truth refined,
The exploring soul, whose eye had read mankind?
Where are the links that twined, with heavenly art,
His country's interest round the patriot's heart? (3)

*   *   *   *   *

Justum bellum quibus necessarium, et pia arma quibus nulla nisi in armis relinquitur spes.—*Livy.*

*   *   *   *   *

Is there no call, no consecrating cause,
Approved by Heaven, ordain'd by nature's laws,

production of painful labour, pausing on every word, and balancing every sentence.

(3) Mr. Moore has discarded the following lines:—
Where is the tongue that scatter'd words of fire?
The spirit breathing through the poet's lyre?
Do those descend with all that tide of fame
Which vainly waters an unfruitful name?—P. E.

Where justice flies the herald of our way,
And truth's pure beams upon the banners play?

Yes, there's a call sweet as an angel's breath
To slumbering babes, or innocence in death;
And urgent as the tongue of Heaven within,
When the mind's balance trembles upon sin.

Oh! 'tis our country's voice, whose claim should meet
An echo in the soul's most deep retreat;
Along the heart's responding chord should run,
Nor let a tone there vibrate—but the one!

VARIETY.

Ask what prevailing pleasing power
  Allures the sportive wandering bee
To roam, untired, from flower to flower,
  He'll tell you, 't is variety.

Look Nature round, her features trace,
  Her seasons, all her changes see;
And own, upon Creation's face,
  The greatest charm's variety.

For me, ye gracious powers above!
  Still let me roam, unfix'd and free;
In all things,—but the nymph I love,
  I'll change, and taste variety.

But, Patty, not a world of charms
  Could e'er estrange my heart from thee;--
No, let me ever seek those arms,
  There still I'll find variety.

TO A BOY, WITH A WATCH.
WRITTEN FOR A FRIEND.

Is it not sweet, beloved youth,
  To rove though Erudition's bowers,
And cull the golden fruits of truth,
  And gather Fancy's brilliant flowers?

And is it not more sweet than this,
  To feel thy parents' hearts approving,
And pay them back in sums of bliss
  The dear, the endless debt of loving?

It must be so to thee, my youth;
  With this idea toil is lighter;
This sweetens all the fruits of truth,
  And makes the flowers of fancy brighter.

The little gift we send thee, boy,
  May sometimes teach thy soul to ponder,
If indolence or siren joy
  Should ever tempt that soul to wander.

'T will tell thee that the winged day
  Can ne'er be chain'd by man's endeavour;

That life and time shall fade away,
  While heaven and virtue bloom for ever!

SONG.

If I swear by that eye, you'll allow,
  Its look is so shifting and new,
That the oath I might take on it now
  The very next glance would undo.

Those babies that nestle so sly
  Such thousands of arrows have got,
That an oath, on the glance of an eye
  Such as yours, may be off in a shot.

Should I swear by the dew on your lip,
  Though each moment the treasure renews,
If my constancy wishes to trip,
  I may kiss off the oath when I choose.

Or a sigh may disperse from that flower
  Both the dew and the oath that are there;
And I'd make a new vow every hour,
  To lose them so sweetly in air.

But clear up the heaven of your brow,
  Nor fancy my faith is a feather;
On my heart I will pledge you my vow,
  And they both must be broken together!

TO . . . .

Remember him thou leavest behind,
  Whose heart is warmly bound to thee,
Close as the tenderest links can bind
  A heart as warm as heart can be.

Oh! I had long in freedom roved,
  Though many seem'd my soul to share;
'T was passion when I thought I loved,
  'T was fancy when I thought them fair.

Even she, my muse's early theme,
  Beguiled me only while she warm'd;
'T was young desire that fed the dream,
  And reason broke what passion form'd.

But thou--ah! better had it been
  If I had still in freedom roved,
If I had ne'er thy beauties seen,
  For then I never should have loved.

Then all the pain which lovers feel
  Had never to this heart been known;
But then, the joys that lovers steal,
  Should they have ever been my own?

Oh! trust me when I swear thee this,
  Dearest! the pain of loving thee,

The very pain is sweeter bliss
  Than passion's wildest ecstasy.

That little cage I would not part,
  In which my soul is prison'd now,
For the most light and winged heart
  That wantons on the passing vow.

Still, my beloved! still keep in mind,
  However far removed from me,
That there is one thou leavest behind,
  Whose heart respires for only thee!

And though ungenial ties have bound
  Thy fate unto another's care,
That arm, which clasps thy bosom round,
  Cannot confine the heart that's there.

No, no! that heart is only mine
  By ties all other ties above,
For I have wed it at a shrine
  Where we have had no priest but Love.

SONG.

When Time, who steals our years away,
  Shall steal our pleasures too,
The memory of the past will stay,
  And half our joys renew.
Then, Julia, when thy beauty's flower
  Shall feel the wintry air,
Remembrance will recall the hour
  When thou alone wert fair.
Then talk no more of future gloom;
  Our joys shall always last;
For Hope shall brighten days to come,
  And Memory gild the past.

Come, Chloe, fill the genial bowl,
  I drink to Love and thee:
Thou never canst decay in soul,
  Thou 'lt still be young for me.
And as thy lips the tear-drop chase
  Which on my cheek they find,
So hope shall steal away the trace
  That sorrow leaves behind.
Then fill the bowl—away with gloom!
  Our joys shall always last;
For Hope shall brighten days to come,
  And Memory gild the past.

But mark, at thought of future years
  When love shall lose its soul,
My Chloe drops her timid tears—
  They mingle with my bowl.
How like this bowl of wine, my fair,
  Our loving life shall fleet;
Though tears may sometimes mingle there,
  The draught will still be sweet.

Then fill the cup—away with gloom!
  Our joys shall always last;
For Hope will brighten days to come,
  And Memory gild the past.

SONG.

Have you not seen the timid tear,
  Steal trembling from mine eye?
Have you not mark'd the flush of fear,
  Or caught the murmur'd sigh?
And can you think my love is chill,
  Nor fix'd on you alone?
And can you rend, by doubting still,
  A heart so much your own?

To you my soul's affections move,
  Devoutly, warmly true;
My life has been a task of love,
  Or along, long thought of you.
If all your tender faith be o'er,
  If still my truth you'll try,
Alas, I know but *one* proof more—
  I'll bless your name, and die!

REUBEN AND ROSE.

A TALE OF ROMANCE.

The darkness that hung upon Willumberg's walls
  Had long been remember'd with awe and dismay;
For years not a sunbeam had play'd in its halls,
  And it seem'd as shut out from the regions of day.

Though the valleys were brighten'd by many a beam,
  Yet none could the woods of that castle illume;
And the lightning which flash'd on the neighbour-
    ing stream
  Flew back, as if fearing to enter the gloom!

"Oh! when shall this horrible darkness disperse?"
  Said Willumberg's lord to the Seer of the Cave.—
"It can never dispel," said the wizard of verse,
  "Till the bright star of chivalry sinks in the wave!"

And who was the bright star of chivalry then?
  Who *could* be but Reuben, the flower of the age?
For Reuben was first in the combat of men,   [page.
  Though Youth had scarce written his name on her

For Willumberg's daughter his young heart had
    beat,—
For Rose, who was bright as the spirit of dawn,
When with wand dropping diamonds, and silvery
    feet,
  It walks o'er the flowers of the mountain and lawn.

Must Rose, then, from Reuben so fatally sever?
  Sad, sad, were the words of the Seer of the Cave,
That darkness should cover that castle for ever,
  Or Reuben be sunk in the merciless wave!

To the wizard she flew, saying, " Tell me, oh, tell!
  Shall my Reuben no more be restored to my eyes?"
" Yes, yes—when a spirit shall toll the great bell
  Of the mouldering abbey, your Reuben shall rise!"

Twice, thrice he repeated " Your Reuben shall rise!"
  And Rose felt a moment's release from her pain ;
And wiped, while she listen'd, the tears from her eyes,
  And hoped she might yet see her hero again.

That hero could smile at the terrors of death,
  When he felt that he died for the sire of his Rose;
To the Oder he flew, and there plunging beneath,
  In the depth of the billows soon found his repose.

How strangely the order of destiny falls!—
  Not long in the waters the warrior lay,
When a sunbeam was seen to glance over the walls,
  And the castle of Willumberg bask'd in the ray !

All, all but the soul of the maid was in light;
  There sorrow and terror lay gloomy and blank:
Two days did she wander, and all the long night,
  In quest of her love, on the wide river's bank.

Oft, oft did she pause for the toll of the bell,
  And heard but the breathings of night in the air ;
Long, long did she gaze on the watery swell,
  And saw but the foam of the white billow there.

And often as midnight its veil would undraw,
  As she look'd at the light of the moon in the stream,
She thought 't was his helmet of silver she saw,
  As the curl of the surge glitter'd high in the beam.

And now the third night was begemming the sky ;
  Poor Rose, on the cold dewy margent reclined,
There wept till the tear almost froze in her eye,
  When—hark !—'t was the bell that came deep in
    the wind !

She startled, and saw, through the glimmering shade,
  A form o'er the waters in majesty glide ; [cay'd,
She knew 't was her love, though his cheek was de-
  And his helmet of silver was wash'd by the tide.

Was this what the Seer of the Cave had foretold?—
  Dim, dim through the phantom the moon shot a
    gleam ;
'T was Reuben, but, ah ! he was deathly and cold,
  And fleeted away like the spell of a dream !

Twice, thrice did he rise, and as often she thought
  From the bank to embrace him, but vain her
    endeavour !
Then, plunging beneath, at a billow she caught,
  And sunk to repose on its bosom for ever !

— o ♦ o —

DID NOT.

'T was a new feeling—something more
Than we had dared to own before,
  Which then we hid not;
We saw it in each other's eye,
And wish'd, in every half-breathed sigh,
  To speak, but did not.

She felt my lips' impassion'd touch—
'T was the first time I dared so much,
  And yet she chid not ;
But whisper'd o'er my burning brow,
" Oh ! do you doubt I love you now ?"
  Sweet soul ! I did not.

Warmly I felt her bosom thrill,
I press'd it closer, closer still,
  Though gently bid not ;
Till—oh ! the world hath seldom heard
Of lovers, who so nearly err'd,
  And yet, who did not.

— o ♦ o —

TO . . . .

That wrinkle, when first I espied it,
  At once put my heart out of pain ;
Till the eye, that was glowing beside it,
  Disturb'd my ideas again.

Thou art just in the twilight at present,
  When woman's declension begins ;
When, fading from all that is pleasant,
  She bids a good night to her sins.

Yet thou still art so lovely to me,
  I would sooner, my exquisite mother !
Repose in the sunset of thee,
  Than bask in the noon of another.

— o ♦ o —

TO MRS. . . . . ,
ON SOME CALUMNIES AGAINST HER CHARACTER.

Is not thy mind a gentle mind?
Is not that heart a heart refined ?
Hast thou not every gentle grace,
We love in woman's mind and face?
And, oh ! art *thou* a shrine for Sin
To hold her hateful worship in?

No, no, be happy—dry that tear—
Though some thy heart hath harbour'd near,
May now repay its love with blame ;
Though man, who ought to shield thy fame,
Ungenerous man, be first to shun thee;
Though all the world look cold upon thee ;
Yet shall thy pureness keep thee still
Unharm'd by that surrounding chill;

Like the famed drop, in crystal found,(1)
Floating, while all was frozen around,—
Unchill'd, unchanging shalt thou be,
Safe in thy own sweet purity.(2)

———o❦o———

ANACREONTIC.

—— in *lachrymas* verterat omne merum.
          Tib., lib. i., eleg. 5.

Press the grape, and let it pour
Around the board its purple shower;
And, while the drops my goblet steep,
I 'll think in woe the clusters weep.

Weep on, weep on, my pouting vine!
Heaven grant no tears, but tears of wine.
Weep on; and, as thy sorrows flow,
I 'll taste the luxury of woe.

———o❦o———

TO . . . .

When I loved you, I can't but allow
I had many an exquisite minute;
But the scorn that I feel for you now
Hath even more luxury in it.

Thus, whether we 're on or we 're off,
Some witchery seems to await you :
To love you was pleasant enough,
And, oh! 't is delicious to hate you !

———o❦o———

TO JULIA.
IN ALLUSION TO SOME ILLIBERAL CRITICISMS.

Why, let the stingless critic chide
With all that fume of vacant pride
Which mantles o'er the pedant fool,
Like vapour on a stagnant pool.
Oh! if the song, to feeling true,
Can please the elect, the sacred few,
Whose souls, by Taste and Nature taught,
Thrill with the genuine pulse of thought—
If some fond feeling maid like thee,
The warm-eyed child of Sympathy,
Shall say, while o'er my simple theme
She languishes in Passion's dream,
"He was, indeed, a tender soul—
No critic law, no chill control,
Should ever freeze, by timid art,
The flowings of so fond a heart !"

Yes, soul of Nature! soul of Love!
That, hovering like a snow-wing'd dove,
Breathed o'er my cradle warblings wild,
And hail'd me Passion's warmest child,—
Grant me the tear from Beauty's eye,
From Feeling's breast the votive sigh;
Oh! let my song, my memory, find
A shrine within the tender mind;
And I will smile when critics chide,
And I will scorn the fume of pride
Which mantles o'er the pedant fool,
Like vapour round some stagnant pool !

———o❦o———

TO JULIA,

Mock me no more with Love's beguiling dream,
   A dream, I find, illusory as sweet :
One smile of friendship, nay, of cold esteem,
   Far dearer were than passion's bland deceit !

I 've heard you oft eternal truth declare ;
   Your heart was only mine, I once believed.
Ah! shall I say that all your vows were air ?
   And *must* I say, my hopes were all deceived ?

Vow, then, no longer that our souls are twined,
   That all our joys are felt with mutual zeal;
Julia!—'t is pity, pity makes you kind;
   You know I love, and you would *seem* to feel.

But shall I still go seek within those arms
   A joy in which affection takes no part?
No, no, farewell! you give me but your charms,
   When I had fondly thought you gave your heart.

———o❦o———

THE SHRINE.
TO . . . . . .

My fates had destined me to rove
A long, long pilgrimage of love ;
And many an altar on my way
Has lured my pious steps to stay;
For, if the saint was young and fair,
I turn'd and sung my vespers there.
This, from a youthful pilgrim's fire,
Is what your pretty saints require :
To pass, nor tell a single bead,
With them would be profane indeed !
But, trust me, all this young devotion
Was but to keep my zeal in motion ;

(1) This alludes to a curious gem, upon which Claudian has left us some very elaborate epigrams. It was a drop of pure water enclosed within a piece of crystal. See Claudian. Epigram. "de Crystallo cui aqua inerat." Addison mentions a curiosity of this kind at Milan; and adds, "It is such a rarity as this that I saw at Vendôme in France, which they there pretend is a tear that our Saviour shed over Lazarus, and was gathered up by an angel, who put it into a little crystal vial, and made a present of it to Mary Magdalen."—*Addison's Remarks on several Parts of Italy.*

(2) This piece has undergone a variety of verbal changes, as will be perceived on comparing the last eight lines with those that formerly occupied their place :—

   Ungenerous man, be first to wound thee;
   Though the whole world may freeze around thee,
   Oh! thou 'lt be like that lucid tear
   Which bright, within the crystal's sphere,
   In liquid purity was found,
   Though all had grown congeal'd around ;
   Floating in frost, it mock'd the chill,
   Was pure, was soft, was brilliant still!—P. E.

And, every humbler altar past,
I now have reach'd THE SHRINE at last!

——o◊◊o——

TO A LADY,

WITH SOME MANUSCRIPT POEMS,

ON LEAVING THE COUNTRY.

WHEN, casting many a look behind,
    I leave the friends I cherish here—
Perchance some other friends to find,
    But surely finding none so dear—

Haply the little simple page,
    Which votive thus I've traced for thee,
May now and then a look engage,
    And steal one moment's thought for me.

But, oh! in pity let not those
    Whose hearts are not of gentle mould,
Let not the eye that seldom flows
    With feeling's tear, my song behold.

For, trust me, they who never melt
    With pity, never melt with love;
And such will frown at all I've felt,
    And all my loving lays reprove.

But if, perhaps, some gentler mind,
    Which rather loves to praise than blame,
Should in my page an interest find,
    And linger kindly on my name;

Tell him—or, oh! if, gentler still,
    By female lips my name be blest:
For, where do all affections thrill
    So sweetly as in woman's breast?—

Tell her, that he, whose loving themes
    Her eye indulgent wanders o'er,
Could sometimes wake from idle dreams,
    And bolder flights of fancy soar;

That Glory oft would claim the lay,
    And Friendship oft his numbers move;
But whisper then, that, "sooth to say,
    His sweetest song was given to Love!"

——o◊◊o——

TO JULIA.

THOUGH Fate, my girl, may bid us part,
    Our souls it cannot, shall not sever;
The heart will seek its kindred heart,
    And cling to it as close as ever.

But must we, must we part indeed?
    Is all our dream of rapture over?
And does not Julia's bosom bleed
    To leave so dear, so fond a lover?

Does *she* too mourn?—Perhaps she may;
    Perhaps she mourns our bliss so fleeting:
But why is Julia's eye so gay,
    If Julia's heart like mine is beating?

I oft have loved that sunny glow
    Of gladness in her blue eye gleaming—
But can the bosom bleed with woe,
    While joy is in the glances beaming?

No, no!—Yet, love, I will not chide;
    Although your heart *were* fond of roving,
Nor that nor all the world beside
    Could keep your faithful boy from loving.

You'll soon be distant from his eye,
    And, with you, all that's worth possessing.
Oh! then it will be sweet to die,
    When life has lost its only blessing!

——o◊◊o——

TO . . . . . .

SWEET lady, look not thus again:
    Those bright deluding smiles recall
A maid remember'd now with pain,
    Who was my love, my life, my all!

Oh! while this heart bewilder'd took
    Sweet poison from her thrilling eye,
Thus would she smile, and lisp, and look,
    And I would hear, and gaze, and sigh!

Yes, I did love her—wildly love—
    She was her sex's best deceiver!
And oft she swore she'd never rove—
    And I was destined to believe her!

Then, lady, do not wear the smile
    Of one whose smile could thus betray;
Alas! I think the lovely wile
    Again could steal my heart away.

For when those spells that charm'd my mind
    On lips so pure as thine I see,
I fear the heart which she resign'd
    Will err again, and fly to thee!

——o◊◊o——

NATURE'S LABELS.

A FRAGMENT.

IN vain we fondly strive to trace
The soul's reflection in the face;
In vain we dwell on lines and crosses,
Crooked mouth, or short proboscis;
Boobies have look'd as wise and bright
As Plato or the Stagirite;
And many a sage and learned skull
Has peep'd through windows dark and dull.

8

Since then, though art do all it can,
We ne'er can reach the inward man,
Nor (howsoe'er "learn'd Thebans" doubt)
The inward woman, from without,
Methinks 't were well if Nature could
(And Nature could, if Nature would)
Some pithy short descriptions write,
On tablets large, in black and white,
Which she might hang about our throttles,
Like labels upon physic-bottles;
And where all men might read—but stay—
As dialectic sages say,
The argument most apt and ample
For common use is the example.
For instance, then, if Nature's care
Had not portray'd, in lines so fair,
The inward soul of Lucy L–nd–n,
This is the label she'd have pinn'd on.

FIRST LABEL.

Within this form there lies enshrined
The purest, brightest gem of mind.
Though Feeling's hand may sometimes throw
Upon its charms the shade of woe,
The lustre of the gem, when veil'd,
Shall be but mellow'd, not conceal'd.

Now, sirs, imagine, if you 're able,
That Nature wrote a second label,
They 're her own words—at least suppose so—
And boldly pin it on Pomposo.

LABEL SECOND.

When I composed the fustian brain
Of this redoubted Captain Vain,
I had at hand but few ingredients,
And so was forced to use expedients.
I put therein some small discerning,
A grain of sense, a grain of learning;
And when I saw the void behind,
I fill'd it up with froth and wind!

＊   ＊   ＊   ＊

TO JULIA,

ON HER BIRTHDAY.

When Time was entwining the garland of years,
Which to crown my beloved was given,
Though some of the leaves might be sullied with tears,
Yet the flowers were all gather'd in heaven.

And long may this garland be sweet to the eye,
May its verdure for ever be new;
Young Love shall enrich it with many a sigh,
And Sympathy nurse it with dew.

A REFLECTION AT SEA.

See how, beneath the moonbeam's smile,
Yon little billow heaves its breast,
And foams and sparkles for a while,—
Then murmuring subsides to rest.

Thus man, the sport of bliss and care,
Rises on time's eventful sea;
And, having swell'd a moment there,
Thus melts into eternity!

CLORIS AND FANNY.

Cloris! if I were Persia's king,
I'd make my graceful queen of thee;
While Fanny, wild and artless thing,
Should but thy humble handmaid be.

There is but *one* objection in it—
That, verily, I'm much afraid
I should, in some unlucky minute,
Forsake the mistress for the maid.

THE SHIELD.

Say, did you not hear a voice of death!
And did you not mark the paly form
Which rode on the silvery mist of the heath,
And sung a ghostly dirge in the storm?

Was it the wailing bird of the gloom,
That shrieks on the house of woe all night?
Or a shivering fiend that flew to a tomb,
To howl and to feed till the glance of light?

'T was *not* the death-bird's cry from the wood,
Nor shivering fiend that hung on the blast;
'T was the shade of Helderic—man of blood—
It screams for the guilt of days that are past.

See how the red, red lightning strays,
And scares the gliding ghosts of the heath!
Now on the leafless yew it plays,
Where hangs the shield of this son of death.

That shield is blushing with murderous stains;
Long has it hung from the cold yew's spray;
It is blown by storms and wash'd by rains,
But neither can take the blood away!

Oft by that yew, on the blasted field,
Demons dance to the red moon's light;
While the damp boughs creak, and the swinging
    shield
Sings to the raving spirit of night!

TO JULIA,

WEEPING.

Oh! if your tears are given to care,
If real woe disturbs your peace,
Come to my bosom, weeping fair!
And I will bid your weeping cease.
But if with Fancy's vision'd fears,
With dreams of woe your bosom thrill;
You look so lovely in your tears,
That I must bid you drop them still.

DREAMS.

TO . . . .

In slumber, I prithee how is it
  That souls are oft taking the air,
And paying each other a visit,
  While bodies are heaven knows where?

Last night, 'tis in vain to deny it,
  Your Soul took a fancy to roam,
For I heard her, on tiptoe so quiet,
  Come ask, whether *mine* was at home.

And mine let her in with delight,
  And they talk'd and they laugh'd the time through;
For, when souls come together at night,
  There is no saying what they mayn't do!

And *your* little Soul, heaven bless her!
  Had much to complain and to say,
Of how sadly you wrong and oppress her
  By keeping her prison'd all day.

" If I happen," said she, " but to steal
  For a peep now and then to her eye,
Or, to quiet the fever I feel,
  Just venture abroad on a sigh;

" In an instant she frightens me in
  With some phantom of prudence or terror,
For fear I should stray into sin,
  Or, what is still worse, into error!

" So, instead of displaying my graces,
  By daylight, in language and mien,
I am shut up in corners and places,
  Where truly I blush to be seen!"

Upon hearing this piteous confession,
  My Soul, looking tenderly at her,
Declared as for grace and discretion,
  He did not know much of the matter;

" But, to-morrow, sweet Spirit!" he said,
  " Be at home after midnight, and then
I will come when your lady 's in bed,
  And we 'll talk o'er the subject again."

So she whisper'd a word in his ear,
  I suppose to her door to direct him,
And, just after midnight, my dear,
  Your polite little Soul may expect him.

TO ROSA.

WRITTEN DURING ILLNESS.

The wisest soul, by anguish torn,
  Will soon unlearn the lore it knew;
And when the shrining casket 's worn,
  The gem within will tarnish too.

But love 's an essence of the soul,
  Which sinks not with this chain of clay;
Which throbs beyond the chill control
  Of withering pain or pale decay.

And surely, when the touch of Death
  Dissolves the spirit's earthly ties,
Love still attends the immortal breath,
  And makes it purer for the skies!

Oh Rosa, when, to seek its sphere,
  My soul shall leave this orb of men,
That love which form'd its treasure here
  Shall be its *best* of treasures then!

And as, in fabled dreams of old,
  Some air-born genius, child of time,
Presided o'er each star that roll'd,
  And track'd it through its path sublime;

So thou, fair planet, not unled,-
  Shall through thy mortal orbit stray;
Thy lover's shade, to thee still wed,
  Shall linger round thy earthly way.

Let other spirits range the sky,
  And play around each starry gem;
I 'll bask beneath that lucid eye,
  Nor envy worlds of suns to them.

And when that heart shall cease to beat,
  And when that breath at length is free,
Then, Rosa, soul to soul we 'll meet,
  And mingle to eternity! (1)

SONG.

The wreath you wove, the wreath you wove,
  Is fair—but oh, how fair,
If Pity's hand had stolen from Love
  One leaf to mingle there!

If every rose with gold were tied,
  Did gems for dew-drops fall,
One faded leaf where Love had sigh'd
  Were sweetly worth them all.

The wreath you wove, the wreath you wove,
  Our emblem well may be;
Its bloom is yours, but hopeless Love
  Must keep its tears for me.

(1) Mr. Moore has omitted in the present edition the
following lines, which originally formed the last verse
but one of the poem:—

    And oh! if airy shapes may steal
     To mingle with a mortal frame,
    Then, then, my love!—but drop the veil!
     Hide, hide from heaven the unholy flame.
                      P. E.

THE SALE OF LOVES.

I DREAMT that, in the Paphian groves,
  My nets by moonlight laying,
I caught a flight of wanton Loves,
  Among the rose-beds playing.
Some just had left their silvery shell
  While some were full in feather;
So pretty a lot of Loves to sell
  Were never yet strung together.
    Come buy my Loves,
    Come buy my Loves,
Ye dames and rose-lipp'd misses!—
    They 're new and bright,
    The cost is light,
For the coin of this isle is kisses.

First Cloris came, with looks sedate,
  The coin on her lips was ready;
"I buy," quoth she, "my Love by weight,
  Full grown, if you please, and steady."
"Let mine be light," said Fanny, "pray—
  Such lasting toys undo one;
A light little Love that will last to-day,—
  To-morrow I 'll sport a new one."
    Come buy my Loves,
    Come buy my Loves,
Ye dames and rose-lipp'd misses!—
    There 's some will keep,
    Some light and cheap,
At from ten to twenty kisses.

The learned Prue took a pert young thing,
  To divert her virgin Muse with,
And pluck sometimes a quill from his wing,
  To indite her billets-doux with.
Poor Cloe would give for a well-fledged pair
  Her only eye, if you 'd ask it;
And Tabitha begg'd, old toothless fair,
  For the youngest Love in the basket.
    Come buy my Loves, etc., etc.

But *one* was left, when Susan came,
  One worth them all together;
At sight of her dear looks of shame,
  He smiled, and pruned his feather.
She wish'd the boy—'t was more than whim—
  Her looks, her sighs betray'd it;
But kisses were not enough for him,
  I ask'd a heart, and she paid it!
    Good-by, my Loves,
    Good-by, my Loves,
'T would make you smile to 've seen us
    First trade for this
    Sweet child of bliss,
And then nurse the boy between us.

———o♦♦o———

TO . . . .

THE world had just begun to steal
  Each hope that led me lightly on;
I felt not as I used to feel,
  And life grew dark and love was gone.

No eye to mingle sorrow's tear,
  No lip to mingle pleasure's breath,
No circling arms to draw me near—
  'T was gloomy, and I wish'd for death.

But when I saw that gentle eye,
  Oh! something seem'd to tell me then,
That I was yet too young to die,
  And hope and bliss might bloom again.

With every gentle smile that crost
  Your kindling cheek, you lighted home
Some feeling, which my heart had lost,
  And peace, which far had learn'd to roam.

'T was then indeed so sweet to live,
  Hope look'd so new and Love so kind,
That, though I mourn, I yet forgive
  The ruin they have left behind.

I could have loved you—oh, so well!—
  The dream, that wishing boyhood knows,
Is but a bright beguiling spell,
  That only lives while passion glows:

But, when this early flush declines,
  When the heart's sunny morning fleets,
You know not then how close it twines
  Round the first kindred soul it meets.

Yes, yes, I could have loved, as one
  Who, while his youth's enchantments fall,
Finds something dear to rest upon,
  Which pays him for the loss of all.

———o♦♦o———

TO . . . .

NEVER mind how the pedagogue proses,
  You want not antiquity's stamp;
A lip, that such fragrance discloses,
  Oh! never should smell of the lamp.

Old Cloe, whose withering kiss
  Hath long set the Loves at defiance,
Now, done with the science of bliss,
  May take to the blisses of science. (1)

(1) On comparing this poem with a copy as originally
published, it will be found that the author has here made
an elision of the following lines:—

  Young Sappho, for want of employments,
    Alone o'er her Ovid may melt,
  Condemn'd but to read of enjoyments
    Which wiser Corinna had felt.— P. E.

But for *you* to be buried in books—
  Ah, Fanny, they 're pitiful sages,
Who could not in *one* of your looks
  Read more than in millions of pages.

Astronomy finds in those eyes
  Better light than she studies above ;
And Music would borrow your sighs
  As the melody fittest for Love. (1)

Your Arithmetic only can trip
  If to count your own charms you endeavour ;
And Eloquence glows on your lip
  When you swear, that you 'll love me for ever.

Thus you see, what a brilliant alliance
  Of arts is assembled in you ;—
A course of more exquisite science
  Man never need wish to pursue.

And, oh !—if a Fellow like me
  May confer a diploma of hearts,
With my lip thus I seal your degree,
  My divine little Mistress of Arts!

—o❦o—

ON THE DEATH OF A LADY.

SWEET spirit! if thy airy sleep
  Nor sees my tears nor hears my sighs,
Then will I weep, in anguish weep,
  Till the last heart's drop fills mine eyes.

But if thy sainted soul can feel,
  And mingles in our misery;
Then, then my breaking heart I 'll seal—
  Thou shalt not hear one sigh from me.

The beam of morn was on the stream,
  But sullen clouds the day deform :
Like thee was that young orient beam,
  Like death, alas, that sullen storm !

Thou wert not form'd for living here,
  So link'd thy soul was with the sky ;
Yet, ah, we held thee all so dear,
  We thought thou wert not form'd to die.

—o❦o—

INCONSTANCY.

AND do I then wonder that Julia deceives me,
  When surely there 's nothing in nature more
    common?

(1) Another elision occurs here :—

  In ethics—'t is you that can check,
    In a minute their doubts and their quarrels ;
  Oh! show but that mole on your neck,
    And 't will soon put an end to their morals.
                       P. E.

She vows to be true, and while vowing she leaves
  me—
  And could I expect any more from a woman?

Oh, woman ! your heart is a pitiful treasure ;
  And Mahomet's doctrine was not too severe,
When he held that you were but materials of
  pleasure,
  And reason and thinking were out of your sphere.

By your heart, when the fond sighing lover can win it,
  He thinks that an age of anxiety 's paid ;
But, oh, while he 's blest, let him die at the minute—
  If he live but a *day*, he 'll be surely betray'd.

—o❦o—

THE NATAL GENIUS.

A DREAM.

TO ....., THE MORNING OF HER BIRTHDAY.

IN witching slumbers of the night,
I dreamt I was the airy sprite
  That on thy natal moment smiled ;
And thought I wafted on my wing
Those flowers which in Elysium spring,
  To crown my lovely mortal child.

With olive-branch I bound thy head,
Heart's-ease along thy path I shed,
  Which was to bloom through all thy years ;
Nor yet did I forget to bind
Love's roses, with his myrtle twined,
  And dew'd by sympathetic tears.

Such was the wild but precious boon
Which Fancy, at her magic noon,
  Bade me to Nona's image pay ;
And were it thus my fate to be
Thy little guardian deity,
  How blest around thy steps I'd play!

Thy life should glide in peace along,
Calm as some lonely shepherd's song
  That 's heard at distance in the grove ;
No cloud should ever dim thy sky,
No thorns along thy pathway lie,
  But all be beauty, peace, and love.

Indulgent Time should never bring
To thee one blight upon his wing,
  So gently o'er thy brow he'd fly ;
And death itself should but be felt
Like that of daybeams, when they melt,
  Bright to the last, in evening's sky ! (2)

(2) This beautiful verse originally stood thus :—

    The wing of time should never brush
    Thy dewy lip's luxuriant flush,
      To bid its roses withering die ;
    Nor age itself, though dim and dark,
    Should ever quench a single spark
      That flashes from my Nona's eye.—P. E.

ELEGIAC STANZAS,

SUPPOSED TO BE WRITTEN BY JULIA,

ON THE DEATH OF HER BROTHER.

THOUGH sorrow long has worn my heart;
  Though every day I 've counted o'er
Hath brought a new and quickening smart
  To wounds that rankled fresh before;

Though in my earliest life bereft
  Of tender links by nature tied ;
Though hope deceived, and pleasure left;
  Though friends betray'd and foes belied ;

I still had hopes—for hope will stay
  After the sunset of delight ;
So like the star which ushers day,
  We scarce can think it heralds night !—

I hoped that, after all its strife,
  My weary heart at length should rest,
And, fainting from the waves of life,
  Find harbour in a brother's breast.

That brother's breast was warm with truth,
  Was bright with honour's purest ray;
He was the dearest, gentlest youth—
  Ah, why then was he torn away?

He should have stay'd, have linger'd here
  To soothe his Julia's every woe ;
He should have chased each bitter tear,
  And not have caused those tears to flow.

We saw within his soul expand
  The fruits of genius, nursed by taste ;
While Science, with a fostering hand,
  Upon his brow her chaplet placed.

We saw, by bright degrees, his mind
  Grow rich in all that makes men dear;—
Enlighten'd, social, and refined,
  In friendship firm, in love sincere.

Such was the youth we loved so well,
  And such the hopes that fate denied ;—
We loved, but ah ! could scarcely tell
  How deep, how dearly, till he died !

Close as the fondest links could strain,
  Twined with my very heart he grew,

(1) This little poem has been curtailed, the author having
suppressed the following stanzas :—

> Our hearts have suffer'd little harm
>   In this short fever of desire;
> You have not lost a single charm,
>   Nor I one spark of feeling fire.
>
> My kisses have not stain'd the rose
>   Which Nature hung upon your lip ;

And by that fate which breaks the chain,
  The heart is almost broken too.

———o&&o———

TO THE LARGE AND BEAUTIFUL MISS......,

IN ALLUSION TO SOME PARTNERSHIP IN A LOTTERY SHARE.

IMPROMPTU.

—Ego pars——*Virgil.*

IN wedlock a species of lottery lies,
  Where in blanks and in prizes we deal;
But how comes it that you, such a capital prize,
  Should so long have remain'd in the wheel?

If ever, by Fortune's indulgent decree,
  To me such a ticket should roll,
A sixteenth, Heaven knows ! were sufficient for me ;
  For what could *I* do with the whole ?

———o&&o———

A DREAM.

I THOUGHT this heart enkindled lay
  On Cupid's burning shrine :
I thought he stole thy heart away,
  And placed it near to mine.

I saw thy heart begin to melt,
  Like ice before the sun ;
Till both a glow congenial felt,
  And mingled into one !

———o&&o———

TO . . . . . .

WITH all my soul, then, let us part,
  Since both are anxious to be free ;
And I will send you home your heart,
  If you will send back mine to me.

We 've had some happy hours together,
  But joy must often change its wing ;
And spring would be but gloomy weather,
  If we had nothing else but spring.

'T is not that I expect to find
  A more devoted, fond, and true one,
With rosier cheek or sweeter mind—
  Enough for me that she 's a new one.

Thus let us leave the bower of love,
  Where we have loiter'd long in bliss ;
And you may down *that* pathway rove,
  While I shall take my way through *this.* (1)

> And still your sigh with nectar flows
>   For many a raptured soul to sip.
>
> Farewell ! and when some other fair
>   Shall call your wanderer to her arms,
> 'T will be my luxury to compare
>   Her spells with your remember'd charms.
>
> " This cheek," I 'll say, " is not so bright
>   As one that used to meet my kiss ;

ANACREONTIC.

"SHE never look'd so kind before—
Yet why the wanton's smile recall?
I 've seen this witchery o'er and o'er,
'T is hollow, vain, and heartless all!"

Thus I said, and sighing, drain'd
The cup which she so late had tasted;
Upon whose rim still fresh remain'd
The breath, so oft in falsehood wasted.

I took the harp, and would have sung
As if 't were not of her I sang;
But still the notes on Lamia hung—
On whom but Lamia *could* they hang?

Those eyes of hers, that floating shine,
Like diamonds in some Eastern river;
That kiss, for which, if worlds were mine,
A world for every kiss I' d give her.

That frame so delicate, yet warm'd
With flushes of love's genial hue;—
A mould transparent, as if form'd
To let the spirit's light shine through. (1)

Of these I sung, and notes and words
Were sweet, as if the very air
From Lamia's lip hung o'er the chords,
And Lamia's voice still warbled there!

But when, alas, I turn'd the theme,
And when of vows and oaths I spoke,
Of truth and hope's seducing dream—
The chord beneath my finger broke.

False harp! false woman!—such, oh, such
Are lutes too frail and hearts too willing;
Any hand, whate'er its touch,
Can set their chords or pulses thrilling. (2)

And when that thrill is most awake,
And when you think Heaven's joys awalt you,
The nymph will change, the chord will break—
Oh Love, oh Music, how I hate you!

> This eye has not such liquid light
> As one that used to talk of bliss!"
> Farewell! and when some future lover
> Shall claim the heart which I resign,
> And in exulting joys discover
> All the charms that once were mine;
> I think I should be sweetly blest,
> If, in a soft imperfect sigh,
> You 'd say, while to his bosom prest,
> He loves not half so well as I!—P. E.

(1) This verse in preceding editions stood thus:—

> That mould so fine, so pearly bright,
> Of which luxurious heaven hath cast her,
> Through which her soul doth beam as white
> As flame through lamps of alabaster!—P. E.

TO JULIA.

I SAW the peasant's hand unkind
From yonder oak the ivy sever;
They seem'd in very being twined;
Yet now the oak is fresh as ever!

Not so the widow'd ivy shines:
Torn from its dear and only stay,
In drooping widowhood it pines,
And scatters all its bloom away.

Thus, Julia, did our hearts entwine,
Till Fate disturb'd their tender ties:
Thus gay indifference blooms in thine,
While mine, deserted, droops and dies!

HYMN OF A VIRGIN OF DELPHI,

AT THE TOMB OF HER MOTHER.

OH, lost, for ever lost—no more
Shall Vesper light our dewy way
Along the rocks of Crissa's shore,
To hymn the fading fires of day;
No more to Tempé's distant vale
In holy musings shall we roam,
Through summer's glow and winter's gale,
To bear the mystic chaplets home.(3)
'T was then my soul's expanding zeal,
By nature warm'd and led by thee,
In every breeze was taught to feel
The breathings of a Deity.
Guide of my heart! still hovering round,
Thy looks, thy words are still my own—
I see thee raising from the ground
Some laurel, by the winds o'erthrown,
And hear thee say, "This humble bough
Was planted for a doom divine;
And, though it droop in languor now,
Shall flourish on the Delphic shrine!
Thus, in the vale of earthly sense,
Though sunk awhile the spirit lies,
A viewless hand shall cull it thence,
To bloom immortal in the skies!"

(2) These four lines have undergone some verbal changes; they were originally—

> False harp! false woman!—such, oh, such
> Are lutes too frail and maids too willing;
> Every hand's licentious touch
> Can learn to wake their wildest thrilling!—P. E.

(3) The laurel, for the common uses of the temple, for adorning the altars and sweeping the pavement, was supplied by a tree near the fountain of Castalia; but upon all important occasions they sent to Tempé for their laurel. We find, in Pausanias, that this valley supplied the branches of which the temple was originally constructed; and Plutarch says, in his Dialogue on Music, "The youth who brings the Tempic laurel to Delphi is always attended

All that the young should feel and know,
  By thee was taught so sweetly well,
Thy words fell soft as vernal snow,
  And all was brightness where they fell!
Fond soother of my infant tear,
  Fond sharer of my infant joy,
Is not thy shade still lingering here?
  Am I not still thy soul's employ?
Oh yes—and, as in former days,
  When, meeting on the sacred mount,
Our nymphs awaked their choral lays,
  And danced around Cassotis' fount;
As then, 't was all thy wish and care,
  That mine should be the simplest mien,
My lyre and voice the sweetest there,
  My foot the lightest o'er the green :
So still, each look and step to mould,
  Thy guardian care is round me spread,
Arranging every snowy fold,
  And guiding every mazy tread.
And, when I lead the hymning choir,
  Thy spirit still, unseen and free,
Hovers between my lip and lyre,
  And weds them into harmony.
Flow, Plistus, flow, thy murmuring wave
Shall never drop its silvery tear
Upon so pure, so blest a grave,
  To memory so entirely dear !

——◦◦◦——

SYMPATHY.

TO JULIA.

—— sine me sit nulla Venus.—*Sulpicia.*

Our hearts, my love, were form'd to be
  The genuine twins of Sympathy,
  They live with one sensation :
In joy or grief, but most in love,
Like chords in unison they move,
  And thrill with like vibration.

How oft I've heard thee fondly say,
Thy vital pulse shall cease to play
  When mine no more is moving ;
Since, now, to feel a joy *alone*
Were worse to thee than feeling none
  So twinn'd are we in loving !(1)

by a player on the flute." Ἀλλα μην και τῳ κατακο-
μιϛουτι παιδι την Τεμπικην δαϕνην εις Δελϕους παρο-
μαρτει αυλητης.

(1) This poem originally consisted of three six-line
verses ; the third, which has been suppressed, was :—

    And, oh ! how often in those eyes,
    Which melting beam'd like azure skies
      In dewy vernal weather—
    How often have I raptured read
    The burning glance, that silent said,
      " Now, love, *we feel together* ?"—P. E.

(2) The preceding eight lines, it will be perceived, are

THE TEAR.

On beds of snow the moonbeam slept,
  And chilly was the midnight gloom,
When by the damp grave Ellen wept—
  Fond maid! it was her Lindor's tomb !

A warm tear gush'd, the wintry air
  Congeal'd it as it flow'd away :
All night it lay an ice-drop there,
  At morn it glitter'd in the ray.

An angel, wandering from her sphere,
  Who saw this bright, this frozen gem,
To dew-eyed Pity brought the tear,
  And hung it on her diadem !

——◦◦◦——

THE SNAKE.

My love and I, the other day,
Within a myrtle arbour lay,
When near us, from a rosy bed,
A little Snake put forth its head.

" See," said the maid with thoughtful eyes—
" Yonder the fatal emblem lies !
Who could expect such hidden harm
Beneath the rose's smiling charm ?"

Never did grave remark occur
Less *à-propos* than this from her.

I rose to kill the snake, but she,
Half-smiling, pray'd it might not be.
" No," said the maiden—and, alas,
  Her eyes spoke volumes, while she said it—
" Long as the snake is in the grass,
  One *may*, perhaps, have cause to dread it : (2)

But, when its wicked eyes appear,
  And when we know for what they wink so,
One must be *very* simple, dear,
  To let it wound one—don't you think so?"

——◦◦◦——

TO ROSA.

Is the song of Rosa mute ?
Once such lays inspired her lute !

not quite the same as those which occupied their place
when this little poem was first given to the public :—

    Never did moral thought occur
      In more unlucky hour than this ;
    For oh ! I just was leading her
      To talk of love and think of bliss.

    I rose to kill the snake, but she
      In pity pray'd, it might not be.

    " No," said the girl,—and many a spark
      Flash'd from her eyelid, as she said it,
    " Under the rose, or in the dark,
      One might, perhaps, have cause to dread it."—P. E.

Never doth a sweeter song
Steal the breezy lyre along,
When the wind, in odours dying,
Woos it with enamour'd sighing.

Is my Rosa's lute unstrung?
Once a tale of peace it sung
To her lover's throbbing breast—
Then was he divinely blest!
Ah! but Rosa loves no more,
Therefore Rosa's song is o'er;
And her lute neglected lies;
And her boy forgotten sighs.
Silent lute—forgotten lover—
Rosa's love and song are over!

ELEGIAC STANZAS.

Sic juvat perire.

WHEN wearied wretches sink to sleep,
How heavenly soft their slumbers lie!
How sweet is death to those who weep,
To those who weep and long to die!

Saw you the soft and grassy bed,
Where flowerets deck the green earth's breast?
'T is there I wish to lay my head,
'T is there I wish to sleep at rest.

Oh, let not tears embalm my tomb,—
None but the dews at twilight given!
Oh, let not sighs disturb the gloom,—
None but the whispering winds of heaven!

LOVE AND MARRIAGE.

Eque brevi verbo ferre perenne malum.
Secundus, eleg. vii.

STILL the question I must parry,
Still a wayward truant prove:
Where I love, I must not marry;
Where I marry, cannot love.

Were she fairest of creation,
With the least presuming mind;
Learned without affectation;
Not deceitful, yet refined;

Wise enough, but never rigid;
Gay, but not too lightly free;
Chaste as snow, and yet not frigid;
Fond, yet satisfied with me;

Were she all this ten times over,
All that heaven to earth allows,
I should be too much her lover
Ever to become her spouse.

Love will never bear enslaving;
Summer garments suit him best;

Bliss itself is not worth having,
If we 're by compulsion blest.

ANACREONTIC.

I FILL'D to thee, to thee I drank,
I nothing did but drink and fill;
The bowl by turns was bright and blank,
'T was drinking, filling, drinking still.

At length I bid an artist paint
Thy image in this ample cup,
That I might see the dimpled saint,
To whom I quaff'd my nectar up.

Behold, how bright that purple lip
Now blushes through the wave at me;
Every roseate drop I sip
Is just like kissing wine from thee.

And still I drink the more for this;
For, ever when the draught I drain,
Thy lip invites another kiss,
And—in the nectar flows again.

So, here 's to thee, my gentle dear,
And may that eyelid never shine
Beneath a darker, bitterer tear
Than bathes it in this bowl of mine!

THE SURPRISE.

CHLORIS, I swear, by all I ever swore,
That from this hour I shall not love thee more.—
" What! love no more? Oh! why this alter'd vow?"
Because I *cannot* love thee *more*—than *now!*

TO MISS . . . . . .,

ON HER ASKING THE AUTHOR WHY SHE HAD SLEEPLESS NIGHTS.

I 'LL ask the sylph who round thee flies,
And in thy breath his pinion dips,
Who suns him in thy radiant eyes,
And faints upon thy sighing lips;

I 'll ask him where 's the veil of sleep
That used to shade thy looks of light;
And why those eyes their vigil keep,
When other suns are sunk in night?

And I will say—her angel breast
Has never throbb'd with guilty sting;
Her bosom is the sweetest nest
Where Slumber could repose his wing!

And I will say—her cheeks that flush,
Like vernal roses in the sun,
Have ne'er by shame been taught to blush,
Except for what her eyes have done!

Then tell me, why, thou child of air!
Does slumber from her eyelids rove?
What is her heart's impassion'd care?—
Perhaps, oh sylph! perhaps, 't is love.

————ο⁕ο————

THE WONDER.

Come, tell me where the maid is found,
  Whose heart can love without deceit,
And I will range the world around,
  To sigh one moment at her feet.

Oh! tell me where 's her sainted home,
  What air receives her blessed sigh;
A pilgrimage of years I 'll roam
  To catch one sparkle of her eye!

And if her cheek be smooth and bright,
  While truth within her bosom lies,
I 'll gaze upon her morn and night,
  Till my heart leave me through my eyes.

Show me on earth a thing so rare,
  I 'll own all miracles are true;
To make one maid sincere and fair,
  Oh, 't is the utmost Heaven can do!

————ο⁕ο————

LYING.

Che con le lor bugie pajon divini.—*Mauro d'Arcano.*

I do confess, in many a sigh,
  My lips have breathed you many a lie;
And who, with such delights in view,
  Would lose them, for a lie or two?

Nay,—look not thus, with brow reproving;
Lies are, my dear, the soul of loving.
If half we tell the girls were true,
If half we swear to think and do,
Were aught but lying's blissful illusion,
This world would be in strange confusion.
If ladies' eyes were, every one,
As lovers swear, a radiant sun,
Astronomy must leave the skies,
To learn her lore in ladies' eyes.
Oh, no—believe me, lovely girl,
When nature turns your teeth to pearl,

Your neck to snow, your eyes to fire,
Your amber locks to golden wire,
Then, only then, can Heaven decree,
That you should live for only me,
Or I for you, as night and morn,
We 've swearing kiss'd, and kissing sworn.

And now, my gentle hints to clear,
For once I 'll tell you truth, my dear.
Whenever you may chance to meet
Some loving youth, whose love is sweet,
Long as you 're false and he believes you,
Long as you trust and he deceives you, ,
So long the blissful bond endures,
And while he lies, his heart is yours:
But, oh! you 've wholly lost the youth
The instant that he tells you truth.

————ο⁕ο————

ANACREONTIC.

Friend of my soul, this goblet sip,
  'T will chase that pensive tear;
'T is not so sweet as woman's lip,
  But, oh! 't is more sincere.
    Like her delusive beam,
    'T will steal away thy mind;
    But, truer than love's dream,
    It leaves no sting behind.

Come, twine the wreath, thy brows to shade;
  These flowers were cull'd at noon;—
Like woman's love the rose will fade,
  But, ah! not half so soon.
    For though the flower 's decay'd,
    Its fragrance is not o'er;
    But once when love 's betray'd,
    Its sweet life blooms no more.

————ο⁕ο————

THE PHILOSOPHER ARISTIPPUS. (1)

TO A LAMP WHICH HAD BEEN GIVEN HIM BY LAIS.

Dulcis conscia lectuli lucerna.
                     Martial., lib. xiv., epig. 39.

" Oh! love the Lamp" (my mistress said),
  " The faithful Lamp that, many a night,
Besides thy Lais' lonely bed
  Has kept its little watch of light.

(1) It does not appear to have been very difficult to become a philosopher amongst the ancients. A moderate store of learning, with a considerable portion of confidence, and just wit enough to produce an occasional apophthegm, seem to have been all the qualifications necessary for the purpose. The principles of moral science were so very imperfectly understood that the founder of a new sect, in forming his ethical code, might consult either fancy or temperament, and adapt it to his own passions and propensities; so that Mahomet, with a little more learning, would have flourished as a philosopher in those days, and would have required but the polish of the schools to become the rival of Aristippus in morality. In

the science of nature, too, though some valuable truths were discovered by them, they seemed hardly to know they were truths, or at least were as well satisfied with errors; and Xenophanes, who asserted that the stars were igneous clouds, lighted up every night and extinguished again in the morning, was thought and styled a philosopher, as generally as he who anticipated Newton in developing the arrangement of the universe.

For this opinion of Xenophanes, see Plutarch. de Placit. Philosoph., lib. ii., cap. 13. It is impossible to read this treatise of Plutarch, without alternately admiring the genius, and smiling at the absurdities of the philosophers.

" Full often has it seen her weep,
And fix her eye upon its flame,
Till, weary, she has sunk to sleep,
Repeating her beloved's name.(1)

" Then love the Lamp—'t will often lead
Thy step through learning's sacred way;
And when those studious eyes shall read,
At midnight, by its lonely ray,
Of things sublime, of nature's birth,
Of all that's bright in heaven or earth,
Oh, think that she by whom 't was given,
Adores thee more than earth or heaven ! "

Yes—dearest Lamp, by every charm
On which thy midnight beam has hung; (2)
The head reclined, the graceful arm
Across the brow of ivory flung ;

The heaving bosom, partly hid,
The sever'd lips' unconscious sighs,
The fringe that from the half-shut lid
Adown the cheek of roses lies :

By these, by all that bloom untold,
And long as all shall charm my heart,
I 'll love my little Lamp of gold—
My Lamp and I shall never part.

And often, as she smiling said,
In fancy's hour, thy gentle rays
Shall guide my visionary tread
Through poesy's enchanting maze.
Thy flame shall light the page refined,
Where still we catch the Chian's breath,
Where still the bard, though cold in death,
Has left his soul unquench'd behind.
Or, o'er thy humbler legend shine,
Oh man of Ascra's dreary glades,(3)
To whom the nightly warbling Nine (4)
A wand of inspiration gave, (5)
Pluck'd from the greenest tree that shades
The crystal of Castalia's wave.

Then, turning to a purer lore,
We 'll cull the sages' deep-hid store,
From Science steal her golden clue,
And every mystic path pursue,
Where Nature, far from vulgar eyes,
Through labyrinths of wonder flies.
'T is thus my heart shall learn to know
How fleeting is this world below,
Where all that meets the morning light,
Is changed before the fall of night !(6)

I 'll tell thee, as I trim thy fire,
" Swift, swift the tide of being runs,
And Time, who bids thy flame expire,
Will also quench yon heaven of suns."

Oh, then, if earth's united power
Can never chain one feathery hour;
If every print we leave to-day
To-morrow's wave will sweep away ;
Who pauses to inquire of heaven
Why were the fleeting treasures given,
The sunny days, the shady nights,
And all their brief but dear delights,
Which heaven has made for man to use,
And man should think it crime to lose ?
Who that has cull'd a fresh-blown rose
Will ask it why it breathes and glows,
Unmindful of the blushing ray,
In which it shines its soul away ;
Unmindful of the scented sigh,
With which it dies, and loves to die ?

Pleasure, thou only good on earth ! (7)
One precious moment given to thee—
Oh ! by my Laïs' lip, 't is worth
The sage's immortality.

Then far be all the wisdom hence,
That would our joys one hour delay !
Alas, the feast of soul and sense
Love calls us to in youth's bright day,
If not soon tasted, fleets away. (8)

---

(1) Mr. Moore has here omitted the following lines,
which found a place in previous editions of this poem :—

"Oft has it known her cheek to burn
With recollections, fondly free,
And seen her turn, impassion'd turn,
To kiss the pillow, love! for thee,
And, in a murmur, wish thee there,
That kiss to feel, that thought to share !—P. E.

(2) The ancients had their lucernæ cubiculariæ, or bed-
chamber lamps, which, as the Emperor Galienus said,
"nil cras meminere ;" and, with the same commendation
of secrecy, Praxagora addresses her lamp in Aristophanes,
Εκκλης. We may judge how fanciful they were, in the
use and embellishment of their lamps, from the famous
symbolic Lucerna, which we find in the Romanum Museum
Mich. Ang. Causei, p.127.

(3) Hesiod, who tells us in melancholy terms of his
father's flight to the wretched village of Ascra. Εργ. και
Ημερ. v. 251.

(4) Εννυχιαι στειχον, περικαλλεα οσσαν ιεισαι. Theog.,
v. 10.

(5) Και μοι σκηπτρον εδον, δαφνης αριθηλεα οδον.
id., v.30.

(6) 'Ρειν τα δια ποταμου δικην, as expressed among
the dogmas of Heraclitus the Ephesian, and with the same
image by Seneca, in whom we find a beautiful diffusion
of the thought. "Nemo est mane, qui fuit pridie. Cor-
pora nostra rapiuntur fluminem more ; quidquid vides
currit cum tempore. Nihil ex his quæ videmus manet.
Ego ipse, dum loquor mutari ipsa, mutatus sum," etc.

(7) Aristippus considered motion as the principle of
happiness, in which idea he differed from the Epicureans,
who looked to a state of repose as the only true volup-
tuousness, and avoided even the too lively agitations of
pleasure, as a violent and ungraceful derangement of the
senses.

(8) The preceding five lines have undergone consider-

Ne'er wert thou form'd, my Lamp, to shed
　Thy splendour on a lifeless page ;—
Whate'er my blushing Lais said
　Of thoughtful lore and studies sage,
'T was mockery all—her glance of joy
　Told me thy dearest, best employ. (1)
And, soon as night shall close the eye
　Of heaven's young wanderer in the west;
When seers are gazing on the sky,
　To find their future orbs of rest ;
Then shall I take my trembling way,
　Unseen but to those worlds above,
And, led by thy mysterious ray,
　Steal to the night-bower of my love. (2)

TO MRS. ———.

ON HER BEAUTIFUL TRANSLATION OF VOITURE'S KISS.

Mon âme sur ma lèvre étoit lors toute entière,
Pour savourer le miel qui sur la vôtre étoit;
Mais, en me retirant, elle resta derrière,
Tant de ce doux plaisir l'amorce l'arrestoit.—*Voiture.*

How heavenly was the poet's doom,
　To breathe his spirit through a kiss;
And lose within so sweet a tomb
　The trembling messenger of bliss!

And sure his soul return'd to feel
　That it *again* could ravish'd be ;
For in the kiss that thou didst steal,
　His life and soul have fled to thee.

RONDEAU.

" GOOD night ! good night !"—And is it so?
　And must I from my Rosa go ?

---

able change since their first publication ; they originally
stood thus :—

> Then far be all the wisdom hence,
> And all the lore, whose tame control
> Would wither joy with chill delays !
> Alas! the fertile fount of sense,
> At which the young, the panting soul
> Drinks life and love, too soon decays !—P. E.

(1) Maupertuis has been still more explicit than this
philosopher, in ranking the pleasures of sense above the
sublimest pursuits of wisdom. Speaking of the infant
man, in his production, he calls him, " une nouvelle
créature, qui pourra comprendre les choses les plus su-
blimes, et, ce qui est bien au-dessus, qui pourra goûter
lès mêmes plaisirs." See his *Vénus physique.* This ap-
pears to be one of the efforts at Fontenelle's gallantry of
manner, for which the learned President is so well and
justly ridiculed in the *Akakia* of Voltaire.

Maupertuis may be thought to have borrowed from the
ancient Aristippus that indiscriminate theory of pleasures
which he has set forth in his *Essai de Philosophie morale,*
and for which he was so very justly condemned. Aristip-
pus, according to Laertius, held μη διαφερειν τε ηδονην
ηδονης, which irrational sentiment has been adopted by
Maupertuis : "Tant qu'on ne considère que l'état présent,
tous les plaisirs sont du même genre," etc., etc.

Oh Rosa, say " Good night!" once more,
And I 'll repeat it o'er and o'er,
Till the first glance of dawning light
Shall find us saying, still, " Good night."

And still " Good night," my Rosa, say—
But whisper still, " a minute stay ; "
And I will stay, and every minute
Shall have an age of transport in it ;
Till Time himself shall stay his flight,
To listen to our sweet "Good night."

" Good night !" you 'll murmur with a sigh,
And tell me it is time to fly :
And I will vow, will swear to go,
While still that sweet voice murmurs " No ! "(3)
Till slumber seal our weary sight—
And then, my love, my soul, "Good night!"

SONG.

WHY does azure deck the sky?
　'T is to be like thy looks of blue;
Why is red the rose's dye ?
　Because it is thy blushes' hue.
All that 's fair, by Love's decree,
Has been made resembling thee !

Why is falling snow so white,
　But to be like thy bosom fair?
Why are solar beams so bright?
　That they may seem thy golden hair!
All that 's bright, by Love's decree,
Has been made resembling thee!

(2) The previous editions of this poem concluded with
the following lines :—

> Calm be her sleep, the gentle dear!
> Nor let her dream of bliss so near,
> Till o'er her cheek she thrilling feel
> My sighs of fire in murmurs steal,
> And I shall lift the locks that flow
> Unbraided o'er her lids of snow,
> And softly kiss those sealed eyes,
> And wake her into sweet surprise !
> Or if she dream, oh ! let her dream
> Of those delights we both have known,
> And felt so truly, that they seem
> Form'd to be felt by us alone!
> And I shall mark her kindling cheek,
> Shall see her bosom warmly move,
> And bear her faintly, lowly speak
> The murmur'd sounds so dear to love!
> Oh ! I shall gaze till even the sigh
> That wafts her very soul be nigh,
> And, when the nymph is all but blest,
> Sink in her arms and share the rest !
> Sweet Laïs ! what an age of bliss
> In that one moment waits for me !
> Oh sages !—think on joy like this,
> And where's your boast of apathy?—P. E.

(3) This and the preceding line were originally given—

> And I will vow to kiss no more,
> Yet kiss you closer than before.—P. E.

Why are nature's beauties felt?
Oh! 't is thine in her we see!
Why has music power to melt?
Oh! because it speaks like thee.
All that 's sweet, by Love's decree,
Has been made resembling thee!

TO ROSA.

Like one who trusts to summer skies,
And puts his little bark to sea,
Is he who, lured by smiling eyes,
Consigns his simple heart to thee.

For fickle is the summer wind,
And sadly may the bark be tost;
For thou art sure to change thy mind,
And then the wretched heart is lost!

WRITTEN IN A COMMONPLACE BOOK,

CALLED "THE BOOK OF FOLLIES;" IN WHICH EVERY ONE
THAT OPENED IT WAS TO CONTRIBUTE SOMETHING.

TO THE BOOK OF FOLLIES.

This tribute 's from a wretched elf,
Who hails thee, emblem of himself.
The book of life, which I have traced,
Has been, like thee, a motley waste
Of follies scribbled o'er and o'er,
One folly bringing hundreds more.
Some have indeed been writ so neat,
In characters so fair, so sweet,
That those who judge not too severely
Have said they loved such follies dearly.
Yet still, O book! the illusion stands,
For these were penn'd by *female* hands,
The rest—alas! I own the truth—
Have all been scribbled so uncouth
That Prudence, with a withering look,
Disdainful flings away the book.
Like thine, its pages here and there
Have oft been stain'd with blots of care;
And sometimes hours of peace, I own,
Upon some fairer leaves have shown,
White as the snowings of that heaven
By which those hours of peace were given.
But now no longer—such, oh, such
The blast of Disappointment's touch!—
No longer now those hours appear;
Each leaf is sullied by a tear;
Blank, blank is every page with care,
Not even a folly brightens there.
Will they yet brighten?—never, never!
Then *shut the book*, O God, for ever!

TO ROSA.

Say, why should the girl of my soul be in tears
At a meeting of rapture like this,

When the glooms of the past and the sorrow of years
Have been paid by one moment of bliss?

Are they shed for that moment of blissful delight,
Which dwells on her memory yet?
Do they flow, like the dews of the love-breathing night,
From the warmth of the sun that has set?

Oh! sweet is the tear on that languishing smile,
That smile, which is loveliest then;
And if such are the drops that delight can beguile,
Thou shalt weep them again and again.

LIGHT SOUNDS THE HARP.

Light sounds the harp when the combat is over,
When heroes are resting, and joy is in bloom;
When laurels hang loose from the brow of the lover,
And Cupid makes wings of the warrior's plume.
But, when the foe returns,
Again the hero burns;
High flames the sword in his hand once more:
The clang of mingling arms
Is then the sound that charms,
And brazen notes of war, that stirring trumpets pour!
Then again comes the harp, when the combat is over—
When heroes are resting, and Joy is in bloom—
When laurels hang loose from the brow of the lover,
And Cupid makes wings of the warrior's plume.

Light went the harp when the War-God, reclining,
Lay lull'd on the white arm of Beauty to rest,
When round his rich armour the myrtle hung
    twining,
And flights of young doves made his helmet their
    But, when the battle came,   [nest.
    The hero's eye breathed flame:
Soon from his neck the white arm was flung;
    While, to his wakening ear,
    No other sounds were dear
But brazen notes of war, by thousand trumpets sung!
But then came the light harp, when danger was ended,
And Beauty once more lull'd the War-God to rest;
When tresses of gold with his laurels lay blended,
And flights of young doves made his helmet their
    nest.

FROM THE GREEK OF MELEAGER.(1)

Fill high the cup with liquid flame,
And speak my Heliodora's name.

(1) Εγχει, και παλιν ειπε, παλιν, παλιν, Ἡλιοδωρας
      Ειπε, συν ακρητω το γλυκυ μισγ' ονομα.
    Και μοι τον βρεχθεντα μυροις και χθιζον εοντα,
      Μναμοσυνον κεινας, αμφιτιθει ςεφανον·
    Δακρυει φιλεραςον ιδου ροδον, ουνεκα κειναν
    Αλλοθι κ' ου κολποις ημετεροις εσορα.
                    Brunck. Analect., tom. i., p. 28.

Repeat its magic o'er and o'er,
And let the sound my lips adore,
Live in the breeze, till every tone,
And word, and breath, speaks her alone.

Give me the wreath that withers there,
    It was but last delicious night
It circled her luxuriant hair,
    And caught her eyes' reflected light.
Oh! haste and twine it round my brow,
'T is all of her that's left me now.
And see—each rosebud drops a tear,
To find the nymph no longer here—
No longer where such heavenly charms
As hers *should* be—within these arms.

——o♦♦o——

SONG.

Fly from the world, O Bessy! to me,
    Thou wilt never find any sincerer;
I 'll give up the world, O Bessy! for thee,
    I can never meet any that's dearer.
Then tell me no more, with a tear and a sigh,
    That our loves will be censured by many;
All, all have their follies, and who will deny
    That ours is the sweetest of any?

When your lip has met mine, in communion so sweet,
    Have we felt as if virtue forbid it?—
Have we felt as if heaven denied them to meet?—
    No, rather 't was heaven that did it.
So innocent, love, is the joy we then sip,
    So little of wrong is there in it,
That I wish all my errors were lodged on your lip,
    And I 'd kiss them away in a minute.

Then come to your lover, oh! fly to his shed,
    From a world which I know thou despisest;
And slumber will hover as light o'er our bed
    As e'er on the couch of the wisest.
And when o'er our pillow the tempest is driven,
    And thou, pretty innocent, fearest,
I 'll tell thee, it is not the chiding of heaven,—
    'T is only our lullaby, dearest.

And, oh! while we lie on our deathbed, my love,
    Looking back on the scene of our errors,
A sigh from my Bessy shall plead then above
    And Death be disarm'd of his terrors.
And each to the other embracing will say,
    " Farewell! let us hope we 're forgiven."
Thy last fading glance will illumine the way,
    And a kiss be our passport to heaven!

(1) In the present edition, the three following verses
have been suppressed :—

> Your eyes!—the eyes of languid doves
>   Were never half so like each other!
> The glances of the baby loves
>   Resemble less their warm-eyed mother!

THE RESEMBLANCE.

—— vo cercand' io,
Donna, quant' è possibile, in altrui
La desiata vostra forma vera.
        Petrarch., Sonett. 14.

Yes, if 't were any common love,
    That led my pliant heart astray,
I grant, there 's not a power above
    Could wipe the faithless crime away.

But, 't was my doom to err with one
    In every look so like to thee,
That, underneath yon blessed sun,
    So fair there are but thou and she.

Both born of beauty, at a birth,
    She held with thine a kindred sway,
And wore the only shape on earth
    That could have lured my soul to stray.(1)

Then blame me not, if false I be,
    'T was love that waked the fond excess;
My heart had been more true to thee,
    Had mine eye prized thy beauty less.

——o♦♦o——

FANNY, DEAREST.

Yes! had I leisure to sigh and mourn,
    Fanny, dearest, for thee I 'd sigh;
And every smile on my cheek should turn
    To tears when thou art nigh.
But, between love, and wine, and sleep,
    So busy a life I live,
That even the time it would take to weep
    Is more than my heart can give.
Then bid me not to despair and pine,
    Fanny, dearest of all the dears!
The Love that 's order'd to bathe in wine
    Would be sure to take cold in tears.

Reflected bright in this heart of mine,
    Fanny, dearest, thy image lies;
But, ah, the mirror would cease to shine,
    If dimm'd too often with sighs.
They lose the half of beauty's light,
    Who view it through sorrow's tear;
And 't is but to see thee truly bright
    That I keep my eye-beam clear.
Then wait no longer till tears shall flow,
    Fanny, dearest—the hope is vain;
If sunshine cannot dissolve thy snow,
    I shall never attempt it with rain.

> Her lip!—oh, call me not false-hearted,
>   When such a lip I fondly press'd;
> 'T was Love some melting cherry parted,
>   Gave thee one half and her the rest!
> And when, with all thy murmuring tone,
>   They sued, half open, to be kiss'd,
> I could as soon resist thine own—
>   And them, Heaven knows! I ne'er resist.—P. E

THE RING.

TO . . . .

No—Lady! Lady! keep the ring:
  Oh! think, how many a future year,
Of placid smile and downy wing,
  May sleep within its holy sphere.

Do not disturb their tranquil dream,
  Though love hath ne'er the mystery warm'd;
Yet heaven will shed a soothing beam,
  To bless the bond itself hath form'd.

But then, that eye, that burning eye,—
  Oh! it doth ask, with witching power,
If heaven can ever bless the tie
  Where love inwreathes no genial flower?

Away, away, bewildering look,
  Or all the boast of virtue's o'er;
Go—hie thee to the sage's book,
  And learn from him to feel no more.

I cannot warn thee: every touch,
  That brings my pulses close to thine,
Tells me I want thy aid as much—
  Even more, alas, than thou dost mine.

Yet, stay,—one hope, one effort yet—
  A moment turn those eyes away,
And let me, if I can, forget
  The light that leads my soul astray.

Thou say'st, that we were born to meet,
  That our hearts bear one common seal;—
Think, Lady, think, how man's deceit
  Can seem to sigh and feign to feel.

When, o'er thy face some gleam of thought,
  Like daybeams through the morning air,
Hath gradual stole, and I have caught
  The feeling ere it kindled there;

The sympathy I then betray'd
  Perhaps was but the child of art,
The guile of one, who long hath play'd
  With all these wily nets of heart.

Oh! thine is not my earliest vow;
  Though few the years I yet have told,
Canst thou believe I've lived till now,
  With loveless heart or senses cold?

(1) The two following verses, which terminated the
poem, have been struck out of the present edition :—

    While thus to mine thy bosom lies,
      While thus our breaths commingling glow,
    'T were more than woman to be wise,
      'T were more than man to wish thee so!

No—other nymphs to joy and pain
  This wild and wandering heart hath moved:
With some it sported, wild and vain,
  While some it dearly, truly, loved.

The cheek to thine I fondly lay,
  To theirs hath been as fondly laid;
The words to thee I warmly say,
  To them have been as warmly said.

Then, scorn at once a worthless heart,
  Worthless alike, or fix'd or free;
Think of the pure bright soul thou art,
  And—love not me, oh love not me.

Enough—now, turn thine eyes again;
  What, still that look and still that sigh!
Dost thou not feel my counsel then?
  Oh! no, beloved,—nor do I.(1)

——◦◦◦——

TO THE INVISIBLE GIRL.

They try to persuade me, my dear little sprite,
That you're *not* a true daughter of ether and light,
Nor have any concern with those fanciful forms
That dance upon rainbows and ride upon storms;
That, in short, you're a woman; your lip and your eye
As mortal as ever drew gods from the sky.(2)
But I *will* not believe them—no, Science, to you
I have long bid a last and a careless adieu:
Still flying from Nature to study her laws,
And dulling delight by exploring its cause,
You forget how superior, for mortals below,
Is the fiction they dream to the truth that they know.
Oh! who, that has e'er enjoy'd rapture complete,
Would ask *how* we feel it, or *why* it is sweet;
How rays are confused, or how particles fly
Through the medium refined of a glance or a sigh;
Is there one, who but once would not rather have
    known it,
Than written, with Harvey, whole volumes upon it?

As for you, my sweet-voiced and invisible love,
You must surely be one of those spirits, that rove
By the bank where, at twilight, the poet reclines,
When the star of the west on his solitude shines,
And the magical fingers of fancy have hung
Every breeze with a sigh, every leaf with a tongue.
Oh! hint to him then, 't is retirement alone
Can hallow his harp or ennoble its tone;
Like you, with a veil of seclusion between,
His song to the world let him utter unseen;
And like you, a legitimate child of the spheres,
Escape from the eye to enrapture the ears.

    Did we not love so true, so dear,
      This lapse could never be forgiven;
    But hearts so fond and lips so near—
      Give me the ring, and now—Oh heaven!—P. E.

(2) These two lines, as they originally appeared, were :—
  That, in short, you're a woman; your lip and your breast
  As mortal as ever were tasted or press'd!—P. E.

Sweet spirit of mystery! how I should love,
In the wearisome ways I am fated to rove,
To have you thus ever invisibly nigh,
Inhaling for ever your song and your sigh!
'Mid the crowds of the world and the murmurs of care,
I might sometimes converse with my nymph of the air,
And turn with distaste from the clamorous crew,
To steal in the pauses one whisper from you,

Then, come and be near me, for ever be mine,
We shall hold in the air a communion divine,
As sweet as, of old, was imagined to dwell
In the grotto of Numa, or Socrates' cell.
And oft, at those lingering moments of night,
When the heart's busy thoughts have put slumber to
    flight,
You shall come to my pillow and tell me of love,
Such as angel to angel might whisper above.
Sweet spirit!—and then, could you borrow the tone
Of that voice, to my ear like some fairy-song known,
The voice of the one upon earth, who has twined
With her being for ever my heart and my mind,
Though lonely and far from the light of her smile,
An exile, and weary and hopeless the while,
Could you shed for a moment her voice on my ear,
I will think, for that moment, that Cara is near;
That she comes with consoling enchantment to speak,
And kisses my eyelid and breathes on my cheek,
And tells me, the night shall go rapidly by,
For the dawn of our hope, of our heaven, is nigh.

Fair spirit! if such be your magical power,
It will lighten the lapse of full many an hour;
And, let fortune's realities frown as they will,
Hope, fancy, and Cara may smile for me still.

—◦❀◦—

THE RING, A TALE. (1)

Annulus ille viri.—*Ovid. Amor.*, lib. ii., eleg. 15.

The happy day at length arrived
  When Rupert was to wed
The fairest maid in Saxony,
  And take her to his bed.

As soon as morn was in the sky,
  The feast and sports began;
The men admired the happy maid,
  The maids the happy man.

In many a sweet device of mirth
  The day was pass'd along;
And some the featly dance amused,
  And some the dulcet song.

(1) I should be sorry to think that my friend had any
serious intentions of frightening the nursery by this
story: I rather hope—though the manner of it leads me
to doubt—that his design was to ridicule that distempered
taste which prefers those monsters of the fancy to the
"speciosa miracula" of true poetic imagination.

The younger maids with Isabel
  Disported through the bowers,
And deck'd her robe, and crown'd her head
  With motley bridal flowers.

The matrons all in rich attire,
  Within the castle walls,
Sat listening to the choral strains
  That echo'd through the halls.

Young Rupert and his friends repair'd
  Unto a spacious court,
To strike the bounding tennis-ball
  In feat and manly sport.

The bridegroom on his finger wore
  The wedding-ring so bright,
Which was to grace the lily hand
  Of Isabel that night.

And fearing he might break the gem,
  Or lose it in the play,
He look'd around the court, to see
  Where he the ring might lay.

Now, in the court a statue stood,
  Which there full long had been;
It might a Heathen goddess be,
  Or else a Heathen queen.

Upon its marble finger then
  He tried the ring to fit;
And, thinking it was safest there,
  Thereon he fasten'd it.

And now the tennis sports went on,
  Till they were wearied all,
And messengers announced to them,
  Their dinner in the hall.

Young Rupert for his wedding-ring
  Unto the statue went;
But, oh, how shock'd was he to find
  The marble finger bent!

The hand was closed upon the ring
  With firm and mighty clasp;
In vain he tried, and tried, and tried,
  He could not loose the grasp!

Then sore surprised was Rupert's mind—
  As well his mind might be;
"I 'll come," quoth he, "at night again,
  When none are here to see."

I find, by a note in the manuscript, that he met with
this story in a German author, *Fromman upon Fascina-*
tion, book iii., part vi., ch. 18. On consulting the work,
I perceive that Fromman quotes it from Beluacensis,
among many other stories equally diabolical and interest-
ing.—E.

He went unto the feast, and much
  He thought upon his ring;
And marvell'd sorely what could mean
  So very strange a thing!

The feast was o'er, and to the court
  He hied without delay,
Resolved to break the marble hand,
  And force the ring away.

But, mark a stranger wonder still—
  The ring was there no more,
And yet the marble hand ungrasp'd,
  And open as before!

He search'd the base, and all the court,
  But nothing could he find;
Then to the castle hied he back
  With sore bewilder'd mind.

Within he found them all in mirth,
  The night in dancing flew;
The youth another ring procured,
  And none the adventure knew.

And now the priest has join'd their hands,
  The hours of love advance:
Rupert almost forgets to think
  Upon the morn's mischance.

Within the bed fair Isabel
  In blushing sweetness lay,
Like flowers, half-open'd by the dawn,
  And waiting for the day.

And Rupert, by her lovely side,
  In youthful beauty glows,
Like Phœbus, when he bends to cast
  His beams upon a rose.

And here my song would leave them both,
  Nor let the rest be told,
If 't were not for the horrid tale
  It yet has to unfold.

Soon Rupert, 'twixt his bride and him,
  A death-cold carcass found;
He saw it not, but thought he felt
  Its arms embrace him round.

He started up, and then return'd,
  But found the phantom still;
In vain he shrunk, it clipp'd him round,
  With damp and deadly chill!

And when he bent, the earthy lips
  A kiss of horror gave;
'T was like the smell from charnel vaults,
  Or from the mouldering grave!

Ill-fated Rupert!—wild and loud
  Then cried he to his wife,
"Oh! save me from this horrid fiend,
  My Isabel! my life!"

But Isabel had nothing seen,
  She look'd around in vain;
And much she mourn'd the mad conceit
  That rack'd her Rupert's brain.

At length from this invisible
  These words to Rupert came;
(Oh God! while he did hear the words
  What terrors shook his frame!)

"Husband, husband, I've the ring
  Thou gavest to day to me;
And thou 'rt to me for ever wed,
  As I am wed to thee!"

And all the night the demon lay
  Cold-chilling by his side,
And strain'd him with such deadly grasp,
  He thought he should have died.

But when the dawn of day was near,
  The horrid phantom fled,
And left the affrighted youth to weep
  By Isabel in bed.

And all that day a gloomy cloud
  Was seen on Rupert's brows;
Fair Isabel was likewise sad,
  But strove to cheer her spouse.

And, as the day advanced, he thought
  Of coming night with fear:
Alas, that he should dread to view
  The bed that should be dear!

At length the second night arrived,
  Again their couch they press'd;
Poor Rupert hoped that all was o'er,
  And look'd for love and rest.

But oh! when midnight came, again
  The fiend was at his side,
And, as it strain'd him in its grasp,
  With howl exulting cried:—

"Husband, husband, I've the ring,
  The ring thou gavest to me;
And thou 'rt to me for ever wed,
  As I am wed to thee!"

In agony of wild despair,
  He started from the bed;
And thus to his bewilder'd wife
  The trembling Rupert said:

10

"Oh Isabel! dost thou not see
  A shape of horrors here,
That strains me to its deadly kiss,
  And keeps me from my dear?"

"No, no, my love! my Rupert, I
  No shape of horrors see;
And much I mourn the phantasy
  That keeps my dear from me."

This night, just like the night before,
  In terrors pass'd away,
Nor did the demon vanish thence
  Before the dawn of day.

Said Rupert then, "My Isabel,
  Dear partner of my woe,
To Father Austin's holy cave
  This instant will I go."

Now Austin was a reverend man,
  Who acted wonders maint—
Whom all the country round believed
  A devil or a saint!

To Father Austin's holy cave
  Then Rupert straightway went;
And told him all, and ask'd him how
  These horrors to prevent.

The father heard the youth, and then
  Retired awhile to pray;
And, having pray'd for half an hour,
  Thus to the youth did say:

"There is a place where four roads meet,
  Which I will tell to thee;
Be there this eve, at fall of night,
  And list what thou shalt see.

"Thou 'lt see a group of figures pass
  In strange disorder'd crowd,
Travelling by torchlight through the roads,
  With noises strange and loud.

"And one that's high above the rest,
  Terrific towering o'er,
Will make thee know him at a glance,
  So I need say no more.

"To him from me these tablets give,
  They'll quick be understood;
Thou need'st not fear, but give them straight,
  I've scrawl'd them with my blood!"

The night-fall came, and Rupert all
  In pale amazement went
To where the cross-roads met, as he
  Was by the Father sent.

And lo! a group of figures came
  In strange disorder'd crowd,
Travelling by torchlight through the roads,
  With noises strange and loud.

And, as the gloomy train advanced,
  Rupert beheld from far
A female form of wanton mien,
  High seated on a car.

And Rupert, as he gazed upon
  The loosely-vested dame,
Thought of the marble statue's look,
  For hers was just the same.

Behind her walk'd a hideous form,
  With eyeballs flashing death;
Whene'er he breathed, a sulphur'd smoke
  Came burning in his breath.

He seem'd the first of all the crowd,
  Terrific towering o'er;
"Yes, yes," said Rupert, "this is he,
  And I need ask no more."

Then slow he went, and to this fiend
  The tablets trembling gave,
Who look'd and read them with a yell
  That would disturb the grave.

And when he saw the blood-scrawl'd name,
  His eyes with fury shine;
"I thought," cries he, "his time was out,
  But he must soon be mine!"

Then darting at the youth a look
  Which rent his soul with fear,
He went unto the female fiend,
  And whisper'd in her ear.

The female fiend no sooner heard
  Than, with reluctant look,
The very ring that Rupert lost
  She from her finger took.

And, giving it unto the youth,
  With eyes that breathed of hell,
She said, in that tremendous voice,
  Which he remember'd well:

"In Austin's name take back the ring,
  The ring thou gavest to me;
And thou 'rt to me no longer wed,
  Nor longer I to thee."

He took the ring, the rabble pass'd,
  He home return'd again;
His wife was then the happiest fair,
  The happiest he of men.

TO . . . .

ON SEEING HER WITH A WHITE VEIL AND A RICH GIRDLE.

Μαργαριται δηλουσι δακρυων ροον.
Ap. Nicephor. in Oneirocritico.

Put off the vestal veil, nor, oh!
Let weeping angels view it;
Your cheeks belie its virgin snow,
And blush repenting through it.

Put off the fatal zone you wear;
The shining pearls around it
Are tears, that fell from Virtue there,
The hour when Love unbound it.

———◦⊙◦———

WRITTEN IN THE BLANK LEAF

OF A LADY'S COMMONPLACE BOOK.

Here is one leaf reserved for me,
From all thy sweet memorials free;
And here my simple song might tell
The feelings thou must guess so well.
But could I thus, within thy mind,
One little vacant corner find,
Where no impression yet is seen,
Where no memorial yet hath been,
Oh! it should be my sweetest care
To *write my name for ever there!*

———◦⊙◦———

TO MRS. BL———.

WRITTEN IN HER ALBUM. (1)

They say that Love had once a book
(The urchin likes to copy you),
Where all who came the pencil took,
And wrote, like us, a line or two.

'T was Innocence, the maid divine,
Who kept this volume bright and fair,
And saw that no unhallow'd line
Or thought profane should enter there;

And daily did the pages fill
With fond device and loving lore,
And every leaf she turn'd was still
More bright than that she turn'd before.

Beneath the touch of Hope, how soft,
How light the magic pencil ran!
Till Fear would come, alas, as oft,
And trembling close what Hope began.

A tear or two had dropp'd from Grief,
And Jealousy would, now and then,
Ruffle in haste some snow-white leaf,
Which Love had still to smoothe again.

But, ah! there came a blooming boy,
Who often turn'd the pages o'er,
And wrote therein such words of joy,
That all who read them sigh'd for more.

And Pleasure was this spirit's name,
And though so soft his voice and look,
Yet Innocence, whene'er he came,
Would tremble for her spotless book.

For oft a Bacchant cup he bore,
With earth's sweet nectar sparkling bright;
And much she fear'd lest, mantling o'er,
Some drops should on the pages light.(2)

And so it chanced, one luckless night,
The urchin let that goblet fall
O'er the fair book, so pure, so white,
And sullied lines and marge and all!

In vain now, touch'd with shame, he tried
To wash those fatal stains away;
Deep, deep had sunk the sullying tide,
The leaves grew darker every day.(3)

And Fancy's sketches lost their hue,
And Hope's sweet lines were all effaced,
And Love himself now scarcely knew
What Love himself so lately traced.

At length the urchin Pleasure fled,
(For how, alas! could Pleasure stay?)
And Love, while many a tear he shed,
Reluctant flung the book away.

The index now alone remains,
Of all the pages spoil'd by Pleasure,
And though it bears some earthy stains,
Yet Memory counts the leaf a treasure.

And oft, they say, she scans it o'er,
And oft, by this memorial aided,
Brings back the pages now no more,
And thinks of lines that long have faded.

(1) Mr. Moore has suppressed the following motto, which preceded this poem in former editions:—

Τουτο δε τι εστι το ποτον; Πλανη, εφη.
Cebetis Tabula.—P. E.

(2) The place of this verse was occupied in former editions by the following:—

For still she saw his playful fingers
Fill'd with sweets and wanton toys;
And well she knew the stain that lingers
After sweets from wanton boys!—P. E.

(3) The following eight lines, which originally appeared here, no longer make part of the poem:—

In vain be sought, with eager lip,
The honey from the leaf to drink,
For still the more the boy would sip,
The deeper still the blot would sink!

Oh! it would make you weep, to see
The traces of this honey flood
Steal o'er a page, where Modesty
Had freshly drawn a rose's bud!—P. E.

I know not if this tale be true,
   But thus the simple facts are stated;
And I refer their truth to you,
   Since Love and you are near related.

———o·00·o———

TO CARA,

AFTER AN INTERVAL OF ABSENCE.

CONCEAL'D within the shady wood
   A mother left her sleeping child,
And flew, to cull her rustic food,
   The fruitage of the forest wild.

But storms upon her pathway rise,
   The mother roams astray and weeping,
Far from the weak appealing cries
   Of him she left so sweetly sleeping.

She hopes, she fears; a light is seen,
   And gentler blows the night wind's breath;
Yet no—'t is gone—the storms are keen,
   The infant may be chill'd to death!

Perhaps, even now, in darkness shrouded,
   His little eyes lie cold and still ;—
And yet, perhaps, they are not clouded,
   Life and love may light them still.

Thus, Cara, at our last farewell,
   When, fearful even thy hand to touch,
I mutely ask'd those eyes to tell
   If parting pain'd thee half so much :

I thought,—and, oh ! forgive the thought,
   For none was e'er by love inspired
Whom fancy had not also taught
   To hope the bliss his soul desired.(1)

Yes, I did think, in Cara's mind,
   Though yet to that sweet mind unknown,
I left one infant wish behind,
   One feeling, which I call'd my own.

Oh blest ! though but in fancy blest,
   How did I ask of Pity's care,
To shield and strengthen, in thy breast,
   The nursling I had cradled there.

And many an hour, beguiled by pleasure,
   And many an hour of sorrow numbering,
I ne'er forgot the new-born treasure
   I left within thy bosom slumbering.

(1) This and the preceding verse have been somewhat
changed; in former editions they appear—
   Thus, when my soul with parting sigh
     Hung on thy hand's bewildering touch,
   And, timid, ask'd that speaking eye,
     If parting pain'd thee half so much:
   I thought, and, oh ! forgive the thought,
     For who, by eyes like thine inspired,

Perhaps, indifference has not chill'd it,
   Haply, it yet a throb may give—
Yet, no—perhaps, a doubt has kill'd it ;
   Say, dearest—does the feeling live ? (2)

———o·00·o———

TO CARA,

ON THE DAWNING OF A NEW YEAR'S DAY.

WHEN midnight came to close the year,
   We sigh'd to think it thus should take
The hours it gave us—hours as dear
   As sympathy and love could make
Their blessed moments,—every sun
Saw us, my love, more closely one.

But, Cara, when the dawn was nigh
   Which came a new year's light to shed,
That smile we caught from eye to eye
   Told us, those moments were not fled:
Oh, no,—we felt, some future sun
Should see us still more closely one.

Thus may we ever, side by side,
   From happy years to happier glide;
And still thus may the passing sigh
   We give to hours, that vanish o'er us,
Be follow'd by the smiling eye,
   That Hope shall shed on scenes before us!

———o·00·o———

TO . . . ., 1801.

To be the theme of every hour
The heart devotes to Fancy's power,
When her prompt magic fills the mind
With friends and joys we've left behind,
And joys return and friends are near,
And all are welcomed with a tear :—
In the mind's purest seat to dwell,
To be remember'd oft and well
By one whose heart, though vain and wild,
By passion led, by youth beguiled,
Can proudly still aspire to be
All that may yet win smiles from thee :—
If thus to live in every part
Of a lone weary wanderer's heart;
If thus to be its sole employ
Can give thee one faint gleam of joy,
Believe it, Mary,—oh ! believe
A tongue that never can deceive,
Though, erring, it too oft betray
Even more than Love should dare to say,—(3)

(2) This line originally read—
   Oh, Cara ! does the infant live?—P. E.
(3) This couplet formerly stood—
   When passion doth not first betray,
   And tinge the thought upon its way.—P. E.

Could e'er resist the flattering fault
   Of fancying what his soul desired ?—P. E.

In Pleasure's dream or Sorrow's hour,
In crowded hall or lonely bower,
The business of my life shall be
For ever to remember thee.
And though that heart be dead to mine,
Since Love is life and wakes not thine,
I'll take thy image, as the form
Of one whom Love had fail'd to warm,(1)
Which, though it yield no answering thrill,
Is not less dear, is worshipp'd still—
I'll take it, wheresoe'er I stray,
The bright cold burden of my way.
To keep this semblance fresh in bloom,
My heart shall be its lasting tomb,
And Memory, with embalming care,
Shall keep it fresh and fadeless there.(2)

—◦◦◦—

THE GENIUS OF HARMONY,

AN IRREGULAR ODE.

Ad harmoniam canere mundum.
Cicero, de Nat. Deor., lib. iii.

THERE lies a shell beneath the waves,
In many a hollow winding wreathed,
Such as of old
Echo'd the breath that warbling sea-maids breathed;
This magic shell,
From the white bosom of a syren fell,
As once she wander'd by the tide that laves
Sicilia's sands of gold.

(1) This line is substituted for the original one—
Of something I should long to warm.—P. E.

(2) The two last lines were originally turned—
And Love shall lend his sweetest care,
With memory to embalm it there!—P. E.

(3) In the *Histoire naturelle des Antilles*, there is an account of some curious shells, found at Curaçoa, on the back of which were lines, filled with musical characters so distinct and perfect, that the writer assures us a very charming trio was sung from one of them. "On le nomme musical, parce qu'il porte sur le dos des lignes noirâtres pleines de notes, qui ont une espéce de clé pour les mettre en chant, de sorte que l'on diroit qu'il ne manque que la lettre à cette tablature naturelle. Ce curieux gentilhomme (M. du Montel) rapporte qu'il en a vu qui avoient cinq lignes, une clé et des notes qui formoient un accord parfait. Quelqu'un y avoit ajouté la lettre, que la nature avoit oubliée, et la faisoit chanter en forme de trio, dont l'air étoit fort agréable."—Chap. xix., art. 11. The author adds, a poet himself imagine that these shells were used by the syrens at their concerts.

(4) According to Cicero, and his commentator, Macrobius, the lunar tone is the gravest and faintest on the planetary heptachord. "Quam ob causam summus ille cœli stellifer cursus, cujus conversio est concitatior, acuto et excitato movetur sono; gravissimo autem hic lunaris atque infimus."—*Somn. Scip.* Because, says Macrobius, "spiritu ut in extremitate languescente jam volvitur, et propter angustias quibus penultimus orbis arctatur impetu leniore convertitur."—In *Somn. Scip.*, lib. ii., cap. 4. In their musical arrangement of the heavenly bodies, the

It bears
Upon its shining side the mystic notes
Of those entrancing airs,(3)
The genii of the deep were wont to swell, [roll'd!
When heaven's eternal orbs their midnight music
Oh! seek it, wheresoe'er it floats;
And, if the power
Of thrilling numbers to thy soul be dear,
Go, bring the bright shell to my bower,
And I will fold thee in such downy dreams
As lap the Spirit of the Seventh Sphere,
When Luna's distant tone falls faintly on his ear!(4)
And thou shalt own,
That, through the circle of creation's zone,
Where matter slumbers or where spirit beams;
From the pellucid tides (5) that whirl
The planets through their maze of song,
To the small rill, that weeps along
Murmuring o'er beds of pearl;
From the rich sigh
Of the sun's arrow through an evening sky,(6)
To the faint breath the tuneful osier yields
On Afric's burning fields; (7)
Thou'lt wondering own this universe divine
Is mine!
That I respire in all, and all in me,
One mighty mingled soul of boundless harmony.
Welcome, welcome, mystic shell!
Many a star has ceased to burn (8),
Many a tear has Saturn's urn

ancient writers are not very intelligible.—See *Ptolem.*, lib. iii.

Leone Ebreo, pursuing the idea of Aristotle, that the heavens are animal, attributes their harmony to perfect and reciprocal love. "Non peró manca fra loro il perfetto e reciproco amore: la causa principale, che ne mostra il loro amore, è la lor amicizia armonica oe la concordanza che perpetuamente si trova in loro."—Dialog. ii. di Amore, p. 58. This "reciproco amore" of Leone is the φιλότη of the ancient Empedocles, who seems, in his Love and Hate of the Elements, to have given a glimpse of the principles of attraction and repulsion. See the fragment to which I allude in Laertius, Άλλοτε μεν φιλότητι, συνερχομεν', κ. τ. λ., lib. viii., cap. 2., n. 12.

(5) Leucippus, the atomist, imagined a kind of vortices in the heavens, which he borrowed from Anaxagoras, and possibly suggested to Descartes.

(6) Heraclides, upon the allegories of Homer, conjectures that the idea of the harmony of the spheres originated with this poet, who, in representing the solar beams as arrows, supposes them to emit a peculiar sound in the air.

(7) In the account of Africa which D'Ablancourt has translated, there is mention of a tree in that country, whose branches when shaken by the hand produce very sweet sounds. "Le même auteur (Abenzégar) dit qu'il y a un certain arbre, qui produit des gaules comme d'osier, et qu'en les prenant à la main et les branlant elles font une espéce d'harmonie fort agréable," etc., etc.—*L'Afrique de Marmol.*

(8) Alluding to the extinction, or at least the disappearance, of some of those fixed stars, which we are taught

O'er the cold bosom of the ocean wept,(1)
    Since thy aërial spell
    Hath in the waters slept.
        Now blest I 'll fly
With the bright treasure to my choral sky,
    Where she, who waked its early swell,
    The Syren of the heavenly choir,
Walks o'er the great string of my Orphic Lyre ;(2)
    Or guides around the burning pole
    The winged chariot of some blissful soul : (3)
        While thou—
Oh son of earth, what dreams shall rise for thee!
        Beneath Hispania's sun,
        Thou 'lt see a streamlet run,
Which I 've imbued with breathing melody;(4)
And there, when night-winds down the current die,
Thou 'lt hear how like a harp its waters sigh :
A liquid chord is every wave that flows,
An airy plectrum every breeze that blows.(5)

    There, by that wondrous stream,
    Go, lay thy languid brow,
And I will send thee such a godlike dream,
As never bless'd the slumbers even of him,(6)
Who, many a night, with his primordial lyre,(7)
    Sate on the chill Pangæan mount,(8)

And, looking to the orient dim,
Watch'd the first flowing of that sacred fount
    From which his soul had drunk its fire.
Oh! think what visions, in that lonely hour,
    Stole o'er his musing breast;
        What pious ecstasy (9)
Wafted his prayer to that eternal Power,
Whose seal upon this new-born world impress'd (10)
The various forms of bright divinity!

Or, dost thou know what dreams I wove,
'Mid the deep horror of that silent bower,(11)
Where the rapt Samian slept his holy slumber ?
    When, free from every earthly chain,
From wreaths of pleasure and from bonds of pain,
    His spirit flew through fields above,
Drank at the source of nature's fontal number,(12)
And saw, in mystic choir, around him move
The stars of song, Heaven's burning minstrelsy !
    Such dreams, so heavenly bright,
        I swear
    By the great diadem that twines my hair,
    And by the seven gems that sparkle there,(13)
        Mingling their beams
In a soft iris of harmonious light,
    Oh, mortal! such shall be thy radiant dreams.

to consider as suns, attended each by its system. Des-
cartes thought that our earth might formerly have been
a sun, which became obscured by a thick incrustation over
its surface. This probably suggested the idea of a central
fire.

(1) Porphyry says, that Pythagoras held the sea to be a
tear, Την Θαλατταν μεν εκαλει ειναι δακρυον (De Vitâ);
and some one else, if I mistake not, has added the planet
Saturn as the source of it. Empedocles, with similar
affectation, called the sea "the sweat of the earth:" ίδρωτα
της γης. See Rittershusius upon Porphyry, Num. 41.

(2) The system of the harmonised orbs was styled by the
ancients the Great Lyre of Orpheus, for which Lucian thus
accounts :—ή δε Λυρη επταμιτος εουσα την των κινου-
μενων αστρων άρμονιαν συνεβαλλετο. κ. τ. λ. in As-
trolog.

(3) Διειλε ψυχας ισαριθμους τοις αστροις, ενειμε Θ'
έκαστην προς έκαστον, και εμβιβασας' ΩΣ ΕΙΣ ΟΧΗΜΑ.
"Distributing the souls severally among the stars, and
mounting each soul upon a star as on its chariot."—Plato,
Timæus.

(4) This musical river is mentioned in the romance of
Achilles Tatius. Επει ποταμον ...ην δε ακουσαι Θελης
του ύδατος λαλουντος. The Latin version, in supplying
the hiatus which is in the original, has placed the river in
Hispania. "In Hispaniâ quoque fluvius est, quem primo
aspectu," etc., etc.

(5) These two lines are translated from the words of
Achilles Tatius. Εαν γαρ ολιγος ανεμος εις τας δινας
εμπεση, το'μεν ύδωρ ως χορδη χρουσται. το δε πνευμα
του ύδατος πληκτρον γινεται. το ρευμα δε ως κιθαρα
λαλει.—Lib. ii.

(6) Orpheus.

(7) They called his lyre αρχαιοτροπον έπταχορδον
Ορφεως. See a curious work by a professor of Greek at

Venice, entitled "Hebdomades, sive septem de septenario
libri."—Lib. iv., cap. 3., p. 177.

(8) Eratosthenes, in mentioning the extreme veneration
of Orpheus for Apollo, says that he was accustomed to go
to the Pangæan mountain at day-break, and there wait
the rising of the sun, that he might be the first to hail its
beams. Επεγειρομενος τε της νυκτος, κατα την έωθινην
επι το ορος το καλουμενον Παγγαιον, προςεμενε τας ανα-
τολας, ίνα ίδη του ' Ηλιου πρωτον.—Καταστεριαμ. 24.

(9) There are some verses of Orpheus preserved to us,
which contain sublime ideas of the unity and magnificence
of the Deity. For instance, those which Justin Martyr has
produced :—

        Ούτος μεν χαλκειον ες ουρανον εστηρικται
        Χρυσεω ενι θρονω, κ. τ. λ.—Ad Græc. Cohortat.

It is thought by some, that these are to be reckoned
amongst the fabrications, which were frequent in the
early times of Christianity. Still, it appears doubtful to
whom they are to be attributed, being too pious for the
Pagans, and too poetical for the Fathers.

(10) In one of the Hymns of Orpheus, he attributes a
figured seal to Apollo, with which he imagines that deity to
have stamped a variety of forms upon the universe.

(11) Alluding to the cave near Samos, where Pythagoras
devoted the greater part of his days and nights to medita-
tion and the mysteries of his philosophy. Iamblich. de
Vit. This, as Holstenius remarks, was in imitation of the
Magi.

(12) The tetractys, or sacred number of the Pythago-
reans, on which they solemnly swore, and which they
called παγκαν αεναοου φυσεως, "the fountain of perennial
nature." Lucian has ridiculed this religious arithmetic
very cleverly in his Sale of Philosophers.

(13) This diadem is intended to represent the analogy
between the notes of music and the prismatic colours.

I found her not—the chamber seem'd
Like some divinely haunted place,
Where fairy forms had lately beam'd,
And left behind their odorous trace!

It felt, as if her lips had shed
A sigh around her, ere she fled,
Which hung, as on a melting lute,
When all the silver chords are mute,
There lingers still a trembling breath
After the note's luxurious death,
A shade of song, a spirit air
Of melodies which had been there.

I saw the veil, which, all the day,
Had floated o'er her cheek of rose;
I saw the couch, where late she lay
In languor of divine repose;

And I could trace the hallow'd print
Her limbs had left, as pure and warm
As if 't were done in rapture's mint,
And Love himself had stamp'd the form.

Oh, my sweet mistress, where wert thou?
In pity fly not thus from me;
Thou art my life, my essence now,
And my soul dies of wanting thee.

———o⚬o———

TO MRS. HENRY TIGHE,

ON READING HER "PSYCHE."

Tell me the witching tale again
For never has my heart or ear
Hung on so sweet, so pure a strain,
So pure to feel, so sweet to hear.

Say, Love, in all thy prime of fame,
When the high heaven itself was thine;
When piety confess'd the flame,
And even thy errors were divine;

We find in Plutarch a vague intimation of this kindred harmony in colours and sounds.—Οψις τε και ακοη, μετα φηνης τε και φωτος των αρμονιαν επιφαινουσι.—De Musica.

Cassiodorus, whose idea I may be supposed to have borrowed, says, in a letter upon music to Boetius, "Ut diadema oculis, varia luce gemmarum, sic cithara diversitate soni, blanditur auditui." This is indeed the only tolerable thought in the letter.—Lib. ii., Variar.

(1)See the story in Apuleius. With respect to this beautiful allegory of Love and Psyche, there is an ingenious idea suggested by the senator Buonarroti, in his "Osservazioni sopra alcuni frammenti di vasi antici." He thinks the fable is taken from some very occult mysteries, which had long been celebrated in honour of Love; and accounts, upon this supposition, for the silence of the more ancient authors upon the subject, as it was not till towards the decline of pagan superstition, that writers could venture to reveal or discuss such ceremonies. Accordingly, observes

Did ever Muse's hand, so fair,
A glory round thy temples spread?
Did ever lip's ambrosial air
Such fragrance o'er thy altars shed?

One maid there was, who round her lyre
The mystic myrtle wildly wreathed;—
But all her sighs were sighs of fire,
The myrtle wither'd as she breathed.

Oh! you, that love's celestial dream,
In all its purity, would know,
Let not the senses' ardent beam
Too strongly through the vision glow.

Love safest lies conceal'd in night,
The night where heaven has bid him lie;
Oh! shed not there unhallow'd light,
Or, Psyche knows, the boy will fly.(1)

Sweet Psyche, many a charmed hour,
Through many a wild and magic waste,
To the fair fount and blissful bower (2)
Have I, in dreams, thy light foot traced!

Where'er thy joys are number'd now,
Beneath whatever shades of rest,
The Genius of the starry brow (3)
Hath bound thee to thy Cupid's breast;

Whether above the horizon dim,
Along whose verge our spirits stray,—
Half sunk beneath the shadowy rim,
Half brighten'd by the upper ray,—(4)

Thou dwellest in a world, all light,
Or, lingering here, dost love to be,
To other souls, the guardian bright
That Love was, through this gloom, to thee;

Still be the song to Pscyhe dear,
The song, whose gentle voice was given

this author, we find Lucian and Plutarch treating, without reserve, of the Dea Syria, as well as of Isis and Osiris; and Apuleius, to whom we are indebted for the beautiful story of Cupid and Psyche, has also detailed some of the mysteries of Isis. See the *Giornale dei Litterari d'Italia*, tom. xxvii., articol. 1. See also the observations upon the ancient gems in the Museum Florentinum, vol. i., p. 156.

I cannot avoid remarking here an error into which the French Encyclopédistes have been led by M. Spon, in their article Psyche. They say. "Pétrone fait un récit de la pompe nuptiale de ces deux amants (Amour et Psyché). Déjà, dit-il," etc.. etc. The Psyche of Petronius, however, is a servant-maid, and the marriage which he describes is that of the young Pannychis. See Spon's *Recherches curieuses*, etc., Dissertat. 5.

(2) Allusions to Mrs. Tighe's Poem.

(3) Constancy.

(4) By this image the Platonists expressed the middle state of the soul between sensible and intellectual existence.

To be, on earth, to mortal ear,
An echo of her own, in heaven.(1)

—————◦◊◊◦—————

FROM THE HIGH PRIEST OF APOLLO,

TO A VIRGIN OF DELPHI. (2)

Cum digno digna......—*Sulpicia.*

"WHO is the maid, with golden hair,
With eye of fire, and foot of air,
Whose harp around my altar swells,
The sweetest of a thousand shells ?"
'T was thus the deity, who treads
The arch of heaven, and proudly sheds
Day from his eyelids—thus he spoke,
As through my cell his glories broke.

Aphelia is the Delphic fair,(3)
With eyes of fire and golden hair,
Aphelia's are the airy feet,
And hers the harp divinely sweet;
For foot so light has never trod
The laurel'd caverns (4) of the god,
Nor harp so soft hath ever given
A sigh to earth or hymn to heaven.

"Then tell the virgin to unfold,
In looser pomp, her locks of gold,
And bid those eyes more fondly shine
To welcome down a Spouse Divine ; (5)

(1) In the present edition the last two verses have undergone some verbal changes; they appeared originally—

Thou risest to a cloudless pole !
Or, lingering here, dost love to mark
The twilight walk of many a soul
Through sunny good and evil dark;

Still be the song to Psyche dear,
The song, whose dulcet tide was given
To keep her name as fadeless here
As nectar keeps her soul in Heaven !—P. E.

(2) This poem, as well as a few others, formed part of a work which I had early projected, and even announced to the public, but which, luckily perhaps, for myself, had been interrupted by my visit to America in the year 1803.

Among those impostures in which the priests of the pagan temples are known to have indulged, one of the most favourite was that of announcing to some fair votary of the shrine, that the God himself had become enamoured of her beauty, and would descend in all his glory, to pay her a visit within the recesses of the fane. An adventure of this description formed an episode in the classic romance which I had sketched out ; and the short fragment

* We here give the continuation of this note, as it appeared in former editions :—

In the temple of Jupiter Belus there was a splendid bed for these occasions. In Egyptian Thebes the same mockery was practised; and at the oracle of Patara in Lycia, the priestess never could prophecy till an interview with the deity was allowed her. The story which we read in *Josephus* (lib. xviii., cap. 3.) of the Roman matron Paulina, whom the priests of Isis, for a bribe, betrayed in this manner to Mundus, is a singular instance of the impudent excess to which credulity suffered these impostures to be carried. This

Since He, who lights the path of years—
Even from the fount of morning's tears
To where his setting splendours burn
Upon the western sea-maid's urn—
Doth not, in all his course, behold
Such eyes of fire, such hair of gold.
Tell her, he comes, in blissful pride,
His lip yet sparkling with the tide
That mantles in Olympian bowls,—
The nectar of eternal souls !
For her, for her he quits the skies,
And to her kiss from nectar flies.
Oh, he would quit his star-throned height,
And leave the world to pine for light,
Might he but pass the hours of shade
Beside his peerless Delphic maid,
She, more than earthly woman blest,
He, more than god on woman's breast !"

There is a cave beneath the deep, (6)
Where living rills of crystal weep
O'er herbage of the loveliest hue
That ever spring begemm'd with dew .
There oft the greensward's glossy tint
Is brighten'd by the recent print
Of many a faun and naiad's feet,—
Scarce touching earth, their step so fleet,—
That there, by moonlight's ray, had trod,
In light dance, o'er the verdant sod.(7)

given above, belongs to an epistle by which the story was to have been introduced.*

(3) In the 9th Pythic of Pindar, where Apollo, in the same manner, requires of Chiron some information respecting the fair Cyrene, the Centaur, in obeying, very gravely apologises for telling the God what his omniscience must know so perfectly already :—

Ει δε γε χρη και παρ σοφον αντιφεριξαι,
Ερεω·

(4) Αλλ' εις δαφνωδη γυαλα βησομαι ταδε.
                                    Euripid., Ion., v. 76.

(5) Changed from—

And bid those eyes with fonder fire
Be kindled for a god's desire.†

(6) The Corycian Cave, which Pausanias mentions. The inhabitants of Parnassus held it sacred to the Corycian nymphs, who were children of the river Plistus.

(7) The preceding six lines originally stood thus—

There oft the green bank's glossy tint
Is brighten'd by the amorous print
Of many a faun and naiad's form,
That still upon the dew is warm,
When virgins come at peep of day
To kiss the sod where lovers lay !

story has been put into the form of a little novel, under the name of *La Pudicitia Schernita,* by the licentious and unfortunate *Pallavicino.* See his *Opere Scelte,* tom. i.—I have made my priest here prefer a cave to the temple.—P. E.

† Nè deve partorir ammiratione ch'egli si pregiasse di haver una Deità concorrente nel possesso della moglie; mentre anche noi nei nostri secoli, non ostante così rigorose leggi d'honore, trovasi chi s'ascrive a gloria il veder la moglie honorata dagl' amplessi di un Principe.—*Pallavicino.*

"There, there," the god impassion'd said,
Soon as the twilight tinge is fled,
And the dim orb of lunar souls (1)
Along its shadowy pathway rolls—
There shall we meet,—and not even He,(2)
The God who reigns immortally,
Where Babel's turrets paint their pride
Upon the Euphrates' shining tide—(3)
Not even when to his midnight loves
In mystic majesty he moves,
Lighted by many an odorous fire,

"And hymn'd by all Chaldæa's choir,—
E'er yet, o'er mortal brow, let shine
Such effluence of Love Divine,
As shall to-night, blest maid, o'er thine."

Happy the maid, whom heaven allows
To break for heaven her virgin vows!
Happy the maid!—her robe of shame (4)
Is whiten'd by a heavenly flame,
Whose glory, with a lingering trace,
Shines through and deifies her race!(5)

(1) It should seem that lunar spirits were of a purer order than spirits in general, as Pythagoras was said by his followers to have descended from the regions of the moon. The heresiarch Manes, in the same manner, imagined that the sun and moon are the residence of Christ, and that the ascension was nothing more than his flight to those orbs.

(2) Instead of this and the succeeding ten lines, the poem originally continued thus :—

There shall we find our bridal bed,
And ne'er did rosy rapture spread,
Not even in Jove's voluptuous bowers,
A bridal bed so bless'd as ours!
"Tell the imperial God, who reigns
Sublime in oriental fanes,
Whose towering turrets paint their pride
Upon Euphrates' pregnant tide;
Tell him, when to his midnight loves
In mystic majesty he moves,
Lighted by many an odorous fire,
And hymn'd by all Chaldæa's choir—
Oh! tell the godhead to confess,
The pompous joy delights him less
(Even though his mighty arms infold
A priestess on a couch of gold)
Than when in love's unholier prank,
By moonlight cave or rustic bank,
Upon his neck some wood-nymph lies,
Exhaling from her lip and eyes
The flame and incense of delight,
To sanctify a dearer rite,
A mystery, more divinely warm'd
Than priesthood ever yet perform'd!"—P. E.

(3) The temple of Jupiter Belus, at Babylon; in one of whose towers there was a large chapel set apart for those celestial assignations. "No man is allowed to sleep here," says Herodotus; "but the apartment is appropriated to a female, whom, if we believe the Chaldæan priests, the deity selects from the women of the country, as his favourite." . Lib. i., cap. 181.

(4) Fontenelle, in his playful rifacimento of the learned materials of Van Dale, has related in his own inimitable manner an adventure of this kind which was detected and exposed at Alexandria. See L'Histoire des Oracles, dissert. 2., chap. vii. Crebillon, too, in one of his most amusing little stories, has made the Génie Mange-Taupes, of the Isle Jonquille, assert this privilege of spiritual beings in a manner rather formidable to the husbands of the island. He says, however, "Les maris ont le plaisir de rester toujours dans le doute; en pareil cas, c'est une ressource."

(5) The following lines, which formerly concluded the poem, have been omitted in the present edition :—

Oh, virgin! what a doom is thine!
To-night, to-night a lip divine
In every kiss shall stamp on thee
A seal of immortality!
Fly to the cave, Aphelia, fly;
There lose the world and wed the sky!

The fragments given below, extracted from the work of which the above poem was to have formed a part, describe the effect of one of those invitations of Apollo upon the mind of a young enthusiastic girl :—

Delphi heard her shrine proclaim,
In oracles, the guilty flame.
Apollo loved my youthful charms,
Apollo woo'd me to his arms!—
Sure, sure when man so oft allows
Religion's wreath to bind his brows,
Weak wondering woman must believe;
Where pride and zeal at once deceive;
When flattery takes a holy vest,
Oh! 't is too much for woman's breast!

How often ere the destined time,
Which was to seal my joys sublime,
How often did I trembling run
To meet, at morn, the mounting sun,
And, while his fervid beam he threw
Upon my lips' luxuriant dew,
I thought—alas! the simple dream—
There burn'd a kiss in every beam;
With parted lips inhaled their heat,
And sigh'd, "Oh God! thy kiss is sweet!"

Oft too, at day's meridian hour,
When to the Naiad's gloomy bower
Our virgins steal, and, blushing, hide
Their beauties in the folding tide,
If, through the grove, whose modest arms
Were spread around my robeless charms,
A wandering sunbeam wanton fell
Where lovers' looks alone should dwell,
Not all a lover's looks of flame
Could kindle such an amorous shame.
It was the sun's admiring glance,
And, as I felt its glow advance
O'er my young beauties, wildly flush'd,
I burn'd and panted, thrill'd and blush'd!

.   .   .   .

No deity at midnight came:
The lamps, that witness'd all my shame,
Reveal'd to these bewilder'd eyes
No other shape than earth supplies;
No solar light, no nectar'd air—
All, all, alas! was human there:
Woman's faint conflict, virtue's fall,
And passion's victory, human all!
How gently must the guilt of love
Be charm'd away by Powers above,
When men possess such tender skill
In softening crime and sweetening ill!
'T was but a night, and morning's rays
Saw me, with fond, forgiving gaze,
Hang o'er the quiet slumbering breast
Of him who ruin'd all my rest;
Him, who had taught these eyes to weep
Their first sad tears, and yet could sleep!

.   .   .   .
                                        —P. E.

FRAGMENT.

Pity me, love! I'll pity thee,
If thou indeed hast felt like me.
All, all my bosom's peace is o'er!
At night, which *was* my hour of calm,
When from the page of classic lore,
From the pure fount of ancient lay,
My soul has drawn the placid balm,
Which charm'd its every grief away,
Ah! there I find that balm no more.
Those spells, which make us oft forget
The fleeting troubles of the day,
In deeper sorrows only whet
The stings they cannot tear away.
When to my pillow rack'd I fly,
With wearied sense and wakeful eye,
While my brain maddens, where, oh, where
Is that serene consoling prayer,
Which once has harbinger'd my rest,
When the still soothing voice of Heaven
Hath seem'd to whisper in my breast,
"Sleep on, thy errors are forgiven!"
No, though I still in semblance pray,
My thoughts are wandering far away,
And even the name of Deity
Is murmur'd out in sighs for thee.

A NIGHT THOUGHT.

How oft a cloud, with envious veil,
Obscures yon bashful light,
Which seems so modestly to steal
Along the waste of night!

'T is thus the world's obtrusive wrongs
Obscure with malice keen
Some timid heart, which only longs
To live and die unseen.

THE KISS.

Grow to my lip, thou sacred kiss,
On which my soul's beloved swore
That there should come a time of bliss,
When she would mock my hopes no more.
And fancy shall thy glow renew,
In sighs at morn, and dreams at night,
And none shall steal thy holy dew
Till thou 'rt absolved by rapture's rite.
Sweet hours, that are to make me blest,
Fly, swift as breezes, to the goal,
And let my love, my more than soul,
Come blushing to this ardent breast.
Then, while in every glance I drink
The rich o'erflowings of her mind,
Oh! let her all-enamour'd sink
In sweet abandonment resign'd,
Blushing for all our struggles past,
And murmuring, "I am thine at last!"

SONG.

Think on that look whose melting ray
For one sweet moment mix'd with mine,
And for that moment seem'd to say,
"I dare not, or I would be thine!"

Think on thy every smile and glance,
On all thou hast to charm and move;
And then forgive my bosom's trance,
Nor tell me it is sin to love.

Oh, *not* to love thee were the sin;
For sure, if Fate's decrees be done,
Thou, thou art destined still to win,
As I am destined to be won!

THE CATALOGUE.

"Come, tell me," says Rosa, as kissing and kiss'd,
One day she reclined on my breast;
"Come, tell me the number, repeat me the list,
"Of the nymphs you have loved and caress'd."—
Oh Rosa! 't was only my fancy that roved,
My heart at the moment was free;
But I 'll tell thee, my girl, how many I 've loved,
And the number shall finish with thee.

My tutor was Kitty; in infancy wild
She taught me the way to be blest;
She taught me to love her,—I loved like a child,
But Kitty could fancy the rest.
This lesson of dear and enrapturing lore
I have never forgot, I allow;
I have had it *by rote* very often before,
But never *by heart* until now.

Pretty Martha was next, and my soul was all flame,
But my head was so full of romance,
That I fancied her into some chivalry dame,
And I was her knight of the lance.
But Martha was not of this fanciful school,
And she laugh'd at her poor little knight;
While I thought her a goddess, she thought me a fool,
And I 'll swear *she* was most in the right.

My soul was now calm, till, by Cloris's looks,
Again I was tempted to rove;
But Cloris, I found, was so learned in books
That she gave me more logic than love.
So I left this young Sappho, and hasten'd to fly
To those sweeter logicians in bliss,
Who argue the point with a soul-telling eye,
And convince us at once with a kiss.

Oh! Susan was then all the world unto me,
But Susan was piously given;
And the worst of it was, we could never agree
On the road that was shortest to heaven.

"Oh, Susan!" I've said, in the moments of mirth,
  "What's devotion to thee or to me?
I devoutly believe there's a heaven on earth,
  And believe that that heaven's in *thee!*"

————

TO . . . .

*Moria pur quando vuol, non è bisogna mutar nè faccia
nè voce per esser un angelo."*(1)

Die when you will, you need not wear
  At Heaven's Court a form more fair
    Than Beauty here on earth has given;
Keep but the lovely looks we see—
The voice we hear—and you will be
  An angel *ready-made* for Heaven!

————

IMITATION OF CATULLUS. (2)

TO HIMSELF.

"Miser Catulle, desinas ineptire," etc.

Cease the sighing fool to play;
Cease to trifle life away;
Nor vainly think those joys thine own,
Which all, alas, have falsely flown.
What hours, Catullus, once were thine,
How fairly seem'd thy day to shine,
When lightly thou didst fly to meet
The girl whose smile was then so sweet—
The girl thou lovedst with fonder pain
Than e'er thy heart can feel again.

Ye met—your souls seem'd all in one,
Like tapers that commingling shone; (3)
Thy heart was warm enough for both,
And hers, in truth, was nothing loth.

Such were the hours that once were thine;
But, ah! those hours no longer shine.
For now the nymph delights no more
In what she loved so much before;
And all Catullus now can do,
Is to be proud and frigid too;
Nor follow where the wanton flies,
Nor sue the bliss that she denies.
False maid! he bids farewell to thee,
To love, and all love's misery;
The heyday of his heart is o'er,
Nor will he court one favour more. (4)

Fly, perjured girl!—but whither fly?
Who now will praise thy cheek and eye?

Who now will drink the syren tone
Which tells him thou art all his own?(5)
Oh, none :—and he who loved before
Can never, never love thee more.

————

"Neither do I condemn thee; go, and sin no more!"
                    St. John, chap. viii.

Oh woman, if through sinful wile
  Thy soul hath stray'd from honour's track,
'T is mercy only can beguile,
  By gentle ways, the wanderer back.

The stain that on thy virtue lies,
  Wash'd by those tears, not long will stay;
As clouds that sully morning skies
  May all be wept in showers away.

Go, go, be innocent,—and live;
  The tongues of men may wound thee sore;
But Heaven in pity can forgive,
  And bids thee "go, and sin no more!"

————

NONSENSE.

Good reader! if you e'er have seen,
  When Phœbus hastens to his pillow,
The mermaids, with their tresses green,
  Dancing upon the western billow:
If you have seen, at twilight dim,
  When the lone spirit's vesper hymn
Floats wild along the winding shore;
If you have seen, through mist of eve,
The fairy train their ringlets weave,
Glancing along the spangled green :—
  If you have seen all this, and more,
God bless me, what a deal you've seen!

————

EPIGRAM,

FROM THE FRENCH.

"I never give a kiss (says Prue),
  "To naughty man, for I abhor it."
She will not *give* a kiss, 't is true;
  She'll *take* one though, and thank you for it.

————

ON A SQUINTING POETESS.

To no *one* Muse does she her glance confine,
But has an eye, at once, to *all* the Nine!

(1) The words addressed by Lord Herbert of Cherbury
to a beautiful Nun at Murano.—*See his Life.*

(2) The following note existed in previous editions :—
Few poets knew better than Catullus what a French writer calls
———— la délicatesse
    D'un voluptueux sentiment;
but his passions too often obscured his imagination.—P. E.

(3) This line has been changed from—
    Sweet little sports were said and done.—P. E.

(4) Four lines of the original poem are here suppressed :
they were—

> But soon he'll see thee droop thy head,
> Doom'd to a lone and loveless bed,
> When none will seek the happy night,
> Or come to traffic in delight!—P. E.

(5) Another elision occurs in this place :—

> Who now will court thy wild delights,
> Thy honey kiss, and turtle bites?—P. E.

TO ROSA.

"A far conserva, e cumulo d'amanti."—*Past. Fido.*

AND are you then a thing of art,
   Seducing all, and loving none?
And have I strove to gain a heart
   Which every coxcomb thinks his own?(1)

Tell me at once if this be true,
   And I will calm my jealous breast;
Will learn to join the dangling crew,
   And share your simpers with the rest.

But if your heart be *not* so free,—
   Oh! if another share that heart,
Tell not the hateful tale to me,
   But mingle mercy with your art.

I'd rather think you "false as hell,"
   Than find you to be all divine,—
Than know that heart could love so well,
   Yet know that heart would *not* be mine!

————

TO PHILLIS.

PHILLIS, you little rosy rake,
   That heart of yours I long to rifle:
Come, give it me, and do not to make
   So much ado about a *trifle!*

————

TO A LADY,

ON HER SINGING.

THY song has taught my heart to feel
   Those soothing thoughts of heavenly love,
Which o'er the sainted spirits steal
   When listening to the spheres above!

When, tired of life and misery,
   I wish to sigh my latest breath,
Oh, Emma! I will fly to thee,
   And thou shalt sing me into death.

And if along thy lip and cheek
   That smile of heavenly softness play,
Which,—ah! forgive a mind that's weak,—
   So oft has stolen my mind away;

Thou 'lt seem an angel of the sky,
   That comes to charm me into bliss;
I 'll gaze and die—who would not die,
   If death were half so sweet as this?

(1) The two following verses have been here suppress-
ed:—

   And do you, like the dotard's fire,
      Which powerless of enjoying any,
   Feeds its abortive sick desire
      By trifling impotent with many?

SONG.

ON THE BIRTHDAY OF MRS. ——

WRITTEN IN IRELAND, 1799.

OF all my happiest hours of joy,
   And even I have had my measure,
When hearts were full, and every eye
   Hath kindled with the light of pleasure,
An hour like this I ne'er was given,
   So full of friendship's purest blisses;
Young Love himself looks down from heaven,
   To smile on such a day as this is.
      Then come, my friends, this hour improve,
         Let's feel as if we ne'er could sever;
      And may the birth of her we love
         Be thus with joy remember'd ever!

Oh! banish every thought to-night,
   Which could disturb our soul's communion;
Abandon'd thus to dear delight,
   We 'll even for once forget the Union!
On that let statesmen try their powers,
   And tremble o'er the rights they 'd die for;
The union of the soul be ours,
   And every union else we sigh for.
         Then come, my friends, etc.

In every eye around I mark
   The feelings of the heart o'erflowing;
From every soul I catch the spark
   Of sympathy, in friendship glowing.
Oh! could such moments ever fly;
   Oh! that we ne'er were doom'd to lose 'em;
And all as bright as Charlotte's eye,
   And all as pure as Charlotte's bosom.
         Then come, my friends, etc.

For me, whate'er my span of years,
   Whatever sun may light my roving;
Whether I waste my life in tears,
   Or live, as now, for mirth and loving;
This day shall come with aspect kind,
   Wherever fate may cast your rover;
He 'll think of those he left behind,
   And drink a health to bliss that 's over!
         Then come, my friends, etc.

————

SONG. (2)

MARY, I believed thee true,
   And I was blest in thus believing;
But now I mourn that e'er I knew
   A girl so fair and so deceiving.
      Fare thee well.

   Do you thus seek to flirt a number,
      And through a round of danglers run,
   Because your heart's insipid slumber
      Could never wake to *feel* for *one?*

(2) These words were written to the pathetic Scotch
air "Galla Water."

Few have ever loved like me,—
  Yes, I have loved thee too sincerely!
And few have e'er deceived like thee,—
  Alas! deceived me too severely.

Fare thee well!—yet think awhile
  On one whose bosom bleeds to doubt thee;
Who now would rather trust that smile,
  And die with thee, than live without thee.

Fare thee well! I 'll think of thee,
  Thou leavest me many a bitter token ;
For see, distracting woman, see,
  My peace is gone, my heart is broken !—
    Fare thee well !

————○○○————

MORALITY.

A FAMILIAR EPISTLE.

ADDRESSED TO J. AT—NS—N, ESQ. M. R. I. A. (1)

THOUGH long at school and college, dosing
O'er books of verse and books of prosing,
And copying from their moral pages
Fine recipes for making sages ;
Though long with those divines at school,
Who think to make us good by rule ;
Who, in methodic forms advancing,
Teaching morality like dancing,
Tell us, for Heaven or money's sake,
What *steps* we are through life to take :
Though thus, my friend, so long employ'd,
With so much midnight oil destroy'd,
I must confess, my searches past,
I 've only learn'd to *doubt* at last.
I find the doctors and the sages
Have differ'd in all climes and ages,
And two in fifty scarce agree
On what is pure morality.
'T is like the rainbow's shifting zone,
And every vision makes its own.

The doctors of the Porch advise,
As modes of being great and wise,
That we should cease to own or know
The luxuries that from feeling flow :—
Reason alone must claim direction,
And Apathy 's the soul's perfection.
Like a dull lake the heart must lie,
Nor passion's gale nor pleasure's sigh,
Though Heaven the breeze, the breath, supplied,
Must curl the wave or swell the tide !"

Such was the rigid Zeno's plan
To form his philosophic man ;
Such were the modes *he* taught mankind
To weed the garden of the mind;

They tore from thence some weeds, 't is true,
But all the flowers were ravaged too!

Now listen to the wily strains,
Which, on Cyrene's sandy plains,
When Pleasure, nymph with loosen'd zone.
Usurp'd the philosophic throne,—
Hear what the courtly sage's (2) tongue
To his surrounding pupils sung :—
" Pleasure 's the only noble end
To which all human powers should tend,
And Virtue gives her heavenly lore,
But to make Pleasure please us more.
Wisdom and she were both design'd
To make the senses more refined,
That man might revel, free from cloying,
Then most a sage when most enjoying!"

Is this morality?—Oh, no!
Even I a wiser path could show.
The flower within this vase confined,
The pure, the unfading flower of mind,
Must not throw all its sweets away
Upon a mortal mould of clay :
No, no,—its richest breath should rise
In virtue's incense to the skies.

But thus it is, all sects we see
Have watchwords of morality :
Some cry out Venus, others Jove ;
Here 't is Religion, there 't is Love.
But while they thus so widely wander,
While mystics dream, and doctors ponder;
And some, in dialectics firm,
Seek virtue in a middle term ;
While thus they strive, in Heaven's defiance,
To chain morality with science;
The plain good man, whose actions teach
More virtue than a sect can preach,
Pursues his course, unsagely blest,
His tutor whispering in his breast;
Nor could he act a purer part,
Though he had Tully all by heart.
And when he drops the tear on woe,
He little knows or cares to know
That Epictetus blamed that tear,
By Heaven approved, to virtue dear !

Oh! when I 've seen the morning beam
Floating within the dimpled stream ;
While Nature, wakening from the night,
Has just put on her robes of light,
Have I, with cold optician's gaze,
Explored the *doctrine* of those rays?
No, pedants, I have left to you
Nicely to separate hue from hue.

(1) Mr. Atkinson, to whom this poem is addressed, is the author of some esteemed works, and was Mr. Moore's particular friend : it was said of him that he was one in whom "the elements were so mixed," that neither in his head nor his heart had nature left any deficiency.—P. E.

(2) Aristippus.

Go, give that moment up to art,
When Heaven and nature claim the heart;
And, dull to all their best attraction,
Go—measure *angles of refraction.*
While I, in feeling's sweet romance,
Look on each daybeam as a glance
From the great eye of Him above,
Wakening his world with looks of love!

—o♦♦o—

THE TELL-TALE LYRE.

I 've heard, there was in ancient days
A Lyre of most melodious spell;
'T was heaven to hear its fairy lays,
If half be true that legends tell.

'T was play'd on by the gentlest sighs,
And to their breath it breathed again
In such entrancing melodies
As ear had never drunk till then!

Not harmony's serenest touch
So stilly could the notes prolong;
They were not heavenly song so much
As they were dreams of heavenly song!

If sad the heart, whose murmuring air
Along the chords in languor stole,
The numbers it awaken'd there
Were eloquence from pity's soul.

Or if the sigh, serene and light,
Was but the breath of fancied woes,
The string, that felt its airy flight,
Soon whisper'd it to kind repose.

And when young lovers talk'd alone,
If, 'mid their bliss that Lyre was near,
It made their accents all its own,
And sent forth notes that heaven might hear.

There was a nymph, who long had loved,
But dared not tell the world how well:
The shades, where she at evening roved,
Alone could know, alone could tell.

'T was there, at twilight time, she stole,
When the first star announced the night,—
With him who claim'd her inmost soul,
To wander by that soothing light.(1)

It chanced that, in the fairy bower
Where blest they woo'd each other's smile,

(1) This verse is altered from—
   'T was there, at twilight time, she stole,
     So oft, to make the dear one bless'd,
   Whom love had given her virgin soul,
     And nature soon gave all the rest!—P. E.
(2) The place of this quatrain was formerly occupied by—
   Here, as thy lover dries the tear
     Yet warm from life's malignant wrongs,

This Lyre, of strange and magic power,
Hung whispering o'er their heads the while.

And as, with eyes commingling fire,
They listen'd to each other's vow,
The youth full oft would make the Lyre
A pillow for the maiden's brow:

And while the melting words she breathed
Were by its echoes wafted round,
Her locks had with the chords so wreathed,
One knew not which gave forth the sound.

Alas, their hearts but little thought,
While thus they talk'd the hours away,
That every sound the Lyre was taught
Would linger long, and long betray.

So mingled with its tuneful soul
Were all their tender murmurs grown,
That other sighs unanswer'd stole,
Nor words it breathed but theirs alone.

Unhappy nymph! thy name was sung
To every breeze that wander'd by;
The secrets of thy gentle tongue
Were breathed in song to earth and sky.

The fatal Lyre, by Envy's hand
Hung high amid the whispering groves,
To every gale by which 't was fann'd,
Proclaim'd the mystery of your loves.

Nor long thus rudely was thy name
To earth's derisive echoes given;
Some pitying spirit downward came,
And took the Lyre and thee to heaven.

There, freed from earth's unholy wrongs,
Both happy in Love's home shall be;
Thou, uttering nought but seraph songs,
And that sweet Lyre still echoing thee!(2)

—o♦♦o—

PEACE AND GLORY.
WRITTEN ON THE APPROACH OF WAR.

WHERE is now the smile, that lighten'd
  Every hero's couch of rest?
Where is now the hope, that brighten'd
  Honour's eye and Pity's breast?

Have we lost the wreath we braided
  For our weary warrior men?

Within his arms thou lovest to hear
  The luckless lyre's remember'd songs.

Still do your happy souls attune
  The notes it learn'd on earth to move;
Still breathing o'er the chords, commune
  In sympathies of angel love!

Is the faithless olive faded?
  Must the bay be pluck'd again?

Passing hour of sunny weather,
  Lovely, in your light awhile,
Peace and Glory, wed together,
  Wander'd through our blessed isle.
And the eyes of Peace would glisten,
  Dewy as a morning sun,
When the timid maid would listen
  To the deeds her chief had done.

Is their hour of dalliance over?
  Must the maiden's trembling feet
Waft her from her warlike lover
  To the desert's still retreat?
Fare you well! with sighs we banish
  Nymph so fair and guests so bright;
Yet the smile, with which you vanish,
  Leaves behind a soothing light;—

Soothing light, that long shall sparkle
  O'er your warrior's sanguined way,
Through the field where horrors darkle,
  Shedding hope's consoling ray.
Long the smile his heart will cherish,
  To its absent idol true;
While around him myriads perish,
  Glory still will sigh for you!

SONG.

Take back the sigh thy lips of art
  In passion's moment breathed to me;
Yet, no—it must not, will not part,
  'T is now the life-breath of my heart,
And has become too pure for thee.

Take back the kiss, that faithless sigh
  With all the warmth of truth imprest;
Yet, no—the fatal kiss may lie,
Upon *thy* lip its sweets would die,
  Or bloom to make a rival blest.

Take back the vows that, night and day,
  My heart received, I thought from thine:
Yet, no—allow them still to stay,
They might some other heart betray,
  As sweetly as they've ruin'd mine.

LOVE AND REASON.

"Quand l'homme commence à raisonner, il cesse de
sentir."—*J. J. Rousseau.*(1)

'T was in the summer time so sweet,
  When hearts and flowers are both in season,
That—who, of all the world, should meet,
  One early dawn, but Love and Reason;

(1) Quoted somewhere in St. Pierre's *Étude de la Nature.*

Love told his dream of yesternight,
  While Reason talk'd about the weather;
The morn, in sooth, was fair and bright,
  And on they took their way together.

The boy in many a gambol flew,
  While Reason, like a Juno, stalk'd,
And from her portly figure threw
  A lengthen'd shadow, as she walk'd.

No wonder Love, as on they pass'd,
  Should find that sunny morning chill,
For still the shadow Reason cast
  Fell o'er the boy, and cool'd him still,

In vain he tried his wings to warm,
  Or find a pathway not so dim,
For still the maid's gigantic form
  Would stalk between the sun and him.

"This must not be," said little Love—
  "The sun was made for more than you."
So, turning through a myrtle grove,
  He bid the portly nymph adieu.

Now gaily roves the laughing boy
  O'er many a mead, by many a stream;
In every breeze inhaling joy,
  And drinking bliss in every beam.

From all the gardens, all the bowers,
  He cull'd the many sweets they shaded,
And ate the fruits and smell'd the flowers,
  Till taste was gone and odour faded.

But now the sun, in pomp of noon,
  Look'd blazing o'er the sultry plains;
Alas! the boy grew languid soon,
  And fever thrill'd through all his veins.

The dew forsook his baby brow,
  No more with healthy bloom he smiled—
Oh! where was tranquil Reason now,
  To cast her shadow o'er the child?

Beneath a green and aged palm,
  His foot at length for shelter turning,
He saw the nymph reclining calm,
  With brow as cool as his was burning.

"Oh! take me to that bosom cold,"
  In murmurs at her feet he said;
And Reason oped her garment's fold,
  And flung it round his fever'd head.

He felt her bosom's icy touch,
  And soon it lull'd his pulse to rest;
For, ah! the chill was quite too much,
  And Love expired on Reason's breast!

Nay, do not weep, my Fanny dear;
While in these arms you lie,
This world hath not a wish, a fear,
That ought to cost that eye a tear,
    That heart, one single sigh.

The world!—ah, Fanny, Love must shun
The paths were many rove;
One bosom to recline upon,
One heart to be his only one,
    Are quite enough for Love.

What can we wish, that is not here
Between your arms and mine?
Is there, on earth, a space so dear
As that within the happy sphere
    Two loving arms entwine?

For me, there's not a lock of jet
Adown your temples curl'd,
Within whose glossy tangling net,
My soul doth not, at once, forget
    All, all this worthless world.

'T is in those eyes, so full of love,
My only worlds I see;
Let but *their* orbs in sunshine move,
And earth below and skies above
    May frown or smile for me.

———o♢♢o———

ASPASIA.

'T was in the fair Aspasia's bower,
That Love and Learning, many an hour,
In dalliance met; and learning smiled
With pleasure on the playful child,
Who often stole, to find a nest
Within the folds of Learning's vest.

There, as the listening statesman hung
In transport on Aspasia's tongue,
The destinies of Athens took
Their colour from Aspasia's look,
Oh happy time, when laws of state,
When all that ruled the country's fate,
Its glory, quiet, or alarms,
Was plann'd between two snow-white arms!

(1) Changed from—

    While lips are balm and looks are flame.—P. E.

(2) It was imagined by some of the ancients that there is
an ethereal ocean above us, and that the sun and moon are
two floating luminous islands, in which the spirits of the
blest reside. Accordingly we find that the word Ωκεανος
was sometimes synonymous with αηρ, and death was not
unfrequently called Ωκεανοιο πορος, or "the passage of
the ocean."

(3) Eunapius, in his life of Iamblichus, tells us of two

Blest times! they could not always last—
And yet, even now they are not past.
Though we have lost the giant mould,
In which their men were cast of old,
Woman, dear woman, still the same,
While beauty breathes through soul or frame, (1)
While man possesses heart or eyes,
Woman's bright empire never dies!

No, Fanny, love, they ne'er shall say,
That beauty's charm hath pass'd away;
Give but the universe a soul
Attuned to woman's soft control,
And Fanny hath the charm, the skill,
To wield a universe at will.

———o♢♢o———

THE GRECIAN GIRL'S DREAM
OF THE BLESSED ISLANDS. (2)
TO HER LOVER.

—ἠχι τε καλος
Πυθαγορης, ὁσσοι τε χορον στηριξαν ερωτος.
    Απολλων περι Πλωτινου.   Oracul. Metric. a
                            Joan. Opsop. collecta.

Was it the moon, or was it morning's ray,
That call'd thee, dearest, from these arms away?
Scarce had'st thou left me, when a dream of night
Came o'er my spirit so distinct and bright,
That, while I yet can vividly recall
Its witching wonders, thou shalt hear them all.
Methought I saw, upon the lunar beam,
Two winged boys, such as thy muse might dream,
Descending from above, at that still hour,
And gliding, with smooth step, into my bower.
Fair as the beauteous spirits that, all day,
In Amatha's warm founts imprison'd stay, (3)
But rise at midnight, from the enchanted rill,
To cool their plumes upon some moonlit hill.

At once I knew their mission;—'t was to bear
My spirit upward, through the paths of air,
To that elysian realm, from whence stray beams
So oft, in sleep, had visited my dreams.
Swift at their touch dissolved the ties, that clung
All earthly round me, and aloft I sprung;
While, heavenward guides, the little genii flew
Thro' paths of light, refresh'd by heaven's own dew,

beautiful little spirits or loves, which Iamblichus raised
by enchantment from the warm springs at Gadara; "di-
cens astantibus (says the author of the *Dii Fatidici*, p. 160,
illos esse loci Genios:" which words, however, are not
in Eunapius.

I find from Cellarius, that Amatha, in the neighbourhood
of Gadara, was also celebrated for its warm springs, and
I have preferred it as a more poetical name than Gadara.
Cellarius quotes Hieronymus. "Est et alia villa in vicinia
Gadarae nomine Amatha, ubi calidae aquae erumpunt."—
Geograph. Antiq., lib. iii., cap. 13.

And fann'd by airs still fragrant with the breath
Of cloudless climes and worlds that know not death.

Thou know'st that, far beyond our nether sky,
And shown but dimly to man's erring eye,
A mighty ocean of blue ether rolls, (1)
Gemm'd with bright islands, where the chosen
   souls,
Who 've pass'd in lore and love their earthly hours,
Repose for ever in unfading bowers.
That very moon, whose solitary light
So often guides thee to my bower at night,
Is no chill planet, but an isle of love,
Floating in splendour through those seas above,
And peopled with bright forms, aërial grown,
Nor knowing aught of earth but love alone.
Thither, I thought, we wing'd our airy way:—
Mild o'er its valleys stream'd a silvery day,
While, all around, on lily beds of rest,
Reclined the spirits of the immortal Blest. (2)
Oh! there I met those few congenial maids,
Whom love hath warm'd, in philosophic shades;
There still Leontium,(3) on her sage's breast,
Found lore and love, was tutor'd and carest ;.
And there the clasp of Pythias'(4) gentle arms
Repald the zeal which deified her charms.

(1) This belief of an ocean in the heavens, or "waters above the firmament," was one of the many physical errors in which the early fathers bewildered themselves. Le P. Baltus, in his *Défenses des Saints Pères accusés de Platonisme*, taking it for granted that the ancients were more correct in their notions (which by no means appears from what I have already quoted), adduces the obstinacy of the fathers, in this whimsical opinion, as a proof of their repugnance to even truth from the hands of the philosophers. This is a strange way of defending the fathers, and attributes much more than they deserve to the philosophers. For an abstract of this work of Baltus (the opposer of Fontenelle, Van Dale, etc., in the famous Oracle controversy), see *Bibliothèque des Auteurs ecclésiast., du* XVIIIe *siècle*, part 1., tom. ii."

(2) There were various opinions among the ancients with respect to their lunar establishment; some made it an elysium, and others a purgatory; while some supposed it to be a kind of *entrepôt* between heaven and earth, where souls which had left their bodies, and those that were on their way to join them, were deposited in the valleys of Hecate, and remained till further orders. Τοις περι σεληνην αερι λεγειν αυτας κατοικειν, και απ' αυτης κατω χωρειν εις την περιγειον γενεσιν.—*Stob.* lib. i., Eclog. Physic.

(3) The pupil and mistress of Epicurus, who called her his "dear little Leontium" (Δεοντιριον), as appears by a fragment of one of his letters in Laertius. This Leontium was a woman of talent; "she had the impudence (says Cicero) to write against Theophrastus ;" and Cicero at the same time gives her a name which is neither polite nor translatable. "Meretricula etiam Leontium contra Theophrastum scribere ausa est."—*De Natur. Deor.* She left a daughter called Danae, who was just as rigid an Epicurean as her mother; something like Wieland's Danae in Agathon.

The Attic Master,(5) in Aspasia's eyes,
Forgot the yoke of less endearing ties,
While fair Theano,(6) innocently fair,
Wreathed playfully her Samian's flowing hair ;(7)
Whose soul now fix'd, its transmigrations past,
Found in those arms a resting-place, at last;
And smiling own'd, whate'er his dreamy thought
In mystic numbers long had vainly sought,
The One that's form'd of Two whom love hath bound
Is the best number gods or men e'er found.

But think, my Theon, with what joy I thrill'd,
When near a fount, which through the valley rill'd,
My fancy's eye beheld a form recline,
Of lunar race, but so resembling thine
That, oh! 't was but fidelity in me,
To fly, to clasp, and worship it for thee.
No aid of words the unbodied soul requires,
To waft a wish or embassy desires;
But by a power, to spirits only given,
A deep mute impulse, only felt in heaven,
Swifter than meteor shaft through summer skies,
From soul to soul the glanced idea flies.

Oh, my beloved, how divinely sweet
Is the pure joy, when kindred spirits meet!

It would sound much better, 1 think, if the name were Leontia, as it occurs the first time in Laertius ; but M. Ménage will not hear of this reading.

(4) Pythias was a woman whom Aristotle loved, and to whom after her death he paid divine honours, solemnising her memory by the same sacrifices which the Athenians offered to the Goddess Ceres. For this impious gallantry the philosopher was, of course, censured; but it would be well if certain of our modern Stagyrites showed a little of this superstition about the memory of their mistresses.

(5) Socrates, who used to console himself in the society of Aspasia for those "less endearing ties" which he found at home with Xantippe. For an account of this extraordinary creature, Aspasia, and her school of erudite luxury at Athens, see *L'Histoire de l'Académie*, etc., tom. XXXI., p. 69. Ségur rather fails on the inspiring subject of Aspasia.—*Les Femmes*, tom. i., p. 122.

The Author of the *Voyage du Monde de Descartes*, has also placed these philosophers in the moon, and has allotted seigneuries to them, as well as to the astronomers (part ii., p. 143); but he ought not to have forgotten their wives and mistresses; "curæ non ipsâ in morte relinquunt."

(6) There are some sensible letters extant under the name of this fair Pythagorean. They are addressed to her female friends upon the education of children, the treatment of servants, etc. One, in particular, to Nicostrata, whose husband had given her reasons for jealousy, contains such truly considerate and rational advice, that it ought to be translated for the edification of all married ladies. See Gale's *Opuscul. Myth. Phys.*, p. 741.

(7) Pythagoras was remarkable for fine hair, and Doctor Thiers (in his *Histoire des Perruques*) seems to take for granted it was all his own ; as he has not mentioned him among those ancients who were obliged to have recourse to the "coma apposititia." *L'Histoire des Perruques*, chap. i.

Like him, the river-god,(1) whose waters flow,
With love their only light, through caves below,
Wafting in triumph all the flowery braids,
And festal rings, with which Olympic maids
Have deck'd his current, as an offering meet
To lay at Arethusa's shining feet.
Think, when he meets at last his fountain-bride,
What perfect love must thrill the blended tide!
Each lost in each, till, mingling into one,
Their lot the same for shadow or for sun,
A type of true love, to the deep they run.
'T was thus—

(1) The river Alpheus, which flowed by Pisa or Olympia,
and into which it was customary to throw offerings of
different kinds, during the celebration of the Olympic
games. In the pretty romance of *Clitophon and Leucippe*,
the river is supposed to carry these offerings as bridal gifts
to the fountain Arethusa. Και επι την Αρεθουσαν ούτω
του Αλφειου νυμφοστολει· όταν ουν ή των ολυμπιων
εορτη, χ. τ. λ. Lib. i.

(2) The changes effected in this poem are at once so
numerous and important, that, instead of attempting to
particularise them, we deem it more expedient to reprint
the original here, leaving it to the reader to remark how
carefully Mr. Moore has excluded every epithet and line
which, at a former period, it is probable he esteemed, if
not the best, at least the most likely to catch the warm
fancy of youth, in the production:—

    Was it the moon, or was it morning's ray,
    That call'd thee, dearest, from these arms away!
    I linger'd still, in all the murmuring rest,
    The languor of a soul too richly blest!
    Upon my breath thy sigh yet faintly hung;
    Thy name yet died in whispers o'er my tongue;
    I heard thy lyre, which thou hadst left behind,
    In amorous converse with the breathing wind;
    Quick to my heart I press'd the shell divine,
    And, with a lip yet glowing warm from thine,
    I kiss'd its every chord, while every kiss
    Shed o'er the chord some dewy print of bliss.
    Then soft to thee I touch'd the fervid lyre,
    Which told such melodies, such notes of fire,
    As none but chords that drank the burning dews
    Of kisses dear as ours could e'er diffuse!
    Oh love! how blissful is the bland repose
    That soothing follows upon rapture's close,
    Like a soft twilight, o'er the mind to shed
    Mild melting traces of the transport fled!

    While thus I lay, in this voluptuous calm,
    A drowsy languor sleep'd my eyes in balm;
    Upon my lap the lyre in murmurs fell,
    While, faintly wandering o'er its silver shell,
    My fingers soon their own sweet requiem play'd,
    And slept in music which themselves had made!
    Then, then, my Theon, what a heavenly dream!
    I saw two spirits on the lunar beam,
    Two winged boys, descending from above,
    And gliding to my bower with looks of love,
    Like the young genii, who repose their wings
    All day in Amatha's luxurious springs,
    And rise at midnight, from the tepid rill,
    To cool their plumes upon some moon-lit hill!
    Soft o'er my brow, which kindled with their sighs,
    Awhile they play'd; then gliding through my eyes
    (Where the bright babies, for a moment, hung,
    Like those thy lip hath kiss'd, thy lyre hath sung),
    To that dim mansion of my breast they stole,
    Where, wreathed in blisses, lay my captive soul.
    Swift at their touch dissolved the ties that clung
    So sweetly round her, and aloft she sprung!

But, Theon, 't is an endless theme,
And thou grow'st weary of my half-told dream.
Oh would, my love, we were together now,
And I would woo sweet patience to thy brow,
And make thee smile at all the magic tales
Of star-lit bowers and planetary vales,
Which my fond soul, inspired by thee and love,
In slumber's loom hath fancifully wove.
But no; no more—soon as to-morrow's ray
O'er soft Ilissus shall have died away,
I 'll come, and, while love's planet in the west
Shines o'er our meeting, tell thee all the rest.(2)

    Exulting guides, the little genii flew
    Through paths of light, refresh'd with starry dew,
    And fann'd by airs of that ambrosial breath,
    On which the free soul banquets after death!

    Thou know'st, my love, beyond our clouded skies,
    As bards have dream'd, the spirits' kingdom lies.
    Through that fair clime a sea of ether rolls,
    Gemm'd with bright islands, where the hallow'd souls,
    Whom life had wearied in its race of hours,
    Repose for ever in unfading bowers!
    That very orb, whose solitary light,
    So often guides thee to my arms at night,
    Is no child planet, but an isle of love,
    Floating in splendour through those seas above!
    Thither, I thought, we wing'd our airy way,
    Mild o'er its valleys stream'd a silvery day,
    While all around, on lily beds of rest,
    Reclined the spirits of the immortal Blest!
    Oh! there I met those few congenial maids,
    Whom love hath warm'd, in philosophic shades;
    There still Leontium, on her sage's breast,
    Found lore and love, was tutor'd and caress'd.
    And there the twine of Pythias' gentle arms
    Repaid the zeal which deified her charms!
    The Attic Master, in Aspasia's eyes,
    Forgot the toil of less endearing ties;
    While fair Theano, innocently fair,
    Play'd with the ringlets of her Samian's hair,
    Who, fix'd by love, at length was all her own,
    And pass'd his spirit through her lips alone!

    Oh Samian sage! whate'er thy glowing thought
    Of mystic Numbers hath divinely wrought,
    The One that 's form'd of two who dearly love
    Is the best number Heaven can boast above!

    But think, my Theon, how this soul was thrill'd,
    When near a fount, which o'er the vale distill'd,
    My fancy's eye beheld a form recline,
    Of lunar race, but so resembling thine,
    That, oh!—'t was but fidelity in me,
    To fly, to clasp, and worship it for thee!
    No aid of words the unbodied soul requires
    To waft a wish, or embassy desires;
    But, by a throb to spirits only given,
    By a mute impulse only felt in heaven,
    Swifter than meteor shaft through summer skies,
    From soul to soul the glanced idea flies!

    We met—like thee the youthful vision smiled;
    But not like thee, when passionately wild,
    Thou wakest the slumbering blushes of my cheek,
    By looking things thyself would blush to speak!
    No; 't was the tender intellectual smile,
    Flush'd with the past and yet serene the while,
    Of that delicious hour when, glowing yet,
    Thou yield'st to nature with a fond regret,
    And thy soul, waking from its wilder'd dream,
    Lights in thine eye a mellower, chaster beam!
    Oh my beloved! how divinely sweet
    Is the pure joy, when kindred spirits meet!

TO CLOE.

IMITATED FROM MARTIAL.

I COULD resign that eye of blue,
  Howe'er its splendour used to thrill me;
And even that cheek of roseate hue,—
  To lose it, Cloe, scarce would kill me.

That snowy neck I ne'er should miss,
  However much I 've raved about it;
And sweetly as that lip can kiss,
  I *think* I could exist without it.(1)

In short, so well I 've learn'd to fast,
  That, sooth my love, I know not whether
I might not bring myself at last
  To—do without you altogether.

———

THE WREATH AND THE CHAIN.

I BRING thee, love, a golden Chain,
  I bring thee too a flowery Wreath;
The gold shall never wear a stain,
  The flowerets long shall sweetly breathe.
Come, tell me which the tie shall be,
To bind thy gentle heart to me.

The Chain is form'd of golden threads,
  Bright as Minerva's yellow hair,
When the last beam of evening sheds
  Its calm and sober lustre there. (2)
The Wreath's of brightest myrtle wove,
  With sun-lit drops of bliss among it,
And many a rose-leaf, cull'd by Love,
  To heal his lip when bees have stung it.
Come, tell me which the tie shall be,
To bind thy gentle heart to me.

Yes, yes, I read that ready eye,
  Which answers when the tongue is loth,

Thou likest the form of either tie,
  And spread'st thy playful hands for both.
Ah!—if there were not something wrong,
  The world would see them blended oft;
The Chain would make the Wreath so strong!
  The Wreath would make the Chain so soft!
Then might the gold, the flowerets be
Sweet fetters for my love and me.

But, Fanny, so unblest they twine,
  That (heaven alone can tell the reason)
When mingled thus they cease to shine,
  Or shine but for a transient season.
Whether the Chain may press too much,
  Or that the Wreath is slightly braided,
Let but the gold the flowerets touch,
  And all their bloom, their glow is faded!(3)
Oh! better to be always free,
Than thus to bind my love to me.

The timid girl now hung her head,
  And, as she turn'd an upward glance,
I saw a doubt its twilight spread
  Across her brow's divine expanse.
Just then, the garland's brightest rose
  Gave one of its love-breathing sighs—
Oh! who can ask how Fanny chose,
  That ever look'd in Fanny's eyes?
" The Wreath, my life, the Wreath shall be
The tie to bind my soul to thee."

———

TO . . . .

AND hast thou mark'd the pensive shade,
  That many a time obscures my brow,
'Midst all the joys, beloved maid,
  Which thou canst give, and only thou?

Oh! 't is not that I then forget
  The bright looks that before me shine; (4)

(1) The first eight lines originally ran—

> I could resign that eye of blue,
>   Howe'er it burn, howe'er it thrill me;
> And, though your lip be rich with dew,
>   To lose it, Cloe, scarce would kill me.
>
> That snowy neck I ne'er should miss,
>   However warm I 've twined about it!
> And though your bosom beat with bliss,
>   I think my soul could live without it.—P. E.

(2) Changed from—

> The Chain is of a splendid thread,
>   Stolen from Minerva's yellow hair,
> Just when the setting sun had shed
>   The sober beam of evening there.—P. E.

(3) The following lines are here elided—

> Sweet Fanny, what would Rapture do,
>   When all her blooms had lost their grace?
> Might she not steal a rose or two
>   From other wreaths, to fill their place?—P. E.

(4) In former editions—

> The endearing charms that round me twine.—P. E.

The Elean god, whose faithful waters flow,
With love their only light, through caves below,
Wafting in triumph all the flowery braids,
And festal rings, with which Olympic maids
Have deck'd their billow, as an offering meet
To pour at Arethusa's crystal feet!
Think, when he mingles with his fountain-bride,
What perfect rapture thrills the blended tide!
Each melts in each, till one pervadin; kiss
Confounds their currents in a sea of bliss!
'T was thus—
                    But, Theon, 't is a weary theme,
And thou delight'st not in my lingering dream.
Oh! that our lips were, at this moment, near,
And I would kiss thee into patience, dear!
And make thee smile at all the magic tales
Of star-lit bowers and planetary vales,
Which my fond soul, inspired by thee and love,
In slumber's loom hath exquisitely wove,
But no; no more—soon as to-morrow's ray
O'er soft Ilissus shall dissolve away,
I 'll fly, my Theon, to thy burning breast,
And there in murmurs tell thee all the rest:
Then, if too weak, too cold the vision seems,
Thy lip shall teach me something more than dreams!—P. E.

For never throbb'd a bosom yet
  Could feel their witchery like mine.

When bashful on my bosom hid,
  And blushing to have felt so blest,
Thou dost but lift thy languid lid,
  Again to close it on my breast;—

Yes,—these are minutes all thine own,
  Thine own to give, and mine to feel;
Yet, even in them, my heart has known
  The sigh to rise, the tear to steal.

For I have thought of former hours,
  When he who first thy soul possess'd,
Like me awaked its witching powers,
  Like me was loved, like me was blest.

Upon *his* name thy murmuring tongue
  Perhaps hath all as sweetly dwelt;
Upon his words thine ear hath hung,
  With transport all as purely felt.(1)

For him—yet why the past recall,
  To damp and wither present bliss?
Thou 'rt now my own, heart, spirit, all,
  And heaven could grant no more than this!

Forgive me, dearest, oh! forgive;
  I would be first, be sole to thee:
Thou shouldst have but begun to live,
  The hour that gave thy heart to me.

Thy book of life till then effaced,
  Love should have kept that leaf alone
On which he first so brightly traced
  That thou wert, soul and all, my own.

TO . . . . . 'S PICTURE.

Go then, if she, whose shade thou art,
  No more will let thee soothe my pain;
Yet, tell her, it has cost this heart
  Some pangs, to give thee back again!

Tell her, the smile was not so dear
  With which she made thy semblance mine,

(1) Formerly—

> For him that snowy lid hath hung
> In ecstasy, as purely felt!—P. E.

(2) Love and Psyche are here considered as the active and passive principles of creation, and the universe is supposed to have received its first harmonising impulse from the nuptial sympathy between these two powers. A marriage is generally the first step in cosmogony. Timæus held Form to be the father, and Matter the mother of the world; Elion and Berouth, I think, are Sanchoniatho's first spiritual lovers, and Manco-Capac and his wife introduced creation amongst the Peruvians. In short,

As bitter is the burning tear
  With which I now the gift resign.

Yet go—and could she still restore,
  As some exchange for taking thee,
The tranquil look which first I wore,
  When her eyes found me calm and free;

Could she give back the careless flow,
  The spirit that my heart then knew—
Yet, no, 't is vain—go, picture, go—
  Smile at me once, and then—adieu!

FRAGMENT

OF A MYTHOLOGICAL HYMN TO LOVE. (2)

BLEST infant of eternity!
Before the day-star learn'd to move,
In pomp of fire, along his grand career,
Glancing the beamy shafts of light
From his rich quiver to the farthest sphere,
  Thou wert alone, oh Love!
Nestling beneath the wings of ancient Night,
  Whose horrors seem'd to smile in shadowing thee.

No form of beauty soothed thine eye,
  As through the dim expanse it wander'd wide;
No kindred spirit caught thy sigh,
  As o'er the watery waste it lingering died.

Unfelt the pulse, unknown the power,
  That latent in his heart was sleeping;—
Oh Sympathy! that lonely hour
  Saw Love himself thy absence weeping.

But look, what glory through the darkness beams!
Celestial airs along the water glide:—
What Spirit art thou, moving o'er the tide
  So beautiful? oh, not of earth,
But, in that glowing hour, the birth
Of the young Godhead's own creative dreams.(3)
    'T is she!
Psyche, the first-born spirit of the air.
  To thee, oh Love, she turns,
  On thee her eyebeam burns:
Blest hour, before all worlds ordain'd to be! (4)

Harlequin seems to have studied cosmogonies, when he said "tutto il mondo è fatto come la nostra famiglia."

(3) The preceding three lines have been substituted for,

> So lovely? art thou but the child
>   Of the young godhead's dreams,
> That mock his hope with fancies strange and wild?
>   Or were his tears, as quick they fell,
>   Collected in so bright a form,
>   Till, kindled by the ardent spell
>   Of his desiring eyes,
> They spring to life in shape so fair and warm?—P. E.

(4) Changed from—

> Blest hour of nuptial ecstasy.—P. E.

They meet—
The blooming god—the spirit fair—
Meet in communion sweet.

Now, Sympathy, the hour is thine;
All nature feels the thrill divine,
The veil of Chaos is withdrawn,
And their first kiss is great Creation's dawn!

———<small>○◆◇○</small>———

TO HIS SERENE HIGHNESS
THE DUKE OF MONTPENSIER,
ON HIS PORTRAIT OF THE LADY ADELAIDE FORBES.

Donington Park, 1802.

To catch the thought, by painting's spell,
    Howe'er remote, howe'er refined,
And o'er the kindling canvas tell
    The silent story of the mind;

O'er nature's form to glance the eye,
    And fix, by mimic light and shade,
Her morning tinges, ere they fly,
    Her evening blushes, ere they fade;—

Yes, these are Painting's proudest powers;
    The gift by which her art divine
Above all others proudly towers,—
    And these, oh Prince! are richly thine.(1)

And yet, when Friendship sees thee trace,
    In almost living truth exprest,
This bright memorial of a face
    On which her eye delights to rest;

(1) These four lines formerly read—

<small>These are the pencil's grandest theme,
Divinest of the powers divine
That light the Muse's flowery dream;
And these, oh Prince! are richly thine!—P. E.</small>

(2) Changed from—

<small>While o'er each line, so brightly true,
Her soul with fond attention roves,
Blessing the hand whose various hue
Could imitate the form it loves.—P. E.</small>

(3) Though I have styled this poem a Dithyrambic Ode, I cannot presume to say that it possesses, in any degree, the characteristics of that species of poetry. The nature of the ancient Dithyrambic is very imperfectly known. According to M. Burette, a licentious irregularity of metre, an extravagant research of thought and expression, and a rude embarrassed construction, are among its most distinguishing features; and in all these respects, I have but too closely, I fear, followed my models. Burette adds, "Ces caractères des dithyrambes se font sentir à ceux qui lisent attentivement les odes de Pindare."—*Mémoires de l'Acad.,* vol. x., p. 306. The same opinion may be collected from Schmidt's dissertation upon the subject. I think, however, if the dithyrambics of Pindar were in our possession, we should find that, however wild and fanciful, they were by no means the tasteless jargon they are represented, and that even their irregularity was what Boileau calls "un beau désordre." Chiabrera, who has been styled the Pindar of Italy, and from whom all its poetry upon the

While o'er the lovely look serene,
    The smile of peace, the bloom of youth,
The cheek that blushes to be seen,
    The eye that tells the bosom's truth;

While o'er each line, so brightly true,
    Our eyes with lingering pleasure rove,
Blessing the touch whose various hue
    Thus brings to mind the form we love;(2)

We feel the magic of thy art,
    And own it with a zest, a zeal,
A pleasure, nearer to the heart
    Than critic taste can *ever* feel.

———<small>○◆◇○</small>———

THE FALL OF HEBE.
A DITHYRAMBIC ODE. (3)

'T WAS on a day
When the immortals at their banquet lay;
    The bowl
    Sparkled with starry dew,
The weeping of those myriad urns of light,
    Within whose orbs, the almighty Power,
    At nature's dawning hour,
Stored the rich fluid of ethereal soul.(4)
    Around,
Soft odorous clouds, that upward wing their flight
    From eastern isles
(Where they have bathed them in the orient ray,
And with rich fragrance all their bosoms fill'd),
    In circles flew, and, melting as they flew,
A liquid daybreak o'er the board distill'd.

Greek model was called Chiabreresco (as Crescimbeni informs us, lib. i., cap. 12), has given, amongst his *Vendemmie,* a Dithyrambic, "all' uso de' Greci;" full of those compound epithets, which, we are told, were a chief characteristic of the style (συνθετους δε λεξιες εποιουν—*Suid.* Διθυραμβοδιδ.); such as—

<small>Briglindorato Pegaso
Nubicalpestator.</small>

But I cannot suppose that Pindar, even amidst all the licence of dithyrambics, would have descended to ballad-language like the following:—

<small>Bella Filli, e bella Clori,
Non più dar pregio a tue bellezze e taci,
Che se Bacco fa vezzi alle mie labbra
Fo le fiche a' vostri baci.
———————— esser vorrei Coppier,
E se troppo desiro
Deh fossi io Bottiglier.
Rime del Chiabrera, part. ii., p. 353.</small>

(4) This is a Platonic fancy. The philosopher supposes, in his Timæus, that, when the Deity had formed the soul of the world, he proceeded to the composition of other souls, in which process, says Plato, he made use of the same cup, though the ingredients he mingled were not quite so pure as for the former; and having refined the mixture with a little of his own essence, he distributed it among the stars, which served as reservoirs of the fluid.— Ταυτ' ειπε και παλιν επι τον προτερον κρατηρα εν ω την του παντος ψυχην κεραννυς εμισγε, κ. τ. λ.

All, all was luxury!
All *must* be luxury, where Lyæus smiles.
His locks divine
Were crown'd
With a bright meteor-braid,
Which, like an ever-springing wreath of vine,
Shot into brilliant leafy shapes,
And o'er his brow in lambent tendrils play'd:
While 'mid the foliage hung,
Like lucid grapes,
A thousand clustering buds of light,
Cull'd from the gardens of the galaxy.

Upon his bosom Cytherea's head
Lay lovely, as when first the Syrens sung
Her beauty's dawn,
And all the curtains of the deep, undrawn,
Reveal'd her sleeping in its azure bed.
The captive deity
Hung lingering on her eyes and lip,
With looks of ecstasy.
Now, on his arm,
In blushes she reposed,
And, while he gazed on each bright charm, (1)
To shade his burning eyes her hand in dalliance stole.

And now she raised her rosy mouth to sip
The nectar'd wave
Lyæus gave,
And from her eyelids, half-way closed,
Sent forth a melting gleam,
Which fell, like sun-dew, in the bowl:
While her bright hair, in mazy flow
Of gold descending
Adown her cheek's luxurious glow,
Hung o'er the goblet's side,
And was reflected in its crystal tide,
Like a bright crocus flower,
Whose sunny leaves, at evening hour

With roses of Cyrene blending, (2)
Hang o'er the mirror of some silvery stream.

The Olympian cup
Shone in the hands
Of dimpled Hebe, as she wing'd her feet
Up
The empyreal mount,
To drain the soul-drops at their stellar fount; (3)
And still
As the resplendent rill
Gush'd forth into the cup with mantling heat,
Her watchful care
Was still to cool its liquid fire
With snow-white sprinklings of that feathery air
The children of the Pole respire,
In those enchanted lands, (4)
Where life is all a spring, and north winds never blow.

But oh!
Bright Hebe, what a tear,
And what a blush were thine,
When, as the breath of every Grace
Wafted thy feet along the studded sphere,
With a bright cup for Jove himself to drink,
Some star, that shone beneath thy tread,
Raising its amorous head
To kiss those matchless feet,
Check'd thy career too fleet;
And all heaven's host of eyes
Entranced, but fearful all,
Saw thee, sweet Hebe, prostrate fall (5)
Upon the bright floor of the azure skies; (6)
Where, 'mid its stars, thy beauty lay,
As blossom, shaken from the spray
Of a spring thorn
Lies 'mid the liquid sparkles of the morn;
Or, as in temples of the Paphian shade,
The worshippers of Beauty's queen behold

(1) Changed from—
    And while her zone resign'd its every charm.—P. E.

(2) We learn from Theophrastus, that the roses of Cyrene were particularly fragrant.—Ευοσματα τα δε τα εν Κυρηνη ῥοδα.

(3 Heraclitus (Physicus) held the soul to be a spark of the stellar essence—"Scintilla stellaris essentiæ."—*Macrobius*, in *Somn. Scip.*, lib. i., cap. 14.

(4) The country of the Hyperboreans. These people were supposed to be placed so far north, that the north wind could not affect them; they lived longer than any other mortals; passed their whole time in music and dancing, etc., etc. But the most extravagant fiction related of them is that to which the two lines preceding allude. It was imagined that, instead of our vulgar atmosphere, the Hyperboreans breathed nothing but feathers! According to Herodotus and Pliny, this idea was suggested by the quantity of snow which was observed to fall in those regions; thus the former: Τα ὡν πτερα εικαδοντας την χιονα τους Σκυθας; τε και τους περιοικους δοκεω λεγειν.

—*Herodot.*, lib. iv., cap. 31. Ovid tells the fable otherwise: see *Metamorph.*, lib. xv.

Mr. O'Halloran, and some other Irish Antiquarians, have been at great expense of learning to prove that the strange country, where they took snow for feathers, was Ireland, and that the famous Abaris was an Irish Druid. Mr. Row land, however, will have it that Abaris was a Welshman, and that his name is only a corruption of Ap Rees!

(5) This and the following line are changed from—
    Saw those luxuriant beauties sink,
  In lapse of loveliness, along the azure skies!—P. E.

(6. It is Servius, I believe, who mentions this unlucky trip which Hebe made in her occupation of cup-bearer; and Hoffman tells it after him: "Cum Hebe pocula Jovi admi nistrans, perque lubricum minus caute incedens, cecidis set," etc.*

* This note was formerly continued thus:—"Revolutisque vesti- bus"—in short, she fell in a very awkward manner, and though (as the Encyclopédistes think) it would have amused Jove at any other time, yet, as he happened to be out of temper on that day, the poor girl was dismissed from her employment.—P. E.

An image of their rosy idol, laid
Upon a diamond shrine.

The wanton wind,
Which had pursued the flying fair,
And sported 'mid the tresses unconfined
Of her bright hair,
Now, as she fell,—oh wanton breeze!
Ruffled the robe, whose graceful flow
Hung o'er those limbs of unsunn'd snow, (1)
Purely as the Eleusinian veil
Hangs o'er the Mysteries!(2)

The brow of Juno flush'd—
Love bless'd the breeze!
The Muses blush'd ;
And every cheek was hid behind a lyre,
While every eye looked laughing through the
strings.

But the bright cup? the nectar'd draught
Which Jove himself was to have quaff'd?
Alas, alas, upturn'd it lay
By the fall'n Hebe's side;
While, in slow lingering drops, the ethereal tide,
As conscious of its own rich essence, ebb'd away.

Who was the Spirit that remember'd Man,
In that blest hour,
And, with a wing of love,
Brush'd off the goblet's scatter'd tears,
As, trembling near the edge of heaven they ran,
And sent them floating to our orb below? (3)
Essence of immortality!
The shower
Fell glowing through the spheres;
While all around new tints of bliss,
New odours and new light,
Enrich'd its radiant flow.
Now, with a liquid kiss,

(1) In former editions these lines read—
And sweetly twined
Its spirit with the breathing rings
Of her ambrosial hair,
Soar'd as she fell, and on its ruffling wings
(Oh wanton wind!)
Wafted the robe whose sacred flow
Shadow'd her kindling charms of snow.—P. E.

(2) The arcane symbols of this ceremony were deposit-
ed in the cista, where they lay religiously concealed from
the eyes of the profane. They were generally carried in
the procession by an ass ; and hence the proverb, which
one may so often apply in the world, "asinus portat my-
steria." See the *Divine Legation*, book ii., sect. 4.

(3) In the *Geoponica*, lib. ii., cap. 17, there is a fable
somewhat like this descent of the nectar to earth. Εν ου-
ρανῳ των θεων ευωχουμενων, και του νεκταρος πολλου
παρακειμενου, ανασκιρτησαι χορεια τον Ερωτα και
συσσεισαι τω πτερω του κρατηρος την βασιν, και περι-
τρεψαι μεν αυτον· το δε νεκταρ εις την γην εκχυθεν,
κ. τ. λ. Vid. *Autor. de Re Rust.* edit. Cantab., 1704.

It stole along the thrilling wire
Of Heaven's luminous Lyre, (4)
Stealing the soul of music in its flight;
And now, amid the breezes bland,
That whisper from the planets as they roll,
The bright libation, softly fann'd
By all their sighs, meandering stole.
They who, from Atlas' height,
Beheld this rosy flame
Descending through the waste of night,
Thought 't was some planet, whose empyreal frame
Had kindled, as it rapidly revolved
Around its fervid axle, and dissolved
Into a flood so bright!

The youthful Day,
Within his twilight bower,
Lay sweetly sleeping
On the flush'd bosom of a lotos-flower ; (5)
When round him, in profusion weeping,
Dropp'd the celestial shower,
Steeping
The rosy clouds, that curl'd
About his infant head,
Like myrrh upon the locks of Cupid shed.
But, when the waking boy
Waved his exhaling tresses through the sky,
O morn of joy!—
The tide divine,
All glorious with the vermil dye
It drank beneath his orient eye,
Distill'd in dews, upon the world,
And every drop was wine, was heavenly WINE!

Blest be the sod, and blest the flower
On which descended first that shower,
All fresh from Jove's nectareous springs;—
Oh far less sweet the flower, the sod,
O'er which the Spirit of the Rainbow flings
The magic mantle of her solar God! (6)

(4) The constellation Lyra. The astrologers attribute
great virtues to this sign in ascendenti, which are enume-
rated by Pontano, in his *Urania :*—

———— Ecce novem cum pectine chordas
Emodulans, mulceique novo vaga sidera cantu,
Quo captæ nascentum animæ concordia ducunt
Pectora, etc.

(5) The Egyptians represented the dawn of day by a
young boy seated upon a lotos. Εστι Αιγυπτους εωρα-
κως αρχην ανατολης παιδιον νεγρον γραφοντας επι
λωτω καθεζομενον.—*Plutarch.* περι του μη χραν εμμετρ.
See also his Treatise *de Isid. et Osir.* Observing that the
lotos showed its head above water at sunrise, and sank
again at his setting, they conceived the idea of consecrat-
ing this flower to Osiris, or the sun.

This symbol of a youth sitting upon a lotos is very fre-
quent on the Abraxases, or Basilidian stones. See *Mont-
faucon*, tom. ii., planche 158, and the *Supplement*, etc.,
tom. ii., lib. vii., cap. 5.

(6) The ancients esteemed those flowers and trees the

RINGS AND SEALS.

' Ωσπερ σφραγιδες τα φιληματα.
Achilles Tatius, lib. ii.

" Go !" said the angry weeping maid,
" The charm is broken!—once betray'd,
Never can this wrong'd heart rely
On word or look, on oath or sigh.
Take back the gifts so fondly given,
With promised faith and vows to heaven;
That little ring which, night and morn,
With wedded truth my hand hath worn;
That seal which oft in moments blest
Thou hast upon my lip imprest,
And sworn its sacred spring should be
A fountain seal'd(1) for only thee:
Take, take them back, the gift and vow,
All sullied, lost, and hateful now! "

I took the ring—the seal I took,
While, oh, her every tear and look
Were such as angels look and shed,
When man is by the world misled.
Gently I whisper'd, " Fanny, dear !
Not half thy lover's gifts are here:
Say, where are all the kisses given,
From morn to noon, from noon to even,—
Those signets of true love, worth more
Than Solomon's own seal of yore,—
Where are those gifts, so sweet, so many?
Come, dearest,—give back all, if any."(2)

While thus I whisper'd, trembling too,
Lest all the nymph had sworn was true,
I saw a smile relenting rise
'Mid the moist azure of her eyes,
Like daylight o'er a sea of blue,
While yet in mid-air hangs the dew.
She let her cheek repose on mine,
She let my arms around her twine;
One kiss was half allow'd, and then—
The ring and seal were hers again.(3)

sweetest upon which the rainbow had appeared to rest;
and the wood they chiefly burned in sacrifices was that
which the smile of Iris had consecrated. *Plutarch. Sympos.,*
lib. iv., cap. 2, where (as Vossius remarks) καιουσι, instead
of καλουσι, is undoubtedly the genuine reading. See
Vossius, for some curious particularities of the rainbow,
De Origin. et Progress. Idololat., lib. iii., cap. 13.

(1) "There are gardens, supposed to be those of King
Solomon, in the neighbourhood of Bethlehem. The friars
show a fountain, which, they say, is the 'sealed fountain'
to which the holy spouse in the Canticles is compared;
and they pretend a tradition, that Solomon shut up these
springs, and put his signet upon the door, to keep them for
his own drinking."—*Maundrell's Journey from Aleppo to
Jerusalem.* See also the notes to Mr. Good's *Translation
of the Song of Solomon.*

TO MISS SUSAN B—CKF—D. (4)

ON HER SINGING.

I MORE than once have heard, at night,
A song, like those thy lip hath given,
And it was sung by shapes of light,
Who look'd and breathed, like thee, of heaven.

But this was all a dream of sleep,
And I have said, when morning shone,
"Why should the night-witch, Fancy, keep
These wonders for herself alone?"

I knew not then that fate had lent
Such tones to one of mortal birth;
I knew not then that Heaven had sent
A voice, a form like thine on earth.

And yet, in all that flowery maze
Through which my path of life has led,
When I have heard the sweetest lays
From lips of rosiest lustre shed;

When I have heard the sweetest lays
From Beauty's lip, in sweetness vying
With music's own melodious bird,
When on the rose's bosom lying;

Though form and song at once combined
Their loveliest bloom and softest thrill,
My heart hath sigh'd, my ear hath pined
For something lovelier, softer still:

Oh, I have found it all, at last,
In thee, thou sweetest living lyre
Through which the soul of song e'er pass'd,
Or feeling breathed its sacred fire.

All that I e'er, in wildest flight
Of fancy's dreams, could hear or see
Of music's sigh or beauty's light,
Is realised, at once, in thee!

(2) The place of the preceding six lines was originally
occupied by—
" Say, where are all the seals he gave
To every ringlet's jetty wave,
And where is every one he printed
Upon that lip so ruby-tinted—
Seals of the purest gem of bliss,
Oh! richer, softer far than this !

" And then the ring—my love! recall
How many rings, delicious all,
His arms around that neck have twisted,
Twining warmer far than this did !
Where are they all, so sweet, so many?
Oh! dearest, give back all, if any !"—P. E.

(3) Changed from—
Oh ! who can tell the bliss one feels
In thus exchanging rings and seals !—P. E.

(4) The present Duchess of Hamilton.

IMPROMPTU, ON LEAVING SOME FRIENDS.

O dulces comitum valete cœtus!—Catullus.

No, never shall my soul forget
  The friends I found so cordial-hearted;
Dear shall be the day we met,
  And dear shall be the night we parted.

If fond regrets, however sweet,
  Must with the lapse of time decay,
Yet still, when thus in mirth you meet,
  Fill high to him that's far away!

Long be the light of memory found
  Alive within your social glass;
Let that be still the magic round,
  O'er which Oblivion dares not pass.

A WARNING,

TO . . . .

Oh fair as heaven and chaste as light!
Did nature mould thee all so bright,
That thou shouldst e'er be brought to weep
O'er languid virtue's fatal sleep,
O'er shame extinguish'd, honour fled,
Peace lost, heart wither'd, feeling dead?

No, no! a star was born with thee,
Which sheds eternal purity.
Thou hast, within those sainted eyes,
So fair a transcript of the skies,
In lines of light such heavenly lore,
That man should read them and adore.
Yet have I known a gentle maid
Whose mind and form were both array'd
In nature's purest light, like thine;—
Who wore that clear celestial sign,
Which seems to mark the brow that's fair
For destiny's peculiar care:
Whose bosom too, like Dian's own,
Was guarded by a sacred zone,
Where the bright gem of virtue shone;
Whose eyes had, in their light, a charm
Against all wrong, and guile, and harm.
Yet, hapless maid, in one sad hour,
These spells have lost their guardian power;(1)
The gem has been beguiled away;
Her eyes have lost their chastening ray;
The modest pride, the guiltless shame,
The smiles that from reflection came,
All, all have fled, and left her mind
A faded monument behind;

(1) The four preceding lines as originally published stood—

Whose eyes were talismans of fire
Against the spell of man's desire!
Yet, hapless girl, in one sad hour
Her charms have shed their radiant flower.
        —P. E.

The ruins of a once pure shrine,
No longer fit for guest divine. (2)
Oh! 'twas a sight I wept to see—
Heaven keep the lost one's fate from thee!

TO . . . .

'Tis time, I feel, to leave thee now,
  While yet my soul is something free;
While yet those dangerous eyes allow
  One minute's thought to stray from thee.

Oh! thou becomest each moment dearer;
  Every chance that brings me nigh thee,
Brings my ruin nearer, nearer,
  I am lost, unless I fly thee.

Nay, if thou dost not scorn and hate me,
  Doom me not thus so soon to fall;
Duties, fame, and hopes await me,—
  But that eye would blast them all!

For thou hast heart as false and cold
  As ever yet allured or sway'd,
And couldst, without a sigh, behold
  The ruin which thyself had made.

Yet,—could I think that, truly fond,
  That eye but once would smile on me,
Even as thou art, how far beyond
  Fame, duty, wealth, that smile would be!

Oh! but to win it, night and day,
  Inglorious at thy feet reclined,
I'd sigh my dreams of fame away,
  The world for thee forgot, resign'd.

But no, 'tis o'er, and—thus we part,
  Never to meet again,—no, never.
False woman, what a mind and heart
  Thy treachery has undone for ever!

WOMAN.

Away, away—you're all the same,
  A smiling, fluttering, jilting throng;
And, wise too late, I burn with shame,
  To think I've been your slave so long.

Slow to be won, and quick to rove,
  From folly kind, from cunning loth,
Too cold for bliss, too weak for love,
  Yet feigning all that's best in both;

(2) This couplet now occupies the place of—

Like some wave-beaten mouldering stone,
To memory raised by hands unknown,
Which, many a wintry hour, has stood
Beside the ford of Tyra's flood,
To tell the traveller, as he cross'd,
That there some loved friend was lost.—P. E.

13

Still panting o'er a crowd to reign,—
  More joy it gives to woman's breast
To make ten frigid coxcombs vain,
  Than one true manly lover blest.

Away, away—your smile 's a curse—
  Oh! blot me from the race of men,
Kind pitying heaven, by death or worse,
  If e'er I love such things again.

———o♦♦o———

TO . . . .

Νοσει τα φιλτατα.—Euripides.

Come, take thy harp—'tis vain to muse
  Upon the gathering ills we see;
Oh! take thy harp, and let me lose
  All thoughts of ill in hearing thee.

Sing to me, love!—though death were near,
  Thy song could make my soul forget—
Nay, nay, in pity, dry that tear,
  All may be well, be happy yet.

Let me but see that snowy arm
  Once more upon the dear harp lie,
And I will cease to dream of harm,
  Will smile at fate while thou art nigh.

Give me that strain of mournful touch
  We used to love long, long ago,
Before our hearts had known as much
  As now, alas! they bleed to know.

Sweet notes! they tell of former peace,
  Of all that look'd so smiling then,
Now vanish'd, lost—oh, pray thee, cease,
  I cannot bear those sounds again.

(1) In Plutarch's *Essay on the Decline of the Oracles,* Cleombrotus, one of the interlocutors, describes an extraordinary man whom he had met with, after long research, upon the banks of the Red Sea. Once in every year this supernatural personage appeared to mortals, and conversed with them; the rest of his time he passed among the Genii and the Nymphs. Περι την ερυθραν θαλασσαν ευρον, ανθρωποις ανα παν ετος απαξ εντυγχανοντα, ταλλα δε συν ταις νυμφαις, νομασι και δαιμοσι, ως εφασκε. He spoke in a tone not far removed from singing, and whenever he opened his lips, a fragrance filled the place: ρθεγγομενου δε του τοπου ευωδια κατειχε, του στοματος ηδιστον αποπνεοντος. From him Cleombrotus learned the doctrine of a plurality of worlds.

(2) In former editions—
    That tower'd upon his brow; as when we see
    The gentle moon and the full radiant sun
    Shining in heaven together. When he spoke, etc.

(3) The celebrated Janus Dousa, a little before his death, imagined that he *heard* a strain of music in the air. See the poem of Heinsius, "In harmoniam quam paulo ante obitum audire sibi visus est Dousa." Page 501.

(4)   ——ενθα μακαρων
  νασον ωκεανιδες

Art *thou,* too, wretched? yes, thou art;
  I see thy tears flow fast with mine—
Come, come to this devoted heart,
  'T is breaking, but it still is thine!

———o♦♦o———

A VISION OF PHILOSOPHY.

'T was on the Red Sea coast, at morn, we met
The venerable man; (1) a healthy bloom
Mingled its softness with the vigorous thought
That tower'd upon his brow; (2) and, when he spoke,
'T was language sweeten'd into song—such holy
  sounds
As oft, they say, the wise and virtuous hear,
Prelusive to the harmony of heaven,
When death is nigh; (3) and still, as he unclosed
His sacred lips, an odour, all as bland
As ocean-breezes gather from the flowers
That blossom in elysium, (4) breathed around.
With silent awe we listen'd, while he told
Of the dark veil which many an age had hung
O'er Nature's form, till, long explored by man,
The mystic shroud grew thin and luminous,
And glimpses of that heavenly form shone through:—
Of magic wonders, that were known and taught
By him (or Cham or Zoroaster named)
Who mused amid the mighty cataclysm,
O'er his rude tablets of primeval lore; (5)
And gathering round him, in the sacred ark,
The mighty secrets of that former globe,
Let not the living star of science (6) sink
Beneath the waters which ingulph'd a world!—
Of visions, by Calliope reveal'd
To him, (7) who traced upon his typic lyre
The diapason of man's mingled frame,
And the grand Doric heptachord of heaven,
With all of pure, of wondrous and arcane,

    κυραι περιπλεουσιν' αν-
θεμα δε χρυσου φλεγει.—Pindar., Olymp. ii.

(5) Cham, the son of Noah, is supposed to have taken with him into the ark the principal doctrines of magical, or rather of natural, science, which he had inscribed upon some very durable substances, in order that they might resist the ravages of the deluge, and transmit the secrets of antediluvian knowledge to his posterity. See the extracts made by Bayle, in his article, Cham. The identity of Cham and Zoroaster depends upon the authority of Berosus (or rather the impostor Annius), and a few more such respectable testimonies. See Naudé's *Apologie pour les Grands Hommes,* etc., chap. viii., where he takes more trouble than is necessary in refuting this gratuitous supposition.

(6) Chamum à posteris hujus artis admiratoribus Zoroastrum, seu vivum astrum, propterea fuisse dictum et pro Deo habitum.—Bochart., *Geograph. Sacr.,* lib. iv., cap. 1.

(7) Orpheus.—Paulinus, in his *Hebdomades,* cap. 2, lib. iii., has endeavoured to show, after the Platonists, that man is a diapason, or octave, made up of a diatesseron, which is his soul, and a diapente, which is his body. Those frequent allusions to music, by which the ancient philoso-

Which the grave sons of Mochus, many a night,
Told to the young and bright-hair'd visitant

phers illustrated their sublime theories, must have tended
very much to elevate the character of the art, and to en-
rich it with associations of the grandest and most interest-
ing nature. See a preceding note, for their ideas upon
the harmony of the spheres. Heraclitus compared the
mixture of good and evil in this world, to the blended
varieties of harmony in a musical instrument (Plutarch.
de Animæ Procreat.); and Euryphamus, the Pythagorean,
in a fragment preserved by Stobæus, describes human life,
in its perfection, as a sweet and well-tuned lyre. Some
of the ancients were so fanciful as to suppose that the
operations of the memory were regulated by a kind of
musical cadence, and that ideas occurred to it "per arsin
et thesin," while others converted the whole man into a
mere harmonised machine, whose motion depended upon
a certain tension of the body analogous to that of the
strings in an instrument. Cicero indeed ridicules Aris-
toxenus for this fancy, and says, "Let him teach singing,
and leave philosophy to Aristotle;" but Aristotle himself,
though decidedly opposed to the harmonic speculations of
the Pythagoreans and Platonists, could sometimes conde-
scend to enliven his doctrines by reference to the beau-
ties of musical science; as, in the treatise Περι κοσμου
attributed to him, Καθαπερ δε εν χορω, κορυφαιου καταρ-
ξαντος, κ. τ. λ.

The Abbé Batteux, in his enquiry into the doctrine of
the Stoics, attributes to those philosophers the same mode
of illustration. "L'âme était cause active, ποιειν αιτιος;
le corps, cause passive, ήδε του πασχειν:—l'une agissant
dans l'autre, et y prenant par son action même un ca-
ractère, des formes, des modifications qu'elle n'avait pas
par elle-même; à peu près comme l'air qui, chassé dans
un instrument de musique, fait connaître, par les différens
sons qu'il produit, les differentes modifications qu'il y
reçoit." See a fine simile founded upon this notion in
Cardinal Polignac's poem, lib. v., v. 734.

(1) Pythagoras is represented in Iamblichus as descend-
ing with great solemnity from Mount Carmel, for which
reason the Carmelites have claimed him as one of their
fraternity. This Mochus or Moschus, with the descendants
of whom Pythagoras conversed in Phœnicia, and from
whom he derived the doctrines of atomic philosophy, is
supposed by some to be the same with Moses. Huett has
adopted this idea, *Démonstration évangélique*, Prop. iv.,
chap. 2, § 7; and Le Clerc, amongst others, has refuted
it. See *Biblioth. choisie*, tom. i., page 75. It is certain,
however, that the doctrine of atoms was known and pro-
mulgated long before Epicurus. "With the fountains of
Democritus," says Cicero, "the gardens of Epicurus were
watered;" and the learned author of the *Intellectual Sys-
tem* has shown, that all the early philosophers, till the
time of Plato, were atomists. We find Epicurus, however,
boasting that his tenets were new and unborrowed, and
perhaps few among the ancients had any stronger claim to
originality. In truth, if we examine their schools of phi-
losophy, notwithstanding the peculiarities which seem to
distinguish them from each other, we may generally ob-
serve that the difference is but verbal and trifling; and
that, among those various and learned heresies, there is
scarcely one to be selected, whose opinions are its own,
original and exclusive. The doctrine of the world's eter-
nity may be traced through all the sects. The continual
metempsychosis of Pythagoras, the grand periodic year of

Of Carmel's sacred mount. (1)—Then, in a flow
Of calmer converse, he beguiled us on

the Stoics, (at the conclusion of which the universe is sup-
posed to return to its original order, and commence a new
revolution,) the successive dissolution and combination of
atoms maintained by the Epicureans—all these tenets are
but different intimations of the same general belief in the
eternity of the world. As explained by St. Austin, the pe-
riodic year of the Stoics disagrees only so far with the idea
of the Pythagoreans, that instead of an endless transmis-
sion of the soul through a variety of bodies, it restores the
same body and soul to repeat their former round of exist-
ence, so that the "identical Plato, who lectured in the
Academy of Athens, shall again and again, at certain in-
tervals, during the lapse of eternity, appear in the same
Academy and resume the same functions—"———sic ea-
dem tempora temporaliumque rerum volumina repeti,
ut v. g. sicut in isto sæculo Plato philosophus in urbe
Atheniensi, in ea schola quæ Academia dicta est, discipulos
docuit, ita per innumerabilia retro sæcula, multum plexis
quidem intervallis, sed certis, et idem Plato, et eadem ci-
vitas, eademque schola, iidemque discipuli repetiti et per
innumerabilia deinde sæcula repetendi sint.—*De Civitat.
Dei*, lib. xii., cap. 13. Vanini, in his dialogues, has given
us a similar explication of the periodic revolutions of the
world. "Eâ de causâ, qui nunc sunt in usu ritus, centies
millies fuerunt, totiesque renascentur quoties cecide-
runt." 52.

The paradoxical notions of the Stoics upon the beauty,
the riches, the dominion of their imaginary sage, are
among the most distinguishing characteristics of their
school, and, according to their advocate Lipsius, were pe-
culiar to that sect. "Priora illa (decreta) quæ passim in
philosophantium scholis ferè obtinent, ista quæ peculiaria
huic sectæ et habent contradictionem : i. e. paradoxa."—
Manduct. ad Stoic. Philos., lib. iii., dissertat. 2. But it is
evident (as the Abbé Garnier has remarked, *Mémoires de
l'Acad.*, tom. xxxv.) that even these absurdities of the Stoics
are borrowed, and that Plato is the source of all their
extravagant paradoxes. We find their dogma, "dives qui
sapiens," (which Clement of Alexandria has transferred
from the Philosopher to the Christian, *Pædagog.*, lib. iii.,
cap. 6.) expressed in the prayer of Socrates at the end of
the *Phædrus*. Ω φιλε Παν τε και αλλοι οσοι τηδε θεοι,
δοιητε μοι καλω γενεσθαι τανδοθεν· ταξωθεν δε οσα εχω,
τοις εντος ειναι μοι φιλα· πλουσιον δε νομιζοιμι τον
σοφον. And many other instances might be adduced from
the Αντεραστα, the Πολιτικος, etc., to prove that these
weeds of paradox were all gathered among the bowers of
the Academy. Hence it is that Cicero, in the preface to
his paradoxes, calls them Socratica; and Lipsius, exulting
in the patronage of Socrates, says "Ille totus est noster."
This is indeed a coalition, which evinces as much as can
be wished the confused similitude of ancient philosophical
opinions : the father of scepticism is here enrolled amongst
the founders of the Portico; he, whose best knowledge was
that of his own ignorance, is called in to authorise the
pretensions of the most obstinate dogmatists in all anti-
quity.

Rutilius, in his *Itinerarium*, has ridiculed the sabbath
of the Jews, as "lassati mollis imago Dei;" but Epicurus
gave an eternal holiday to his gods, and, rather than dis-
turb the slumbers of Olympus, denied at once the inter-
ference of a Providence. He does not, however, seem to
have been singular in this opinion. Theophilus of Antioch,

Through many a maze of Garden and of Porch,
Through many a system, where the scatter'd light

If he deserve any credit, imputes a similar belief to Pythagoras:—φησι (Πυθαγορας) τε των παντων Θεους ανθωρπων μηδεν φροντιζειν. And Plutarch, though so hostile to the followers of Epicurus, has unaccountably adopted the very same theological error. Thus, after quoting the opinions of Anaxagoras and Plato upon divinity, he adds, Κοινως ουν αμαρτανουσιν αμφοτεροι, οτι τον Θεον εποιησαν επιςφερομενον των ανθρωπινων. De Placit. Philosoph., lib. i., cap. 7. Plato himself has attributed a degree of indifference to the gods, which is not far removed from the apathy of Epicurus's heaven; as thus, in his Philebus, where Protarchus asks, Ουκουν εικος γε ουτε χαιρειν Θεους, ουτε το εναντιον; and Socrates answers, Πανυ μεν ουν εικος, ασχημον γουν αυτων εκατερον γιγνομενον εστιν;—while Aristotle supposes a still more absurd neutrality, and concludes, by no very flattering analogy, that the deity is as incapable of virtue as of vice. Και γαρ ωσπερ ουδεν θηριου εςι κακια, ουδ' αρετη, ουτως ουδε Θεου.—Ethic. Nicomach., lib. vii., cap. 1. In truth, Aristotle, upon the subject of Providence, was little more correct than Epicurus. He supposed the moon to be the limit of divine interference, excluding of course this sublunary world from its influence. The first definition of the world, in his treatise Περι Κοσμου (if this treatise be really the work of Aristotle) agrees, almost verbum verbo, with that in the letter of Epicurus to Pythocles; and both omit the mention of a deity. In his Ethics, too, he intimates a doubt whether the gods feel any interest in the concerns of mankind.—Ει γαρ τις επιμελεια των ανθρωπινων υπο Θεων γινεται. It is true, he adds, 'Ωσπερ δοκει; but even this is very sceptical.

In these erroneous conceptions of Aristotle, we trace the cause of that general neglect which his philosophy experienced among the early Christians. Plato is seldom much more orthodox, but the obscure enthusiasm of his style allowed them to accommodate all his fancies to their own purpose. Such glowing steel was easily moulded, and Platonism became a sword in the hands of the fathers.

The Providence of the Stoics, so vaunted in their school, was a power as contemptibly inefficient as the rest. All was fate in the system of the Portico. The chains of destiny were thrown over Jupiter himself, and their deity was, like the Borgia of the epigrammatist, "et Cæsar et nihil." Not even the language of Seneca can reconcile this degradation of divinity. "Ille ipse omnium conditor ac rector scripsit quidem fata, sed sequitur; semper paret, semel jussit."—Lib. de Providentia, cap. 5.

With respect to the difference between the Stoics, Peripatetics and Academicians, the following words of Cicero prove that he saw but little to distinguish them from each other:—"Peripateticos et Academicos, nominibus differentes, re congruentes; a quibus Stoici ipsi verbis magis quam sententiis dissenserunt."—Academic., lib. ii., 5; and perhaps what Reid has remarked upon one of their points of controversy might be applied as effectually to the reconcilement of all the rest. "The dispute between the Stoics and Peripatetics was probably all for want of definition. The one said they were good under the control of reason, the other that they should be eradicated."—Essays,

Of heavenly truth lay like a broken beam
From the pure sun, which, though refracted all

vol. iii. In short, it appears a no less difficult matter to establish the boundaries of opinion between any two of the philosophical sects, than it would be to fix the landmarks of those estates in the moon, which Ricciolus so generously allotted to his brother astronomers. Accordingly we observe some of the greatest men of antiquity passing without scruple from school to school, according to the fancy or convenience of the moment. Cicero, the father of Roman philosophy, is sometimes an Academician, sometimes a Stoic; and, more than once, he acknowledges a conformity with Epicurus; "non sine causa igitur Epicurus ausus est dicere semper in pluribus bonis esse sapientem, quia semper sit in voluptatibus."—Tusculan. Quæst., lib. v. Though often pure in his theology, Cicero sometimes smiles at futurity as a fiction; thus, in his Oration for Cluentius, speaking of punishments in the life to come, he says, "Quæ si falsa sunt, id quod omnes intelligunt, quid ei tandem aliud mors eripuit, præter sensum doloris?"—though here we should, perhaps, do him but justice by agreeing with his commentator Sylvius, who remarks upon this passage, "Hæc autem dixit, ut causæ suæ subserviret." The poet Horace roves like a butterfly through the schools, and now wings along the walls of the Porch, now basks among the flowers of the Garden; while Virgil, with a tone of mind strongly philosophical, has yet left us wholly uncertain as to the sect which he espoused. The balance of opinion declares him to have been an Epicurean, but the ancient author of his life asserts that he was an Academician; and we trace through his poetry the tenets of almost all the leading sects. The same kind of eclectic indifference is observable in most of the Roman writers. Thus Propertius, in the fine elegy to Cynthia, on his departure for Athens,—

Illic vel studiis animum emendare Platonis,
Incipiam, aut hortis, docte Epicure, tuis.
                                Lib. iii., Eleg. 21.

Though Broeckhusius here reads, "dux Epicure," which seems to fix the poet under the banners of Epicurus. Even the Stoic Seneca, whose doctrines have been considered so orthodox, that St. Jerome has ranked him amongst the ecclesiastical writers, while Boccaccio doubts (in consideration of his supposed correspondence with St. Paul) whether Dante should have placed him in Limbo with the rest of the Pagans—even the rigid Seneca has bestowed such commendations on Epicurus, that if only those passages of his works were preserved to us, we could not hesitate, I think, in pronouncing him a confirmed Epicurean. With similar inconsistency, we find Porphyry, in his work upon abstinence, referring to Epicurus as an example of the most strict Pythagorean temperance; and Lancelotti (the author of Farfalloni degli antici Istorici) has been seduced by this grave reputation of Epicurus into the absurd error of associating him with Chrysippus, as a chief of the Stoic school. There is no doubt, indeed, that however the Epicurean sect might have relaxed from its original purity, the morals of its founder were as correct as those of any among the ancient philosophers; and his doctrines upon pleasure, as explained in the letter to Menœceus, are rational, amiable, and consistent with our nature. A late writer, De Sablons, in his Grands Hommes vengés, expresses strong indignation against the Encyclopédistes for their just and animated praises of Epicurus, and discussing the question, "si ce philosophe était vertueux," denies it upon no other authority than the calumnies col-

Into a thousand hues, is sunshine still, (1)
And bright through every change!—he spoke of Him
The lone (2) eternal One, who dwells above,
And of the soul's untraceable descent
From that high fount of spirit, through the grades
Of intellectual being, till it mix
With atoms vague, corruptible, and dark;
Nor yet even then, though sunk in earthly dross,
Corrupted all, nor its ethereal touch
Quite lost, but tasting of the fountain still.
As some bright river, which has roll'd along
Through meads of flowery light and mines of gold,
When pour'd at length into the dusky deep,
Disdains to take at once its briny taint,
But keeps unchanged awhile the lustrous tinge,
Or balmy freshness, of the scenes it left. (3)

And here the old man ceased—a winged train
Of nymphs and genii bore him from our eyes.
The fair illusion fled! and, as I waked,
'T was clear that my rapt soul had roam'd, the while,
To that bright realm of dreams, that spirit-world,
Which mortals know by its long track of light
O'er midnight's sky, and call the Galaxy. (4)

————◦◦◦————

TO MRS. ......

To see thee every day that came,
And find thee still each day the same;
In pleasure's smile, or sorrow's tear,
To me still ever kind and dear;—
To meet thee early, leave thee late,
Has been so long my bliss, my fate,
That life, without this cheering ray,
Which came, like sunshine, every day,
And all my pain, my sorrow chased,
Is now a lone and loveless waste.

Where are the chords she used to touch?
The airs, the songs she loved so much?
Those songs are hush'd, those chords are still,
And so, perhaps, will every thrill
Of feeling soon be lull'd to rest,
Which late I waked in Anna's breast.
Yet, no—the simple notes I play'd
From memory's tablets soon may fade;
The songs, which Anna loved to hear,
May vanish from her heart and ear;
But friendship's voice shall ever find
An echo in that gentle mind,
Nor memory lose, nor time impair,
The sympathies that tremble there.

————◦◦◦————

THE DEVIL AMONG THE SCHOLARS, (5)

A FRAGMENT.

Τι κακον ὁ γελως;
Chrysost. Homil. in Epist. ad Hebræos.

•   •   •   •   •

BUT, whither have these gentle ones,
These rosy nymphs and black-eyed nuns,
With all of Cupid's wild romancing,
Led my truant brains a dancing?
Instead of studying tomes scholastic,
Ecclesiastic, or monastic,
Off I fly, careering far
In chase of Pollys, prettier far
Than any of their namesakes are,—
The Polymaths and Polyhistors,
Polyglots and all their sisters. (6)
So have I known a hopeful youth
Sit down in quest of lore and truth,
With tomes sufficient to confound him,
Like Tohu Bohu, heap'd around him,—

lected by Plutarch, who himself confesses that, on this particular subject, he consulted only opinion and report, without pausing to investigate their truth.—Αλλα την δοξαν, ου την αληθειαν σκοπουμεν. To the factious zeal of his illiberal rivals, the Stoics, Epicurus chiefly owed these gross misrepresentations of the life and opinions of himself and his associates, which, notwithstanding the learned exertions of Gassendi, have still left an odium on the name of his philosophy; and we ought to examine the ancient accounts of this philosopher with about the same degree of cautious belief which, in reading ecclesiastical history, we yield to the invectives of the fathers against the heretics,—trusting as little to Plutarch upon a dogma of Epicurus, as we would to the vehement St. Cyril upon a tenet of Nestorius. (1801.)

The preceding remarks, I wish the reader to observe, were written at a time when I thought the studies to which they refer much more important as well as more amusing than, I freely confess, they appear to me at present.

(1) Lactantius asserts that all the truths of Christianity may be found dispersed through the ancient philosophical sects, and that any one who would collect these scattered fragments of orthodoxy might form a code in no respect differing from that of the Christian. " Si extitisset aliquis, qui veritatem sparsam per singulos per sectasque

diffusam colligeret in unum, ac redigeret in corpus, is profecto non dissentiret a nobis."—Inst., lib. vi., c. 7.

(2) Το μονον και ερημον.

(3) This bold Platonic image I have taken from a passage in Father Bouchet's letter upon the Metempsychosis, inserted in Picart's Cérém. Relig., tom. iv.

(4) According to Pythagoras, the people of Dreams are souls collected together in the Galaxy.—Δημος δε ονειρων, κατα Πυθαγοραν, αι ψυχαι ἁς συναγεσθαι φησιν εις τον γαλαξιαν.—Porphyr. de Antro Nymph.

(5) The title of this amusing production was formerly accompanied by the following note:—

" I promised that I would give the remainder of this poem, but as my critics do not seem to relish the sublime learning which it contains, they shall have no more of it. With a view, however, to the edification of these gentlemen, I have prevailed on an industrious friend of mine, who has read a great number of these unnecessary books, to illuminate the extract with a little of his precious erudition."—P. E.

(6) The following lines have been struck out of the present edition :—

The instant I have got the whim in,
Off I fly with nuns and women,
Like epic poets, ne'er at ease
Until I 've stolen " in medias res !"—P. E.

Mamurra(1) stuck to Theophrastus,
And Galen tumbling o'er Bombastus, (2)
When lo! while all that's learn'd and wise
Absorbs the boy, he lifts his eyes,
And through the window of his study
Beholds some damsel fair and ruddy,
With eyes as brightly turn'd upon him as
The angel's (3) were on Hieronymus. (4)
Quick fly the folios, widely scatter'd
Old Homer's laurel'd brow is batter'd,
And Sappho, headlong sent, flies just in
The reverend eye of St. Augustin. (5)
Raptured he quits each dosing sage,
Oh woman, for thy lovelier page:
Sweet book!—unlike the books of art,—
Whose errors are thy fairest part;
In whom the dear errata column
Is the best page in all the volume!(6)

But to begin my subject rhyme—
'T was just about this devilish time,
When scarce there happen'd any frolics
That were not done by Diabolics,
A cold and loveless son of Lucifer,
Who woman scorn'd, nor saw the use of her,

A branch of Dagon's family,
(Which Dagon, whether He or She,
Is a dispute that vastly better is
Referr'd to Scaliger (7) et cæteris,)
Finding that, in this cage of fools,
The wisest sots adorn the schools,
Took it at once his head Satanic in,
To grow a great scholastic manikin,—
A doctor, quite as learn'd and fine as
Scotus John or Tom Aquinas,(8)
Lully, Hales Irrefragabilis,
Or any doctor of the rabble is.
In languages, (9) the Polyglots,
Compared to him, were Babel sots;
He chatter'd more than ever Jew did;—
Sanhedrim and Priest included,
Priest and holy Sanhedrim
Were one-and-seventy fools to him.
But chief the learned demon felt a
Zeal so strong for gamma, delta,
That, all for Greek and learning's glory, (10)
He nightly tippled "Græco more,"
And never paid a bill or balance
Except upon the Grecian Kalends:—

(1) Mamurra, a dogmatic philosopher, who never doubted about any thing, except who was his father.—"Nullà de re unquam præterquam de patre dubitavit."—*In Vit.* He was very learned—"Là dedans, (that is, in his head when it was opened,) le Punique heurte le Persan, l'Hébreu choque l'Arabique, pour ne point parler de la mauvaise intelligence du Latin avec le Grec," etc.—See *L'Histoire de Montmaur,* tom. ii., p. 91.

(2) Bombastus was one of the names of that great scholar and quack Paracelsus.—"Philippus Bombastus latet sub splendido tegmine Aureoli Theophrasti Paracelsi," says Stadelius de circumforaneâ Literatorum vanitate.—He used to fight the devil every night with a broadsword, to the no small terror of his pupil Oporinus, who has recorded the circumstance. (Vide Oporin., *Vit. apud Christian. Gryph.Vit. Select. quorundam Eruditissimorum,* etc.) Paracelsus had but a poor opinion of Galen :—"My very beard (says he in his *Paragrœnum*) has more learning in it than either Galen or Avicenna."

(3) The angel who scolded St. Jerome for reading Cicero, as Gratian tells the story in his *Concordantia discordantium Canonum,* and says, that for this reason bishops were not allowed to read the Classics : "Episcopus Gentilium libros non legat."—*Distinct.* 37. But Gratian is notorious for lying—besides, angels, as the illustrious pupil of Pantenus assures us, have got no tongues. Ουχ ὡς ἡμιν τα ωτα, οὑτως εκεινοις ἡ γλωττα· ουδ' οι οργανα τις δοῃ φωνης αγγελοις.—Clem. Alexand. *Stromat.**

(4) The following couplet is here omitted—
   Saying, 't was just as sweet to kiss her—oh!
   Far more sweet than reading Cicero !—P. E.

(5) Changed from—
   And Sappho's skin to Tully's leather,
   All are confused and toss'd together !—P. E.

(6) The idea of the Rabbins, respecting the origin of

* This note formerly terminated by the reflection—"Now, how an angel could scold without a tongue, I shall leave the angelic Mrs. — — to determine."—P. E.

woman, is not a little singular. They think that man was originally formed with a tail, like a monkey, but that the Deity cut off this appendage. and made woman of it. Upon this extraordinary supposition the following reflection is founded :—

   If such is the tie between women and men,
      The ninny who weds is a pitiful elf,
   For he takes to his tail like an idiot again,
      And thus makes a deplorable ape of himself.
   Yet, if we may judge as the fashions prevail,
      Every husband remembers the original plan,
   And, knowing his wife is no more than his tail,
      Why he—leaves her behind him as much as he can.

(7) Scaliger. *de Emendat. Tempor.*—Dagon was thought by others to be a certain sea-monster, who came every day out of the Red Sea to teach the Syrians husbandry.—See Jaques Gaffarel (*Curiosités inouïes,* chap. i.), who says he thinks this story of the sea-monster "carries little show of probability with it."

(8) I wish it were known with any degree of certainty whether the *Commentary on Bœthius* attributed to Thomas Aquinas be really the work of this Angelic Doctor. There are some bold assertions hazarded in it : for instance, he says that Plato kept school in a town called Academia, and that Alcibiades was a very beautiful woman whom some of Aristotle's pupils fell in love with :—"Alcibiades mulier fuit pulcherrima, quam videntes quidam discipuli Aristotelis," etc.—See Freytag *Adparat. Litterar.*, art. 86, tom. i.

(9) The following compliment was paid to Laurentius Valla, upon his accurate knowledge of the Latin language:

   Nunc postquam manes defunctus Valla petivit,
      Non audet Pluto verba Latina loqui.
   Since Val arrived in Pluto's shade,
      His nouns and pronouns all so pat in,
   Pluto himself would be afraid
      To say his soul's his own, in Latin!

See for these lines the "*Auctorum Censio*" of Du Verdier (page 29).

(10) It is much to be regretted that Martin Luther, with

From whence your scholars,when they want tick,
Say, to be *Attic*'s to be *on* tick.
In logics, he was quite Ho Panu ; (1)
Knew as much as ever man knew.
He fought the combat syllogistic
With so much skill and art eristic,
That though you were the learned Stagyrite,
At once upon the hip he had you right. (2)
In music, though he had no ears
Except for that amongst the spheres,
(Which most of all, as he averr'd it,
He dearly loved, 'cause no one heard it,)
Yet aptly he, at sight, could read
Each tuneful diagram in Bede,
And find, by Euclid's corollaria,
The ratios of a jig or aria.
But, as for all your warbling Delias,
Orpheuses and Saint Cecilias,
He own'd he thought them much surpass'd
By that redoubted Hyaloclast (3)
Who still contrived by dint of throttle,
Where'er he went, to crack a bottle.

Likewise to show his mighty knowledge, he,
On things unknown in physiology,

all his talents for reforming, should yet be vulgar enough
to laugh at Camerarius for writing to him in Greek.
"Master Joachim (says he) has sent me some dates and
some raisins, and has also written me two letters in
Greek. As soon as I am recovered, I shall answer them
in Turkish, that he too may have the pleasure of reading
what he does not understand." "Græca sunt, legi non
possunt," is the ignorant speech attributed to Accursius ;
but very unjustly :—for, far from asserting that Greek
could not be read, that worthy jurisconsult upon the
Law 6. D. de Bonor. Possess. expressly says, "Græcæ li-
teræ possunt intelligi et legi." (Vide *Nov. Libror. Rarior.
Collection.*, fascic. iv.)—Scipio Carteromachus seems to
have been of opinion that there is no salvation out of the
pale of Greek Literature : " Via prima salutis Graiä pan-
detur ab urbe :" and the zeal of Laurentius Rhodomannus
cannot be sufficiently admired, when he exhorts his coun-
trymen, "per gloriam Christi, per salutem patriæ, per
reipublicæ decus et emolumentum," to study the Greek
language. Nor must we forget Phavorinus, the excellent
Bishop of Nocera, who, careless of all the usual commen-
dations of a Christian, required no further eulogium on
his tomb than,"Here lieth a Greek Lexicographer."

(1) 'Ο παινυ.—The introduction of this language into
English poetry has a good effect, and ought to be more
universally adopted. A word or two of Greek in a stanza
would serve as ballast to the most "light o' love" verses.
Ausonius, among the ancients, may serve as a model :—

Ου γαρ μοι Σεμις εστιν in hac regione μενοντι
Αξιον ab nostris επιδευεα esse καμηγαις.

Ronsard, the French poet, has enriched his sonnets and
od.s with many an exquisite morsel from the Lexicon.
His "chère Entelechie," in addressing his mistress, can
only be equalled by Cowley's "Antiperistasis."

(2) The following lines of the original poem are sup-
pressed in the present edition—

Sometimes indeed his speculations
Were view'd as dangerous innovations.

Wrote many a chapter to divert us,
(Like that great little man Albertus,)
Wherein he show'd the reason why,
When children first are heard to cry,
If boy the baby chance to be,
He cries O A !—if girl, O E !—
Which are, quoth he, exceeding fair hints
Respecting their first sinful parents;
" Oh Eve!" exclaimeth little madam, (4)
While little master cries " Oh Adam!" (5)

But, 't was in Optics and Dioptrics,
Our dæmon play'd his first and top tricks.
He held that sunshine passes quicker
Through wine than any other liquor ; (6)
And though he saw no great objection
To steady light and clear reflection,
He thought the aberrating rays,
Which play about a bumper's blaze,
Were by the Doctors look'd, in common, on
As a more rare and rich phenomenon.
He wisely said that the sensorium
Is for the eyes a great emporium,
To which these noted picture-stealers
Send all they can, and meet with dealers.

As thus—the Doctor's house did harbour a
Sweet blooming girl, whose name was Barbara :
Oft, when his heart was in a merry key,
He taught this maid his esoterics,
And sometimes, as a cure for hectics,
Would lecture her in dialectics.
How far their zeal let him and her go
Before they came to sealing Ergo,
Or how they placed the medius terminus,
Our chronicles do not determine us ;
But so it was—by some confusion
In this their logical prælusion,
The Doctor wholly spoil'd, they say,
The figure * of young Barbara ;
And thus, by many a snare sophistic,
And enthymeme paralogistic,
Beguiled a maid, who could not give,
To save her life, a negative. † —P. E.

(3) Or Glass-Breaker—Morhofius has given an account
of this extraordinary man, in a work, published 1682.—
De vitreo scypho fracto, etc.

(4) Translated almost literally from a passage in *Albertus
de Secretis*, etc.

(5) Another hiatus in the original poem occurs here :—

In point of science astronomical,
It seem'd to him extremely comical
That, once a-year, the frolic sun
Should call at Virgo's house for fun,
And stop a month and blase around her,
Yet leave her Virgo, as he found her !—P. E.

(6) Couplet here suppressed—

That glasses are the best utensils
To catch the eyes bewilder'd pencils.—P. E.

* The first figure of simple syllogisms, to which Barbara belongs,
together with Celarent, Darii, and Ferio.

† Because the three propositions in the mood of Barbara are
universal affirmatives.—The poet borrowed this equivoque upon
Barbara from a curious Epigram which Menckenius gives in a note
upon his *Essays de Charlataneria Eruditorum*. In the *Nup ie Peri-
pateticæ* of Caspar Barlæus, the reader will find some facetious ap-
plications of the terms of logic to matrimony. Crambe's *Treatise
on Syllogisms*, in Martinus Scriblerus, is borrowed chiefly from
the *Nuptiæ Peripateticæ* of Barlæus.

In many an optical proceeding
The brain, he said, show'd great good breeding;
For instance, when we ogle women
(A trick which Barbara tutor'd him in),
Although the dears are apt to get in a
Strange position on the retina,
Yet instantly the modest brain
Doth set them on their legs again! (1)

Our doctor thus, with "stuff'd sufficiency"
Of all omnigenous omniciency
Began (as who would not begin
That had, like him, so much within?)
To let it out in books of all sorts;
Folios, quartos, large and small sorts;
Poems, so very deep and sensible
That they were quite incomprehensible; (2)
Prose, which had been at learning's Fair,
And bought up all the trumpery there,
The tatter'd rags of every vest,
In which the Greeks and Romans drest,
And o'er her figure swoll'n and antic
Scatter'd them all with airs so frantic,
That those who saw what fits she had,
Declared unhappy Prose was mad!
Epics he wrote, and scores of rebusses,
All as neat as old Turnebus's;
Eggs and altars, cyclopædias,
Grammars, prayer-books—Oh! 'twere tedious,
Did I but tell thee half, to follow me;
Not the scribbling bard of Ptolemy,
No—nor the hoary Trismegistus,   [us,)
(Whose writings all, thank heaven! have miss'd
E'er fill'd with lumber such a ware-room
As this great "porcus literarum!"
　　　　*　　　*　　　*　　　*

———o✦o———

TO LADY HEATHCOTE,

ON AN OLD RING FOUND AT TUNBRIDGE-WELLS.

"Tunnebridge est à la même distance de Londres que
Fontainebleau l'est de Paris. Ce qu'il y a de beau et de
galant dans l'un et dans l'autre sexe s'y rassemble au temps
des eaux. La compagnie," etc., etc.—See *Mémoires de
Grammont*, Second part., chap. iii.

　　　　　　　　　Tunbridge Wells, August, 1805.

WHEN Grammont graced these happy springs,
And Tunbridge saw, upon her Pantiles,

(1) Alluding to that habitual act of the judgment, by
which, notwithstanding the inversion of the image upon
the retina, a correct impression of the object is conveyed
to the sensorium.

(2) Under this description, I believe *the Devil among
the Scholars* may be included. Yet Leibnitz found out
the uses of incomprehensibility, when he was appointed
secretary to a society of philosophers at Nuremberg,
chiefly for his ingenuity in writing a cabalistical letter, not
one word of which either they or himself could interpret.
See the *Eloge historique de M. de Leibnitz, l'Europe sa-
vante.*—People in all ages have loved to be puzzled. We

The merriest wight of all the kings
That ever ruled these gay gallant isles;

Like us, by day they rode they walk'd,
At eve they did as we may do;
And Grammont just like Spencer talk'd,
And lovely Stewart smiled like you.

The only different trait is this,
That woman then, if man beset her,
Was rather given to saying "yes,"
Because,—as yet, she knew no better.

Each night they held a coterie,
Where, every fear to slumber charm'd,
Lovers were all they ought to be,
And husbands not the least alarm'd.

Then call'd they up their school-day pranks,
Nor thought it much their sense beneath
To play at riddles, quips, and cranks,
And lords show'd wit, and ladies teeth.

As—"Why are husbands like the mint?"
Because, forsooth, a husband's duty
Is but to set the name and print
That give a currency to beauty.

"Why is a rose in nettles hid
Like a young widow, fresh and fair?"
Because 't is sighing to be rid
Of *weeds*, that "have no business there!" (3)

And thus they miss'd and thus they hit,
And now they struck and now they parried;
And some lay in of full-grown wit,
While others of a pun miscarried.

'T was one of those facetious nights
That Grammont gave this forfeit ring
For breaking grave conundrum-rites,
Or punning ill, or some such thing:—

From whence it can be fairly traced,
Through many a branch and many a bough,
From twig to twig, until it graced,
The snowy hand that wears it now.

find Cicero thanking Atticus for having sent him a work
of Serapion, "ex quo (says he) quidem ego(quod inter nos
liceat dicere) millesimam partem vix intelligo." Lib. ii.,
epist. 4. And we know that Avicen, the learned Arabian,
read Aristotle's Metaphysics forty times over for the mere
pleasure of being able to inform the world that he could
not comprehend one syllable throughout them. (Nicolas
Massa *in Vit. Avicen.*)

(3) This verse formerly read—
　　"Why is a garden's wilder'd maze
　　　Like a young widow, fresh and fair?"
　　Becau e ii wants some hand to raise
　　　The weeds, which have no business there!—P. E.

All this I'll prove, and then, to you,
  Oh Tunbridge! and your springs *ironical*,
I swear by Heathcote's eye of blue
  To dedicate the important chronicle.

Long may your ancient inmates give
  Their mantles to your modern lodgers,
And Charles's loves in Heathcote live,
  And Charles's bards revive in Rogers.

Let no pedantic fools be there;
  For ever be those fops abolish'd,
With heads as wooden as thy ware,
  And, Heaven knows! not half so polish'd.

But still receive the young, the gay,
  The few who know the rare delight
Of reading Grammont every day,
  And acting Grammont every night.

₊ In addition to the numerous changes already pointed out, we find that the author has entirely omitted the following, which formed part of the collection published under the pseudonyme of "Thomas Little, Esq."

TO MRS. ———.

IF, in the dream that hovers
  Around my sleeping mind,
Fancy thy form discovers,
  And paints thee melting kind:

If joys from sleep I borrow,
  Sure thou'lt forgive me this;
For he who wakes to sorrow
  At least may dream of bliss!

Oh! if thou art, in seeming,
  All that I've e'er required;
Oh! if I feel, in dreaming,
  All that I've e'er desired;

Wilt thou forgive my taking
  A kiss, or something more?
What thou deny'st me waking,
  Oh! let me slumber o'er!

———o⊕o———

TO JULIA.

WELL, Julia, if to love, and live
'Mid all the pleasures love can give,
  Be crimes that bring damnation;
You—you and I have given such scope
To loves and joys, we scarce can hope
  In heaven the least salvation!

And yet, I think, did Heaven design
That blisses dear, like yours and mine,
  Should be our own undoing,
It had not made my soul so warm,
Nor given you such a witching form,
  To bid me dote on ruin!

Then wipe away that timid tear;
Sweet truant! you have nought to fear;
  Though you were whelm'd in sin,
Stand but at heaven's gate awhile,
And you *so like an angel* smile,
  They can't but *let you in.*

EPIGRAM. (1)

YOUR mother says, my little Venus,
There's *something not correct* between us,
  And you're in fault as much as I:
Now, on my soul, my little Venus,
I think 't would not be right between us
  To let your mother tell a lie!

———o⊕o———

SONG.

SWEET seducer! blandly smiling;
Charming still, and still beguiling!
Oft I swore to love thee never,
Yet I love thee more than ever!

Why that little wanton blushing,
Glancing eye, and bosom flushing!
Flushing warm, and wily glancing—
All is lovely, all entrancing!

Turn away those lips of blisses—
I am poison'd by thy kisses!
Yet, again, ah! turn them to me,
Ruin's sweet when they undo me!

Oh! be less, be less enchanting;
Let some little grace be wanting;
Let my eyes, when I'm expiring,
Gaze awhile without admiring!

———o⊕o———

SONG.

WHY, the world are all thinking about it;
  And, as for myself, I can swear,
If I fancied that heaven were without it,
  I'd scarce feel a wish to go there.

If Mahomet would but receive me,
  And Paradise be as he paints,
I'm greatly afraid, God forgive me!
  I'd worship the eyes of his saints.

(1) I believe this epigram is originally French.—E.

14

But why should I think of a trip,
    To the Prophet's seraglio above,
When Phillida gives me her lip,
    As my own little heaven of love?

Oh, Phillis! that kiss may be sweeter
    Than ever by mortal was given;
But your lip, love! is only St. Peter,
    And keeps but the key to your heaven!

IMPROMPTU.

Look in my eyes, my blushing fair!
Thou 'lt see thyself reflected there;
And, as I gaze on thine, I see
Two little miniatures of me:
Thus in our looks some propagation lies,
For we *make babies* in each other's eyes!

TO MRS. ——.

——amore
In canuti pensier si disconviene.—*Guarini.*

Yes, I think I once heard of an amorous youth
    Who was caught in his grandmother's bed;
But I own I had ne'er such a liquorish tooth
    As to wish to be there in his stead.

'T is for you, my dear madam, such conquests to make:
    Antiquarians may value you high;
But I swear I can't love for antiquity's sake,
    Such a poor virtuoso am I.

I have seen many ruins all gilded with care,
    But the cracks were still plain to the eye:
And I ne'er felt a passion to venture in there,
    But turn'd up my nose, and pass'd by!

I perhaps might have sigh'd in your magical chain
    When your lip had more freshness to deck it:
But I 'd hate even Dian herself *in the wane,*—
    She might then *go to hell for a Hecate!*

No, no! when my heart 's in these amorous faints,
    Which is seldom, thank Heaven! the case—
For, by reading the *Fathers,* and *Lives of the Saints,*
    I keep up a stock of good grace:

But then 't is the creature luxuriant and fresh
    That my passion with ecstasy owns:
For indeed, my dear madam, though fond *of the flesh,*
    I never was partial to *bones!*

TO JULIA.

Sweet is the dream, divinely sweet,
    When absent souls in fancy meet!

(1) I believe Mr. Little alluded here to a famous question among the early schoolmen: "How many thousand angels could dance upon the point of a very fine needle, without

At midnight, love, I 'll think of thee!
At midnight, love! oh think of me!
Think that thou givest thy dearest kiss,
And I will think I feel the bliss;
Then, if thou blush, that blush be mine,
And, if I weep, the tear be thine!

TO ——.

Can I again that form caress,
    Or on that lip in rapture twine?
No, no! the lip that all may press
    Shall never more be press'd by mine.

Can I again that look recall
    Which once could make me die for thee?
No, no! the eye that burns on all
    Shall never more be prized by me!

SONG.

Away with this pouting and sadness!
    Sweet girl! will you never give o'er!
I love you, by Heaven! to madness,
    And what can I swear to you more?
Believe not the old woman's fable,
    That oaths are as short as a kiss;
I 'll love you as long as I 'm able,
    And swear for no longer than this.

Then waste not the time with professions;
    For *not* to be blest when we can
Is one of the darkest transgressions
    That happen 'twixt woman and man.
Pretty moralist! why thus beginning
    My innocent warmth to reprove?
Heaven knows that I never loved *sinning*—
    Except little sinnings in love!

If swearing, however, will do it,
    Come, bring me the calendar, pray—
I vow by that lip I 'll go through it,
    And not miss a saint on my way.
The angels shall help me to wheedle;
    I 'll swear upon every one
That e'er danced on the point of a needle,(1)
    Or rode on a beam of the sun!

Oh! why should Platonic control, love,
    Enchain an emotion so free?
Your soul, though a very sweet soul, love,
    Will ne'er be sufficient for me.
If you think, by this coolness and scorning,
    To seem more angelic and bright,
Be an angel, my love, in the morning,
    But, oh! *be a woman to–night!*

jostling one another?" If he *could* have been thinking of the schools while he was writing this song, we cannot say " can it *indoctum.*"

AN ARGUMENT,

TO ANY PHILLIS OR CLOE.

I 'VE oft been told by learned friars,
That wishing and the crime are one,
And Heaven punishes desires
As much as if the deed were done.

If wishing damns us, you and I
Are damn'd to all our heart's content;
Come then, at least we may enjoy
Some pleasure for our punishment!

———o◉o———

THE KISS.

Illa nisi in lecto nusquam potuere doceri.
Ovid, lib. ii., eleg. 5.

GIVE me, my love, that billing kiss
I taught you one delicious night,
When, turning epicures in bliss,
We tried inventions of delight.

Come, gently steal my lips along,
And let your lips in murmurs move;—
Ah, no!—again—that kiss was wrong,—
How can you be so dull, my love?

" Cease, cease!" the blushing girl replied—
And in her milky arms she caught me—
" How can you thus your pupil chide;
You know 't was in the dark you taught me!"

———o◉o———

ELEGIAC STANZAS.(1)

How sweetly could I lay my head
Within the cold grave's silent breast;
Where Sorrow's tears no more are shed,
No more the ills of life molest.

For, ah! my heart, how very soon
The glittering dreams of youth are past!
And, long before it reach its noon,
The sun of life is overcast.

———o◉o———

LOVE IN A STORM.

Quam juvat immites ventos audire cubantem,
Et dominam tenero continuisse sinu.—*Tibullus.*

LOUD sang the wind in the ruins above,
Which murmur'd the warnings of time o'er our
head;
While fearless we offer'd devotions to Love,
The rude rock our pillow, the rushes our bed.

(1) This poem, and some others of the same pensive
cast, we may suppose, were the result of the *few* melan-
choly moments which a life so short and so pleasant as
that of the author could have allowed.—E.

Damp was the chill of the wintry air,
But it made us cling closer, and warmly unite;
Dread was the lightning, and horrid its glare,
But it show'd me my Julia in languid delight.

To my bosom she nestled, and felt not a fear, [frown:
Though the shower did beat, and the tempest did
Her sighs were as sweet, and her murmurs as dear,
As if she lay lull'd on a pillow of down!

———o◉o———

SONG.

JESSY on a bank was sleeping,
A flower beneath her bosom lay;
Love upon her slumber creeping,
Stole the flower and flew away!

Pity, then, poor Jessy's ruin,
Who, becalm'd by Slumber's wing,
Never felt what Love was doing—
Never dream'd of such a thing.

———o◉o———

TO A SLEEPING MAID.

WAKE, my life! thy lover's arms
Are twined around thy sleeping charms:
Wake, my love! and let desire
Kindle those opening orbs of fire.

Yet, sweetest, though the bliss delight thee,
If the guilt, the shame affright thee,
Still those orbs in darkness keep;
Sleep, my girl, or *seem to sleep.*

———o◉o———

SONG.

WHEN the heart's feeling
Burns with concealing,
Glances will tell what we fear to confess:
Oh! what an anguish
Silent to languish,
Could we not look all we wish to express!

When half-expiring,
Restless, desiring,
Lovers wish something, but must not say what,
Looks tell the wanting,
Looks tell the granting,
Looks betray all that the heart would be at.

———o◉o———

THE BALLAD. (2)

THOU hast sent me a flowery band,
And told me 't was fresh from the field;
That the leaves were untouch'd by the hand,
And the purest of odours would yield.

(2) This ballad was probably suggested by the following
Epigram in Martial—
Intactas quare mittis mihi, Polla, coronas,
A te vexatas malo tenere rosas.—Epig. 1c., lib. 2.—E.

And indeed it was fragrant and fair;
　But, if it were handled by thee,
It would bloom with a livelier air,
　And would surely be sweeter to me!

Then take it, and let it entwine
　Thy tresses, so flowing and bright;
And each little floweret will shine
　More rich than a gem to my sight.

Let the odorous gale of thy breath
　Embalm it with many a sigh;
Nay, let it be wither'd to death
　Beneath the warm noon of thine eye.

And instead of the dew that it bears,
　The dew dropping fresh from the tree,
On its leaves let me number the tears
　That affection has stolen from thee!

——◦❀◦——

WRITTEN IN A COMMON-PLACE BOOK,
CALLED "THE BOOK OF FOLLIES."
IMPROMPTU, TO THE PRETTY LITTLE MRS. ——.

Magis venustatem an brevitatem mireris incertum est.
　　　　Macrob., Sat., lib. ii., cap. 2.

THIS journal of folly's an emblem of me;
But what book shall we find emblematic of thee?
Oh! shall we not say thou art *Love's duodecimo?*
None can be prettier, few can be less, you know.
Such a volume in *sheets* were a volume of charms,
Or, if *bound*, it should only be *bound in our arms!*

——◦❀◦——

SONG.

DEAR! in pity do not speak;
　In your eyes I read it all,
In the flushing of your cheek,
　In those tears that fall.
Yes, yes, my soul! I see
You love, you live for only me!

Beam, yet beam that killing eye,
　Bid me expire in luscious pain;
But kiss me, kiss me while I die,
　And, oh! I live again!
Still, my love! with looking kill,
And, oh! revive with kisses still!

——◦❀◦——

TO ———.

In bona cur quisquam tertius ista venit?—Ovid.

So! Rosa turns her back on me,
Thou walking monument! for thee!
Whose visage, like a grave-stone scribbled,
With vanity bedaub'd, befribbled,
Tells only to the *reading* eye,
That underneath corrupting lie,
Within thy heart's contagious tomb
(As in a cemetery's gloom),

Suspicion, rankling to infection,
And all the worms of black reflection!

And thou art Rosa's dear elect,
　And thou hast won the lovely trifle;
And I must bear repulse, neglect,
　And I must all my anguish stifle:
While thou for ever linger'st nigh,
　Scowling, muttering, gloating, mumming,
Like some sharp, busy, fretful fly,
　About a twinkling taper humming.

——◦❀◦——

TO MRS. ———.

YES, Heaven can witness how I strove
To love thee with a spirit's love;
To make thy purer wish my own,
And mingle with thy mind alone.
Oh! I appeal to those pure dreams
In which my soul has hung on thee,
And I've forgot thy witching form,
And I've forgot the liquid beams
That eye diffuses, thrilling warm—
Yes, yes, forgot each sensual charm,
Each maddening spell of luxury,
That could seduce my soul's desires,
And bid it throb with guiltier fires.
Such *was* my love, and many a time,
When sleep has given thee to my breast,
And thou hast seem'd to share the crime
Which made thy lover wildly blest;
E'en then, in all that rich delusion,
When, by voluptuous visions fired,
My soul, in rapture's warm confusion,
Has on a phantom's lip expired!
E'en *then* some purer thoughts would steal
Amid my senses' warm excess;
And at the moment—oh! e'en *then*
I've started from thy melting press,
And blush'd for all I've dared to feel,
Yet sigh'd to feel it all again!—
Such *was* my love, and still, O still
I might have calm'd the unholy thrill:
My heart might be a taintless shrine,
And thou its votive saint should be:
There, there I'd make thee all divine,
Myself divine in honouring thee.
But, oh! that night! that fatal night!
When both bewilder'd, both betray'd,
We sank beneath the flow of soul,
Which for a moment mock'd control;
And on the dangerous kiss delay'd,
And almost yielded to delight!
God! how I wish'd in that wild hour,
That lips alone, thus stamp'd with heat,
Had for a moment all the power
To make our souls effusing meet!
That we might mingle by the breath
In all of love's delicious death;

And in a kiss at once be blest,
As, oh! we trembled at the rest!(1)

———o◍◌o———

FANNY OF TIMMOL.

A MAIL-COACH ADVENTURE.

Quadrigis petimus bene vivere.—Horace.

SWEET Fanny of Timmol! when first you came in
  To the close little carriage in which I was hurl'd,
I thought to myself, if it were not a sin,
  I could teach you the prettiest tricks in the world.

For your dear little lips, to their destiny true, [other,
  Seem'd to know they were born for the use of an-
And to put me in mind of what I ought to do,
  Were eternally biting and kissing each other.

And then you were darting from eyelids so sly,—
  Half open, half shutting,—such tremulous light;
Let them say what they will, I could read in your eye
  More comical things than I ever shall write.

And oft, as we mingled our legs and our feet,
  I felt a pulsation, and cannot tell whether
In yours or in mine—but I know it was sweet,
  And I think we both felt it and trembled together.

At length when arrived, at our supper we sat,
  I heard with a sigh, which had something of pain,
That perhaps our last moment of meeting was that,
  And Fanny should go back to Timmol again.

Yet I swore not that I was in love with you, Fanny,—
  Oh, no! for I felt it could never be true;
I but said—what I 've said very often to many—
  There's few I would rather be kissing than you.

Then first I did learn that you once had believed
  Some lover, the dearest and falsest of men;
And so gently you spoke of the youth who deceived,
  That I thought you perhaps might be tempted again.

But you told me that passion, a moment amused,
  Was follow'd too oft by an age of repenting;
And check'd me so softly, that, while you refused,
  Forgive me, dear girl, if I thought 't was consenting!

And still I entreated, and still you denied,
  Till I almost was made to believe you sincere;
Though I found that, in bidding me leave you, you
    sigh'd,
  And when you repulsed me, 't was done with a tear.

In vain did I whisper, "There's nobody nigh;"
  In vain with the tremors of passion implore:
Your excuse was a kiss, and a tear your reply—
  I acknowledged them both, and I ask'd for no more.

(1) This warm effusion was, in former editions, termi-
nated by the lines headed "Fragment." page 82.—P. E.
(2) Cœnam, non sine candida puella.—*Cat.*, Carm. xiii.

Was I right?—oh! I cannot believe I was wrong.
  Poor Fanny is gone back to Timmol again;
And may Providence guide her uninjured along,
  Nor scatter her path with repentance and pain!

By Heaven! I would rather for ever forswear
  The Elysium that dwells on a beautiful breast,
Than alarm for a moment the *peace* that is there,
  Or banish the *dove* from so hallow'd a nest!

———o◍◌o———

AN INVITATION TO SUPPER.

TO MRS. ——.

MYSELF, dear Julia! and the Sun,
Have now two years of rambling run,
And he before his wheels has driven
The grand menagerie of heaven,
While I have met on earth, I swear,
As many bruies as he has there.
The only difference I can see
Betwixt the flaming god and me
Is, that his ways are periodic,
And mine, I fear, are simply *oddic.*
But, dearest girl! 't is now a lapse
Of two short years, or less, perhaps,
Since you to me, and I to you,
Vow'd to be ever fondly true;—
Ah, Julia! those were pleasant times!
You loved me for my amorous rhymes,
And I loved you, because I thought
'T was so delicious to be taught
By such a charming guide as you,
With eyes of fire and lips of dew,
All I had often fancied o'er,
But never, never felt before:
The day flew by, and night was short
For half our blisses, half our sport!

I know not how we changed, or why,
Or if the first was you or I:
Yet so 't is now, we meet each other,
And I'm no more than Julia's brother;
While she's so like my prudent sister,
There's few would think how close I've kiss'd her.

But, Julia, let those matters pass!
If you will brim a sparkling glass
To vanish'd hours of true delight,
Come to me after dusk to-night.
I'll have no other guest to meet you,
But here alone I'll *tête à tête* you,
Over a little Attic feast,
As full of cordial soul at least
As those where Delia met Tibullus,
Or Lesbia wanton'd with Catullus.(2)

I'll sing you many a roguish sonnet
About it, at it, and upon it;

And songs address'd, as if I loved,
To all the girls with whom I 've roved.
Come, pr'ythee come, you 'll find me here,
Like Horace, waiting for his dear. (1)
There shall not be to-night, on earth,
Two souls more elegant in mirth;
And, though our hey-day passion's fled,
The *spirit* of the love that 's dead
Shall hover wanton o'er our head ; ~
Like souls that round the grave will fly,
In which their late possessors lie:
And who, my pretty Julia, knows,
But when our warm remembrance glows,
The *ghost of Love* may act anew,
What Love *when living* used to do !

AN ODE UPON MORNING.

Turn to me, love! the morning rays
Are glowing o'er thy languid charms;
Take one luxurious parting gaze,
While yet I linger in thine arms.

'T was long before the noon of night
I stole into thy bosom, dear !
And now the glance of dawning light
Has found me still in dalliance here.

Turn to me, love! the trembling gleams
Of morn along thy white neck stray;
Away, away, you envious beams,
I 'll chase you with my lips away!

Oh ! is it not divine to think,—
While all around were lull'd in night,
While even the planets seem'd to wink,—
We kept our vigils of delight?

The heart, that little world of ours,
Unlike the drowsy world of care,
Then, then awaked its sweetest powers,
And all was animation there!

Kiss me once more, and then I fly,
Our parting would to noon-day last;
There, close that languid trembling eye,
And sweetly dream of all the past !

As soon as Night shall fix her seal
Upon the eyes and lips of men,
Oh, dearest ! I will panting steal
To nestle in thine arms again !

Our joy shall take their stolen flight,
Secret as those celestial spheres
Which make sweet music all the night,
Unheard by drowsy mortal ears !

(1)   puellam
     Ad mediam noctem expecto.
              Hor., lib. i., sat. 5.
(2) There are many spurious copies of this song in cir-

SONG. (2)

Oh ! nothing in life can sadden us,
While we have wine and good humour in store;
With this, and a little of love to madden us,
Show me the fool that can labour for more!
Come, then, bid Ganymede fill every bowl for you,
Fill them up brimmers, and drink as I call :
I 'm going to toast every nymph of my soul for you,
Ay, on my soul, I'm in love with them all!

Dear creatures ! we can't live without them,
They 're all that is sweet and seducing to man!
Looking, sighing about and about them,
We dote on them, die for them, all that we can.

Here's Phillis !—whose innocent bosom
Is always agog for some novel desires ;
To-day to get lovers, to-morrow to lose 'em,
Is all that the innocent Phillis requires.—
Here's to the gay little Jessy!—who simpers
So vastly good–humour'd whatever is done; [pers,
She 'll kiss you, and that without whining or whim-
And do what you please with you—all out of fun !
                Dear creatures, etc.

A bumper to Fanny!—I know you will scorn her,
Because she 's a prude, and her nose is so curl'd;
But if ever you chatted with Fan in a corner,
You 'd say she 's the best little girl in the world!—
Another to Lyddy !—still struggling with duty,
And asking her conscience still, "whether she should;"
While her eyes, in the silent confession of beauty,
Say, " Only for *something* I certainly would !"
                Dear creatures, etc.

Fill for Cloe!—bewitchingly simple,
Who angles the heart without knowing her lure;
Still wounding around with a blush or a dimple,
Nor seeming to feel that she also could cure!—
Here's pious Susan!—the saint, who alone, sir,
Could ever have made me religious outright:
For had I such a dear little saint of my own, sir,
I 'd pray on my knees to her half the long night !
                Dear creatures, etc.

JULIA'S KISS.

When infant Bliss in roses slept,
Cupid upon his slumber crept;
And, while a balmy sigh he stole,
Exhaling from the infant's soul,
He smiling said," With this, with this
I 'll scent my Julia's burning kiss !"

culation, and it is universally attributed to a gentleman
who has no more right than the Editor of these Poems to
any share whatever in the composition.—E.

Nay, more ; he stole to Venus' bed,
Ere yet the sanguine flush had fled,
Which Love's divinest, dearest flame
Had kindled through her panting frame.
Her soul still dwelt on memory's themes,
Still floated in voluptuous dreams ;
And every joy she felt before
In slumber now was acting o'er.
From her ripe lips, which seem'd to thrill
As in the war of kisses still,
And amorous to each other clung,
He stole the dew that trembling hung,
And smiling said, " With this, with this,
I 'll bathe my Julia's burning kiss."

—————o◦◦◦o—————

A FRAGMENT.

TO ————.

'T is night, the spectred hour is nigh!
Pensive I hear the moaning blast
Passing, with sad sepulchral sigh,
My lyre that hangs neglected by,
And seems to mourn for pleasures past!
That lyre was once attuned for thee
To many a lay of fond delight,
When all thy days were given to me,
And mine was every blissful night.
How oft I 've languish'd by thy side,
And while my heart's luxuriant tide
Ran in wild riot through my veins,
I 've waked such sweetly-maddening strains,
As if by inspiration's fire
My soul was blended with my lyre!
Oh! while in every fainting note
We heard the soul of passion float ;
While in thy blue dissolving glance,
I 've raptured read thy bosom's trance,
I 've sung and trembled, kiss'd and sung ;
Till, as we mingle breath with breath,
Thy burning kisses parch my tongue,
My hands drop listless on the lyre,
And, murmuring like a swan in death,
Upon thy bosom I expire!
Yes, I indeed remember well
Those hours of pleasure past and o'er :
Why have I lived their sweets to tell?
To tell, but never feel them more!
I should have died, have sweetly died,
In one of those impassion'd dreams,
When languid, silent on thy breast,
Drinking thine eyes' delicious beams,
My soul has flutter'd from its nest,
And on thy lip just parting sigh'd!
Oh! dying thus a death of love,
To heaven how dearly should I go!
He well might hope for joys above,
Who had begun them here below!

*   *   *   *   *

(1) All these songs were adapted to airs which Mr. Little composed, and sometimes sang, for his friends: this may

SONG.

A CAPTIVE thus to thee, my girl,
How sweetly shall I pass my age,
Contented, like the playful squirrel,
To wanton up and down my cage.

When Death shall envy joy like this,
And come to shade our sunny weather,
Be our last sigh the sigh of bliss,
And both our souls exhaled together!

—————o◦◦◦o—————

SONG. (1)

SWEETEST love! I 'll not forget thee ;
Time shall only teach my heart
Fonder, warmer, to regret thee,
Lovely, gentle as thou art!
Farewell, Bessy!

Yet, oh! yet again we 'll meet, love,
And repose our hearts at last :
Oh! sure 't will then be sweet, love,
Calm to think on sorrows past.
Farewell, Bessy!

Yes, my girl, the distant blessing
Mayn't be always sought in vain ;
And the moment of possessing—
Will 't not, love, repay our pain?
Farewell, Bessy!

Still I feel my heart is breaking,
When I think I stray from thee,
Round the world that quiet seeking,
Which I fear is not for me!
Farewell, Bessy!

Calm to peace thy lover's bosom—
Can it, dearest! must it be?
Thou within an hour shalt lose him,
He for ever loses thee!
Farewell, Bessy!

—————o◦◦◦o—————

SONG.

WHERE is the nymph, whose azure eye
Can shine through rapture's tear?
The sun has sunk, the moon is high,
And yet she comes not here!

Was that her footstep on the hill—
Her voice upon the gale?—
No, 't was the wind, and all is still :
Oh maid of Marlivale!

Come to me, love, I 've wander'd far,
'T is past the promised hour :
Come to me, love, the twilight star
Shall guide thee to my bower.

account for the peculiarity of metre observable in many of them.—E.

POEMS RELATING TO AMERICA.

PREFACE.

THE Poems suggested to me by my visit to Bermuda, in the year 1803, as well as by the tour which I made subsequently, through some parts of North America, have been hitherto very injudiciously arranged;—any distinctive character they may possess having been disturbed and confused by their being mixed up not only with trifles of a much earlier date, but also with some portions of a classical story, in the form of Letters, which I had made some progress in before my departure from England. In the present edition, this awkward jumble has been remedied; and all the Poems relating to my Transatlantic voyage will be found classed by themselves. As, in like manner, the line of route by which I proceeded through some parts of the States and the Canadas, has been left hitherto to be traced confusedly through a few detached notes, I have thought that, to future readers of these poems, some clearer account of the course of that journey might not be unacceptable,—together with such vestiges as may still linger in my memory of events now fast fading into the back ground of time.

For the precise date of my departure from England, in the *Phaeton* frigate, I am indebted to the "*Naval Recollections* of Captain Scott," then a midshipman of that ship. "We were soon ready," says this gentleman, "for sea, and a few days saw Mr. Merry and suite embarked on board. Mr. Moore likewise took his passage with us on his way to Bermuda. We quitted Spithead on the 25th of September (1803), and in a short week lay becalmed under the lofty peak of Pico."

During the voyage, I dined very frequently with the officers of the gun-room; and it was not a little gratifying to me to learn, from this gentleman's volume, that the cordial regard these social and openhearted men inspired in me was not wholly unreturned on their part. After mentioning our arrival at Norfolk, in Virginia, Captain Scott says, "Mr. and Mrs. Merry left the *Phaeton*, under the usual salute, accompanied by Mr. Moore;" then, adding some kind compliments on the score of talents, etc., he concludes with a sentence which it gave me tenfold more pleasure to read,—" The gun-room mess witnessed the day of his departure with genuine sorrow." From Norfolk, after a stay of about ten days, under the hospitable roof of the British Consul, Colonel Hamilton, I proceeded, in the *Driver* sloop of war, to Bermuda.

There was then on that station another youthful sailor, who has since earned for himself a distinguished name among English writers of travels, Captain Basil Hall,—then a midshipman on board the *Leander*. In his "*Fragments of Voyages and*

Travels," this writer has called up some agreeable reminiscences of that period; in perusing which—so full of life and reality are his sketches—I found all my own naval recollections brought freshly to my mind. The very names of the different ships, then so familiar to my ears—the *Leander*, the *Boston*, the *Cambrian*—transported me back to the season of youth and those Summer Isles once more.

The testimony borne by so competent a witness as Captain Hall to the truth of my sketches of the beautiful scenery of Bermuda is of far too much value to me, in my capacity of traveller, to be here omitted by me, however conscious I must feel of but ill deserving the praise he lavishes on me, as a poet. Not that I pretend to be at all indifferent to such kind tributes; —on the contrary, those are always the most alive to praise, who feel inwardly less confidence in the soundness of their own title to it. In the present instance, however, my vanity (for so this uneasy feeling is always called) seeks its food in a different direction. It is not as a poet I invoke the aid of Captain Hall's opinion, but as a traveller and observer; it is not to my invention I ask him to bear testimony, but to my matter-of-fact.

"The most pleasing and most exact description which I know of Bermuda," says this gentleman, "is to be found in Moore's *Odes and Epistles*, a work published many years ago. The reason why his account excels in beauty as well as in precision that of other men probably is, that the scenes described lie so much beyond the scope of ordinary observation in colder climates, and the feelings which they excite in the beholder are so much higher than those produced by the scenery we have been accustomed to look at, that, unless the imagination be deeply drawn upon, and the diction sustained at a correspondent pitch, the words alone strike the ear, while the listener's fancy remains where it was. In Moore's account there is not only no exaggeration, but, on the contrary, a wonderful degree of temperance in the midst of a feast which, to his rich fancy, must have been peculiarly tempting. He has contrived, by a magic peculiarly his own, yet without departing from the truth, to sketch what was before him with a fervour which those who have never been on the spot might well be excused for setting down as the sport of the poet's invention." (1)

How truly politic it is in a poet to connect his verse with well known and interesting localities,— to wed his song to scenes already invested with fame, and thus lend it a chance of sharing the charm which encircles them,—I have myself, in more than one instance, very agreeably experienced. Among the memorials of this description, which,

(1) *Fragments of Voyages and Travels*, vol. ii., chap. 6.

as I learn with pleasure and pride, still keep me remembered in some of those beautiful regions of the West which I visited, I shall mention but one slight instance, as showing how potently the Genius of the Place may lend to song a life and imperishableness to which, in itself, it boasts no claim or pretension. The following lines, in one of my Bermudian Poems,—

'T was there, in the shade of the Calabash Tree,
With a few who could feel and remember like me,

still live in memory, I am told, on those fairy shores, connecting my name with the picturesque spot they describe, and the noble old tree which I believe still adorns it. One of the few treasures (of *any* kind) I possess, is a goblet formed of one of the fruit-shells of this remarkable tree, which was brought from Bermuda, a few years since, by Mr. Dudley Costello, and which that gentleman, having had it tastefully mounted as a goblet, very kindly presented to me; the following words being part of the inscription which it bears :—" To Thomas Moore, Esq., this cup, formed of a calabash which grew on the tree that bears his name, near Walsingham, Bermuda, is inscribed by one who," etc., etc.

From Bermuda I proceeded in the *Boston*, with my friend Captain (now Admiral) J. E. Douglas, to New York, from whence, after a short stay, we sailed for Norfolk, in Virginia; and about the beginning of June, 1804, I set out from that city on a tour through part of the States. At Washington, I passed some days with the English minister, Mr. Merry; and was, by him, presented at the levee of the President, Jefferson, whom I found sitting with General Dearborn and one or two other officers, and in the same homely costume, comprising slippers and Connemara stockings, in which Mr. Merry had been received by him—much to that formal minister's horror—when waiting upon him, in full dress, to deliver his credentials. My single interview with this remarkable person was of very short duration ; but to have seen and spoken with the man who drew up the Declaration of American Independence was an event not to be forgotten.

At Philadelphia, the society I was chiefly made acquainted with, and to which (as the verses addressed to "Delaware's green banks"(1) sufficiently testify) I was indebted for some of my most agreeable recollections of the United States, consisted entirely of persons of the Federalist or Anti-Democratic party. Few and transient, too, as had been my opportunities of judging for myself of the political or social state of the country, my mind was left open too much to the influence of the feelings and prejudices of those I chiefly consorted with; and certainly, in no quarter was I so sure to find decided hostility, both to the men and the principles then dominant throughout the Union, as among officers

of the British navy, and in the ranks of an angry Federalist opposition. For any bias, therefore, that, under such circumstances, my opinions and feelings may be thought to have received, full allowance, of course, is to be made in appraising the weight due to my authority on the subject. All I can answer for, is the perfect sincerity and earnestness of the actual impressions, whether true or erroneous, under which my Epistles from the United States were written; and so strong, at the time, I confess, were those impressions, that it was the only period of my past life during which I have found myself at all sceptical as to the soundness of that liberal creed of politics, in the profession and advocacy of which I may be almost literally said to have begun life, and shall most probably end it.

Reaching, for the second time, New York, I set out from thence on the now familiar and easy enterprise of visiting the Falls of Niagara. It is but too true, of all grand objects, whether in nature or art, that facility of access to them much diminishes the feeling of reverence they ought to inspire. Of this fault, however, the route to Niagara, at that period —at least the portion of it which led through the Genesee country—could not justly be accused. The latter part of the journey, which lay chiefly through yet but half-cleared wood, we were obliged to perform on foot; and a slight accident I met with, in the course of our rugged walk, laid me up for some days at Buffalo. To the rapid growth, in that wonderful region, of, at least, the materials of civilisation,— however ultimately they may be turned to account, —this flourishing town, which stands on Lake Erie, bears most ample testimony. Though little better, at the time when I visited it, than a mere village, consisting chiefly of huts and wigwams, it is now, by all accounts, a populous and splendid city, with five or six churches, town-hall, theatre, and other such appurtenances of a capital.

In adverting to the comparatively rude state of Buffalo at that period, I should be ungrateful were I to omit mentioning, that, even then, on the shores of those far lakes, the title of " Poet,"—however unworthily in that instance bestowed,—bespoke a kind and distinguishing welcome for its wearer; and that the Captain who commanded the packet in which I crossed Lake Ontario, (2) in addition to other marks of courtesy, begged, on parting with me, to be allowed to decline payment for my passage.

When we arrived, at length, at the inn, in the neighbourhood of the Falls, it was too late to think of visiting them that evening ; and I lay awake almost the whole night with the sound of the cataract in my ears. The day following I consider as a sort of era in my life; and the first glimpse I caught of that wonderful cataract gave me a feeling which nothing in this world can ever awaken again.(3) It

(1) See Epistle to Mr. W. R. Spencer.
(2) The Commodore of the Lakes, as he is styled.
(3) The two first sentences of the above paragraph, as

well as a succeeding passage of this Preface, stood originally as part of the Notes on one of the American Poems.

was through an opening among the trees, as we approached the spot where the full view of the Falls was to burst upon us, that I caught this glimpse of the mighty mass of waters folding smoothly over the edge of the precipice; and so overwhelming was the notion it gave me of the awful spectacle I was approaching, that during the short interval that followed, imagination had far outrun the reality; and, vast and wonderful as was the scene that then opened upon me, my first feeling was that of disappointment. It would have been impossible, indeed, for any thing real to come up to the vision I had, in these few seconds, formed of it; and those awful scriptural words, "The fountains of the great deep were broken up," can alone give any notion of the vague wonders for which I was prepared.

But, in spite of the start thus got by imagination, the triumph of reality was, in the end, but the greater; for the gradual glory of the scene that opened upon me soon took possession of my whole mind; presenting, from day to day, some new beauty or wonder, and, like all that is most sublime in nature or art, awakening sad as well as elevating thoughts. I retain in my memory but one other dream—for such do events so long past appear—which can in any respect be associated with the grand vision I have just been describing; and, however different the nature of their appeals to the imagination, I should find it difficult to say on which occasion I felt most deeply affected, when looking on the Falls of Niagara, or when standing by moonlight among the ruins of the Coliseum.

Some changes, I understand, injurious to the beauty of the scene, have taken place in the shape of the Falls since the time of my visit to them; and among these is the total disappearance, by the gradual crumbling away of the rock, of the small leafy island which then stood near the edge of the Great Fall, and whose tranquillity and unapproachableness, in the midst of so much turmoil, lent it an interest which I thus tried to avail myself of, in a Song of the Spirit of that region : (1)

> There, amid the island-sedge,
> Just above the cataract's edge,
> Where the foot of living man
> Never trod since time began,
> Lone I sit at close of day, etc., etc.

Another characteristic feature of the vicinity of the Falls, which, I understand, no longer exists, was the interesting settlement of the Tuscarora Indians. With the gallant Brock,(2) who then commanded at Fort George, I passed the greater part of my time during the few weeks I remained at Niagara, and a visit I paid to these Indians, in company with him and his brother officers, on his going to distribute

among them the customary presents and prizes, was not the least curious of the many new scenes I witnessed. These people received us in all their ancient costume. The young men exhibited for our amusement in the race, the bat-game, and other sports, while the old and the women sat in groups under the surrounding trees; and the whole scene was as picturesque and beautiful as it was new to me. It is said that West, the American painter, when he first saw the Apollo, at Rome, exclaimed instantly, "A young Indian warrior!"—and, however startling the association may appear, some of the graceful and agile forms which I saw that day among the Tuscaroras were such as would account for its arising in the young painter's mind.

After crossing "the fresh-water ocean" of Ontario, I passed down the St. Lawrence to Montreal and Quebec, staying for a short time at each of these places, and this part of my journey, as well as my voyage on from Quebec to Halifax, is sufficiently traceable through the few pieces of poetry that were suggested to me by scenes and events on the way. And here I must again venture to avail myself of the valuable testimony of Captain Hall to the truth of my descriptions of some of those scenes through which his more practised eye followed me; taking the liberty to omit in my extracts, as far as may be done without injury to the style or context, some of that generous surplusage of praise in which friendly criticism delights to indulge.

In speaking of an excursion he had made up the river Ottawa,—"a stream," he adds, "which has a classical place in every one's imagination from Moore's Canadian Boat Song," Captain Hall proceeds as follows:—"While the poet above alluded to has retained all that is essentially characteristic and pleasing in these boat songs, and rejected all that is not so, he has contrived to borrow his inspiration from numerous surrounding circumstances, presenting nothing remarkable to the dull senses of ordinary travellers. Yet these highly poetical images, drawn in this way, as it were carelessly and from every hand, he has combined with such graphic—I had almost said geographical—truth, that the effect is great even upon those who have never, with their own eyes, seen the 'Utawa's tide,' nor 'flown down the Rapids,' nor heard the 'bell of St. Anne's' toll its evening chime; while the same lines give to distant regions, previously consecrated in our imagination, a vividness of interest, when viewed on the spot, of which it is difficult to say how much is due to the magic of the poetry, and how much to the beauty of the real scene."(3)

While on the subject of the Canadian Boat Song, an anecdote connected with that once popular ballad

---

(1) Introduced in the Epistle to Lady Charlotte Rawdon.
(2) This brave and amiable officer was killed at Queenston, in Upper Canada, soon after the commencement of the war with America, in the year 1812. He was in the

act of cheering on his men when he fell. The inscription on the monument raised to his memory, on Queenston Heights, does but due honour to his manly character.
(3) "It is singularly gratifying," the author adds, "to

may, for my musical readers at least, possess some interest. A few years since, while staying in Dublin, I was presented, at his own request, to a gentleman who told me that his family had in their possession a curious relic of my youthful days,—being the first notation I had made, in pencilling, of the air and words of the Canadian Boat Song, while on my way down the St. Lawrence,—and that it was their wish I should add my signature to attest the authenticity of the autograph. I assured him with truth that I had wholly forgotten even the existence of such a memorandum; that it would be as much a curiosity to myself as it could be to any one else, and that I should feel thankful to be allowed to see it. In a day or two after my request was complied with, and the following is the history of this musical "relic."

In my passage down the St. Lawrence, I had with me two travelling companions, one of whom, named Harkness, the son of a wealthy Dublin merchant, has been some years dead. To this young friend, on parting with him, at Quebec, I gave, as a keepsake, a volume I had been reading on the way,—Priestley's *Lectures on History;* and it was upon a fly-leaf of this volume I found I had taken down, in pencilling, both the notes and a few of the words of the original song by which my own boat-glee had been suggested. The following is the form of my memorandum of the original air:—

Then follows, as pencilled down at the same moment, the first verse of my Canadian Boat Song, with air and words as they are at present. From all this it will be perceived, that, in my own setting of the air, I departed in almost every respect but the time from the strain our *voyageurs* had sung to us, leaving the music of the glee nearly as much my own as the words. Yet, how strongly impressed I had become with the notion that this was the identical air sung by the boatmen—how closely it linked itself in my imagination with the scenes and sounds amidst which it had occurred to me,—may be seen by reference to a note appended to the glee as first published, which will be found in the following pages.

To the few desultory, and, perhaps, valueless recollections I have thus called up, respecting the contents of these productions, I have only to add, that the heavy storm of censure and criticism—some of it, I fear, but too well deserved—which, both in America and in England, the publication of my *Odes and Epistles* drew down upon me, was fol-

discover that, to this hour, the Canadian *voyageurs* never omit their offerings to the shrine of St. Anne, before engaging in any enterprise; and that, during its performance, they omit no opportunity of keeping up so propi-

lowed by results which have far more than compensated for any pain such attacks at the time may have inflicted. In the most formidable of all my censors, at that period,—the great master of the art of criticism, in our day,—I have found ever since one of the most cordial and highly valued of all my friends; while the good-will I have experienced from more than one distinguished American sufficiently assures me, that any injustice I may have done to that land of freemen, if not long since wholly forgotten, is now remembered only to be forgiven.

As some consolation to me for the onsets of criticism, I received, shortly after the appearance of my volume, a letter from Stockholm, addressed to "the author of *Epistles, Odes, and other Poems*," and informing me that "the Princes, Nobles, and Gentlemen, who composed the General Chapter of the most Illustrious, Equestrian, Secular, and Chapteral Order of St. Joachim," had elected me as a Knight of this Order. Notwithstanding the grave and official style of the letter, I regarded it, I own, at first, as a mere ponderous piece of pleasantry; and even suspected that in the name of St. Joachim, I could detect the low and irreverent pun of St. Jokehim.

On a little inquiry, however, I learned that there actually existed such an order of knighthood; that the title, insignia, etc., conferred by it had, in the instances of Lord Nelson, the Duke of Bouillon, and Colonel Imhoff, who were all Knights of St. Joachim, been authorised by the British Court; but that since then, this sanction of the Order had been withdrawn. Of course, to the reduction thus caused in the value of the honour was owing its descent in the scale of distinction to "such small deer" of Parnassus as myself. I wrote a letter, however, full of grateful acknowledgment, to Monsieur Hanson, the Vice Chancellor of the Order, saying that I was unconscious of having entitled myself, by any public service, to a reward due only to the benefactors of mankind, and therefore begged leave most respectfully to decline it.

———❦❀❧———

DEDICATION.

TO FRANCIS EARL OF MOIRA,

GENERAL IN HIS MAJESTY'S FORCES, MASTER-GENERAL OF THE ORDNANCE, CONSTABLE OF THE TOWER, ETC.

MY LORD,

It is impossible to think of addressing a Dedication to your Lordship without calling to mind the well-known reply of the Spartan to a rhetorician who proposed to pronounce an eulogium on Hercules. "On Hercules!" said the honest Spartan; " who ever thought of blaming Hercules?" In a similar manner the concurrence of public opinion has left to the

tious an intercourse. The flourishing village which surrounds the church on the 'Green Isle' in question owes its existence and support entirely to these pious contributions."

panegyrist of your Lordship a very superfluous task. I shall, therefore, be silent on the subject, and merely entreat your indulgence to the very humble tribute of gratitude which I have here the honour to present.

I am, my Lord,
With every feeling of attachment and respect,
Your Lordship's very devoted Servant,
THOMAS MOORE.

27, *Bury Street, St. James's,*
April 10, 1806.

----o❦❦❦o----

PREFACE.(1)

THE principal poems in the following collection were written during an absence of fourteen months from Europe. Though curiosity was certainly not the motive of my voyage to America, yet it happened that the gratification of curiosity was the only advantage which I derived from it. Finding myself in the country of a new people, whose infancy had promised so much, and whose progress to maturity has been an object of such interesting speculation, I determined to employ the short period of time, which my plan of return to Europe afforded me, in travelling through a few of the States, and acquiring some knowledge of the inhabitants.

The impression which my mind received from the character and manners of these republicans suggested the Epistles which are written from the city of Washington and Lake Erie. (2) How far I was right in thus assuming the tone of a satirist against a people whom I viewed but as a stranger and a visiter, is a doubt which my feelings did not allow me time to investigate. All I presume to answer for is the fidelity of the picture which I have given; and though prudence might have dictated gentler language, truth, I think, would have justified severer.

I went to America with prepossessions by no means unfavourable, and indeed rather indulged in many of those illusive ideas, with respect to the purity of the government and the primitive happiness of the people, which I had early imbibed in my native country, where, unfortunately, discontent at home enhances every distant temptation, and the western world has long been looked to as a retreat from real or imaginary oppression; as, in short, the elysian Atlantis, where persecuted patriots might find their visions realised, and be welcomed by kindred spirits to liberty and repose. In all these flattering expectations I found myself completely disappointed, and felt inclined to say to America, as Horace says to his mistress, "intentata nites." Brissot, in the preface

to his travels, observes, that "freedom in that country is carried to so high a degree as to border upon a state of nature;" and there certainly is a close approximation to savage life, not only in the liberty which they enjoy, but in the violence of party spirit and of private animosity which results from it. This illiberal zeal embitters all social intercourse; and, though I scarcely could hesitate in selecting the party whose views appeared to me the more pure and rational, yet I was sorry to observe that, in asserting their opinions, they both assume an equal share of intolerance; the Democrats, consistently with their principles, exhibiting a vulgarity of rancour, which the Federalists too often are so forgetful of their cause as to imitate.

The rude familiarity of the lower orders, and indeed the unpolished state of society in general, would neither surprise nor disgust if they seemed to flow from that simplicity of character, that honest ignorance of the gloss of refinement, which may be looked for in a new and inexperienced people. But when we find them arrived at maturity in most of the vices and all the pride of civilisation, while they are still so far removed from its higher and better characteristics, it is impossible not to feel that this youthful decay, this crude anticipation of the natural period of corruption, must repress every sanguine hope of the future energy and greatness of America.

I am conscious that, in venturing these few remarks, I have said just enough to offend, and by no means sufficient to convince; for the limits of a preface prevent me from entering into a justification of my opinions, and I am committed on the subject as effectually as if I had written volumes in their defence. My reader, however, is apprised of the very cursory observation upon which these opinions are founded, and can easily decide for himself upon the degree of attention or confidence which they merit.

With respect to the poems in general, which occupy the following pages, I know not in what manner to apologise to the public for intruding upon their notice such a mass of unconnected trifles, such a world of epicurean atoms as I have here brought in conflict together. (3) To say that I have been tempted by the liberal offers of my bookseller, is an excuse which can hope for but little indulgence from the critic; yet I own that, without this seasonable inducement, these poems very possibly would never have been submitted to the world. The glare of publication is too strong for such imperfect productions: they should be shown but to the eye of friendship,

---

(1) This preface, as well as the Dedication which precedes it, were prefixed originally to the volume entitled *Odes and Epistles,* of which, hitherto, the poems relating to the American tour have formed a part. The following mottoes were prefixed to the original edition:—
        Tanti non es, ais. Sapis, Luperce.
                    Martial, Lib. i., Epig. 118.

ΠΕΡΙΠΛΕΥΣΑΙ ΜΕΝ ΠΟΛΛΑΣ ΠΟΛΕΙΣ ΚΑΛΟΝ,
ΕΝΟΙΚΗΣΑΙ ΔΕ ΤΗ ΚΡΑΤΙΣΤΗ ΧΡΗΣΙΜΟΝ.

Plutarch. περι παιδων αγωγης.

(2) Episles VI., VII., and VIII.

(3) See the foregoing Note.

in that dim light of privacy which is as favourable to poetical as to female beauty, and serves as a veil for faults, while it enhances every charm which it displays. Besides, this is not a period for the idle occupations of poetry, and times like the present require talents more active and more useful. Few have now the leisure to read such trifles, and I sincerely regret that I have had the leisure to write them.

------⚬🕱⚬------

POEMS RELATING TO AMERICA.

TO LORD VISCOUNT STRANGFORD.
ABOARD THE PHAETON FRIGATE, OFF THE AZORES,
BY MOONLIGHT.

SWEET Moon! if, like Crotona's sage, (1)
By any spell my hand could dare
To make thy disk its ample page,
And write my thoughts, my wishes there;
How many a friend, whose careless eye
Now wanders o'er that starry sky,
Should smile, upon thy orb to meet
The recollection, kind and sweet,
The reveries of fond regret,
The promise, never to forget,
And all my heart and soul would send
To many a dear-loved distant friend.

How little, when we parted last,
I thought those pleasant times were past,
For ever past, when brilliant joy
Was all my vacant heart's employ:
When, fresh from mirth to mirth again,
We thought the rapid hours too few;
Our only use for knowledge then
To gather bliss from all we knew.
Delicious days of whim and soul!
When, mingling lore and laugh together,
We lean'd the book on Pleasure's bowl,
And turn'd the leaf with Folly's feather.
Little I thought that all were fled,
That, ere that summer's bloom was shed,
My eye should see the sail unfurl'd
That wafts me to the western world.

And yet, 't was time;—in youth's sweet days,
To cool that season's glowing rays,
The heart awhile, with wanton wing,
May dip and dive in Pleasure's spring;
But, if it wait for winter's breeze,
The spring will chill, the heart will freeze.

(1) Pythagoras; who was supposed to have a power of writing upon the Moon by the means of a magic mirror. —See *Bayle*, art. *Pythag.*

(2) Alluding to these animated lines in the 44th Carmen of Catulius:—

Jam mens prætrepidans avet vagari,
Jam læti studio pedes vigescunt!

And then, that Hope, that fairy Hope,—
Oh! she awaked such happy dreams,
And gave my soul such tempting scope
For all its dearest, fondest schemes,
That not Verona's child of song,
When flying from the Phrygian shore,
With lighter heart could bound along,
Or pant to be a wanderer more! (2)

Even now delusive hope will steal
Amid the dark regrets I feel,
Soothing, as yonder placid beam
Pursues the murmurers of the deep,
And lights them with consoling gleam,
And smiles them into tranquil sleep.
Oh! such a blessed night as this,
I often think, if friends were near,
How we should feel, and gaze with bliss
Upon the moon-bright scenery here!
The sea is like a silvery lake,
And o'er its calm the vessel glides
Gently, as if it fear'd to wake
The slumber of the silent tides.
The only envious cloud that lowers
Hath hung its shade on Pico's height,(3)
Where dimly, 'mid the dusky, he towers,
And, scowling at this heaven of light,
Exults to see the infant storm
Cling darkly round his giant form!

Now, could I range those verdant isles,
Invisible, at this soft hour,
And see the looks, the beaming smiles,
That brighten many an orange bower;
And could I lift each pious veil,
And see the blushing cheek it shades,—
Oh! I should have full many a tale,
To tell of young Azorian maids. (4)
Yes, Strangford, at this hour, perhaps,
Some lover (not too idly blest,
Like those, who in their ladies' laps
May cradle every wish to rest,)
Warbles, to touch his dear one's soul,
Those madrigals, of breath divine,
Which Camoens' harp from Rapture stole,
And gave, all glowing warm to thine. (5)
Oh! could the lover learn from thee,
And breathe them with thy graceful tone,
Such sweet beguiling minstrelsy
Would make the coldest nymph his own.

(3) A very high mountain on one of the Azores, from which the island derives its name. It is said by some to be as high as the Peak of Teneriffe.

(4) I believe it is Guthrie who says, that the inhabitants of the Azores are much addicted to gallantry. This is an assertion in which even Guthrie may be credited.

(5) These islands belong to the Portuguese.

But, hark!—the boatswain's pipings tell
'T is time to bid my dream farewell :
Eight bells :—the middle watch is set;
Good night, my Strangford!—ne'er forget
That, far beyond the western sea (1)
Is one, whose heart remembers thee.

——◦♦◦——

TO THE FLYING-FISH. (2)

WHEN I have seen thy snow-white wing
From the blue wave at evening spring,
And show those scales of silvery white,
So gaily to the eye of light,
As if thy frame were form'd to rise,
And live amid the glorious skies ;
Oh! it has made me proudly feel,
How like thy wing's impatient zeal
Is the pure soul, that rests not, pent
Within this world's gross element,
But takes the wing that God has given,
And rises into light and heaven !

But when I see that wing, so bright,
Grow languid with a moment's flight,
Attempt the paths of air in vain,
And sink into the waves again ;
Alas! the flattering pride is o'er ;
Like thee, awhile, the soul may soar,
But erring man must blush to think,
Like thee, again the soul may sink.

Oh Virtue! when thy clime I seek,
Let not my spirit's flight be weak : ·
Let me not, like this feeble thing,
With brine still dropping from its wing,
Just sparkle in the solar glow
And plunge again to depths below;
But, when I leave the grosser throng
With whom my soul hath dwelt so long,
Let me, in that aspiring day,
Cast every lingering stain away,
And, panting for thy purer air,
Fly up at once and fix me there.

——◦♦◦——

TO MISS MOORE,

FROM NORFOLK, IN VIRGINIA, NOVEMBER, 1803.

IN days, my Kate, when life was new,
When, lull'd with innocence and you,
I heard, in home's beloved shade,
The din the world at distance made;

When, every night my weary head
Sunk on its own unthorned bed,
And, mild as evening's matron hour
Looks on the faintly shutting flower,
A mother saw our eyelids close,
And bless'd them into pure repose;
Then, haply if a week, a day,
I linger'd from that home away,
How long the little absence seem'd!
How bright the look of welcome beam'd,
As mute you heard, with eager smile,
My tales of all that pass'd the while!

Yet now, my Kate, a gloomy sea
Rolls wide between that home and me ;
The moon may thrice be born and die,
Ere even that seal can reach mine eye,
Which used so oft, so quick to come,
Still breathing all the breath of home,—
As if, still fresh, the cordial air
From lips beloved were lingering there.
But now, alas,—far different fate!
It comes o'er ocean, slow and late,
When the dear hand that fill'd its fold
With words of sweetness may lie cold.

But hence that gloomy thought! at last,
Beloved Kate, the waves are past:
I tread on earth securely now,
And the green cedar's living bough
Breathes more refreshment to my eyes
Than could a Claude's divinest dyes.
At length I touch the happy sphere
To liberty and virtue dear,
Where man looks up, and, proud to claim
His rank within the social frame,
Sees a grand system round him roll,
Himself its centre, sun, and soul !
Far from the shocks of Europe—far
From every wild elliptic star
That, shooting with a devious fire,
Kindled by heaven's avenging ire,
So oft hath into chaos hurl'd
The systems of the ancient world.

The warrior here, in arms no more,
Thinks of the toil, the conflict o'er,
And glorying in the freedom won
For hearth and shrine, for sire and son,
Smiles on the dusky webs that hide
His sleeping sword's remember'd pride.

(1) The following note has been suppressed in the present edition :—
" From Captain Cockburn, who commanded the *Phaeton*, I received such kind attentions as I must ever remember with gratitude. As some of the journalists have gravely asserted that I went to America to speculate in lands, it may not be impertinent to state, that the object of this voyage across the Atlantic was my appointment to the office of Registrar of the Vice-Admiralty Court of Bermuda."—P. E.

(2) It is the opinion of St. Austin upon Genesis, and I believe of nearly all the Fathers, that birds, like fish, were originally produced from the waters ; in defence of which idea they have collected every fanciful circumstance which can tend to prove a kindred similitude between them: ευγγενειαν τοις πετομενοις προς τα νηκτα. With this thought in our minds, when we first see the Flying-Fish, we could almost fancy that we are present at the moment of creation, and witness the birth of the first bird from the waves.

While Peace, with sunny cheeks of toil,
Walks o'er the free unlorded soil,
Effacing with her splendid share
The drops that war had sprinkled there.
Thrice-happy land! where he who flies
From the dark ills of other skies,
From scorn, or want's unnerving woes,
May shelter him in proud repose :
Hope sings along the yellow sand
His welcome to a patriot land ;
The mighty wood, with pomp, receives
The stranger in its world of leaves,
Which soon their barren glory yield
To the warm shed and cultured field ;
And he, who came, of all bereft,
To whom malignant fate had left
Nor home nor friends nor country dear,
Finds home and friends and country here.

Such is the picture, warmly such,
That fancy long, with florid touch,
Had painted to my sanguine eye
Of man's new world of liberty.
Oh! ask me not, if Truth have yet
Her seal on fancy's promise set;
If even a glimpse my eyes behold
Of that imagined age of gold;—
Alas, not yet one gleaming trace! (1)
Never did youth, who loved a face
As sketch'd by some fond pencil's skill,
And made by fancy lovelier still,
Shrink back with more of sad surprise,
When the live model met his eyes,
Than I have felt, in sorrow felt,
To find a dream on which I 've dwelt
From boyhood's hour, thus fade and flee
At touch of stern reality ! (2)

But, courage, yet, my wavering heart!
Blame not the temple's meanest part, (3)

(1) Such romantic works as *The American Farmer's Letters*, and the *Account of Kentucky* by Imlay, would seduce us into a belief, that innocence, peace, and freedom had deserted the rest of the world for Martha's Vineyard and the banks of the Ohio. The French travellers, too, almost all from revolutionary motives, have contributed their share to the diffusion of this flattering misconception. A visit to the country is, however, quite sufficient to correct even the most enthusiastic prepossession.

(2) By comparing the following extract from the original poem with the passage commencing, "Oh! ask me not if truth have yet," and terminating "at touch of stern reality," it will be perceived that Mr. Moore has not limited himself to merely verbal changes. The same remark holds good with respect to the concluding lines of the epistle, but the alterations are not sufficiently important to render the quotation of them necessary :—

Oh! ask me not if Truth will seal
The reveries of Fancy's zeal,
If yet my charmed eyes behold
These features of an age of gold—

Till thou hast traced the fabric o'er:—
As yet, we have beheld no more
Than just the porch to Freedom's fane;
And, though a sable spot may stain
The vestibule, 't is wrong, 't is sin
To doubt the godhead reigns within!
So here I pause—and now, my Kate,
To you, and those dear friends, whose fate
Touches more near this home-sick soul
Than all the Powers from pole to pole,
One word at parting,—in the tone
Most sweet to you, and most my own.
The simple strain I send you here, (4)
Wild though it be, would charm your ear,
Did you but know the trance of thought
In which my mind its numbers caught.
'T was one of those half-waking dreams,
That haunt me oft, when music seems
To bear my soul in sound along,
And turn its feelings all to song.
I thought of home, the according lays
Came full of dreams of other days;
Freshly in each succeeding note
I found some young remembrance float,
Till following, as a clue, that strain,
I wander'd back to home again.

Oh! love the song, and let it oft
Live on your lip, in accents soft.
Say that it tells you, simply well,
All I have bid its wild notes tell,—
Of Memory's dream, of thoughts that yet
Glow with the light of joy that 's set,
And all the fond heart keeps in store
Of friends and scenes beheld no more.
And now, adieu!—this artless air,
With a few rhymes, in transcript fair,
Are all the gifts I yet can boast
To send you from Columbia's coast;
But when the sun, with warmer smile,
Shall light me to my destined isle, (5)

No—yet, alas ! no gleaming trace !
Never did youth, who loved a face
From portrait's rosy flattering art,
Recoil with more regret of heart,
To find an owlet eye of grey
Where painting pour'd the sapphire's ray,
Than I have felt, indignant felt,
To think the glorious dreams should melt
Which oft, in boyhood's witching time,.
Have wrapt me to this wondrous clime !—P. E.

(3) Norfolk, it must be owned, presents an unfavourable specimen of America. The characteristics of Virginia in general are not such as can delight either the politician or the moralist, and at Norfolk they are exhibited in their least attractive form. At the time when we arrived the yellow fever had not yet disappeared, and every odour that assailed us in the streets very strongly accounted for its visitation.

(4) A trifling attempt at musical composition accompanied this Epistle.

(5) Bermuda.

You shall have many a cowslip-bell,
Where Ariel slept, and many a shell,
In which that gentle spirit drew
From honey flowers the morning dew.

———◦❉◦———

A BALLAD:

THE LAKE OF THE DISMAL SWAMP.

WRITTEN AT NORFOLK, IN VIRGINIA.

" They tell of a young man, who lost his mind upon the
death of a girl he loved, and who, suddenly disappearing
from his friends, was never afterwards heard of. As he
had frequently said, in his ravings, that the girl was not
dead, but gone to the Dismal Swamp, it is supposed he had
wandered into that dreary wilderness, and had died of hun-
ger, or been lost in some of its dreadful morasses."—*Anon.*

" La Poésie a ses monstres comme la nature."
                                   —*D'Alembert.*

" THEY made her a grave too cold and damp
    For a soul so warm and true;
And she 's gone to the Lake of the Dismal Swamp,(1)
Where, all night long, by a fire-fly lamp,
    She paddles her white canoe.

" And her fire-fly lamp I soon shall see,
    And her paddle I soon shall hear;
Long and loving our life shall be,
And I 'll hide the maid in a cypress tree,
    When the footstep of death is near."

Away to the Dismal Swamp he speeds—
    His path was rugged and sore,
Through tangled juniper, beds of reeds,
Through many a fen, where the serpent feeds,
    And man never trod before.

And when, on the earth, he sunk to sleep,
    If slumber his eyelids knew,
He lay where the deadly vine doth weep
Its venomous tear, and nightly steep
    The flesh with blistering dew!

And near him the she-wolf stirr'd the brake,
    And the copper-snake breathed in his ear,
Till he starting cried, from his dream awake,
" Oh! when shall I see the dusky Lake,
    And the white canoe of my dear?"

He saw the Lake, and a meteor bright
    Quick over its surface play'd—
" Welcome," he said, " my dear-one's light!"
And the dim shore echo'd, for many a night,
    The name of the death-cold maid.

(1) The Great Dismal Swamp is ten or twelve miles
distant from Norfolk, and the Lake in the middle of it
(about seven miles long) is called Drummond's Pond.

(2) This poem formerly opened—
    Lady, where'er you roam, whatever beam
    Of bright creation warms your mimic dream;
    Whether you trace the valley's golden meads,
    Where mazy Linth his lingering current leads.—P. E.

(3) Lady Donegall, I had reason to suppose, was at this

Till he hollow'd a boat of the birchen bark,
    Which carried him off from shore;
Far, far he follow'd the meteor spark,
The wind was high and the clouds were dark,
    And the boat return'd no more.

But oft, from the Indian hunter's camp,
    This lover and maid so true
Are seen, at the hour of midnight damp,
To cross the Lake by a fire-fly lamp,
    And paddle their white canoe.

———◦❉◦———

TO THE MARCHIONESS DOWAGER OF DONEGALL.

FROM BERMUDA, JANUARY, 1804.

LADY! where'er you roam, whatever land
Woos the bright touches of that artist hand;(2)
Whether you sketch the valley's golden meads,
Where mazy Linth his lingering current leads;(3)
Enamour'd catch the mellow hues that sleep,
At eve, on Meillerie's immortal steep;
Or musing o'er the Lake, at day's decline,
Mark the last shadow on that holy shrine,(4)
Where, many a night, the shade of Tell complains,
Of Gallia's triumph and Helvetia's chains;
Oh! lay the pencil for a moment by,
Turn from the canvas that creative eye,
And let its splendour, like the morning ray,
Upon a shepherd's harp, illume my lay.

Yet, Lady, no—for song so rude as mine,
Chase not the wonders of your art divine;
Still, radiant eye, upon the canvas dwell;
Still, magic finger, weave your potent spell;
And, while I sing the animated smiles
Of fairy nature in these sun-born isles,
Oh, might the song awake some bright design,
Inspire a touch, or prompt one happy line,
Proud were my soul, to see its humble thought
On painting's mirror so divinely caught;
While wondering Genius, as he lean'd to trace
The faint conception kindling into grace,
Might love my numbers for the spark they threw,
And bless the lay that lent a charm to you.

Say, have you ne'er, in nightly vision, stray'd
To those pure isles of ever-blooming shade,
Which bards of old, with kindly fancy, placed
For happy spirits in the Atlantic waste? (5)

time still in Switzerland, where the well-known powers
of her pencil must have been frequently awakened.

(4) The chapel of William Tell on the Lake of Lucerne.

(5) M. Gebelin says, in his *Monde Primitif,* "Lorsque
Strabon crut que les anciens théologiens et poëtes pla-
çoient les champs élysées dans les isles de l'Océan Atlan-
tique, il n'entendit rien à leur doctrine." M. Gebelin's
supposition, I have no doubt, is the more correct; but that
of Strabo is, in the present instance, most to my purpose,

There listening, while, from earth, each breeze that
Brought echoes of their own undying fame,(1) [came
In eloquence of eye, and dreams of song,
They charm'd their lapse of nightless hours along:—
Nor yet in song, that mortal ear might suit,
For every spirit was itself a lute,
Where Virtue waken'd, with elysian breeze,
Pure tones of thought and mental harmonies.

Believe me, Lady, when the zephyrs bland
Floated our bark to this enchanted land,—
These leafy isles upon the ocean thrown,
Like studs of emerald o'er a silver zone,—
Not all the charm that ethnic fancy gave
To blessed arbours o'er the western wave,
Could wake a dream, more soothing or sublime,
Of bowers ethereal, and the Spirit's clime.

Bright rose the morning, every wave was still,
When the first perfume of a cedar hill
Sweetly awaked us, and, with smiling charms,
The fairy harbour woo'd us to its arms. (2)
Gently we stole, before the whispering wind,
Through plantain shades, that round, like awnings,
          twined
And kiss'd on either side the wanton sails,
Breathing our welcome to these vernal vales;
While, far reflected o'er the wave serene,
Each wooded island shed so soft a green,
That the enamour'd keel, with whispering play,
Through liquid herbage seem'd to steal its way.

Never did weary bark more gladly glide,
Or rest its anchor in a lovelier tide!
Along the margin many a shining dome,
White as the palace of a Lapland gnome,
Brighten'd the wave;—in every myrtle grove
Secluded bashful, like a shrine of love,
Some elfin mansion sparkled through the shade;
And, while the foliage interposing play'd,
Lending the scene an ever-changing grace,
Fancy would love, in glimpses vague, to trace
The flowery capital, the shaft, the porch,(3)
And dream of temples, till her kindling torch
Lighted me back to all the glorious days
Of Attic genius; and I seem'd to gaze

On marble, from the rich Pentelic mount,
Gracing the umbrage of some Naiad's fount.

Then thought I, too, of thee, most sweet of all
The spirit race that come at poet's call,
Delicate Ariel! (4) who, in brighter hours,
Lived on the perfume of these honey'd bowers,
In velvet buds, at evening, loved to lie,
And win with music every rose's sigh,
Though weak the magic of my humble strain
To charm your spirit from its orb again,
Yet, oh, for her, beneath whose smile I sing,
For her (whose pencil, if your rainbow wing
Were dimm'd or ruffled by a wintry sky,
Could smooth its feather and relume its dye,)
Descend a moment from your starry sphere,
And, if the lime-tree grove that once was dear,
The sunny wave, the bower, the breezy hill,
The sparkling grotto, can delight you still,
Oh cull their choicest tints, their softest light,
Weave all these spells into one dream of night,
And while the lovely artist slumbering lies,
Shed the warm picture o'er her mental eyes;
Take for the task her own creative spells,
And brightly show what song but faintly tells.

—o⋈o—
STANZAS.

Θυμος, δε ποτ' εμος————
————με προςφωνει ταδε·
Γινωσκε ταυθρωπεια μη σεβειν αγαν.
                    Æschyl., Fragment.

A beam of tranquillity smiled in the west,
    The storms of the morning pursued us no more;
And the wave, while it welcomed the moment of rest,
    Still heaved, as remembering ills that were o'er.

Serenely my heart took the hue of the hour,
    Its passions were sleeping, were mute as the dead,
And the spirit becalm'd but remember'd their power,
    As the billow the force of the gale that was fled.

I thought of those days, when to pleasure alone
    My heart ever granted a wish or a sigh;
When the saddest emotion my bosom had known
    Was pity for those who were wiser than I.

---

(1) In former editions—
      There, as eternal gales, with fragrance warm,
      Breathed from Elysium through each shadowy form.—P. E.
(2) Nothing can be more romantic than the little har-
bour of St. George's. The number of beautiful islets,
the singular clearness of the water, and the animated play
of the graceful little boats, gliding for ever between the
islands, and seeming to sail from one cedar-grove into
another, formed altogether as lovely a miniature of na-
ture's beauties as can well be imagined.

(3) This is an illusion which, to the few who are fanciful
enough to indulge in it, renders the scenery of Bermuda
particularly interesting. In the short but beautiful twilight
of their spring evenings, the white cottages, scattered over

the islands, and but partially seen through the trees that
surround them, assume often the appearance of little
Grecian temples, and a vivid fancy may embellish the
poor fisherman's hut with columns such as the pencil of a
Claude might imitate. I had one favourite object of this
kind in my walks, which the hospitality of its owner robbed
me of by asking me to visit him. He was a plain good
man, and received me well and warmly, but I could never
turn his house into a Grecian temple again.

(4) The following note is omitted in the present edition:—

Ariel. Among the many charms which Bermuda has for a poetic
eye, we cannot for an instant forget that it is the scene of Shak-
speare's Tempest, and that here he conjured up the "delicate Ariel,"
who alone is worth the whole heaven of ancient mythology.—P. E.

16

I reflected, how soon in the cup of Desire
  The pearl of the soul may be melted away;
How quickly, alas, the pure sparkle of fire [clay. (1)
  We inherit from heaven may be quench'd in the

And I pray'd of that Spirit who lighted the flame,
  That Pleasure no more might its purity dim;
So that, sullied but little, or brightly the same,
  I might give back the boon I had borrow'd from him.

How blest was the thought! it appear'd as if Heaven
  Had already an opening to Paradise shown;
As if, passion all chasten'd and error forgiven,
  My heart then began to be purely its own.

I look'd to the west, and the beautiful sky
  Which morning had clouded was clouded no more:
"Oh! thus," I exclaim'd, "may a heavenly eye
  Shed light on the soul that was darken'd before."

—————◦◦◦◦—————

TO GEORGE MORGAN, ESQ.

OF NORFOLK, VIRGINIA. (2)

FROM BERMUDA, JANUARY, 1804.

Κεινη δ' ηνεμοεσσα και ατροπος, οια θ' αλιπληξ,
Αιθυιης και μαλλον επιδρομος νεπερ ιπποις,
Ποντω ενεστηρικται.
        Callimach., Hymn, in Del., v. 11.

Oh, what a sea of storm we've pass'd!—(3)
  High mountain waves and foamy showers,
And battling winds, whose savage blast
  But ill agrees with one whose hours
Have pass'd in old Anacreon's bowers.
Yet think not poesy's bright charm
Forsook me in this rude alarm: (4)—

(1) This verse, in its original form, stood thus:—
    I felt how the pure intellectual fire
    In luxury loses its heavenly ray;
    How soon, in the lavishing cup of Desire,
    The pearl of the soul may be melted away!—P. E.

(2) This gentleman is attached to the British consulate
at Norfolk. His talents are worthy of a much higher
sphere; but the excellent dispositions of the family with
whom he resides, and the cordial repose he enjoys amongst
some of the kindest hearts in the world, should be almost
enough to atone to him for the worst caprices of fortune.
The consul himself, Colonel Hamilton, is one among the
very few instances of a man, ardently loyal to his king,
and yet beloved by the Americans. His house is the very
temple of hospitality; and I sincerely pity the heart of that
stranger who, warm from the welcome of such a board,
could sit down to write a libel on his host, in the true
spirit of a modern philosophist. See the *Travels* of the
Duke de la Rochefoucault Liancourt, vol ii.

(3) The opening of this poem has undergone some
change; in former editions it commenced—
    Oh, what a tempest whirl'd us hither!
    Winds whose savage breath could wither
    All the light and languid flowers
    That bloom in Epicurus' bowers!
    Yet think not, George, that Fancy's charm
    Forsook me in this rude alarm.—P. E.

(4) We were seven days on our passage from Norfolk to

When close they reef'd the timid sail,
  When, every plank complaining loud,
We labour'd in the midnight gale,
  And even our haughty mainmast bow'd,
Even then, in that unlovely hour,
  The Muse still brought her soothing power,
And, 'midst the war of waves and wind,
  In song's Elysium lapp'd my mind.
Nay, when no numbers of my own
Responded to her wakening tone,
She open'd, with her golden key,
  The casket where my memory lays
Those gems of classic poesy
  Which time has saved from ancient days.

Take one of these, to Laïs sung—
I wrote it while my hammock swung,
As one might write a dissertation
Upon "Suspended Animation!"

Sweet(5) is your kiss, my Laïs dear,
But with that kiss I feel a tear
Gush from your eyelids, such as start
When those who've dearly loved must part.
Sadly you lean your head to mine,
And mute those arms around me twine,
Your hair adown my bosom spread,
All glittering with the tears you shed.
In vain I've kiss'd those lids of snow,
For still, like ceaseless founts they flow,
Bathing our cheeks, whene'er they meet.
Why is it thus? do, tell me, sweet!
Ah, Laïs! are my bodings right?
Am I to lose you? is to-night

Bermuda, during three of which we were forced to lay-to
in a gale of wind. The *Driver* sloop of war, in which I went,
was built at Bermuda of cedar, and is accounted an excel-
lent sea-boat. She was then commanded by my very re-
gretted friend, Captain Compton, who in July last was
killed aboard the *Lily*, in an action with a French pri-
vateer. Poor Compton! he fell a victim to the strange
impolicy of allowing such a miserable thing as the *Lily* to
remain in the service; so small, crank, and unmanageable,
that a well-manned merchantman was at any time a match
for her.

(5) This epigram is by Paul the Silentiary, and may be
found in the *Analecta* of Brunck, vol. iii., p. 72. As the
reading there is somewhat different from what I have fol-
lowed in this translation, I shall give it as I had it in my
memory at the time, and as it is in Heinsius, who, I be-
lieve, first produced the epigram. See his *Poemata*.

'Ηδυ μεν εςι φιλημα το Λαιδος' ηδυ δε αυτων
  Ηπιοδινητων δακρυ χεεις βλεφαρων,
Και πολυ κιχλιδουσα σοβεις ευδοςρυχον αιγλην,
  'Ημετερα κεφαλην δηρον ερεισαμενη.
Μυρομενην δ' εφιλησα· τα δ' ως δροσερης απο πηγης,
  Δακρυα μιγνυμενων πιπτε κατα ςοματων·
Ειπε δ' ανειρομενω, τινος ουνεκα δακρυα λειβεις;
  Δειδια μη με λιπης· εςε γαρ ορκαπαται.

Our last——go, false to heaven and me!
Your very tears are treachery.

———

Such, while in air I floating hung,
  Such was the strain, Morgante mio!
The muse and I together sung,
  With Boreas to make out the trio.
But, bless the little fairy isle!
How sweetly after all our ills,
We saw the sunny morning smile
  Serenely o'er its fragrant hills;
And felt the pure delicious flow
Of airs, that round this Eden blow
Freshly as even the gales that come
O'er our own healthy hills at home.

Could you but view the scenery fair,
  That now beneath my window lies,
You'd think that nature lavish'd there
  Her purest wave, her softest skies,
To make a heaven for love to sigh in, ·
  For bards to live and saints to die in.
Close to my wooded bank below,
  In glassy calm the waters sleep,
And to the sunbeam proudly show
  The coral rocks they love to steep. (1)
The fainting breeze of morning fails;
  The drowsy boat moves slowly past,
And I can almost touch its sails
  As loose they flap around the mast.
The noontide sun a splendour pours
That lights up all these leafy shores;
While his own heaven, its clouds and beams,
  So pictured in the waters lie,
That each small bark, in passing, seems
  To float along a burning sky.

Oh for the pinnace lent to thee, (2)
  Blest dreamer, who, in vision bright,
Didst sail o'er heaven's solar sea,
  And touch at all its isles of light.
Sweet Venus, what a clime he found
Within thy orb's ambrosial round! (3)
There spring the breezes, rich and warm,
  That sigh around thy vesper car;

And angels dwell, so pure of form
  That each appears a living star. (4)
These are the sprites, celestial queen!
  Thou sendest nightly to the bed
Of her I love, with touch unseen
  Thy planet's brightening tints to shed;
To lend that eye a light still clearer,
  To give that cheek one rose-blush more,
And bid that blushing lip be dearer,
  Which had been all too dear before.

But, whither means the muse to roam?
'T is time to call the wanderer home.
Who could have thought the nymph would perch her
Up in the clouds with Father Kircher?
So, health and love to all your mansion!
Long may the bowl that pleasures bloom in,
  The flow of heart, the soul's expansion,
  Mirth and song, your board illumine.
At all your feasts, remember too,
  When cups are sparkling to the brim,
That here is one who drinks to you,
  And, oh! as warmly drink to him.

———◦◦◦———

LINES,
WRITTEN IN A STORM AT SEA.

That sky of clouds is not the sky
To light a lover to the pillow
  Of her he loves—
The swell of yonder foaming billow
Resembles not the happy sigh
  That rapture moves.

Yet do I feel more tranquil far
Amid the gloomy wilds of ocean,
  In this dark hour,
Than when, in passion's young emotion,
I've stolen, beneath the evening star,
  To Julia's bower.

Oh! there's a holy calm profound
In awe like this, that ne'er was given
  To Pleasure's thrill;
'T is as a solemn voice from heaven,
And the soul, listening to the sound,
  Lies mute and still.

(1) The water is so clear around the island, that the rocks are seen beneath to a very great depth; and, as we entered the harbour, they appeared to us so near the surface that it seemed impossible we should not strike on them. There is no necessity, of course, for heaving the lead; and the negro pilot, looking down at the rocks from the bow of the ship, takes her through this difficult navigation, with a skill and confidence which seem to astonish some of the oldest sailors.
Iam commoditati tuæ præparatam."—*Itinerar.* l., Dial. i.,
(2) In Kircher's *Ecstatic Journey to Heaven*, Cosmiel, the genius of the world, gives Theodidactus a boat of asbestos, with which he embarks into the regions of the sun. "Vides (says Cosmiel) hanc asbestinam navicu-

cap. 5. This work of Kircher abounds with strange fancies.
(3) When the Genius of the world and his fellow-traveller arrive at the planet Venus, they find an island of loveliness, full of odours and intelligences, where angels preside, who shed the cosmetic influence of this planet over the earth; such being, according to astrologers, the "vis influxiva" of Venus. When they are in this part of the heavens, a casuistical question occurs to Theodidactus, and he asks, "Whether baptism may be performed with the waters of Venus?" "An aquis globi Veneris baptismus institui possit?" to which the Genius answers, "Certainly."
(4) This idea is Father Kircher's. "Tot animatos soles dixisses."—*Itinerar.* l., Dial. i., cap. 5.

'T is true, it talks of danger nigh,
Of slumbering with the dead to-morrow
    In the cold deep,
Where pleasure's throb or tears of sorrow
No more shall wake the heart or eye,
    But all must sleep.

Well !—there are some, thou stormy bed,
To whom thy sleep would be a treasure;
    Oh ! most to him
Whose lip hath drain'd life's cup of pleasure,
Nor left one honey drop to shed
    Round sorrow's brim.

Yes—*he* can smile serene at death :
Kind heaven, do thou but chase the weeping
    Of friends who love him ;
Tell them that he lies calmly sleeping
Where sorrow's sting or envy's breath
    No more shall move him.

ODES TO NEA ;

WRITTEN AT BURMUDA.

NEA τυραννει.—*Euripid.*, Medea, v. 967.

Nay, tempt me not to love again :
    There was a time when love was sweet,
Dear Nea! had I known thee then,
    Our souls had not been slow to meet.
But, oh, this weary heart hath run,
    So many a time, the rounds of pain,
Not even for thee, thou lovely one,
    Would I endure such pangs again.

If there be climes, where never yet
    The print of beauty's foot was set,
Where man may pass his loveless nights,
    Unfever'd by her false delights,
Thither my wounded soul would fly,
    Where rosy cheek or radiant eye
Should bring no more their bliss or pain,
    Nor fetter me to earth again.

Dear absent girl ! whose eyes of light,
    Though little prized when all my own,
Now float before me, soft and bright
    As when they first enamouring shone,—
What hours and days have I seen glide,
While fix'd, enchanted, by thy side, (1)
Unmindful of the fleeting day,
I 've let life's dream dissolve away.
Oh bloom of youth profusely shed !
Oh moments ! simply, vainly sped,
Yet sweetly too—for Love perfumed
The flame which thus my life consumed ;

(1) Changed from—
    How many hours of idle waste
    Within those witching arms embraced.—P. E.

And brilliant was the chain of flowers,
In which he led my victim hours.

Say, Nea, say, couldst thou, like her,
When warm to feel and quick to err,
Of loving fond, of roving fonder,
This thoughtless soul might wish to wander,—
Couldst thou, like her, the wish reclaim,
    Endearing still, reproaching never,
Till even this heart should burn with shame,
    And be thy own more fix'd than ever ?
No, no—on earth there 's only one
    Could bind such faithless folly fast ;
And sure on earth but one alone
    Could make such virtue false at last

Nea, the heart which she forsook,
    For thee were but a worthless shrine—
Go, lovely girl, that angel look
    Must thrill a soul more pure than mine
Oh ! thou shalt be all else to me,
    That heart can feel or tongue can feign ;
I 'll praise, admire, and worship thee,
    But must not, dare not, love again.

—— Tale iter omne cave.
    Propert., lib. iv., Eleg. 8.

I pray you, let us roam no more
Along that wild and lonely shore,
    Where late we thoughtless stray'd ;
'T was not for us, whom Heaven intends
To be no more than simple friends,
    Such lonely walks were made.

That little bay, where turning in
From ocean's rude and angry din,
    As lovers steal to bliss,
The billows kiss the shore, and then
Flow back into the deep again,
    As though they did not kiss.

Remember, o'er its circling flood
In what a dangerous dream we stood—
    The silent sea before us,
Around us, all the gloom of grove,
That ever lent its shade to love,
    No eye but Heaven's o'er us !

I saw you blush, you felt me tremble,
In vain would formal art dissemble
    All we then look'd and thought ;
'T was more than tongue could dare reveal,
'T was every thing that young hearts feel,
    By Love and Nature taught. (2)

(2) In the original—
    'T was more than virtue ought to feel,
    But all that passion ought !—P. E.

I stoop'd to cull with faltering hand,
A shell that on the golden sand
   Before us faintly gleam'd;
I trembling raised it, and when you
Had kiss'd the shell, I kiss'd it too—
   How sweet, how wrong it seem'd! (1)

Oh, trust me, 'twas a place, an hour,
The worst that e'er the tempter's power
   Could tangle me or you in;
Sweet Nea, let us roam no more
Along that wild and lonely shore,
   Such walks may be our ruin.

—o&o—

You read it in these spell-bound eyes,
   And there alone should love be read;
You hear me say it all in sighs,
   And thus alone should love be said.

Then dread no more: I will not speak:
   Although my heart to anguish thrill,
I'll spare the burning of your cheek,
   And look it all in silence still.

Heard you the wish I dared to name,
   To murmur on that luckless night,
When passion broke the bonds of shame,
   And love grew madness in your sight?

Divinely through the graceful dance,
   You seem'd to float in silent song,
Bending to earth that sunny glance,
   As if to light your steps along.

Oh! how could others dare to touch
   That hallow'd form with hand so free,
When but to look was bliss too much,
   Too rare for all but Love and me!

With smiling eyes, that little thought
   How fatal were the beams they threw,
My trembling hands you lightly caught,
   And round me, like a spirit, flew.

Heedless of all, but you alone—
   And you, at least, should not condemn,
If, when such eyes before me shone,
   My soul forgot all eyes but them,—

I dared to whisper passion's vow,—
   For love had even of thought bereft me,—

(1) There are some verbal changes here:—
   I raised it to your lips of dew,
   You kiss'd the shell, I kiss'd it too—
   Good heaven! how sweet it seem'd!—P. E.

(2) The original ode read—
   Heedless of all, I wildly turn'd,
   My soul forgot—nor, oh! condemn,
   That when such eyes before me burn'd,
   My soul forgot all eyes but them!

Nay, half-way bent to kiss that brow,
   But, with a bound, you blushing left me. (2)

Forget, forget that night's offence,
   Forgive it, if, alas! you can;
'Twas love, 'twas passion—soul and sense—
   'Twas all that's best and worst in man.

That moment, did the assembled eyes
   Of heaven and earth my madness view,
I should have seen, through earth and skies,
   But you alone—but only you.

Did not a frown from you reprove,
   Myriads of eyes to me were none;
Enough for me to win your love,
   And die upon the spot, when won. (3)

—o&o—

A DREAM OF ANTIQUITY.

I just had turn'd the classic page,
   And traced that happy period over,
When blest alike were youth and age,
   And love inspired the wisest sage,
   And wisdom graced the tenderest lover.

Before I laid me down to sleep,
   Awhile I from the lattice gazed
Upon that still and moonlight deep,
   With isles like floating gardens raised,
For Ariel there his sports to keep;
While, gliding 'twixt their leafy shores,
The lone night-fisher plied his oars.

I felt—so strongly Fancy's power
   Came o'er me in that witching hour—
As if the whole bright scenery there
   Were lighted by a Grecian sky,
And I then breathed the blissful air
   That late had thrill'd to Sappho's sigh.

Thus, waking, dreamt I,—and when Sleep
   Came o'er my sense, the dream went on;
Nor, through her curtain dim and deep,
   Hath ever lovelier vision shone.
I thought that, all enrapt, I stray'd
Through that serene luxurious shade, (4)
Where Epicurus taught the Loves
   To polish Virtue's native brightness,—

   I dared to speak in sobs of bliss,
   Rapture of every thought bereft me;
   I would have clasp'd you—oh, even this!—
   But, with a bound, you blushing left me.—P. E.

(3) The last two lines of this quatrain in former editions stand—
   I should have—oh, my only love!
   My life!—what should I not have done?—P. E.

(4 Gassendi thinks that the gardens, which Pausanias

As pearls, we're told, that fondling doves
  Have play'd with, wear a smoother white-
'T was one of those delicious nights   [ness. (1)
  So common in the climes of Greece,
When day withdraws but half its lights,
  And all is moonshine, balm, and peace.
And thou wert there, my own beloved,
And by thy side I fondly roved
Through many a temple's reverend gloom,
And many a bower's seductive bloom,
Where Beauty learn'd what Wisdom taught,
And sages sigh'd and lovers thought;
Where schoolmen conn'd no maxims stern,
  But all was form'd to soothe or move,
To make the dullest love to learn,
  To make the coldest learn to love. (2)

And now the fairy pathway seem'd
  To lead us through enchanted ground,
Where all that bard has ever dream'd
  Of love or luxury bloom'd around.
Oh! 't was a bright bewildering scene—
  Along the alley's deepening green,
Soft lamps, that hung like burning flowers,
And scented and illumed the bowers,
Seem'd, as to him, who darkling roves
Amid the lone Hercynian groves,

mentions, in his first book, were those of Epicurus; and
Stuart says, in his *Antiquities of Athens*, "Near this convent
(the convent of Hagios Asomatos) is the place called at
present Kepoi, or the Gardens; and Ampelos Kepos, or
the Vineyard Garden: these were probably the gardens
which Pausanias visited." Vol. i., chap. 2.

(1) This method of polishing pearls, by leaving them
awhile to be played with by doves, is mentioned by the
fanciful Cardanus, *De Rerum Varietat.*, lib. vii., cap. 34.

(2) This beautiful Dream has been carefully retouched
by the author in the present edition, as will be perceived
on comparing the introductory lines with the following:—

  I just had turn'd the classic page,
    And traced that happy period over
  When love could warm the proudest sage,
    And wisdom grace the tenderest lover!
  Before I laid me down to sleep,
    Upon the bank awhile I stood,
  And saw the vestal planet weep
    Her tears of light on Ariel's flood.
  My heart was full of Fancy's dream,
    And, as I watch'd the playful stream,
  Entangling in its net of smiles
  So fair a group of elfin isles,
  I felt as if the scenery there
    Were lighted by a Grecian sky—
  As if I breathed the blissful air
    That yet was warm with Sappho's sigh!

  And now the downy hand of rest
    Her signet on my eyes imprest,
  And still the bright and balmy spell,
    Like star-dew, o'er my fancy fell!
  I thought that, all enrapt, I stray'd
  Through that serene luxurious shade,
  Where Epicurus taught the Loves
    To polish Virtue's native brightness,
  Just as the beak of playful doves
    Can give to pearls a smoother whiteness!

Appear those countless birds of light,
That sparkle in the leaves at night,
And from their wings diffuse a ray
Along the traveller's weary way. (3)
'T was light of that mysterious kind,
  Through which the soul perchance may roam,
When it has left this world behind,
  And gone to seek its heavenly home.
And, Nea, thou wert by my side,
Through all this heaven-ward path my guide. (4)

But, lo, as wandering thus we ranged
That upward path, the vision changed;
And now, methought, we stole along
  Through halls of more voluptuous glory
Than ever lived in Telan song,
  Or wanton'd in Milesian story. (5)
And nymphs were there, whose very eyes
Seem'd soften'd o'er with breath of sighs;
Whose every ringlet, as it wreathed,
A mute appeal to passion breathed. (6)
Some flew, with amber cups, around,
  Pouring the flowery wines of Crete; (7)
And, as they pass'd with youthful bound,
  The onyx shone beneath their feet. (8)
While others, waving arms of snow
  Entwined by snakes of burnish'd gold, (9)

    'T was one of those delicious nights
      So common in the climes of Greece,
    When day withdraws but half its lights,
      And all is moonshine, balm, and peace!
    And thou wert there, my own beloved!
    And dearly by thy side I roved
    Through many a temple's reverend gloom,
    And many a bower's seductive bloom,
    Where Beauty blush'd and Wisdom taught,
    Where lovers sigh'd and sages discern,
    Where hearts might feel or heads discern,
      And all was form'd to soothe or move,
    To make the dullest love to learn,
      To make the coldest learn to love!—P. E.

(3) "In Hercynio Germaniæ saltu inusitata genera alitum
accepimus quarum plumæ, ignium modo, colluceant noc-
tibus."—*Plin.*, lib. x., cap. 47.

(4) Changed from—

    And, Nea, thou didst look and move,
      Like any blooming soul of bliss,
    That wanders to its home above
      Through mild and shadowy light like this!—P. E.

(5) The Milesiacs, or Milesian fables, had their origin in
Miletus, a luxurious town of Ionia. Aristides was the
most celebrated author of these licentious fictions. See
Plutarch (in Crasso), who calls them ακολασα βιβλια.

(6) In the original poem—

    And nymphs were there, whose very eyes
      Seem'd almost to exhale in sighs;
    Whose every little ringlet thrill'd,
      As if with soul and passion fill'd!—P. E.

(7) "Some of the Cretan wines, which Athenæus calls
οινος ανθοσμιας, from their fragrancy resembling that of
the finest flowers."—*Barry on Wines*, chap. vii.

(8) It appears that in very splendid mansions, the floor
or pavement was frequently of onyx. Thus Martial : "Cal-
catusque tuo sub pede lucet onyx." Epig. 50., lib. xii.

(9) Bracelets of this shape were a favourite ornament

And showing charms, as loth to show,
  Through many a thin Tarentian fold, (1)
Glided among the festal throng,
Bearing rich urns of flowers along,
Where roses lay, in languor breathing,   [ing,
And the young bee-grape, (2) round them wreath-
Hung on their blushes warm and meek,
Like curls upon a rosy cheek.

Oh, Nea! why did morning break
  The spell that thus divinely bound me?
Why did I wake? how *could* I wake,
  With thee my own and heaven around me!

—————♦♦♦○—————

WELL—peace to thy heart, though another's it be,
And health to that cheek, though it bloom not for me!
To-morrow I sail for those cinnamon groves, (3)
Where nightly the ghost of the Carribee roves,
And, far from the light of those eyes, I may yet
Their allurements forgive and their splendour forget.

Farewell to Bermuda, (4) and long may the bloom
Of the lemon and myrtle its valleys perfume ;
May spring to eternity hallow the shade,
Where Ariel has warbled and Waller (5) has stray'd.
And thou—when, at dawn, thou shalt happen to roam
Through the lime-cover'd alley that leads to thy home,
Where oft, when the dance and the revel were done,
And the stars were beginning to fade in the sun,
I have led thee along, and have told by the way
What my heart all the night had been burning to say—
Oh! think of the past—give a sigh to those times,
And a blessing for me to that alley of limes.

—————♦♦♦○—————

IF I were yonder wave, my dear,
  And thou the isle it clasps around,
I would not let a foot come near
  My land of bliss, my fairy ground.

If I were yonder conch of gold,
  And thou the pearl within it placed,
I would not let an eye behold
  The sacred gem my arms embraced.

If I were yonder orange-tree,
  And thou the blossom blooming there,
I would not yield a breath of thee
  To scent the most imploring air.

Oh! bend not o'er the water's brink,
  Give not the wave that odorous sigh,
Nor let its burning mirror drink
  The soft reflection of thine eye.

That glossy hair, that glowing cheek,
  So pictured in the waters seem,
That I could gladly plunge to seek
  Thy image in the glassy stream. (6)

Blest fate! at once my chilly grave
  And nuptial bed that stream might be ;
I'll wed thee in its mimic wave,
  And die upon the shade of thee.

Behold the leafy mangrove, bending
  O'er the waters blue and bright,
Like Nea's silky lashes, lending
  Shadow to her eyes of light.

Oh! my beloved! where'er I turn,
  Some trace of thee enchants mine eyes ;
In every star thy glances burn ;
  Thy blush on every floweret lies.

Nor find I in creation aught
  Of bright, or beautiful, or rare,
Sweet to the sense, or pure to thought,
  But thou art found reflected there. (7)

among the women of antiquity. Οἱ ἐπικαρπιοι ὀφεις και
αἱ χρυσαι πεδαι Θαιδος και Αριςαγορας και Λαιδος
φαρμακα.—*Philostrat.*, Epist. xl. Lucian, too, tells us of
the βραχιοισι δρακοντες. See his *Amores*, where he
describes the dressing-room of a Grecian lady, and we
find the "silver vase," the rouge, the tooth-powder, and
all the "mystic order" of a modern toilet.

(1) Ταραντινιδιων, διαφανες ενδυμα, ωνομασμενον απο
της Ταραντινων χρησεως και τρυφης.—*Pollux.*

(2) Apiana, mentioned by Pliny, lib. xiv., and "now
called the Muscatell (a muscarum telis," says Pancirollus,
book I., sect. i., chap. 47.

(3) I had, at this time, some idea of paying a visit to the
West Indies.

(4) The inhabitants pronounce the name as if it were
written Bermooda. See the commentators on the words
"still-vex'd Bermoothes," in the *Tempest.*—I wonder it
did not occur to some of those all-reading gentlemen that,
possibly, the discoverer of this "island of hogs and devils"
might have been no less a personage than the great John

Bermudez, who, about the same period (the beginning of
the sixteenth century), was sent Patriarch of the Latin
church to Ethiopia, and has left us most wonderful stories
of the Amazons and the Griffins which he encountered.—
Travels of the Jesuits, vol. i. I am afraid, however, it
would take the Patriarch rather too much out of his way.

(5) Johnson does not think that Waller was ever at Ber-
muda; but the *Account of the European Settlements in
America* affirms it confidently. (Vol. ii.) I mention this
work, however, less for its authority than for the pleasure
I feel in quoting an unacknowledged production of the
great Edmund Burke.

(6) As first published—

  That glossy hair, that glowing cheek,
    Upon the billows poor their beam
  So warmly, that my soul could seek
    Its Nea in the painted stream.—P. E.

(7) Instead of the last verse, the poem formerly termi-
nated thus :—

  But then thy breath !—not all the fire
    That lights the lone Semenda's death

THE SNOW SPIRIT. (1)

No, ne'er did the wave in its element steep
    An island of lovelier charms ;
It blooms in the giant embrace of the deep,
    Like Hebe in Hercules' arms.
The blush of your bowers is light to the eye,
    And their melody balm to the ear;
But the fiery planet of day is too nigh,
    And the Snow Spirit never comes here.

The down from his wing is as white as the pearl
    That shines through thy lips when they part,
And it falls on the green earth as melting, my girl,
    As a murmur of thine on the heart.
Oh! fly to the clime, where he pillows the death,
    As he cradles the birth of the year;
Bright are your bowers and balmy their breath,
    But the Snow Spirit cannot come here.

How sweet to behold him when, born on the gale,
    And brightening the bosom of morn,
He flings, like the priest of Diana, a veil
    O'er the brow of each virginal thorn.
Yet think not the veil he so chillingly casts
    Is the veil of a vestal severe;
No, no, thou wilt see what a moment it lasts,
    Should the Snow Spirit ever come here.

But fly to his region—lay open thy zone,
    And he 'll weep all his brilliancy dim,
To think that a bosom, as white as his own,
    Should not melt in the daybeam like him.
Oh! lovely the print of those delicate feet
    O'er his luminous path will appear—
Fly, my beloved! this island is sweet,
    But the Snow Spirit cannot come here.

———o**H**o———

Ενταυθα δε καθωρμισαι ημιν. και ὁ, τι μεν ονομα τη
νησω, ουκ οιδα· χρυση δ' αν προς γε εμου ονομαδοιτο.
    —*Philostrat.*, Icon. 17., lib. ii.

I STOLE along the flowery bank,
    While many a bending sea-grape (2) drank
The sprinkle of the feathery oar
    That wing'd me round this fairy shore.

      In eastern climes, could e'er respire
        An odour like thy dulcet breath ! *

      I pray thee, on those lips of thine
        To wear this rosy leaf for me,
      And breathe of something not divine,
        Since nothing human breathes of thee!

      All other charms of thine I meet
        In nature, but thy sigh alone;
      Then take, oh ! take, though not so sweet,
        The breath of roses for thine own !

      So while I walk the flowery grove,
        The bud that gives, through morning dew,

   * Referunt tamen quidam in interiore India avem esse, nomine
Semendam, etc. Cardan. 10 de *Subtilitat.* Cæsar Scaliger seems
to think Semenda but another name for the Phœnix. *Exercitat.* 233.

'T was noon; and every orange bud
Hung languid o'er the crystal flood,
Faint as the lids of maiden's eyes
When love-thoughts in her bosom rise.
Oh, for a naiad's sparry bower,
To shade me in that glowing hour!

A little dove, of milky hue,
Before me from a plantain flew,
And, light along the water's brim,
I steer'd my gentle bark by him ;
For fancy told me, Love had sent
This gentle bird with kind intent
To lead my steps, where I should meet—
I knew not what, but something sweet.

And—bless the little pilot dove!
He had indeed been sent by Love,
To guide me to a scene so dear
As fate allows but seldom here;
One of those rare and brilliant hours,
That, like the aloe's (3) lingering flowers,
May blossom to the eye of man
But once in all his weary span.

Just where the margin's opening shade
A vista from the waters made,
My bird reposed his silver plume
Upon a rich banana's bloom.
Oh vision bright ! oh spirit fair !
What spell, what magic raised her there ?
'T was Nea ! slumbering calm and mild,
And bloomy as the dimpled child,
Whose spirit in elysium keeps
Its playful sabbath, while he sleeps.

The broad banana's green embrace
Hung shadowy round each tranquil grace;
One little beam alone could win
The leaves to let it wander in,
And, stealing over all her charms,
From lip to cheek, from neck to arms,
New lustre to each beauty lent,—
Itself all trembling as it went ! (4)

      The lustre of the lips I love,
        May seem to give their perfume too !—P. E.

(1) The motto to this ode has been suppressed:—

      Tu potes insolitas, Cynthia, ferre nives?
               Propert., Lib. i., Eleg.8.—P. E.

(2) The sea-side or mangrove grape, a native of the West
Indies.

(3) The Agave. This, I am aware, is an erroneous no-
tion, but it is quite true enough for poetry. Plato, I think,
allows a poet to be "three removes from truth ;" τριτα-
τος απο της αληθειας.

(4) Changed from—

      It glanced around a fiery kiss,
      All trembling, as it went, with bliss !—P. E.

Dark lay her eyelid's jetty fringe
Upon that cheek whose roseate tinge
Mix'd with its shade, like evening's light
Just touching on the verge of night. (1)
Her eyes, though thus in slumber hid,
Seem'd glowing through the ivory lid,
And, as I thought, a lustre threw
Upon her lip's reflecting dew,—
Such as a night-lamp, left to shine
Alone on some secluded shrine,
May shed upon the votive wreath,
Which pious hands have hung beneath. (2)

Was ever vision half so sweet!
Think, think how quick my heart-pulse beat,
As o'er the rustling bank I stole ;—
Oh! ye, that know the lover's soul,
It is for you alone to guess,
That moment's trembling happiness. (3)

———◦◉◦———

A STUDY FROM THE ANTIQUE. (4)

BEHOLD, my love, the curious gem
Within this simple ring of gold ;
'T is hallow'd by the touch of them
Who lived in classic hours of old.

Some fair Athenian girl, perhaps,
Upon her hand this gem display'd,
Nor thought that time's succeeding lapse
Should see it grace a lovelier maid.

Look, dearest, what a sweet design !
The more we gaze, it charms the more ;
Come—closer bring that cheek to mine,
And trace with me its beauties o'er.

Thou seest, it is a simple youth
By some enamour'd nymph embraced—
Look, as she leans, and say, in sooth
Is not that hand most fondly placed ?

Upon his curled head behind
It seems in careless play to lie, (5)
Yet presses gently, half inclined
To bring the truant's lip more nigh.

Oh happy maid ! too happy boy !
The one so fond and little loth,

The other yielding slow to joy—
Oh rare, indeed, but blissful both.

Imagine, love, that I am he,
And just as warm as he is chilling ;
Imagine, too, that thou art she,
But quite as coy as she is willing :

So may we try the graceful way
In which their gentle arms are twined,
And thus, like her, my hand I lay
Upon thy wreathed locks behind :

And thus I feel thee breathing sweet,
As slow to mine thy head I move ;
And thus our lips together meet,
And thus,—and thus,—I kiss thee, love.

———◦◉◦———

— λιβανωτῳ εικασεν, ὁτι απολλυμενον ευφραινει.
Aristot., Rhetor., lib. iii., cap. 4.

THERE 's not a look, a word of thine,
My soul hath e'er forgot ;
Thou ne'er hast bid a ringlet shine,
Nor given thy locks one graceful twine
Which I remember not.

There never yet a murmur fell
From that beguiling tongue,
Which did not, with a lingering spell,
Upon my charmed senses dwell,
Like songs from Eden sung.

Ah ! that I could at once forget
All, all that haunts me so—
And yet, thou witching girl—and yet,
To die were sweeter than to let
The loved remembrance go.

No ; if this slighted heart must see
Its faithful pulse decay,
Oh let it die, remembering thee,
And like the burnt aroma be
Consumed in sweets away.

———◦◉◦———

TO JOSEPH ATKINSON, ESQ.

FROM BERMUDA. (6)

" THE daylight is gone—but, before we depart,
One cup shall go round to the friend of my heart,

---

(1) In the original—
> Her eyelid's black and silken fringe
> Lay on her cheek, of vermil tinge,
> Like the first ebon cloud that closes
> Dark on evening's Heaven of roses !—P. E.

(2) These four lines have undergone some slight varia-
tion :—
> Such as, declining dim and faint,
> The lamp of some beloved saint
> Doth shed upon a flowery wreath,
> Which pious hands have hung beneath.—P. E.

(3) This couplet originally appeared—
> It is for you to dream the bliss,
> The tremblings of an hour like this !—P. E.

(4) This ode formerly appeared under the title of "A
kiss à l'antique."—P. E.

(5) Somewhat like the symplegma of Cupid and Psyche
at Florence, in which the position of Psyche's hand is
finely and delicately expressive of affection. See the
Museum Florentinum, tom. ii., tab. 43, 44. There are
few subjects on which poetry could be more interestingly
employed than in illustrating some of these ancient statues
and gems.

(6) Pinkerton has said that "a good history and descrip-
tion of the Bermudas might afford a pleasing addition to
the geographical library;" but there certainly are not

17

The kindest, the dearest—oh! judge by the tear
I now shed while I name him, how kind and how
   dear."

'T was thus in the shade of the Calabash Tree,
With a few, who could feel and remember like me,
The charm that, to sweeten my goblet, I threw,
Was a sigh to the past and a blessing on you.

Oh! say, is it thus, in the mirth-bringing hour,
When friends are assembled, when wit in full flower,
Shoots forth from the lip, under Bacchus's dew,
In blossoms of thought ever springing and new—
Do you sometimes remember, and hallow the brim
Of your cup with a sigh, as you crown it to him
Who is lonely and sad in these valleys so fair,
And would pine in elysium, if friends were not there!

Last night, when we came from the Calabash Tree,
When my limbs were at rest and my spirit was free,
The glow of the grape and the dreams of the day
Set the magical springs of my fancy in play,
And oh,—such a vision as haunted me then
I would slumber for ages to witness again.
The many I like and the few I adore,
The friends who were dear and beloved before,
But never till now so beloved and dear,
At the call of my Fancy surrounded me here;
And soon,—oh, at once, did the light of their smiles
To a paradise brighten this region of isles;
More lucid the wave, as they look'd on it, flow'd,
And brighter the rose, as they gather'd it, glow'd.

Not the valleys Hernæan (though water'd by rills
Of the pearliest flow, from those pastoral hills, (1)
Where the Song of the Shepherd, primeval and wild,
Was taught to the nymphs by their mystical child,)
Could boast such a lustre o'er land and o'er wave
As the magic of love to this paradise gave.

Oh, magic of love! unembellish'd by you,
Hath the garden a blush or the landscape a hue?
Or shines there a vista in nature or art,
Like that which love opes through the eye to the heart?

Alas, that a vision so happy should fade!
That, when morning around me in brilliancy play'd,
The rose and the stream I had thought of at night
Should still be before me, unfadingly bright;
While the friends, who had seem'd to hang over the
   stream,
And to gather the roses, had fled with my dream.

But look, where, all ready, in sailing array,
The bark that's to carry these pages away (2)
Impatiently flutters her wing to the wind,
And will soon leave these islets of Ariel behind.
What billows, what gales is she fated to prove,
Ere she sleep in the lee of the land that I love!
Yet pleasant the swell of the billows would be,
And the roar of those gales would be music to me.
Not the tranquillest air that the winds ever blew,
Not the sunniest tears of the summer-eve dew,
Were as sweet as the storm, or as bright as the foam
Of the surge, that would hurry your wanderer home.

materials for such a work. The island, since the time of its discovery, has experienced so very few vicissitudes, the people have been so indolent, and their trade so limited, that there is but little which the historian could amplify into importance; and, with respect to the natural productions of the country, the few which the inhabitants can be induced to cultivate are so common in the West Indies, that they have been described by every naturalist who has written any account of those islands.

It is often asserted by the trans-Atlantic politicians that this little colony deserves more attention from the mother-country than it receives, and it certainly possesses advantages of situation, to which we should not be long insensible, if it were once in the hands of an enemy. I was told by a celebrated friend of Washington, at New York, that they had formed a plan for its capture towards the conclusion of the American war; "with the intention (as he expressed himself) of making it a nest of hornets for the annoyance of British trade in that part of the world." And there is no doubt it lies so conveniently in the track to the West Indies, that an enemy might with ease convert it into a very harassing impediment.

The plan of Bishop Berkeley for a college at Bermuda, where American savages might be converted and educated, though concurred in by the government of the day, was a wild and useless speculation. Mr. Hamilton, who was governor of the island some years since, proposed if I mistake not, the establishment of a marine academy for the instruction of those children of West Indians, who

might be intended for any nautical employment. This was a more rational idea, and for something of this nature the island is admirably calculated. But the plan should be much more extensive, and embrace a general system of education; which would relieve the colonists from the alternative to which they are reduced at present, of either sending their sons to England for instruction, or intrusting them to colleges in the states of America, where ideas, by no means favourable to Great Britain, are very sedulously inculcated.

The women of Bermuda, though not generally handsome, have an affectionate languor in their look and manner, which is always interesting. What the French imply by their epithet *aimante* seems very much the character of the young Bermudian girls—that predisposition to loving, which, without being awakened by any particular object, diffuses itself through the general manner in a tone of tenderness that never fails to fascinate. The men of the island, I confess, are not very civilised; and the old philosopher, who imagined that, after this life, men would be changed into mules, and women into turtle-doves, would find the metamorphosis in some degree anticipated at Bermuda.

(1) Mountains of Sicily, upon which Daphnis, the first inventor of bucolic poetry, was nursed by the nymphs. See the lively description of these mountains in *Diodorus Siculus*, lib. iv. Ἡραια γαρ ορη κατα την Σικελιαν εστιν, ἁ φασι καλλει, κ. τ. λ.

(2 A ship, ready to sail for England.

THE STEERSMAN'S SONG,

WRITTEN ABOARD THE BOSTON FRIGATE, 28TH APRIL. (1)

WHEN freshly blows the northern gale,
And under courses snug we fly ;
Or when light breezes swell the sail,
And royals proudly sweep the sky ;
'Longside the wheel, unwearied still
I stand, and, as my watchful eye
Doth mark the needle's faithful thrill,
I think of her I love, and cry,
Port, my boy ! port.

When calms delay, or breezes blow
Right from the point we wish to steer ;
When by the wind close haul'd we go,
And strive in vain the port to near ;
I think 't is thus the fates defer
My bliss with one that's far away,
And while remembrance springs to her,
I watch the sails and sighing say,
Thus, my boy ! thus.

But see the wind draws kindly aft,
All hands are up the yards to square,
And now the floating stu'n-sails waft
Our stately ship through waves and air.
Oh ! then I think that yet for me,
Some breeze of fortune thus may spring,
Some breeze to waft me, love, to thee—
And in that hope I smiling sing,
Steady, boy ! so.

—→⧆○—

TO THE FIRE-FLY. (2)

AT morning, when the earth and sky
Are glowing with the light of spring,
We see thee not, thou humble fly !
Nor think upon thy gleaming wing.

But when the skies have lost their hue,
And sunny lights no longer play,
Oh then we see and bless thee too
For sparkling o'er the dreary way.

Thus let me hope, when lost to me
The lights that now my life illume,
Some milder joys may live, like thee,
To cheer, if not to warm, the gloom !

TO THE LORD VISCOUNT FORBES.

FROM THE CITY OF WASHINGTON. (3)

IF former times had never left a trace
Of human frailty in their onward race,
Nor o'er their pathway written, as they ran,
One dark memorial of the crimes of man ;
If every age, in new unconscious prime,
Rose, like a phœnix, from the fires of time,
To wing its way unguided and alone,
The future smiling and the past unknown ;
Then ardent man would to himself be new,
Earth at his foot and heaven within his view :
Well might the novice hope, the sanguine scheme
Of full perfection prompt his daring dream,
Ere cold experience, with her veteran lore,
Could tell him, fools had dreamt as much before.
But, tracing as we do, through age and clime,
The plans of virtue 'midst the deeds of crime,
The thinking follies and the reasoning rage
Of man, at once the idiot and the sage ;
When still we see, through every varying frame
Of arts and polity, his course the same,
And know that ancient fools but died, to make
A space on earth for modern fools to take ;
'T is strange, how quickly we the past forget ;
That Wisdom's self should not be tutor'd yet,
Nor tire of watching for the monstrous birth
Of pure perfection 'midst the sons of earth !

Oh ! nothing but that soul which God has given
Could lead us thus to look on earth for heaven ;
O'er dross without to shed the light within,
And dream of virtue while we see but sin.

Even here, beside the proud Potowmac's stream,
Might sages still pursue the flattering theme
Of days to come, when man shall conquer fate,
Rise o'er the level of his mortal state,
Belie the monuments of frailty past,
And plant perfection in this world at last !
" Here," might they say, " shall power's divided reign
Evince that patriots have not bled in vain.
Here godlike liberty's herculean youth,
Cradled in peace, and nurtured up by truth,
To full maturity of nerve and mind,
Shall crush the giants that bestride mankind. (4)
Here shall religion's pure and balmy draught
In form no more from cups of state be quaff'd,

(1) I left Bermuda in the *Boston* about the middle of
April, in company with the *Cambrian* and *Leander*,
aboard the latter of which was the Admiral, Sir Andrew
Mitchell, who divides his year between Halifax and Ber-
muda, and is the very soul of society and good-fellowship
to both. We separated in a few days, and the *Boston* after
a short cruise proceeded to New York.

(2) The lively and varying illumination, with which
these fire-flies light up the woods at night, gives quite an
idea of enchantment. " Puis ces mouches se developpant
de l'obscurite de ces arbres et s'approchant de nous, nous

les voyions sur les orangers voisins, qu'ils mettoient tout
en feu, nous rendant la vue de leurs beaux fruits dorés
que la nuit avoit ravie," etc., etc.—See *L'Histoire des
Antilles*, art. 2, chap. 4, liv. i.

(3) The following motto was formerly prefixed to this
epistle :—

Και μη Θαυμασης μητ' ει μακροτεραν γεγραφα την
επιςολην, μηδ' ει τι περιεργοτερον η πρεσβυτικωτε-
ρον ειρηκαμεν ἑαυτη.—*Isocrat.*, epist. iv.—P. E.

(4) Thus Morse. "Here the sciences and the arts of

But flow for all, through nation, rank, and sect,
Free as that heaven its tranquil waves reflect.
Around the columns of the public shrine
Shall grow:ng arts their gradual wreath entwine,
Nor breathe corruption from the flowering braid,
Nor mine that fabric which they bloom to shade.
No longer here shall Justice bound her view,
Or wrong the many, while she rights the few;
But take her range through all the social frame,
Pure and pervading as that vital flame
Which warms at once our best and meanest part,
And thrills a hair while it expands a heart!"

Oh golden dream! what soul that loves to scan
The bright disk rather than the dark of man,
That owns the good, while smarting with the ill,
And loves the world with all its frailty still,—
What ardent bosom does not spring to meet
The generous hope, with all that heavenly heat,
Which makes the soul unwilling to resign
The thoughts of growing, even on earth, divine!
Yes, dearest friend, I see thee glow to think
The chain of ages yet may boast a link
Of purer texture than the world has known,
And fit to bind us to a Godhead's throne.

But, is it thus? doth even the glorious dream
Borrow from truth that dim uncertain gleam,
Which tempts us still to give such fancies scope
As shock not reason, while they nourish hope?
No, no, believe me, 't is not so—even now,
While yet upon Columbia's rising brow,
The showy smile of young presumption plays,
Her bloom is poison'd and her heart decays.
Even now, in dawn of life, her sickly breath
Burns with the taint of empires near their death;
And, like the nymphs of her own withering
      clime,
She 's old in youth, she 's blasted in her prime. (1)

Already has the child of Gallia's school,
The foul Philosophy that sins by rule,
With all her train of reasoning, damning arts,
Begot by brilliant heads on worthless hearts,

Like things that quicken after Nilus' flood,
The venom'd birth of sunshine and of mud,—
Already has she pour'd her poison here
O'er every charm that makes existence dear;
Already blighted, with her blackening trace,
The opening bloom of every social grace,
And all those courtesies, that love to shoot
Round virtue's stem, the flowerets of her fruit.

And, were these errors but the wanton tide
Of young luxuriance or unchasten'd pride,
The fervid follies and the faults of such
As wrongly feel because they feel too much;
Then might experience make the fever less,
Nay, graft a virtue on each warm excess.
But no; 't is heartless speculative ill,
All youth's transgression with all age's chill;
The apathy of wrong, the bosom's ice,
A slow and cold stagnation into vice.

Long has the love of gold, that meanest rage,
And latest folly of man's sinking age,
Which, rarely venturing in the van of life,
While nobler passions wage their heated strife,
Comes skulking last, with selfishness and fear,
And dies, collecting lumber in the rear,—
Long has it palsied every grasping hand
And greedy spirit through this bartering land;
Turn'd life to traffic, set the demon gold
So loose abroad that virtue's self is sold,
And conscience, truth, and honesty are made
To rise and fall, like other wares of trade. (2)

Already in this free, this virtuous state,
Which, Frenchmen tell us, was ordain'd by fate,
To show the world what high perfection springs
From rabble senators and merchant kings,—
Even here already patriots learn to steal
Their private perquisites from public weal,
And, guardians of the country's sacred fire,
Like Afric's priests, let out the flame for hire.
Those vaunted demagogues, who nobly rose
From England's debtors to be England's foes, (3)
Who could their monarch in their purse forget,
And break allegiance, but to cancel debt, (4)

civilised life are to receive their highest improvements:
here civil and religious liberty are to flourish, unchecked
by the cruel hand of civil or ecclesiastical tyranny: here
genius, aided by all the improvements of former ages, is
to be exerted in humanising mankind, in expanding and
enriching their minds with religious and philosophical
knowledge," etc., etc.—P. 569.

(1) "What will be the old age of this government, if it
is thus early decrepit?" Such was the remark of Fauchet,
the French minister at Philadelphia, in that famous de-
spatch to his government, which was intercepted by one
of our cruisers in the year 1794. This curious memorial
may be found in *Porcupine's Works*, vol. i., p. 279. It
remains a striking monument of republican intrigue on
one side and republican profligacy on the other: and I
would recommend the perusal of it to every honest

politician, who may labour under a moment's delusion
with respect to the purity of American patriotism.

(2) "Nous voyons que dans les pays où l'on n'est affecté
que de l'esprit de commerce, on trafique de toutes les
actions humaines et de toutes les vertus morales."—*Mon-
tesquieu de l'Esprit des lois*, liv. xx., chap. 2.

(3) I trust I shall not be suspected of a wish to justify
those arbitrary steps of the English government which
the colonies found it so necessary to resist; my only object
here is to expose the selfish motives of some of the lead-
ing American demagogues.

(4) The most persevering enemy to the interests of this
country, amongst the politicians of the western world,
has been a Virginian merchant, who, finding it easier to
settle his conscience than his debts, was one of the first to
raise the standard against Great Britain, and has ever

Have proved at length the mineral's tempting hue,
Which makes a patriot, can unmake him too. (1)
Oh! Freedom, Freedom, how I hate thy cant!
Not Eastern bombast, not the savage rant
Of purpled madmen, were they number'd all
From Roman Nero down to Russian Paul,
Could grate upon my ear, so mean, so base,
As the rank jargon of that factious race,
Who, poor of heart and prodigal of words,
Form'd to be slaves, yet struggling to be lords,
Strut forth, as patriots, from their negro-marts,
And shout for rights, with rapine in their hearts. (2)

Who can, with patience, for a moment see
The medley mass of pride and misery,
Of whips and charters, manacles and rights,
Of slaving blacks and democratic whites, (3)
And all the piebald polity that reigns
In free confusion o'er Columbia's plains?
To think that man, thou just and gentle God!
Should stand before thee with a tyrant's rod
O'er creatures like himself, with souls from thee,
Yet dare to boast of perfect liberty!
Away, away—I'd rather hold my neck
By doubtful tenure from a sultan's beck,
In climes where liberty has scarce been named,
Nor any right but that of ruling claim'd,
Than thus to live, where bastard Freedom waves
Her fustian flag in mockery over slaves ;
Where—motley laws admitting no degree
Betwixt the vilely slaved and madly free—
Alike the bondage and the licence suit
The brute made ruler and the man made brute!

But, while I thus, my friend, in flowerless song,
So feebly paint what yet I feel so strong,
The ills, the vices of the land, where first
Those rebel fiends, that rack the world, were nurst,
Where treason's arm by royalty was nerved, [served,
And Frenchmen learn'd to crush the throne they
Thou, calmly lull'd in dreams of classic thought,
By bards illumined and by sages taught,
Pant'st to be all, upon this mortal scene,
That bard hath fancied or that sage hath been.
Why should I wake thee? why severely chase
The lovely forms of virtue and of grace,
That dwell before thee, like the pictures spread
By Spartan matrons round the genial bed,

since endeavoured to revenge upon the whole country the
obligations which he lies under to a few of its merchants.
(1. See Porcupine's account of the Pennsylvania insurrec-
tion in 1794. In short, see Porcupine's works throughout, for
ample corroboration of every sentiment which I have ven-
tured to express. In saying this, I refer less to the com-
ments of that writer than to the occurrences which he has
related and the documents which he has preserved. Opi-
nion may be suspected of bias, but facts speak for themselves.
(2) This couplet has been changed from—
    But pant for licence, while they spurn control,
    And shout for rights, with rapine in their soul !—P. E.

Moulding thy fancy, and with gradual art
Brightening the young conceptions of thy heart.

Forgive me, Forbes—and should the song destroy
One generous hope, one throb of social joy,
One high pulsation of the zeal for man,
Which few can feel, and bless that few who can,—
Oh! turn to him, beneath whose kindred eyes
Thy talents open and thy virtues rise,
Forget where nature has been dark or dim,
And proudly study all her lights in him.
Yes, yes, in him the erring world forget,
And feel that man *may* reach perfection yet.

———◦◦◦———

LINES

WRITTEN ON LEAVING PHILADELPHIA.

——Τηνδε την πολιν φιλως
Ε(πων· επαξια γαρ.
Sophocl., Œdip. Colon., v. 758.

ALONE by the Schuylkill a wanderer roved,
    And bright were its flowery banks to his eye;
But far, very far, were the friends that he loved,
    And he gazed on its flowery banks with a sigh.

Oh Nature, though blessed and bright are thy rays,
    O'er the brow of creation enchantingly thrown,
Yet faint are they all to the lustre that plays
    In a smile from the heart that is fondly our own.

Nor long did the soul of the stranger remain
    Unblest by the smile he had languish'd to meet;
Though scarce did he hope it would soothe him again,
    Till the threshold of home had been press'd by his
        feet.

But the lays of his boyhood had stolen to their ear,
    And they loved what they knew of so humble a name;
And they told him, with flattery welcome and dear,
    That they found in his heart something better than
        fame.

Nor did woman—oh woman! whose form and whose
        soul
    Are the spell and the light of each path we pursue ;
Whether sunn'd in the tropics or chill'd at the pole,
    If woman be there, there is happiness too:—

(3) In Virginia the effects of this system begin to be felt
rather seriously. While the master raves of liberty, the
slave cannot but catch the contagion, and accordingly
there seldom elapses a month without some alarm of in-
surrection amongst the negroes. The accession of Loui-
siana, it is feared, will increase this embarrassment; as
the numerous emigrations, which are expected to take
place, from the southern states to this newly-acquired
territory, will considerably diminish the white population,
and thus strengthen the proportion of negroes, to a degree
which must ultimately be ruinous.

Nor did she her enamouring magic deny,—
  That magic his heart had relinquish'd so long,—
Like eyes he had loved was *her* eloquent eye,
  Like them did it soften and weep at his song.

Oh, blest be the tear, and in memory oft
  May its sparkle be shed o'er the wanderer's dream;
Thrice blest be that eye, and may passion, as soft
  As free from a pang, ever mellow its beam!

The stranger is gone—but he will not forget,
  When at home he shall talk of the toils he has
    known,
To tell, with a sigh, what endearments he met,
  As he stray'd by the wave of the Schuylkill
    alone.

———◦∙◦◦∙◦———

TO THOMAS HUME, ESQ., M.D.

FROM THE CITY OF WASHINGTON.

Διηγησομαι δοηγηματα ισως απιστα, κοινωνα ων πεπονθα
ουκ εχων.—*Xenophont.*, Ephes. Ephesiac., lib. v.

'T is evening now ; beneath the western star
Soft sighs the lover through his sweet segar,
And fills the ears of some consenting she
With puffs and vows, with smoke and constancy.
The patriot, fresh from Freedom's councils come,
Now pleased retires to lash his slaves at home ;
Or woo, perhaps, some black Aspasia's charms,(1)
And dream of Freedom in his bondsmaid's arms.(2)

(1) The "black Aspasia" of the present .... of the
United States, inter Avernales haud ignotissima nymphas,
has given rise to much pleasantry among the anti-democrat
wits in America.

(2) This epistle formerly commenced thus :—

  'T is evening now : the beats and cares of day
  In twilight dews are calmly wept away.
  The lover now, beneath the western star,
  Sighs through the medium of his sweet cigar,
  And fills the ears of some consenting she
  With puffs and vows, with smoke and constancy !
  The weary statesman for repose hath fled
  From halls of council to his negro's shed,
  Where blest he woos some black Aspasia's grace,
  And dreams of freedom in his slave's embrace!—P. E.

(3) "On the original location of the ground now allotted
for the seat of the Federal City (says Mr. Weld), the iden-
tical spot on which the capitol now stands was called Rome.
This anecdote is related by many as a certain prognostic of
the future magnificence of this city, which is to be, as it
were, a second Rome."—*Weld's Travels*, letter iv.

(4) A little stream runs through the city, which, with
intolerable affectation, they have styled the Tiber. It was
originally called Goose-Creek.

(5) "To be under the necessity of going through a deep
wood for one or two miles, perhaps, in order to see a
next-door neighbour, and in the same city, is a curious
and, I believe, a novel circumstance."—*Weld*, letter iv.
The Federal City (if it must be called a city) has not been
much increased since Mr. Weld visited it. Most of the
public buildings, which were then in some degree of
forwardness, have been since utterly suspended. The

In Fancy now, beneath the twilight gloom,
Come, let me lead thee o'er this " second Rome !"(3)
Where tribunes rule, where dusky Davi bow,
And what was Goose-Creek once is Tiber now :—(4)
This embryo capital, where Fancy sees
Squares in morasses, obelisks in trees ;
Which second-sighted seers, even now, adorn
With shrines unbuilt and heroes yet unborn,
Though nought but woods (5) and J————n they
    see,
Where streets should run and sages *ought* to be.

  And look, how calmly in yon radiant wave,
The dying sun prepares his golden grave.
Oh mighty river ! oh ye banks of shade !
Ye matchless scenes, in nature's morning made,
While still, in all the exuberance of prime,
She pour'd her wonders lavishly sublime,
Nor yet had learn'd to stoop, with humbler care,
From grand to soft, from wonderful to fair ;—
Say, were your towering hills, your boundless floods,
Your rich savannas and majestic woods,
Where bards should meditate and heroes rove,
And woman charm, and man deserve her love,—
Oh say, was world so bright but born to grace
Its own half-organised, half-minded race (6)
Of weak barbarians, swarming o'er its breast,
Like vermin gender'd on the lion's crest?
Were none but brutes to call that soil their home,
Where none but demigods should dare to roam?

hotel is already a ruin ; a great part of its roof has fallen
in, and the rooms are left to be occupied gratuitously by
the miserable Scotch and Irish emigrants. The Presi-
dent's house, a very noble structure, is by no means
suited to the philosophical humility of its present posses-
sor, who inhabits but a corner of the mansion himself,
and abandons the rest to a state of uncleanly desolation,
which those who are not philosophers cannot look at
without regret. This grand edifice is encircled by a very
rude paling, through which a common rustic stile intro-
duces the visiters of the first man in America. With
respect to all that is within the house, I shall imitate the
prudent forbearance of Herodotus, and say, τα δε εν
απορρητῳ.
The private buildings exhibit the same characteristic
display of arrogant speculation and premature ruin ; and
the few ranges of houses which were begun some years
ago have remained so long waste and unfinished that they
are now for the most part dilapidated.

(6) The picture which Buffon and De Pauw have drawn
of the American Indian, though very humiliating, is, as
far as I can judge, much more correct than the flattering
representations which Mr. Jefferson has given us. See
the Notes on Virginia, where this gentleman endeavours
to disprove in general the opinion maintained so strongly
by some philosophers, that nature (as Mr. Jefferson ex-
presses it) *be-littles* her productions in the western world.
M. de Pauw attributes the imperfection of animal life in
America to the ravages of a very recent deluge, from
whose effects upon its soil and atmosphere it has not yet
sufficiently recovered.—*Recherches sur les Américains*,
part i., tom. i., p. 102.

Or worse, thou wondrous world! oh! doubly worse,
Did heaven design thy lordly land to nurse
The motley dregs of every distant clime,
Each blast of anarchy and taint of crime
Which Europe shakes from her perturbed sphere,
In full malignity to rankle here?

But, hold,—observe yon little mount of pines,
Where the breeze murmurs and the fire-fly shines,
There let thy fancy raise, in bold relief,
The sculptured image of that veteran chief (1)
Who lost the rebel's in the hero's name,
And climb'd o'er prostrate loyalty to fame;
Beneath whose sword Columbia's patriot train
Cast off their monarch, that their mob might reign.

How shall we rank thee upon glory's page?
Thou more than soldier and just less than sage!
Of peace too fond to act the conqueror's part,
Too long in camps to learn a statesman's art,
Nature design'd thee for a hero's mould,
But, ere she cast thee, let the stuff grow cold.

While loftier souls command, nay, make their fate,
Thy fate made thee, and forced thee to be great.
Yet Fortune, who so oft, so blindly sheds
Her brightest halo round the weakest heads,
Found *thee* undazzled, tranquil as before,
Proud to be useful, scorning to be more;
Less moved by glory's than by duty's claim,
Renown the meed, but self-applause the aim;
All that thou *wert* reflects less fame on thee,
Far less, than all thou didst *forbear to be.*
Nor yet the patriot of one land alone,—
For thine's a name all nations claim their own;
And every shore, where breathed the good and brave,
Echo'd the plaudits thy own country gave.

Now look, my friend, where faint the moonlight falls
On yonder dome, and, in those princely halls,—
If thou canst hate, as sure that soul must hate,
Which loves the virtuous, and reveres the great,—
If thou canst loathe and execrate with me
The poisonous drug of French philosophy,

That nauseous slaver of these frantic times,
With which false liberty dilutes her crimes,—
If thou hast got, within thy freeborn breast,
One pulse that beats more proudly than the rest,
With honest scorn for that inglorious soul,
Which creeps and winds beneath a mob's control,
Which courts the rabble's smile, the rabble's nod,
And makes, like Egypt, every beast its god,
There, in those walls—but, burning tongue, forbear!
Rank must be reverenced, even the rank that's there:
So here I pause—and now, dear Hume, we part;
But oft again, in frank exchange of heart,
Thus let us meet, and mingle converse dear
By Thames at home, or by Potowmac here.
O'er lake and marsh, through fevers and through fogs,
'Midst bears and yankees, democrats and frogs,
Thy foot shall follow me, thy heart and eyes
With me shall wonder, and with me despise. (2)
While I, as oft, in fancy's dream shall rove,
With thee conversing, through that land I love,
Where, like the air that fans her fields of green,
Her freedom spreads, unfever'd and serene;
And sovereign man can condescend to see
The throne and laws more sovereign still than he.

————

LINES

WRITTEN AT THE COHOS, OR FALLS OF MOHAWK RIVER. (3)

Già era in loco ove s' udia 'l rimbombo
 Dell' acqua——.—*Dante.*

FROM rise of morn till set of sun
I've seen the mighty Mohawk run;
And as I mark'd the woods of pine
Along his mirror darkly shine,
Like tall and gloomy forms that pass
Before the wizard's midnight glass;
And as I view'd the hurrying pace
With which he ran his turbid race,
Rushing, alike untired and wild,
Through shades that frown'd and flowers that
Flying by every green recess   [smiled,
That woo'd him to its calm caress,
Yet sometimes turning with the wind,
As if to leave one look behind,—

(1) On a small hill near the capitol there is to be an equestrian statue of General Washington.

(2) In the ferment which the French revolution excited among the democrats of America, and the licentious sympathy with which they shared in the wildest excesses of jacobinism, we may find one source of that vulgarity of vice, that hostility to all the graces of life, which distinguishes the present demagogues of the United States, and has become indeed too generally the characteristic of their countrymen. But there is another cause of the corruption of private morals, which, encouraged as it is by the government, and identified with the interests of the community, seems to threaten the decay of all honest principle in America. I allude to those fraudulent violations of neutrality to which they are indebted for the most lucrative part of their commerce, and by which they have

so long infringed and counteracted the maritime rights and advantages of this country. This unwarrantable trade is necessarily abetted by such a system of collusion, imposture, and perjury, as cannot fail to spread rapid contamination around it.

(3) There is a dreary and savage character in the country immediately about these Falls, which is much more in harmony with the wildness of such a scene than the cultivated lands in the neighbourhood of Niagara. See the drawing of them in Mr. Weld's book. According to him, the perpendicular height of the Cohos Fall is fifty feet; but the Marquis de Chastellux makes it seventy-six.

The fine rainbow, which is continually forming and dissolving, as the spray rises into the light of the sun, is perhaps the most interesting beauty which these wonderful cataracts exhibit.

Oft have I thought, and thinking sigh'd,
How like to thee, thou restless tide,
May be the lot, the life of him
Who roams along thy water's brim;
Through what alternate wastes of woe
And flowers of joy my path may go;
How many a shelter'd calm retreat
May woo the while my weary feet,
While still pursuing, still unblest,
I wander on, nor dare to rest;
But, urgent as the doom that calls
Thy water to its destined falls,
I feel the world's bewildering force
Hurry my heart's devoted course
From lapse to lapse, till life be done,
And the spent current cease to run.

One only prayer I dare to make,
As onward thus my course I take;—
Oh, be my falls as bright as thine!
May heaven's relenting rainbow shine
Upon the mist that circles me,
As soft as now it hangs o'er thee!

SONG

OF THE EVIL SPIRIT OF THE WOODS. (1)

Qua via difficilis, quaque est via nulla.
    Ovid., Metam., lib. iii., v. 227.

Now the vapour, hot and damp,
Shed by day's expiring lamp,
Through the misty ether spreads
Every ill the white man dreads;
Fiery fever's thirsty thrill,
Fitful ague's shivering chill!

Hark! I hear the traveller's song,
As he winds the woods along:—
Christian, 't is the song of fear;
Wolves are round thee, night is near,
And the wild thou darest to roam—
Think, 't was once the Indian's home! (2)

Hither, sprites, who love to harm,
Wheresoe'er you work your charm,

By the creeks, or by the brakes,
Where the pale witch feeds her snakes,
And the cayman (3) loves to creep,
Torpid, to his wintry sleep:
Where the bird of carrion flits,
And the shuddering murderer sits, (4)
Lone beneath a roof of blood;
While upon his poison'd food,
From the corpse of him he slew
Drops the chill and gory dew.

Hither bend ye, turn ye hither,
Eyes that blast and wings that wither!
Cross the wandering Christian's way,
Lead him, ere the glimpse of day,
Many a mile of maddening error
Through the maze of night and terror,
Till the morn behold him lying
On the damp earth, pale and dying.
Mock him, when his eager sight
Seeks the cordial cottage-light;
Gleam then, like the lightning-bug,
Tempt him to the den that's dug
For the foul and famish'd brood
Of the she-wolf, gaunt for blood;
Or, unto the dangerous pass
O'er the deep and dark morass,
Where the trembling Indian brings
Belts of porcelain, pipes, and rings,
Tributes, to be hung in air,
To the Fiend presiding there! (5)

Then, when night's long labour past,
Wilder'd, faint, he falls at last,
Sinking where the causeway's edge
Moulders in the slimy sedge,
There let every noxious thing
Trail its filth and fix its sting;
Let the bull-toad taint him over,
Round him let musquitoes hover,
In his ears and eyeballs tingling,
With his blood their poison mingling,
Till, beneath the solar fires,
Rankling all, the wretch expires!

(1) The idea of this poem occurred to me in passing through the very dreary wilderness between Batavia, a new settlement in the midst of the woods, and the little village of Buffalo upon Lake Erie. This is the most fatiguing part of the route through the Genesee country to Niagara.

(2) "The Five Confederated Nations (of Indians) were settled along the banks of the Susquehannah and the adjacent country, until the year 1779, when General Sullivan, with an army of 4000 men, drove them from their country to Niagara, where, being obliged to live on salted provisions, to which they were unaccustomed, great numbers of them died. 200 were buried in one grave, where they had encamped."—*Morse's Amer. Geog.*

(3) The alligator, who is supposed to lie in a torpid state all the winter, in the bank of some creek or pond, having previously swallowed a large number of pine-knots, which are his only sustenance during the time.

(4) This was the mode of punishment for murder (as Charlevoix tells us) among the Hurons. "They laid the dead body upon poles at the top of a cabin, and the murderer was obliged to remain several days together, and to receive all that dropped from the carcass, not only on himself but on his food."

(5) "We find also collars of porcelain, tobacco, ears of maize, skins, etc., by the side of difficult and dangerous ways, on rocks, or by the side of the falls; and these are so many offerings made to the spirits which preside in these places."—See *Charlevoix's Letter on the Traditions and the Religion of the Savages of Canada.*

Father Hennepin too mentions this ceremony; he also says, "We took notice of one barbarian, who made a kind of sacrifice upon an oak at the Cascade of St. Antony of Padua, upon the river Mississippi."—See *Hennepin's Voyage into North America.*

TO THE HONOURABLE W. R. SPENCER.

FROM BUFFALO, UPON LAKE ERIE.

Nec venit ad duros musa vocata Getas.
Ovid., ex Ponto, lib. i., ep. 5.

Thou oft hast told me of the happy hours
Enjoy'd by thee in fair Italia's bowers,
Where, lingering yet, the ghost of ancient wit
'Midst modern monks profanely dares to flit, (1)
And pagan spirits, by the Pope unlaid,
Haunt every stream and sing through every shade.
There still the bard who (if his numbers be
His tongue's light echo) must have talk'd like thee,—
The courtly bard, from whom thy mind has caught
Those playful sunshine holidays of thought,
In which the spirit baskingly reclines;
Bright without effort, resting while it shines,—
There still he roves, and laughing loves to see
How modern priests with ancient rakes agree ;
How, 'neath the cowl, the festal garland shines,
And Love still finds a niche in Christian shrines. (2)

There still, too, roam those other souls of song,
With whom thy spirit hath communed so long,
That, quick as light, their rarest gems of thought,
By Memory's magic to thy lip are brought.
But here, alas ! by Erie's stormy lake,
As, far from such bright haunts my course I take,
No proud remembrance o'er the fancy plays,
No classic dream, no star of other days
Hath left that visionary light behind,
That lingering radiance of immortal mind,
Which gilds and hallows even the rudest scene,
The humblest shed, where Genius once has been !

All that creation's varying mass assumes
Of grand or lovely, here aspires and blooms ;
Bold rise the mountains, rich the gardens glow,
Bright lakes expand, and conquering (3) rivers flow ;

(1) This epistle has undergone some verbal changes in its commencement—

Thou oft hast told me of the fairy hours
Thy heart has number'd, in those classic bowers
Where fancy sees the ghost of ancient wit
'Mid cowls and cardinals profanely flit.—P. E.

(2) Changed from—

How mitres hang where ivy wreaths might twine,
And heathen Massic 's damn'd for stronger wine !—P. E.

(3) This epithet was suggested by Charlevoix's striking description of the confluence of the Missouri with the Mississippi. " I believe this is the finest confluence in the world. The two rivers are much of the same breadth, each about half a league ; but the Missouri is by far the most rapid, and seems to enter the Mississippi like a conqueror, through which it carries its white waves to the opposite shore, without mixing them : afterwards it gives its colour to the Mississippi, which it never loses again, but carries quite down to the sea."—Letter xxvii.

But mind, immortal mind, without whose ray
This world 's a wilderness and man but clay,
Mind, mind alone, in barren still repose,
Nor blooms, nor rises, nor expands, nor flows.
Take Christians, Mohawks, democrats, and all
From the rude wigwam to the congress-hall,
From man the savage, whether slaved or free,
To man the civilised, less tame than he,—
'T is one dull chaos, one unfertile strife
Betwixt half-polish'd and half-barbarous life ;
Where every ill the ancient world could brew
Is mix'd with every grossness of the new ;
Where all corrupts, though little can entice,
And nought is known of luxury, but its vice !

Is this the region then, is this the clime
For soaring fancies ? for those dreams sublime,
Which all their miracles of light reveal
To heads that meditate and hearts that feel ?
Alas ! not so—the Muse of Nature lights
Her glories round ; she scales the mountain heights,
And roams the forests ; every wondrous spot
Burns with her step, yet man regards it not. (4)
She whispers round, her words are in the air,
But lost, unheard, they linger freezing there, (5)
Without one breath of soul, divinely strong,
One ray of mind, to thaw them into song.

Yet, yet forgive me, oh ye sacred few,
Whom late by Delaware's green banks I knew ;
Whom, known and loved through many a social eve,
'T was bliss to live with, and 't was pain to leave.(6)
Not with more joy the lonely exile scann'd
The writing traced upon the desert's sand,
Where his lone heart but little hoped to find
One trace of life, one stamp of human kind,
Than did I hail the pure, the enlighten'd zeal,
The strength to reason and the warmth to feel,
The manly polish and the illumined taste,
Which—'mid the melancholy heartless waste

(4) In former editions—

No, no—the Muse of inspiration plays
O'er every scene ; she walks the forest-maze,
And climbs the mountain ; every blooming spot
Burns with her step, yet man regards it not !—P. E.

(5) Alluding to the fanciful notion of "words congealed in northern air."

(6) In the society of Mr. Dennie and his friends, at Philadelphia, I passed the few agreeable moments which my tour through the States afforded me. Mr. Dennie has succeeded in diffusing through this cultivated little circle that love for good literature and sound politics, which he feels so zealously himself, and which is so very rarely the characteristic of his countrymen. They will not, I trust, accuse me of illiberality for the picture which I have given of the ignorance and corruption that surround them. If I did not hate, as I ought, the rabble to which they are opposed, I could not value, as I do, the spirit with which they defy it; and in learning from them what Americans *can be,* I but see with the more indignation what Americans *are.*

18

My foot has traversed—oh you sacred few!
I found by Delaware's green banks with you.

Long may you loathe the Gallic dross that runs
Through your fair country, and corrupts its sons;
Long love the Arts, the glories which adorn
Those fields of Freedom where your sires were born.
Oh! if America can yet be great,
If neither chain'd by choice, nor doom'd by fate
To the mob-mania which imbrutes her now,
She yet can raise the crown'd yet civic brow
Of single majesty, can add the grace
Of Rank's rich capital to Freedom's base,
Nor fear the mighty shaft will feebler prove
For the fair ornament that flowers above;
If yet, released from all that pedant throng,
So vain of error and so pledged to wrong,
Who hourly teach her, like themselves, to hide
Weakness in vaunt, and barrenness in pride,
She yet can rise, can wreathe the Attic charms
Of soft refinement round the pomp of arms,
And see her poets flash the fires of song,
To light her warriors' thunderbolts along;
It is to you, to souls that favouring heaven
Has made like yours, the glorious task is given:
Oh! but for *such,* Columbia's days were done;
Rank without ripeness, quicken'd without sun,
Crude at the surface, rotten at the core,
Her fruits would fall before her spring were o'er.

Believe me, Spencer, while I wing'd the hours
Where Schuylkill winds his way through banks of
    flowers;
Though few the days, the happy evenings few,
So warm with heart, so rich with mind they flew,
That my charm'd soul forgot its wish to roam,
And rested there, as in a dream of home,
And looks I met, like looks I'd loved before,
And voices too, which, as they trembled o'er
The chord of memory, found full many a tone
Of kindness there in concord with their own.
Yes,—we had nights of that communion free,
That flow of heart, which I have known with thee

(1) I wrote these words to an air which our boatmen
sung to us frequently. The wind was so unfavourable
that they were obliged to row all the way, and we were
five days in descending the river from Kingston to Mont-
real, exposed to an intense sun during the day, and at
night forced to take shelter from the dews in any miser-
able hut upon the banks that would receive us. But the
magnificent scenery of the St. Lawrence repays all such
difficulties.
    Our *voyageurs* had good voices, and sung perfectly in
tune together. The original words of the air, to which I
adapted these stanzas, appeared to be a long incoherent
story, of which I could understand but little, from the
barbarous pronunciation of the Canadians. It begins—

    Dans mon chemin j'ai rencontré
    Deux cavaliers très bien montés;

And the *refrain* to every verse was,

    A l'ombre d'un bois je m'en vais jouer,
    A l'ombre d'un bois je m'en vais danser.

So oft, so warmly; nights of mirth and mind,
Of whims that taught, and follies that refined.
When shall we both renew them? when, restored
To the gay feast and intellectual board,
Shall I once more enjoy with thee and thine
Those whims that teach, those follies that refine?
Even now, as, wandering upon Eçie's shore,
I hear Niagara's distant cataract roar,
I sigh for home,—alas! these weary feet
Have many a mile to journey, ere we meet.

Ω ΠΑΤΡΙΣ, 'ΩΣ ΣΟΥ ΚΑΡΤΑ ΝΥΝ ΜΝΕΙΑΝ ΕΧΩ.
                                    Euripides.

------⟶●◑◐○------

BALLAD STANZAS.

I KNEW by the smoke, that so gracefully curl'd
    Above the green elms, that a cottage was near,
And I said, "If there's peace to be found in the world,
    A heart that was humble might hope for it here!"

It was noon, and on flowers that languish'd around
    In silence reposed the voluptuous bee;
Every leaf was at rest, and I heard not a sound
    But the woodpecker tapping the hollow-beech tree.

And, "Here in this lone little wood," I exclaim'd,
    "With a maid who was lovely to soul and to eye,
Who would blush when I praised her, and weep if I
        blamed,
    How blest could I live, and how calm could I die!

"By the shade of yon sumach, whose red berry dips
    In the gush of the fountain, how sweet to recline,
And to know that I sigh'd upon innocent lips,
    Which had never been sigh'd on by any but mine!"

----⟶●◑◐●○----

A CANADIAN BOAT SONG.

WRITTEN ON THE RIVER ST. LAWRENCE. (1)

Et remigem cantus hortatur.—*Quintilian.*

FAINTLY as tolls the evening chime
Our voices keep tune and our oars keep time.

I ventured to harmonise this air, and have published
it. Without that charm which association gives to every
little memorial of scenes or feelings that are past, the
melody may, perhaps, be thought common and trifling;
but I remember when we have entered, at sunset, upon
one of those beautiful lakes, into which the St. Lawrence
so grandly and unexpectedly opens, I have heard this
simple air with a pleasure which the finest compositions
of the first masters have never given me; and now there
is not a note of it which does not recall to my memory
the dip of our oars in the St. Lawrence, the flight of our
boat down the Rapids, and all those new and fanciful im-
pressions to which my heart was alive during the whole
of this very interesting voyage.
    The above stanzas are supposed to be sung by those
voyageurs who go to the Grand Portage by the Utawas
River. For an account of this wonderful undertaking, see
Sir Alexander Mackenzie's *General History of the Fur
Trade,* prefixed to his Journal.

Soon as the woods on shore look dim,
We'll sing at St. Ann's our parting hymn.(1)
Row, brothers, row, the stream runs fast,
The Rapids are near and the daylight's past.

Why should we yet our sail unfurl?
There is a not a breath the blue wave to curl.
But, when the wind blows off the shore,
Oh! sweetly we'll rest our weary oar.
Blow, breezes, blow, the stream runs fast,
The Rapids are near and the daylight's past.

Utawas' tide! this trembling moon
Shall see us float over thy surges soon.
Saint of this green isle! hear our prayers,
Oh, grant us cool heavens and favouring airs.
Blow, breezes, blow, the stream runs fast,
The Rapids are near and the daylight's past.

— —◦◦◦◦— —

TO THE LADY CHARLOTTE RAWDON.

FROM THE BANKS OF THE ST. LAWRENCE.

Not many months have now been dream'd away,
Since yonder sun, beneath whose evening ray
Our boat glides swiftly past these wooded shores,
Saw me where Trent his mazy current pours,
And Donington's old oaks, to every breeze,
Whisper the tale of by-gone centuries;—
Those oaks, to me as sacred as the groves,
Beneath whose shade the pious Persian roves,
And hears the spirit-voice of sire, or chief,
Or loved mistress, sigh in every leaf.(2)
There, oft, dear Lady, while thy lip hath sung
My own unpolish'd lays, how proud I've hung
On every tuneful accent! proud to feel
That notes like mine should have the fate to steal,
As o'er thy hallowing lip they sigh'd along,
Such breath of passion and such soul of song.
Yes,—I have wonder'd, like some peasant boy
Who sings, on Sabbath-eve, his strains of joy,
And when he hears the wild untutor'd note
Back to his ear on softening echoes float,
Believes it still some answering spirit's tone,
And thinks it all too sweet to be his own!

I dreamt not then that, ere the rolling year
Had fill'd its circle, I should wander here

In musing awe; should tread this wondrous world,
See all its store of inland waters hurl'd
In one vast volume down Niagara's steep,
Or calm behold them, in transparent sleep,
Where the blue hills of old Toronto shed
Their evening shadows o'er Ontario's bed:
Should trace the grand Cadaraqui, and glide
Down the white rapids of his lordly tide
Through massy woods, 'mid islets flowering fair,
And blooming glades, where the first sinful pair
For consolation might have weeping trod,
When banish'd from the garden of their God.
Oh, Lady! these are miracles, which man,
Caged in the bounds of Europe's pigmy span,
Can scarcely dream of,—which his eye must see
To know how wonderful this world can be!

But lo,—the last tints of the west decline,
And night falls dewy o'er these banks of pine.
Among the reeds, in which our idle boat
Is rock'd to rest, the wind's complaining note
Dies like a half-breathed whispering of flutes;
Along the wave the gleaming porpoise shoots,
And I can trace him, like a watery star,(3)
Down the steep current, till he fades afar
Amid the foaming breakers' silvery light,
Where yon rough rapids sparkle through the night.
Here, as along this shadowy bank I stray,
And the smooth glass-snake,(4) gliding o'er my way,
Shows the dim moonlight through his scaly form,
Fancy, with all the scene's enchantment warm,
Hears in the murmur of the nightly breeze
Some Indian Spirit warble words like these:—

From the land beyond the sea,
Whither happy spirits flee;
Where, transform'd to sacred doves, (5)
Many a blessed Indian roves
Through the air on wing, as white
As those wondrous stones of light,(6)
Which the eye of morning counts
On the Apallachian mounts,—
Hither oft my flight I take
Over Huron's lucid lake,
Where the wave, as clear as dew,
Sleeps beneath the light canoe,
Which, reflected, floating there,
Looks as if it hung in air.(7)

---

(1) "At the Rapid of St. Ann they are obliged to take out part, if not the whole, of their lading. It is from this spot the Canadians consider they take their departure, as it possesses the last church on the island, which is dedicated to the tutelar saint of voyagers."—*Mackenzie, General History of the Fur Trade.*

(2) "Avendo essi per costume di avere in venerazione gli alberi grandi ed antichi, quasi che siano spesso ricettaccoli di anime beate."—*Pietro della Valle*, part. second., lettera 16, dai giardini di Sciraz.

(3) Anburey, in his *Travels*, has noticed this shooting illumination which porpoises diffuse at night through the river St. Lawrence.—Vol. i., p. 29.

(4) The glass-snake is brittle and transparent.

(5) "The departed spirit goes into the Country of Souls, where, according to some, it is transformed into a dove." —*Charlevoix, upon the Traditions and the Religion of the Savages of Canada.* See the curious fable of the American Orpheus in Lafitau, tom. i., p. 402.

(6) "The mountains appeared to be sprinkled with white stones, which glistened in the sun, and were called by the Indians manetoe aseniah, or spirit-stones."—*Mackenzie's Journal.*

(7) These lines were suggested by Carver's description of one of the American lakes. "When it was calm," he says, "and the sun shone bright, I could sit in my canoe,

Then, when I have stray'd a while
Through the Manataulin isle, (1)
Breathing all its holy bloom,
Swift I mount me on the plume
Of my wakon–bird, (2) and fly
Where, beneath a burning sky,
O'er the bed of Erie's lake
Slumbers many a water–snake,
Wrapt within the web of leaves,
Which the water–lily weaves. (3)
Next I chase the floweret–king
Through his rosy realm of spring;
See him now, while diamond hues
Soft his neck and wings suffuse,
In the leafy chalice sink,
Thirsting for his balmy drink ;
Now behold him all on fire,
Lovely in his looks of ire,
Breaking every infant stem,
Scattering every velvet gem,
Where his little tyrant lip
Had not found enough to sip.

Then my playful hand I steep
Where the gold–thread (4) loves to creep,
Cull from thence a tangled wreath,
Words of magic round it breathe,
And the sunny chaplet spread
O'er the sleeping fly–bird's head, (5)
Till, with dreams of honey blest,
Haunted, in his downy nest,
By the garden's fairest spells,
Dewy buds and fragrant bells,
Fancy all his soul embowers
In the fly–bird's heaven of flowers.

Oft, when hoar and silvery flakes
Melt along the ruffled lakes,

When the grey moose sheds his horns,
When the track, at evening, warns
Weary hunters of the way
To the wigwam's cheering ray,
Then, aloft through freezing air,
With the snow–bird (6) soft and fair
As the fleece that heaven flings
O'er his little pearly wings,
Light above the rocks I play,
Where Niagara's starry spray,
Frozen on the cliff, appears
Like a giant's starting tears.
There, amid the island–sedge,
Just upon the cataract's edge,
Where the foot of living man
Never trod since time began,
Lone I sit, at close of day,
While, beneath the golden ray,
Icy columns gleam below,
Feather'd round with falling snow,
And an arch of glory springs,
Sparkling as the chain of rings
Round the neck of virgins hung,—
Virgins (7) who have wander'd young
O'er the waters of the west
To the lands where spirits rest !

Thus have I charm'd, with visionary lay,
The lonely moments of the night away;
And now, fresh daylight o'er the water beams !
Once more, embark'd upon the glittering streams,
Our boat flies light along the leafy shore,
Shooting the falls, without a dip of oar
Or breath of zephyr, like the mystic bark
The poet saw, in dreams divinely dark,
Borne without sails along the dusky flood, (8)
While on its deck a pilot angel stood,

where the depth was upwards of six fathoms, and plainly see huge piles of stone at the bottom, of different shapes, some of which appeared as if they had been hewn ; the water was at this time as pure and transparent as air, and my canoe seemed as if it hung suspended in that element. It was impossible to look attentively through this limpid medium, at the rocks below, without finding, before many minutes were elapsed, your head swim and your eyes no longer able to behold the dazzling scene."

(1) "Après avoir traversé plusieurs isles peu considérables, nous en trouvâmes le quatrième jour une fameuse nommée l'isle de Manitoualin."—*Voyages du baron de Lahontan*, tom. i., let. 15. Manataulin signifies a Place of Spirits, and this island in Lake Huron is held sacred by the Indians.

(2) "The wakon–bird, which probably is of the same species with the bird of Paradise, receives its name from the ideas the Indians have of its superior excellence ; the wakon–bird being, in their language, the Bird of the Great Spirit."—*Morse.*

(3) The islands which stud the bosom of Lake Erie are surrounded, to a considerable distance, by the large pond–lily, whose leaves spread thickly over the surface of the

lake, and form a kind of bed for the water–snakes in summer.

(4) "The gold thread is of the vine kind, and grows in swamps. The roots spread themselves just under the surface of the morasses, and are easily drawn out by handfuls. They resemble a large entangled skein of silk, and are of a bright yellow."—*Morse.*

(5) "L'oiseau–mouche, gros comme un hanneton, est de toutes couleurs, vives et changeantes : il tire sa subsistance des fleurs comme les abeilles ; son nid est fait d'un coton très fin suspendu à une branche d'arbre."—*Voyages aux Indes Occidentales, par M. Bossu,* seconde part., lett. xx.

(6) Emberiza hyemalis.—See *Imlay's Kentucky,* p. 280.

(7) Lafitau supposes that there was an order of vestals established among the Iroquois Indians.—*Mœurs des Sauvages Américains, etc.,* tom. i., p. 173.

(8)   Vedi che sdegna gli argomenti umani ;
    Si che remo non vuol, nè altro velo,
    Che l' ale sue tra liti si lontani.

    Vedi come l' ha dritte verso 'l cielo
    Trattando l' aere con l' eterne penne ;
    Che non si mutan, come mortal pelo.
            Dante, Purgator., cant. ii.

And, with his wings of living light unfurl'd,
Coasted the dim shores of another world!

Yet, oh! believe me, 'mid this mingled maze
Of nature's beauties, where the fancy strays
From charm to charm, where every floweret's hue
Hath something strange, and every leaf is new,—
I never feel a joy so pure and still,
So inly felt, as when some brook or hill,
Or veteran oak, like those remember'd well,
Some mountain echo or some wild-flower's smell,
(For who can say by what small fairy ties
The memory clings to pleasure as it flies?)
Reminds my heart of many a sylvan dream
I once indulged by Trent's inspiring stream ;
Of all my sunny morns and moonlight nights
On Donington's green lawns and breezy heights.

Whether I trace the tranquil moments o'er
When I have seen thee cull the fruits of lore,
With him, the polish'd warrior, by thy side,
A sister's idol and a nation's pride!
When thou hast read of heroes, trophied high
In ancient fame, and I have seen thine eye
Turn to the living hero, while it read,
For pure and brightening comments on the dead ;—
Or whether memory to my mind recalls
The festal grandeur of those lordly halls,
When guests have met around the sparkling board,
And welcome warm'd the cup that luxury pour'd ;
When the bright future Star of England's throne,
With magic smile, hath o'er the banquet shone,
Winning respect, nor claiming what he won,
But tempering greatness, like an evening sun
Whose light the eye can tranquilly admire,
Radiant, but mild, all softness, yet all fire ;—
Whatever hue my recollections take,
Even the regret, the very pain they wake
Is mix'd with happiness ;—but, ah! no more—
Lady! adieu—my heart has linger'd o'er
Those vanish'd times, till all that round me lies,
Stream, banks, and bowers have faded on my eyes !

—————

IMPROMPTU,

AFTER A VISIT TO MRS. ——, OF MONTREAL.

'Twas but for a moment—and yet in that time
She crowded the impressions of many an hour :
Her eye had a glow, like the sun of her clime,
Which waked every feeling at once into flower.

(1) This is one of the Magdalen Islands, and, singular
enough, is the property of Sir Isaac Coffin. The above
lines were suggested by a superstition very common among
sailors, who call this ghost-ship, I think, "the flying
Dutchman."

We were thirteen days on our passage from Quebec to
Halifax, and I had been so spoiled by the truly splendid
hospitality of my friends of the *Phaeton* and *Boston,* that I

Oh! could we have borrow'd from Time but a day,
To renew such impressions again and again,
The things we should look, and imagine, and say,
Would be worth all the life we had wasted till then.

What we had not the leisure or language to speak,
We should find some more spiritual mode of re-
vealing,
And, between us, should feel just as much in a week
As others would take a milennium in feeling.

—————

WRITTEN ON PASSING DEADMAN'S ISLAND,(1)

IN THE GULF OF ST. LAWRENCE,

LATE IN THE EVENING, SEPTEMBER, 1804.

SEE you, beneath yon cloud so dark,
Fast gliding along a gloomy bark ?
Her sails are full,—though the wind is still,
And there blows not a breath her sails to fill!

Say, what doth that vessel of darkness bear ?
The silent calm of the grave is there,
Save now and again a death-knell rung,
And the flap of the sails with night-fog hung.

There lieth a wreck on the dismal shore
Of cold and pitiless Labrador ;
Where, under the moon, upon mounts of frost,
Full many a mariner's bones are tost.

Yon shadowy bark hath been to that wreck,
And the dim blue fire, that lights her deck,
Doth play on as pale and livid a crew
As ever yet drank the church-yard dew.

To Deadman's Isle, in the eye of the blast,
To Deadman's Isle she speeds her fast ;
By skeleton shapes her sails are furl'd,
And the hand that steers is not of this world!

Oh! hurry thee on—oh! hurry thee on,
Thou terrible bark, ere the night be gone,
Nor let morning look on so foul a sight
As would blanch for ever her rosy light !

—————

TO THE BOSTON FRIGATE,(2)

ON LEAVING HALIFAX FOR ENGLAND, OCTOBER, 1805.

Νοστου προφασις γλυκερου.—*Pindar.*, Pyth. 4.

WITH triumph this morning, oh *Boston!* I hail
The stir of thy deck and the spread of thy sail,

was but ill prepared for the miseries of a Canadian vessel.
The weather, however, was pleasant, and the scenery
along the river delightful. Our passage through the Gut
of Canso, with a bright sky and a fair wind, was particu-
larly striking and romantic.

(2) Commanded by Captain J. E. Douglas, with whom I
returned to England, and to whom I am indebted for
many, many kindnesses. In truth, I should but offend

For they tell me I soon shall be wafted, in thee,
To the flourishing isle of the brave and the free.
And that chill Nova-Scotia's unpromising strand (1)
Is the last I shall tread of American land.
Well—peace to the land! may her sons know, at length,
That in high-minded honour lies liberty's strength,
That though man be as free as the fetterless wind,
As the wantonest air that the north can unbind,
Yet, if health do not temper and sweeten the blast,
If no harvest of mind ever sprung where it pass'd,
Then unblest is such freedom, and baleful its might,—
Free only to ruin, and strong but to blight! (2)

Farewell to the few I have left with regret;
May they sometimes recall, what I cannot forget,
The delight of those evenings,—too brief a delight!
When in converse and song we have stolen on the
        night; (3)
When they 've ask'd me the manners, the mind, or
        the mien
Of some bard I had known or some chief I had seen,
Whose glory, though distant, they long had adored,
Whose name had oft hallow'd the wine-cup they
        pour'd;
And still as, with sympathy humble but true,
I have told of each bright son of fame all I knew,
They have listen'd, and sigh'd that the powerful stream
Of America's empire should pass, like a dream,
Without leaving one relic of genius, to say
How sublime was the tide which had vanish'd away!
Farewell to the few—though we never may meet
On this planet again, it is soothing and sweet

To think that, whenever my song or my name
Shall recur to their ear, they 'll recall me the same
I have been to them now, young, unthoughtful, and
        blest,
Ere hope had deceived me or sorrow deprest.

But, Douglas! while thus I recall to my mind
The elect of the land we shall soon leave behind,
I can read in the weather-wise glance of thine eye,
As it follows the rack flitting over the sky,
That the faint coming breeze will be fair for our flight,
And shall steal us away, ere the falling of night.
Dear Douglas! thou knowest, with thee by my side,
With thy friendship to soothe me, thy courage to
        guide,
There is not a bleak isle in those summerless seas,
Where the day comes in darkness, or shines but to
        freeze,
Not a tract of the line, not a barbarous shore,
That I could not with patience, with pleasure explore!
Oh think then how gladly I follow thee now,
When Hope smooths the billowy path of our prow,
And each prosperous sigh of the west-springing wind
Takes me nearer the home where my heart is en-
        shrined;
Where the smile of a father shall meet me again,
And the tears of a mother turn bliss into pain;
Where the kind voice of sisters shall steal to my heart,
And ask it, in sighs, how we ever could part?—

But see!—the bent top-sails are ready to swell—
To the boat—I am with thee—Columbia, farewell!

. Among the Poems which, in former editions of the Author's works, appeared under the title of
EPISTLES, ODES, AND OTHER POEMS, and which are now given under the designation of POEMS RELATING
TO AMERICA, were the following. Why they have been refused a place in the new edition is left unexplained.

TO MISS ——.

WITH woman's form and woman's tricks
So much of man you seem to mix,
One knows not where to take you :
I pray you, if 'tis not too far,
Go, ask of Nature *which* you are,
Or what she meant to make you.

Yet stay—you need not take the pains—
With neither beauty, youth, nor brains,

For man or maid's desiring;
Pert as female, fool as male,
As boy too green, as girl too stale—
The thing 's not worth inquiring!

——o§§o——

THE SENSES.

A DREAM.

EMBOWER'D in the vernal shades,
And circled all by rosy fences,
I saw the five luxurious maids,
Whom mortals love, and call The Senses.

(1) Sir John Wentworth, the Governor of Nova-Scotia,
very kindly allowed me to accompany him on his visit to
the College, which they have lately established at Windsor,
about forty miles from Halifax, and I was indeed most
pleasantly surprised by the beauty and fertility of the
country which opened upon us after the bleak and rocky
wilderness by which Halifax is surrounded.—I was told
that, in travelling onwards, we should find the soil and

the delicacy of my friend Douglas, and, at the same time,
do injustice to my own feelings of gratitude, did I attempt
to say how much I owe to him.

the scenery improve, and it gave me much pleasure to
know that the worthy Governor has by no means such an
"inamabile regnum" as I was, at first sight, inclined to
believe.

(2) Originally given—
        Yet if health do not sweeten the blast with her bloom,
        Nor virtue's aroma its pathway perfume,
        Unblest is the freedom and dreary the flight,
        That but wanders to ruin and wantons to blight!—P. E.

(3) Changed from—
        That communion of heart and that parley of soul,
        Which has lengthen'd our nights and illumined our bowl.—P. E.

Many and blissful were the ways
　In which they seem'd to pass their hours—
One wander'd through the garden's maze,
　Inhaling all the soul of flowers;

Like those who live upon the smell
　Of roses, by the Ganges' stream,(1)
With perfume from the floweret's bell,
　She fed her life's ambrosial dream.

Another touch'd the silvery lute,
　To chain a charmed sister's ear,
Who hung beside her, still and mute,
　Gazing as if her eyes could hear!

The nymph who thrill'd the warbling wire
　Would often raise her ruby lip,
As if it pouted with desire
　Some cooling nectar'd draught to sip.

Nor yet was she who heard the lute
　Unmindful of the minstrel maid,
But press'd the sweetest, richest fruit,
　To bathe her ripe lip as she play'd!

But, oh! the fairest of the group
　Was one who in the sunshine lay,
And oped the cincture's golden loop
　That hid her bosom's panting play!

And still her gentle hand she stole
　Along the snows, so smoothly orb'd,
And look'd the while as if her soul
　Were in that heavenly touch absorb'd!

Another nymph, who linger'd nigh,
　And held a prism of various light,
Now put the rainbow wonder by,
　To look upon this lovelier sight.

And still as one's enamour'd touch
　Adown the lapsing ivory fell,
The other's eye, entranced as much,
　Hung giddy o'er its radiant swell!

Too wildly charm'd, I would have fled—
　But she who in the sunshine lay,
Replaced her golden loop, and said,
　" We pray thee for a moment stay.

" If true my counting pulses beat,
　It must be now almost the hour
When Love, with visitation sweet,
　Descends upon our bloomy bower.

" And with him from the sky he brings
　Our sister-nymph who dwells above—

(1) Circa fontem Gangis Astomorum gentem——halitu
tantum viventum et odore quem naribus trahant.
　　　　　　Plin., lib. vii., cap 2.

Oh! never may she haunt these springs
　With any other god but Love!

" When he illumes her magic urn,
　And sheds his own enchantments in it,
Though but a minute's space it burn,
　'T is heaven to breathe it but a minute!

" Not all the purest power we boast,
　Nor silken touch, nor vernal dye,
Nor music, when it thrills the most,
　Nor balmy cup, nor perfume's sigh,

" Such transport to the soul can give,
　Though felt till time itself shall wither,
As in that one dear moment live,
　When Love conducts our sister hither!"

She ceased—the air respired of bliss—
　A languor slept in every eye;
And now the scent of Cupid's kiss
　Declared the melting power was nigh!

I saw them come—the nymph and boy,
　In twisted wreaths of rapture bound;
I saw her light the urn of joy,
　While all her sisters languish'd round!

A sigh from every bosom broke—
　I felt the flames around me glide,
Till with the glow I trembling woke,
　And found myself by Fanny's side!

————o••o————

THE VASE.

THERE was a vase of odour lay
　For many an hour on Beauty's shrine,
So sweet that Love went every day
　To banquet on its breath divine.

And not an eye had ever seen
　The fragrant charm the vase conceal'd:
Oh Love! how happy 't would have been,
　If thou hadst ne'er that charm reveal'd!

But Love, like every other boy,
　Would know the spell that lurks within;
He wish'd to break the crystal toy,
　But Beauty murmur'd," 't was a sin!"

He swore, with many a tender plea,
　That neither Heaven nor earth forbad it;
She told him, Virtue kept the key,
　And look'd as if—she wish'd he had it!

He stole the key when Virtue slept
　(Even she can sleep, if Love but ask it),
And Beauty sigh'd, and Beauty wept,
　While silly Love unlock'd the casket.

Oh dulcet air that vanish'd then!
　Can Beauty's sigh recall thee ever!
Can Love himself inhale again
　A breath so precious—never, never!

Go, maiden, weep—the tears of woe
　By Beauty to repentance given,
Though bitterly on earth they flow,
　Shall turn to fragrant balm in Heaven!

————◦••◦————

TO ————,

Sine Venere friget Apollo.—*Ægid., Menagius.*

How can I sing of fragrant sighs
　I ne'er have felt from thee?
How can I sing of smiling eyes
　That ne'er have smiled on me?

The heart, 'tis true, may fancy much,
　But, oh! 'tis cold and seeming—
One moment's real rapturous touch
　Is worth an age of dreaming!

Think'st thou, when Julia's lip and breast
　Inspired my youthful tongue,
I coldly spoke of lips unprest,
　Nor felt the heaven I sung!

No, no; the spell that warm'd so long
　Was still my Julia's kiss,
And still the girl was paid in song
　What she had given in bliss!

Then beam one burning smile on me,
　And I will sing those eyes;
Let me but feel a breath from thee,
　And I will praise thy sighs.

That rosy mouth alone can bring
　What makes the bard divine—
Oh! Lady! how my lip would sing,
　If once 't were prest to thine!

ON SEEING AN INFANT IN NEA'S ARMS.

The first ambrosial child of bliss
　That Psyche to her bosom press'd,
Was not a brighter babe than this,
　Nor blush'd upon a lovelier breast!
His little snow-white fingers, straying
　Along her lip's luxuriant flower,
Look'd like a flight of ringdoves playing,
　Silvery through a roseate bower!

And when, to shade the playful boy,
　Her dark hair fell, in mazes bright,
Oh! 't was a type of stolen joy,
　'T was love beneath the veil of night!
Soft as she smiled, he smiled again;
　They seem'd so kindred in their charms,
That one might think the babe had then
　Just budded in her blooming arms!

————◦••◦————

FRAGMENTS OF A JOURNAL TO G. M. ESQ. (1)
FROM FREDERICKSBURG, VIRGINIA, JUNE 2. (2)

DEAR George! though every bone is aching,
　　After the shaking
I 've had this week, over ruts and ridges, (3)
　　And bridges
Made of a few uneasy planks, (4)
　　In open ranks,
Like old women's teeth, all loosely thrown
Over rivers of mud, whose names alone
Would make the knees of stoutest man knock,
　　Rappahannock,
Occoquan—the Heavens may harbour us!
Who ever heard of names so barbarous!
Worse than M****'s Latin,
　　Or the smooth codicil
To a witch's will, where she brings her cat in!
　　I treat my goddess ill,
(My muse I mean) to make her speak 'em;
　　Like the Verbum Græcum,

---

(1) These fragments form but a small part of a ridiculous medley of prose and doggerel, into which, for my amusement, I threw some of the incidents of my journey. If it were even in a more rational form, there is yet much of it too allusive and too personal for publication.

(2) Having remained about a week at New York, where I saw Madame Jerome Bonaparte, and felt a slight shock of an earthquake (the only things that particularly awakened my attention), I sailed again in the *Boston* for Norfolk, from whence I proceeded on my tour to the northward, through Williamsburgh, Richmond, etc. At Richmond there are a few men of considerable talents. Mr. Wickham, one of their celebrated legal characters, is a gentleman whose manners and mode of life would do honour to the most cultivated societies. Judge Marshall, the author of *Washington's Life*, is another very distinguished ornament of Richmond. These gentlemen, I must observe, are of that respectable, but at present unpopular, party, the Federalists.

(3) What Mr. Weld says of the continual necessity of balancing or trimming the stage, in passing over some of the wretched roads in America, is by no means exaggerated. "The driver frequently had to call to the passengers in the stage, to lean out of the carriage, first at one side then at the other, to prevent it from oversetting in the deep ruts with which the road abounds! 'Now, gentlemen, to the right;' upon which the passengers all stretched their bodies half way out of the carriage, to balance it on that side. 'Now, gentlemen, to the left;' and so on."—*Weld's Travels,* letter 3.

(4) Before the stage can pass one of these bridges, the driver is obliged to stop and arrange the loose planks, of which it is composed, in the manner that best suits his ideas of safety: and, as the planks are again disturbed by the passing of the coach, the next travellers who arrive have of course a new arrangement to make. Mahomet (as Sale tells us) was at some pains to imagine a precarious kind of bridge for the entrance of Paradise, in order to enhance the pleasures of arrival: a Virginian bridge, I think, would have answered his purpose completely.

Spermagoraiolekitholakanopolides, (1)
Words that ought only be said upon holidays,
When one has nothing else to do.

But, dearest George, though every bone is
aching
　　After this shaking,
And trying to regain the socket,
From which the stage thought fit to rock it,
I fancy I shall sleep the better
For having scrawl'd a kind of letter
　　To you.
It seems to me like—"George, good-night!"
Though far the spot I date it from;
To which I fancy, while I write,
You answer back—"Good-night t' ye, Tom."
But do not think that I shall turn all
　　Sorts of quiddities,
　　And insipidities,
　　Into my journal;
That I shall tell you the different prices
Of eating, drinking, and such other vices,
To "contumace your appetite's acidities."(2)
No, no; the Muse too delicate-bodied is
　　For such commodities!
Neither suppose, like fellow of college, she
　　Can talk of conchology,
　　Or meteorology:
Or that a nymph, who wild as comet errs,
　　Can discuss barometers,
Farming-tools, statistic histories,
Geography, law, or such like mysteries,
For which she doesn't care three skips of
Prettiest flea, that e'er the lips of
Catherine Roache (3) look'd smiling upon,
When bards of France all, one by one,
Declared, that never did hand approach
Such a flea as was caught upon Catherine Roache!
　　*　　*　　*　　*　　*

Sentiment, George, I'll talk, when I've got any,
　　And botany—
Oh! Linnæus has made such a prig o' me,
Cases I'll find of such polygamy

Under every bush,
　As would make the "shy curcuma" (4) blush;
Vice under every name and shape,
From adulterous gardens to fields of rape!
I'll send you some Dionæa Muscipula,
And, into Bartram's book if you dip, you'll a
Pretty and florid description find of
This "ludicrous, lobed, carnivorous, kind of—"(5)
　　The Lord deliver us!
Think of a vegetable being "carnivorous!"
　　And George, be sure·
I'll treat you too, like Liancourt (6)
　　(Nor thou be risible),
With all the views, so striking and romantic,
　Which one *might* have of the Atlantic,
　　If it were visible.
　　*　　*　　*　　*　　*

And now, to tell you the gay variety
　　Of my stage society;
There was a quaker, who room for twenty took,
Pious and big as a Polyglot Pentateuch!
There was his niece too, sitting so fair by,
Like a neat testament, kept to swear by.
　　What pity, blooming girl!
　That lips, so ready for a lover,
Should not beneath their ruby casket cover
　　One tooth of pearl!(7)
But, like a rose beside the church-yard stone,
Bedoom'd to blush o'er many a mouldering bone!
　　There was　*　　*　　*

There was a student of the college, too,
　　Who said
Much more about the riches of his head,
Than, if there were an income-tax on brains,
His head could venture to acknowledge to.
　　I ask'd the Scholar
　If his—what d' ye call her?—
　Alma mater and her Bishop
Properly follow'd the Marquis's wish up, (8)
　　And were much advancing
　　In dancing?
　　*　　*　　*　　*

<hr>

(1) Σπερμαγοραιολεκιθολαχανοπωλιδες. — From the *Lysistrata* of Aristophanes, v. 458.

(2) This phrase is taken verbatim from an account of an expedition to Drummond's Pond, by one of those many Americans who profess to think that the English language, as it has been hitherto written, is deficient in what they call republican energy. One of the *savants* of Washington is far advanced in the construction of a new language for the United States, which is supposed to be a mixture of Hebrew and Mikmak.

(3) Alluding to a collection of poems, called *La Puce de grands-jours de Poitiers*. They were all written upon a flea, which Stephen Pasquier found on the bosom of the famous Catherine des Roches, one morning during the *grands-jours* of Poitiers. I ask pardon of the learned Catherine's memory, for my vulgar alteration of her most respectable name.

(4) "Curcuma, cold and shy."—*Darwin.*

(5) "Observed likewise in these savannas abundance of the ludicrous Dionæa Muscipula."—*Bartram's Travels in North America.* For his description of this "carnivorous vegetable," see introduction, p. 13.

(6) This philosophical Duke, describing the view from Mr. Jefferson's house, says, "The Atlantic might be seen, were it not for the greatness of the distance, which renders that prospect impossible."—See his *Travels.*

(7) Polygnotus was the first painter, says Pliny, who showed the teeth in his portraits. He would scarcely, I think, have been tempted to such an innovation in America.

(8) The Marquis de Chastellux, in his wise letter to Mr. Maddison, Professor of Philosophy in the College of William and Mary, at Williamsburgh, dwells with much earnestness on the attention which should be paid to

The evening now grew dark and still;
    The whip-poor-will
Sung pensively on every tree;
And straight I fell into a reverie
Upon that man of gallantry and pith,
    Captain Smith. (1)
And very strange it seem'd to me,
That, after having kiss'd so grand a
Dame as Lady Trabigzanda,
        By any chance he
        Could take a fancy
To a nymph, with such a copper front as
        Pocahuntas!

And now, as through the gloom so dark,
The fire-flies scatter'd many a fiery spark,
To one, that glitter'd on the quaker's bonnet,
        I wrote a sonnet.
    *   *   *   *   *

And——
        two lines more had just completed it;
    But, at the moment I repeated it,
        Our stage
Which good Brissot, with brain so critical
        And sage,
Calleth the true " machine political," (2)
With all its load of uncles, scholars, nieces,
        Together jumbled,
        Tumbled
Into a rut and fell to pieces!
    *   *   *   *   *

Good night!—my bed must be,
By this time, warm enough for me,
Because I find old Ephram Steady
And Miss his niece are there already!

Some cavillers
Object to sleep with fellow-travellers;
    But   *   *   *   *
Saints protect the pretty quaker,
Heaven forbid that I should wake her!

————o**o————

ON THE LOSS OF A LETTER FOR NEA.

On! it was fill'd with words of flame,
    With all the wishes wild and dear,
Which love may write, but dares not name,
    Which woman reads, but must not hear!

Of many a nightly dream it told,
    When all that chills the heart by day,
The wordly doubt, the caution cold,
    In Fancy's fire dissolve away!

When soul and soul divinely meet,
    Free from the senses' guilty shame,
And mingle in a sigh so sweet,
    As Virtue's self would blush to blame!

How could he lose such tender words!
    Words! that of themselves should spring
To Nea's ear, like panting birds,
    With heart and soul upon their wing!

Oh! fancy what they dared to speak;
    Think all a virgin's shame can dread,
Nor pause until thy conscious cheek
    Shall burn with thinking all they said!

And I shall feign, shall fancy, too,
    Some dear reply thou might'st have given;
Shall make that lip distil its dew
    In promise bland and hopes of heaven!

dancing.—See his *Travels.* This college, the only one in the state of Virginia, and the first which I saw in America, gave me but a melancholy idea of republican seats of learning. That contempt for the elegancies of education, which the American democrats affect, is no where more grossly conspicuous than in Virginia: the young men, who look for advancement, study rather to be demagogues than politicians; and as every thing that distinguishes from the multitude is supposed to be invidious and unpopular, the levelling system is applied to education, and has had all the effect which its partisans could desire, by producing a most extensive equality of ignorance. The Abbé Raynal, in his prophetic admonitions to the Americans, directing their attention very strongly to learned establishments, says, "When the youth of a country are seen depraved, the nation is on the decline." I know not what the Abbé Raynal would pronounce of this nation now, were he alive to know the morals of the students at Williamsburgh! But when he wrote, his countrymen had not yet introduced the "doctrinam deos spernentem" into America.

(1) John Smith, a famous traveller, and by far the most enterprising of the first settlers in Virginia. How much he was indebted to the interesting young Pocahuntas, daughter of King Powhatan, may be seen in all the histories of this colony. In the Dedication of his own work to the Duchess of Richmond, he thus enumerates his *bonnes fortunes:*—"Yet my comfort is, that heretofore honourable and vertuous Ladies, and comparable but among themselves, have offered me rescue and protection in my greatest dangers. Even in forraine parts I have felt reliefe from that sex. The beauteous Lady Trabigzanda, when I was a slave to the Turks, did all she could to secure me. When I overcame the Bashaw of Nalbrits in Tartaria, the charitable Lady Callamata supplyed my necessities. In the utmost of my extremities, that blessed Pokahuntas, the great King's daughter of Virginia, oft saved my life."
Davis, in his whimsical *Travels through America,* has manufactured into a kind of romance the loves of Mr. Rolfe with this "opaci maxima mundi," Pocahuntas.

(2) "The American stages are the true political carriage."—*Brissot's Travels,* letter 6th.—There is nothing more amusing than the philosophical *singeries* of these French travellers. In one of the letters of Clavière, prefixed to those of Brissot, upon their plan for establishing a republic of philosophers in some part of the western world, he entreats Brissot to be particular in choosing a place "where there are no musquitoes:" forsooth, ne quid respublica detrimenti caperet!

Shall think it tells of future days,
When the averted cheek will turn,
When eye with eye shall mingle rays,
And lip to lip shall closely burn!

Ah! if this flattery is not thine,
If colder hope thy answer brings,
I 'll wish thy words were lost like mine,
Since I can dream such dearer things!

———o••o———

"Errare malo cum Platone, quam cum aliis recte sentire."—*Cic.*

I would rather think wrongly with Plato, than rightly with any one else.

1802.

Fanny, my love, we ne'er were sages,
But, trust me, all that Tully's zeal
Express'd for Plato's glowing pages,
All that, and more, for thee I feel!

Whate'er the heartless world decree,
Howe'er unfeeling prudes condemn,
Fanny! I 'd rather sin with thee,
Than live and die a saint with them!

———o••o———

TO A FRIEND.

When next you see the black-eyed *Caty*,
The loving languid girl of Hayti, (1)
Whose finger so expertly plays
Amid the ribbon's silken maze,
Just like Aurora, when she ties
A rainbow round the morning skies!

Say, that I hope, when winter 's o'er,
On Norfolk's bank again to rove,
And then shall search the ribbon store
For some of *Caty's* softest *love.*

I should not like the gloss were past,
Yet want it not entirely new;
But bright and strong enough to last
About—suppose a week or two.

However frail, however light,
'T will do, at least to wear at night :
And so you 'll tell our black-eyed *Caty*—
The loving languid girl of Hayti!

———o••o———

SONG.

I ne'er on that lip for a minute have gazed,
But a thousand temptations beset me,
And I 've thought, as the dear little rubies you raised,
How delicious 't would be—if you 'd let me!

(1) Among the West-Indian French at Norfolk, there are some very interesting St. Domingo girls, who in the day sell millinery, etc., and at night assemble in little cotillon parties, where they dance away the remembrance of their unfortunate country, and forget the miseries which "les amis des noirs" have brought upon them.

Then be not so angry for what I have done,
Nor say that you 've sworn to forget mê;
They were buds of temptation too pouting to shun,
And I thought that—you could not but let me!

When your lip with a whisper came close to my cheek,
Oh think how bewitching it met me!
And, plain as the eye of a Venus could speak,
Your eye seem'd to say—you would let me!

Then forgive the transgression, and bid me remain,
For, in truth, if I go, you 'll regret me;
Or, oh!—let me try the transgression again,
And I 'll do all you wish—will you let me?

———o••o———

ON A BEAUTIFUL EAST-INDIAN.

If all the daughters of the sun
Have loving looks and hearts of flame,
Go, tell me not that *she* is one—
'T was from the wintry moon she came!

And yet, sweet eye! thou ne'er wert given
To kindle what thou dost not feel;
And yet, thou flushing lip—by Heaven!
Thou ne'er wert made for Dian's seal!

Oh! for a sunbeam, rich and warm,
From thy own Ganges' fervid haunts,
To light thee up, thou lovely form!
To all my soul adores and wants:

To see thee burn—to faint and sigh
Upon that bosom as it blazed,
And be, myself the first to die,
Amid the flame myself had raised.

———o••o———

TO———.

I know that none can smile like thee,
But there is one, a gentler one,
Whose heart, though young and wild it be,
Would ne'er have done as thine has done.

When we were left alone to-day,
When every curious eye was fled,
And all that love could look or say,
We might have look'd, we might have said :

Would *she* have felt me trembling press,
Nor trembling press to me again?
Would *she* have had the power to bless,
Yet want the heart to bless me then?

Her tresses, too, as soft as thine—
Would she have idly paused to twine

Their scatter'd locks, with cold delay,
While, oh! such minutes pass'd away,
As Heaven has made for those who love?
For those who love, and long to steal
What none but hearts of ice reprove,
What none but hearts of fire can feel!

Go, go—an age of vulgar years
May now be pined, be sigh'd away,
Before one blessed hour appears,
Like that which we have lost to-day!

———o&o———

FROM THE GREEK. (1)

I 've press'd her bosom oft and oft;
  In spite of many a pouting check,
Have touch'd her lip in dalliance soft,
  And play'd around her silvery neck.

But, as for more, the maid 's so coy,
  That saints or angels might have seen us;
She 's now for prudence, now for joy,
  Minerva half, and half a Venus.

When Venus makes her bless me near,
  Why then, Minerva makes her loth,
And—oh the sweet tormenting dear!
  She makes me mad between them both!

———o&o———

AT NIGHT. (2)

At night, when all is still around,
How sweet to hear the distant sound
Of footstep, coming soft and light!
What pleasure in the anxious beat
With which the bosom flies to meet
That foot that comes so soft at night!

And then, at night, how sweet to say,
" 'T is late, my love!" and chide delay,
  Though still the western clouds are bright;
Oh! happy too the silent press,
The eloquence of mute caress,
  With those we love exchanged at night!

At night, what dear employ to trace,
In fancy, every glowing grace
  That 's hid by darkness from the sight!
And guess, by every broken sigh,
What tales of bliss the shrouded eye
  Is telling from the soul, at night!

———o&o———

TO ———.

I often wish that thou wert dead,
  And I beside thee calmly sleeping;
Since love is o'er and passion fled,
  And life has nothing worth our keeping!

No—common souls may bear decline
  Of all that throbb'd them once so high;
But hearts that beat like thine and mine
  Must still love on, love on or die!

'T is true, our early joy was such
  That nature could not bear the excess!
It was too much—for life too much—
  Though life be all a blank with less!

To see that eye, so cold, so still,
  Which once, oh God! could melt in bliss—
No, no, I cannot bear the chill!
  Hate, burning hate, were heaven to this!

CORRUPTION AND INTOLERANCE.

TWO POEMS. (3)

ADDRESSED TO AN ENGLISHMAN BY AN IRISHMAN.

PREFACE.

The following satirical Poems were published ori-
ginally without the author's name; "Corruption"
and "Intolerance" in the year 1808, and "The
Sceptic" in the year following. The political opinions
adopted in the first of these Satires—the Poem on

Corruption—was chiefly caught up, as is intimated
in the Original Preface, from the writings of Boling-
broke, Sir William Wyndham, and other statesmen
of that factious period, when the same sort of alliance
took place between Toryism and what is now called
Radicalism, which is always likely to ensue on the
ejection of the Tory party from power. (4)   In this

(1) Μαδους χερσιν εχω, ϛοματι ϛομα, δε περι δειρην
  Ασχετα λυσσωων βοσκομαι αργυρεην·
Ουπω δ' αφρογενειαν ὁλην ἑλον· αλλ' ετι καμνων
  Παρθενον αμφιεπον λεχρον αναινομενην.
Ἡμισυ γαρ Παφιη, το δ' αρ' ἡμισυ δωκεν Αθηνη·
  Αυταρ εγω μεσσος τηκομαι αμφοτερων.
                              Paulus Silentiarius.

(2) These lines allude to a curious lamp, which has for its

device a Cupid, with the words "at night" written over him.

(3) In preparing this new edition for press, Mr. Moore
has, in a variety of instances, abridged the notes which
originally illustrated the text of these satirical Poems. We
have deemed it proper, in the Paris edition, to supply
the passages so expunged, which will be readily recog-
nised by their being enclosed within brackets [   ].—P. E.

(4) Bolingbroke himself acknowledges that "both parties
were become factions, in the strict sense of the word."

somewhat rash effusion, it will be seen that neither of the two great English parties is handled with much respect; and I remember being taken to task, by one of the few of my Whig acquaintances that ever looked into the poem, for the following allusion to the silencing effects of official station on certain orators :—

As bees, on flowers alighting, cease their hum,
So, settling upon places, Whigs grow dumb.

But these attempts of mine, in the stately Juvenalian style of satire, met with but little success,—never having attained, I believe, even the honours of a second edition; and I found that lighter form of weapon, to which I afterwards betook myself, not only more easy to wield, but, from its very lightness, perhaps, more sure to reach its mark.

It is right my readers should here be apprized, that the plan of classing my Poetical Works according to the order of their first publication is pursued no further than as regards the preceding poems; and that, therefore, the arrangement of the contents of the succeeding pages, though not, in a general way, departing much from this rule, is not to be depended upon as observing it.

ORIGINAL PREFACE.

THE practice which has been lately introduced into literature, of writing very long notes upon very indifferent verses, appears to me rather a happy invention; as it supplies us with a mode of turning dull poetry to account; and as horses too heavy for the saddle may yet serve well enough to draw lumber, so Poems of this kind make excellent beasts of burden, and will bear notes, though they may not bear reading. Besides, the comments in such cases are so little under the necessity of paying any servile deference to the text, that they may even adopt that Socratic dogma, " Quod supra nos nihil ad nos."

In the first of the two following Poems, I have ventured to speak of the Revolution of 1688, in language which has sometimes been employed by Tory writers, and which is therefore neither very new nor popular. But however an Englishman might be reproached with ingratitude, for depreciating the merits and results of a measure, which he is taught to regard as the source of his liberties—however ungrateful it might appear in Alderman B—rch to question for a moment the purity of that glorious era, to which he is indebted for the seasoning of so many orations—yet an Irishman, who has none of these obligations to acknowledge; to whose country the Revolution brought nothing but injury and insult, and who recollects that the book of Molyneux was burned, by order of William's Whig Parliament, for daring to extend to unfortunate Ireland those principles on which the Revolution was professedly founded—an Irishman may be allowed to criticise freely the measures of that period, without exposing

himself either to the imputation of ingratitude, or to the suspicion of being influenced by any Popish remains of Jacobitism. No nation, it is true, was ever blessed with a more golden opportunity of establishing and securing its liberties for ever than the conjuncture of Eighty-Eight presented to the people of Great Britain. But the disgraceful reigns of Charles and James had weakened and degraded the national character. The bold notions of popular right, which had arisen out of the struggles between Charles the First and his Parliament, were gradually supplanted by those slavish doctrines for which Lord H—kesb—ry eulogises the churchmen of that period; and as the Reformation had happened too soon for the purity of religion, so the Revolution came too late for the spirit of liberty. Its advantages accordingly were for the most part specious and transitory, while the evils which it entailed are still felt and still increasing. By rendering unnecessary the frequent exercise of Prerogative,—that unwieldly power which cannot move a step without alarm,—it diminished the only interference of the Crown, which is singly and independently exposed before the people, and whose abuses therefore are obvious to their senses and capacities. Like the myrtle over a celebrated statue in Minerva's temple at Athens, it skilfully veiled from the public eye the only obtrusive feature of royalty. At the same time, however, that the Revolution abridged this unpopular attribute, it amply compensated by the substitution of a new power, as much more potent in its effect as it is more secret in its operations. In the disposal of an immense revenue and the extensive patronage annexed to it, the first foundations of this power of the Crown were laid; the innovation of a standing army at once increased and strengthened it, and the few slight barriers which the Act of Settlement opposed to its progress have all been gradually removed during the whiggish reigns that succeeded; till at length this spirit of influence has become the vital principle of the state,—an agency, subtle and unseen, which pervades every part of the Constitution, lurks under all its forms, and regulates all its movements, and, like the invisible sylph or grace which presides over the motions of beauty,

" Illam, quicquid agit, quoquo vestigia flectit,
Componit furtim subsequiturque."

The cause of Liberty and the Revolution are so habitually associated in the minds of Englishmen, that probably in objecting to the latter I may be thought hostile or indifferent to the former. But assuredly nothing could be more unjust than such a suspicion. The very object, indeed, which my humble animadversions would attain is, that in the crisis to which I think England is now hastening, and between which and foreign subjugation she may soon be compelled to choose, the errors and omissions of 1688 should be remedied; and, as it was then her fate to experience a Revolution without Reform, so she may now endeavour to accomplish a Reform without Revolution.

In speaking of the parties which have so long agitated England, it will be observed that I lean as little to the Whigs as to their adversaries. Both factions have been equally cruel to Ireland, and perhaps equally insincere in their efforts for the liberties of England. There is one name, indeed, connected with whiggism, of which I can never think but with veneration and tenderness. As justly, however, might the light of the sun be claimed by any particular nation, as the sanction of that name be monopolised by any party whatsoever. Mr. Fox belonged to mankind, and they have lost in him their ablest friend.

With respect to the few lines upon Intolerance, which I have subjoined, they are but the imperfect beginning of a long series of Essays, with which I here menace my readers, upon the same important subject. I shall look to no higher merit in the task than that of giving a new form to claims and remonstrances, which have often been much more eloquently urged, and which would long ere now have produced their effect, but that the minds of some of our statesmen, like the pupil of the human eye, contract themselves the more, the stronger light there is shed upon them.

CORRUPTION.

AN EPISTLE.

Νυν δ' απανθ' ωσπερ εξ αγορας εκπεπραται ταυτα· αντεισηκται δε αντι τουτων, υφ' ων απολωλε και νενοσηκεν η Ελλας. Ταυτα δ' εστι τι; ζηλος, ει τις ειληφε τι· γελως, αν ομολογη· συγγνωμη τοις ελεγχομενοις· μισος, αν τουτοις τις επιτιμα· ταλλα παντα, οσα εκ του δωροδοκειν ηρτηται.—Demosth., Philipp. iii.

Boast on, my friend—though stript of all beside, Thy struggling nation still retains her pride: (1)

(1) Angli suos ac sua omnia impense mirantur; cæteras nationes despectui habent.—*Barclay* (as quoted in one of Dryden's *prefaces*).

(2) England began very early to feel the effects of cruelty towards her dependencies. "The severity of her government (says Macpherson) contributed more to deprive her of the continental dominions of the family of Plantagenet than the arms of France."—*History*, vol. i.

(3) "By the total reduction of the kingdom of Ireland in 1691 (says Burke), the ruin of the native Irish, and in a great measure, too, of the first races of the English, was completely accomplished. The new English interest was settled with as solid a stability as any thing in human affairs can look for. All the penal laws of that unparalleled code of oppression, which were made after the last event, were manifestly the effects of national hatred and scorn towards a conquered people, whom the victors delighted to trample upon, and were not at all afraid to provoke." Yet this is the era to which the wise Common

That pride, which once in genuine glory woke When Marlborough fought, and brilliant St. John spoke: That pride which still, by time and shame unstung, Outlives even Wh—tel—cke's sword and H—wk—s-b'ry's tongue!

Boast on, my friend, while in this humbled isle, (2) Where Honour mourns and Freedom fears to smile, Where the bright light of England's fame is known But by the shadow o'er our fortunes thrown; Where, doom'd ourselves to nought but wrongs and slights, (3) We hear you boast of Britain's glorious rights, As wretched slaves, that under hatches lie, Hear those on deck extol the sun and sky! Boast on, while wandering through my native haunts, I coldly listen to thy patriot vaunts; And feel, though close our wedded countries twine, More sorrow for my own than pride from thine.

Yet pause a moment—and if truths severe Can find an inlet to that courtly ear, Which hears no news but W—rd's gazetted lies, And loves no politics in rhyme but Pye's,— If aught can please thee but the good old saws [laws," Of "Church and State," and "William's matchless And "Acts and Rights of glorious Eighty-eight,"— Things, which though now a century out of date, Still serve to ballast, with convenient words, A few crank arguments for speeching lords,—(4) Turn, while I tell how England's freedom found, Where most she look'd for life, her deadliest wound; How brave she struggled, while her foe was seen, How faint since Influence lent that foe a screen: How strong o'er James and Popery she prevail'd, How weakly fell, when Whigs and gold assail'd.(5)

While kings were poor, and all those schemes unknown Which drain the people, to enrich the throne; Ere yet a yielding Commons had supplied Those chains of gold by which themselves are tied;

Council of Dublin refer us for "invaluable blessings," etc. [And this is the era which such Governors as his Grace the Duke of R—chm—nd think it politic to commemorate, in the eyes of my insulted countrymen, by an annual procession round the statue of King William!

An unvarying trait of the policy of Great Britain towards Ireland has been her selection of such men to govern us as were least likely to deviate into justice and liberality, and the alarm which she has taken when any conscientious Viceroy has shown symptoms of departure from the old code of prejudice and oppression. Our most favourite Governors have accordingly been our shortest visitors, and the first moments of their popularity have in general been the last of their government. Thus Sir Anthony Bellingham, after the death of Henry the Eighth, was recalled "for not sufficiently consulting the English interests." or. in other words, for not shooting the requisite quantity of wild Irish. The same kind of delinquency led to the recall of Sir John Perrot, in Elizabeth's time,

Then proud Prerogative, untaught to creep
With bribery's silent foot on Freedom's sleep, (6)

and to that of the Earl of Radnor, in the reign of Charles
the Second, of whom Lord Orford says, "We are not told
how he disappointed the King's expectations, probably not
by too great complaisance, nor why his administration,
which Burnet calls *just*, was disliked. If it is true that he
was a good governor, the presumption will be that his
rule was not disliked by those *to* whom but *from* whom he
was sent."—*Royal and Noble Authors.*
We are not without instances of the same illiberal po-
licy in our own times.]

(4) It never seems to occur to those orators and address-
ers who round off so many sentences and paragraphs with
the Bill of Rights, the Act of Settlement, etc., that most of
the provisions which these Acts contained for the preser-
vation of parliamentary independence have been long
laid aside as romantic and troublesome. [The Revolution,
as its greatest admirers acknowledge, was little more than
a recognition of ancient privileges, a restoration of that
old Gothic structure which was brought from the woods
of Germany into England. Edward the First had long
before made a similar recognition, and had even more
expressly reverted to the first principles of the constitu-
tion, by declaring that "the people should have their laws,
liberties, and free customs, as largely and wholly as they
have used to have the same at any time they had them."
But, luckily for the Crown and its interests, the conces-
sions both of Edward and of William have been equally
vague and verbal, equally theoretical and insincere. The
feudal system was continued, notwithstanding the former,
and Lord M——'s honest head is upon his shoulders, in
spite of the latter.] I never meet, I confess, with a poli-
tician who quotes seriously the Declaration of Rights, etc.,
to prove the actual existence of English liberty, that I do
not think of that marquis, whom Montesquieu mentions,*
who set about looking for mines in the Pyrenees, on the
strength of authorities which he had read in some ancient
authors. The poor marquis toiled and searched in vain.
He quoted his authorities to the last, but found no mines
after all.

(5) The chief, perhaps the only advantage which has
resulted from the system of influence, is that tranquil
course of uninterrupted action which it has given to the
administration of government. If kings *must* be para-
mount in the state (and their ministers for the time being
always think so), the country is indebted to the Revolu-
tion for enabling them to become so quietly, and for
removing skilfully the danger of those shocks and colli-
sions which the alarming efforts of prerogative never
failed to produce.

[It is the nature of a people in general to attend but to
the externals of Government. Having neither leisure nor
ability to discuss its measures, they look no deeper than the
surface for their utility and no farther than the present for
their consequences. Mrs. Macaulay has said of a certain
period, "The people at this time were, as the people of Great
Britain always are, half-stupid, half-drunk, and half-asleep;"
and however we may dissent from this petulant effusion of
a Scotchwoman, it must be owned that the reasoning
powers of John Bull are not very easily called into action,
and that even where he does condescend to exert them, it
is like Dogberry's display of his reading and writing,
"where there is no need of such vanity:" as upon that
deep question about the dangers of the church, which was

* Liv. xxi., chap. 2.

Frankly avow'd his bold enslaving plan,
And claim'd a right from God to trample man!

submitted for his discussion by Mr. P-rc-v-l at the late
elections. It follows, however, from this apathy of the
people, that as long as no glaring exertion of power, no
open violation of forms is obtruded upon them, it is of
very little consequence how matters are managed behind
the curtain; and a few quiet men, getting close to the ear
of the Throne, may whisper away the salvation of the
country so inaudibly, that ruin will be divested of half its
alarming preparatives. If, in addition to this slumber of
the people, a great majority of those whom they have
deputed to watch for them can be induced, by any irre-
sistible argument, to prefer the safety of the government
to the integrity of the constitution, and to think a conni-
vance at the encroachments of power less troublesome
than the difficulties which would follow reform, I cannot
imagine a more tranquil state of affairs than must neces-
sarily result from such general and well-regulated ac-
quiescence.] Instead of vain and disturbing efforts to
establish that speculative balance of the constitution,
which, perhaps, has never existed but in the pages of
Montesquieu * and De Lolme, a preponderance is now
silently yielded to one of the three estates, which carries
the other two almost insensibly, but still effectually, along
with it; and even though the path may lead eventually to
destruction, yet its specious and gilded smoothness almost
atones for the danger; and like Milton's bridge over
Chaos, it may be said to lead,

"Smooth, easy, inoffensive, down to ——."

(6) [Though the Kings of England were most unroyally
harassed and fettered in all their pursuits by pecuniary
difficulties, before the provident enactments of William's
reign had opened to the Crown its present sources of
wealth, yet we must not attribute to the Revolutionary
Whigs the credit altogether of inventing this art of go-
vernment. Its advantages had long been understood by
ministers and favourites, though the limits of the royal
revenue prevented them from exercising it with effect. In
the reign of Mary, indeed, the gold of Spain, being added
to the usual resources of the Throne, produced such a
spirit of ductility in her Parliaments, that the price for
which each member had sold himself was publicly ascer-
tained: and if Charles the First could have commanded a
similar supply, it is not too much to suppose that the
Commonwealth never would have existed. But it was
during the reign of the second Charles that the nearest
approaches were made to that pecuniary system which
our debt, our funds, and our taxes, have since brought to
such perfection; and Clifford and Danby would not dis-
grace even the present times of political venality. Still,
however, the experiment was but partial and imperfect, †
and attended with scarcely any other advantage than that
of suggesting the uses to which the power of the purse has
been since converted, just as the fulminating dust of the
chemists may have prepared the way for the invention of
gunpowder.]

* [Montesquieu seems not a little satisfied with his own inge-
nuity in finding out the character of the English from the nature
of their political institutions; but it appears to me somewhat like
that easy sagacity by which Lavater has discovered the genius of
Shakspeare in his features.

† [See Preface to a *Collection of Debates*, etc., in 1694 and 1695,
for an account of the public tables kept at Westminster, in Charles
the Second's time, "to feed the betrayers of their country." The
payment of each day's work was left under their respective plates.]

But Luther's schism had too much roused mankind
For Hampden's truths to linger long behind ;
Nor then, when king-like popes had fallen so low
Could pope-like kings (1) escape the levelling blow.
That ponderous sceptre (in whose place we bow
To the light talisman of influence now),
Too gross, too visible to work the spell
Which modern power performs, in fragments fell ;
In fragments lay, till, patch'd and painted o'er
With fleurs-de-lys, it shone and scourged once more.

'T was then, my friend, thy kneeling nation quaff'd
Long, long and deep, the churchman's opiate draught
Of passive, prone obedience—then took flight
All sense of man's true dignity and right ; (2)
And Britons slept so sluggish in their chain,
That Freedom's watch-voice call'd almost in vain.
Oh, England ! England ! what a chance was thine,
When the last tyrant of that ill-starr'd line

(1) The drivelling correspondence between James I. and
his "dog Steenie" (the Duke of Buckingham), which we
find among the *Hardwicke Papers*, sufficiently shows, if
we wanted any such illustration, into what doting idiotic
brains the plan of arbitrary power may enter.

(2) In former editions—
　　Of tame obedience—till her sense of right
　　And pulse of glory seem'd extinguish'd quite.—P. E.

(3) Tacitus has expressed his opinion, in a passage very
frequently quoted, that such a distribution of power as
the theory of the British constitution exhibits is merely a
subject of bright speculation, "a system more easily
praised than practised, and which, even could it happen
to exist, would certainly not prove permanent ;" and, in
truth, a review of England's annals would dispose us to
agree with the great historian's remark. For we find that
at no period whatever has this balance of the three estates
existed ; that the nobles predominated till the policy of
Henry VII., and his successor reduced their weight by
breaking up the feudal system of property ; that the power
of the Crown became then supreme and absolute, till the
bold encroachments of the Commons subverted the fa-
bric altogether ; that the alternate ascendency of preroga-
tive and privilege distracted the period which followed
the Restoration ; and that, lastly, the Acts of 1688, by laying
the foundation of an unbounded court-influence, have
secured a preponderance to the Throne, which every suc-
ceeding year increases. So that the vaunted British con-
stitution has never perhaps existed but in mere theory.

(4) The monarchs of Great Britain can never be suffi-
ciently grateful for that accommodating spirit which led
the Revolutionary Whigs to give away the crown, without
imposing any of those restraints or stipulations which
other men might have taken advantage of so favourable a
moment to enforce, and in the framing of which they had
so good a model to follow as the limitations proposed by
the Lords Essex and Halifax, in the debate upon the
Exclusion Bill. They not only condescended, however, to
accept of places, but took care that these dignities should
be no impediment to their "voice potential" in affairs of
legislation ; and although an Act was after many years suf-
fered to pass, which by one of its articles disqualified place-
men from serving as members of the House of Commons,
it was yet not allowed to interfere with the influence of
the reigning monarch, nor with that of his successor Anne.

Fled from his sullied crown, and left thee free
To found thy own eternal liberty !
How nobly high, in that propitious hour,
Might patriot hands have raised the triple tower (3)
Of British freedom, on a rock divine
Which neither force could storm nor treachery mine !
But no—the luminous, the lofty plan,
Like mighty Babel, seem'd too bold for man ;
The curse of jarring tongues again was given
To thwart a work which raised men nearer hea-
　　ven.
While Tories marr'd what Whigs had scarce begun,
While Whigs undid what Whigs themselves had
　　done,(4)
The hour was lost, and William, with a smile,
Saw Freedom weeping o'er the unfinish'd pile !

Hence all the ills you suffer,—hence remain
Such galling fragments of that feudal chain, (5)

The purifying clause, indeed, was not to take effect till
after the decease of the latter sovereign, and she very
considerately repealed it altogether. So that, as repre-
sentation has continued ever since, if the king were simple
enough to send to foreign courts ambassadors who were
most of them in the pay of those courts, he would be just
as honestly and faithfully represented as are his people.
It would be endless to enumerate all the favours which
were conferred upon William by those "apostate Whigs."
They complimented him with the first suspension of the
Habeas Corpus Act which had been hazarded since the
confirmation of that privilege ; and this example of our
Deliverer's reign has not been lost upon any of his suc-
cessors. They promoted the establishment of a standing
army, and circulated in its defence the celebrated *Balan-
cing Letter*, in which it is insinuated that England, even
then, in her boasted hour of regeneration, was arrived at
such a pitch of faction and corruption, that nothing could
keep her in order but a Whig ministry and a standing
army. They refused, as long as they could, to shorten the
duration of parliaments ; and though, in the Declaration of
Rights, the necessity of such a reform was acknowledged,
they were able, by arts not unknown to modern ministers,
to brand those as traitors and republicans who urged it. *
But the grand and distinguishing trait of their measures
was the power they bestowed on the Crown of almost
annihilating the freedom of elections,—of turning from its
course, and for ever defiling that great stream of Repre-
sentation which had, even in the most agitated periods,
reflected some features of the people, but which from
thenceforth became the Pactolus, the "aurifer amnis " of
the court, and served as a mirror of the national will
and popular feeling no longer. We need but consult the
writings of that time, to understand the astonishment then
excited by measures, which the practice of a century has
rendered not only familiar but necessary. See a pamphlet
called *The Danger of mercenary Parliaments*, 1698 ; *State
Tracts*, Will. III., vol. ii. ; see also *Some Paradoxes pre-
sented as a New Year's Gift* (State Poems, vol. iii.).

(5) The last great wound given to the feudal system was

* See a pamphlet published in 1693, upon the King's refusing to
sign the Triennial Bill, called *A Discourse between a Yeoman of Kent
and a Knight of a Shire.*—" Hereupon (says the Yeoman) the gentle-
man grew angry, and said that I talked like a base commons-
wealth man."

Whose links, around you by the Norman flung,
Though loosed and broke so often, still have clung.
Hence sly Prerogative, like Jove of old,
Has turn'd his thunder into showers of gold,
Whose silent courtship wins securer joys, (1)
Taints by degrees, and ruins without noise.
While Parliaments, no more those sacred things
Which make and rule the destiny of kings,
Like loaded dice by ministers are thrown,
And each new set of sharpers cog their own.

the Act of the 12th of Charles II., which abolished the tenure of knight's service *in capite*, and which Blackstone compares, for its salutary influence upon property, to the boasted provisions of Magna Charta itself. Yet even in this Act we see the effects of that counteracting spirit which has contrived to weaken every effort of the English nation towards liberty [which allowed but half the errors of Popery to be removed at the Reformation, and which planted more abuses than it suffered to be rooted out at the Revolution]. The exclusion of copyholders from their share of elective rights was permitted to remain as a brand of feudal servitude, and as an obstacle to the rise of that strong counterbalance which an equal representation of property would oppose to the weight of the Crown. If the managers of the Revolution had been sincere in their wishes for reform, they would not only have taken this fetter off the rights of election, but would have renewed the mode adopted in Cromwell's time of increasing the number of knights of the shire, to the exclusion of those rotten insignificant boroughs, which have tainted the whole mass of the constitution. Lord Clarendon calls this measure of Cromwell's "an alteration fit to be more warrantable made, and in a better time." It formed part of Mr. Pitt's plan in 1783; but Pitt's plan of reform was, a kind of announced dramatic piece, about as likely to be ever acted as Mr. Sheridan's "*Foresters*."

(1) —— fore enim tutum iter et patens
       Converso in pretium Deo.
    Aurum per medios ire satellites, etc.—*Horat.*

[The Athenians considered seduction so much more dangerous than force, that the penalty for a rape was merely a pecuniary fine, while the guilt of seduction was punished with death. And though it must be owned that, during the reign of that ravisher Prerogative, the poor constitution was treated like Miss Cunegund among the Bulgarians, yet I agree with the principle of the Athenian law that her present state of willing self-abandonment is much more hopeless and irreclaimable, and calls for a more signal vengeance upon her seducers.]

It would be a task not uninstructive to trace the history of Prerogative from the date of its strength under the Tudor princes, when Henry VII. and his successors "taught the people (as Nathaniel Bacon says) * to dance to the tune of Allegiance," to the period of the Revolution, when the Throne, in its attacks upon liberty, began to exchange the noisy explosions of Prerogative for the silent and effectual air-gun of Influence. In following its course, too, since that memorable era, we shall find that, while the royal power has been abridged in branches where it might be made conducive to the interests of the people, it has been left in full and unshackled vigour against almost every point where the integrity of the Constitution is vulnerable. For instance, the power of

* *Historic. and Politic. Discourse,* etc., part. ii., p. 114.

Hence the rich oil, that from the Treasury steals,
Drips smooth o'er all the Constitution's wheels,
Giving the old machine such pliant play, (2)
That Court and Commons jog one joltless way,
While Wisdom trembles for the crazy car,
So gilt, so rotten, carrying fools so far;
And the duped people, hourly doom'd to pay
The sums that bribe their liberties away,—(3)
Like a young eagle, who has lent his plume
To fledge the shaft by which he meets his doom,—

chartering boroughs, to whose capricious abuse in the hands of the Stuarts we are indebted for most of the present anomalies of representation, might, if suffered to remain, have in some degree atoned for its mischief, by restoring the old unchartered boroughs to their rights, and widening more equally the basis of the legislature. But, by the Act of Union with Scotland, this part of the prerogative was removed, lest Freedom should have a chance of being healed, even by the rust of the spear which had formerly wounded her. The dangerous power, however, of creating peers, which has been so often exercised *for* the government *against* the constitution, is still left in free and unqualified activity; notwithstanding the example of that celebrated Bill for the limitation of this ever-budding branch of prerogative, which was proposed in the reign of George I., under the peculiar sanction and recommendation of the Crown, but which the Whigs, thought right to reject, with all that characteristic delicacy, which, in general, prevents them, when enjoying the sweets of office themselves, from taking any uncourtly advantage of the Throne. It will be recollected, however, that the creation of the twelve peers by the Tories in Anne's reign (a measure which Swift, like a true party man, defends) gave these upright Whigs all possible alarm for their liberties.

With regard to the generous fit about his prerogative which seized so unroyally the good king George I., historians have hinted that the paroxysm originated far more in hatred to his son than in love to the Constitution.† This, of course, however, is a calumny: no loyal person, acquainted with the annals of the three Georges, could possibly suspect any *one* of those gracious monarchs either of ill-will to his heir, or indifference for the constitution.

(2. "They drove so fast (says Welwood of the ministers of Charles I.), that it was no wonder that the wheels and chariot broke."—(*Memoirs,* p. 35.) But this fatal accident, if we may judge from experience, is to be imputed far less to the folly and impetuosity of the drivers, than to the want of that suppling oil from the Treasury which has been found so necessary to make a government like that of England run smoothly. Had Charles been as well provided with this article as his successors have been since the happy Revolution, his Commons would never have merited from him the harsh appellation of "seditious vipers," but would have been (as they now are, and I trust always will be) "dutiful Commons," "loyal Commons," etc., etc., and would have given him ship-money, or any other sort of money he might have fancied.

(3 [The period that immediately succeeds a coronation has been called very aptly the Honey-moon of a reign; and if we suppose the Throne to be the wife, and the People the husband, § I know no better model of a matri-

† Coxe says that this Bill was projected by Sunderland.

§ This is contrary to the symbolical language of prophecy, in
20

See their own feathers pluck'd, to wing the
   dart
Which rank corruption destines for their heart !
But soft! methinks I hear thee proudly say,
" What ! shall I listen to the impious lay,
That dares, with Tory licence, to profane
The bright bequests of William's glorious reign ?
Shall the great wisdom of our patriot sires,
Whom H—wks—b—y quotes and savoury B—rch
   admires,
Be slander'd thus? shall honest St—le agree
With virtuous R—se to call us pure and free,

Yet fail to prove it ?   Shall our patent pair
Of wise state-poets waste their words in air,
And P—e unheeded breathe his prosperous strain,
And C—nn—ng *take the people's sense* in vain?"(1)

   The people ! ah, that Freedom's form should
     stay
Where Freedom's spirit long hath pass'd away !
That a false smile should play around the dead,
And flush the features when the soul hath fled !(2)
When Rome had lost her virtue with her rights,
When her foul tyrant sat on Capreæ's heights (3)

---

monial transaction, nor one that I would sooner recom-
mend to a woman of spirit, than that which the arrange-
ments of 1688 afford. In the first place, she must not
only obtain from her husband an allowance of pin-money,
or civil-list establishment, sufficient to render her inde-
pendent of his caprice, but she must also prevail on him
to make her the steward of his estates, and to intrust her
with the management of all his pecuniary concerns. I
need not tell a woman of sense to what spirited uses she
may turn such concessions. He will soon become so
tame and docile under her hands, that she may make him
play the strangest and most amusing tricks, such as quar-
relling with his nearest and dearest relations about a dish
of tea,* a turban,† or a wafer ;‡ preparing his house for
defence against robbers, by putting fetters and hand-
cuffs on two thirds of its inmates ; employing C—nn—g and
P—rc—v—l in his sickest moments to read to him alter-
nately *Joe Miller* and the *Catechism*, with a thousand other
diverting inconsistencies. If her spouse have still enough
of sense remaining to grumble at the ridiculous exhibition
which she makes of him, let her withhold from him now
and then the rights of the Habeas Corpus Act (a mode of
proceeding which the women of Athens once adopted\, §
and if the good man loves such privileges, the interruption
will soon restore him to submission. If his former wife
were a Papist, or had any tendency that way, I would
advise my fair Sovereign, whenever he begins to argue
with her unpleasantly, to shout out "No Popery, no
Popery!" as loud as she can, into his ears, and it is asto-
nishing what an effect it will have in disconcerting all his
arguments. This method was tried lately by an old woman
at Northampton, and with much success.] Among those
auxiliaries which the Revolution of 1688 marshalled on
the side of the Throne, the bugbear of Popery has not
been the least convenient and serviceable. Those unskil-
ful tyrants, Charles and James, instead of profiting by
that useful subserviency which has always distinguished
the ministers of our religious establishment, were so in-
fatuated as to plan the ruin of this best bulwark of their
power, and, moreover, connected their designs upon the
Church so undisguisedly with their attacks upon the Con-
stitution, that they identified in the minds of the people
the interests of their religion and their liberties. During

which (according to Sir Isaac Newton) the King is the husband, and
the people the wife. See Faber, on the Prophecies.—I would beg
leave to suggest to Mr. Faber, that his friend Sir B—ch—d M—sgr—ve
can, in his own proper person, supply him with an exposition of
" the Horns of the Beast."
   * America.   + India.   + Ireland.
  § See the Lysistrata of Aristophanes.—The following is the form
of suspension, as he gives it :—

  'Οπως αν ανηρ επιτυρη μαλιϛα μου
  Κουδεποϑ' εκουσα τ' ανδρι τῳ 'μῳ πεισομαι.

those times, therefore, "No Popery" was the watchword
of freedom, and served to keep the public spirit awake
against the invasions of bigotry and prerogative. The Re-
volution, however, by removing this object of jealousy, has
produced a reliance on the orthodoxy of the Throne, of
which the Throne has not failed to take advantage ; and the
cry of "No Popery," having thus lost its power of alarming
the people against the inroads of the Crown, has served
ever since the very different purpose of strengthening the
Crown against the pretensions and struggles of the people.
The danger of the Church from Papists and Pretenders
was the chief pretext for the repeal of the Triennial Bill, for
the adoption of a standing army, for the numerous suspen-
sions of the Habeas Corpus Act, and, in short, for all those
spirited infractions of the Constitution by which the reigns
of the last century were so eminently distinguished. We
have seen very lately, too, how the Throne has been
enabled, by the same scarecrow sort of alarm, to select
its ministers from among men, whose servility is their
only claim to elevation, and who are pledged (if such an
alternative *could* arise) to take part with the scruples of
the King against the salvation of the empire.

  (1) Somebody has said. " Quand tous les poëtes seraient
noyés, ce ne serait pas grand dommage ;" but I am aware
that this is not fit language to be held at a time when our
birth-day odes and state-papers are written by such pretty
poets as Mr. P—e and Mr. C—nn—ng. [I can assure the
latter, too, that I think him (like his water-proof colleague
Lord C—stl—r—gh) reserved for a very different fate from
that which the author I have just quoted imagines for his
poetical fraternity.] All I wish is, that the latter gentle-
man would change places with his brother P—e, by
which means we should have somewhat less prose in our
odes, and certainly less poetry in our politics.

  (2) "It is a scandal (said Sir Charles Sedley in William's
reign) that a government so sick at heart as ours is should
look so well in the face ;" and Edmund Burke has said, in
the present reign, "When the people conceive that laws
and tribunals, and even popular assemblies, are perverted
from the ends of their institution, they find in these names
of degenerated establishments only new motives to dis-
content. Those bodies which, when full of life and beauty,
lay in their arms and were their joy and comfort, when
dead and putrid become more loathsome from remem-
brance of former endearments."—*Thoughts on the present
Discontents*, 1770.

  (3)   —— Tutor haberi
  Principis, Augustâ Caprearum in rupe sedentis
  Cum grege Chaldæo.   *Juvenal*, Sat. x., v. 92.
The senate still continued, during the reign of Tiberius,
to manage all the business of the nation ; the money was
then and long after coined by their authority, and every
other public affair received their sanction.

Amid his ruffian spies, and doom'd to death
Each noble name they blasted with their breath,—
Even then, (in mockery of that golden time,
When the Republic rose revered, sublime,
And her proud sons, diffused from zone to zone,
Gave kings to every nation but their own,)
Even then the senate and the tribunes stood,
Insulting marks, to show how high the flood
Of Freedom flow'd, in glory's by–gone day,
And how it ebb'd,—for ever ebb'd away!(1)

Look but around—though yet a tyrant's sword
Nor haunts our sleep nor glitters o'er our board,
Though blood be better drawn, by modern quacks,
With Treasury leeches, than with sword or axe;
Yet say, could even a prostrate tribune's power,
Or a mock senate, in Rome's servile hour,
Insult so much the claims, the rights of man,
As doth that fetter'd mob, that free divan,
Of noble tools and honourable knaves,
Of pension'd patriots and privileged slaves ;—
That party-colour'd mass, which nought can warm
But rank Corruption's heat—whose quicken'd swarm
Spread their light wings in Bribery's golden sky,
Buzz for a period, lay their eggs, and die ;—
That greedy vampire, which from Freedom's tomb
Comes forth, with all the mimicry of bloom
Upon its lifeless cheek, and sucks and drains
A people's blood to feed its putrid veins!

Thou start'st, my friend, at picture drawn so dark—
"Is there no light?" thou ask'st—"no lingering spark

We are told by Tacitus of a certain race of men, who
made themselves particularly useful to the Roman em-
perors, and were therefore called "instrumenta regni,"
or "court tools." From this it appears, that my Lords
M-lgr-ve, Ch-th-m, etc., etc., are by no means things of
modern invention.

(1) There is something very touching in what Tacitus
tells us of the hopes that revived in a few patriot bosoms,
when the death of Augustus was near approaching, and
already began with which they already began
"bona libertatis incassum disserere."

According to Ferguson, Cæsar's interference with the
rights of election "made the subversion of the Republic
more felt than any of the former acts of his power."—
Roman Republic, book v., chap. i.

(2) Andrew Marvell, the honest opposer of the court
during the reign of Charles the Second, and the last
member of parliament who, according to the ancient mode,
took wages from his constituents. The Commons have,since
then, much changed their pay-masters. See the *State Poems*
for some rude but spirited effusions of Andrew Marvell.

(3) The following artless speech of Sir Francis Win-
nington, in the reign of Charles the Second, will amuse
those who are fully aware of the perfection we have since
attained in that system of government whose humble
beginnings so much astonished the worthy baronet. "I
did observe (says he) that all those who had pensions, and
most of those who had offices, voted all of a side, as they
were directed by some great officer, exactly as if their
business in this House had been to preserve their pensions

Of ancient fire to warm us? Lives there none,
To act a Marvell's part?" (2)—alas ! not one.
To place and power all public spirit tends;
In place and power all public spirit ends ;(3)
Like hardy plants, that love the air and sky,
When *out*, 't will thrive—but taken *in*, 't will die !

Not bolder truths of sacred Freedom hung
From Sidney's pen, or burn'd on Fox's tongue,
Than upstart Whigs produce each market-night,
While yet their conscience, as their purse, is light;
While debts at home excite their care for those
Which, dire to tell, their much-loved country owes,
And loud and upright, till their prize be known,
They thwart the King's supplies to raise their own.
But bees, on flowers alighting, cease their hum—
So, settling upon places, Whigs grow dumb.
And, though most base is he who, 'neath the shade
Of Freedom's ensign (4) plies Corruption's trade, (5)
And makes the sacred flag he dares to show
His passport to the market of her foe,
Yet, yet, I own, so venerably dear
Are Freedom's grave old anthems to my ear,
That I enjoy them, though by traitors sung,
And reverence Scripture even from Satan's tongue.
Nay, when the Constitution has expired,
I 'll have such men, like Irish wakers, hired
To chant old "Habeas Corpus" by its side,
And ask, in purchased ditties, why it died? (6)

See yon smooth lord, whom nature's plastic pains
Would seem to 've fashion'd for those Eastern reigns

and offices, and not to make laws for the good of them who
sent them here."—He alludes to that parliament which
was called, *par excellence*, the Pensionary Parliament.
[A distinction, however, which it has long lost, and which
we merely give it just as we say *The* Irish Rebellion.]

(4) Changed from—
> And though I feel as if indignant Heaven
> Must think that wretch too foul to be forgiven,
> Who basely hangs the bright protecting shade
> Of Freedom's ensign o'er Corruption's trade.—P. E.

(5) ["While they promise them liberty, they themselves
are the servants of corruption." 2 Pet. ii.—I suggest,
with much deference, to the expounders of Scripture-
Prophecy, whether Mr. C-nn-ng is not at present fulfilling
the prediction of "the scoffers," who were to come "in
the last days."]

(6) [I believe it is in following the corpse to the grave,
and not at the wakes (as we call the watching of the dead),
that this elegiac howl of my countrymen is performed.
Spenser says, that our howl "is heathenish, and proceeds
from a despair of salvation." If so, I think England may
join in chorus with us at present.—The Abbe de Moiraye
tells us, that the Jews in the East address their dead in a
similar manner, and say, "Hu! Hu! Hu! why did you die?
Had'nt you a wife? Had'nt you a long pipe?" etc., etc.
(See his *Travels*.) I thought for a long time with Vallen-
cey, that we were a colony of Carthaginians, but from
this passage of De Moiraye, and from the way in which
Mr. P-rc-v-l would have us treated, I begin to suspect we
are no better than Jews.]

When eunuchs flourish'd, and such nerveless things
As men rejected were the chosen of kings;—(1)
Even *he*, forsooth, (oh fraud, of all the worst!)
Dared to assume the patriot's name at first—(2)
Thus Pitt began, and thus begin his apes;
Thus devils, when *first* raised, take pleasing shapes.
But oh, poor Ireland! if revenge be sweet
For centuries of wrong, for dark deceit
And withering insult—for the Union thrown
Into thy bitter cup,(3) when that alone
Of slavery's draught was wanting (4)— if for this
Revenge be sweet, thou *hast* that dæmon's bliss;
For, sure, 't is more than hell's revenge to see
That England trusts the men who 've ruin'd thee;—
That, in these awful days, when every hour
Creates some new or blasts some ancient power,
When proud Napoleon, like the enchanted shield (5)
Whose light compell'd each wondering foe to yield,

(1) According to Xenophon, the chief circumstance which
recommended these creatures to the service of Eastern
princes was the ignominious station they held in society,
and the probability of their being, upon this account,
more devoted to the will and caprice of a master, from
whose notice alone they der'ved consideration, and in
whose favour they might seek refuge from the general
contempt of mankind.—Ἀδοξοι οντες οἱ ευνουχοι παρα
τοις αλλοις ανθρωποις και δια τουτο δεσποτου επικου-
ρου προσδεονται. *—But I doubt whether even an Eastern
prince would have chosen an entire administration upon
this principle.

(2) [Does Lord C-stl-r—gh remember the reforming
Resolutions of his early days?]

(3) "And in the cup an *Union* shall be thrôwn."—*Hamlet.*

[Three C's were branded in the Sibylline books, as fatal
to the peace and liberties of Rome. Τρια καππα κακιστα
Cornelius Sylla, Cornelius Cinna, and Cornelius Len-
tulus).† And three C's will be remembered in Ireland as
long as C-md-n and cruelty, Cl-re and corruption, C-stl-
r—gh and contempt, are alliteratively and appropriately
associated.]

(4) Among the many measures which, since the Revo-
lution, have contributed to increase the influence of the
Throne, and to feed up this "Aaron's serpent" of the
constitution to its present healthy and respectable magni-
tude, there have been few more nutritive than the Scotch
and Irish Unions. Sir John Packer said, in a debate upon
the former question, that "he would submit it to the
House, whether men who had basely betrayed their trust,
by giving up their independent constitution, were fit to
be admitted into the English House of Commons." But
Sir John would have moved, If he had not been out of
place at the time, that the pliancy of such materials was
not among the least of their recommendations. Indeed,
the promoters of the Scotch Union were by no means
disappointed in the leading object of their measure, for
the triumphant majorities of the court-party in parliament
may be dated from the admission of the 45 and the 16.
Once or twice, upon the alteration of their law of treason
and the imposition of the malt-tax (measures which were
in direct violation of the Act of Union), these worthy North

* [See a pamphlet on the Union, by "a Philosopher."]

† [See a *Treatise* by Pontus De Thiard, " *De recta Nominum im-
positione*," p. 43.]

With baleful lustre blinds the brave and free,
And dazzles Europe into slavery,—
That, in this hour, when patriot zeal should guide,
When Mind should rule, and—Fox should *not* have
died,
All that devoted England can oppose
To enemies made fiends and friends made foes,
Is the rank refuse, the despised remains (6)
Of that unpitying power, whose whips and chains
Drove Ireland first to turn, with harlot glance,
Towards other shores, and woo the embrace of
France;—
Those hack'd and tainted tools, so foully fit
For the grand artisan of mischief, P—tt,
So useless ever but in vile employ,
So weak to save, so vigorous to destroy—
Such are the men that guard thy threaten'd shore,
Oh England! sinking England! (7) boast no more.

Britons arrayed themselves in opposition to the court;
but finding this effort for their country unavailing, they
prudently determined to think thenceforward of them-
selves, and few men have ever kept to a laudable reso-
lution more firmly. The effect of Irish representation on
the liberties of England will be no less perceptible and
permanent.

——Ουδ' ὁγε Ταυροι
Λειπεται αντελλουτος. §

The infusion of such cheap and useful ingredients as my
Lord L., Mr. D. B., etc., etc., into the legislature, cannot
but act as a powerful alterative on the constitution, and
clear it by degreesof all troublesome humours of honesty.

(5) The magician's shield in Ariosto:—
E tolto per vertù dello splendore
La libertate a loro.—Cant. 2.

We are told that Cæsar's code of morality was contained
in the following lines of Euripides, which that great man
frequently repeated:—

Ειπερ γαρ αδικειν χρη τυραννιδος περι
Καλλιστον αδικειν· τ' αλλα δ' ευσεβειν χρεων.

This is also, as it appears, the moral code of Napoleon.

(6) [When the Duke of Buckingham was assassinated,
Charles the First, as a tribute to his memory, continued
all his creatures in the same posts and favours which they
had enjoyed under their patron ; and much in the same
manner do we see the country sacrificed to the manes of
a Minister at present.

It is invidious perhaps to look for parallels in the reign
of Charles the First, but the expedient of threatening the
Commons with dissolution, which has lately been played
off with so much éclat, appears to have been frequently
resorted to at that period. In one instance Hume tells
us, that the King sent his Lord Keeper (*not his Jester*) to
menace the House, that, unless they dispatched a certain
Bill for subsidies, they must expect to sit no longer. By
similar threats the excise upon beer and ale was carried
in Charles the Second's reign. It is edifying to know, that
though Mr. C-nn-ng despises Puffendorf, he has no objec-
tion to precedents derived from the Courts of the Stuarts.

(7) The following prophetic remarks occur in a letter

§ From Aratus (v. 715.) a poet who wrote upon Astronomy,
though, as Cicero assures us, he knew nothing whatever about the
subject: just as the great Harvey wrote "*De Generatione*," though
he had as little to do with the matter as my Lord Viscount C.

INTOLERANCE.

A SATIRE.

"This clamour, which pretends to be raised for the safety of religion, has almost worn out the very appearance of it, and rendered us not only the most divided, but the most immoral people upon the face of the earth."

Addison, Freeholder, No. 37.

START not, my friend, nor think the Muse will stain
Her classic fingers with the dust profane
Of Bulls, Decrees, and all those thundering scrolls,
Which took such freedom once with royal souls, (1)
When heaven was yet the pope's exclusive trade,
And kings were *damn'd* as fast as now they're *made*.
No, no—let D—gen—n search the papal chair (2)
For fragrant treasures long forgotten there;
And, as the witch of sunless Lapland thinks
That little swarthy gnomes delight in stinks,

Let sallow P—rc—v—l snuff up the gale
Which wizard D—gen—n's gather'd sweets ex-
    hale.
Enough for me, whose heart has learn'd to scorn
Bigots alike in Rome or England born,
Who loathe the venom, whencesoe'er it springs,
From popes or lawyers, (3) pastry-cooks or kings,—
Enough for me to laugh and weep by turns,
As mirth provokes, or indignation burns,
As C—nn—ng vapours, or as France succeeds,
As H—wk—sb'ry proses, or as Ireland bleeds!

And thou, my friend, if, in these headlong
    days,
When bigot Zeal her drunken antics plays
So near a precipice, that men the while
Look breathless on and shudder while they smile—
If, in such fearful days, thou'lt dare to look
To hapless Ireland, to this rankling nook

written by Sir Robert Talbot, who attended the Duke of Bedford to Paris in 1762. Talking of states which have grown powerful in commerce, he says, "According to the nature and common course of things, there is a confede-racy against them, and consequently in the same propor-tion as they increase in riches, they approach to destruction. The address of our King William, in making all Europe take the alarm at France, has brought that country before us near that inevitable period. We must necessarily have our turn, and Great Britain will attain it as soon as France shall have a declaimer with organs as proper for that po-litical purpose as were those of our William the Third. . . . . Without doubt, my Lord, Great Britain must lower her flight. Europe will remind us of the balance of commerce, as she has reminded France of the balance of power. The address of our statesmen will immortalise them by contriving for us a descent which shall not be a fall, by making us rather resemble Holland than Carthage and Venice."—*Letters on the French Nation.*

(1) The king-deposing doctrine, notwithstanding its many mischievous absurdities, was of no little service to the cause of political liberty, by inculcating the right of resist-ance to tyrants, and asserting the will of the people to be the only true fountain of power. Bellarmine, the most violent of the advocates for papal authority, was one of the first to maintain (*De Pontif.*, lib. i., cap. 7), "that kings have not their authority or office immediately from God nor his law, but only from the law of nations;" and in King James's "*Defence of the Rights of Kings against Cardinal Perron,*" we find his Majesty expressing strong indignation against the Cardinal for having asserted "that to the deposing of a king the consent of the people must be obtained"—"for by these words (says James) the people are exalted above the king, and made the judges of the king's deposing," p. 424.—Even in Mariana's celebrated book, where the nonsense of bigotry does not interfere, there may be found many liberal and enlightened views of the principles of government, of the restraints which should be imposed upon royal power, of the subordination of the Throne to the interests of the people, etc., etc., (*De Rege et Regis Institutione.* See particularly lib. i., cap. 6, 8, and 9.)—It is rather remarkable, too, that England should be indebted to another Jesuit for the earliest de-fence of that principle upon which the Revolution was

founded, namely, the right of the people to change the succession.—(See Doleman's *Conferences,* written in sup-port of the title of the Infanta of Spain against that of James I.)—When Englishmen, therefore, say that Popery is the religion of slavery, they should not only recollect that their own boasted constitution is the work and bequest of popish ancestors; they should not only remember the laws of Edward III., "under whom (says Bolingbroke) the constitution of our parliaments, and the whole form of our government, became reduced into better form;" but they should know that even the errors charged on Popery have leaned to the cause of liberty, and that Papists were the first promulgators of the doctrines which led to the Revo-lution.—In general, however, the political principles of the Roman Catholics have been described as happened to suit the temporary convenience of their oppressors, and have been represented alternately as slavish or refractory, according as a pretext for tormenting them was wanting. The same inconsistency has marked every other imputa-tion against them. They are charged with laxity in the observance of oaths, though an oath has been found suf-ficient to shut them out from all worldly advantages. If they reject certain decisions of their church, they are said to be sceptics and bad Christians; if they admit those very decisions, they are branded as bigots and bad subjects. We are told that confidence and kindness will make them enemies to the government, though we know that exclu-sion and injuries have hardly prevented them from being its friends. In short, nothing can better illustrate the mi-sery of those shifts and evasions by which a long course of cowardly injustice must be supported, than the whole history of Great Britain's conduct towards the Catholic part of her empire.

(2) The "Sella *Stercoraria*" of the popes.—The Right Honourable and learned Doctor will find an engraving of this chair in Spanheim's *Disquisitio Historica de Papâ Foeminâ* (p. 118); and I recommend it as a model for the fashion of that seat which the Doctor is about to take in the privy council of Ireland.

(3) When Innocent X. was entreated to decide the con-troversy between the Jesuits and the Jansenists, he an-swered, that "he had been bred a lawyer, and had there-fore nothing to do with divinity."—It were to be wished that some of our English pettifoggers knew their own fit element as well as Pope Innocent X.

Which Heaven hath freed from poisonous things in
   vain,
While G—ff—rd's tongue and M—sgr—ve's pen re-
   main—
If thou hast yet no golden blinkers got
To shade thine eyes from this devoted spot,
Whose wrongs, though blazon'd o'er the world they
   be,
Placemen alone are privileged *not* to see—
Oh! turn awhile, and, though the shamrock wreathes
My homely harp, yet shall the song it breathes
Of Ireland's slavery, and of Ireland's woes,
Live, when the memory of her tyrant foes
Shall but exist, all future knaves to warn,
Embalm'd in hate and canonised by scorn.
When C—stl—r—gh,(1) in sleep still more profound
Than his own opiate tongue now deals around,
Shall wait the impeachment of that awful day
Which even *his* practised hand can't bribe away.

Yes, my dear friend, wert thou but near me now,
To see how Spring lights up on Erin's brow
Smiles that shine out, unconquerably fair, [there,—
Even through the blood-marks left by C—md—n(2)
Couldst thou but see what verdure paints the sod
Which none but tyrants and their slaves have trod,
And didst thou know the spirit, kind and brave,
That warms the soul of each insulted slave,
Who, tired with struggling, sinks beneath his lot,
And seems by all but watchful France forgot. (3)
Thy heart would burn—yes, even thy Pittite heart
Would burn, to think that such a blooming part
Of the world's garden, rich in nature's charms,
And fill'd with social souls and vigorous arms,
Should be the victim of that canting crew,
So smooth, so godly,—yet so devilish too;
Who, arm'd at once with prayer-books and with
   whips,(4)
Blood on their hands and Scripture on their lips,

---

(1) [The breach of faith which the managers of the Irish Union have been guilty of in disappointing those hopes of emancipation which they excited in the bosoms of the Catholics, is no new trait in the annals of English policy. A similar deceit was practised to facilitate the Union with Scotland, and hopes were held out of exemption from the Corporation and Test Acts, in order to divert the Parliament of that country from encumbering the measure with any stipulation to that effect.]

(2) Not the C—md—n who speaks thus of Ireland:—
"To wind up all, whether we regard the fruitfulness of the soil, the advantage of the sea, with so many commodious havens, or the natives themselves, who are warlike, ingenious, handsome, and well-complexioned, soft-skinned and very nimble, by reason of the pliantness of their muscles, this Island is in many respects so happy, that Giraldus might very well say, 'Nature had regarded with more favourable eyes than ordinary this Kingdom of Zephyr.'"

(3) The example of toleration, which Bonaparte has held forth, will, I fear, produce no other effect than that of determining the British government to persist, from the very spirit of opposition, in their own old system of intolerance and injustice; just as the Siamese blacken their teeth, "because," as they say, "the devil has white ones." *

(4) One of the unhappy results of the controversy between Protestants and Catholics is the mutual exposure which their criminations and recriminations have produced. In vain do the Protestants charge the Papists with closing the door of salvation upon others, while many of their own writings and articles breathe the same uncharitable spirit. No canon of Constance or Lateran ever damned heretics more effectually than the eighth of the Thirty-nine Articles consigns to perdition every single member of the Greek church; and I doubt whether a more sweeping clause of damnation was ever proposed in the most bigoted council, than that which the Calvinistic theory of predestination in the seventeenth of these Articles exhibits. It is true that no liberal Protestant avows such exclusive opinions; that every honest clergyman must feel a pang while he subscribes to them; that some even assert the Athanasian Creed to be the forgery

*See *l'Histoire Naturelle et Politique du Royaume de Siam*, etc.

of one Vigilius Tapsensis, in the beginning of the sixth century, and that eminent divines, like Jortin, have not hesitated to say, "There are propositions contained in our Liturgy and Articles, which no man of common sense among us believes."† But while all this is freely conceded to Protestants; while nobody doubts their sincerity, when they declare that their articles are not essentials of faith, but a collection of opinions which have been promulgated by fallible men, and from many of which they feel themselves justified in dissenting,—while so much liberty of retractation is allowed to Protestants upon their own declared and subscribed Articles of Religion, is it not strange that a similar indulgence should be so obstinately refused to the Catholics, upon tenets which their church has uniformly resisted and condemned, in every country where it has independently flourished? When the Catholics say, "The Decree of the Council of Lateran, which you object to us, has no claim whatever upon either our faith or our reason; it did not even profess to contain any doctrinal decision, but was merely a judicial proceeding of that assembly; and it would be as fair for us to impute a *wife-killing* doctrine to the Protestants, because their first pope, Henry VIII., was sanctioned in an indulgence of that propensity, as for you to conclude that we have inherited a king-deposing taste from the *acts* of the Council of Lateran, or the secular pretensions of our popes. With respect, too, to the Decree of the Council of Constance, upon the strength of which you accuse us of breaking faith with heretics, we do not hesitate to pronounce that Decree a calumnious forgery, a forgery, too, so obvious and ill-fabricated, that none but our enemies have ever ventured to give it the slightest credit for authenticity." When the Catholics make these declarations (and they are almost weary with making them), when they show, too, by their conduct, that these declarations are sincere, and that their faith and morals are no more regulated by the absurd decrees of old councils and popes, than their science is influenced by the papal anathema against that Irishman § who first found out the Antipodes,—is it not strange that

† *Strictures on the Articles, Subscriptions,* etc.

§ Virgilius, surnamed Solivagus, a native of Ireland, who maintained, in the 8th century, the doctrine of the Antipodes, and was anathematised accordingly by the Pope. John Scotus Erigena, another Irishman, was the first that ever wrote against transubstantiation.

Tyrants by creed, and torturers by text,
Make *this* life hell, in honour of the *next!*
Your R—desd—les, P—re—v—ls,—great, glorious
　　Heaven,
If I'm presumptuous, be my tongue forgiven,
When here I swear, by my soul's hope of rest,
I'd rather have been born, ere man was blest
With the pure dawn of Revelation's light,
Yes,—rather plunge me back in Pagan night,
And take my chance with Socrates for bliss, (1)
Than be the Christian of a faith like this,

Which builds on heavenly cant its earthly sway,
And in a convert mourns to lose a prey;
Which, grasping human hearts with double hold,(2)
Like Danae's lover mixing god and gold,—(3)
Corrupts both state and church, and makes an
　　oath
The knave and atheist's passport into both;
Which, while it dooms dissenting souls to know
Nor bliss above nor liberty below,
Adds the slave's suffering to the sinner's fear,
And, lest he 'scape hereafter, racks him here!(4)

so many still wilfully distrust what every good man is so much interested in believing? That so many should prefer the dark-lantern of the 13th century to the sunshine of intellect which has since overspread the world, and that every dabbler in theology, from Mr. Le Mesurier down to the Chancellor of the Exchequer, should dare to oppose the rubbish of Constance and Lateran to the bright and triumphant progress of justice, generosity, and truth?

(1) In a singular work, written by one Franciscus Collius, "upon the Souls of the Pagans," the author discusses, with much coolness and erudition, all the probable chances of salvation upon which a heathen philosopher might calculate. Consigning to perdition without much difficulty Plato, Socrates, etc., the only sage at whose fate he seems to hesitate is Pythagoras, in consideration of his golden thigh, and the many miracles which he performed. But, having balanced a little his claims, and finding reason to father all these miracles on the devil, he at length, in the twenty-fifth chapter, decides upon damning him also. (*De Animabus Paganorum*, lib. iv., cap. 20 and 25.—The poet Dante compromises the matter with the Pagans, and gives them a neutral territory or limbo of their own, where their employment, it must be owned, is not very enviable —"Senza speme vivemo in desio."—Cant. iv.—Among the numerous errors imputed to Origen, he is accused of having denied the eternity of future punishment; and, if he never advanced a more irrational doctrine, we may venture, I think, to forgive him. He went so far, however, as to include the devil himself in the general hell-delivery which he supposed would one day or other take place, and in this St. Augustin thinks him rather too merciful—"Misericordior profecto fuit Origines, qui et ipsum diabolum," etc. (*De Civitat. Dei*, lib. xxi., cap. 17.)— According to St. Jerome, it was Origen's opinion, that "the devil himself, after a certain time, will be as well off as the angel Gabriel"—" Id ipsum fore Gabrielem quod diabolum." (See his *Epistle to Pammachius*.) But Halloix, in his *Defence of Origen*, denies strongly that this learned father had any such misplaced tenderness for the devil. [I take the liberty of recommending these *notitiæ* upon damnation to the particular attention of the learned Chancellor of the Exchequer.]

(2) In former editions—

　　Which, binding polity in spiritual chains,
　　And tainting piety with temporal stains.—P. E.

(3) Mr. Fox, in his Speech on the Repeal of the Test Act (1790), thus condemns the intermixture of religion with the political constitution of a state :—" What purpose (he asks) can it serve, except the baleful purpose of communicating and receiving contamination? Under such an alliance corruption must alight upon the one, and slavery overwhelm the other."

Locke, too, says of the connection between church and state," The boundaries on both sides are fixed and immoveable. He jumbles heaven and earth together, the things most remote and opposite, who mixes these two societies, which are in their original, end, business, and in every thing, perfectly distinct and infinitely different from each other."—*First Letter on Toleration.*

The corruptions introduced into Christianity may be dated from the period of its establishment under Constantine, nor could all the splendour which it then acquired atone for the peace and purity which it lost.

(4) There has been, after all, quite as much intolerance among Protestants as among Papists. According to the hackneyed quotation—

　　Iliacos intra muros peccatur et extra.

Even the great champion of the Reformation, Melanchthon, whom Jortin calls "a divine of much mildness and *good-nature*," thus expresses his approbation of the burning of Servetus : "Legi (he says to Bullinger) quæ de Serveti blasphemiis respondistis, et pietatem ac judicia vestra probo. Judico etiam senatum Genevensem rectè fecisse, quod hominem pertinacem et non omissurum blasphemias sustulit; ac miratus sum esse qui severitatem illam improbent."—I have great pleasure in contrasting with these "mild and good-natured" sentiments the following words of the Papist Baluze, in addressing his friend Conringius : "Interim amemus, mi Conringi, et tametsi diversas opiniones tuemur in causa religionis, moribus tamen diversi non simus, qui eadem literarum studia sectamur."—*Herman. Conring. Epistol.*, par. secund., p. 56.

Hume tells us that the Commons, in the beginning of Charles the First's reign, "attacked Montague, one of the King's chaplains, on account of a moderate book which he had lately composed, and which, to their great disgust saved virtuous Catholics, as well as other Christians, from eternal torments."—In the same manner a complaint was lodged before the Lords of the Council against that excellent writer Hooker, for having, in a Sermon against Popery, attempted to save many of his Popish ancestors for *ignorance.*—To these examples of Protestant toleration I shall beg leave to oppose the following extract from a letter of old Roger Ascham (the tutor of Queen Elizabeth), which is preserved among the *Harrington papers*, and was written in 1566, to the Earl of Leicester, complaining of the Archbishop Young, who had taken away his prebend in the church of York: "Master Bourne * did never grieve me half so moche in offering me wrong, as Mr. Dudley and the Byshopp of York doe, in taking away my right. No byshopp in Q. Mary's time would have so dealt with me; not Mr. Bourne himself, when Winchester lived, durst have so dealt with me. For suche good estimation in those dayes even the learnedst and wysest men, as Gar-

* Sir John Bourne, Principal Secretary of State to Queen Mary.

But no—far other faith, far milder beams
Of heavenly justice warm, the Christian's dreams;
His creed is writ on Mercy's page above,
By the pure hands of all-atoning Love;
He weeps to see abused Religion twine
Round Tyranny's coarse brow her wreath divine;
And *he*, while round him sects and nations raise
To the one God their varying notes of praise,
Blesses each voice, whate'er its tone may be,
That serves to swell the general harmony. (1)

Such was the spirit, gently, grandly bright,
That fill'd, oh Fox! thy peaceful soul with light;
While free and spacious as that ambient air
Which folds our planet in its circling care,
The mighty sphere of thy transparent mind
Embraced the world, and breathed for all mankind.
Last of the great, farewell!—yet *not* the last—
Though Britain's sunshine hour with thee be past,
Ierne still one ray of glory gives,
And feels but half thy loss while Grattan lives.

────●❀❖❀●────

APPENDIX.

To the foregoing Poem, as first published, were
subjoined, in the shape of a Note, or Appendix, the
following remarks on the History and Music of Ire-
land. This fragment was originally intended to
form part of a Preface to the Irish Melodies; but
afterwards, for some reason which I do not now re-
collect, was thrown aside.

    *   *   *   *

Our history, for many centuries past, is credit-
able neither to our neighbours nor ourselves, and
ought not to be read by any Irishman who wishes
either to love England or to feel proud of Ireland.
The loss of independence very early debased our
character; and our feuds and rebellions, though
frequent and ferocious, but seldom displayed that
generous spirit of enterprise with which the pride of
an independent monarchy so long dignified the
struggles of Scotland. It is true this island has given

dener and Cardinal Poole, made of my poore service, that
although they knewe perfectly that in religion, both by
open wrytinge and pryvie talke, I was contrarye unto
them; yea, when Sir Francis Englefield by name did note
me speciallye at the councill-board, Gardener would not
suffer me to be called thither, nor touched ellswheare,
saiinge suche words of me in a lettre, as, though lettres
cannot, I blushe to write them to your lordshipp. Win-
chester's good-will stoode not in speaking faire and wish-
ing well, but he did in deede that for me,* whereby my
wife and children shall live the better when I am gone."
(See *Nugæ Antiquæ*, vol. i., pp. 98, 99.)—If men who
acted thus were bigots, what shall we call Mr. P-rc-v-l.
In Sutcliffe's *Survey of Popery* there occurs the following
assertion:—"Papists, that positively hold the heretical and
false doctrines of the modern church of Rome, cannot
possibly be saved."—As a contrast to this and other speci-
mens of Protestant liberality, which it would be much

* By Gardener's favour Ascham long held his fellowship, though
not resident.

birth to heroes who, under more favourable circum-
stances, might have left in the hearts of their coun-
trymen recollections as dear as those of a Bruce or a
Wallace; but success was wanting to consecrate re-
sistance, their cause was branded with the disheart-
ening name of treason, and their oppressed country
was such a blank among nations, that, like the ad-
ventures of those woods which Rinaldo wished to
explore, the fame of their actions was lost in the ob-
scurity of the place where they achieved them.

> ────— Errando in quelli boschi
> Trovar potria strane avventure e molte,
> Ma come i luoghi i fatti ancor son foschi,
> Che non se'n ha notizia le più volte.(2)

Hence is it that the annals of Ireland, through a
lapse of six hundred years, exhibit not one of those
shining names, not one of those themes of national
pride, from which poetry borrows her noblest in-
spiration; and that history, which ought to be the
richest garden of the Muse, yields no growth to her
in this hapless island but cypress and weeds. In
truth, the poet who would embellish his song with
allusions to Irish names and events, must be con-
tented to seek them in those early periods when our
character was yet unalloyed and original, before
the impolitic craft of our conquerors had divided,
weakened, and disgraced us. The sole traits of he-
roism, indeed, which he can venture at this day to
commemorate, either with safety to himself, or
honour to his country, are to be looked for in those
ancient times when the native monarchs of Ireland
displayed and fostered virtues worthy of a better
age; when our Malachies wore around their necks
collars of gold which they had won in single combat
from the invader, (3) and our Brians deserved and
won the warm affections of a people by exhibiting all
the most estimable qualities of a king. It may be
said that the magic of tradition has shed a charm
over this remote period, to which it is in reality but
little entitled, and that most of the pictures, which
we dwell on so fondly, of days when this island was

more easy than pleasant to collect, I refer my reader to
the Declaration of Le Père Courayer, doubting not that,
while he reads the sentiments of this pious man upon
toleration, he will feel inclined to exclaim with Belsham,
"Blush, ye Protestant bigots! and be confounded at the
comparison of your own wretched and malignant preju-
dices with the generous and enlarged ideas, the noble and
animated language, of this Popish priest."—*Essays*, xxvii.,
p. 86.

(1) "La tolérance est la chose du monde la plus propre
à ramener le siècle d'or, et à faire un concert et une har-
monie de plusieurs voix et instruments de différents tons
et notes, aussi agréable pour le moins que l'uniformité
d'une seule voix." *Bayle*, *Commentaire Philosophique*, etc.,
part. ii., chap. vi.—Both Bayle and Locke would have
treated the subject of Toleration in a manner much more
worthy of themselves and of the cause, if they had written
in an age less distracted by religious prejudices.

(2) *Ariosto*, canto iv.

(3) See Warner's *History of Ireland*, vol. i., book ix.

distinguished amidst the gloom of Europe by the sanctity of her morals, the spirit of her knighthood, and the polish of her schools, are little more than the inventions of national partiality,—that bright but spurious offspring which vanity engenders upon ignorance, and with which the first records of every people abound. But the sceptic is scarcely to be envied who would pause for stronger proofs than we already possess of the early glories of Ireland; and were even the veracity of all these proofs surrendered, yet who would not fly to such flattering fictions from the sad degrading truths which the history of later times presents to us?

The language of sorrow, however, is, in general, best suited to our Music, and with themes of this nature the poet may be amply supplied. There is scarcely a page of our annals that will not furnish him a subject, and while the national Muse of other countries adorns her temple proudly with trophies of the past, in Ireland her melancholy altar, like the shrine of Pity at Athens, is to be known only by the tears that are shed upon it; "*lacrymis altaria sudant.*" (1)

There is a well-known story, related of the Antiochians under the reign of Theodosius, which is not only honourable to the powers of music in general, but which applies so peculiarly to the mournful melodies of Ireland, that I cannot resist the temptation of introducing it here.—The piety of Theodosius would have been admirable, had it not

been stained with intolerance; but under his reign was, I believe, first set the example of a disqualifying penal code enacted by Christians against Christians. (2) Whether his interference with the religion of the Antiochians had any share in the alienation of their loyalty is not expressly ascertained by historians; but severe edicts, heavy taxation, and the rapacity and insolence of the men whom he sent to govern them, sufficiently account for the discontents of a warm and susceptible people. Repentance soon followed the crimes into which their impatience had hurried them; but the vengeance of the Emperor was implacable, and punishments of the most dreadful nature hung over the city of Antioch, whose devoted inhabitants, totally resigned to despondence, wandered through the streets and public assemblies, giving utterance to their grief in dirges of the most touching lamentation. (3) At length, Flavianus, their bishop, whom they had sent to intercede with Theodosius, finding all his entreaties coldly rejected, adopted the expedient of teaching these songs of sorrow which he had heard from the lips of his unfortunate countrymen to the minstrels who performed for the Emperor at table. The heart of Theodosius could not resist this appeal; tears fell fast into his cup while he listened, and the Antiochians were forgiven.—Surely, if music ever spoke the misfortunes of a people, or could ever conciliate forgiveness for their errors, the music of Ireland ought to possess those powers.

THE SCEPTIC,

A PHILOSOPHICAL SATIRE.

Νομον παντων βασιλεα. —*Pindar. ap. Herodot.*, lib. iii.

PREFACE.

THE Sceptical Philosophy of the Ancients has been no less misrepresented than the Epicurean. Pyrrho may perhaps have carried it to rather an irrational excess; but we must not believe, with Beattie, all the absurdities imputed to this philosopher; and it appears to me that the doctrines of the school, as explained by Sextus Empiricus,(4) are far more suited

to the wants and infirmities of human reason, as well as more conducive to the mild virtues of humility and patience, than any of those systems of philosophy which preceded the introduction of Christianity. The Sceptics may be said to have held a middle path between the Dogmatists and Academicians; the former of whom boasted that they had attained the truth, while the latter denied that any attainable truth existed. The Sceptics, however,

(1) *Statius, Thebaid.*, lib. xii.

(2) "A sort of civil excommunication (says Gibbon), which separated them from their fellow-citizens by a peculiar brand of infamy; and this declaration of the supreme magistrate tended to justify, or at least to excuse, the insults of a fanatic populace. The sectaries were gradually disqualified for the possession of honourable or lucrative employments, and Theodosius was satisfied with his own justice when he decreed, that, as the Eunomians distinguished the nature of the Son from that of the Father, they should be incapable of making their wills, or of receiving any advantage from testamentary donations."

(3) Μελη τινα ολοφυρμου πληρη και συμπαθειας συν-

θεμενοι, ταις μελωδιαις επηδον.—*Nicephor.*, lib. xii., cap. 43. This story is told also in *Sozomen*, lib. vii., cap. 23; but unfortunately Chrysostom says nothing whatever about it, and he not only had the best opportunities of information, but was too fond of music, as appears by his praises of psalmody (*Exposit. in Psalm* xli.', to omit such a flattering illustration of its powers. He imputes their reconciliation to the interference of the Antiochian solitaries, while Zozimus attributes it to the remonstrances of the sophist Libanius.—Gibbon, I think, does not even allude to this story of the musicians.

(4) *Pyrrh. Hypoth.*—The reader may find a tolerably clear abstract of this work of Sextus Empiricus in *La Vérité des Sciences*, by Mersenne, liv. i., chap. ii., etc.

without either asserting or denying its existence, professed to be modestly and anxiously in search of it; or, as St. Augustine expresses it, in his liberal tract against the Manichæans, "nemo nostrum dicat jam se invenisse veritatem; sic eam quæramus quasi ab utrisque nesciatur." (1) From this habit of impartial investigation, and the necessity which it imposed upon them, of studying not only every system of philosophy, but every art and science, which professed to lay its basis in truth, they necessarily took a wider range of erudition, and were far more travelled in the regions of philosophy than those whom conviction or bigotry had domesticated in any particular system. It required all the learning of dogmatism to overthrow the dogmatism of learning; and the Sceptics may be said to resemble, in this respect, that ancient incendiary, who stole from the altar the fire with which he destroyed the temple. This advantage over all the other sects is allowed to them even by Lipsius, whose treatise on the miracles of the Virgo Hallensis will sufficiently save him from all suspicion of scepticism. "Labore, ingenio, memoria," he says, "supra omnes pene philosophos fuisse.—Quid nonne omnia aliorum secta tenere debuerunt et inquirere, si poterunt refellere? res dicit. Nonne orationes varias, raras, subtiles inveniri ad tam receptas, claras, certas (ut videbatur) sententias evertendas?" etc., etc.(2)—*Manuduct. ad Philosoph. Stoic.*, Dissert. 4.

Between the scepticism of the ancients and the moderns the great difference is, that the former doubted for the purpose of investigating, as may be exemplified by the third book of Aristotle's *Metaphysics*, (3) while the latter investigate for the purpose of doubting, as may be seen through most of the philosophical works of Hume. (4) Indeed the Pyrrhonism of latter days is not only more subtle than that of antiquity, but, it must be confessed, more dangerous in its tendency. The happiness of a Christian depends so essentially upon his belief, that it is but natural he should feel alarm at the progress of doubt, lest it should steal by degrees into that region from which he is most interested in excluding it, and poison at last the very spring of his consolation and hope. Still, however, the abuses of doubt-

(1) *Lib. contra Epist. Manichæi quam vocant Fundamenti*, Op. Paris., tom. vi.

(2) See *Martin. Schoockius de Scepticismo*, who endeavours,—weakly, I think,—to refute this opinion of Lipsius.

(3) Εστι δε τοις ευπορησαι βουλομενοις προυργου το διαπορησαι καλως.—*Metaphys.*, lib. iii., cap. 1.

(4) Neither Hume, however, nor Berkeley, are to be judged by the misrepresentations of Beattie, whose book, however amiably intended, puts forth a most unphilosophical appeal to popular feelings and prejudices, and is a continued *petitio principii* throughout.

(5) Lib. iii., cap. 1.

(6) "The particular bulk, number, figure, and motion of the parts of fire or snow are really in them, whether

ing ought not to deter a philosophical mind from indulging mildly and rationally in its use; and there is nothing, surely, more consistent with the meek spirit of Christianity, than that humble scepticism which professes not to extend its distrust beyond the circle of human pursuits, and the pretensions of human knowledge. A follower of this school may be among the readiest to admit the claims of a superintending Intelligence upon his faith and adoration: it is only to the wisdom of this weak world that he refuses, or at least delays, his assent;—it is only in passing through the shadow of earth that his mind undergoes the eclipse of scepticism. No follower of Pyrrho has ever spoken more strongly against the dogmatists than St. Paul himself, in the First Epistle to the Corinthians; and there are passages in Ecclesiastes and other parts of Scripture, which justify our utmost diffidence in all that human reason originates. Even the Sceptics of antiquity refrained carefully from the mysteries of theology, and, in entering the temples of religion, laid aside their philosophy at the porch. Sextus Empiricus thus declares the acquiescence of his sect in the general belief of a divine and fore-knowing Power :—Τῳ μεν βιῳ κατακολουθουντες αδοξαστως φαμεν ειναι θεους και σεβομεν θεους και προνοειν αυτους φαμεν. (5) In short, it appears to me, that this rational and well-regulated scepticism is the only daughter of the Schools that can safely be selected as a handmaid for Piety. He who distrusts the light of reason will be the first to follow a more luminous guide; and if, with an ardent love for truth, he has sought her in vain through the ways of this life, he will but turn with the more hope to that better world, where all is simple, true, and everlasting: for there is no parallax at the zenith;—it is only near our troubled horizon that objects deceive us into vague and erroneous calculations.

THE SCEPTIC.

As the gay tint, that decks the vernal rose, (6)
Not in the flower, but in our vision glows;
As the ripe flavour of Falernian tides
Not in the wine, but in our taste resides;

any one perceive them or not, and therefore they may be called real qualities, because they really exist in those bodies; but light, heat, whiteness, or coldness, are no more really in them than sickness or pain is in manna. Take away the sensation of them; let not the eye see light or colours, nor the ears hear sounds; let the palate not taste, nor the nose smell, and all colours, tastes, odours, and sounds, as they are such particular ideas, vanish and cease."—Locke, book ii., chap. 8.

Bishop Berkeley, it is well known, extended this doctrine even to primary qualities, and supposed that matter itself has but an ideal existence. But how are we to apply his theory to that period which preceded the formation of man, when our system of sensible things was produced, and the sun shone, and the waters flowed, without

So when, with heartfelt tribute, we declare
That Marco 's honest and that Susan 's fair,
'T is in our minds, and not in Susan's eyes
Or Marco's life, the worth or beauty lies :
For she, in flat-nosed China, would appear
As plain a thing as Lady Anne is here ;
And one light joke at rich Loretto's dome
Would rank good Marco with the damn'd at Rome.

There 's no deformity so vile, so base,
That 't is not somewhere thought a charm, a
   grace ;
No foul reproach, that may not steal a beam
From other suns, to bleach it to esteem. (1)
Ask, who is wise?—you'll find the self-same man
A sage in France, a madman in Japan ;
And here some head beneath a mitre swells,
Which there had tingled to a cap and bells :

any sentient being to witness them? The spectator, whom
Whiston supplies, will scarcely solve the difficulty : " To
speak my mind freely," says he, "I believe that the Mes-
sias was there actually present."—See *Whiston of the
Mosaic Creation.*

(1 Boetius employs this argument of the Sceptics among
his consolatory reflections upon the emptiness of fame.
" Quid quod diversarum gentium mores inter se atque
instituta discordant, ut quod apud alios laude, apud alios
supplicio dignum judicetur?"—Lib. ii., prosa 7. Many
amusing instances of diversity, in the tastes, manners,
and morals of different nations, may be found throughout
the works of that amusing sceptic Le Mothe le Vayer.—
See his *Opuscule Sceptique,* his Treatise *De la Secte Scep-
tique,* and, above all, those *Dialogues,* not to be found in
his works, which he published under the name of Horatius
Tubero.—The chief objection to these writings of Le Vayer
(and it is a blemish which may be felt also in the *Esprit
des Lois*), is the suspicious obscurity of the sources from
whence he frequently draws his instances, and the indis-
criminate use made by him of the lowest populace of the
library,—those lying travellers and wonder-mongers, of
whom Shaftesbury, in his *Advice to an Author,* complains,
as having tended in his own time to the diffusion of a very
shallow and vicious sort of scepticism.—Vol. i., p. 352.
The Pyrrhonism of Le Vayer, however, is of the most in-
nocent and playful kind; and Villemandy, the author of
Scepticismus Debellatus, exempts him specially in the de-
claration of war which he denounces against the other
armed neutrals of the sect, in consideration of the or-
thodox limits within which he confines his incredulity.

(2) This was the creed also of those modern Epicureans,
whom Ninon de l'Enclos collected around her in the rue
des Tournelles, and whose object seems to have been to
decry the faculty of reason, as tending only to embarrass
our wholesome use of pleasures, without enabling us, in
any degree, to avoid their abuse. Madame des Houlières,
the fair pupil of Des Barreaux in the arts of poetry and
gallantry, has devoted most of her verses to this laudable
purpose, and is even such a determined foe to reason,
that, in one of her pastorals, she congratulates her sheep
on the want of it. St. Evremont speaks thus upon the
subject :—

    " Un mélange incertain d'esprit et de matière
    Nous fait vivre avec trop ou trop peu de lumière.
    •   •   •   •   •   •

Nay, there may yet some monstrous region be,
Unknown to Cook, and from Napoleon free,
Where C—stl—r—gh would for a patriot pass,
And mouthing M——ve scarce be deem'd an ass!

   " List not to reason (Epicurus cries),
But trust the senses,—*there* conviction lies :"—(2)
Alas! *they* judge not by a purer light,
Nor keep their fountains more untinged and bright :
Habit so mars them, that the Russian swain
Will sigh for train-oil, while he sips Champagne;
And health so rules them, that a fever's heat
Would make even Sh—r—d—n think water sweet.

Just as the mind the erring sense (3) believes,
The erring mind, in turn, the sense deceives;
And cold disgust can find but wrinkles there,
Where passion fancies all that 's smooth and fair.

    Nature, élève-nous à la clarté des anges,
    Ou nous abaisse au sens des simples animaux."

Which may be thus paraphrased :—

    Had man been made, at nature's birth,
    Of only flame or only earth,
    Had he been form'd a perfect whole
    Of purely *that,* or grossly *this,*
    Then sense would ne'er have clouded soul,
    Nor soul restrain'd the sense's bliss.
    Oh happy, had his light been strong,
    Or had he never shared a light
    Which shines enough to show he 's wrong,
    But *not* enough to lead him right.

(3) See, among the fragments of Petronius, those verses
beginning " Fallunt nos oculi," etc. The most sceptical
of the ancient poets was Euripides; and it would, I think,
puzzle the whole school of Pyrrho to produce a doubt
more startling than the following :—

    Τις δ' οιδεν ει ζην τουθ' ὁ κεκληται θανειν,
    Το ζην δε θνησκειν εστι;

See *Laert. in Pyrrh.*

Socrates and Plato where the grand sources of ancient
scepticism. According to Cicero (*de Orator.,* lib. iii.),
they supplied Arcesilas with the doctrines of the Middle
Academy ; and how closely these resembled the tenets of
the Sceptics, may be seen even in Sextus Empiricus (lib.
i., cap. 33.), who, with all his distinctions, can scarcely
prove any difference. It appears strange that Epicurus
should have been a dogmatist; and his natural temper
would most probably have led him to the repose of scep-
ticism, had not the Stoics, by their violent opposition to
his doctrines, compelled him to be as obstinate as them-
selves. Plutarch, indeed, in reporting some of his opi-
nions, represents him as having delivered them with con-
siderable hesitation.—Επικουρος ουδεν απογινωσκει του-
των, εχομενος του ενδεχομενου.—*De Placit. Philosoph.,*
lib. ii., cap. 13. See also the 21st and 22d chapters. But
that the leading characteristics of the sect were self-suffi-
ciency and dogmatism, appears from what Cicero says of
Velleius, *De Natur. Deor.*—" Tum Velleius, fidenter sané,
ut solent isti, nihil tam verens quam ne dubitare aliquâ de
re videretur."

P * * * *, who sees, upon his pillow laid,
A face for which ten thousand pounds were paid,
Can tell, how quick before a jury flies
The spell that mock'd the warm seducer's eyes.

Self is the medium through which Judgment's
      ray
Can seldom pass without being turn'd astray. (1)
The smith of Ephesus (2) thought Dian's shrine,
By which his craft most throve, the most divine;
And even the *true* faith seems not half so true,
When link'd with *one* good living as with *two*.
Had W—le—t first been pension'd by the throne,
Kings would have suffer'd by his praise alone;
And P—ine perhaps, for something snug per ann.,
Had laugh'd, like W—ll—sley, at all Rights of Man.

But 't is not only individual minds,—
Whole nations, too, the same delusion blinds. (3)
Thus England, hot from Denmark's smoking meads,
Turns up her eyes at Gallia's guilty deeds;
Thus, self-pleased still, the same dishonouring chain
She binds in Ireland, she would break in Spain;
While praised at distance, but at home forbid,
Rebels in Cork are patriots at Madrid.

If Grotius be thy guide, shut, shut the book,—
In force alone for Laws of Nations look. (4)

(1) Formerly given thus—
    Self is the medium least refined of all
    Through which opinion's searching beam can fall;
    And, passing there, the clearest, steadiest ray
    Will tinge its light and turn its line astray.
    The Ephesian smith a holier charm espied
    In Dian's toe, than all his heaven beside;
    And true religion shines not half so true
    On *one* good living as it shines on *two*.—P. E.

(2) [See Acts, chap. xix., where every line reminds one of
those reverend craftsmen who are so ready to cry out—
"The church is in danger!"]

"For a certain man named Demetrius, a silversmith
which made silver shrines for Diana, brought no small
gain unto the craftsmen:

["Whom he called together, with the workmen of like
occupation, and said, Sirs, ye know that by this craft we
have our wealth:

. . . .

"So that not only this our craft is likely to be set at
nought, but also that the temple of the great goddess Diana
should be despised," etc., etc.]

(3) This couplet is a condensation of the original lines—
    But 't is not only individual minds
    That habit tinctures, or that interest blinds;
    Whole nations, fool'd by falsehood, fear, or pride,
    Their ostrich-heads in self-illusion hide.—P. E.

(4) Formerly turned thus—
    Oh! trust me, Self can cloud the brightest cause,
    Or gild the worst;—and then, for nation's laws!
    Go, good civilian, shut thy useless book,
    In force alone for laws of nations look.—P. E.

(5) [With most of this writer's latter politics I confess I
feel a most hearty concurrence, and perhaps, if I were

Let shipless Danes and whining yankees dwell
On naval rights, with Grotius and Vattel,
While C—bb—t's (5) pirate code alone appears
Sound moral sense to England and Algiers.

Woe to the Sceptic, in these party days,
Who wafts to neither shrine his puffs of praise!
For him no pension pours its annual fruits,
No fertile sinecure spontaneous shoots;   [rhyme,
Not *his* the meed that crown'd Don H—kh—m's
Nor sees he e'er, in dreams of future time,
Those shadowy forms of sleek reversions rise,
So dear to Scotchmen's second-sighted eyes.
Yet who, that looks to History's damning leaf,
Where Whig and Tory, thief opposed to thief,
On either side in lofty shame are seen, (6)
While Freedom's form hangs crucified between—
Who, B—rd—tt, who such rival rogues can see,
But flies from *both* to Honesty and thee?

If, weary of the world's bewildering maze, (7)
Hopeless of finding, through its weedy ways,
One flower of truth, the busy crowd we shun,
And to the shades of tranquil learning run,
How many a doubt pursues! (8) how oft we sigh,
When histories charm, to think that histories lie!!
That all are grave romances, at the best,
And M—sgr—ve's (9) but more clumsy than the rest.

an Englishman, my pride might lead me to acquiesce in
that system of lawless unlimited sovereignty, which he
claims so boldly for his country at sea; but, viewing the
question somewhat more disinterestedly, and as a friend
to the common rights of mankind, I cannot help thinking
that the doctrines which he maintained upon the Copen-
hagen expedition, and the differences with America, would
establish a species of maritime tyranny, as discreditable
to the character of England, as it would be galling and
unjust to the other nations of the world.]

(6) "Those two thieves," says Ralph, "between whom
the nation is crucified."—*Use and Abuse of Parliaments.*

(7) The agitation of the ship is one of the chief difficul-
ties which impede the discovery of the longitude at sea;
and the tumult and hurry of life are equally unfavourable
to that calm level of mind which is necessary to an in-
quirer after truth.

In the mean time, our modest Sceptic, in the absence
of truth, contents himself with probabilities, resembling
in this respect those suitors of Penelope, who, on finding
that they could not possess the mistress herself, very
wisely resolved to put up with her maids; Τη Πηνελοπη
πλησιαδειν μη δυναμενοι, ταις ταυτης εμιγνυντο Θερα-
παιναις.—*Plutarch,* Περι Παιδων Αγωγης.

(8) See a curious work, entitled *Reflections upon Learn-
ing,* written on the plan of Agrippa's *De Vanitate Scien-
tiarum,* but much more honestly and skilfully executed.

(9) This historian of the Irish rebellions has outrun even
his predecessor in the same task, Sir John Temple, for
whose character with respect to veracity the reader may
consult *Carte's Collection of Ormond's Original Papers,*
p. 207. See also Dr. Nalson's account of him, in the in-
troduction to the second volume of his *Historic. Collect.*

By Tory Hume's seductive page beguiled,
We fancy Charles was just and Strafford mild; (1)
And Fox himself, with party pencil, draws
Monmouth a hero, "for the good old cause!" (2)
Then rights are wrongs, and victories are defeats,
As French or English pride the tale repeats;
And, when they tell Corunna's story o'er,
They 'll disagree in all, but honouring Moore:
Nay, future pens, to flatter future courts,
May cite perhaps the Park-guns' gay reports,
To prove that England triumph'd on the morn
Which found her Junot's jest and Europe's scorn.

In science, too—how many a system, raised
Like Neva's icy domes, awhile hath blazed
With lights of fancy and with forms of pride,
Then, melting, mingled with the oblivious tide!
Now Earth usurps the centre of the sky,
Now Newton puts the paltry planet by;
Now whims revive beneath Descartes's(3) pen,
Which *now*, assail'd by Locke's, expire again.
And when, perhaps, in pride of chemic powers,
We think the keys of Nature's kingdom ours,
Some Davy's magic touch the dream unsettles,
And turns at once our alkalis to metals.
Or, should we roam, in metaphysic maze,
Through fair-built theories of former days,

Some Dr—mm—d (4) from the north, more ably
        skill'd,
Like other Goths, to ruin than to build,
Tramples triumphant through our fanes o'erthrown,
Nor leaves one grace, one glory of his own.

Oh Learning, whatsoe'er thy pomp and boast,
Unletter'd minds have taught and charm'd men
        most.
The rude unread Columbus was our guide
To worlds, which learn'd Lactantius had denied;
And one wild Shakspeare, following Nature's
        lights,
Is worth whole planets, fill'd with Stagyrites.

See grave Theology, when once she strays
From Revelation's path, what tricks she plays;
What various heavens,—all fit for bards to sing,—
Have churchmen dream'd, from Papias (5) down to
        King! (6)
While hell itself, in India nought but smoke, (7)
In Spain 's a furnace, and in France—a joke.

Hail, modest Ignorance, thou goal and prize,
Thou last, best knowledge of the simply wise!
Hail, humble Doubt, when error's waves are past,
How sweet to reach thy shelter'd port (8) at last,

---

(1) He defends Strafford's conduct as "innocent and even laudable." In the same spirit, speaking of the arbitrary sentences of the Star Chamber, he says,—"The severity of the Star Chamber, which was generally ascribed to Laud's passionate disposition, was perhaps, in itself, somewhat blameable."

(2) That flexibility of temper and opinion, which the habits of scepticism are so calculated to produce, are thus pleaded for by Mr. Fox, in the very sketch of Monmouth to which I allude; and this part of the picture the historian may be thought to have drawn from himself. "One of the most conspicuous features in his character seems to have been a remarkable, and, as some think, a culpable degree of flexibility. That such a disposition is preferable to its opposite extreme will be admitted by all, who think that modesty, even in excess, is more nearly allied to wisdom than conceit and self-sufficiency. He who has attentively considered the political, or indeed the general concerns of life, may possibly go still further, and may rank a willingness to be convinced, or, in some cases, even without conviction, to concede our own opinion to that of other men, among the principal ingredients in the composition of practical wisdom."—It is right to observe, however, that the Sceptic's readiness of concession arises rather from uncertainty than conviction, more from a suspicion that his own opinion may be wrong, than from any persuasion that the opinion of his adversary is right. "It may be so," was the courteous and sceptical formula, with which the Dutch were accustomed to reply to the statements of ambassadors. See *Lloyd's State Worthies*, art. *Sir Thomas Wyat.*

[To the historical fragment of Mr. Fox, we may apply what Pliny says of the last unfinished works of celebrated artists—"In Ienocinio commendationis dolor est manus, cum id ageret, extinctæ." Lib. xxxv., cap. 2.]

(3) Descartes, who is considered as the parent of modern scepticism, says, that there is nothing in the whole range of philosophy which does not admit of two opposite opinions, and which is not involved in doubt and uncertainty. "In Philosophia nihil adhuc reperiri, de quo non in utramque partem disputatur, hoc est, quod non sit incertum et dubium." Gassendi is likewise to be added to the list of modern Sceptics; and Wedderkopff, in his Dissertation *De Scepticismo profano et sacro* (Argentorat., 1666), has denounced Erasmus also as a follower of Pyrrho, for his opinions upon the Trinity, and some other subjects. To these if we add the names of Bayle, Mallebranche, Dryden, Locke, etc., etc., I think there is no one who need be ashamed of doubting in such company.

(4) See this gentleman's *Academic Questions.*

(5) Papias lived about the time of the apostles, and is supposed to have given birth to the heresy of the Chiliastæ, whose heaven was by no means of a spiritual nature, but rather an anticipation of the Prophet of Hera's elysium. See *Eusebius, Hist. Ecclesiast.*, lib. iii., cap. 33, and *Hieronym. de Scriptor. Ecclesiast.*—From all I can find in these authors concerning Papias, it seems hardly fair to impute to him those gross imaginations in which the believers of the sensual milennium indulged.

(6) King, in his *Morsels of Criticism*, vol. i., supposes the sun to be the receptacle of blessed spirits.

(7) The Indians call hell "the House of Smoke." See *Picart upon the Religion of the Banians.* The reader who is curious about infernal matters, may be edified by consulting *Rusca de Inferno*, particularly lib. ii., cap. 7, 8, where he will find the precise sort of fire ascertained in which wicked spirits are to be burned hereafter.

(8) "Chère Sceptique, douce pâture de mon âme, et l'unique port de salut à un esprit qui aime le repos!"—*La Mothe le Vayer.*

And, there, by changing skies nor lured nor awed,
Smile at the battling winds that roar abroad. (1)
There gentle Charity, who knows how frail
The bark of Virtue, even in summer's gale,
Sits by the nightly fire, whose beacon glows
For all who wander, whether friends or foes.
There Faith retires, and keeps her white sail furl'd,
Till call'd to spread it for a better world;

While Patience, watching on the weedy shore,
And, mutely waiting till the storm be o'er,
Oft turns to Hope, who still directs her eye
To some blue spot, just breaking in the sky!

Such are the mild, the blest associates given
To him who doubts, — and trusts in nought but
Heaven!

INTERCEPTED LETTERS; OR, THE TWOPENNY POST-BAG.

BY THOMAS BROWN, THE YOUNGER.

Elapsæ manibus secidére tabellæ.—Ovid.

PREFACE.

It would almost seem, that the same unembittered spirit, the same freedom from all real malice, with which, in most instances, the sort of squib-warfare waged by me was carried on, and during which the following satirical and humorous poems were produced, was felt, in some degree, even by those who were themselves the objects of it;—so generously forgiving have I, in most instances, found them. Even the high Personage against whom the earliest and perhaps most successful of my lighter missiles were launched, could refer to and quote them, as I learn from an incident mentioned in the *Life of Sir Walter Scott*, with a degree of good-humour and playfulness which was creditable alike to his temper and good sense. At a memorable dinner given by the Regent to Sir Walter in the year 1815, Scott, among other stories with which his royal host was much amused, told of a sentence passed by an old friend of his, the Lord Justice Clerk Braxfield, attended by circumstances in which the cruelty of this waggish judge was even more conspicuous than his humour. "The Regent laughed heartily," says the biographer, "at this specimen of Braxfield's brutal humour; and "I' faith, Walter," said he, "this old big-wig seems to have taken things as coolly as my tyrannical self. Don't you remember Tom Moore's description of me at breakfast?—

"'The table spread with tea and toast,
Death-warrants, and the *Morning Post.*'"

In reference to this, and other less exalted instances, of the good-humoured spirit in which my "innocui sales" have in general been taken, I shall venture to cite here a few flattering sentences which, coming as they did from a political adversary and a stranger, touched me far more by their generosity

than even by their praise. In speaking of the pension which had just then been conferred upon me, and expressing, in warm terms, his approval of the grant, the editor of a leading Tory journal (2) thus liberally expresses himself:—"We know that some will blame us for our prejudice—if it be prejudice,—in favour of Mr. Moore; but we cannot help it. As he tells us himself,

"'Wit a diamond brings
That cuts its bright way through'

the most obdurate political antipathies. * * * We do not believe that any one was ever hurt by libels so witty as those of Mr. Moore:—great privilege of wit, which renders it impossible even for those whose enemies wits are, to hate them!"

To return to the period of the Regency:—In the numerous attacks from the government press, which my vollies of small shot against the Court used to draw down upon me, it was constantly alleged, as an aggravation of my misdeeds, that I had been indebted to the Royal personage thus assailed by me for many kind and substantial services. Luckily, the list of the benefits showered upon me from that high quarter may be despatched in a few sentences. At the request of Lord Moira, one of my earliest and best friends, his Royal Highness graciously permitted me to dedicate to him my Translation of the *Odes of Anacreon*. I was twice, I think, admitted to the honour of dining at Carlton House, and when the Prince, on his being made Regent in 1811, gave his memorable fête, I was one of the crowd—about 1500, I believe, in number —who enjoyed the privilege of being his guests on the occasion.

There occur some allusions, indeed, in the *Twopenny Post-Bag*, to the absurd taste displayed in the ornaments of the Royal supper table at that fête; (3) and this violation—for such, to a certain extent, I

(1) Changed from—
    And, gently rock'd in undulating doubt,
    Smile at the sturdy winds which war without!—P. E.

(2) The *Standard*, August 24, 1835.

(3)   The same *fauteuils* and girandoles—
    The same gold asses, pretty souls,

    That, in this rich and classic dome,
    Appear so perfectly at home;
    The same bright river, 'mong the dishes,
    But not—ah! not the same dear fishes.
    Late hours and claret kill'd the old ones;—
    So, 'stead of silver and of gold ones,

allow it to have been—of the reverence due to the rites of the Hospitable Jove, (1) which, whether administered by prince or peasant, ought to be sacred from such exposure, I am by no means disposed to defend. But, whatever may be thought of the taste or prudence of some of these satires, there exists no longer, I apprehend, much difference of opinion respecting the character of the Royal personage against whom they were aimed. Already, indeed, has the stern verdict which the voice of History cannot but pronounce upon him been in some degree anticipated, (2) in a sketch of the domestic events of his reign, supposed to have proceeded from the pen of one who was himself an actor in some of its most painful scenes, and who, from his professional position, commanded a near insight into the character of that exalted individual, both as husband and father. To the same high authority I must refer for an account of the mysterious "Book," (3) to which allusion is more than once made in the following pages.

One of the first and most successful of the numerous trifles I wrote at that period, was the Parody on the Regent's celebrated Letter, announcing to the world that he "had no predilections," etc. This very opportune squib was, at first, circulated privately; my friend, Mr. Perry, having for some time hesitated to publish it. He got some copies of it, however, printed off for me, which I sent round to several members of the Whig party; and, having to meet a number of them at dinner immediately after, found it no easy matter to keep my countenance while they were discussing among them the merits of the Parody. One of the party, I recollect, having

> (It being rather hard to raise
> Fish of that *specie* now-a-days)
> Some sprats have been, by Y—rm—h's wish,
> Promoted into silver fish,
> And gudgeons so V—ns—tt—t told
> The Reg—t! are as good as gold.
>
> *Twopenny Post-Bag.*

(1) Ante fores stabat Jovis Hospitis ara.—*Ovid.*

(2) *Edinburgh Review*, No. cxxiv., *George the Fourth and Queen Caroline.*—"When the Prince entered upon public life he was found to have exhausted the resources of a career of pleasure; to have gained followers without making friends; to have acquired much envy and some admiration among the unthinking multitude of polished society; but not to command in any quarter either respect or esteem. * * * The portrait which we have painted of him is undoubtedly one of the darkest shade, and most repulsive form."

(3) "There is no doubt whatever that *The Book*, written by Mr. Perceval, and privately printed at his house, under Lord Eldon's superintendence and his own, was prepared in concert with the King, and was intended to sound the alarm against Carlton House and the Whigs."— *Ed. Review, ib.*

(4) *Twopenny Post-Bag.* I avail myself of the mention

quoted to me the following description of the state of both King and Regent, at that moment,—

> " A straight waistcoat on *him*, and restrictions on *me*,
> A more limited monarchy could not well be,"

grew rather provoked with me for not enjoying the fun of the parody as much as himself.

While thus the excitement of party feeling lent to the political trifles contained in these pages a relish and pungency not their own, an effect has been attributed to two squibs, wholly unconnected with politics—the Letter from the Dowager Countess of Corke, and from Messrs. Lackington and Co. (4)—of which I myself had not the slightest notion till I found it thus alluded to in Mr. Lockhart's *Life of Sir Walter Scott.* In speaking of the causes which were supposed to have contributed to the comparative failure of the Poem of *Rokeby*, the biographer says, " It is fair to add that, among the London circles, at least, some sarcastic flings, in Mr. Moore's *Twopenny Post-Bag*, must have had an *unfavourable* influence on this occasion."(5)

Among the translations that have appeared on the Continent, of the greater part of my poetical works, there has been no attempt, as far as I can learn, to give a version of any of my satirical writings,—with the single exception of a squib, entitled "*Little Man and Little Soul*,"(6) of which there is a translation into German verse, by the late distinguished oriental scholar, Professor Von Bohlen.(7) Though unskilled, myself, in German, I can yet perceive—sufficiently to marvel at it—the dexterity and ease with which the Old Ballad metre of the original is adopted and managed in the translation. As this

here of this latter squib, to recant a correction which I too hastily made in the two following lines of it :—

> And, though statesmen may glory in being unbought,
> In an author, we think, sir, that 's rather a fault.

Forgetting that Pope's ear was satisfied with the sort of rhyme here used, I foolishly altered (and spoiled) the whole couplet to ged rid of it.

(5) "See, for instance," says Mr. Lockhart, "the Epistle of Lady Corke ; or that of Messrs. Lackington, booksellers, to one of their dandy authors :—

> " ' Should you feel any touch of *poetical* glow,
> We 've a scheme to suggest :—Mr. Sc—tt, you must know,
> (Who, we 're *sorry* to say it, now works for *the Row*,) *
> Having quitted the Borders, to seek new renown,
> Is coming, by long Quarto stages, to Town ;
> And beginning with Rokeby (the job 's sure to pay)
> Means to *do* all the Gentlemen's Seats on the way.
> Now, the scheme is (though none of our hackneys can beat him)
> To start a fresh Poet through Highgate to *meet* him ;
> Who, by means of quick proofs—no revises—long coaches—
> May do a few villas, before Sc—tt approaches.
> Indeed, if our Pegasus be not curst shabby,
> He 'll reach, without foundering, at least Woburn Abbey.' "

(6) Alluding to a speech delivered in the year 1813 by the Right Hon. Charles Abbot (then Speaker) against Mr. Grattan's motion for a Committee on the Claims of the Catholics.

(7) Author of *The Ancient Indian.*

* Paternoster Row.

trifle may be considered curious, not only in itself, but still more as connected with so learned a name, I shall here present it to my readers, premising that the same eminent Professor has left a version also of one of my very early *facetiæ*, "*The Rabbinical Origin of Woman.*"

"THERE WAS A LITTLE MAN."

(*Translated by Professor von Bohlen.*)

Es war ein kleiner Mann
Und der hatt'n kleinen Geist
Und er sprach: kleiner Geist sehn wir zu, zu, zu.
Ob uns möglich wohl wird seyn
So ein kleiness Redelein
Das wir halten, kleiner ich und kleiner du, du, du,
Das wir halten, kleiner ich und kleiner du.

Und der kleine Geist. der brach
Aus dem Loche nun und sprach:
Ich behaupte, kleiner Mann, du bist keck, keck, keck,
Nimm nicht übel meine Zweifel,
Aber sage mir, zum Teufel,
Hat die kleine, kleine Red' einen zweck, zweck, zweck,
Hat die kleine kleine Red' einen zweck?

Der kleine Mann darauf
Blies die Bäcklein mächtig auf,
Und er sprach: kleiner Geist sey gescheut, scheut, scheut;
Kleiner ich und kleiner du
Sind berufen ja dazu
Zu verdammen und bekehren alle Leut', Leut', Leut',
Zu verdammen und bekehren alle Leut'.

Und sie fingen beide an
Der kleine Geist und kleine Mann,
Paukten ab ihre Rede so klein, klein, klein;
Und die ganze Welt für wahr
Meint, das aufgeblas'ne Paar
Musst ein winziges Pfäffelein nur seyn, seyn, seyn,
Musst ein winziges Pfäffelein, nur seyn.

I have thus brought together, as well from the records of others as from my own recollection, whatever incidental lights could be thrown from those sources, on some of the satirical effusions contained in the following pages.

DEDICATION.

TO STEPHEN WOOLRICHE, ESQ.

MY DEAR WOOLRICHE,

IT is now about seven years since I promised (and I grieve to think it is almost as long since we met) to dedicate to you the very first Book, of whatever size or kind, I should publish. Who could have thought that so many years would elapse, without my giving the least signs of life upon the subject of this important promise? Who could have imagined that a volume of doggerel, after all, would be the first offering that Gratitude would lay upon the shrine of Friendship?

If you continue, however, to be as much interested about me and my pursuits as formerly, you will be happy to hear that doggerel is not my *only* occupa-

(1) *Ariosto*, canto 35.

tion; but that I am preparing to throw my name to the Swans of the Temple of Immortality, (1) leaving it, of course, to the said Swans to determine whether they ever will take the trouble of picking it from the stream.

In the mean time, my dear Woolriche, like an orthodox Lutheran, you must judge of me rather by my *faith* than my *works;* and however trifling the tribute which I here offer, never doubt the fidelity with which I am and always shall be,

Your sincere
and attached friend,

THE AUTHOR.

245, *Piccadilly, March* 4, 1813.

ORIGINAL PREFACE.

THE Bag, from which the following Letters are selected, was dropped by a Twopenny Postman about two months since, and picked up by an emissary of the Society for the Suppression of Vice, who, supposing it might materially assist the private researches of that Institution, immediately took it to his employers, and was rewarded handsomely for his trouble. Such a treasury of secrets was worth a whole host of informers; and, accordingly, like the Cupids of the Poet (if I may use so profane a simile) who "fell at odds about the sweet-bag of a bee," (2) those venerable Suppressors almost fought with each other for the honour and delight of first ransacking the Post-Bag. Unluckily, however, it turned out, upon examination, that the discoveries of profligacy which it enabled them to make lay chiefly in those upper regions of society, which their well-bred regulations forbid them to molest or meddle with.—In consequence, they gained but very few victims by their prize, and, after lying for a week or two under Mr. Hatchard's counter, the Bag, with its violated contents, was sold for a trifle to a friend of mine.

It happened that I had been just then seized with an ambition (having never tried the strength of my wing but in a Newspaper) to publish something or other in the shape of a Book; and it occurred to me that, the present being such a letter-writing era, a few of these Twopenny-Post Epistles, turned into easy verse, would be as light and popular a task as I could possibly select for a commencement. I did not, however, think it prudent to give too many Letters at first, and, accordingly, have been obliged (in order to eke out a sufficient number of pages) to reprint some of those trifles which had already appeared in the public journals. As in the battles of ancient times, the shades of the departed were sometimes seen among the combatants, so I thought I might manage to remedy the thinness of my ranks, by conjuring up a few dead and forgotten ephemerons to fill them.

(2) Herrick.

Such are the motives and accidents that led to the present publication; and as this is the first time my Muse has ever ventured out of the go-cart of a News-paper, though I feel all a parent's delight at seeing little Miss go alone, I am also not without a parent's anxiety, lest an unlucky fall should be the consequence of the experiment; and I need not point how many living instances might be found, of Muses that have suffered very severely in their heads, from taking rather too early and rashly to their feet. Besides, a Book is so very different a thing from a Newspaper!—in the former, your doggerel, without either company or shelter, must stand shivering in the middle of a bleak page by itself; whereas, in the latter, it is comfortably backed by advertisements, and has sometimes even a Speech of Mr. St—ph—n's, or something equally warm, for a *chauffe-pied*—so that, in general, the very reverse of "laudatur et alget" is its destiny.

Ambition, however, must run some risks, and I shall be very well satisfied if the reception of these few Letters should have the effect of sending me to the Post-Bag for more.

———◦➒◘⑊◦———

PREFACE TO FOURTEENTH EDITION.

BY A FRIEND OF THE AUTHOR.

In the absence of Mr. Brown, who is at present on a tour through ———, I feel myself called upon, as his friend, to notice certain misconceptions and mis-representations, to which this little volume of Trifles has given rise.

In the first place, it is not true that Mr. Brown has had any accomplices in the work. A note, in-deed, which has hitherto accompanied his Preface, may very naturally have been the origin of such a supposition; but that note, which was merely the coquetry of an author, I have, in the present edition, taken upon myself to remove, and Mr. Brown must therefore be considered, like the mother of that unique production, the Centaur, μονα και μονον, (1) as alone responsible for the whole contents of the volume.

In the next place it has been said that, in conse-quence of this graceless little book, a certain distin-guished Personage prevailed upon another distin-guished Personage to withdraw from the author that notice and kindness with which he had so long and so liberally honoured him. In this story there is not one syllable of truth. For the magnanimity of the *former* of these persons I would, indeed, in no case answer too rashly: but of the conduct of the

(1) *Pindar, Pyth.* 2.—My friend certainly cannot add ουτ' εν ανδρασι γεραισφορον.

(2) Bishop of Casæ Nigræ, in the fourth century.

(3) A new reading has been suggested in the original of the Ode of Horace, freely translated by Lord Eld—n. In the line "Sive per Syrteis iter æstuosas," it is proposed,

latter towards my friend, I have a proud gratification in declaring, that it has never ceased to be such as he must remember with indelible gratitude—a gra-titude the more cheerfully and warmly paid, from its not being a debt incurred solely on his own account, but for kindness shared with those nearest and dearest to him.

To the charge of being an Irishman, poor Mr. Brown pleads guilty; and I believe it must also be acknow-ledged that he comes of a Roman Catholic family: an avowal which I am aware is decisive of his utter reprobation, in the eyes of those exclusive patentees of Christianity, so worthy to have been the followers of a certain enlightened Bishop, Donatus, (2) who held "that God is in Africa, *and not elsewhere.*" But from all this it does not necessarily follow that Mr. Brown is a Papist; and, indeed, I have the strongest reasons for suspecting that they who say so are somewhat mistaken. Not that I presume to have ascertained his opinions upon such subjects. All I profess to know of his orthodoxy is, that he has a Protestant wife and two or three little Protestant children, and that he has been seen at church every Sunday, for a whole year together, listening to the sermons of his truly reverend and amiable friend, Dr. ————, and behaving there as well and as orderly as most people.

There are yet a few other mistakes and falsehoods about Mr. Brown, to which I had intended, with all becoming gravity, to advert; but I begin to think the task is quite as useless as it is tiresome. Misrepre-sentations and calumnies of this sort are, like the arguments and statements of Dr. Duigenan,—not at all the less vivacious or less serviceable to their fabri-cators, for having been refuted and disproved a thou-sand times over. They are brought forward again, as good as new, whenever malice or stupidity may be in want of them; and are quite as useful as the old broken lantern, in Fielding's *Amelia*, which the watchman always keeps ready by him, to produce, in proof of riotous conduct, against his victims. I shall, there-fore give up the fruitless toil of vindication, and would even draw my pen over what I have already written, had I not promised to furnish my publisher with a Preface, and know not how else I could con-trive to eke it out.

I have added two or three more trifles to this edi-tion, which I found in the *Morning Chronicle,* and knew to be from the pen of my friend. The rest of the volume remains (3) in its original state.

April 20, 1814.

by a very trifling alteration, to read "*Surtees,*" instead of "Syrteis," which brings the Ode, it is said, more home to the noble translator, and gives a peculiar force and apiness to the epithet "æstuosas." I merely throw out this emen-dation for the learned, being unable myself to decide upon its merits.

22

INTERCEPTED LETTERS, Etc.

LETTER I.

FROM THE PR—NC—SS CH—RL—E OF W—L—S TO
THE LADY B—RB—A ASHL—Y. (1)

My dear Lady Bab, you 'll be shock'd, I'm afraid,
When you hear the sad rumpus your Ponies have
    made;
Since the time of horse-consuls (now long out of date),
No nags ever made such a stir in the state.
Lord Eld—n first heard—and as instantly pray'd he
To " God and his King "—that a Popish young Lady
(For though you 've bright eyes and twelve thousand
    a-year,
It is still but too true you 're a Papist, my dear,)
Had insidiously sent, by a tall Irish groom,
Two priest-ridden Ponies, just landed from Rome,
And so full, little rogues, of pontifical tricks,
That the dome of St. Paul's was scarce safe from
    their kicks.

Off at once to Papa, in a flurry he flies—
For Papa always does what these statesmen advise,
On condition that they 'll be, in turn, so polite
As in no case whate'er to advise him *too right*—
"Pretty doings are here, Sir (he angrily cries, [wise)—
While by dint of dark eyebrows he strives to look
" 'T is a scheme of the Romanists, so help me God !
To ride over your *most* Royal Highness rough-shod—
Excuse, Sir, my tears—they 're from loyalty's source—
Bad enough 't was for Troy to be sack'd by a *Horse*,
But for us to be ruin'd by *Ponies* still worse !"
Quick a Council is call'd—the whole Cabinet sits—
The Archbishops declare, frighten'd out of their wits,
That if once Popish Ponies should eat at my manger,
From that awful moment the Church is in danger !
As, give them but stabling, and shortly no stalls
Will suit their proud stomachs but those at St. Paul's.

The Doctor, (2) and he, the devout man of Lea-
    ther, (3)
V—ns—tt—t, now laying their Saintheads together,
Declare that these skittish young *a*-bominations
Are clearly foretold in Chap. vi., Revelations—
Nay, they verily think they could point out the one
Which the Doctor's friend Death was to canter upon.

Lord H—rr—by, hoping that no one imputes
To the Court any fancy to persecute brutes,
Protests, on the word of himself and his cronies,
That had these said creatures been Asses, not Ponies,
The Court would have started no sort of objection,
As Asses were, *there*, always sure of protection.

(1) This young Lady, who is a Roman Catholic, had
lately made a present of some beautiful Ponies to the
Pr—nc—ss.
(2) Mr. Addington, so nicknamed.
(3 Alluding to a tax lately laid upon leather.

" If the Pr—nc—ss *will* keep them (says Lord
    C—stl—r—gh),
To make them quite harmless, the only true way
Is (as certain Chief Justices do with their wives)
To flog them within half an inch of their lives.
If they 've any bad Irish blood lurking about,
This (he knew by experience) would soon draw it out."
Should this be thought cruel, his Lordship proposes
" The new *Veto* snaffle (4) to bind down their noses—
A pretty contrivance, made out of old chains,
Which appears to indulge, while it doubly restrains;
Which, however high-mettled, their gamesomeness
    checks   [necks !"
(Adds his Lordship humanely), or else breaks their

This proposal received pretty general applause
From the Statesmen around—and the neck-breaking
    clause
Had a vigour about it, which soon reconciled
Even Eld—n himself to a measure so mild.
So the snaffles, my dear, were agreed to *nem. con.*,
And my Lord C—stl—r—gh, having so often shone
In the *fettering* line, is to buckle them on.

I shall drive to your door in these *Vetos* some day,
But, at present, adieu !—I must hurry away
To go see my Mamma, as I 'm suffer'd to meet her
For just half an hour by the Qu—n's best repeater.
           C.H—RL—TTE.

—◦◦◦◦—

LETTER II.

FROM COLONEL M'M—H—N TO G—LD FR—NC—S
    L—CKIE, ESQ.

Dear Sir, I've just had time to look
Into your very learned Book, (5)
Wherein—as plain as man can speak,
Whose English is half modern Greek—
You prove that we can ne'er intrench
Our happy isles against the French,
Till Royalty in England's made
A much more independent trade ;—
In short, until the House of Guelph
Lays Lords and Commons on the shelf,
And boldly sets up for itself.

All that can well be understood,
In this said Book, is vastly good ;
And, as to what 's incomprehensible,
I dare be sworn 't is full as sensible.

But, to your work's immortal credit,
The Pr—n—e, good Sir, the Pr—n—e has read it

(4) The question whether a Veto was to be allowed to
the Crown in the appointment of Irish Catholic Bishops
was, at this time, very generally and actively agitated.
(5) For an account of this extraordinary work of Mr.
Leckie, see the *Edinburgh Review*, vol. xx.

(The only Book, himself remarks,
Which he has read since Mrs. Clarke's).
Last levee-morn he look'd it through,
During that awful hour or two
Of grave tonsorial preparation,
Which, to a fond admiring nation,
Sends forth, announced by trump and drum,
The best-wigg'd Pr—n—e in Christendom.

He thinks with you the imagination
Of *partnership* in legislation
Could only enter in the noddles
Of dull and ledger-keeping twaddles,
Whose heads on *firms* are running so,
They even must have a King and Co.,
And hence, most eloquently show forth
On *checks* and *balances*, and so forth.

But now, he trusts, we 're coming near a
Far more royal, loyal era;
When England's monarch need but say,
" Whip me those scoundrels, C—stl—r—gh!"
Or," Hang me up those Papists, Eld—n,"
And 't will be done—ay, faith, and well done.

With view to which, I 've his command
To beg, Sir, from your travell'd hand,
(Round which the foreign graces swarm)(1)
A Plan of radical Reform;
Compiled and chosen, as best you can,
In Turkey or at Ispahan,
And quite upturning, branch and root,
Lords, Commons, and Burdett to boot.

But, pray, whate'er you may impart, write
Somewhat more brief than Major C—rtwr—ght:
Else, though the Pr——e be long in rigging,
'T would take, at least, a fortnight's wigging,—
Two wigs to every paragraph—
Before he well could get through half.

You'll send it also speedily—
As truth to say, 'twixt you and me,
His Highness, heated by your work,
Already thinks himself Grand Turk!
And you'd have laugh'd, had you seen how
He scared the Ch—nc—ll—r just now,
When (on his Lordship's entering puff'd) he
Slapp'd his back and call'd him " Mufti!"

The tailors too have got commands,
To put directly into hands

(1) " The truth indeed seems to be, that having lived so long abroad as evidently to have lost, in a great degree, the use of his native language, Mr. Leckie has gradually come not only to speak, but to feel, like a foreigner."—*Edinburgh Review.*
(2) The learned Colonel must allude here to a description of the Mysterious Isle, in the *History of Abdalla, Son of Hanif,* where such inversions of the order of nature

All sorts of Dulimans and Pouches,
With Sashes, Turbans, and Paboutches
(While Y—rm—th's sketching out a plan
Of new *Moustaches à l'Ottomane*),
And all things fitting and expedient
To *turkify* our gracious R—g—nt!

You, therefore, have no time to waste—
So, send your System.—
Yours, in haste.

POSTSCRIPT.
BEFORE I send this scrawl away,
I seize a moment, just to say,
There 's some parts of the Turkish system
So vulgar, 't were as well you miss'd 'em.
For instance—in *Seraglio* matters—
Your Turk, whom girlish fondness flatters,
Would fill his Haram (tasteless fool !)
With tittering red-cheek'd things from school.
But, *here* (as in that fairy land,
Were Love and Age went hand in hand; (2)
Where lips, till sixty, shed no honey,
And Grandams were worth any money,)
Our Sultan has much riper notions—
So, let your list of *she*-promotions
Include those only, plump and sage,
Who 've reach'd the *regulation*-age;
That is, (as near as one can fix
From Peerage dates) full fifty-six.

This rule 's for *fav'rites*—nothing more—
For, as to *wives*, a Grand Signor,
Though not decidedly *without* them,
Need never care one curse about them.

—◦••◦—

LETTER III.
FROM G—GE PR—CE R—G—T TO THE E—— OF Y——TH. (3)
WE miss'd you last night at the "hoary old sinner's,"
Who gave us, as usual, the cream of good dinners;
His soups scientific—his fishes quite *prime*—
His pâtés superb—and his cutlets sublime!
In short, 't was the snug sort of dinner to stir a
Stomachic orgasm in my Lord El—b—gh,
Who *set to,* to be sure, with miraculous force, [coarse!
And exclaim'd, between mouthfuls," a *He*—Cook, of
While you live—(what 's there under that cover? pray,
look)— [Cook.
While you live—(I 'll just taste it)—ne'er keep a She-
'T is a sound Salic Law—(a small bit of that toast)—
Which ordains that a female shall ne'er rule the roast,

are said to have taken place.—" A score of old women and the same number of old men played here and there in the court, some at chuck-farthing, others at tip-cat or at cockles."—And again, " There is nothing, believe me, more engaging than those lovely wrinkles," etc., etc.—See *Tales of the East,* vol. iii., pp. 607, 608.
(3) This letter, as the reader will perceive, was written the day after a dinner given by the M—rq—s of H—d—t.

For Cookery's a secret—(this turtle's uncommon)—
Like Masonry, never found out by a woman!"

The dinner, you know, was in gay celebration
Of *my* brilliant triumph and H—nt's condemnation;
A compliment, too, to his Lordship the Judge [grudge
For his Speech to the Jury—and zounds! who would
Turtle soup, though it came to five guineas a-bowl,
To reward such a loyal and complaisant soul?
We were all in high gig—Roman Punch and Tokay
Travell'd round, till our heads travell'd just the same
way;   [nor
And we cared not for Juries or Libels—no—damme!
Even for the threats of last Sunday's *Examiner!*

More good things were eaten than said—but Tom
T—rrh—t
In quoting Joe Miller, you know, has some merit;
And, hearing the sturdy Justiciary Chief
Say—sated with turtle—"I'll now try the beef,"
Tommy whisper'd him (giving his Lordship a sly hit)
I fear 't will be *hung*-beef, my Lord, if you *try* it!"

And C—md—n was there, who that morning, had
To fit his new Marquis's coronet on;   [gone
And the dish set before him—oh dish well-devised!—
Was what old Mother Glass calls, "a calf's head
surprised!"
The *brains* were near Sh—ry, and *once* had been fine,
But, of late, they had lain so long soaking in wine,
That, though we, from courtesy, still chose to call
These brains very fine, they were no brains at all.

When the dinner was over, we drank, every one
In a bumper, "the venial delights of Crim. Con.;"
At which H—df—t with warm reminiscences gloated,
And E—b'r—h chuckled to hear himself quoted.

Our next round of toasts was a fancy quite new,
For we drank—and you'll own 't was benevolent too—
To those well-meaning husbands, cits, parsons, or
peers,   [dears:
Whom we've, any time, honour'd by courting their
This museum of wittols was comical rather;
Old H—df—t gave M—ss—y, and *I* gave your f—th—r.

In short, not a soul till this morning would budge—
We were all fun and frolic,—and even the J——e
Laid aside, for a time, his juridical fashion,
And through the whole night wasn't *once* in a passion!

I write this in bed, while my whiskers are airing,
And M—c(1) has a sly dose of jalap preparing

(1) Colonel M'Mahon.
(2) This letter, which contained some very heavy en-
closures, seems to have been sent to London by a private
hand, and then put into the Twopenny Post-Office, to save
trouble. See the *Appendix.*
(3) In sending this sheet to the Press, however, I learn

For poor T—mmy T—rr—t at breakfast to quaff—
As I feel I want something to give me a laugh,
And there 's nothing so good as old T—mmy, kept close
To his Cornwall accounts, after taking a dose.

———✥———

LETTER IV.

Dublin. .2)

LAST week, dear N—ch—l, making merry
At dinner with our Secretary,
When all were drunk, or pretty near
(The time for doing business here),
Says he to me, "Sweet Bully Bottom!
These Papist dogs—hiccup—'od rot 'em!—
Deserve to be bespatter'd—hiccup—
With all the dirt even *you* can pick up.
But, as the Pr—ce (here 's to him—fill—
Hip, hip, hurra!)—is trying still
To humbug them with kind professions,
And as *you* deal in *strong* expressions—
'Rogue'—'traitor'—hiccup—and all that—
You must be muzzled, Doctor Pat!—
You must indeed—hiccup—that's flat."

Yes—"muzzled" was the word, Sir John—
These fools have clapp'd a muzzle on
The boldest mouth that e'er ran o'er
With slaver of the times of yore!(3)—
Was it for this that back I went
As far as Lateran and Trent,
To prove that they, who damn'd us then,
Ought now, in turn, be damn'd again?—
The silent victim still to sit
Of Gr—tt—n's fire and C—nn—g's wit,
To hear even noisy M—th—w gabble on,
Nor mention once the W—e of Babylon!
Oh! 't is too much—who now will be
The Nightman of No-Popery?
What Courtier, Saint, or even Bishop,
Such learned filth will ever fish up?
If there among our ranks be one
To take my place, 't is *thou*, Sir John;
Thou, who, like me, art dubb'd Right Hon.
Like me, too, art a Lawyer Civil
That wishes Papists at the devil.

To whom then but to thee, my friend,
Should Patrick (4) his Portfolio send?
Take it—'t is thine—his learn'd Portfolio,
With all its theologic olio

that the "muzzle" has been taken off, and the Right Hon.
Doctor again let loose!
(4) A bad name for poetry; but D—gen—n is still worse.
—As Prudentius says upon a very different subject—
Torquetur Apollo
Nomine percussus.

Of Bulls, half Irish and half Roman—
Of Doctrines, now believed by no man—
Of Councils, held for men's salvation,
Yet always ending in damnation—
(Which shows that, since the world's creation,
Your Priests, whate'er their gentle shamming,
Have always had a taste for damning,)
And many more such pious scraps,
To prove (what *we 've* long proved, perhaps,)
That, mad as Christians used to be
About the Thirteenth Century,
There still are Christians to be had
In this, the Nineteenth, just as mad!

Farewell—I send with this, dear N—ch—l,
A rod or two I 've had in pickle
Wherewith to trim old Gr—tt—n's jacket.—
The rest shall go by Monday's packet.   P. D.

*Among the Enclosures in the foregoing Letter was
the following " Unanswerable Argument against
the Papists."*

   *   *   *   *

WE'RE told the ancient Roman nation
Made use of spittle in lustration ; (1)
(*Vide* Lactantium ap. Gallæum—(2)
i. e. you need not *read* but *see* 'em ;)
Now, Irish Papists, fact surprising,
Make use of spittle in baptising:
Which proves them all, O'Finns, O'Fagans,
Connors, and Tooles, all downright Pagans.
This fact 's enough :—let no one tell us
To free such sad *salivous* fellows.—
No, no—the man, baptised with spittle,
Hath no truth in him—not a tittle!

   *   *   *   *

—⊶⊷—

LETTER V.

FROM THE COUNTESS DOWAGER OF C—RK TO LADY——.

MY dear Lady ——! I 've been just sending out
About five hundred cards for a snug little Rout—
(By the by, you 've seen *Rokeby?* this moment got
   mine—
The Mail-Coach Edition (3)—prodigiously fine!)
But I can't conceive how, in this very cold weather,
I 'm ever to bring my five hundred together;
As, unless the thermometer 's near boiling heat,
One can never get half of one's hundreds to meet.
(Apropos—you 'd have laugh'd to see Townsend last
Escort to their chairs, with his staff, so polite, [night,
The " three maiden Miseries," all in a fright;
Poor Townshend, like Mercury, filling two posts,
Supervisor of *thieves,* and chief-usher of *ghosts!*)

(1) ——— Lustralibus antè salivis
    Expiat.   *Pers.,* sat. 2.
(2) I have taken the trouble of examining the Doctor's
reference here, and find him, for once, correct. The fol-
lowing are the words of his indignant referee Gallæus—
" Asserere non veremur sacrum baptismum a Papistis

But, my dear Lady ——, can 't you hit on some
   notion,
At least for one night to set London in motion ?—
As to having the R—g—nt, *that* show is gone by—
Besides, I 've remark'd that (between you and I)
The Marchesa and he, inconvenient in more ways,
Have taken much lately to whispering in doorways ;
Which—considering, you know, dear, the *size* of the
   two—   [through;
Makes a block that one's company *cannot* get.
And a house such as mine is, with doorways so small,
Has no room for such cumbersome love-work at all.—
(Apropos, though of love-work—you 've heard it, I
   hope,
That Napoleon's old mother 's to marry the Pope,—
What a comical pair!)—but, to stick to my Rout,
'T will be hard if some novelty can't be struck out.
Is there no Algerine, no Kamchatkan arrived?
No Plenipo-Pacha, three-tail'd and ten-wived?
No Russian, whose dissonant consonant name
Almost rattles to fragments the trumpet of fame?

I remember the time, three or four winters back,
When—provided their wigs were but decently black—
A few Patriot monsters, from Spain, were a sight
That would people one's house for one night after night,
But—whether the Ministers *paw'd* them too much—
(And you know how they spoil whatsoever they
   touch)   [town]
Or, whether Lord G—rge (the young man about
Has, by dint of bad poetry, written them down,
One has certainly lost one's *peninsular* rage;
And the only stray Patriot seen for an age
Has been at such places (think how the fit cools!)
As old Mrs. V—gh—n's or Lord L—v—rp—l's.

But, in short, my dear, names like Wintztschit-
   stopschinzoudhoff   [off :
Are the only things now make an evening go smooth
So, get me a Russian—till death I 'm your debtor—
If he brings the whole Alphabet, so much the better.
And—Lord ! if he would but *in character* sup
Off his fish-oil and candles, he 'd quite set me up!

Au revoir, my sweet girl—I must leave you in haste,
Little Gunter has brought me the Liqueurs to taste.

POSTSCRIPT.

BY the bye, have you found any friend that can
   construe
That Latin account, t'other day, of a Monster? (4)
If we can't get a Russian, and *that thing* in Latin
Be not *too* improper, I think I 'll bring that in.

profanari, et spoti usum in peccatorum expiatione a Pa-
ganis non a Christianis *mandsse."*
(3) See Mr. **Murray's** Advertisement about the Mail-
Coach copies of *Rokeby.*
(4) Alluding, I suppose, to the Latin Advertisement of a
Lusus Naturæ in the Newspapers lately.

LETTER VI.

FROM ABDALLAH, (1) IN LONDON, TO MOHASSAN,
IN ISPAHAN.

WHILST thou, Mohassan, (happy thou!)
Dost daily bend thy loyal brow
Before our King—our Asia's treasure!
Nutmeg of Comfort! Rose of Pleasure!—
And bear'st as many kicks and bruises
As the said Rose and Nutmeg chooses;
Thy head still near the bowstring's borders,
And but left on till further orders—
Through London streets, with turban fair,
And caftan, floating to the air,
I saunter on, the admiration
Of this short-coated population—
This sew'd up race—this button'd nation—
—Who, while they boast their laws so free,
Leave not one limb at liberty,
But live, with all their lordly speeches,
The slaves of buttons and tight breeches.

Yet, though they thus their knee-pans fetter
(They're Christians, and they know no better), (2)
In *some* things they're a thinking nation;
And, on Religious Toleration,
I own I like their notions *quite,*
They are so Persian and so right!
You know our Sunnites, (3)—hateful dogs!
Whom every pious Shiite flogs,
Or longs to flog (4)—'t is true, they pray
To God, but in an ill-bred way;
With neither arms, nor legs, nor faces
Stuck in their right canonic places. (5)
'T is true, they worship Ali's name—(6)
Their Heaven and *ours* are just the same—
(A Persian's Heaven is easily made,
'T is but black eyes and lemonade.)
Yet, though we 've tried for centuries back—
We can't persuade this stubborn pack,
By bastinadoes, screws, or nippers,
To wear the establish'd pea-green slippers. (7)

Then, only think, the libertines!
They wash their toes—they comb their chins, (8)
With many more such deadly sins;
And (what 's the worst, though last I rank it)
Believe the Chapter of the Blanket!

Yet, spite of tenets so flagitious,
(Which *must,* at bottom, be seditious;
Since no man living would refuse
Green slippers, but from treasonous views;
Nor wash his toes, but with intent
To overturn the government,)—
Such is our mild and tolerant way,
We only curse them twice a-day
(According to a Form that 's set,)
And, far from torturing, only let
All orthodox believers beat 'em,
And twitch their beards, where'er they meet 'em.

As to the rest, they 're free to do
Whate'er their fancy prompts them to,
Provided they make nothing of it
Towards rank or honour, power or profit;
Which things, we naturally expect,
Belong to us, the Establish'd sect,
Who disbelieve (the Lord be thanked!)
The aforesaid Chapter of the Blanket.

The same mild views of Toleration
Inspire, I find, this button'd nation,
Whose Papists (full as given to rogue,
And only Sunnites with a brogue)
Fare just as well, with all their fuss,
As rascal Sunnites do with us.

The tender Gazel I enclose
Is for my love, my Syrian Rose—
Take it when night begins to fall,
And throw it o'er her mother's wall.

GAZEL.

REMEMBEREST thou the hour we past,—
That hour the happiest and the last?

(1) I have made many inquiries about this Persian gentleman, but cannot satisfactorily ascertain who he is. From his notions of Religious Liberty, however, I conclude that he is an importation of Ministers; and he has arrived just in time to assist the P——e and Mr. L——ck—e in their new Oriental Plan of Reform.—See the second of these Letters.—How Abdallah's epistle to Ispahan found its way into the Twopenny Post-Bag is more than I can pretend to account for.

(2) "C'est un honnête homme," said a Turkish governor of De Ruyter; "c'est grand dommage qu'il soit Chrétien."

(3) *Sunnites* and *Shiites* are the two leading sects into which the Mahometan world is divided; and they have gone on cursing and persecuting each other, without any intermission, for about eleven hundred years. The *Sunni* is the established sect in Turkey, and the *Shia* in Persia; and the differences between them turn chiefly upon those important points which our pious friend Abdallah, in the true spirit of Shiite Ascendency, reprobates in this Letter.

(4) "Les Sunnites, qui étoient comme les Catholiques de Musulmanisme."—*D'Herbelot.*

(5) "In contradistinction to the Sounis, who in their prayers cross their hands on the lower part of the breast, the Schiahs drop their arms in straight lines; and as the Sounis, at certain periods of the prayer, press their foreheads on the ground or carpet, the Schiahs," etc., etc.—*Forster's Voyage.*

(6) "Les Turcs ne détestent pas Ali réciproquement; au contraire, ils le reconnoissent," etc., etc.—*Chardin.*

(7) "The Shiites wear green slippers, which the Sunnites consider as a great abomination."—*Mariti.*

(8) For these points of difference, as well as for the Chapter of the Blanket, I must refer the reader (not having the book by me) to Picart's *Account of the Mahometan Sects.*

Oh! not so sweet the Siha thorn
To summer bees, at break of morn,
Not half so sweet, through dale and dell,
To Camel's ears the tinkling bell,
As is the soothing memory
Of that one precious hour to me.

How can we live, so far apart?
Oh! why not rather, heart to heart,
    United live and die—
Like those sweet birds, that fly together,
With feather always touching feather,
    Link'd by a hook and eye! (1)

———∘❦∘———

LETTER VII.

FROM MESSRS. L—CK—GT—N AND CO.
TO ——————, ESQ. (2)

PER Post, Sir, we send your MS.—look'd it thro'—
Very sorry—but can't undertake—'t would n't do.
Clever work, Sir, would *get up* prodigiously well—
Its only defect is—it never would sell.
And though *Statesmen* may glory in being *unbought*,
In an *Author* 't is not so desirable thought.

Hard times, Sir,—most books are too dear to be
    read—
Though the *gold* of Good-sense and Wit's *small-
    change* are fled,
Yet the *paper* we publishers pass, in their stead,
Rises higher each day, and ('tis frightful to think it)
Not even such names as F—tzg—r—d's can sink it!

However, Sir—if you 're for trying again,
And at somewhat that 's vendible—we are your
    men.

Since the Chevalier C—rr (3) took to marrying
    lately,
The Trade is in want of a *Traveller* greatly—
No job, Sir, more easy—your *Country* once plann'd,
A month aboard ship and a fortnight on land
Puts your Quarto of Travels, Sir, clean out of hand.

An East-India pamphlet's a thing that would tell—
And a lick at the Papists is *sure* to sell well,
Or supposing you 've nothing *original* in you—
Write Parodies, Sir, and such fame it will win you,
You 'll get to the Blue-stocking Routs of Albinia! (4)

(1) This will appear strange to an English reader, but it
is literally translated from Abdallah's Persian, and the
curious bird to which he alludes is the *Juftak*, of which I
find the following account in Richardson:—"A sort of
bird, that is said to have but one wing; on the opposite
side to which the male has a hook and the female a ring,
so that, when they fly, they are fastened together."
(2) From motives of delicacy, and, indeed, of *fellow-
feeling*, I suppress the name of the Author, whose re-
jected manuscript was inclosed.—See the *Appendix*.

(Mind—*not* to her *dinners*—a *second-hand* Muse
Must n't think of aspiring to mess with the *Blues*.)
Or—in case nothing else in this world you can do—
The deuce is in 't, Sir, if you cannot *review!*

Should you feel any touch of *poetical* glow,
We 've a Scheme to suggest—Mr. Sc—tt, you must
    know,   [Row,) (5)
(Who, we 're sorry to say it, now works for *the*
Having quitted the Borders, to seek new renown,
Is coming, by long Quarto stages to Town;
And beginning with Rokeby (the job 's sure to pay)
Means to *do* all the Gentlemen's Seats on the way.
Now, the Scheme is (though none of our hackneys
    can beat him)
To start a fresh Poet through Highgate to *meet* him;
Who, by means of quick proofs—no revises—long
    coaches—
May do a few Villas before Sc—tt approaches—
Indeed, if our Pegasus be not curst shabby, [Abbèy.
He 'll reach, without foundering, at least Woburn-
Such, Sir, is our plan—if you 're up to the freak,
'T is a match! and we 'll put you *in* training next
    week.
At present, no more—in reply to this Letter, a
Line will oblige very much
    Temple of the Muses.   Yours, et cetera.

———∘❦∘———

LETTER VIII.

FROM COLONEL TH—M—S TO ——————
SK—FF—NGT—N, ESQ.

COME to our Fête, (6) and bring with thee
Thy newest, best embroidery;
Come to our Fête, and show again
That pea-green coat, thou pink of men,
Which charm'd all eyes that last survey'd it;
When Br—mm—l's self inquired, "who made
    it?"—
When Cits came wondering from the East,
And thought thee Poet Pye *at least!*

Oh! come, (if haply 't is thy week
For looking pale,) with paly cheek;
Though more we love thy roseate days,
When the rich rouge-pot pours its blaze
Full o'er thy face, and, amply spread,
Tips even thy whisker-tops with red—
Like the last tints of dying day
That o'er some darkling grove delay.

(3) Sir John Carr, the author of *Tours in Ireland,
Holland, Sweden*, etc., etc.
(4) This alludes, I believe, to a curious correspondence,
which is said to have passed lately between Alb—n—a,
Countess of B—ck—gh—ms—e, and a certain ingenious
Parodist.
(5) Paternoster Row.
(6) This Letter enclosed a Card for the Grand Fête of
the 5th of February.

Bring thy best lace, thou gay Philander,
(That lace, like H—rry Al—x—nd—r,
Too precious to be wash'd,)—thy rings,
Thy seals—in short, thy prettiest things!
Put all thy wardrobe's glories on,
And yield in frogs and fringe to none
But the great R——t's self alone;
Who—by particular desire—
For that night only, means to hire
A dress from Romeo C—tes, Esquire. (1)
Hail, first of Actors! (2) best of R—g—ts!
Born for each other's fond allegiance!
Both gay Lotharios—both good dressers—
Of serious farce *both* learn'd Professors—
Both circled round, for use or show,
With cock's combs, wheresoe'er they go! (3)

Thou know'st the time, thou man of lore!
It takes to chalk a ball-room floor—
Thou know'st the time, too, well-a-day!
It takes to dance that chalk away. (4)
The Ball-room opens—far and nigh
Comets and suns beneath us lie;
O'er snow-white moons and stars we walk,
And the floor seems one sky of chalk!
But soon shall fade that bright deceit,
When many a maid, with busy feet
That sparkle in the lustre's ray,
O'er the white path shall bound and play
Like Nymphs along the Milky Way:
With every step a star hath fled,
And suns grow dim beneath their tread!
So passeth life—(thus Sc—tt would write,
And spinsters read him with delight,)—
Hours are not feet, yet hours trip on,
Time is not chalk, yet time's soon gone! (5)

But, hang this long digressive flight!
I meant to say, thou 'lt see, that night,
What falsehood rankles in their hearts,
Who say the Pr——e neglects the arts—
Neglects the arts?—no, Str—hl—g, (6) no;
Thy Cupids answer "'t is not so;"

(1) An amateur actor of much risible renown.

(2)   Quem tu, Melpomene, semel
       Nascentem *placido lumine*, videris, etc.—*Horat.*
The Man, upon whom thou hast deign'd to look funny,
Oh Tragedy's Muse! at the hour of his birth—
Let them say what they will, that's the Man for *my* money,
Give others thy tears, but let *me* have thy mirth!
[The assertion that follows, however, is not verified in
the instance before us.
       Illum ———————————
       ————— non equus impiger
       Curru ducet Achaico.]

(3) The crest of Mr. C—tes, the very amusing amateur
tragedian here alluded to, was a cock; and most profusely
were his liveries, harness, etc., covered with this ornament.
(4) To those who neither go to balls nor read the
Morning Post it may be necessary to mention, that the

And every floor, that night, shall tell
How quick thou daubest, and how well.
Shine as thou may'st, in French vermillion,
Thou 'rt *best*, beneath a French cotillion;
And still comest off, whate'er thy faults,
With *flying colours* in a Waltz.
Nor need'st thou mourn the transient date
To thy best works assign'd by fate.
While *some* chefs-d'œuvre live to weary one,
Thine boast a short life and a merry one;
Their hour of glory past and gone
With "Molly put the kettle on!" (7)

But, bless my soul! I've scarce a leaf
Of paper left—so must be brief.

This festive Fête, in fact, will be
The former Fête's *fac-simile;* (8)
The same long Masquerade of Rooms,
All trick'd up in such odd costumes,
(These, P—rt—r, (9) are thy glorious works!)
You'd swear Egyptians, Moors, and Turks,
Bearing Good-Taste some deadly malice,
Had clubb'd to raise a Pic-Nic Palace;
And each to make the ollo pleasant
Had sent a State-Room as a present.
The same *fauteuils* and girondoles—
The same gold asses (10) pretty souls!
That in this rich and classic dome
Appear so perfectly at home.
The same bright river 'mong the dishes,
But *not*—ah! not the same dear fishes—
Late hours and claret kill'd the old ones—
So 'stead of silver and of gold ones,
(It being rather hard to raise
Fish of that *specie* now-a-days)
Some sprats have been by Y—rm—th's wish.
Promoted into *Silver* Fish,
And Gudgeons (so V—ns—tt—t told
The R—g—t) are as good as *Gold!*

So, prithee, come—our Fête will be
But half a Fête if wanting thee.   J. T.

floors of ball-rooms, in general, are chalked, for safety
and for ornament, with various fanciful devices.
(5)   Hearts are not flint, yet flints are rent,
       Hearts are not steel, yet steel is bent.
After all, however, Mr. Sc—tt may well say to the Colonel,
(and, indeed, to much better wags than the Colonel,)
ῥᾷον μωμεῖσθαι ἢ μιμεῖσθαι.
(6) A foreign artist much patronised by the Prince Regent.
(7) The name of a popular country-dance.
(8) "C—rl—t—n H——e will exhibit a complete *fac-
simile*, in respect to interior ornament, to what it did at
the last Fête. The same splendid draperies," etc., etc.—
Morning Post.
(9 Mr. Walsh Porter, to whose taste was left the fur-
nishing of the rooms of Carlton House.
(10 The salt-cellars on the Pr——e's *own* table were in
the form of an Ass with panniers.

APPENDIX.

LETTER IV. Page 172.

AMONG the papers, enclosed in Dr. D—g—n—n's Letter, was found an Heroic Epistle in Latin verse, from Pope Joan to her Lover, of which, as it is rather a curious document, I shall venture to give some account. This female Pontiff was a native of England, (or, according to others, of Germany,) who, at an early age, disguised herself in male attire, and followed her lover, a young ecclesiastic, to Athens, where she studied with such effect, that, upon her arrival at Rome, she was thought worthy of being raised to the Pontificate. This Epistle is addressed to her Lover (whom she had elevated to the dignity of Cardinal,) soon after the fatal *accouchement* by which her Fallibility was betrayed.

She begins by reminding him tenderly of the time when they were together at Athens—when, as she says,

———" by Ilissus' stream
We whispering walk'd along, and learn'd to speak
The tenderest feelings in the purest Greek;
Ah, then, how little did we think or hope,
Dearest of men, that I should e'er be Pope!(1)
That I, the humble Joan, whose house-wife art
Seem'd just enough to keep thy house and heart,
(And those, alas, at sixes and at sevens,)
Should soon keep all the keys of all the heavens!"

Still less (she continues to say) could they have foreseen, that such a catastrophe as had happened in Council would befall them—that she

" Should thus surprise the Conclave's grave decorum,
And let a *little Pope* pop out before 'em—
Pope *Innocent!* alas, the only one
That name could e'er be justly fix'd upon."

She then very pathetically laments the downfall of her greatness, and enumerates the various treasures to which she is doomed to bid farewell for ever:—

" But oh, more dear, more precious ten times over—
Farewell my Lord, my Cardinal, my Lover!
I made *thee* Cardinal—thou madest *me*—ah!
Thou madest the Papa (2) of the world Mamma!"

I have not time at present to translate any more of this Epistle; but I presume the argument which the Right Hon. Doctor and his friends mean to de-

(1) Spanheim attributes the unanimity with which Joan was elected to that innate and irresistible charm, by which her sex, though latent, operated upon the instinct of the Cardinals—"Non vi aliquâ, sed concorditer, omnium in se converso desiderio, quæ sunt blandientis sexus artes, latentes in hâc quanquam!"

(2) This is an anachronism, for it was not till the eleventh century that the Bishop of Rome took the title of Papa, or Universal Father.

(3) There was, in like manner, a mysterious Book, in the 16th Century, which employed all the anxious curiosity of the Learned of that time. Every one spoke of it; many wrote against it; though it does not appear that any body

duce from it is, (in their usual convincing strain) that Romanists must be unworthy of Emancipation *now*, because they had a Petticoat Pope in the Ninth Century. Nothing can be more logically clear, and I find that Horace had exactly the same views upon the subject:

Romanus (eheu posteri negabitis!)
Emancipatus FŒMINÆ
Fert vallum !

LETTER VII. Page 175.

THE Manuscript, found enclosed in the Bookseller's Letter, turns out to be a Melo-Drama, in two Acts, entitled " *The Book,*"(3) of which the Theatres, of course, had had the refusal, before it was presented to Messrs. L—ck—ngt—n and Co. This rejected Drama, however, possesses considerable merit, and I shall take the liberty of laying a sketch of it before my Readers.

The first Act opens in a very awful manner—*Time*, three o'clock in the morning—*Scene*, the Bourbon Chamber (4) in C—rlton House.—Enter the P——e R—g—t solus—After a few broken sentences, he thus exclaims:—

Away—Away—
Thou haunt'st my fancy so, thou devilish Book,
I meet thee—trace thee, wheresoe'er I look.
I see thy damned *ink* in Eld—n's brows—
I see thy *foolscap* on my H—rtf—d's Spouse—
V—ns—tt—t's head recalls thy *leathern* case,
And all thy *blank-leaves* stare from R—d—r's face!
While, turning here (*laying his hand on his heart*),
    I find, ah wretched elf,
Thy *List* of dire *Errata* in myself.
    (*Walks the stage in considerable agitation.*)
Oh Roman Punch! oh potent Curaçoa!
Oh Mareschino! Mareschino oh!
Delicious drams! why have you not the art
To kill this gnawing *Book-worm* in my heart?

He is here interrupted in his Soliloquy by perceiving on the ground some scribbled fragments of paper, which he instantly collects, and " by the light of two magnificent candelabras " discovers the following unconnected words, "*Wife neglected*"—"*the Book*" —"*Wrong Measures* "—" *the Queen*"—" *Mr. Lambert*"—" *the* R—g—t."

Ha! treason in my house!—Curst words, that wither

had ever seen it; and Grotius is of opinion that no such Book ever existed. It was entitled "Liber de tribus impostoribus." (See *Morhof., Cap. de Libris damnatis.*)— Our more modern mystery of "the Book" resembles this in many particulars; and, if the number of Lawyers employed in drawing it up be stated correctly, a slight alteration of the title into " *à tribus impostoribus*" would produce a coincidence altogether very remarkable.

(4) The same Chamber, doubtless, that was prepared for the reception of the Bourbons at the first Grand Fête, and which was ornamented (all " for the Deliverance of Europe") with *fleurs de lis.*

23

My princely soul, (*shaking the papers violently*)
what Demon brought you hither?
"My Wife;"—"the Book" too!—stay—a nearer look—
(*holding the fragments closer to the candelabras*)
Alas! too plain, B, double O, K, Book—
Death and destruction!
He here rings all the bells, and a whole legion of
valets enter. A scene of cursing and swearing (very
much in the German style) ensues, in the course of
which messengers are despatched, in different direc-
tions, for the L—rd Ch—nc—ll—r, the D—e of
C—b—l—d, etc. etc. The intermediate time is
filled up by another Soliloquy, at the conclusion of
which the aforesaid Personages rush on alarmed;
the D—ke with his stays only half-laced, and the
Ch—nc—ll—r with his wig thrown hastily over an
old red night-cap, "to maintain the becoming splen-
dour of his office." (1) The R—g—t produces the
appalling fragments, upon which the Ch—nc—ll—r
breaks out into exclamations of loyalty and tender-
ness, and relates the following portentous dream.

'T is scarcely two hours since
I had a fearful dream of thee, my P———c!—
Methought I heard thee, 'midst a courtly crowd,
Say from thy throne of gold, in mandate loud, [there
"Worship my whiskers!"—(*weeps*) not a knee was
But bent and worshipp'd the Illustrious Pair,
Which curl'd in conscious majesty! (*pulls out his
handkerchief*)—while cries
Of "Whiskers, whiskers!" shook the echoing skies.—
Just in that glorious hour, methought, there came,
With looks of injured pride, a princely Dame,
And a young maiden, clinging by her side,
As if she fear'd some tyrant would divide
Two hearts that nature and affection tied!
The Matron came—within her *right* hand glow'd
A radiant torch! while from her *left* a load   [veil—
Of Papers hung—(*wipes his eyes*)—collected in her
The venal evidence, the slanderous tale,
The wounding hint, the current lies that pass
From *Post* to *Courier*, form'd the motley mass;
Which, with disdain, before the throne she throws,
And lights the Pile beneath thy princely nose. (*Weeps.*)
Heavens, how it blazed!—I 'd ask no livelier fire,
(*With animation*) To roast a Papist by, my gracious
Sire!   [see—
But ah! the Evidence—(*weeps again*) I mourn'd to
Cast, as it burn'd, a deadly light on thee:
And Tales and Hints their random sparkles flung,
And hiss'd and crackled, like an old maid's tongue;
While *Post* and *Courier*, faithful to their fame,
Made up in stink for what they lack'd in flame.
When, lo, ye Gods! the fire ascending brisker,
Now singes *one*, now lights the *other* whisker.

(1) "To enable the individual, who holds the office of
Chancellor, to maintain it in becoming splendour." (*A
loud laugh.*)—Lord Castlereagh's *Speech upon the Vice-
Chancellor's Bill.*

(2) Mr. Leigh Hunt and his brother.

Ah! where was then the Sylphid that unfurls
Her fairy standard in defence of curls?
Throne, Whiskers, Wig soon vanish'd into smoke,
The watchman cried "Past One," and—I awoke.

Here his Lordship weeps more profusely than ever,
and the R—g—t (who has been very much agitated
during the recital of the Dream) by a movement as
characteristic as that of Charles XII. when he was
shot, claps his hands to his whiskers to feel if all be
really safe. A Privy Council is held—all the Servants,
etc. are examined, and it appears that a Tailor, who
had come to measure the R—g—t for a Dress (which
takes three whole pages of the best superfine *clin-
quant* in describing) was the only person who had
been in the Bourbon Chamber during the day. It is,
accordingly, determined to seize the Tailor, and the
Council breaks up with a unanimous resolution to
be vigorous.

The commencement of the Second Act turns chiefly
upon the Trial and Imprisonment of two Brothers(2)
—but as this forms the *under-plot* of the Drama, I
shall content myself with extracting from it the fol-
lowing speech, which is addressed to the two Bro-
thers, as they "exeunt severally" to Prison:

Go to your prisons—though the air of Spring
No mountain coolness to your cheeks shall bring;
Though Summer flowers shall pass unseen away,
And all your portion of the glorious day
May be some solitary beam that falls,
At morn or eve, upon your dreary walls—
Some beam that enters, trembling as if awed,
To tell how gay the young world laughs abroad!
Yet go—for thoughts as blessed as the air
Of Spring or Summer flowers await you there;
Thoughts such as He, who feasts his courtly crew
In rich conservatories, never knew;
Pure self-esteem—the smiles that light within—
The Zeal, whose circling charities begin
With the few loved ones Heaven has placed it near,
And spread, till all mankind are in its sphere;
The Pride, that suffers without vaunt or plea,
And the fresh Spirit, that can warble free,
Through prison-bars its hymn to Liberty!

The Scene next changes to a Tailor's Work-shop,
and a fancifully-arranged group of these Artists is
discovered upon the Shop-board—their task evi-
dently of a *royal* nature, from the profusion of gold
lace, frogs, etc., that lie about—They all rise and
come forward, while one of them sings the following
Stanzas to the tune of "*Derry down.*"

My brave brother Tailors, come, straighten your knees,
For a moment, like gentlemen, stand up at ease,
While I sing of our P———e (and a fig for his railers),
The Shop-board's delight! the Mæcenas of Tailors!
    Derry down, down, down Derry down.

Some monarchs take roundabout ways into note,
While *His* short cut to fame is—the cut of his coat;

Philip's Son thought the World was too small for his
    Soul,
But our R—g—t's finds room in a laced button-hole.
                    Derry down, etc.

Look through all Europe's Kings—those, at least,
    who go loose—
Not a King of them all 's such a friend to the Goose,
So, God keep him increasing in size and renown,
Still the fattest and best-fitted P——e about town!
                    Derry down, etc.

During the "Derry down" of this last verse, a messenger from the S—c—t—y of S——e's Office rushes on, and the singer (who, luckily for the effect of the scene, is the very Tailor suspected of the mysterious fragments) is interrupted in the midst of his laudatory exertions, and hurried away, to the no small surprise and consternation of his comrades. The Plot now hastens rapidly in its developement—the management of the Tailor's examination is highly skilful, and the alarm which he is made to betray is natural without being ludicrous. The explana-

tion, too, which he finally gives is not more simple than satisfactory. It appears that the said fragments formed part of a self-exculpatory note, which he had intended to send to Colonel M'M——n upon subjects purely professional, and the corresponding bits (which still lie luckily in his pocket) being produced, and skilfully laid beside the others, the following billet-doux is the satisfactory result of their juxtaposition.

Honour'd Colonel—my Wife, who 's the Queen of
    all slatterns,
Neglected to put up the Book of new Patterns.
She sent the wrong Measures too—shamefully wrong—
They 're the same used for poor Mr. Lambert, when
    young;
But, bless you! they wouldn't go half round the
    R—g—t—
So, hope you 'll excuse yours till death, most obe-
    dient.

This fully explains the whole mystery—the R—g—t resumes his wonted smiles, and the Drama terminates, as usual, to the satisfaction of all parties.

SATIRICAL AND HUMOROUS POEMS.

ΣΧΟΛΑΖΟΝΤΟΣ ΑΣΧΟΛΙΑ.

THE INSURRECTION OF THE PAPERS.

A DREAM.

"It would be impossible for his Royal Highness to disengage his person from the accumulating pile of papers that encompassed it."—Lord Castlereagh's *Speech upon Colonel M'Mahon's Appointment. April* 14, 1812.

Last night I toss'd and turn'd in bed,
But could not sleep—at length I said,
"I 'll think of Viscount C—stl—r—gh.
And of his speeches—that 's the way."
And so it was, for instantly
I slept as sound as sound could be.
And then I dreamt—so dread a dream!
Fuseli has no such theme;
Lewis never wrote or borrow'd
Any horror half so horrid!

    Methought the Pr——e, in whisker'd state,
Before me at his breakfast sate;
On one side lay unread Petitions,
On t' other, Hints from five Physicians;
Here tradesmen's bills,—official papers,
Notes from my Lady, drams for vapours—
There plans of saddles, tea and toast,
Death-warrants and the *Morning Post.*

    When lo! the Papers, one and all,
'As if at some magician's call,
Began to flutter of themselves
From desk and table, floor and shelves,

And, cutting each some different capers,
Advanced, oh jacobinic papers!
As though they said, "Our sole design is
To suffocate his Royal Highness!"
The Leader of this vile sedition
Was a huge Catholic Petition,
With grievances so full and heavy,
It threaten'd worst of all the bevy.
Then Common-Hall Addresses came
In swaggering sheets, and took their aim
Right at the R—g—t's well-dress'd head,
As if *determined* to be read.
Next Tradesmen's Bills began to fly,
And Tradesmen's Bills, we know, mount
    high;
Nay, even Death-warrants thought they 'd best
Be lively too, and join the rest.

    But, oh the basest of defections!
His Letter about "predilections"—
His own dear Letter, void of grace,
Now flew up in its parent's face!
Shock'd with this breach of filial duty,
He just could murmur "*et* Tu, *Brute!*"
Then sunk, subdued upon the floor
At Fox's bust, to rise no more!

I waked—and pray'd, with lifted hand,
    "Oh! never may this Dream prove true;
Though paper overwhelms the land,
    Let it not crush the Sovereign too!"

PARODY OF A CELEBRATED LETTER. (1)

AT length, dearest Freddy, the moment is nigh,
When, with P—rc—v—l's leave, I may throw my
     chains by;
And, as time now is precious, the first thing I do,
Is to sit down and write a wise letter to you.

      *   *   *   *

      *   *   *   *

      *   *   *   *

      *   *   *   *

I meant before now to have sent you this Letter,
But Y—rm—th and I thought perhaps 'twould be
     better
To wait till the Irish affairs were decided—
(That is, till both Houses had prosed and divided,
With all due appearance of thought and digestion)—
For, though H—rtf—rd House had long settled the
     question,
I thought it but decent, between me and you,
That the two other Houses should settle it too.

I need not remind you how cursedly bad
Our affairs were all looking, when Father went
     mad; (2)
A straight waistcoat on him and restrictions on me,
A more limited Monarchy could not well be.
I was call'd upon then, in that moment of puzzle,
To choose my own Minister—just as they muzzle
A playful young bear, and then mock his disaster,
By bidding him choose out his own dancing-master.

I thought the best way, as a dutiful son,
Was to do as Old Royalty's self would have done. (3)
So I sent word to say, I would keep the whole batch in,
The same chest of tools, without cleansing or patching;
For tools of this kind, like Martinus's sconce, (4)
Would lose all their beauty, if purified once;
And think—only think—if our Father should find,
Upon graciously coming again to his mind, (5)
That improvement had spoil'd any favourite adviser—
That R—se was grown honest, or W—stm—rel—nd
     wiser—
That R—d—r was, even by one twinkle, the brighter—
Or L—v—rp—l's speeches but half a pound lighter—
What a shock to his old royal heart it would be!
No!—far were such dreams of improvement from me:

(1) Letter from his Royal Highness the Prince Regent to
the Duke of York, Feb. 13, 1812.
(2) "I think it hardly necessary to call your recollection
to the recent circumstances under which I assumed the
authority delegated to me by Parliament."—Prince's Letter.
(3) "My sense of duty to our Royal father solely decided
that choice."—Ibid.
(4) The antique shield of Martinus Scriblerus, which,
upon scouring, turned out to be only an old sconce.
(5) "I waved any personal gratification, in order that

And it pleased me to find, at the House, where, you
     know, (6)   [coa, (7)
There's such good mutton cutlets, and strong cura-
That the Marchioness call'd me a duteous old boy,
And my Y—rm—th's red whiskers grew redder for joy.

You know, my dear Freddy, how oft, if I would,
By the law of last Sessions I might have done good.
I might have withheld these political noodles
From knocking their heads against hot Yankee
     Doodles;
I might have told Ireland I pitied her lot, [did not.
Might have soothed her with hope—but you know I
And my wish is, in truth, that the best of old fellows
Should not, on recovering, have cause to be jealous,
But find that, while he has been laid on the shelf,
We've been all of us nearly as mad as himself.
You smile at my hopes—but the Doctors and I
Are the last that can think the K—ng ever will die. (8)

A new era's arrived (9)—though you'd hardly
     believe it—
And all things, of course, must be new to receive it.
New villas, new fêtes (which even Waithman at-
     tends)—   [friends?
New saddles, new helmets, and—why not new

      *   *   *   *

I repeat it, "New Friends"—for I cannot describe
The delight I am in with this P—rc—v—l tribe.
Such capering!—such vapouring!—such rigour!—
     such vigour!
North, South, East, and West, they have cut such a
     figure,   [ears,
That soon they will bring the whole world round our
And leave us no friends—but Old Nick and Algiers.

When I think of the glory they've beam'd on my
     chains,
'Tis enough quite to turn my illustrious brains.
It is true we are bankrupts in commerce and riches,
But think how we find our Allies in new breeches!
We've lost the warm hearts of the Irish, 'tis granted,
But then we've got Java, an island much wanted,
To put the last lingering few who remain
Of the Walcheren warriors out of their pain.
Then how Wellington fights! and how squabbles his
     brother!
For Papists the one, and with Papists the other;

his Majesty might resume, on his restoration to health,
every power and prerogative," etc.—Prince's Letter.
(6) "And I have the satisfaction of knowing that such was
the opinion of persons for whose judgment," etc.—Ibid.
(7) The letter-writer's favourite luncheon.
(8) "I certainly am the last person in the kingdom to
whom it can be permitted to despair of our royal father's
recovery."—Prince's Letter.
(9) "A new era is now arrived, and I cannot but reflect
with satisfaction," etc.—Ibid.

One crushing Napoleon by taking a City,
While t' other lays waste a whole Catholic Committee.
Oh deeds of renown !—shall I boggle or flinch,
With such prospects before me? by Jove, not an inch.
No—let *England's* affairs go to rack, if they will,
We 'll look after the affairs of the *Continent* still ;
And, with nothing at home but starvation and riot,
Find Lisbon in bread, and keep Sicily quiet.

I am proud to declare I have no predilections ;(1)
My heart is a sieve, where some scatter'd affections
Are just danced about for a moment or two,
And the *finer* they are, the more sure to run through :
Neither feel I resentments, nor wish there should
        come ill   [m—l,
To mortal—except (now I think on 't) Beau Br—m-
Who threaten'd last year, in a superfine passion,
To cut *me*, and bring the old K—ng into fashion.
This is all I can lay to my conscience at present ;
When such is my temper, so neutral, so pleasant ;
So royally free from all troublesome feelings,
So little encumber'd by faith in my dealings
(And that I 'm consistent the world will allow,
What I was at Newmarket the same I am now).
When such are my merits (you know I hate cracking)
I hope, like the Vender of Best Patent Blacking,
" To meet with the generous and kind approbation
Of a candid, enlighten'd, and liberal nation."

By the by, ere I close this magnificent Letter,
(No man, except Pole, could have writ you a better,)
'T would please me if those, whom I 've humbugg'd
        so long (2)   [wrong,
With the notion (good men !) that I knew right from
Would a few of then join me—mind, only a few—
To let *too* much light in on me never would do.
But even Grey's brightness shan't make me afraid,
While I 've C—md—n and Eld—n to fly to for shade;
Nor will Holland's clear intellect do us much harm,
While there 's W—stm—rel—nd near him to weaken
        the charm.
As for Moira's high spirit, if aught can subdue it,
Sure joining with H—rtf—rd and Y—rm—th will
        do it !
Between R—d—r and Wh—rt—n let Sheridan sit,
And the fogs will soon quench even Sheridan's wit :
And against all the pure public feeling that glows
Even in Whitbread himself we 've a Host in G—rge
        R—se!
So, in short, if they wish to have Places, they may,
And I 'll thank you to tell all these matters to Grey,(3)

Who,I doubt not,will write(as there 's no time to lose)
By the twopenny post to tell Grenville the news ;
And now, dearest Fred (though I 've no predilection),
Believe me yours always with truest affection.

P.S. A copy of this is to P—rc—l going—(4)
Good Lord, how St. Stephen's will ring with his
        crowing!

—o⊕o—

ANACREONTIC.

TO A PLUMASSIER.

Fine and feathery artisan,
Best of Plumists (if you can
With your art so far presume),
Make for me a Pr—ce's Plume—
Feathers soft and feathers rare,
Such as suits a Pr—ce to wear.

First, thou downiest of men,
Seek me out a fine Pea-hen ;
Such a Hen, so tall and grand,
As by Juno's side might stand,
If there were no cocks at hand.
Seek her feathers, soft as down,
Fit to shine on Pr—ce's crown ;
If thou canst not find them, stupid !
Ask the way of Prior's Cupid.(5)

Ranging these in order due,
Pluck me next an old Cuckoo ;.
Emblem of the happy fates
Of easy, kind, cornuted mates.
Pluck him well—be sure you do—
Who wouldn't be an old Cuckoo,
Thus to have his plumage blest,
Beaming on a R—y—l crest ?

Bravo, Plumist!—now what bird
Shall we find for Plume the third?
You must get a learned Owl,
Bleakest of black-letter fowl—
Bigot bird, that hates the light, (6)
Foe to all that 's fair and bright.
Seize his quills, (so form'd to pen
Books, (7) that shun the search of men ;
Books that, far from every eye,
In " swelter'd venom sleeping" lie,)
Stick them in between the two,
Proud Pea-hen and Old Cuckoo.
Now you have the triple feather,
Bind the kindred stems together

(1) " I have no predilections to indulge,—no resent-
ments to gratify.—*Prince's Letter.*
(2) " I cannot conclude without expressing the gratifi-
cation I should feel if some of those persons with whom
the early habits of my public life were formed would
strengthen my hands, and constitute a part of my go-
vernment."—*Ibid.*
(3) " You are authorised to communicate these senti-

ments to Lord Grey, who, I have no doubt, will make them
known to Lord Grenville."—*Ibid.*
(4 " I shall send a copy of this letter immediately to
Mr. Perceval."—*Ibid.*
(5 See Prior's poem, entitled " *The Dove.*"
(6) P—rc—v—l.
(7) In allusion to " the Book" which created such a
sensation at that period.

With a silken tie, whose hue
Once was brilliant Buff and Blue;
Sullied now—alas, how much!
Only fit for Y—rm—th's touch.

There—enough—thy task is done;
Present worthy G——ge's Son;
Now, beneath, in letters neat,
Write "I SERVE," and all's complete.

————o⊕o————

EPIGRAM.

WHAT news to-day?—"Oh! worse and worse—
Mac(1) is the Pr—ce's Privy Purse!"—
The Pr—ce's *Purse!* no, no, you fool,
You mean the Pr—ce's *Ridicule.*

————o⊕o————

EXTRACTS

FROM THE DIARY OF A POLITICIAN.

Wednesday.

THROUGH M—nch—st—r Square took a canter just
        now—
Met the *old yellow chariot,* (2) and made a low bow.
This I did, of course, thinking 't was loyal and civil,
But got such a look—oh 't was black as the devil!
How unlucky!—*incog.* he was travelling about,
And I, like a noodle, must go find him out.

Mem.—when next by the old yellow chariot I ride,
To remember there *is* nothing princely inside.

Thursday.

At Levee to-day made another sad blunder—
What *can* be come over me lately, I wonder?
The Pr—ce was as cheerful, as if, all his life,
He had never been troubled with Friends or a Wife.
"Fine weather," says he—to which I, who *must* prate,
Answer'd, "Yes, Sir, but *changeable* rather, of late."
He took it, I fear, for he look'd somewhat gruff,
And handled his new pair of whiskers so rough,
That before all the courtiers I fear'd they'd come off,
And then, Lord, how Geramb (3) would triumph-
        antly scoff!

Mem.—to buy for son Dicky some unguent or lotion
To nourish his whiskers—sure road to promotion!(4)

Saturday.

Last night a Concert—vastly gay—
Given by Lady C—stl—r—gh.

(1) Colonel M—cm—h—n.
(2) The *incog.* vehicle of the Pr—ce.
(3) Baron Geramb, the rival of his R. H. in whiskers.
(4) England is not the only country where merit of this
kind is noticed and rewarded. "I remember," says Ta-
vernier, "to have seen one of the King of Persia's porters,
whose mustaches were so long that he could tie them
behind his neck, for which reason he had a double pen-
sion."

My Lord loves music, and, we know,
Has "*two strings always to his bow.*" (5)
In choosing songs, the R—g—t named
"*Had I a heart for falsehood framed;*"
While gentle H—rtf—d begg'd and pray'd
For "*Young I am, and sore afraid.*"

————o⊕o————

KING CRACK (6) AND HIS IDOLS.

WRITTEN AFTER THE LATE NEGOTIATION FOR A NEW
M—N—STRY.

KING CRACK was the best of all possible Kings,
    (At least, so his Courtiers would swear to you
        gladly,)
But Crack now and then would do heterodox things,
And, at last, took to worshipping *Images* sadly.

Some broken-down Idols, that long had been placed
    In his father's old *Cabinet,* pleased him so much,
That he knelt down and worshipp'd, though—such
        was his taste!—
    They were monstrous to look at, and rotten to
        touch.

And these were the beautiful Gods of King Crack!—
    But his People, disdaining to worship such things,
Cried aloud, one and all, "Come, your Godships
        must pack—
    You'll not do for *us,* though you *may* do for *Kings.*"

Then, trampling these images under their feet,
    They sent Crack a petition, beginning "Great
        Cæsar!
We're willing to worship; but only entreat
    That you'll find us some *decenter* Godheads than
        these are."

"I'll try," says King Crack—so they furnish'd him
        models
    Of better-shaped Gods, but he sent them all back;
Some were chisell'd too fine, some had heads 'stead
        of noddles,
    In short, they were all *much* too godlike for Crack.

So he took to his darling old Idols again,
    And, just mending their legs and new bronzing
        their faces,
In open defiance of Gods and of men,
    Set the monsters up grinning once more in their
        places.

(5) A rhetorical figure used by Lord C—stl—r—gh, in
one of his speeches.
(6) One of those antediluvian Princes, with whom Ma-
netho and Whiston seem so intimately acquainted. If we
had the Memoirs of Thoth, from which Manetho compiled
his History, we should find, I dare say, that Crack was
only a Regent, and that he, perhaps, succeeded Typhon,
who (as Whiston says) was the last King of the Antedilu-
vian dynasty.

WHAT'S MY THOUGHT LIKE?

Quest. Why is a Pump like V—sc—nt C—stl—r—gh?
Answ. Because it is a slender thing of wood,
That up and down its awkward arm doth sway,
And coolly spout and spout and spout away,
In one weak, washy, everlasting flood!

————◦◦◦————

EPIGRAM.

DIALOGUE BETWEEN A CATHOLIC DELEGATE AND HIS
R—Y—L H—GHN—SS THE D—E OF C—B—L—D.

SAID his Highness to Ned, (1) with that grim face of his,
    " Why refuse us the *Veto*, dear Catholic Neddy? "
" Because, Sir," said Ned, looking full in his phiz,
    " You 're *forbidding* enough, in all conscience,
        already!"

————◦◦◦————

WREATHS FOR THE MINISTERS.

AN ANACREONTIC.

HITHER, Flora, Queen of Flowers!
Haste thee from Old Brompton's bowers—
Or (if sweeter that abode)
From the King's well-odour'd Road,
Where each little nursery bud
Breathes the dust and quaffs the mud.
Hither come, and gaily twine
Brightest herbs and flowers of thine
Into wreaths for those who rule us,
Those who rule, and (some say) fool us—
Flora, sure, will love to please
England's Household Deities! (2)
First you must then, willy-nilly,
Fetch me many an orange lily—
Orange of the darkest dye
Irish G—ff—rd can supply;—
Choose me out the longest sprig,
And stick it in old Eld—n's wig.

Find me next a Poppy posy,
Type of his harangues so dosy,
Garland gaudy, dull and cool,
To crown the head of L—v—rp—l.
'T will console his brilliant brows
For that loss of laurel boughs,
Which they suffer'd (what a pity!)
On the road to Paris City.

(1) Edward Byrne, the head of the Delegates of the Irish
Catholics.
(2) The ancients, in like manner, crowned their Lares,
or Household Gods. See *Juvenal*, Sat. 9, v. 138.—Plu-
tarch, too, tells us that Household Gods were then, as they
are now, "much given to War and penal Statutes."—
ερινυωδεις και ποινιμους δαιμονας.
(3) Certain tinsel imitations of the Shamrock which are
distributed by the Servants of C———n House every Pa-
trick's Day.
(4) The *sobriquet* given to Lord Sidmouth.

Next, our C—stl—r—gh to crown,
Bring me from the County Down,
Wither'd Shamrocks, which have been
Gilded o'er, to hide the green—
(Such as H—df—t brought away
From Pall-Mall last Patrick's Day—(3)
Stitch the garland through and through
With shabby threads *of every hue;*—
And as, Goddess!—*entre nous*—
His Lordship loves (though best of men)
A little *torture*, now and then,
Crimp the leaves, thou first of Syrens,
Crimp them with thy curling-irons.

That's enough—away, away—
Had I leisure, I could say
How the *oldest rose* that grows
Must be pluck'd to deck Old Rose—
How the Doctor's (4) brow should smile
Crown'd with wreaths of camomile.
But time presses—to thy taste
I leave the rest, so, prithee, haste!

————◦◦◦————

EPIGRAM.

DIALOGUE BETWEEN A DOWAGER AND HER MAID ON
THE NIGHT OF LADY G—TH'S FÊTE.

" I WANT the Court Guide," said my lady, " to look
If the House, Seymour Place, be at 30 or 20."
"We 've lost the *Court Guide*, Ma'am, but here's *the
        Red Book,*   [plenty!"
Where you 'll find, I dare say, Seymour *Places* in

————◦◦◦————

HORACE, ODE XI., LIB. II.

FREELY TRANSLATED BY THE PR—CE R—G—T. (5)

(6) COME, Y—rm—th, my boy, never trouble your
        brains,
        About what your old crony,
        The Emperor Boney,
Is doing or brewing on Muscovy's plains;
(7) Nor tremble, my lad, at the state of our granaries:
        Should there come famine,
        Still plenty to cram in   [naries.
You always shall have, my dear Lord of the Stan-

Brisk let us revel, while revel we may;
(8) For the gay bloom of fifty soon passes away,

(5 This and the following are extracted from a Work,
which may, some time or other, meet the eye of the Public
—entitled " Odes of Horace, done into English by several
Persons of Fashion."
    (6)   Quid bellicosus Cantaber, et Scythes,
            Hirpine Quincti, cogitet, Hadria
                Divisus objecto, remittas
                    Quærere.
    (7)   Nec trepides in usum
            Poscentis ævi pauca.
    (8)   Fugit retro
            Levis juventas et decor.

And then people get fat,
    And infirm, and—all that,
(1) And a wig (I confess it) so clumsily sits,
    That it frightens the little Loves out of their wits.

(2) Thy whiskers, too, Y—rm—th!—alas, even they,
    Though so rosy they burn,
    Too quickly must turn
    (What a heart-breaking change for thy whiskers!)
      to Grey.   [fidget
(3) Then why, my Lord Warden, oh! why should you
    Your mind about matters you don't understand?
    Or why should you write yourself down for an
      idiot,
      Because " *you*," forsooth, " *have the pen in*
      your hand ! "

    Think, think how much better
      Than scribbling a letter,
    (Which both you and I
    Should avoid by the by,)
(4) How much pleasanter 't is to sit under the bust
    Of old Charley,(5) my friend here, and drink
      like a new one;
    While Charley looks sulky and frowns at me, just
      As the Ghost in the Pantomime frowns at Don
      Juan.

    (6) To crown us, Lord Warden,
      In C—mb—rl—nd's garden
    Grows plenty of *monk's-hood* in venomous sprigs.
      While Otto of Roses
      Refreshing all noses
    Shall sweetly exhale from our whiskers and wigs.

(7) What youth of the Household will cool our Noyau
    In that streamlet delicious,

(1)   Pellente lascivos amores
         Canitie.
2)   Neque uno Luna *rubens* nitet
         Vultu.
(3)   Quid æternis *minorem*
         Consiliis animum fatigas?
(4)   Cur non sub alta vel platano, vel hac
         Pinu jacentes sic temere.
(5) Charles Fox.
(6)   Rosâ
    Canos odorati capillos,
      Dum licet, Assyriaque nardo
    Potamus uncti.
(7)   Quis puer ocius
    Restinguet ardentis Falerni
      Pocula *prætereunte lympha?*
(8)   Quis . . . . . . eliciet domo
    Lyden?
9)   Eburna, dic age, cum lyra   qu. *liar-a*)
    Maturet.
(10)   Incomtam Lacænæ
    More comam religata nodo.
(11)   Integer vitæ scelerisque purus.

That down 'midst the dishes,
    All full of gold fishes,
    Romantic doth flow?—
(8) Or who will repair
    Unto M——ch——r Sq——e,
And see if the gentle *Marchesa* be there?
    Go—bid her haste hither,
(9) And let her bring with her
    The newest No-Popery Sermon that 's going—
(10) Oh ! let her come, with her dark tresses flow-
      ing,
    All gentle and juvenile, curly and gay,
    In the manner of—Ackermann's Dresses for May !

---o§§o---

HORACE, ODE XXII., LIB. I.

FREELY TRANSLATED BY LORD ELD—N.

(11) The man who keeps a conscience pure,
      (If not his own, at least his Prince's,)
    Through toil and danger walks secure,
      Looks big and black, and never winces.

(12) No want has he of sword or dagger,
      Cock'd hat, or ringlets of Gerumb;
    Though Peers may laugh, and Papists swagger,
      He does n't care one single d—mn.

(13) Whether 'midst Irish chairmen going,
      Or through St. Giles's alleys dim,
    'Mid drunken Sheelahs, blasting, blowing,
      No matter, 't is all one to him.

(14) For instance, I, one evening late,
      Upon a gay vacation sally,
    Singing the praise of Church and State,
      Got (God knows how) to Cranbourne Alley.

(12)   Non eget Mauri jaculis, neque arcu,
      Nec venenatis gravida sagittis,
         Fusce, pharetra.
(13)   Sive per Syrtes iter æstuosas,
    Sive facturus per inhospitalem
    Caucasum, vel quæ loca fabulosus
      Lambit Hydaspes.

The Noble Translator had, at first, laid the scene of
these imagined dangers of his Man of Conscience among
the Papists of Spain, and had translated the words "quæ
loca *fabulosus lambit* Hydaspes" thus—"The *fabling*
Spaniard *licks* the French;" but, recollecting that it is
our interest just now to be respectful to *Spanish* Catholics
(though there is certainly no earthly reason for our being
even commonly civil to *Irish* ones), he altered the pas-
sage as it stands at present.

(14)   Namque me silvâ lupus in Sabinâ,
    Dum meam canto Lalagen, et ultra
    Terminum curis vagor expeditis,
      Fugit inermen.

I cannot help calling the reader's attention to the pecu-
liar ingenuity with which these lines are paraphrased.
Not to mention the happy conversion of the Wolf into a

When lo! an Irish Papist darted
Across my path, gaunt, grim, and big—
I did but frown, and off he started,
Scared at me, even without my wig.

(1) Yet a more fierce and raw-boned dog
Goes not to Mass in Dublin City,
Nor shakes his brogue o'er Allen's Bog,
Nor spouts in Catholic Committee.

(2) Oh! place me 'midst O'Rourkes, O'Tooles,
The ragged royal blood of Tara;
Or place me where Dick M—rt—n rules
The houseless wilds of Connemara;

(3) Of Church and State I'll warble still, [grumble;
Though even Dick M—rt—n's self should
Sweet Church and State, like Jack and Jill,
(4) So lovingly upon a hill—
Ah! ne'er like Jack and Jill to tumble!

———o⊶o———

THE NEW COSTUME OF THE MINISTERS.

——Nova monstra creavit.—*Ovid.,Metamorph.*,l. i., v. 437.

Having sent off the troops of brave Major Camac,
With a swinging horse-tail at each valorous back,
And such helmets, God bless us! as never deck'd any
Male creature before, except Signor Giovanni—
"Let's see," said the R—g—t (like Titus, perplex'd
With the duties of empire,) " whom *shall* I dress
next?"

He looks in the glass—but perfection is there,
Wig, whiskers, and chin-tufts all right to a hair; (5)
Not a single *ex*-curl on his forehead he traces—
For curls are like Ministers, strange as the case is,
The *falser* they are, the more firm in their places.
His coat he next views—but the coat who could doubt?
For his Y—rm—th's own Frenchified hand cut it out;

Papist, (seeing that Romulus was suckled by a wolf, that
Rome was founded by Romulus, and that the Pope has
always reigned at Rome,) there is something particularly
neat in supposing "*ultra terminum*" to mean vacation-
time; and then the modest consciousness with which the
Noble and Learned Translator has avoided touching upon
the words "*curis expeditis*," (or, as it has been otherwise
read, "*causis expeditis*,") and the felicitous idea of his
being "*inermis*" when "without his wig," are altogether
the most delectable specimens of paraphrase in our lan-
guage.
  (1)   Quale portentum neque militaris
         Daunias latis alit æsculetis,
         Nec Jubæ tellus generat leonum
             Arida nutrix.
  (2)   Pone me pigris ubi nulla campis
         Arbor æstiva recreatur aura:
         Quod latus mundi, nebulæ, malusque
             Jupiter urget.
I must here remark, that the said Dick M—rt—n being
a very good fellow, it was not at all fair to make a "*malus
Jupiter*" of him.

Every pucker and seam were made matters of state,
And a Grand Household Council was held on each plait.

Then whom shall he dress? shall he new-rig his
    brother,   [other?
Great C—mb—rl—d's Duke, with some kickshaw or
And kindly invent him more Christian-like shapes
For his feather-bed neckcloths and pillory capes?
Ah! no—here his ardour would meet with delays,
For the Duke had been lately pack'd up in new Stays,
So complete for the winter, he saw very plain
'T would be devilish hard work to *unpack* him again.

So, what's to be done? — there's the Ministers,
    bless 'em!—
As he *made* the puppets, why should n't he *dress* 'em?
"An excellent thought!—call the tailors—be nimble—
Let Cum. bring his spy-glass, and H—rtf—d her
    thimble;
While Y—rm—th shall give us, in spite of all quizzers,
The last Paris cut with his true Gallic scissors."

So saying, he calls C—stl—r—gh, and the rest
Of his heaven-born statesmen, to come and be drest.
While Y—rm—th, with snip-like and brisk expedition,
Cuts up, all at once, a large Catholic Petition [done!")
In long tailors' measures, (the P—e crying "Well-
And first *puts in hand* my Lord Chancellor Eld—n.

*   *   *   *   *   *   *

———o⊶o———

CORRESPONDENCE
BETWEEN A LADY AND GENTLEMAN,
UPON THE ADVANTAGE OF (WHAT IS CALLED)
" HAVING LAW (6) ON ONE'S SIDE. "

The Gentleman's Proposal.
"Legge aurea,
S'ei piace, ei lice."

Come, fly to these arms, nor let beauties so bloomy
To one frigid owner be tied;

(3)   Dulce ridentem Lalagen amabo,
           Dulce loquentem.
(4) There cannot be imagined a more happy illustration
of the inseparability of Church and State, and their (what
is called) "standing and falling together," than this an-
cient apologue of Jack and Jill. Jack, of course, repre-
sents the State in this ingenious little Allegory.
       Jack fell down,
           And broke his *Crown*,
       And Jill came tumbling after.
(5) That model of Princes, the *Emperor Commodus*, was
particularly luxurious in the dressing and ornamenting
of his hair. His conscience, however, would not suffer
him to trust himself with a barber, and he used, accord-
ingly, to burn off his beard—"timore tonsoris," says
Lampridius. (*Hist. August. Scriptor.*) — The dissolute
Ælius Verus, too, was equally attentive to the decoration
of his wig. (See *Jul. Capitolin.*)—Indeed, this was not the
only princely trait in the character of Verus, as he had
likewise a most hearty and dignified contempt for his
wife.—See his insulting answer to her in *Spartianus.*
(6) In allusion to Lord Ell—nb—gh.
                                                        24

Your prudes may revile, and your old ones look gloomy,
　But, dearest, we've *Law* on our side.

Oh! think the delight of two lovers congenial,
　Whom no dull decorums divide;
Their error how sweet, and their raptures how *venial*,
　When once they've got Law on their side.

'Tis a thing, that in every King's reign has been
　done, too:
Then why should it now be decried?
If the Father has done it, why shouldn't the Son, too?
　For so argues Law on our side.

And even should our sweet violation of duty
　By cold-blooded jurors be tried,
They can *but* bring it in "a misfortune," my beauty,
　As long as we've Law on our side.

The Lady's Answer.

HOLD, hold, my good Sir, go a little more slowly;
　For, grant me so faithless a bride,
Such sinners as we are a little too *lowly*,
　To hope to have Law on our side.

Had you been a great Prince, to whose star shining
　o'er 'em
The People should look for their guide,
Then your Highness (and welcome!) might kick
　down decorum—
　You'd always have Law on your side.

Were you even an old Marquis, in mischief grown
　hoary,
Whose heart, though it long ago died
To the *pleasures* of vice, is alive to its *glory*—
　You still would have Law on your side.

But for *you*, Sir, Crim. Con. is a path full of troubles;
　By *my* advice therefore abide,
And leave the pursuit to those Princes and Nobles
　Who have *such* a *Law* on their side.

———o♯♭o———

OCCASIONAL ADDRESS

FOR THE OPENING OF THE NEW THEATRE OF ST. ST—PH—N.

INTENDED TO HAVE BEEN SPOKEN BY THE PROPRIE-
TOR IN FULL COSTUME, ON THE 24TH OF NOVEM-
BER, 1812.

THIS day a New House, for your edification,
We open, most thinking and right-headed nation!
Excuse the materials—though rotten and bad, [had;
They're the best that for money just now could be
And, if *echo* the charm of such houses should be,
You will find it shall *echo* my speech to a T.

As for actors, we've got the old Company yet,
The same motley, odd, tragi-comical set;
And considering they all were but clerks t' other day,
It is truly surprising how well they can play,

Our Manager,(1) (he, who in Ulster was nurst,
And sung *Erin go Brah* for the galleries first,
But, on finding *Pitt*-interest a much better thing,
Changed his note of a sudden, to *God save the King,*)
Still wise as he's blooming, and fat as he's clever,
Himself and his speeches as *lengthy* as ever,
Here offers you still the full use of his breath,
Your devoted and long-winded proser till death.

You remember last season, when things went per-
We had to engage (as a block to rehearse on) [verse on,
One Mr. V—ns—tt—t, a good sort of person,
Who's also employ'd for this season to play,
In "*Raising the Wind,*" and "*the Devil to Pay.*"(2)
We expect too—at least we've been plotting and
　planning—
To get that great actor from Liverpool, C—nn—g;
And, as at the Circus there's nothing attracts
Like a good *single combat* brought in 'twixt the acts,
If the Manager should, with the help of Sir P—ph—m,
Get up new *diversions* and C—nn—g should stop 'em,
Who knows but we'll have to announce in the papers,
"Grand fight—second time—with additional capers."

Be your taste for the ludicrous, humdrum, or sad,
There is plenty of each in this house to be had.
Where our Manager ruleth there weeping will be,
For a *dead hand at tragedy* always was he;
And there never was dealer in dagger and cup,
Who so *smilingly* got all his tragedies up.
His powers poor Ireland will never forget,
And the widows of Walcheren weep o'er them yet.

So much for the actors;—for secret machinery,
Traps, and deceptions, and shifting of scenery,
Y—rm—th and Cum. are the best we can find,
To transact all that trickery business behind.
The former's employ'd too to teach us French jigs,
Keep the whiskers in curl, and look after the wigs.

In taking my leave now, I've only to say,
A few *Seats in the House*, not as yet sold away,
May be had of the Manager, Pat C—stl—r—gh.

———o♯♭o———

LITTLE MAN AND LITTLE SOUL.

A BALLAD.

To the tune of "There was a little man, and he woo'd
a little maid."

DEDICATED TO THE RT. HON. CH—RL—S ABB—T.

Arcades ambo
Et *cant*-are pares.   1813.

THERE was a little Man, and he had a little Soul,
　And he said, "Little Soul, let us try, try, try,
　　Whether it's within our reach
　　To make up a little Speech,

———

(1) Lord C—stl—r—gh.
(2) He had recently been appointed Chancellor of the
Exchequer.

Just between little you and little I, I, I,
Just between little you and little I!"—

Then said his little Soul,
Peeping from her little hole,
"I protest, little Man, you are stout, stout, stout,
But, if it's not uncivil,
Pray tell me, what the devil
Must our little, little speech be about, bout, bout,
Must our little, little speech be about?"

The little Man look'd big,
With the assistance of his wig,
And he call'd his little Soul to order, order, order,
Till she fear'd he'd make her jog in
To gaol, like Thomas Croggan,
(As she was n't Duke or Earl) to reward her,
    ward her, ward her,
As she was n't Duke or Earl, to reward her.

The little Man then spoke,
"Little soul, it is no joke,   [sup,
For as sure as J—cky F—ll—r loves a sup, sup,
I will tell the Prince and People
What I think of Church and Steeple,   [up, up,
And my little patent plan to prop them up,
And my little patent plan to prop them up."

Away then, cheek by jowl,
Little Man and little Soul   [tittle, tittle;
Went and spoke their little speech to a tittle,
And the world all declare
That this priggish little pair   [little.
Never yet in all their lives look'd so little, little,
Never yet in all their lives look'd so little!
    —◦◦◦—

THE SALE OF THE TOOLS.
Instrumenta regni.—*Tacitus.*

HERE's a choice set of Tools for you, Gemmen and
    Ladies,
They'll fit you quite handy, whatever your trade is ;
(Except it be *Cabinet-making;*—no doubt,
In that delicate service they're rather worn out ;
Though their owner, bright youth! if he'd had his
    own will,
Would have bungled away with them joyously still.)
You can see they've been pretty well *hack'd*—and
    alack !
What tool is there job after job will not hack?
Their edge is but dullish, it must be confess'd,
And their temper, like E——nb'r——h's, none of
    the best ;   [trying,
But you'll find them good hard-working Tools, upon
Wer't but for their *brass*, they are well worth the
    buying ;   [screens,
They're famous for making *blinds, sliders,* and
And are, some of them, excellent *turning* machines.

The first Tool I'll put up (they call it a *Chancellor*)
Heavy concern to both purchaser *and* seller.
Though made of pig iron, yet worthy of note 'tis,
'Tis ready to *melt* at a half minute's notice. (1)
Who bids? Gentle buyer ! 'twill turn as thou shapest ;
'T will make a good thumb-screw to torture a Papist ;
Or else a cramp-iron, to stick in the wall
Of some church that old women are fearful will fall ;
Or better, perhaps, (for I'm guessing at random)
A heavy *drag-chain* for some Lawyer's old *Tandem.*
Will nobody bid ? It is cheap, I am sure, Sir—
Once, twice,—going, going,—thrice, gone! it is
    yours, Sir.
To pay ready money you sha'n't be distrest,
As a *bill* at *long date* suits the Chancellor best.

Come, where's the next Tool?—Oh! 't is here in
    a trice,—
This implement, Gemmen, at first was a *Vice ;*
(A tenacious and close sort of tool, that will let
Nothing out of its grasp it once happens to get ;)
But it since has received a new *coating* of *Tin,*
Bright enough for a Prince to behold himself in.
Come, what shall we say for it? briskly ! bid on,
We'll the sooner get rid of it—going—quite gone.
God be with it, such tools, if not quickly knock'd
    down,
Might at last cost their owner—how much? why, a
    Crown!

The next Tool I'll set up has hardly had handsel or
Trial as yet, and is *also* a Chancellor—
Such dull things as these should be sold by the gross ;
Yet, dull as it is, 't will be found to *shave close,*
And like *other* close shavers, some courage to gather,
This *blade* first began by a flourish on *leather.* (2)
You shall have it for nothing—then, marvel with me
At the terrible *tinkering* work there must be,
Where a Tool such as this is (I'll leave you to judge it)
Is placed by ill-luck at the top of *the Budget!*
    —◦◦◦—

REINFORCEMENTS FOR LORD WELLINGTON.
Suosque tibi commendat Troja Penates,
Hos cape fatorum comites.—*Virgil.*
                                    1813.

As recruits in these times are not easily got,
And the Marshal *must* have them—pray, why should
    we not,
As the last and, I grant it, the worst of our loans to
    him,
Ship off the Ministry, body and bones, to him ?
There's not in all England, I'd venture to swear,
Any men we could half so conveniently spare ;
And, though they've been helping the French for
    years past,
We may thus make them useful to England at last.

(1) An allusion to Lord Eld—n's lachrymose tendencies.
(2) "Of the taxes proposed by Mr. Vansittart, that prin-
cipally opposed in Parliament was the additional duty on
leather."—*Annual Register.*

C—stl—r—gh in our sieges might save some dis-
graces,
Being used to the *taking* and *keeping* of *places;*
And Volunteer C—nn—g, still ready for joining,
Might show off his talent for sly *undermining.*
Could the Household but spare us its glory and pride,
Old H—df—t at *horn-works* again might be tried,
And the Ch—f J—st—e make a *bold charge* at his
side :
While V—ns—tt—t could victual the troops *upon tick,*
And the doctor look after the baggage and sick.

Nay, I do not see why the great R—g—t himself
Should, in times such as these, stay at home on the
shelf :
Though through narrow defiles he 's not fitted to pass,
Yet who could resist, if he bore down *en masse?*
And though oft, of an evening, perhaps he might prove,
Like our Spanish confederates, "unable to move,"(1)
Yet there 's *one* thing in war of advantage unbounded,
Which is, that he could not with ease be *surrounded.*

In my next I shall sing of their arms and equipment;
At present no more, but—good luck to the shipment!

———o**o———

HORACE, ODE I., LIB. III.

A FRAGMENT.

Odi profanum vulgus et arceo :
Favete linguis: carmina non prius
   Audita Musarum sacerdos
     Virginibus puerisque canto.
Regum timendorum in proprios greges,
Reges in ipsos imperium est Jovis.

1813.

I HATE thee, oh, **Mob,** as my Lady hates delf ;
To Sir Francis I 'll give up thy claps and thy hisses,
Leave old Magna Charta to shift for itself,
   And, like G—dw—n, write books for young
   masters and misses.
Oh ! it *is* not high rank that can make the heart merry,
   Even monarchs themselves are not free from
   mishap :

(1) The character given to the Spanish soldier, in Sir
John Murray's memorable despatch.
(2) The literal closeness of the version here cannot but
be admired. The Translator has added a long, erudite,
and flowery note upon *Roses,* of which I can merely give
a specimen at present. In the first place, he ransacks
the *Rosarium Politicum* of the Persian poet Sadi, with the
hope of finding some *Political* Roses, to match the gentle-
man in the text—but in vain : he then tells us that Cicero
accused Verres of reposing upon a cushion "Melitensi
rosâ fartum," which, from the odd mixture of words, he
supposes to be a kind of *Irish* Bed of Roses, like Lord
Castlereagh's. The learned Clerk next favours us with

Though the Lords of Westphalia must quake before
   Jerry,
Poor Jerry himself has to quake before Nap.
   *   *   *   *   *

———o**o———

HORACE, ODE XXXVIII., LIB. I.

A FRAGMENT.

Persicos odi, puer, adparatus;
Displicent nexæ philyra coronæ;
Mitte sectari, Rosa *quo locorum*
     Sera moretur.

TRANSLATED BY A TREASURY CLERK, WHILE WAITING
DINNER FOR THE RIGHT HON. G—RGE R—SE.

Boy, tell the Cook that I hate all nick-nackeries,
Fricassees, vol-au-vents, puffs, and gim-crackeries—
Six by the Horse-Guards!—old Georgy is late—
But come—lay the table-cloth—zounds ! do not wait,
Nor stop to inquire, while the dinner is staying,
At which of his places Old R—e is delaying ! (2)
   *   *   *   *   *

———o**o———

IMPROMPTU,

UPON BEING OBLIGED TO LEAVE A PLEASANT PARTY,
FROM THE WANT OF A PAIR OF BREECHES TO DRESS
FOR DINNER IN.

1810.

BETWEEN Adam and me the great difference is,
   Though a paradise each has been forced to resign,
That he never wore breeches till turn'd out of his,
   While, for want of my breeches, I 'm banish'd from
   mine.

———o**o———

LORD WELLINGTON AND THE MINISTERS.

So gently in peace Alcibiades smiled,
   While in battle he shone forth so terribly grand,
That the emblem they graved on his seal was a child,
   With a thunderbolt placed in its innocent hand.

Oh Wellington, long as such Ministers wield
   Your magnificent arm, the same emblem will do;
For while *they* 're in the Council and *you* in the Field,
   We 've the *babies* in *them,* and the *thunder* in *you !*

some remarks upon a well-known punning epitaph on
fair Rosamond, and expresses a most loyal hope, that, if
"Rosa munda" mean "a Rose with clean hands," it may
be found applicable to the Right Honourable Rose in
question. He then dwells at some length upon the "Rosa
aurea," which, though descriptive, in one sense, of the
old Treasury Statesman, yet, as being consecrated and
worn by the Pope, must, of course, not be brought into
the same atmosphere with him. Lastly, in reference to
the words "*old* Rose," he winds up with the pathetic la-
mentation of the Poet "consenuisse Rosas." The whole
note indeed shows a knowledge of Roses that is quite
edifying.

———o⊗€o———

IRISH MELODIES.

PREFACE.

The recollections connected, in my mind, with that early period of my life, when I first thought of interpreting in verse the touching language of my country's music, tempt me to advert to those long past days; and, even at the risk of being thought to indulge overmuch in what Colley Cibber calls "the great pleasure of writing about one's self all day," to notice briefly some of those impressions and influences under which the attempt to adapt words to our ancient Melodies was for some time meditated by me, and at last undertaken.

There can be no doubt that to the zeal and industry of Mr. Bunting his country is indebted for the preservation of her old national airs. During the prevalence of the Penal Code, the music of Ireland was made to share in the fate of its people. Both were alike shut out from the pale of civilised life; and seldom any where but in the huts of the proscribed race could the sweet voice of the songs of other days be heard. Even of that class, the itinerant harpers, among whom for a long period our ancient music had been kept alive, there remained but few to continue the precious tradition; and a great music-meeting held at Belfast in the year 1792, at which the two or three still remaining of the old race of wandering harpers assisted, exhibited the last public effort made by the lovers of Irish music to preserve to their country the only grace or ornament left to her, out of the wreck of all her liberties and hopes. Thus what the fierce legislature of the Pale had endeavoured vainly through so many centuries to effect, —the utter extinction of Ireland's Minstrelsy,—the deadly pressure of the Penal Laws had nearly, at the close of the eighteenth century, accomplished; and, but for the zeal and intelligent research of Mr. Bunting, at that crisis, the greater part of our musical treasures would probably have been lost to the world. It was in the year 1796 that this gentleman published his first volume; and the national spirit and hope then wakened in Ireland, by the rapid spread of the democratic principle throughout Europe, could not but insure a most cordial reception for such a work;—flattering as it was to the fond dreams of Erin's early days, and containing in itself, indeed, remarkable testimony to the truth of her claims to an early date of civilisation.

It was in the year 1797 that, through the medium of Mr. Bunting's book, I was first made acquainted with the beauties of our native music. A young friend of our family, Edward Hudson, the nephew of an eminent dentist of that name, who played with much taste and feeling on the flute, and, unluckily for himself, was but too deeply warmed with the patriotic ardour then kindling around him, was the first who made known to me this rich mine of our country's melodies;—a mine, from the working of which my humble labours as a poet have since derived their sole lustre and value. About the same period I formed an acquaintance, which soon grew into intimacy, with young Robert Emmet. He was my senior, I think, by one class, in the university; for when, in the first year of my course, I became a member of the Debating Society,—a sort of nursery to the authorised Historical Society—I found him in full reputation, not only for his learning and eloquence, but also for the blamelessness of his life, and the grave suavity of his manners.

Of the political tone of this minor school of oratory, which was held weekly at the rooms of different resident members, some notion may be formed from the nature of the questions proposed for discussion, —one of which, I recollect, was, "Whether an Aristocracy or a Democracy is most favourable to the advancement of science and literature?" while another, bearing even more pointedly on the relative position of the government and the people, at this crisis, was thus significantly propounded:—"Whether a soldier was bound, on all occasions, to obey the orders of his commanding officer?" On the former of these questions the effect of Emmet's eloquence upon his young auditors was, I recollect, most striking. The prohibition against touching upon modern politics, which it was subsequently found necessary to enforce, had not yet been introduced; and Emmet, who took of course ardently the side of Democracy in the debate, after a brief review of the republics of antiquity, showing how much they had all done for the advancement of science and the arts, proceeded, lastly, to the grand and perilous example, then passing before all eyes, the young Republic of France. Referring to the circumstance told of Cæsar, that, in swimming across the Rubicon, he contrived to carry with him his Commentaries and his sword, the young orator said, "Thus France wades through a sea of storm and blood; but while, in one hand, she wields the sword against her aggressors, with the other she upholds the glories of science and literature unsullied by the ensanguined tide through which she struggles." In another of his remarkable speeches, I remember his saying, "When a people, advancing rapidly in knowledge and power, perceive at last how far their government is lagging behind them, what then, I ask, is to be done in such a case? What, but to pull the government up to the people?"

In a few months after, both Emmet and myself were admitted members of the greater and recognised institution, called the Historical Society; and, even here, the political feeling so rife abroad contrived to mix up its restless spirit with all our debates and proceedings, notwithstanding the constant watchfulness of the college authorities, as well as of a strong party within the Society itself, devoted adherents to the policy of the government, and taking invariably part with the Provost and Fellows in all their restrictive and inquisitorial measures. The most distinguished and eloquent of these supporters of power were a young man named Sargent, of whose fate in after days I know nothing, and Jebb, the late Bishop of Limerick, who was then, as he continued to be through life, much respected for his private worth and learning.

Of the popular side, in the Society, the chief champion and ornament was Robert Emmet; and though every care was taken to exclude from the subjects of debate all questions verging towards the politics of the day, it was always easy enough, by a side-wind of digression or allusion, to bring Ireland and the prospects then opening upon her within the scope of the orator's view. So exciting and powerful, in this respect, were Emmet's speeches, and so little were even the most eloquent of the adverse party able to cope with his powers, that it was at length thought advisable, by the higher authorities, to send among us a man of more advanced standing, as well as belonging to a former race of renowned speakers, in that Society, in order that he might answer the speeches of Emmet, and endeavour to obviate the mischievous impression they were thought to produce. The name of this mature champion of the higher powers it is not necessary here to record; but the object of his mission among us was in some respect gained; as it was in replying to a long oration of his, one night, that Emmet, much to the mortification of us who gloried in him as our leader, became suddenly embarrassed in the middle of his speech, and, to use the parliamentary phrase, broke down. Whether from a momentary confusion in the thread of his argument, or possibly from diffidence in encountering an adversary so much his senior,—for Emmet was as modest as he was high-minded and brave,—he began, in the full career of his eloquence, to hesitate and repeat his words, and then, after an effort or two to recover himself, sate down.

It fell to my own lot to be engaged, about the same time, in a brisk struggle with the dominant party in the Society, in consequence of a burlesque poem which I gave in, as candidate for the Literary Medal, entitled *An Ode upon Nothing, with Notes, by Trismegistus Rustifustius, D. D.*, etc., etc. For this squib against the great Dons of learning, the medal was voted to me by a triumphant majority. But a motion was made in the following week to rescind this vote; and a fierce contest between the two parties ensued, which I at last put an end to by voluntarily withdrawing my composition from the Society's Book.

I have already adverted to the period when Mr. Bunting's valuable volume first became known to me. There elapsed no very long time before I was myself the happy proprietor of a copy of the work, and, though never regularly instructed in music, could play over the airs with tolerable facility on the pianoforte. Robert Emmet used sometimes to sit by me, when I was thus engaged; and I remember one day his starting up as from a reverie, when I had just finished playing that spirited tune called the *Red Fox*, (1) and exclaiming, "Oh that I were at the head of twenty thousand men, marching to that air!"

How little did I then think that in one of the most touching of the sweet airs I used to play to him, his own dying words would find an interpreter so worthy of their sad but proud feeling; (2) or that another of those mournful strains, (3) would long be associated, in the hearts of his countrymen, with the memory of her (4) who shared with Ireland his last blessing and prayer.

Though fully alive, of course, to the feelings which such music could not but inspire, I had not yet undertaken the task of adapting words to any of the airs; and it was, I am ashamed to say, in dull and turgid prose, that I made my first appearance in print as a champion of the popular cause. Towards the latter end of the year 1797, the celebrated newspaper called *The Press* was set up by Arthur O'Connor, Thomas Addis Emmet, and other chiefs of the United Irish conspiracy, with the view of preparing and ripening the public mind for the great crisis then fast approaching. This memorable journal, according to the impression I at present retain of it, was far more distinguished for earnestness of purpose and intrepidity, than for any great display of literary talent;—the bold letters written by Emmet (the elder), under the signature of "Montanus," being the only compositions I can now call to mind, as entitled to praise for their literary merit. It required, however, but a small sprinkling of talent to make bold writing, at that time, palatable; and, from the experience of my own home, I can answer for the avidity with which every line of this daring journal was devoured. It used to come out, I think, twice a-week, and, on the evening of publication, I always read it aloud to our small circle after supper.

It may easily be conceived that, what with my ardour for the national cause, and a growing consciousness of some little turn for authorship, I was naturally eager to become a contributor to those patriotic and popular columns. But the constant anxiety about me which I knew my own family felt, —a feeling more wakeful far than even their zeal in the public cause,—withheld me from hazarding any step that might cause them alarm. I had ventured,

(1) "Let Erin remember the days of old."
(2) "Oh, breathe not his name."

(3) "She is far from the land where her young hero sleeps."   (4) Miss Curran.

indeed, one evening, to pop privately into the letter-box of *The Press* a short Fragment in imitation of Ossian. But this, though inserted, passed off quietly; and nobody was, in *any* sense of the phrase, the wiser for it. I was soon tempted, however, to try a more daring flight. Without communicating my secret to any one but Edward Hudson, I addressed a long Letter, in prose, to the * * * * * of * * * *, in which a profusion of bad flowers of rhetoric was enwreathed plentifully with that weed which Shakspeare calls "the cockle of rebellion," and, in the same manner as before, committed it tremblingly to the chances of the letter-box. I hardly expected my prose would be honoured with insertion, when, lo, on the next evening of publication, when, seated as usual in my little corner by the fire, I unfolded the paper for the purpose of reading it to my select auditory, there was my own Letter staring me full in the face, being honoured with so conspicuous a place as to be one of the first articles my audience would expect to hear. Assuming an outward appearance of ease, while every nerve within me was trembling, I contrived to accomplish the reading of the Letter without raising in either of my auditors a suspicion that it was my own. I enjoyed the pleasure, too, of hearing it a good deal praised by them; and might have been tempted by this to acknowledge myself the author, had I not found that the language and sentiments of the article were considered by both to be "very bold."(1)

I was not destined, however, to remain long undetected. On the following day, Edward Hudson,(2) —the only one, as I have said, entrusted with my secret, called to pay us a morning visit, and had not been long in the room, conversing with my mother, when, looking significantly at me, he said, "Well, you saw——" Here he stopped; but the mother's eye had followed his, with the rapidity of lightning, to mine, and at once she perceived the whole truth. "That Letter was yours, then?" she asked of me eagerly; and, without hesitation, of course, I acknowledged the fact; when in the most earnest manner she entreated of me never again to have any connexion with that paper; and, as every wish of hers was to me law, I readily pledged the solemn promise she required.

Though well aware how easily a sneer may be raised at the simple details of this domestic scene,

I have yet ventured to put it on record, as affording an instance of the gentle and womanly watchfulness,—the Providence, as it may be called, of the little world of home,—by which, although placed almost in the very current of so headlong a movement, and living familiarly with some of the most daring of those who propelled it, I yet was guarded from any participation in their secret oaths, counsels, or plans, and thus escaped all share in that wild struggle to which so many far better men than myself fell victims.

In the mean while, this great conspiracy was hastening on, with fearful precipitancy, to its outbreak; and vague and shapeless as are now known to have been the views, even of those who were engaged practically in the plot, it is not any wonder that to the young and uninitiated like myself it should have opened prospects partaking far more of the wild dreams of poesy than of the plain and honest prose of real life. But a crisis was then fast approaching, when such self-delusions could no longer be indulged, and when the mystery which had hitherto hung over the plans of the conspirators was to be rent asunder by the stern hand of power.

Of the horrors that fore-ran and followed the frightful explosion of the year 1798, I have neither inclination nor, luckily, occasion to speak. But among these introductory scenes, which had somewhat prepared the public mind for such a catastrophe, there was one, of a painful description, which, as having been myself an actor in it, I may be allowed briefly to notice.

It was not many weeks, I think, before this crisis, that, owing to information gained by the college authorities of the rapid spread, among the students, not only of the principles but the organisation of the Irish Union,(3) a solemn Visitation was held by Lord Clare, the vice-chancellor of the University, with the view of inquiring into the extent of this branch of the plot, and dealing summarily with those engaged in it.

Imperious and harsh as then seemed the policy of thus setting up a sort of Inquisitorial tribunal, armed with the power of examining witnesses on oath, and in a place devoted to the instruction of youth, I cannot but confess that the facts which came out in the course of the evidence went far towards justifying even this arbitrary proceeding; and

(1) So thought higher authorities, among the extracts from *The Press* quoted by the Secret Committee of the House of Commons, to show how formidable had been the designs of the United Irishmen, there are two or three paragraphs cited from this redoubtable Letter.

(2) Of the depth and extent to which Hudson had involved himself in the conspiracy, none of our family had harboured the least notion; till, on the seizure of the thirteen Leinster delegates, at Oliver Bond's, in the month of March, 1798, we found, to our astonishment and sorrow, that he was one of the number.

To those unread in the painful history of this period, it is right to mention that almost all the leaders of the United Irish conspiracy were Protestants. Among those companions of my own alluded to in these pages, I scarcely remember a single Catholic.

(3) In the Report from the Secret Committee of the Irish House of Lords, this extension of the plot to the College is noticed as "a desperate project of the same faction to corrupt the youth of the country by introducing their organised system of treason into the University."

to the many who, like myself, were acquainted only with the general views of the Union leaders, without even knowing, even from conjecture, who those leaders were, or what their plans or objects, it was most startling to hear the disclosures which every succeeding witness brought forth. There were a few,—and among that number, poor Robert Emmet, John Brown, and the two * * * * * *'s, (1) whose total absence from the whole scene, as well as the dead silence that, day after day, followed the calling out of their names, proclaimed how deep had been their share in the unlawful proceedings inquired into by this tribunal.

But there was one young friend of mine, * * * * * * *, whose appearance among the suspected and examined as much surprised as it deeply and painfully interested me. He and Emmet had long been intimate and attached friends;—their congenial fondness for mathematical studies having been, I think, a far more binding sympathy between them than any arising out of their political opinions. From his being called up, however, on this day, when, as it appeared afterwards, all the most important evidence was brought forward, there could be little doubt that, in addition to his intimacy with Emmet, the college authorities must have possessed some information which led them to suspect him of being an accomplice in the conspiracy. In the course of his examination, some questions were put to him which he refused to answer,—most probably from their tendency to involve or inculpate others, and he was accordingly dismissed, with the melancholy certainty that his future prospects in life were blasted; it being already known that the punishment for such contumacy was not merely expulsion from the University, but exclusion from all the learned professions.

The proceedings, indeed, of this whole day had been such as to send me to my home in the evening with no very agreeable feelings or prospects. I had heard evidence given affecting even the lives of some of those friends whom I had long regarded with admiration as well as affection; and what was still worse than even their danger,—a danger ennobled, I thought, by the cause in which they suffered,—was the shameful spectacle exhibited by those who had appeared in evidence against them. Of these witnesses, the greater number had been themselves involved in the plot, and now came forward either as voluntary informers, or else were driven by the fear of the consequences of refusal to secure their own safety at the expense of companions and friends.

I well remember the gloom, so unusual, that hung over our family circle on that evening, as, talking

(1) One of these brothers has long been a general in the French army; having taken a part in all those great enterprises of Napoleon which have now become matter of history. Should these pages meet the eye of General * * * * * *, they will call to his mind the days we passed

together of the events of the day, we discussed the likelihood of my being among those who would be called up for examination on the morrow. The deliberate conclusion to which my dear honest advisers came, was that, overwhelming as the consequences were to all their plans and hopes for me, yet, if the questions leading to criminate others, which had been put to almost all examined on that day, and which poor * * * * * * * * alone had refused to answer, I must, in the same manner, and at all risks, return a similar refusal. I am not quite certain whether I received any intimation, on the following morning, that I was to be one of those examined in the course of the day; but I rather think some such notice had been conveyed to me;—and, at last, my awful turn came, and I stood in presence of the formidable tribunal. There sate, with severe look, the vice-chancellor, and, by his side, the memorable Doctor Duigenan,—memorable for his eternal pamphlets against the Catholics.

The oath was proffered to me. "I have an objection, my Lord," said I, "to taking this oath." "What is your objection?" he asked sternly. "I have no fears, my Lord, that any thing I might say would criminate myself, but it might tend to involve others, and I despise the character of the person who could be led, under any such circumstances, to inform against his associates." This was aimed at some of the revelations of the preceding day; and, as I learned afterwards, was so understood. "How old are you, Sir?" he then asked. "Between seventeen and eighteen, my Lord." He then turned to his assessor, Duigenan, and exchanged a few words with him, in an under tone of voice. "We cannot," he resumed, again addressing me, "suffer any one to remain in our University, who refuses to take this oath." "I shall, then, my Lord," I replied, "take the oath,—still reserving to myself the power of refusing to answer any such questions as I have just described." "We do not sit here to argue with you, Sir," he rejoined sharply; upon which I took the oath, and seated myself in the witnesses' chair.

The following are the questions and answers that then ensued. After adverting to the proved existence of United Irish Societies in the University, he asked, " Have you ever belonged to any of these societies?" "No, my Lord." "Have you ever known of any of the proceedings that took place in them?" "No, my Lord." "Did you ever hear of a proposal at any of their meetings, for the purchase of arms and ammunition?" "Never, my Lord." "Did you ever hear a proposition made, in one of these societies, with respect to the expediency of assassination?" "Oh no, my Lord." He then

together in Normandy, a few summers since;—more especially our excursion to Bayeux, when, as we talked on the way of old college times and friends, all the eventful and stormy scenes he had passed through since seemed forgotten.

turned again to Duigenan, and, after a few words with him, said to me:—" When such are the answers you are able to give, (1) pray what was the cause of your great repugnance to taking the oath?" "I have already told your Lordship my chief reason; in addition to which, it was the first oath I ever took, and the hesitation was, I think, natural."(2)

I was now dismissed without any further questioning; and, thus, having had been this short operation, was amply repaid for it by the kind zeal with which my young friends and companions flocked to congratulate me; not so much, I was inclined to hope, on my acquittal by the court, as on the manner in which I had acquitted *myself*. Of my reception, on returning home, after the fears entertained of so very different a result, I will not attempt any description;—it was all that *such* a home alone could furnish.

I have been induced thus to continue, down to the very verge of the warning outbreak of 1798, the slight sketch of my early days which I ventured to commence in the Preface to the *Odes of Anacreon:* nor could I have furnished the *Irish Melodies* with any more pregnant illustration, as it was in those times, and among the events then stirring, that the feeling which afterwards found a voice in my country's music, was born and nurtured.

I shall now string together such detached notices and memoranda respecting this work, as I think may be likely to interest my readers.

Of the few songs written with a concealed political feeling,—such as " When he who adores thee," and one or two more,—the most successful, in its day, was " When first I met thee warm and young," which alluded, in its hidden sense, to the Prince Regent's desertion of his political friends. It was little less, I own, than profanation to disturb the sentiment of so beautiful an air by any connexion with such a subject. The great success of this song, soon after I wrote it, among a large party staying

(1) There had been two questions put to all those examined on the first day,—" Were you ever asked to join any of these societies?"—and " By whom were you asked?" —which I should have refused to answer, and must, of course, have declined the consequences.

(2) For the correctness of the above report of this short examination, I can pretty confidently answer. It may amuse, therefore, my readers,—as showing the manner in which biographers make the most of small facts,—to see an extract or two from another account of this affair, published not many years since by an old and zealous friend of our family. After stating with tolerable correctness one or two of my answers, the writer thus proceeds:—" Upon this, Lord Clare repeated the question, and young Moore made such an appeal, as caused his lordship to relax, austere and rigid as he was. The words I cannot exactly remember; the substance was as follows: —that he entered college to receive the education of a scholar and a gentleman; that he knew not how to compromise these characters by informing against his college companions; that his own speeches in the debating society

at Chatsworth, is thus alluded to in one of Lord Byron's letters to me:—" I have heard from London that you have left Chatsworth and all there full of ' entusymusy'...... and, in particular, that ' When first I met thee' has been quite overwhelming in its effect. I told you it was one of the best things you ever wrote, though that dog **** wanted you to omit part of it."

It has been sometimes supposed that " Oh, breathe not his name," was meant to allude to Lord Edward Fitzgerald: but this is a mistake; the song having been suggested by the well-known passage in Robert Emmet's dying speech, " Let no man write my epitaph . . . . . let my tomb remain uninscribed, till other times and other men shall learn to do justice to my memory."

The feeble attempt to commemorate the glory of our great Duke—"When History's Muse," etc.—is in so far remarkable, that it made up amply for its want of poetical spirit, by an outpouring, rarely granted to bards in these days, of the spirit of prophecy. It was in the year 1815 that the following lines first made their appearance :—

And still the last crown of thy toils is remaining,
 The grandest, the purest even *thou* hast yet known;
Though proud was thy task, other nations unchaining,
 Far prouder to heal the deep wounds of thy own.
At the foot of that throne, for whose weal thou hast stood,
Go, plead for the land that first cradled thy fame, etc.

About fourteen years after these lines were written, the Duke of Wellington recommended to the throne the great measure of Catholic Emancipation.

The fancy of the " Origin of the Irish Harp " was (as I have elsewhere acknowledged)(3) suggested by a drawing made under peculiarly painful circumstances, by the friend so often mentioned in this sketch, Edward Hudson.

In connexion with another of these matchless airs— one that defies all poetry to do it justice—I find the following singular and touching statement in an ar-

had been ill construed, when the worst that could be said of them was, if truth had been spoken, that they were patriotic . . . . that he was aware of the high-minded nobleman he had the honour of appealing to, and if his lordship could for a moment condescend to step from his high station and place himself in his situation, then say how he would act under such circumstances,—it would be his guidance."—*Herbert's Irish Varieties.* London, 1836.

(3) "When, in consequence of the compact entered into between government and the chief leaders of the conspiracy, the State Prisoners, before proceeding into exile, were allowed to see their friends, I paid a visit to Edward Hudson, in the jail of Kilmainham, where he had then lain immured for four or five months, hearing of friend after friend being led out to death, and expecting every week his own turn to come. I found that to amuse his solitude he had made a large drawing with charcoal on the wall of his prison, representing that fancied origin of the Irish Harp which, some years after, I adopted as the subject of one of the ' Melodies.'"—*Life and Death of Lord Edward Fitzgerald,* vol. i.

ticle of the *Quarterly Review.* Speaking of a young and promising poetess, Lucretia Davidson, who died very early from nervous excitement, the Reviewer says, "She was particularly sensitive to music. There was one song (it was Moore's Farewell to his Harp) to which she took a special fancy. She wished to hear it only at twilight,—thus (with that same perilous love of excitement which made her place the Æolian harp in the window when she was composing), seeking to increase the effect which the song produced upon a nervous system, already diseasedly susceptible; for it is said that whenever she heard this song, she became cold, pale, and almost fainting; yet it was her favourite of all songs, and gave occasion to those verses addressed in her fifteenth year to her sister."(1)

With the Melody entitled "Love, Valour, and Wit," an incident is connected, which awakened feelings in me of proud but sad pleasure, to think that my songs had reached the hearts of some of the descendants of those great Irish families, who found themselves forced, in the dark days of persecution, to seek in other lands a refuge from the shame and ruin of their own;—those, whose story I have thus associated with one of their country's most characteristic airs:—

Ye Blakes and O'Donnells, whose fathers resign'd
The green hills of their youth, among strangers to find
That repose which at home they had sigh'd for in vain.

From a foreign lady, of this ancient extraction,—whose names, could I venture to mention them, would lend to the incident an additional Irish charm,—I received, about two years since, through the hands of a gentleman to whom it had been entrusted, a large portfolio, adorned inside with a beautiful drawing, representing Love, Wit, and Valour, as described in the song. In the border that surrounds the drawing are introduced the favourite emblems of Erin, the harp, the shamrock, the mitred head of St. Patrick, together with scrolls containing each, inscribed in letters of gold, the name of some favourite melody of the fair artist.

This present was accompanied by the following letter from the lady herself; and her Irish race, I fear, is but too discernible in the generous indiscretion with which, in this instance, she allows praise so much to outstrip desert:—

"Monsieur,   "*Le* 25 *Août*, 1836.
"Si les poëtes n'étoient en quelque sorte une propriété intellectuelle dont chacun prend sa part à raison de la puissance qu'ils exercent, je ne saurois en vérité comment faire pour justifier mon courage!—car il en falloit beaucoup pour avoir osé consacrer mon pauvre talent d'amateur à vos délicieuses poësies, et plus encore pour en renvoyer le pâle reflet à son véritable auteur.

"J'espère toutefois que ma sympathie pour l'Irlande vous fera juger ma foible production avec cette heureuse partialité qui impose silence à la critique: car, si je n'ap-

(1) *Quarterly Review,* vol. xli., p. 294.

partiens pas à l'Ile Verte par ma naissance, ni mes relations, je puis dire que je m'y intéresse avec un cœur irlandais, et que j'ai conservé plus que le nom de mes pères. Cela seul me fait espérer que mes petits voyageurs ne subiront pas le triste noviciat des étrangers. Puissent-ils remplir leur mission sur le sol natal, en agissant conjointement et toujours pour la cause irlandaise, et amener enfin une ère nouvelle pour cette héroïque et malheureuse nation :—le moyen de vaincre de tels adversaires s'ils ne font qu'un?

"Vous dirai-je, Monsieur, les doux momentsque je dois à vos ouvrages? ce seroit répéter une fois de plus ce que vous entendez tous les jours et de tous les coins de la terre. Aussi j'ai garde de vous ravir un temps trop précieux par l'écho de ces vieilles vérités.

"Si jamais mon étoile me conduit en Irlande, je ne m'y croirai pas étrangère. Je sais que le passé y laisse de longs souvenirs, et que la conformité des désirs et des espérances rapproche en dépit de l'espace et du temps.

"Jusque là, recevez, je vous prie, l'assurance de ma parfaite considération, avec laquelle j'ai l'honneur d'être,
"Monsieur,
"Votre très humble servante,
"La Comtesse * * * * *"

Of the translations that have appeared of the Melodies in different languages, I shall here mention such as have come to my knowledge.

Latin.—"Cantus Hibernici," Nicholas Lee Torre, London, 1835.

Italian.—G. Flechia, Torino, 1836.—Adele Custi, Milano, 1836.

French.—Madame Belloc, Paris, 1823.—Loeve Veimars, Paris, 1829.

Russian.—Several detached Melodies, by the popular Russian poet Kozlof.

Polish.—Selections, in the same manner, by Niemcewich, Kosmian, and others.

I have now exhausted, not so much my own recollections, as the patience, I fear, of my readers on this subject. We are told of painters calling those last touches of the pencil which they give to some favourite picture the "ultima basia;" and with the same sort of affectionate feeling do I now take leave of the *Irish Melodies,*—the only work of my pen, as I very sincerely believe, whose fame (thanks to the sweet music in which it is embalmed) may boast a chance of prolonging its existence to a day much beyond our own.

DEDICATION.

TO THE MARCHIONESS DOWAGER OF DONEGAL.

It is now many years since, in a Letter prefixed to the Third Number of the *Irish Melodies,* I had the pleasure of inscribing the Poems of that work to your Ladyship, as to one whose character reflected honour on the country to which they relate, and whose friendship had long been the pride and happiness of their Author. With the same feelings of affection and respect, confirmed if not increased by the experience of every succeeding year, I now place those

Poems in their present new form under your protection, and am, With perfect sincerity,
Your Ladyship's ever attached friend,
THOMAS MOORE.

ORIGINAL PREFACE.

THOUGH an edition of the Poetry of the *Irish Melodies*, separate from the Music, has long been called for, yet, having, for many reasons, a strong objection to this sort of divorce, I should with difficulty have consented to a disunion of the words from the airs, had it depended solely upon me to keep them quietly and indissolubly together. But, besides the various shapes in which these, as well as my other lyrical writings, have been published throughout America, they are included, of course, in all the editions of my works printed on the Continent, and have also appeared, in a volume full of typographical errors, in Dublin. I have therefore readily acceded to the wish expressed by the Proprietor of the *Irish Melodies*, for a revised and complete edition of the poetry of the Work, though well aware that my verses must lose even more than the "*animæ dimidium*" in being detached from the beautiful airs to which it was their good fortune to be associated.

The Advertisements which were prefixed to the different numbers, the Prefatory Letter upon Music, etc., will be found in an Appendix.

IRISH MELODIES.

GO WHERE GLORY WAITS THEE.
AIR—*Maid of the Valley.*

Go where glory waits thee,
But while fame elates thee,
Oh! still remember me.
When the praise thou meetest
To thine ear is sweetest,
Oh! then remember me.
Other arms may press thee,
Dearer friends caress thee,
All the joys that bless thee,
Sweeter far may be;
But when friends are nearest,
And when joys are dearest,
Oh! then remember me!

When, at eve, thou rovest
By the star thou lovest,
Oh! then remember me.

(1) Brien Boromhe, the great monarch of Ireland, who was killed at the battle of Clontarf, in the beginning of the 11th century, after having defeated the Danes in twenty-five engagements.
2 Munster. (3) The palace of Brien.
(4) This alludes to an interesting circumstance related of the Dalgais, the favourite troops of Brien, when they were interrupted in their return from the battle of Clontarf, by Fitzpatrick, prince of Ossory. The wounded men

Think, when home returning,
Bright we've seen it burning,
Oh! thus remember me.
Oft as summer closes,
When thine eye reposes
On its lingering roses,
Once so loved by thee,
Think of her who wove them,
Her who made thee love them,
Oh! then remember me.

When, around thee dying,
Autumn leaves are lying,
Oh! then remember me.
And, at night, when gazing
On the gay hearth blazing,
Oh! still remember me.
Then should music, stealing
All the soul of feeling,
To thy heart appealing,
Draw one tear from thee;
Then let memory bring thee
Strains I used to sing thee,—
Oh! then remember me.

WAR SONG.
REMEMBER THE GLORIES OF BRIEN THE BRAVE. (1)
AIR—*Molly Macalpin.*

REMEMBER the glories of Brien the brave,
Though the days of the hero are o'er;
Though lost to Mononia (2) and cold in the grave,
He returns to Kinkora (3) no more.
That star of the field, which so often hath pour'd
Its beam on the battle, is set;
But enough of its glory remains on each sword,
To light us to victory yet.

Mononia! when Nature embellish'd the tint
Of thy fields, and thy mountains so fair,
Did she ever intend that a tyrant should print
The footstep of slavery there?
No! Freedom, whose smile we shall never resign,
Go, tell our invaders, the Danes,
That 't is sweeter to bleed for an age at thy shrine,
Than to sleep but a moment in chains.

Forget not our wounded companions who stood (4)
In the day of distress by our side; [blood,
While the moss of the valley grew red with their
They stirr'd not, but conquer'd and died.

entreated that they might be allowed to fight with the rest.—"*Let stakes* (they said) *be stuck in the ground, and suffer each of us, tied to and supported by one of these stakes, to be placed in his rank by the side of a sound man.*" "Between seven and eight hundred wounded men (adds O'Halloran), pale, emaciated, and supported in this manner, appeared mixed with the foremost of the troops;—never was such another sight exhibited."—*History of Ireland*, book xii., chap. i.

That sun which now blesses our arms with his light,
  Saw them fall upon Ossory's plain ;—
Oh ! let him not blush, when he leaves us to-night,
  To find that they fell there in vain.

THE HARP THAT ONCE THROUGH TARA'S HALLS.

Air—*Gramachree.*

THE harp that once through Tara's halls
  The soul of music shed,
Now hangs as mute on Tara's walls,
  As if that soul were fled.—
So sleeps the pride of former days,
  So glory's thrill is o'er,
And hearts, that once beat high for praise,
  Now feel that pulse no more.

No more to chiefs and ladies bright
  The harp of Tara swells ;
The chord alone, that breaks at night,
  Its tale of ruin tells.
Thus Freedom now so seldom wakes,
  The only throb she gives,
Is when some heart indignant breaks,
  To show that still she lives.

OH ! BREATHE NOT HIS NAME.

Air—*The Brown Maid.*

OH ! breathe not his name, let it sleep in the shade,
Where cold and unhonour'd his relics are laid :
Sad, silent, and dark, be the tears that we shed,
As the night-dew that falls on the grass o'er his head.

But the night-dew that falls, though in silence it
    weeps,
Shall brighten with verdure the grave where he sleeps;
And the tear that we shed, though in secret it rolls,
Shall long keep his memory green in our souls.

WHEN HE, WHO ADORES THEE.

Air—*The Fox's Sleep.*

WHEN he, who adores thee, has left but the name
  Of his fault and his sorrows behind,
Oh ! say wilt thou weep, when they darken the fame
  Of a life that for thee was resign'd ?
Yes, weep, and however my foes may condemn,
  Thy tears shall efface their decree ;
For Heaven can witness, though guilty to them,
  I have been but too faithful to thee.

With thee were the dreams of my earliest love ;
  Every thought of my reason was thine ;
In my last humble prayer to the Spirit above,
  Thy name shall be mingled with mine.
Oh ! blest are the lovers and friends who shall live
  The days of thy glory to see ;
But the next dearest blessing that Heaven can give
  Is the pride of thus dying for thee.

ERIN ! THE TEAR AND THE SMILE IN THINE EYES.

Air—*Aileen Aroon.*

ERIN ! the tear and the smile in thine eyes
Blend like the rainbow that hangs in thy skies !
  Shining through sorrow's stream,
  Saddening through pleasure's beam,
  Thy suns with doubtful gleam,
    Weep while they rise.

Erin, thy silent tear never shall cease,
Erin, thy languid smile ne'er shall increase,
  Till, like the rainbow's light,
  Thy various tints unite,
  And form in heaven's sight
    One arch of peace !

FLY NOT YET.

Air—*Planxty Kelly.*

FLY not yet, 'tis just the hour,
  When pleasure, like the midnight flower
That scorns the eye of vulgar light,
Begins to bloom for sons of night,
    And maids who love the moon.
'T was but to bless these hours of shade
That beauty and the moon were made ;
'T is then their soft attractions glowing
Set the tides and goblets flowing.
    Oh ! stay,—Oh ! stay,—
Joy so seldom weaves a chain
Like this to-night, that oh, 'tis pain
    To break its links so soon.

Fly not yet, the fount that play'd
In times of old through Ammon's shade, (1)
Though icy cold by day it ran,
Yet still, like souls of mirth, began
    To burn when night was near.
And thus, should woman's heart and looks
At noon be cold as winter brooks,
Nor kindle till the night, returning,
Brings their genial hour for burning.
    Oh ! stay,—Oh ! stay,—
When did morning ever break,
And find such beaming eyes awake
    As those that sparkle here ?

OH ! THINK NOT MY SPIRITS ARE ALWAYS AS LIGHT.

Air—*John O'Reilly the Active.*

OH ! think not my spirits are always as light,
  And as free from a pang as they seem to you now,
Nor expect that the heart-beaming smile of to-night
  Will return with to-morrow to brighten my brow.

(1) Solis Fons, near the Temple of Ammon.

No :—life is a waste of wearisome hours,
  Which seldom the rose of enjoyment adorns ;
And the heart that is soonest awake to the flowers,
  Is always the first to be touch'd by the thorns.
But send round the bowl, and be happy awhile—
  May we never meet worse, in our pilgrimage
    here,
Than the tear that enjoyment may gild with a smile,
  And the smile that compassion can turn to a tear.

The thread of our life would be dark, Heaven knows
  If it were not with friendship and love intertwined ;
And I care not how soon I may sink to repose,
  When these blessings shall cease to be dear to my
    mind.
But they who have loved the fondest, the purest,
  Too often have wept o'er the dream they believed ;
And the heart that has slumber'd in friendship se-
  curest
Is happy indeed if 't was never deceived.
But send round the bowl ; while a relic of truth
  Is in man or in woman, this prayer shall be mine,—
That the sunshine of love may illumine our youth,
  And the moonlight of friendship console our
    decline.

—◦∗∘—

THOUGH THE LAST GLIMPSE OF ERIN WITH SORROW I SEE.

Air—*Coulin.*

Though the last glimpse of Erin with sorrow I see,
Yet wherever thou art shall seem Erin to me ;
In exile thy bosom shall still be my home,
And thine eyes make my climate wherever we roam.

To the gloom of some desert or cold rocky shore,
Where the eye of the stranger can haunt us no more,
I will fly with my Coulin, and think the rough wind
Less rude than the foes we leave frowning behind.

And I 'll gaze on thy gold hair as graceful it wreathes,
And hang o'er thy soft harp, as wildly it breathes ;
Nor dread that the cold-hearted Saxon will tear
One chord from that harp, or one lock from that
  hair.(1)

(1) "In the twenty-eighth year of the reign of Henry VIII.
an Act was made respecting the habits, and dress in ge-
neral, of the Irish, whereby all persons were restrained
from being shorn or shaven above the ears, or from
wearing Glibbes, or *Coulins* (long locks), on their heads,
or hair on their upper lip, called Crommeal. On this
occasion a song was written by one of our bards, in which
an Irish virgin is made to give the preference to her dear
Coulin (or the youth with the flowing locks) to all strangers
(by which the English were meant), or those who wore
their habits. Of this song, the air alone has reached us,
and is universally admired."—*Walker's Historical Me-
moirs of Irish Bards.* p. 134. About this period, harsh
measures were taken against the Irish Minstrels.

RICH AND RARE WERE THE GEMS SHE WORE. (2)

Air—*The Summer is coming.*

Rich and rare were the gems she wore,
And a bright gold ring on her wand she bore ;
But oh ! her beauty was far beyond
Her sparkling gems, or snow-white wand.

"Lady ! dost thou not fear to stray,
So lone and lovely through this bleak way ?
Are Erin's sons so good or so cold,
As not be tempted by woman or gold ? "

" Sir Knight ! I feel not the least alarm,
No son of Erin will offer me harm :—
For though they love woman and golden store,
Sir Knight ! they love honour and virtue more ! "

On she went, and her maiden smile
In safety lighted her round the green isle ;
And blest for ever is she who relied
Upon Erin's honour and Erin's pride.

—◦∗∘—

AS A BEAM O'ER THE FACE OF THE WATERS MAY GLOW.

Air—*The Young Man's Dream.*

As a beam o'er the face of the waters may glow
While the tide runs in darkness and coldness below,
So the cheek may be tinged with a warm sunny
  smile,
Though the cold heart to ruin runs darkly the while.

One fatal remembrance, one sorrow that throws
Its bleak shade alike o'er our joys and our woes,
To which life nothing darker or brighter can bring,
For which joy has no balm and affliction no sting—

Oh ! this thought in the midst of enjoyment will stay,
Like a dead, leafless branch in the summer's bright
  ray ;
The beams of the warm sun play round it in vain ;
It may smile in his light, but it blooms not again.

(2) This ballad is founded upon the following anecdote :
—" The people were inspired with such a spirit of honour,
virtue, and religion, by the great example of Brien, and
by his excellent administration, that, as a proof of it, we
are informed that a young lady of great beauty, adorned
with jewels and a costly dress, undertook a journey alone,
from one end of the kingdom to the other, with a wand
only in her hand, at the top of which was a ring of ex-
ceeding great value ; and such an impression had the laws
and government of this Monarch made on the minds of
all the people, that no attempt was made upon her honour,
nor was she robbed of her clothes or jewels."—*Warner's
History of Ireland,* vol. i., book x.

THE MEETING OF THE WATERS. (1)
Air—*The Old Head of Denis.*

THERE is not in the wide world a valley so sweet
As that vale in whose bosom the bright waters
    meet; (2)
Oh! the last rays of feeling and life must depart,
Ere the bloom of that valley shall fade from my heart.

Yet it *was* not that nature had shed o'er the scene
    Her purest of crystal and brightest of green;
'T was *not* her soft magic of streamlet or hill,
Oh! no,—it was something more exquisite still.

'T was that friends, the beloved of my bosom, were
    near,   [dear,
Who made every dear scene of enchantment more
And who felt how the best charms of nature improve,
When we see them reflected from looks that we love.

Sweet vale of Avoca! how calm could I rest
In thy bosom of shade, with the friends I love best,
Where the storms that we feel in this cold world
    should cease,
And our hearts, like thy waters, be mingled in peace.

—◦❈◦—

HOW DEAR TO ME THE HOUR.
Air—*The Twisting of the Rope.*

How dear to me the hour when daylight dies,
    And sunbeams melt along the silent sea,
For then sweet dreams of other days arise,
    And memory breathes her vesper sigh to thee.

And, as I watch the line of light, that plays
    Along the smooth wave toward the burning west,
I long to tread that golden path of rays,
    And think 't would lead to some bright isle of rest.

—◦❈◦—

TAKE BACK THE VIRGIN PAGE.
WRITTEN ON RETURNING A BLANK BOOK.
Air—*Dermott.*

TAKE back the virgin page,
    White and unwritten still;
Some hand, more calm and sage,
    The leaf must fill.
Thoughts come, as pure as light,
    Pure as even *you* require;
But, oh! each word I write
    Love turns to fire.

Yet let me keep the book:
    Oft shall my heart renew,
When on its leaves I look,
    Dear thoughts of you.
Like you, 't is fair and bright;
    Like you, too bright and fair
To let wild passion write
    One wrong wish there.

Haply, when from those eyes
    Far, far away I roam,
Should calmer thoughts arise
    Towards you and home;
Fancy may trace some line,
    Worthy those eyes to meet,
Thoughts that not burn, but shine,
    Pure, calm, and sweet.

And as, o'er ocean far,
    Seamen their records keep,
Led by some hidden star
    Through the cold deep;
So may the words I write
    Tell through what storms I stray—
You still the unseen light,
    Guiding my way.

—◦❈◦—

ST. SENANUS AND THE LADY.
Air—*The Brown Thorn.*
ST. SENANUS.

" OH! haste, and leave this sacred Isle,
Unholy bark, ere morning smile;
For on thy deck, though dark it be,
    A female form I see;
And I have sworn this sainted sod
Shall ne'er by woman's feet be trod!"

THE LADY.

"Oh! Father, send not hence my bark
Through wintry winds and billows dark,
I come, with humble heart, to share
    Thy morn and evening prayer;
Nor mine the feet, oh! holy Saint,
The brightness of thy sod to taint."

The lady's prayer Senanus spurn'd;
The winds blew fresh, the bark return'd.
But legends hint, that had the maid
    Till morning's light delay'd,
And given the saint one rosy smile,
She ne'er had left his lonely isle.

---

(1) "The Meeting of the Waters" forms a part of that beautiful scenery which lies between Rathdrum and Arklow, in the county of Wicklow, and these lines were suggested by a visit to this romantic spot, in the summer of the year 1807.

(2) The rivers Avon and Avoca.

(3) In a metrical life of St. Senanus, taken from an old Kilkenny MS. and which may be found among the *Acta Sanctorum Hiberniæ*, we are told of his flight to the island of Scattery, and his resolution not to admit any woman of the party; he refused to receive even a sister

saint, St. Cannera, whom an angel had taken to the island for the express purpose of introducing her to him. The following was the ungracious answer of Senanus, according to his poetical biographer:—

    Cui Præsul, quid fœminis
    Commune est cum monachis?
    Nec te nec ullam aliam
    Admittemus in insulam.

        See the *Acta Sanct. Hib.*, page 610.

According to Dr. Ledwich, St. Senanus was no less a personage than the river Shannon; but O'Connor, and other antiquarians, deny this metamorphosis indignantly.

THE LEGACY.

Air—*Unknown.*

WHEN in death I shall calmly recline,
O bear my heart to my mistress dear,
Tell her it lived upon smiles and wine
Of the brightest hue, while it linger'd here.
Bid her not shed one tear of sorrow
To sully a heart so brilliant and light;
But balmy drops of the red grape borrow,
To bathe the relic from morn till night.

When the light of my song is o'er,
Then take my harp to your ancient hall;
Hang it up at that friendly door,
Where weary travellers love to call. (1)
Then if some bard, who roams forsaken,
Revive its soft note in passing along,
Oh! let one thought of its master waken
Your warmest smile for the child of song.

Keep this cup, which is now o'erflowing,
To grace your revel, when I'm at rest;
Never, oh! never its balm bestowing
On lips that beauty hath seldom blest.
But when some warm devoted lover
To her he adores shall bathe its brim,
Then, then my spirit around shall hover,
And hallow each drop that foams for him.

HOW OFT HAS THE BENSHEE CRIED.

Air—*The Dear Black Maid.*

How oft has the Benshee cried,
How oft has death untied
Bright links that Glory wove,
Sweet bonds entwined by Love!
Peace to each manly soul that sleepeth!
Rest to each faithful eye that weepeth;
Long may the fair and brave,
Sigh o'er the hero's grave.

We're fallen upon gloomy days! (2)
Star after star decays.
Every bright name, that shed
Light o'er the land, is fled.
Dark falls the tear of him who mourneth
Lost joy, or hope that ne'er returneth:
But brightly flows the tear,
Wept o'er a hero's bier.

Quench'd are our beacon lights—
Thou, of the Hundred Fights! (3)

(1) In every house was one or two harps, free to all travellers, who were the more caressed, the more they excelled in music.—*O'Halloran.*

(2) I have endeavoured here, without losing that Irish character which it is my object to preserve throughout the *Irish Melodies,* to allude to the sad and ominous fatality, by which England has been deprived of so many great and good men, at a moment when she most requires all the aids of talent and integrity.

Thou, on whose burning tongue
Truth, peace, and freedom hung!(4)
Both mute,—but long as valour shineth,
Or mercy's soul at war repineth,
So long shall Erin's pride
Tell how they lived and died.

WE MAY ROAM THROUGH THIS WORLD.

Air—*Garyone.*

WE may roam through this world, like a child at a
feast,
Who but sips of a sweet, and then flies to the rest;
And, when pleasure begins to grow dull in the east,
We may order our wings and be off to the west:
But if hearts that feel, and eyes that smile,
Are the dearest gifts that heaven supplies,
We never need leave our own green isle,
For sensitive hearts, and for sun-bright eyes,
Then, remember, wherever your goblet is crown'd,
Through this world, whether eastward or westward you roam,
When a cup to the smile of dear woman goes round,
Oh! remember the smile which adorns her at home.

In England, the garden of Beauty is kept
By a dragon of prudery placed within call;
But so oft this unamiable dragon has slept,
That the garden's but carelessly watch'd after all.
Oh! they want the wild sweet-briery fence
Which round the flowers of Erin dwells;
Which warns the touch, while winning the sense,
Nor charms us least when it most repels.
Then remember, wherever your goblet is crown'd,
Through this world, whether eastward or westward you roam,
When a cup to the smile of dear woman goes round,
Oh! remember the smile that adorns her at home.

In France, when the heart of a woman sets sail,
On the ocean of wedlock its fortune to try,
Love seldom goes far in a vessel so frail,
But just pilots her off, and then bids her good-bye.
While the daughters of Erin keep the boy,
Ever smiling beside his faithful oar,
Through billows of woe, and beams of joy,
The same as he look'd when he left the shore.
Then remember, wherever your goblet is crown'd,
Through this world, whether eastward or westward you roam,
When a cup to the smile of dear woman goes round,
Oh! remember the smile that adorns her at home.

(3) This designation, which has been before applied to Lord Nelson, is the title given to a celebrated Irish hero, in a Poem by O'Guive, the bard of O'Niel, which is quoted in the *Philosophical Survey of the South of Ireland,* page 433. "Con, of the hundred Fights, sleep in thy grass-grown tomb, and upbraid not our defeats with thy victories."

(4) Fox, "Romanorum ultimus."

EVELEEN'S BOWER.
Air—*Unknown.*

Oh! weep for the hour,
    When to Eveleen's bower
The Lord of the Valley with false vows came;
    The moon hid her light,
    From the heavens that night,
And wept behind her clouds o'er the maiden's shame.

The clouds pass'd soon
    From the chaste cold moon,
And heaven smiled again with her vestal flame;
    But none will see the day,
    When the clouds shall pass away,
Which that dark hour left upon Eveleen's fame.

The white snow lay
    On the narrow path-way,
When the Lord of the Valley cross'd over the moor;
    And many a deep print
    On the white snow's tint
Show'd the track of his footstep to Eveleen's door.

The next sun's ray
    Soon melted away
Every trace on the path where the false Lord came;
    But there's a light above,
    Which alone can remove
That stain upon the snow of fair Eveleen's fame.

LET ERIN REMEMBER THE DAYS OF OLD.
Air—*The Red Fox.*

Let Erin remember the days of old,
    Ere her faithless sons betray'd her;
When Malachi wore the collar of gold, (1)
    Which he won from her proud invader,
When her kings, with standard of green unfurl'd,
    Led the Red-Branch Knights to danger! (2)
Ere the emerald gem of the western world
    Was set in the crown of a stranger.

(1) "This brought on an encounter between Malachi (the Monarch of Ireland in the tenth century) and the Danes, in which Malachi defeated two of their champions, whom he encountered successively, hand to hand, taking a collar of gold from the neck of one, and carrying off the sword of the other, as trophies of his victory."—*Warner's History of Ireland*, vol. i., book ix.

(2) "Military orders of knights were very early established in Ireland : long before the birth of Christ we find an hereditary order of Chivalry in Ulster, called *Curaidhe na Craiobhe ruadh*, or the Knights of the Red Branch, from their chief seat in Emania, adjoining to the palace of the Ulster kings, called *Teagh na Craiobhe ruadh*, or the Academy of the Red Branch; and contiguous to which was a large hospital, founded for the sick knights and soldiers, called *Bronbhearg*, or the House of the Sorrowful Soldier."—*O'Halloran's Introduction, etc.*, part i., chap. 5.

(3) It was an old tradition, in the time of Giraldus, that Lough Neagh had been originally a fountain, by whose sudden overflowing the country was inundated, and a

On Lough Neagh's bank as the fisherman strays,
    When the clear cold eve's declining,
He sees the round towers of other days
    In the wave beneath him shining:
Thus shall memory often, in dreams sublime,
    Catch a glimpse of the days that are over;
Thus, sighing, look through the waves of time,
    For the long-faded glories they cover. (2)

THE SONG OF FIONNUALA. (4)
Air—*Arrah my dear Eveleen.*

Silent, oh Moyle, be the roar of thy water,
    Break not, ye breezes, your chain of repose,
While, murmuring mournfully, Lir's lonely daughter
    Tells to the night-star her tale of woes.
When shall the swan, her death-note singing,
    Sleep, with wings in darkness furl'd?
When will heaven, its sweet bell ringing,
    Call my spirit from this stormy world?

Sadly, oh Moyle, to thy winter-wave weeping,
    Fate bids me languish long ages away;
Yet still in her darkness doth Erin lie sleeping,
    Still doth the pure light its dawning delay.
When will that day-star, mildly springing,
    Warm our isle with peace and love?
When will heaven, its sweet bell ringing,
    Call my spirit to the fields above?

COME, SEND ROUND THE WINE.
Air—*We brought the Summer with us.*

Come, send round the wine, and leave points of belief
    To simpleton sages and reasoning fools;
This moment's a flower too fair and brief,
    To be wither'd and stain'd by the dust of the schools.
Your glass may be purple, and mine may be blue,
    But, while they are fill'd from the same bright bowl,
The fool who would quarrel for difference of hue,
    Deserves not the comfort they shed o'er the soul.

whole region, like the Atlantis of Plato, overwhelmed. He says that the fishermen, in clear weather, used to point out to strangers the tall ecclesiastical towers under the water. *Piscatores aquæ illius turres ecclesiasticas, quæ more patriæ arctæ sunt et altæ, necnon et rotundæ, sub undis manifeste sereno tempore conspiciunt, et extraneis transeuntibus, reique causas admirantibus, frequenter ostendunt.—Topogr. Hib.*, dist. 2., c. 9.

(4) To make this story intelligible in a song would require a much greater number of verses than any one is authorised to inflict upon an audience at once; the reader must therefore be content to learn, in a note, that Fionnuala, the daughter of Lir, was, by some supernatural power, transformed into a swan, and condemned to wander, for many hundred years, over certain lakes and rivers in Ireland, till the coming of Christianity, when the first sound of the mass-bell was to be the signal of her release.—I found this fanciful fiction among some manuscript translations from the Irish, which were begun under the direction of that enlightened friend of Ireland, the late Countess of Moira.

Shall I ask the brave soldier, who fights by my side
In the cause of mankind, if our creeds agree?
Shall I give up the friend I have valued and tried,
If he kneel not before the same altar with me?
From the heretic girl of my soul should I fly,
To seek somewhere else a more orthodox kiss?
No, perish the hearts, and the laws that try
Truth, valour, or love, by a standard like this!

SUBLIME WAS THE WARNING.
AIR—*The Black Joke.*

SUBLIME was the warning that Liberty spoke,
And grand was the moment when Spaniards awoke
Into life and revenge from the conqueror's chain.
Oh, Liberty! let not this spirit have rest,
Till it move, like a breeze, o'er the waves of the west—
Give the light of your look to each sorrowing spot,
Nor, oh, be the Shamrock of Erin forgot
While you add to your garland the Olive of Spain!

If the fame of our fathers, bequeathed with their rights,
Give to country its charm, and to home its delights;
If deceit be a wound, and suspicion a stain,
Then, ye men of Iberia, our cause is the same!
And oh! may his tomb want a tear and a name,
Who would ask for a nobler, a holier death,
Than to turn his last sigh into victory's breath,
For the Shamrock of Erin and Olive of Spain!

Ye Blakes and O'Donnels, whose fathers resign'd
The green hills of their youth, among strangers to find
That repose which, at home, they had sigh'd for in vain,
Join, join in our hope that the flame, which you light,
May be felt yet in Erin, as calm and as bright,
And forgive even Albion while blushing she draws,
Like a truant, her sword, in the long-slighted cause
Of the Shamrock of Erin and Olive of Spain!

God prosper the cause!—oh, it cannot but thrive,
While the pulse of one patriot heart is alive,
Its devotion to feel, and its rights to maintain,
Then, how sainted by sorrow its martyrs will die!
The finger of Glory shall point where they lie;
While, far from the footstep of coward or slave,
The young spirit of Freedom shall shelter their grave,
Beneath Shamrocks of Erin and Olives of Spain!

BELIEVE ME, IF ALL THOSE ENDEARING
YOUNG CHARMS.
AIR—*My Lodging is on the cold Ground.*

BELIEVE me, if all those endearing young charms,
Which I gaze on so fondly to-day,

Were to change by to-morrow, and fleet in my arms,
Like fairy-gifts fading away,
Thou wouldst still be adored, as this moment thou art,
Let thy loveliness fade as it will,
And around the dear ruin each wish of my heart,
Would entwine itself verdantly still.

It is not while beauty and youth are thine own,
And thy cheeks unprofaned by a tear,
That the fervour and faith of a soul can be known,
To which time will but make thee more dear:
No, the heart that has truly loved never forgets,
But as truly loves on to the close,
As the sun-flower turns on her god, when he sets,
The same look which she turn'd when he rose.

ERIN, OH ERIN.
AIR—*Thamama Halla.*

LIKE the bright lamp, that shone in Kildare's holy
fane, (1)
And burn'd through long ages of darkness and storm,
Is the heart that sorrows have frown'd on in vain,
Whose spirit outlives them, unfading and warm.
Erin, oh Erin, thus bright through the tears
Of a long night of bondage, thy spirit appears.

The nations have fallen, and thou still art young,
Thy sun is but rising, when others are set; [hung,
And though slavery's cloud o'er thy morning hath
The full noon of freedom shall beam round thee yet.
Erin, oh Erin, though long in the shade,
Thy star will shine out when the proudest shall fade.

Unchill'd by the rain, and unwaked by the wind,
The lily lies sleeping through winter's cold hour,
Till Spring's light touch her fetters unbind,
And daylight and liberty bless the young flower. (2)
Thus Erin, oh Erin, *thy* winter is past,
And the hope that lived through it shall blossom at last.

DRINK TO HER.
AIR—*Heigh ho! my Jackey.*

DRINK to her who long
Hath waked the poet's sigh,
The girl who gave to song
What gold could never buy.
Oh! woman's heart was made
For minstrel hands alone;
By other fingers play'd,
It yields not half the tone.
Then here's to her who long
Hath waked the poet's sigh,
The girl who gave to song
What gold could never buy.

(1) The inextinguishable fire of St. Bridget, at Kildare, which Giraldus mentions:—"Apud Kildariam occurrit Ignis Sanctæ Brigidæ, quem inextinguibilem vocant; non quod extingui non possit, sed quod tam solicite moniales et sanctæ mulieres ignem, suppetente materia, fovent et

nutriunt, ut a tempore virginis per tot annorum curricula semper mansit inextinctus."—*Girald. Camb. de Mirabil. Hibern.*, dist. 2, c. 34.
(2) Mrs. H. Tighe, in her exquisite lines on the lily, has applied this image to a still more important object.

26

At Beauty's door of glass,
   When Wealth and Wit once stood,
They ask'd her, "*which* might pass?"
   She answer'd, "he who could."
With golden key Wealth thought
   To pass—but 't would not do :
While Wit a diamond brought,
   Which cut his bright way through.
So here's to her who long
   Hath waked the poet's sigh,
The girl who gave to song
   What gold could never buy.

The love that seeks a home
   Where wealth or grandeur shines,
Is like the gloomy gnome,
   That dwells in dark gold mines.
But oh ! the poet's love
   Can boast a brighter sphere ;
Its native home 's above,
   Though woman keeps it here.
Then drink to her who long
   Hath waked the poet's sigh,
The girl who gave to song
   What gold could never buy,

—o⧫o—

OH! BLAME NOT THE BARD. (1)

Air—*Kitty Tyrrel.*

Oh ! blame not the bard, if he fly to the bowers
  Where Pleasure lies, carelessly smiling at Fame ;
He was born for much more, and in happier hours
  His soul might have burn'd with a holier flame.
The string, that now languishes loose o'er the lyre,
  Might have bent a proud bow to the warrior's
         dart ; (2)   [sire,
And the lip, which now breathes but the song of de-
  Might have pour'd the full tide of a patriot's heart.

But alas for his country !—her pride is gone by,
  And that spirit is broken which never would bend ;
O'er the ruin her children in secret must sigh,
  For 'tis treason to love her, and death to defend.
Unprized are her sons, till they've learn'd to betray ;
  Undistinguish'd they live, if they shame not their
    sires ;

And the torch, that would light them through dig-
  nity's way,   [expires.
Must be caught from the pile where their country

Then blame not the bard, if in pleasure's soft dream
  He should try to forget what he never can heal :
Oh ! give but a hope—let a vista but gleam
  Through the gloom of his country, and mark how
    he 'll feel !
That instant, his heart at her shrine would lay down
  Every passion it nursed, every bliss it adored ;
While the myrtle, now idly entwined with his crown,
  Like the wreath of Harmodius, should cover his
      [sword. (3)

But though glory be gone, and though hope fade away,
  Thy name, loved Erin, shall live in his songs ;
Not even in the hour when his heart is most gay
  Will he lose the remembrance of thee and thy
    wrongs.
The stranger shall hear thy lament on his plains ;
  The sigh of thy harp shall be sent o'er the deep,
Till thy masters themselves, as they rivet thy chains,
  Shall pause at the song of their captive, and weep !

—o⧫o—

WHILE GAZING ON THE MOON'S LIGHT.

Air—*Oonagh.*

While gazing on the moon's light,
  A moment from her smile I turn'd,
To look at orbs that, more bright,
  In lone and distant glory burn'd.
    But *too* far
    Each proud star,
For me to feel its warming flame ;
    Much more dear
    That mild sphere,
Which near our planet smiling came ; (4)
Thus, Mary, be but thou my own,
  While brighter eyes unheeded play,
I 'll love those moonlight looks alone
  That bless my home and guide my way.

The day had sunk in dim showers,
  But midnight now, with lustre meet,
Illumined all the pale flowers,
  Like hope upon a mourner's cheek.

(1) We may suppose this apology to have been uttered by one of those wandering bards, whom Spenser so severely, and perhaps truly, describes in his State of Ireland, and whose poems, he tells us, "were sprinkled with some pretty flowers of their natural device, which gave good grace and comeliness unto them, the which it is great pity to see abused to the gracing of wickedness and vice, which, with good usage, would serve to adorn and beautify virtue."

(2) It is conjectured by Wormius, that the name of Ireland is derived from Yr, the Runic for a bow, in the use of which weapon the Irish were once very expert. This derivation is certainly more creditable to us than the following : "So that Ireland, called the land of Ire, from

the constant broils therein for 400 years, was now become the land of concord."—*Lloyd's State Worthies,* art. *The Lord Grandison.*

(3) See the Hymn, atributed to Alcæus, Εν μυρτου κλαδι το ξιφος φορησω—"I will carry my sword, hidden in myrtles, like Harmodius and Aristogiton," etc.

(4) "Of such celestial bodies as are visible, the sun excepted, the single moon, as despicable as it is in comparison to most of the others, is much more beneficial than they all put together."—*Whiston's Theory, etc.*

In the *Entretiens d'Ariste,* among other ingenious emblems, we find a starry sky without a moon, with these words, *Non mille, quod absens.*

I said (while
The moon's smile
Play'd o'er a stream, in dimpling bliss,)
"The moon looks
On many brooks,
The brook can see no moon but this ;" (1)
And thus, I thought, our fortunes run,
For many a lover looks to thee,
While oh! I feel there is but *one*,
One Mary in the world for me.

----◦••◦----

ILL OMENS.

AIR—*Kitty of Coleraine; or, Paddy's Resource.*

WHEN daylight was yet sleeping under the billow,
And stars in the heavens still lingering shone,
Young Kitty, all blushing, rose up from her pillow,
The last time she e'er was to press it alone.
For the youth whom she treasured her heart and her soul in
Had promised to link the last tie before noon ;
And when once the young heart of a maiden is stolen,
The maiden herself will steal after it soon.

As she look'd in the glass, which a woman ne'er misses,
Nor ever wants time for a sly glance or two,
A butterfly,(2) fresh from the night-flower's kisses,
Flew over the mirror, and shaded her view.
Enraged with the insect for hiding her graces,
She brush'd him—he fell, alas! never to rise:
" Ah! such," said the girl, "is the pride of our faces,
For which the soul's innocence too often dies."

While she stole through the garden, where heart's-ease was growing,
She cull'd some, and kiss'd off its night-fallen dew ;
And a rose, further on, look'd so tempting and glowing,
That, spite of her haste, she must gather it too :
But while o'er the roses too carelessly leaning,
Her zone flew in two, and the heart's-ease was lost :
" Ah! this means," said the girl (and she sigh'd at its meaning),
"That love is scarce worth the repose it will cost!"

----◦••◦----

BEFORE THE BATTLE.

AIR—*The Fairy Queen.*

BY the hope within us springing,
Herald of to-morrow's strife ;
By that sun, whose light is bringing
Chains or freedom, death or life—
Oh! remember life can be
No charm for him, who lives not free!

(1) This image was suggested by the following thought, which occurs somewhere in Sir William Jones's works : "The moon looks upon many night-flowers ; the night-flower sees but one moon."
(2) An emblem of the soul.

Like the day-star in the wave;
Sinks a hero in his grave,
'Midst the dew-fall of a nation's tears.

Happy is he o'er whose decline
The smiles of home may soothing shine,
And light him down the steep of years :
But oh, how blest they sink to rest,
Who close their eyes on victory's breast!

O'er his watch-fire's fading embers
Now the foeman's cheek turns white,
When his heart that field remembers,
Where we tamed his tyrant might.
Never let him bind again
A chain like that we broke from then.
Hark! the horn of combat calls—
Ere the golden evening falls,
May we pledge that horn in triumph round!(3)

Many a heart that now beats high,
In slumber cold at night shall lie,
Nor waken even at victory's sound :—
But oh how blest that hero's sleep,
O'er whom a wondering world shall weep!

----◦••◦----

AFTER THE BATTLE.

AIR—*Thy Fair Bosom.*

NIGHT closed around the conqueror's way,
And lightnings show'd the distant hill,
Where those who lost that dreadful day
Stood few and faint, but fearless still.
The soldier's hope, the patriot's zeal,
For ever dimm'd, for ever crost—
Oh! who shall say what heroes feel,
When all but life and honour 's lost?

The last sad hour of freedom's dream,
And valour's task, moved slowly by,
While morn they watch'd, till morning's beam
Should rise and give them light to die.
There 's yet a world, where souls are free,
Where tyrants taint not nature's bliss ;—
If death that world's bright opening be,
Oh! who would live a slave in this?

----◦••◦----

'TIS SWEET TO THINK.

AIR—*Thady, you Gander.*

'TIS sweet to think that, where'er we rove,
We are sure to find something blissful and dear,
And that, when we 're far from the lips we love,
We've but to make love to the lips we are near.(4)

(3) " The Irish Corna was not entirely devoted to martial purposes. In the heroic ages, our ancestors quaffed Meadh out of them, as the Danish hunters do their beverage at this day."—*Walker.*
(4) I believe it is Marmontel who says, "*Quand on n'a*

The heart, like a tendril, accustom'd to cling,
    Let it grow where it will, cannot flourish alone,
But will lean to the nearest and loveliest thing
    It can twine with itself, and make closely its own.
Then oh! what pleasure, where'er we rove,
    To be sure to find something, still, that is dear,
And to know, when far from the lips we love,
    We 've but to make love to the lips we are near.

'T were a shame, when flowers around us rise,
    To make light of the rest, if the rose is n't there;
And the world's so rich in resplendent eyes,
    'T were a pity to limit one's love to a pair.
Love's wing and the peacock's are nearly alike,
    They are both of them bright, but they 're change-
        able too,
And wherever a new beam of beauty can strike,
    It will tincture Love's plume with a different hue.
Then oh! what pleasure, where'er we rove,
    To be sure to find something, still, that is dear,
And to know, when far from the lips we love,
    We 've but to make love to the lips we are near.

IT IS NOT THE TEAR AT THIS MOMENT SHED.(1)

Air—*The Sixpence.*

It is not the tear at this moment shed,
    When the cold turf has just been laid o'er him,
That can tell how beloved was the friend that's fled,
    Or how deep in our hearts we deplore him.
'T is the tear, through many a long day wept,
    'T is life's whole path o'ershaded;
'T is the one remembrance, fondly kept,
    When all lighter griefs have faded.

Thus his memory, like some holy light,
    Kept alive in our hearts, will improve them,
For worth shall look fairer, and truth more bright,
    When we think how he lived but to love them.
And as fresher flowers the sod perfume
    Where buried saints are lying,
So our hearts shall borrow a sweetening bloom
    From the image he left there in dying!

THE IRISH PEASANT TO HIS MISTRESS. (2)

Air —————.

Through grief and through danger thy smile hath
      cheer'd my way,   [me lay;
Till hope seem'd to bud from each thorn that round
The darker our fortune, the brighter our pure love
      burn'd,
Till shame into glory, till fear into zeal was turn'd;

Yes, slave as I was, in thy arms my spirit felt free,
    And bless'd even the sorrows that made me more
      dear to thee.

Thy rival was honour'd, while thou wert wrong'd
      and scorn'd,
Thy crown was of briers, while gold her brows
      adorn'd;
She woo'd me to temples, while thou lay'st hidin caves,
    Her friends were all masters, while thine, alas! were
      slaves;
Yet cold in the earth, at thy feet, I would rather be,
    Than wed what I loved not, or turn one thought from
                    [thee.
They slander thee sorely, who say thy vows are frail—
    Hadst thou been a false one, thy cheek had look'd
      less pale.   [chains—
They say, too, so long thou hast worn those lingering
    That deep in thy heart they have printed their servile
      stains—   [subdue—
Oh! foul is the slander—no chain could that soul
Where shineth *thy* spirit, there liberty shineth too!(3)

ON MUSIC.

Air—*Banks of Banna.*

When through life unblest we rove,
    Losing all that made life dear,
Should some notes we used to love,
    In days of boyhood, meet our ear,
Oh! how welcome breathes the strain!
    Wakening thoughts that long have slept,
Kindling former smiles again
    In faded eyes that long have wept.

Like the gale, that sighs along
    Beds of oriental flowers,
Is the grateful breath of song,
    That once was heard in happier hours;
Fill'd with balm the gale sighs on,
    Though the flowers have sunk in death;
So, when pleasure's dream is gone,
    Its memory lives in Music's breath.

Music, oh how faint, how weak,
    Language fades before thy spell!
Why should Feeling ever speak,
    When thou canst breathe her soul so well?
Friendship's balmy words may feign,
    Love's are even more false than they;
Oh! 'tis only music's strain
    Can sweetly soothe, and not betray.

---

pas ce que l'on aime, il faut aimer ce que l'on a."—There are so many matter-of-fact people, who take such *jeux d'esprit* as this defence of inconstancy to be the actual and genuine sentiments of him who writes them, that they compel one, in self-defence, to be as matter-of-fact as themselves, and to remind them, that Democritus was not the worse physiologist for having playfully contended

that snow was black; nor Erasmus in any degree the less wise, for having written an ingenious encomium of folly.

(1) These lines were occasioned by the loss of a very near and dear relative, who had died lately at Madeira.

(2) Meaning, allegorically, the ancient Church of Ireland.

(3) "Where the Spirit of the Lord is, there is liberty."
—*St. Paul, 2 Corinthians,* iii., 17.

THE ORIGIN OF THE HARP.

Air—*Gage Fane.*

'Tis believed that this Harp, which I wake now for thee,
Was a Siren of old, who sung under the sea; [thee,
And who often, at eve, through the bright waters roved,
To meet, on the green shore, a youth whom she loved.

But she loved him in vain, for he left her to weep,
And in tears, all the night, her gold tresses to steep;
Till heaven look'd with pity on true-love so warm,
And changed to this soft Harp the sea-maiden's form.

Still her bosom rose fair—still her cheeks smiled the
    same—   [frame;
While her sea-beauties gracefully form'd the light
And her hair, as, let loose, o'er her white arm it fell,
Was changed to bright chords uttering melody's
    spell.(1)
                                                [known
Hence it came, that this soft Harp so long hath been
To mingle love's language with sorrow's sad tone;
Till *thou* didst divide them, and teach the fond lay
To speak love when I'm near thee, and grief when
    away.

LOVE'S YOUNG DREAM.

Air—*The Old Woman.*

Oh! the days are gone, when Beauty bright
    My heart's chain wove;
When my dream of life, from morn till night,
    Was love, still love.
    New hope may bloom,
    And days may come,
Of milder calmer beam,
But there's nothing half so sweet in life
As love's young dream:
No, there's nothing half so sweet in life
As love's young dream.

Though the bard to purer fame may soar,
    When wild youth's past;
Though he win the wise, who frown'd before,
    To smile at last;
    He'll never meet
    A joy so sweet,
In all his noon of fame,
As when first he sung to woman's ear
    His soul-felt flame,
And, at every close, she blush'd to hear
    The one loved name.

No,—that hallow'd form is ne'er forgot
    Which first love traced;
Still it lingering haunts the greenest spot
    On memory's waste.

(1) This thought was suggested by an ingenious design, prefixed to an ode upon St. Cecilia, published some years since, by Mr. Hudson of Dublin.—P. E.

'T was odour fled
    As soon as shed;
'T was morning's winged dream;
'T was a light, that ne'er can shine again
    On life's dull stream:
Oh! 't was light that ne'er can shine again
    On life's dull stream.

THE PRINCE'S DAY. (2)

Air—*St. Patrick's Day.*

Though dark are our sorrows, to-day we'll forget them,
    And smile through our tears, like a sunbeam in
        showers:
There never were hearts, if our rulers would let them,
    More form'd to be grateful and blest than ours.
        But just when the chain
        Has ceased to pain,
    And hope has enwreathed it round with flowers,
        There comes a new link,
        Our spirits to sink—
Oh! the joy that we taste, like the light of the poles,
    Is a flash amid darkness, too brilliant to stay;
But, though't were the last little spark in our souls,
    We must light it up now, on our Prince's Day.

Contempt on the minion who calls you disloyal!
    Though fierce to your foe, to your friends you are
        true;
And the tribute most high to a head that is royal,
    Is love from a heart that loves liberty too.
        While cowards, who blight
        Your fame, your right,
Would shrink from the blaze of the battle array,
        The Standard of Green
        In front would be seen—
Oh, my life on your faith! were you summon'd this
        minute,
    You'd cast every bitter remembrance away,
And show what the arm of old Erin has in it,
    When roused by the foe, on her Prince's Day.

He loves the Green Isle, and his love is recorded
    In hearts which have suffer'd too much to forget;
And hope shall be crown'd, and attachment rewarded,
    And Erin's gay jubilee shine out yet.
        The gem may be broke
        By many a stroke,
    But nothing can cloud its native ray;
        Each fragment will cast
        A light to the last—
And thus, Erin, my country, though broken thou art,
    There's a lustre within thee, that ne'er will decay;
A spirit which beams through each suffering part,
    And now smiles at all pain on the Prince's Day.

(2) This song was written for a fête in honour of the Prince of Wales's Birthday, given by my friend, Major Bryan, at his seat in the county of Kilkenny.

WEEP ON, WEEP ON.
Air—*The Song of Sorrow.*

WEEP on, weep on, your hour is past,
　Your dreams of pride are o'er;
The fatal chain is round you cast,
　And you are men no more.
In vain the hero's heart hath bled;
　The sage's tongue hath warn'd in vain;
Oh, Freedom! once thy flame hath fled,
　It never lights again!

Weep on—perhaps in after days,
　They'll learn to love your name,
When many a deed may wake in praise
　That long hath slept in blame.
And when they tread the ruin'd isle,
　Where rest, at length, the lord and slave,
They'll wondering ask, how hands so vile
　Could conquer hearts so brave?

"'T was fate," they'll say, "a wayward fate
　Your web of discord wove;
And while your tyrants join'd in hate,
　You never join'd in love.
But hearts fell off that ought to twine,
　And man profaned what God had given;
Till some were heard to curse the shrine
　Where others knelt to heaven!"

LESBIA HATH A BEAMING EYE.
Air—*Nora Creina.*

LESBIA hath a beaming eye,
　But no one knows for whom it beameth;
Right and left its arrows fly,
　But what they aim at no one dreameth.
Sweeter 't is to gaze upon
　My Nora's lid that seldom rises;
Few its looks, but every one,
　Like unexpected light, surprises!
　　Oh, my Nora Creina, dear,
　　My gentle, bashful Nora Creina,
　　　Beauty lies
　　　In many eyes,
　　But Love in yours, my Nora Creina.

Lesbia wears a robe of gold,
　But all so close the nymph hath laced it,
Not a charm of beauty's mould
　Presumes to stay where Nature placed it.
Oh! my Nora's gown for me,
　That floats as wild as mountain breezes,
Leaving every beauty free
　To sink or swell as Heaven pleases.

(1) I have here made a feeble effort to imitate that exquisite inscription of Shenstone's, "Heu! quanto minus est cum reliquis versari quam tui meminisse!"
(2) This ballad is founded upon one of the many stories related of St. Kevin, whose bed in the rock is to be seen

Yes, my Nora Creina, dear,
My simple, graceful Nora Creina,
　　Nature's dress
　　Is loveliness—
The dress *you* wear, my Nora Creina.

Lesbia hath a wit refined,
　But, when its points are gleaming round us,
Who can tell if they're design'd
　To dazzle merely, or to wound us?
Pillow'd on my Nora's heart,
　In safer slumber Love reposes—
Bed of peace! whose roughest part
　Is but the crumpling of the roses.
　　Oh! my Nora Creina, dear,
　　My mild, my artless Nora Creina!
　　　Wit, though bright,
　　　Hath no such light
　　As warms your eyes, my Nora Creina.

I SAW THY FORM IN YOUTHFUL PRIME.
Air—*Domhnall.*

I SAW thy form in youthful prime,
　Nor thought that pale decay
Would steal before the steps of Time,
　And waste its bloom away, Mary!
Yet still thy features wore that light,
　Which fleets not with the breath;
And life ne'er look'd more truly bright
　Than in thy smile of death, Mary!

As streams that run o'er golden mines,
　Yet humbly, calmly glide,
Nor seem to know the wealth that shines
　Within their gentle tide, Mary!
So veil'd beneath the simplest guise,
　Thy radiant genius shone,
And that which charm'd all other eyes
　Seem'd worthless in thy own, Mary!

If souls could always dwell above,
　Thou ne'er hadst left that sphere;
Or could we keep the souls we love,
　We ne'er had lost thee here, Mary!
Though many a gifted mind we meet,
　Though fairest forms we see,
To live with them is far less sweet
　Than to remember thee, Mary!" (1)

BY THAT LAKE, WHOSE GLOOMY SHORE. (2)
Air—*The Brown Irish Girl.*

BY that Lake, whose gloomy shore
Sky-lark never warbles o'er, (3)

at Glendalough, a most gloomy and romantic spot in the county of Wicklow.
(3) There are many other curious traditions concerning this Lake, which may be found in Giraldus, Colgan, etc.

Where the cliff hangs high and steep,
Young Saint Kevin stole to sleep.
" Here, at least," he calmly said,
" Woman ne'er shall find my bed."
Ah! the good Saint little knew
What that wily sex can do.

'T was from Kathleen's eyes he flew—
Eyes of most unholy blue!
She had loved him well and long,
Wish'd him hers, nor thought it wrong.
Wheresoe'er the Saint would fly,
Still he heard her light foot nigh;
East or west, where'er he turn'd,
Still her eyes before him burn'd.

On the bold cliff's bosom cast,
Tranquil now he sleeps at last;
Dreams of heaven, nor thinks that e'er
Woman's smile can haunt him there.
But nor earth nor heaven is free
From her power, if fond she be:
Even now, while calm he sleeps,
Kathleen o'er him leans and weeps.

Fearless she had track'd his feet
To this rocky wild retreat;
And when morning met his view,
Her mild glances met it too.
Ah, your Saints have cruel hearts!
Sternly from his bed he starts,
And with rude repulsive shock
Hurls her from the beetling rock.

Glendalough, thy gloomy wave
Soon was gentle Kathleen's grave!
Soon the Saint (yet ah! too late,)
Felt her love, and mourn'd her fate.
When he said, " Heaven rest her soul!"
Round the Lake light music stole;
And her ghost was seen to glide,
Smiling, o'er the fatal tide.

———◦◦◦———

SHE IS FAR FROM THE LAND.

Air—Open the Door.

She is far from the land where her young hero sleeps,
And lovers are round her, sighing;
But coldly she turns from their gaze, and weeps,
For her heart in his grave is lying.

She sings the wild song of her dear native plains,
Every note which he loved awaking;—

Ah! little they think, who delight in her strains,
How the heart of the Minstrel is breaking.

He had lived for his love, for his country he died,
They were all that to life had entwined him;
Nor soon shall the tears of his country be dried,
Nor long will his Love stay behind him.

Oh! make her a grave where the sunbeams rest,
When they promise a glorious morrow;
They'll shine o'er her sleep, like a smile from the West,
From her own loved Island of sorrow.

———◦◦◦———

NAY, TELL ME NOT, DEAR.

Air—Dennis, don't be threatening.

Nay, tell me not, dear, that the goblet drowns
One charm of feeling, one fond regret;
Believe me, a few of thy angry frowns
Are all I 've sunk in its bright wave yet.
Ne'er hath a beam
Been lost in the stream
That ever was shed from thy form or soul;
The spell of those eyes,
The balm of thy sighs,
Still float on the surface, and hallow my bowl.
Then fancy not, dearest, that wine can steal
One blissful dream of the heart from me;
Like founts that awaken the pilgrim's zeal,
The bowl but brightens my love for thee.

They tell us that Love in his fairy bower
Had two blush-roses, of birth divine;
He sprinkled the one with a rainbow's shower,
But bathed the other with mantling wine.
Soon did the buds
That drank of the floods
Distill'd by the rainbow decline and fade;
While those which the tide
Of ruby had dyed
All blush'd into beauty, like thee, sweet maid!
Then fancy not, dearest, that wine can steal
One blissful dream of the heart from me;
Like founts that awaken the pilgrim's zeal,
The bowl but brightens my love for thee.

———◦◦◦———

AVENGING AND BRIGHT.

Air—Crooghan a Venee.

Avenging and bright fall the swift sword of Erin (1)
On him who the brave sons of Usna betray'd!—
For every fond eye he hath waken'd a tear in [blade.
A drop from his heart-wounds shall weep o'er her

(1) The words of this song were suggested by the very
ancient Irish story called "Deirdri, or the Lamentable
Fate of the Sons of Usnach," which has been translated
literally from the Gaelic, by Mr. O'Flanagan (see vol. i. of
Transactions of the Gaelic Society of Dublin), and upon
which it appears that the " Darthula of Macpherson " is
founded. The treachery of Conor, King of Ulster, in put-

ting to death the three sons of Usna, was the cause of a
desolating war against Ulster, which terminated in the
destruction of Eman. " This story (says Mr. O'Flanagan)
has been, from time immemorial, held in high repute as
one of the three tragic stories of the Irish. These are,
' The death of the children of Touran ;' ' The death of the
children of Lear' (both regarding Tuatha de Danans', and

By the red cloud that hung over Conor's dark
   dwelling,(1)   [gore—
When Ulad's(2) three champions lay sleeping in
By the billows of war, which so often, high swelling,
Have wafted these heroes to victory's shore—

We swear to revenge them!— no joy shall be tasted,
   The harp shall be silent, the maiden unwed,
Our halls shall be mute, and our fields shall lie wasted,
   Till vengeance is wreak'd on the murderer's head.

Yes, monarch! though sweet are our home recollec-
   tions,   [fall;
Though sweet are the tears that from tenderness
Though sweet are our friendships, our hopes, our
   Revenge on a tyrant is sweetest of all! [affections,

WHAT THE BEE IS TO THE FLOWERET.

AIR—*The Yellow Horse.*

He.—WHAT the bee is to the floweret,
   When he looks for honey-dew,
   Through the leaves that close embower it,
   That, my love, I'll be to you.

She.—What the bank, with verdure glowing,
   Is to waves that wander near,
   Whispering kisses, while they're going,
   That I'll be to you, my dear.

She.—But they say, the bee's a rover,
   Who will fly, when sweets are gone;
   And, when once the kiss is over,
   Faithless brooks will wander on.

He.—Nay, if flowers *will* lose their looks,
   If sunny banks *will* wear away,
   'T is but right that bees and brooks
   Should sip and kiss them, while they may.

LOVE AND THE NOVICE.

AIR—*Cean Dubh Delish.*

"HERE we dwell, in holiest bowers,
   Where angels of light o'er our orisons bend;
Where sighs of devotion and breathings of flowers
   To heaven in mingled odour ascend.
     Do not disturb our calm, oh Love!
     So like is thy form to the cherubs above,
   It well might deceive such hearts as ours."

Love stood near the Novice and listen'd,
   And Love is no novice in taking a hint;

His laughing blue eyes soon with piety glisten'd;
   His rosy wing turn'd to heaven's own tint.
    "Who would have thought," the urchin cries,
    "That Love could so well, so gravely disguise
His wandering wings, and wounding eyes?"

Love now warms thee, waking and sleeping,
   Young Novice, to him all thy orisons rise.
He tinges the heavenly fount with his weeping,
   He brightens the censer's flame with his sighs.
     Love is the Saint enshrined in thy breast,
     And angels themselves would admit such a guest,
   If he came to them clothed in Piety's vest.

THIS LIFE IS ALL CHEQUER'D WITH PLEASURES AND WOES.

AIR—*The Bunch of Green Rushes that grew at the Brim.*

THIS life is all chequer'd with pleasures and woes,
   That chase one another like waves of the deep—
Each brightly or darkly, as onward it flows,
   Reflecting our eyes, as they sparkle or weep.
So closely our whims on our miseries tread,
   That the laugh is awaked ere the tear can be dried;
And, as fast as the rain-drop of Pity is shed,
   The goose-plumage of Folly can turn it aside.
     But pledge me the cup—if existence would cloy,
     With hearts ever happy, and heads ever wise,
     Be ours the light Sorrow, half-sister to Joy,
     And the light brilliant Folly that flashes and dies.

When Hylas was sent with his urn to the fount, [play,
   Through fields full of light, and with heart full of
Light rambled the boy, over meadow and mount,
   And neglected his task for the flowers on the way.(3)
Thus many, like me, who in youth should have tasted
   The fountain that runs by Philosophy's shrine,
Their time with the flowers on the margin have wasted,
   And left their light urns all as empty as mine.
     But pledge me the goblet;—while Idleness weaves
     These flowerets together, should Wisdom but see
     One bright drop or two that has fall'n on the leaves
     From her fountain divine, 't is sufficient for me.

OH, THE SHAMROCK.

AIR—*Alley Croker.*

THROUGH Erin's Isle
   To sport awhile
As Love and Valour wander'd,
     With Wit, the sprite,
     Whose quiver bright
A thousand arrows squander'd;

---

this, ' The death of the children of Usnach,' which is a
Milesian story." It will be recollected, that among these
Melodies, there is a ballad upon the story of the children
of Lear or Lir; "Silent, oh Moyle!" etc.

Whatever may be thought of those sanguine claims to
antiquity which Mr. O'Flanagan and others advance for
the literature of Ireland, it would be a lasting reproach
upno our nationality, if the Gaelic researches of this gen-

tleman did not meet with all the liberal encouragement
they so well merit.

(1) "Oh Nasi! view that cloud that I here see in the sky!
I see over Eman-green a chilling cloud of blood-tinged
red."—*Deirdri's Song.*

(2) Ulster.

(3) Proposito florem præbulit officio.—*Propert.*, lib. i.,
eleg. 20.

Where'er they pass,
    A triple grass (1)
Shoots up, with dew-drops streaming,
    As softly green
    As emeralds seen
Through purest crystal gleaming.
Oh the Shamrock, the green, immortal Shamrock!
        Chosen leaf
        Of Bard and Chief,
    Old Erin's native Shamrock!

Says Valour, "See,
    They spring for me,
Those leafy gems of morning!"—
    Says Love, "No, no,
    For me they grow,
My fragrant path adorning."
    But Wit perceives
    The triple leaves,
And cries, "Oh! do not sever
    A type that blends
    Three godlike friends,
Love, Valour, Wit, for ever!"
Oh the Shamrock, the green, immortal Shamrock!
    Chosen leaf, etc.

So firmly fond
    May last the bond
They wove that morn together,
    And ne'er may fall
    One drop of gall
On Wit's celestial feather.
    May Love, as twine
    His flowers divine,
Of thorny falsehood weed 'em;
    May Valour ne'er
    His standard rear
Against the cause of Freedom!
Oh the Shamrock, the green, immortal Shamrock!
    Chosen leaf, etc.

AT THE MID HOUR OF NIGHT.

Air—*Molly, my dear.*

At the mid hour of night, when stars are weeping,
        I fly
To the lone vale we loved, when life shone warm in
        thine eye;
    And I think oft, if spirits can steal from the regions
        of air,
    To revisit past scenes of delight, thou wilt come
        to me there,
And tell me our love is remember'd, even in the sky.

(1) It is said that St. Patrick, when preaching the Tri-
nity to the Pagan Irish, used to illustrate his subject by
reference to that species of trefoil called in Ireland by the
name of the Shamrock; and hence, perhaps, the Island of
Saints adopted this plant as her national emblem. Hope,
among the ancients, was sometimes represented as a

Then I sing the wild song 't was once such pleasure
    to hear!
When our voices commingling breathed, like one, on
    the ear;
    And, as Echo far off through the vale my sad
        orison rolls,
    I think, oh my love! 't is thy voice from the King-
        dom of Souls, (2)
Faintly answering still the notes that once were so
    dear.

ONE BUMPER AT PARTING.

Air—*Moll Roe in the Morning.*

One bumper at parting!—though many
    Have circled the board since we met,
The fullest, the saddest of any
    Remains to be crown'd by us yet.
The sweetness that pleasure hath in it
    Is always so slow to come forth,
That seldom, alas, till the minute
    It dies, do we know half its worth.
But come—may our life's happy measure
    Be all of such moments made up;
They 're born on the bosom of Pleasure,
    They die 'midst the tears of the cup.

As onward we journey, how pleasant
    To pause and inhabit awhile
Those few sunny spots, like the present,
    That 'mid the dull wilderness smile!
But Time, like a pitiless master,
    Cries "Onward!" and spurs the gay hours—
Ah, never doth Time travel faster
    Than when his way lies among flowers.
But come—may our life's happy measure
    Be all of such moments made up;
They 're born on the bosom of Pleasure,
    They die 'midst the tears of the cup.

We saw how the sun look'd in sinking,
    The waters beneath him how bright;
And now, let our farewell of drinking
    Resemble that farewell of light.
You saw how he finish'd by darting
    His beam o'er a deep billow's brim—
So, fill up, let 's shine at our parting,
    In full liquid glory, like him.
And oh! may our life's happy measure
    Of moments like this be made up,
'T was born on the bosom of Pleasure,
    It dies 'mid the tears of the cup.

beautiful child, standing upon tip-toes, and a trefoil or
three-coloured grass in her hand.
(2) "There are countries," says Montaigne, "where they
believe the souls of the happy live in all manner of liberty,
in delightful fields; and that it is those souls, repeating
the words we utter, which we call Echo."
                                                    27

'T IS THE LAST ROSE OF SUMMER.

Air—*Groves of Blarney.*

'T is the last rose of summer
　Left blooming alone;
All her lovely companions
　Are faded and gone:
No flower of her kindred,
　No rose-bud is nigh,
To reflect back her blushes,
　Or give sigh for sigh.

I 'll not leave thee, thou lone one!
　To pine on the stem;
Since the lovely are sleeping,
　Go, sleep thou with them.
Thus kindly I scatter
　Thy leaves o'er the bed,
Where thy mates of the garden
　Lie scentless and dead.

So soon may *I* follow,
　When friendships decay,
And from Love's shining circle
　The gems drop away.
When true hearts lie wither'd,
　And fond ones are flown,
Oh! who would inhabit
　This bleak world alone?

THE YOUNG MAY MOON.

Air—*The Dandy O!*

The young May moon is beaming, love,
The glow-worm's lamp is gleaming, love,
　　How sweet to rove
　　Through Morna's grove, (1)
When the drowsy world is dreaming, love!
Then awake!—the heavens look bright, my dear,
'T is never too late for delight, my dear,
　　And the best of all ways
　　To lengthen our days
Is to steal a few hours from the night, my dear!

Now all the world is sleeping, love,
But the Sage, his star-watch keeping, love,
　　And I, whose star,
　　More glorious far,
Is the eye from that casement peeping, love.

(1) "Steals silently to Morna's grove."—See, in Mr. Bunt-ing's collection, a poem translated from the Irish, by the late John Brown, one of my earliest college companions and friends, whose death was as singularly melancholy and unfortunate as his life had been amiable, honourable, and exemplary.

(2) These stanzas are founded upon an event of most melancholy importance to Ireland, if, as we are told by our Irish historians, it gave England the first opportunity of profiting by our divisions and subduing us. The fol-lowing are the circumstances, as related by O'Halloran:—"The king of Leinster had long conceived a violent affection for Dearbhorgil, daughter to the king of Meath, and though she had been for some time married to O Ruark, prince of Breffni, yet it could not restrain his passion.

Then awake!—till rise of sun, my dear,
The Sage's glass we'll shun, my dear,
　　Or, in watching the flight
　　Of bodies of light,
He might happen to take thee for one, my dear.

THE MINSTREL-BOY.

Air—*The Moreen.*

The Minstrel-Boy to the war is gone,
　In the ranks of death you 'll find him;
His father's sword he has girded on,
　And his wild harp slung behind him.
"Land of song!" said the warrior-bard,
　"Though all the world betrays thee,
One sword, at least, thy rights shall guard,
　One faithful harp shall praise thee!"

The Minstrel fell!—but the foeman's chain
　Could not bring his proud soul under;
The harp he loved ne'er spoke again,
　For he tore its chords asunder;
And said, "No chains shall sully thee,
　Thou soul of love and bravery!
Thy songs were made for the pure and free,
　They shall never sound in slavery."

THE SONG OF O'RUARK,

PRINCE OF BREFFNI. (2)

Air—*The Pretty Girl milking her Cow.*

The valley lay smiling before me,
　Where lately I left her behind;
Yet I trembled, and something hung o'er me,
　That sadden'd the joy of my mind.
I look'd for the lamp which, she told me,
　Should shine when her Pilgrim return'd;
But, though darkness began to infold me,
　No lamp from the battlements burn'd!

I flew to her chamber—'t was lonely,
　As if the loved tenant lay dead;—
Ah, would it were death, and death only!
　But no, the young false one had fled.
And there hung the lute that could soften
　My very worst pains into bliss;
While the hand that had waked it so often
　Now throbb'd to a proud rival's kiss.

They carried on a private correspondence, and she in-formed him that O'Ruark intended soon to go on a pil-grimage (an act of piety frequent in those days), and con-jured him to embrace that opportunity of conveying her from a husband she detested to a lover she adored. Mac Murchad too punctually obeyed the summons, and had the lady conveyed to his capital of Ferns."—The monarch Ro-derick espoused the cause of O'Ruark, while Mac Murchad fled to England, and obtained the assistance of Henry II.

"Such," adds Giraldus Cambrensis (as I find him in an old translation), "is the variable and fickle nature of woman, by whom all mischief in the world (for the most part) do happen and come, as may appear by Marcus An-tonius, and by the destruction of Troy."

There *was* a time, falsest of women,
　When Breffni's good sword would have sought
That man, through a million of foemen,
　Who dared but to wrong thee *in thought !*
While now—oh degenerate daughter
　Of Erin, how fallen is thy fame!
And through ages of bondage and slaughter,
　Our country shall bleed for thy shame.

Already the curse is upon her,
　And strangers her valleys profane;
They come to divide, to dishonour,
　And tyrants they long will remain.
But onward!—the green banner rearing,
　Go, flesh every sword to the hilt;
On *our* side is Virtue and Erin,
　On *theirs* is the Saxon and Guilt.

———❦———

OH! HAD WE SOME BRIGHT LITTLE ISLE OF OUR OWN.

Air—*Sheela na Guira.*

On! had we some bright little isle of our own,
In a blue summer ocean, far off and alone,
Where a leaf never dies in the still blooming bowers,
And the bee banquets on through a whole year of
　　Where the sun loves to pause　[flowers;
　　　With so fond a delay,
　　　That the night only draws
　　　A thin veil o'er the day;
Where simply to feel that we breathe, that we live,
Is worth the best joy that life elsewhere can give.

There, with souls ever ardent and pure as the clime,
We should love, as they loved in the first golden time;
The glow of the sunshine, the balm of the air,
Would steal to our hearts, and make all summer
　　there.
　　　With affection as free
　　　From decline as the bowers,
　　　And, with hope, like the bee,
　　　Living always on flowers,
Our life should resemble a long day of light,
And our death come on, holy and calm as the night.

———❦———

FAREWELL!—BUT WHENEVER YOU WELCOME THE HOUR.

Air—*Moll Roone.*

Farewell! but whenever you welcome the hour
That awakens the night-song of mirth in your bower,
Then think of the friend who once welcomed it too,
And forgot his own griefs to be happy with you.
His griefs may return, not a hope may remain
Of the few that have brighten'd his pathway of pain,
But he ne'er will forget the short vision, that threw
Its enchantment around him, while lingering with
　you.

And still on that evening, when pleasure fills up
To the highest top sparkle each heart and each cup,

Where'er my path lies, be it gloomy or bright,
My soul, happy friends, shall be with you that night;
Shall join in your revels, your sports, and your wiles,
And return to me, beaming all o'er with your smiles—
Too blest, if it tells me that, 'mid the gay cheer,
Some kind voice had murmur'd, " I wish he were
　here!"

Let Fate do her worst, there are relics of joy,
Bright dreams of the past, which she cannot destroy;
Which come in the night-time of sorrow and care,
And bring back the features that joy used to wear.
Long, long be my heart with such memories fill'd!
Like the vase, in which roses have once been distill'd—
You may break, you may shatter the vase, if you will,
But the scent of the roses will hang round it still.

———❦———

OH! DOUBT ME NOT.

Air—*Yellow Wat and the Fox.*

On! doubt me not—the season
　Is o'er when Folly made me rove,
And now the vestal, Reason,
　Shall watch the fire awaked by Love.
Although this heart was early blown,
　And fairest hands disturb'd the tree,
They only shook some blossoms down—
　Its fruit has all been kept for thee.
Then doubt me not—the season
　Is o'er when Folly made me rove,
And now the vestal, Reason,
　Shall watch the fire awaked by Love.

And though my lute no longer
　May sing of Passion's ardent spell,
Yet, trust me, all the stronger
　I feel the bliss I do not tell.
The bee through many a garden roves,
　And hums his lay of courtship o'er,
But when he finds the flower he loves,
　He settles there, and hums no more.
Then doubt me not—the season
　Is o'er when Folly kept me free,
And now the vestal, Reason,
　Shall guard the flame awaked by thee.

———❦———

YOU REMEMBER ELLEN.(1)

Air—*Were 1 a Clerk.*

You remember Ellen, our hamlet's pride,
　How meekly she bless'd her humble lot,
When the stranger, William, had made her his bride,
　And love was the light of their lowly cot.
Together they toil'd through winds and rains,
　Till William, at length, in sadness said,
" We must seek our fortune on other plains;"—
　Then, sighing, she left her lowly shed.

(1) This ballad was suggested by a well-known and interesting story told of a certain noble family in England.

They roam'd a long and a weary way,
  Nor much was the maiden's heart at ease,
When now, at close of one stormy day,
  They see a proud castle among the trees.
"To-night," said the youth,"we'll shelter there ;
  The wind blows cold, the hour is late : "
So he blew the horn with a chieftain's air,
  And the porter bow'd, as they pass'd the gate.

" Now, welcome, Lady," exclaim'd the youth,—
  This castle is thine, and these dark woods all!"
She believed him crazed, but his words were truth,
  For Ellen is Lady of Rosna Hall !
And dearly the Lord of Rosna loves
  What William the stranger woo'd and wed ;
And the light of bliss, in these lordly groves,
  Shines pure as it did in the lowly shed.

I'D MOURN THE HOPES.

Air—*The Rose-Tree.*

I 'D mourn the hopes that leave me,
  If thy smiles had left me too ;
I 'd weep when friends deceive me,
  If thou wert, like them, untrue.
But while I've thee before me,
  With heart so warm and eyes so bright,
No clouds can linger o'er me,
  That smile turns them all to light.

'T is not in fate to harm me,
  While fate leaves thy love to me :
'T is not in joy to charm me,
  Unless joy be shared with thee.
One minute's dream about thee
  Were worth a long, an endless year
Of waking bliss without thee,
  My own love, my only dear !

And though the hope be gone, love,
  That long sparkled o'er our way,
Oh! we shall journey on, love,
  More safely, without its ray.
Far better lights shall win me,
  Along the path I've yet to roam—
The mind that burns within me,
  And pure smiles from thee at home.

Thus, when the lamp that lighted
  The traveller at first goes out,
He feels awhile benighted,
  And looks round in fear and doubt.
But soon, the prospect clearing,
  By cloudless starlight on he treads,
And thinks no lamp so cheering
  As that light which Heaven sheds.

(1) Our Wicklow Gold Mines, to which this verse alludes, deserve, I fear, but too well the character given of them.
(2) " The bird, having got its prize, settled not far off,

COME O'ER THE SEA.

Air—*Cuishlih ma Chree.*

COME o'er the sea,
  Maiden, with me,
Mine through sunshine, storm, and snows ;
  Seasons may roll,
  But the true soul
Burns the same, where'er it goes.
Let fate frown on, so we love and part not ;
'T is life where *thou* art,'t is death where thou art not.
  Then come o'er the sea,
  Maiden, with me,
Come wherever the wild wind blows ;
  Seasons may roll,
  But the true soul
Burns the same, where'er it goes.

  Was not the sea
  Made for the Free,
Land for courts and chains alone ?.
  Here we are slaves,
  But, on the waves,
Love and Liberty's all our own.
No eye to watch, and no tongue to wound us,
All earth forgot, and all heaven around us—
  Then come o'er the sea,
  Maiden, with me,
Mine through sunshine, storms, and snows ;
  Seasons may roll,
  But the true soul
Burns the same, where'er it goes.

HAS SORROW THY YOUNG DAYS SHADED.

Air—*Sly Patrick.*

HAS sorrow thy young days shaded,
  As clouds o'er the morning fleet?
Too fast have those young days faded
  That, even in sorrow, were sweet?
Does Time with his cold wing wither
  Each feeling that once was dear ?—
Then, child of misfortune, come hither,
  I 'll weep with thee, tear for tear.

Has love to that soul, so tender,
  Been like our Lagenian mine,(1)
Where sparkles of golden splendour
  All over the surface shine—
But, if in pursuit we go deeper,
  Allured by the gleam that shone,
Ah! false as the dream of the sleeper,
  Like Love, the bright ore is gone.

Has Hope, like the bird in the story, (2)
  That flitted from tree to tree

with the talisman in his mouth. The prince drew near it, hoping it would drop it; but, as he approached, the bird took wing, and settled again," etc.—*Arabian Nights.*

With the talisman's glittering glory—
Has Hope been that bird to thee?
On branch after branch alighting,
The gem did she still display,
And, when nearest and most inviting,
Then waft the fair gem away?

If thus the young hours have fleeted,
When sorrow itself look'd bright;
If thus the fair hope hath cheated,
That led thee along so light;
If thus the cold world now wither
Each feeling that once was dear—
Come, child of misfortune, come hither,
I'll weep with thee, tear for tear.

NO, NOT MORE WELCOME.
Air—*Luggelaw.*

No, not more welcome the fairy numbers
Of music fall on the sleeper's ear,
When half awaking from fearful slumbers,
He thinks the full quire of heaven is near—
Than came that voice, when, all forsaken,
This heart long had sleeping lain,
Nor thought its cold pulse would ever waken
To such benign blessed sounds again.

Sweet voice of comfort! 't was like the stealing
Of summer wind through some wreathed shell—
Each secret winding, each inmost feeling
Of all my soul echoed to its spell.
'T was whisper'd balm—'t was sunshine spoken!—
I'd live years of grief and pain
To have my long sleep of sorrow broken
By such benign blessed sounds again.

WHEN FIRST I MET THEE.
Air—*O Patrick! fly from me.*

When first I met thee, warm and young,
There shone such truth about thee,
And on thy lip such promise hung,
I did not dare to doubt thee.
I saw thee change, yet still relied,
Still clung with hope the fonder,
And thought, though false to all beside,
From me thou couldst not wander.
But go, deceiver! go,
The heart, whose hopes could make it
Trust one so false, so low,
Deserves that thou shouldst break it.

When every tongue thy follies named,
I fled the unwelcome story;
Or found, in even the faults they blamed,
Some gleams of future glory.
I still was true, when nearer friends
Conspired to wrong, to slight thee;
The heart that now thy falsehood rends
Would then have bled to right thee.

But go, deceiver! go—
Some day, perhaps, thou'lt waken
From pleasure's dream, to know
The grief of hearts forsaken.

Even now, though youth its bloom has shed,
No lights of age adorn thee;
The few who loved thee once have fled,
And they who flatter scorn thee.
Thy midnight cup is pledged to slaves,
No genial ties enwreath it;
The smiling there, like light on graves,
Has rank cold hearts beneath it.
Go—go—though worlds were thine,
I would not now surrender
One taintless tear of mine
For all thy guilty splendour!

And days may come, thou false one! yet,
When even those ties shall sever!
When thou wilt call, with vain regret,
On her thou'st lost for ever;
On her who, in thy fortune's fall,
With smiles had still received thee,
And gladly died to prove thee all
Her fancy first believed thee.
Go—go—'t is vain to curse,
'T is weakness to upbraid thee;
Hate cannot wish thee worse
Than guilt and shame have made thee.

WHILE HISTORY'S MUSE.
Air—*Paddy Whack.*

While History's Muse the memorial was keeping
Of all that the dark hand of Destiny weaves,
Beside her the Genius of Erin stood weeping,
For hers was the story that blotted the leaves.
But oh! how the tear in her eyelids grew bright,
When, after whole pages of sorrow and shame,
She saw History write,
With a pencil of light   [name.
That illumed the whole volume, her Wellington's

"Hail, Star of my Isle!" said the Spirit, all sparkling
With beams, such as break from her own dewy
skies—
"Through ages of sorrow, deserted and darkling,
I've watch'd for some glory like thine to arise.
For, though heroes I've number'd, unblest was
their lot,
And unhallow'd they sleep in the cross-ways of
Fame;—
But oh! there is not
One dishonouring blot
On the wreath that encircles my Wellington's name.

"Yet still the last crown of thy toils is remaining,
The grandest, the purest, even *thou* hast yet
known;

Though proud was thy task, other nations unchain-
　　ing,
　Far prouder to heal the deep wounds of thy own.
At the foot of that throne, for whose weal thou hast
　　stood,
Go, plead for the land that first cradled thy fame,
　　And, bright o'er the flood
　　Of her tears and her blood,
Let the rainbow of Hope be her Wellington's name!"

THE TIME I'VE LOST IN WOOING.

Air—*Peas upon a Trencher.*

The time I've lost in wooing,
In watching and pursuing
　　The light that lies
　　In woman's eyes,
Has been my heart's undoing.
Though Wisdom oft has sought me,
I scorn'd the lore she brought me,
　　My only books
　　Were woman's looks,
And folly's all they've taught me.

Her smile when Beauty granted,
I hung with gaze enchanted,
　　Like him the Sprite,(1)
　　Whom maids by night
Oft meet in glen that's haunted.
Like him, too, Beauty won me,
But while her eyes were on me,
　　If once their ray
　　Was turn'd away,
O! winds could not outrun me.

And are those follies going?
And is my proud heart growing
　　Too cold or wise
　　For brilliant eyes
Again to set it glowing?
No, vain, alas! the endeavour
From bonds so sweet to sever;
　　Poor Wisdom's chance
　　Against a glance
Is now as weak as ever.

WHERE IS THE SLAVE.

Air—*Sios agus sios liom.*

Oh, where's the slave so lowly,
Condemn'd to chains unholy,
　　Who, could he burst
　　His bonds at first,
Would pine beneath them slowly?

(1) This alludes to a kind of Irish fairy, which is to be
met with, they say, in the fields at dusk. As long as you
keep your eyes upon him, he is fixed, and in your power;
—but the moment you look away (and he is ingenious in
furnishing some inducement) he vanishes. I had thought

What soul, whose wrongs degrade it,
Would wait till time decay'd it,
　　When thus its wing
　　At once may spring
To the throne of Him who made it?

Farewell, Erin,—farewell, all,
Who live to weep our fall!

Less dear the laurel growing,
Alive, untouch'd and blowing,
　　Than that whose braid
　　Is pluck'd to shade
The brows with victory glowing.
We tread the land that bore us,
Her green flag glitters o'er us,
　　The friends we've tried
　　Are by our side,
And the foe we hate before us.

Farewell, Erin,—farewell, all,
Who live to weep our fall!

COME, REST IN THIS BOSOM.

Air—*Lough Sheeling.*

Come, rest in this bosom, my own stricken deer,
Though the herd have fled from thee, thy home is
　　still here;
Here still is the smile, that no cloud can o'ercast,
And a heart and a hand all thy own to the last.

Oh! what was love made for, if 'tis not the same
Through joy and through torment, through glory and
I know not, I ask not, if guilt's in that heart? [shame?
I but know that I love thee, whatever thou art.

Thou hast call'd me thy Angel in moments of bliss,
And thy Angel I'll be, 'mid the horrors of this,—
Through the furnace, unshrinking, thy steps to pursue,
And shield thee, and save thee,—or perish there too!

'T IS GONE, AND FOR EVER.

Air—*Savournah Deelish.*

'T is gone, and for ever, the light we saw breaking,
　Like Heaven's first dawn o'er the sleep of the dead—
When Man, from the slumber of ages awaking,
　Look'd upward, and bless'd the pure ray, ere it fled.
'T is gone, and the gleams it has left of its burning,
But deepen the long night of bondage and mourning,
That dark o'er the kingdoms of earth is returning,
　And darkest of all, hapless Erin, o'er thee.

For high was thy hope, when those glories were darting
　Around thee, through all the gross clouds of the
　　world;

that this was the sprite which we call the Leprechaun;
but a high authority upon such subjects, Lady Morgan, (in
a note upon her national and interesting novel, *O'Donnel*,)
has given a very different account of that goblin.

When Truth, from her fetters indignantly starting,
  At once, like a sun-burst, her banner unfurl'd.(1)
Oh! never shall earth see a moment so splendid!
Then, then—had one Hymn of Deliverance blended
The tongues of all nations—how sweet had ascended
  The first note of liberty, Erin, from thee!

But, shame on those tyrants who envied the blessing!
  And shame on the light race, unworthy its good,
Who, at Death's rocking altar, like furies, caressing
  The young hope of Freedom, baptised it in blood.
Then vanish'd for ever that fair sunny vision,
Which, spite of the slavish, the cold heart's derision,
Shall long be remember'd, pure, bright, and elysian,
  As first it arose, my lost Erin, on thee.

FILL THE BUMPER FAIR.

Air—*Bob and Joan.*

Fill the bumper fair!
  Every drop we sprinkle
O'er the brow of Care
  Smooths away a wrinkle.
Wit's electric flame
  Ne'er so swiftly passes,
As when through the frame
  It shoots from brimming glasses.
Fill the bumper fair!
  Every drop we sprinkle
O'er the brow of Care
  Smooths away a wrinkle.

Sages can, they say,
  Grasp the lightning's pinions,
And bring down its ray
  From the starr'd dominions:
So we, Sages, sit,
  And, 'mid bumpers brightening,
From the Heaven of Wit
  Draw down all its lightning.
      Fill the bumper, etc.

Wouldst thou know what first
  Made our souls inherit
This ennobling thirst
  For wine's celestial spirit?
It chanced, upon that day,
  When, as bards inform us,
Prometheus stole away
  The living fires that warm us:
      Fill the bumper, etc.

The careless Youth, when up
  To Glory's fount aspiring,

Took nor urn nor cup
  To hide the pilfer'd fire in.—
But oh, his joy, when, round
  The halls of heaven spying,
Among the stars he found,
  A bowl of Bacchus lying!
      Fill the bumper, etc.

Some drops were in that bowl,
  Remains of last night's pleasure,
With which the Sparks of Soul
  Mix'd their burning treasure.
Hence the goblet's shower
  Hath such spells to win us;
Hence its mighty power
  O'er that flame within us.
Fill the bumper fair!
  Every drop we sprinkle
O'er the brow of Care
  Smooths away a wrinkle.

IN THE MORNING OF LIFE.

Air—*The little Harvest Rose.*

In the morning of life, when its cares are unknown,
  And its pleasures in all their new lustre begin,
When we live in a bright-beaming world of our own,
  And the light that surrounds us is all from within;
Oh 'tis not, believe me, in that happy time
  We can love, as in hours of less transport we
      may;—
Of our smiles, of our hopes, 'tis the gay sunny prime,
  But affection is truest when these fade away.

When we see the first glory of youth pass us by,
  Like a leaf on the stream that will never return;
When our cup, which had sparkled with pleasure so
    high,
  First tastes of the *other,* the dark-flowing urn;
Then, then is the time when affection holds sway
  With a depth and a tenderness joy never knew;
Love, nursed among pleasures, is faithless as they,
  But the love born of Sorrow, like Sorrow, is true.

In climes full of sunshine, though splendid the
    flowers,   [worth;
  Their sighs have no freshness, their odour no
'Tis the cloud and the mist of our own Isle of showers
  That call the rich spirit of fragrancy forth.
So it is not 'mid splendour, prosperity, mirth,
  That the depth of Love's generous spirit appears;
To the sunshine of smiles it may first owe its birth,
  But the soul of its sweetness is drawn out by
    tears. (2)

---

(1) "The Sun-burst" was the fanciful name given by
the ancient Irish to the Royal Banner.
(2) The termination of this song, it will be perceived, has
undergone some change since its original publication:—
  In climes full of sunshine, though splendid their dyes,
    Yet faint is the odour the flowers shed about;

'T is the clouds and the mists of our own weeping skies
  That call the full spirit of fragrancy out.

So the wild glow of passion may kindle from mirth,
  But 't is only in grief true affection appears;—
And, even though to smiles it may first owe its birth,
  All the soul of its sweetness is drawn out by tears.—P. E.

I SAW FROM THE BEACH.

Air—*Miss Molly.*

I saw from the beach, when the morning was shining,
  A bark o'er the waters move gloriously on ;
I came when the sun o'er that beach was declining,
  The bark was still there, but the waters were gone.

And such is the fate of our life's early promise,
  So passing the spring-tide of joy we have known ;
Each wave that we danced on at morning ebbs from us,
  And leaves us, at eve, on the bleak shore alone.

Ne'er tell me of glories, serenely adorning
  The close of our day, the calm eve of our night ;—
Give me back, give me back the wild freshness of
    Morning,
  Her clouds and her tears are worth Evening's best
    light.

Oh, who would not welcome that moment's returning
  When passion first waked a new life through his
    frame,
And his soul, like the wood that grows precious in
    burning,
  Gave out all its sweets to love's exquisite flame.

DEAR HARP OF MY COUNTRY.

Air—*New Langolee.*

Dear Harp of my Country ! in darkness I found thee,
  The cold chain of Silence had hung o'er thee long,(1)
When proudly, my own Island Harp, I unbound thee,
  And gave all thy chords to light, freedom, and song !
The warm lay of love and the light note of gladness
  Have waken'd thy fondest, thy liveliest thrill,
But, so oft hast thou echoed the deep sigh of sadness,
  That even in thy mirth it will steal from thee still.

Dear Harp of my country! farewell to thy numbers,
  This sweet wreath of song is the last we shall twine!
Go, sleep with the sunshine of Fame on thy slumbers,
  Till touch'd by some hand less unworthy than
    mine.
If the pulse of the patriot, soldier, or lover,
  Have throbb'd at our lay, 't is thy glory alone ;
I was *but* as the wind, passing heedlessly over,
  And all the wild sweetness I waked was thy own.

MY GENTLE HARP.

Air—*The Coina, or Dirge.*

My gentle Harp, once more I waken
  The sweetness of thy slumbering strain ;

(1) In that rebellious but beautiful song, " When Erin
first rose," there is, if I recollect right, the following
line :—
  " The dark chain of Silence was thrown o'er the deep."
The chain of Silence was a sort of practical figure of
rhetoric among the ancient Irish. Walker tells us of " a
celebrated contention for precedence between Finn and

In tears our last farewell was taken,
  And now in tears we meet again.
No light of joy hath o'er thee broken,
  But, like those harps whose heavenly skill
Of slavery, dark as thine, hath spoken,
  Thou hang'st upon the willows still.

And yet, since last thy chord resounded,
  An hour of peace and triumph came,
And many an ardent bosom bounded
  With hopes—that now are turn'd to shame.
Yet even then, while Peace was singing
  Her halcyon song o'er land and sea,
Though joy and hope to others bringing,
  She only brought new tears to thee.

Then, who can ask for notes of pleasure,
  My drooping Harp, from chords like thine?
Alas, the lark's gay morning measure
  As ill would suit the swan's decline !
Or how shall I, who love, who bless thee,
  Invoke thy breath for Freedom's strains,
When even the wreaths in which I dress thee
  Are sadly mix'd—half flowers, half chains ?

But come—if yet thy frame can borrow
  One breath of joy, oh, breathe for me,
And show the world, in chains and sorrow,
  How sweet thy music still can be ;
How gaily, even 'mid gloom surrounding,
  Thou yet canst wake at pleasure's thrill--
Like Memnon's broken image sounding,
  'Mid desolation tuneful still! (2)

AS SLOW OUR SHIP.

Air—*The Girl I left behind me.*

As slow our ship her foamy track
  Against the wind was cleaving,
Her trembling pennant still look'd back
  To that dear Isle 't was leaving.
So loath we part from all we love,
  From all the links that bind us ;
So turn our hearts as on we rove,
  To those we've left behind us.

When, round the bowl, of vanish'd years
  We talk, with joyous seeming,—
With smiles that might as well be tears,
  So faint, so sad their beaming ;
While memory brings us back again
  Each early tie that twined us,
Oh, sweet's the cup that circles then
  To those we've left behind us.

Gaul, near Finn's palace at Almhaim, where the attending
Bards, anxious, if possible, to produce a cessation of hos-
tilities, shook the chain of Silence, and flung themselves
among the ranks." See also the *Ode to Gaul, the son of
Morni,* in Miss Brooke's *Reliques of Irish Poetry.*
  (2) Dimidio magicæ resonant ubi Memnone chordæ.—
Juvenal.

And when, in other climes, we meet
 Some isle, or vale enchanting,
Where all looks flowery, wild, and sweet,
 And nought but love is wanting;
We think how great had been our bliss,
 If Heaven had but assign'd us
To live and die in scenes like this,
 With some we 've left behind us!

As travellers oft look back at eve,
 When eastward darkly going,
To gaze upon that light they leave
 Still faint behind them glowing—
So, when the close of pleasure's day
 To gloom hath near consign'd us,
We turn to catch one fading ray
 Of joy that 's left behind us.

—⟶⊷∘⟵—

WHEN COLD IN THE EARTH.

AIR—*Limerick's Lamentation.*

WHEN cold in the earth lies the friend thou hast
 loved,
 Be his faults and his follies forgot by thee then;
Or, if from their slumber the veil be removed,
 Weep o'er them in silence, and close it again.
And oh! if 'tis pain to remember how far
 From the pathways of light he was tempted to
 roam,
Be it bliss to remember that thou wert the star
 That arose on his darkness, and guided him home.

From thee and thy innocent beauty first came
 The revealings, that taught him true love to adore,
To feel the bright presence, and turn him with
 shame
 From the idols he blindly had knelt to before.
O'er the waves of a life, long benighted and wild,
 Thou camest, like a soft golden calm o'er the sea;
And if happiness purely and glowingly smiled
 On his evening horizon, the light was from thee.

And though sometimes the shades of past folly
 might rise,
 And though falsehood again would allure him to
 stray,
He but turn'd to the glory that dwelt in those eyes,
 And the folly, the falsehood, soon vanish'd away.
As the Priests of the Sun, when their altar grew dim,
 At the day-beam alone could its lustre repair,
So, if virtue a moment grew languid in him,
 He but flew to that smile and rekindled it there.

—⟶⊷∘⟵—

REMEMBER THEE!

AIR—*Castle Tirowen.*

REMEMBER thee! yes, while there 's life in this heart,
It shall never forget thee, all lorn as thou art;
More dear in thy sorrow, thy gloom, and thy showers,
Than the rest of the world in their sunniest hours.

Wert thou all that I wish thee, great, glorious, and
 free,
First flower of the earth, and first gem of the sea,
I might hail thee with prouder, with happier brow,
But oh! could I love thee more deeply than now?

No, thy chains as they rankle, thy blood as it runs,
But make thee more painfully dear to thy sons—
Whose hearts, like the young of the desert-bird's nest,
Drink love in each life-drop that flows from thy
 breast.

—⟶⊷∘⟵—

WREATH THE BOWL.

AIR—*Nora Kista.*

WREATH the bowl
 With flowers of soul,
The brightest Wit can find us;
 We 'll take a flight
 Towards heaven to-night,
And leave dull earth behind us.

Should Love amid
 The wreaths be hid
That Joy, the enchanter, brings us,
 No danger fear,
 While wine is near—
We'll drown him if he stings us.
 Then, wreath the bowl
 With flowers of soul,
The brightest Wit can find us;
 We'll take a flight
 Towards heaven to-night,
And leave dull earth behind us.

'T was nectar fed
 Of old, 'tis said,
Their Junos, Joves, Apollos;
 And man may brew
 His nectar too,
The rich receipt's as follows:
 Take wine like this,
 Let looks of bliss
Around it well be blended,
 Then bring Wit's beam
 To warm the stream,
And there's your nectar, splendid!
 So, wreath the bowl,
 With flowers of soul,
The brightest Wit can find us;
 We 'll take a flight
 Towards heaven to-night,
And leave dull earth behind us.

Say, why did Time
 His glass sublime
Fill up with sands unsightly,
 When wine, he knew,
 Runs brisker through,
And sparkles far more brightly?

28

Oh, lend it us,
And, smiling thus,
The glass in two we'll sever,
Make pleasure glide
In double tide,
And fill both ends for ever!
Then, wreath the bowl
With flowers of soul
The brightest Wit can find us;
We'll take a flight
Towards heaven to-night,
And leave dull earth behind us.

———o♦o———

WHENE'ER I SEE THOSE SMILING EYES.

AIR—*Father Quinn.*

WHENE'ER I see those smiling eyes,
So full of hope, and joy, and light,
As if no cloud could ever rise,
To dim a heaven so purely bright—
I sigh to think how soon that brow
In grief may lose its every ray,
And that light heart, so joyous now,
Almost forget it once was gay.

For time will come with all its blights,
The ruin'd hope, the friend unkind,
And love, that leaves, where'er it lights,
A chill'd or burning heart behind:
While youth, that now like snow appears,
Ere sullied by the darkening rain,
When once 't is touch'd by sorrow's tears,
Can never shine so bright again.

———o♦o———

IF THOU'LT BE MINE.

AIR—*The Winnowing Sheet.*

IF thou 'lt be mine, the treasures of air,
Of earth, and sea, shall lie at thy feet;
Whatever in Fancy's eye looks fair,
Or in Hope's sweet music sounds *most* sweet,
Shall be ours—if thou wilt be mine, love!

Bright flowers shall bloom wherever we rove,
A voice divine shall talk in each stream;
The stars shall look like worlds of love,
And this earth be all one beautiful dream
In our eyes—if thou wilt be mine, love!

And thoughts, whose source is hidden and high,
Like streams that come from heaven-ward hills,
Shall keep our hearts, like meads, that lie
To be bathed by those eternal rills,
Ever green, if thou wilt be mine, love!

All this and more the Spirit of Love
Can breathe o'er them who feel his spells;
That heaven, which forms his home above,
He can make on earth, wherever he dwells,
As thou 'lt own,—if thou wilt be mine, love!

TO LADIES' EYES.

AIR—*Fague a Ballagh.*

To Ladies' eyes a round, boy,
We can't refuse, we can't refuse;
Though bright eyes so abound, boy,
'T is hard to choose, 't is hard to choose.
For thick as stars that lighten
Yon airy bowers, yon airy bowers,
The countless eyes that brighten
This earth of ours, this earth of ours.
But fill the cup—where'er, boy,
Our choice may fall, our choice may fall,
We're sure to find Love there, boy,
So drink them all! so drink them all!

Some looks there are so holy,
They seem but given, they seem but given,
As shining beacons, solely,
To light to heaven, to light to heaven.
While some—oh! ne'er believe them—
With tempting ray, with tempting ray,
Would lead us (God forgive them!)
The other way, the other way.
But fill the cup—where'er, boy,
Our choice may fall, our choice may fall,
We're sure to find Love there, boy;
So drink them all! so drink them all!

In some, as in a mirror,
Love seems pourtray'd, Love seems pourtray'd;
But shun the flattering error,
'T is but his shade, 't is but his shade.
Himself has fix'd his dwelling
In eyes we know, in eyes we know,
And lips—but this is telling—
So here they go! so here they go!
Fill up, fill up—where'er, boy,
Our choice may fall, our choice may fall,
We're sure to find Love there, boy;
So drink them all! so drink them all!

———o♦o———

FORGET NOT THE FIELD.

AIR—*The Lamentation of Aughrim.*

FORGET not the field where they perish'd,
The truest, the last of the brave,
All gone—and the bright hope we cherish'd
Gone with them, and quench'd in their grave!

Oh! could we from death but recover
Those hearts as they bounded before,
In the face of high heaven to fight over
That combat for freedom once more ;—

Could the chain for an instant be riven
Which Tyranny flung round us then,
No, 't is not in Man, nor in Heaven,
To let Tyranny bind it again!

But 't is past—and, though blazon'd in story
  The name of our Victor may be,
Accurst is the march of that glory
  Which treads o'er the hearts of the free.

Far dearer the grave or the prison,
  Illumed by one patriot name,
Than the trophies of all who have risen
  On Liberty's ruins to fame.

—◦●◦—

SAIL ON, SAIL ON.

Air—*The Humming of the Ban.*

Sail on, sail on, thou fearless bark—
  Wherever blows the welcome wind,
It cannot lead to scenes more dark,
  More sad than those we leave behind.
Each wave that passes seems to say,
  " Though death beneath our smile may be,
Less cold we are, less false than they,
  Whose smiling wreck'd thy hopes and thee."

Sail on, sail on—through endless space—
  Through calm—through tempest—stop no more:
The stormiest sea 's a resting-place
  To him who leaves such hearts on shore.
Or—if some desert land we meet,
  Where never yet false-hearted men
Profaned a world, that else were sweet—
  Then rest thee, bark, but not till then.

—◦●◦—

NE'ER ASK THE HOUR.

Air—*My husband's a journey to Portugal gone.*

Ne'er ask the hour—what is it to us
  How Time deals out his treasures ?
The golden moments lent us thus
  Are not *his* coin, but Pleasure's.
If counting them o'er could add to their blisses,
  I 'd number each glorious second :
But moments of joy are, like Lesbia's kisses,
  Too quick and sweet to be reckon'd.
Then fill the cup—what is it to us
  How time his circle measures ?
The fairy hours we call up thus
  Obey no wand but Pleasure's.

Young Joy ne'er thought of counting hours,
  Till Care, one summer's morning,
Set up, among his smiling flowers,
  A dial, by way of warning.
But Joy loved better to gaze on the sun,
  As long as its light was glowing,
Than to watch with old Care how the shadow
  And how fast that light was going.   [stole on,
So fill the cup—what is it to us
  How Time his circle measures ?
The fairy hours we call up thus
  Obey no wand but Pleasure's.

† Tous les habitants de Mercure sont vifs.—*Pluralité des Mondes.*

THEY MAY RAIL AT THIS LIFE.

Air—*Noch bonin shin doe.*

They may rail at this life—from the hour I began it
  I found it a life full of kindness and bliss;
And, until they can show me some happier planet,
  More social and bright, I 'll content me with this.
As long as the world has such lips and such eyes
  As before me this moment enraptured I see,
They may say what they will of their orbs in the skies,
  But this earth is the planet for you, love, and me.

In Mercury's star, where each moment can bring them
  New sunshine and wit from the fountain on high,
Though the nymphs may have livelier poets to sing them, (1)
  They 've none, even there, more enamour'd than I.
And, as long as this harp can be waken'd to love,
  And that eye its divine inspiration shall be,
They may talk as they will of their Edens above,
  But this earth is the planet for you, love, and me.

In that star of the west, by whose shadowy splendour,
  At twilight so often we 've roam'd through the dew,
There are maidens, perhaps, who have bosoms as tender,
  And look, in their twilights, as lovely as you. (2)
But though they were even more bright than the queen
  Of that isle they inhabit in heaven's blue sea,
As I never those fair young celestials have seen,
  Why—this earth is the planet for you, love, and me.

As for those chilly orbs on the verge of creation,
  Where sunshine and smiles must be equally rare,
Did they want a supply of cold hearts for that station,
  Heaven knows we have plenty on earth we could spare.
Oh ! think what a world we should have of it here,
  If the haters of peace, of affection and glee,
Were to fly up to Saturn's comfortless sphere,
  And leave earth to such spirits as you, love, and me.

—◦●◦—

OH FOR THE SWORDS OF FORMER TIME !

Air—*Name unknown.*

Oh for the swords of former time !
  Oh for the men who bore them,
When, arm'd for Right, they stood sublime,
  And tyrants crouch'd before them :
When free yet, ere courts began
  With honours to enslave him,
The best honours worn by Man
  Were those which Virtue gave him.
Oh for the swords, etc., etc.

Oh for the Kings who flourish'd then !
  Oh for the pomp that crown'd them,

2) La Terre pourra être pour Venus l'étoile du berger et la mère des amours, comme Venus l'est pour nous.—*Ib.*

When hearts and hands of freeborn men
  Were all the ramparts round them.
When, safe built on bosoms true,
  The throne was but the centre,
Round which Love a circle drew
  That Treason durst not enter.
Oh for the Kings who flourish'd then !
  Oh for the pomp that crown'd them,
When hearts and hands of freeborn men
  Were all the ramparts round them !

THE PARALLEL.

AIR—*I would rather than Ireland.*

YES, sad one of Sion, (1) if closely resembling,
  In shame and in sorrow, thy wither'd-up heart—
If drinking deep, deep, of the same "cup of trembling"
  Could make us thy children, our parent thou art.

Like thee doth our nation lie conquer'd and broken,
  And fall'n from her head is the once royal crown ;
In her streets, in her halls, Desolation hath spoken,
  And "while it is day yet, her sun hath gone
    down." (2)

Like thine doth her exile, 'mid dreams of returning,
  Die far from the home it were life to behold ;
Like thine do her sons, in the day of their mourning,
  Remember the bright things that bless'd them of old.

Ah, well may we call her, like thee, "the Forsaken,"(3)
  Her boldest are vanquish'd, her proudest are slaves ;
And the harps of her minstrels, when gayest they
  waken,   [graves !
Have tones 'mid their mirth like the wind over

Yet hadst thou thy vengeance—yet came there the
  morrow,
That shines out, at last, on the longest dark night,
When the sceptre, that smote thee with slavery and
  sorrow,
  Was shiver'd at once, like a reed, in thy sight.

When that cup, which for others the proud Golden
  City (4)   [lips ;
Had brimm'd full of bitterness, drench'd her own
And the world she had trampled on heard, without pity,
  The howl in her halls, and the cry from her ships.

When the curse Heaven keeps for the haughty came
  Her merchants rapacious, her rulers unjust,   [over
And a ruin at last for the earthworm to cover, (5)
  The Lady of Kingdoms (6) lay low in the dust.

(1) These verses were written after the perusal of a
treatise by Mr. Hamilton, professing to prove that the
Irish were originally Jews.
(2) "Her sun is gone down while it was yet day."—
Jer., xv. 9.
(3) "Thou shalt no more be termed Forsaken."—
Isaiah, lxii. 4.

DRINK OF THIS CUP.

AIR—*Paddy O'Rafferty.*

DRINK of this cup ;—you 'll find there 's a spell in
  Its every drop 'gainst the ills of mortality ;
Talk of the cordial that sparkled for Helen !
  Her cup was a fiction, but this is reality.
Would you forget the dark world we are in,
  Just taste of the bubble that gleams on the top of it ;
But would you rise above earth, till akin
  To immortals themselves, you must drain every
    drop of it !
Send round the cup—for oh there 's a spell in
  Its every drop 'gainst the ills of mortality ;
Talk of the cordial that sparkled for Helen !
  Her cup was a fiction, but this is reality.

Never was philter form'd with such power
  To charm and bewilder as this we are quaffing ;
Its magic began when, in Autumn's rich hour,
  A harvest of gold in the fields it stood laughing.
There having, by Nature's enchantment, been fill'd
  With the balm and the bloom of her kindliest
    weather,
This wonderful juice from its core was distill'd
  To enliven such hearts as are here brought to-
    gether.
Then drink of the cup—you 'll find there 's a spell in
  Its every drop 'gainst the ills of mortality ;
Talk of the cordial that sparkled for Helen !
  Her cup was a fiction, but this is reality.

And though, perhaps—but breathe it to no one—
  Like liquor the witch brews at midnight so awful,
This philter in secret was first taught to flow on,
  Yet 't is n't less potent for being unlawful.
And, even though it taste of the smoke of that flame
  Which in silence extracted its virtue forbidden—
Fill up—there 's a fire in some hearts I could name,
  Which may work too its charm, though as lawless
    and hidden.
So drink of the cup—for oh there 's a spell in
  Its every drop 'gainst the ills of mortality ;
Talk of the cordial that sparkled for Helen !
  Her cup was a fiction, but this is reality.

THE FORTUNE-TELLER.

AIR—*Open the Door softly.*

DOWN in the valley come meet me to-night,
  And I 'll tell you your fortune truly
As ever 't was told, by the new-moon 's light,
  To a young maiden, shining as newly.

(4) "How hath the oppressor ceased ! the golden city
ceased !"—*Isaiah*, xiv. 11.
(5) "Thy pomp is brought down to the grave . . . .
and the worms cover thee."—*Isaiah*, xiv., 4.
(6) "Thou shalt no more be called the Lady of King-
doms."—*Isaiah*, xlvii. 5.

But, for the world, let no one be nigh,
Lest haply the stars should deceive me;
Such secrets between you and me and the sky
Should never go farther, believe me.

If at that hour the heavens be not dim,
My science shall call up before you
A male apparition—the image of him
Whose destiny 't is to adore you.

And if to that phantom you 'll be kind,
So fondly around you he 'll hover,
You 'll hardly, my dear, any difference find
'Twixt him and a true living lover.

Down at your feet, in the pale moonlight,
He 'll kneel, with a warmth of devotion—
An ardour, of which such an innocent sprite
You 'd scarcely believe had a notion.

What other thoughts and events may arise,
As in destiny's book I 've not seen them,
Must only be left to the stars and your eyes
To settle, ere morning, between them.

———o+o———

OH, YE DEAD!

Air—*Plough Tune.*

Oh, ye Dead! oh, ye Dead! (1) whom we know by
the light you give
From your cold gleaming eyes, though you move
like men who live,
Why leave you thus your graves,
In far off fields and waves,
Where the worm and the sea-bird only know your bed,
To haunt this spot where all
Those eyes that wept your fall,   [dead?
And the hearts that wail'd you, like your own, lie

It is true, it is true, we are shadows cold and wan;
And the fair and the brave whom we loved on earth
But still thus even in death,   [are gone;
So sweet the living breath
Of the fields and the flowers in our youth we wan-
That ere, condemn'd, we go   [der'd o'er,
To freeze 'mid Hecla's snows,
We would taste it awhile, and think we live once more!

(1) Paul Zealand mentions that there is a mountain in
some part of Ireland, where the ghosts of persons who
have died in foreign lands walk about and converse with
those they meet, like living people. If asked why they
do not return to their homes, they say they are obliged to
go to Mount Hecla, and disappear immediately.

(2) The particulars of the tradition respecting O'Do-
nohue and his White Horse, may be found in Mr. Weld's
Account of Killarney, or more fully detailed in Derrick's
Letters. For many years after his death, the spirit of this
hero is supposed to have been seen on the morning of
May-day, gliding over the lake on his favourite white

O'DONOHUE'S MISTRESS.

Air—*The Little and Great Mountain.*

Of all the fair months, that round the sun
In light-link'd dance their circles run,
Sweet May, shine thou for me;
For still, when thy earliest beams arise,
That youth, who beneath the blue lake lies,
Sweet May, returns to me.

Of all the bright haunts, where daylight leaves
Its lingering smile on golden eves,
Fair lake, thou 'rt dearest to me;
For when the last April sun grows dim,
Thy Naiads prepare his steed (2) for him
Who dwells, bright lake, in thee.

Of all the proud steeds that ever bore
Young plumed Chiefs on sea or shore,
White Steed, most joy to thee;
Who still, with the first young glance of spring,
From under that glorious lake dost bring
My love, my chief, to me.

While, white as the sail some bark unfurls,
When newly launch'd, thy long mane (3) curls,
Fair Steed, as white and free;
And spirits, from all the lake's deep bowers,
Glide o'er the blue wave scattering flowers,
Around my love and thee.

Of all the sweet deaths that maidens die,
Whose lovers beneath the cold wave lie,
Most sweet that death will be,
Which, under the next May evening's light,
When thou and thy steed are lost to sight,
Dear love, I 'll die for thee.

———o+o———

ECHO.

Air—*The Wren.*

How sweet the answer Echo makes
To music at night,
When, roused by lute or horn, she wakes,
And far away, o'er lawns and lakes,
Goes answering light.

Yet Love hath echoes truer far,
And far more sweet,

horse, to the sound of sweet unearthly music, and pre-
ceded by groups of youths and maidens, who flung wreaths
of delicate spring flowers in his path.

Among other stories, connected with this Legend of the
Lakes, it is said that there was a young and beautiful girl
whose imagination was so impressed with the idea of this
visionary chieftain, that she fancied herself in love with
him, and at last, in a fit of insanity, on a May morning
threw herself into the lake.

(3) The boatmen at Killarney call those waves which
come on a windy day, crested with foam, "O'Donohue's
white horses."

Than e'er beneath the moonlight's star,
Of horn or lute, or soft guitar,
  The songs repeat.

'T is when the sigh, in youth sincere,
  And only then—
The sigh that 's breathed for one to hear,
Is by that one, that only dear,
  Breathed back again!

OH, THE SIGHT ENTRANCING.

Air—*Planxty Sudley*

Oh, the sight entrancing,
When morning's beam is glancing
    O'er files array'd
    With helm and blade,
And plumes in the gay wind dancing!
When hearts are all high beating
And the trumpet's voice repeating
    That song, whose breath
    May lead to death,
But never to retreating.
Oh, the sight entrancing,
When morning's beam is glancing
    O'er files array'd
    With helm and blade,
And plumes in the gay wind dancing!

Yet, 'tis not helm or feather—
For ask yon despot, whether
    His plumed bands
    Could bring such hands
And hearts as ours together.
Leave pomps to those who need 'em—
Give man but heart and freedom,
    And proud he braves
    The gaudiest slaves
That crawl where monarchs lead 'em.
The sword may pierce the beaver,
Stone walls in time may sever,
    'T is mind alone,
    Worth steel and stone,
That keeps men free for ever.
Oh, that sight entrancing,
When the morning's beam is glancing,
    O'er files array'd
    With helm and blade,
And in Freedom's cause advancing!

THEE, THEE, ONLY THEE.

Air—*The Market-Stake.*

The dawning of morn, the daylight's sinking,
The night's long hours still find me thinking
  Of thee, thee, only thee.
When friends are met, and goblets crown'd,
And smiles are near, that once enchanted,
Unreach'd by all that sunshine round,
  My soul, like some dark spot, is haunted
  By thee, thee, only thee.

Whatever in fame's high path could waken
My spirit once, is now forsaken
  For thee, thee, only thee.
Like shores, by which some headlong bark
  To the ocean hurries, resting never,
Life's scenes go by me, bright or dark,
  I know not, heed not, hastening ever
    To thee, thee, only thee.

I have not a joy but of thy bringing,
And pain itself seems sweet when springing
    From thee, thee, only thee.
Like spells, that nought on earth can break,
  Till lips, that know the charm, have spoken,
This heart, howe'er the world may wake
  Its grief, its scorn, can but be broken
    By thee, thee, only thee.

SHALL THE HARP THEN BE SILENT.

Air—*Macfarlane's Lamentation.*

Shall the Harp then be silent, when he who first gave
  To our country a name, is withdrawn from all eyes?
Shall a Minstrel of Erin stand mute by the grave
  Where the first—where the last of her Patriots lies?

No—faint though the death-song may fall from his lips,
  Though his Harp, like his soul, may with shadows
    be crost,
Yet, yet shall it sound, 'mid a nation's eclipse,
  And proclaim to the world what a star hath been
    lost;—(1)

What a union of all the affections and powers
  By which life is exalted, embellish'd, refined,
Was embraced in that spirit—whose centre was ours,
  While its mighty circumference circled mankind.

Oh, who that loves Erin, or who that can see,
  Through the waste of her annals, that epoch sub-
    lime—
Like a pyramid raised in the desert—where he
  And his glory stand out to the eyes of all time;

That *one* lucid interval, snatch'd from the gloom
  And the madness of ages, when fill'd with his soul,
A Nation o'erleap'd the dark bounds of her doom,
  And for *one* sacred instant, touch'd Liberty's goal?

Who, that ever hath heard him—hath drank at the
    source
  Of that wonderful eloquence, all Erin's own,
In whose high-thoughted daring, the fire, and the force,
  And the yet untamed spring of her spirit are
    shown?

(1) These lines were written on the death of our great
patriot, Grattan, in the year 1820. It is only the two first
verses that are either intended or fitted to be sung.

An eloquence rich, wheresoever its wave
  Wander'd free and triumphant, with thoughts that
    shone through
As clear as the brook's "stone of lustre," and gave,
  With the flash of the gem, its solidity too.
                        [crowd,
Who, that ever approach'd him, when free from the
  In a home full of love, he delighted to tread
'Mong the trees which a nation had given, and which
    bow'd,
  As if each brought a new civic crown for his
    head—(1)

Is there one, who hath thus, through his orbit of life
  But at distance observed him—through glory,
    through blame,
In the calm of retreat, in the grandeur of strife,
  Whether shining or clouded, still high and the
    same?—(2)

Oh no, not a heart that e'er knew him but mourns
  Deep, deep, o'er the grave where such glory is
    shrined—
O'er a monument Fame will preserve 'mong the urns
Of the wisest, the bravest, the best of mankind !

—◦❀◦—

SWEET INNISFALLEN.

Air—*The Captivating Youth.*

Sweet Innisfallen, fare thee well,
  May calm and sunshine long be thine!
How fair thou art let others tell—
  To *feel* how fair shall long be mine.

Sweet Innisfallen, long shall dwell
  In memory's dream that sunny smile,
Which o'er thee on that evening fell,
  When first I saw thy fairy isle.

'T was light, indeed, too blest for one,
  Who had to turn to paths of care—
Through crowded haunts again to run,
  And leave thee bright and silent there ; (3)

No more unto thy shores to come,
  But, on the world's rude ocean tost,
Dream of thee sometimes as a home
  Of sunshine he had seen and lost.

(1) The following verse is here omitted :—
That home, where—like him, who, as fable hath told, *
Put the rays from his brow, that his child might come near-
Every glory forgot, the most wise of the old
  Became all that the simplest and youngest hold dear.—P. E.

(2) Another elision occurs here :—
  Such a union of all that enriches life's hour,
    Of the sweetness we love and the greatness we praise,
  As that type of simplicity blended with power,
    A child with a thunderbolt, only pourtrays.—P. E.

* Apollo, in his interview with Phaëton, as described by Ovid,—
"*Opposuit radios propiusque accedere jussit.*"

Far better in thy weeping hour
  To part from thee, as I do now,
When mist is o'er thy blooming bowers,
  Like sorrow's veil on beauty's brow.

For, though unrivall'd still thy grace,
  Thou dost not look, as then, *too* blest,
But, thus in shadow, seem'st a place
  Where erring man might hope to rest—

Might hope to rest, and find in thee
  A gloom like Eden's, on the day
He left its shade, when every tree,
  Like thine, hung weeping o'er his way.

Weeping or smiling, lovely isle!
  And all the lovelier for thy tears—
For though but rare thy sunny smile,
  'T is heaven's own glance when it appears.

Like feeling hearts whose joys are few,
  But, when *indeed* they come, divine—
The brightest light the sun e'er threw
  Is lifeless to one gleam of thine !

—◦❀◦—

'T WAS ONE OF THOSE DREAMS. (4)

Air—*The Song of the Woods.*

'T was one of those dreams, that by music are
  brought,
Like a bright summer haze, o'er the poet's warm
  thought—
When, lost in the future, his soul wanders on,
And all of this life, but its sweetness, is gone.

The wild notes he heard o'er the water were those
He had taught to sing Erin's dark bondage and woes,
And the breath of the bugle now wafted them o'er
From Dinis' green isle, to Glena's wooded shore.

He listen'd—while, high o'er the eagle's rude nest,
The lingering sounds on their way loved to rest ;
And the echoes sung back from their full mountain
  quire,
As if loath to let song so enchanting expire.

It seem'd as if every sweet note that died here
Was again brought to life in some airier sphere,

(3) In the original edition the two preceding verses
read—

    Sweet Innisfallen, fare thee well,
      And long may light around thee smile,
    As soft as on that evening fell
      When first I saw thy fairy isle !

    Thou wert too lovely then for one
      Who had to turn to paths of care—
    Who had through vulgar crowds to run,
      And leave thee bright and silent there.—P. E.

(4) Written during a visit to Lord Kenmare, at Killar-
ney.

Some heaven in those hills, where the soul of the
 strain
That had ceased upón earth was awaking again !

Oh forgive, if, while listening to music, whose breath
Seem'd to circle his name with a charm against death,
He should feel a proud spirit within him proclaim,
" Even so shalt thou live in the echoes of Fame:

"Even so, though thy memory should now die away,
'T will be caught up again in some happier day,
And the hearts and the voices of Erin prolong,
Through the answering Future, thy name and thy
 song."

———o♦♦o———

OH, BANQUET NOT.

Air—*Planxty Irwine.*

Oh, banquet not in those shining bowers,
 Where Youth resorts, but come to me,
For mine's a garden of faded flowers,
 More fit for sorrow, for age, and thee.
And there we shall have our feast of tears,
 And many a cup in silence pour ;
Our guests, the shades of former years,
 Our toasts, to lips that bloom no more.

There, while the myrtle's withering boughs
 Their lifeless leaves around us shed,
We'll brim the bowl to broken vows
 To friends long lost, the changed, the dead.
Or, while some blighted laurel waves
 Its branches o'er the dreary spot,
We'll drink to those neglected graves
 Where valour sleeps, unnamed, forgot.

———o♦♦o———

FAIREST ! PUT ON AWHILE.

Air—*Cummilum.*

Fairest ! put on awhile
 These pinions of light I bring thee,
And o'er thy own green isle
 In fancy let me wing thee.
Never did Ariel's plume,
 At golden sunset, hover
O'er scenes so full of bloom
 As I shall waft thee over.

Fields, where the Spring delays
 And fearlessly meets the ardour
Of the warm Summer's gaze,
 With only her tears to guard her ;
Rocks, through myrtle boughs
 In grace majestic frowning,
Like some bold warrior's brows
 That Love hath just been crowning.

Islets, so freshly fair,
 That never hath bird como nigh them,
But, from his course through air,
 He hath been won down by them ;—(1)
Types, sweet maid, of thee,
 Whose look, whose blush inviting,
Never did Love yet see
 From heaven, without alighting.

Lakes, where the pearl lies hid, (2)
 And caves, where the gem is sleeping,
Bright as the tears thy lid
 Lets fall in lonely weeping.
Glens, (3) where Ocean comes,
 To 'scape the wild wind's rancour ;
And harbours, worthiest homes
 Where Freedom's fleet can anchor.

Then, if, while scenes so grand,
 So beautiful, shine before thee,
Pride for thy own dear land
 Should haply be stealing o'er thee,
Oh, let grief come first,
 O'er pride itself victorious—
Thinking how man hath curst
 What Heaven had made so glorious

———o♦♦o———

QUICK ! WE HAVE BUT A SECOND.

Air—*Paddy Snap.*

Quick ! we have but a second,
 Fill round the cup while you may ;
For time, the churl, hath beckon'd,
 And we must away, away!
Grasp the pleasure that's flying,
 For oh, not Orpheus' strain
Could keep sweet hours from dying,
 Or charm them to life again.
 Then, quick ! we have but a second,
 Fill round the cup while you may!
 For Time, the churl, hath beckon'd,
 And we must away, away !

See the glass, how it flushes,
 Like some young Hebe's lip,
And half meets thine, and blushes
 That thou shouldst delay to sip.
Shame, oh shame unto thee,
 If ever thou see'st that day,
When a cup or lip shall woo thee,
 And turn untouch'd away !
 Then, quick ! we have but a second,
 Fill round, fill round while you may ;
 For Time, the churl, hath beckon'd,
 And we must away, away !

(1) In describing the Skeligs (islands of the Barony of
Forth), Dr. Keating says, "There is a certain attractive
virtue in the soil which draws down all the birds that
attempt to fly over it, and obliges them to light upon the
rock."

(2) "Kennius, a British writer of the ninth century,

mentions the abundance of pearls in Ireland. Their
princes, he says, hung them behind their ears : and this
we find confirmed by a present made A. C. 1094, by Gilbert,
Bishop of Limerick, to Anselm, Archbishop of Canterbury,
of a considerable quantity of Irish pearls."—*O'Halloran.*

(3) Glengariff.

AND DOTH NOT A MEETING LIKE THIS.

Air—*Unknown.*

And doth not a meeting like this make amends
    For all the long years I 've been wandering away—
To see thus around me my youth's early friends,
    As smiling and kind as in that happy day?
Though haply o'er some of your brows, as o'er mine,
    The snow-fall of time may be stealing—what then?
Like Alps in the sunset, thus lighted by wine,
    We 'll wear the gay tinge of youth's roses again.

What soften'd remembrances come o'er the heart,
    In gazing on those we 've been lost to so long!
The sorrows, the joys, of which once they were part,
    Still round them, like visions of yesterday, throng.
As letters some hand hath invisibly traced,
    When held to the flame, will steal out on the sight,
So many a feeling, that long seem'd effaced,
    The warmth of a meeting like this brings to light.

And thus, as in memory's bark we shall glide,
    To visit the scenes of our boyhood anew,
Though oft we may see, looking down on the tide,
    The wreck of full many a hope shining through;
Yet still, as in fancy we point to the flowers,
    That once made a garden of all the gay shore,
Deceived for a moment, we 'll think them still ours,
    And breathe the fresh air of life's morning once
       more. (1)

So brief our existence, a glimpse, at the most,
    Is all we can have of the few we hold dear;
And oft even joy is unheeded and lost,
    For want of some heart, that could echo it, near.
Ah, well may we hope, when this short life is gone,
    To meet in some world of more permanent bliss,
For a smile, or a grasp of the hand, hastening on,
    Is all we enjoy of each other in this. (2)

But, come, the more rare such delights to the heart,
    The more we should welcome and bless them the
       more ;
They 're ours when we meet—they are lost when
       we part,
Like birds that bring Summer, and fly when 't is
       o'er.
Thus circling the cup, hand in hand, ere we drink,
    Let Sympathy pledge us, through pleasure, through
       pain,
That, fast as a feeling but touches one link,
    Her magic shall send it direct through the chain.

(1) Jours charmants, quand je songe à vos heureux instants,
    Je pense remonter le fleuve de mes ans;
    Et mon cœur enchanté, sur sa rive fleurie,
    Respire encor l'air pur du matin de la vie.
(2) The same thought has been happily expressed by my friend, Mr. Washington Irving, in his *Bracebridge Hall,* vol. i., p. 213. The sincere pleasure which I feel in call-

THE MOUNTAIN SPRITE.

Air—*The Mountain Sprite.*

In yonder valley there dwelt, alone,
A youth, whose moments had calmly flown,
'Till spells came o'er him, and, day and night,
He was haunted and watch'd by a Mountain Sprite.

As once, by moonlight, he wander'd o'er
The golden sands of that island shore,
A foot-print sparkled before his sight—
'T was the fairy foot of the Mountain Sprite!

Beside a fountain, one sunny day,
As bending over the stream he lay,
There peep'd down o'er him two eyes of light,
And he saw in that mirror the Mountain Sprite.

He turn'd, but, lo, like a startled bird,
That spirit fled!—and the youth but heard
Sweet music, such as marks the flight
Of some bird of song, from the Mountain Sprite.

One night, still haunted by that bright look,
The boy, bewilder'd, his pencil took,
And, guided only by memory's light,
Drew the once-seen form of the Mountain Sprite.

" Oh thou, who lovest the shadow," cried
A voice, low whispering by his side,
" Now turn and see,"—here the youth's delight
Seal'd the rosy lips of the Mountain Sprite.

" Of all the Sprits of land and sea,"
Then rapt he murmur'd," there's none like thee,
And oft, oh oft, may thy foot thus light
In this lonely bower, sweet Mountain Sprite !"

—◦◦◦—

AS VANQUISH'D ERIN.

Air—*The Boyne Water.*

As vanquish'd Erin wept beside
    The Boyne's ill-fated river,
She saw where Discord, in the tide,
    Had dropp'd his loaded quiver.
" Lie hid," she cried, " ye venom'd darts,
    Where mortal eye may shun you;
Lie hid—the stain of manly hearts,
    That bled for me, is on you."

But vain her wish, her weeping vain—
    As Time too well hath taught her—

ing this gentleman my friend is much enhanced by the reflection, that he is too good an American to have admitted me so readily to such a distinction, if he had not known that my feelings towards the great and free country that gave him birth have been long such as every real lover of the liberty and happiness of the human race must entertain.

29

Each year the Fiend returns again,
  And dives into that water;
And brings, triumphant, from beneath
  His shafts of desolation,
And sends them, wing'd with worse than death,
  Through all her maddening nation.

Alas for her who sits and mourns,
  Even now, beside that river—
Unwearied still the Fiend returns,
  And stored is still his quiver.
"When will this end, ye Powers of Good?"
  She weeping asks for ever;
But only hears, from out that flood,
  The Demon answer,"Never!"

DESMOND'S SONG. (1)
AIR—*Unknown.*

By the Feal's wave benighted,
  No star in the skies,
To thy door by Love lighted,
  I first saw those eyes.
Some voice whisper'd o'er me,
  As the threshold I cross'd,
There was ruin before me,
  If I loved, I was lost.

Love came, and brought sorrow
  Too soon in his train;
Yet so sweet, that to-morrow
  'T were welcome again.
Though misery's full measure
  My portion should be,
I would drain it with pleasure,
  If pour'd out by thee.

You, who call it dishonour
  To bow to this flame,
If you 're eyes, look but on her,
  And blush while you blame.
Hath the pearl less whiteness
  Because of its birth?
Hath the violet less brightness
  For growing near earth?

No—Man for his glory
  To ancestry flies;
But Woman's bright story
  Is told in her eyes.
While the Monarch but traces
  Through mortals his line,
Beauty, born of the Graces,
  Ranks next to Divine!

THEY KNOW NOT MY HEART.
AIR—*Coolon Das.*

They know not my heart, who believe there can be
One stain of this earth in its feelings for thee;
Who think, while I see thee in beauty's young hour,
As pure as the morning's first dew on the flower,
I could harm what I love—as the sun's wanton ray
But smiles on the dew-drop to waste it away.

No—beaming with light as those young features are,
There 's a light round thy heart which is lovelier far:
It *is* not that cheek—'t is the soul dawning clear
Through its innocent blush makes thy beauty so dear:
As the sky we look up to, though glorious and fair,
Is look'd up to the more, because Heaven lies there!

I WISH I WAS BY THAT DIM LAKE.
AIR—*I wish I was on yonder Hill.*

I wish I was by that dim Lake, (2)
Where sinful souls their farewell take
Of this vain world, and half-way lie
In death's cold shadow, ere they die.
There, there, far from thee,
Deceitful world, my home should be;
Where, come what might of gloom and pain,
False hope should ne'er deceive again.

The lifeless sky, the mournful sound
Of unseen waters falling round;
The dry leaves, quivering o'er my head,
Like man, unquiet even when dead!
These, ay, these shall wean
My soul from life's deluding scene,
And turn each thought, o'ercharged with gloom,
Like willows, downward towards the tomb.

(1) "Thomas, the heir of the Desmond family, had accidentally been so engaged in the chase, that he was benighted near Tralee, and obliged to take shelter at the Abbey of Feal, in the house of one of his dependents, called Mac Cormac. Catherine, a beautiful daughter of his host, instantly inspired the Earl with a violent passion, which he could not subdue. He married her, and by this inferior alliance alienated his followers, whose brutal pride regarded this indulgence of his love as an unpardonable degradation of his family."—*Leland,* vol. ii.

(2) These verses are meant to allude to that ancient haunt of superstition, called Patrick's Purgatory. "In the midst of these gloomy regions of Donegall (says Dr. Campbell) lay a lake, which was to become the mystic theatre of this fabled and intermediate state. In the lake were several islands; but one of them was dignified with that called the Mouth of Purgatory, which, during the dark ages, attracted the notice of all Christendom, and was the resort of penitents and pilgrims from almost every country in Europe."

"It was," as the same writer tells us, "one of the most dismal and dreary spots in the North, almost inaccessible, through deep glens and rugged mountains, frightful with impending rocks, and the hollow murmurs of the western winds in dark caverns, peopled only with such fantastic beings as the mind, however gay, is, from strange association, wont to appropriate to such gloomy scenes."—*Strictures on the Ecclesiastical and Literary History of Ireland.*

As they, who to their couch at night
Would win repose, first quench the light,
So must the hopes, that keep this breast
Awake, be quench'd, ere it can rest.
Cold, cold, this heart must grow,
Unmoved by either joy or woe,
Like freezing founts, where all that's thrown
Within their current turns to stone.

SHE SUNG OF LOVE.

Air—*The Munster Man.*

She sung of Love, while o'er her lyre
The rosy rays of evening fell,
As if to feed with their soft fire
The soul within that trembling shell.
The same rich light hung o'er her cheek,
And play'd around those lips that sung
And spoke, as flowers would sing and speak,
If Love could lend their leaves a tongue.

But soon the West no longer burn'd,
Each rosy ray from heaven withdrew;
And, when to gaze again I turn'd,
The minstrel's form seem'd fading too.
As if her light and heaven's were one,
The glory all had left that frame;
And from her glimmering lips the tone,
As from a parting spirit, came. (1)

Who ever loved, but had the thought
That he and all he loved must part?
Fill'd with this fear, I flew and caught
The fading image to my heart—
And cried, "Oh Love! is this thy doom?
Oh light of youth's resplendent day!
Must ye then lose your golden bloom,
And thus, like sunshine, die away."

SING—SING—MUSIC WAS GIVEN.

Air—*The Humours of Ballamaguiry ; or the Old Langolee.*

Sing—sing—Music was given
To brighten the gay, and kindle the loving;
Souls here, like planets in heaven,
By harmony's laws alone are kept moving.
Beauty may boast of her eyes and her cheeks,
But Love from the lips his true archery wings;
And she, who but feathers the dart when she speaks,
At once sends it home to the heart when she sings.
Then sing—sing—Music was given,
To brighten the gay, and kindle the loving;
Souls here, like planets in heaven,
By harmony's laws alone are kept moving.

(1) The thought here was suggested by some beautiful
lines in Mr. Rogers's Poem of *Human Life*, beginning—
"Now in the glimmering dying light she grows
Less and less earthly."
I would quote the entire passage, did I not fear to put
my own humble imitation of it out of countenance.

When Love, rock'd by his mother,
Lay sleeping as calm as slumber could make him
"Hush, hush," said Venus, "no other
Sweet voice but his own is worthy to wake him.'
Dreaming of music he slumber'd the while,
Till faint from his lip a soft melody broke,
And Venus, enchanted, look'd on with a smile,
While Love to his own sweet singing awoke.
Then sing—sing—Music was given,
To brighten the gay, and kindle the loving
Souls here, like planets in heaven,
By harmony's laws alone are kept moving

THOUGH HUMBLE THE BANQUET.

Air—*Farewell, Eamon.*

Though humble the banquet to which I invite thee
Thou'lt find there the best a poor bard can command
Eyes, beaming with welcome, shall throng round, to
light thee,
And Love serve the feast with his own willing hand
[the dwelling
And though Fortune may seem to have turn'd from
Of him thou regardest her favouring ray,
Thou wilt find there a gift, all her treasures excelling
Which, proudly he feels, hath ennobled his way

'T is that freedom of mind, which no vulgar dominion
Can turn from the path a pure conscience approves
Which, with hope in the heart, and no chain on the
pinion,
Holds upwards its course to the light which it loves

'T is this makes the pride of his humble retreat,
And with this, though of all other treasures be
reaved,
The breeze of his garden to him is more sweet
Than the costliest incense that Pomp e'er received

Then, come, if a board so untempting hath power
To win thee from grandeur, its best shall be thine
And there 's one, long the light of the bard's happy
bower,
Who, smiling, will blend her bright welcome with
mine.

SING, SWEET HARP.

Air—*Unknown.*

Sing, sweet Harp, oh sing to me
Some song of ancient days,
Whose sounds, in this sad memory,
Long-buried dreams shall raise ;—
Some lay that tells of vanish'd fame,
Whose light once round us shone ;
Of noble pride, now turn'd to shame,
And hopes for ever gone.
Sing, sad Harp, thus sing to me ;
Alike our doom is cast,
Both lost to all but memory,
We live but in the past.

How mournfully the midnight air
　Among thy chords doth sigh,
As if it sought some echo there
　Of voices long gone by;—
Of Chieftains, now forgot, who seem'd
　The foremost then in fame;
Of Bards who, once immortal deem'd,
　Now sleep without a name.
In vain, sad Harp, the midnight air
　Among thy chords doth sigh;
In vain it seeks an echo there
　Of voices long gone by.

Couldst thou but call those spirits round,
　Who once, in bower and hall,
Sate listening to thy magic sound,
　Now mute and mouldering all;—
But, no; they would but wake to weep
　Their children's slavery;
Then leave them in their dreamless sleep,
　The dead, at least, are free!
Hush, hush, sad Harp, that dreary tone,
　That knell of Freedom's day;
Or, listening to its death-like moan,
　Let me, too, die away.

———◦◦◦◦———

SONG OF THE BATTLE EVE.

TIME—THE NINTH CENTURY.

AIR—*Cruiskeen Lawn.*

TO-MORROW, comrade, we
On the battle-plain must be,
　There to conquer, or both lie low!
The morning star is up—
But there 's wine still in the cup,
　And we 'll take another quaff, ere we go, boy, go;
　We 'll take another quaff, ere we go.

'T is true, in manliest eyes
A passing tear will rise,
　When we think of the friends we leave lone;
But what can wailing do?
See, our goblet 's weeping too!　　　[our own;
　With its tears we 'll chase away our own, boy,
　With its tears we 'll chase away our own.

But daylight 's stealing on;
The last that o'er us shone
　Saw our children around us play;
The next—ah! where shall we
And those rosy urchins be?　　　[boy, away;
　But—no matter—grasp thy sword and away,
　No matter—grasp thy sword and away!

Let those, who brook the chain
Of Saxon or of Dane,
　Ignobly by their fire-sides stay;
One sigh to home be given,
One heartfelt prayer to heaven,　　　[hurra!
　Then, for Erin and her cause, boy, hurra! hurra!
　Then, for Erin and her cause, hurra!

THE WANDERING BARD.

AIR—*Planxty O'Reilly.*

WHAT life like that of the bard can be—
The wandering bard, who roams as free
As the mountain lark that o'er him sings,
And, like that lark a music brings,
Within him, where'er he comes or goes—
A fount that for ever flows!
The world 's to him like some play-ground,
Where fairies dance their moonlight round;—
Il dimm'd the turf where late they trod,
The elves but seek some greener sod;
So, when less bright his scene of glee,
To another away flies he!

Oh, what would have been young Beauty's doom,
Without a bard to fix her bloom?
They tell us, in the moon's bright round,
Things lost in this dark world are found;
So charms, on earth long pass'd and gone,
In the poet's lay live on.—
Would ye have smiles that ne'er grow dim?
You 've only to give them all to him,
Who, with but a touch of Fancy's wand,
Can lend them life, this life beyond,
And fix them high, in Poesy's sky—
Young stars that never die!

Then, welcome the bard where'er he comes,
For, though he hath countless airy homes,
To which his wing excursive roves,
Yet still, from time to time, he loves
To light upon earth and find such cheer
As brightens our banquet here.
No matter how far, how fleet he flies,
You 've only to light up kind young eyes,
Such signal-fires as here are given—
And down he 'll drop from Fancy's heaven,
The minute such call to love or mirth
Proclaims he 's wanting on earth!

———◦◦◦———

ALONE IN CROWDS TO WANDER ON.

AIR—*Shule Aroon.*

ALONE in crowds to wander on,
And feel that all the charm is gone
Which voices dear and eyes beloved
Shed round us once, where'er we roved—
This, this the doom must be
Of all who 've loved, and lived to see
The few bright things they thought would stay
For ever near them, die away.

Though fairer forms around us throng,
Their smiles to others all belong,
And want that charm which dwells alone
Round those the fond heart calls its own.
Where, where the sunny brow?
The long-known voice—where are they now?
Thus ask I still, nor ask in vain,
The silence answers all too plain.

Oh, what is Fancy's magic worth,
If all her art cannot call forth
One bliss like those we felt of old
From lips now mute, and eyes now cold?
No, no—her spell is vain—
As soon could she bring back again
Those eyes themselves from out the grave,
As wake again one bliss they gave.

—◦••◦—

I 'VE A SECRET TO TELL THEE.

AIR—*Oh! Southern Breeze.*

I 'VE a secret to tell thee, but hush! not here—
  Oh! not where the world its vigil keeps:
I 'll seek, to whisper it in thine ear,
  Some shore where the Spirit of Silence sleeps;
Where Summer's wave unmurmuring dies,
  Nor fay can hear the fountain's gush;
Where, if but a note her night-bird sighs,
  The rose saith, chidingly, "Hush, sweet, hush!"

There, amid the deep silence of that hour,
  When stars can be heard in ocean dip,
Thyself shall, under some rosy bower,
  Sit mute, with thy finger on thy lip:
Like him, the boy,(1) who, born among
  The flowers that on the Nile-stream blush,
Sits ever thus—his only song
  To earth and heaven, "Hush, all, hush!"

—◦••◦—

SONG OF INNISFAIL.

AIR—*Peggy Bawn.*

THEY came from a land beyond the sea,
  And now o'er the western main
Set sail, in their good ships, gallantly,
  From the sunny land of Spain.
" Oh, where 's the Isle we 've seen in dreams,
  Our destined home or grave?" (2)
Thus sang they as, by the morning's beams,
  They swept the Atlantic wave.

And lo, where afar o'er ocean shines
  A sparkle of radiant green,
As though in that deep lay emerald mines,
  Whose light through the wave was seen.
" 'T is Innisfail (3)—'t is Innisfail!"
  Rings o'er the echoing sea;
While, bending to heaven, the warriors hail
  That home of the brave and free.

Then turn'd they unto the Eastern wave,
  Where now their Day-God's eye
A look of such sunny omen gave
  As lighted up sea and sky.

(1) The God of Silence, thus pictured by the Egyptians.
(2) "Milesius remembered the remarkable prediction o
the principal Druid, who foretold that the posterity of Ga-

Nor frown was seen through sky or sea.
  Nor tear o'er leaf or sod,
When first on their Isle of Destiny
  Our great forefathers trod.

—◦••◦—

THE NIGHT DANCE.

AIR—*The Nightcap.*

STRIKE the gay harp! see the moon is on high,
  And, as true to her beam as the tides of the ocean,
Young hearts, when they feel the soft light of her
    eye,
  Obey the mute call, and heave into motion.
Then, sound notes—the gayest, the lightest,
  That ever took wing, when heaven look'd brightest
    Again! Again!
Oh! could such heart-stirring music be heard
  In that City of Statues described by romancers,
So wakening its spell, even stone would be stirr'd,
  And statues themselves all start into dancers!

Why then delay, with such sounds in our ears,
  And the flower of Beauty's own garden before us—
While stars overhead leave the song of their spheres,
  And, listening to ours, hang wondering o'er us?
Again, that strain!—to hear it thus sounding
  Might set even Death's cold pulses bounding—
    Again! Again!
Oh, what delight when the youthful and gay
  Each with eye like a sunbeam and foot like a
    feather,
Thus dance, like the Hours to the music of May,
  And mingle sweet song and sunshine together!

—◦••◦—

THERE ARE SOUNDS OF MIRTH.

AIR—*The Priest in his Boots.*

THERE are sounds of mirth in the night-air ringing,
  And lamps from every casement shown;
While voices blithe within are singing,
  That seem to say "Come," in every tone.
Ah! once how light, in Life's young season,
  My heart had leap'd at that sweet lay;
Nor paused to ask of greybeard Reason
  Should I the syren call obey.

And, see—the lamps still livelier glitter,
  The syren lips more fondly sound;
No, seek, ye nymphs, some victim fitter
  To sink in your rosy bondage bound.
Shall a bard, whom not the world in arms,
  Could bend to tyranny's rude controul,
Thus quail, at sight of woman's charms,
  And yield to a smile his freeborn soul?

delus should obtain the possession of a Western Island
(which was Ireland), and there inhabit."—*Keating.*
(3) The Island of Destiny, one of the ancient names of
Ireland.

Thus sung the sage, while, slyly stealing,
  The nymphs their fetters around him cast,
And—their laughing eyes, the while, concealing—
  Led Freedom's Bard their slave at last.
For the Poet's heart, still prone to loving,
  Was like that rock of the Druid race, (1)
Which the gentlest touch at once set moving,
  But all earth's power couldn't cast from its base.

OH! ARRANMORE, LOVED ARRANMORE.

Air—*Killdroughalt Fair.*

Oh! Arranmore, loved Arranmore,
  How oft I dream of thee,
And of those days when, by thy shore,
  I wander'd young and free.
Full many a path I've tried, since then,
  Through pleasure's flowery maze,
But ne'er could find the bliss again
  I felt in those sweet days.

How blithe upon thy breezy cliffs
  At sunny morn I've stood,
With heart as bounding as the skiffs
  That danced along thy flood;
Or, when the western wave grew bright
  With daylight's parting wing,
Have sought that Eden in its light
  Which dreaming poets sing;(2)

That Eden where the immortal brave
  Dwell in a land serene—
Whose bowers beyond the shining wave,
  At sunset, oft are seen.
Ah, dream too full of saddening truth!
  Those mansions o'er the main
Are like the hopes I built in youth—
  As sunny and as vain!

LAY HIS SWORD BY HIS SIDE.

Air—*If the Sea were Ink.*

Lay his sword by his side (3)—it hath served him
  Not to rest near his pillow below;   [too well
To the last moment true, from his hand ere it fell,
  Its point was still turn'd to a flying foe.
Fellow-labourers in life, let them slumber in death,
  Side by side, as becomes the reposing brave—
That sword which he loved still unbroke in its sheath,
  And himself unsubdued in his grave.

(1) The Rocking Stones of the Druids, some of which no force is able to dislodge from their stations.

(2) "The inhabitants of Arranmore are still persuaded that, in a clear day, they can see from this coast Hy Brysail, or the Enchanted Island, the Paradise of the Pagan Irish, and concerning which they relate a number of romantic stories."—*Beaufort's Ancient Topography of Ireland.*

(3) It was the custom of the ancient Irish, in the manner of the Scythians, to bury the favourite swords of their heroes along with them.

Yet pause—for, in fancy, a still voice I hear,
  As if breathed from his brave heart's remains;—
Faint echo of that which, like a talisman seal'd,
  Once sounded the war-word, "Burst your chains!"
And it cries, from the grave where the hero lies deep,
  "Though the day of your Chieftain for ever hath set,
Oh leave not his sword thus inglorious to sleep—
  It hath victory's life in it yet!

"Should some alien, unworthy such weapon to wield,
  Dare to touch thee, my own gallant sword,
Then rest in thy sheath, like a talisman seal'd,
  Or return to the grave of thy chainless lord.
But, if grasp'd by a hand that hath learn'd the proud use
  Of a falchion, like thee, on the battle-plain—
Then, at Liberty's summons, like lightning let loose,
  Leap forth from thy dark sheath again!"

THE WINE-CUP IS CIRCLING.

Air—*Michael Hoy.*

The wine-cup is circling in Almhin's hall, (4)
  And its Chief, 'mid his heroes reclining,
Looks up, with a sigh, to the trophied wall,
  Where his sword hangs idly shining.
    When, hark! that shout
    From the vale without—
"Arm ye quick, the Dane, the Dane is nigh!"
    Every Chief starts up
    From his foaming cup,
And "To battle, to battle!" is the Finian's cry.

The minstrels have seized their harps of gold,
  And they sing such thrilling numbers—
'Tis like the voice of the Brave, of old,
  Breaking forth from their place of slumbers!
    Spear to buckler rang,
    As the minstrels sang,
And the Sun-burst (5) o'er them floated wide;
    While remembering the yoke
    Which their fathers broke,
"On for liberty, for liberty!" the Finians cried.

Like clouds of the night the Northmen came,
  O'er the valley of Almhin lowering;
While onward moved, in the light of its fame,
  That banner of Erin, towering.
    With the mingling shock
    Rung cliff and rock,

(4) The Palace of Fin Mac-Cumhal (the Fingal of Macpherson) in Leinster. It was built on the top of the hill, which has retained from thence the name of the Hill of Allen, in the county of Kildare. The Finians, or Fenii, were the celebrated National Militia of Ireland, which this Chief commanded. The introduction of the Dance in the above song is an anachronism common to most of the Finian and Ossianic legends.

(5) The name given to the banner of the Irish.

While, rank on rank, the invaders die:
And the shout, that last
O'er the dying pass'd,
Was "victory! victory!"—the Finian's cry.

—o♦♦o—

OH, COULD WE DO WITH THIS WORLD OF OURS.

Air—*Basket of Oysters.*

Oh, could we do with this world of ours
As thou dost with thy garden bowers,
Reject the weeds and keep the flowers,
   What a heaven on earth we 'd make it!
So bright a dwelling should be our own,
So warranted free from sigh or frown,
That angels soon would be coming down,
   By the week or month to take it.

Like those gay flies that wing through air,
And in themselves a lustre bear,
A stock of light, still ready there,
   Whenever they wish to use it;
So, in this world I'd make for thee,
Our hearts should all like fire-flies be,
And the flash of wit or poesy
   Break forth whenever we choose it.

While every joy that glads our sphere
Hath still some shadow hovering near,
In this new world of ours, my dear,
   Such shadows will all be omitted:—
Unless they're like that graceful one,
Which, when thou 'rt dancing in the sun,
Still near thee, leaves a charm upon
   Each spot where it hath flitted!

—o♦♦o—

FROM THIS HOUR THE PLEDGE IS GIVEN.

Air—*Renardine.*

From this hour the pledge is given,
From this hour my soul is thine:
Come what will, from earth or heaven,
   Weal or woe, thy fate be mine.
When the proud and great stood by thee,
   None dared thy rights to spurn;
And if now they 're false and fly thee,
   Shall I, too, basely turn?
No;—whate'er the fires that try thee,
   In the same this heart shall burn.

Though the sea, where thou embarkest,
   Offers now no friendly shore,
Light may come where all looks darkest,
   Hope hath life, when life seems o'er.

And, of those past ages dreaming,
   When glory deck'd thy brow,
Oft I fondly think, though seeming
   So fallen and clouded now,
Thou 'lt again break forth, all beaming—
   None so bright, so blest as thou!

—o♦♦o—

THE DREAM OF THOSE DAYS. (1)

Air—*I love you above all the rest.*

The dream of those days when first I sung thee is o'er,
Thy triumph hath stain'd the charm thy sorrows
   then wore;   [chains,
And even of the light which Hope once shed o'er thy
Alas, not a gleam to grace thy freedom remains.

Say, is it that slavery sunk so deep in thy heart,
That still the dark brand is there, though chainless
   thou art;
And Freedom's sweet fruit, for which thy spirit long
   burn'd,
Now, reaching at last thy lip, to ashes hath turn'd?

Up Liberty's steep by Truth and Eloquence led,
With eyes on her temple fix'd, how proud was thy
   tread!
Ah, better thou ne'er hadst lived that summit to gain,
Or died in the porch, than thus dishonour the fane.

—o♦♦o—

SILENCE IS IN OUR FESTAL HALLS.

Air—*The green Woods of Truigha.*

Silence is in our festal halls—
   Sweet son of song!(2) thy course is o'er;
In vain on thee sad Erin calls,
   Her minstrel's voice responds no more;—
All silent as the Eolian shell
   Sleeps at the close of some bright day,
When the sweet breeze, that waked its swell
   At sunny morn, hath died away.

Yet, at our feasts, thy spirit long,
   Awaked by music's spell, shall rise;
For, name so link'd with deathless song
   Partakes its charm and never dies:
And even within the holy fane,
   When music wafts the soul to heaven,
One thought to him, whose earliest strain
   Was echoed there, shall long be given.

But where is now the cheerful day,
   The social night, when by thy side,
He who now weaves this parting lay
   His skilless voice with thine allied;

---

(1) Written in one of those moods of hopelessness and disgust which come occasionally over the mind, in contemplating the present state of Irish patriotism.

(2) It is hardly necessary, perhaps, to inform the reader,

that these lines are meant as a tribute of sincere friendship to the memory of an old and valued colleague in this work, Sir John Stevenson.

And sung those songs whose every tone,
   When bard and minstrel long have past,
Shall still, in sweetness all their own,
   Embalm'd by fame, undying last.

Yes, Erin, thine alone the fame—
   Or, if thy bard have shared the crown,
From thee the borrow'd glory came,
   And at thy feet is now laid down.
Enough, if Freedom still inspire
   His latest song, and still there be,
As evening closes round his lyre,
   One ray upon its chords from thee.

— ◦➋✿➏◦ —

APPENDIX:

CONTAINING

THE ADVERTISEMENTS ORIGINALLY PREFIXED TO
THE DIFFERENT NUMBERS, AND THE PREFA-
TORY LETTER ON IRISH MUSIC.

ADVERTISEMENT PREFIXED TO THE FIRST AND SECOND NUMBERS.

Power takes the liberty of announcing to the Public a Work which has long been a *Desideratum* in this country. Though the beauties of the National Music of Ireland have been very generally felt and acknowledged, yet it has happened, through the want of appropriate English words, and of the arrangement necessary to adapt them to the voice, that many of the most excellent compositions have hitherto remained in obscurity. It is intended, therefore, to form a Collection of the best Original Irish Melodies, with characteristic Symphonies and Accompaniments; and with Words containing, as frequently as possible, allusions to the manners and history of the country. Sir John Stevenson has very kindly consented to undertake the arrangement of the airs; and the lovers of Simple National Music may rest secure that, in such tasteful hands, the native charms of the original melody will not be sacrificed to the ostentation of science.

In the poetical Part, Power has had promises of assistance from several distinguished Literary Characters; particularly from Mr. Moore, whose lyrical talent is so peculiarly suited to such a task, and whose zeal in the undertaking will be best understood from the following Extract of a Letter which he has addressed to Sir J. Stevenson on the subject:—

"I feel very anxious that a work of this kind should be undertaken. We have too long neglected the only talent for which our English neighbours ever deigned to allow us any credit. Our National Music has never been properly collected; (1) and, while the composers of the Continent have enriched their Operas and Sonatas with Melodies borrowed from Ireland—very often without even the honesty of acknowledgment—we have left these treasures, in a great degree, unclaimed and fugitive. Thus our Airs, like too many of our countrymen, have, for want of protection at home, passed into the service of foreigners. But we are come, I hope, to a better period of both Politics and Music; and how much they are connected, in Ireland at least, appears too plainly in the tone of sorrow and depression which characterises most of our early Songs.

"The task which you propose to me, of adapting words to these airs, is by no means easy. The Poet, who would follow the various sentiments which they express, must feel and understand that rapid fluctuation of spirits, that unaccountable mixture of gloom and levity, which composes the character of my countrymen, and has deeply tinged their Music. Even in their liveliest strains we find some melancholy note intrude—some minor Third or flat Seventh—which throws its shade as it passes, and makes even mirth interesting. If Burns had been an Irishman (and I would willingly give up all our claims upon Ossian for him), his heart would have been proud of such music, and his genius would have made it immortal.

"Another difficulty (which is, however, purely mechanical) arises from the irregular structure of many of those airs, and the lawless kind of metre which it will in consequence be necessary to adapt to them. In these instances the poet must write, not to the eye, but to the ear; and must be content to have his verses of that description which Cicero mentions, '*Quos si cantu spoliaveris nuda remanebit oratio!*' That beautiful Air, '*The Twisting of the Rope,*' which has all the romantic character of the Swiss *Ranz des Vaches*, is one of those wild and sentimental rakes which it will not be very easy to tie down in sober wedlock with Poetry. However, notwithstanding all these difficulties, and the very moderate portion of talent which I can bring to surmount them, the design appears to me so truly National, that I shall feel much pleasure in giving it all the assistance in my power.

"*Leicestershire, Feb.,* 1807."

ADVERTISEMENT TO THE THIRD NUMBER.

In presenting the Third Number of this work to the Public, Power begs leave to offer his acknowledgments for the very liberal patronage with which it has been honoured; and to express a hope that the unabated zeal of those who have hitherto so admirably conducted it, will enable him to continue it through many future Numbers with equal spirit, variety, and taste. The stock of popular Melodies is far from being exhausted; and there is still in

---

(1) The writer here forgot, that the public are indebted to Mr. Bunting for a very valuable collection of Irish Music; and that the patriotic genius of Miss Owenson has been employed upon some of our finest airs.

reserve an abundance of beautiful Airs, which call upon Mr. Moore, in the language he so well understands, to save them from the oblivion to which they are hastening.

Power respectfully trusts he will not be thought presumptuous in saying, that he feels proud, as an Irishman, in even the very subordinate share which he can claim, in promoting a Work so creditable to the talents of the Country—a Work which, from the spirit of nationality it breathes, will do more, he is convinced, towards liberalising the feelings of society, and producing that brotherhood of sentiment which it is so much our interest to cherish, than could ever be effected by the mere arguments of well-intentioned but uninteresting politicians.

LETTER
TO
THE MARCHIONESS DOWAGER OF DONEGAL,
PREFIXED TO THE THIRD NUMBER.

WHILE the publisher of these Melodies very properly inscribes them to the Nobility and Gentry of Ireland in general, I have much pleasure in selecting one from that number, to whom my share of the Work is particularly dedicated. I know that, though your Ladyship has been so long absent from Ireland, you still continue to remember it well and warmly—that you have not suffered the attractions of English society to produce, like the taste of the lotus, any forgetfulness of your own country, but that even the humble tribute which I offer derives its chief claim upon your interest and sympathy from the appeal which it makes to your patriotism. Indeed, absence, however fatal to some affections of the heart, rather tends to strengthen our love for the land where we were born; and Ireland is the country, of all others, which an exile from it must remember with most enthusiasm. Those few darker and less amiable traits with which bigotry and misrule have stained her character, and which are too apt to disgust us upon a nearer intercourse, become at a distance softened, or altogether invisible. Nothing is remembered but her virtues and her misfortunes—the zeal with which she has always loved liberty, and the barbarous policy which has always withheld it from her—the ease with which her generous spirit might be conciliated, and the cruel ingenuity which has been exerted to "wring her into undutifulness." (1)

It has been often remarked, and still oftener felt, that in our music is found the truest of all comments upon our history. The tone of defiance, succeeded by the languor of despondency—a burst of turbulence dying away into softness—the sorrows of one moment lost in the levity of the next—and all that romantic mixture of mirth and sadness, which is naturally produced by the efforts of a lively temperament to shake off, or forget, the wrongs which lie upon it. Such are the features of our history and character, which we find strongly and faithfully reflected in our music; and there are even many airs, which it is difficult to listen to, without recalling some period or event to which their expression seems applicable. Sometimes, for instance, when the strain is open and spirited, yet here and there shaded by a mournful recollection, we can fancy that we behold the brave allies of Montrose, (2) marching to the aid of the royal cause, notwithstanding all the perfidy of Charles and his ministers, and remembering just enough of past sufferings to enhance the generosity of their present sacrifice. The plaintive melodies of Carolan take us back to the times in which he lived, when our poor countrymen were driven to worship their God in caves, or to quit for ever the land of their birth—like the bird that abandons the nest which human touch has violated. In many of these mournful songs we seem to hear the last farewell of the exile, (3) mingling regret for the ties which he leaves at home, with sanguine hopes of the high honours that await him abroad—such honours as were won on the field of Fontenoy, where the valour of Irish Catholics turned the fortune of the day, and extorted from George the Second that memorable exclamation, " Cursed be the laws which deprive me of such subjects! "

Though much has been said of the antiquity of our music, it is certain that our finest and most popular airs are modern; and perhaps we may look no further than the last disgraceful century for the origin of most of those wild and melancholy strains, which were at once the offspring and solace of grief, and were applied to the mind as music was formerly to

(1) A phrase which occurs in a Letter from the Earl of Desmond to the Earl of Ormond, in Elizabeth's time.—*Scrinia Sacra*, as quoted by Curry.

(2) There are some gratifying accounts of the gallantry of these Irish auxiliaries in " *The Complete History of the Wars in Scotland under Montrose*" (1660). See particularly, for the conduct of an Irishman at the battle of Aberdeen, chap. vi., p. 49; and for a tribute to the bravery of Colonel O'Kyan, chap. vii., p. 55. Clarendon owns that the Marquis of Montrose was indebted for much of his miraculous success to the small band of Irish heroes under Macdonnell.

(3) The associations of the Hindu music, though more obvious and defined, were far less touching and charac-teristic. They divided their songs according to the seasons of the year, by which (says Sir William Jones) "they were able to recall the memory of autumnal merriment, at the close of the harvest, or of separation and melancholy during the cold months," etc.—*Asiatic Transactions*, vol iii., on the Musical Modes of the Hindus.—What the Abbé du Bos says of the symphonies of Lully, may be asserted, with much more probability, of our bold and impassioned airs:—"Elles auroient produit de ces effets, qui nous paroissent fabuleux dans le récit des anciens, si on les avoit fait entendre à des hommes d'un naturel aussi vif, que les Athéniens."—*Réflex. sur la Peinture*, etc., tom. i., sect. 45.

the body, "decantare loca dolentia." Mr. Pinkerton
is of opinion (1) that none of the Scotch popular airs
are as old as the middle of the sixteenth century ;
and though musical antiquaries refer us, for some
of our melodies, to so early a period as the fifth
century, I am persuaded that there are few, of a
civilised description (and by this I mean to exclude
all the savage Ceanans, Cries, (2) etc.,) which can
claim quite so ancient a date as Mr. Pinkerton allows
to the Scotch. But music is not the only subject
upon which our taste for antiquity has been rather
unreasonably indulged ; and, however heretical it
may be to dissent from these romantic speculations,
I cannot help thinking that it is possible to love our
country very zealously, and to feel deeply interested
in her honour and happiness, without believing that
Irish was the language spoken in Paradise ; (3) that
our ancestors were kind enough to take the trouble
of polishing the Greeks, (4) or that Abaris, the Hyper-
borean, was a native of the North of Ireland. (5)

By some of these zealous antiquarians it has been
imagined that the Irish were early acquainted with
counter-point ; (6) and they endeavour to support
this conjecture by a well-known passage in Giraldus,
where he dilates, with such elaborate praise, upon

(1) Dissertation, prefixed to the 2d volume of his Scot-
tish Ballads.

(2) Of which some genuine specimens may be found at
the end of Mr. Walker's Work upon the Irish bards. Mr.
Bunting has disfigured his last splendid volume by too
many of these barbarous rhapsodies.

(3) See advertisement to the Transactions of the Gaelic
Society of Dublin.

(4) O'Halloran, vol. i., part iv., chap. vii.

(5) Id., ib., chap. vi.

(6) It is also supposed, but with as little proof, that they
understood the diésis, or enharmonic interval. — The
Greeks seem to have formed their ears to this delicate
gradation of sound ; and, whatever difficulties or objec-
tions may lie in the way of its *practical* use, we must
agree with Mersenne, (*Préludes de l'Harmonie*, quest. 7,)
that the *theory* of Music would be imperfect without it.
Even in practice, too, as Tosi, among others, very justly
remarks, (*Observations on Florid Song*, chap. i., sect. 16,)
there is no good performer on the violin who does not
make a sensible difference between D sharp and E flat,
though, from the imperfection of the instrument, they are
the same notes upon the piano-forte. The effect of modu-
lation by enharmonic transitions is also very striking and
beautiful.

(7) The words ποικιλια and ετεροφωνια, in a passage
of Plato, and some expressions of Cicero in Fragment,
lib. ii., *de Republ.*, induced the Abbé Fraguier to maintain
that the ancients had a knowledge of counter-point. M.
Burette, however, has answered him, I think, satisfacto-
rily. (*Examen d'un Passage de Platon*, in the 3d vol. of
Histoire de l'Acad.) M. Huet is of opinion (*Pensées
Diverses*), that what Cicero says of the music of the spheres,
in his dream of Scipio, is sufficient to prove an acquaint-
ance with harmony; but one of the strongest passages,
which I recollect, in favour of this supposition, occurs in
the Treatise (Περι Κοσμου) attributed to Aristotle.—
Μουσικη δε οξεις αμα και βαρεις, κ. τ. λ.

the beauties of our national minstrelsy. But the
terms of this eulogy are much too vague, too deficient
in technical accuracy, to prove that even Giraldus
himself knew any thing of the artifice of counter-
point. There are many expressions in the Greek
and Latin writers which might be cited, with much
more plausibility, to prove that they understood the
arrangement of music in parts; (7) and it is in general
now conceded, I believe, by the learned, that, however
grand and pathetic the melody of the ancients may
have been, it was reserved for the ingenuity of mo-
dern Science to transmit the " light of Song" through
the variegating prism of Harmony.

Indeed, the irregular scale of the early Irish (in
which, as in the music of Scotland, the interval of
the fourth was wanting, (8) must have furnished but
wild and refractory subjects to the harmonist. It
was only when the invention of Guido began to be
known, and the powers of the harp (9) were enlarged
by additional strings, that our airs can be supposed
to have assumed the sweet character which interests
us at present; and while the Scotch persevered in
the old mutilation of the scale, (10) our music became
by degrees more amenable to the laws of harmony
and counter-point.

(8) Another lawless peculiarity of our music is the fre-
quent occurrence of, what composers call, consecutive
fifths; but this, I must say, is an irregularity which can
hardly be avoided by persons not conversant with all the
rules of composition. If I may venture, indeed, to cite
my own wild attempts in this way, it is a fault which I find
myself continually committing, and which has even, at
times, appeared so pleasing to my ear, that I have surren-
dered it to the critic with no small reluctance. May there
not be a little pedantry in adhering too rigidly to this rule?
—I have been told that there are instances in Haydn, of
an undisguised succession of fifths; and Mr. Shield, in his
Introduction to Harmony, seems to intimate that Handel
has been sometimes guilty of the same irregularity.

(9) A singular oversight occurs in an Essay upon the
Irish Harp, by Mr. Beauford, which is inserted in the Ap-
pendix to Walker's *Historical Memoirs* :—"The Irish (says
he), according to Bromton, in the reign of Henry II. had
two kinds of Harps, 'Hibernici tamen in duobus musici
generis instrumentis, quamvis præcipitem et velocem,
suavem tamen et jucundum :' the one greatly bold and
quick, the other soft and pleasing."—How a man of Mr.
Beauford's learning could so mistake the meaning, and
mutilate the grammatical construction of this extract, is
unaccountable. The following is the passage as I find it
entire in Bromton; and it requires but little Latin to per-
ceive the injustice which has been done to the words of
the old Chronicler :—" Et cum Scotia, hujus terræ filia,
utatur lyrâ, tympano et choro, ac Wallia cythara, tubis et
choro Hibernici tamen .in duobus musici generis instru-
mentis, *quamvis præcipitem et velocem, suavem tamen
et jucundum*, crispatis modulis et intricatis notulis, *effi-
ciunt harmoniam*."—*Hist. Anglic. Script.*, page 1075. I
should not have thought this error worth remarking, but
that the compiler of the Dissertation on the Harp, pre-
fixed to Mr. Bunting's last Work, has adopted it implicitly.

(10) The Scotch lay claim to some of our best airs, but
there are strong traits of difference between their melo-

While profiting, however, by the improvements of the moderns, our style still keeps its original character sacred from their refinements; and though Carolan, it appears, had frequent opportunities of hearing the works of Geminiani and other great masters, we but rarely find him sacrificing his native simplicity to any ambition of their ornaments, or affectation of their science. In that curious composition, indeed, called his Concerto, it is evident that he laboured to imitate Corelli; and this union of manners, so very dissimilar, produces the same kind of uneasy sensation which is felt at a mixture of different styles of architecture. In general, however, the artless flow of our music has preserved itself free from all tinge of foreign innovation; (1) and the chief corruptions of which we have to complain arise from the unskilful performance of our own itinerant musicians, from whom, too frequently, the airs are noted down, encumbered by their tasteless decorations, and responsible for all their ignorant anomalies. Though it be sometimes impossible to trace the original strain, yet, in most of them, " auri per ramos *aura* refulget, (2) the pure gold of the melody shines through the ungraceful foliage which surrounds it — and the most delicate and difficult duty of a compiler is to endeavour, by retrenching these inelegant superfluities, and collating the various methods of playing or singing each air, to restore the regularity of its form, and the chaste simplicity of its character.

I must again observe, that in doubting the antiquity of our music, my scepticism extends but to those polished specimens of the art, which it is difficult to conceive anterior to the dawn of modern improvement; and that I would by no means invalidate the claims of Ireland to as early a rank in the annals of minstrelsy, as the most zealous antiquary may be inclined to allow her. In addition, indeed, to the power which music must always have possessed over the minds of a people so ardent and susceptible, the stimulus of persecution was not wanting to quicken our taste into enthusiasm: the charms of song were ennobled with the glories of martyrdom, and the acts against minstrels, in the reigns of Henry VIII. and Elizabeth, were as successful, I doubt not, in making my countrymen musicians, as the penal laws have been in keeping them Catholics.

With respect to the verses which I have written for these Melodies, as they are intended rather to be sung than read, I can answer for their sound with somewhat more confidence than for their sense. Yet it would be affectation to deny that I have given much attention to the task, and that it is not through any want of zeal or industry, if I unfortunately disgrace the sweet airs of my country, by poetry altogether unworthy of their taste, their energy, and their tenderness.

Though it be the humble nature of my contributions to this work may exempt them from the rigours of literary criticism, it was not to be expected that those touches of political feeling, those tones of national complaint, in which the poetry sometimes sympathises with the music, would be suffered to pass without censure or alarm. It has been accordingly said, that the tendency of this publication is mischievous, (3) and that I have chosen these airs but as a vehicle of dangerous politics—as fair and precious vessels (to borrow an image of St. Augustin,) (4) from which the wine of error might be administered. To those who identify nationality with treason, and who see, in every effort for Ireland, a system of hostility towards England—to those, too, who, nursed in the gloom of prejudice, are alarmed by the faintest gleam of liberality that threatens to disturb their darkness—like that Demophon of old, who, when the sun shone upon him, shivered, (5) —to such men I shall not condescend to offer an apology for the too great warmth of any political sentiment which may occur in the course of these pages. But as there are many, among the more wise and tolerant, who, with feeling enough to mourn over the wrongs of their country, and sense enough to perceive all the danger of not redressing them, may yet be of opinion that allusions, in the least degree inflammatory, should be avoided in a publication of this popular description—I beg of these respected persons to believe, that there is no one who more sincerely deprecates than I do any appeal to the passions of an ignorant and angry multitude; but that it is not through that gross and inflammable

---

dies and ours. They had formerly the same passion for robbing us of our Saints, and the learned Dempster was for this offence called "The Saint Stealer." It must have been some Irishman, I suppose, who, by way of reprisal, stole Dempster's beautiful wife from him at Pisa.—See this anecdote in the *Pinacotheca* of Erythræus, part i., page 25.

(1) Among other false refinements of the art, our music (with the exception perhaps of the air called "*Mamma, Mamma,*" and one or two more of the same ludicrous description,) has avoided that puerile mimicry of natural noises, motions, etc., which disgraces so often the works of even Handel himself. D'Alembert ought to have had better taste than to become the patron of this imitative affectation.—*Discours Préliminaire de l'Encyclopédie.* The

reader may find some good remarks on the subject in Avison upon Musical Expression; a work which, though under the name of Avison, was written, it is said, by Dr. Brown.

(2) Virgil, *Æneid,* lib. vi., verse 204.

(3) See Letters, under the signatures of Timæus, etc., in the *Morning Post, Pilot,* and other papers.

(4) "Non accuso verba, quasi vasa electa atque pretiosa; sed vinum erroris quod cum eis nobis propinatur."— lib. i., Confess., chap. xvi.

(5) This emblem of modern bigots was head-butler (τραπεδοποιος) to Alexander the Great.—*Sext. Empir. Pyrrh. Hypoth.,* lib. i.

region of society a work of this nature could ever have been intended to circulate. It looks much higher for its audience and readers—it is found upon the piano-fortes of the rich and the educated—of those who can afford to have their national zeal a little stimulated, without exciting much dread of the excesses into which it may hurry them; and of many whose nerves may be, now and then, alarmed with advantage, as much more is to be gained by their fears, than could ever be expected from their justice.

Having thus adverted to the principal objection, which has been hitherto made to the poetical part of this work, allow me to add a few words in defence of my ingenious coadjutor, Sir John Stevenson, who has been accused of having spoiled the simplicity of the airs by the chromatic richness of his symphonies, and the elaborate variety of his harmonies. We might cite the example of the admirable Haydn, who has sported through all the mazes of musical science, in his arrangement of the simplest Scottish melodies; but it appears to me, that Sir John Stevenson has brought to this task an innate and national feeling, which it would be vain to expect from a foreigner, however tasteful or judicious. Through many of his own compositions we trace a vein of Irish sentiment, which points him out as peculiarly suited to catch the spirit of his country's music; and, far from agreeing with those fastidious critics who think that his symphonies have nothing kindred with the airs which they introduce, I would say that, on the contrary, they resemble, in general, those illuminated initials of old manuscripts, which are of the same character with the writing which follows, though more highly coloured and more curiously ornamented.

In those airs which he has arranged for voices, his skill has particularly distinguished itself, and though it cannot be denied that a single melody most naturally expresses the language of feeling and passion, yet often, when a favourite strain has been dismissed, as having lost its charm of novelty for the ear, it returns, in a harmonised shape, with new claims on our interest and attention; and to those who study the delicate artifices of composition, the construction of the inner parts of these pieces must afford, I think, considerable satisfaction. Every voice has an air to itself, a flowing succession of notes, which might be heard with pleasure, independently of the rest;—so artfully has the harmonist (if I may thus express it) *gavelled* the melody, distributing an equal portion of its sweetness to every part,

If your Ladyship's love of Music were not well known to me, I should not have hazarded so long a letter upon the subject; but as, probably, I may have presumed too far upon your partiality, the best revenge you now can take is to write me just as long a letter upon Painting; and I promise to attend to your theory of the art, with a pleasure only surpassed by that which I have so often derived from your practice

of it.—May the mind which such talents adorn continue calm as it is bright, and happy as it is virtuous! Believe me, your Ladyship's

Grateful Friend and Servant,

Dublin, January, 1810. THOMAS MOORE.

ADVERTISEMENT TO THE FOURTH NUMBER.

THIS Number of the Melodies ought to have appeared much earlier; and the writer of the words is ashamed to confess, that the delay of its publication must be imputed chiefly, if not entirely, to him. He finds it necessary to make this avowal, not only for the purpose of removing all blame from the Publisher, but in consequence of a rumour, which has been circulated industriously in Dublin, that the Irish Government had interfered to prevent the continuance of the Work.

This would be, indeed, a revival of Henry the Eighth's enactments against Minstrels, and it is flattering to find that so much importance is attached to our compilation, even by such persons as the inventors of the report. Bishop Lowth, it is true, was of opinion, that *one* song, like the *Hymn to Harmodius*, would have done more towards rousing the spirit of the Romans, than *all* the Philippics of Cicero. But we live in wiser and less musical times; ballads have long lost their revolutionary powers, and we question if even a "*Lillibullero*" would produce any very *serious* consequences at present. It is needless, therefore, to add, that there is no truth in the report; and we trust that whatever belief it obtained was founded more upon the character of *the Government* than of *the Work*.

The Airs of the last Number, though full of originality and beauty, were, in general, perhaps, too curiously selected to become all at once as popular as, we think, they deserve to be. The public are apt to be reserved towards new acquaintances in music, and this, perhaps, is one of the reasons why many modern composers introduce none but old friends to their notice. It is, indeed, natural that persons, who love music only by association, should be somewhat slow in feeling the charms of a new and strange melody; while those, on the other hand, who have a quick sensibility for this enchanting art, will as naturally seek and enjoy novelty, because in every variety of strain they find a fresh combination of ideas; and the sound has scarcely reached the ear, before the heart has rapidly rendered it into imagery and sentiment. After all, however, it cannot be denied that the most popular of our National Airs are also the most beautiful; and it has been our wish, in the present Number, to select from those Melodies only which have long been listened to and admired. The least known in the collection is the Air of "*Love's Young Dream;*" but it will be found, I think, one of those easy and artless strangers whose merit the heart instantly acknowledges.

Bury Street, St. James's, Nov., 1811. T. M.

ADVERTISEMENT TO THE FIFTH NUMBER.

It is but fair, to those who take an interest in this Work, to state that it is now very near its termination, and that the Sixth Number, which shall speedily appear, will, most probably, be the last of the series. Three volumes will then have been completed, according to the original plan, and the Proprietors desire me to say that a List of Subscribers will be published with the concluding Number.

It is not so much, I must add, from a want of materials, and still less from any abatement of zeal or industry, that we have adopted the resolution of bringing our task to a close; but we feel so proud, still more for our country's sake than our own, of the general interest which this purely Irish Work has excited, and so anxious lest a particle of that interest should be lost by too long a protraction of its existence, that we think it wiser to take away the cup from the lip, while its flavour is yet, we trust, fresh and sweet, than to risk any further trial of the charm, or give so much as not to leave some wish for more. In speaking thus, I allude entirely to the Airs, which are, of course, the main attraction of these Volumes; and though we have still a great many popular and delightful Melodies to produce, (1) it cannot be denied that we should soon experience considerable difficulty in equalling the richness and novelty of the earlier numbers, for which, as we had the choice of all before us, we naturally selected only the most rare and beautiful. The Poetry, too, would be sure to sympathise with the decline of the Music; and, however feebly my words have kept pace with the *excellence* of the Airs, they would follow their *falling off*, I fear, with wonderful alacrity. Both pride and prudence, therefore, counsel us to come to a close, while yet our Work is, we believe, flourishing and attractive, and thus, in the imperial attitude, "*stantes mori*," before we incur the charge either of altering for the worse, or, what is equally unpardonable, continuing too long the same.

We beg to say, however, that it is only in the event of our failing to find Airs as good as most of those we have given, that we mean thus to anticipate the natural period of dissolution (like those Indians who when their relatives become worn out, put them to death); and they who are desirous of retarding this Euthanasia of the Irish Melodies cannot better effect their wish than by contributing to our collection—not what are called curious Airs, for we have abundance of such, and they are, in general, *only* curious—but any real sweet and expressive Songs of our Country, which either chance or research may have brought into their hands. T. M.

Mayfield Cottage, Ashbourne, December, 1813.

(1) Among these is *Savourna Deelish*, which I have been hitherto only withheld from selecting by the diffidence I feel in treading upon the same ground with Mr. Campbell, whose beautiful words to this fine Air have taken too

ADVERTISEMENT TO THE SIXTH NUMBER.

In presenting this Sixth Number to the public as our last, and bidding adieu to the Irish Harp for ever, we shall not answer very confidently for the strength of our resolution, nor feel quite sure that it may not turn out to be one of those eternal farewells which a lover takes occasionally of his mistress, merely to enhance, perhaps, the pleasure of their next meeting. Our only motive, indeed, for discontinuing the Work was a fear that our treasures were nearly exhausted, and a natural unwillingness to descend to the gathering of mere seed-pearl, after the really precious gems it has been our lot to string together. The announcement, however, of this intention, in our Fifth Number, has excited a degree of anxiety in the lovers of Irish Music, not only pleasant and flattering, but highly useful to us; for the various contributions we have received in consequence have enriched our collection with so many choice and beautiful Airs, that should we adhere to our present resolution of publishing no more, it would certainly furnish an instance of forbearance unexampled in the history of poets and musicians. To one gentleman in particular, who has been for many years resident in England, but who has not forgot, among his various pursuits, either the language or the melodies of his native country, we beg to offer our best thanks for the many interesting communications with which he has favoured us. We trust that neither he nor any other of our kind friends will relax in those efforts by which we have been so considerably assisted; for, though our work must now be looked upon as defunct, yet—as Reaumur found out the art of making the cicada sing after it was dead — it is just possible that we may, some time or other, try a similar experiment upon the *Irish Melodies*. T. M.

Mayfield, Ashbourne, March, 1815.

ADVERTISEMENT TO THE SEVENTH NUMBER.

Had I consulted only my own judgment, this Work would not have extended beyond the Six Numbers already published; which contain the flower, perhaps, of our national melodies, and have now attained a rank in public favour, of which I would not willingly risk the forfeiture, by degenerating, in any way, from those merits that were its source. Whatever treasures of our music were still in reserve, (and it will be seen, I trust, that they are numerous and valuable,) I would gladly have left to future poets to glean, and, with the ritual words "*tibi trado*," would have delivered up the torch into other hands, before it had lost much of its light in my own. But the call for a continuance of the work has been, as I understand from the Publisher, so general, and we

strong possession of all ears and hearts, for me to think of following in his footsteps with any success. I suppose, however, as a matter of duty, I must attempt the air for our next Number.

have received so many contributions of old and beautiful airs (1) — the suppression of which, for the enhancement of those we have published, would too much resemble the policy of the Dutch in burning their spices — that I have been persuaded, though not without much diffidence in my success, to commence a new series of the *Irish Melodies*.

T. M.

DEDICATION

TO THE MARCHIONESS OF HEADFORT,

PREFIXED TO THE TENTH NUMBER.

It is with a pleasure, not unmixed with melancholy, that I dedicate the last Number of the *Irish Melodies* to your Ladyship; nor can I have any doubt that the feelings with which you receive the tribute will be of the same mingled and saddened tone. To you — who, though but little beyond the season of childhood, when the earlier numbers of this work appeared—lent the aid of your beautiful voice, and, even then, exquisite feeling for music, to the happy circle who met, to sing them together, under your father's roof, the gratification, whatever it may be, which this humble offering brings, cannot be otherwise than darkened by the mournful reflection, how many of the voices, which then joined with ours, are now silent in death!

I am not without hope that, as far as regards the grace and spirit of the Melodies, you will find this closing portion of the work not unworthy of what has preceded it. The Sixteen Airs, of which the Number and the Supplement consists, have been selected from the immense mass of Irish music, which has been for years past accumulating in my hands; and it was from a desire to include all that appeared most worthy of preservation, that the four supplementary songs which follow this Tenth Number have been added.

Trusting that I may yet again, in remembrance of old times, hear our voices together in some of the harmonised airs of this Volume, I have the honour to subscribe myself,

Your Ladyship's faithful Friend and Servant,
THOMAS MOORE.

Sloperton Cottage, May, 1834.

NATIONAL AIRS.

ADVERTISEMENT.

It is Cicero, I believe, who says *"naturâ ad modos ducimur;"* and the abundance of wild indigenous airs, which almost every country, except England, possesses, sufficiently proves the truth of his assertion. The lovers of this simple but interesting kind of music are here presented with the first number of a collection, which, I trust, their contributions will enable us to continue. A pretty air without words resembles one of those *half* creatures of Plato, which are described as wandering in search of the remainder of themselves through the world. To supply this other half, by uniting with congenial words the many fugitive melodies which have hitherto had none — or only such as are unintelligible to the generality of their hearers — is the object and ambition of the present work.

Neither is it our intention to confine ourselves to what are strictly called National Melodies, but, wherever we meet with any wandering and beautiful air, to which poetry has not yet assigned a worthy home, we shall venture to claim it as an *estray* swan, and enrich our humble Hippocrene with its song.

*   *   *   *   *

T. M.

(1) One Gentleman, in particular, whose name I shall feel happy in being allowed to mention, has not only sent as nearly forty ancient airs, but has communicated many curious fragments of Irish poetry, and some interesting traditions current in the country where he resides, illustrated by sketches of the romantic scenery to which they refer; all of which, though too late for the present Number, will be of infinite service to us in the prosecution of our task.

A TEMPLE TO FRIENDSHIP. (1)

Spanish Air.

"A Temple to Friendship," said Laura, enchanted,
  "I'll build in this garden—the thought is divine!"
Her temple was built, and she now only wanted
  An image of Friendship to place on the shrine.
She flew to a sculptor, who set down before her
  A Friendship, the fairest his art could invent;
But so cold and so dull, that the youthful adorer
  Saw plainly this was not the idol she meant.

"Oh! never," she cried, "could I think of enshrining
  An image whose looks are so joyless and dim ;—
But yon little god, upon roses reclining,
  We'll make, if you please, Sir, a Friendship of him."
So the bargain was struck ; with the little god laden
  She joyfully flew to her shrine in the grove :
"Farewell," said the sculptor, " you're not the first maiden
  Who came but for Friendship and took away Love."

—◦◦◦◦—

FLOW ON, THOU SHINING RIVER.

Portuguese Air.

Flow on, thou shining river ;
  But, ere thou reach the sea,

(2) The thought is taken from a song by Le Prieur, called *La Statue de l'Amitié.*

Seek Ella's bower, and give her
  The wreaths I fling o'er thee.
And tell her thus, if she'll be mine,
  The current of our lives shall be,
With joys along their course to shine,
  Like those sweet flowers on thee.

But if, in wandering thither,
  Thou find'st she mocks my prayer,
Then leave those wreaths to wither
  Upon the cold bank there;
And tell her thus, when youth is o'er,
  Her lone and loveless charms shall be
Thrown by upon life's weedy shore,
  Like those sweet flowers from thee.

ALL THAT'S BRIGHT MUST FADE.
Indian Air.

ALL that's bright must fade—
  The brightest still the fleetest;
All that's sweet was made,
  But to be lost when sweetest.
Stars that shine and fall—
  The flower that drops in springing—
These, alas! are types of all
  To which our hearts are clinging.
All that's bright must fade—
  The brightest still the fleetest;
All that's sweet was made
  But to be lost when sweetest!

Who would seek or prize
  Delights that end in aching?
Who would trust to ties
  That every hour are breaking?
Better far to be
  In utter darkness lying,
Than to be bless'd with light, and see
  That light for ever flying.
All that's bright must fade—
  The brightest still the fleetest;
All that's sweet was made
  But to be lost when sweetest!

SO WARMLY WE MET.
Hungarian Air.

So warmly we met and so fondly we parted,
  That which was the sweeter even I could not tell—
That first look of welcome her sunny eyes darted,
  Or that tear of passion, which bless'd our farewell.
To meet was a heaven, and to part thus another—
  Our joy and our sorrow seem'd rivals in bliss;
Oh! Cupid's two eyes are not liker each other
  In smiles and in tears, than that moment to this.

The first was like day-break, new, sudden, delicious—
  The dawn of a pleasure scarce kindled up yet;

The last like the farewell of daylight, more precious,
  More glowing and deep, as 't is nearer its set.
Our meeting, though happy, was tinged by a sorrow
  To think that such happiness could not remain;
While our parting, though sad, gave a hope that to-
    morrow
  Would bring back the bless'd hour of meeting again.

THOSE EVENING BELLS.
AIR—*The Bells of St. Petersburgh.*

THOSE evening bells! those evening bells!
How many a tale their music tells,
Of youth, and home, and that sweet time,
When last I heard their soothing chime.

Those joyous hours are past away;
And many a heart, that then was gay,
Within the tomb now darkly dwells,
And hears no more those evening bells.

And so 't will be when I am gone;
That tuneful peal will still ring on,
While other bards shall walk these dells,
And sing your praise, sweet evening bells!

SHOULD THOSE FOND HOPES.
Portuguese Air.

SHOULD those fond hopes e'er forsake thee, (1)
  Which now so sweetly thy heart employ;
Should the cold world come to wake thee
  From all thy visions of youth and joy;
Should the gay friends, for whom thou wouldst banish
  Him who once thought thy young heart his own,
All, like spring birds, falsely vanish,
  And leave thy winter unheeded and lone;—

Oh! 'tis then that he thou hast slighted
  Would come to cheer thee, when all seem'd o'er;
Then the truant, lost and blighted,
  Would to his bosom be taken once more.
Like that dear bird we both can remember,
  Who left us while summer shone round,
But, when chill'd by bleak December,
  On our threshold a welcome still found.

REASON, FOLLY, AND BEAUTY.
Italian Air.

REASON, and Folly, and Beauty, they say,
Went on a party of pleasure one day:
  Folly play'd
  Around the maid,
The bells of his cap rung merrily out;
  While Reason took
  To his sermon-book—
Oh! which was the pleasanter no one need doubt,
Which was the pleasanter no one need doubt.

(1) This is one of the many instances among my lyrical poems—though the above, it must be owned, is an ex- | treme case—where the metre has been necessarily sacrificed to the structure of the air.

Beauty, who likes to be thought very sage,
Turn'd for a moment to Reason's dull page,
　　Till Folly said,
　　"Look here, sweet maid!"—
The sight of his cap brought her back to herself;
　　While Reason read
　　His leaves of lead,
With no one to mind him, poor sensible elf!
No—no one to mind him, poor sensible elf!

Then Reason grew jealous of Folly's gay cap;
Had he that on, her heart might entrap—
　　　"There it is,"
　　Quoth Folly, "old quiz!"
(Folly was always good-natured, 'tis said,)
　　" Under the sun
　　There 's no such fun,
As Reason with my cap and bells on his head,
Reason with my cap and bells on his head!"

But Reason the head-dress so awkwardly wore,
That Beauty now liked him still less than before;
　　While Folly took
　　Old Reason's book,
And twisted the leaves in a cap of such *ton*,
　　That Beauty vow'd
　　(Though not aloud),
She liked him still better in that than his own,
Yes—liked him still better in that than his own.

——◦❋◦——

FARE THEE WELL, THOU LOVELY ONE!
Sicilian Air.

FARE thee well, thou lovely one!
　Lovely still, but dear no more;
Once his soul of truth is gone,
　Love's sweet life is o'er.
Thy words, whate'er their flattering spell,
　Could scarce have thus deceived;
But eyes that acted truth so well
　Were sure to be believed.
Then, fare thee well, thou lovely one!
　Lovely still, but dear no more;
Once his soul of truth is gone,
　Love's sweet life is o'er.

Yet those eyes look constant still,
　True as stars they keep their light;
Still those cheeks their pledge fulfil
　Of blushing always bright.
'T is only on thy changeful heart
　The blame of falsehood lies;
Love lives in every other part,
　But there, alas! he dies.
Then, fare thee well, thou lovely one!
　Lovely still, but dear no more;
Once his soul of truth is gone,
　Love's sweet life is o'er.

(1) The thought in this verse is borrowed from the original Portuguese words.

DOST THOU REMEMBER.
Portuguese Air.

DOST thou remember that place so lonely,
A place for lovers, and lovers only,
　Where first I told thee all my secret sighs?
When as the moonbeam, that trembled o'er thee,
Illumed thy blushes, I knelt before thee,
　And read my hope's sweet triumph in those eyes?
Then, then, while closely heart was drawn to heart,
Love bound us—never, never more to part!

And when I call'd thee by names the dearest (1)
That love could fancy, the fondest, nearest—
　"My life, my only life!" among the rest;
In those sweet accents that still inthral me,
Thou saidst, "Ah! wherefore thy life thus call me?
　Thy soul, thy soul's the name that I love best;
For life soon passes—but how bless'd to be
That soul which never, never parts from thee!"

——◦❋◦——

OH, COME TO ME WHEN DAYLIGHT SETS.
Venetian Air.

OH, come to me when daylight sets;
　Sweet! then come to me,
When smoothly go our gondolets
　O'er the moonlight sea.
When Mirth 's awake, and Love begins,
　Beneath that glancing ray,
With sound of lutes and mandolins,
　To steal young hearts away.
Then, come to me when daylight sets;
　Sweet! then come to me,
When smoothly go our gondolets
　O'er the moonlight sea.

Oh, then 's the hour for those who love,
　Sweet, like thee and me;
When all 's so calm below, above,
　In Heaven and o'er the sea.
When maidens sing sweet barcarolles, (2)
　And Echo sings again
So sweet, that all with ears and souls
　Should love and listen then.
So, come to me when daylight sets;
　Sweet! then come to me,
When smoothly go our gondolets
　O'er the moonlight sea.

——◦❋◦——

OFT, IN THE STILLY NIGHT.
Scotch Air.

OFT, in the stilly night,
　Ere Slumber's chain has bound me,
Fond Memory brings the light
　Of other days around me;
　　The smiles, the tears,
　　Of boyhood's years,

(2) Barcarolles, sorte de chansons en langue Vénitienne, que chantent les gondoliers à Venise.—*Rousseau.*

The words of love then spoken;
  The eyes that shone,
  Now dimm'd and gone,
The cheerful hearts now broken!
Thus, in the stilly night,
  Ere Slumber's chain has bound me,
Sad Memory brings the light
  Of other days around me.

When I remember all
  The friends, so link'd together,
I've seen around me fall,
  Like leaves in wintry weather;
    I feel like one
    Who treads alone
Some banquet-hall deserted,
    Whose lights are fled,
    Whose garlands dead,
And all but he departed!
Thus, in the stilly night,
  Ere Slumber's chain has bound me,
Sad Memory brings the light
  Of other days around me.

———o♦♦o———

HARK! THE VESPER HYMN IS STEALING.
Russian Air.

HARK! the vesper hymn is stealing
  O'er the waters soft and clear;
Nearer yet and nearer pealing,
    Jubilate, Amen.
Farther now, now farther stealing,
  Soft it fades upon the ear,
    Jubilate, Amen.

Now, like moonlight waves retreating
  To the shore, it dies along;
Now, like angry surges meeting,
  Breaks the mingled tide of song,
    Jubilate, Amen.
Hush! again, like waves retreating
  To the shore, it dies along,
    Jubilate, Amen.

———o♦♦o———

THERE COMES A TIME.
German Air.

THERE comes a time, a dreary time,
  To him whose heart hath flown
O'er all the fields of youth's sweet prime,
  And made each flower its own.
'T is when his soul must first renounce
  Those dreams so bright, so fond;
Oh! then's the time to die at once,
  For life has nought beyond.

When sets the sun on Afric's shore,
  That instant all is night;
And so should life at once be o'er,
  When Love withdraws his light;—

Nor like our northern day, gleam on
  Through twilight's dim delay,
The cold remains of lustre gone,
  Of fire long pass'd away.

———o♦♦o———

LOVE AND HOPE.
Swiss Air.

AT morn, beside yon summer sea,
  Young Hope and Love reclined;
But scarce had noon-tide come, when he
Into his bark leap'd smilingly,
  And left poor Hope behind.

"I go," said Love, "to sail awhile
  Across this sunny main;"
And then so sweet his parting smile,
That Hope, who never dreamt of guile,
  Believed he'd come again.

She linger'd there till evening's beam
  Along the waters lay;
And o'er the sands, in thoughtful dream,
Oft traced his name, which still the stream
  As often wash'd away.

At length a sail appears in sight,
  And toward the maiden moves!
'T is Wealth that comes, and gay and bright,
His golden bark reflects the light,
  But ah! it is not Love's.

Another sail—'t was Friendship show'd
  Her night-lamp o'er the sea;
And calm the light that lamp bestow'd;
But Love had lights that warmer glow'd,
  And where, alas! was he?

Now fast around the sea and shore
  Night threw her darkling chain;
The sunny sails were seen no more,
Hope's morning dreams of bliss were o'er—
  Love never came again!

———o♦♦o———

MY HARP HAS ONE UNCHANGING THEME.
Swedish Air.

MY harp has one unchanging theme,
  One strain that still comes o'er
Its languid chord, as 't were a dream
  Of joy that's now no more.
In vain I try, with livelier air,
  To wake the breathing string;
That voice of other times is there,
  And saddens all I sing.

Breathe on, breathe on, thou languid strain,
  Henceforth be all my own;
Though thou art oft so full of pain,
  Few hearts can bear thy tone.

31

Yet oft thou 'rt sweet, as if the sigh,
 The breath that Pleasure's wings
Gave out, when last they wanton'd by,
 Were still upon thy strings.

OH, NO—NOT E'EN WHEN FIRST WE LOVED.
Cashmerian Air.

Oh, no—not e'en when first we loved,
 Wert thou as dear as now thou art;
Thy beauty then my senses moved,
 But now thy virtues bind my heart.
What was but Passion's sigh before,
 Has since been turn'd to Reason's vow;
And, though I then might love thee *more*,
 Trust me, I love thee *better* now.

Although my heart in earlier youth
 Might kindle with more wild desire,
Believe me, it has gain'd in truth
 Much more than it has lost in fire.
The flame now warms my inmost core
 That then but sparkled o'er my brow,
And, though I seem'd to love thee more,
 Yet, oh, I love thee better now.

PEACE BE AROUND THEE.
Scotch Air.

Peace be around thee, wherever thou rovest;
 May life be for thee one summer's day,
And all that thou wishest, and all that thou lovest,
 Come smiling around thy sunny way!
If sorrow e'er this calm should break,
 May even thy tears pass off so lightly,
Like spring-showers, they 'll only make
 The smiles that follow shine more brightly.

May Time, who sheds his blight o'er all,
 And daily dooms some joy to death,
O'er thee let years so gently fall,
 They shall not crush one flower beneath.
As half in shade and half in sun
 This world along its path advances,
May that side the sun 's upon
 Be all that e'er shall meet thy glances!

COMMON SENSE AND GENIUS.
French Air.

While I touch the string,
 Wreathe my brows with laurel,
For the tale I sing
 Has, for once, a moral.
Common Sense, one night,
 Though not used to gambols,
Went out by moonlight,
 With Genius, on his rambles.
  While I touch the string, etc.

Common Sense went on,
 Many wise things saying;
While the light that shone
 Soon set Genius straying.
One his eye ne'er raised
 From the path before him;
T'*other* idly gazed
 On each night-cloud o'er him.
  While I touch the string, etc.

So they came, at last,
 To a shady river;
Common Sense soon pass'd,
 Safe, as he doth ever;
While the boy, whose look
 Was in Heaven that minute,
Never saw the brook,
 But tumbled headlong in it!
  While I touch the string, etc.

How the Wise One smiled,
 When safe o'er the torrent,
At that youth, so wild,
 Dripping from the current!
Sense went home to bed;
 Genius left to shiver
On the bank, 'tis said,
 Died of that cold river!
  While I touch the string, etc.

THEN, FARE THEE WELL.
Old English Air.

Then, fare thee well, my own dear love,
 This world has now for us
No greater grief, no pain above
 The pain of parting thus,
  Dear love!
 The pain of parting thus.

Had we but known, since first we met,
 Some few short hours of bliss,
We might, in numbering them, forget
 The deep, deep pain of this,
  Dear love!
 The deep, deep pain of this.

But no, alas, we 've never seen
 One glimpse of pleasure's ray,
But still there came some cloud between,
 And chased it all away,
  Dear love!
 And chased it all away.

Yet, even could those sad moments last,
 Far dearer to my heart
Were hours of grief, together past,
 Than years of mirth apart,
  Dear love!
 Than years of mirth apart.

Farewell! our hope was born in fears,
   And nursed 'mid vain regrets ;
Like winter suns, it rose in tears,
   Like them in tears it sets,
     Dear love!
   Like them in tears it sets.

—◦♦◦—

GAILY SOUNDS THE CASTANET.

Maltese Air.

GAILY sounds the castanet,
   Beating time to bounding feet,
When, after daylight's golden set,
   Maids and youths by moonlight meet.
Oh, then, how sweet to move
   Through all that maze of mirth,
Led by light from eyes we love
   Beyond all eyes on earth.

Then, the joyous banquet spread
   On the cool and fragrant ground,
With heaven's bright sparklers overhead,
   And still brighter sparkling round.
Oh, then, how sweet to say
   Into some loved one's ear,
Thoughts reserved through many a day
   To be thus whisper'd here.

When the dance and feast are done,
   Arm in arm as home we stray,
How sweet to see the dawning sun
   O'er her cheek's warm blushes play !
Then, too, the farewell kiss—
   The words, whose parting tone
Lingers still in dreams of bliss,
   That haunt young hearts alone.

—◦♦◦—

JOYS OF YOUTH, HOW FLEETING!

Portuguese Air.

WHISPERINGS, heard by wakeful maids,
   To whom the night-stars guide us ;
Stolen walks through moonlight shades,
   With those we love beside us,
     Hearts beating,
     At meeting ;
     Tears starting,
     At parting :
Oh, sweet youth, how soon it fades !
Sweet joys of youth, how fleeting '

Wanderings far away from home,
   With life all new before us ;
Greetings warm, when home we come,
   From hearts whose prayers watch'd o'er us.
     Tears starting,
     At parting ;
     Hearts beating,
     At meeting :
Oh, sweet youth, how lost on some !
   To some, how bright and fleeting!

COME, CHASE THAT STARTING TEAR AWAY.

French Air.

COME, chase that starting tear away,
   Ere mine to meet it springs ;
To-night, at least, to-night be gay,
   Whate'er to-morrow brings.
Like sun-set gleams, that linger late
   When all is darkening fast,
Are hours like these we snatch from Fate—
   The brightest, and the last.
     Then, chase that starting tear, etc.

To gild the deepening gloom, if Heaven
   But one bright hour allow,
Oh, think that one bright hour is given,
   In all its splendour, now.
Let's live it out—then sink in night,
   Like waves that from the shore
One minute swell, are touch'd with light,
   Then lost for evermore !
     Come, chase that starting tear, etc.

—◦♦◦—

LOVE IS A HUNTER-BOY.

Languedocian Air.

LOVE is a hunter-boy,
   Who makes young hearts his prey ;
And, in his nets of joy,
   Ensnares them night and day.
In vain conceal'd they lie—
   Love tracks them every where ;
In vain aloft they fly—
   Love shoots them flying there.

But 'tis his joy most sweet,
   At early dawn to trace
The print of Beauty's feet,
   And give the trembler chase.
And if, through virgin snow,
   He tracks her footsteps fair,
How sweet for Love to know,
   None went before him there. (1)

—◦♦◦—

HEAR ME BUT ONCE.

French Air.

HEAR me but once, while o'er the grave,
   In which our Love lies cold and dead,
I count each flattering hope he gave
   Of joys, now lost, and charms now fled.

Who could have thought the smile he wore,
   When first we met, would fade away ?
Or that a chill would e'er come o'er
   Those eyes so bright through many a day ?
     Hear me but once, etc.

(1) These four lines originally read—
    And most he loves through snow
     To trace those footsteps fair,
    For then the boy doth know
     None track'd before him there.—P. E.

WHEN LOVE WAS A CHILD.
Swedish Air.

WHEN Love was a child, and went idling round,
'Mong flowers, the whole summer's day,
One morn in the valley a bower he found,
So sweet, it allured him to stay.

O'erhead, from the trees, hung a garland fair,
A fountain ran darkly beneath;—
'T was Pleasure had hung up the flowerets there;
Love knew it, and jump'd at the wreath.

But Love did n't know—and, at *his* weak years,
What urchin was likely to know?—
That Sorrow had made of her own salt tears
The fountain that murmur'd below.

He caught at the wreath—but with too much haste,
As boys when impatient will do—
It fell in those waters of briny taste,
And the flowers were all wet through.

This garland he now wears night and day;
And, though it all sunny appears
With Pleasure's own light, each leaf, they say,
Still tastes of the Fountain of Tears.

SAY, WHAT SHALL BE OUR SPORT TO-DAY?
Sicilian Air.

SAY, what shall be our sport to-day?
There's nothing on earth, in sea, or air,
Too bright, too high, too wild, too gay
For spirits like mine to dare!
'T is like the returning bloom
Of those days, alas, gone by,
When I loved, each hour—I scarce knew whom—
And was bless'd—I scarce knew why.

Ay—those were days when life had wings,
And flew, oh flew so wild a height,
That, like the lark which sunward springs,
'T was giddy with too much light.
And, though of some plumes bereft,
With that sun, too, nearly set,
I've enough of light and wing still left
For a few gay soarings yet.

BRIGHT BE THY DREAMS.
Welsh Air.

BRIGHT be thy dreams—may all thy weeping
Turn into smiles while thou art sleeping.
May those by death or seas removed,
The friends, who in thy spring-time knew thee,
All thou hast ever prized or loved,
In dreams come smiling to thee!

There may the child, whose love lay deepest,
Dearest of all, come while thou sleepest;

Still as she was—no charm forgot—
No lustre lost that life had given;
Or, if changed, but changed to what
Thou'lt find her yet in Heaven!

GO, THEN—'T IS VAIN.
Sicilian Air.

Go, then—'t is vain to hover
Thus round a hope that 's dead;
At length my dream is over:
'T was sweet—'t was false—'t is fled!
Farewell! since nought it moves thee,
Such truth as mine to see—
Some one, who far less loves thee,
Perhaps more bless'd will be.

Farewell, sweet eyes, whose brightness
New life around me shed;
Farewell, false heart, whose lightness
Now leaves me death instead.
Go, now, those charms surrender
To some new lover's sigh—
One who, though far less tender,
May be more bless'd than I.

THE CRYSTAL-HUNTERS.
Swiss Air.

O'ER mountains bright
With snow and light,
We Crystal-Hunters speed along;
While rocks and caves,
And icy waves,
Each instant echo to our song;
And, when we meet with store of gems,
We grudge not kings their diadems.
O'er mountains bright
With snow and light,
We Crystal-Hunters speed along;
While grots and caves,
And icy waves,
Each instant echo to our song.

Not half so oft the lover dreams
Of sparkles from his lady's eyes,
As we of those refreshing gleams
That tell where deep the crystal lies;
Though, next to crystal, we too grant,
That ladies' eyes may most enchant.
O'er mountains bright, etc.

Sometimes, when on the Alpine rose
The golden sunset leaves its ray,
So like a gem the floweret glows,
We thither bend our headlong way;
And, though we find no treasure there,
We bless the rose that shines so fair.
O'er mountains bright
With snow and light,

We Crystal–Hunters speed along;
　　While rocks and caves,
　　And icy waves,
Each instant echo to our song.

ROW GENTLY HERE.
Venetian Air.

Row gently here,
　　My gondolier,
So softly wake the tide,
　　That not an ear,
　　On earth, may hear,
But hers to whom we glide.
Had Heaven but tongues to speak, as well
　　As starry eyes to see,
Oh, think what tales 't would have to tell
　　Of wandering youths like me!

Now rest thee here,
　　My gondolier;
Hush, hush, for up I go,
　　To climb yon light
　　Balcony's height,
While thou keep'st watch below.
Ah! did we take for Heaven above
　　But half such pains as we
Take, day and night, for woman's love,
　　What angels we should be.

OH, DAYS OF YOUTH.
French Air.

OH, days of youth and joy, long clouded,
　Why thus for ever haunt my view?
When in the grave your light lay shrouded,
　Why did not Memory die there too?
Vainly doth Hope her strain now sing me,
　Telling of joys that yet remain—
No, never more can this life bring me
　One joy that equals youth's sweet pain.

Dim lies the way to death before me,
　Cold winds of Time blow round my brow;
Sunshine of youth! that once fell o'er me,
　Where is your warmth, your glory now?
'T is not that then no pain could sting me;
　'T is not that now no joys remain;
Oh, 'tis that life no more can bring me
　One joy so sweet as that worst pain.

WHEN FIRST THAT SMILE.
Venetian Air.

WHEN first that smile, like sunshine, bless'd my
　Oh what a vision then came o'er me!　[sight,
Long years of love, of calm and pure delight,
　Seem'd in that smile to pass before me.
Ne'er did the peasant dream of summer skies,
　Of golden fruit, and harvests springing,
With fonder hope than I of those sweet eyes,
　And of the joy their light was bringing.

Where now are all those fondly–promised hours?
　Ah! woman's faith is like her brightness—
Fading as fast as rainbows, or day–flowers,
　Or aught that's known for grace and lightness.
Short as the Persian's prayer, at close of day,
　Should be each vow of Love's repeating;
Quick let him worship Beauty's precious ray—
　Even while he kneels, that ray is fleeting!

PEACE TO THE SLUMBERERS!
Catalonian Air.

PEACE to the slumberers!
　They lie on the battle–plain,
With no shroud to cover them;
　The dew and the summer rain
Are all that weep over them.
　Peace to the slumberers!

Vain was their bravery!—
　The fallen oak lies where it lay,
Across the wintry river;
　But brave hearts, once swept away,
Are gone, alas, for ever.
　Vain was their bravery!

Woe to the conqueror!
　Our limbs shall lie as cold as theirs
Of whom his sword bereft us,
　Ere we forget the deep arrears
Of vengeance they have left us!
　Woe to the conqueror!

WHEN THOU SHALT WANDER.
Sicilian Air.

WHEN thou shalt wander by that sweet light
　We used to gaze on so many an eve,
When love was new and hope was bright,
　Ere I could doubt or thou deceive—
Oh, then, remembering how swift went by
Those hours of transport, even *thou* may'st sigh.

Yes, proud one! even thy heart may own
　That love like ours was far too sweet
To be, like summer garments, thrown
　Aside, when pass'd the summer's heat;
And wish in vain to know again
Such days, such nights, as bless'd thee then.

WHO 'LL BUY MY LOVE–KNOTS?
Portuguese Air.

HYMEN, late, his love–knots selling,
Call'd at many a maiden's dwelling:
None could doubt, who saw or knew them,
Hymen's call was welcome to them.
　" Who 'll buy my love–knots?
　Who 'll buy my love–knots?"
Soon as that sweet cry resounded,
How his baskets were surrounded!

Maids, who now first dreamt of trying
These gay knots of Hymen's tying ;
Dames, who long had sat to watch him,
Passing by, but ne'er could catch him ;—
    " Who 'll buy my love-knots ?
    Who 'll buy my love-knots ?"
All at that sweet cry assembled ;
Some laugh'd, some blush'd, and some trembled.

" Here are knots," said Hymen, taking
Some loose flowers, " of Love's own making ;
Here are gold ones—you may trust 'em"—
(These, of course, found ready custom).
    " Come, buy my love-knots !
    Come, buy my love-knots !
Some are labell'd ' Knots to tie men—
Love the maker—Bought of Hymen.' "

Scarce their bargains were completed,
When the nymphs all cried, " We're cheated !
See these flowers—they 're drooping sadly ;
This gold-knot, too, ties but badly—
    Who 'd buy such love-knots ?
    Who 'd buy such love-knots ?
Even this tie, with Love's name round it—
All a sham—He never bound it."

Love, who saw the whole proceeding,
Would have laugh'd, but for good breeding ;
While old Hymen, who was used to
Cries like that these dames gave loose to—
    " Take back our love-knots !
    Take back our love-knots !"
Coolly said, " There 's no returning
Wares on Hymen's hands—Good morning !"

————o❦o————

SEE, THE DAWN FROM HEAVEN.

To an Air sung at Rome, on Christmas Eve.

SEE, the dawn from Heaven is breaking
        O'er our sight,
And Earth, from sin awaking,
        Hails the light !
See those groups of angels, winging
        From the realms above,
On their brows, from Eden, bringing
        Wreaths of Hope and Love.

Hark, their hymns of glory pealing
        Through the air,
To mortal ears revealing·
        Who lies there !
In that dwelling, dark and lowly,
        Sleeps the Heavenly Son,
He, whose home 's above—the Holy,
        Ever Holy One !

NETS AND CAGES. (1)

Swedish Air.

COME, listen to my story, while
    Your needle's task you ply ;
At what I sing some maids will smile,
    While some, perhaps, may sigh.
Though Love 's the theme, and Wisdom blames
    Such florid songs as ours,
Yet Truth sometimes, like Eastern dames,
    Can speak her thoughts by flowers.
Then listen, maids, come listen, while,
    Your needle's task you ply ;
At what I sing there 's some may smile,
    While some, perhaps, will sigh.

Young Cloe, bent on catching Loves,
    Such nets had learn'd to frame,
That none, in all our vales and groves,
    E'er caught so much small game :
But gentle Sue, less given to roam,
    While Cloe's nets were taking
Such lots of Loves, sat still at home,
    One little Love-cage making.
        Come, listen, maids, etc.

Much Cloe laugh'd at Susan's task ;
    But mark how things went on :
These light-caught Loves, ere you could ask
    Their name and age, were gone !
So weak poor Cloe's nets were wove,
    That, though she charm'd into them
New game each hour, the youngest Love
    Was able to break through them.
        Come, listen, maids, etc.

Meanwhile, young Sue, whose cage was wrought
    Of bars too strong to sever,
One love with golden pinions caught,
    And caged him there for ever ;
Instructing, thereby, all coquettes,
    Whate'er their looks or ages,
That, though 't is pleasant weaving Nets,
    'T is wiser to make Cages.

Thus, maidens, thus, do I beguile
    The task your fingers ply ;—
May all who hear like Susan smile,
    And not, like Cloe, sigh !

————o❦o————

WHEN THROUGH THE PIAZZETTA.

Venetian Air.

WHEN through the Piazzetta
    Night breathes her cool air,
Then, dearest Ninetta,
    I 'll come to thee there.

(1 Suggested by the following remark of Swift's :—" The reason why so few marriages are happy is, because young ladies spend their time in making nets, not in making cages."

Beneath thy mask shrouded,
 I 'll know thee afar,
As Love knows, though clouded,
 His own Evening Star.

In garb, then, resembling
 Some gay gondolier,
I 'll whisper thee, trembling,
 " Our bark, love, is near ':
Now, now, while there hover
 Those clouds o'er the moon,
'T will waft thee safe over
 Yon silent Lagoon."

—o▰o—

GO, NOW, AND DREAM.

Sicilian Air.

Go, now, and dream o'er that joy in thy slumber—
Moments so sweet again ne'er shalt thou number.
Of Pain's bitter draught the flavour ne'er flies,
While Pleasure's scarce touches the lip ere it dies.
 Go, then, and dream, etc.

That moon, which hung o'er your parting, so splendid,
Often will shine again, bright as she then did—
But never more will the beam she saw burn
In those happy eyes, at your meeting, return.
 Go, then, and dream, etc.

—o▰o—

TAKE HENCE THE BOWL.

Neapolitan Air.

TAKE hence the bowl—though beaming
 Brightly as bowl e'er shone,
Oh, it but sets me dreaming
 Of happy days now gone.
There, in its clear reflection,
 As in a wizard's glass,
Lost hopes and dead affection,
 Like shades, before me pass.

Each cup I drain brings hither
 Some scene of bliss gone by ;—
Bright lips, too bright to wither,
 Warm hearts, too warm to die.
Till, as the dream comes o'er me
 Of those long vanish'd years,
Alas, the wine before me
 Seems turning all to tears !

—o▰o—

FAREWELL, THERESA!

Venetian Air.

FAREWELL, Theresa! yon cloud that over
Heaven's pale night-star gathering we see,
Will scarce from that pure orb have pass'd, ere thy
  lover
Swift o'er the wide wave shall wander from thee.

Long, like that dim cloud, I 've hung around thee,
Darkening thy prospects, saddening thy brow ;

With gay heart, Theresa, and bright cheek I found
  thee ;
 Oh, think how changed, love, how changed art
  thou now !

But here I free thee : like one awaking
 From fearful slumber, thou break'st the spell ;
'T is over—the moon, too, her bondage is breaking—
 Past are the dark clouds ; Theresa, farewell !

—o▰o—

OFT, WHEN THE WATCHING STARS.

Savoyard Air.

OFT, when the watching stars grow pale,
 And round me sleeps the moonlight scene,
To hear a flute through yonder vale
 I from my casement lean.
" Come, come, my love !" each note then seems to say,
" Oh, come, my love ! the night wears fast away ! "
 Never to mortal ear,
  Could words, though warm they be,
 Speak Passion's language half so clear
  As do those notes to me.

Then quick my own light lute I seek,
 And strike the chords with loudest swell ;
And, though they nought to others speak,
 He knows their language well.
"I come, my love," each note then seems to say,
"I come, my love !—thine, thine till break of day."
 Oh, weak the power of words,
  The hues of painting dim,
 Compared to what those simple chords
  Then say and paint to him !

—o▰o—

WHEN THE FIRST SUMMER BEE.

German Air.

WHEN the first summer bee
 O'er the young rose shall hover,
 Then, like that gay rover,
  I 'll come to thee.
He to flowers, I to lips, full of sweets to the brim—
What a meeting, what a meeting for me and for him !
 When the first summer bee, etc.

Then to every bright tree
 In the garden he 'll wander ;
 While I, oh, much fonder,
  Will stay with thee.   [run,
In search of new sweetness through thousands he 'll
While I find the sweetness of thousands in one.
 Then, to every bright tree, etc.

—o▰o—

THOUGH 'T IS ALL BUT A DREAM.

French Air.

THOUGH 't is all but a dream at the best,
 And still, when happiest, soonest o'er,
Yet, even in a dream to be bless'd
 Is so sweet, that I ask for no more.

The bosom that opes
　With earliest hopes,
The soonest finds those hopes untrue ;
　As flowers that first
　In spring-time burst
The earliest wither too !
　Ay—'t is all but a dream, etc.

Though by friendship we oft are deceived,
　And find love's sunshine soon o'ercast,
Yet friendship will still be believed,
　And love trusted on to the last.
　　The web 'mong the leaves
　　The spider weaves
Is like the charm Hope hangs o'er men ;
　Though often she sees
　'T is broke by the breeze,
She spins the bright tissue again.
　Ay—'t is all but a dream, etc.

WHEN THE WINE-CUP IS SMILING.
Italian Air.

WHEN the wine-cup is smiling before us,
　And we pledge round to hearts that are true, boy,
　　true,
Then the sky of this life opens o'er us,
　And heaven gives a glimpse of its blue.
Talk of Adam in Eden reclining,
　We are better, far better off thus, boy, thus :
For *him* but *two* bright eyes were shining—
　See what numbers are sparkling for us!

When on *one* side the grape-juice is dancing,
　While on t'other a blue eye beams, boy, beams,
'T is enough, 'twixt the wine and the glancing,
　To disturb even a saint from his dreams.
Yet, though life like a river is flowing,
　I care not how fast it goes on, boy, on,
So the grape on its bank is still growing,
　And Love lights the waves as they run.

WHERE SHALL WE BURY OUR SHAME?
Neapolitan Air.

WHERE shall we bury our shame?
　Where, in what desolate place,
Hide the last wreck of a name
　Broken and stain'd by disgrace?
Death may dissever the chain,
　Oppression will cease when we're gone ;
But the dishonour, the stain,
　Die as we may, will live on.

Was it for this we sent out
　Liberty's cry from our shore?
Was it for this that her shout
　Thrill'd to the world's very core?
Thus to live cowards and slaves!—
　Oh, ye free hearts that lie dead,
Do you not, even in your graves,
　Shudder, as o'er you we tread?

NE'ER TALK OF WISDOM'S GLOOMY SCHOOLS.
Mahratta Air.

NE'ER talk of Wisdom's gloomy schools ;
　Give me the sa_e who's able
To draw his moral thoughts and rules
　From the study of the table ;—
Who learns how lightly, fleetly pass
　This world and all that 's in it,
From the bumper that but crowns his glass,
　And is gone again next minute!

The diamond sleeps within the mine,
　The pearl beneath the water ;
While Truth, more precious, dwells in wine,
　The grape 's own rosy daughter.
And none can prize her charms like him,
　Oh, none like him obtain her,
Who thus can, like Leander, swim
　Through sparkling floods to gain her !

HERE SLEEPS THE BARD.
Highland Air.

HERE sleeps the Bard who knew so well
All the sweet windings of Apollo's shell ;
Whether its music roll'd like torrents near,
Or died, like distant streamlets, on the ear.
Sleep, sleep, mute bard ; alike unheeded now
The storm and zephyr sweep thy lifeless brow ;—
That storm, whose rush is like thy martial lay ;
That breeze which, like thy love-song, dies away !

DO NOT SAY THAT LIFE IS WANING.
Danish Air.

Do not say that life is waning,
　Or that hope's sweet day is set ;
While I 've thee and love remaining,
　Life is in the horizon yet.

Do not think those charms are flying,
　Though thy roses fade and fall ;
Beauty hath a grace undying,
　Which in thee survives them all.

Not for charms, the newest, brightest,
　That on other cheeks may shine,
Would I change the least, the slightest,
　That is lingering now o'er thine.

THE GAZELLE.
Hindoo Air.

Dost thou not hear the silver bell,
　Through yonder lime-trees ringing?
'Tis my lady's light gazelle,
　To me her love thoughts bringing,
All the while that silver bell
　Around his dark neck ringing.

See, in his mouth he bears a wreath,
  My love hath kist in tying;
Oh, what tender thoughts beneath
  Those silent flowers are lying—
Hid within the mystic wreath,
  My love hath kist in tying!

Welcome, dear gazelle, to thee,
  And joy to her, the fairest,
Who thus hath breathed her soul to me,
  In every leaf thou bearest;
Welcome, dear gazelle, to thee,
  And joy to her the fairest!

Hail, ye living, speaking flowers,
  That breathe of her who bound ye;
Oh, 't was not in fields, or bowers,
  'T was on her lips, she found ye;—
Yes, ye blushing, speaking flowers,
  'T was on her lips she found ye.

——o♦♦o——

NO—LEAVE MY HEART TO REST.
Spanish Air.

No—leave my heart to rest, if rest it may,
When youth, and love, and hope, have pass'd
    away.
Couldst thou, when summer hours are fled,
To some poor leaf that's fall'n and dead,
Bring back the hue it wore, the scent it shed?
No—leave this heart to rest, if rest it may,
When youth, and love, and hope, have pass'd away.

Oh, had I met thee then, when life was bright,
Thy smile might still have fed its tranquil light;
But now thou comest like sunny skies,
Too late to cheer the seaman's eyes,
When wreck'd and lost his bark before him lies!
No—leave this heart to rest, if rest it may,
Since youth, and love, and hope, have pass'd away.

——o♦♦o——

WIND THY HORN, MY HUNTER BOY.
German Air.

Wind thy horn, my hunter boy,
  And leave thy lute's inglorious sighs;
Hunting is the hero's joy,
  Till war his nobler game supplies.
Hark! the hound-bells ringing sweet,
While hunters shout, and the woods repeat,
          Hilli-ho! hilli-ho!

Wind again thy cheerful horn,
  Till echo, faint with answering, dies.
Burn, bright torches, burn till morn,
  And lead us where the wild boar lies.
Hark! the cry, "He's found, he's found,"
While hill and valley our shouts resound,
          Hilli-ho! hilli-ho!

WHERE ARE THE VISIONS.
Air Unknown.

"Where are the visions that round me once hover'd,
  Forms that shed grace from their shadows alone;
Looks fresh as light from a star just discover'd,
  And voices that Music might take for her own?"

Time, while I spoke, with his wings resting o'er me,
  Heard me say, "Where are those visions, oh where?"
And pointing his wand to the sunset before me,
  Said, with a voice like the hollow wind, "There."

Fondly I look'd, when the wizard had spoken,
  And there, 'mid the dim-shining ruins of day,
Saw, by their light, like a talisman broken,
  The last golden fragments of hope melt away. (1)

——o♦♦o——

OH, GUARD OUR AFFECTION.
Scotch Air.

Oh, guard our affection, nor e'er let it feel
The blight that this world o'er the warmest will steal:
While the faith of all round us is fading or past,
Let ours, ever green, keep its bloom to the last.

Far safer for Love 't is to wake and to weep,
As he used in his prime, than go smiling to sleep;
For death on his slumber, cold death follows fast,
While the love that is wakeful lives on to the last.

And though, as Time gathers his clouds o'er our head,
A shade somewhat darker o'er life they may spread,
Transparent, at least, be the shadow they cast,
So that Love's soften'd light may shine through to
    the last.

——o♦♦o——

SLUMBER, OH SLUMBER.
Air Unknown.

"Slumber, oh slumber; if sleeping thou makest
My heart beat so wildly, I'm lost if thou wakest."
      Thus sung I to a maiden,
        Who slept one summer's day,
      And, like a flower o'erladen
        With too much sunshine, lay.
          Slumber, oh slumber, etc.

"Breathe not, oh breathe not, ye winds, o'er her
    cheeks;   [speaks."
If mute thus she charm me, I'm lost when she
      Thus sing I, while, awaking,
        She murmurs words that seem
      As if her lips were taking
        Farewell of some sweet dream.
          Breathe not, oh breathe not, etc.

(1 The following quatrain has been here omitted:—
    "Oh lend me thy wings, Time," I hastily utter'd,
      Impatient to catch the last glimmer that shone;
    But scarcely again had the dark wizard flutter'd
      His wing o'er my head, ere the light all was gone.—P. E.
                                                        32

BRING THE BRIGHT GARLANDS HITHER.
Russian Air.

BRING the bright garlands hither,
Ere yet a leaf is dying;
If so soon they must wither,
Ours be their last sweet sighing.
Hark, that low dismal chime!
'T is the dreary voice of Time.
Oh, bring beauty, bring roses,
Bring all that yet is ours;
Let life's day, as it closes,
Shine to the last through flowers.

Haste, ere the bowl's declining,
Drink of it now or never;
Now, while beauty is shining,
Love, or she's lost for ever.
Hark! again that dull chime,
'T is the dreary voice of Time.
Oh, if life be a torrent,
Down to oblivion going,
Like this cup be its current,
Bright to the last drop flowing!

IF IN LOVING, SINGING.
Spanish Air.

IF in loving, singing, night and day
We could trifle merrily life away,
Like atoms dancing in the beam,
Like day-flies skimming o'er the stream,
Or summer blossoms, born to sigh
Their sweetness out, and die—
How brilliant, thoughtless, side by side,
Thou and I could make our minutes glide!
No atoms ever glanced so bright,
No day-flies ever danced so light,
Nor summer blossoms mix'd their sigh,
So close, as thou and I!

WHEN ABROAD IN THE WORLD.
Italian Air.

WHEN abroad in the world thou appearest,
And the young and the lovely are there,
To my heart while of all thou'rt the dearest,
To my eyes thou 'rt of all the most fair.
They pass, one by one,
Like waves of the sea,
That say to the Sun,
"See, how fair we can be."
But where's the light like thine,
In sun or shade to shine?
No—no, 'mong them all, there is nothing like thee,
Nothing like thee.

Oft, of old, without farewell or warning,
Beauty's self used to steal from the skies;
Fling a mist round her head, some fine morning,
And post down to earth in disguise;

But, no matter what shroud
Around her might be,
Men peep'd through the cloud,
And whisper'd, "'T is She."
So thou, where thousands are,
Shinest forth the only star;—
Yes, yes, 'mong them all, there is nothing like thee,
Nothing like thee.

THOU LOVEST NO MORE.
French Air.

Too plain, alas, my doom is spoken,
Nor canst thou veil the sad truth o'er;
Thy heart is changed, thy vow is broken,
Thou lovest no more—thou lovest no more.

Though kindly still those eyes behold me,
The smile is gone, which once they wore;
Though fondly still those arms enfold me,
'T is not the same—thou lovest no more.

Too long my dream of bliss believing,
I've thought thee all thou wert before;
But now—alas! there's no deceiving,
'T is all too plain, thou lovest no more.

Oh, thou as soon the dead couldst waken
As lost affection's life restore,
Give peace to her that is forsaken,
Or bring back him who loves no more.

KEEP THOSE EYES STILL PURELY MINE.
German Air.

KEEP those eyes still purely mine,
Though far off I be:
When on others most they shine,
Then think they're turn'd on me.

Should those lips as now respond
To sweet minstrelsy,
When their accents seem most fond,
Then think they 're breathed for me.

Make what hearts thou wilt thy own,
If when all on thee
Fix their charmed thoughts alone,
Thou think'st the while on me.

HOPE COMES AGAIN.
Old English Air.

HOPE comes again, to this heart long a stranger,
Once more she sings me her flattering strain;
But hush, gentle syren—for, ah, there's less danger
In still suffering on, than in hoping again.

Long, long, in sorrow. too deep for repining,
Gloomy, but tranquil, this bosom hath lain;

And joy coming now, like a sudden light shining
O'er eyelids long darken'd, would bring me but
[pain.
Fly then, ye visions, that Hope would shed o'er me,
Lost to the future, my sole chance of rest
Now lies not in dreaming of bliss that 's before me,
But, ah—in forgetting how once I was blest.

—◦◦◦—

O SAY, THOU BEST AND BRIGHTEST.
Spanish Air.

O SAY, thou best and brightest,
My first love and my last,
When he, whom now thou slightest,
From life's dark scene hath past,
Will kinder thoughts then move thee?
Will pity wake one thrill
For him who lived to love thee,
And dying loved thee still?

If when, that hour recalling
From which he dates his woes,
Thou feel'st a tear-drop falling,
Ah, blush not while it flows:
But, all the past forgiving,
Bend gently o'er his shrine,
And say, "This heart, when living,
With all its faults, was mine."

—◦◦◦—

WHEN NIGHT BRINGS THE HOUR.
Florentine Air.

WHEN night brings the hour
Of starlight and joy,
There comes to my bower
A fairy-wing'd boy;
With eyes so bright,
So full of wild arts,
Like nets of light,
To tangle young hearts;
With lips, in whose keeping
Love's secret may dwell,
Like Zephyr asleep in
Some rosy sea-shell.
Guess who he is,
Name but his name,
And his best kiss,
For reward, you may claim.

Where'er o'er the ground
He prints his light feet,
The flowers there are found
Most shining and sweet:
His looks, as soft
As lightning in May,
Though dangerous oft,
Ne'er wound but in play:
And oh, when his wings
Have brush'd o'er my lyre,
You 'd fancy its strings
Were turning to fire.

Guess who he is,
Name but his name,
And his best kiss,
For reward, you may claim.

—◦◦◦—

I WOULD TELL HER I LOVE HER. (1)
Italian Air.

I WOULD tell her I love her,
Did I know but the way;
Could my lips but discover
What a lover should say—
Could my lips but discover
What a lover should say.
Though I swear to adore her
Every morning I rise,
Yet, when once I'm before her,
All my eloquence flies.
Oh, ye gods! did ye ever
Such a simpleton know?
I'm in love, and yet never
Have the heart to say so—
No, no, ne'er have the heart to say so—
No, no, ne'er have the heart to say so.

Having pluck'd up a spirit
One moonshiny night,
Then, thought I, "I'll defer it
Till to-morrow's daylight—
Yes," thought I, "I'll defer it
Till to-morrow's daylight."
But, alas! the pale moon-beam
Could not frighten me more,
For I found by the noon-beam
I was dumb as before.
Oh, ye gods! did ye ever
Such a simpleton know?
I'm in love, and yet never
Have the heart to say so—
No, no, ne'er have the heart to say so—
No, no, ne'er have the heart to say so.

—◦◦◦—

LIKE ONE WHO, DOOM'D.
Indian Air.

LIKE one who, doom'd o'er distant seas
His weary path to measure,
When home at length, with favouring breeze,
He brings the far-sought treasure;

His ship, in sight of shore, goes down,
That shore to which he hasted;
And all the wealth he thought his own
Is o'er the waters wasted!

Like him, this heart, through many a track
Of toil and sorrow straying,
One hope alone brought fondly back,
Its toil and grief repaying.

(1) This song, which formed part of the "*National Airs*"
as originally published, is omitted in the new London edi-
tion.—P. E.

Like him, alas, I see that ray
  Of hope before me perish,
And one dark minute sweep away
  What years were given to cherish.

—o**o—

FEAR NOT THAT, WHILE AROUND THEE.
French Air.

FEAR not that, while around thee
  Life's varied blessings pour,
One sigh of hers shall wound thee,
  Whose smile thou seek'st no more.
No, dead and cold for ever
  Let our past love remain;
Once gone, its spirit never
  Shall haunt thy rest again.

May the new ties that bind thee
  Far sweeter, happier prove,
Nor e'er of me remind thee,
  But by their truth and love.
Think how, asleep or waking,
  Thy image haunts me yet;
But, how this heart is breaking
  For thy own peace forget.

—o**o—

WHEN LOVE IS KIND.
Austrian Air.

WHEN Love is kind,
  Cheerful and free,
Love's sure to find
  Welcome from me.

But when Love brings
  Heartache or pang,
Tears, and such things—
  Love may go hang!

If Love can sigh
  For one alone,
Well pleased am I
  To be that one.

But should I see
  Love given to rove
To two or three,
  Then—good-by, Love!

Love must, in short,
  Keep fond and true,
Through good report,
  And evil too.

Else here I swear,
  Young Love may go,
For aught I care—
  To Jericho. (1)

(1) Suggested by the old song, "*Prudence may go to Je-
richo.*"

THE GARLAND I SEND THEE.
Italian Air.

THE Garland I send thee was cull'd from those
  bowers
Where thou and I wander'd in long-vanish'd hours;
Not a leaf or a blossom its bloom here displays,
But bears some remembrance of those happy days.

The roses were gather'd by that garden gate,
Where our meetings, though early, seem'd always
  too late;
Where lingering full oft, through a summer-night's
  moon,
Our partings, though late, appear'd always too soon.

The rest were all cull'd from the banks of that glade,
Where, watching the sunset, so often we've stray'd,
And mourn'd, as the time went, that Love had no
To bind in his chain even one happy hour.   [power

—o**o—

SPRING AND AUTUMN. (2)
French Air.

EVERY season hath its pleasure;
  Spring may boast her flowery prime,
Yet the vineyard's ruby treasures
  Brighten Autumn's soberer time.
So Life's year begins and closes;
  Days, though shortening, still can shine;
What though youth gave love and roses,
  Age still leaves us friends and wine.

Phillis, when she might have caught me,
  All the Spring look'd coy and shy,
Yet herself in Autumn sought me,
  When the flowers were all gone by.
Ah, too late;—she found her lover
  Calm and free beneath his vine,
Drinking to the Spring-time over,
  In his best autumnal wine.

Thus may we, as years are flying,
  To their flight our pleasures suit,
Nor regret the blossoms dying,
  While we still may taste the fruit.
No, while days like this are ours,
  Where's the lip that dares repine?
Spring may take our loves and flowers,
  So Autumn leaves us friends and wine.

—o**o—

HOW SHALL I WOO?
Italian Air.

IF I speak to thee in friendship's name,
  Thou think'st I speak too coldly;
If I mention Love's devoted flame,
  Thou say'st I speak too boldly.

(2) Partly borrowed from the "*Printemps et l'Automne*"
of Berenger.

Between these two unequal fires,
　Why doom me thus to hover?
I 'm a friend, if such thy heart requires ;
　If more thou seek'st, a lover.
Which shall it be? How shall I woo?
Fair one, choose between the two.

Though the wings of Love will brightly play
　When first he comes to woo thee,
There 's a chance that he may fly away
　As fast as he flies *to* thee.
While Friendship, though on foot she come,
　No flights of fancy trying,
Will, therefore, oft be found at home,
　When Love abroad is flying.
Which shall it be? How shall I woo?
Dear one, choose between the two.

If neither feeling suits thy heart,
　Let 's see, to please thee, whether
We may not learn some precious art
　To mix their charms together ;
One feeling, still more sweet, to form
　From two so sweet already—
A friendship that like love is warm,
　A love like friendship steady.
Thus let it be, thus let me woo,
Dearest, thus we 'll join the two.

LOVE ALONE.
French Air.

IF thou wouldst have thy charms enchant our eyes,
First win our hearts, for there thy empire lies :

Beauty in vain would mount a heartless throne—
Her Right Divine is given by Love alone.

What would the rose with all her pride be worth
Were there no sun to call her brightness forth?
Maidens, unloved, like flowers in darkness thrown,
Wait but that light which comes from Love alone.

Fair as thy charms in yonder glass appear,
Trust not their bloom, they 'll fade from year to year :
Would'st thou they still should shine as first they shone,
Go, fix thy mirror in Love's eyes alone.

HARK! I HEAR A SPIRIT SING. (1)
Hindostanee Air.

HARK!—I hear a spirit sing from yonder vale
With voice as sweet as summer's rosy gale.
" Come, sweetheart," it seems to say, " with me away,
　To Beauty's bower away, away."
Who art thou? and whence thy birth?
" Pleasure I 'm call'd, and born on earth."
　No, no!
Though full of charms thy pathway be,
Oh, Pleasure, thou art not for me.

Hark!—I hear another voice from yonder height,
That now is bathed in heaven's calmest light :
" Come, pure heart," it seems to say, " with me away,
　From Pleasure's call away, away!
Who art thou? and what thy name?
" Virtue I 'm call'd—from heaven I came."
　Yes, yes!
Though rude and steep thy pathway be,
Oh, Virtue, I will fly to thee.

SACRED SONGS.

TO EDWARD TUITE DALTON, ESQ.
THIS FIRST NUMBER OF SACRED SONGS (2)
IS INSCRIBED BY HIS SINCERE AND AFFECTIONATE FRIEND,
Mayfield Cottage, Ashbourne, May, 1816. 　T. MOORE.

THOU ART, O GOD.
AIR—*Unknown.* (3)

" The day is thine ; the night also is thine : thou hast
prepared the light and the sun.
" Thou hast set all the borders of the earth : thou hast
made summer and winter."—*Psalm* lxxiv., 16, 17.

THOU art, O GOD, the life and light
　Of all this wondrous world we see ;
Its glow by day, its smile by night,
　Are but reflections caught from Thee.

Where'er we turn thy glories shine,
And all things fair and bright are Thine !

When Day, with farewell beam, delays
　Among the opening clouds of Even,
And we can almost think we gaze
　Through golden vistas into Heaven—
Those hues, that make the Sun's decline
So soft, so radiant, LORD ! are Thine.

When Night, with wings of starry gloom,
　O'ershadows all the earth and skies,
Like some dark beauteous bird, whose plume
　Is sparkling with unnumber'd eyes—
That sacred gloom, those fires divine,
So grand, so countless, LORD ! are Thine.

(1) This is a second song which has been omitted in the
new London edition of the " *National Airs.*"—P. E.

(2) The " *Sacred Songs* " originally appeared in two
numbers, to the first of which was prefixed the above de-
dication, while the second, which appeared some years
later, was thus inscribed:

" To the Rev. Thomas Parkinson, D.D., Archdeacon of Leicester,
Chancellor of Chester, and Rector of Kegworth, this number of
" *Sacred Songs* " is inscribed by his obliged and faithful friend,
　　　　　　　　　　" THOMAS MOORE. P.E.
" *Sloperton Cottage, Devizes, May,* 22, 1824."
(3) This air by the late Mrs. Sheridan is sung to the beau-
tiful old words, " I do confess thou 'rt smooth and fair."

When youthful Spring around us breathes,
　Thy Spirit warms her fragrant sigh;
And every flower the Summer wreathes
　Is born beneath that kindling eye.
Where'er we turn, thy glories shine,
　And all things fair and bright are Thine.

—⊙₩⊙—

THE BIRD, LET LOOSE.

AIR—*Beethoven.*

THE bird, let loose in eastern skies, (1)
　When hastening fondly home,
Ne'er stoops to earth her wing, nor flies
　Where idle warblers roam.
But high she shoots through air and light,
　Above all low delay,
Where nothing earthly bounds her flight,
　Nor shadow dims her way.

So grant me, GOD, from every care
　And stain of passion free,
Aloft, through Virtue's purer air,
　To hold my course to Thee!
No sin to cloud, no lure to stay
　My soul, as home she springs;—
Thy Sunshine on her joyful way,
　Thy Freedom in her wings!

—⊙₩⊙—

FALLEN IS THY THRONE.

AIR—*Martini.*

FALLEN is thy Throne, oh Israel!
　Silence is o'er thy plains,
Thy dwellings all lie desolate,
　Thy children weep in chains.
Where are the dews that fed thee
　On Etham's barren shore?
That fire from Heaven which led thee,
　Now lights thy path no more.

LORD! thou didst love Jerusalem—
　Once she was all thy own;
Her love thy fairest heritage, (2)
　Her power thy glory's throne. (3)
Till evil came, and blighted
　Thy long-loved olive tree;—(4)
And Salem's shrines were lighted
　For other gods than Thee.

Then sunk the star of Solyma—
　Then pass'd her glory's day,
Like heath that, in the wilderness, (5)
　The wild wind whirls away.
Silent and waste her bowers,
　Where once the mighty trod,
And sunk those guilty towers,
　While Baal reign'd as God.

" Go"—said the LORD—" Ye Conquerors!
　Steep in her blood your swords,
And raze to earth her battlements, (6)
　For they are not the LORD's.
Till Zion's mournful daughter
　O'er kindred bones shall tread,
And Hinnom's vale of slaughter (7)
　Shall hide but half her dead !"

—⊙₩⊙—

WHO IS THE MAID?

ST. JEROME'S LOVE. (8)

AIR—*Beethoven.*

WHO is the Maid my spirit seeks,
　Through cold reproof and slander's blight?
Has *she* Love's roses on her cheeks?
　Is *hers* an eye of this world's light?
No—wan and sunk with midnight prayer
　Are the pale looks of her I love;
Or if, at times, a light be there,
　Its beam is kindled from above.

I chose not her, my heart's elect,
　From those who seek their Maker's shrine
In gems and garlands proudly deck'd,
　As if themselves were things divine.
No—Heaven but faintly warms the breast
　That beats beneath a broider'd veil;
And she who comes in glittering vest
　To mourn her frailty, still is frail. (9)

Not so the faded form I prize
　And love, because its bloom is gone;
The glory in those sainted eyes
　Is all the grace her brow puts on.
And ne'er was Beauty's dawn so bright,
　So touching as that form's decay,
Which, like the altar's trembling light,
　In holy lustre wastes away.

(1) The carrier-pigeon, it is well known, flies at an elevated pitch, in order to surmount every obstacle between her and the place to which she is destined.

(2) "I have left mine heritage; I have given the dearly-beloved of my soul into the hands of her enemies."—*Jeremiah,* xii. 7.

(3) "Do not disgrace the throne of thy glory."—*Jer.,* xiv. 21.

(4) "The LORD called thy name a green olive-tree; fair and of goodly fruit," etc.—*Jer.,* xi. 16.

(5) "For he shall be like the heath in the desert."—*Jer.,* xvii. 6.

(6) "Take away her battlements; for they are not the LORD's."—*Jer.,* v. 10.

(7) "Therefore, behold, the days come, saith the LORD, that it shall no more be called Tophet, nor the Valley of the Son of Hinnom, but the Valley of Slaughter; for they shall bury in Tophet till there be no place."—*Jer.,* vii. 32.

(8) These lines were suggested by a passage in one of St. Jerome's Letters, replying to some calumnious remarks that had been circulated respecting his intimacy with the matron Paula:—"Numquid me vestes sericæ, nitentes gemmæ, picta facies, aut auri rapuit ambitio? Nulla fuit alia Romæ matronarum, quæ meam possit edomare mentem, nisi lugens atque jejunans, fletu pene cæcata."—*Epist.,* "*Si tibi putem.*"

(9) Ου γαρ χρυσοφορειν την δακρυουσαν δει.—*Chrysost. Homil.* 8., *in Epist. ad Tim.*

THIS WORLD IS ALL A FLEETING SHOW.
Air—*Stevenson.*

THIS world is all a fleeting show,
For man's illusion given;
The smiles of Joy, the tears of Woe,
Deceitful shine, deceitful flow—
There's nothing true but Heaven !

And false the light on Glory's plume,
As fading hues of Even;
And Love and Hope, and Beauty's bloom,
Are blossoms gather'd for the tomb—
There's nothing bright but Heaven !

Poor wanderers of a stormy day,
From wave to wave 're driven,
And Fancy's flash, and Reason's ray,
Serve but to light the troubled way—
There's nothing calm but Heaven !

—o**o—

WEEP NOT FOR THOSE.
Air—*Avison.*

WEEP not for those whom the veil of the tomb,
In life's happy morning, hath hid from our eyes,
Ere sin threw a blight o'er the spirit's young bloom,
Or earth had profaned what was born for the skies.
Death chill'd the fair fountain, ere sorrow had stain'd
'T was frozen, in all the pure light of its course, [it;
And but sleeps till the sunshine of Heaven has un-
chain'd it,
To water that Eden where first was its source.
Weep not for those whom the veil of the tomb,
In life's happy morning, hath hid from our eyes,
Ere sin threw a blight o'er the spirit's young bloom,
Or earth had profaned what was born for the skies.

Mourn not for her, the young Bride of the Vale, (1)
Our gayest and loveliest, lost to us now,
Ere life's early lustre had time to grow pale,
And the garland of Love was yet fresh on her brow.
Oh, then was her moment, dear spirit, for flying
From this gloomy world, while its gloom was un-
known—
And the wild hymns she warbled so sweetly, in dying,
Were echoed in Heaven by lips like her own.
Weep not for her—in her spring-time she flew
To that land where the wings of the soul are unfurl'd;
And now, like a star beyond evening's cold dew,
Looks radiantly down on the tears of this world.

—o@o—

THE TURF SHALL BE MY FRAGRANT SHRINE.
Air—*Stevenson.*

THE turf shall be my fragrant shrine;
My temple, LORD ! that Arch of thine;

(1) This second verse, which I wrote long after the first,
alludes to the fate of a very lovely and amiable girl, the
daughter of the late Colonel Bainbrigge, who was married
in Ashbourne church, October 31, 1815, and died of a fever
in a few weeks after: the sound of her marriage-bells
seemed scarcely out of our ears when we heard of her

My censer's breath the mountain airs,
And silent thoughts my only prayers. (2)

My choir shall be the moonlight waves,
When murmuring homeward to their caves,
Or when the stillness of the sea,
Even more than music, breathes of Thee !

I'll seek, by day, some glade unknown,
All light and silence, like thy Throne;
And the pale stars shall be, at night,
The only eyes that watch my rite.

Thy Heaven, on which 't is bliss to look,
Shall be my pure and shining book,
Where I shall read, in words of flame,
The glories of thy wondrous name.

I'll read thy anger in the rack
That clouds awhile the day-beam's track;
Thy mercy in the azure hue
Of sunny brightness, breaking through.

There's nothing bright, above, below,
From flowers that bloom to stars that glow,
But in its light my soul can see
Some feature of thy Deity.

There's nothing dark, below, above,
But in its gloom I trace thy Love,
And meekly wait that moment, when
Thy touch shall turn all bright again !

—o**o—

OH THOU WHO DRY'ST THE MOURNER'S TEAR.
Air—*Haydn.*

"He healeth the broken in heart, and bindeth up their
wounds."—*Psalm* cxlvii. 3.

OH Thou who dry'st the mourner's tear,
How dark this world would be,
If, when deceived and wounded here,
We could not fly to Thee.
The friends who in our sunshine live,
When Winter comes are flown;
And he who has but tears to give,
Must weep those tears alone.
But Thou wilt heal that broken heart,
Which, like the plants that throw
Their fragrance from the wounded part,
Breathes sweetness out of woe.

When joy no longer soothes or cheers,
And even the hope that threw
A moment's sparkle o'er our tears,
Is dimm'd and vanish'd too,

death. During her last delirium she sung several hymns,
in a voice even clearer and sweeter than usual, and among
them were some from the present collection, (particularly,
"There's nothing bright but Heaven,") which this very in-
teresting girl had often heard me sing during the summer.
(2) Pii orant tacitê.

Oh, who would bear life's stormy doom,
　Did not thy Wing of Love
Come, brightly wafting through the gloom
　Our Peace-branch from above?
Then sorrow, touch'd by Thee, grows bright
　With more than rapture's ray;
As darkness shows us worlds of light
　We never saw by day.

——o♦♦o——

SOUND THE LOUD TIMBREL.

MIRIAM'S SONG.

AIR—*Avison*. (1)

"And Miriam, the Prophetess, the sister of Aaron, took
a timbrel in her hand; and all the women went out after
her, with timbrels and with dances."—*Exod.*, xv. 20.

SOUND the loud Timbrel o'er Egypt's dark sea!
JEHOVAH has triumph'd—his people are free.
Sing—for the pride of the Tyrant is broken,
　His chariots, his horsemen, all splendid and brave—
How vain was their boast, for the LORD hath but
　　spoken,
　And chariots and horsemen are sunk in the wave.
Sound the loud Timbrel o'er Egypt's dark sea!
JEHOVAH has triumph'd—his people are free.

Praise to the Conqueror, praise to the LORD!
His word was our arrow, his breath was our sword.—
Who shall return to tell Egypt the story
　Of those she sent forth in the hour of her pride?
For the LORD hath look'd out from his pillar of
　　glory, (2)
　And all her brave thousands are dash'd in the tide.
Sound the loud Timbrel o'er Egypt's dark sea!
JEHOVAH has triumph'd—his people are free.

——o♦♦o——

WERE NOT THE SINFUL MARY'S TEARS.

AIR—*Stevenson*.

WERE not the sinful Mary's tears
　An offering worthy Heaven,
When, o'er the faults of former years,
　She wept—and was forgiven?

When, bringing every balmy sweet
　Her day of luxury stored,
She o'er her Saviour's hallow'd feet
　The precious odours pour'd;—

And wiped them with that golden hair,
　Where once the diamond shone;
Though now those gems of grief were there
　Which shine for GOD alone!

(1) I have so much altered the character of this air, which
is from the beginning of one of Avison's old-fashioned
concertos, that, without this acknowledgment, it could
hardly, I think, be recognised.

(2) "And it came to pass, that, in the morning watch,

Were not those sweets, so humbly shed—
　That hair—those weeping eyes—
And the sunk heart, that inly bled—
　Heaven's noblest sacrifice?

Thou, that hast slept in error's sleep,
　Oh, wouldst thou wake in Heaven,
Like Mary kneel, like Mary weep,
　"Love much" (3) and be forgiven!

——o♦♦o——

GO, LET ME WEEP.

AIR—*Stevenson*.

Go, let me weep—there's bliss in tears,
　When he who sheds them inly feels
Some lingering stain of early years
　Effaced by every drop that steals.
The fruitless showers of worldly woe
　Fall dark to earth, and never rise;
While tears that from repentance flow
　In bright exhalement reach the skies.
　　Go, let me weep.

Leave me to sigh o'er hours that flew
　More idly than the summer's wind,
And, while they pass'd, a fragrance threw,
　But left no trace of sweets behind.—
The warmest sigh that pleasure heaves
　Is cold, is faint to those that swell
The heart, where pure repentance grieves
　O'er hours of pleasure, loved too well.
　　Leave me to sigh.

——o♦♦o——

AS DOWN IN THE SUNLESS RETREATS.

AIR—*Haydn*.

As down in the sunless retreats of the Ocean,
　Sweet flowers are springing no mortal can see,
So, deep in my soul the still prayer of devotion,
　Unheard by the world, rises silent to Thee,
　　My GOD! silent, to Thee—
　　Pure, warm, silent, to Thee.

As still to the star of its worship, though clouded,
　The needle points faithfully o'er the dim sea,
So, dark as I roam, in this wintry world shrouded,
　The hope of my spirit turns trembling, to Thee,
　　My GOD! trembling to Thee,
　　True, fond, trembling, to Thee.

——o♦♦o——

COME NOT, OH LORD.

AIR—*Haydn*.

COME not, oh LORD, in the dread robe of splendour
Thou worest on the Mount, in the day of thine ire;
Come veil'd in those shadows, deep, awful, but tender,
　Which Mercy flings over thy features of fire!

the LORD looked unto the host of the Egyptians, through
the pillar of fire and of the cloud, and troubled the host of
the Egyptians."—*Exod.*, xiv. 24.

(3) "Her sins, which are many, are forgiven; for she
loved much."—*St. Luke*, vii. 47.

Lord, thou rememberest the night, when thy na-
    tion (1)
  Stood fronting her Foe by the red-rolling stream ;
O'er Egypt thy pillar shed dark desolation,
  While Israel bask'd all the night in its beam.

So, when the dread clouds of anger enfold Thee,
  From us, in thy mercy, the dark side remove ;
While shrouded in terrors the guilty behold Thee,
  Oh, turn upon us the mild light of thy Love !

BUT WHO SHALL SEE.

AIR—*Stevenson.*

But who shall see the glorious day
  When, throned on Zion's brow,
The Lord shall rend that veil away
  Which hides the nations now ? (2)
When earth no more beneath the fear
  Of his rebuke shall lie ; (3)
When pain shall cease, and every tear
  Be wiped from every eye.(4)

Then, Judah, thou no more shalt mourn
  Beneath the heathen's chain ;
Thy days of splendour shall return,
  But all be new again. (5)
The Fount of Life shall then be quaff'd
  In peace, by all who come ;(6)
And every wind that blows shall waft
  Some long-lost exile home.

ALMIGHTY GOD !

CHORUS OF PRIESTS.

AIR—*Mozart.*

Almighty God ! when round thy shrine
The Palm-tree's heavenly branch we twine, (7)
(Emblem of Life's eternal ray,
  And Love that " fadeth not away,")

We bless the flowers, expanded all, (8)
We bless the leaves that never fall,
And trembling say,—" In Eden thus
The Tree of Life may flower for us ! "

When round thy Cherubs—smiling calm,
Without their flames (9)—we wreathe the Palm,
Oh God ! we feel the emblem true—
Thy Mercy is eternal too.
Those Cherubs, with their smiling eyes,
That crown of Palm which never dies,
Are but the types of Thee above—
Eternal Life, and Peace, and Love !

OH FAIR ! OH PUREST !

SAINT AUGUSTIN TO HIS SISTER. (10)

AIR—*Moore.*

Oh fair ! oh purest ! be thou the dove
That flies alone to some sunny grove,
And lives unseen, and bathes her wing,
All vestal white, in the limpid spring.
There, if the hovering hawk be near,
That limpid spring in its mirror clear
Reflects him, ere he reach his prey,
And warns the timorous bird away.
    Be thou this dove ;
Fairest, purest, be thou this dove.

The sacred pages of God's own book
Shall be the spring, the eternal brook
In whose holy mirror, night and day,
Thou 'lt study Heaven's reflected ray ;—
And should the foes of virtue dare,
Thou wilt see how dark their shadows lie
Between Heaven and thee, and trembling fly !
    Be thou that dove ;
Fairest, purest, be thou that dove.

(1) "And it came between the camp of the Egyptians and the camp of Israel ; and it was a cloud and darkness to them, but it gave light by night to these."—*Ex.*, xiv. 20. My application of this passage is borrowed from some late prose writer whose name I am ungrateful enough to forget.

(2) "And he will destroy, in this mountain, the face of the covering cast over all people, and the veil that is spread over all nations."—*Isaiah*, xxv. 7.

(3) "The rebuke of his people shall he take away from off all the earth."—*Ib.*, xxv. 8.

(4) "And God shall wipe away all tears from their eyes ; neither shall there be any more pain."—*Rev.*, xxi. 4.

(5) "And he that sat upon the throne said, Behold, I make all things new."—*Ib.*, xxi. 5.

(6) "And whosoever will, let him take the water of life freely."—*Ib.*, xxii. 17.

(7) "The Scriptures having declared that the Temple of Jerusalem was a type of the Messiah, it is natural to conclude that the Palms, which made so conspicuous a figure in that structure, represented that *Life* and *Immortality* which were brought to light by the Gospel."—*Observations on the Palm, as a sacred Emblem,* by W. Tighe.

(8) "And he carved all the walls of the house round about with carved figures of cherubims, and palm-trees, and *open flowers.*"—1 *Kings,* vi. 29.

(9) "When the passover of the tabernacles was revealed to the great lawgiver in the mount, then the cherubic images which appeared in that structure were no longer surrounded by flames ; for the tabernacle was a type of the dispensation of mercy, by which Jehovah confirmed his gracious covenant to redeem mankind."—*Observations on the Palm.*

(10) In St. Augustin's Treatise upon the advantages of a solitary life, addressed to his sister, there is the following fanciful passage, from which, the reader will perceive, the thought of this song was taken :—" Te, soror nunquam nolo esse securam, sed timere semperque tuam fragilitatem habere suspectam, ad instar pavidæ columbæ frequentare rivos aquarum et quasi in speculo accipiuris cernere supervolantis effigiem et cavere. Rivi aquarum sententiæ sunt scripturarum, quæ de limpidissimo sapientiæ fonte profluentes," etc., etc.—*De Vit. Eremit. ad Sororem.*

33

ANGEL OF CHARITY.

Air—*Handel.*

Angel of Charity, who, from above,
　Comest to dwell a pilgrim here,
Thy voice is music, thy smile is love,
　And Pity's soul is in thy tear.
When on the shrine of God were laid
　First-fruits of all most good and fair
That ever bloom'd in Eden's shade,
　Thine was the holiest offering there.

Hope and her sister, Faith, were given
　But as our guides to yonder sky;
Soon as they reach the verge of heaven,
　There, lost in perfect bliss, they die. (1)
But, long as Love, Almighty Love,
　Shall on his throne of thrones abide,
Thou, Charity, shalt dwell above,
　Smiling for ever by His side !

—⁂—

LORD, WHO SHALL BEAR THAT DAY.

Air—*Dr. Boyce.*

Lord, who shall bear that day, so dread, so splendid,
　When we shall see thy Angel, hovering o'er
This sinful world, with hand to heaven extended,
　And hear him swear by Thee that Time's no
　　more? (2)
When Earth shall feel thy fast consuming ray—
Who, Mighty God, oh who shall bear that day ?

When through the world thy awful call hath
　sounded—
　"Wake, all ye Dead, to judgment wake, ye
　　Dead!" (3)
And from the clouds, by seraph eyes surrounded,
　The Saviour shall put forth his radiant head ; (4)
While Earth and Heaven before Him pass away—(5)
Who, Mighty God, oh who shall bear that day ?

When, with a glance, the Eternal Judge shall sever
　Earth's evil spirits from the pure and bright,
And say to *those*, "Depart from me for ever!"
　To *these*, "Come, dwell with me in endless
　　light!" (6)
When each and all in silence take their way—
Who, Mighty God, oh who shall bear that day ?

(1) "Then Faith shall fail, and holy Hope shall die,
　　One lost in certainty, and one in joy."—*Prior.*
(2) "And the Angel which I saw stand upon the sea and
upon the earth lifted up his hand to heaven, and sware by
Him that liveth for ever and ever, that there should be time
no longer."—*Rev.*, x. 5, 6.
(3) "Awake, ye Dead, and come to judgment."
(4) "They shall see the Son of Man coming in the clouds
of heaven—and all the angels with him."—*Matt.*, xxiv. 30.,
and xxv. 31.

BEHOLD THE SUN.

Air—*Lord Mornington.*

Behold the Sun, how bright
　From yonder East he springs,
As if the soul of life and light
　Were breathing from his wings.

So bright the Gospel broke
　Upon the souls of men ;
So fresh the dreaming world awoke
　In Truth's full radiance then.

Before yon Sun arose,
　Stars cluster'd through the sky—
But oh how dim, how pale were those,
　To His one burning eye!

So Truth lent many a ray,
　To bless the Pagan's night—
But, Lord, how weak, how cold were they
　To Thy One glorious Light!

—⁂—

OH, TEACH ME TO LOVE THEE.

Air—*Haydn.*

On, teach me to love Thee, to feel what thou art,
Till, fill'd with the one sacred image, my heart
　Shall all other passions disown ;
Like some pure temple, that shines apart,
　Reserved for Thy worship alone.

　　　　　　　　　　　　　　　[blame,
In joy and in sorrow, through praise and through
Thus still let me, living and dying the same,
　In *Thy* service bloom and decay—
Like some lone altar, whose votive flame
　In holiness wasteth away.

Though born in this desert, and doom'd by my birth
To pain and affliction, to darkness and dearth,
　On Thee let my spirit rely—
Like some rude dial, that, fix'd on earth,
　Still looks for its light from the sky.

—⁂—

LIKE MORNING, WHEN HER EARLY BREEZE.

Air—*Beethoven.*

Like morning, when her early breeze
　Breaks up the surface of the seas,

(5) "From his face the earth and the heaven fled away."
—*Rev.*, xx. 11.
(6) "And before Him shall be gathered all nations, and
He shall separate them one from another.
　"Then shall the King say unto them on his right hand,
Come, ye blessed of my Father, inherit the kingdom pre-
pared for you, etc.
　"Then shall He say also unto them on the left hand, De-
part from me, ye cursed, etc.
　"And these shall go away into everlasting punishment;
but the righteous into life eternal."—*Matt.*, xxv. 32, *et seq.*

That, in those furrows, dark with night,
Her hand may sow the seeds of light—

Thy Grace can send its breathings o'er
The Spirit, dark and lost before,
And, freshening all its depths, prepare
For Truth divine to enter there.

Till David touch'd his sacred lyre,
In silence lay the unbreathing wire ;
But when he swept its chords along,
Even Angels stoop'd to hear that song.

So sleeps the soul, till Thou, oh LORD,
Shalt deign to touch its lifeless chord—
Till, waked by Thee, its breath shall rise
In music, worthy of the skies !

—◦◦◦◦◦—

WEEP, CHILDREN OF ISRAEL.
AIR—*Stevenson.*

WEEP, weep for him, the Man of GOD— (1)
In yonder vale he sunk to rest ;
But none of earth can point the sod (2)
That flowers above his sacred breast.
    Weep, children of Israel, weep !

His doctrine fell like Heaven's rain, (3)
His words refresh'd like Heaven's dew—
'Oh, ne'er shall Israel see again
A Chief, to GOD and her so true.
    Weep, children of Israel, weep !

Remember ye his parting gaze,
His farewell song by Jordan's tide,
When, full of glory and of days,
He saw the promised land—and died. (4)
    Weep, children of Israel, weep !

Yet died he not as men who sink,
Before our eyes, to soulless clay ;
But, changed to spirit, like a wink
Of summer lightning, pass'd away.(5)
    Weep, children of Israel, weep !

(1) " And the children of Israel wept for Moses in the plains of Moab."—*Deut.*, xxxiv. 8.

(2) " And he buried him in a valley in the land of Moab : but no man knoweth of his sepulchre unto this day."—*Ib.*, ver. 6.

(3) " My doctrine shall drop as the rain, my speech shall distil as the dew."—*Moses' Song.*

(4) " I have caused thee to see it with thine eyes, but thou shalt not go over thither."—*Deut.*, xxxiv. 4.

(5) " As he was going to embrace Eleazer and Joshua, and was still discoursing with them, a cloud stood over him on the sudden, and he disappeared in a certain valley, although he wrote in the Holy Books that he died, which was done out of fear, lest they should venture to say that,

COME, YE DISCONSOLATE.
AIR—*German.*

COME, ye disconsolate, where'er you languish,
Come, at God's altar fervently kneel ;
Here bring your wounded hearts, here tell your an-
    guish—
Earth has no sorrow that Heaven cannot heal.

Joy of the desolate, Light of the straying,
Hope, when all others die, fadeless and pure,
Here speaks the Comforter, in God's name saying—
    " Earth has no sorrow that Heaven cannot cure."

Go, ask the infidel, what boon he brings us,
What charm for aching hearts *he* can reveal,
Sweet as that heavenly promise Hope sings us—
    " Earth has no sorrow that GOD cannot heal."

—◦◦◦◦◦—

AWAKE, ARISE, THY LIGHT IS COME.
AIR—*Stevenson.*

AWAKE, arise, thy light come ; (6)
The nations, that before outshone thee,
Now at thy feet lie dark and dumb—
    The glory of the LORD is on thee !

Arise—the Gentiles to thy ray,
From every nook of earth shall cluster ;
And kings and princes haste to pay
    Their homage to thy rising lustre. (7)

Lift up thine eyes around, and see,
O'er foreign fields, o'er farthest waters,
Thy exiled sons return to thee,
    To thee return thy home-sick daughters. (8)

And camels rich, from Midian's tents,
Shall lay their treasures down before thee ;
And Saba bring her gold and scents,
    To fill thy air, and sparkle o'er thee. (9)

See, who are these that, like a cloud, (10)
Are gathering from all earth's dominions,
Like doves, long absent, when allow'd
    Homeward to shoot their trembling pinions.

because of his extraordinary virtue, he went to GOD."—*Josephus*, book iv., chap. viii.

(6) " Arise, shine ; for thy light is come, and the glory of the LORD is risen upon thee."—*Isaiah*, lx.

(7) "And the Gentiles shall come to thy light, and kings to the brightness of thy rising."—*Ib.*

(8) "Lift up thine eyes round about and see ; all they gather themselves together, they come to thee : thy sons shall come from afar, and thy daughters shall be nursed at thy side."—*Ib.*

(9) "The multitude of camels shall cover thee ; the dromedaries of Midian and Ephah ; all they from Sheba shall come ; they shall bring gold and incense."—*Ib.*

(10) "Who are these that fly as a cloud, and as the doves to their windows?"—*Ib.*

Surely the isles shall wait for me, (1)
  The ships of Tarshish round will hover,
To bring thy sons across the sea,
  And waft their gold and silver over.

And Lebanon thy pomp shall grace—(2)
  The fir, the pine, the palm victorious
Shall beautify our Holy Place,
  And make the ground I tread on glorious.

No more shall Discord haunt thy ways, (3)
  Nor ruin waste thy cheerless nation;
But thou shalt call thy portals Praise,
  And thou shalt name thy walls Salvation.

The sun no more shall make thee bright, (4)
  Nor moon shall lend her lustre to thee;
But GOD, Himself, shall be thy Light,
  And flash eternal glory through thee.

Thy sun shall never more go down;
  A ray, from heaven itself descended,
Shall light thy everlasting crown—
  Thy days of mourning all are ended. (5)

My own, elect, and righteous Land!
  The Branch, for ever green and vernal,
Which I have planted with this hand—
  Live thou shalt in Life Eternal. (6)

THERE IS A BLEAK DESERT.
AIR—*Crescentini.*

THERE is a bleak Desert, where daylight grows weary
Of wasting its smile on a region so dreary—
    What may that Desert be?
'Tis life, cheerless Life, where the few joys that come
Are lost, like that daylight, for 'tis not their home.

There is a lone Pilgrim, before whose faint eyes
The water he pants for but sparkles and flies—
    Who may that Pilgrim be?
'Tis man, hapless Man, through this life tempted on
By fair shining hopes, that in shining are gone.
             [stealing
There is a bright Fountain, through that Desert
To pure lips alone its refreshment revealing—
    What may that Fountain be?

'Tis Truth, holy Truth, that, like springs under
  ground,
By the gifted of Heaven alone can be found. (7)

There is a fair Spirit, whose wand hath the spell
To point where those waters in secrecy dwell—
    Who may that Spirit be?   [where'er
'Tis Faith, humble Faith, who hath learn'd that,
Her wand bends to worship, the Truth must be
    there!

SINCE FIRST THY WORD.
AIR—*Nicholas Freeman.*

SINCE first Thy Word awaked my heart,
  Like new life dawning o'er me,
Where'er I turn mine eyes, Thou art,
  All light and love before me.
Nought else I feel, or hear, or see—
  All bonds of earth I sever—
Thee, O GOD, and only Thee
  I live for, now and ever.

Like him whose fetters dropp'd away
  When light shone o'er his prison, (8)
My spirit, touch'd by Mercy's ray,
  Hath from her chains arisen.
And shall a soul Thou bidd'st be free,
  Return to bondage?—never!
Thee, O GOD, and only Thee
  I live for, now and ever.

HARK! 'T IS THE BREEZE.
AIR—*Rousseau.*

HARK! 'tis the breeze of twilight, calling
  Earth's weary children to repose;
While, round the couch of Nature falling,
  Gently the night's soft curtains close.
Soon o'er a world, in sleep reclining,
  Numberless stars, through yonder dark,
Shall look, like eyes of Cherubs shining
  From out the veils that hid the Ark.

Guard us, oh Thou, who never sleepest,
  Thou who, in silence throned above,
Throughout all time, unwearied, keepest,
  Thy watch of Glory, Power, and Love.

---

(1) "Surely the isles shall wait for me, and the ships of Tarshish first, to bring thy sons from far, their silver and their gold with them."—*Isaiah*, lx.

(2) "The glory of Lebanon shall come unto thee; the fir-tree, the pine-tree, and the box together, to beautify the place of my sanctuary, and I will make the place of my feet glorious."—*Ib.*

(3) "Violence shall no more be heard in thy land, wasting nor destruction within thy borders; but thou shalt call thy walls Salvation, and thy gates Praise."—*Ib.*

(4) "Thy sun shall be no more thy light by day; neither for brightness shall the moon give light unto thee: but

the LORD shall be unto thee an everlasting light, and thy GOD thy glory."—*Isaiah*, lx.

(5) "Thy sun shall no more go down; for the LORD shall be thine everlasting light, and the days of thy mourning shall be ended."—*Ib.*

(6) "Thy people also shall be all righteous; they shall inherit the land for ever, the branch of my planting, the work of my hands."—*Ib.*

(7) In singing, the following line had better be adopted,—
    " Can but by the gifted of Heaven be found."

(8) "And, behold, the angel of the LORD came upon him, and a light shined in the prison, and his chains fell off from his hands."—*Acts*, xii. 7.

Grant that, beneath thine eye, securely,
Our souls, awhile from life withdrawn,
May, in their darkness, stilly, purely,
Like " sealed fountains," rest till dawn.

—◦❈◦—

WHERE IS YOUR DWELLING, YE SAINTED?

Air—*Hasse.*

Where is your dwelling, ye Sainted?
Through what Elysium more bright
Than fancy or hope ever painted,
Walk ye in glory and light?
Who the same kingdom inherits?
Breathes there a soul that may dare
Look to that world of Spirits,
Or hope to dwell with you there?

Sages! who, even in exploring
Nature through all her bright ways,
Went, like the Seraphs, adoring,
And veil'd your eyes in the blaze—
Martyrs! who left for our reaping
Truths you had sown in your blood—
Sinners! whom long years of weeping
Chasten'd from evil to good—

Maidens! who, like the young Crescent,
Turning away your pale brows
From earth, and the light of the Present,
Look'd to your Heavenly Spouse—
Say, through what region enchanted
Walk ye, in Heaven's sweet air?
Say, to what spirits 'tis granted,
Bright souls, to dwell with you there?

—◦❈◦—

HOW LIGHTLY MOUNTS THE MUSE'S WING.

Air—*Anonymous.*

How lightly mounts the Muse's wing
Whose theme is in the skies—
Like morning larks, that sweeter sing
The nearer Heaven they rise.

Though Love his magic lyre may tune,
Yet ah, the flowers he round it wreathes
Were pluck'd beneath pale Passion's moon,
Whose madness in their odour breathes.

How purer far the sacred lute,
Round which Devotion ties
Sweet flowers that turn to heavenly fruit,
And palm that never dies.

(1) "And that they should publish and proclaim in all their cities, and in Jerusalem, saying, Go forth unto the mount, and fetch olive-branches," etc, etc.—*Neh.,* viii. 15.
(2) "For since the days of Joshua the son of Nun unto that day had not the children of Israel done so : and there was very great gladness."—*Ib.,* 17.
(3) "Sun, stand thou still upon Gibeon ; and thou, Moon, in the valley of Ajalon."—*Josh.,* x. 12.

Though War's high-sounding harp may be
Most welcome to the hero's ears,
Alas, his chords of victory
Are wet, all o'er, with human tears.

How far more sweet their numbers run,
Who hymn, like Saints above,
No victor, but the Eternal One!
No trophies but of Love!

—◦❈◦—

GO FORTH TO THE MOUNT.

Air—*Stevenson.*

Go forth to the Mount—bring the olive-branch
home, (1)
And rejoice, for the day of our Freedom is come!
From that time, (2) when the moon upon Ajalon's vale,
Looking motionless down, (3) saw the kings of the
earth,
In the presence of God's mighty Champion, grow
pale—
Oh, never had Judah an hour of such mirth!
Go forth to the Mount—bring the olive-branch home,
And rejoice, for the day of our Freedom is come!

Bring myrtle and palm—bring the boughs of each tree
That's worthy to wave o'er the tents of the Free. (4)
From that day, when the footsteps of Israel shone,
With a light not their own, through the Jordan's
deep tide,
Whose waters shrunk back as the Ark glided on— (5)
Oh, never had Judah an hour of such pride!
Go forth to the Mount—bring the olive-branch home,
And rejoice, for the day of our Freedom is come!

—◦❈◦—

IS IT NOT SWEET TO THINK, HEREAFTER.

Air—*Haydn.*

Is it not sweet to think, hereafter,
When the Spirit leaves this sphere,
Love, with deathless wing, shall waft her
To those she long hath mourn'd for here?

Hearts, from which 't was death to sever,
Eyes, this world can ne'er restore,
There as warm, as bright as ever,
Shall meet us and be lost no more.

When wearily we wander, asking
Of earth and heaven, where are they
Beneath whose smile we once lay basking,
Blest, and thinking bliss would stay?

(4) "Fetch olive-branches and pine-branches, and myrtle-branches, and palm-branches, and branches of thick trees, to make booths."—*Neh.,* viii. 15.
(5) "And the priests that bare the ark of the covenant of the LORD stood firm on dry ground in the midst of Jordan, and all the Israelites passed over on dry ground."—*Josh.,* iii. 17.

Hope still lifts her radiant finger
  Pointing to the eternal Home,
Upon whose portal yet they linger,
  Looking back for us to come.

Alas, alas—doth Hope deceive us?
  Shall friendship—love—shall all those ties
That bind a moment, and then leave us,
  Be found again where nothing dies?

Oh, if no other boon were given,
  To keep our hearts from wrong and stain,
Who would not try to win a Heaven
  Where all we love shall live again?

———<small>◦╫◦</small>———

WAR AGAINST BABYLON.

AIR—*Novello.*

" WAR against Babylon!" shout we around, (1)
Be our banners through earth unfurl'd;

Rise up, ye nations, ye kings, at the sound— (2)
  "War against Babylon !" shout through the world !
Oh thou, that dwellest on many waters, (3)
  Thy day of pride is ended now ;
And the dark curse of Israel's daughters
  Breaks, like a thunder-cloud, over thy brow !
    War, war, war against Babylon !

Make bright the arrows, and gather the shields, (4)
  Set the standard of GOD on high ;
Swarm we, like locusts, o'er all her fields,
  " Zion " our watchword, and " vengeance " our
    cry !
Woe ! woe !—the time of thy visitation (5)
  Is come, proud Land, thy doom is cast—
And the black surge of desolation
  Sweeps o'er thy guilty head, at last !
    War, war, war against Babylon !

LEGENDARY BALLADS.

PREFACE.

IN spite of the satirist's assertion, that

  " next to singing, the most foolish thing
  Is gravely to harangue on what we sing,"—

I shall yet venture on a few observations, not relating so much to my own Songs, as to my thoughts and recollections respecting song-writing in general. The close alliance known to have existed between poetry and music, during the infancy of both these arts, has sometimes led to the conclusion that they are essentially kindred to each other, and that the true poet ought to be, if not practically, at least in taste and ear, a musician. That such was the case in the early times of ancient Greece, and that her poets then not only set their own verses to music, but sung them at public festivals, there is every reason, from all we know on the subject, to believe. A similar union between the two arts attended the dawn of modern literature, in the twelfth century, and was, in a certain degree, continued down as far as the time of Petrarch, when, as it appears from his own memorandums, that poet used to sing his verses, in composing them ; (6) and when it was the custom with all writers of sonnets and *canzoni* to prefix to their poems a sort of key-note, by which the intonation in reciting or chanting them was to be regulated.

As the practice of uniting in one individual— whether Bard, Scald, or Troubadour— the character and functions both of musician and poet, is known to have been invariably the mark of a rude state of society, so the gradual separation of these two callings, in accordance with that great principle of Political Economy, the division of labour, has been found an equally sure index of improving civilisation. So far, in England, indeed, has this partition of workmanship been carried, that, with the signal exception of Milton, there is not to be found, I believe, among all the eminent poets of England, a single musician. It is but fair, at the same time, to acknowledge, that out of the works of these very poets might be produced a select number of songs, surpassing, in fancy, grace, and tenderness, all that the language, perhaps, of any other country could furnish.

We witness, in our own times — as far as the knowledge or practice of music is concerned — a similar divorce between the two arts ; and my friend and neighbour, Mr. Bowles, is the only distinguished poet of our day whom I can call to mind as being also a musician. (7) Not to dwell further, however, on living writers, the strong feeling, even to tears, with which I have seen Byron listen to some favourite melody, has been elsewhere described by me ; and

(1) "Shout against her round about."—*Jer.*, l. 15.
(2) "Set up a standard in the land, blow the trumpet among the nations, prepare the nations against her, call together against her the kingdoms," etc., etc.—*Ib.*, li. 27.
(3) "Oh thou that dwellest upon many waters is come."—*Ib.*, 13.
(4) "Make bright the arrows ; gather the shields ..... set the standard upon the walls of Babylon."—*Ib.*, li. 11, 12.
(5) "Woe unto them! for their day is come, the time of their visitation !"—*Ib.*, l. 27.
(6) The following is a specimen of these memorandums, as given by Foscolo :—"I must make these two verses over

again, singing them, and I must transpose them—3 o'clock, A. M. 19th October." Frequently to sonnets of that time such notices as the following were prefixed :—*Intonatum per Francum*"—"Scriptor dedit *sonum.*"
(7) The late Rev. William Crowe, author of the noble poem of "*Lewisden Hill,*" was likewise a musician, and has left a Treatise on English Versification, to which his knowledge of the sister art lends a peculiar interest.

So little does even the origin of the word "lyrick," as applied to poetry, seem to be present to the minds of some writers, that the poet Young has left us an Essay on Lyric Poetry, in which there is not a single allusion to Music.

the musical taste of Sir Walter Scott I ought to be the last person to call in question, after the very cordial tribute he has left on record to my own untutored minstrelsy. (1) But I must say, that, pleased as my illustrious friend appeared really to be, when I first sung for him at Abbotsford, it was not till an evening or two after, at his own hospitable supper-table, that I saw him in his true sphere of musical enjoyment. No sooner had the *quaigh* taken its round, after our repast, than his friend, Sir Adam, was called upon, with the general acclaim of the whole table, for the song of "Hey tuttie tattie," and gave it out to us with all the true national relish. But it was during the chorus that Scott's delight at this festive scene chiefly showed itself. At the end of every verse, the whole company rose from their seats, and stood round the table with arms crossed, so as to grasp the hand of the neighbour on each side. Thus interlinked, we continued to keep measure to the strain, by moving our arms up and down, all chanting forth vociferously, "Hey tuttie tattie, hey tuttie tattie." Sir Walter's enjoyment of this old Jacobite chorus—a little increased, doubtless, by seeing how I entered into the spirit of it—gave to the whole scene, I confess, a zest and charm in my eyes such as the finest musical performance could not have bestowed on it.

Having been thus led to allude to this visit, I am tempted to mention a few other circumstances connected with it. From Abbotsford I proceeded to Edinburgh, whither Sir Walter, in a few days after, followed; and during my short stay in that city an incident occurred, which, though already mentioned by Scott in his Diary, (2) and owing its chief interest to the connexion of his name with it, ought not to be omitted among these memoranda. As I had expressed a desire to visit the Edinburgh theatre, which opened but the evening before my departure, it was proposed to Sir Walter and myself, by our friend Jeffrey, that we should dine with him at an early hour, for that purpose, and both were good-natured enough to accompany me to the theatre. Having found, in a volume (3) sent to me by some anonymous correspondent, a more circumstantial account of the scene of that evening than Sir Walter has given in his Diary, I shall here avail myself of its graphic and (with one exception) accurate details. After adverting to the sensation produced by the appearance of the late Duchess of St. Alban's in one of the boxes, the writer thus proceeds :—"There was a general buzz and stare, for a few seconds; the audience then turned their backs to the lady, and their attention to the stage, to wait till the first piece should be over

ere they intended staring again. Just as it terminated, another party quietly glided into a box near that filled by the Duchess. One pleasing female was with the three male comers. In a minute the cry ran round :—'Eh, yon 's Sir Walter, wi' Lockhart an' his wife; (4) and wha 's the wee bit bodie wi' the pawkie een ? Wow, but it's Tam Moore, just—Scott, Scott! Moore, Moore!'—with shouts, cheers, bravos, and applause. But Scott would not rise to appropriate these tributes. One could see that he urged Moore to do so; and *he*, though modestly reluctant, at last yielded, and bowed hand on heart, with much animation. The cry for Scott was then redoubled. He gathered himself up, and, with a benevolent bend, acknowledged this deserved welcome. The orchestra played alternately Scotch and Irish Melodies."

Among the choicest of my recollections of that flying visit to Edinburgh, are the few days I passed with Lord Jeffrey, at his agreeable retreat, Craig-Crook. I had then recently written the words and music of a glee, "Ship a-hoy!" which there won its first honours. So often, indeed, was I called upon to repeat it, that the upland echoes of Craig-Crook ought long to have had its burden by heart.

Having thus got on Scottish ground, I find myself awakened to the remembrance of a name which, whenever song-writing is the theme, ought to rank second to none in that sphere of poetical fame. Robert Burns was wholly unskilled in music; yet the rare art of adapting words successfully to notes, of wedding verse in congenial union with melody, which, were it not for his example, I should say none but a poet versed in the sister-art ought to attempt, has yet, by him, with the aid of a music to which my own country's strains are alone comparable, been exercised with so workmanly a hand, as well as with so rich a variety of passion, playfulness, and power, as no song-writer, perhaps, but himself, has ever yet displayed.

That Burns, however untaught, was yet, in ear and feeling, a musician, (5) is clear from the skill with which he adapts his verse to the structure and character of each different strain. Still more strikingly did he prove his fitness for this peculiar task, by the sort of instinct with which, in more than one instance, he discerned the real and innate sentiment which an air was calculated to convey, though always before associated with words expressing a totally different feeling. Thus the air of a ludicrous old song, "Fee him, father, fee him," has been made the medium of one of Burns's most pathetic effusions ; while, still more marvellously, "Hey tuttie tattie"

(1) Life by Lockhart, vol. vi., p. 128.

(2) "We went to the theatre together, and the house being luckily a good one, received T. M. with rapture. I could have hugged them, for it paid back the debt of the kind reception I met with in Ireland."

(3) Written by Mr. Benson Hill.

(4) The writer was here mistaken. There was one lady of

our party ; but neither Mr. nor Mrs. Lockhart was present.

(5) It appears certain, notwithstanding, that he was, in his youth, wholly insensible to music. In speaking of him and his brother, Mr. Murdoch, their preceptor, says, "Robert's ear, in particular, was remarkably dull, and his voice untunable. It was long before I could get him to distinguish one tune from another."

has been elevated by him into that heroic strain, "Scots, wha hae wi' Wallace bled;"—a song which, in a great national crisis, would be of more avail than all the eloquence of a Demosthenes. (1)

It was impossible that the example of Burns, in these, his higher inspirations, should not materially contribute to elevate the character of English song-writing, and even to lead to a re-union of the gifts which it requires, if not, as of old, in the same individual, yet in that perfect sympathy between poet and musician which almost amounts to identity, and of which we have seen, in our own times, so interesting an example in the few songs bearing the united names of those two sister muses, Mrs. Arkwright and the late Mrs. Hemans.

Very different was the state of the song-department of English poesy at the time when first I tried my novice hand at the lyre. The divorce between song and sense had then reached its utmost range; and to all verses connected with music, from a Birth-day Ode down to the *libretto* of the last new opera, might fairly be applied the solution Figaro gives of the quality of the words of songs, in general,—" Ce qui ne vaut pas la peine d'être dit, on le chante."

It may here be suggested that the convivial lyrics of Captain Morris present an exception to the general character I have given of the songs of this period; and assuredly, had Morris written much that at all approached the following verses of his "Reasons for Drinking," (which I quote from recollection,) few would have equalled him either in fancy, or in that lighter kind of pathos, which comes, as in this instance, like a few melancholy notes in the middle of a gay air, throwing a soft and passing shade over mirth :—

> "My muse, too, when her wings are dry,
> 　No frolic flights will take ;
> But round a bowl she'll dip and fly,
> 　Like swallows round a lake.
> If then the nymph must have her share,
> 　Before she 'll bless her swain,
> Why, *that* I think 's a reason fair
> 　To fill my glass again.
>
> "Then, many a lad I liked is dead,
> 　And many a lass grown old ;
> And, as the lesson strikes my head,
> 　My weary heart grows cold.
> But wine awhile holds off despair,
> 　Nay, bids a hope remain ;—
> And that I think 's a reason fair
> 　To fill my glass again."

(1) I know not whether it has ever been before remarked, that the well-known lines in one of Burns's most spirited songs,—

> " The title 's but the guinea's stamp,
> 　The man 's the gold for a' that,"

may possibly have been suggested by the following passage in Wycherley's play, the "*Country Wife*:"—"I weigh the *man*, not his *title*; 'tis not the King's *stamp* can make the metal better."

How far my own labours in this field—if, indeed, the gathering of such idle flowers may be so designated—have helped to advance, or even kept pace with, the progressive improvement I have here described, it is not for me to presume to decide. I only know that in a strong and inborn feeling for music lies the source of whatever talent I may have shown for poetical composition; and that it was the effort to translate into language the emotions and passions which music appeared to me to express, that first led to my writing any poetry at all deserving of the name. Dryden has happily described music as being "inarticulate poetry;" and I have always felt, in adapting words to an expressive air, that I was but bestowing upon it the gift of articulation, and thus enabling it to speak to others all that was conveyed, in its wordless eloquence, to myself.

Accustomed as I have always been to consider my songs as a sort of compound creations, in which the music forms no less essential a part than the verses, it is with a feeling which I can hardly expect my unlyrical readers to understand, that I see such a swarm of songs as crowd these pages all separated from the beautiful airs which have formed hitherto their chief ornament and strength—their "decus et tutamen." But, independently of this uneasy feeling, or fancy, there is yet another inconvenient consequence of the divorce of the words from the music, which will be more easily, perhaps, comprehended, and which, in justice to myself, as a metre-monger, ought to be noticed. Those occasional breaches of the laws of rhythm, which the task of adapting words to airs demands of the poet, though very frequently one of the happiest results of his skill, become blemishes when the verse is separated from the melody, and require, to justify them, the presence of the music to whose wildness or sweetness the sacrifice had been made.

I have already mentioned a Treatise by the late Rev. Mr. Crowe, on English versification ; and I remember his telling me, in reference to the point I have just touched upon, that, should another edition of that work be called for, he meant to produce, as examples of new and anomalous forms of versification, the following songs from the *Irish Melodies ;*—" Oh the days are gone when Beauty bright "—" At the dead hour of night, when stars are weeping, I fly,"—and, "Through grief and through danger thy smile hath cheered my way." (2)

(2) I shall avail myself of this opportunity of noticing the charge brought by Mr. Bunting against Sir John Stevenson, of having made alterations in many of the airs that formed our Irish Collection. Whatever changes of this kind have been ventured upon (and they are but few and slight,) the responsibility for them rests solely with me ; as, leaving the Harmonist's department to my friend Stevenson, I reserved the selection and management of the melodies entirely to myself.

━━ ◦❀❀◦ ━━

LEGENDARY BALLADS.

TO THE MISS FIELDINGS,

THESE BALLADS ARE INSCRIBED,

BY THEIR FAITHFUL FRIEND AND SERVANT,

THOMAS MOORE.

THE VOICE.

It came o'er her sleep, like a voice of those days,
When love, only love, was the light of her ways;
And, soft as in moments of bliss long ago,
It whisper'd her name from the garden below.

"Alas," sigh'd the maiden, "how fancy can cheat!
The world once had lips that could whisper thus
　　sweet;
But cold now they slumber in yon fatal deep,
Where, oh that beside them this heart too could
　　sleep!"

She sunk on her pillow—but no, 't was in vain
To chase the illusion, that Voice came again!
She flew to the casement—but, hush'd as the grave,
In moonlight lay slumbering woodland and wave.

"Oh sleep, come and shield me," in anguish she said,
"From that call of the buried, that cry of the Dead!"
And sleep came around her—but, starting, she woke,
For still from the garden that spirit Voice spoke!

"I come," she exclaim'd, "be thy home where it
　　may,
On earth or in heaven, that call I obey;
Then forth through the moonlight, with heart beat-
　　ing fast
And loud as a death-watch, the pale maiden pass'd.

Still round her the scene all in loneliness shone;
And still, in the distance, that Voice led her on;
But whither she wander'd, by wave or by shore,
None ever could tell, for she came back no more.

No, ne'er came she back—but the watchman who
　　stood,
That night, in the tower which o'ershadows the
　　flood,
Saw dimly, 't is said, o'er the moon-lighted spray,
A youth on a steed bear the maiden away.

CUPID AND PSYCHE.

They told her that he, to whose vows she had
　　listen'd
Through night's fleeting hours, was a Spirit un-
　　blest;—
Unholy the eyes that beside her had glisten'd,
And evil the lips she in darkness had prest.

"When next in thy chamber the bridegroom re-
　　clineth,
Bring near him thy lamp, when in slumber he lies,
And there, as the light o'er his dark features shin-
　　eth,
Thou'lt see what a demon hath won all thy sighs!"

Too fond to believe them, yet doubting, yet fearing,
When calm lay the sleeper she stole with her light;
And saw—such a vision!—no image, appearing
To bards in their day-dreams, was ever so bright.

A youth, but just passing from childhood's sweet
　　morning,
While round him still linger'd its innocent ray;
Though gleams from beneath his shut eyelids, gave
　　warning
Of summer-noon lightnings that under them lay.

His brow had a grace more than mortal around it,
While, glossy as gold from a fairy-land mine,
His sunny hair hung, and the flowers that crown'd it
Seem'd fresh from the breeze of some garden divine.

Entranced stood the bride, on that miracle gazing,
What late was but love is idolatry now;
But, ah—in her tremor the fatal lamp raising—
A sparkle flew from it and dropp'd on his brow.

All's lost—with a start from his rosy sleep waking,
The Spirit flash'd o'er her his glances of fire;
Then, slow from the clasp of her snowy arms break-
　　ing,
Thus said, in a voice more of sorrow than ire:

"Farewell—what a dream thy suspicion hath broken!
Thus ever Affection's fond vision is crost;
Dissolved are her spells when a doubt is but spoken,
And love, once distrusted, for ever is lost!"

HERO AND LEANDER.

"The night-wind is moaning with mournful sigh,
There gleameth no moon in the misty sky,
　　No star over Helle's sea;
Yet, yet there is shining one holy light,
One love-kindled star through the deep of night,
　　To lead me, sweet Hero, to thee!"

Thus saying, he plunged in the foamy stream,
Still fixing his gaze on that distant beam
　　No eye but a lover's could see;
And still, as the surge swept over his head,
"To-night," he said tenderly, "living or dead,
　　Sweet Hero, I'll rest with thee!"

But fiercer around him the wild waves speed;
Oh, Love! in that hour of thy votary's need,

34

Where, where could thy Spirit be?
He struggles—he sinks—while the hurricane's breath
Bears rudely away his last farewell in death—
"Sweet Hero, I die for thee!"

———o♦♦c———

THE LEAF AND THE FOUNTAIN.

"TELL me, kind Seer, I pray thee,
So may the stars obey thee,
   So may each airy
   Moon-elf and fairy
Nightly their homage pay thee!
Say, by what spell, above, below,
In stars that wink or flowers that blow,
   I may discover,
   Ere night is over,
Whether my love loves me or no,
Whether my love loves me."

"Maiden, the dark tree nigh thee
Hath charms no gold could buy thee;
   Its stem enchanted,
   By moon-elves planted,
Will all thou seek'st supply thee.
Climb to yon boughs that highest grow,
Bring thence their fairest leaf below;
   And thou 'lt discover,
   Ere night is over,
Whether thy love loves thee or no,
Whether thy love loves thee."

"See, up the dark tree going,
With blossoms round me blowing,
   From thence, oh Father,
   This leaf I gather,
Fairest that there is growing.
Say, by what sign I now shall know
If in this leaf lie bliss or woe,
   And thus discover,
   Ere night is over,
Whether my love loves me or no,
Whether my love loves me."

"Fly to yon fount that's welling
Where moonbeam ne'er had dwelling,
   Dip in its water
   That leaf, oh Daughter,
And mark the tale 't is telling; (1)
Watch thou if pale or bright it grow,
List thou, the while, that fountain's flow,
   And thou 'lt discover
   Whether thy lover,
Loved as he is, loves thee or no,
Loved as he is, loves thee."

(1) The ancients had a mode of divination somewhat similar to this; and we find the Emperor Adrian, when he went to consult the Fountain of Castalia, plucking a bay-leaf and dipping it into the sacred water.
(2) The air to which I have adapted these words was

Forth flew the nymph, delighted,
To seek that fount benighted;
   But, scarce a minute
   The leaf lay in it,
When, lo, its bloom was blighted!
And as she ask'd, with voice of woe—
Listening, the while, that fountain's flow—
   "Shall I recover
   My truant lover?"
The fountain seem'd to answer, "No;"
The fountain answered, "No."

———o♦♦c———

CEPHALUS AND PROCRIS.

A HUNTER once in that grove reclined,
   To shun the noon's bright eye,
And oft he wooed the wandering wind,
   To cool his brow with its sigh.
While mute lay even the wild bee's hum,
   Nor breath could stir the aspen's hair,
His song was still "Sweet air, oh come!"
   While Echo answered, "Come, sweet air!"

But, hark, what sounds from the thicket rise?
   What meaneth that rustling spray?
"'T is the white-horn'd doe," the hunter cries,
   "I have sought since break of day."
Quick o'er the sunny glade he springs,
   The arrow flies from his sounding bow,
"Hilliho—hilliho!" he gaily sings,
   While Echo sighs forth "hilliho!"

Alas, 't was not the white-horn'd doe
   He saw in the rustling grove,
But the bridal veil, as pure as snow,
   Of his own young wedded love.
And, ah, too sure that arrow sped,
   For pale at his feet he sees her lie;—
"I die, I die," was all she said,
   While Echo murmur'd, "I die, I die!"

———ɔ♦♦c———

YOUTH AND AGE. (2)

"TELL me, what 's Love?" said Youth, one day,
To drooping Age, who cross'd his way.—
"It is a sunny hour of play,
For which repentance dear doth pay;
   Repentance! Repentance!
And this is Love, as wise men say."

"Tell me, what 's Love?" said Youth once more,
Fearful, yet fond, of Age's lore.—
"Soft as a passing summer's wind,
Wouldst know the blight it leaves behind?
   Repentance! Repentance!
And this is Love—when love is o'er."

composed by Mrs. Arkwright to some old verses, "Tell me what 's love, kind shepherd, pray?" and it has been my object to retain as much of the structure and phraseology of the original words as possible.

"Tell me, what's Love?" said Youth again,
Trusting the bliss, but not the pain.
"Sweet as a May tree's scented air—
Mark ye what bitter fruit 't will bear,
    Repentance! Repentance!
This, this is Love—sweet Youth, beware."

Just then, young Love himself came by,
And cast on Youth a smiling eye;
Who could resist that glance's ray?
In vain did Age his warning say,
    "Repentance! Repentance!"
Youth laughing went with Love away.

THE DYING WARRIOR.

A WOUNDED Chieftain, lying
    By the Danube's leafy side,
Thus faintly said, in dying,
    "Oh! bear, thou foaming tide,
    This gift to my lady-bride."

'T was then, in life's last quiver,
    He flung the scarf he wore
Into the foaming river,
    Which, ah, too quickly, bore
    That pledge of one no more!

With fond impatience burning,
    The Chieftain's lady stood,
To watch her love returning
    In triumph down the flood,
    From that day's field of blood.

But, field, alas, ill-fated!
    The lady saw, instead
Of the bark whose speed she waited,
    Her hero's scarf, all red
    With the drops his heart had shed.

One shriek—and all was over—
    Her life-pulse ceased to beat;
The gloomy waves now cover
    That bridal-flower so sweet,
    And the scarf is her winding sheet!

THE MAGIC MIRROR.

" COME, if thy magic Glass have power
    To call up forms we sigh to see;
Show me my love, in that rosy bower,
    Where last she pledged her truth to me."

The Wizard show'd him his Lady bright,
    Where lone and pale in her bower she lay;
"True-hearted maid," said the happy Knight,
    "She's thinking of one, who is far away."

But, lo! a page, with looks of joy,
    Brings tidings to the Lady's ear;
" 'T is," said the Knight," the same bright boy,
    Who used to guide me to my dear."

The Lady now, from her favourite tree,
    Hath, smiling, pluck'd a rosy flower;
"Such," he exclaim'd, "was the gift that she
    Each morning sent me from that bower!"

She gives her page the blooming rose,
    With looks that say, "Like lightning, fly!"
"Thus," thought the Knight," she soothes her woes,
    By fancying, still, her true-love nigh."

But the page returns, and—oh, what a sight,
    For trusting lover's eyes to see!—
Leads to that bower another Knight,
    As young and, alas, as loved as he!

"Such," quoth the Youth, "is Woman's love!"
    Then, darting forth, with furious bound,
Dash'd at the Mirror his iron glove,
    And strew'd it all in fragments round.

MORAL.

Such ills would never have come to pass,
    Had he ne'er sought that fatal view;
The Wizard would still have kept his Glass,
    And the Knight still thought his Lady true.

THE PILGRIM.

STILL thus, when twilight gleam'd,
Far off his Castle seem'd,
    Traced on the sky;
And still, as fancy bore him
To those dim towers before him,
He gazed, with wishful eye,
    And thought his home was nigh.

"Hall of my Sires!" he said,
"How long, with weary tread,
    Must I toil on?
Each eve, as thus I wander,
Thy towers seem rising yonder,
But, scarce hath daylight shone,
    When, like a dream, thou 'rt gone!"

So went the Pilgrim still,
Down dale and over hill,
    Day after day;
That glimpse of home, so cheering,
At twilight still appearing,
But still, with morning's ray,
    Melting, like mist, away!

Where rests the Pilgrim now?
Here, by this cypress bough,
    Closed his career;
That dream, of fancy's weaving,
No more his steps deceiving,
Alike past hope and fear,
    The Pilgrim's home is here.

THE HIGH-BORN LADYE.

In vain all the Knights of the Underwald wooed her,
    Though brightest of maidens, the proudest was
        she;   [they sued her,
Brave chieftains they sought, and young minstrels
But worthy were none of the high-born Ladye.

"Whomsoever I wed," said this maid, so excelling,
    "That Knight must the conqueror of conquerors be;
He must place me in halls fit for monarchs to dwell in;
    None else shall be Lord of the high-born Ladye!"

Thus spoke the proud damsel, with scorn looking
        round her
On Knights and on Nobles of highest degree;
Who humbly and hopelessly left as they found her,
    And worshipp'd at distance the high-born Ladye.

At length came a Knight from a far land to woo her,
    With plumes on his helm like the foam of the sea;
His vizor was down—but, with voice that thrill'd
        through her,
    He whisper'd his vows to the high-born Ladye.

" Proud maiden! I come with high spousals to grace
        thee,
    In me the great conqueror of conquerors see;
Enthroned in a hall fit for monarchs I'll place thee,
    And mine thou'rt for ever, thou high-born
        Ladye!"

The maiden she smiled, and in jewels array'd her,
    Of thrones and tiaras already dreamt she;   [her
And proud was the step, as her bridegroom convey'd
    In pomp to his home, of that high-born Ladye.

"But whither," she, starting, exclaims, "have you
        led me?
Here's nought but a tomb and a dark cypress tree;
Is *this* the bright palace in which thou wouldst wed
        me?"
    With scorn in her glance said the high-born Ladye.

"'T is the home," he replied, "of earth's loftiest
        creatures"—
Then lifted his helm for the fair one to see;
But she sunk on the ground—'t was a skeleton's
        features,
    And Death was the Lord of the high-born Ladye!

—◦◦◦—

THE INDIAN BOAT.

'T was midnight dark,
    The seaman's bark
Swift o'er the waters bore him,
    When, through the night,
    He spied a light
Shoot o'er the wave before him.

" A sail! a sail!" he cries;
    " She comes from the Indian shore,
And to-night shall be our prize,
    With her freight of golden ore:
        Sail on ! sail on !"
    When morning shone
He saw the gold still clearer;
    But, though so fast
    The waves he pass'd,
That boat seem'd never the nearer.

Bright daylight came,
    And still the same
Rich bark before him floated·
    While on the prize
    His wishful eyes
Like any young lover's doated:
"More sail! more sail!" he cries,
    While the waves o'ertop the mast:
And his bounding galley flies,
    Like an arrow before the blast.
    Thus on, and on,
    Till day was gone,
And the moon through heaven did hie her,
    He swept the main,
    But all in vain,
That boat seem'd never the nigher.

And many a day
    To night gave way,
And many a morn succeeded :
    While still his flight,
    Through day and night,
That restless mariner speeded.
Who knows—who knows what seas
    He is now careering o'er?
Behind, the eternal breeze,
    And that mocking bark before!
    For, oh, till sky
    And earth shall die,
And their death leave none to rue it,
    That boat must flee
    O'er the boundless sea,
And that ship in vain pursue it.

—◦◦◦—

THE STRANGER.

Come list, while I tell of the heart-wounded Stranger
    Who sleeps her last slumber in this haunted
        ground ;
Where often, at midnight, the lonely wood-ranger
    Hears soft fairy music re-echo around.

None e'er knew the name of that heart-stricken lady,
    Her language, though sweet, none could e'er un-
        derstand ;
But her features so sunn'd, and her eyelash so shady,
    Bespoke her a child of some far Eastern land.

'T was one summer night, when the village lay sleep-
　　ing,
　A loft strain of melody came o'er our ears; [ing,
So sweet, but so mournful, half song and half weep-
Like music that Sorrow had steep'd in her tears.

We thought 't was an anthem some angel had sung
　　us;—
　But, soon as the day-beams had gush'd from on
　　high,
With wonder we saw this bright stranger among us,
　All lovely and lone, as if stray'd from the sky.

Nor long did her life for this sphere seem intended,
　For pale was her cheek, with that spirit-like hue
Which comes when the day of this world is nigh
　　ended,
　And light from another already shines through.

Then her eyes, when she sung—oh, but once to
　　have seen them—
　Left thoughts in the soul that can never depart;
While her looks and her voice made a language
　　between them,
　That spoke more than holiest words to the heart.

But she pass'd like a day-dream, no skill could re-
　　store her—
　Whate'er was her sorrow, its ruin came fast;
She died with the same spell of mystery o'er her,
　That song of past days on her lips to the last.

Nor even in the grave is her sad heart reposing—
　Still hovers the spirit of grief round her tomb;
For oft, when the shadows of midnight are closing,
　The same strain of music is heard through the
　　gloom.

SET OF GLEES.

MUSIC BY MOORE.

TO MRS. JEFFREY,

IN REMEMBRANCE OF THE PLEASANT HOURS PASSED AT
CRAIG-CROOK, WITH HER AND MY VALUED FRIEND,
HER HUSBAND, I HAVE GREAT PLEASURE IN
INSCRIBING THE FOLLOWING GLEES.

THOMAS MOORE.

THE MEETING OF THE SHIPS.

WHEN o'er the silent seas, alone
For days and nights we 've cheerless gone,
Oh they who 've felt it know how sweet,
Some sunny morn a sail to meet.

Sparkling at once is every eye,
" Ship ahoy!" our joyful cry;
While answering back the sounds we hear,
" Ship ahoy! what cheer? what cheer?"

Then sails are back'd, we nearer come,
Kind words are said of friends and home;
And soon, too soon, we part with pain,
To sail o'er silent seas again.

HIP, HIP, HURRAH.

COME, fill round a bumper, fill up to the brim,
He who shrinks from a bumper I pledge not to him;
Here 's the girl that each loves, be her eye of what hue,
Or lustre, it may, so her heart is but true.
　　Charge! (drinks) hip, hip, hurra, hurra!

Come, charge high, again, boy, nor let the full wine
Leave a space in the brimmer, where daylight may
　　shine;

Here 's " the friends of our youth—though of some
　　we 're bereft,
May the links that are lost but endear what are left!"
　　　　Charge! (drinks) hip, hip, hurra, hurra!

Once more fill a bumper—ne'er talk of the hour;
On hearts thus united old Time has no power.
May our lives, though, alas! like the wine of to-night,
They must soon have an end, to the last flow as bright.
　　　Charge! (drinks) hip, hip, hurra, hurra!
　　　　　　　　　　　　　　　　[will run
Quick, quick, now, I 'll give you, since Time's glass
Even faster than ours doth, three bumpers in one;
Here 's the poet who sings,—here 's the warrior who
　　fights—
Here 's the statesman who speaks, in the cause of
　　men's rights!
　　　Charge! (drinks) hip, hip, hurra, hurra!
　　　　　　　　　　　　　　　　[please,
Come, once more, a bumper!—then drink as you
Though who could fill half-way to toast such as these?
Here 's our next joyous meeting—and oh, when we
　　meet,
May our wine be as bright and our union as sweet!
　　　Charge! (drinks) hip, hip, hurra, hurra!

HUSH, HUSH!

" HUSH, hush!"—how well
　That sweet word sounds,
When Love, the little sentinel,
　Walks his night-rounds;
Then, if a foot but dare
　One rose-leaf crush,
Myriads of voices in the air
　Whisper, " Hush, hush!"

"Hark, hark, 'tis he!"
  The night elves cry,
And hush their fairy harmony,
    While he steals by;
But if his silvery feet
    One dew-drop brush,
Voices are heard in chorus sweet,
  Whispering, "Hush, hush!"

THE EVENING GUN.

Remember'st thou that setting sun,
  The last I saw with thee,
When loud we heard the evening gun
  Peal o'er the twilight sea?
Boom!—the sounds appear'd to sweep
  Far o'er the verge of day,
Till, into realms beyond the deep,
  They seem'd to die away.

Oft, when the toils of day are done,
  In pensive dreams of thee,
I sit to hear that evening gun,
  Peal o'er the stormy sea.
Boom!—and while, o'er billows curl'd,
  The distant sounds decay,
I weep, and wish from this rough world
  Like them to die away.

THE WATCHMAN.

A TRIO.

WATCHMAN.

Past twelve o'clock—past twelve.

Good night, good night, my dearest—
  How fast the moments fly!
'T is time to part, thou hearest
  That hateful watchman's cry.

WATCHMAN.

Past one o'clock—past one.

Yet stay a moment longer—
  Alas! why is it so,
The wish to stay grows stronger,
  The more 't is time to go?

WATCHMAN.

Past two o'clock—past two.

Now wrap thy cloak about thee—
  The hours must sure go wrong,
For when they 're pass'd without thee,
  They 're, oh, ten times as long.

WATCHMAN.

Past three o'clock—past three.

Again that dreadful warning!
  Had ever time such flight?
And see the sky, 't is morning—
  So now, *indeed*, good night.

WATCHMAN.

Past three o'clock—past three.

Good night, good night.

SAY, WHAT SHALL WE DANCE?

Say, what shall we dance?
Shall we bound along the moonlight plain,
To music of Italy, Greece, or Spain?
    Say, what shall we dance?
Shall we, like those who rove
Through bright Grenada's grove,
To the light Bolero's measures move?
Or choose the Guaracia's languishing lay,
And thus to its sound die away?

    Strike the gay chords,
Let us hear each strain from every shore
That music haunts or young feet wander o'er.
Hark! 't is the light march, to whose measured time,
The Polish lady, by her lover led,
Delights through gay saloons with step untired to
    tread;
Or sweeter still, through moonlight walks
Whose shadows serve to hide
The blush that 's raised by him who talks
Of love the while by her side.
Then comes the smooth waltz, to whose flouting
    sound
Like dreams we go gliding around,
Say, which shall we dance? which shall we dance?

THE PARTING BEFORE THE BATTLE.

HE.

On to the field, our doom is seal'd,
  To conquer or be slaves;
This sun shall see our nation free,
  Or set upon our graves.

SHE.

Farewell, oh farewell, my love,
  May Heaven thy guardian be,
And send bright angels from above,
  To bring thee back to me.

HE.

On to the field, the battle-field,
  Where freedom's standard waves,
This sun shall see our tyrant yield,
  Or shine upon our graves. (1)

(1) The following lines, which originally formed part
of this glee, have been suppressed:—

> Hark! the trumpet's signal blast—
>   Take this last farewell!
> Yet, oh! not the last;
>   On to the field!

For hope whispers fondly that hearts so united,
  So happy, even death would be loath to destroy,
And, checking his dark hand, would pause ere he blighted
  A love but just opening in sunshine and joy.

> Onward to the battle-field,
>   Where freedom's standard waves!
> This sun shall see our tyrant yield,
>   Or shine upon our graves!—P. E.

BALLADS, SONGS, Etc.

TO-DAY, DEAREST! IS OURS.

To-day, dearest! is ours;
  Why should Love carelessly lose it?
This life shines or lowers
  Just as we, weak mortals, use it.
'T is time enough, when its flowers decay,
  To think of the thorns of Sorrow;
And Joy, if left on the stem to-day,
  May wither before to-morrow.

Then why, dearest! so long
  Let the sweet moments fly over?
Though now, blooming and young,
  Thou hast me devoutly thy lover,
Yet Time from both, in his silent lapse,
  Some treasure may steal or borrow;
Thy charms may be less in bloom, perhaps,
  Or I less in love to-morrow.

—◦❀◦—

WHEN ON THE LIP THE SIGH DELAYS.

When on the lip the sigh delays,
  As if 't would linger there for ever;
When eyes would give the world to gaze,
  Yet still look down, and venture never;
When, though with fairest nymphs we rove,
  There 's one we dream of more than any —
If all this is not real love,
  'T is something wondrous like it, Fanny!

To think and ponder, when apart,
  On all we 've got to say at meeting;
And yet when near, with heart to heart,
  Sit mute, and listen to their beating;
To see but one bright object move,
  The only moon, where stars are many—
If all this is not downright love,
  I prithee say what is, my Fanny!

When Hope foretells the brightest, best,
  Though Reason on the darkest reckons;
When Passion drives us to the west,
  Though Prudence to the eastward beckons;
When all turns round, below, above,
  And our own heads the most of any—
If this is not stark, staring love,
  Then you and I are sages, Fanny.

—◦❀◦—

HERE, TAKE MY HEART.

Here, take my heart—'t will be safe in thy keeping,
  While I go wandering o'er land and o'er sea;
Smiling or sorrowing, waking or sleeping,
  What need I care, so my heart is with thee?

If, in the race we are destined to run, love,
  They who have light hearts the happiest be,
Then, happier still must be they who have none, love,
  And that will be my case when mine is with thee.

It matters not where I may now be a rover,
  I care not how many bright eyes I may see;
Should Venus herself come and ask me to love her,
  I 'd tell her I could n't—my heart is with thee.

And there let it lie, growing fonder and fonder—
  For, even should Fortune turn truant to me,
Why, let her go—I 've a treasure beyond her,
  As long as my heart 's out at interest with thee!

—◦❀◦—

OH, CALL IT BY SOME BETTER NAME.

Oh, call it by some better name,
  For Friendship sounds too cold,
While Love is now a worldly flame,
  Whose shrine must be of gold;
And Passion, like the sun at noon,
  That burns o'er all he sees,
Awhile as warm, will set as soon—
  Then, call it none of these.

Imagine something purer far,
  More free from stain of clay
Than Friendship, Love, or Passion are,
  Yet human still as they:
And if thy lip, for love like this,
  No mortal word can frame,
Go, ask of angels what it is,
  And call it by that name.

—◦❀◦—

POOR WOUNDED HEART.

Poor wounded heart, farewell!
  Thy hour of rest is come;
  Thou soon wilt reach thy home,
Poor wounded heart, farewell!
The pain thou 'lt feel in breaking
  Less bitter far will be,
Than that long deadly aching,
  This life has been to thee.

There—broken heart, farewell!
  The pang is o'er—
  The parting pang is o'er;
Thou now wilt bled no more,
Poor broken heart, farewell!
No rest for thee but dying—
  Like waves, whose strife is past,
On death's cold shore thus lying,
  Thou sleep'st in peace at last—
Poor broken heart, farewell!

THE EAST INDIAN.

Come, May, with all thy flowers,
　Thy sweetly-scented thorn,
Thy cooling evening showers,
　Thy fragrant breath at morn:
When May-flies haunt the willow,
　When May-buds tempt the bee,
Then o'er the shining billow
　My love will come to me.

From Eastern Isles she's winging
　Through watery wilds her way,
And on her cheek is bringing
　The bright sun's orient ray:
Oh, come and court her hither,
　Ye breezes mild and warm—
One winter's gale would wither
　So soft, so pure a form.

The fields where she was straying
　Are blest with endless light,
With zephyrs always playing
　Through gardens always bright.
Then now, sweet May! be sweeter
　Than e'er thou'st been before;
Let sighs from roses meet her
　When she comes near our shore.

———

POOR BROKEN FLOWER.

Poor broken flower! what art can now recover thee?
　Torn from the stem that fed thy rosy breath—
　　In vain the sun-beams seek
　　To warm that faded cheek;　　　　[thee,
The dews of heaven, that once like balm fell over
Now are but tears, to weep thy early death.

So droops the maid whose lover hath forsaken her—
　Thrown from his arms, as lone and lost as thou;
　　In vain the smiles of all
　　Like sun-beams round her fall;
The only smile that could from death awaken her,
That smile, alas! is gone to others now.

———

THE PRETTY ROSE-TREE.

　　Being weary of love,
　　I flew to the grove,
And chose me a tree of the fairest;
　　Saying, "Pretty Rose-tree,
　　Thou my mistress shalt be,
And I'll worship each bud thou bearest.
For the hearts of this world are hollow,
And fickle the smiles we follow;
　　And 'tis sweet, when all
　　Their witch'ries pall
To have a pure love to fly to:
　　So, my pretty Rose-tree,
　　Thou my mistress shalt be,
And the only one now I shall sigh to."

　　When the beautiful hue
　　Of thy cheek through the dew
Of morning is bashfully peeping,
　　"Sweet tears," I shall say
　　(As I brush them away),
"At least there's no art in this weeping."
Although thou shouldst die to-morrow,
'T will not be from pain or sorrow;
　　And the thorns of thy stem
　　Are not like them
With which men wound each other:
　　So, my pretty Rose-tree,
　　Thou my mistress shalt be,
And I'll ne'er again sigh to another.

———

SHINE OUT, STARS!

Shine out, Stars! let Heaven assemble
　Round us every festal ray,
Lights that move not, lights that tremble,
　All to grace this Eve of May.
Let the flower-beds all lie waking,
　And the odours shut up there,
From their downy prisons breaking,
　Fly abroad through sea and air.

And would Love, too, bring his sweetness,
　With our other joys to weave,
Oh what glory, what completeness,
　Then would crown this bright May Eve!
Shine out, Stars! let night assemble
　Round us every festal ray,
Lights that move not, lights that tremble,
　To adorn this Eve of May.

———

THE YOUNG MULETEERS OF GRENADA.

Oh, the joys of our evening posada,
　Where, resting at close of day,
We, young Muleteers of Grenada,
　Sit and sing the sunshine away!
So merry, that even the slumbers,
　That round us hung, seem gone;
Till the lute's soft drowsy numbers
　Again beguile them on.
　　Oh, the joys, etc.

Then as each to his loved sultana
　In sleep still breathes the sigh,
The name of some black-eyed Tirana
　Escapes our lips as we lie.
Till, with morning's rosy twinkle,
　Again we're up and gone—
While the mule-bell's drowsy tinkle
　Beguiles the rough way on.
Oh, the joys of our merry posada,
　Where, resting at close of day,
We, young Muleteers of Grenada,
　Thus sing the gay moments away.

TELL HER, OH, TELL HER.

TELL her, oh, tell her, the lute she left lying
Beneath the green arbour is still lying there ;
And breezes, like lovers, around it are sighing,
But not a soft whisper replies to their prayer.

Tell her, oh, tell her, the tree that, in going,
Beside the green arbour she playfully set,
As lovely as ever is blushing and blowing,
And not a bright leaflet has fallen from it yet.

So, while away from that arbour forsaken
The maiden is wandering, still let her be
As true as the lute, that no sighing can waken,
And blooming for ever, unchanged as the tree!

—◦◉◦—

NIGHTS OF MUSIC.

NIGHTS of music, nights of loving,
Lost too soon, remember'd long,
When we went by moonlight roving,
Hearts all love and lips all song.
When this faithful lute recorded
All my spirit felt to thee ;
And that smile the song rewarded—
Worth whole years of fame to me!

Nights of song, and nights of splendour,
Fill'd with joys too sweet to last—
Joys that, like the star-light, tender,
While they shone, no shadow cast.
Though all other happy hours
From my fading memory fly,
Of that star-light, of those bowers,
Not a beam, a leaf shall die!

—◦◉◦—

OUR FIRST YOUNG LOVE.

OUR first young love resembles
That short but brilliant ray,
Which smiles, and weeps, and trembles
Through April's earliest day.
And not all life before us,
Howe'er its lights may play,
Can shed a lustre o'er us
Like that first April ray.

Our summer sun may squander
A blaze serener, grander ;
Our autumn beam
May, like a dream
Of heaven, die calm away ;
But, no—let life before us
Bring all the light it may,
'T will ne'er shed lustre o'er us
Like that first youthful ray.

—◦◉◦—

BLACK AND BLUE EYES.

THE brilliant black eye
May in triumph let fly

All its darts. without caring who feels 'em ;
But the soft eye of blue,
Though it scatter wounds too,
Is much better pleased when it heals 'em—
Dear Fanny!
Is much better pleased when it heals 'em.

The black eye may say,
" Come and worship my ray—
By adoring, perhaps you may move me ! "
But the blue eye, half hid,
Says, from under its lid,
" I love, and am yours, if you love me!"
Yes, Fanny!
The blue eye, half hid,
Says, from under its lid,
" I love, and am yours, if you love me!"

Come tell me, then, why,
In that lovely blue eye,
Not a charm of its tint I discover ;
Oh why should you wear
The only blue pair
That ever said "No" to a lover ?
Dear Fanny!
Oh, why should you wear
The only blue pair
That ever said "No" to a lover ?

—◦◉◦—

DEAR FANNY.

" SHE has beauty, but still you must keep your heart
cool ;
She has wit, but you must n't be caught so : "
Thus Reason advises, but Reason 's a fool,
And 'tis not the first time I have thought so,
Dear Fanny!
'Tis not the first time I have thought so.

" She is lovely ; then love her, nor let the bliss fly ;
'T is the charm of youth's vanishing season : "
Thus Love has advised me, and who will deny
That Love reasons much better than Reason?
Dear Fanny!
Love reasons much better than Reason.

—◦◉◦—

FROM LIFE WITHOUT FREEDOM.

FROM life without freedom, say, who would not fly ?
For one day of freedom, oh ! who would not die?
Hark!—hark ! 't is the trumpet! the call of the brave,
The death-song of tyrants, the dirge of the slave.
Our country lies bleeding—haste, haste to her aid ;
One arm that defends is worth hosts that invade.

In death's kindly bosom our last hope remains—
The dead fear no tyrants, the grave has no chains.
On, on to the combat! the heroes that bleed
For virtue and mankind are heroes indeed.
And oh, even if.Freedom from this world be driven,
Despair not—at least we shall find her in heaven.

HERE 'S THE BOWER.

HERE 's the bower she loved so much,
　And the tree she planted;
Here 's the harp she used to touch—
　Oh, how that touch enchanted!
Roses now unheeded sigh;
　Where 's the hand to wreathe them?
Songs around neglected lie;
　Where 's the lip to breathe them?
　　　　Here 's the bower, etc.

Spring may bloom, but she we loved
　Ne'er shall feel its sweetness;
Time, that once so fleetly moved,
　Now hath lost its fleetness.
Years were days when here she stray'd,
　Days were moments near her;
Heaven ne'er form'd a brighter maid,
　Nor Pity wept a dearer!
　　　　Here 's the bower, etc.

—◦◦◦—

LOVE AND THE SUN-DIAL.

YOUNG Love found a Dial once, in a dark shade,
Where man ne'er had wander'd nor sunbeam play'd;
" Why thus in darkness lie?" whisper'd young Love,
" Thou, whose gay hours in sunshine should move."
" I ne'er," said the Dial, " have seen the warm sun,
So noonday and midnight to me, Love, are one."

Then Love took the Dial away from the shade,
And placed her where Heaven's beam warmly play'd.
There she reclined, beneath Love's gazing eye,
While, mark'd all with sunshine, her hours flew by.
" Oh, how," said the Dial, " can any fair maid,
That 's born to be shone upon, rest in the shade?"

But night now comes on, and the sunbeam 's o'er,
And Love stops to gaze on the Dial no more.
Alone and neglected, while bleak rain and winds
Are storming around her, with sorrow she finds
That Love had but number'd a few sunny hours—
Then left the remainder to darkness and showers!

—◦◦◦—

I SAW THE MOON RISE CLEAR.

A FINLAND LOVE SONG.

I SAW the moon rise clear
　O'er hills and vales of snow,
Nor told my fleet rein-deer
　The track I wish'd to go.
Yet quick he bounded forth;
　For well my rein-deer knew
I 've but one path on earth—
　The path which leads to you.

The gloom that Winter cast
　How soon the heart forgets,
When Summer brings, at last,
　Her sun that never sets!

So dawn'd my love for you;
　So, fix'd through joy and pain;
Than summer sun more true,
　'T will never set again.

—◦◦◦—

LOVE AND TIME.

'T IS said—but whether true or not
　Let bards declare who 've seen 'em—
That Love and Time have only got
　One pair of wings between 'em.
In courtship's first delicious hour,
　The boy full oft can spare 'em;
So, loitering in his lady's bower,
　He lets the grey-beard wear 'em.
　　　Then is Time's hour of play;
　　　Oh, how he flies, flies away!

But short the moments, short as bright,
　When he the wings can borrow;
If Time to-day has had his flight,
　Love takes his turn to morrow.
Ah! Time and Love, your change is then
　The saddest and most trying,
When one begins to limp again,
　And t' other takes to flying.
　　　Then is Love's hour to stray;
　　　Oh, how he flies, flies away!

But there 's a nymph, whose chains I feel,
　And bless the silken fetter,
Who knows, the dear one, how to deal
　With Love and Time much better.
So well she checks their wanderings,
　So peacefully she pairs 'em,
That Love with her ne'er thinks of wings,
　And Time for ever wears 'em.
　　　This is Time's holiday;
　　　Oh, how he flies, flies away!

—◦◦◦—

LOVE'S LIGHT SUMMER-CLOUD.

PAIN and sorrow shall vanish before us—
　Youth may wither, but feeling shall last;
All the shadow that e'er shall fall o'er us
　Love's light summer-cloud only shall cast.
　　　Oh, if to love thee more
　　　Each hour I number o'er—
　　　If this a passion be
　　　Worthy of thee,
Then be happy, for thus I adore thee.
　Charms may wither, but feeling shall last;
All the shadow that e'er shall fall o'er thee,
　Love's light summer-cloud sweetly shall cast.

Rest, dear bosom, no sorrows shall pain thee,
　Sighs of pleasure alone shalt thou steal;
Beam, bright eyelid, no weeping shall stain thee,
　Tears of rapture alone shalt thou feel.
　　　Oh, if there be a charm
　　　In love, to banish harm—

If pleasure's truest spell
    Be to love well,
Then be happy, for thus I adore thee.
Charms may wither, but feeling shall last:
All the shadow that e'er shall fall o'er thee,
Love's light summer-cloud sweetly shall cast.

LOVE, WANDERING THROUGH THE GOLDEN MAZE.

Love, wandering through the golden maze
    Of my beloved's hair,
Traced every lock with fond delays,
    And, doting, linger'd there.
And soon he found 't were vain to fly;
    His heart was close confined,
For every ringlet was a tie—
    A chain by beauty twined.

MERRILY EVERY BOSOM BOUNDETH.

THE TYROLESE SONG OF LIBERTY.

Merrily every bosom boundeth,
    Merrily, oh!
Where the song of Freedom soundeth,
    Merrily, oh!
    There the warrior's arms
      Shed more splendour;
    There the maiden's charms
      Shine more tender;
Every joy the land surroundeth,
    Merrily, oh! merrily, oh!

Wearily every bosom pineth,
    Wearily, oh!
Where the bond of slavery twineth
    Wearily, oh!
    There the warrior's dart
      Hath no fleetness;
    There the maiden's heart
      Hath no sweetness—
Every flower of life declineth,
    Wearily, oh! wearily, oh!

Cheerily then from hill and valley,
    Cheerily, oh!
Like your native fountains sally,
    Cheerily, oh!
    If a glorious death,
      Won by bravery,
    Sweeter be than breath
      Sigh'd in slavery,
Round the flag of Freedom rally,
    Cheerily, oh! cheerily, oh!

REMEMBER THE TIME.

THE CASTILIAN MAID.

Remember the time, in La Mancha's shades,
    When our moments so blissfully flew;
When you call'd me the flower of Castilian maids,
    And I blush'd to be call'd so by you:

When I taught you to warble the gay seguadille,
    And to dance to the light castanet;
Oh, never, dear youth, let you roam where you will,
    The delight of those moments forget.

They tell me, you lovers from Erin's green isle,
    Every hour a new passion can feel;
And that soon, in the light of some lovelier smile,
    You 'll forget the poor maid of Castile.
But they know not how brave in the battle you are,
    Or they never could think you would rove;
For 't is always the spirit most gallant in war
    That is fondest and truest in love.

LOVE THEE.

Love thee?—so well, so tenderly
    Thou 'rt loved, adored by me,
Fame, fortune, wealth, and liberty,
    Were worthless without thee.
Though brimm'd with blessings, pure and rare,
    Life's cup before me lay,
Unless thy love were mingled there,
    I 'd spurn the draught away.
Love thee?—so well, so tenderly
    Thou 'rt loved, adored by me,
Fame, fortune, wealth, and liberty,
    Were worthless without thee.

Without thy smile, the monarch's lot
    To me were dark and lone,
While, *with* it, even the humblest cot
    Were brighter than his throne. (1)
Those worlds, for which the conqueror sighs,
    For me would have no charms:
My only world thy gentle eyes—
    My throne thy circling arms!
Oh, yes, so well, so tenderly
    Thou 'rt loved, adored by me,
Whole realms of light and liberty
    Were worthless without thee.

OH, SOON RETURN.

Our white sail caught the evening ray,
    The wave beneath us seem'd to burn,
When all the weeping maid could say
    Was, " Oh, soon return!"
Through many a clime our ship was driven,
    O'er many a billow rudely thrown;
Now chill'd beneath a northern heaven,
    Now sunn'd in summer's zone:
And still, where 'er we bent our way,
    When evening bid the west wave burn,
I fancied still I heard her say,
    " Oh, soon return!

(1) These four lines originally appeared—
    Without thy smile how joylessly
    All glory's meeds I see!
    And even the wreath of victory
    Must owe its bloom to thee.—P. E.

If ever yet my bosom found
  Its thoughts one moment turn'd from thee,
'T was when the combat raged around,
  And brave men look'd to me.
But though the war-field's wild alarm
  For gentle Love was all unmeet,
He lent to Glory's brow the charm
  Which made even danger sweet.
And still, when victory's calm came o'er
  The hearts where rage had ceased to burn,
Those parting words I heard once more,
  "Oh, soon return!—Oh, soon return!"

ONE DEAR SMILE.

Couldst thou look as dear as when
  First I sigh'd for thee;
Couldst thou make me feel again
Every wish I breathed thee then,
  Oh, how blissful life would be!
Hopes, that now beguiling leave me,
  Joys, that lie in slumber cold—
All would wake, couldst thou but give me
  One dear smile like those of old.

No—there's nothing left us now
  But to mourn the past:
Vain was every ardent vow—
Never yet did Heaven allow
  Love so warm, so wild, to last.
Not even hope could now deceive me—
  Life itself looks dark and cold:
Oh, thou never more canst give me
  One dear smile like those of old.

YES, YES, WHEN THE BLOOM.

Yes, yes, when the bloom of Love's boyhood is o'er,
He'll turn into friendship that feels no decay;
And, though Time may take from him the wings he
    once wore,
The charms that remain will be bright as before,
And he'll lose but his young trick of flying away.

Then let it console thee, if Love should not stay,
  That Friendship our last happy moments will
    crown:
Like the shadows of morning, Love lessens away,
While Friendship, like those at the closing of day,
  Will linger and lengthen as life's sun goes down.

WHEN 'MIDST THE GAY I MEET.

When 'midst the gay I meet
  That gentle smile of thine,
Though still on me it turns most sweet,
  I scarce can call it mine:
But when to me alone
  Your secret tears you show,
Oh, then I feel those tears my own,
  And claim them while they flow.

Then still with bright looks bless
  The gay, the cold, the free;
Give smiles to those who love you less,
  But keep your tears for me.

The snow on Jura's steep
  Can smile in many a beam,
Yet still in chains of coldness sleep,
  How bright soe'er it seem.
But, when some deep-felt ray,
  Whose touch is fire, appears,
Oh, then the smile is warm'd away,
  And, melting, turns to tears.
Then still with bright looks bless
  The gay, the cold, the free;
Give smiles to those who love you less,
  But keep your tears for me.

THE DAY OF LOVE.

The beam of morning trembling
  Stole o'er the mountain brook,
With timid ray resembling
  Affection's early look.
Thus love begins—sweet morn of love!

The noon-tide ray ascended,
  And o'er the valley's stream
Diffused a glow as splendid
  As passion's riper dream.
Thus love expands—warm noon of love!

But evening came, o'ershading
  The glories of the sky,
Like faith and fondness fading
  From passion's alter'd eye.
Thus love declines—cold eve of love!

LUSITANIAN WAR-SONG.

The song of war shall echo through our mountains,
  Till not one hateful link remains
  Of slavery's lingering chains;
  Till not one tyrant tread our plains,
  Nor traitor lip pollute our fountains.
No! never till that glorious day
Shall Lusitania's sons be gay,
Or hear, oh Peace, thy welcome lay
Resounding through her sunny mountains.

The song of war shall echo through our mountains,
  Till Victory's self shall, smiling, say,
  "Your cloud of foes hath pass'd away.
  And Freedom comes, with new-born ray,
To gild your vines and light your fountains."
Oh, never till that glorious day
Shall Lusitania's sons be gay,
Or hear, sweet Peace, thy welcome lay
Resounding through her sunny mountains.

THE YOUNG ROSE.

THE young rose I give thee, so dewy and bright,
Was the floweret most dear to the sweet bird of night,
Who oft, by the moon, o'er her blushes hath hung,
And thrill'd every leaf with the wild lay he sung.

Oh, take thou this young rose, and let her life be
Prolong'd by the breath she will borrow from thee:
For, while o'er her bosom thy soft notes shall thrill,
She'll think the sweet night-bird is courting her still.

—◦◦◦—

WHEN TWILIGHT DEWS.

WHEN twilight dews are falling soft
    Upon the rosy sea, love,
I watch the star, whose beam so oft
    Has lighted me to thee, love.
And thou too, on that orb so dear,
    Dost often gaze at even,
And think, though lost for ever here,
    Thou 'lt yet be mine in heaven.

There's not a garden walk I tread,
    There's not a flower I see, love,
But brings to mind some hope that's fled,
    Some joy that's gone with thee, love.
And still I wish that hour was near,
    When, friends and foes forgiven,
The pains, the ills we've wept through here,
    May turn to smiles in heaven.

—◦◦◦—

YOUNG JESSICA.

YOUNG Jessica sat all the day,
    With heart o'er idle love-thoughts pining;
Her needle bright beside her lay,
    So active once!—now idly shining.
Ah, Jessy, 'tis in idle hearts
    That love and mischief are most nimble;
The safest shield against the darts
    Of Cupid is Minerva's thimble.

The child who with a magnet plays,
    Well knowing all its arts, so wily,
The tempter near a needle lays,
    And laughing says, "We'll steal it slily."
The needle, having nought to do,
    Is pleased to let the magnet wheedle;
Till closer, closer come the two,
    And—off, at length, elopes the needle.

Now, had this needle turn'd its eye
    To some gay reticule's construction,
It ne'er had stray'd from duty's tie,
    Nor felt the magnet's sly seduction.
Thus, girls, would you keep quiet hearts,
    Your snowy fingers must be nimble;
The safest shield against the darts
    Of Cupid is Minerva's thimble.

HOW HAPPY, ONCE.

How happy, once, though wing'd with sighs,
    My moments flew along,
While looking on those smiling eyes,
    And listening to thy magic song!
But vanish'd now, like summer dreams,
    Those moments smile no more;
For me that eye no longer beams,
    That song for me is o'er.
Mine the cold brow,
That speaks thy alter'd vow,
While others feel thy sunshine now.

Oh, could I change my love like thee,
    One hope might yet be mine—
Some other eyes as bright to see,
    And hear a voice as sweet as thine:
But never, never can this heart
    Be waked to life again;
With thee it lost its vital part,
    And wither'd then!
Cold its pulse lies,
And mute are even its sighs,
All other grief it now defies.

—◦◦◦—

I LOVE BUT THEE.

IF, after all, you still will doubt and fear me,
    And think this heart to other loves will stray,
If I must swear, then, lovely doubter, hear me;
    By every dream I have when thou 'rt away,
By every throb I feel when thou art near me,
    I love but thee—I love but thee!

By those dark eyes, where light is ever playing,
    Where Love, in depth of shadow, holds his throne,
And by those lips, which give whate'er thou 'rt saying,
    Or grave or gay, a music of its own,
A music far beyond all minstrel's playing,
    I love but thee—I love but thee!

By that fair brow, where Innocence reposes,
    As pure as moonlight sleeping upon snow,
And by that cheek, whose fleeting blush discloses
    A hue too bright to bless this world below,
And only fit to dwell on Eden's roses,
    I love but thee—I love but thee!

—◦◦◦—

LET JOY ALONE BE REMEMBER'D NOW.

LET thy joys alone be remember'd now,
    Let thy sorrows go sleep awhile;
Or if thought's dark cloud come o'er thy brow,
    Let Love light it up with his smile.
For thus to meet, and thus to find,
    That Time, whose touch can chill
Each flower of form, each grace of mind,
    Hath left thee blooming still—

Oh, joy alone should be thought of now,
  Let our sorrows go sleep awhile;
Or, should thought's dark cloud come o'er thy brow,
  Let Love light it up with his smile.

When the flowers of life's sweet garden fade,
  If but *one* bright leaf remain
Of the many that once its glory made,
  It is not for us to complain.
But thus to meet and thus to wake
  In all Love's early bliss;
Oh, Time all other gifts may take,
  So he but leaves us this!
Then let joy alone be remember'd now,
  Let our sorrows go sleep awhile;
Or if thought's dark cloud come o'er the brow,
  Let Love light it up with his smile!

———⊰✿⊱———

LOVE THEE, DEAREST? LOVE THEE?

Love thee, dearest? love thee?
  Yes, by yonder star I swear,
Which through tears above thee
  Shines so sadly fair;
Though often dim,
With tears, like him,
Like him my truth will shine,
  And—love thee, dearest? love thee?
Yes, till death I 'm thine.

Leave thee, dearest? leave thee?
  No, that star is not more true;
When my vows deceive thee,
  He will wander too.
A cloud of night
May veil his light,
And death shall darken mine—
  But—leave thee, dearest? leave thee?
No, till death I 'm thine.

———⊶❀⊷———

MY HEART AND LUTE.

I give thee all—I can no more—
  Though poor the offering be;
My heart and lute are all the store
  That I can bring to thee.
A lute whose gentle song reveals
  The soul of love full well;
And, better far, a heart that feels
  Much more than lute could tell.

Though love and song may fail, alas!
  To keep life's clouds away,
At least 't will make them lighter pass,
  Or gild them if they stay.
And even if Care, at moments, flings
  A discord o'er life's happy strain,
Let Love but gently touch the strings,
  'T will all be sweet again!

PEACE, PEACE TO HIM THAT 'S GONE!

When I am dead,
  Then lay my head
In some lone distant dell,
  Where voices ne'er
  Shall stir the air,
Or break its silent spell.

If any sound
  Be heard around,
Let the sweet bird alone,
  That weeps in song,
  Sing all night long,
" Peace, peace to him that's gone!"

Yet, oh, were mine
  One sigh of thine,
One pitying word from thee,
  Like gleams of heaven,
  To sinners given,
Would be that word to me.

Howe'er unblest,
  My shade would rest
While listening to that tone;—
  Enough 't would be
  To hear from thee,
" Peace peace, to him that 's gone!"

———⊶❀⊷———

ROSE OF THE DESERT.

Rose of the Desert! thou, whose blushing ray,
Lonely and lovely, fleets unseen away;
No hand to cull thee, none to woo thy sigh—
In vestal silence left to live and die—
Rose of the Desert! thus should woman be,
Shining uncourted, lone and safe, like thee.

Rose of the Garden, how unlike thy doom!
Destined for others, not thyself, to bloom:
Cull'd ere thy beauty lives through half its day;
A moment cherish'd, and then cast away:
Rose of the Garden! such is woman's lot—
Worshipp'd while blooming—when she fades, forgot.

———⊶❀⊷———

'T IS ALL FOR THEE.

If life for me hath joy or light,
  'T is all from thee;
My thoughts by day, my dreams by night,
  Are but of thee, of only thee.
Whate'er of hope or peace I know,
My zest in joy, my balm in woe,
To those dear eyes of thine I owe—
  'T is all from thee.

My heart, even ere I saw those eyes,
  Seem'd doom'd to thee;
Kept pure till then from other ties,
  'T was all for thee, for only thee.

Like plants that sleep, till sunny May
Calls forth their life, my spirit lay,
Till, touch'd by Love's awakening ray,
    It lived for thee, it lived for thee.

When Fame would call me to her heights,
    She speaks by thee;
And dim would shine her proudest lights,
    Unshared by thee, unshared by thee.
Whene'er I seek the Muse's shrine,
Where Bards have hung their wreaths divine,
And wish those wreaths of glory mine,
    'T is all for thee, for only thee.

—o♦♦o—

WAKE THEE, MY DEAR.

WAKE thee, my dear—thy dreaming
    Till darker hours will keep;
While such a moon is beaming,
    'T is wrong towards Heaven to sleep.

Moments there are we number,
    Moments of pain and care,
Which to oblivious slumber
    Gladly the wretch would spare.
But now—who 'd think of dreaming
    When Love his watch should keep?
While such a moon is beaming,
    'T is wrong towards Heaven to sleep.

If e'er the fates should sever,
    My life and hopes from thee, love,
The sleep that lasts for ever
    Would then be sweet to me, love.
But now—away with dreaming!
    Till darker hours 't will keep;
While such a moon is beaming.
    'T is wrong towards Heaven to sleep.

—o♦♦o—

THE SONG OF THE OLDEN TIME. (1)

THERE's a song of the olden time,
    Falling sad o'er the ear,
Like the dream of some village chime,
    Which in youth we loved to hear.
And even amidst the grand and gay,
    When Music tries her gentlest art,
I never hear so sweet a lay,
    Or one that hangs so round my heart,
As that song of the olden time,
    Falling sad o'er the ear,
Like the dream of some village chime,
    Which in youth we loved to hear.

And when all of this life is gone,
    Even the hope, lingering now,

Like the last of the leaves left on
    Autumn's sere and faded bough,
'T will seem as still those friends were near,
    Who loved me in youth's early day,
If in that parting hour I hear
    The same sweet notes, and die away—
To that song of the olden time,
    Breathed, like Hope's farewell strain,
To say, in some brighter clime,
    Life and youth will shine again !

—o♦♦o—

THE BOY OF THE ALPS. (2)

LIGHTLY, Alpine rover,
Tread the mountains over;
Rude is the path thou'st yet to go;
    Snow cliffs hanging o'er thee,
    Fields of ice before thee,
While the hid torrent moans below.
Hark, the deep thunder,
Through the vales yonder !
'T is the huge avalanche downward cast;
    From rock to rock
    Rebounds the shock.
But courage, boy! the danger 's past!
    Onward, youthful rover,
    Tread the glacier over,
Safe shalt thou reach thy home at last.

On, ere light forsake thee,
Soon will dusk o'ertake thee :
O'er yon ice-bridge lies thy way !
    Now, for the risk prepare thee;
    Safe it yet may bear thee,
Though 't will melt in morning's ray.

Hark, that dread howling !
'T is the wolf prowling—
Scent of thy track the foe hath got,
    And cliff and shore
    Resound his roar.
But, courage, boy !—the danger 's past!
    Watching eyes have found thee,
    Loving arms are round thee,
Safe hast thou reach'd thy father's cot.

—o♦♦o—

FOR THEE ALONE.

FOR thee alone I brave the boundless deep,
    Those eyes my light through every distant sea ;
My waking thoughts, the dream that gilds my sleep,
    The noon-tide reverie, are all given to thee,
        To thee alone, to thee alone.

Though future scenes present to Fancy's eye
    Fair forms of light that crowd the distant air,

(1) In this song, which is one of the many set to music by myself, the occasional lawlessness of the metre arises, I need hardly say, from the peculiar structure of the air.
(2) This and the Songs that follow (as far as and includ-

ing the one, "The dawn is breaking o'er us", have been published, with music, by Messrs. Addison and Beale, Regent Street.

When nearer view'd, the fairy phantoms fly,
  The crowds dissolve, and thou alone art there,
    Thou, thou alone.

To win thy smile, I speed from shore to shore,
  While Hope's sweet voice is heard in every blast,
Still whispering on, that when some years are o'er,
  One bright reward shall crown my toil at last—
    Thy smile alone, thy smile alone.

Oh place beside the transport of that hour
  All earth can boast of fair, of rich, and bright,
Wealth's radiant mines, the lofty thrones of power—
  Then ask where first thy lover's choice would light?
    On thee alone, on thee alone.

—————

HER LAST WORDS, AT PARTING.

Her last words, at parting, how *can* I forget?
  Deep treasured through life, in my heart they shall
    stay;
Like music, whose charm in the soul lingers yet,
  When its sounds from the ear have long melted away.
Let Fortune assail me, her threatenings are vain;
  Those still-breathing words shall my talisman be—
" Remember, in absence, in sorrow, and pain,
  There's one heart, unchanging, that beats but for
    thee."

From the desert's sweet well though the pilgrim must
    hie,
  Never more of that fresh-springing fountain to taste,
He hath still of its bright drops a treasured supply,
  Whose sweetness lends life to his lips through the
    waste.
So, dark as my fate is still doom'd to remain,
  These words shall my well in the wilderness be—
" Remember, in absence, in sorrow, and pain,
  There's one heart, unchanging, that beats but for
    thee."

—————

LET 'S TAKE THIS WORLD AS SOME WIDE SCENE.

Let 's take this world as some wide scene,
  Through which, in frail but buoyant boat,
With skies now dark and now serene,
  Together thou and I must float;
Beholding oft, on either shore,
  Bright spots where we should love to stay;
But Time plies swift his flying oar,
  And away we speed, away, away.

Should chilling winds and rains come on,
  We'll raise our awning 'gainst the shower;
Sit closer till the storm is gone,
  And, smiling, wait a sunnier hour.
And if that sunnier hour should shine,
  We'll know its brightness cannot stay,
But happy, while 't is thine and mine,
  Complain not when it fades away.

So shall we reach at last that Fall
  Down which life's currents all must go—
The dark, the brilliant, destined all
  To sink into the void below.
Nor even that hour shall want its charms
  If, side by side, still fond we keep,
And calmly, in each other's arms
  Together link'd, go down the sleep.

—————

LOVE'S VICTORY.

Sing to Love—for oh, 't was he
  Who won the glorious day;
Strew the wreaths of victory
  Along the conqueror's way.
Yoke the Muses to his car,
  Let them sing each trophy won;
While his mother's joyous star
  Shall light the triumph on.

Hail to Love, to mighty Love,
  Let spirits sing around;
While the hill, the dale, and grove,
  With " mighty Love " resound.
Or, should a sigh of sorrow steal
  Amid the sounds thus echo'd o'er,
'T will but teach the god to feel
  His victories the more.

See his wings, like amethyst
  Of sunny Ind their hue;
Bright as when, by Pysche kiss'd,
  They trembled through and through.
Flowers spring beneath his feet;
  Angel forms beside him run;
While unnumber'd lips repeat
  " Love's victory is won! "
    Hail to Love, to mighty Love, etc.

—————

SONG OF HERCULES TO HIS DAUGHTER. (1)

" I 've been, oh, sweet daughter,
  To fountain and sea,
To seek in their water
  Some bright gem for thee.
Where diamonds were sleeping,
  Their sparkle I sought,
Where crystal was weeping,
  Its tears I have caught.

" The sea-nymph I 've courted
  In rich coral halls;
With Naiads have sported
  By bright waterfalls.
But, sportive or tender,
  Still sought I around
That gem, with whose splendour
  Thou yet shalt be crown'd.

(1) Founded on the fable reported by Arrian (in *Indicis*)
of Hercules having searched the Indian Ocean, to find the
pearl with which he adorned his daughter Pandæa.

" And see, while I'm speaking,
 Yon soft light afar;—
The pearl I've been seeking
 There floats like a star!
In the deep Indian Ocean
 I see the gem shine,
And quick as light's motion
 Its wealth shall be thine."

Then eastward, like lightning,
 The hero-god flew,
His sunny looks bright'ning
 The air he went through.
And sweet was the duty,
 And hallow'd the hour,
Which saw thus young Beauty
 Embellish'd by Power.

—⟶••◦—

THE DREAM OF HOME.

WHO has not felt how sadly sweet ·
 The dream of home, the dream of home,
Steals o'er the heart, too soon to fleet,
 When far o'er sea or land we roam?
Sunlight more soft may o'er us fall,
 To greener shores our bark may come;
But far more bright, more dear than all,
 That dream of home, that dream of home.

Ask of the sailor youth when far
 His light bark bounds o'er ocean's foam,
What charms him most, when evening's star
 Smiles o'er the wave? to dream of home.
Fond thoughts of absent friends and loves
 At that sweet hour around him come;
His heart's best joy where'er he roves,
 That dream of home, that dream of home.

—◦••◦—

THE YOUNG INDIAN MAID.

THERE came a nymph dancing
 Gracefully, gracefully,
Her eye a light glancing
 Like the blue sea;
And while all this gladness
 Around her steps hung,
Such sweet notes of sadness
 Her gentle lips sung,
That ne'er while I live from my memory shall fade
The song, or the look, of that young Indian maid.

Her zone of bells ringing
 Cheerily, cheerily,
Chimed to her singing
 Light echoes of glee;
But in vain did she borrow
 Of mirth the gay tone,
Her voice spoke of sorrow,
 And sorrow alone.
Nor e'er while I live from my memory shall fade
The song or the look of that young Indian maid.

THEY TELL ME THOU 'RT THE FAVOUR'D GUEST. (1)

THEY tell me thou 'rt the favour'd guest
 Of every fair and brilliant throng;
No wit like thine to wake the jest,
 No voice like thine to breathe the song:
And none could guess, so gay thou art,
That thou and I are far apart.

Alas! alas! how different flows
 With thee and me the time away!
Not that I wish thee sad—Heaven knows—
 Still, if thou can'st, be light and gay;
I only know, that without thee
The sun himself is dark to me.

Do I thus haste to hall and bower,
 Among the proud and gay to shine?
Or deck my hair with gem and flower,
 To flatter other eyes than thine?
Ah, no, with me love's smiles are past—
Thou hadst the first, thou hadst the last.

— ⟶••◦—

THE HOMEWARD MARCH.

BE still, my heart: I hear them come:
 Those sounds announce my lover near:
The march that brings our warriors home
 Proclaims he'll soon be here.

 Hark, the distant tread,
 O'er the mountain's head,
While hills and dales repeat the sound;
 And the forest deer
 Stand still to hear,
As those echoing steps ring round.

Be still, my heart, I hear them come,
 Those sounds that speak my soldier near;
Those joyous steps seem'd wing'd for home—
 Rest, rest, he'll soon be here.

But hark, more faint the footsteps grow,
 And now they wind to distant glades;
Not here their home—alas, they go
 To gladden happier maids!

 Like sounds in a dream,
 The footsteps seem,
As down the hills they die away;
 And the march, whose song
 So peal'd along,
Now fades like a funeral lay.

(1) Part of a translation of some Latin verses, supposed
to have been addressed by Hippolyta Taurella to her
husband, during his absence at the gay court of Leo the
Tenth. The verses may be found in the Appendix to
Roscoe's Work.

36

'T is past, 't is o'er—hush, heart, thy pain!
And though not here, alas, they come,
Rejoice for those, to whom that strain
Brings sons and lovers home.

WAKE UP, SWEET MELODY.

WAKE up, sweet melody!
    Now is the hour
    When young and loving hearts
    Feel most thy power.
One note of music, by moonlight's soft ray—
Oh, 't is worth thousands heard coldly by day.
    Then wake up, sweet melody!
    Now is the hour
    When young and loving hearts
    Feel most thy power.

    Ask the fond nightingale
    When his sweet flower
Loves most to hear his song,
    In her green bower?
Oh, he will tell thee, through summer-nights long,
Fondest she lends her whole soul to his song.
    Then wake up, sweet melody!
    Now is the hour
    When young and loving hearts
    Feel most thy power.

CALM BE THY SLEEP.

CALM be thy sleep as infants' slumbers!
Pure as angel thoughts thy dreams!
May every joy this bright world numbers
Shed o'er thee their mingled beams!
Or if, where Pleasure's wing hath glided,
    There ever must some pang remain,
Still be thy lot with me divided—
    Thine all the bliss, and mine the pain!

Day and night my thoughts shall hover
    Round thy steps where'er they stray;
As, even when clouds his idol cover,
    Fondly the Persian tracks its ray.
If this be wrong, if Heaven offended
    By worship to its creature be,
Then let my vows to both be blended,
    Half breathed to Heaven and half to thee.

THE FANCY FAIR.

COME, maids and youths, for here we sell
    All wondrous things of earth and air;
Whatever wild romancers tell,
    Or poets sing, or lovers swear,
    You'll find at this our Fancy Fair.

Here eyes are made like stars to shine,
    And kept, for years, in such repair,
That even when turn'd of thirty-nine,
    They'll hardly look the worse for wear,
    If bought at this our Fancy Fair.

We've lots of tears for bards to shower,
    And hearts that such ill usage bear,
That, though they're broken every hour,
    They'll still in rhyme fresh breaking bear,
    If purchased at our Fancy Fair.

As fashions change in every thing,
    We've goods to suit each season's air,
Eternal friendships for the spring,
    And endless loves for summer wear—
    All sold at this our Fancy Fair.

We've reputations white as snow,
    That long will last, if used with care,
Nay, safe through all life's journey go,
    If pack'd and mark'd as " brittle ware"—
    Just purchased at the Fancy Fair.

THE EXILE.

NIGHT waneth fast, the morning star
    Saddens with light the glimmering sea,
Whose waves shall soon to realms afar
    Waft me from hope, from love, and thee.
Coldly the beam from yonder sky
    Looks o'er the waves that onward stray;
But colder still the stranger's eye
    To him whose home is far away.

Oh, not at hour so chill and bleak,
    Let thoughts of me come o'er thy breast;
But of the lost one think and speak,
    When summer suns sink calm to rest.
So, as I wander, Fancy's dream
    Shall bring me, o'er the sunset seas,
Thy look in every melting beam,
    Thy whisper in each dying breeze.

IF THOU WOULDST HAVE ME SING AND PLAY.

IF thou wouldst have me sing and play
    As once I play'd and sung,
First take this time-worn lute away,
    And bring one freshly strung.
Call back the time when pleasure's sigh
    First breathed among the strings;
And Time himself, in flitting by,
    Made music with his wings.

But how is this? though new the lute,
    And shining fresh the chords,
Beneath this hand they slumber mute,
    Or speak but dreamy words.
In vain I seek the soul that dwelt
    Within that once sweet shell,
Which told so warmly what it felt,
    And felt what nought could tell.

Oh, ask not then for passion's lay
    From lyre so coldly strung;
With this I ne'er can sing or play
    As once I play'd and sung.

No, bring that long-loved lute again—
　Though chill'd by years it be,
If *thou* wilt call the slumbering strain,
　'T will wake again for thee.

Though time have frozen the tuneful stream
　Of thoughts thàt gush'd along,
One look from thee, like Summer's beam,
　Will thaw them into song.
Then give, oh give, that wakening ray,
　And, once more blithe and young,
Thy bard again will sing and play
　As once he play'd and sung.

—◁ ❦ ▷—

STILL WHEN DAYLIGHT.

STILL, when daylight o'er the wave
Bright and soft its farewell gave,
I used to hear, while light was falling,
O'er the wave a sweet voice calling,
　Mournfully at distance calling.

Ah! once how blest that maid would come,
To meet her sea-boy hastening home;
And through the night those sounds repeating,
Hail his bark with joyous greeting,
　Joyously his light bark greeting.

But one sad night, when winds were high,
Nor earth, nor heaven, could hear her cry,
She saw his boat come tossing over
Midnight's wave—but not her lover!
　No, never more her lover.

And still that sad dream loath to leave,
She comes with wandering mind at eve,
And oft we hear, when night is falling,
Faint her voice through twilight calling,
　Mournfully at twilight calling.

—◁ ❦ ▷—

THE SUMMER WEBS.

THE summer webs that float and shine,
　The summer dews that fall,
Though light they be, this heart of mine
　Is lighter still than all.
It tells me, every cloud is past
　Which lately seem'd to lour;
That Hope hath wed young Joy at last,
　And now 's their nuptial hour!

With light thus round, within, above,
　With nought to wake one sigh,
Except the wish, that all we love
　Were at this moment nigh—
It seems as if life's brilliant sun
　Had stopp'd in full career,
To make this hour its brightest one,
　And rest in radiance here.

MIND NOT THOUGH DAYLIGHT.

MIND not though daylight around us is breaking—
Who 'd think now of sleeping when morn 's but just
　waking?
Sound the merry viol, and, daylight or not,
Be all for one hour in the gay dance forgot.

See young Aurora, up heaven's hill advancing,
Though fresh from her pillow, even she too is dancing:
While thus all creation, earth, heaven, and sea,
Are dancing around us, oh, why should not we?

Who 'll say that moments we use thus are wasted?
Such sweet drops of time only flow to be tasted;
While hearts are high beating, and harps full in tune,
The fault is all morning's for coming so soon.

—◁ ❦ ▷—

THEY MET BUT ONCE.

THEY met but once, in youth's sweet hour,
　And never since that day
Hath absence, time, or grief had power
　To chase that dream away.
They 've seen the suns of other skies,
　On other shores have sought delight;
But never more, to bless their eyes,
　Can come a dream so bright!
They met but once—a day was all
　Of Love's young hopes they knew;
And still their hearts that day recall,
　As fresh as then it flew.

Sweet dream of youth! oh, ne'er again
　Let either meet the brow
They left so smooth and smiling then,
　·Or see what it is now.
For, Youth, the spell was only thine;
　From thee alone the enchantment flows,
That makes the world around thee shine
　With light thyself bestows.
They met but once;—oh, ne'er again
　Let either meet the brow
They left so smooth and smiling then,
　Or see what it is now.

—◁ ❦ ▷—

CHILD'S SONG. FROM A MASQUE.

I HAVE a garden of my own,
　Shining with flowers of every hue;
I loved it dearly while alone,
　But I shall love it more with you:
And there the golden bees shall come,
　In summer-time at break of morn,
And wake us with their busy hum
　Around the Siha's fragrant thorn.

I have a fawn from Aden's land,
　On leafy buds and berries nurst;
And you shall feed him from your hand,
　Though he may start with fear at first.

And I will lead you where he lies
For shelter in the noon-tide heat;
And you may touch his sleeping eyes,
And feel his little silvery feet.

—o◆◆o—

WITH MOONLIGHT BEAMING.

WITH moonlight beaming
   Thus o'er the deep,
Who'd linger dreaming
   In idle sleep? ·
Leave joyless souls to live by day—
Our life begins with yonder ray;
   And while thus brightly
      The moments flee,
   Our barks skim lightly
      The shining sea.

To halls of splendour
   Let great ones hie;
Through light more tender
   Our pathways lie:
While round, from banks of brook or lake,
Our company blithe echoes make;
   And, as we lend 'em
      Sweet word or strain,
   Still back they send 'em,
      More sweet, again.

—o◆◆o—

THE HALCYON HANGS O'ER OCEAN.

THE halcyon hangs o'er ocean,
   The sea-lark skims the brine;
This bright world's all in motion,
   No heart seems sad but mine.

To walk through sun-bright places,
   With heart all cold the while;
To look in smiling faces,
   When we no more can smile;

To feel, while earth and heaven
   Around thee shine with bliss,
To thee no light is given—
   Oh, what a doom is this!

—o◆◆o—

THE WORLD WAS HUSH'D.

THE world was hush'd, the moon above
Sail'd through ether slowly,
When, near the casement of my love,
   Thus I whisper'd lowly—
"Awake, awake, how canst thou sleep?
   The field I seek to-morrow
Is one where man hath fame to reap,
   And woman gleans but sorrow."

"Let battle's field be what it may,"
   Thus spoke a voice replying,
"Think not thy love, while thou 'rt away,
   Will here sit idly sighing.

No—woman's soul, if not for fame,
   For love can brave all danger!"
Then forth from out the casement came
   A plumed and armed stranger.

A stranger? No; 't was she, the maid,
   Herself before me beaming,
With casque array'd, and falchion blade
   Beneath her girdle gleaming!
Close side by side, in freedom's fight,
   That blessed morning found us;
In Victory's light we stood ere night,
   And Love, the morrow, crown'd us!

—o◆◆o—

THE TWO LOVES.

THERE are two Loves, the poet sings,
   Both born of Beauty at a birth:
The one, akin to heaven, hath wings,
   The other, earthly, walks on earth.
With *this* through bowers below we play,
   With *that* through clouds above we soar;
With both, perchance, may lose our way :—
      Then, tell me which,
   Tell me which shall we adore?

The one when tempted down from air,
   At Pleasure's fount to lave his lip,
Nor lingers long, nor oft will dare
   His wing within the wave to dip.
While, plunging deep and long beneath,
   The other bathes him o'er and o'er
In that sweet current, even to death :—
      Then, tell me which,
   Tell me which shall we adore?

The boy of heaven, even while he lies,
   In Beauty's lap, recalls his home;
And when most happy, inly sighs
   For something happier still to come.
While he of earth, too fully blest
   With this bright world to dream of more,
Sees all his heaven on Beauty's breast :—
      Then, tell me which,
   Tell me which shall we adore?

The maid who heard the poet sing
   These twin-desires of earth and sky,
And saw, while one inspired his string,
   The other glisten'd in his eye—
To name the earthlier boy ashamed,
   To choose the other fondly loath,
At length, all blushing, she exclaim'd—
      "Ask not which,
   Oh, ask not which—we 'll worship both.

"The extremes of each thus taught to shun,
   With hearts and souls between them given,
When weary of this earth with one,
   We 'll with the other wing to heaven."

Thus pledged the maid her vow of bliss;
And while *one* Love wrote down the oath,
The other seal'd it with a kiss;
    And Heaven look'd on,
Heaven look'd on; and hallow'd both.

—◦◦◦—

THE LEGEND OF PUCK THE FAIRY.

WOULDST know what tricks, by the pale moonlight,
Are play'd by me, the merry little Sprite,
Who wing through air from the camp to the court,
From king to clown, and of all make sport;
    Singing, I am the Sprite
    Of the merry midnight,
Who laugh at weak mortals, and love the moonlight.

To a miser's bed, where he snoring slept
And dreamt of his cash, I slily crept;
Chink, chink o'er his pillow like money I rang,
And he waked to catch—but away I sprang,
    Singing, I am the Sprite, etc.

I saw through the leaves, in a damsel's bower,
She was waiting her love at that starlight hour:
" Hist—hist! " quoth I, with an amorous sigh,
And she flew to the door, but away flew I,
    Singing, I am the Sprite, etc.

While a bard sat inditing an ode to his love,
Like a pair of blue meteors I stared from above,
And he swoon'd—for he thought 't was the ghost,
    poor man!
Of his lady's eyes—while away I ran,
    Singing, I am the Sprite, etc.

—◦◦◦—

BEAUTY AND SONG.

    DOWN in yon summer vale,
      Where the rill flows,
    Thus said a Nightingale
      To his loved Rose:—
    " Though rich the pleasures
    Of song's sweet measures,
    Vain were its melody,
    Rose, without thee."

    Then from the green recess
      Of her night-bower,
    Beaming with bashfulness,
      Spoke the bright flower:—
    " Though morn should lend her
    Its sunniest splendour,
    What would the Rose be,
    Unsung by thee? "

(1) On the Tower of the Winds, at Athens, there is a conch-shell placed in the hands of Boreas.—See *Stuart's Antiquities.* " The north wind," says Herodotus, in speaking of the Hyperboreans, " never blows with them."
(2) " Sub ipso siderum cardine jacent."—*Pompon. Mela.*

Thus still let Song attend
    Woman's bright way;
Thus still let woman lend
    Light to the lay.
Like stars, through heaven's sea
Floating in harmony,
Beauty should glide along
    Circled by Song.

—◦◦◦—

SONG OF A HYPERBOREAN.

I COME from a land in the sun-bright deep,
    Were golden gardens grow;
Where the winds of the north, becalm'd in sleep,
    Their conch-shells never blow. (1)
      Haste to that holy Isle with me,
        Haste—haste!

So near the track of the stars are we, (2)
    That oft, on night's pale beams,
The distant sounds of their harmony
    Come to our ear, like dreams.
      Then, haste to that holy Isle with me, etc.

The Moon, too, brings her world so nigh, (3)
    That when the night-seer looks
To that shadowless orb, in a vernal sky,
    He can number its hills and brooks.
        Then, haste, etc., etc.

To the Sun-god all our hearts and lyres (4)
    By day, by night, belong;
And the breath we draw from his living fires,
    We give him back in song.
        Then, haste, etc., etc.

From us descends the maid who brings
    To Delos gifts divine;
And our wild bees lend their rainbow wings
    To glitter on Delphi's shrine. (5)
      Then, haste to that holy Isle with me,
        Haste—haste!

—◦◦◦—

WHEN THOU ART NIGH.

WHEN thou art nigh, it seems
    A new creation round;
The sun hath fairer beams,
    The lute a softer sound.
Though thee alone I see,
    And hear alone thy sigh,
'Tis light, 't is song to me,
    'T is all—when thou art nigh.

When thou art nigh, no thought
    Of grief comes o'er my heart;

(3) " They can show the moon very near."—*Diodor. Sicul.*
(4) Hecatæus tells us, that this Hyperborean island was dedicated to Apollo; and most of the inhabitants were either priests or songsters.
(5) Pausan.

I only think—could aught
But joy be where thou art?
Life seems a waste of breath
When far from thee I sigh;
And death—ay, even death
Were sweet, if thou wert nigh.

—◦◦◦—

CUPID ARMED.

PLACE the helm on thy brow,
In thy hand take the spear;—
Thou art arm'd, Cupid, now,
And thy battle-hour is near.
March on! march on! thy shaft and bow
Were weak against such charms;
March on! march on! so proud a foe
Scorns all but martial arms.

See the darts in her eyes,
Tipt with scorn, how they shine!
Every shaft, as it flies,
Mocking proudly at thine.
March on! march on! thy feather'd darts
Soft bosoms soon might move;
But ruder arms to ruder hearts
Must teach what 't is to love.

Place the helm on thy brow;
In thy hand take the spear—
Thou art arm'd, Cupid, now,
And thy battle-hour is near.

—◦◦◦—

ROUND THE WORLD GOES.

ROUND the world goes, by day and night,
While with it also round go we;
And in the flight of one day's light
An image of all life's course we see.
Round, round, while thus we go round,
The best thing a man can do,
Is to make it, at least, a *merry*-go-round,
By—sending the wine round too.

Our first gay stage of life is when
Youth, in its dawn, salutes the eye—
Season of bliss! Oh, who would n't then
Wish to cry, "Stop!" to earth and sky?
But, round, round, both boy and girl
Are whisk'd through that sky of blue;
And much would their hearts enjoy the whirl,
If—their heads did n't whirl round too.

Next, we enjoy our glorious noon,
Thinking all life a life of light;
But shadows come on, 'tis evening soon,
And, ere we can say, "How short!"—'t is night.
Round, round, still all goes round,
Even while I 'm thus singing to you;
And the best way to make it a *merry*-go-round,
Is to—chorus my song round too.

THOU BIDST ME SING.

THOU bidst me sing the lay I sung to thee
In other days, ere joy had left this brow;
But think, though still unchanged the notes may be,
How different feels the heart that breathes them
now!
The rose thou wear'st to-night is still the same
We saw this morning on its stem so gay;
But, ah! that dew of dawn, that breath which came
Like life o'er all its leaves, hath pass'd away.

Since first that music touch'd thy heart and mine,
How many a joy and pain o'er both have past!—
The joy, a light too precious long to shine,
The pain, a cloud whose shadows always last.
And though that lay would, like the voice of home,
Breathe o'er our ear, 't would waken now a sigh—
Ah! not, as then, for fancied woes to come,
But, sadder far, for real bliss gone by.

—◦◦◦—

OH, DO NOT LOOK SO BRIGHT AND BLEST.

OH, do not look so bright and blest,
For still there comes a fear,
When brow like thine looks happiest,
That grief is then most near.
There lurks a dread in all delight,
A shadow near each ray,
That warns us then to fear their flight,
When most we wish their stay.
Then look not thou so bright and blest,
For ah! there comes a fear,
When brow like thine looks happiest,
That grief is then most near.

Why is it thus that fairest things
The soonest fleet and die?—
That when most light is on their wings,
They 're then but spread to fly?
And, sadder still, the pain will stay—
The bliss no more appears;
As rainbows take their light away,
And leave us but the tears!
Then look not thou so bright and blest,
For ah! there comes a fear,
When brow like thine looks happiest,
That grief is then most near.

—◦◦◦—

THE MUSICAL BOX.

"Look here," said Rose, with laughing eyes,
"Within this box, by magic hid,
A tuneful Sprite imprison'd lies,
Who sings to me whene'er he 's bid.
Though roving once his voice and wing,
He 'll now lie still the whole day long;
Till thus I touch the magic spring—
Then hark, how sweet and blithe his song!"
                              (*A symphony.*)

"Ah, Rose," I cried, "the poet's lay
    Must ne'er even Beauty's slave become;
Through earth and air his song may stray,
    If all the while his heart's at home.
And though in freedom's air he dwell,
    Nor bond nor chain his spirit knows,
Touch but the spring thou know'st so well,
    And—hark, how sweet the love-song flows!"
                        (*A symphony.*)

Thus pleaded I for freedom's right;
    But when young Beauty takes the field,
And wise men seek defence in flight,
    The doom of poets is to yield.
No more my heart the enchantress braves,
    I'm now in Beauty's prison hid;
The Sprite and I are fellow-slaves,
    And I, too, sing whene'er I'm bid.

—◦❈◦—

WHEN TO SAD MUSIC SILENT YOU LISTEN.

WHEN to sad Music silent you listen,
    And tears on those eyelids tremble like dew,
Oh, then there dwells in those eyes as they glisten
    A sweet holy charm that mirth never knew.
But when some lively strain resounding
    Lights up the sunshine of joy on that brow,
Then the young rein-deer o'er the hills bounding
    Was ne'er in its mirth so graceful as thou.

When on the skies at midnight thou gazest,
    A lustre so pure thy features then wear,
That, when on some star that bright eye thou raisest,
    We feel 't is thy home thou 'rt looking for there.
But, when the word for the gay dance is given,
    So buoyant thy spirit, so heartfelt thy mirth,
Oh then we exclaim, "Ne'er leave earth for heaven,
    But linger still here, to make heaven of earth."

—◦❈◦—

THE DAWN IS BREAKING O'ER US.

THE dawn is breaking o'er us,
    See, heaven hath caught its hue!
We 've day's long light before us,
    What sport shall we pursue?
The hunt o'er hill and lea?
The sail o'er summer sea?
Oh let not hour so sweet
Unwing'd by pleasure fleet.
The dawn is breaking o'er us,
    See, heaven hath caught its hue!
We 've day's long light before us,
    What sport shall we pursue?

But see, while we 're deciding
    What morning sport to play,

The dial's hand is gliding,
    And morn hath pass'd away!
Ah, who 'd have thought that noon
    Would o'er us steal so soon—
That morn's sweet hour of prime
    Would last so short a time?
But come, we 've day before us,
    Still heaven looks bright and blue;
Quick, quick, ere eve comes o'er us,
    What sport shall we pursue?

Alas! why thus delaying?
    We 're now at evening's hour;
Its farewell beam is playing
    O'er hill and wave and bower.
That light we thought would last,
Behold, even now, 't is past;
And all our morning dreams
Have vanish'd with its beams!
But come! 't were vain to borrow
    Sad lessons from this lay,
For man will be to-morrow—
    Just what he 's been to-day.

—◦❈◦—

THE LANGUAGE OF FLOWERS.

FLY swift, my light gazelle,
    To her who now lies waking,
To hear thy silver bell
    The midnight silence breaking.
And, when thou comest, with gladsome feet,
    Beneath her lattice springing,
Ah, well she 'll know how sweet
    The words of love thou 'rt bringing.

Yet, no—not words, for they
    But half can tell love's feeling;
Sweet flowers alone can say
    What passion fears revealing.
A once bright rose's wither'd leaf,
    A towering lily broken—
Oh, these may paint a grief
    No words could e'er have spoken.

Not such, my gay gazelle,
    The wreath thou speedest over
Yon moonlight dale, to tell
    My lady how I love her.
And, what to her will sweeter be
    Than gems the richest, rarest—
From Truth's immortal tree(1)
    One fadeless leaf thou bearest.

(1) The tree called in the East Amrita, or the Immortal.

—◦❈◦—

UNPUBLISHED SONGS, ETC.

ASK NOT IF STILL I LOVE.

Ask not if still I love,
    Too plain these eyes have told thee;
Too well their tears must prove
    How near and dear I hold thee.
If, where the brightest shine,
    To see no form but thine,
    To feel that earth can show
      No bliss above thee—
If this be love, then know
    That thus, that thus, I love thee.

'T is not in pleasure's idle hour
    That thou canst know affection's power:
No, try its strength in grief or pain;
    Attempt, as now, its bonds to sever,
Thou 'lt find true love's a chain
    That binds for ever!

—◦✸◦—

DEAR? YES.

Dear? yes, though mine no more,
    Even this but makes thee dearer;
And love, since hope is o'er,
    But draws thee nearer.

Change as thou wilt to me,
The same thy charm must be;
New loves may come to weave
    Their witchery o'er thee,
Yet still, though false, believe
    That I adore thee—yes, still adore thee.
Think'st thou that aught but death could end
A tie not falsehood's self can rend?
No, when alone far off I die,
    No more to see, no more caress thee,
Even then, my life's last sigh
    Shall be to bless thee—yes, still to bless thee.

—◦✦◦—

UNBIND THEE, LOVE.

Unbind, love, unbind thee, love,
    From those dark ties unbind thee;
Though fairest hand the chain hath wove,
    Too long its links have twined thee.
Away from earth!—thy wings were made
    In yon mid-sky to hover,
With earth beneath their dove-like shade,
    And heaven all radiant over.

Awake thee, boy, awake thee, boy,
    Too long thy soul is sleeping;
And thou may'st from this minute's joy
    Wake to eternal weeping.
Oh, think, this world is not for thee;
    Though hard its links to sever;
Though sweet and bright and dear they be,
    Break, or thou 'rt lost for ever.

THERE'S SOMETHING STRANGE.

A BUFFO SONG.

There 's something strange, I know not what,
    Come o'er me,
Some phantom I 've for ever got
    Before me.
I look on high, and in the sky
    'T is shining;
On earth, its light with all things bright
    Seems twining.
In vain I try this goblin's spells
    To sever;
Go where I will, it round me dwells
    For ever.

And then what tricks by day and night
    It plays me,
In every shape the wicked sprite
    Waylays me.
Sometimes like two bright eyes of blue
    'T is glancing;
Sometimes like feet, in slippers neat,
    Comes dancing.
By whispers round of every sort
    I 'm taunted.
Never was mortal man, in short,
    So haunted.

—◦✦◦—

NOT FROM THEE.

Not from thee the wound should come,
    No, not from thee.
I care not what or whence my doom,
    So not from thee!
Cold triumph! first to make
    This heart thy own;
And then the mirror break
    Where fix'd thou shinest alone.
Not from thee the wound should come,
    Oh, not from thee.
I care not what, or whence, my doom,
    So not from thee.

Yet no—my lips that wish recall;
    From thee, from thee,
If ruin o'er this head must fall,
    'T will welcome be.
Here to the blade I bare
    This faithful heart;
Wound deep—thou 'lt find that there,
    In every pulse, thou art.
Yes from thee I 'll bear it all:
    If ruin be
The doom that o'er this heart must fall,
    'T were sweet from thee.

GUESS, GUESS.

I LOVE a maid, a mystic maid,
 Whose form no eyes but mine can see;
She comes in light, she comes in shade,
 And beautiful in both is she.
Her shape in dreams I oft behold,
 And oft she whispers in my ear
Such words as, when to others told,
 Awake the sigh, or wring the tear.
 Then guess, guess, who she,
 The lady of my love, may be.

I find the lustre of her brow
 Come o'er me in my darkest ways;
And feel as if her voice, even now,
 Were echoing far off my lays.
There is no scene of joy or woe
 But she doth gild with influence bright;
And shed o'er all so rich a glow
 As makes even tears seem full of light.
 Then guess, guess, who she,
 The lady of my love, may be.

WHEN LOVE, WHO RULED.

WHEN Love, who ruled as Admiral o'er
 His rosy mother's isles of light,
Was cruising off the Paphian shore,
 A sail at sunset hove in sight.
"A chase! a chase! my Cupids all!"
Said Love, the little Admiral.

Aloft the winged sailors sprung,
 And, swarming up the mast like bees,
The snow-white sails expanding flung,
 Like broad magnolias to the breeze.
"Yo ho, yo ho, my Cupids all!"
Said Love, the little Admiral.

The chase was o'er—the bark was caught,
 The winged crew her freight explored;
And found 't was just as Love had thought,
 For all was contraband aboard.
"A prize, a prize, my Cupids all!"
Said Love, the little Admiral.

Safe stow'd in many a package there,
 And labell'd slyly o'er as "Glass,"
Were lots of all the illegal ware
 Love's Custom-House forbids to pass.
"O'erhaul, o'erhaul, my Cupids all!"
Said Love, the little Admiral.

False curls they found, of every hue,
 With rosy blushes ready made;
And teeth of ivory, good as new,
 For veterans in the smiling trade.
"Ho ho, ho ho, my Cupids all!"
Said Love, the little Admiral.

Mock sighs, too—kept in bags for use,
 Like breezes bought of Lapland seers—

Lay ready here to be let loose,
 When wanted, in young spinsters' ears.
"Ha ha, ha ha, my Cupids all!"
Said Love, the little Admiral.

False papers next on board were found,
 Sham invoices of flames and darts,
Professedly for Paphos bound,
 But meant for Hymen's golden marts.
"For shame, for shame, my Cupids all!"
Said Love, the little Admiral.

Nay, still to every fraud awake,
 Those pirates all Love's signals knew,
And hoisted oft his flag, to make
 Rich wards and heiresses *bring-to*. (1)
"A foe, a foe, my Cupids all!"
Said Love, the little Admiral.

"This must not be," the boy exclaims;
 "In vain I rule the Paphian seas,
If Love's and Beauty's sovereign names
 Are lent to cover frauds like these.
Prepare, prepare, my Cupids all!"
Said Love, the little Admiral.

Each Cupid stood with lighted match—
 A broadside struck the smuggling foe,
And swept the whole unhallow'd batch
 Of Falsehood to the depths below.
"Huzza, huzza! my Cupids all!"
Said Love, the little Admiral.

STILL THOU FLIEST.

STILL thou fliest, and still I woo thee,
 Lovely phantom—all in vain;
Restless ever, my thoughts pursue thee,
 Fleeting ever, thou mock'st their pain.
Such doom, of old, that youth betided,
 Who wooed, he thought, some angel's charms,
But found a cloud that from him glided—
 As thou dost from these out-stretch'd arms.

Scarce I 've said, "How fair thou shinest,"
 Ere thy light hath vanish'd by;
And 't is when thou look'st divinest
 Thou art still most sure to fly.
Even as the lightning, that, dividing
 The clouds of night, saith, "Look on me;"
Then flits again; its splendour hiding—
 Even such the glimpse I catch of thee.

THEN FIRST FROM LOVE.

THEN first from Love, in Nature's bowers,
 Did Painting learn her fairy skill,
And cull the hues of loveliest flowers,
 To picture woman lovelier still.
For vain was every radiant hue,
 Till passion lent a soul to art,

(1) "To *Bring-to*, to check the course of a ship." *Falconer*
37

And taught the painter, ere he drew,
To fix the model in his heart.

Thus smooth his toil awhile went on,
Till, lo, one touch his art defies ;
The brow, the lip, the blushes shone,
But who could dare to paint those eyes?
'T was all in vain the painter strove;
So turning to that boy divine,
"Here take," he said, " the pencil, Love:
No hand should paint such eyes, but thine."

HUSH, SWEET LUTE.

HUSH, sweet Lute, thy songs remind me
Of past joys, now turn'd to pain;
Of ties that long have ceased to bind me,
But whose burning marks remain.
In each tone, some echo falleth
On my ear of joys gone by;
Every note some dream recalleth
Of bright hopes but born to die.

Yet, sweet Lute, though pain it bring me,
Once more let thy numbers thrill ;
Though death were in the strain they sing me,
I must woo its anguish still.
Since no time can e'er recover
Love's sweet light when once 't is set,
Better to weep such pleasures over,
Than smile o'er any left us yet.

BRIGHT MOON.

BRIGHT moon, that high in heaven art shining,
All smiles, as if within thy bower to-night
Thy own Endymion lay reclining,
And thou wouldst wake him with a kiss of light!—
By all the bliss thy beam discovers,
By all those visions far too bright for day,
Which dreaming bards and waking lovers
Behold, this night, beneath thy lingering ray—

I pray thee, queen of that bright heaven,
Quench not to-night thy love-lamp in the sea,
Till Anthe, in this bower, hath given
Beneath thy beam, her long-vow'd kiss to me.
Guide hither, guide her steps benighted,
Ere thou, sweet moon, thy bashful crescent hide;
Let Love but in this bower be lighted,
Then shroud in darkness all the world beside.

LONG YEARS HAVE PASS'D.

LONG years have pass'd, old friend, since we
First met in life's young day;
And friends, long loved by thee and me,
Since then have dropp'd away.
But enough remain to cheer us on,
And sweeten, when thus we're met,
The glass we fill to the many gone,
And the few who're left us yet.

Our locks, old friend, now thinly grow,
And some hang white and chill;
While some, like flowers 'mid Autumn's snow,
Retain youth's colour still.
And so, in our hearts, though one by one,
Youth's sunny hopes have set,
Thank heaven, not all their light is gone—
We 've some to cheer us yet.

Then here's to thee, old friend, and long
May thou and I thus meet,
To brighten still with wine and song
This short life, ere it fleet.
And still as death comes stealing on,
Let 's never, old friend, forget,
Even while we sigh o'er blessings gone,
How many are left us yet.

DREAMING FOR EVER.

DREAMING for ever, vainly dreaming,
Life to the last pursues its flight;
Day hath its visions fairly beaming,
But false as those of night.
The one illusion, the other real,
But both the same brief dreams at last ;
And when we grasp the bliss ideal,
Soon as it shines, 'tis past.

Here, then, by this dim lake reposing,
Calmly I'll watch, while light and gloom
Flit o'er its face till night is closing—
Emblem of life's short doom!
But though, by turns, thus dark and shining,
'T is still unlike man's changeful day,
Whose light returns not, once declining—
Whose cloud, once come, will stay.

THE RUSSIAN LOVER.

FLEETLY o'er the moonlight snows
Speed we to my lady's bower ;
Swift our sledge as lightning goes,
Nor shall stop till morning's hour.
Bright, my steed, the northern star
Lights us from yon jewell'd skies ;
But, to greet us, brighter far,
Morn shall bring my lady's eyes.

Lovers, lull'd in sunny bowers,
Sleeping out their dream of time,
Know not half the bliss that's ours,
In this snowy, icy clime.
Like yon star that livelier gleams
From the frosty heavens around,
Love himself the keener beams
When with snows of coyness crown'd.

Fleet then on, my merry steed,
Bound, my sledge, o'er hill and dale;—
What can match a lover's speed?
See, 'tis daylight, breaking pale !

Brightly hath the northern star
Lit us from yon radiant skies ;
But, behold, how brighter far
Yonder shine my lady's eyes!

———❦———

THOUGH LIGHTLY SOUNDS THE SONG
I SING.

A SONG OF THE ALPS.

Though lightly sounds the song I sing to thee,
Though like the lark's its soaring music be,
Thou'lt find even here some mournful note that tells
How near such April joy to weeping dwells.

'T is 'mong the gayest scenes that oftenest steal
Those saddening thoughts we fear, yet love to feel ;
And music never half so sweet appears
As when her mirth forgets itself in tears.

Then say not thou this Alpine song is gay—
It comes from hearts that, like their mountain-lay,
Mix joy with pain, and oft when pleasure's breath
Most warms the surface, feel most sad beneath.
The very beam in which the snow-wreath wears
Its gayest smile is that which wins its tears ;
And passion's power can never lend the glow
Which wakens bliss, without some touch of woe.

SONGS FROM THE GREEK ANTHOLOGY.

HERE AT THY TOMB. (1)
BY MELEAGER.

Here, at thy tomb, those tears I shed,
 Tears, which though vainly now they roll,
Are all love hath to give the dead,
 And wept o'er thee with all love's soul ;—

Wept in remembrance of that light
 Which nought on earth, without thee, gives,
Hope of my heart! now quench'd in night,
 But dearer, dead, than aught that lives.

Where is she ? where the blooming bough
 That once my life's sole lustre made?
Torn off by death, 't is withering now,
 And all its flowers in dust are laid.

Oh, earth! that to thy matron breast
 Hast taken all those angel charms,
Gently, I pray thee, let her rest,—
 Gently, as in a mother's arms.

———❦———

SALE OF CUPID. (2)
BY MELEAGER.

Who'll buy a little boy? Look, yonder is he,
Fast asleep, sly rogue, on his mother's knee ;
So bold a young imp 't is n't safe to keep,
So I'll part with him now, while he's sound asleep.
See his arch little nose, how sharp 't is curl'd,
His wings, too, even in sleep unfurl'd ;
And those fingers, which still ever ready are found
For mirth or for mischief, to tickle or wound.

He'll try with his tears your heart to beguile,
But never you mind—he's laughing all the while ;
For little he cares, so he has his own whim,
And weeping or laughing are all one to him.

His eye is as keen as the lightning's flash,
His tongue like the red bolt quick and rash,
And so savage is he, that his own dear mother
Is scarce more safe in his hands than another.

In short, to sum up this darling's praise,
He's a downright pest in all sorts of ways ;
And if any one wants such an imp to employ,
He shall have a dead bargain of this little boy.
But see, the boy wakes—his bright tears flow—
His eyes seem to ask could I sell him ? oh no,
Sweet child no, no—though so naughty you be,
You shall live evermore with my Lesbia and me.

———❦———

TO WEAVE A GARLAND FOR THE ROSE. (3)
BY PAUL, THE SILENTIARY.

To weave a garland for the rose,
 And think thus crown'd 't would lovelier be,
Were far less vain than to suppose
 That silks and gems add grace to thee.
Where is the pearl whose orient lustre
 Would not, beside thee, look less bright ?
What gold could match the glossy cluster
 Of those young ringlets full of light?

Bring from the land, where fresh it gleams,
 The bright blue gem of India's mine,
And see how soon, though bright its beams,
 'T will pale before one glance of thine ;
Those lips, too, when their sounds have blest us
 With some divine, mellifluous air,
Who would not say that Beauty's cestus
 Had let loose all its witcheries there ? (4)

Here, to this conquering host of charms,
 I now give up my spell-bound heart,
Nor blush to yield even Reason's arms,
 When thou her bright-eyed conqueror art.

---

(1) Δακρυα σοι και νερθε δια χθονος, Ηλιοδωρα.
                                        Ap. Brunck.
(2) Πωλεισθω, και ματρος ετ' εν κολποισι καθευδων.
                          Ap. Brunck., Analect. xcv.

(3) Ουτε ῥαδων στεφανων επιδευεσαι, ουτε συ πεπλων.
                                    Ap. Brunck., xvii.
(4) ——και ἡ μελιφυρτος εκεινη
     Ηθεος ἁρμονιη, κεστος ερυ Παφιης.

Thus to the wind all fears are given;
Henceforth those eyes alone I see,
Where Hope, as in her own blue heaven,
Sits beckoning me to bliss and thee!

—◦❀◦—

WHY DOES SHE SO LONG DELAY?(1)
BY PAUL, THE SILENTIARY.

WHY does she so long delay?
Night is waning fast away;
Thrice have I my lamp renew'd,
Watching here in solitude.
Where can she so long delay?
    Where, so long delay?

Vainly now have two lamps shone;
See the third is nearly gone: (2)
Oh that Love would, like the ray
Of that weary lamp, decay!
But no, alas, it burns still on,
    Still, still, burns on.

Gods, how oft the traitress dear
Swore, by Venus, she 'd be here!
But to one so false as she
What is man or deity?
Neither doth this proud one fear—
    No, neither doth she fear.

—◦❀◦—

TWINEST THOU WITH LOFTY WREATH THY BROW? (3)
BY PAUL, THE SILENTIARY.

TWINEST thou with lofty wreath thy brow?
Such glory then thy beauty sheds,
I almost think, while awed I bow,
'T is Rhea's self before me treads.
Be what thou wilt—this heart
Adores whate'er thou art!

Dost thou thy loosen'd ringlets leave,
Like sunny waves, to wander free?
Then, such a chain of charms they weave
As draws my inmost soul from me.
Do what thou wilt—I must
Be charm'd by all thou dost!

Even when, enwrapp'd in silvery veils,(4)
Those sunny locks elude the sight—
Oh, not even then their glory fails
To haunt me with its unseen light.
Change as thy beauty may,
It charms in every way.

(1) Δηθυνει Κλεοφαντις.—Ap. Brunck., xxviii.
(2)   ὁ δε τριτος αρχεται ηδε
        Λυχνος ὑποκλαξειν.
(3)   Κεκρυφαλοι σφιγγουσι τεην τριχα;
                    Ap. Brunck., xxxiv.
(4) Αργενναις οθονηισι κατηορα βοστρυχα κευθεις.

For thee the Graces still attend,
Presiding o'er each new attire,
And lending every dart they send
Some new peculiar touch of fire.
Be what thou wilt—this heart
Adores whate'er thou art!

—◦❀◦—

WHEN THE SAD WORD. (5)
BY PAUL, THE SILENTIARY.

WHEN the sad word, "Adieu," from my lip is nigh falling,
And with it Hope passes away,
Ere the tongue hath half breathed it, my fond heart, recalling
That fatal farewell, bids me stay.
For oh !'t is a penance so weary
One hour from thy presence to be,
That death to this soul were less dreary,
    Less dark, than long absence from thee.

Thy beauty, like Day, o'er the dull world breaking,
Brings life to the heart it shines o'er,
And, in mine, a new feeling of happiness waking,
Made light what was darkness before.
But mute is the Day's sunny glory,
While thine hath a voice, (6) on whose breath,
More sweet than the Syren's sweet story, (7)
My hopes hang, through life and through death!

—◦❀◦—

MY MOPSA IS LITTLE. (8)
BY PHILODEMUS.

MY Mopsa is little, my Mopsa is brown,
But her cheek is as smooth as the peach's soft down,
And, for blushing, no rose can come near her;
In short, she has woven such nets round my heart,
That I ne'er from my dear little Mopsa can part—
    Unless I can find one that 's dearer.

Her voice hath a music that dwells on the ear,
And her eye from its orb gives a daylight so clear,
That I 'm dazzled whenever I meet her;
Her ringlets, so curly, are Cupid's own net,
And her lips, oh their sweetness I ne'er shall forget—
    Till I light upon lips that are sweeter.

But 't is not her beauty that charms me alone,
'T is her mind, 't is that language whose eloquent tone
From the depths of the grave could revive one:
In short, here I swear, that if death were her doom,
I would instantly join my dead love in the tomb—
    Unless I could meet with a live one.

(5) Σωζεο σοι μελλων ενεπειν.—Ap. Brunck., xxxix.
(6) Ηματι γαρ σεο φεγγος ομοιον. αλλα το μεν που
        Αφθογγον.
(7)   Συ δ'εμοι και το λαδημα φερεις
        Κεινο, το Σειρηνων γλυκυερωτερον.
(8) Μικκη και μελανευσα Φιλιννιον.—Ap. Brunck., x.

STILL, LIKE DEW IN SILENCE FALLING. (1)

BY MELEAGER.

STILL, like dew in silence falling,
　Drops for thee the nightly tear;
Still that voice, the past recalling,
　Dwells, like echo, on my ear,
　　Still, still!

Day and night the spell hangs o'er me,
　Here for ever fix'd thou art;
As thy form first shone before me,
　So 't is graven on this heart,
　　Deep, deep!

Love, oh Love, whose bitter sweetness,
　Dooms me to this lasting pain,
Thou who camest with so much fleetness,
　Why so slow to go again? (2)
　　Why? why?

—o o o—

UP, SAILOR BOY, 'T IS DAY!

UP, sailor boy, 'tis day!
　The west wind blowing,
　The spring-tide flowing,
Summon thee hence away.
Didst thou not hear yon soaring swallow sing?
Chirp, chirp—in every note he seem'd to say
'T is Spring, 't is Spring.
Up, boy, away—
Who 'd stay on land to-day?
　The very flowers
　Would from their bowers
Delight to wing away!

Leave languid youths to pine
　On silken pillows;
　But be the billows
Of the great deep thine.
Hark, to the sail the breeze sings, "Let us fly;"
While soft the sail, replying to the breeze,
Says, with a yielding sigh,
" Yes, where you please."
Up, boy! the wind, the ray,
　The blue sky o'er thee,
　The deep before thee,
All cry aloud, "Away!"

—o o o—

IN MYRTLE WREATHS.

BY ALCÆUS.

IN myrtle wreaths my votive sword I 'll cover,
　Like them of old, whose one immortal blow
Struck off the galling fetters that hung over
　Their own bright land, and laid her tyrant low.
Yes, loved Harmodius, thou 'rt undying;
　Still 'midst the brave and free,
In isles, o'er ocean lying,
　Thy home shall ever be.

In myrtle leaves my sword shall hide its lightning,
　Like his, the youth, whose ever-glorious blade
Leap'd forth like flame, the midnight banquet
　　brightening,
　And in the dust a despot victim laid.
Blest youths, how bright in Freedom's story
　Your wedded names shall be;
A tyrant's death your glory,
　Your meed, a nation free!

EVENINGS IN GREECE.

TO MRS. ROBERT ARKWRIGHT,
THIS PRODUCTION IS, WITH THE WARMEST ADMIRATION
OF HER MUSICAL TALENTS, INSCRIBED, BY HER
VERY OBLIGED AND FAITHFUL SERVANT,
　　　　　THOMAS MOORE.

—o o o—

ADVERTISEMENT.

IN thus connecting together a series of Songs by
a thread of poetical narrative, my chief object has
been to combine Recitation with Music, so as to en-
able a greater number of persons to join in the per-
formance, by enlisting, as readers, those who may
not feel willing or competent to take a part, as singers.
　The Island of Zea, where the scene is laid, was
called by the ancients Ceos, and was the birth-place
of Simonides, Bacchylides, and other eminent per-
sons. An account of its present state may be found
in the *Travels* of Dr. Clarke, who says, that "it ap-
peared to him to be the best cultivated of any of the
Grecian Isles."—Vol. vi., p. 174.　　　T. M.

(1) Αιει μοι δυνει μεν εν ουασιν ηχος Ερωτος.
　　　　　Ap. Brunck., liii.

FIRST EVENING.

" THE sky is bright—the breeze is fair,
　And the mainsail flowing, full and free—
Our farewell word is woman's prayer,
　And the hope before us—Liberty!
　　Farewell, farewell.
To Greece we give our shining blades,
And our hearts to you, young Zean Maids!

" The moon is in the heavens above,
　And the wind is on the foaming sea—
Thus shines the star of woman's love
　On the glorious strife of Liberty!
　　Farewell, farewell.
To Greece we give our shining blades,
And our hearts to you, young Zean Maids!"

Thus sung they from the bark, that now
Turn'd to the sea its gallant prow,

(2) Ω πτανοι, μη και ποτ' εφιπτασθαι μεν, Ερωτες,
　Οιδατ', αποπτηναι δ' ουδ ὁσον ισχυετε.

Bearing within it hearts as brave,
As e'er sought Freedom o'er the wave;
And leaving on that islet's shore,
  Where still the farewell beacons burn,
Friends, that shall many a day look o'er
  The long dim sea for their return.

Virgin of Heaven! speed their way—
  Oh, speed their way—the chosen flower
Of Zea's youth, the hope and stay
  Of parents in their wintry hour,
The love of maidens, and the pride
Of the young, happy, blushing bride,
Whose nuptial wreath has not yet died—
All, all are in that precious bark,
  Which now, alas, no more is seen—
Though every eye still turns to mark
  The moonlight spot where it had been.

Vainly you look, ye maidens, sires,
  And mothers—your beloved are gone!—
Now may you quench those signal fires,
  Whose light they long look'd back upon
From their dark deck—watching the flame
As fast it faded from their view,
With thoughts that, but for manly shame,
  Had made them droop and weep like you.
Home to your chambers! home, and pray
For the bright coming of that day,
When, blessed by heaven, the cross shall sweep
  The Crescent from the Ægean deep;
And your brave warriors, hastening back,
Will bring such glories in their track,
As shall, for many an age to come,
Shed light around their name and home.

There is a Fount on Zea's isle,
Round which, in soft luxuriance, smile
All the sweet flowers, of every kind,
  On which the sun of Greece looks down,
Pleased as a lover on the crown
His mistress for her brow hath twined,
When he beholds each floweret there
Himself had wish'd her most to wear.
Here bloom'd the laurel-rose, (1) whose wreath
Hangs radiant round the Cypriot shrines,
And here those bramble-flowers, that breathe
  Their odour into Zante's wines: (2)
The splendid woodbine, that, at eve,
  To grace their floral diadems,
The lovely maids of Patmos weave:—(3)
And that fair plant, whose tangled stems

Shine like a Nereid's hair; (4) when spread
Dishevell'd, o'er her azure bed;—
All these bright children of the clime,
(Each at its own most genial time,
The Summer, or the year's sweet prime,)
Like beautiful earth-stars, adorn
The Valley where that Fount is born:
While round, to grace its cradle green,
Groups of Velani oaks are seen,
Towering on every verdant height—
Tall, shadowy, in the evening light,
Like genii, set to watch the birth
Of some enchanted child of earth—
Fair oaks, that over Zea's vales,
  Stand with their leafy pride unfurl'd;
While Commerce, from her thousand sails,
  Scatters their fruit throughout the world! (5)

'T was here—as soon as prayer and sleep
(Those truest friends to all who weep)
Had lighten'd every heart, and made
Even sorrow wear a softer shade—
'T was here, in this secluded spot,
  Amid whose breathings calm and sweet
Grief might be soothed, if not forgot,
  The Zean nymphs resolved to meet
ᵉach evening now, by the same light
That saw their farewell tears that night;
And try, if sound of lute and song,
  If wandering 'mid the moonlight flowers
In various talk, could charm along
  With lighter step, the lingering hours,
Till tidings of that bark should come,
Or Victory waft their warriors home!

When first they met—the wonted smile
Of greeting having gleam'd awhile—
'T would touch even Moslem heart to see
The sadness that came suddenly
O'er their young brows, when they look'd round
Upon that bright enchanted ground;
And thought, how many a time, with those
Who now were gone to the rude wars,
They there had met, at evening's close,
  And danced till morn outshone the stars!

But seldom long doth hang the eclipse
  Of sorrow o'er such youthful breasts—
The breath from her own blushing lips,
  That on the maiden's mirror rests,
Not swifter, lighter from the glass,
Than sadness from her brow doth pass.

---

(1) "Nerium Oleander. In Cyprus it retains its ancient
name, Rhodadaphne, and the Cypriots adorn their churches
with the flowers on feast-days."—*Journal of Dr. Sibthorpe,
Walpole's Turkey.*   (2) *Id.*

(3) Lonicera Caprifolium, used by the girls of Patmos
for garlands.

(4) Cuscuta Europæa. "From the twisting and twining
of the stems, it is compared by the Greeks to the dishevel-
led hair of the Nereids."—*Walpole's Turkey*

(5) "The produce of the island in these acorns alone
amounts annually to 15,000 quintals."—*Clarke's Travels.*

Soon did they now, as round the Well
  They sat, beneath the rising moon—
And some, with voice of awe, would tell
Of midnight fays, and nymphs who dwell
  In holy founts—while some would tune
Their idle lutes, that now had lain,
For days, without a single strain ;—
And others, from the rest apart,
With laugh that told the lighten'd heart,
Sat, whispering in each other's ear,
Secrets, that all in turn would hear ;—
Soon did they find this thoughtless play
So swiftly steal their griefs away,
  That many a nymph, though pleased the while,
  Reproach'd her own forgetful smile,
And sigh'd to think she *could* be gay.

Among these maidens there was one,
Who to Leucadia (1) late had been—
Had stood, beneath the evening sun,
  On its white towering cliffs, and seen
The very spot were Sappho sung
Her swan-like music, ere she sprung
(Still holding, in that fearful leap,
  By her loved lyre,) Into the deep,
And dying quench'd the fatal fire,
At once, of both her heart and lyre.

Mutely they listen'd all—and well
Did the young travell'd maiden tell
Of the dread height to which that steep
  Beetles above the eddying deep—(2)
Of the lone sea-birds, wheeling round
The dizzy edge with mournful sound—
And of those scented lilies (3) found
  Still blooming on that fearful place—(4)
As if call'd up by Love, to grace
The immortal spot, o'er which the last
Bright footsteps of his martyr pass'd !

While fresh to every listener's thought
These legends of Leucadia brought
All that of Sappho's hapless flame
Is kept alive, still watch'd by Fame—
The maiden, tuning her soft lute,
While all the rest stood round her, mute,
Thus sketch'd the languishment of soul,
That o'er the tender Lesbian stole ;
And, in a voice, whose thrilling tone
Fancy might deem the Lesbian's own,
One of those fervid fragments gave,
  Which still—like sparkles of Greek Fire,

(1) Now Santa Maura, whence Sappho leaped into the sea.

(2) The precipice, which is fearfully dizzy, is about one
hundred and fourteen feet from the water, which is of a
profound depth, as appears from the dark blue colour and
the eddy that plays round the pointed and projecting
rocks."—*Goodisson's Ionian Isles.*

(3) For details connected with the subject of these
lines, see Mr. Goodisson's very interesting description of
all the circumstances.

Undying, even beneath the wave,—
Burn on through Time, and ne'er expire.

SONG.

As o'er her loom the Lesbian Maid
  In love-sick languor hung her head,
Unknowing where her fingers stray'd,
  She weeping turn'd away, and said,
"Oh, my sweet Mother—'tis in vain—
  I cannot weave, as once I wove—
So wilder'd is my heart and brain
  With thinking of that youth I love !" (5)

Again the web she tried to trace,
  But tears fell o'er each tangled thread ;
While, looking in her mother's face,
  Who watchful o'er her lean'd, she said,
"Oh, my sweet Mother—'tis in vain—
  I cannot weave, as once I wove—
So wilder'd is my heart and brain
  With thinking of that youth I love !"

A silence follow'd this sweet air,
  As each in tender musing stood,
Thinking, with lips that moved in prayer,
  Of Sappho and that fearful flood:
While some, who ne'er till now had known
  How much their hearts resembled hers,
Felt as they made her griefs their own,
  That *they*, too, were Love's worshippers.

At length a murmur, all but mute,
So faint it was, came from the lute
Of a young melancholy maid,
Whose fingers all uncertain play'd
From chord to chord, as if in chase
  Of some lost melody, some strain
Of other times, whose faded trace
  She sought among those chords again.
Slowly the half-forgotten theme
(Though born in feelings ne'er forgot)
Came to her memory—as a beam
  Falls broken o'er some shaded spot ;—
And while her lute's sad symphony
Fill'd up each sighing pause between ;
And Love himself might weep to see
  What ruin comes where he hath been—
As wither'd still the grass is found
Where fays have danced their merry round—
Thus simply to the listening throng
She breathed her melancholy song :—

(4) This and the preceding line originally read—
  And of those scented lilies (some
    Of whose white flowers, the Zean said,
  Herself had gather'd and brought home,
    In memory of the minstrel maid),
  Still blooming, etc.—P. E.

(5) I have attempted, to give some idea of that beauti-
ful fragment of Sappho, beginning Γλυκεῖα μᾶτερ, which
represents so truly (as Warton remarks) "the languor
and listlessness of a person deeply in love."

SONG.

Weeping for thee, my love, through the long day,
Lonely and wearily life wears away.
Weeping for thee, my love, through the long night—
No rest in darkness, no joy in light!
Nought left but Memory, whose dreary tread
Sounds through this ruin'd heart, where all lies
    dead—
Wakening the echoes of joy long fled!

    Of many a stanza, this alone
    Had 'scaped oblivion—like the one
    Stray fragment of a wreck, which thrown,
    With the lost vessel's name, ashore,
    Tells who they were that live no more.
      When thus the heart is in a vein
    Of tender thought, the simplest strain
    Can touch it with peculiar power—
      As when the air is warm, the scent
    Of the most wild and rustic flower
      Can fill the whole rich element—
    And, in such moods, the homeliest tone
    That 's link'd with feelings, once our own—
    With friends or joys gone by—will be
    Worth choirs of loftiest harmony!

But some there were, among the group
    Of damsels there, too light of heart
To let their spirits longer droop,
    Even under music's melting art;
And one, upspringing with a bound,
From a low bank of flowers, look'd round
With eyes that, though so full of light,
Had still a trembling tear within;
And, while her fingers, in swift flight,
Flew o'er a fairy mandolin,
Thus sung the song her lover late
Had sung to her—the eve before
That joyous night, when, as of yore,
All Zea met, to celebrate
The Feast of May, on the sea-shore.

        SONG.

    When the Balaika (1)
      Is heard o'er the sea,
    I 'll dance the Romaika
      By moonlight with thee.
    If waves then, advancing,
      Should steal on our play,
    Thy white feet in dancing,
      Shall chase them away. (2)

(1) This word is defrauded here, I suspect, of a syllable; Dr. Clarke, if I recollect right, makes it "Balalaika."

(2) "I saw above thirty parties engaged in dancing the Romaika upon the sand; in some of those groups, the girl who led them chased the retreating wave."—*Douglas on the Modern Greeks.*

(3) "In dancing the Romaika (says Mr. Douglas) they begin in slow and solemn step till they have gained the

    When the Balaika
      Is heard o'er the sea,
    Thou 'lt dance the Romaika,
      My own love, with me.

    Then, at the closing
      Of each merry lay,
    How sweet 't is reposing,
      Beneath the night ray!
    Or if, declining,
      The moon leave the skies,
    We 'll talk by the shining
      Of each other's eyes.

    Oh then, how featly
      The dance we'll renew,
    Treading so fleetly
      Its light mazes through: (3)
    Till stars looking o'er us
      From heaven's high bowers,
    Would change their bright chorus
      For one dance of ours!
    When the Balaika
      Is heard o'er the sea,
    Thou 'lt dance the Romaika,
      My own love, with me.

How changingly for ever veers
The heart of youth, 'twixt smiles and tears!
Even as in April, the light vane
Now points to sunshine, now to rain.
Instant this lively lay dispell'd
    The shadow from each blooming brow,
    And Dancing, joyous Dancing, held
    Full empire o'er each fancy now.

But say—*what* shall the measure be?
    " Shall we the old Romaika tread,
(Some eager ask'd) " as anciently
    'T was by the maids of Delos led,
When, slow at first, then circling fast,
As the gay spirits rose—at last,
With hand in hand, like links, enlock'd,
    Through the light air they seem'd to flit
In labyrinthine maze, that mock'd
    The dazzled eye that follow'd it?"
Some call'd aloud "the Fountain Dance!"—
    While one young dark-eyed Amazon,
Whose step was air-like, and whose glance
    Flash'd, like a sabre in the sun,
Sportively said, " Shame on these soft
And languid strains we hear so oft,

time, but by degrees the air becomes more sprightly ; the conductress of the dance sometimes setting to her partner, sometimes darting before the rest, and leading them through the most rapid evolutions; sometimes crossing under the hands, which are held up to let her pass, and giving as much liveliness and intricacy as she can to the figures, into which she conducts her companions, while their business is to follow her in all her movements, without breaking the chain, or losing the measure."

Daughters of Freedom! have not we
    Learn'd from our lovers and our sires
The dance of Greece, while Greece was free—
    That Dance, where neither flutes nor lyres,
But sword and shield clash on the ear
A music tyrants quake to hear? (1)
Heroïnes of Zea, arm with me,
And dance the dance of Victory!"

Thus saying, she, with playful grace,
    Loosed the wide hat, that o'er her face
(From Anatolia (2) came the maid)
    Hung, shadowing each sunny charm;
And, with a fair young armourer's aid,
    Fixing it on her rounded arm,
A mimic shield with pride display'd;
    Then, springing towards a grove that spread
    Its canopy of foliage near,
Pluck'd off a lance–like twig, and said,
    "To arms, to arms!" while o'er her head
She waved the light branch as a spear.

Promptly the laughing maidens all
Obey'd their Chief's heroic call;—
    Round the shield-arm of each was tied
    Hat, turban, shawl, as chance might be;
    The grove, their verdant armoury,
Falchion and lance (3) alike supplied;
    And as their glossy locks, let free,
    Fell down their shoulders carelessly,
You might have dreamed you saw a throng
    Of youthful Thyads, by the beam
Of a May moon, bounding along
    Peneus' silver-eddied (4) stream!

And now they stepp'd, with measured tread,
    Martially, o'er the shining field;
Now, to the mimic combat led
    (A heroine at each squadron's head),
    Struck lance to lance and sword to shield:
While still, through every varying feat,
    Their voices, heard in contrast sweet
With some, of deep but soften'd sound,
    From lips of aged sires around,
Who smiling watch'd their children's play—
Thus sung the ancient Pyrrhic lay:—

SONG.
"Raise the buckler—poise the lance—
Now here—now there—retreat—advance!"

Such were the sounds, to which the warrior boy
    Danced in those happy days, when Greece was free;
When Sparta's youth, even in the hour of joy,
    Thus train'd their steps to war and victory.

(1) For a description of the Pyrrhic Dance see De
Guys, etc.—It appears from Apuleius (lib. x.) that this
war-dance was, among the ancients, sometimes performed
by females.
(2) See the *costume* of the Greek women of Natolia in
Castellan's Mœurs des Ottomans.

"Raise the buckler—poise the lance—
Now here—now there—retreat—advance!"
Such was the Spartan warriors' dance.

"Grasp the falchion—gird the shield—
Attack—defend—do all but yield."

Thus did thy sons, oh Greece, one glorious night,
    Dance by a moon like this, till o'er the sea
That morning dawn'd by whose immortal light
    They nobly died for thee and liberty!(5)
"Raise the buckler—poise the lance—
Now here—now there—retreat—advance!"
Such was the Spartan heroes' dance.

———

Scarce had they closed this martial lay
    When, flinging their light spears away,
The combatants, in broken ranks, .
    All breathless from the war-field fly;
And down, upon the velvet banks
    And flowery slopes, exhausted lie,
Like rosy huntresses of Thrace,
Resting at sunset from the chase.

"Fond girls!" an aged Zean said—
One who, himself, had fought and bled,
And now, with feelings, half delight,
Half sadness, watch'd their mimic fight—
"Fond maids! who thus with War can jest—
Like Love, in Mars's helmet drest,
When, in his childish innocence,
    Pleased with the shade that helmet flings,
He thinks not of the blood that thence
    Is dropping o'er his snowy wings.
Ay—true it is, young patriot maids,
    If Honour's arm still won the fray,
If luck but shone on righteous blades,
    War were a game for gods to play!
But, no, alas!—hear one, who well
    Hath track'd the fortunes of the brave—
Hear *me*, in mournful ditty, tell
    What glory waits the patriot's grave:"—

SONG.
As by the shore, at break of day,
A vanquish'd Chief expiring lay,
Upon the sands, with broken sword,
    He traced his farewell to the Free;
And, there, the last unfinish'd word
    He dying wrote was "Liberty!"

At night a Sea-bird shriek'd the knell
Of him who thus for Freedom fell;
The words he wrote, ere evening came,
    Were cover'd by the sounding sea;—

(3) The sword was the weapon chiefly used in this
dance.
(4) Homer, *Iliad*, 2, 753.
(5) It is said that Leonidas and his companions employed
themselves, on the eve of the battle, in music and the
gymnastic exercises of their country.

38

So pass away the cause and name
  Of him who dies for Liberty!

That tribute of subdued applause
A charm'd, but timid, audience pays,
That murmur, which a minstrel draws
From hearts that feel, but fear to praise,
Follow'd this song, and left a pause
Of silence after it, that hung
Like a fix'd spell on every tongue.
  At length, a low and tremulous sound
Was heard from midst a group, that round
A bashful maiden stood, to hide
Her blushes, while the lute she tried—
Like roses, gathering round to veil
The song of some young nightingale,
Whose trembling notes steal out between
The cluster'd leaves, herself unseen.
And, while that voice, in tones that more
  Through feeling than through weakness err'd,
Came, with a stronger sweetness, o'er
  The attentive ear, this strain was heard :—

SONG.

I saw, from yonder silent cave, (1)
  Two Fountains running, side by side,
The one was Memory's limpid wave,
  The other cold Oblivion's tide.
" Oh Love!" said I, in thoughtless mood,
  As deep I drank of Lethe's stream,
" Be all my sorrows in this flood
  Forgotten like a vanish'd dream!" (2)

But who could bear that gloomy blank,
  Where joy was lost as well as pain?
Quickly of Memory's fount I drank,
  And brought the past all back again
And said, " Oh Love! whate'er my lot,
  Still let this soul to thee be true—
Rather than have one bliss forgot,
  Be all my pains remember'd too!"

The group that stood around, to shade
  The blushes of that bashful maid,
Had, by degrees, as came the lay
More strongly forth, retired away,
Like a fair shell, whose valves divide,
To show the fairer pearl inside :
For such she was—a creature, bright
  And delicate as those day-flowers,
Which, while they last, make up, in light
  And sweetness, what they want in hours.

So rich upon the ear had grown
  Her voice's melody—its tone

(1) "This morning we paid our visit to the Cave of Tro-
phonius, and the Fountains of Memory and Oblivion, just
upon the water of Hercyna, which flows through stupen-
dous rocks."—*Williams's Travels in Greece.*

(2) Originally written—

  " Oh, Love!" said I, in thoughtless dream,
    As o'er my lips the Lethe pass'd,

Gathering new courage, as it found
An echo in each bosom round—
That, ere the nymph, with downcast eye
Still on the chords, her lute laid by,
" Another song," all lips exclaim'd,
And each some matchless favourite named;
While blushing, as her fingers ran
O'er the sweet chords, she thus began :—

SONG.

Oh, Memory, how coldly
  Thou paintest joy gone by :
Like rainbows, thy pictures
  But mournfully shine and die.
Or, if some tints thou keepest,
  That former days recall,
As o'er each line thou weepest,
  Thy tears efface them all.

But, Memory, too truly
  Thou paintest grief that's past;
Joy's colours are fleeting,
  But those of Sorrow last.
And, while thou bring'st before us
  Dark pictures of past ill,
Life's evening, closing o'er us,
  But makes them darker still.

So went the moonlight hours along,
In this sweet glade ; and so, with song
And witching sounds—not such as they,
  The cymbalists of Ossa, play'd,
To chase the moon's eclipse away, (3)
  But soft and holy—did each maid
Lighten her heart's eclipse awhile,
And win back Sorrow to a smile.

Not far from this secluded place,
  On the sea-shore a ruin stood ;—
A relic of the extinguish'd race,
  Who once look'd o'er that foamy flood,
When fair Ioulis, (4) by the light
Of golden sunset, on the sight
Of mariners who sail'd that sea,
Rose, like a city of chrysolite,
  Call'd from the wave by witchery.
This ruin—now by barbarous hands
Debased into a motley shed,
Where the once splendid column stands
Inverted on its leafy head—
Form'd, as they tell, in times of old,
  The dwelling of that bard, whose lay
Could melt to tears the stern and cold,
  And sadden, 'mid their mirth, the gay—

  " Here, in this dark and chilly stream,
    Be all my pains forgot at last."—P. E.

(3) This superstitious custom of the Thessalians exists
also, as Pietro della Valle tells us, among the Persians.

(4) Ancient city of Zea, the walls of which were of marble.
Its remains (says Clarke) "extend from the shore, quite
into a valley watered by the streams of a fountain, whence
Ioulis received its name."

Simonides, (1) whose fame through years,
    And ages past, still bright appears—
Like Hesperus, a star of tears!

'T was hither now—to catch a view
    Of the white waters, as they play'd
Silently in the light—a few
    Of the more restless damsels stray'd;
And some would linger 'mid the scent
    Of hanging foliage, that perfumed
The ruin'd walls; while others went,
    Culling whatever floweret bloom'd
In the lone leafy space between,
    Where gilded chambers once had been,
Or, turning sadly to the sea,
    Sent o'er the wave a sigh unblest
To some brave champion of the Free—
    Thinking, alas, how cold might be,
        At that still hour, his place of rest!

Meanwhile there came a sound of song
    From the dark ruins—a faint strain,
As if some echo, that among
Those minstrel halls had slumber'd long,
    Were murmuring into life again.

But, no—the nymphs knew well the tone—
    A maiden of their train, who loved,
Like the night-bird, to sing alone,
    Had deep into those ruins roved,
And there, all other thoughts forgot,
    Was warbling o'er, in lone delight,
A lay that, on that very spot,
    Her lover sung one moonlight night:—

SONG.

Ah! where are they, who heard, in former hours,
The voice of song in these neglected bowers?
        They are gone—all gone!
The youth, who told his pain in such sweet tone,
That all, who heard him, wish'd his pain their own—
        He is gone—he is gone!
And she, who, while he sung, sat listening by,
And thought, to strains like these 't were sweet to
    die—
        She is gone—she too is gone!

'T is thus, in future hours, some bard will say
Of her, who hears, and him, who sings this lay—
        They are gone—they both are gone!

(1) **Zea** was the birth-place of this poet, whose verses
are by Catullus called "tears."
(2) These "Songs of the Well," as they were called among
the ancients, still exist in Greece. *De Guys* tells us that
he has seen "the young women in Prince's Island, as-
sembled in the evening at a public well, suddenly strike
up a dance, while others sung in concert to them."
(3) "The inhabitants of Syra, both ancient and modern,
may be considered as the worshippers of water. The old

The moon was now, from heaven's steep,
    Bending to dip her silvery urn
Into the bright and silent deep—
    And the young nymphs, on their return
From those romantic ruins, found
    Their other playmates, ranged around
The sacred Spring, prepared to tune
    Their parting hymn, (2) ere sunk the moon,
To that fair Fountain, by whose stream
    Their hearts had form'd so many a dream.

Who has not read the tales, that tell
    Of old Eleusis' sacred Well,
Or heard what legend-songs recount
    Of Syra, and its holy Fount, (3)
Gushing, at once, from the hard rock
    Into the laps of living flowers—
Where village maidens loved to flock,
    On summer-nights, and, like the Hours,
Link'd in harmonious dance and song,
    Charm'd the unconscious night along;
While holy pilgrims, on their way
    To Delos' isle, stood looking on,
Enchanted with a scene so gay,
    Nor sought their boats, till morning shone.

Such was the scene this lovely glade
And its fair inmates now display'd,
As round the Fount, in linked ring,
    They went, in cadence slow and light,
And thus to that enchanted Spring
    Warbled their Farewell for the night:—

SONG.

Here, while the moonlight dim
Falls on that mossy brim,
Sing we our Fountain Hymn,
    Maidens of Zea!
Nothing but Music's strain,
When Lovers part in pain,
Soothes, till they meet again,
    Oh, Maids of Zea!

Bright Fount, so clear and cold,
Round which the nymphs of old
Stood, with their locks of gold,
    Fountain of Zea!
Not even Castaly,
Famed though its streamlet be,
Murmurs or shines like thee,
    Oh, Fount of Zea!

fountain, at which the nymphs of the island assembled in
the earliest ages, exists in its original state; the same
rendezvous as it was formerly, whether of love and gal-
lantry, or of gossiping and tale-telling. It is near to the
town, and the most limpid water gushes continually from
the solid rock. It is regarded by the inhabitants with a
degree of religious veneration; and they preserve a tra-
dition, that the pilgrims of old time, in their way to Delos,
resorted hither for purification."—*Clarke.*

Thou, while our hymn we sing,
Thy silver voice shalt bring,
Answering, answering,
   Sweet Fount of Zea!
For of all rills that run,
Sparkling by moon or sun,
Thou art the fairest one,
   Bright Fount of Zea!

Now, by those stars that glance
Over heaven's still expanse,
Weave we our mirthful dance,
   Daughters of Zea!
Such as, in former days,
Danced they, by Dian's rays,
Where the Eurotas strays, (1)
   Oh, Maids of Zea!

But when to merry feet
Hearts with no echo beat,
Say, can the dance be sweet?
   Maidens of Zea!
No, nought but Music's strain,
When lovers part in pain,
Soothes, till they meet again,
   Oh, Maids of Zea!

—◦❀◦—

SECOND EVENING.

SONG.

When evening shades are falling
O'er Ocean's sunny sleep,
To pilgrims' hearts recalling
   Their home beyond the deep;
When, rest o'er all descending,
   The shores with gladness smile,
And lutes, their echoes blending,
Are heard from isle to isle,
Then, Mary, Star of the Sea (2)
We pray, we pray, to thee!

The noon-day tempest over,
   Now Ocean toils no more,
And wings of halcyons hover,
   Where all was strife before.
Oh thus may life, in closing
   Its short tempestuous day,
Beneath heaven's smile reposing,
   Shine all its storms away:
Thus, Mary, Star of the Sea,
We pray, we pray, to thee!

On Helle's sea the light grew dim,
As the last sounds of that sweet hymn
   Floated along its azure tide—
Floated in light, as if the lay
Had mix'd with sunset's fading ray,
   And light and song together died.

So soft through evening's air had breathed
That choir of youthful voices, wreathed
   In many-linked harmony,
That boats, then hurrying o'er the sea,
Paused, when they reach'd this fairy shore,
And linger'd till the strain was o'er.

Of those young maids who've met to fleet
In song and dance this evening's hours,
Far happier now the bosoms beat
   Than when they last adorn'd the bowers;
For tidings of glad sound had come,
   At break of day, from the far isles—
Tidings like breath of life to some—
That Zea's sons would soon wing home,
   Crown'd with the light of Victory's smiles,
To meet that brightest of all meeds
That wait on high heroic deeds,
When gentle eyes that scarce, for tears,
   Could trace the warrior's parting track,
Shall, like a misty morn that clears,
When the long-absent sun appears,
   Shine out, all bliss, to hail him back.

How fickle still the youthful breast!—
   More fond of change than a young moon,
No joy so new was e'er possest
   But Youth would leave for newer soon.
These Zean nymphs, though bright the spot,
   Where first they held their evening play,
As ever fell to fairy's lot
   To wanton o'er by midnight's ray,
Had now exchanged that shelter'd scene
For a wide glade beside the sea—
A lawn, whose soft expanse of green
Turn'd to the west sun smilingly,
As though, in conscious beauty bright,
It joy'd to give him light for light.

And ne'er did evening more serene
Look down from heaven on lovelier scene.
Calm lay the flood around, while fleet,
   O'er the blue shining element,
Light barks, as if with fairy feet
   That stirr'd not the hush'd waters, went;
Some that, ere rosy eve fell o'er
   The blushing wave, with mainsail free,
Had put forth from the Attic shore,
   Or the near Isle of Ebony;—
Some, Hydriot barks, that, deep in caves
   Beneath Colonna's pillar'd cliffs,
Had all day lurk'd, and o'er the waves
   Now shot their long and dart-like skiffs.
Woe to the craft, however fleet,
These sea-hawks in their course shall meet,
Laden with juice of Lesbian vines,
Or rich from Naxos' emery mines;
For not more sure, when owlets flee
O'er the dark crags of Pendelee,

---

(1) "Qualis in Eurotæ ripis, aut per juga Cynthi
Exercet Diana choros."—*Virgil.*

(2) One of the titles of the Virgin:—"Maria illuminatrix,
sive stella Maris."—*Isidor.*

Doth the night-falcon mark his prey,
Or pounce on it more fleet than they.

And what a moon now lights the glade
  Where these young island nymphs are met!
Full-orb'd, yet pure; as if no shade
  Had touch'd its virgin lustre yet;
And freshly bright, as if just made
  By Love's own hands, of new-born light
Stolen from his mother's star to-night.

On a bold rock, that o'er the flood
Jutted from that soft glade, there stood
A Chapel, fronting towards the sea—
Built in some by-gone century—
Where, nightly, as the seaman's mark,
When waves rose high or clouds were dark,
A lamp, bequeath'd by some kind Saint,
Shed o'er the wave its glimmer faint,
Waking in way-worn men a sigh
And prayer to heaven, as they went by.
'T was there, around that rock-built shrine,
  A group of maidens and their sires
Had stood to watch the day's decline,
  And, as the light fell o'er their lyres,
Sung to the Queen-Star of the Sea
That soft and holy melody.

But lighter thoughts and lighter song
Now woo the coming hours along.
For, mark, where smooth the herbage lies,
  Yon gay pavilion, curtain'd deep
With silken folds, through which bright eyes,
  From time to time, are seen to peep;
While twinkling lights that, to and fro,
Beneath those veils, like meteors, go,
Tell of some spells at work, and keep
Young fancies chain'd in mute suspense,
Watching what next may shine from thence.
Nor long the pause, ere hands unseen
  That mystic curtain backward drew,
And all, that late but shone between,
  In half-caught gleams, now burst to view.
A picture 't was of the early days
Of glorious Greece, ere yet those rays
Of rich immortal Mind were hers
That made mankind her worshippers;
While, yet unsung, her landscapes shone
With glory lent by heaven alone;
Nor temples crown'd her nameless hills,
Nor Muse immortalised her rills;
Nor aught but the mute poesy
Of sun, and stars, and shining sea
Illumed that land of bards to be.
While, prescient of the gifted race
  That yet would realm so blest adorn,
Nature took pains to deck the place
  Where glorious Art was to be born.

(1) "Violet-crowned Athens."—*Pindar.*
(2) The whole of this scene was suggested by Pliny's

Such was the scene that mimic stage
  Of Athens and her hills portray'd;
Athens in her first youthful age,
  Ere yet the simple violet braid, (1)
Which then adorn'd her, had shone down
The glory of earth's loftiest crown.
While yet undream'd, her seeds of Art
  Lay sleeping in the marble mine—
Sleeping till Genius bade them start
  To all but life, in shapes divine;
Till deified the quarry shone,
And all Olympus stood in stone!

There, in the foreground of that scene,
On a soft bank of living green,
Sate a young nymph, with her lap full
  Of newly gather'd flowers, o'er which
She graceful lean'd, intent to cull
  All that was there of hue most rich,
To form a wreath, such as the eye
Of her young lover, who stood by,
With pallet mingled fresh, might choose
To fix by Painting's rainbow hues.

The wreath was form'd; the maiden raised
  Her speaking eyes to his, while he—
Oh *not* upon the flowers now gazed—
  But on that bright look's witchery.
While quick as if but then the thought,
Like light, had reach'd his soul, he caught
His pencil up, and, warm and true
As life itself, that love-look drew:
And, as his raptured task went on,
And forth each kindling feature shone,
Sweet voices, through the moonlight air,
  From lips as moonlight fresh and pure,
Thus hail'd the bright dream passing there,
  And sung the Birth of Portraiture. (2)

SONG.

As once a Grecian maiden wove
  Her garland 'mid the summer bowers,
There stood a youth, with eyes of love,
  To watch her while she wreathed the flowers.
The youth was skill'd in Painting's art,
  But ne'er had studied woman's brow,
Nor knew what magic hues the heart
  Can shed o'er Nature's charms, till now.

CHORUS.

Blest be Love, to whom we owe
All that's fair and bright below.

His hand had pictured many a rose,
  And sketch'd the rays that light the brook;
But what were these, or what were those,
  To woman's blush, to woman's look?
"Oh, if such magic power there be,
  This, this," he cried, "is all my prayer,

account of the artist Pausias and his mistress Glycera,
Lib. 35, c. 40.

To paint that living light I see,
And fix the soul that sparkles there.

His prayer, as soon as breathed, was heard;
His pallet, touch'd by Love, grew warm,
And Painting saw her hues transferr'd
From lifeless flowers to woman's form.
Still as from tint to tint he stole,
The fair design shone out the more,
And there was now a life, a soul,
Where only colours glow'd before.

Then first carnations learn'd to speak,
And lilies into life were brought;
While, mantling on the maiden's cheek,
Young roses kindled into thought.
Then hyacinths their darkest dyes
Upon the locks of Beauty threw;
And violets, transform'd to eyes,
Inshrined a soul within their blue.

CHORUS.

Blest be Love, to whom we owe
All that's fair and bright below.
Song was cold and Painting dim
Till Song and Painting learn'd from him.

Soon as the scene had closed, a cheer
Of gentle voices, old and young,
Rose from the groups that stood to hear
This tale of yore so aptly sung;
And while some nymphs, in haste to tell
The workers of that fairy spell,
How crown'd with praise their task had been,
Stole in behind the curtain'd scene,
The rest, in happy converse stray'd—
Talking that ancient love-tale o'er—
Some to the groves that skirt the glade,
Some, to the chapel by the shore,
To look what lights were on the sea,
And think of the absent silently.

But soon that summons, known so well
Through bower and hall, in Eastern lands,
Whose sound, more sure than gong or bell,
Lovers and slaves alike commands—
The clapping of young female hands,
Calls back the groups from rock and field
To see some new-form'd scene reveal'd;—
And fleet and eager, down the slopes
Of the green glade, like antelopes,

When, in their thirst, they hear the sound
Of distant rills, the light nymphs bound.

Far different now the scene—a waste
Of Libyan sands, by moonlight's ray;
An ancient well, whereon were traced
The warning words, for such as stray
Unarmed there, "Drink and away!"(1)
While, near it, from the night-ray screen'd,
And like his bells, in hush'd repose,
A camel slept—young as if wean'd
When last the star, Canopus, rose. (2)

Such was the back-ground's silent scene;—
While nearer lay, fast slumbering too,
In a rude tent, with brow serene,
A youth whose cheeks of way-worn hue
And pilgrim-bonnet, told the tale
That he had been to Mecca's Vale:
Haply in pleasant dreams, even now
Thinking the long-wish'd hour is come
When, o'er the well-known porch at home,
His hand shall hang the aloe bough—
Trophy of his accomplish'd vow. (3)

But brief his dream—for now the call
Of the camp-chiefs from rear to van,
"Bind on your burdens," (4) wakes up all
The widely slumbering caravan;
And thus meanwhile, to greet the ear
Of the young pilgrim as he wakes,
The song of one who, lingering near,
Had watch'd his slumber, cheerly breaks:

SONG.

Up and march! the timbrel's sound
Wakes the slumbering camp around;
Fleet thy hour of rest hath gone,
Armed sleeper, up, and on!
Long and weary is our way
O'er the burning sands to-day;
But to pilgrim's homeward feet
Even the desert's path is sweet.

When we lie at dead of night,
Looking up to heaven's light,
Hearing but the watchman's tone
Faintly chanting "God is one," (5)

(1) The traveller Shaw mentions a beautiful rill in Barbary, which is received into a large bason called *Shrub we krub*, "Drink and away"—there being great danger of meeting with thieves and assassins in such places.

(2) The Arabian shepherd has a peculiar ceremony in weaning the young camel: when the proper time arrives, he turns the camel towards the rising star, Canopus, and says, "Do you see Canopus? from this moment you taste not another drop of milk."—*Richardson.*

(3) "Whoever returns from a pilgrimage to Mecca hangs this plant (the mitre-shaped aloe) over his street door, as

a token of his having performed this holy journey."—*Hasselquist.*

(4) This form of notice to the caravans to prepare for marching was applied by Hafiz to the necessity of relinquishing the pleasures of this world, and preparing for death:—"'For me what room is there for pleasure in the bower of Beauty, when every moment the bell makes proclamation, 'Bind on your burdens?'"

(5) The watchmen, in the camp of the caravans, go their rounds, crying one after another, "God is one," etc., etc.

Oh what thoughts then o'er us come
Of our distant village home,
Where that chant, when evening sets,
Sounds from all the minarets.

Cheer thee!—soon shall signal lights,
Kindling o'er the Red Sea heights,
Kindling quick from man to man,
Hail our coming caravan : (1)
Think what bliss that hour will be!
Looks of home again to see,
And our names again to hear
Murmur'd out by voices dear.

So pass'd the desert dream away,
Fleeting as his who heard this lay.
Nor long the pause between, nor moved
    The spell-bound audience from that spot ;
While still, as usual, Fancy roved
    On to the joy that yet was not,—
Fancy, who hath no present home,
But builds her bower in scenes to come,
Walking for ever in a light
That flows from regions out of sight.

But see, by gradual dawn descried,
    A mountain realm—rugged as e'er
Upraised to heaven its summits bare,
Or told to earth, with frown of pride,
    That Freedom's falcon nest was there,
Too high for hand of lord or king
To hood her brow, or chain her wing.

'T is Maina's land—her ancient hills,
The abode of nymphs (2)—her countless rills
And torrents, in their downward dash,
    Shining, like silver, through the shade
Of the sea-pine and flowering ash—
    All with a truth so fresh pourtray'd
As wants but touch of life to be
A world of warm reality.

And now, light bounding forth, a band
    Of mountaineers, all smiles, advance—
Nymphs with their lovers, hand in hand,
    Link'd in the Ariadne dance ; (3)
And while, apart from that gay throng,
A minstrel youth, in varied song,
Tells of the loves, the joys, the ills
Of these wild children of the hills,
The rest by turns, of fierce or gay,
As war or sport inspires the lay,
Follow each change that wakes the strings,
And act what thus the lyrist sings :—

SONG.

No life is like the mountaineer's,
    His home is near the sky,
Where throned above this world, he hears
    Its strife at distance die.

(1) "It was customary," says Irwin, "to light up fires on
the mountains, within view of Cosseir, to give notice of
the approach of the caravans that came from the Nile."

Or, should the sound of hostile drum
Proclaim below, "We come—we come,"
Each crag that towers in air
Gives answer, "Come who dare!"
While, like bees, from dell and dingle,
Swift the swarming warriors mingle,
And their cry "Hurra!" will be,
"Hurra, to victory!"

Then, when battle's hour is over,
See the happy mountain lover,
With the nymph, who'll soon be bride,
Seated blushing by his side,
Every shadow of his lot
In her sunny smile forgot.
Oh, no life is like the mountaineer's,
    His home is near the sky,
Where, throned above this world, he hears
    Its strife at distance die.
Nor only thus through summer suns
His blithe existence cheerly runs—
    Even Winter, bleak and dim,
    Brings joyous hours to him ;
When, his rifle behind him flinging,
He watches the roe-buck springing,
And away, o'er the hills away
Re-echoes his glad "hurra."

Then how blest, when night is closing,
By the kindled hearth reposing,
To his rebeck's drowsy song
He beguiles the hour along ;
Or, provoked by merry glances,
To a brisker movement dances,
Till, weary at last, in slumber's chain,
He dreams o'er chase and dance again,
    Dreams, dreams them o'er again.

As slow that minstrel, at the close,
Sunk, while he sung, to feign'd repose,
Aptly did they, whose mimic art
    Follow'd the changes of his lay,
Pourtray the lull, the nod, the start,
    Through which, as faintly died away
His lute and voice, the minstrel pass'd,
Till voice and lute lay hush'd at last.

But now far other song came o'er
    Their startled ears—song that, at first,
As solemnly the night-wind bore
    Across the wave its mournful burst,
Seem'd to the fancy like a dirge
    Of some lone Spirit of the Sea,
Singing o'er Helle's ancient surge
    The requiem of her Brave and Free.

Sudden, amid their pastime, pause
    The wondering nymphs ; and as the sound

(2)   ———virginibus bacchata Laconis
          Taygeta.—Virg.
(3) See, for an account of this dance, De Guy's Travels.

Of that strange music nearer draws,
  With mute enquiring eye look round,
Asking each other what can be
The source of this sad minstrelsy?
Nor longer can they doubt, the song
  Comes from some island-bark, which now
Courses the bright waves swift along,
  And soon, perhaps, beneath the brow
Of the Saint's Rock will shoot its prow.

Instantly all, with hearts that sigh'd
  'Twixt fear's and fancy's influence,
Flew to the rock, and saw from thence
A red-sail'd pinnace towards them glide,
  Whose shadow, as it swept the spray,
Scatter'd the moonlight's smiles away.
Soon as the mariners saw that throng
  From the cliff gazing, young and old,
Sudden they slack'd their sail and song,
  And, while their pinnace idly roll'd
On the light surge, these tidings told :—

'T was from an isle of mournful name,
From Missolonghi, last they came—
Sad Missolonghi, sorrowing yet
O'er him, the noblest Star of Fame
That e'er in life's young glory set !—
And now were on their mournful way,
  Wafting the news through Helle's isles ;—
News that would cloud even Freedom's ray,
  And sadden Victory 'mid her smiles.

Their tale thus told, and heard, with pain,
Out spread the galliot's wings again ;
And, as she sped her swift career,
Again that Hymn rose on the ear—
"Thou art not dead—thou art not dead !"
As oft 't was sung, in ages flown,
Of him, the Athenian, who, to shed
  A tyrant's blood, pour'd out his own,

SONG.

Thou art not dead—thou art not dead! (1)
  No, dearest Harmodius, no.
Thy soul, to realms above us fled,
Though, like a star, it dwells o'er head,
  Still lights this world below.
Thou art not dead—thou art not dead !
  No, dearest Harmodius, no.

Through isles of light, where heroes tread
  And flowers ethereal blow,
Thy god-like Spirit now is led,
Thy lip with life ambrosial fed,
  Forgets all taste of woe.
Thou art not dead—thou art not dead !
  No, dearest Harmodius, no.

The myrtle, round that falchion spread
  Which struck the immortal blow,
Throughout all time, with leaves unshed—

The patriot's hope, the tyrant's dread—
  Round Freedom's shrine shall grow.
Thou art not dead—thou art not dead !
  No, dearest Harmodius, no.

Where hearts like thine have broke or bled,
  Though quench'd the vital glow,
Their memory lights a flame instead,
Which, even from out the narrow bed
  Of death its beams shall throw.
Thou art not dead—thou art not dead !
  No, dearest Harmodius, no.

Thy name, by myriads sung and said,
  From age to age shall go,
Long as the oak and ivy wed,
As bees shall haunt Hymettus' head,
  Or Helle's waters flow.
Thou art not dead—thou art not dead !
  No, dearest Harmodius, no.

———

'Mong those who linger'd listening there—
  Listening, with ear and eye, as long
As breath of night could towards them bear
  A murmur of that mournful song—
A few there were, in whom the lay
Had call'd up feelings far too sad
To pass with the brief strain away,
  Or turn at once to theme more glad ;
And who, in mood untuned to meet
  The light laugh of the happier train,
Wander'd to seek some moonlight seat
Where they might rest, in converse sweet,
  Till vanish'd smiles should come again.
And seldom e'er hath noon of night
To sadness lent more soothing light.
On one side, in the dark blue sky,
Lonely and radiant, was the eye
Of Jove himself, while, on the other,
  'Mong tiny stars that round her gleam'd,
The young moon, like the Roman mother,
  Among her living "jewels," beam'd.

Touch'd by the lovely scenes around,
  A pensive maid—one who, though young,
Had known what 't was to see unwound
  The ties by which her heart had clung—
Waken'd her soft tamboura's sound,
  And to its faint accords thus sung ;—

SONG.

Calm as, beneath its mother's eyes,
In sleep the smiling infant lies,
So, watch'd by all the stars of night,
Yon landscape sleeps in light.
And while the night-breeze dies away,
  Like relics of some faded strain,
Loved voices, lost for many a day,
  Seem whispering round again.

(1) Φιλταθ' Ἁρμοδι' ουπω τεθνηκας.

Oh youth! oh love! ye dreams, that shed
Such glory once—where are ye fled?

Pure ray of light that, down the sky,
    Art pointing, like an angel's wand,
As if to guide to realms that lie
    In that bright sea beyond:
Who knows but in some brighter deep
    Than even that tranquil moon-lit main,
Some land may lie, where those who weep
    Shall wake to smile again!

With cheeks that had regain'd their power
    And play of smiles—and each bright eye,
Like violets after morning's shower,
    The brighter for the tears gone by,
Back to the scene such smiles should grace
These wandering nymphs their path retrace,
And reach the spot, with rapture new,
Just as the veils asunder flew,
And a fresh vision burst to view.

There, by her own bright Attic flood,
The blue-eyed Queen of Wisdom stood;—
Not as she haunts the sage's dreams,
    With brow unveil'd, divine, severe;
But soften'd, as on bards she beams,
    When fresh from Poesy's high sphere,
A music, not her own, she brings,
And, through the veil which Fancy flings
O'er her stern features, gently sings.

But who is he—that urchin nigh,
    With quiver on the rose-trees hung,
Who seems just dropp'd from yonder sky,
And stands to watch that maid, with eye
    So full of thought, for one so young?—
That child—but, silence! lend thine ear,
And thus in song the tale thou 'lt hear :—

SONG.

As Love, one summer eve, was straying,
    Who should he see, at that soft hour,
But young Minerva, gravely playing
    Her flute within an olive bower.
I need not say, 'tis Love's opinion
    That, grave or merry, good or ill,
The sex all bow to his dominion,
    As woman will be woman still.

Though seldom yet the boy hath given
    To learned dames his smiles or sighs,
So handsome Pallas look'd, that even
    Love quite forgot the maid was wise.
Besides, a youth of his discerning
    Knew well that, by a shady rill,
At sunset hour, whate'er her learning,
    A woman will be woman still.

Her flute he praised in terms extatic—
    Wishing it dumb, nor cared how soon;—

For Wisdom's notes, howe'er chromatic,
    To Love seem always out of tune.
But long as he found face to flatter,
    The nymph found breath to shake and thrill;
As, weak or wise—it does n't matter—
    Woman, at heart, is woman still.

Love changed his plan, with warmth exclaim-
        ing,
    "How rosy was her lips' soft dye!"
And much that flute, the flatterer, blaming,
    For twisting lips so sweet awry.
The nymph look'd down, beheld her features
    Reflected in the passing rill,
And started, shock'd—for, ah, ye creatures!
    Even when divine, you 're women still.

Quick from the lips it made so odious,
    That graceless flute the Goddess took,
And, while yet fill'd with breath melodious,
    Flung it into the glassy brook;
Where as its vocal life was fleeting
    Adown the current, faint and shrill,
'T was heard in plaintive tone repeating,
    "Woman, alas, vain woman still!"

An interval of dark repose—
Such as the summer lightning knows,
'Twixt flash and flash, as still more bright
The quick revealment comes and goes,
Opening 'each time the veils of night,
To show, within, a world of light—
Such pause, so brief, now pass'd between
This last gay vision and the scene,
    Which now its depth of light disclosed.
A bower it seem'd, an Indian bower,
    Within whose shade a nymph reposed,
Sleeping away noon's sunny hour—
Lovely as she, the Sprite, who weaves
Her mansion of sweet Durva leaves,
And there, as Indian legends say,
Dreams the long summer hours away.
And mark, how charm'd this sleeper seems
With some hid fancy—she, too, dreams!
Oh for a wizard's art to tell
    The wonders that now bless her sight!
'T is done—a truer, holier spell
    Than e'er from wizard's lip yet fell
    Thus brings her vision all to light :—

SONG.

    " Who comes so gracefully
        Gliding along,
    While the blue rivulet
        Sleeps to her song;
    Song, richly vying
    With the faint sighing
    Which swans, in dying,
        Sweetly prolong?"

                                            39

So sung the shepherd-boy
   By the stream's side,
Watching that fairy-boat
   Down the flood glide,
Like a bird winging,
Through the waves bringing
That Syren, singing
   To the hush'd tide.

"Stay," said the shepherd-boy,
   " Fairy-boat, stay,
Linger, sweet minstrelsy,
   Linger a day."
But vain his pleading,
Past him, unheeding,
Song and boat, speeding,
   Glided away.

So to our youthful eyes
   Joy and hope shone;
So, while we gazed on them,
   Fast they flew on;—
Like flowers declining
Even in the twining,
One moment shining,
   And, the next, gone!

Soon as the imagined dream went by,
Uprose the nymph, with anxious eye
Turn'd to the clouds, as though some boon
   She waited from that sun-bright dome,
And marvell'd that it came not soon
   As her young thoughts would have it come.

But joy is in her glance!—the wing
   Of a white bird is seen above;
And oh, if round his neck he bring
   The long-wish'd tidings from her love,
Not half so precious in her eyes
   Even that high-omen'd bird (1) would be
Who dooms the brow o'er which he flies
   To wear a crown of Royalty.

She had herself, last evening, sent
   A winged messenger, whose flight
Through the clear roseate element,
   She watch'd till, lessening out of sight,
Far to the golden West it went,
   Wafting to him, her distant love,
A missive in that language wrought
   Which flowers can speak, when aptly wove,
Each hue a word, each leaf a thought.

And now—oh speed of pinion, known
   To Love's light messengers alone!—
Ere yet another evening takes
   Its farewell of the golden lakes,
She sees another envoy fly,
   With the wish'd answer, through the sky.

SONG.

Welcome, sweet bird, through the sunny air winging,
   Swift hast thou come o'er the far-shining sea,
Like Seba's dove, on thy snowy neck bringing
   Love's written vows from my lover to me.
Oh, in thy absence, what hours did I number!—
   Saying oft, " Idle bird, how could he rest ?"
But thou art come at last, take now thy slumber,
   And lull thee in dreams of all thou lovest best.

Yet dost thou droop—even now while I utter
   Love's happy welcome, thy pulse dies away;
Cheer thee, my bird—were it life's ebbing flutter,
   This fondling bosom should woo it to stay.
But no—thou'rt dying—thy last task is over—
   Farewell, sweet martyr to Love and to me!
The smiles thou hast waken'd by news from my lover,
   Will now all be turn'd into weeping for thee.

While thus this scene of song (their last
   For the sweet summer season) pass'd,
A few presiding nymphs, whose care
   Watch'd over all, invisibly,
As do those guardian sprites of air,
   Whose watch we feel, but cannot see,
Had from the circle—scarcely miss'd,
   Ere they were sparkling there again—
Glided, like fairies, to assist
   Their handmaids on the moonlit plain,
Where, hid by intercepting shade
   From the stray glance of curious eyes,
A feast of fruits and wines was laid—
   Soon to shine out, a glad surprise!

And now the moon, her ark of light
   Steering through heaven, as though she bore
In safety, through that deep of night,
   Spirits of earth, the good, the bright,
   To some remote immortal shore,
Had half-way sped her glorious way,
   When, round reclined on hillocks green,
In groups, beneath that tranquil ray,
   The Zeans at their feast were seen.
Gay was the picture—every maid
Whom late the lighted scene display'd,
Still in her fancy garb array'd;—
The Arabian pilgrim, smiling here
   Beside the nymph of India's sky;
While there the Mainiote mountaineer
   Whisper'd in young Minerva's ear,
   And urchin Love stood laughing by.

Meantime the elders round the board,
   By mirth and wit themselves made young,
High cups of juice Zacynthian pour'd,
   And, while the flask went round, thus sung:—

(1) The Huma.

SONG.

Up with the sparkling brimmer,
    Up to the crystal rim;
Let not a moon-beam glimmer
    'Twixt the flood and brim.
When hath the world set eyes on
    Aught to match this light,
Which, o'er our cup's horizon,
    Dawns in bumpers bright?

Truth in a deep well lieth—
    So the wise aver:
But Truth the fact denieth—
    Water suits not her.
No, her abode's in brimmers,
    Like this mighty cup—
Waiting till we, good swimmers,
    Dive to bring her up.

Thus circled round the song of glee,
And all was tuneful mirth the while,
Save on the cheeks of some, whose smile,
As fix'd they gaze upon the sea,
Turns into paleness suddenly!
What see they there? a bright blue light
That, like a meteor, gliding o'er
The distant wave, grows on the sight,
As though 't were wing'd to Zea's shore.

To some, 'mong those who came to gaze,
    It seem'd the night-light, far away,
Of some lone fisher, by the blaze
    Of pine torch, luring on his prey;
While others, as, 'twixt awe and mirth,
    They breathed the bless'd Panaya's (1) name,
Vow'd that such light was not of earth,
    But of that drear ill-omen'd flame,
Which mariners see on sail or mast,
When Death is coming in the blast.
While marvelling thus they stood, a maid,
    Who sate apart, with downcast eye,
Not yet had, like the rest, survey'd
    That coming light which now was nigh,
Soon as it met her sight, with cry
    Of pain-like joy, "'Tis he! 'tis he!"
Loud she exclaim'd, and, hurrying by
    The assembled throng, rush'd towards the sea.
At burst so wild, alarm'd, amazed,
All stood, like statues, mute, and gazed
Into each other's eyes, to seek
What meant such mood, in maid so meek?

Till now, the tale was known to few,
But now from lip to lip it flew:—
A youth, the flower of all the band,
    Who late had left this sunny shore,
When last he kiss'd that maiden's hand,
    Lingering, to kiss it o'er and o'er,
By his sad brow too plainly told
    The ill-omen'd thought which cross'd him then,

(1) The name which the Greeks give to the Virgin Mary.

That once those hands should lose their hold,
    They ne'er would meet on earth again!
In vain his mistress, sad as he,
But with a heart from self as free
As generous woman's only is,
Veil'd her own fears to banish his.—
With frank rebuke, but still more vain,
    Did a rough warrior, who stood by,
Call to his mind this martial strain,
    His favourite once, ere Beauty's eye
    Had taught his soldier-heart to sigh:—

SONG.

March! nor heed those arms that hold thee,
    Though so fondly close they come;
Closer still will they enfold thee,
    When thou bring'st fresh laurels home.
Dost thou dote on woman's brow?
    Dost thou live but in her breath?
March!—one hour of victory now
    Wins thee woman's smile till death.

Oh what bliss, when war is over,
    Beauty's long-miss'd smile to meet,
And, when wreaths our temples cover,
    Lay them shining at her feet.
Who would not, that hour to reach,
    Breathe out life's expiring sigh—
Proud as waves that on the beach
    Lay their war-crests down, and die.

There! I see thy soul is burning—
    She herself, who clasps thee so,
Paints, even now, thy glad returning,
    And, while clasping, bids thee go.
One deep sigh, to passion given,
    One last glowing tear, and then—
March!—nor rest thy sword, till Heaven
    Brings thee to those arms again.

Even then, e'er loath their hands could part,
    A promise the youth gave, which bore
Some balm unto the maiden's heart,
    That soon as the fierce fight was o'er,
To home he'd speed, if safe and free—
    Nay, even if dying, still would come,
So the blest word of "Victory!"
    Might be the last he'd breathe at home.
"By day," he cried, "thou'lt know my bark;
But, should I come through midnight dark,
A blue light on the prow shall tell
That Greece hath won, and all is well!"

Fondly the maiden, every night
Had stolen to seek that promised light;
Nor long her eyes had now been turn'd
From watching, when the signal burn'd.
Signal of joy—for her, for all—
    Fleetly the boat now nears the land,
While voices, from the shore-edge, call
    For tidings of the long-wish'd band.

Oh the blest hour, when those who've been
Through peril's paths by land or sea,
Lock'd in our arms again are seen
Smiling in glad security;
When heart to heart we fondly strain,
Questioning quickly o'er and o'er—
Then hold them off, to gaze again,
And ask, though answer'd oft before,
If they, *indeed,* are ours once more?

Such is the scene, so full of joy,
Which welcomes now this warrior-boy,
As fathers, sisters, friends all run
Bounding to meet him—all but one,
Who, slowest on his neck to fall,
Is yet the happiest of them all.

And now behold him, circled round
With beaming faces, at that board,
While cups, with laurel foliage crown'd,
Are to the coming warriors pour'd—
Coming, as he, their herald, told,
With blades from victory scarce yet cold,
With hearts untouch'd by Moslem steel,
And wounds that home's sweet breath will heal.

"Ere morn," said he—and, while he spoke,
Turn'd to the east, where, clear and pale,
The star of dawn already broke—
"We 'll greet, on yonder wave, their sail!"
Then, wherefore part? all, all agree
To wait them here, beneath this bower;
And thus, while even amidst their glee,
Each eye is turn'd to watch the sea,
With song they cheer the anxious hour.

SONG.

"'Tis the Vine! 'tis the Vine!" said the cup-loving
As he saw it spring bright from the earth, [boy,
And call'd the young Genii of Wit, Love, and Joy,
To witness and hallow its birth.
The fruit was full grown, like a ruby it flamed
Till the sun-beam that kiss'd it look'd pale:
"'Tis the Vine! 'tis the Vine!" every Spirit exclaim'd,
"Hail, hail to the Wine-tree, all hail!"

First, fleet as a bird, to the summons Wit flew,
While a light on the vine-leaves there broke,
In flashes so quick and so brilliant, all knew
'T was the light from his lips as he spoke.
"Bright tree! let thy nectar but cheer me," he cried,
"And the fount of Wit never can fail:"
"'T is the Vine! 'tis the Vine!" hills and valleys reply
"Hail, hail to the Wine-tree, all hail!"

Next, Love, as he lean'd o'er the plant to admire
Each tendril and cluster it wore,
From his rosy mouth sent such a breath of desire,
As made the tree tremble all o'er.
Oh, never did flower of the earth, sea, or sky,
Such a soul-giving odour inhale:
"'T is the Vine! 'tis the Vine!" all re-echo the cry,
"Hail, hail to the Vine-tree, all hail!"

Last, Joy, without whom even Love and Wit die,
Came to crown the bright hour with his ray;
And scarce had that mirth-waking tree met his eye,
When a laugh spoke what Joy could not say;—
A laugh of the heart, which was echo'd around
Till, like music, it swell'd on the gale; [resound,
"'Tis the Vine! 'tis the Vine!" laughing myriads
"Hail, hail to the Wine-tree, all hail!"

THE SUMMER FÊTE.

PREFACE.

Some recollections respecting the gala at Boyle Farm, by which the *Summer Fête* was suggested, may be here introduced without impropriety. In an old letter of my own, to which I have had access, giving an account of this brilliant festival to a friend in Ireland, I find some memorandums which, besides their reference to the subject of the poem, contain some incidents also connected with the first appearance before the public of one of the most successful of all my writings, the story of the *Epicurean.* I shall give my extracts from this letter, in their original diary-like form, without alteration or dressing:—

June 30, 1827.—Day threatening for the Fête. Was with Lord Essex (1) at three o'clock, and started about half an hour after. The whole road swarming with carriages and four all the way to Boyle Farm, which Lady de Roos has lent, for the occa-

sion, to Henry;—the five givers of the Fête, being Lords Chesterfield, Castlereagh, Alvanley, Henry de Roos, and Robert Grosvenor, subscribing four or five hundred pounds each towards it. The arrangements all in the very best taste. The pavilion for quadrilles, on the bank of the river, with steps descending to the water, quite eastern—like what one sees in Daniel's pictures. Towards five the *élite* of the gay world was assembled—the women all looking their best, and scarce a single ugly face to be found. About half past five, sat down to dinner, 450 under a tent on the lawn, and fifty to the Royal Table in the conservatory. The Tyrolese musicians sung during dinner, and there were, after dinner, gondo-

(1) I cannot let pass the incidental mention here of this social and public-spirited nobleman, without expressing my strong sense of his kindly qualities, and lamenting the loss which not only society, but the cause of sound and progressive Political Reform, has sustained by his death.

las on the river, with Caradori, De Begnis, Velluti, etc., singing barcarols and rowing off occasionally, so as to let their voices die away and again return. After these succeeded a party in dominoes, Madame Vestris, Fanny Ayton, etc., who rowed about in the same manner and sung, among other things, my gondola song, "Oh come to me when daylight sets." The evening was delicious, and, as soon as it grew dark, the groves were all lighted up with coloured lamps, in different shapes and devices. A little lake near a grotto took my fancy particularly, the shrubs all round being illuminated, and the lights reflected in the water. Six-and-twenty of the prettiest girls of the world of fashion, the F****t*rs, Br* d***ll, De R**s's, Miss F**ld**g, Miss F*x, Miss R*ss*ll, Miss B**ly, were dressed as Rosières, and opened the quadrilles in the pavilion . . . . . . While talking with D—n (Lord P.'s brother), he said to me, "I never read any thing so touching as the death of your heroine." "What," said I, "have you got so far already?"(1) "Oh, I read it in the *Literary Gazette*." This anticipation of my catastrophe is abominable. Soon after, the Marquis P—lm—a said to me, as he and I and B—m stood together, looking at the gay scene, "This is like one of your fêtes." "Oh yes," said B—m, thinking he alluded to *Lalla Rookh*, "quite oriental. "Non, non," replied P—lma, "je veux dire cette fête d'Athènes, dont j'ai lu la description dans la gazette d'aujourd'hui."

———◦❦◦———

DEDICATION

TO THE HONOURABLE MRS. NORTON.

For the groundwork of the following Poem I am indebted to a memorable Fête, given some years since, at Boyle Farm, the seat of the late Lord Henry Fitzgerald. In commemoration of that evening—of which the lady to whom these pages are inscribed was, I well recollect, one of the most distinguished ornaments—I was induced at the time to write some verses, which were afterwards, however, thrown aside unfinished, on my discovering that the same task had been undertaken by a noble poet,(2) whose playful and happy *jeu-d'esprit* on the subject has since been published. It was but lately, that, on finding the fragments of my own sketch among my papers, I thought of founding on them such a description of an imaginary Fête as might furnish me with situations for the introduction of music.

Such is the origin and object of the following Poem, and to Mrs. NORTON it is, with every feeling of admiration and regard, inscribed by her father's warmly-attached friend.

THOMAS MOORE.

Sloperton Cottage, November, 1831.

(1) The *Epicurean* had been published but the day before.
(2) Lord Francis Egerton.

THE SUMMER FÊTE.

WHERE are ye now, ye summer days,
That once inspired the poet's lays?
Blest time! ere England's nymphs and swains,
  For lack of sunbeams, took to coals—
Summers of light, undimm'd by rains,
Whose only mocking trace remains
  In watering-pots and parasols."

Thus spoke a young Patrician maid,
  As, on the morning of that Fête
  Which bards unborn shall celebrate,
She backward drew her curtain's shade,
And, closing one half-dazzled eye,
Peep'd with the other at the sky—
The important sky, whose light or gloom
Was to decide, this day, the doom
Of some few hundred beauties, wits,
Blues, dandies, swains, and exquisites.

Faint were her hopes; for June had now
  Set in with all his usual rigour!
Young Zephyr yet scarce knowing how
To nurse a bud, or fan a bough,
  But Eurus in perpetual vigour;
And, such the biting summer air,
That she, the nymph now nestling there—
Snug as her own bright gems recline,
At night, within their cotton shrine—
Had, more than once, been caught of late
Kneeling before her blazing grate,
Like a young worshipper of fire,
  With hands uplifted to the flame,
Whose glow, as if to woo them nigher,
  Through the white fingers flushing came.

But oh, the light, the unhoped-for light,
  That now illumed this morning's heaven!
Up sprung Ianthe at the sight,
  Though—hark!—the clocks but strike eleven,
And rarely did the nymph surprise
Mankind so early with her eyes.

Who now will say that England's sun
  (Like England's self, these spendthrift days)
His stock of wealth hath near outrun,
  And must retrench his golden rays—
Pay for the pride of sunbeams past,
And to mere moonshine come at last?

"Calumnious thought!" Ianthe cries,
  While coming mirth lit up each glance,
And, prescient of the ball, her eyes
  Already had begun to dance:
For brighter sun than that which now
  Sparkled o'er London's spires and towers,
Had never bent from heaven his brow
  To kiss Firenze's City of Flowers.

What must it be—if thus so fair
'Mid the smoked groves of Grosvenor Square—
What must it be where Thames is seen
Gliding between his banks of green,
While rival villas, on each side,
Peep from their bowers to woo his tide,
And, like a Turk between two rows
Of Harem beauties, on he goes—
A lover, loved for even the grace
With which he slides from their embrace.

In one of those enchanted domes,
    One, the most flowery, cool, and bright
Of all by which that river roams,
    The Fête is to be held to-night—
That Fête already link'd to fame,
    Whose cards, in many a fair one's sight
(When look'd for long, at last they came,)
    Seem'd circled with a fairy light;—
That Fête to which the cull, the flower
Of England's beauty, rank, and power,
From the young spinster, just come *out*,
    To the old Premier, too long *in*—
From legs of far-descended gout,
    To the last new-mustachio'd chin—
All were convoked by Fashion's spells
To the small circle where she dwells,
    Collecting nightly, to allure us,
    Live atoms, which, together hurl'd,
She, like another Epicurus,
    Sets dancing thus, and calls "the World."

Behold how busy in those bowers
(Like May-flies, in and out of flowers,)
The countless menials swarming run,
To furnish forth, ere set of sun,
The banquet-table richly laid
Beneath yon awning's lengthen'd shade,
Where fruits shall tempt, and wines entice,
    And Luxury's self, at Gunter's call,
Breathe from her summer-throne of ice
    A spirit of coolness over all.

And now the important hour drew nigh,
When, 'neath the flush of evening's sky,
The west-end " world" for mirth let loose,
And moved, as he of Syracuse (1)
Ne'er dreamt of moving worlds, by force
    Of four-horse power, had all combined
Through Grosvenor Gate to speed their course,
    Leaving that portion of mankind,
    Whom they call "Nobody," behind;—
No star for London's feasts to-day,
No moon of beauty, new this May,
To lend the night her crescent ray ;—

Nothing, in short, for ear or eye,
But veteran belles, and wits gone by,
The relics of a past beau-monde,
A world, like Cuvier's, long dethroned!
Even Parliament this evening nods
Beneath the harangues of minor gods,
    On half its usual opiate's share ;
The great dispensers of repose,
The first-rate furnishers of prose,
    Being all call'd to—prose elsewhere.

Soon as through Grosvenor's lordly square—(2)
    That last impregnable redoubt,
Where, guarded with Patrician care,
    Primeval Error still holds out—
Where never gleam of gas must dare
    'Gainst ancient Darkness to revolt,
Nor smooth Macadam hope to spare
    The dowagers one single jolt ;—
Where, far too stately and sublime
To profit by the lights of time,
Let Intellect march how it will,
They stick to oil and watchmen still :—
Soon as through that illustrious square
    The first epistolary bell,
Sounding by fits upon the air,
    Of parting pennies rung the knell ;
Warn'd by that tell-tale of the hours,
    And by the day-light's westering beam,
The young Ianthe, who, with flowers
    Half crown'd, had sat in idle dream
Before her glass, scarce knowing where
Her fingers roved through that bright hair,
    While, all capriciously, she now
    Dislodged some curl from her white brow,
And now again replaced it there ;—
As though her task was meant to be
One endless change of ministry—
A routing-up of Loves and Graces,
But to plant others in their places.

Meanwhile—what strain is that which floats
Through the small boudoir near—like notes
Of some young bird, its task repeating
For the next linnet music-meeting?
A voice it was, whose gentle sounds
Still kept a modest octave's bounds,
Nor yet had ventured to exalt
Its rash ambition to B *alt*,
That point towards which when ladies rise,
The wise man takes his hat and—flies.
Tones of a harp, too, gently play'd,
    Came with this youthful voice communing;
Tones true, for once, without the aid
    Of that inflictive process, tuning—

(1) Archimedes.
(2) I am not certain whether the Dowagers of this Square
have yet yielded to the innovations of Gas and Police, but
at the time when the above lines were written they still
obstinately persevered in their old *régime;* and would not
suffer themselves to be either well guarded or well lighted.

A process which must oft have given
 Poor Milton's ears a deadly wound;
So pleased, among the joys of Heaven,
 He specifies "harps *ever* tuned."(1)
She who now sang this gentle strain
 Was our young nymph's still younger sister—
Scarce ready yet for Fashion's train
 In their light legions to enlist her,
But counted on, as sure to bring
 Her force into the field next Spring.

The song she thus, like Jubal's shell,
 Gave forth " so sweetly and so well,"
Was one in *Morning Post* much famed,
 From a *divine* collection, named,
 " Songs of the Toilet "—every Lay
Taking for subject of its Muse,
 Some branch of feminine array,
Some item, with full scope, to choose,
 From diamonds down to dancing shoes;
From the last hat that Herbault's hands
 Bequeathed to an admiring world,
Down to the latest flounce that stands
Like Jacob's Ladder—or expands
 Far forth, tempestuously unfurl'd.

Speaking of one of these new Lays,
The *Morning Post* thus sweetly says :—
" Not all that breathes from Bishop's lyre,
 That Barnett dreams, or Cooke conceives,
Can match for sweetness, strength, or fire,
 This fine Cantata upon Sleeves.
The very notes themselves reveal
 The cut of each new sleeve so well;
A *flat* betrays the *Imbéciles*, (2)
 Light fugues the flying lappets tell;
While rich cathedral chords awake
Our homage for the *Manches d'Évéque*."

'T was the first opening song—the Lay
 Of all least deep in toilet-lore,
That the young nymph, to while away
 The tiring-hour, thus warbled o'er :—

SONG.

Array thee, love, array thee, love,
 In all thy best array thee;
The sun 's below—the moon 's above—
 And Night and Bliss obey thee.
Put on thee all that 's bright and rare,
 The zone, the wreath, the gem,
Not so much gracing charms so fair,
 As borrowing grace from them.
Array thee, love, array thee, love,
 In all that 's bright array thee;
The sun 's below—the moon 's above—
 And Night and Bliss obey thee.

Put on the plumes thy lover gave,
 The plumes that, proudly dancing,
Proclaim to all, where'er they wave,
 Victorious eyes advancing.
Bring forth the robe, whose hue of heaven
 From thee derives such light,
That Iris would give all her seven
 To boast but *one* so bright.
 Array thee, love, etc.

Now hie thee, love, now hie thee, love,
 Through Pleasure's circles hie thee,
And hearts, where'er thy footsteps move,
 Will beat when they come nigh thee.
Thy every word shall be a spell,
 Thy every look a ray,
And tracks of wondering eyes shall tell
 The glory of thy way!
Now hie thee, love, now hie thee, love,
 Through Pleasure's circles hie thee,
And hearts, where'er thy footsteps move,
 Shall beat when they come nigh thee.

Now in his Palace of the West,
 Sinking to slumber, the bright Day,
Like a tired monarch fann'd to rest,
 'Mid the cool airs of Evening lay;
While round his couch's golden rim
 The gaudy clouds, like courtiers, crept—
Struggling each other's light to dim,
 And catch his last smile e'er he slept.
How gay, as o'er the gliding Thames
 The golden eve its lustre pour'd,
Shone out the high-born knights and dames
 Now group'd around that festal board ;
A living mass of plumes and flowers,
 As though they 'd robb'd both birds and bowers—
A peopled rainbow, swarming through
 With habitants of every hue;
While, as the sparkling juice of France
 High in the crystal brimmers flow'd,
Each sunset ray that mix'd by chance
 With the wine's sparkles, show'd
 How sunbeams may be taught to dance.

If not in written form exprest,
 'T was known, at least, to every guest,
That, though not bidden to parade
 Their scenic powers in masquerade,
 (A pastime little found to thrive
 In the bleak fog of England's skies,
Where wit 's the thing we best contrive,
 As masqueraders, to *disguise*,)
It yet was hoped—and well that hope
 Was answer'd by the young and gay—
That, in the toilet's task to-day,
Fancy should take her wildest scope;—

(1) ———their golden harps they took—
Harps ever tuned.—*Paradise Lost*, book iii.

(2) The name given to those large sleeves that hang
loosely.

That the rapt milliner should be
Let loose through fields of poesy,
The tailor, in inventive trance,
  Up to the height of Epic clamber,
And all the regions of Romance
  Be ransacked by the *femme de chambre*.

Accordingly, with gay Sultanas,
Rebeccas, Sapphos, Roxalanas—
Circassian slaves whom Love would pay
  Half his maternal realms to ransom—
Young nuns, whose chief religion lay
  In looking most profanely handsome—
Muses in muslin—pastoral maids
  With hats from the *Arcade-ian* shades—
And fortune-tellers, rich, 't was plain,
As fortune-*hunters* form'd their train.

With these, and more such female groups,
Were mixed no less fantastic troops
Of male exhibiters—all willing
To look, even more than usual, killing;—
Beau tyrants, smock-faced braggadocios,
And brigands, charmingly ferocious;—
M. P.s turn'd Turks, good Moslems then,
  Who, last night, voted for the Greeks;
And Friars, staunch No-Popery men,
  In close confab with Whig Caciques.

But where is she—the nymph, whom late
  We left before her glass delaying,
Like Eve, when by the lake she sate,
  In the clear wave her charms surveying,
And saw in that first glassy mirror
The first fair face that lured to error.
"Where is she?" ask'st thou ;—watch all looks
  As centring to one point they bear,
Like sun-flowers by the sides of brooks,
  Turn'd to the sun—and she is there.
Even in disguise, oh never doubt
By her own light you 'd track her out:
As when the moon, close shawl'd in fog,
Steals, as she thinks, through heaven *incog.*,
Though hid herself, some sidelong ray,
At every step, detects her way.

But not in dark disguise to-night
Hath our young heroine veil'd her light;
For see, she walks the earth, Love's own,
  His wedded bride, by holiest vow
Pledged in Olympus, and made known
  To mortals by the type which now
Hangs glittering on her snowy brow,
That butterfly, mysterious trinket,
Which means the Soul (tho' few would think it),
And sparkling thus on brow so white,
Tells us we 've Psyche here to-night!

But hark! some song hath caught her ears—
  And, lo, how pleased, as though she 'd ne'er

Heard the Grand Opera of the Spheres,
  Her goddess-ship approves the air;
And to a mere terrestrial strain,
Inspired by nought but pink champagne,
  Her butterfly as gaily nods
As though she sate with all her train
  At some great Concert of the Gods,
With Phœbus, leader—Jove, director,
And half the audience drunk with nectar.

From a male group the carol came—
  A few gay youths, whom round the board
The last-tried flask's superior fame
  Had lured to taste the tide it pour'd;
And one, who, from his youth and lyre,
Seem'd grandson to the Teian sire,
Thus gaily sung, while, to his song,
Replied in chorus the gay throng :—

SONG.

Some mortals there may be, so wise, or so fine,
  As in evenings like this no enjoyment to see;
But, as *I 'm* not particular—wit, love, and wine,
  Are for one night's amusement sufficient for me.
Nay—humble and strange as my tastes may appear—
  If driven to the worst, I could manage, thank
      Heaven,
To put up with eyes such as beam round me here,
  And such wine as we 're sipping, six days out of
      seven.
So pledge *me* a bumper—your sages profound
  May be blest, if they will, on their own patent plan;
But as we are *not* sages, why—send the cup round—
  We must only be happy the best way we can.

A reward by some king was once offer'd, we 're told,
  To whoe'er could invent a new bliss for mankind;
But, talk of *new* pleasures!—give me but the old,
  And I 'll leave your inventors all new ones they find.
Or should I, in quest of fresh realms of bliss,
  Set sail in the pinnace of Fancy some day,
Let the rich rosy sea I embark on be this,
  And such eyes as we 've here be the stars of my way!
In the mean time, a bumper—your Angels, on high,
  May have pleasures unknown to life's limited span;
But, as we are *not* Angels, why—let the flask fly—
  We must only be happy *all* ways that we can.

Now nearly fled was sunset's light,
  Leaving but so much of its beam
As gave to objects, late so bright,
  The colouring of a shadowy dream;
And there was still where Day had set
  A flush that spoke him loath to die—
A last link of his glory yet,
  Binding together earth and sky.
Say, why is it that twilight best
Becomes even brows the loveliest?
That dimness, with its softening touch,
  Can bring out grace, unfelt before,

And charms we ne'er can see too much,
  When seen but half enchant the more?
Alas, it is that every joy
In fulness finds its worst alloy,
And half a bliss, but hoped or guess'd,
Is sweeter than the whole possess'd;—
That Beauty, when least shone upon,
  A creature most ideal grows;
And there's no light from moon or sun
Like that Imagination throws;—
It is, alas, that Fancy shrinks
  Even from a bright reality,
And, turning inly, feels and thinks
  Far heavenlier things than e'er will *be*.

Such was the effect of twilight's hour
  On the fair groups that, round and round,
From glade to grot, from bank to bower,
  Now wander'd through this fairy ground.
And thus did Fancy—and champagne—
  Work on the sight their dazzling spells,
Till nymphs that look'd, at noon-day, plain,
  Now brighten'd, in the gloom, to belles:
And the brief interval of time,
  'Twixt after dinner and before,
To dowagers brought back their prime,
  And shed a halo round two-score.

Meanwhile, new pastimes for the eye,
  The ear, the fancy, quick succeed;
And now along the waters fly
  Light gondoles, of Venetian breed,
With knights and dames, who, calm reclined,
  Lisp out love-sonnets as they glide—
Astonishing old Thames to find
  Such doings on his moral tide.

So bright was still that tranquil river,
  With the last shaft from Daylight's quiver,
That many a group, in turn, were seen
Embarking on its wave serene;
And, 'mong the rest, in chorus gay,
.A band of mariners, from the isles
Of sunny Greece, all song and smiles,
As smooth they floated, to the play
Of their oar's cadence, sung this lay:—

TRIO.
Our home is on the sea, boy,
  Our home is on the sea;
    When Nature gave
    The ocean-wave,
    She mark'd it for the Free.
Whatever storms befall, boy,
  Whatever storms befall,
    The island bark
    Is Freedom's ark,
    And floats her safe through all.

Behold yon sea of isles, boy,
  Behold yon sea of isles,

    Where every shore
    Is sparkling o'er
    With Beauty's richest smiles.
For us hath Freedom claim'd, boy,
  For us hath Freedom claim'd
    Those ocean-nests
    Where Valour rests
    His eagle wing untamed.

And shall the Moslem dare, boy,
  And shall the Moslem dare,
    While Grecian hand
    Can wield a brand,
    To plant his Crescent there?
No—by our fathers, no, boy,
  No, by the Cross we show—
    From Maina's rills
    To Thracia's hills
    All Greece re-echoes "No!"

Like pleasant thoughts that o'er the mind
  A minute come, and go again,
Even so, by snatches, in the wind,
  Was caught and lost that choral strain,
Now full, now faint upon the ear,
As the bark floated far or near.
At length when, lost, the closing note
  Had down the waters died away,
Forth from another fairy boat,
  Freighted with Music, came this song:—

SONG.
Smoothly flowing through verdant vales,
  Gentle river, thy current runs,
Shelter'd safe from winter gales,
  Shaded cool from summer suns.
Thus our Youth's sweet moments glide,
  Fenced with flowery shelter round;
No rude tempest wakes the tide,
  All its path is fairy ground.

But, fair river, the day will come,
  When, woo'd by whispering groves in vain,
Thou 'lt leave those banks, thy shaded home,
  To mingle with the stormy main.
And thou, sweet Youth, too soon wilt pass
  Into the world's unshelter'd sea,
Where, once thy wave hath mix'd, alas,
  All hope of peace is lost for thee.

Next turn we to the gay saloon, ·
  Resplendent as a summer noon,
  Where, 'neath a pendent wreath of lights,
  A Zodiac of flowers and tapers—
(Such as in Russian ball-rooms sheds
  Its glory o'er young dancers' heads)—
  Quadrille performs her mazy rites,
And reigns supreme o'er slides and capers;—
Working to death each opera strain,
  As, with a foot that ne'er reposes,

40

She jigs through sacred and profane,
   From *Maid and Magpie* up to *Moses;*"—(1)
Wearing out tunes as fast as shoes,
   Till fagg'd Rossini scarce respires;
Till Meyerbeer for mercy sues,
   And Weber at her feet expires.

And now the set hath ceased—the bows
   Of fiddlers taste a brief repose,
While light along the painted floor,
   Arm within arm, the couples stray,
Talking their stock of nothings o'er,
   Till nothing 's left, at last, to say.
When, lo! most opportunely sent—
   Two Exquisites, a he and she,
Just brought from Dandyland, and meant
   For Fashion's grand Menagerie,
Enter'd the room—and scarce were there
When all flock'd round them, glad to stare
At *any* monsters, *any* where.

Some thought them perfect, to their tastes;
While others hinted that the waists
(That in particular of the *he* thing)
Left far too ample room for breathing:
Whereas, to meet these critic's wishes,
   The isthmus there should be so small,
That Exquisites, at last, like fishes,
   Must manage not to breathe at all.
The female (these same critics said),
   Though orthodox from toe to chin,
Yet lack'd that spacious width of head
   To hat of toadstool much akin—
That build of bonnet, whose extent
Should, like a doctrine of dissent,
   Puzzle church-doors to let it in.

However—sad as 't was, no doubt,
That nymph so smart should go about,
With head unconscious of the place
It *ought* to fill in Infinite Space—
Yet all allow'd that, of *her kind,*
A prettier show 't was hard to find;
While of that doubtful genus, "dressy men,"
The male was thought a first-rate specimen.
Such *Savants,* too, as wish'd to trace
The manners, habits of this race—
To know what rank (if rank at all)
'Mong reasoning things to them should fall—
What sort of notions heaven imparts
To high-built heads and tight-laced hearts,
And how far Soul, which, Plato says,
Abhors restraint, can act in stays—
Might now, if gifted with discerning,
Find opportunities of learning:
As these two creatures—from their pout
And frown, 't was plain—had just fallen out;

And all their little thoughts, of course,
Were stirring in full fret and force;
Like mites, through microscope espied,
A world of nothings magnified.

But mild the vent such beings seek,
The tempest of their souls to speak;
As Opera swains to fiddles sigh,
To fiddles fight, to fiddles die,
Even so this tender couple set
Their well-bred woes to a Duet.

WALTZ DUET. (2)

HE.

Long as I waltz'd with only thee,
   Each blissful Wednesday that went by,
Nor stylish Stultz, nor neat Nugee
   Adorn'd a youth so blest as I.
     Oh! ah! ah! oh!
Those happy days are gone—heighho!

SHE.

Long as with thee I skimm'd the ground,
   Nor yet was scorn'd for Lady Jane,
No blither nymph teetotum'd round
   To Collinet's immortal strain.
     Oh! ah! etc.
Those happy days are gone—heighho!

HE.

With Lady Jane now whirl'd about,
   I know no bounds of time or breath;
And should the charmer's head hold out,
   My heart and heels are hers till death.
     Oh! ah! etc.
Still round and round through life we 'll go.

SHE.

To Lord Fitznoodle's eldest son,
   A youth renown'd for waistcoats smart,
I now have given (excuse the pun)
   A vested interest in my heart.
     Oh! ah! etc.
Still round and round with him I 'll go.

HE.

What if, by fond remembrance led
   Again to wear our mutual chain,
For me thou cut'st Fitznoodle dead,
   And I *levant* from Lady Jane.
     Oh! ah! etc.
Still round and round again we 'll go.

SHE.

Though he the Noodle honours give,
   And thine, dear youth, are not so high,
With thee in endless waltz I 'd live,
   With thee, to Weber's Stop-Waltz, die!
     Oh! ah! etc.
Thus round and round through life we 'll go.
          [Exeunt waltzing.

---

(1) In England the *partition* of this opera of Rossini was transferred to the story of Peter the Hermit; by which means the indecorum of giving such names as "Moïse," "Pharaon," etc., to the dances selected from it (as was done in Paris), has been avoided.

(2) It is hardly necessary to remind the reader that this Duet is a parody of the often-translated and parodied ode of Horace, "Donec gratus eram tibi," etc.

While thus, like motes that dance away
Existence in a summer ray,
These gay things, born but to quadrille,
The circle of their doom fulfil—
(That dancing room, whose law decrees
    That they should live, on the alert toe,
A life of ups-and-downs, like keys
Of Broadwood's in a long concerto:—)
While thus the fiddle's spell, *within*,
    Calls up its realm of restless sprites,
Without, as if some Mandarin
    Were holding there his Feast of Lights,
Lamps of all hues, from walks and bowers,
Broke on the eye, like kindling flowers,
Till, budding into light, each tree
Bore its full fruit of brilliancy.

Here shone a garden—lamps all o'er,
    As though the Spirits of the Air
Had taken it in their heads to pour
    A shower of summer meteors there ;—
While here a lighted shrubbery led
    To a small lake that sleeping lay,
Cradled in foliage, but, o'er-head,
    Open to heaven's sweet breath and ray ;
While round its rim there burning stood
Lamps, with young flowers beside them bedded,
That shrunk from such warm neighbourhood ;
And, looking bashful in the flood,
    Blush'd to behold themselves so wedded.

Hither, to this embower'd retreat,
    Fit but for nights so still and sweet ;
Nights, such as Eden's calm recall
    In its first lonely hour, when all
So silent is, below, on high,
    That if a star falls down the sky,
You almost think you hear it fall—
Hither, to this recess, a few,
    To shun the dancers' wildering noise,
And give an hour, ere night-time flew,
    To music's more ethereal joys,
Came, with their voices—ready all
As Echo, waiting for a call—
In hymn or ballad, dirge or glee,
To weave their mingling minstrelsy.

And first, a dark-eyed nymph, array'd—
Like her, whom Art hath deathless made,
Bright Mona Lisa, (1) with that braid
Of hair across the brow, and one
Small gem that in the centre shone —
With face, too, in its form resembling
Da Vinci's Beauties—the dark eyes,
Now lucid, as through crystal trembling,
    Now soft, as if suffused with sighs—
Her lute, that hung beside her, took,
And, bending o'er it with shy look,
More beautiful in shadow thus,
Than when with life most luminous,
Pass'd her light finger o'er the chords,
And sung to them these mournful words :—

SONG.

Bring hither, bring thy lute, while day is dying —
    Here will I lay me, and list to thy song ;
Should tones of other days mix with its sighing,
    Tones of a light heart, now banish'd so long,
Chase them away—they bring but pain,
And let thy theme be woe again.

Sing on, thou mournful lute—day is fast going,
    Soon will its light from thy chords die away ;
One little gleam in the west is still glowing,
    When that hath vanish'd, farewell to thy lay.
Mark, how it fades !—see, it is fled !
Now, sweet lute, be thou, too, dead.

The group, that late, in garb of Greeks,
    Sung their light chorus o'er the tide—
Forms, such as up the wooded creeks
    Of Helle's shore at noon-day glide,
Or, nightly, on her glistening sea,
    Woo the bright waves with melody—
Now link'd their triple league again
Of voices sweet, and sung a strain,
Such as, had Sappho's tuneful ear
But caught it on the fatal steep,
She would have paused, entranced, to hear,
    And, for that day, defer'd her leap.

SONG AND TRIO.

On one of those sweet nights that oft
    Their lustre o'er the Ægean fling,
Beneath my casement, low and soft,
    I heard a Lesbian lover sing;
And, listening both with ear and thought,
These sounds upon the night-breeze caught—
    " Oh, happy as the Gods is he,
    Who gazes at this hour on thee ! "

The song was one by Sappho sung,
    In the first love-dreams of her lyre,
When words of passion from her tongue
    Fell like a shower of living fire.
And still, at close of every strain,
I heard these burning words again—
    " Oh, happy as the gods is he,
    Who listens at this hour to thee ! "

Once more to Mona Lisa turn'd
    Each asking eye—nor turn'd it in vain;
Though the quick transient blush that burn'd
    Bright o'er her cheek, and died again,
Show'd with what inly shame and fear
Was utter'd what all loved to hear.
Yet not to sorrow's languid lay
    Did she her lute-song now devote;
But thus, with voice that, like a ray
    Of southern sunshine, seem'd to float—
So rich with climate was each note—

(1) The celebrated portrait by Leonardo da Vinci, which
he is said to have occupied four years in painting.—
Vasari, vol. vii.

Call'd up in every heart a dream
Of Italy with this soft theme:—

SONG.

Oh, where art thou dreaming,
  On land, or on sea?
In my lattice is gleaming
  The watch-light for thee:
And this fond heart is glowing
  To welcome thee home,
And the night is fast going,
  But thou art not come:
    No, thou comest not!

'Tis the time when night-flowers
  Should wake from their rest;
'Tis the hour of all hours
  When the lute singeth best.
But the flowers are half sleeping
  Till *thy* glance they see;
And the hush'd lute is keeping
  Its music for thee:
    Yet, thou comest not!

Scarce had the last word left her lip,
When a light boyish form, with trip
Fantastic, up the green walk came,
Prank'd in gay vest, to which the flame
Of every lamp he pass'd, or blue,
Or green, or crimson, lent its hue;
As though a live cameleon's skin
He had despoil'd, to robe him in.
A zone he wore of clattering shells,
  And from his lofty cap, where shone
A peacock's plume, there dangled bells
  That rang as he came dancing on.
Close after him, a page—in dress
And shape, his miniature express—
An ample basket, fill'd with store
Of toys and trinkets, laughing bore;
Till, having reach'd this verdant seat,
He laid it at his master's feet,
Who, half in speech and half in song,
Chaunted this invoice to the throng:—

SONG.

Who'll buy?—'t is Folly's shop, who'll buy?—
  We've toys to suit all ranks and ages;
Besides our usual fools' supply,
  We've lots of playthings, too, for sages.
For reasoners, here's a juggler's cup,
  That fullest seems when nothing's in it;
And nine-pins set, like systems, up,
  To be knock'd down the following minute.
    Who'll buy?—'t is Folly's shop, who'll buy?

Gay caps we here of foolscap make,
  For bards to wear in dog-day weather;
Or bards the bells alone may take,
  And leave to wits the cap and feather.
Teetotums we've for patriots got,
  Who court the mob with antics humble;

Like theirs the patriot's dizzy lot,
  A glorious spin, and then—a tumble.
    Who'll buy, etc., etc.

Here, wealthy misers to inter,
  We've shrouds of neat post-obit paper;
While for their heirs, we've *quick*silver,
  That, fast as they can wish, will caper.
For aldermen we've dials true,
  That tell no hour but that of dinner;
For courtly parsons sermons new,
  That suit alike both saint and sinner.
    Who'll buy, etc., etc.

No time we've now to name our terms,
  But, whatsoe'er the whims that seize you,
This oldest of all mortal firms,
  Folly and Co., will try to please you.
Or, should you wish a darker hue
  Of goods than *we* can recommend you,
Why then (as we with lawyers do)
  To Knavery's shop next door we'll send you.
    Who'll buy, etc., etc.

While thus the blissful moments roll'd,
  Moments of rare and fleeting light,
That show themselves, like grains of gold
  In the mine's refuse, few and bright;
Behold where, opening far away,
  The long Conservatory's range,
Stripp'd of the flowers it wore all day,
  But gaining lovelier in exchange,
Presents, on Dresden's costliest ware,
A supper such as Gods might share.
Ah, much-loved Supper!—blithe repast
Of other times, now dwindling fast,
Since Dinner far into the night
Advanced the march of appetite;
Deploy'd his never-ending forces
Of various vintage and three courses,
And, like those Goths who play'd the dickens
With Rome and all her sacred chickens,
Put Supper and her fowls so white,
Legs, wings, and drumsticks, all to flight.

Now waked once more by wine—whose tide
Is the true Hippocrene, where glide
The Muse's swans with happiest wing,
Dipping their bills, before they sing—
The minstrels of the table greet
The listening ear with descant sweet:—

SONG AND TRIO.

THE LEVEE AND COUCHEE.

Call the Loves around,
  Let the whispering sound
Of their wings be heard alone,
  Till soft to rest
  My Lady blest
At this bright hour hath gone.
  Let Fancy's beams
  Play o'er her dreams,

Till, touch'd with light all through,
　　Her spirit be
Like a summer sea,
Shining and slumbering too.
And, while thus hush'd she lies,
Let the whisper'd chorus rise—　　　[eyes."
" Good evening, good evening, to our Lady's bright

　　But the day-beam breaks,
　　　See, our Lady wakes!
Call the Loves around once more,
　　　Like stars that wait
　　　At morning's gate,
Her first steps to adore.
　　Let the veil of night
　　From her dawning sight
All gently pass away,
　　Like mists that flee
　　From a summer sea,
Leaving it full of day.
And, while her last dream flies,
Let the whisper'd chorus rise—　　　[eyes."
" Good morning, good morning, to our Lady's bright

SONG.

If to see thee be to love thee,
　If to love thee be to prize
Nought of earth or heaven above thee,
　Nor to live but for those eyes :
If such love to mortal given
Be wrong to earth, be wrong to heaven,
'T is not for thee the fault to blame,
For from those eyes the madness came.
Forgive but thou the crime of loving,
　In this heart more pride 't will raise
To be thus wrong, with thee approving,
　Than right, with all a world to praise !

But say, while light these songs resound,
What means that buzz of whispering round,
From lip to lip—as if the Power
Of Mystery, in this gay hour,
Had thrown some secret (as we fling
Nuts among children) to that ring
Of rosy restless lips, to be
Thus scrambled for so wantonly?
And, mark ye, still as each reveals
The mystic news, her hearer steals
A look towards yon enchanted chair,
　Where, like the Lady of the Masque,
A nymph, as exquisitely fair
　As Love himself for bride could ask,
Sits blushing deep, as if aware
Of the wing'd secret circling there.
Who is this nymph? and what, oh Muse,
　What, in the name of all odd things
That woman's restless brain pursues,
　What mean these mystic whisperings?
Thus runs the tale :—yon blushing maid,
Who sits in beauty's light array'd,

While o'er her leans a tall young Dervise,
(Who from her eyes, as all observe, is
Learning by heart the Marriage Service,)
Is the bright heroine of our song—
The Love-wed Psyche, whom so long
We've miss'd among this mortal train,
We thought her wing'd to heaven again.

But no—earth still demands her smile;
Her friends, the Gods, must wait awhile.
And if, for maid of heavenly birth,
　A young Duke's proffer'd heart and hand
Be things worth waiting for on earth,
　Both are, this hour, at her command.
To-night, in yonder half-lit shade,
　For love concerns expressly meant,
The fond proposal first was made,
　And love and silence blush'd consent.
Parents and friends (all here, as Jews,
Enchanters, house-maids, Turks, Hindoos,)
Have heard, approved, and blest the tie;
And now, hadst thou a poet's eye,
Thou might'st behold, in the air, above
That brilliant brow, triumphant Love,
Holding, as if to drop it down
Gently upon her curls, a crown
Of Ducal shape—but, oh, such gems !
Pilfer'd from Peri diadems,
And set in gold like that which shines
To deck the Fairy of the Mines :
In short, a crown all glorious—such as
Love orders when he makes a Duchess.

But see, 'tis morn in heaven; the Sun
Up the bright orient hath begun
To canter his immortal team;
　And, though not yet arrived in sight,
His leaders' nostrils send a steam
　Of radiance forth, so rosy bright
　As makes their onward path all light.
What 's to be done? if Sol will be
So deuced early, so must we;
And when the day thus shines outright,
Even dearest friends must bid good night.
So, farewell, scene of mirth and masking,
　Now almost a by-gone tale;
Beauties, late in lamp-light basking,
　Now, by daylight, dim and pale;
Harpers, yawning o'er your harps,.
Scarcely knowing flats from sharps;
Mothers who, while bored you keep
Time by nodding, nod to sleep;
Heads of hair, that stood last night
Crêpé, crispy, and upright,
But have now, alas, one sees, a
Leaning like the tower of Pisa;
Fare ye well—thus sinks away
　All that 's mighty, all that 's bright;
Tyre and Sidon had their day,
　And even a Ball—has but its night!

LALLA ROOKH.

PREFACE.

THE Poem, or Romance, of *Lalla Rookh*, having now reached, I understand, its twentieth edition, a short account of the origin and progress of a work which has been hitherto so very fortunate in its course, may not be deemed, perhaps, superfluous or misplaced.

It was about the year 1812 that, far more through the encouraging suggestions of friends than from any confident promptings of my own ambition, I conceived the design of writing a Poem upon some Oriental subject, and of those quarto dimensions which Scott's successful publications in that form had then rendered the regular poetical standard. A negotiation on the subject was opened with the Messrs. Longman, and, in the same year; but, from some causes which I cannot now recollect, led to no decisive result; nor was it till a year or two after, that any further steps were taken in the matter—their house being the only one, it is right to add, with which, from first to last, I held any communication upon the subject.

On this last occasion, Mr. Perry kindly offered himself as my representative in the treaty; and, what with the friendly zeal of my negotiator on the one side, and the prompt and liberal spirit with which he was met on the other, there has seldom, I think, occurred any transaction in which Trade and Poesy have shone out so advantageously in each other's eyes. The short discussion that then took place, between the two parties, may be comprised in a very few sentences. " I am of opinion," said Mr. Perry —enforcing his view of the case by arguments which it is not for me to cite—"that Mr. Moore ought to receive for his Poem the largest price that has been given, in our day, for such a work." "That was," answered the Messrs. Longman, "three thousand guineas." "Exactly so," replied Mr. Perry, "and no less a sum ought he to receive."

It was then objected, and very reasonably, on the part of the firm, that they had never yet seen a single line of the Poem; and that a perusal of the work ought to be allowed to them, before they embarked so large a sum in the purchase. But, no;—the romantic view which my friend, Perry, took of the matter was, that this price should be given as a tribute to reputation already acquired, without any condition for a previous perusal of the new work. This high tone, I must confess, not a little startled and alarmed me; but, to the honour and glory of Romance—as well on the publishers' side as the poet's—this very generous view of the transaction was, without any difficulty, acceded to, and the firm agreed, before we separated, that I was to receive three thousand guineas for my Poem.

At the time of this agreement, but little of the work, as it stands at present, had yet been written. But the ready confidence of my success shown by others made up for the deficiency of that requisite feeling within myself; while a strong desire not wholly to disappoint this "auguring hope " became almost a substitute for inspiration. In the year 1815, therefore, having made some progress in my task, I wrote to report the state of the work to the Messrs. Longman, adding, that I was now most willing and ready, should they desire it, to submit the manuscript for their consideration. Their answer to this offer was as follows :—"We are certainly impatient for the perusal of the Poem; but solely for our gratification. Your sentiments are always honourable."(1)

I continued to pursue my task for another year, being likewise occasionally occupied with the *Irish Melodies*, two or three numbers of which made their appearance during the period employed in writing Lalla Rookh. At length, in the year 1816, I found my work sufficiently advanced to be placed in the hands of the publishers. But the state of distress to which England was reduced, in that dismal year, by the exhausting effects of the series of wars she had just then concluded, and the general embarrassment of all classes both agricultural and commercial, rendered it a juncture the least favourable that could well be conceived for the first launch into print of so light and costly a venture as *Lalla Rookh*. Feeling conscious, therefore, that, under such circumstances, I should act but honestly in putting it in the power of the Messrs. Longman to re-consider the terms of their engagement with me—leaving them free to postpone, modify, or even, should such be their wish, relinquish it altogether, I wrote them a letter to that effect, and received the following answer :—" We shall be most happy in the pleasure of seeing you in February. We agree with you, indeed, that the times are most inauspicious for ' poetry and thousands;' but we believe that your poetry would do more than that of any other living poet at the present moment." (2)

The length of time I employed in writing the few stories strung together in *Lalla Rookh* will appear, to some persons, much more than was necessary for the production of such easy and "light o' love " fictions. But, besides that I have been, at all times, a far more slow and pains-taking workman than would ever be guessed, I fear, from the result, I felt that, in this instance, I had taken upon myself a more than ordinary responsibility, from the immense stake risked by others on my chance of success. For a long time, therefore, after the agreement had been concluded, though generally at work with a view to this task, I made but very little real progress in it; and I have still by me the beginnings of several

(1) April 10, 1815.   (2) November 9, 1816.

stories, continued, some of them, to the length of three or four hundred lines, which, after in vain endeavouring to mould them into shape, I threw aside, like the tale of Cambuscan, "left half-told." One of these stories, entitled The Peri's Daughter, was meant to relate the loves of a nymph of this aërial extraction with a youth of mortal race, the rightful Prince of Ormuz, who had been, from his infancy, brought up, in seclusion, on the banks of the river Amou, by an aged guardian named Mohassan. The story opens with the first meeting of these destined lovers, then in their childhood; the Peri having wafted her daughter to this holy retreat, in a bright enchanted boat, whose first appearance is thus described :—

> For, down the silvery tide afar,
> There came a boat, as swift and bright
> As shines, in heaven, some pilgrim-star,
> That leaves its own high home, at night,
> To shoot to distant shrines of light.

> "It comes, it comes," young Orian cries,
> And panting to Mohassan flies.
> Then, down upon the flowery grass
> Reclines to see the vision pass ;
> With partly joy and partly fear,
> To find its wondrous light so near,
> And hiding oft his dazzled eyes
> Among the flowers on which he lies.

> Within the boat a baby slept,
> Like a young pearl within its shell ;
> While one, who seem'd of riper years,
> But not of earth, or earth-like spheres,
> Her watch beside the slumberer kept ;
> Gracefully waving, in her hand,
>   The feathers of some holy bird,
>   With which, from time to time, she stirr'd
> The fragrant air, and coolly fann'd
> The baby's brow, or brush'd away
> The butterflies that, bright and blue
> As on the mountains of Malay,
>   Around the sleeping infant flew.

> And now the fairy boat hath stopp'd
> Beside the bank, the nymph has dropp'd
> Her golden anchor in the stream ;

A song is sung by the Peri in approaching, of which the following forms a part :—

> My child she is but half divine,
> Her father sleeps in the Caspian water ;
>   Sea-weeds twine
>   His funeral shrine,
> But he lives again in the Peri's daughter.
> Fain would I fly from mortal sight
> To my own sweet bowers of Peristan ;
> But there, the flowers are all too bright
> For the eyes of a baby born of man.
> On flowers of earth her feet must tread ;
>   So hither my light-wing'd bark hath brought her ;
>   Stranger, spread
>   Thy leafiest bed,
> To rest the wandering Peri's daughter.

In another of these inchoate fragments, a proud female saint, named Banou, plays a principal part ; and her progress through the streets of Cufa, on the night of a great illuminated festival, I find thus described :—

> It was a scene of mirth that drew
> A smile from even the Saint Banou,
> As, through the hush'd admiring throng,
> She went with stately steps along,
> And counted o'er, that all might see,
> The rubies of her rosary.
> But none might see the worldly smile
> That lurk'd beneath her veil, the while :
> Alla forbid ! for, who would wait
> Her blessing at the temple's gate—
> What holy man would ever run
> To kiss the ground she knelt upon,
> If once, by luckless chance, he knew
> She look'd and smiled as others do.
> Her hands were join'd, and from each wrist
> By threads of pearl and golden twist
> Hung relics of the saints of yore,
> And scraps of talismanic lore—
> Charms for the old, the sick, the frail,
> Some made for use, and all for sale.
> On either side, the crowd withdrew,
> To let the Saint pass proudly through ;
> While turban'd heads, of every hue,
> Green, white, and crimson, bow'd around,
> And gay tiaras touch'd the ground—
> As tulip-bells, when o'er their beds
> The musk-wind passes, bend their heads.
> Nay, some there were, among the crowd
> Of Moslem heads that round her bow'd,
> So fill'd with zeal, by many a draught
> Of Shiraz wine profanely quaff'd,
> That, sinking low in reverence then,
> They never rose till morn again.

There are yet two more of these unfinished sketches, one of which extends to a much greater length than I was aware of, and, as far as I can judge from a hasty renewal of my acquaintance with it, is not incapable of being yet turned to account.

In only one of these unfinished sketches, the tale of The Peri's Daughter, had I yet ventured to invoke that most home-felt of all my inspirations, which has lent to the story of The Fire-worshippers its main attraction and interest. That it was my intention, in the concealed Prince of Ormuz, to shadow out some impersonation of this feeling, I take for granted from the prophetic words supposed to be addressed to him by his aged guardian :—

> Bright child of destiny ! even now
> I read the promise on that brow,
> That tyrants shall no more defile
> The glories of the Green-Sea Isle,
> But Ormuz shall again be free,
> And hail her native Lord in thee !

In none of the other fragments do I find any trace of this sort of feeling, either in the subject or the personages of the intended story ; and this was the reason, doubtless, though hardly known at the time to myself, that, finding my subjects so slow in kindling my own sympathies, I began to despair of their ever touching the hearts of others; and felt often inclined to say,

" Oh no, I have no voice or hand
For such a song, in such a land."

Had this series of disheartening experiments been carried on much further, I must have thrown aside the work in despair. But, at last, fortunately, as it proved, the thought occurred to me of founding a story on the fierce struggle so long maintained between the Ghebers, (1) or ancient Fire-worshippers of Persia, and their haughty Moslem masters. From that moment, a new and deep interest in my whole task took possession of me. The cause of tolerance was again my inspiring theme; and the spirit that had spoken in the melodies of Ireland soon found itself at home in the East.

Having thus laid open the secrets of the work-shop to account for the time expended in *writing* this work, I must also, in justice to my own industry, notice the pains I took in long and laboriously *reading* for it. To form a store-house, as it were, of illustration purely Oriental, and so familiarise myself with its various treasures, that, as quick as Fancy required the aid of fact, in her spiritings, the memory was ready, like another Ariel, at her "strong bidding," to furnish materials for the spell-work—such was, for a long while, the sole object of my studies; and whatever time and trouble this preparatory process may have cost me, the effects resulting from it, as far as the humble merit of truthfulness is concerned, have been such as to repay me more than sufficiently for my pains. I have not forgotten how great was my pleasure, when told by the late Sir James Mackintosh, that he was once asked by Colonel W——s, the historian of British India, "whether it was true that Moore had never been in the East?" "Never," answered Mackintosh. "Well, that shows me," replied Colonel W——s, "that reading over D'Herbelot is as good as riding on the back of a camel."

I need hardly subjoin to this lively speech, that although D'Herbelot's valuable work was, of course, one of my manuals, I took the whole range of all such Oriental reading as was accessible to me; and became, for the time, indeed, far more conversant with all relating to that distant region, than I have ever been with the scenery, productions, or modes of life of any of those countries lying most within my reach. We know that D'Anville, though never in his life out of Paris, was able to correct a number of errors in a plan of the Troad taken by De Choiseul, on the spot; and, for my own very different, as well as far inferior, purposes, the knowledge I had thus acquired of distant localities, seen only by me in my day dreams, was no less ready and useful.

(1) Voltaire, in his tragedy of *Les Guébres*, written with a similar under-current of meaning, was accused of having transformed his Fire-worshippers into Jansenists: — "Quelques figuristes," he says, "prétendent que les Guébres sont les Jansénistes."

An ample reward for all this pains-taking has been found in such welcome tributes as I have just now cited; nor can I deny myself the gratification of citing a few more of the same description. From another distinguished authority on Eastern subjects, the late Sir John Malcolm, I had myself the pleasure of hearing a similar opinion publicly expressed;— that eminent person, in a speech spoken by him at a Literary Fund Dinner, having remarked, that together with those qualities of a poet which he much too partially assigned to me was combined also "the truth of the historian."

Sir William Ouseley, another high authority, in giving his testimony to the same effect, thus notices an exception to the general accuracy for which he gives me credit:—"Dazzled by the beauties of this composition, (2) few readers can perceive, and none surely can regret, that the poet, in his magnificent castastrophe, has forgotten, or boldly and most happily violated, the precept of Zoroaster, above noticed, which held it impious to consume any portion of a human body by fire, especially by that which glowed upon their altars." Having long lost, I fear, most of my Eastern learning, I can only cite, in defence of my catastrophe, an old Oriental tradition, which relates, that Nimrod, when Abraham refused, at his command, to worship the fire, ordered him to be thrown into the midst of the flames. (3) A precedent so ancient for this sort of use of the worshipped element, would appear, for all purposes at least of poetry, fully sufficient.

In addition to these agreeable testimonies, I have also heard, and need hardly add, with some pride and pleasure, that parts of this work have been rendered into Persian, and have found their way to Ispahan. To this fact, as I am willing to think it, allusion is made in some lively verses, written many years since, by my friend, Mr. Luttrell:—

" I'm told, dear Moore, your lays are sung,
(Can it be true, you lucky man?)
By moonlight, in the Persian tongue,
Along the streets of Ispahan."

That some knowledge of the work may have really reached that region appears not improbable, from a passage in the *Travels* of Mr. Frazer, who says, that "being delayed for some time at a town on the shores of the Caspian, he was lucky enough to be able to amuse himself with a copy of Lalla Rookh, which a Persian had lent him."

Of the description of Balbec, in "*Paradise and the Peri*," Mr. Carne, in his Letters from the East, thus speaks: "The description in Lalla Rookh of the plain and the ruins is exquisitely faithful. The minaret is on the declivity near at hand, and there

(2) The Fire-worshippers.

(3) Tradunt autem Hebræi hanc fabulam quod Abraham in ignem missus sit quia ignem adorare noluit.—St. Hieron, *in quæst. in Genesim.*

wanted only the muezzin's cry to break the silence."

I shall now tax my reader's patience with but one more of these generous vouchers. Whatever of vanity there may be in citing such tributes, they show, at least, of what great value, even in poetry, is that prosaic quality, Industry; since, as the reader of the foregoing pages is now fully apprized, it was in a slow and laborious collection of small facts, that the first foundations of this fanciful Romance were laid.

The friendly testimony I have just referred to appeared, some years since, in the form in which I now give it, and, if I recollect right, in the *Athenæum:*—

" I embrace this opportunity of bearing my individual testimony (if it be of any value) to the extraordinary accuracy of Mr. Moore, in his topographical, antiquarian, and characteristic details, whether of costume, manners, or less-changing monuments, both in his *Lalla Rookh* and in the *Epicurean.* It has been my fortune to read his Atlantic, Bermudean, and American Odes and Epistles, in the countries and among the people to which and to whom they related ; I enjoyed also the exquisite delight of reading his *Lalla Rookh* in Persia itself: and I have perused the *Epicurean*, while all my recollections of Egypt and its still existing wonders are as fresh as when I quitted the banks of the Nile for Arabia :—I owe it, therefore, as a debt of gratitude (though the payment is most inadequate), for the great pleasure I have derived from his productions, to bear my humble testimony to their local fidelity.
"J. S. B."

Among the incidents connected with this work, I must not omit to notice the splendid Divertissement, founded upon it, which was acted at the Château Royal of Berlin, during the visit of the Grand Duke Nicholas to that capital, in the year 1822. The different stories composing the work were represented in Tableaux Vivans and songs ; and among the crowd of royal and noble personages engaged in the performances, I shall mention those only who represented the principal characters, and whom I find thus enumerated in the published account of the Divertissement. (1)

" Fadladin, Grand-Nasir,	Comte Haack, (*maréchal de cour*).
Aliris, Roi de Bucharie	. S. A. I. Le *Grand-Duc.*
Lallah Roûkh	. S. A. I. La *Grande-Duchesse.*
Aurungzeb, le Grand Mogol	S. A. R. *le prince Guillaume, frère du roi.*
Abdallah, père d'Aliris	S. A. R. *le duc de Cumberland.*
La Reine, son épouse	S. A. R. *la princesse Louise Radzivill.*"

Besides these and other leading personages, there were also brought into action, under the various denominations of Seigneurs et Damas de Bucharie, Dames de Cachemire, Seigneurs et Dames dansans à la Fête des Roses, nearly 150 persons.

Of the manner and style in which the Tableaux of the different stories are described in the work from

(1) *Lalla Roûkh*, Divertissement mêlé de chants et de danses, Berlin, 1822. The work contains a series of coloured engravings, representing groups, processions, etc., in different Oriental costumes.

which I cite, the following account of the performance of Paradise and the Peri will afford some specimen :—

" La décoration représentoit les portes brillantes du Paradis, entourées de nuages. Dans le premier tableau on voyait la Péri, triste et désolée, couchée sur le seuil des portes fermées, et l'Ange de lumière qui lui adresse des consolations et des conseils. Le second représente le moment où la Péri, dans l'espoir que ce don lui ouvrira l'entrée du Paradis, recueille la dernière goutte de sang que vient de verser le jeune guerrier Indien. . . . . . .

"La Péri et l'Ange de lumière répondoient pleinement à l'image et à l'idée qu'on est tenté de se faire de ces deux individus, et l'impression qu'a faite généralement la suite des tableaux de cet épisode délicat et intéressant est loin de s'effacer de notre souvenir."

In this grand Fête, it appears, originated the translation of *Lalla Rookh* into German verse, by the Baron de la Motte Fouqué ; and the circumstances which led him to undertake the task are described by himself, in a Dedicatory Poem to the Empress of Russia, which he has prefixed to his translation. As soon as the performance, he tells us, had ended, Lalla Rookh (the Empress herself) exclaimed, with a sigh, " Is it, then, all over? are we now at the close of all that has given us so much delight? and lives there no poet who will impart to others, and to future times, some notion of the happiness we have enjoyed this evening ?" On hearing this appeal, a Knight of Cashmere (who is no other than the poetical Baron himself) comes forward and promises to attempt to present to the world " the Poem itself in the measure of the original:" whereupon Lalla Rookh, it is added, approvingly smiled.

— ◦❊◦ —

TO SAMUEL ROGERS, ESQ.
THIS EASTERN ROMANCE
IS INSCRIBED BY HIS VERY GRATEFUL AND AFFECTIONATE
FRIEND,
May 19, 1817. THOMAS MOORE.
— ◦❊◦ —

LALLA ROOKH.

In the eleventh year of the reign of Aurungzebe, Abdalla, King of the Lesser Bucharia, a lineal descendant from the Great Zingis, having abdicated the throne in favour of his son, set out on a pilgrimage to the Shrine of the Prophet ; and, passing into India through the delightful valley of Cashmere, rested for a short time at Delhi on his way. He was entertained by Aurungzebe in a style of magnificent hospitality, worthy alike of the visiter and the host, and was afterwards escorted with the same splendour to Surat, where he embarked for Arabia. (2) During the stay of the Royal Pilgrim at Delhi, a marriage was agreed upon between the Prince, his son, and the youngest daughter of the Emperor, Lalla Rookh ; (3) — a

(2) These particulars of the visit of the King of Bucharia to Aurungzebe are found in *Dow's History of Hindoostan*, vol. iii., p. 392.
(3) Tulip cheek.

41

Princess described by the poets of her time as more
beautiful than Leila, (1) Shirine, (2) Dewildé, (3) or
any of those heroines whose names and loves em-
bellish the songs of Persia and Hindostan. It was
intended that the nuptials should be celebrated at
Cashmere; where the young King, as soon as the
cares of empire would permit, was to meet, for the
first time, his lovely bride, and, after a few months'
repose in that enchanting valley, conduct her over
the snowy hills into Bucharia.

The day of Lalla Rookh's departure from Delhi
was as splendid as sunshine and pageantry could
make it. The bazaars and baths were all covered
with the richest tapestry; hundreds of gilded barges
upon the Jumna floated with their banners shining
in the water; while through the streets groups of
beautiful children went strewing the most delicious
flowers around, as in that Persian festival called the
Scattering of the Roses; (4) till every part of the city
was as fragrant as if a caravan of musk from Khoten
had passed through it. The Princess, having taken
leave of her kind father, who at parting hung a cor-
nelian of Yemen round her neck, on which was in-
scribed a verse from the Koran, and having sent a
considerable present to the Fakirs, who kept up the
Perpetual Lamp in her sister's tomb, meekly ascended
the palankeen prepared for her; and, while Aurung-
zebe stood to take a last look from his balcony, the
procession moved slowly on the road to Lahore.

Seldom had the Eastern world seen a cavalcade so
superb. From the gardens in the suburbs to the
Imperial palace, it was one unbroken line of splen-
dour. The gallant appearance of the Rajahs and
Mogul lords, distinguished by those insignia of
the Emperor's favour, (5) the feathers of the egret
of Cashmere in their turbans, and the small silver-

rimm'd kettle-drums at the bows of their saddles;
—the costly armour of their cavaliers, who vied,
on this occasion, with the guards of the great Keder
Khan, (6) in the brightness of their silver battle-
axes and the massiness of their maces of gold;—
the glittering of the gilt pine-apples (7) on the tops
of the palankeens;—the embroidered trappings of
the elephants, bearing on their backs small turrets,
in the shape of little antique temples, within which
the Ladies of Lalla Rookh lay as it were enshrined
—the rose-coloured veils of the Princess's own sump-
tuous litter, (8) at the front of which a fair young
female slave sat fanning her through the curtains,
with feathers of the Argus pheasant's wing; (9)—
and the lovely troop of Tartarian and Cashmerian
maids of honour, whom the young King had sent to
accompany his bride, and who rode on each side of
the litter, upon small Arabian horses;—all was
brilliant, tasteful, and magnificent, and pleased even
the critical and fastidious Fadladeen, Great Nazir
or Chamberlain of the Haram, who was borne in his
palankeen immediately after the Princess, and con-
sidered himself not the least important personage of
the pageant.

Fadladeen was a judge of every thing—from the
pencilling of a Circassian's eyelids to the deepest
questions of science and literature; from the mix-
ture of a conserve of rose-leaves to the composition
of an epic poem: and such influence had his opinion
upon the various tastes of the day, that all the cooks
and poets of Delhi stood in awe of him. His po-
litical conduct and opinions were founded upon that
line of Sadi,—"Should the Prince at noon-day say,
It is night, declare that you behold the moon and
stars."—And his zeal for religion, of which Aurung-
zebe was a munificent protector, (10) was about as

---

(1) The mistress of Mejnoun, upon whose story so many
Romances in all the languages of the East are founded.

(2) For the loves of this celebrated beauty with Khosrou
and with Ferhad, see *D'Herbelot, Gibbon, Oriental Collec-
tions,* etc.

(3) "The history of the loves of Dewildé and Chizer,
the son of the Emperor Alla, is written in an elegant
poem, by the noble Chusero."—*Ferishta.*

(4) Gul Reazee.

(5) "One mark of honour or knighthood bestowed by
the Emperor is the permission to wear a small kettle-drum
at the bows of their saddles, which at first was invented
for the training of hawks, and to call them to the lure,
and is worn in the field by all sportsmen to that end."—
Fryer's Travels.

"Those on whom the King has conferred the privilege
must wear an ornament of jewels on the right side of the
turban, surmounted by a high plume of the feathers of a
kind of egret. This bird is found only in Cashmere, and
the feathers are carefully collected for the King, who
bestows them on his nobles."—*Elphinstone's Account of
Caubul.*

(6) "Khedar Khan, the Khakan, or King of Turquestan,
beyond the Gihon (at the end of the eleventh century),
whenever he appeared abroad was preceded by seven

hundred horsemen with silver battle-axes, and was fol-
lowed by an equal number bearing maces of gold. He
was a great patron of poetry, and it was he who used to
preside at public exercises of genius, with four basins of
gold and silver by him to distribute among the poets who
excelled."—*Richardson's Dissertation,* prefixed to his Dic-
tionary.

(7) "The kubdeh, a large golden knob, generally in the
shape of a pine-apple, on the top of the canopy over the
litter or palanquin."—*Scott's Notes on the Bahardanush.*

(8) In the Poem of *Zohair,* in the *Moallakat,* there is the
following lively description of "a company of maidens
seated on camels."

"They are mounted in carriages covered with costly
awnings, and with rose-coloured veils, the linings of
which have the hue of crimson Andem-wood.

"When they ascend from the bosom of the vale, they sit
forward on the saddle-cloth, with every mark of a volup-
tuous gaiety.

"Now, when they have reached the brink of yon blue-
gushing rivulet, they fix the poles of their tents like the
Arab with a settled mansion."

(9) See *Bernier's* description of the attendants on Rau-
chanara-Begum, in her progress to Cashmere.

(10) This hypocritical Emperor would have made a worthy

disinterested as that of the goldsmith who fell in love with the diamond eyes of the idol of Jaghernaut. (1)

During the first days of their journey, Lalla Rookh, who had passed all her life within the shadow of the Royal Gardens of Delhi, (2) found enough in the beauty of the scenery through which they passed to interest her mind, and delight her imagination ; and when at evening, or in the heat of the day, they turned off from the high road to those retired and romantic places which had been selected for her encampments — sometimes on the banks of a small rivulet, as clear as the waters of the Lake of Pearl ; (3) sometimes under the sacred shade of a Banyan tree, from which the view opened upon a glade covered with antelopes ; and often in those hidden embowered spots, described by one from the Isles of the West, (4) as "places of melancholy, delight, and safety, where all the company around was wild peacocks and turtle-doves ;"—she felt a charm in these scenes, so lovely and so new to her, which, for a time, made her in different to every other amusement. But Lalla Rookh was young, and the young love variety ; nor could the conversation of her Ladies and the Great Chamberlain, Fadladeen, (the only persons, of course, admitted to her pavilion,) sufficiently enliven those many vacant hours, which were devoted neither to the pillow nor the palankeen. There was a little Persian slave who sung sweetly to the Vina, and who, now and then, lulled the Princess to sleep

with the ancient ditties of her country, about the loves of Wamak and Ezra, (5) the fair-haired Zal and his mistress Rodahver ; (6) not forgetting the combat of Rustam with the terrible white Demon. (7)   At other times she was amused by those graceful dancing girls of Delhi, who had been permitted by the Bramins of the Great Pagoda to attend her, much to the horror of the good Mussulman Fadladeen, who could see nothing graceful or agreeable in idolaters, and to whom the very tinkling of their golden anklets (8) was an abomination.

But these and many other diversions were repeated till they lost all their charm, and the nights and noon-days were beginning to move heavily, when, at length, it was recollected that, among the attendants sent by the bridegroom, was a young poet of Cashmere, much celebrated throughout the Valley for his manner of reciting the stories of the East, on whom his Royal Master had conferred the privilege of being admitted to the pavilion of the Princess, that he might help to beguile the tediousness of the journey by some of his most agreeable recitals.   At the mention of a poet, Fadladeen elevated his critical eyebrows, and, having refreshed his faculties with a dose of that delicious opium (9) which is distilled from the black poppy of the Thebais, gave orders for the minstrel to be forthwith introduced into the presence.

The Princess, who had one.. in her life seen a poet from behind the screens of gauze in her father's

---

associate of certain Holy Leagues.—" He held the cloak of religion (says Dow) between his actions and the vulgar ; and impiously thanked the Divinity for a success which he owed to his own wickedness. When he was murdering and persecuting his brothers and their families, he was building a magnific nt mosque at Delhi, as an offering to God for his assistance to him in the civil war. He acted as high priest at the consecration of this temple ; and made a practice of attending divine service there, in the humble dress of a Fakeer. But when he lifted one hand to the Divinity, he, with the other, signed warrants for the assassination of his relations."—*History of Hindostan*, vol. iii., p. 335. See also the curious letter of Aurungzebe, given in the *Oriental Collections*, vol. i., p. 320.

(1) " The idol at Jaghernaut has two fine diamonds for eyes. No goldsmith is suffered to enter the Pagoda, one having stole one of these eyes, being locked up all night with the Idol."—*Tavernier*.

(2) See a description of these royal Gardens in " *An Account of the present state of Delhi*, by Lieut. W. Franklin."—*Asiat. Research.*, vol. iv., p. 417.

(3) " In the neighbourhood is Notte Gill, or the Lake of Pearl, which receives this name from its pellucid water."—*Pennant's Hindoostan*.

"Nasir Jung, encamped in the vicinity of the Lake of Tonoor, amused himself with sailing on that clear and beautiful water, and gave it the fanciful name of Motee Talab, 'the Lake of Pearls,' which it still retains."—*Wilks's South of India*.

(4) Sir Thomas Roe, Ambassador from James I. to Jehanguire.

(5) " The romance *Wemakweazra*, written in Persian

verse, which contains the loves of Wamak and Ezra, two celebrated lovers who lived before the time of Mahomet."—*Note on the Oriental Tales*.

(6) Their amour is recounted in the Shah-Namèh of Ferdousi ; and there is much beauty in the passage which describes the slaves of Rodahver sitting on the bank of the river, and throwing flowers into the stream, in order to draw the attention of the young Hero who is encamped on the opposite side.—See *Champion's* translation.

(7) Rustam is the Hercules of the Persians. For the particulars of his victory over the Sepeed Deeve, or White Demon, see *Oriental Collections*, vol. ii., p. 45.—Near the city of Shiraz is an immense quadrangular monument, in commemoration of this combat, called the Kelaat-i-Deev Sepeed, or castle of the White Giant, which Father Angelo, in his Gazophilacium Persicum, p. 127, declares to have been the most memorable monument of antiquity which he had seen in Persia.—See *Ouseley's Persian Miscellanies*.

(8) " The women of the Idol, or dancing girls of the Pagoda, have little golden bells, fastened to their feet, the soft harmonious tinkling of which vibrates in unison with the exquisite melody of their voices."—*Maurice's Indian Antiquities*.

" The Arabian courtesans, like the Indian women, have little golden bells fastened round their legs, neck, and elbows, to the sound of which they dance before the King. The Arabian princesses wear golden rings on their fingers, to which little bells are suspended, as well as in the flowing tresses of their hair, that their superior rank may be known, and they themselves receive in passing the homage due to them."—See *Calmet's Dictionary*, art. Bells.

(9) "Abou-Tige, ville de la Thébaïde, où il croît beaucoup de pavot noir, dont se fait le meilleur opium."—*D'Herbelot*.

hull, and had conceived from that specimen no very favourable ideas of the caste, expected but little in this new exhibition to interest her;—she felt inclined, however, to alter her opinion on the very first appearance of Feramorz. He was a youth about Lalla Rookh's own age, and graceful as that idol of women, Crishna (1) — such as he appears to their young imaginations, heroic, beautiful, breathing music from his very eyes, and exalting the religion of his worshippers into love. His dress was simple, yet not without some marks of costliness; and the Ladies of the Princess were not long in discovering that the cloth, which encircled his high Tartaria-cap was of the most delicate kind that the shawl-goats of Tibet supply. (2) Here and there, too, over his vest, which was confined by a flowered girdle of Kashan, hung strings of fine pearl, disposed with an air of studied negligence; — nor did the exquisite embroidery of his sandals escape the observation of these fair critics; who, however they might give way to Fadladeen upon the unimportant topics of religion and government, had the spirit of martyrs in every thing relating to such momentous matters as jewels and embroidery.

For the purpose of relieving the pauses of recitation by music, the young Cashmerian held in his hand a kitar;—such as, in old times, the Arab maids of the West used to listen to by moonlight in the gardens of the Alhambra—and, having premised, with much humility, that the story he was about to relate was founded on the adventures of that Veiled Prophet of Khorassan, (3) who, in the year of the Hegira 163, created such alarm throughout the Eastern Empire, made an obeisance to the Princess, and thus began :—

THE VEILED PROPHET OF KHORASSAN. (4)

In that delightful Province of the Sun,
The first of Persian lands he shines upon,

(1) The Indian Apollo.—"He and the three Rámas are described as youths of perfect beauty; and the princesses of Hindustán were all passionately in love with Crishna, who continues to this hour the darling God of the Indian women."—*Sir W. Jones, on the Gods of Greece, Italy, and India.*

(2) See *Turner's Embassy* for a description of this animal, "the most beautiful among the whole tribe of goats." The material for the shawls (which is carried to Cashmere) is found next the skin.

(3) For the real history of this Impostor, whose original name was Hakem ben Haschem, and who was called Mokanna from the veil of silver gauze (or, as others say, golden) which he always wore, see *D'Herbelot.*

(4) Khorassan signifies, in the old Persian language, Province or Region of the Sun.—*Sir W. Jones.*

(5) "The fruits of Meru are finer than those of any other place; and one cannot see in any other city such palaces with groves, and streams, and gardens."—*Ebn Haukal's Geography.*

(6) One of the royal cities of Khorassan.

(7) Moses.

(8) "Ses disciples assuroient qu'il se couvroit le visage,

Where all the loveliest children of his beam,
Flowerets and fruits blush over every stream, (5)
And, fairest of all streams, the Murga roves
Among Merou's (6) bright palaces and groves;
There on that throne, to which the blind belief
Of millions raised him, sat the Prophet-Chief,
The Great Mokanna. O'er his features hung
The Veil, the Silver Veil, which he had flung
In mercy there, to hide from mortal sight
His dazzling brow, till man could bear its light.
For, far less luminous, his votaries said,
Were even the gleams, miraculously shed [he trod,
O'er Moussa's (7) cheek, (8) when down the Mount
All glowing from the presence of his God!

On either side, with ready hearts and hands,
His chosen guard of bold Believers stands;
Young fire-eyed disputants, who deem their swords,
On points of faith, more eloquent than words;
And such their zeal, there's not a youth with brand
Uplifted there, but, at the Chief's command,
Would make his own devoted heart its sheath,
And bless the lips that doom'd so dear a death!
In hatred to the Caliph's hue of night, (9)
Their vesture, helms and all, is snowy white;
Their weapons various—some equipp'd, for speed,
With javelins of the light Kathaian reed; (10)
Or bows of buffalo horn and shining quivers
Fill'd with the stems (11) that bloom on Iran's rivers; (12)
While some, for war's more terrible attacks,
Wield the huge mace and ponderous battle-axe;
And as they wave aloft in morning's beam
The milk-white plumage of their helms, they seem
Like a chenar-tree grove (13) when Winter throws
O'er all its tufted heads his feathering snows.

Between the porphyry pillars that uphold
The rich moresque-work of the roof of gold,

pour ne pas éblouir ceux qui l'approchoient par l'éclat de son visage comme Moïse."—*D'Herbelot.*

(9) Black was the colour adopted by the Caliphs of the House of Abbas, in their garments, turbans, and standards.—"Il faut remarquer ici, touchant les habits blancs des disciples de Hakem, que la couleur des habits, des coëffures, et des étendarts des Khalifes Abasides étant la noire, ce chef de rebelles ne pouvait pas en choisir une qui lui fut plus opposée."—*D'Herbelot.*

(10) "Our dark javelins, exquisitely wrought of Khathaian reeds, slender and delicate."—*Poem of Amru.*

(11) Pichula, used anciently for arrows by the Persians.

(12) The Persians call this plant Gaz. The celebrated shaft of Isfendiar, one of their ancient heroes, was made of it.—"Nothing can be more beautiful than the appearance of this plant in flower during the rains on the banks of rivers, where it is usually interwoven with a lovely twining asclepias."—*Sir W. Jones, Botanical Observations on Select Indian Plants.*

(13) The oriental plane. "The chenar is a delightful tree; its bole is of a fine white and smooth bark; and its foliage, which grows in a tuft at the summit, is of a bright green."—*Morier's Travels.*

Aloft the Haram's curtain'd galleries rise,
Where through the silken net-work, glancing eyes,
From time to time, like sudden gleams that glow
Through autumn clouds, shine o'er the pomp below.
What impious tongue, ye blushing saints, would dare
To hint that aught but Heaven hath placed you there?
Or that the loves of this light world could bind,
In their gross chain, your Prophet's soaring mind!
No—wrongful thought!—commission'd from above
To people Eden's bowers with shapes of love,
(Creatures so bright, that the same lips and eyes
They wear on earth will serve in Paradise,)
There to recline among Heaven's native maids,
And crown the Elect with bliss that never fades —
Well hath the Prophet-Chief his bidding done;
And every beauteous race beneath the sun,
From those who kneel at Brahma's burning fount, (1)
To the fresh nymphs bounding o'er Yemen's mounts;
From Persia's eyes of full and fawn-like ray,
To the small half-shut glances of Kathay; (2)
And Georgia's bloom, and Azab's darker smiles,
And the gold ringlets of the Western Isles ;
All, all are there;—each Land its flower hath given,
To form that fair young Nursery for Heaven!

But why this pageant now? this arm'd array?
What triumph crowds the rich Divan to-day
With turban'd heads, of every hue and race,
Bowing before that veil'd and awful face,
Like tulip-beds, (3) of different shape and dyes,
Bending beneath the invisible West-wind's sighs!
What new-made mystery now, for Faith to sign,
And blood to seal, as genuine and divine,
What dazzling mimickry of God's own power,
Hath the bold Prophet plann'd to grace this hour?

Not such the pageant now, though not less proud;
Yon warrior youth, advancing from the crowd,
With silver bow, with belt of broider'd crape,
And fur-bound bonnet of Bucharian shape, (4)
So fiercely beautiful in form and eye,
Like war's wild planet in a summer sky;
That youth to-day—a proselyte, worth hordes
Of cooler spirits and less practised swords—
Is come to join, all bravery and belief,
The creed and standard of the heaven-sent Chief.

Though few his years, the West already knows
Young Azim's fame;—beyond the Olympian snows,
Ere manhood darken'd o'er his downy cheek,
O'erwhelm'd in fight and captive to the Greek, (5)
He linger'd there, till peace dissolved his chains ;—
Oh, who could, even in bondage, tread the plains
Of glorious Greece, nor feel his spirit rise
Kindling within him? who, with heart and eyes,
Could walk where Liberty had been, nor see
The shining foot-prints of her Deity,
Nor feel those god-like breathings in the air,
Which mutely told her spirit had been there?
Not he, that youthful warrior—no, too well
For his soul's quiet work'd the awakening spell ;
And now, returning to his own dear land,
Full of those dreams of good that, vainly grand,
Haunt the young heart—proud views of human-
Of men to Gods exalted and refined—   [kind,
False views, like that horizon's fair deceit,
Where earth and heaven but *seem*, alas, to meet!—
Soon as he heard an Arm Divine was raised
To right the nations, and beheld, emblazed
On the white flag Mokanna's host unfurl'd,
Those words of sunshine, "Freedom to the World,"
At once his faith, his sword, his soul, obey'd
The inspiring summons ; every chosen blade
That fought beneath that banner's sacred text
Seem'd doubly edged, for this world and the next ;
And ne'er did Faith with her smooth bandage bind
Eyes more devoutly willing to be blind,
In virtue's cause :—never was soul inspired,
With livelier trust in what it most desired,
Than his, the enthusiast there, who kneeling, pale
With pious awe, before that Silver Veil,
Believes the form, to which he bends his knee,
Some pure redeeming angel, sent to free
This fetter'd world from every bond and stain,
And bring its primal glories back again !

Low as young Azim knelt, that motley crowd
Of all earth's nations sunk the knee and bow'd,
With shouts of "Alla!" echoing long and loud ;
While high in air, above the Prophet's head,
Hundreds of banners, to the sunbeam spread,
Waved, like the wings of the white birds that fan
The flying throne of star-taught Soliman. (6)

(1) The burning fountains of Brahma near Chittogong,
esteemed as holy.—*Turner.*   (2) China.
(3) "The name of tulip is said to be of Turkish extrac-
tion, and given to the flower on account of its resembling
a turban."—*Beckmann's History of Inventions.*
(4) The inhabitants of Bucharia wear a round cloth
bonnet, shaped much after the Polish fashion, having a
large fur border. They tie their kaftans about the middle
with a girdle of a kind of silk crape, several times round
the body.—*Account of Independent Tartary, in Pinker-
ton's Collection.*
(5) In the war of the Caliph Mahadi against the Empress
Irene, for an account of which vide *Gibbon*, vol. x.
(6) This wonderful Throne was called The Star of the

Genii. For a full description of it, see the fragment,
translated by Captain Franklin, from a Persian MS. entitled,
"*The History of Jerusalem,*" *Oriental Collections*, vol. i.,
p. 235.—When Soliman travelled, the eastern writers say,
"he had a carpet of green silk on which his throne was
placed, being of a prodigious length and breadth, and suf-
ficient for all his forces to stand upon, the men placing
themselves on his right hand, and the spirits on his left;
and that when all were in order, the wind, at his command,
took up the carpet, and transported it, with all that were
upon it, wherever he pleased; the army of birds at the
same time flying over their heads, and forming a kind of
canopy to shade them from the sun."—*Sale's Koran*,
vol. ii., p. 214, note.

Then thus he spoke:—" Stranger, though new the
     frame
Thy soul inhabits now, I've track'd its flame
For many an age, (1) in every chance and change
Of that existence, through whose varied range—
As through a torch-race, where from hand to hand
The flying youths transmit their shining brand,
From frame to frame the unextinguish'd soul
Rapidly passes, till it reach the goal!

   " Nor think 'tis only the gross Spirits, warm'd
With duskier fire and for earth's medium form'd,
That run this course;—Beings, the most divine,
Thus deign through dark mortality to shine.
Such was the Essence that in Adam dwelt,
To which all Heaven, except the Proud One, knelt: (2)
Such the refined Intelligence that glow'd
In Moussa's (3) frame—and, thence descending
     flow'd
Through many a Prophet's breast; (4)—in Issa (5)
     shone,
And in Mohammed burn'd; till, hastening on,
(As a bright river that, from fall to fall
In many a maze descending, bright through all,
Finds some fair region where, each labyrinth past,
In one full lake of light it rests at last)
That Holy Spirit, settling calm and free
From lapse or shadow, centres all in me !"

   Again, throughout the assembly at these words,
Thousands of voices rung : the warriors' swords
Were pointed up to heaven; a sudden wind
In the open banners play'd, and from behind
Those Persian hangings, that but ill could screen
The Haram's loveliness, white hands were seen
Waving embroider'd scarves, whose motion gave
A perfume forth—like those the Houris wave
When beckoning to their bowers the immortal
     Brave.

   "But these," pursued the Chief, " are truths
     sublime,
That claim a holier mood and calmer time
Than earth allows us now ;—this sword must first
The darkling prison-house of Mankind burst,
Ere Peace can visit them, or Truth let in
Her wakening daylight on a world of sin.
But then—celestial warriors, then, when all
Earth's shrines and thrones before our banner fall ;
When the glad Slave shall at these feet lay down
His broken chain, the tyrant Lord his crown,

The Priest his book, the Conqueror his wreath,
And from the lips of Truth one mighty breath
Shall, like a whirlwind, scatter in its breeze
That whole dark pile of human mockeries;—
Then shall the reign of mind commence on earth,
And starting fresh as from a second birth,
Man, in the sunshine of the world's new spring,
Shall walk transparent, like some holy thing !
Then, too, your Prophet from his angel brow
Shall cast the Veil that hides its splendours now,
And gladden'd Earth shall, through her wide ex-
     panse,
Bask in the glories of this countenance!

   "For thee, young warrior, welcome !—thou hast yet
Some tasks to learn, some frailties to forget,
Ere the white war-plume o'er thy brow can wave;—
But, once my own, mine all till in the grave !"

The pomp is at an end—the crowds are gone—
Each ear and heart still haunted by the tone
Of that deep voice, which thrill'd like Alla's own !
The Young all dazzled by the plumes and lances,
The glittering throne, and Haram's half-caught
     glances ;
The Old deep pondering on the promised reign
Of peace and truth ; and all the female train
Ready to risk their eyes, could they but gaze
A moment on that brow's miraculous blaze!

   But there was one, among the chosen maids,
Who blush'd behind the gallery's silken shades,
One to whose soul the pageant of to-day
Has been like death :—you saw her pale dismay,
Ye wondering sisterhood, and heard the burst
Of exclamation from her lips, when first
She saw that youth, too well, too dearly known,
Silently kneeling at the Prophet's throne.

Ah Zelica ! there *was* a time, when bliss
Shone o'er thy heart from every look of his ;
When but to see him, hear him, breathe the air
In which he dwelt, was thy soul's fondest prayer ;
When round him hung such a perpetual spell,
Whate'er he did, none ever did so well.
Too happy days ! when, if he touch'd a flower
Or gem of thine, 'twas sacred from that hour ;
When thou didst study him, till every tone
And gesture and dear look became thy own—
Thy voice like his, the changes of his face
In thine reflected with still lovelier grace,

(1) The transmigration of souls was one of his doctrines.
—Vide D'Herbelot.
(2. "And when we said unto the angels, Worship Adam,
they all worshipped him except Eblis (Lucifer), who re-
fused."—The Koran, chap. ii.
(3) Moses.
(4) This is according to D'Herbelot's account of the doc-
trines of Mokanna :—"Sa doctrine étoit, que Dieu avoit
pris une forme et figure humaine, depuis qu'il eut com-

mandé aux anges d'adorer Adam, le premier des hommes.
Qu'après la mort d'Adam, Dieu étoit apparu sous la figure
de plusieurs prophètes, et autres grands hommes qu'il
avoit choisis, jusqu'à ce qu'il prît celle d'Abu Moslem,
prince de Khorassan, lequel professoit l'erreur de la Te-
nassukhiah ou Metempsychose ; et qu'après la mort de ce
prince, la Divinité étoit passée, et descendue en sa per
sonne."
(5) Jesus.

Like echo, sending back sweet music, fraught
With twice the aërial sweetness it had brought!
Yet now he comes—brighter than even he
E'er beam'd before—but, ah! not bright for thee;
No—dread, unlook'd for, like a visitant
From the other world, he comes as if to haunt
Thy guilty soul with dreams of lost delight,
Long lost to all but memory's aching sight:—
Sad dreams! as when the Spirit of our Youth
Returns in sleep, sparkling with all the truth
And innocence once ours, and leads us back,
In mournful mockery, o'er the shining track
Of our young life, and points out every ray
Of hope and peace we've lost upon the way!

Once happy pair!—In proud Bokhara's groves,
Who had not heard of their first youthful loves?
Born by that ancient flood, (1) which from its spring
In the dark Mountains swiftly wandering,
Enrich'd by every pilgrim brook that shines
With relics from Bucharia's ruby mines,
And, lending to the Caspian half its strength,
In the cold Lake of Eagles sinks at length;—
There, on the banks of that bright river born,
The flowers, that hung above its wave at morn,
Bless'd not the waters, as they murmur'd by,
With holier scent and lustre, than the sigh
And virgin-glance of first affection cast
Upon their youth's smooth current, as it pass'd!
But war disturb'd this vision—far away
From her fond eyes summon'd to join the array
Of Persia's warriors on the hills of Thrace,
The youth exchanged his sylvan dwelling-place
For the rude tent and war-field's deathful clash;
His Zelica's sweet glances for the flash
Of Grecian wild-fire, and Love's gentle chains
For bleeding bondage on Byzantium's plains.

Month after month, in widowhood of soul
Drooping, the maiden saw two Summers roll
Their suns away—but, ah, how cold and dim
Even summer suns, when not beheld with him!
From time to time ill-omen'd rumours came,
Like spirit-tongues, muttering the sick man's name,
Just ere he dies:—at length those sounds of dread
Fell withering on her soul, "Azim is dead!"
Oh Grief, beyond all other griefs, when fate
First leaves the young heart lone and desolate
In the wide world, without that only tie
For which it loved to live or fear'd to die;—
Lorn as the hung-up lute, that ne'er hath spoken
Since the sad day its master-chord was broken!

Fond maid, the sorrow of her soul was such,
Even reason sunk—blighted beneath its touch;
And though, ere long, her sanguine spirit rose
Above the first dead pressure of its woes,
Though health and bloom return'd, the delicate chain
Of thought, once tangled, never clear'd again.

Warm, lively, soft as in youth's happiest day,
The mind was still all there, but turn'd astray;—
A wandering bark, upon whose pathway shone
All stars of heaven, except the guiding one!
Again she smiled, nay, much and brightly smiled,
But 'twas a lustre, strange, unreal, wild;
And when she sung to her lute's touching strain,
'T was like the notes, half ecstasy, half pain,
The bulbul (2) utters, ere her soul depart,
When, vanquish'd by some minstrel's powerful art,
She dies upon the lute whose sweetness broke her
heart!

Such was the mood in which that mission found
Young Zelica—that mission, which around
The Eastern world, in every region blest
With woman's smile, sought out its loveliest,
To grace that galaxy of lips and eyes
Which the Veil'd Prophet destined for the skies:—
And such quick welcome as a spark receives
Dropp'd on a bed of Autumn's wither'd leaves,
Did every tale of these enthusiasts find
In the wild maiden's sorrow-blighted mind.
All fire at once the maddening zeal she caught;—
Elect of Paradise! blest, rapturous thought!
Predestined bride, in heaven's eternal dome,
Of some brave youth—ha! durst they say "of some?"
No—of the one, one only object traced
In her heart's core too deep to be effaced;
The one whose memory, fresh as life, is twined
With every broken link of her lost mind;
Whose image lives, though Reason's self be wreck'd,
Safe 'mid the ruins of her intellect!

Alas, poor Zelica! it needed all
The fantasy, which held thy mind in thrall,
To see in that gay Haram's glowing maids
A sainted colony for Eden's shades;
Or dream that he—of whose unholy flame
Thou wert too soon the victim—shining came
From Paradise, to people its pure sphere
With souls like thine, which he hath ruin'd here!
No—had not reason's light totally set,
And left thee dark, thou hadst an amulet
In the loved image, graven on thy heart,
Which would have saved thee from the tempter's art,
And kept alive, in all its bloom of breath,
That purity, whose fading is love's death!—
But lost, inflamed—a restless zeal took place
Of the mild virgin's still and feminine grace;
First of the Prophet's favourites, proudly first
In zeal and charms—too well the Impostor nursed
Her soul's delirium, in whose active flame,
Thus lighting up a young luxuriant frame,

(1) The Amoo, which rises in the Belur Tag, or Dark
Mountains, and, running nearly from east to west, splits
into two branches; one of which falls into the Caspian
sea, and the other into Aral Nahr, or the Lake of Eagles.
(2) The nightingale.

He saw more potent sorceries to bind
To his dark yoke the spirits of mankind,
More subtle chains than hell itself e'er twined.
No art was spared, no witchery;—all the skill
His demons taught him was employ'd to fill
Her mind with gloom and ecstasy by turns—
That gloom, through which Frenzy but fiercer burns;
That ecstasy, which from the depth of sadness
Glares like the maniac's moon, whose light is mad-
        ness!

'T was from a brilliant banquet, where the sound
Of poesy and music breathed around,
Together picturing to her mind and ear
The glories of that heaven, her destined sphere,
Where all was pure, where every stain that lay
Upon the spirit's light should pass away,
And, realising more than youthful love
E'er wish'd or dream'd, she should for ever rove
Through fields of fragrance by her Azim's side,
His own bless'd, purified, eternal bride!—
'T was from a scene, a witching trance like this,
He hurried her away, yet breathing bliss,
To the dim charnel-house;—through all its steams
Of damp and death, led only by those gleams
Which foul Corruption lights, as with design
To show the gay and proud *she* too can shine—
And, passing on through upright ranks of Dead,
Which to the maiden, doubly crazed by dread,
Seem'd, through the bluish death-light round them
        cast,
To move their lips in mutterings as she pass'd—
There, in that awful place, when each had quaff'd
And pledged in silence such a fearful draught,
Such—oh! the look and taste of that red bowl
Will haunt her till she dies—he bound her soul
By a dark oath, in hell's own language framed,
Never, while earth his mystic presence claim'd,
While the blue arch of day hung o'er them both,
Never, by that all-imprecating oath,
In joy or sorrow from his side to sever.—
She swore, and the wide charnel echo'd, "Never,
        never!"

From that dread hour, entirely, wildly given
To him and—she believed, lost maid!—to heaven;
Her brain, her heart, her passions all inflamed,
How proud she stood, when in full Haram named
The Priestess of the Faith!—how flash'd her eyes
With light, alas, that was not of the skies,
When round, in trances, only less than hers,
She saw the Haram kneel, her prostrate worshippers.
Well might Mokanna think that form alone
Had spells enough to make the world his own :—
Light lovely limbs, to which the spirit's play
Gave motion, airy as the dancing spray,
When from its stem the small bird wings away :
Lips in whose rosy labyrinth, when she smiled,
The soul was lost; and blushes, swift and wild

As are the momentary meteors sent
Across the uncalm but beauteous firmament.
And then her look—oh! where 's the heart so wise
Could unbewilder'd meet those matchless eyes?
Quick, restless, strange, but exquisite withal,
Like those of angels, just before their fall;
Now shadow'd with the shames of earth—now crost
By glimpses of the Heaven her heart had lost;
In every glance there broke, without controul,
The flashes of a bright but troubled soul,
Where sensibility still wildly play'd,
Like lightning, round the ruins it had made!

And such was now young Zelica—so changed
From her who, some years since, delighted ranged
The almond groves that shade Bokhara's tide,
All life and bliss, with Azim by her side!
So alter'd was she now, this festal day,
When, 'mid the proud Divan's dazzling array,
The vision of that Youth whom she had loved,
Had wept as dead, before her breathed and moved;—
When—bright, she thought, as if from Eden's track
But half-way trodden, he had wander'd back
Again to earth, glistening with Eden's light—
Her beauteous Azim shone before her sight.

O Reason! who shall say what spells renew,
When least we look for it, thy broken clew!
Through what small vistas o'er the darken'd brain
Thy intellectual day-beam bursts again!
And how, like forts, to which beleaguerers win
Unhoped-for entrance through some friend within,
One clear idea, wakened in the breast
By memory's magic, lets in all the rest!
Would it were thus, unhappy girl, with thee!
But though light came, it came but partially;
Enough to show the maze in which thy sense
Wander'd about—but not to guide it thence;
Enough to glimmer o'er the yawning wave,
But not to point the harbour which might save.
Hours of delight and peace, long left behind,
With that dear form came rushing o'er her mind;
But, oh! to think how deep her soul had gone
In shame and falsehood since those moments shone;
And, then, her oath—*there* madness lay again,
And, shuddering, back she sunk into her chain
Of mental darkness, as if blest to flee
From light, whose every glimpse was agony!
Yet, *one* relief this glance of former years
Brought, mingled with its pain—tears, floods of tears,
Long frozen at her heart, but now like rills
Let loose in spring-time from the snowy hills,
And gushing warm, after a sleep of frost,
Through valleys where their flow had long been lost.

Sad and subdued, for the first time her frame
Trembled with horror, when the summons came
(A summons proud and rare, which all but she,
And, she till now, had heard with ecstasy,)

To meet Mokanna at his place of prayer,
A garden oratory, cool and fair,
By the stream's side, where still at close of day
The Prophet of the Veil retired to pray;
Sometimes alone—but, oftener far, with one,
One chosen nymph to share his orison.

Of late none found such favour in his sight
As the young Priestess; and though, since that night
When the death-caverns echo'd every tone
Of the dire oath that made her all his own,
The Impostor, sure of his infatuate prize,
Had, more than once, thrown off his soul's disguise,
And utter'd such unheavenly monstrous things,
As even across the desperate wanderings
Of a weak intellect, whose lamp was out,
Threw startling shadows of dismay and doubt;—
Yet zeal, ambition, her tremendous vow,
The thought, still haunting her, of that bright
      brow,
Whose blaze, as yet from mortal eye conceal'd,
Would soon, proud triumph! be to her reveal'd,
To her alone;—and then the hope, most dear,
Most wild of all, that her transgression here
Was but a passage through earth's grosser fire,
From which the spirit would at last aspire,
Even purer than before—as perfumes rise
Through flame and smoke, most welcome to the
      skies—
And that when Azim's fond divine embrace
Should circle her in heaven, no darkening trace
Would on that bosom he once loved remain,
But all be bright, be pure, be *his* again!—
These were the wildering dreams, whose curst deceit
Had chain'd her soul beneath the tempter's feet,
And made her think even damning falsehood sweet.
But now that Shape, which had appall'd her view,
That Semblance—oh how terrible, if true!
Which came across her frenzy's full career
With shock of consciousness, cold, deep, severe,
As when, in northern seas, at midnight dark,
An isle of ice encounters some swift bark,
And, startling all its wretches from their sleep,
By one cold impulse hurls them to the deep;—

So came that shock not frenzy's self could bear,
And waking up each long-lull'd image there,
But check'd her headlong soul, to sink it in despair!

Wan and dejected, through the evening dusk,
She now went slowly to that small kiosk,
Where, pondering alone his impious schemes,
Mokanna waited her—too wrapt in dreams
Of the fair-ripening future's rich success,
To heed the sorrow, pale and spiritless,
That sat upon his victim's downcast brow,
Or mark how slow her step, how alter'd now
From the quick ardent Priestess, whose light bound
Came like a spirit's o'er the unechoing ground—
From that wild Zelica, whose every glance
Was thrilling fire, whose every thought a trance!

Upon his couch the Veil'd Mokanna lay,
While lamps around—not such as lend their ray,
Glimmering and cold, to those who nightly pray
In holy Koom, (1) or Mecca's dim arcades—
But brilliant, soft, such lights as lovely maids
Look loveliest in, shed their luxurious glow
Upon his mystic Veil's white glittering flow.
Beside him, stead of beads and books of prayer,
Which the world fondly thought he mused on there,
Stood vases, fill'd with Kishmee's (2) golden wine,
And the red weepings of the Shiraz vine;
Of which his curtain'd lips full many a draught
Took zealously, as if each drop they quaff'd,
Like Zemzem's Spring of Holiness, (3) had power
To freshen the soul's virtues into flower!
And still he drank and ponder'd—nor could see
The approaching maid, so deep his reverie;
At length, with fiendish laugh, like that which broke
From Eblis at the Fall of Man, he spoke:—
"Yes, ye vile race, for hell's amusement given,
Too mean for earth, yet claiming kin with heaven;
God's images, forsooth!—such gods as he
Whom India serves, the monkey deity;—(4)
Ye creatures of a breath, proud things of clay,
To whom if Lucifer, as grandams say,
Refused, though at the forfeit of heaven's light,
To bend in worship, Lucifer was right!—(5)

(1 The cities of Com (or Koom) and Cashan are full of
mosques, mausoleums, and sepulchres of the descendants
of Ali, the Saints of Persia.—*Chardin.*
      (2) An island in the Persian Gulf, noted for its white wine.
      (3) The miraculous well at Mecca; so called, says Sale,
from the murmuring of its waters.
      (4 The god Hannaman.—"Apes are in many parts of
India highly venerated, out of respect to the God Hanna-
man, a deity partaking of the form of that race."—*Pen-
nant's Hindoostan.*
      See a curious account, in *Stephen's Persia*, of a solemn
embassy from some part of the Indies to Goa, when the
Portuguese were there, offering vast treasures for the re-
covery of a monkey's tooth, which they held in great ve-
neration, and which had been taken away upon the con-
quest of the kingdom of Jafanapatan.

(5) This resolution of Eblis not to acknowledge the new
creature, man, was, according to Mahometan tradition,
thus adopted:—"The earth (which God had selected for the
materials of his work) was carried into Arabia to a place
between Mecca and Tayef, where, being first kneaded by
the angels, it was afterwards fashioned by God himself
into a human form, and left to dry for the space of forty
days, or, as others say, as many years; the angels, in the
mean time, often visiting it, and Eblis (then one of the
angels nearest to God's presence, afterwards the devil)
among the rest; but he, not contented with looking at it,
kicked it with his foot till it rung; and knowing God de-
signed that creature to be his superior, took a secret re-
solution never to acknowledge him as such."—*Sale* on the
Koran.
                                                      42

Soon shall I plant this foot upon the neck
Of your foul race, and, without fear or check,
Luxuriating in hate, avenge my shame,
My deep-felt, long-nurst loathing of man's name!—
Soon at the head of myriads, blind and fierce
As hooded falcons, through the universe
I'll sweep my darkening desolating way,
Weak man my instrument, curst man my prey!

"Ye wise, ye learn'd, who grope your dull way on
By the dim twinkling gleams of ages gone,
Like superstitious thieves, who think the light
From dead men's marrow guides them best at
    night— (1)
Ye shall have honours—wealth—yes, Sages, yes—
I know, grave fools, your wisdom's nothingness;
Undazzled it can track yon starry sphere,
But a gilt stick, a bawble blinds it here.
How I shall laugh, when trumpeted along
In lying speech, and still more lying song,
By these learn'd slaves, the meanest of the throng;
Their wits bought up, their wisdom shrunk so small,
A sceptre's puny point can wield it all!

"Ye too, believers of incredible creeds,
Whose faith enshrines the monsters which it breeds;
Who, bolder even than Nemrod, think to rise,
By nonsense heap'd on nonsense, to the skies;
Ye shall have miracles, ay, sound ones too,
Seen, heard, attested, every thing—but true.
Your preaching zealots, too inspired to seek
One grace of meaning for the things they speak;
Your martyrs, ready to shed out their blood,
For truths too heavenly to be understood;
And your State Priests, sole vendors of the lore
That works salvation—as, on Ava's shore,
Where none *but* priests are privileged to trade
In that best marble of which Gods are made; (2)
They shall have mysteries—ay, precious stuff
For knaves to thrive by—mysteries enough;
Dark tangled doctrines, dark as fraud can weave,
Which simple votaries shall on trust receive,
While craftier feign belief, till they believe.
A Heaven too ye must have, ye lords of dust—
A splendid Paradise—pure souls, ye must:
That Prophet ill sustains his holy call,
Who finds not heavens to suit the tastes of all;
Houris for boys, omniscience for sages,
And wings and glories for all ranks and ages.
Vain things!—as lust or vanity inspires,
The heaven of each is but what each desires,
And, soul or sense, whate'er the object be,
Man would be man to all eternity!

(1) A kind of lantern formerly used by robbers, called
the Hand of Glory, the candle for which was made of the
fat of a dead malefactor. This, however, was rather a
western than an eastern superstition.
(2) The material of which images of Gaudma (the Birman

So let him—Eblis! grant this crowning curse,
But keep him what he is, no Hell were worse."

"Oh, my lost soul!" exclaim'd the shuddering
    maid,
Whose ears had drunk like poison all he said.—
Mokanna started—not abash'd, afraid—
He knew no more of fear than one who dwells
Beneath the tropics knows of icicles!
But, in those dismal words that reach'd his ear,
"Oh, my lost soul!" there was a sound so drear,
So like that voice, among the sinful dead,
In which the legend o'er Hell's Gate is read,
That, new as 't was from her, whom nought could
    dim
Or sink till now, it startled even him.

"Ha, my fair Priestess!"—thus, with ready wile,
The impostor turn'd to greet her—"thou, whose
    smile
Hath inspiration in its rosy beam
Beyond the Enthusiast's hope or Prophet's dream;
Light of the Faith! who twinest religion's zeal
So close with love's, men know not which they feel,
Nor which to sigh for in their trance of heart,
The heaven thou preachest or the heaven thou art!
What should I be without thee? without thee
How dull were power, how joyless victory!
Though borne by angels, if that smile of thine
Bless'd not my banner, 't were but half divine.
But—why so mournful, child? those eyes, that shone
All life last night—what!—is their glory gone?
Come, come—this morn's fatigue hath made them
    pale,
They want rekindling—suns themselves would fail
Did not their comets bring, as I to thee,
From light's own fount supplies of brilliancy.
Thou seest this cup—no juice of earth is here,
But the pure waters of that upper sphere,
Whose rills o'er ruby beds and topaz flow,
Catching the gem's bright colour, as they go.
Nightly my Genii come and fill these urns—
Nay, drink—in every drop life's essence burns;
'T will make that soul all fire, those eyes all light—
Come, come, I want thy loveliest smiles to-night.
There is a youth—why start?—thou saw'st him then;
Look'd he not nobly? such the godlike men
Thou 'lt have to woo thee in the bowers above;—
Though *he*, I fear, hath thoughts too stern for love,
Too ruled by that cold enemy of bliss
The world calls virtue—we must conquer this.
Nay, shrink not, pretty sage! 't is not for thee
To scan the mazes of Heaven's mystery:

Deity) are made is held sacred. "Birmans may not
purchase the marble in mass, but are suffered, and indeed
encouraged, to buy figures of the Deity ready made."—
Symes's Ava, vol. ii., p. 376.

The steel must pass through fire, ere it can yield
Fit instruments for mighty hands to wield.
This very night I mean to try the art
Of powerful beauty on that warrior's heart.
All that my Haram boasts of bloom and wit,
Of skill and charms, most rare and exquisite,
Shall tempt the boy;—young Mirzala's blue eyes,
Whose sleepy lid like snow on violets lies;
Arouya's cheeks, warm as a spring-day sun,
And lips that, like the seal of Solomon,
Have magic in their pressure; Zeba's lute,
And Lilla's dancing feet, that gleam and shoot
Rapid and white as sea-birds o'er the deep—
All shall combine their witching powers to steep
My convert's spirit in that softening trance,
From which to heaven is but the next advance—
That glowing, yielding fusion of the breast,
On which Religion stamps her image best.
But hear me, Priestess!—though each nymph of these
Hath some peculiar practised power to please,
Some glance or step which, at the mirror tried,
First charms herself, then all the world beside;
There still wants *one*, to make the victory sure,
One who in every look joins every lure;
Through whom all beauty's beams concentred pass,
Dazzling and warm, as through love's burning-glass;
Whose gentle lips persuade without a word;
Whose words, even when unmeaning, are adored,
Like inarticulate breathings from a shrine,
Which our faith takes for granted are divine!
Such is the nymph we want, all warmth and light,
To crown the rich temptations of to-night;
Such the refined enchantress that must be
This hero's vanquisher—and thou art she!"

With her hands clasp'd, her lips apart and pale,
The maid had stood, gazing upon the Veil
From which these words, like south winds through a fence
Of Kerzrah flowers, came fill'd with pestilence; (1)
So boldly utter'd too! as if all dread
Of frowns from her, of virtuous frowns, were fled,
And the wretch felt assured that, once plunged in,
Her woman's soul would know no pause in sin!

At first, though mute she listen'd, like a dream
Seem'd all he said; nor could her mind, whose beam
As yet was weak, penetrate half his scheme.
But when, at length, he utter'd, "Thou art she!"
All flash'd at once, and shrieking piteously,
"Oh not for worlds!" she cried—"Great God! to whom
I once knelt innocent, is this my doom?
Are all my dreams, my hopes of heavenly bliss,
My purity, my pride, then come to this—
To live the wanton of a fiend! to be
The pander of his guilt—oh infamy!
And sunk myself as low as hell can steep
In its hot flood, drag others down as deep!

Others—ha!-yes—that youth who came to-day—
Not him I loved—not him—oh! I do but say,
But swear to me this moment 't is not he,
And I will serve, dark fiend, will worship even thee!"

"Beware, young raving thing!—in time beware,
Nor utter what I cannot, must not bear,
Even from *thy* lips. Go—try thy lute, thy voice,
The boy must feel their magic;—I rejoice
To see those fires, no matter whence they rise,
Once more illuming my fair Priestess' eyes; [warm,
And should the youth, whom soon those eyes shall
Indeed resemble thy dead lover's form,
So much the happier wilt thou find thy doom,
As one warm lover, full of life and bloom,
Excels ten thousand cold ones in the tomb. [made
Nay, nay, no frowning, sweet!—those eyes were
For love, not anger—I must be obey'd."

"Obey'd!—'t is well—yes, I deserve it all—
On me, on me Heaven's vengeance cannot fall
Too heavily—but Azim, brave and true
And beautiful—must *he* be ruin'd too?
Must *he* too, glorious as he is, be driven
A renegade like me from Love and Heaven?
Like me?—weak wretch, I wrong him—not like me;
No—he's all truth and strength and purity!
Fill up your maddening hell-cup to the brim,
Its witchery, fiend, will have no charm for him.
Let loose your glowing wantons from their bowers,
He loves, he loves, and can defy their powers!
Wretch as I am, in *his* heart still I reign
Pure as when first we met, without a stain!
Though ruin'd—lost—my memory, like a charm
Left by the dead, still keeps his soul from harm.
Oh! never let him know how deep the brow
He kiss'd at parting is dishonour'd now;—
Ne'er tell him how debased, how sunk is she,
Whom once he loved—once!—*still* loves dotingly.
Thou laugh'st, tormentor;—what!—thou 'lt brand my name?
Do, do—in vain—he'll not believe my shame;
He thinks me true, that nought beneath God's sky
Could tempt or change me, and—so once thought I.
But this is past—though worse than death my lot,
Than hell—'t is nothing while *he* knows it not.
Far off to some benighted land I'll fly,
Where sunbeam ne'er shall enter till I die;
Where none will ask the lost one whence she came,
But I may fade and fall without a name,
And thou—curst man or fiend, whate'er thou art,
Who found'st this burning plague-spot in my heart,
And spread'st it—oh, so quick!—through soul and frame,
With more than demon's art, till I became
A loathsome thing, all pestilence, all flame!—

(1) "It is commonly said in Persia, that if a man breathe
in the hot south wind, which in June or July passes over
that flower (the Kerzereh), it will kill him."—*Thevenot.*

If, when I'm gone——"
      "Hold, fearless maniac, hold,
Nor tempt my rage—by Heaven, not half so bold
The puny bird, that dares with teasing hum
Within the crocodile's stretch'd jaws to come! (1)
And so thou'lt fly, forsooth?—what !—give up all
Thy chaste dominion in the Haram Hall,
Where now to Love and now to Alla given,
Half mistress and half saint, thou hang'st as even
As doth Medina's tomb, 't wixt hell and heaven!
Thou'lt fly?—as easily may reptiles run,
The gaunt snake once hath fix'd his eyes upon;
As easily, when caught, the prey may be
Pluck'd from his loving folds, as thou from me.
No, no, 'tis fix'd—let good or ill betide,
Thou 'rt mine till death, till death Mokanna's bride!
Hast thou forgot thy oath?"—
      At this dread word,
The Maid, whose spirit his rude taunts had stirr'd
Through all its depths, and roused an anger there
That burst and lighten'd even through her despair—
Shrunk back, as if a blight were in the breath
That spoke that word, and stagger'd pale as death.

"Yes, my sworn bride, let others seek in bowers
Their bridal place—the charnel vault was ours!
Instead of scents and balms, for thee and me
Rose the rich steams of sweet mortality;
Gay flickering death-lights shone while we were
    wed,
And, for our guests, a row of goodly Dead,
(Immortal spirits in their time, no doubt,)
From reeking shrouds upon the rite look'd out!
That oath thou heard'st more lips than thine repeat—
That cup—thou shudderest, Lady—was it sweet?
That cup we pledged, the charnel's choicest wine,
Hath bound thee—aye, body and soul—all mine;
Bound thee by chains that, whether blest or curst
No matter now, not hell itself shall burst!
Hence, woman, to the Haram, and look gay,
Look wild, look—any thing but sad : yet stay—
One moment more—from what this night hath
    pass'd,
I see thou know'st me, know'st me well at last.
Ha! ha! and so, fond thing, thou thought'st all true,
And that I love mankind?—I do, I do—

(1) The humming-bird is said to run this risk for the
purpose of picking the crocodile's teeth. The same cir-
cumstance is related of the lapwing, as a fact to which he
was witness, by *Paul Lucas, Voyage fait en* 1714.
  The ancient story concerning the Trochilus, or hum-
ming-bird, entering with impunity into the mouth of the
crocodile, is firmly believed at Java.—*Barrow's Cochin-
China.*
  (2) Circum easdem ripas (Nili, viz.)ales est Ibis. Ea ser-
pentium populatur ova, gratissimamque ex his escam nidis
suis refert.—*Solinus.*
  (3) "The feast of Lanterns is celebrated at Yamtcheou
with more magnificence than any where else; and the re-
port goes, that the illuminations there are so splendid,

As victims, love them; as the sea-dog dotes
Upon the small sweet fry that round him floats;
Or, as the Nile-bird loves the slime that gives
That rank and venomous food on which she
    lives?—(2)

"And, now thou seest my *soul's* angelic hue,
'T is time these *features* were uncertain'd too—
This brow, whose light—oh rare celestial light!
Hath been reserved to bless thy favour'd sight;
These dazzling eyes, before whose shrouded might
Thou 'st seen immortal Man kneel down and quake—
Would that they *were* heaven's lightnings for his
    sake!—
But turn and look—then wonder, if thou wilt,
That I should hate, should take revenge, by guilt,
Upon the hand, whose mischief or whose mirth
Sent me thus maim'd and monstrous upon earth;
And on that race who, though more vile they be
Than mowing apes, are demi-gods to me!
Here—judge if hell, with all its power to damn,
Can add one curse to the foul thing I am!"

He raised his veil— the Maid turn'd slowly round,
Look'd at him—shriek'd—and sunk upon the ground!

On their arrival, next night, at the place of en-
campment, they were surprised and delighted to
find the groves all around illuminated; some artists
of Yamtcheou (3) having been sent on previously
for the purpose. On each side of the green alley,
which led to the Royal Pavilion, artificial sceneries
of bamboo-work (4) were erected, representing
arches, minarets, and towers, from which hung
thousands of silken lanterns, painted by the most
delicate pencils of Canton. Nothing could be more
beautiful than the leaves of the mango-trees and
acacias, shining in the light of the bamboo scenery,
which shed a lustre round as soft as that of the
nights of Peristan.
  Lalla Rookh, however, who was too much occupied
by the sad story of Zelica and her lover, to give a
thought to any thing else, except, perhaps, him who
related it, hurried on through this scene of splen-
dour to her pavilion—greatly to the mortification of
the poor artists of Yamtcheou —and was followed

that an Emperor once, not daring openly to leave his
Court to go thither, committed himself with the Queen
and several princesses of his family into the hands of a
magician, who promised to transport them thither in a
trice. He made them in the night to ascend magnificent
thrones that were borne up by swans, which in a moment
arrived at Yamtcheou. The Emperor saw at his leisure
all the solemnity, being carried upon a cloud that hovered
over the city and descended by degrees; and came back
again with the same speed and equipage, nobody at court
perceiving his absence."—*The Present State of China,*
p. 156.
  (4) See a description of the nuptials of Vizier Alee in
the *Asiatic Annual Register of* 1804.

with equal rapidity by the Great Chamberlain, cursing, as he went, that ancient Mandarin, whose parental anxiety in lighting up the shores of the lake, where his beloved daughter had wandered and been lost, was the origin of these fantastic Chinese illuminations. (1)

Without a moment's delay, young Feramorz was introduced, and Fadladeen, who could never make up his mind as to the merits of a poet, till he knew the religious sect to which he belonged, was about to ask him whether he was a Shia or a Sooni, when Lalla Rookh impatiently clapped her hands for silence, and the youth, being seated upon the musnud near her, proceeded:—

Prepare thy soul, young Azim!—thou hast braved
The bands of Greece, still mighty though enslaved;
Hast faced her phalanx, arm'd with all its fame,
Her Macedonian pikes and globes of flame;
All this hast fronted, with firm heart and brow,
But a more perilous trial waits thee now—
Woman's bright eyes, a dazzling host of eyes
From every land where woman smiles or sighs;
Of every hue, as Love may chance to raise
His black or azure banner in their blaze;
And each sweet mode of warfare, from the flash
That lightens boldly through the shadowy lash,
To the sly stealing splendours, almost hid,
Like swords half-sheath'd, beneath the downcast lid,
Such, Azim, is the lovely luminous host
Now led against thee; and, let conquerors boast
Their fields of fame, he who in virtue arms
A young warm spirit against beauty's charms,
Who feels her brightness, yet defies her thrall,
Is the best, bravest, conqueror of them all.

Now, through the Haram chambers, moving lights
And busy shapes proclaim the toilet's rites ;—
From room to room the ready handmaids hie,
Some skill'd to wreathe the turban tastefully,

Or hang the veil, in negligence of shade,
O'er the warm blushes of the youthful maid,
Who, if between the folds but *one* eye shone,
Like Seba's Queen could vanquish with that one :—(2)
While some bring leaves of Henna, to imbue
The fingers' ends with a bright roseate hue, (3)
So bright, that in the mirror's depth they seem
Like tips of coral branches in the stream :
And others mix the Kohol's jetty dye,
To give that long dark languish to the eye, (4)
Which makes the maids, whom kings are proud to cull
From fair Circassia's vales, so beautiful.
All is in motion ; rings and plumes and pearls
Are shining every where :—some younger girls
Are gone by moonlight to the garden-beds,
To gather fresh cool chaplets for their heads ;—
Gay creatures! sweet, though mournful, 'tis to see
How each prefers a garland from that tree
Which brings to mind her childhood's innocent day,
And the dear fields and friendships far away.
The maid of India, blest again to hold
In her full lap the Champac's leaves of gold, (5)
Thinks of the time when, by the Ganges' flood,
Her little play-mates scatter'd many a bud
Upon her long black hair, with glossy gleam
Just dripping from the consecrated stream;
While the young Arab, haunted by the smell
Of her own mountain flowers, as by a spell—
The sweet Elcaya, (6) and that courteous tree
Which bows to all who seek its canopy, (7)
Sees, call'd up round her by these magic scents,
The well, the camels, and her father's tents ;
Sighs for the home she left with little pain,
And wishes even its sorrows back again !

Meanwhile, through vast illuminated halls,
Silent and bright, where nothing but the falls
Of fragrant waters, gushing with cool sound
From many a jasper fount, is heard around,

---

(1) "The vulgar ascribe it to an accident that happened in the family of a famous mandarin, whose daughter, walking one evening upon the shore of a lake, fell in and was drowned; this afflicted father, with his family, ran thither, and, the better to find her, he caused a great company of lanterns to be lighted. All the inhabitants of the place thronged after him with torches. The year ensuing they made fires upon the shores the same day ; they continued the ceremony every year, every one lighted his lantern, and by degrees it commenced into a custom."—*Present State of China.*

(2) "Thou hast ravished my heart with one of thine eyes."—*Solomon's Song.*

(3) "They tinged the ends of her fingers scarlet with Henna, so that they resembled branches of coral."—*Story of Prince Futtun in Bahardanush.*

(4) "The women blacken the inside of their eyelids with a powder named the black Kohol."—*Russel.*

"None of these ladies," says *Shaw*, "take themselves to be completely dressed, till they have tinged the hair and edges of their eyelids with the powder of lead ore. Now,

as this operation is performed by dipping first into the powder a small wooden bodkin of the thickness of a quill, and then drawing it afterwards through the eyelids over the ball of the eye, we shall have a lively image of what the Prophet (Jer. iv., 30.) may be supposed to mean by *rending the eyes with painting.* This practice is no doubt of great antiquity ; for besides the instance already taken notice of, we find that where Jezebel is said (2 Kings ix., 30.) *to* I *ave painted her face,* the original words are, *she adjusted her eyes with the powder of lead-ore.*"—*Shaw's Travels.*

(5) "The appearance of the blossoms of the gold-coloured Campac on the black hair of the Indian women has supplied the Sanscrit Poets with many elegant allusions."—See *Asiatic Researches,* vol. iv.

(6) A tree famous for its perfume, and common on the hills of Yemen.—*Niebuhr.*

(7) Of the genus mimosa, "which droops its branches whenever any person approaches it, seeming as if it saluted those who retire under its shade."—*Niebuhr.*

Young Azim roams bewilder'd—nor can guess
What means this maze of light and loneliness.
Here, the way leads, o'er tesselated floors
Or mats of Cairo, through long corridors,
Where, ranged in cassolets and silver urns,
Sweet wood of aloe or of sandal burns ;
And spicy rods, such as illume at night
The bowers of Tibet, (1) send forth odorous light,
Like Peris' wands, when pointing out the road
For some pure Spirit to its blest abode :
And here, at once, the glittering saloon
Bursts on his sight, boundless and bright as noon ;
Where, in the midst, reflecting back the rays
In broken rainbows, a fresh fountain plays
High as the enamell'd cupola, which towers
All rich with arabesques of gold and flowers ;
And the mosaic floor beneath shines through
The sprinkling of that fountain's silvery dew,
Like the wet glistening shells, of every dye,
That on the margin of the Red Sea lie.

Here too he traces the kind visitings
Of woman's love, in those fair living things
Of land and wave, whose fate—in bondage thrown
For their weak loveliness—is like her own !
On one side gleaming with a sudden grace
Through water, brilliant as the crystal vase
In which it undulates, small fishes shine,
Like golden ingots from a fairy mine ;—
While, on the other, latticed lightly in
With odoriferous woods of Comorin, (2)
Each brilliant bird that wings the air is seen ;—
Gay sparkling loories, such as gleam between
The crimson blossoms of the coral tree (3)
In the warm isles of India's sunny sea ;
Mecca's blue sacred pigeon, (4) and the thrush
Of Hindostan, (5) whose holy warblings gush,
At evening, from the tall pagoda's top ;—
Those golden birds that, in the spice-time, drop
About the gardens, drunk with that sweet food (6)
Whose scent hath lured them o'er the summer flood ;(7)
And those that under Araby's soft sun
Build their high nests of budding cinnamon ; (8)
In short, all rare and beauteous things, that fly
Through the pure element, here calmly lie

Sleeping in light, like the green birds (9) that dwell
In Eden's radiant fields of asphodel !

So on, through scenes past all imagining,
More like the luxuries of that impious King, (10)
Whom Death's dark Angel, with his lightning torch,
Struck down and blasted even in Pleasure's porch,
Than the pure dwelling of a Prophet sent,
Arm'd with Heaven's sword, for man's enfranchise-
            ment—
Young Azim wander'd, looking sternly round,
His simple garb and war-boots' clanking sound
But ill according with the pomp and grace
And silent lull of that voluptuous place.

"Is this, then," thought the youth, " is this the way
To free man's spirit from the deadening sway
Of worldly sloth—to teach him, while he lives,
To know no bliss but that which virtue gives,
And when he dies, to leave his lofty name
A light, a landmark on the cliffs of fame?
It was not so, Land of the generous thought
And daring deed, thy god-like sages taught ;
It was not thus, in bowers of wanton ease,
Thy Freedom nursed her sacred energies :
Oh ! not beneath the enfeebling withering glow
Of such dull luxury did those myrtles grow,
With which she wreathed her sword, when she would
            dare
Immortal deeds ; but in the bracing air
Of toil—of temperance—of that high, rare,
Ethereal virtue, which alone can breathe
Life, health, and lustre into Freedom's wreath.
Who that surveys this span of earth we press—
This speck of life in time's great wilderness,
This narrow isthmus 'twixt two boundless seas,
The past, the future, two eternities !—
Would sully the bright spot, or leave it bare,
When he might build him a proud temple there,
A name, that long shall hallow all its space,
And be each purer soul's high resting-place.
But no—it cannot be, that one, whom God
Has sent to break the wizard Falsehood's rod—
A Prophet of the Truth, whose mission draws
Its rights from Heaven, should thus profane its cause

---

(1) "Cloves are a principal ingredient in the composi-
tion of the perfumed rods, which men of rank keep con-
stantly burning in their presence."—*Turner's Tibet.*

(2) " C'est d'où vient le bois d'aloës, que les Arabes
appellent Oud Comari, et celui du sandal, qui s'y trouve
en grande quantité."—*D'Herbelot.*

(3) "Thousands of variegated loories visit the coral-
trees."—*Barrow.*

(4) "In Mecca there are quantities of blue pigeons,
which none will affright or abuse, much less kill.'—*Pitt's
Account of the Mahometans.*

(5) "The Pagoda Thrush is esteemed among the first
choristers of India. It sits perched on the sacred pagodas,
and from thence delivers its melodious song."—*Pennant's
Hindoostan.*

(6) *Tavernier* adds, that while the Birds of Paradise lie
in this intoxicated state, the emmets come and eat off
their legs; and that hence it is they are said to have no
feet.

(7) Birds of Paradise, which, at the nutmeg season come
in flights from the southern isles to India; and "the
strength of the nutmeg," says *Tavernier,* "so intoxicates
them that they fall dead drunk to the earth."

(8) "That bird which liveth in Arabia, and buildeth its
nest with cinnamon."—*Brown's Vulgar Errors.*

(9) "The spirits of the martyrs will be lodged in the
crops of green birds."—*Gibbon,* vol. ix., p. 421.

(10) Shedad, who made the delicious gardens of Irim, in
imitation of Paradise, and was destroyed by lightning the
first time he attempted to enter them.

With the world's vulgar pomps;—no no—I see—
He thinks me weak—this glare of luxury
Is but to tempt, to try the eaglet gaze
Of my young soul—shine on, 't will stand the blaze!"

So thought the youth;—but, even while he
    defied
This witching scene, he felt its witchery glide
Through every sense. The perfume breathing
    round,
Like a pervading spirit;—the still sound
Of falling waters, lulling as the song
Of Indian bees at sunset, when they throng
Around the fragrant Nilica, and deep
In its blue blossoms hum themselves to sleep; (1)
And music, too—dear music! that can touch
Beyond all else the soul that loves it much—
Now heard far off, so far as but to seem
Like the faint exquisite music of a dream;
All was too much for him, too full of bliss,
The heart could nothing feel: that felt not this;
Soften'd he sunk upon a couch, and gave
His soul up to sweet thoughts, like wave on wave
Succeeding in smooth seas, when storms are laid;
He thought of Zelica, his own dear maid,
And of the time when, full of blissful sighs,
They sat and look'd into each other's eyes,
Silent and happy—as if God had given
Nought else worth looking at on this side heaven.

" Oh, my loved mistress, thou, whose spirit still
Is with me, round me, wander where I will—
It is for thee, for thee alone I seek
The paths of glory; to light up thy cheek
With warm approval—in that gentle look,
To read my praise, as in an angel's book,
And think all toils rewarded, when from thee
I gain a smile worth immortality!
How shall I bear the moment, when restored
To that young heart where I alone am lord,
Though of such bliss unworthy—since the best
Alone deserve to be the happiest :—
When from those lips, unbreathed upon for years,
I shall again kiss off the sould-felt tears,
And find those tears warm as when last they started,
Those sacred kisses pure as when we parted.
O my own life!—why should a single day,
A moment, keep me from those arms away?"

While thus he thinks, still nearer on the breeze
Come those delicious, dream-like harmonies,

Each note of which but adds new downy links
To the soft chain in which his spirit sinks.
He turns him toward the sound, and far away
Through a long vista, sparkling with the play
Of countless lamps—like the rich track which Day
Leaves on the waters, when he sinks from us,
So long the path, its light so tremulous;—
He sees a group of female forms advance,
Some chain'd together in their mazy dance
By fetters, forged in the green sunny bowers,
As they were captives to the King of Flowers; (2)
And some disporting round, unlink'd and free,
Who seem'd to mock their sisters' slavery,
And round and round them still, in wheeling flight
Went, like gay moths about a lamp at night;
While others waked, as gracefully along
Their feet kept time, the very soul of song
From psaltery, pipe, and lutes of heavenly thrill,
Or their own youthful voices, heavenlier still.
And now they come, now pass before his eye,
Forms such as Nature moulds, when she would
    vie
With Fancy's pencil, and give birth to things
Lovely beyond its fairest picturings.

Awhile they dance before him, then divide,
Breaking, like rosy clouds at even-tide
Around the rich pavilion of the sun,
Till silently dispersing, one by one,
Through many a path, that from the chamber leads
To gardens, terraces, and moonlight meads,
Their distant laughter comes upon the wind,
And but one trembling nymph remains behind—
Beckoning them back in vain, for they are gone,
And she is left in all that light alone;
No veil to curtain o'er her beauteous brow,
In its young bashfulness more beauteous now;
But a light golden chain-work round her hair, (3)
Such as the maids of Yezd (4) and Shiras wear,
From which, on either side, gracefully hung
A golden amulet, in the Arab tongue,
Engraven o'er with some immortal line
From Holy Writ, or bard scarce less divine;
While her left hand, as shrinkingly she stood,
Held a small lute of gold and sandal-wood,
Which, once or twice, she touch'd with hurried
    strain,
Then took her trembling fingers off again.
But when at length a timid glance she stole
At Azim, the sweet gravity of soul
She saw through all his features calm'd her fear,
And, like a half-tamed antelope, more near,

(1) "My Pandits assure me that the plant before us (the Nilica) is their Sephalica, thus named because the bees are supposed to sleep on its blossoms."—*Sir W. Jones.*

(2) "They deferred it till the King of Flowers should ascend his throne of enamelled foliage."—*The Bahar-danush.*

(3) "One of the head-dresses of the Persian women is composed of a light golden chain-work, set with small

pearls, with a thin gold plate pendant, about the bigness of a crown-piece, on which is impressed an Arabian prayer, and which hangs upon the cheek below the ear."—*Hanway's Travels.*

(4) "Certainly the women of Yezd are the handsomest women in Persia. The proverb is, that to live happy a man must have a wife of Yezd, eat the bread of Yezdecas, and drink the wine of Shiraz."—*Tavernier.*

Though shrinking still, she came;—then sat her down
Upon a musnud's (1) edge, and, bolder grown,
In the pathetic mode of Isfahan (2)
Touch'd a preluding strain, and thus began :—

There's a bower of roses by Bendemeer's (3) stream.
  And the nightingale sings round it all the day long;
In the time of my childhood 't was like a sweet dream,
  To sit in the roses and hear the bird's song.

That bower and its music I never forget,
  But oft when alone, in the bloom of the year,
I think—is the nightingale singing there yet?
  Are the roses still bright by the calm Bendemeer?

No, the roses soon wither'd that hung o'er the wave,
  But some blossoms were gather'd, while freshly
    they shone,
And a dew was distill'd from their flowers, that gave
  All the fragrance of Summer, when Summer was
    gone.

Thus memory draws from delight, ere it dies,
  An essence that breathes of it many a year;
Thus bright to my soul, as 't was then to my eyes,
  Is that bower on the banks of the calm Bendemeer!

  "Poor maiden!" thought the youth, " if thou wert
    sent,
With thy soft lute and beauty's blandishment,
To wake unholy wishes in this heart,
Or tempt its truth, thou little know'st the art.
For though thy lip should sweetly counsel wrong,
Those vestal eyes would disavow its song.
But thou hast breathed such purity, thy lay
Returns so fondly to youth's virtuous day,
And leads thy soul—if e'er it wander'd thence—
So gently back to its first innocence,
That I would sooner stop the unchain'd dove,
When swift returning to its home of love,
And round its snowy wing new fetters twine,
Than turn from virtue one pure wish of thine!"

  Scarce had this feeling pass'd, when, sparkling
    through
The gently open'd curtains of light blue
That veil'd the breezy casement, countless eyes,
Peeping like stars through the blue evening skies,
Look'd laughing in, as if to mock the pair
That sat so still and melancholy there.—

And now the curtains fly apart, and in
From the cool air, 'mid showers of jessamine
Which those without fling after them in play,
Two lightsome maidens spring—lightsome as they
Who live in the air on odours—and around
The bright saloon, scarce conscious of the ground,
Chase one another, in a varying dance
Of mirth and languor, coyness and advance,
Too eloquently like love's warm pursuit ;—
While she, who sung so gently to the lute
Her dream of home, steals timidly away,
Shrinking as violets do in Summer's ray—
But takes with her from Azim's heart that sigh
We sometimes give to forms that pass us by
In the world's crowd, too lovely to remain,
Creatures of light we never see again!

  Around the white necks of the nymphs who danced
Hung carcanets of orient gems, that glanced
More brilliant than the sea-glass glittering o'er
The hills of crystal on the Caspian shore; (4)
While from their long dark tresses, in a fall
Of curls descending, bells as musical
As those that, on the golden-shafted trees
Of Eden, shake in the eternal breeze, (5)
Rung round their steps, at every bound more sweet,
As 't were the extatic language of their feet.
At length the chase was o'er, and they stood wreathed
Within each other's arms; while soft there breathed
Through the cool casement, mingled with the sighs
Of moonlight flowers, music that seem'd to rise
From some still lake, so liquidly it rose ;
And, as it swell'd again at each faint close,
The ear could track through all that maze of chords
And young sweet voices, these impassion'd words:—

  A Spirit there is, whose fragrant sigh
    Is burning now through earth and air ;
  Where cheeks are blushing, the Spirit is nigh,
    Where lips are meeting, the Spirit is there!

  His breath is the soul of flowers like these,
    And his floating eyes—oh! they resemble(6)
  Blue water-lilies, (7) when the breeze
    Is making the stream around them tremble.

  Hail to thee, hail to thee, kindling power!
    Spirit of Love, Spirit of Bliss!
  Thy holiest time is the moonlight hour,
    And there never was moonlight so sweet as this.

  (1) Musnuds are cushioned seats, usually reserved for
persons of distinction.
  (2) The Persians, like the ancient Greeks, call their
musical modes or perdas by the names of different
countries or cities, as the mode of Isfahan, the mode of
Irak, etc.
  (3) A river which flows near the ruins of Chilminar.
  (4) "To the north of us (on the coast of the Caspian,
near Badku,) was a mountain, which sparkled like
diamonds, arising from the sea-glass and crystals with

which it abounds."—Journey of the Russian Ambassador
to Persia, 1746.
  (5) "To which will be added the sound of the bells,
hanging on the trees, which will be put in motion by the
wind proceeding from the throne of God, as often as the
blessed wish for music."—Sale.
  (6) "Whose wanton eyes resemble blue water-lilies,
agitated by the breeze."—Jayadeva.
  (7) The blue lotos, which grows in Cashmere and in
Persia.

By the fair and brave
    Who blushing unite,
Like the sun and wave,
    When they meet at night;

By the tear that shows
    When passion is nigh,
As the rain-drop flows
    From the heat of the sky;

By the first love-beat
    Of the youthful heart,
By the bliss to meet,
    And the pain to part;

By all that thou hast
    To mortals given,
Which—oh, could it last,
    This earth were heaven!

We call thee hither, entrancing Power!
    Spirit of Love! Spirit of Bliss!
Thy holiest time is the moonlight hour,
    And there never was moonlight so sweet as this.

Impatient of a scene, whose luxuries stole,
Spite of himself, too deep into his soul,
And where midst all that the young heart loves most,
Flowers, music, smiles, to yield was to be lost,
The youth had started up, and turn'd away
From the light nymphs, and their luxurious lay,
To muse upon the pictures that hung round, (1)
Bright images, that spoke without a sound,
And views, like vistas into fairy ground.
But here again new spells came o'er his sense :—
All that the pencil's mute omnipotence
Could call up into life, of soft and fair.
Of fond and passionate, was glowing there;

Nor yet too warm, but touch'd with that fine art
Which paints of pleasure but the purer part;
Which knows even Beauty when half-veil'd is best—
Like her own radiant planet of the west,
Whose orb when half retired looks loveliest. (2)
There hung the history of the Genii-King,
Traced through each gay voluptuous wandering
With her from Saba's bowers, in whose bright eyes
He read that to be blest is to be wise ;— (3)
Here fond Zuleika (4) woos with open arms
The Hebrew boy, who flies from her young charms,
Yet, flying, turns to gaze, and, half undone,
Wishes that Heaven and she could *both* be won ;
And here, Mohammed, born for love and guile,
Forgets the Koran in his Mary's smile ;—
Then beckons some kind angel from above
With a new text to consecrate their love. (5)

    With rapid step, yet pleased and lingering eye,
Did the youth pass these pictured stories by,
And hasten'd to a casement, where the light
Of the calm moon came in, and freshly bright
The fields without were seen, sleeping as still
As if no life remain'd in breeze or rill.
Here paused he, while the music, now less near,
Breathed with a holier language on his ear,
As though the distance, and that heavenly ray
Through which the sounds came floating, took away
All that had been too earthly in the lay.

    Oh! could he listen to such sounds unmoved,
And by that light—nor dream of her he loved?
Dream on, unconscious boy! while yet thou ma st ;
'Tis the last bliss thy soul shall ever taste.
Clasp yet awhile her image to thy heart,
Ere all the light, that made it dear, depart.
Think of her smiles as when thou saw'st th m last,
Clear, beautiful, by nought of earth o'ercast,

---

(1) It has been generally supposed that the Mahometans prohibit all pictures of animals; but *Toderini* shows that, though the practice is forbidden by the Koran, they are not more averse to painted figures and images than other people. From Mr. Murphy's work, too, we find that the Arabs of Spain had no objection to the introduction of figures into painting.

(2) This is not quite astronomically true. "Dr. Hadley (says Keil) has shown that Venus is brightest when she is about forty degrees removed from the sun; and that then but *only a fourth part* of her lucid disk is to be seen from the earth."

(3) For the loves of King Solomon (who was supposed to preside over the whole race of Genii) with Balkis, the Queen of Sheba or Saba, see *D'Herbelot*, and the *Notes on the Koran*, chap. 2.

"In the palace which Solomon ordered to be built against the arrival of the Queen of Saba, the floor or pavement was of transparent glass, laid over running water, in which fish were swimming." This led the Queen into a very natural mistake, which the Koran has not thought beneath its dignity to commemorate. "It was said unto her, 'Enter the palace.' And when she saw it she imagined it to be a great water; and she discovered her legs, by lifting up her robe to pass through it. Whereupon Solomon said to her, 'Verily, this is the place evenly floored with glass.'"—Chap. 27.

(4) The wife of Potiphar, thus named by the Orientals. Her adventure with the patriarch Joseph is the subject of many of their poems and romances.

The *sura*, or chapter of the *Alcoran*, contains the history of Joseph, and which for elegance of style surpasses every other of the Prophet's books. Some Arabian writers also call her Rail. The passion which this frail beauty of antiquity conceived for her young Hebrew slave has given rise to a much-esteemed poem in the Persian language, entitled *Yusef vau Zelikha*, by *Noweddin Jami*; the manuscript copy of which, in the Bodleian Library at Oxford, is supposed to be the finest in the whole world."—*Note upon Nott's Translation of Hafez.*

(5) The particulars of Mahomet's amour with Mary, the Coptic girl, in justification of which he added a new chapter to the Koran, may be found in *Gagnier's Notes upon Abulfeda*, p. 151.

43

Recall her tears, to thee at parting given,
Pure as they weep, *if* angels weep, in heaven.
Think, in her own still bower she waits thee now,
With the same glow of heart and bloom of brow,
Yet shrined in solitude—thine all, thine only,
Like the one star above thee, bright and lonely.
Oh! that a dream so sweet, so long enjoy'd,
Should be so sadly, cruelly destroy'd!

   The song is hush'd, the laughing nymphs are
     flown,
And he is left, musing of bliss, alone;—
Alone?—no, not alone—that heavy sigh,
That sob of grief, which broke from some one
     nigh—
Whose could it be?—alas! is misery found
Here, even here, on this enchanted ground?
He turns, and sees a female form, close veil'd,
Leaning, as if both heart and strength had fail'd,
Against a pillar near;—not glittering o'er
With gems and wreaths, such as the others wore,
But in that deep-blue melancholy dress, (1)
Bokhara's maidens wear in mindfulness
Of friends or kindred, dead or far away;—
And such as Zelica had on that day
He left her—when, with heart too full to speak,
He took away her last warm tears upon his cheek.

   A strange emotion stirs within him—more
Than mere compassion ever waked before:
Unconsciously he opes his arms, while she
Springs forward, as with life's last energy,
But, swooning in that one convulsive bound,
Sinks, ere she reach his arms, upon the ground;—
Her veil falls off—her faint hands clasp his knees—
'T is she herself!—'t is Zelica he sees!
But, ah, so pale, so changed—none but a lover
Could in that wreck of beauty's shrine discover
The once-adored divinity—even he
Stood for some moments mute, and doubtingly;
Put back the ringlets from her brow, and gazed
Upon those lids, where once such lustre blazed,
Ere he could think she was *indeed* his own,
Own darling maid, whom he so long had known
In joy and sorrow, beautiful in both;
Who, even when grief was heaviest—when loath
He left her for the wars—in that worst hour
Sat in her sorrow like the sweet night-flower, (2)
When darkness brings its weeping glories out,
And spreads its sighs like frankincense about.

   "Look up, my Zelica—one moment show
Those gentle eyes to me, that I may know
Thy life, thy loveliness is not all gone,
But *there*, at least, shines as it ever shone.

(1) "Deep blue is their mourning colour."—*Hanway.*
(2) The sorrowful nyctanthes, which begins to spread
its rich odour after sunset.
(3) "Concerning the vipers, which Pliny says were fre-

Come, look upon thy Azim—one dear glance,
Like those of old, were heaven! whatever chance
Hath brought thee here, oh, 't was a blessed one!
There—my loved lips—they move—that kiss hath run
Like the first shoot of life through every vein,
And now I clasp her, mine, all mine again.
Oh the delight—now, in this very hour,
When, had the whole rich world been in my power,
I should have singled out thee, only thee,
From the whole world's collected treasury—
To have thee here—to hang thus fondly o'er
My own, best, purest Zelica once more!"

   It was indeed the touch of those fond lips
Upon her eyes that chased their short eclipse,
And, gradual as the snow, at Heaven's breath,
Melts off and shows the azure flowers beneath,
Her lids unclosed, and the bright eyes were seen
Gazing on his—not, as they late had been,
Quick, restless, wild, but mournfully serene;
As if to lie, even for that tranced minute,
So near his heart, had consolation in it;
And thus to wake in his beloved caress
Took from her soul one half its wretchedness.
But, when she heard him call her good and pure,
Oh, 't was too much—too dreadful to endure!
Shuddering she broke away from his embrace,
And, hiding with both hands her guilty face,
Said, in a tone whose anguish would have riven
A heart of very marble, "Pure!—oh Heaven!"——

   That tone—those looks so changed—the withering
     blight,
That sin and sorrow leave where'er they light;
The dead despondency of those sunk eyes,
Where once, had he thus met her by surprise,
He would have seen himself, too happy boy,
Reflected in a thousand lights of joy;
And then the place—that bright unholy place,
Where vice lay hid beneath each winning grace
And charm of luxury, as the viper weaves
Its wily covering of sweet balsam leaves—(3)
All struck upon his heart, sudden and cold
As death itself;—it needs not to be told—
No, no—he sees it all, plain as the brand
Of burning shame can mark—whate'er the hand,
That could from Heaven and him such brightness
     sever,
'T is done—to Heaven and him she 's lost for ever!
It was a dreadful moment; not the tears,
The lingering, lasting misery of years
Could match that minute's anguish—all the worst
Of sorrow's elements in that dark burst
Broke o'er his soul, and, with one crash of fate,
Laid the whole hopes of his life desolate.

quent among the balsam-trees, I made very particular
inquiry; several were brought me alive both to Yambo
and Jidda."—*Bruce.*

" Oh ! curse me not," she cried, as wild he toss'd
His desperate hand towards Heaven — " though I am
  lost,
Think not that guilt, that falsehood made me fall,
No, no—'t was grief, 't was madness did it all !
Nay, doubt me not—though all thy love hath ceased—
I know it hath—yet, yet believe, at least,
That every spark of reason's light must be
Quench'd in this brain, ere I could stray from thee.
They told me thou wert dead—why, Azim, why
Did we not, both of us, that instant die
When we were parted? Oh ! couldst thou but know
With what a deep devotedness of woe
I wept thy absence—o'er and o'er again
Thinking of thee, still thee, till thought grew
  pain,
And memory, like a drop that, night and day,
Falls cold and ceaseless, wore my heart away.
Didst thou but know how pale I sat at home,
My eyes still turn'd the way thou wert to come,
And, all the long, long night of hope and fear,
Thy voice and step still sounding in my ear —
Oh God! thou wouldst not wonder that, at last,
When every hope was all at once o'ercast,
When I heard frightful voices round me say
Axim is dead!—this wretched brain gave way,
And I became a wreck, at random driven,
Without one glimpse of reason or of Heaven—
All wild—and even this quenchless love within
Turn'd to foul fires to light me into sin !—
Thou pitiest me—I knew thou wouldst—that sky
Hath nought beneath it half so lorn as I.
The fiend, who lured me hither—hist ! come near,
Or thou too, *thou* art lost, if he should hear—
Told me such things—oh ! with such devilish art,
As would have ruin'd even a holier heart—
Of thee, and of that ever-radiant sphere,
Where bless'd at length, if I but served *him* here,
I should for ever live in thy dear sight,
And drink from those pure eyes eternal light.
Think, think how lost, how madden'd I must be,
To hope that guilt could lead to God or thee !
Thou weep'st for me—do weep—oh, that I durst
Kiss off that tear ! but, no—these lips are curst,
They must not touch thee ;—one divine caress,
One blessed moment of forgetfulness
I 've had within those arms, and *that* shall lie,
Shrined in my soul's deep memory till I die;
The last of joy's last relics here below,
The one sweet drop, in all this waste of woe,
My heart has treasured from affection's spring,
To soothe and cool its deadly withering !
But thou—yes, thou must go—for ever go ;
This place is not for thee—for thee ! oh no,
Did I but tell thee half, thy tortured brain
Would burn like mine, and mine go wild again !
Enough, that Guilt reigns here—that hearts, once
  good,
Now tainted, chill'd, and broken, are his food.—

Enough, that we are parted—that there rolls
A flood of headlong fate between our souls,
Whose darkness severs me as wide from thee
As hell from heaven, to all eternity !"

  " Zelica, Zelica !" the youth exclaim'd,
In all the tortures of a mind inflamed
Almost to madness—" by that sacred Heaven,
Where yet, if prayers can move, thou 'lt be for-
  given,
As thou art here—here, in this writhing heart,
All sinful, wild, and ruin'd as thou art !
By the remembrance of our once pure love,
Which, like a church-yard light, still burns above
The grave of our lost souls—which guilt in thee
Cannot extinguish, nor despair in me!
I do conjure, implore thee to fly hence—
If thou hast yet once spark of innocence,
Fly with me from this place————"
                    " With thee! oh bliss!
'T is worth whole years of torment to hear this.
What ! take the lost one with thee?—let her rove
By thy dear side, as in those days of love,
When we were both so happy, both so pure—
Too heavenly dream ! if there's on earth a cure
For the sunk heart, 't is this—day after day
To be the blest companion of thy way;
To hear thy angel eloquence—to see
Those virtuous eyes for ever turn'd on me;
And, in their light re-chasten'd silently,
Like the stain'd web that whitens in the sun,
Grow pure by being purely shone upon !
And thou wilt pray for me—I know thou wilt—
At the dim vesper hour, when thoughts of guilt
Come heaviest o'er the heart, thou 'lt lift thine
  eyes,
Full of sweet tears, unto the darkening skies,
And plead for me with Heaven, till I can dare
To fix my own weak sinful glances there;
Till the good angels, when they see me cling
For ever near thee, pale and sorrowing,
Shall for thy sake pronounce my soul forgiven,
And bid thee take thy weeping slave to heaven !
Oh yes, I 'll fly with thee————"
                    Scarce had she said
These breathless words, when a voice deep and dread
As that of Monker, waking up the dead
From their first sleep—so startling 't was to both—
Rung through the casement near, " Thy oath ! thy
  oath !"
Oh Heaven, the ghastliness of that Maid's look !—
" 'T is he," faintly she cried, while terror shook
Her inmost core, nor durst she lift her eyes,
Though through the casement, now, nought but the
  skies
And moonlight fields were seen, calm as before—
" 'T is he, and I am his—all, all is o'er—
Go—fly this instant, or thou 'rt ruin'd too—
My oath, my oath, oh God ! 't is all too true,

True as the worm in this cold heart it is—
I am Mokanna's bride—his, Azim, his!
The Dead stood round us, while I spoke that vow,
Their blue lips echo'd it—I hear them now!
Their eyes glared on me, while I pledged that bowl,
'T was burning blood—I feel it in my soul!
And the Veil'd Bridegroom—hist! I 've seen to-night
What angels know not of—so foul a sight,
So horrible—oh! never may'st thou see
What *there* lies hid from all but hell and me!
But I must hence—off, off—I am not thine,
Nor Heaven's, nor Love's, nor aught that is divine—
Hold me not—ha! think'st thou the fiends that sever
Hearts, cannot sunder hands?—thus, then—for ever!"

With all that strength, which madness lends the
    weak,
She flung away his arm; and, with a shriek,
Whose sound, though he should linger out more years
Than wretch e'er told, can never leave his ears—
Flew up through that long avenue of light,
Fleetly as some dark ominous bird of night,
Across the sun, and soon was out of sight!

LALLA ROOKH could think of nothing all day but the
misery of these two young lovers. Her gaiety was
gone, and she looked pensively even upon Fadladeen.
She felt, too, without knowing why, a sort of
uneasy pleasure in imagining that Azim must have
been just such a youth as Feramorz; just as worthy
to enjoy all the blessings, without any of the pangs,
of that illusive passion, which too often, like the
sunny apples of Istkahar, (1) is all sweetness on one
side, and all bitterness on the other.

As they passed along a sequestered river after
sunset, they saw a young Hindoo girl upon the
bank, (2) whose employment seemed to them so
strange, that they stopped their palankeens to ob-
serve her. She had lighted a small lamp, filled with
oil of cocoa, and placing it in an earthen dish,

(1) " In the territory of Istkahar there is a kind of apple,
half of which is sweet and half sour."—*Ebn Haukal.*

(2) For an account of this ceremony, see *Grandpré's,
Voyage in the Indian Ocean.*

(3) " The place where the Whangho, a river of Tibet,
rises, and where there are more than a hundred springs,
which sparkle like stars; whence it is called Hotun-nor,
that is, the Sea of Stars."—*Description of Tibet in Pin-
kerton.*

(4) "The Lescar or Imperial camp is divided, like a re-
gular town, into squares, alleys, and streets, and from a
rising ground furnishes one of the most agreeable prospects
in the world. Starting up in a few hours in an uninha-
bited plain, it raises the idea of a city built by enchant-
ment. Even those who leave their houses in cities to
follow the prince in his progress are frequently so charmed
with the Lescar, when situated in a beautiful and conve-
nient place, that they cannot prevail with themselves to
remove. To prevent this inconvenience to the court,

adorned with a wreath of flowers, had committed it
with a trembling hand to the stream; and was now
anxiously watching its progress down the current,
heedless of the gay cavalcade which had drawn up
beside her. Lalla Rookh was all curiosity;—when
one of her attendants, who had lived upon the banks
of the Ganges, (where this ceremony is so frequent,
that often, in the dusk of the evening, the river is
seen glittering all over with lights, like the Oton-
tala or Sea of Stars,) (3) informed the Princess that
it was the usual way, in which the friends of those
who had gone on dangerous voyages offered up vows
for their safe return. If the lamp sunk immediately,
the omen was disastrous; but if it went shining
down the stream, and continued to burn till entirely
out of sight, the return of the beloved object was
considered as certain.

Lalla Rookh, as they moved on, more than once
looked back, to observe how the young Hindoo's
lamp proceeded; and, while she saw with pleasure
that it was still unextinguished, she could not help
fearing that all the hopes of this life were no better
than that feeble light upon the river. The remainder
of the journey was passed in silence. She now, for
the first time, felt that shade of melancholy, which
comes over the youthful maiden's heart, as sweet
and transient as her own breath upon a mirror; nor
was it till she heard the lute of Feramorz, touched
lightly at the door of her pavilion, that she waked
from the reverie in which she had been wandering.
Instantly her eyes were lighted up with pleasure;
and, after a few unheard remarks from Fadladeen
upon the indecorum of a poet seating himself in
presence of a Princess, every thing was arranged as
on the preceding evening, and all listened with
eagerness, while the story was thus continued :—

Whose are the gilded tents that crowd the way,
Where all was waste and silent yesterday?
This City of War which, in a few short hours,
Hath sprung up here, (4) as if the magic powers

the Emperor, after sufficient time is allowed to the
tradesmen to follow, orders them to be burnt out of their
tents.—*Dow's Hindostan.*

Colonel Wilks gives a lively picture of an Eastern en-
campment :—"His camp, like that of most Indian armies,
exhibited a motley collection of covers from the scorching
sun and dews of the night, variegated according to the
taste or means of each individual, by extensive inclosures
of coloured calico surrounding superb suites of tents;
by ragged cloths. or blankets stretched over sticks or
branches; palm leaves hastily spread over similar sup-
ports; handsome tents and splendid canopies; horses,
oxen, elephants, and camels; all intermixed without any
exterior mark of order or design, except the flags of the
chiefs, which usually mark the centres of a congeries of
these masses; the only regular part of the encampment
being the streets of shops, each of which is constructed
nearly in the manner of a booth at an English fair."—*His-
torical Sketches of the South of India.*

Of Him who, in the twinkling of a star,
Built the high pillar'd halls of Chilminar, (1)
Had conjured up, far as the eye can see, [armory:
This world of tents, and domes, and sun-bright
Princely pavilions, screen'd by many a fold
Of crimson cloth, and topp'd with balls of gold:—
Steeds, with their housings of rich silver spun,
Their chains and poitrels glittering in the sun;
And camels, tufted o'er with Yemen's shells, (2)
Shaking in every breeze their light-toned bells!

But yester-eve, so motionless around,
So mute was this wide plain, that not a sound
But the far torrent, or the locust bird (3)
Hunting among the thickets, could be heard;—
Yet hark! what discords now, of every kind,
Shouts, laughs, and screams are revelling in the wind;
The neigh of cavalry;—the tinkling throngs
Of laden camels and their drivers' songs;—(4)
Ringing of arms, and flapping in the breeze
Of streamers from ten thousand canopies;—
War-music, bursting out from time to time,
With gong and tymbalon's tremendous chime;—
Or, in the pause, when harsher sounds are mute,
The mellow breathings of some horn or flute,
That far off, broken by the eagle note
Of the Abyssinian trumpet, (5) swell and float.

Who leads this mighty army?—ask ye "who?"
And mark ye not those banners of dark hue,
The Night and Shadow, (6) over yonder tent?—
It is the Caliph's glorious armament.
Roused in his palace by the dread alarms,
That hourly came, of the false Prophet's arms,
And of his host of infidels, who hurl'd
Defiance fierce at Islam (7) and the world,—
Though worn with Grecian warfare, and behind
The veils of his bright palace calm reclined,

Yet brook'd he not such blasphemy should stain,
Thus unrevenged, the evening of his reign;
But, having sworn upon the Holy Grave (8)
To conquer or to perish, once more gave
His shadowy banners proudly to the breeze,
And with an army, nursed in victories,
Here stands to crush the rebels that o'er-run
His blest and beauteous Province of the Sun.

Ne'er did the march of Mahadi display
Such pomp before;—not even when on his way
To Mecca's Temple, when both land and sea
Were spoil'd to feed the Pilgrim's luxury; (9)
When round him, 'mid the burning sands, he saw
Fruits of the North in icy freshness thaw,
And cool'd his thirsty lip, beneath the glow
Of Mecca's sun, with urns of Persian snow:—(10)
Nor e'er did armament more grand than that
Pour from the kingdoms of the Caliphat.
First, in the van, the People of the Rock, (11)
On their light mountain steeds, of royal stock: (12)
Then, chieftains of Damascus, proud to see
The flashing of their swords' rich marquetry; (13)
Men, from the regions near the Volga's mouth,
Mix'd with the rude black archers of the South;
And Indian lancers, in white-turban'd ranks,
From the far Sinde, or Attock's sacred banks,
With dusky legions from the Land of Myrrh, (14)
And many a mace-arm'd Moor and Mid-sea islander.

Nor less in number, though more new and rude
In warfare's school, was the vast multitude
That, fired by zeal, or by oppression wrong'd,
Round the white standard of the impostor throng'd.
Beside his thousands of Believers—blind,
Burning and headlong as the Samiel wind—
Many who felt, and more who fear'd to feel
The bloody Islamite's converting steel,

---

(1) The edifices of Chilminar and Balbec are supposed to have been built by the Genii, acting under the orders of Jan ben Jan, who governed the world long before the time of Adam.

(2) "A superb camel, ornamented with strings and tufts of small shells."—*Ali Bey.*

(3) A Native of Khorassan, and allured southward by means of the water of a fountain between Shiraz and Ispahan, called the Fountain of Birds, of which it is so fond that it will follow wherever that water is carried.

(4) "Some of the camels have bells about their necks, and some about their legs, like those which our carriers put about their fore-horses' necks, which together with the servants (who belong to the camels, and travel on foot,) singing all night, make a pleasant noise, and the journey passes away delightfully."—*Pitt's Account of the Mahometans.*

"The camel-driver follows the camels singing, and sometimes playing upon his pipe; the louder he sings and pipes, the faster the camels go. Nay, they will stand still when he gives over his music."—*Tavernier.*

(5) "This trumpet is often called, in Abyssinia, *nesser*

cano, which signifies the Note of the Eagle."—*Note of Bruce's Editor.*

(6) The two black standards borne before the Caliphs of the House of Abbas were called, allegorically, The Night and the Shadow.—See *Gibbon.*

(7) The Mahometan religion.

(8) "The Persians swear by the Tomb of Shah Besade, who is buried at Casbin; and when one desires another to asseverate a matter, he will ask him, if he dare swear by the Holy Grave."—*Struy.*

(9) Mahadi, in a single pilgrimage to Mecca, expended six millions of dinars of gold.

(10) Nivem Meccam apportavit, rem ibi aut nunquam aut raro visam.—*Abulfeda.*

(11) The inhabitants of Hejaz or Arabia Petræa, called by an Eastern writer "The People of the Rock.—*Ebn Haukal.*

(12) "Those horses, called by the Arabians Kochlani, of whom a written genealogy has been kept for 2000 years. They are said to derive their origin from King Solomon's steeds."—*Niebuhr.*

(13) "Many of the figures on the blades of their swords are wrought in gold or silver, or in marquetry with small gems."—*Asiat. Misc.*, v. i.   14 Azab or Saba.

Flock'd to his banner;—chiefs of the Uzbek race,
Waving their heron crests with martial grace; (1)
Turkomans, countless as their flocks, led forth
From the aromatic pastures of the North;
Wild warriors of the turquoise hills, (2)—and those
Who dwell beyond the everlasting snows
Of Hindoo Kosh, (3) in stormy freedom bred,
Their fort the rock, their camp the torrent's bed.
But none, of all who own'd the Chief's command,
Rush'd to that battle-field with bolder hand,
Or sterner hate, than Iran's outlaw'd men,
Her Worshippers of Fire (4)—all panting then
For vengeance on the accursed Saracen;
Vengeance at last for their dear country spurn'd,
Her throne usurp'd, and her bright shrines o'er-
   turn'd.
From Yezd's (5) eternal Mansion of the Fire,
Where aged saints in dreams of Heaven expire:
From Badku, and those fountains of blue flame
That burn into the Caspian, (6) fierce they came,
Careless for what or whom the blow was sped,
So vengeance triumph'd, and their tyrants bled.

Such was the wild and miscellaneous host,
That high in air their motley banners tost
Around the Prophet-Chief—all eyes still bent
Upon that glittering Veil, where'er it went,
That beacon through the battle's stormy flood,
That rainbow of the field, whose showers were blood!

Twice hath the sun upon their conflict set,
And risen again, and found them grappling yet;
While streams of carnage in his noontide blaze
Smoke up to Heaven—hot as that crimson haze,
By which the prostrate Caravan is awed, (7)
In the red Desert, when the wind's abroad.
" On, Swords of God!" the panting Caliph calls—
" Thrones for the living — Heaven for him who
   falls!"—
" On, brave avengers, on!" Mokanna cries,
" And Eblis blast the recreant slave that flies!"

Now comes the brunt, the crisis of the day—
They clash—they strive—the Caliph's troops give
   way!
Mokanna's self plucks the black banner down,
And now the Orient world's imperial crown
Is just within his grasp—when, hark, that shout!
Some hand hath check'd the flying Moslem's rout;
And now they turn, they rally—at their head
A warrior, (like those angel youths who led,
In glorious panoply of Heaven's own mail,
The Champions of the Faith through Beder's vale,)(8)
Bold as if gifted with ten thousand lives,
Turns on the fierce pursuers' blades, and drives
At once the multitudinous torrent back—
While hope and courage kindle in his track;
And, at each step, his bloody falchion makes
Terrible vistas through which victory breaks!
In vain Mokanna, midst the general flight,
Stands, like the red moon, on some stormy night,
Among the fugitive clouds that, hurrying by,
Leave only her unshaken in the sky—
In vain he yells his desperate curses out,
Deals death promiscuously to all about,
To foes that charge and coward friends that fly,
And seems of all the Great Arch-enemy.
The panic spreads—" A miracle!" throughout
The Moslem ranks, " a miracle!" they shout,
All gazing on that youth, whose coming seems
A light, a glory, such as breaks in dreams;
And every sword, true as o'er billows dim
The needle tracks the load-star, following him!

Right towards Mokanna now he cleaves his path,
Impatient cleaves, as though the bolt of wrath
He bears from Heaven withheld its awful burst
From weaker heads, and souls but half-way curst,
To break o'er Him, the mightiest and the worst!
But vain his speed—though, in that hour of blood,
Had all God's seraphs round Mokanna stood,
With swords of fire, ready like fate to fall,
Mokanna's soul would have defied them all,

(1) " The chiefs of the Uzbek Tartars wear a plume of
white heron's feathers in their turbans."—*Account of In-
dependent Tartary.*
(2) In the mountains of Nishapour and Tous (in Khoras-
san) they find turquoises.—*Ebn Haukal.*
(3) For a description of these stupendous ranges of
mountains, see *Elphinstone's Caubul.*
(4) The Ghebers or Guebres, those original natives of
Persia, who adhered to their ancient faith, the religion of
Zoroaster, and who, after the conquest of their country
by the Arabs, were either persecuted at home, or forced
to become wanderers about.
(5) " Yezd, the chief residence of those ancient natives,
who worship the Sun and the Fire, which latter they have
carefully kept lighted, without being once extinguished
for a moment, about 3000 years, on a mountain near
Yezd, called Ater Quedah, signifying the House or Mansion
of the Fire. He is reckoned very unfortunate who dies
off that mountain."—*Stephen's Persia.*

(6) " When the weather is hazy, the springs of Naphtha
(on an island near Baku) boil up the higher, and the
Naphtha often takes fire on the surface of the earth, and
runs in a flame into the sea to a distance almost incre-
dible."—*Hanway on the Everlasting Fire at Baku.*

(7) *Savary* says of the south wind, which blows in Egypt
from February to May, " Sometimes it appears only in
the shape of an impetuous whirlwind, which passes rapidly,
and is fatal to the traveller, surprised in the middle of the
deserts. Torrents of burning sand roll before it, the fir-
mament is enveloped in a thick veil, and the sun appears
of the colour of blood. Sometimes whole caravans are
buried in it."

(8) In the great victory gained by Mahomed at Beder
he was assisted, say the Mussulmans, by three thousand
angels, led by Gabriel, mounted on his horse Hiazum.—
See *The Koran and its Commentators.*

Yet now, the rush of fugitives, too strong
For human force, hurries even *him* along;
In vain he struggles 'mid the wedged array
Of flying thousands—he is borne away;
And the sole joy his baffled spirit knows,
In this forced flight, is—murdering as he goes!
As a grim tiger, whom the torrent's might
Surprises in some parch'd ravine at night,
Turns, even in drowning, on the wretched flocks,
Swept with him in that snow-flood from the rocks,
And, to the last, devouring on his way,
Bloodies the stream he hath not power to stay.

" Alla illa Alla!"—the glad shout renew—
"Alla Akbar!" (1)—the Caliph 's in Merou.
Hang out your gilded tapestry in the streets,
And light your shrines and chaunt your ziraleets.(2)
The Swords of God have triumph'd—on his throne
Your Caliph sits, and the Veil'd Chief hath flown.
Who does not envy that young warrior now,
To whom the Lord of Islam bends his brow,
In all the graceful gratitude of power,
For his throne's safety in that perilous hour?
Who doth not wonder, when, amidst the acclaim
Of thousands, heralding to heaven his name—
'Mid all those holier harmonies of fame,
Which sound along the path of virtuous souls,
Like music round a planet as it rolls—
He turns away—coldly, as if some gloom
Hung o'er his heart no triumphs can illume—
Some sightless grief, upon whose blasted gaze
Though glory's light may play, in vain it plays.
Yes, wretched Azim! thine is such a grief,
Beyond all hope, all terror, all relief;
A dark cold calm, which nothing now can break,
Or warm or brighten—like that Syrian Lake,(3)
Upon whose surface morn and Summer shed
Their smiles in vain, for all beneath is dead!—
Hearts there have been, o'er which this weight of
woe
Came by long use of suffering, tame and slow;
But thine, lost youth! was sudden—over thee
It broke at once, when all seem'd ecstasy;
When Hope look'd up, and saw the gloomy Past
Melt into splendour, and Bliss dawn at last—
'T was then, even then, o'er joys so freshly blown,
This mortal blight of misery came down;
Even then, the full warm gushings of thy heart
Were check'd—like fount-drops, frozen as they
start—
And there, like them, cold sunless relics hang,
Each fix'd and chill'd into a lasting pang.

One sole desire, one passion now remains
To keep life's fever still within his veins,
Vengeance!—dire vengeance on the wretch who
cast
O'er him and all he loved that ruinous blast.
For this, when rumours reach'd him in his flight
Far, far away, after that fatal night—
Rumours of armies, thronging to the attack
Of the Veil'd Chief—for this he wing'd him back,
Fleet as the vulture speeds to flags unfurl'd,
And, when all hope seem'd desperate, wildly hurl'd
Himself into the scale, and saved a world.
For this he still lives on, careless of all
The wreaths that Glory on his path lets fall;
For this alone exists—like lightning-fire,
To speed one bolt of vengeance, and expire!

But safe as yet that Spirit of Evil lives;
With a small band of desperate fugitives,
The last sole stubborn fragment, left unriven,
Of the proud host that late stood fronting Heaven,
He gain'd Merou—breathed a short curse of blood
O'er his lost throne—then pass'd the Jihon's flood,(4)
And gathering all, whose madness of belief
Still saw a Saviour in their down-fallen Chief,
Raised the white banner within Neksheb's gates,(5)
And there, untamed, the approaching conqueror
waits.

Of all his Haram, all that busy hive
With music and with sweets sparkling alive,
He took but one, the partner of his flight,
One—not for love—not for her beauty's light—
No, Zelica stood withering 'midst the gay,
Wan as the blossom that fell yesterday
From the Alma tree and dies, while overhead
To-day's young flower is springing in its stead. (6)
Oh, not for love—the deepest damn'd must be
Touch'd with heaven's glory, ere such fiends as he
Can feel one glimpse of Love's divinity.
But no, she is his victim;—*there* lie all
Her charms for him—charms that can never pall,
As long as hell within his heart can stir,
Or one faint trace of Heaven is left in her.
To work an angel's ruin—to behold
As white a page as Virtue e'er unroll'd
Blacken, beneath his touch, into a scroll
Of damning sins, seal'd with a burning soul—
This is his triumph; this the joy accurst,
That ranks him among demons all but first:
This gives the victim, that before him lies
Blighted and lost, a glory in his eyes,

---

(1) The **Tecbir**, or cry of the Arabs. " Alla Acbar :" says
Ockley, means, " God is most mighty."

(2) The **ziraleet** is a kind of chorus, which the women
of the East sing upon joyful occasions.—*Russell.*

(3) The **Dead Sea, which** contains neither animal nor
vegetable life.

(4) The ancient **Oxus.** (5) A city of **Transoxiana.**

(6) " You never can cast your eyes on this tree, but you
meet there either blossoms or fruit; and as the blossom
drops underneath on the ground (which is frequently
covered with these purple-coloured flowers), others come
forth in their stead," etc., etc.—*Nieuhoff.*

A light like that with which hell–fire illumes
The ghastly writhing wretch whom it consum s

  But other tasks now wait him—tasks that need
All the deep daringness of thought and deed
With which the Dives (1) have gifted him—for mark
Over yon plains, which night had else made dark,
Those lanterns, countless as the winged lights
That spangle India's fields on showery nights—(2)
Far as their formidable gleams they shed,
The mighty tents of the beleaguerer spread,
Glimmering along the horizon's dusky line,
And thence in nearer circles, till they shine
Among the founts and groves, o'er which the town
In all its arm'd magnificence looks down.
Yet, fearless, from his lofty battlements
Mokanna views that multitude of tents;
Nay, smiles to think that, though entoil'd, beset,
Not less than myriads dare to front him yet;—
That friendless, throneless, he thus stands at bay,
Even thus a match for myriads such as they.
" Oh, for a sweep of that dark Angel's wing,
Who brush'd the thousands of the Assyrian King (3)
To darkness in a moment, that I might
People hell's chambers with yon host to-night!
But, come what may, let who will grasp the throne,
Caliph or Prophet, man alike shall groan; .
Let who will torture him, Priest—Caliph—King—
Alike this loathsome world of his shall ring
With victims' shrieks and howlings of the slave—
Sounds, that shall glad me even within my grave!"
Thus, to himself—but to the scanty train
Still left around him, a far different strain:—
" Glorious Defenders of the sacred Crown
I bear from Heaven, whose light nor blood shall
    drown
Nor shadow of earth eclipse;—before whose gems
The paly pomp of this world's diadems,
The crown of Gerashid, the pillar'd throne
Of Parviz, (4) and the heron crest that shone, (5)

Magnificent, o'er Ali's beauteous eyes, (6)
Fade like the stars when morn is in the skies :
Warriors, rejoice—the port to which we've pass'd
O'er Destiny's dark wave beams out at last!
Victory 's our own—'tis written in that book
Upon whose leaves none but the angels look,
That Islam's sceptre shall beneath the power
Of her great foe fall broken in that hour,
When the moon's mighty orb, before all eyes,
From Neksheb's Holy Well portentously shall rise!
Now turn and see!"——
              They turn'd, and, as he spoke,
A sudden splendour all around them broke,
And they beheld an orb, ample and bright,
Rise from the Holy Well, (7) and cast its light
Round the rich city and the plain for miles—(8)
Flinging such radiance o'er the gilded tiles
Of many a dome and fair-roof'd imaret
As autumn suns shed round them when they set.
Instant from all who saw the illusive sign
A murmur broke—"Miraculous! divine!"
The Gheber bow'd, thinking his idol star
Had waked, and burst impatient through the bar
Of midnight, to inflame him to the war;
While he of Moussa's creed saw, in that ray,
The glorious light which, in his freedom's day,
Had rested on the Ark, (9) and now again
Shone out to bless the breaking of his chain.

  "To victory!" is at once the cry of all—
Nor stands Mokanna loitering at that call,
But instant the huge gates are flung aside,
And forth, like a diminutive mountain-tide
Into the boundless sea, they speed their course
Right on into the Moslem's mighty force.
The watchmen of the camp—who, in their rounds,
Had paused, and even forgot the punctual sounds
Of the small drum with which they count the
    night, (10)
To gaze upon that supernatural light—

---

(1) The Demons of the Persian mythology.

(2) Carreri mentions the fire–flies in India during the rainy season.—See his *Travels*.

(3) Sennacherib, called by the Orientals King of Moussal.—*D'Herbelot*.

(4) Chosroes.   For the description of his Throne or Palace, see *Gibbon* and *D'Herbelot*.
  There were said to be under this Throne or Palace of Khosrou Parviz a hundred vaults filled with "treasures so immense, that some Mahometan writers tell us, their Prophet, to encourage his disciples, carried them to a rock, which at his command opened, and gave them a prospect through it of the treasures of Khosrou."—*Universal History*.

(5) "The crown of Gerashid is cloudy and tarnished before the heron tuft of thy turban."—From one of the elegies or songs in praise of Ali, written in characters of gold round the gallery of Abbas's tomb.—See *Chardin*.

(6) The beauty of Ali's eyes was so remarkable, that whenever the Persians would describe any thing as very

lovely, they say it is Ayn Hali, or the eyes of Ali.—*Chardin*.

(7) We are not told more of this trick of the impostor, than that it was "une machine, qu'il disoit être la Lune." According to Richardson, the miracle is perpetuated in Neksheb.—"Nakshab, the name of a city in Transoxiania, where they say there is a well, in which the appearance of the moon is to be seen night and day."

(8) "Il amusa pendant deux mois le peuple de la ville de Nekhscheb, en faisant sortir toutes les nuits du fond d'un puits un corps lumineux semblable à la Lune, qui portoit sa lumière jusqu'à la distance de plusieurs milles."—*D'Herbelot*. Hence he was called Sazendéhmah, or the Moon-maker.

(9) The Shechinah, called Sakinat in the Koran.—See *Sale's Note*, chap. ii.

(10) The parts of the night are made known as well by instruments of music, as by the rounds of the watchmen with cries and small drums.—See *Burder's Oriental Customs*, vol. i., p. 119.

Now sink beneath an unexpected arm,
And in a death-groan give their last alarm.
"On for the lamps that light yon lofty screen, (1)
Nor blunt your blades with massacre so mean;
There rests the Caliph—speed—one lucky lance
May now achieve mankind's deliverance."
Desperate the die—such as they only cast
Who venture for a world, and stake their last.
But Fate's no longer with him—blade for blade
Springs up to meet them through the glimmering
    shade,
And, as the clash is heard, new legions soon
Pour to the spot, like bees of Kauzeroon (2)
To the shrill timbrel's summons—till, at length,
The mighty camp swarms out in all its strength,
And back to Neksheb's gates, covering the plain
With random slaughter, drives the adventurous
    train;
Among the last of whom the Silver Veil
Is seen glittering at times, like the white sail
Of some toss'd vessel, on a stormy night,
Catching the tempest's momentary light!

And hath not *this* brought the proud spirit low?
Nor dash'd his brow, nor check'd his daring? No.
Though half the wretches, whom at night he led
To thrones and victory, lie disgraced and dead,
Yet morning hears him, with unshrinking crest,
Still vaunt of thrones and victory to the rest;—
And they believe him!—oh, the lover may
Distrust that look which steals his soul away;—
The babe may cease to think that it can play
With Heaven's rainbow;—alchymists may doubt
The shining gold their crucible gives out;
But Faith, fanatic Faith, once wedded fast
To some dear falsehood, hugs it to the last.

And well the Impostor knew all lures and arts,
That Lucifer e'er taught to tangle hearts;
Nor, 'mid these last bold workings of his plot
Against men's souls, is Zelica forgot.
Ill-fated Zelica! had reason been
Awake, through half the horrors thou hast seen,
Thou never couldst have borne it—Death had come
At once, and taken thy wrung spirit home.

(1) The Serrapurda, high screens of red cloth, stiffened
with cane, used to enclose a considerable space round the
royal tents.—*Notes on the Bahardanush.*
    The tents of Princes were generally illuminated. Kor-
den tells us that the tent of the Bey of Girge was distin-
guished from the other tents by forty lanterns being sus-
pended before it.—See *Harmer's Observations on Job.*
(2) "From the groves of orange trees at Kauzeroon the
bees cull a celebrated honey."—*Morier's Travels.*
(3) "A custom still subsisting at this day, seems to me
to prove that the Egyptians formerly sacrificed a young
virgin to the God of the Nile; for they now make a statue
of earth in shape of a girl, to which they give the name of
the Betrothed Bride, and throw it into the river."—*Savary.*
(4) That they knew the secret of the Greek fire among

But 'twas not so—a torpor, a suspense
Of thought, almost of life, came o'er the intense
And passionate struggles of that fearful night,
When her last hope of peace and heaven took flight:
And though, at times, a gleam of frenzy broke—
As through some dull volcano's veil of smoke
Ominous flashings now and then will start,
Which show the fire's still busy at its heart;
Yet was she mostly wrapp'd in solemn gloom—
Not such as Azim's, brooding o'er its doom,
And calm without, as is the brow of death,
While busy worms are gnawing underneath—
But in a blank and pulseless torpor, free
From thought or pain, a seal'd-up apathy,
Which left her oft, with scarce one living thrill,
The cold pale victim of her torturer's will.

Again, as in Merou, he had her deck'd
Gorgeously out, the Priestess of the sect;
And led her glittering forth before the eyes
Of his rude train, as to a sacrifice—
Pallid as she, the young devoted Bride
Of the fierce Nile, when, deck'd in all the pride
Of nuptial pomp, she sinks into his tide. (3)
And while the wretched maid hung down her head,
And stood, as one just risen from the dead,
Amid that gazing crowd, the fiend would tell
His credulous slaves it was some charm or spell
Possess'd her now—and from that darken'd trance
Should dawn ere long their Faith's deliverance.
Or if, at times, goaded by guilty shame,
Her soul was roused, and words of wildness came,
Instant the bold blasphemer would translate
Her ravings into oracles of fate,
Would hail Heaven's signals in her flashing eyes,
And call her shrieks the language of the skies!

But vain at length his arts—despair is seen
Gathering around; and famine comes to glean
All that the sword had left unreap'd:—in vain
At morn and eve across the northern plain
He looks impatient for the promised spears
Of the wild Hordes and Tartar mountaineers;
They come not—while his fierce beleaguerers pour
Engines of havoc in, unknown before, (4)

the Mussulmans early in the eleventh century, appears
from *Dow's Account of Mamood I.* "When he arrived at
Moulton, finding that the country of the Jits was defended
by great rivers, he ordered fifteen hundred boats to be
built, each of which he armed with six iron spikes, pro-
jecting from their prows and sides, to prevent their being
boarded by the enemy, who were very expert in that kind
of war. When he had launched this fleet, he ordered
twenty archers into each boat, and five others with fire-
balls, to burn the craft of the Jits, and naphtha to set the
whole river on fire."
    The *agnee aster*, too, in Indian poems the Instrument
of Fire, whose flame cannot be extinguished, is supposed
to signify the Greek Fire.—See *Wilks's South of India*
vol. i., p. 471.—And in the curious Javan poem, the *Brata*

44

And horrible as new; (1)—javelins, that fly
Enwreathed with smoky flames through the dark
    sky,
And red-hot globes, that, opening as they mount,
Discharge, as from a kindled naphtha fount, (2)
Showers of consuming fire o'er all below;
Looking, as through the illumined night they go,
Like those wild birds (3) that by the Magians oft,
At festivals of fire, were sent aloft
Into the air, with blazing faggots tied
To their huge wings, scattering combustion wide.
All night the groans of wretches who expire,
In agony, beneath these darts of fire,
Ring through the city—while, descending o'er
Its shrines and domes and streets of sycamore—
Its lone bazars, with their bright cloths of gold,
Since the last peaceful pageant left unroll'd—
Its beauteous marble baths, whose idle jets
Now gush with blood—and its tall minarets,
That late have stood up in the evening glare
Of the red sun, unhallow'd by a prayer:—
O'er each, in turn, the dreadful flame-bolts fall,
And death and conflagration throughout all
The desolate city hold high festival!

    Mokanna sees the world is his no more;—
One sting at parting, and his grasp is o'er.
"What! drooping now?"—thus, with unblushing
    cheek,
He hails the few, who yet can hear him speak,
Of all those famish'd slaves around him lying,
And by the light of blazing temples dying;—
"What!—drooping now?—now, when at length we
Home o'er the very threshold of success;   [press
When Alla from our ranks hath thinn'd away
Those grosser branches, that kept out his ray

Of favour from us, and we stand at length
Heirs of his light and children of his strength,
The chosen few, who shall survive the fall
Of Kings and Thrones, triumphant over all!
Have you then lost, weak murmurers as you are,
All faith in him, who was your Light, your Star?
Have you forgot the eye of glory, hid
Beneath this Veil, the flashing of whose lid
Could, like a sun-stroke of the desert, wither
Millions of such as yonder Chief brings hither?
Long have its lightnings slept—too long—but now
All earth shall feel the unveiling of this brow!
To-night—yes, sainted men! this very night,
I bid you all to a fair festal rite,
Where—having deep refresh'd each weary limb
With viands, such as feast Heaven's cherubim,
And kindled up your souls, now sunk and dim,
With that pure wine the Dark-eyed Maids above
Keep, seal'd with precious musk, for those they
I will myself uncurtain in your sight,   [love—(4)
The wonders of this brow's ineffable light;
Then lead you forth, and with a wink disperse
Yon myriads, howling through the universe!"

    Eager they listen—while each accent darts
New life into their chill'd and hope-sick hearts;
Such treacherous life as the cool draught supplies
To him upon the stake, who drinks and dies!
Wildly they point their lances to the light
Of the fast-sinking sun, and shout "To-night!"—
"To-night!" their Chief re-echoes in a voice
Of fiend-like mockery that bids hell rejoice.
Deluded victims!—never hath this earth
Seen mourning half so mournful as their mirth.
Here, to the few, whose iron frames had stood,
This racking waste of famine and of blood,

<hr/>

Tudha, given by *Sir Stamford Raffles* in his *History of
Iava*, we find, "He aimed at the heart of Soéta with the
sharp-pointed Weapon of Fire."
    The mention of gunpowder as in use among the Ara-
bians, long before its supposed discovery in Europe, is
introduced by *Ebn Fadhl*, the Egyptian geographer, who
lived in the thirteenth century. "Bodies," he says, "in
the form of scorpions, bound round and filled with nitrous
powder, glide along, making a gentle noise; then, ex-
ploding, they lighten, as it were, and burn. But there
are others which, cast into the air, stretch along like a
cloud, roaring horribly, as thunder roars, and on all sides
vomiting out flames, burst, burn, and reduce to cinders
whatever comes in their way." The historian *Ben Abdalla*,
in speaking of the sieges of Abulualid, in the year of the
Hegira 712, says, "A fiery globe, by means of combustible
matter, with a mighty noise suddenly emitted, strikes
with the force of lightning, and shakes the citadel."—See
the extracts from *Casiri's Biblioth. Arab. Hispan.*, in the
Appendix to *Berington's Literary History of the Middle
Ages*.
    (1) The Greek fire, which was occasionally lent by the
emperors to their allies. "It was," says Gibbon, "either
launched in red-hot balls of stone and iron, or darted in
arrows and javelins, twisted round with flax and tow,
which had deeply imbibed the inflammable oil."

(2) See *Hanway's Account of the Springs of Naphtha at
Baku* (which is called by *Lieutenant Pottinger* Joala
Mookee, or, the Flaming Mouth,) taking fire and running
into the sea. *Dr. Cooke*, in his *Journal*, mentions some
wells in Circassia, strongly impregnated with this inflam-
mable oil, from which issues boiling water. "Though
the weather," he adds, "was now very cold, the warmth
of these wells of hot water produced near them the ver-
dure and flowers of Spring."
    Major Scott Waring says, that naphtha is used by the
Persians, as we are told it was in hell, for lamps.
    . . . . many a row
    Of starry lamps and blazing cressets, fed
    With naphtha and asphaltus, yielding light
    As from a sky.
    (3) "At the great festival of fire, called the Sheb Sezé,
they used to set fire to large bunches of dry combustibles,
fastened round wild beasts and birds, which being then
let loose, the air and earth appeared one great illumina-
tion; and as these terrified creatures naturally fled to the
woods for shelter, it is easy to conceive the conflagrations
they produced."—*Richardson's Dissertation*.
    (4) "The righteous shall be given to drink of pure
wine, sealed; the seal whereof shall be musk."—*Koran*,
chap. lxxxiii.

Faint dying wretches clung, from whom the shout
Of triumph like a maniac's laugh broke out;—
There, others, lighted by the smouldering fire,
Danced, like wan ghosts about a funeral pyre,
Among the dead and dying, strew'd around;—
While some pale wretch look'd on, and from his
    wound
Plucking the fiery dart by which he bled,
In ghastly transport waved it o'er his head!

'Twas more than midnight now—a fearful pause
Had follow'd the long shouts, the wild applause,
That lately from those Royal Gardens burst,
Where the Veil'd demon held his feast accurst,
When Zelica—alas, poor ruin'd heart,
In every horror doom'd to bear its part!—
Was bidden to the banquet by a slave,
Who, while his quivering lip the summons gave,
Grew black, as though the shadows of the grave
Compass'd him round, and, ere he could repeat
His message through, fell lifeless at her feet!
Shuddering she went—a soul-felt pang of fear,
A presage that her own dark doom was near,
Roused every feeling, and brought Reason back
Once more, to writhe her last upon the rack.
All round seem'd tranquil—even the foe had ceased,
As if aware of that demoniac feast,
His fiery bolts; and though the heavens look'd red,
'T was but some distant conflagration's spread,
But hark—she stops—she listens—dreadful tone!
'T is her Tormentor's laugh—and now, a groan,
A long death-groan comes with it:—can this be
The place of mirth, the bower of revelry?
She enters—Holy Alla, what a sight
Was there before her! By the glimmering light
Of the pale dawn, mix'd with the flare of brands
That round lay burning, dropp'd from lifeless hands,
She saw the board, in splendid mockery spread,
Rich censers breathing—garlands overhead—
The urns, the cups, from which they late had quaff'd
All gold and gems, but—what had been the draught?
Oh! who need ask, that saw those livid guests,
With their swollen heads sunk blackening on their
    breasts,
Or looking pale to Heaven with glassy glare,
As if they sought but saw no mercy there;
As if they felt, though poison rack'd them through,
Remorse the deadlier torment of the two!
While some, the bravest, hardiest in the train
Of their false Chief, who on the battle-plain
Would have met death with transport by his side,
Here mute and helpless gasp'd;—but, as they died,
Look'd horrible vengeance with their eyes' last strain,
And clench'd the slackening hand at him in vain.

(1) "The Afghauns believe each of the numerous soli-
tudes and deserts of their country to be inhabited by a
lonely demon, whom they call the Ghoolee Beeabau, or
Spirit of the Waste. They often illustrate the wildness of
any sequestered tribe, by saying, they are wild as the
Demon of the Waste."—*Elphinstone's Caubul.*

Dreadful it was to see the ghastly stare,
The stony look of horror and despair,
Which some of these expiring victims cast
Upon their soul's tormentor to the last—
Upon that mocking Fiend, whose Veil, now raised,
Show'd them, as in death's agony they gazed,
Not the long-promised light, the brow, whose beam-
    ing
Was to come forth, all conquering, all redeeming,
But features horribler than Hell e'er traced
On its own brood;—no Demon of the Waste,(1)
No church-yard Ghole, caught lingering in the light
Of the blest sun, e'er blasted human sight
With lineaments so foul, so fierce as those
The Impostor now, in grinning mockery, shows :—
" There, ye wise Saints, behold your Light, your
    Star—
Ye *would* be dupes and victims, and ye *are*.
Is it enough? or must I, while a thrill
Lives in your sapient bosoms, cheat you still?
Swear that the burning death ye feel within
Is but the trance with which Heaven's joys begin;
That this foul visage, foul as e'er disgraced
Even monstrous man, is—after God's own taste;
And that—but see!—ere I have half-way said
My greetings through, the uncourteous souls are fled.
Farewell, sweet spirits! not in vain ye die,
If Eblis loves you half so well as I.—
Ha, my young bride!—'t is well—take thou thy seat;
Nay, come—no shuddering—didst thou never meet
The Dead before?—they graced our wedding, sweet;
And these, my guests to-night, have brimm'd so
    true
Their parting cups, that *thou* shalt pledge one too.
But—how is this?—all empty? all drunk up?
Hot lips have been before thee in the cup,
Young bride—yet stay—one precious drop remains,
Enough to warm a gentle Priestess' veins ;—
Here, drink—and should thy lover's conquering
    arms
Speed hither, ere thy lip lose all its charms,
Give him but half this venom in thy kiss,
And I 'll forgive my haughty rival's bliss !

"For *me*—I too must die—but not like these
Vile rankling things, to fester in the breeze;
To have this brow in ruffian triumph shown,
With all death's grimness added to its own,
And rot to dust beneath the taunting eyes
Of slaves, exclaiming, ' There his Godship lies !'
No, cursed race!—since first my soul drew breath,
They 've been my dupes, and *shall* be even in death.
Thou see'st yon cistern in the shade—'t is fill'd
With burning drugs, for this last hour distill'd :—(2)

(2) "Il donna du poison dans le vin à tous ses gens, et
se jetta lui-même ensuite dans une cuve pleine de drogues
brûlantes et consumantes, afin qu'il ne restât rien de tous
les membres de son corps, et que ceux qui restoient de
sa secte puissent croire qu'il étoit monté au ciel, ce qui
ne manqua pas d'arriver."—*D'Herbelot.*

There will I plunge me, in that liquid flame—
Fit bath to lave a dying Prophet's frame!—
There perish, all—ere pulse of thine shall fail—
Nor leave one limb to tell mankind the tale.
So shall my votaries, wheresoe'er they rave,
Proclaim that Heaven took back the Saint it gave ;—
That I 've but vanish'd from this earth awhile,
To come again, with bright unshrouded smile!
So shall they build me altars in their zeal,
Where knaves shall minister, and fools shall kneel ;
Where Faith may mutter o'er her mystic spell,
Written in blood—and Bigotry may swell
The sail he spreads for Heaven with blasts from hell !
So shall my banner, through long ages, be
The rallying sign of fraud and anarchy ;
Kings yet unborn shall rue Mokanna's name,
And though I die, my spirit, still the same,
Shall walk abroad in all the stormy strife,
And guilt, and blood, that were its bliss in life !
But, hark ! their battering engine shakes the wall—
Why *let* it shake—thus I can brave them all.
No trace of me shall greet them, when they come,
And I can trust thy faith, for—thou 'lt be dumb.
Now mark how readily a wretch like me,
In one bold plunge, commences Deity !"

He sprung and sunk, as the last words were said—
Quick closed the burning waters o'er his head,
And Zelica was left—within the ring
Of those wide walls the only living thing ;
The only wretched one, still cursed with breath,
In all that frightful wilderness of death !
More like some bloodless ghost—such as, they tell,
In the Lone Cities of the Silent (1) dwell,
And there, unseen of all but Alla, sit
Each by its own pale carcass, watching it.

But morn is up, and a fresh warfare stirs
Throughout the camp of the beleaguerers.
Their globes of fire (the dread artillery lent
By Greece to conquering Mahadi) are spent ;
And now the scorpion's shaft, the quarry sent
From high balistas, and the shielded throng
Of soldiers swinging the huge ram along,
All speak the impatient Islamite's intent
To try, at length, if tower and battlement
And bastion'd wall be not less hard to win,
Less tough to break down, than the hearts within.
First in impatience and in toil is he,
The burning Azim—oh ! could he but see
The Impostor once alive within his grasp,
Not the gaunt lion's hug, nor boa's clasp,
Could match that gripe of vengeance, or keep pace
With the fell heartiness of Hate's embrace !

Loud rings the ponderous ram against the walls ;
Now shake the ramparts, now a buttress falls,
But still no breach—" Once more, one mighty swing
Of all your beams, together thundering !"

There—the wall shakes—the shouting troops exult,
" Quick, quick discharge your weightiest catapult
Right on that spot, and Neksheb is our own !"
'T is done—the battlements come crashing down,
And the huge wall, by that stroke riven in two,
Yawning, like some old crater, rent anew,
Shows the dim desolate city smoking through.
But strange ! no signs of life—nought living seen
Above, below—what can this stillness mean?
A minute's pause suspends all hearts and eyes—
" In through the breach," impetuous Azim cries ;
But the cool Caliph, fearful of some wile
In this blank stillness, checks the troops awhile.—
Just then, a figure, with slow step, advanced
Forth from the ruin'd walls, and, as there glanced
A sunbeam over it, all eyes could see
The well-known Silver Veil !—" 'T is He, 't is He,
" Mokanna, and alone !" they shout around ;
Young Azim from his steed springs to the ground—
" Mine, Holy Caliph ! mine," he cries, " the task
To crush yon daring wretch—'t is all I ask."
Eager he darts to meet the demon foe,
Who still across wide heaps of ruin slow
And falteringly comes, till they are near ;
Then, with a bound, rushes on Azim's spear,
And, casting off the Veil in falling, shows—
Oh !—'t is his Zelica's life-blood that flows !

" I meant not, Azim," soothingly she said,
As on his trembling arm she lean'd her head,
And, looking in his face, saw anguish there
Beyond all wounds the quivering flesh can bear—
" I meant not *thou* shouldst have the pain of
this ;—
Though death, with thee thus tasted, is a bliss
Thou wouldst not rob me of, didst thou but know
How oft I 've pray'd to God I might die so!
But the Fiend's venom was too scant and slow ;—
To linger on were maddening—and I thought
If once that Veil—nay, look not on it—caught
The eyes of your fierce soldiery, I should be
Struck by a thousand death-darts instantly.
But this is sweeter—oh ! believe me, yes—
I would not change this sad but dear caress,
This death within thy arms I would not give
For the most smiling life the happiest live !
All, that stood dark and drear before the eye
Of my stray'd soul, is passing swiftly by ;
A light comes o'er me from those looks of love,
Like the first dawn of mercy from above ;
And if thy lips but tell me I 'm forgiven,
Angels will echo the blest words in heaven !
But live, my Azim ;—oh ! to call thee mine
Thus once again ! *my* Azim—dream divine !

(1) " They have all a great reverence for burial-grounds,
which they sometimes call by the poetical name of Cities
of the Silent, and which they people with the ghosts of the
departed, who sit each at the head of his own grave, invi-
sible to mortal eyes."—*Elphinstone.*

Live, if thou ever lovedst me, if to meet
Thy Zelica hereafter would be sweet,
Oh, live to pray for her—to bend the knee
Morning and night before that Deity,
To whom pure lips and hearts without a stain,
As thine are, Azim, never breathed in vain—
And pray that He may pardon Her—may take
Compassion on her soul for thy dear sake,
And, nought remembering but her love to thee,
Make her all thine, all His eternally!
Go to those happy fields where first we twined
Our youthful hearts together—every wind
That meets thee there, fresh from the well-known
    flowers,
Will bring the sweetness of those innocent hours
Back to thy soul, and thou may'st feel again
For thy poor Zelica, as thou didst then.
So shall thy orisons, like dew that flies
To Heaven upon the morning's sunshine, rise
With all love's earliest ardour to the skies!
And should they—but, alas, my senses fail—
Oh for one minute!—should thy prayers prevail—
If pardon'd souls may, from that World of Bliss,
Reveal their joy to those they love in this—
I 'll come to thee—in some sweet dream—and tell—
Oh Heaven—I die—dear love! farewell, farewell.''

Time fleeted—years on years had pass'd away,
And few of those who, on that mournful day,
Had stood, with pity in their eyes, to see
The maiden's death, and the youth's agony,
Were living still—when, by a rustic grave,
Beside the swift Amoo's transparent wave,
An aged man, who had grown aged there
By that lone grave, morning and night in prayer,
For the last time knelt down—and, though the shade
Of death hung darkening over him, there play'd
A gleam of rapture on his eye and cheek,
That brighten'd even Death—like the last streak
Of intense glory on the horizon's brim,
When night o'er all the rest hangs chill and dim.
His soul had seen a Vision, while he slept;
She, for whose spirit he had pray'd and wept
So many years, had come to him all drest
In angel smiles, and told him she was blest!
For this the old man breathed his thanks, and
    died.—
And there, upon the banks of that loved tide,
He and his Zelica sleep side by side.

THE story of the Veiled Prophet of Khorassan
being ended, they were now doomed to hear Fadladeen's criticisms upon it. A series of disappointments and accidents had occurred to this learned
Chamberlain during the journey. In the first place,
those couriers stationed, as in the reign of Shah
Jehan, between Delhi and the Western coast of India,
to secure a constant supply of mangoes for the Royal
Table, had by some cruel irregularity failed in their
duty; and to eat any mangoes but those of Mazagong
was, of course, impossible. (1) In the next place,
the elephant, laden with his fine antique porcelain, (2)
had, in an unusual fit of liveliness, shattered the
whole set to pieces :—an irreparable loss, as many of
the vessels were so exquisitely old, as to have been
used under the Emperors Yan and Chun, who
reigned many ages before the dynasty of Tang. His
Koran, too, supposed to be the identical copy between
the leaves of which Mahomet's favourite pigeon used
to nestle, had been mislaid by his Koran-bearer
three whole days ; not without much spiritual alarm
to Fadladeen, who, though professing to hold with
other loyal and orthodox Mussulmans, that salvation
could only be found in the Koran, was strongly suspected of believing in his heart, that it could only be
found in his own particular copy of it. When to all
these grievances is added the obstinacy of the cooks,
in putting the pepper of Canara into his dishes instead of the cinnamon of Serendib, we may easily
suppose that he came to the task of criticism with, at
least, a sufficient degree of irritability for the purpose.

"In order," said he, importantly swinging about
his chaplet of pearls, "to convey with clearness my
opinion of the story this young man has related, it
is necessary to take a review of all the stories that
have ever——''—"My good Fadladeen!" exclaimed
the Princess, interrupting him, " we really do not
deserve that you should give yourself so much
trouble. Your opinion of the poem we have just
heard will, I have no doubt, be abundantly edifying,
without any further waste of your valuable erudition."—"If that be all," replied the critic—evidently
mortified at not being allowed to show how much
he knew about every thing, but the subject immediately before him—"if that be all that is required,
the matter is easily despatched." He then proceeded
to analyse the poem, in that strain (so well known
to the unfortunate bards of Delhi), whose censures
were an infliction from which few recovered, and

(1) "The celebrity of Mazagong is owing to its mangoes,
which are certainly the best fruit I ever tasted. The parenttree, from which all those of this species have been grafted,
is honoured during the fruit-season by a guard of sepoys;
and, in the reign of Shah Jehan, couriers were stationed
between Delhi and the Mahratta coast, to secure an abundant and fresh supply of mangoes for the royal table."—
Mrs. Graham's Journal of a Residence in India.

(2) This old porcelain is found in digging, and "if it is
esteemed, it is not because it has acquired any new degree

of beauty in the earth, but because it has retained its ancient beauty; and this alone is of great importance in
China, where they give large sums for the smallest vessels
which were used under the Emperors Yan and Chun, who
reigned many ages before the dynasty of Tang, at which
time porcelain began to be used by the Emperors" (about
the year 442).—*Dunn's Collection of Curious Observations*, etc.;—a bad translation of some parts of the *Lettres
Edifiantes et Curieuses* of the Missionary Jesuits.

whose very praises were like the honey extracted from the bitter flowers of the aloe. The chief personages of the story were, if he rightly understood them, an ill-favoured gentleman, with a veil over his face;—a young lady, whose reason went and came, acording as it suited the poet's convenience to be sensible or otherwise;—and a youth in one of those hideous Bucharian bonnets who took the aforesaid gentleman in a veil for a Divinity. "From such materials," said he, "what can be expected? —after rivalling each other in long speeches and absurdities, through some thousands of lines as indigestible as the filberts of Berdaa, our friend in the veil jumps into a tub of aquafortis; the young lady dies in a set speech, whose only recommendation is that it is her last; and the lover lives on to a good old age, for the laudable purpose of seeing her ghost, which he at last happily accomplishes, and expires. This, you will allow, is a fair summary of the story; and if Nasser, the Arabian merchant, told no better, our Holy Prophet (to whom be all honour and glory!) had no need to be jealous of his abilities for story-telling. (1)

With respect to the style, it was worthy of the matter;—it had not even those politic contrivances of structure, which make up for the commonness of the thoughts by the peculiarity of the manner, nor that stately poetical phraseology by which sentiments mean in themselves, like the blacksmith's (2) apron converted into a banner, are so easily gilt and embroidered into consequence. Then, as to the versification, it was, to say no worse of it, execrable: it had neither the copious flow of Ferdosi, the sweetness of Hafez, nor the sententious march of Sadi; but appeared to him, in the uneasy heaviness of its movement, to have been modelled upon the gait of a very tired dromedary. The licences, too, in which it indulged, were unpardonable;—for instance this line, and the poem abounded with such;—

Like the faint exquisite music of a dream.

"What critic that can count," said Fadladeen, "and has his full complement of fingers to count withal, would tolerate for an instant such syllabic superfluities?"—He here looked round, and discovered that most of his audience were asleep; while the glimmering lamps seemed inclined to follow their example. It became necessary, therefore, however

painful to himself, to put an end to his valuable animadversions for the present, and he accordingly concluded, with an air of dignified candour, thus: —"Notwithstanding the observations which I have thought it my duty to make, it is by no means my wish to discourage the young man;—so far from it, indeed, that if he will but totally alter his style of writing and thinking, I have very little doubt·that I shall be vastly pleased with him."

Some days elapsed, after this harangue of the Great Chamberlain, before Lalla Rookh could venture to ask for another story. The youth was still a welcome guest in the pavilion—to one heart, perhaps, too dangerously welcome;—but all mention of poetry was; as if by common consent, avoided. Though none of the party had much respect for Fadladeen, yet his censures, thus magisterially delivered, evidently made an impression on them all. The Poet, himself, to whom criticism was quite a new operation, (being wholly unknown in that Paradise of the Indies, Cashmere,) felt the shock as it is generally felt at first, till use has made it more tolerable to the patient;—the Ladies began to suspect that they ought not to be pleased, and seemed to conclude that there must have been much good sense in what Fadladeen said, from its having set them all so soundly to sleep;—while the self-complacent Chamberlain was left to triumph in the idea of having, for the hundred and fiftieth time in his life, extinguished a Poet. Lalla Rookh alone—and Love knew why—persisted in being delighted with all she had heard, and in resolving to hear more as speedily as possible. Her manner, however, of first returning to the subject was unlucky. It was while they rested during the heat of noon near a fountain, on which some hand had rudely traced those well-known words from the Garden of Sadi,—"Many, like me, have viewed this fountain, but they are gone, and their eyes are closed for ever!"—that she took occasion, from the melancholy beauty of this passage, to dwell upon the charms of poetry in general. "It is true," she said, "few poets can imitate that sublime bird, which flies always in the air, and never touches the earth: (3)—it is only once in many ages a Genius appears, whose words, like those on the Written Mountain, last for ever: (4)—but still there are some, as delightful, perhaps, though not so wonderful,

(1) "La lecture de ces Fables plaisoit si fort aux Arabes, que, quand Mahomet les entretenoit de l'Histoire de l'Ancien Testament, il les méprisoient, lui disant que celles que Nasser leur racontoient étoient beaucoup plus belles. Cette préférence attira à Nasser la malédiction de Mahomet et de tous ses disciples."—D'Herbelot.

(2) The blacksmith Gao, who successfully resisted the tyrant Zohak, and whose apron became the Royal Standard of Persia.

(3) "The huma, a bird peculiar to the East. It is supposed to fly constantly in the air, and never touch the ground; it is looked upon as a bird of happy omen; and that every head it overshades will in time wear a crown." —Richardson.

In the terms of alliance made by Fuzzel Oola Khan with Hyder in 1760, one of the stipulations was, "that he should have the distinction of two honorary attendants standing behind him, holding fans composed of the feathers of the humma, according to the practice of his family."— Wilks's South of India. He adds in a note;—"The humma is a fabulous bird. The head over which its shadow once passes will assuredly be circled with a crown. The splendid little bird suspended over the throne of Tippoo Sultaun, found at Seringapatam in 1799, was intended to represent this poetical fancy."

(4) "To the pilgrims to Mount Sinai we must attribute the inscriptions, figures, etc., on those rocks, which have

who, if not stars over our head, are at least flowers along our path, and whose sweetness of the moment we ought gratefully to inhale, without calling upon them for a brightness and a durability beyond their nature. In short," continued she, blushing, as if conscious of being caught in an oration, "it is quite cruel that a poet cannot wander through his regions of enchantment, without having a critic for ever, like the old Man of the Sea, upon his back!" (1)— Fadladeen, it was plain, took this last luckless allusion to himself, and would treasure it up in his mind as a whetstone for his next criticism. A sudden silence ensued; and the Princess, glancing a look at Feramorz, saw plainly she must wait for a more courageous moment.

But the glories of Nature, and her wild fragrant airs, playing freshly over the current of youthful spirits, will soon heal even deeper wounds than the dull Fadladeens of this world can inflict. In an evening or two after, they came to the small Valley of Gardens, which had been planted by order of the Emperor, for his favourite sister Rochinara, during their progress to Cashmere, some years before; and never was there a more sparkling assemblage of sweets, since the Gulzar-e-Irem, or Rose-bower of Irem. Every precious flower was there to be found, that poetry, or love, or religion has ever consecrated; from the dark hyacinth, to which Hafez compares his mistress's hair, (2) to the cámalatá, by whose rosy blossoms the heaven of Indra is scented. (3) As they sat in the cool fragrance of this delicious spot, and Lalla Rookh remarked that she could fancy it the abode of that Flower-loving Nymph whom they worship in the temples of Kathay, (4) or of one of those Peris, those beautiful creatures of the air, who live upon perfumes, and to whom a place like this might make some amends for the Paradise they have lost—the young Poet, in whose eyes she appeared, while she spoke, to be one of the bright spiritual creatures she was describing, said hesitatingly that he remembered a Story of a Peri, which, if the Princess had no objection, he would venture to relate. "It is," said he, with an appealing look to Fadladeen, "in a lighter and humbler strain than the other:" then, striking a few careless but melancholy chords on his kitar, he thus began:—

PARADISE AND THE PERI.

ONE morn a Peri at the gate
Of Eden stood, disconsolate;
And as she listen'd to the Springs
Of Life within, like music flowing,
And caught the light upon her wings
Through the half-open portal glowing,
She wept to think her recreant race
Should e'er have lost that glorious place!

" How happy," exclaim'd this child of air,
" Are the holy Spirits who wander there,
'Mid flowers that never shall fade or fall;
Though mine are the gardens of earth and sea,
And the stars themselves have flowers for me,,
One blossom of Heaven out-blooms them all!

" Though sunny the Lake of cool Cashmere,
With its plane-tree Isle reflected clear, (5)
And sweetly the founts of that Valley fall;
Though bright are the waters of Sing-su-hay,
And the golden floods that thitherward stray, (6)
Yet—oh, 'tis only the Blest can say
How the waters of Heaven outshine them all!

" Go, wing thy flight from star to star,
From world to luminous world, as far
As the universe spreads its flaming wall:
Take all the pleasures of all the spheres,
And multiply each through endless years,
One minute of Heaven is worth them all!"

The glorious Angel, who was keeping
The gates of Light, beheld her weeping;
And, as he nearer drew and listen'd
To her sad song, a tear-drop glisten'd
Within his eyelids, like the spray
From Eden's fountain, when it lies
On the blue flower, which—Bramins say—
Blooms nowhere but in Paradise. (7)

---

from thence acquired the name of the Written Mountain."—*Volney.* M. Gebelin and others have been at much pains to attach some mysterious and important meaning to these inscriptions; but Niebuhr, as well as Volney, thinks that they must have been executed at idle hours by the travellers to Mount Sinai, "who were satisfied with cutting the unpolished rock with any pointed instrument; adding to their names and the date of their journeys some rude figures, which bespeak the hand of a people but little skilled in the arts."—*Niebuhr.*

(1) The Story of Sinbad. (2) See *Nott's Hafez*, Ode v.

(3) "The Cámalatá (called by Linnæus, Ipomæa) is the most beautiful of its order, both in the colour and form of its leaves and flowers; its elegant blossoms are ' celestial rosy red, Love's proper hue,' and have justly procured it the name of Cámalatá, or Love's Creeper."—*Sir W. Jones.*

" Cámalatá may also mean a mythological plant, by which all desires are granted to such as inhabit the heaven of Indra; and if ever flower was worthy of paradise, it is 'our charming Ipomæa."—*Ib.*

(4) " According to Father Premare, in his tract on Chinese Mythology, the mother of Fo-hi was the daughter of heaven, surnamed Flower-loving; and as the nymph was walking alone on the bank of a river, she found herself encircled by a rainbow, after which she became pregnant, and, at the end of twelve years, was delivered of a son radiant as herself."—*Asiat. Res.*

(5) "Numerous small islands emerge from the Lake of Cashmere. One is called Char Chenaur, from the plane trees upon it."—*Foster.*

(6) " The Altan Kol or Golden River of Tibet, which runs into the Lakes of Sing-su-hay, has abundance of gold in its sands, which employs the inhabitants all the Summer in gathering it."—*Description of Tibet in Pinkerton.*

(7) " The Brahmins of this province insist that the blue campac flowers only in Paradise."—*Sir W. Jones.* It ap-

" Nymph of a fair but erring line!"
Gently he said—" One hope is thine.
'T is written in the Book of Fate,
    The Peri yet may be forgiven
Who brings to this Eternal gate
    The Gift that is most dear to Heaven!
Go, seek it, and redeem thy sin—
'T is sweet to let 'the Pardon'd in."

Rapidly as comets run
To the embraces of the Sun ;—
Fleeter than the starry brands
Flung at night from angel hands (1)
At those dark and daring sprites
Who would climb the empyreal heights,
Down the blue vault the Peri flies,
    And, lighted earthward by a glance
That just then broke from morning's eyes,
    Hung hovering o'er our world's expanse.

But whither shall the Spirit go
To find this gift for Heaven ?—" I know
The wealth," she cries, "of every urn,
In which unnumber'd rubies burn,
Beneath the pillars of Chilminar; (2)
I know where the Isles of Perfume are (3)
Many a fathom down in the sea,
To the south of sun-bright Araby ; (4)
I know, too, where the Genii hid
The jewell'd cup of their King Jamshid, (5)
With Life's elixir sparkling high—
But gifts like these are not for the sky.
Where was there ever a gem that shone
Like the steps of Alla's wonderful Throne?

An   he Drops of Life — oh! what would
    they be
In the boundless Deep of Eternity?"

While thus she mused, her pinions fann'd
The air of that sweet Indian land,
Whose air is balm; whose ocean spreads
O'er coral rocks, and amber beds; (6)
Whose mountains, pregnant by the beam
Of the warm sun, with diamonds teem ;
Whose rivulets are like rich brides,
Lovely, with gold beneath their tides;
Whose sandal groves and bowers of spice
Might be a Peri's Paradise !
But crimson now her rivers ran
    With human blood—the smell of death
Came reeking from those spicy bowers,
And man, the sacrifice of man,
    Mingled his taint with every breath
Upwafted from the innocent flowers.
Land of the Sun ! what foot invades
Thy Pagods and thy pillar'd shades, (7)
Thy cavern shrines, and Idol stones,
Thy Monarchs and their thousand Thrones ? (8)
'T is He of Gazna (9)—fierce in wrath
He comes, and India's diadems
Lie scatter'd in his ruinous path.—
    His bloodhounds he adorns with gems,
    Torn from the violated necks
Of many a young and loved Sultana ; (10)
    Maidens, within their pure Zenana,
    Priests in the very fane he slaughters,
And choaks up with the glittering wrecks
    Of golden shrines the sacred waters !

pears, however, from a curious letter of the Sultan of
Menangcabow, given by Marsden, that one place on earth
may lay claim to the possession of it. " This is the Sultan,
who keeps the flower champaka that is blue, and to be
found in no other country but his, being yellow elsewhere."
—*Marsden's Sumatra.*

(1) " The Mahometans suppose that falling stars are the
fire-brands wherewith the good angels drive away the
bad, when they approach too near the empyrean or verge
of the heavens."—*Fryer.*

(2) The Forty Pillars; so the Persians call the ruins of
Persepolis. It is imagined by them that this palace and
the edifices at Balbec were built by Genii, for the pur-
pose of hiding in their subterraneous caverns immense
treasures, which still remain there.—*D'Herbelot, Volney.*

(3) *Diodorus* mentions the Isle of Panchaia, to the south
of Arabia Felix, where there was a temple of Jupiter.
This island, or rather cluster of isles, has disappeared,
"sunk (says *Grandpré*) in the abyss made by the fire be-
neath their foundations."—*Voyage to the Indian Ocean.*

(4) The isles of Panchaia.

(5) " The cup of Jamshid, discovered, they say, when
digging for the foundations of Persepolis."—*Richardson.*

(6) " It is not like the Sea of India, whose bottom is rich
with pearls and ambergris, whose mountains of the coast
are stored with gold and precious stones, whose gulfs

breed creatures that yield ivory, and among the plants of
whose shores are ebony, red wood, and the wood of
Hairzan, aloes, camphor, cloves, sandal-wood, and all
other spices and aromatics; where parrots and peacocks
are birds of the forest, and musk and civet are collected
upon the lands."—*Travels of Two Mohammedans.*

(7) . . . . in the ground
    The bended twigs take root, and daughters grow
    About the mother-tree, *a pillar'd shade,*
    High over-arch'd, and echoing walks between.
                                    Milton.
For a particular description and plate of the Banyan-
tree, see *Cordiner's Ceylon.*

(8) " With this immense treasure Mamood returned to
Ghizni, and in the year 400 prepared a magnificent fes-
tival, where he displayed to the people his wealth in
golden thrones and in other ornaments, in a great plain
without the city of Ghizni."—*Ferishta.*

(9) " Mahmood of Gazna, or Ghizni, who conquered In-
dia in the beginning of the 11th century."—See his History
in *Dow* and *Sir J. Malcolm.*

(10) " It is reported that the hunting equipage of the
Sultan Mahmood was so magnificent, that he kept 400
greyhounds and bloodhounds, each of which wore a collar
set with jewels, and a covering edged with gold and
pearls."—*Universal History,* vol. iii.

Downward the Peri turns her gaze,
And, through the war-field's bloody haze,
Beholds a youthful warrior stand,
  Alone beside his native river—
The red blade broken in his hand,
  And the last arrow in his quiver.

"Live," said the Conqueror, "live to share
The trophies and the crowns I bear!"
Silent that youthful warrior stood—
Silent he pointed to the flood
All crimson with his country's blood,
Then sent his last remaining dart,
For answer, to the Invader's heart.

False flew the shaft, though pointed well;
The Tyrant lived, the Hero fell!
Yet mark'd the Peri where he lay,
  And, when the rush of war was past,
Swiftly descending on a ray
  Of morning light, she caught the last—
Last glorious drop his heart had shed,
Before its free-born spirit fled!

"Be this," she cried, as she wing'd her flight,
"My welcome gift at the Gates of Light.
Though foul are the drops that oft distil
  On the field of warfare, blood like this,
For Liberty shed, so holy is, (1)
It would not stain the purest rill,
  That sparkles among the Bowers of Bliss!
Oh, if there be, on this earthly sphere,
A boon, an offering Heaven holds dear,
'T is the last libation Liberty draws
From the heart that bleeds and breaks in her
    cause!"

  "Sweet," said the Angel, as she gave
    The gift into his radiant hand,
  "Sweet is our welcome of the Brave
    Who die thus for their native Land.—
But see—alas!—the crystal bar
Of Eden moves not—holier far

Than even this drop the boon must be,
That opes the Gates of Heaven for thee!"

Her first fond hope of Eden blighted,
  Now among Afric's lunar mountains, (2)
Far to the south, the Peri lighted;
  And sleek'd her plumage at the fountains
Of that Egyptian tide—whose birth
Is hidden from the sons of earth
Deep in those solitary woods,
Where oft the Genii of the Floods
Dance round the cradle of their Nile,
And hail the new-born Giant's smile. (3)
Thence over Egypt's palmy groves,
  Her grots, and sepulchres of Kings, (4)
The exiled Spirit sighing roves;
And now hangs listening to the doves
In warm Rosetta's vale (5)—now loves
  To watch the moonlight on the wings
Of the white pelicans that break
The azure calm of Mœris' Lake. (6)
'T was a fair scene—a land more bright
  Never did mortal eye behold!
Who could have thought, that saw this night
  Those valleys and their fruits of gold
Basking in Heaven's serenest light;—
Those groups of lovely date-trees bending
  Languidly their leaf-crown'd heads,
Like youthful maids, when sleep descending
  Warns them to their silken beds;—(7)
Those virgin lilies, all the night
  Bathing their beauties in the lake,
That they may rise more fresh and bright,
  When their beloved Sun 's awake;—
Those ruin'd shrines and towers that seem
  Amid whose fairy loneliness
Nought but the lapwing's cry is heard,
Nought seen but (when the shadows, flitting
  Fast from the moon, unsheath its gleam,)
Some purple-wing'd Sultana (8) sitting
  Upon a column, motionless,
  And glittering like an Idol bird!—

(1) Objections may be made to my use of the word Liberty in this, and more especially in the story that follows it, as totally inapplicable to any state of things that has ever existed in the East; but though I cannot, of course, mean to employ it in that enlarged and noble sense which is so well understood at the present day, and, I grieve to say, so little acted upon, yet it is no disparagement to the word to apply it to that national independence, that freedom from the interference and dictation of foreigners, without which, indeed, no liberty of any kind can exist; and for which both Hindoos and Persians fought against their Mussulman invaders with, in many cases, a bravery that deserved much better success.

(2) "The Mountains of the Moon, or the Montes Lunæ of antiquity, at the foot of which the Nile is supposed to arise."—*Bruce.*

  "Sometimes called," says *Jackson,* "Jibbel Kumrie, or the white or lunar-coloured mountains; so a white horse is called by the Arabians a moon-coloured horse."

(3) "The Nile, which the Abyssinians know by the names of Abey and Alawy, or the Giant."—*Asiat. Res.,* vol. i., p. 387.

(4) See Perry's *View of the Levant* for an account of the sepulchres in Upper Thebes, and the numberless grots, covered all over with hieroglyphics, in the mountains of Upper Egypt.

  (5) "The orchards of Rosetta are filled with turtle-doves."—*Sonnini.*

(6) Savary mentions the pelicans upon Lake Mœris.

(7) "The superb date-tree, whose head languidly reclines, like that of a handsome woman overcome with sleep."—*Dafard el Hadad.*

(8) "That beautiful bird, with plumage of the finest shining blue, with purple beak and legs, the natural and living ornament of the temples and palaces of the Greeks and Romans, which, from the stateliness of its port, as well as the brilliancy of its colours, has obtained the title of Sultana."—*Sonnini.*   45

Who could have thought, that there, even there,
　Amid those scenes so still and fair,
The Demon of the Plague hath cast
From his hot wing a deadlier blast,
More mortal far than ever came
From the red Desert's sands of flame!
So quick, that every living thing
Of human shape, touch'd by his wing,
Like plants, where the Simoom hath past,
At once falls black and withering!

The sun went down on many a brow,
　Which, full of bloom and freshness then,
Is rankling in the pest-house now,
　And ne'er will feel that sun again.
And, oh! to see the unburied heaps
On which the lonely moonlight sleeps—
The very vultures turn away,
And sicken at so foul a prey!
Only the fierce hyæna stalks (1)
Throughout the city's desolate walks (2)
At midnight, and his carnage plies:—
　Woe to the half-dead wretch, who meets
The glaring of those large blue eyes (3)
　Amid the darkness of the streets!

"Poor race of men!" said the pitying Spirit,
　"Dearly ye pay for your primal Fall—
Some flowerets of Eden ye still inherit,
　But the trail of the Serpent is over them all!'
She wept—the air grew pure and clear
　Around her, as the bright drops ran;
For there's a magic in each tear
　Such kindly Spirits weep for man!

Just then beneath some orange trees,
Whose fruit and blossoms in the breeze
Were wantoning together, free,
Like age at play with infancy—
Beneath that fresh and springing bower,
　Close by the Lake, she heard the moan
Of one who, at this silent hour,
　Had thither stolen to die alone;
One who in life, where'er he moved,
　Drew after him the hearts of many;
Yet now, as though he ne'er were loved,
　Dies here unseen, unwept by any!
None to watch near him—none to slake
　The fire that in his bosom lies,
With even a sprinkle from that lake
　Which shines so cool before his eyes.

No voice, well known through many a day,
　To speak the last, the parting word,
Which, when all other sounds decay,
　Is still like distant music heard—
That tender farewell on the shore
Of this rude world, when all is o'er,
Which cheers the spirit, ere its bark
Puts off into the unknown Dark.

Deserted youth! one thought alone
　Shed joy around his soul in death—
That she, whom he for years had known,
And loved, and might have call'd his own,
　Was safe from this foul midnight's breath—
Safe in her father's princely halls,
Where the cool airs from fountain falls,
Freshly perfumed by many a brand
Of the sweet wood from India's land,
Were pure as she whose brow they fann'd.

But see—who yonder comes by stealth, (4)
　This melancholy bower to seek,
Like a young envoy, sent by Health,
　With rosy gifts upon her cheek?
'Tis she—far off, through moonlight dim
He knew his own betrothed bride,
She, who would rather die with him,
　Than live to gain the world beside!—
Her arms are round her lover now,
　His livid cheek to hers she presses,
And dips, to bind his burning brow,
　In the cool lake her loosen'd tresses.
Ah! once, how little did he think
An hour would come, when he should
　　shrink
With horror from that dear embrace,
　Those gentle arms, that were to him
Holy as is the cradling place
　Of Eden's infant cherubim!
And now he yields—now turns away,
Shuddering as if the venom lay
All in those proffer'd lips alone—
Those lips that, then so fearless grown,
Never until that instant came
Near his unask'd or without shame.
"Oh! let me only breathe the air,
　The blessed air, that's breathed by thee,
And, whether on its wings it bear
　Healing or death, 'tis sweet to me!
There—drink my tears, while yet they fall—
　Would that my bosom's blood were balm,

(1) Jackson, speaking of the plague that occurred in West Barbary, when he was there, says, "The birds of the air fled away from the abodes of men. The hyænas, on the contrary, visited the cemeteries," etc.

(2) "Gondar was full of hyænas from the time it turned dark, till the dawn of day, seeking the different pieces of slaughtered carcasses which this cruel and unclean people expose in the streets without burial, and who firmly be-

lieve that these animals are Falashta from the neighbouring mountains, transformed by magic, and come down to eat human flesh in the dark in safety."—*Bruce.*

(3) *Bruce.*

(4) This circumstance has been often introduced into poetry;—by Vincentius Fabricius, by Darwin, and lately with very powerful effect, by Mr. Wilson.

And, well thou know'st, I'd shed it all,
  To give thy brow one minute's calm.
Nay, turn not from me that dear face—
  Am I not thine—thy own loved bride—
The one, the chosen one, whose place
  In life or death is by thy side?
Think'st thou that she, whose only light,
  In this dim world, from thee hath shone,
Could bear the long, the cheerless night,
  That must be hers when thou art gone?
That I can live, and let thee go,
Who art my life itself?—No, no—
When the stem dies, the leaf that grew
Out of its heart must perish too!
Then turn to me, my own love, turn;
Before, like thee, I fade and burn;
Cling to these yet cool lips, and share
The last pure life that lingers there!"
She fails—she sinks—as dies the lamp
In charnel airs, or cavern–damp,
So quickly do his baleful sighs
Quench all the sweet light of her eyes.
One struggle—and his pain is past—
  Her lover is no longer living!
One kiss the maiden gives, one last,
  Long kiss, which she expires in giving!

"Sleep," said the Peri, as softly she stole
The farewell sigh of that vanishing soul,
As true as e'er warm'd a woman's breast—
"Sleep on, in visions of odour rest,
In balmier airs than ever yet stirr'd
The enchanted pile of that lonely bird,
Who sings at the last his own death–lay,(1)
And in music and perfume dies away!"
Thus saying, from her lips she spread
  Unearthly breathings through the place,
And shook her sparkling wreath, and shed
  Such lustre o'er each paly face,
That like two lovely saints they seem'd,
  Upon the eve of doomsday taken
From their dim graves, in odour sleeping;
  While that benevolent Peri beam'd
Like their good angel, calmly keeping
  Watch o'er them till their souls would waken.

But morn is blushing in the sky;
  Again the Peri soars above,
Bearing to Heaven that precious sigh
  Of pure self-sacrificing love.

High throbb'd her heart, with hope elate,
  The Elysian palm she soon shall win,
For the bright Spirit at the gate
  Smiled as she gave that offering in;
And she already hears the trees
  Of Eden, with their crystal bells
Ringing in that ambrosial breeze
  That from the throne of Alla swells;
And she can see the starry bowls
  That lie around that lucid lake,
Upon whose banks admitted Souls
  Their first sweet draught of glory take!(2)

But, ah! even Peris' hopes are vain—
  Again the Fates forbade, again
The immortal barrier closed—"Not yet,"
  The Angel said, as, with regret,
He shut from her that glimpse of glory—
  "True was the maiden, and her story,
Written in light o'er Alla's head,
  By seraph eyes shall long be read.
But, Peri, see—the crystal bar
  Of Eden moves not—holier far
Than even this sigh the boon must be
That opes the Gates of Heaven for thee."

  Now, upon Syria's land of roses (3)
Softly the light of Eve reposes,
And, like a glory, the broad sun
Hangs over sainted Lebanon;
Whose head in wintry grandeur towers,
  And whitens with eternal sleet,
While Summer, in a vale of flowers,
  Is sleeping rosy at his feet.

To one, who look'd from upper air
O'er all the enchanted regions there,
How beauteous must have been the glow,
The life, the sparkling from below!
Fair gardens, shining streams, with ranks
Of golden melons on their banks,
More golden where the sun–light falls;—
Gay lizards, glittering on the walls (4)
Of ruin'd shrines, busy and bright
As they were all alive with light;
And, yet more splendid, numerous flocks
Of pigeons, settling on the rocks,
With their rich restless wings, that gleam
Variously in the crimson beam

(1) "In the East, they suppose the Phœnix to have fifty orifices in his bill, which are continued to his tail; and that, after living one thousand years, he builds himself a funeral pile, sings a melodious air of different harmonies through his fifty organ pipes, flaps his wings with a velocity which sets fire to the wood, and consumes himself."—*Richardson.*

(2) "On the shores of a quadrangular lake stand a thousand goblets, made of stars, out of which souls predestined to enjoy felicity drink the crystal wave."—*From Chateaubriand's* Description of the Mahometan Paradise, in his *Beauties of Christianity.*

(3) Richardson thinks that Syria had its name from Suri, a beautiful and delicate species of rose, for which that country has been always famous;—hence, Suristan, the Land of Roses.

(4) "The number of lizards I saw one day in the great court of the Temple of the Sun at Balbec amounted to many thousands; the ground, the walls, and stones of the ruined buildings, were covered with them."—*Bruce.*

Of the warm West—as if inlaid
With brilliants from the mine, or made
Of tearless rainbows, such as span
The unclouded skies of Peristan.
And then the mingling sounds that come
Of shepherd's ancient reed, (1) with hum
Of the wild bees of Palestine, (2)
  Banquetting through the flowery vales;
And, Jordan, those sweet banks of thine,
  And woods, so full of nightingales. (3)

But nought can charm the luckless Peri;
  Her soul is sad—her wings are weary—
Joyless she sees the Sun look down
On that great Temple, once his own, (4)
  Whose lonely columns stand sublime,
  Flinging their shadows from on high,
Like dials, which the wizard, Time,
  Had raised to count his ages by!

Yet haply there may lie conceal'd
  Beneath those Chambers of the Sun,
Some amulet of gems, anneal'd
In upper fires, some tablet seal'd
  With the great name of Solomon,
Which, spell'd by her illumined eyes,
May teach her where, beneath the moon,
In earth or ocean, lie the boon,
The charm, that can restore so soon
  An erring Spirit to the skies.

Cheer'd by this hope, she bends her thither;—
  Still laughs the radiant eye of Heaven,
Nor have the golden bowers of Even
In the rich West begun to wither;—
When, o'er the vale of Balbec winging
  Slowly, she sees a child at play,
Among the rosy wild flowers singing,
  As rosy and as wild as they;
Chasing, with eager hands and eyes,
  The beautiful blue damsel flies, (5)
That flutter'd round the jasmine stems,
  Like winged flowers or flying gems:—

And, near the boy, who tired with play
Now nestling 'mid the roses lay,
  She saw a wearied man dismount
    From his hot steed, and on the brink
Of a small imaret's rustic fount (6)
  Impatient fling him down to drink.
Then swift his haggard brow he turn'd
  To the fair child, who fearless sat,
Though never yet hath day-beam burn'd
  Upon a brow more fierce than that—
Sullenly fierce—a mixture dire,
Like thunder-clouds, of gloom and fire;
In which the Peri's eye could read
Dark tales of many a ruthless deed;
The ruin'd maid—the shrine profaned—
Oaths broken—and the threshold stain'd
With blood of guests!—*there* written, all,
Black as the damning drops that fall
From the denouncing Angel's pen,
Ere Mercy weeps them out again.

Yet tranquil now that man of crime
  (As if the balmy evening time
  Soften'd his spirit), look'd and lay,
  Watching the rosy infant's play;—
Though still, whene'er his eye by chance
  Fell on the boy's, its lurid glance
  Met that unclouded, joyous gaze,
  As torches, that have burnt all night
Through some impure and godless rite,
  Encounter morning's glorious rays.

But, hark! the vesper call to prayer,
  As slow the orb of daylight sets,
Is rising sweetly on the air,
  From Syria's thousand minarets!
The boy has started from the bed
Of flowers, where he had laid his head,
And down upon the fragrant sod
  Kneels, (7) with his forehead to the south,
Lisping the eternal name of God
  From Purity's own cherub mouth,

---

(1) "The · yrinx, or Pan's pipe, is still a pastoral instrument in Syria."—*Russell.*

(2) "Wild bees, frequent in Palestine, in hollow trunks or branches of trees, and the clefts of rocks. Thus it is said (Psalm lxxxi.), '*honey out of the stony rock.*'"—*Border's Oriental Customs.*

(3) "The river Jordan is on both sides beset with little thick, and pleasant woods, among which thousands o nightingales warble all together."—*Thevenot.*

(4) The Temple of the Sun at Balbec.

(5) "You behold there a considerable number of a remarkable species of beautiful insects, the elegance of whose appearance and their attire procured for them the name of Damsels."—*Sonnini.*

(6) Imaret, "hospice où on loge et nourrit, gratis, les pélerins pendant trois jours."—*Toderini, translated by the Abbé de Cournand.*—See also *Castellan's Mœurs des Othomans,* tom. v., p. 145.

(7) "Such Turks as at the common hours of prayer are on the road, or so employed as not to find convenience to attend the mosques, are still obliged to execute that duty; nor are they ever known to fail, whatever business they are then about, but pray immediately when the hour alarms them, whatever they are about, in that very place they chance to stand on; insomuch that when a janissary, whom you have to guard you up and down the city, hears the notice which is given him from the steeples, he will turn about, stand still, and beckon with his hand, to tell his charge he must have patience for awhile; when, taking out his handkerchief, he spreads it on the ground, sits cross-legged thereupon, and says his prayers, though in the open market, which, having ended, he leaps briskly up, salutes the person whom he undertook to convey, and renews his journey with the mild expression of *Ghell gohnnum ghell,* or Come, dear, follow me."—*Aaron Hill's Travels.*

And looking, while his hands and eyes
Are lifted to the glowing skies,
Like a stray babe of Paradise,
Just lighted on that flowery plain,
And seeking for its home again.
Oh! 't was a sight—that Heaven—that child—
A scene which might have well beguiled
Even haughty Eblis of a sigh
For glories lost and peace gone by!

And how felt *he*, the wretched man
Reclining there—while memory ran
O'er many a year of guilt and strife,
Flew o'er the dark flood of his life,
Nor found one sunny resting-place,
Nor brought him back one branch of grace?
"There *was* a time," he said, in mild
Heart-humbled tones—"thou blessed child!
When, young and haply pure as thou,
I look'd and pray'd like thee—but now—"
He hung his head—each nobler aim,
And hope, and feeling, which had slept
From boyhood's hour, that instant came
Fresh o'er him, and he wept—he wept!

Blest tears of soul-felt penitence!
In whose benign redeeming flow
Is felt the first, the only sense
Of guiltless joy that guilt can know.
"There's a drop," said the Peri, "that down
from the moon
Falls through the withering airs of June
Upon Egypt's land, (1) of so healing a power,
So balmy a virtue, that even in the hour
That drop descends, contagion dies,
And health re-animates earth and skies!—
Oh, is it not thus, thou man of sin,
The precious tears of repentance fall?
Though foul thy fiery plagues within,
One heavenly drop hath dispell'd them all!"

And now—behold him kneeling there,
By the child's side, in humble prayer,
While the same sunbeam shines upon
The guilty and the guiltless one,
And hymns of joy proclaim through Heaven
The triumph of a Soul Forgiven!

'T was when the golden orb had set,
While on their knees they linger'd yet,

There fell a light more lovely far
Than ever came from sun or star,
Upon the tear that, warm and meek,
Dew'd that repentant sinner's cheek.
To mortal eye this light might seem
A northern flash or meteor beam—
But well the enraptured Peri knew
'T was a bright smile the Angel threw
From Heaven's gate, to hail that tear
Her harbinger of glory near!

"Joy, joy for ever! my task is done—
The Gates are pass'd, and Heaven is won!
Oh! am I not happy? I am, I am—
To thee, sweet Eden! how dark and sad
Are the diamond turrets of Shadukiam, (2)
And the fragrant bowers of Amberabad!

"Farewell, ye odours of Earth, that die,
Passing away like a lover's sigh;—
My feast is now of the Tooba Tree, (3)
Whose scent is the breath of Eternity!

"Farewell, ye vanishing flowers, that shone
In my fairy wreath, so bright and brief;—
Oh! what are the brightest that e'er have blown,
To the lote-tree, springing by Alla's throne,(4)
Whose flowers have a soul in every leaf.
Joy, joy for ever!—my task is done—
The Gates are pass'd, and Heaven is won!"

"AND this," said the Great Chamberlain, "is
poetry! this flimsy manufacture of the brain,
which, in comparison with the lofty and durable
monuments of genius, is as the gold filigree-work
of Zamara beside the eternal architecture of Egypt!"
After this gorgeous sentence, which, with a few
more of the same kind, Fadladeen kept by him for
rare and important occasions, he proceeded to the
anatomy of the short poem just recited. The lax
and easy kind of metre in which it was written ought
to be denounced, he said, as one of the leading
causes of the alarming growth of poetry in our
times. If some check were not given to this law-
less facility, we should soon be over-run by a race
of bards as numerous and as shallow as the hun-
dred and twenty thousand Streams of Basra. (5)
They who succeeded in this style deserved chastise-
ment for their very success;—as warriors have been
punished, even after gaining a victory, because they
had taken the liberty of gaining it in an irregular or

(1) The Nucta, or Miraculous Drop, which falls in Egypt precisely on St. John's day, in June, and is supposed to have the effect of stopping the plague.
(2) The Country of Delight—the name of a province in the kingdom of Jinnistan, or Fairy Land, the capital of which is called the City of Jewels. Amberabad is another of the cities of Jinnistan.
(3 The tree Tooba, that stands in Paradise, in the palace of Mahomet. See *Sale's Prelim. Disc.*—Tooba, says *D'Herbelot*, signifies beatitude, or eternal happiness.

(4) Mahomet is described, in the 53d chapter of the Koran, as having seen the angel Gabriel "by the lote-tree, beyond which there is no passing: near it is the Garden of Eternal abode." This tree, say the commentators, stands in the seventh Heaven, on the right hand of the Throne of God.
(5) "It is said that the rivers or streams of Basra were reckoned in the time of Pelal ben Abi Bordeh, and amounted to the number of one hundred and twenty thousand streams."—*Ebn Haukal.*

unestablished manner. What, then, was to be said to those who failed? to those who presumed, as in the present lamentable instance, to imitate the licence and ease of the bolder sons of song, without any of that grace or vigour which gave a dignity even to negligence;—who, like them, flung the jereed (1) carelessly, but not, like them, to the mark;—"and who," said he, raising his voice to excite a proper degree of wakefulness in his hearers, "contrive to appear heavy and constrained in the midst of all the latitude they allow themselves, like one of those young pagans that dance before the Princess, who is ingenious enough to move as if her limbs were fettered, in a pair of the lightest and loosest drawers of Masulipatam!"

It was but little suitable, he continued, to the grave march of criticism to follow this fantastical Peri, of whom they had just heard, through all her flights and adventures between earth and heaven; but he could not help adverting to the puerile conceitedness of the Three Gifts which she is supposed to carry to the skies,—a drop of blood, forsooth, a sigh, and a tear! How the first of these articles was delivered into the Angel's "radiant hand" he professed himself at a loss to discover; and as to the safe carriage of the sigh and the tear, such Peris and such poets were beings by far too incomprehensible for him even to guess how they managed such matters. "But, in short," said he, "it is a waste of time and patience to dwell longer upon a thing so incurably frivolous—puny even among it own puny race, and such as only the Banyan Hospital (2) for Sick Insects should undertake."

In vain did Lalla Rookh try to soften this inexorable critic; in vain did she resort to her most eloquent common-places—reminding him that poets were a timid and sensitive race, whose sweetness was not to be drawn forth, like that of the fragrant grass near the Ganges, by crushing and trampling upon them; (3)—that severity often extinguished every chance of the perfection which it demanded; and that, after all, perfection was like the Mountain of the Talisman—no one had ever yet reached its summit. (4) Neither these gentle axioms, nor the still gentler looks with which they were inculcated, could lower for one instant the elevation of Fadladeen's eyebrows, or charm him into any thing like

encouragement, or even toleration, of her poet. Toleration, indeed, was not among the weaknesses of Fadladeen:—he carried the same spirit into matters of poetry and of religion, and, though little versed in the beauties or sublimities of either, was a perfect master of the art of persecution in both. His zeal was the same, too, in either pursuit; whether the game before him was pagans or poetasters—worshippers of cows, or writers of epics.

They had now arrived at the splendid city of Lahore, whose mausoleums and shrines, magnificent and numberless, where Death appeared to share equal honours with Heaven, would have powerfully affected the heart and imagination of Lalla Rookh, if feelings more of this earth had not taken entire possession of her already. She was here met by messengers, despatched from Cashmere, who informed her that the King had arrived in the Valley, and was himself superintending the sumptuous preparations that were then making in the Saloons of the Shalimar for her reception. The chill she felt on receiving this intelligence—which to a bride whose heart was free and light would have brought only images of affection and pleasure—convinced her that her peace was gone for ever, and that she was in love, irretrievably in love, with young Feramorz. The veil had fallen off in which this passion at first disguises itself, and to know that she loved was now as painful as to love *without* knowing it had been delicious. Feramorz, too—what misery would be his, if the sweet hours of intercourse so imprudently allowed them should have stolen into his heart the same fatal fascination as into hers;—if notwithstanding his rank, and the modest homage he always paid to it, even *he* should have yielded to the influence of those long and happy interviews, where music, poetry, the delightful scenes of nature—all had tended to bring their hearts close together, and to waken by every means that too ready passion, which often, like the young of the desert-bird, is warmed into life by the eyes alone! (5) She saw but one way to preserve herself from being culpable as well as unhappy, and this, however painful, she was resolved to adopt. Feramorz must no more be admitted to her presence. To have strayed so far into the dangerous labyrinth was wrong, but to linger in it, while the clue was yet in

(1) The name of the javelin with which the Easterns exercise. See *Castellan, Mœurs des Othomans*, tom. iii., p. 161.

(2) "This account excited a desire of visiting the Banyan Hospital, as I had heard much of their benevolence to all kinds of animals that were either sick, lame, or infirm, through age or accident. On my arrival, there were presented to my view many horses, cows, and oxen, in one apartment; in another, dogs, sheep, goats, and monkeys, with clean straw for them to repose on. Above stairs were depositories for seeds of many sorts, and flat broad dishes for water, for the use of birds and insects."—*Parsons's Travels.*

It is said that all animals know the Banyans, that the

most timid approach them, and that birds will fly nearer to them than to other people.—See *Grandpré.*

(3) "A very fragrant grass from the banks of the Ganges, near Heridwar, which in some places covers whole acres, and diffuses, when crushed, a strong odour."—*Sir W. Jones on the Spikenard of the Ancients.*

(4) "Near this is a curious hill, called Koh Talism, the Mountain of the Talisman, because, according to the traditions of the country, no person ever succeeded in gaining its summit."—*Kinneir.*

(5) "The Arabians believe that the ostriches hatch their young by only looking at them."—*P. Vanslebe, Relat. d'Egypte.*

her hand, would be criminal. Though the heart she had to offer to the King of Bucharia might be cold and broken, it should at least be pure; and she must only endeavour to forget the short dream of happiness she had enjoyed—like that Arabian shepherd, who, in wandering into the wilderness, caught a glimpse of the Gardens of Irim, and then lost them again for ever! (1)

The arrival of the young Bride at Lahore was celebrated in the most enthusiastic manner. The Rajas and Omras in her train, who had kept at a certain distance during the journey, and never encamped nearer to the Princess than was strictly necessary for her safeguard, here rode in splendid cavalcade through the city, and distributed the most costly presents to the crowd. Engines were erected in all the squares, which cast forth showers of confectionary among the people; while the artisans, in chariots (2) adorned with tinsel and flying streamers, exhibited the badges of their respective trades through the streets. Such brilliant displays of life and pageantry among the palaces, and domes, and gilded minarets of Lahore, made the city altogether like a place of enchantment; —particularly on the day when Lalla Rookh set out again upon her journey, when she was accompanied to the gate by all the fairest and richest of the nobility, and rode along between ranks of beautiful boys and girls, who kept waving over their heads plates of gold and silver flowers, (3) and then threw them around to be gathered by the populace.

For many days after their departure from Lahore, a considerable degree of gloom hung over the whole party. Lalla Rookh, who had intended to make illness her excuse for not admitting the young minstrel, as usual, to the pavilion, soon found that to feign indisposition was unnecessary;—Fadladeen felt the loss of the good road they had hitherto travelled, and was very near cursing Jehan-Guire (of blessed memory!) for not having continued his delectable alley of trees, (4) at least as far as the mountains of Cashmere;—while the Ladies, who had nothing now to do all day but to be fanned by peacocks' feathers and listen to Fadladeen, seemed heartily weary of the life they led, and, in spite of all the Great Chamberlain's criticisms, were so tasteless as to wish for the poet again. One evening, as they were proceeding to their place of rest for the night, the Princess, who, for the freer enjoyment of the air, had mounted her favourite Arabian palfrey, in passing by a small grove heard the notes of

a lute from within its leaves, and a voice, which she but too well knew, singing the following words:—

> Tell me not of joys above,
>   If that world can give no bliss
> Truer, happier than the Love
>   Which enslaves our souls in this.
>
> Tell me not of Houris' eyes;—
>   Far from me their dangerous glow,
> If those looks that light the skies
>   Wound like some that burn below.
>
> Who that feels what Love is here,
>   All its falsehood—all its pain—
> Would, for even Elysium's sphere,
>   Risk the fatal dream again?
>
> Who that, 'midst a desert's heat,
>   Sees the waters fade away,
> Would not rather die than meet
>   Streams again as false as they?

The tone of melancholy defiance in which these words were uttered went to Lalla Rookh's heart; —and, as she reluctantly rode on, she could not help feeling it to be a sad but still sweet certainty, that Feramorz was to the full as enamoured and miserable as herself.

The place where they encamped that evening was the first delightful spot they had come to since they left Lahore. On one side of them was a grove full of small Hindoo temples, and planted with the most graceful trees of the East; where the tamarind, the cassia, and the silken plantains of Ceylon were mingled in rich contrast with the high fan-like foliage of the Palmyra—that favourite tree of the luxurious bird that lights up the chambers of its nest with fire-flies. (5) In the middle of the lawn where the pavilion stood there was a tank surrounded by small mangoe-trees, on the clear cold waters of which floated multitudes of the beautiful red lotus; (6) while at a distance stood the ruins of a strange and awful-looking tower, which seemed old enough to have been the temple of some religion no longer known, and which spoke the voice of desolation in the midst of all that bloom and loveliness. This singular ruin excited the wonder and conjectures of all. Lalla Rookh guessed in vain, and the all-pretending Fadladeen, who had never till this journey

---

(1) See *Sale's Koran*, note, vol. ii., p. 484.

(2) Oriental Tales.

(3) Ferishta. "Or rather," says *Scott*, upon the passage of Ferishta, from which this is taken, "small coins, stamped with the figure of a flower. They are still used in India to distribute in charity, and, on occasion, thrown by the purse-bearers of the great among the populace."

(4) The fine road made by the Emperor Jehan-Guire from Agra to Lahore, planted with trees on each side. This road is 250 leagues in length. It has "little pyramids

or turrets," says *Bernier*, "erected every half league, to mark the ways, and frequent wells to afford drink to passengers, and to water the young trees."

(5) The Baya, or Indian Gross-Beak.—*Sir W. Jones*.

(6) "Here is a large pagoda by a tank, on the water of which float multitudes of the beautiful red lotus: the flower is larger than that of the white water-lily, and is the most lovely of the nymphæas I have seen."—*Mrs. Graham's Journal of a Residence in India*.

been beyond the precincts of Delhi, was proceeding most learnedly to show that he knew nothing whatever about the matter, when one of the Ladies suggested that perhaps Feramorz could satisfy their curiosity. They were now approaching his native mountains, and this tower might perhaps be a relic of some of those dark superstitions which had prevailed in that country before the light of Islam dawned upon it. The Chamberlain, who usually preferred his own ignorance to the best knowledge that any one else could give him, was by no means pleased with this officious reference; and the Princess, too, was about to interpose a faint word of objection, but, before either of them could speak, a slave was despatched for Feramorz, who, in a very few minutes, made his appearance before them—looking so pale and unhappy in Lalla Rookh's eyes, that she repented already of her cruelty in having so long excluded him.

That venerable tower, he told them, was the remains of an ancient Fire-Temple, built by those Ghebers or Persians of the old religion, who, many hundred years since, had fled hither from their Arab conquerors, (1) preferring liberty and their altars in a foreign land to the alternative of apostasy or persecution in their own. It was impossible, he added, not to feel interested in the many glorious but unsuccessful struggles which had been made by these original natives of Persia to cast off the yoke of their bigoted conquerors. Like their own Fire in the Burning Field at Bakou, (2) when suppressed in one place, they had but broken out with fresh flame in another; and, as a native of Cashmere, of that fair and holy Valley, which had in the same manner become the prey of strangers, (3) and seen her ancient shrines and native princes swept away before the march of her intolerant invaders, he felt a sympathy, he owned, with the sufferings of the persecuted Ghebers, which every monument like this before them but tended more powerfully to awaken.

It was the first time that Feramorz had ever ventured upon so much *prose* before Fadladeen, and it may easily be conceived what effect such prose as this must have produced upon that most orthodox and most pagan-hating personage. He sat for some minutes aghast, ejaculating only at intervals, "Bi-

goted conquerors!—sympathy with Fire-worshippers! (4)—while Feramorz, happy to take advantage of this almost speechless horror of the Chamberlain, proceeded to say that he knew a melancholy story, connected with the events of one of those struggles of the brave Fire-worshippers against their Arab masters, which, if the evening was not too far advanced, he should have much pleasure in being allowed to relate to the Princess. It was impossible for Lalla Rookh to refuse;—he had never before looked half so animated; and when he spoke of the Holy Valley his eyes had sparkled, she thought, like the talismanic characters on the scimitar of Solomon. Her consent was therefore most readily granted; and while Fadladeen sat in unspeakable dismay, expecting treason and abomination in every line, the poet thus began his story of the Fire-worshippers:—

THE FIRE-WORSHIPPERS.

'T is moonlight over Oman's Sea; (5)
 Her banks of pearl and palmy isles
Bask in the night-beam beauteously,
 And her blue waters sleep in smiles.
'T is moonlight in Harmozia's (6) walls,
And through her Emir's porphyry halls,
Where, some hours since, was heard the swell
Of trumpet and the clash of zel, (7)
Bidding the bright-eyed sun farewell;—
The peaceful sun, whom better suits
 The music of the bulbul's nest,
Or the light touch of lovers' lutes,
 To sing him to his golden rest.
All hush'd—there's not a breeze in motion;
The shore is silent as the ocean.
If zephyrs come, so light they come,
 Nor leaf is stirr'd nor wave is driven;—
The wind-tower on the Emir's dome(8)
 Can hardly win a breath from heaven.

Even he, that tyrant Arab, sleeps
Calm, while a nation round him weeps;
While curses load the air he breathes,
And falchions from unnumber'd sheaths
Are starting to avenge the shame
His race hath brought on Iran's (9) name.

---

(1) "On les voit persécutés par les Kalifes se retirer dans les montagnes du Kerman: plusieurs choisirent pour retraite la Tartarie et la Chine; d'autres s'arrêtèrent sur les bords du Gange, à l'est de Delhi."—*M. Anquetil, Mémoires de l'Académie,* tom. xxxi., p. 346.

(2) The "Ager ardens" described by *Kempfer, Amœnitat. Exot.*

(3) "Cashmere (says its historians) had its own princes 4000 years before its conquest by Akbar in 1585. Akbar would have found some difficulty to reduce this paradise of the Indies, situated as it is within such a fortress of mountains, but its monarch, Yusef Khan, was basely betrayed by his Omrahs."—*Pennant.*

(4) Voltaire tells us that in his Tragedy, "Les Guèbres,"

he was generally supposed to have alluded to the Jansenists. I should not be surprised if this story of the Fire-worshippers were found capable of a similar doubleness of application.

(5) The Persian Gulf, sometimes so called, which separates the shores of Persia and Arabia.

(6) The present Gombaroon, a town on the Persian side of the Gulf.

(7) A Moorish instrument of music.

(8) "At Gombaroon and other places in Persia, they have towers for the purpose of catching the wind, and cooling the houses."—*Le Bruyn.*

(9) "Iran is the true general name for the empire of Persia."—*Asiat. Res., Disc. 5.*

Hard, heartless Chief, unmoved alike
'Mid eyes that weep, and swords that strike;—
One of that saintly, murderous brood,
To carnage and the Koran given,
Who think through unbelievers' blood
Lies their directest path to heaven;—
One, who will pause and kneel unshod
In the warm blood his hand hath pour'd,
To mutter o'er some text of God
  Engraven on his reeking sword;—(1)
Nay, who can coolly note the line,
The letter of those words divine,
To which his blade, with searching art,
Had sunk into its victim's heart!

Just Alla! what must be thy look,
  When such a wretch before thee stands
Unblushing, with thy Sacred Book—
  Turning the leaves with blood-stain'd hands,
And wresting from its page sublime
His creed of lust, and hate, and crime;—
Even as those bees of Trebizond,
  Which, from the sunniest flowers that glad
With their pure smile the gardens round,
  Draw venom forth that drives men mad. (2)

Never did fierce Arabia send
  A satrap forth more direly great;
Never was Iran doom'd to bend
  Beneath a yoke of deadlier weight.
Her throne had fallen—her pride was crush'd—
Her sons were willing slaves, nor blush'd,
In their own land—no more their own—
To crouch beneath a stranger's throne.
Her towers, where Mithra once had burn'd,
To Moslem shrines—oh shame!—were turn'd,
Where slaves, converted by the sword,
Their mean apostate worship pour'd,
And cursed the faith their sires adored.
Yet has she hearts, 'mid all this ill,
O'er all this wreck high buoyant still
With hope and vengeance;—hearts that yet—
  Like gems, in darkness, issuing rays
They 've treasured from the sun that 's set—
  Beam all the light of long-lost days!
And swords she hath, nor weak nor slow
  To second all such hearts can dare;
As he shall know, well, dearly know,
  Who sleeps in moonlight luxury there,

Tranquil as if his spirit lay
Becalm'd in Heaven's approving ray.
Sleep on—for purer eyes than thine
Those waves are hush'd, those planets shine;
Sleep on, and be thy rest unmoved
  By the white moonbeam's dazzling power;—
None but the loving and the loved
  Should be awake at this sweet hour.

And see—where, high above those rocks
  That o'er the deep their shadows fling,
Yon turret stands;—where ebon locks,
  As glossy as a heron's wing
  Upon the turban of a king, (3)
Hang from the lattice, long and wild—
'T is she, that Emir's blooming child,
All truth and tenderness and grace,
Though born of such ungentle race;—
An image of Youth's radiant Fountain
Springing in a desolate mountain! (4)

Oh what a pure and sacred thing
  Is Beauty, curtain'd from the sight
Of the gross world, illumining
  One only mansion with her light!
Unseen by man's disturbing eye—
  The flower that blooms beneath the sea,
Too deep for sunbeams, doth not lie
  Hid in more chaste obscurity.
So, Hinda, have thy face and mind,
Like holy mysteries, lain enshrined.
And oh, what transport for a lover
  To lift the veil that shades them o'er!—
Like those who, all at once, discover
  In the lone deep some fairy shore,
Where mortal never trod before,
And sleep and wake in scented airs
No lip had ever breathed but theirs.

Beautiful are the maids that glide,
  On summer-eves, through Yemen's (5) dales,
And bright the glancing looks they hide
  Behind their litters' roseate veils;—
And brides, as delicate and fair
As the white jasmine flowers they wear,
Hath Yemen in her blissful clime,
  Who, lull'd in cool kiosk or bower, (6)
Before their mirrors count the time,(7)
  And grow still lovelier every hour.

(1) "On the blades of their scimitars some verse from the Koran is usually inscribed."—*Russel.*

(2) "There is a kind of Rhododendros about Trebizond, whose flowers the bee feeds upon, and the honey thence drives people mad."—*Tournefort.*

(3) "Their kings wear plumes of black herons' feathers upon the right side, as a badge of sovereignty."—*Hanway.*

(4) "The Fountain of Youth, by a Mahometan tradition, is situated in some dark region of the East."—*Richardson.*

(5) Arabia Felix.

(6) "In the midst of the garden is the chiosk, that is, a large room, commonly beautified with a fine fountain in the midst of it. It is raised nine or ten steps, and inclosed with gilded lattices, round which vines, jessamines, and honeysuckles make a sort of green wall; large trees are planted round this place, which is the scene of their greatest pleasures."—*Lady M. W. Montagu.*

(7) The women of the East are never without their looking-glasses. "In Barbary," says *Shaw* "they are so fond of their looking-glasses, which they hang upon their

But never yet hath bride or maid
　　In Araby's gay Haram smiled,
Whose boasted brightness would not fade
　　Before Al Hassan's blooming child.

Light as the angel shapes that bless
An infant's dream, yet not the less
Rich in all woman's loveliness ;—
With eyes so pure, that from their ray
Dark Vice would turn abash'd away,
Blinded like serpents, when they gaze
Upon the emerald's virgin blaze ;—(1)
Yet fill'd with all youth's sweet desires,
Mingling the meek and vestal fires
Of other worlds with all the bliss,
The fond weak tenderness of this :
A soul, too, more than half divine,
　　Where, through some shades of earthly feel-
　　　　ing,
Religion's soften'd glories shine,
　　Like light through summer foliage stealing,
Shedding a glow of such mild hue,
So warm, and yet so shadowy too,
As makes the very darkness there
More beautiful than light elsewhere.

Such is the maid who, at this hour,
　　Hath risen from her restless sleep,
And sits alone in that high bower,
　　Watching the still and shining deep.
Ah ! 't was not thus—with tearful eyes
　　And beating heart, she used to gaze
On the magnificent earth and skies,
　　In her own land, in happier days.
Why looks she now so anxious down
Among those rocks, whose rugged frown
Blackens the mirror of the deep ?
Whom waits she all this lonely night ?
Too rough the rocks, too bold the steep,
For man to scale that turret's height !—

So deem'd at least her thoughtful sire,
　　When high, to catch the cool night-air,
After the day-beam's withering fire, (2)
　　He built her bower of freshness there,
And had it deck'd with costliest skill,
　　And fondly thought it safe as fair :—
Think, reverend dreamer ! think so still,
　　Nor wake to learn what Love can dare ;—
Love, all-defying Love, who sees
No charm in trophies won with ease ;—
Whose rarest, dearest fruits of bliss
Are pluck'd on Danger's precipice !
Bolder than they, who dare not dive
For pearls, but when the sea 's at rest,
Love, in the tempest most alive,
Hath ever held that pearl the best
He finds beneath the stormiest water.
Yes—Araby's unrivall'd daughter,
Though high that tower, that rock-way rude,
There 's one who, but to kiss thy cheek,
Would climb the untrodden solitude
　　Of Ararat's tremendous peak, (3)
And think its steeps, though dark and dread,
Heaven's pathways, if to thee they led !
Even now thou seest the flashing spray,
That lights his oar's impatient way ;—
Even now thou hear'st the sudden shock
Of his swift bark against the rock,
And stretchest down thy arms of snow,
As if to lift him from below !
Like her to whom, at dead of night,
The bridegroom, with his locks of light, (4)
Came, in the flush of love and pride,
And scaled the terrace of his bride ;—
When, as she saw him rashly spring,
And midway up in danger cling,
She flung him down her long black hair,
Exclaiming, breathless, " There, love, there !"
And scarce did manlier nerve uphold
　　The hero Zal in that fond hour,

---

breasts, that they will not lay them aside, even when after the drudgery of the day they are obliged to go two or three miles with a pitcher or a goat's skin to fetch water."—*Travels.*

In other parts of Asia they wear little looking-glasses on their thumbs. "Hence (and from the lotus being considered the emblem of beauty) is the meaning of the following mute intercourse of two lovers before their parents :—

"'He with salute of deference due,
　　A lotus to his forehead press'd ;
She raised her mirror to his view,
　　Then turn'd it inward to her breast.'"
　　　　　　　　Asiatic Miscellany, vol. ii.

(1) "They say that if a snake or serpent fix his eyes on the lustre of those stones (emeralds), he immediately becomes blind."—*Ahmed ben Abdalaziz, Treatise on Jewels.*

(2) "At Gombaroon and the Isle of Ormus it is sometimes so hot, that the people are obliged to lie all day in the water."—*Marco Polo.*

(3) This mountain is generally supposed to be inacces-

sible. *Struy* says, "I can well assure the reader that their opinion is not true, who suppose this mount to be inaccessible." He adds, that "the lower part of the mountain is cloudy, misty, and dark, the middlemost part very cold, and like clouds of snow, but the upper regions perfectly calm."—It was on this mountain that the Ark was supposed to have rested after the Deluge, and part of it, they say, exists there still, which Struy thus gravely accounts for :—"Whereas none can remember that the air on the top of the hill did ever change or was subject either to wind or rain, which is presumed to be the reason that the Ark has endured so long without being rotten."—See *Carreri's Travels,* where the doctor laughs at this whole account of Mount Ararat.

(4) In one of the books of the Shâh Nâmeh, when Zal (a celebrated hero of Persia, remarkable for his white hair,) comes to the terrace of his mistress Rodahver at night, she lets down her long tresses to assist him in his ascent ; —he, however, manages it in a less romantic way by fixing his crook in a projecting beam.—See *Champion's Ferdosi.*

Than wings the youth who, fleet and bold,
  Now climbs the rocks to Hinda's bower.
See—light as up their granite steeps
  The rock-goats of Arabia clamber,(1)
Fearless from crag to crag he leaps,
  And now is in the maiden's chamber.

She loves—but knows not whom she loves,
  Nor what his race, nor whence he came;—
Like one who meets, in Indian groves,
  Some beauteous bird without a name,
Brought by the last ambrosial breeze,
From isles in the undiscover'd seas,
To show his plumage for a day
To wondering eyes, and wing away!
Will *he* thus fly—her nameless lover?
  Alla forbid! 't was by a moon
As fair as this, while singing over
  Some ditty to her soft Kanoon,(2)
Alone, at this same witching hour,
  She first beheld his radiant eyes
Gleam through the lattice of the bower,
  Where nightly now they mix their sighs;
And thought some spirit of the air
(For what could waft a mortal there?)
Was pausing on his moonlight way
To listen to her lonely lay!
This fancy ne'er hath left her mind:
  And—though, when terror's swoon had past,
She saw a youth, of mortal kind,
  Before her in obeisance cast—
Yet often since, when he hath spoke
Strange awful words—and gleams have broken
  From his dark eyes, too bright to bear,
  Oh! she hath fear'd her soul was given
To some unhallow'd child of air,
  Some erring Spirit cast from heaven,
Like those angelic youths of old,
Who burn'd for maids of mortal mould,
Bewilder'd left the glorious skies,
And lost their heaven for woman's eyes.
Fond girl! nor fiend nor angel he
Who woos thy young simplicity;
But one of earth's impassion'd sons,
  As warm in love, as fierce in ire
As the best heart whose current runs
  Full of the Day-God's living fire.

But quench'd to-night that ardour seems,
  And pale his cheek, and sunk his brow;—
Never before, but in her dreams,
  Had she beheld him pale as now:
And those were dreams of troubled sleep,
From which 't was joy to wake and weep;
Visions, that will not be forgot,
  But sadden every waking scene,

Like warning ghosts, that leave the spot
  All wither'd where they once have been.

  " How sweetly," said the trembling maid,
Of her own gentle voice afraid,
So long had they in silence stood,
Looking upon that tranquil flood—
" How sweetly does the moon-beam smile
To-night upon yon leafy isle!
Oft, in my fancy's wanderings,
I 've wish'd that little isle had wings,
And we, within its fairy bowers,
  Were wafted off to seas unknown,
Where not a pulse should beat but ours,
  And we might live, love, die alone!
Far from the cruel and the cold—
  Where the bright eyes of angels only
Should come around us, to behold
  A paradise so pure and lonely.
Would this be world enough for thee?"
Playful she turn'd that he might see
  The passing smile her cheek put on;
But when she mark'd how mournfully
  His eye met hers, that smile was gone;
And, bursting into heart-felt tears,
" Yes, yes," she cried, " my hourly fears,
My dreams have boded all too right—
We part—for ever part—to-night!
I knew, I knew, it *could* not last—
'T was bright, 't was heavenly, but 'tis past!
Oh! ever thus, from childhood's hour,
I 've seen my fondest hopes decay;
I never loved a tree or flower,
  But 't was the first to fade away.
I never nursed a dear gazelle,
  To glad me with its soft black eye,
But when it came to know me well,
  And love me, it was sure to die!
Now too—the joy most like divine
  Of all I ever dreamt or knew,
To see thee, hear thee, call thee mine—
  Oh misery! must I lose *that* too?
Yet go—on peril's brink we meet;—
  Those frightful rocks—that treacherous sea—
No, never come again—though sweet,
  Though heaven, it may be death to thee!
Farewell—and blessings on thy way,
  Where'er thou go'st, beloved stranger!
Better to sit and watch that ray,
And think thee safe, though far away,
  Than have thee near me, and in danger!"

  " Danger!—oh, tempt me not to boast—"
The youth exclaim'd—" thou little know'st
What he can brave, who, born and nurst
In Danger's paths, has dared her worst;

---

1) " On the lofty hills of Arabia Petræa are rock-goats.".
  —Niebuhr.
(2) " Canun, espèce de psalterion, avec des cordes de bo-
yaux; les dames en touchent dans le serrail, avec des dé-
cailles armées de pointes de coco."—*Toderini, translated
by De Cournand.*

Upon whose ear the signal word
Of strife and death is hourly breaking;
Who sleeps with head upon the sword
His fever'd hand must grasp in waking.
Danger!—"
  " Say on—thou fear'st not then,
And we may meet—oft meet again?"

" Oh! look not so—beneath the skies
I now fear nothing but those eyes.
If aught on earth could charm or force
My spirit from its destined course—
If aught could make this soul forget
The bond to which its seal is set,
'T would be those eyes;—they, only they,
Could melt that sacred seal away!
But no—'t is fix'd—*my* awful doom
Is fix'd—on this side of the tomb
We meet no more;—why, why did Heaven
Mingle two souls that earth has riven,
Has rent asunder wide as ours?
Oh, Arab maid, as soon the Powers
Of Light and Darkness may combine,
As I be link'd with thee or thine!
Thy Father——"
  " Holy Alla save
His grey head from that lightning glance!
Thou know'st him not—he loves the brave;
 Nor lives there under heaven's expanse
One who would prize, would worship thee
And thy bold spirit, more than he.
Oft when, in childhood, I have play'd
With the bright falchion by his side,
I 've heard him swear his lisping maid
In time should be a warrior's bride.
And still, whene'er at Haram hours,
I take him cool sherbets and flowers,
He tells me, when in playful mood,
 A hero shall my bridegroom be,
Since maids are best in battle woo'd,
 And won with shouts of victory!
Nay, turn not from me—thou alone
Art form'd to make both hearts thy own.
Go—join his sacred ranks—thou know'st
The unholy strife these Persians wage:—

Good Heaven, that frown!—even now thou glow'st
 With more than mortal warrior's rage.
Haste to the camp by morning's light,
And, when that sword is raised in fight,
Oh, still remember Love and I
Beneath its shadow trembling lie!
One victory o'er those Slaves of Fire,
Those impious Ghebers, whom my sire
Abhors——"
  " Hold, hold—thy words are death"—
The stranger cried, as wild he flung
His mantle back, and show'd beneath
 The Gheber belt that round him clung. —(1)
" Here, maiden, look—weep—blush to see
All that thy sire abhors in me!
Yes—*I* am of that impious race,
 Those Slaves of Fire who, morn and even,
Hail their Creator's dwelling-place
 Among the living lights of heaven: (2)
Yes—*I* am of that outcast few,
To Iran and to vengeance true,
Who curse the hour your Arabs came
To desolate our shrines of flame,
And swear, before God's burning eye,
To break our country's chains, or die!
Thy bigot sire—nay, tremble not—
 He, who gave birth to those dear eyes,
With me is sacred as the spot
 From which our fires of worship rise!
But know—'t was he that night
 When, from my watch-boat on the sea,
I caught this turret's glimmering light,
 And up the rude rocks desperately
Rush'd to my prey—thou know'st the rest—
I climb'd the gory vulture's nest,
And found a trembling dove within;—
Thine, thine the victory—thine the sin—
If Love hath made one thought his own
That Vengeance claims first—last—alone!
Oh! had we never, never met,
Or could this heart even now forget
How link'd, how bless'd we might have been,
Had fate not frown'd so dark between!
Hadst thou been born a Persian maid,
 In neighbouring valleys had we dwelt,

(1) " They (the Ghebers) lay so much stress on their cu-
shee or girdle, as not to dare to be an instant without it."
—*Grose's Voyage.*—"Le jeune homme nia d'abord la
chose; mais, ayant été dépouillé de sa robe, et la large
ceinture qu'il portoit comme Ghèbre," etc., etc.—*D'Herbe-
lot,* art. *Agduani.* "Pour se distinguer des Idolatres de
l'Inde, les Guèbres se ceignent tous d'un cordon de laine,
ou de poil de chameau."—*Encyclopédie Françoise.*
D'Herbelot says this belt was generally of leather.
(2) "They suppose the Throne of the Almighty is seated
in the sun, and hence their worship of that luminary."—
Hanway. "As to fire, the Ghebers place the spring-
head of it in that globe of fire, the Sun, by them called
Mythras, or Mihir, to which they pay the highest reve-
rence, in gratitude for the manifold benefits flowing from

its ministerial omniscience. But they are so far from
confounding the subordination of the Servant with the
majesty of its Creator, that they not only attribute no
sort of sense or reasoning to the sun or fire in any of its
operations, but consider it as a purely passive blind instru-
ment, directed and governed by the immediate impression
on it of the will of God; but they do not even give that lu-
minary, all-glorious as it is, more than the second rank
amongst his works, reserving the first for that stupen-
dous production of divine power, the mind of man."—
Grose. The false charges brought against the religion
of these people by their Mussulman tyrants is but one
proof among many of the truth of this writer's remark,
that " calumny is often added to oppression, if but for the
sake of justifying it."

Through the same fields in childhood play'd,
  At the same kindling altar knelt—
Then, then, while all those nameless ties,
In which the charm of Country lies,
Had round our hearts been hourly spun,
Till Iran's cause and thine were one;
While in thy lute's awakening sigh
I heard the voice of days gone by,
And saw, in every smile of thine,
Returning hours of glory shine;—
While the wrong'd Spirit of our Land
  Lived, look'd, and spoke her wrongs through
    thee—
God! who could then this sword withstand?
  Its very flash were victory.
But now—estranged, divorced for ever,
Far as the grasp of Fate can sever;
Our only ties what love has wove—
  In faith, friends, country, sunder'd wide;
And then, then only, true to love,
  When false to all that 's dear beside!
Thy Father Iran's deadliest foe—
Thyself, perhaps, even now—but no—
Hate never look'd so lovely yet!
  No—sacred to thy soul will be
The land of him who could forget
  All but that bleeding land for thee.
When other eyes shall see, unmoved,
  Her widows mourn, her warriors fall,
Thou 'lt think how well one Gheber loved,
  And for his sake thou 'lt weep for all!
But look——"
            With sudden start he turn'd
And pointed to the distant wave,
Where lights, like charnel meteors, burn'd
  Bluely, as o'er some seaman's grave;
And fiery darts, at intervals, (1)
  Flew up all sparkling from the main,
As if each star that nightly falls,
  Were shooting back to heaven again.

"My signal lights!—I must away—
Both, both are ruin'd if I stay.
Farewell—sweet life! thou cling'st in vain—
Now, Vengeance, I am thine again!"
Fiercely he broke away, nor stopp'd,
Nor look'd—but from the lattice dropp'd

Down 'mid the pointed crags beneath,
As if he fled from love to death.
While pale and mute young Hinda stood,
Nor moved, till in the silent flood
A momentary plunge below
Startled her from her trance of woe;—
Shrieking she to the lattice flew,
  "I come—I come—if in that tide
Thou sleep'st to-night, I 'll sleep there too,
  In death's cold wedlock, by thy side.
Oh! I would ask no happier bed
  Than the chill wave my love lies under:—
Sweeter to rest together dead,
  Far sweeter, than to live asunder!"
But no—their hour is not yet come—
  Again she sees his pinnace fly,
Wafting him fleetly to his home,
  Where'er that ill-starr'd home may lie;
And calm and smooth it seem'd to win
  Its moonlight way before the wind,
As if it bore all peace within,
  Nor left one breaking heart behind!

THE Princess, whose heart was sad enough already,
could have wished that Feramorz had chosen a less
melancholy story; as it is only to the happy that
tears are a luxury. Her Ladies, however, were by
no means sorry that love was once more the Poet's
theme; for, whenever he spoke of love, they said,
his voice was as sweet as if he had chewed the leaves
of that enchanted tree, which grows over the tomb
of the musician, Tan-Sein. (2)
  Their road all the morning had lain through a
very dreary country;—through valleys, covered with
a low bushy jungle, where, in more than one place,
the awful signal of the bamboo staff, (3) with the
white flag at its top, reminded the traveller that, in
that very spot, the tiger had made some human
creature his victim. It was, therefore, with much
pleasure that they arrived at sunset in a safe and
lovely glen, and encamped under one of those holy
trees, whose smooth columns and spreading roofs
seem to destine them for natural temples of religion.
Beneath this spacious shade, some pious hands had
erected a row of pillars ornamented with the most
beautiful porcelain, (4) which now supplied the use
of mirrors to the young maidens, as they adjusted

(1) "The Mameluks that were in the other boat, when
it was dark, used to shoot up a sort of fiery arrows into
the air, which in some measure resembled lightning or
falling stars."—Baumgarten.
(2) "Within the enclosure which surrounds this monu-
ment (at Gualior) is a small tomb to the memory of Tan-
Sein, a musician of incomparable skill, who flourished at
the court of Akbar. The tomb is overshadowed by a tree,
concerning which a superstitious notion prevails, that
the chewing of its leaves will give an extraordinary me-
lody to the voice."—Narrative of a Journey from Agra to
Ouzein, by W. Hunter, Esq.
(3) "It is usual to place a small white triangular flag,

fixed to a bamboo staff of ten or twelve feet long, at the
place where a tiger has destroyed a man. It is common
for the passengers also to throw each a stone or brick near
the spot, so that in the course of a little time a pile equal
to a good waggon-load is collected. The sight of these
flags and piles of stones imparts a certain melancholy,
not altogether void of apprehension."—Oriental Field
Sports, vol. ii.
(4) The Ficus Indica is called the Pagod Tree and Tree
of Councils; the first from the idols placed under its shade;
the second, because meetings were held under its cool
branches. In some places it is believed to be the haunt
of spectres, as the ancient spreading oaks of Wales have

their hair in descending from the palankeens.
Here, while, as usual, the Princess sat listening
anxiously, with Fadladeen in one of his loftiest
moods of criticism by her side, the young Poet,
leaning against a branch of the tree, thus continued
his story :—

THE morn hath risen clear and calm,
  And o'er the Green Sea (1) palely shines,
Revealing Bahrein's (2) groves of palm,
  And lighting Kishma's (2) amber vines.
Fresh smell the shores of Araby,
While breezes from the Indian sea
Blow round Selama's (3) sainted cape,
  And curl the shining flood beneath—
Whose waves are rich with many a grape,
  And cocoa-nut and flowery wreath,
Which pious seamen, as they pass'd,
Had toward that holy headland cast—
Oblations to the Genii there
For gentle skies and breezes fair!
The nightingale now bends her flight (4)
From the high trees, where all the night
  She sung so sweet, with none to listen;
And hides her from the morning star
  Where thickets of pomegranate glisten
In the clear dawn—bespangled o'er
  With dew, whose night-drops would not stain
The best and brightest scimitar (5)
  That ever youthful Sultan wore
    On the first morning of his reign.

And see—the Sun himself!—on wings
Of glory up the East he springs.
Angel of Light! who from the time
Those heavens began their march sublime,
  Hath first of all the starry choir
Trod in his Maker's steps of fire!
Where are the days, thou wondrous sphere,
When Iran, like a sun-flower, turn'd
To meet that eye where'er it burn'd?—
  When, from the banks of Bendemeer
To the nut-groves of Samarcand,
Thy temples flamed o'er all the land?

Where are they? ask the shades of them
  Who, on Cadessia's (6) bloody plains,
Saw fierce invaders pluck the gem
From Iran's broken diadem,
  And bind her ancient faith in chains :—
Ask the poor exile, cast alone
On foreign shores, unloved, unknown,
Beyond the Caspian's iron Gates, (7)
  Or on the snowy Mossian mountains,
Far from his beauteous land of dates,
  Her jasmine bowers and sunny fountains:
Yet happier so than if he trod
His own beloved, but blighted, sod,
  Beneath a despot stranger's nod!—
Oh, he would rather houseless roam
  Where Freedom and his God may lead,
Than be the sleekest slave at home
  That crouches to the conqueror's creed!

Is Iran's pride then gone for ever,
  Quench'd with the flame in Mithra's
    caves?—
No—she has sons, that never—never—
  Will stoop to be the Moslem's slaves,
  While heaven has light or earth has graves;—
Spirits of fire, that brood not long,
  But flash resentment back for wrong;
And hearts where, slow but deep, the seeds
  Of vengeance ripen into deeds,
Till, in some treacherous hour of calm,
They burst, like Zeilan's giant palm, (8)
Whose buds fly open with a sound
That shakes the pigmy forests round!

Yes, Emir! he, who scaled that tower,
  And, had he reach'd thy slumbering breast,
Had taught thee, in a Gheber's power
  How safe even tyrant heads may rest—
Is one of many, brave as he,
Who loathe thy haughty race and thee;
Who, though they know the strife is vain,
Who, though they know the riven chain
Snaps but to enter in the heart
Of him who rends its links apart,

been of fairies; in others are erected beneath the shade
pillars of stone, or posts, elegantly carved, and orna-
mented with the most beautiful porcelain, to supply the
use of mirrors."—*Pennant.*

(1) The Persian Gulf.—"To dive for pearls in the Green
Sea, or Persian Gulf."—*Sir W. Jones.*

(2) Islands in the Gulf.

(3) Or Selemeh, the genuine name of the headland at
the entrance of the Gulf commonly called Cape Musseldom.
"The Indians, when they pass the promontory, throw
cocoa-nuts, fruits, or flowers into the sea, to secure a pro-
pitious voyage."—*Morier.*

(4) "The nightingale sings from the pomegranate-
groves in the day-time, and from the loftiest trees at
night."—*Russel's Aleppo.*

(5) In speaking of the climate of Shiraz, Francklin says,

"The dew is of such a pure nature, that if the brightest
scimitar should be exposed to it all night, it would not re-
ceive the least rust."

(6) The place where the Persians were finally defeated
by the Arabs, and their ancient monarchy destroyed.

(7) Derbend.—"Les Turcs appellent cette ville Demir
Capi, Porte de Fer; ce sont les Caspiæ Portæ des anciens."
—*D'Herbelot.*

(8) The Talpot or Talipot tree. "This beautiful palm-
tree, which grows in the heart of the forests, may be
classed among the loftiest trees, and becomes still higher
when on the point of bursting forth from its leafy summit.
The sheath which then envelopes the flower is very large,
and, when it bursts, makes an explosion like the report of
a cannon."—*Thunberg.*

Yet dare the issue—blest to be
Even for one bleeding moment free,
And die in pangs of liberty!
Thou know'st them well—'t is some moons since
Thy turban'd troops and blood-red flags,
Thou satrap of a bigot Prince,
Have swarm'd among these Green Sea crags;
Yet here, even here, a sacred band,
Aye, in the portal of that land
Thou, Arab, darest to call thy own,
Their spears across thy path have thrown;
Here—ere the winds half wing'd thee o'er—
Rebellion braved thee from the shore.

Rebellion! foul dishonouring word,
  Whose wrongful blight so oft has stain'd
The holiest cause that tongue or sword
  Of mortal ever lost or gain'd.
How many a spirit, born to bless,
  Hath sunk beneath that withering name,
Whom but a day's, an hour's success
  Had wafted to eternal fame!
As exhalations, when they burst
From the warm earth, if chill'd at first,
If check'd in soaring from the plain,
Darken to fogs and sink again;—
But, if they once triumphant spread
Their wings above the mountain-head,
Become enthroned in upper air,
And turn to sun-bright glories there!

And who is he, that wields the might
Of Freedom on the Green Sea brink,
Before whose sabre's dazzling light (1)
  The eyes of Yemen's warriors wink?
Who comes, embower'd in the spears
Of Kerman's hardy mountaineers?—
Those mountaineers that truest, last,
  Cling to their country's ancient rites,
As if that God, whose eyelids cast
  Their closing gleam on Iran's heights,
Among her snowy mountains threw
The last light of his worship too!

'T is Hafed—name of fear, whose sound
  Chills like the muttering of a charm!—
Shout but that awful name around,
  And palsy shakes the manliest arm.
'T is Hafed, most accursed and dire
(So rank'd by Moslem hate and ire)
Of all the rebel Sons of Fire;

Of whose malign tremendous power
The Arabs, at their mid-watch hour,
Such tales of fearful wonder tell,
That each affrighted sentinel
Pulls down his cowl upon his eyes,
Lest Hafed in the midst should rise!
A man, they say, of monstrous birth,
A mingled race of flame and earth,
Sprung from those old enchanted kings, (2)
  Who in their fairy helms, of yore
A feather from the mystic wings
  Of the Simoorgh resistless wore;
And gifted by the Fiends of Fire,
Who groan'd to see their shrines expire,
With charms that, all in vain withstood,
Would drown the Koran's light in blood!

Such were the tales that won belief,
  And such the colouring Fancy gave
To a young, warm, and dauntless Chief—
  One who, no more than mortal brave,
Fought for the land his soul adored,
  For happy homes and altars free—
His only talisman, the sword,
  His only spell-word, Liberty!
One of that ancient hero line,
Along whose glorious current shine
Names, that have sanctified their blood;
As Lebanon's small mountain-flood
Is render'd holy by the ranks
Of sainted cedars on its banks. (3)
'T was not for him to crouch the knee
Tamely to Moslem tyranny;
'T was not for him, whose soul was cast
In the bright mould of ages past,
Whose melancholy spirit, fed
With all the glories of the dead,
Though framed for Iran's happiest years,
Was born among her chains and tears!—
'T was not for him to swell the crowd
Of slavish heads, that shrinking bow'd
Before the Moslem, as he pass'd,
Like shrubs beneath the poison-blast—
No—far he fled—indignant fled
  The pageant of his country's shame;
While every tear her children shed
  Fell on his soul like drops of flame;
And, as a lover hails the dawn
Of a first smile, so welcomed he
The sparkle of the first sword drawn
For vengeance and for liberty!

(1) "When the bright cimitars make the eyes of our heroes wink."—*The Moallakat, Poem of Amru.*
(2) Tahmuras, and other ancient Kings of Persia; whose adventures in Fairy-land among the Peris and Dives may be found in Richardson's curious *Dissertation.* The griffin Simoorgh, they say, took some feathers from her breast for Tahmuras, with which he adorned his helmet, and transmitted them afterwards to his descendants.
(3) This rivulet, says Dandini, is called the Holy River

from the "cedar-saints" among which it takes its source. In the *Lettres Édifiantes,* there is a different cause assigned for its name of Holy. "In these are deep caverns, which formerly served as so many cells for a great number of recluses, who had chosen these retreats as the only witnesses upon earth of the severity of their penance. The tears of these pious penitents gave the river of which we have just treated the name of the Holy River."—See *Chateaubriand's Beauties of Christianity.*

But vain was valour—vain the flower
Of Kerman, in that deathful hour,
Against Al Hassan's whelming power.—
In vain they met him, helm to helm,
Upon the threshold of that realm
He came in bigot pomp to sway,
And with their corpses block'd his way—
In vain—for every lance they raised,
Thousands around the conqueror blazed ;
　For every arm that lined their shore,
Myriads of slaves were wafted o'er—
A bloody, bold, and countless crowd,
Before whose swarm as fast they bow'd
As dates beneath the locust cloud.

There stood—but one short league away
From old Harmozia's sultry bay—
A rocky mountain, o'er the Sea
Of Oman beetling awfully ; (1)
A last and solitary link
Of those stupendous chains that reach
From the broad Caspian's reedy brink
　Down winding to the Green Sea beach.
Around its base the bare rocks stood,
Like naked giants, in the flood,
　As if to guard the Gulf across ;
While, on its peak, that braved the sky,
A ruin'd Temple tower'd, so high
That oft the sleeping albatross (2)
Struck the wild ruins with her wing,
And from her cloud-rock'd slumbering
Started—to find man's dwelling there
In her own silent fields of air !
Beneath, terrific caverns gave
Dark welcome to each stormy wave
That dash'd, like midnight revellers, in ;—
And such the strange mysterious din
At times throughout those caverns roll'd—
And such the fearful wonders told
Of restless sprites imprison'd there,
That bold were Moslem who would dare,
At twilight hour, to steer his skiff
Beneath the Gheber's lonely cliff. (3)

On the land side, those towers sublime,
That seem'd above the grasp of time,
Were sever'd from the haunts of men
By a wide, deep, and wizard glen,
So fathomless, so full of gloom,
　No eye could pierce the void between ;
It seem'd a place where Gholes might come
With their foul banquets from the tomb,
　And in its caverns feed unseen.
Like distant thunder, from below,
　The sound of many torrents came,
Too deep for eye or ear to know
If 't were the sea's imprison'd flow,
　Or floods of ever-restless flame.
For, each ravine, each rocky spire
Of that vast mountain stood on fire ; (4)
And, though for ever past the days
When God was worshipp'd in the blaze
That from its lofty altar shone—
Though fled the priests, the votaries gone,
Still did the mighty flame burn on, (5)
Through chance and change, through good
　　　　　and ill,
Like its own God's eternal will,
Deep, constant, bright, unquenchable!

Thither the vanquish'd Hafed led
　His little army's last remains ;—
"Welcome, terrific glen !" he said,
" Thy gloom, that Eblis' self might dread,
　Is Heaven to him who flies from chains !"
O'er a dark narrow bridge-way, known
To him and to his Chiefs alone,
They cross'd the chasm and gain'd the towers—
"This home," he cried," at least is ours ;—
Here we may bleed, unmock'd by hymns
　Of Moslem triumph o'er our head ;
Here we may fall, nor leave our limbs
　To quiver to the Moslem's tread.
Stretch'd on this rock, while vultures' beaks
Are whetted on our yet warm cheeks,
Here—happy that no tyrant's eye
Gloats on our torments—we may die !"—

(1) This mountain is my own creation, as the "stupendous chain," of which I suppose it a link, does not extend quite so far as he shores of the Persian Gulf. "This long and lofty range of mountains formerly divided Media from Assyria, and now forms the boundary of the Persian and Turkish empires. It runs parallel with the river Tigris and Persian Gulf, and almost disappearing in the vicinity of Gomberoon (Harmozia) seems once more to rise in the southern districts of Kerman, and following an easterly course, through the centre of Meckraun and Balouchistan, is entirely lost in the deserts of Sinde."—Kinnier's Persian Empire.

(2) These birds sleep in the air. They are most common about the Cape of Good Hope.

(3 "There is an extraordinary hill in this neighbourhood, called Kohé Gubr, or the Guebre's mountain. It rises in the form of a lofty cupola, and on the summit of

it, they say, are the remains of an Atush Kudu or Fire Temple. It is superstitiously held to be the residence of Deeves or Sprites, and many marvellous stories are recounted of the injury and witchcraft suffered by those who essayed in former days to ascend or explore it."—Pottinger's Beloochistan.

(4) The Ghebers generally built their temples over subterraneous fires.

(5 " At the city of Yezd, in Persia, which is distinguished by the appellation of the Darúb Abadut, or seat of Religion, the Guebres are permitted to have an Atush Kudu or Fire Temple (which, they assert, has had the sacred fire in it since the days of Zoroaster) in their own compartment of the city ; but for this indulgence they are indebted to the avarice, not the tolerance, of the Persian government, which taxes them at twenty-five rupees each man."—Pottinger's Beloochistan.

'T was night when to those towers they came,
And gloomily the fitful flame,
That from the ruin'd altar broke,
Glared on his features, as he spoke :—
"'T is o'er—what men could do we've done—
If Iran will look tamely on,
And see her priests, her warriors driven
   Before a sensual bigot's nod,
A wretch who shrines his lusts in heaven,
   And makes a pander of his God ;
If her proud sons, her high-born souls,
   Men, in whose veins—oh, last disgrace !
The blood of Zal and Rustam (1) rolls—
   If they *will* court this upstart race,
And turn from Mithra's ancient ray,
To kneel at shrines of yesterday ;
If they *will* crouch to Iran's foes,
   Why, let them—till the land's despair
Cries out to Heaven, and bondage grows
   Too vile for even the vile to bear !
Till shame at last, long hidden, burns
Their inmost core, and conscience turns
Each coward tear the slave lets fall
Back on his heart in drops of gall.
But *here*, at least, are arms unchain'd,
And souls that thraldom never stain'd ;—
   This spot, at least, no foot of slave
Or satrap ever yet profaned ;
   And though but few—though fast the wave
Of life is ebbing from our veins,
Enough for vengeance still remains.
As panthers, after set of sun,
Rush from the roots of Lebanon
Across the dark-sea robber's way, (2)
We'll bound upon our startled prey ;
And when some hearts that proudest swell
Have felt our falchion's last farewell ;
When Hope's expiring throb is o'er,
And even Despair can prompt no more,
This spot shall be the sacred grave
Of the last few who, vainly brave,
Die for the land they cannot save !"

His Chiefs stood round—each shining blade
Upon the broken altar laid—
And though so wild and desolate
Those courts, where once the Mighty sate ;

Nor longer on those mouldering towers
Was seen the feast of fruits and flowers,
With which of old the Magi fed
The wandering Spirits of their Dead ; (3)
Though neither priest nor rites were there,
   Nor charmed leaf of pure pomegranate ; (4)
Nor hymn, nor censer's fragrant air,
   Nor symbol of their worshipp'd planet ; (5)
Yet the same God that heard their sires
Heard *them*, while on that altar's fires
They swore (6) the latest, holiest deed
Of the few hearts, still left to bleed,
Should be, in Iran's injured name,
To die upon that Mount of Flame—
The last of all her patriot line,
Before her last untrampled Shrine !

Brave suffering souls ! they little knew
How many a tear their injuries drew .
From one meek maid, one gentle foe,
Whom love first touch'd with others' woe—
Whose life, as free from thought as sin,
Slept like a lake, till Love threw in
His talisman, and woke the tide,
And spread its trembling circles wide.
Once, Emir ! thy unheeding child,
'Mid all this havoc, bloom'd and smiled—
Tranquil as on some battle plain
   The Persian lily shines and towers, (7)
Before the combat's reddening stain
   Hath fallen upon her golden flowers.
Light-hearted maid, unawed, unmoved,
While Heaven but spared the sire she loved,
Once at thy evening tales of blood
Unlistening and aloof she stood—
And oft, when thou hast paced along
Thy Haram halls with furious heat,
Hast thou not cursed her cheerful song,
   That came across thee, calm and sweet,
Like lutes of angels, touch'd so near
   Hell's confines, that the damn'd can hear?
Far other feelings Love hath brought—
   Her soul all flame, her brow all sadness,
She now has but the one dear thought,
   And thinks that o'er, almost to madness !
Oft doth her sinking heart recall
His words—" for *my* sake weep for all ;"

(1) Ancient heroes of Persia. "Among the Guebres are some who boast a descent from Rustam."—*Stephens.*

(2) See Russel's account of the panther's attacking travellers in the night on the sea-shore about the roots of Lebanon.

(3) "Among other ceremonies, the Magi used to place upon the tops of high towers various kinds of rich viands, upon which it was supposed the Peris and the spirits of their departed heroes regaled themselves."—*Richardson.*

(4) In the ceremonies of the Ghebers round their Fire, as described by Lord, "the Daroo," he says, "giveth them water to drink, and a pomegranate leaf to chew in the mouth, to cleanse them from inward uncleanness."

(5) "Early in the morning, they (the Parsees or Ghebers at Oulam) go in crowds to pay their devotions to the Sun, to whom upon all the altars there are spheres consecrated, made by magic, resembling the circles of the sun, and when the sun rises these orbs seem to be inflamed, and to turn round with a great noise. They have every one a censer in their hands, and offer incense to the sun."—*Rabbi Benjamin.*

(6) "Nul d'entre eux oseroit se parjurer, quand il a pris à témoin cet élément terrible et vengeur."—*Encyclopédie.*

(7) "A vivid verdure succeeds the autumnal rains, and the ploughed fields are covered with the Persian lily, of a resplendent yellow colour."—*Russel's Aleppo.*

47

And bitterly, as day on day
    Of rebel carnage fast succeeds,
She weeps a lover snatch'd away
    In every Gheber wretch that bleeds.
There's not a sabre meets her eye
    But with his life-blood seems to swim;
There's not an arrow wings the sky
    But fancy turns its point to him.
No more she brings with footstep light
Al Hassan's falchion for the fight;
And—had he look'd with clearer sight,
Had not the mists, that ever rise
From a foul spirit, dimm'd his eyes—
He would have mark'd her shuddering frame,
When from the field of blood he came,
The faltering speech—the look estranged—
Voice, step, and life, and beauty changed—
He would have mark'd all this, and known
Such change is wrought by Love alone!

Ah! not the Love, that should have bless'd
So young, so innocent a breast;
Not the pure, open, prosperous Love,
That, pledged on earth and seal'd above,
Grows in the world's approving eyes,
    In friendship's smile and home's caress,
Collecting all the heart's sweet ties
    Into one knot of happiness!
No, Hinda, no—thy fatal flame
Is nursed in silence, sorrow, shame;—
    A passion, without hope or pleasure,
In thy soul's darkness buried deep,
    It lies, like some ill-gotten treasure—
Some idol, without shrine or name,
O'er which its pale-eyed votaries keep
Unholy watch, while others sleep.

    Seven nights have darken'd Oman's sea,
    Since last, beneath the moonlight ray,
She saw his light oar rapidly
    Hurry her Gheber's bark away—
And still she goes, at midnight hour,
To weep alone in that high bower,
And watch, and look along the deep
For him whose smiles first made her weep;—
But watching, weeping, all was vain,
She never saw his bark again.
The owlet's solitary cry,
The night-hawk, flitting darkly by,
    And oft the hateful carrion bird,
Heavily flapping his clogg'd wing,
Which reek'd with that day's banquetting—
    Was all she saw, was all she heard.

'T is the eighth morn—Al Hassan's brow
    Is brighten'd with unusual joy—
What mighty mischief glads him now,
    Who never smiles but to destroy?
The sparkle upon Herkend's sea,
    When toss'd at midnight furiously, (1)
Tells not of wreck and ruin nigh
More surely than that smiling eye!
"Up, daughter, up—the Kerna's (2) breath
Has blown a blast would waken death,
And yet thou sleep'st—up, child, and see
This blessed day for Heaven and me,
A day more rich in Pagan blood
Than ever flash'd o'er Oman's flood.
Before another dawn shall shine,
His head—heart—limbs—will all be mine;
This very night his blood shall steep
These hands all over ere I sleep!"

"His blood!" she faintly scream'd—her mind
Still singling one from all mankind.
"Yes—spite of his ravines and towers,
Hafed, my child, this night is ours.
Thanks to all-conquering treachery,
    Without whose aid the links accurst,
That bind these impious slaves, would be
    Too strong for Alla's self to burst!
That rebel fiend, whose blade has spread
My path with piles of Moslem dead,
Whose baffling spells had almost driven
Back from their course the Swords of Heaven,
This night, with all his band shall know
How deep an Arab's steel can go,
When God and Vengeance speed the blow.
And—Prophet! by that holy wreath
Thou worest on Ohod's field of death, (3)
I swear, for every sob that parts
In anguish from these heathen hearts,
A gem from Persia's plundered mines
Shall glitter on thy Shrine of Shrines.
But, ha!—she sinks—that look so wild—
Those livid lips—my child, my child,
This life of blood befits not thee,
And thou must back to Araby.
Ne'er had I risk'd thy timid sex
In scenes that man himself might dread,
Had I not hoped our every tread
    Would be on prostrate Persian necks—
Curst race, they offer swords instead!
But cheer thee, maid—the wind that now
Is blowing o'er thy feverish brow,
To-day shall waft thee from the shore;
And, ere a drop of this night's gore

(1) "It is observed, with respect to the Sea of Herkend, that when it is tossed by tempestuous winds it sparkles like fire."—Travels of Two Mohammedans.
(2) A kind of trumpet;—it "was that used by Tamerlane, the sound, of which is described as so dreadful, and so loud,

as to be heard at several miles distance."—Richardson.
(3) "Mohammed had two helmets, an interior and exterior one; the latter of which, called Al Mawashah, the fillet, wreath, or wreathed garland, he wore at the battle of Ohod."—Universal History.

Have time to chill in yonder towers,
Thou 'lt see thy own sweet Arab bowers!"

His bloody boast was all too true;
There lurk'd one wretch among the few
Whom Hafed's eagle eye could count,
Around him on that Fiery Mount—
One miscreant, who for gold betray'd
The pathway through the valley's shade
To those high towers, where Freedom stood
In her last hold of flame and blood.
Left on the field last dreadful night,
When, sallying from their sacred height,
The Ghebers fought hope's farewell fight,
He lay—but died not with the brave;
That sun, which should have gilt his grave,
Saw him a traitor and a slave;—
And, while the few, who thence return'd
To their high rocky fortress, mourn'd
For him among the matchless dead
They left behind on glory's bed,
He lived, and, in the face of morn,
Laugh'd them and Faith and Heaven to scorn.

Oh for a tongue to curse the slave,
  Whose treason, like a deadly blight,
Comes o'er the councils of the brave,
  And blasts them in their hour of might!
May Life's unblessed cup for him
Be drugg'd with treacheries to the brim,
  With hopes that but allure to fly,
  With joys that vanish while he sips,
Like Dead-Sea fruits, that tempt the eye,
  But turn to ashes on the lips!(1)

(1) "They say that there are apple-trees upon the sides of this sea, which bear very lovely fruit, but within are full of ashes."—*Thevenot*. The same is asserted of the oranges there; v. *Witman's Travels in Asiatic Turkey*.

"The Asphalt Lake, known by the name of the Dead Sea, is very remarkable on account of the considerable proportion of salt which it contains. In this respect it surpasses every other known water on the surface of the earth. This great proportion of bitter-tasted salts is the reason why neither animal nor plant can live in this water."—*Klaproth's Chemical Analysis of the Water of the Dead Sea, Annals of Philosophy, January, 1813*. *Hasselquist*, however, doubts the truth of this last assertion, as there are shell-fish to be found in the lake.

Lord Byron has a similar allusion to the fruits of the Dead Sea, in that wonderful display of genius, his third Canto of *Childe Harold*—magnificent beyond any thing, perhaps, that even *he* has ever written.

(2 "The Suhrab, or Water of the Desert, is said to b caused by the rarefaction of the atmosphere from extreme heat; and, which augments the delusion, it is most frequent in hollows, where water might be expected to lodge. I have seen bushes and trees reflected in it, with as much accuracy as though it had been the face of a clear and still lake."—*Pottinger*.

"As to the unbelievers, their works are like a vapour in a plain, which the thirsty traveller thinketh to be wa-

His country's curse, his children's shame,
Outcast of virtue, peace, and fame,
May he, at last, with lips of flame
On the parch'd desert thirsting die—
While lakes, that shone in mockery nigh, (2)
Are fading off, untouch'd, untasted,
Like the once glorious hopes he blasted!
And, when from earth his spirit flies,
  Just Prophet, let the damn'd one dwell
Full in the sight of Paradise,
  Beholding heaven, and feeling hell!

LALLA ROOKH had, the night before, been visited by a dream, which, in spite of the impending fate of poor Hafed, made her heart more than usually cheerful during the morning, and gave her cheeks all the freshened animation of a flower that the Bid-musk has just passed over. (3) She fancied that she was sailing on that Eastern Ocean, where the sea-gipsies, who live for ever on the water, (4) enjoy a perpetual summer in wandering from isle to isle, when she saw a small gilded bark approaching her. It was like one of those boats which the Maldivian islanders send adrift, at the mercy of winds and waves, loaded with perfumes, flowers, and odoriferous wood, as an offering to the Spirit whom they call King of the Sea. At first this little bark appeared to be empty, but, on coming nearer—

She had proceeded thus far in relating the dream to her Ladies, when Feramorz appeared at the door of the pavilion. In his presence, of course, every thing else was forgotten, and the continuance of the story was instantly requested by all. Fresh wood of aloes was set to burn in the cassolets;—the violet

ter, until when he cometh thereto he findeth it to be nothing."—*Koran*, chap. xxiv.

(3) "A wind which prevails in February, called Bidmusk, from a small and odoriferous flower of that name."—"The wind which blows these flowers commonly lasts till the end of the month."—*Le Bruyn*.

(4) "The Biajus are of two races: the one is settled on Borneo, and are a rude but warlike and industrious nation, who reckon themselves the original possessors of the island of Bornen. The other is a species of sea-gipsies, or itinerant fishermen, who live in small covered boats, and enjoy a perpetual summer on the eastern ocean, shifting to leeward from island to island, with the variations of the monsoon. In some of their customs this singular race resemble the natives of the Maldivia islands. The Maldivians annually launch a small bark, loaded with perfumes, gums, flowers, and odoriferous wood, and turn it adrift at the mercy of winds and waves, as an offering to the *Spirit of the Winds*; and sometimes similar offerings are made to the spirit whom they term *the King of the Sea*. In like manner the Biajus perform their offering to the god of evil, launching a small bark, loaded with all the sins and misfortunes of the nation, which are imagined to fall on the unhappy crew that may be so unlucky as first to meet with it."—*Dr. Leyden on the Languages and Literature of the Indo-Chinese Nations*.

sherbets (1) were hastily handed round, and after a
short prelude on his lute, in the pathetic measure of
Nava, (2) which is always used to express the lamen-
tations of absent lovers, the Poet thus continued:—

THE day is lowering—stilly black
Sleeps the grim wave, while heaven's rack,
Dispersed and wild, 'twixt earth and sky
Hangs like a shatter'd canopy.
There 's not a cloud in that blue plain
  But tells of storm to come or past;—
Here, flying loosely as the mane
  Of a young war-horse in the blast;
There, roll'd in masses dark and swelling,
As proud to be the thunder's dwelling!
While some, already burst and riven,
Seem melting down the verge of heaven;
As though the infant storm had rent
  The mighty womb that gave him birth,
And, having swept the firmament,
  Was now in fierce career for earth.

On earth 't was yet all calm around,
A pulseless silence, dread, profound,
More awful than the tempest's sound.
The diver steer'd for Ormus' bowers,
And moor'd his skiff till calmer hours;
The sea-birds, with portentous screech,
Flew fast to land;—upon the beach
The pilot oft had paused, with glance
Turn'd upward to that wild expanse;—
And all was boding, drear, and dark
As her own soul, when Hinda's bark
Went slowly from the Persian shore.—
No music timed her parting oar, (3)
  Nor friends upon the lessening strand
Linger'd, to wave the unseen hand,
Or speak the farewell, heard no more:—
But lone, unheeded, from the bay
The vessel takes its mournful way,
Like some ill-destined bark that steers
In silence through the Gate of Tears. (4)
And where was stern Al Hassan then?
Could not that saintly scourge of men

From bloodshed and devotion spare
One minute for a farewell there?
No—close within, in changeful fits
Of cursing and of prayer, he sits
In savage loneliness to brood
Upon the coming night of blood—
  With that keen second-scent of death,
By which the vulture snuffs his food
  In the still warm and living breath! (5)
While o'er the wave his weeping daughter
Is wafted from these scenes of slaughter.—
As a young bird of Babylon, (6)
Let loose to tell of victory won,
Flies home, with wing, ah! not unstain'd
By the red hands that held her chain'd.

And does the long-left home she seeks
Light up no gladness on her cheeks?
The flowers she nursed—the well-known groves,
Where oft in dreams her spirit roves—
Once more to see her dear gazelles
Come bounding with their silver bells;
Her birds' new plumage to behold;
  And the gay gleaming fishes count,
She left, all filleted with gold,
  Shooting around their jasper fount; (7)
Her little garden mosque to see,
  And once again, at evening hour,
To tell her ruby rosary (8)
  In her own sweet acacia bower.—
Can these delights, that wait her now,
Call up no sunshine on her brow?
No—silent, from her train apart—
As if even now she felt at heart
The chill of her approaching doom—
She sits, all lovely in her gloom
As a pale Angel of the Grave;
And o'er the wide tempestuous wave,
Looks, with a shudder, to those towers,
Where, in a few short awful hours,
Blood, blood, in streaming tides shall run,
Foul incense for to-morrow's sun!
"Where art thou, glorious stranger! thou,
So loved, so lost, where art thou now?

(1) "The sweet-scented violet is one of the plants
most esteemed, particularly for its great use in sorbet,
which they make of violet sugar."—*Hasselquist.*
  "The sherbet they most esteem, and which is drunk by
the Grand Signor, is made of violets and sugar."—*Tavernier.*
  (2) "Last of all she took a guitar, and sung a pathetic
air in the measure called Nava, which is always used to
express the lamentations of absent lovers."—*Persian Tales.*
  (3) "The Easterns used to set out on their longer
voyages with music."—*Harmer.*
  (4) "The Gate of Tears, or straits or passage into the
Red Sea, commonly called Babelmandel. It received
this name from the old Arabians on account of the danger
of the navigation, and the number of shipwrecks by which
it was distinguished; which induced them to consider as
dead, and to wear mourning for, all who had the boldness

to hazard the passage through it into the Ethiopic ocean."
—*Richardson.*
  (5) "I have been told that whensoever an animal falls
down dead, one or more vultures, unseen before, in-
stantly appear."—*Pennant.*
  (6) "They fasten some writing to the wings of a Bagdat
or Babylonian pigeon."—*Travels of Certain Englishmen.*
  (7) "The Empress of Jehan-Guire used to divert herself
with feeding tame fish in her canals, some of which were
many years afterwards known by fillets of gold, which she
caused to be put round them."—*Harris.*
  (8) "Le Tespih qui est un chapelet, composé de 99 pe-
tites boules d'agathe, de jaspe, d'ambre, de corail, ou
d'autres matières précieuses. J'en ai vu un superbe au sei-
gneur Jerpos; il étoit de belles et grosses perles par-
faites et égales, estimé trente mille piastres."—*Toderini.*

Foe—Gheber—infidel—whate'er
The unhallow'd name thou'rt doom'd to bear,
Still glorious—still to this fond heart
Dear as its blood, whate'er thou art!
Yes—Alla, dreadful Alla! yes—
If there be wrong, be crime in this,
Let the black waves that round us roll,
Whelm me this instant, ere my soul,
Forgetting faith—home—father—all—
Before its earthly idol fall,
Nor worship even Thyself above him—
For, oh, so wildly do I love him,
Thy Paradise itself were dim
And joyless, if not shared with him!"
Her hands were clasp'd—her eyes upturn'd,
    Dropping their tears like moonlight rain;
And, though her lip, fond raver! burn'd
    With words of passion, bold, profane,
Yet was there light around her brow,
    A holiness in those dark eyes,
Which show'd — though wandering earthward
        now,
Her spirit's home was in the skies.
Yes—for a spirit pure as hers
Is always pure, even while it errs;
As sunshine, broken in the rill,
Though turn'd astray, is sunshine still!

So wholly had her mind forgot
All thoughts but one, she heeded not
The rising storm—the wave that cast
A moment's midnight, as it pass'd—
Nor heard the frequent shout, the tread—
Of gathering tumult o'er her head—
Clash'd swords, and tongues that seem'd to vie
With the rude riot of the sky.—
But, hark!—that war-whoop on the deck—
    That crash, as if each engine there,
Mast, sails, and all, were gone to wreck,
'Mid yells and stampings of despair!

Merciful Heaven! what *can* it be?
'T is not the storm, though fearfully
The ship has shudder'd as she rode
O'er mountain-waves—"Forgive me, God!
Forgive me"—shriek'd the maid, and knelt,
Trembling all over—for she felt
As if her judgment-hour was near;
While crouching round, half dead with fear,
Her handmaids clung, nor breathed, nor stirr'd—
When, hark!—a second crash—a third—
And now, as if a bolt of thunder
Had riven the labouring planks asunder,
The deck falls in—what horrors then!
Blood, waves, and tackle, swords and men
Come mix'd together through the chasm—
Some wretches in their dying spasm
Still fighting on—and some that call ·
"For God and Iran!" as they fall!

Whose was the hand that turn'd away
The perils of the infuriate fray,
And snatch'd her breathless from beneath
This wilderment of wreck and death?
She knew not—for a faintness came
Chill o'er her, and her sinking frame
Amid the ruins of that hour
Lay, like a pale and scorched flower,
Beneath the red volcano's shower.
But, oh! the sights and sounds of dread
That shock'd her ere her senses fled!
The yawning deck—the crowd that strove
Upon the tottering planks above—
The sail, whose fragments, shivering o'er
The strugglers' heads, all dash'd with gore,
Flutter'd like bloody flags—the clash
Of sabres, and the lightning's flash
Upon their blades, high toss'd about
Like meteor brands (1)—as if throughout
    The elements one fury ran,
One general rage, that left a doubt
    Which was the fiercer, Heaven or Man!

Once too—but no—it could not be—
    'T was fancy all—yet once she thought
While yet her fading eyes could see,
    High on the ruin'd deck she caught
A glimpse of that unearthly form,
    That glory of her soul—even then,
Amid the whirl of wreck and storm,
    Shining above his fellow-men;
As on some black and troublous night,
The Star of Egypt, (2) whose proud light
Never hath beam'd on those who rest
In the White Islands of the West, (3)
Burns through the storm with looks of flame
That put Heaven's cloudier eyes to shame.
But no—'t was but the minute's dream—
A fantasy—and ere the scream
Had half-way pass'd her pallid lips,
A death-like swoon, a chill eclipse
Of soul and sense its darkness spread,
Around her, and she sunk, as dead.

How calm, how beautiful comes on
The stilly hour, when storms are gone;
When warring winds have died away,
And clouds, beneath the glancing ray,
Melt off, and leave the land and sea
Sleeping in bright tranquillity—
Fresh as if Day again were born,
Again upon the lap of Morn!—
When the light blossoms, rudely torn
And scatter'd at the whirlwind's will,
Hang floating in the pure air still,

(1) The meteors that Pliny calls "faces."
(2) "The brilliant Canopus, unseen in European cli
mates." — *Brown.*
(3) See Wilford's learned *Essays on the Sacred Isles in
the West.*

Filling it all with precious balm,
In gratitude for this sweet calm;—
And every drop the thunder-showers
Have left upon the grass and flowers
Sparkles, as 't were that lightning-gem!(1)
Whose liquid flame is born of them!
When, 'stead of one unchanging breeze,
    There blow a thousand gentle airs,
    And each a different perfume bears—
As if the loveliest plants and trees
Had vassal breezes of their own
To watch and wait on them alone,
    And waft no other breath than theirs:
When the blue waters rise and fall,
In sleepy sunshine mantling all;
And even that swell the tempest leaves
Is like the full and silent heaves
Of lovers' hearts, when newly blest,
Too newly to be quite at rest.

Such was the golden hour that broke
Upon the world, when Hinda woke
From her long trance, and heard around
No motion but the water's sound
Rippling against the vessel's side,
As slow it mounted o'er the tide.—
But where is she?—her eyes are dark,
Are wilder'd still—is this the bark,
The same, that from Harmozia's bay
Bore her at morn—whose bloody way
The sea-dog track'd?—no—strange and new
Is all that meets her wondering view.
Upon a galliot's deck she lies,
    Beneath no rich pavilion's shade—
No plumes to fan her sleeping eyes,
    Nor jasmine on her pillow laid.
But the rude litter, roughly spread
With war-cloaks, is her homely bed,
And shawl and sash, on javelins hung,
For awning o'er her head are flung.
Shuddering she look'd around—there lay
A group of warriors in the sun,
Resting their limbs, as for that day
Their ministry of death were done.
Some gazing on the drowsy sea,
Lost in unconscious reverie;
And some, who seem'd but ill to brook
That sluggish calm, with many a look
To the slack sail impatient cast,
As loose it flagg'd around the mast.

Blest Alla! who shall save her now?
There 's not in all that warrior band

One Arab sword, one turban'd brow
From her own Faithful Moslem land.
Their garb—the leathern belt (2) that wraps
    Each yellow vest (3)—that rebel hue—
The Tartar fleece upon their caps (4)—
    Yes—yes—her fears are all too true,
And Heaven hath, in this dreadful hour,
Abandon'd her to Hafed's power;—
Hafed, the Gheber!—at the thought
    Her very heart's blood chills within;
He, whom her soul was hourly taught
To loathe, as some foul fiend of sin,
Some minister, whom Hell had sent
To spread its blast where'er he went,
And fling, as o'er our earth he trod,
His shadow betwixt man and God!
And she is now his captive—thrown
In his fierce hands, alive, alone;
His the infuriate band she sees,
All infidels—all enemies!
What was the daring hope that then
Cross'd her like lightning as again,
With boldness that despair had lent,
    She darted through that armed crowd
A look so searching, so intent,
    That even the sternest warrior bow'd
Abash'd, when he her glances caught,
As if he guess'd whose form they sought.
But no—she sees him not—'t is gone,
The vision that before her shone
Through all the maze of blood and storm
Is fled—'t was but a phantom form—
One of those passing rainbow dreams,
Half light, half shade, which Fancy's beams
Paint on the fleeting mists that roll
In trance or slumber round the soul.

But now the bark, with livelier bound,
    Scales the blue wave—the crew 's in mo-
        tion,
The oar are out, and with light sound
    Break the bright mirror of the ocean,
Scattering its brilliant fragments round.
And now she sees—with horror sees,
Their course is toward that mountain-hold—
Those towers, that make her life-blood freeze,
    Where Mecca's godless enemies
Lie, like beleaguer'd scorpions, roll'd
    In their last deadly venomous fold!
Amid the illumined land and flood
Sunless that mighty mountain stood;
Save where, above its awful head,
There shone a flaming cloud, blood-red,

(1) A precious stone of the Indies, called by the ancients Ceraunium, because it was supposed to be found in places where thunder had fallen. Tertullian says it has a glittering appearance, as if there had been fire in it; and the author of the *Dissertation in Harris's Voyages* supposes it to be the opal.

(2) *D'Herbelot*, art. *Agduani*.

(3) " The Guebres are known by a dark yellow colour, which the men affect in their clothes." — *Thevenot.*

(4) "The Kolah, or cap, worn by the Persians, is made of the skin of the sheep of Tartary." —*Waring*.

As 't were the flag of destiny
Hung out to mark where death would be'

Had her bewilder'd mind the power
Of thought in this terrific hour,
She well might marvel where or how
Man's foot could scale that mountain's brow,
Since ne'er had Arab heard or known
Of path but through the glen alone.
But every thought was lost in fear,
When, as their bounding bark drew near
The craggy base, she felt the waves
Hurry them toward those dismal caves,
That from the Deep in windings pass
Beneath that Mount's volcanic mass ,—
And loud a voice on deck commands
To lower the mast and light the brands!—
Instantly o'er the dashing tide
Within a cavern's mouth they glide,
Gloomy as that eternal Porch
    Through which departed spirits go :—
Not even the flare of brand and torch
    Its flickering light could further throw
    Than the thick flood that boil'd below.
Silent they floated—as if each
Sat breathless, and too awed for speech
In that dark chasm, where even sound
Seem'd dark—so sullenly around
The goblin echoes of the cave
Mutter'd it o'er the long black wave,
As 't were some secret of the grave'

But soft— they pause—the current turns
    Beneath them from its onward track;—
Some mighty unseen barrier spurns
    The vexed tide, all foaming, back.
And scarce the oars' redoubled force
Can stem the eddy's whirling course;
When, hark!—some desperate foot has sprung
Among the rocks—the chain is flung—
The oars are up—the grapple clings,
And the toss'd bark in moorings swings.

Just then, a day-beam through the shade
Broke tremulous—but, ere the maid
Can see from whence the brightness steals,
Upon her brow she shuddering feels
A viewless hand, that promptly ties
A bandage round her burning eyes,
While the rude litter where she lies,
Uplifted by the warrior throng,
O'er the steep rocks is borne along.
Blest power of sunshine!—genial Day,
What balm, what life is in thy ray
To feel thee is such real bliss,
That had the world no joy but this,
To sit in sunshine calm and sweet—
It were a world too exquisite
For man to leave it for the gloom,
The deep cold shadow of the tomb.

Even Hinda, though she saw not where
    Or whither wound the perilous road,
Yet knew by that awakening air,
    Which suddenly around her glow'd,
That they had risen from darkness then,
And breathed the sunny world again!

But soon this balmy freshness fled—
For now the steepy labyrinth led
Through damp and gloom —'mid crash of boughs,
And fall of loosen'd crags that rouse
The leopard from his hungry sleep,
    Who, starting, thinks each crag a prey,
And long is heard, from steep to steep,
    Chasing them down their thundering way !
The jackal's cry—the distant moan
Of the hyæna, fierce and lone—
And that eternal saddening sound
Of torrents in the glen beneath,
As 't were the ever-dark Profound
    That rolls beneath the Bridge of Death!
All, all is fearful—even to see,
    To gaze on those terrific things
She now but blindly hears, would be
    Relief to her imaginings ;
Since never yet was shape so dread,
But Fancy, thus in darkness thrown,
And by such sounds of horror fed,
    Could frame more dreadful of her own.

But does she dream? has Fear again
Perplex'd the workings of her brain?
Or did a voice, all music, then
Come from the gloom, low whispering near—
" Tremble not, love, thy Gheber 's here?"
She *does* not dream—all sense, all ear,
She drinks the words, " Thy Gheber 's here."
'T was his own voice—she could not err—
    Throughout the breathing world's extent
There was but *one* such voice for her,
    So kind, so soft, so eloquent!
Oh, sooner shall the rose of May
    Mistake her own sweet nightingale,
And to some meaner minstrel's lay
    Open her bosom's glowing veil, (1)
Than Love shall ever doubt a tone,
A breath of the beloved one!
Though blest, 'mid all her ills, to think
    She has that one beloved near,
Whose smile, though met on ruin's brink,
    Hath power to make even ruin dear—
Yet soon this gleam of rapture, crost
By fears for him, is chill'd and lost.
How shall the ruthless Hafed brook
That one of Gheber blood should look,

(1 A frequent image among the oriental poets. "The
nightingales warbled their enchanting notes, and rent
the thin veils of the rose-bud and the rose."—*Jami.*

With aught but curses in his eye,
On her—a maid of Araby—
A Moslem maid—the child of him
  Whose bloody banner's dire success
Hath left their altars cold and dim,
  And their fair land a wilderness!
And, worse than all, that night of blood
Which comes so fast—Oh! who shall stay
The sword, that once hath tasted food
  Of Persian hearts, or turn its way?
What arm shall then the victim cover,
Or from her father shield her lover?

"Save him, my God!" she inly cries—
  "Save him this night—and if thine eyes
  Have ever welcomed with delight
The sinner's tears, the sacrifice
  Of sinners' hearts—guard him this night,
And here, before thy throne, I swear
From my heart's inmost core to tear
Love, hope, remembrance, though they be
Link'd with each quivering life-string there,
  And give it bleeding all to Thee!
Let him but live—the burning tear,
The sighs, so sinful, yet so dear,
Which have been all too much his own,
Shall from this hour be Heaven's alone.
Youth pass'd in penitence, and age
In long and painful pilgrimage,
Shall leave no traces of the flame
That wastes me now—nor shall his name
E'er bless my lips, but when I pray
For his dear spirit, that away
Casting from its angelic ray
The eclipse of earth, he, too, may shine
Redeem'd, all glorious and all thine!
Think—think what victory to win
One radiant soul like his from sin—
One wandering star of virtue back
To its own native, heaven-ward track!
Let him but live, and both are thine,
  Together thine—for, blest or crost,
  Living or dead, his doom is mine,
    And, if he perish, both are lost!"

THE next evening Lalla Rookh was entreated by
her Ladies to continue the relation of her wonderful
dream; but the fearful interest that hung round the
fate of Hinda and her lover had completely removed
every trace of it from her mind;—much to the
disappointment of a fair seer or two in her train,
who prided themselves on their skill in interpreting
visions, and who had already remarked, as an

unlucky omen, that the Princess, on the very morn-
ing after the dream, had worn a silk dyed with the
blossoms of the sorrowful tree, Nilica. (1)
  Fadladeen, whose indignation had more than once
broken out during the recital of some parts of this
heterodox poem, seemed at length to have made up
his mind to the infliction; and took his seat this
evening with all the patience of a martyr, while the
Poet resumed his profane and seditious story as fol-
lows :—

  To tearless eyes and hearts at ease
  The leafy shores and sun-bright seas,
  That lay beneath that mountain's height,
  Had been a fair enchanting sight.
  'T was one of those ambrosial eves
  A day of storm so often leaves
  At its calm setting—when the West
  Opens her golden bowers of rest,
  And a moist radiance from the skies
  Shoots trembling down, as from the eyes
  Of some meek penitent, whose last
  Bright hours atone for dark ones past,
  And whose sweet tears, o'er wrong forgiven,
  Shine, as they fall, with light from heaven!

  'T was stillness all—the winds that late
    Had rush'd through Kerman's almond groves,
  And shaken from her bowers of date
    That cooling feast the traveller loves, (2)
  Now, lull'd to languor, scarcely curl
    The Green Sea wave, whose waters gleam
  Limpid, as if her mines of pearl
    Were melted all to form the stream :
  And her fair islets, small and bright,
    With their green shores reflected there,
  Look like those Peri isles of light,
    That hang by spell-work in the air.

  But vainly did those glories burst
  On Hinda's dazzled eyes, when first
  The bandage from her brow was taken,
  And, pale and awed as those who waken
  In their dark tombs—when, scowling near,
  The Searchers of the Grave (3) appear—
  She shuddering turn'd to read her fate
    In the fierce eyes that flash'd around ;
  And saw those towers all desolate,
    That o'er her head terrific frown'd,
  As if defying even the smile
  Of that soft heaven to gild their pile.
  In vain, with mingled hope and fear,
  She looks for him whose voice so dear
  Had come, like music, to her ear—

---

(1) "Blossoms of the sorrowful Nyctanthes give a dur-
able colour to silk."—*Remarks on the Husbandry of Bengal,*
p. 200. Nilica is one of the Indian names of this flower.
—*Sir W. Jones.* The Persians call it Gul.—*Carreri.*

(2) "In parts of Kerman, whatever dates are shaken

from the trees by the wind they do not touch, but leave for
those who have not any, or for travellers."—*Ebn Haukal.*
(3) The two terrible angels, Monkir and Nakir, who are
called the "Searchers of the Grave" in the "Creed of
the orthodox Mahometans" given by Ockley, vol ii.

Strange, mocking dream! again 'tis fled.
And oh, the shoots, the pangs of dread
That through her inmost bosom run,
When voices from without proclaim
" Hafed, the Chief "—and, one by one,
The warriors shout that fearful name!
He comes—the rock resounds his tread—
How shall she dare to lift her head,
Or meet those eyes whose scorching glare
Not Yemen's boldest sons can bear?
In whose red beam, the Moslem tells,
Such rank and deadly lustre dwells,
As in those hellish fires that light
The mandrake's charnel leaves at night. (1)
How shall she bear that voice's tone,
At whose loud battle-cry alone
Whole squadrons oft in panic ran,
Scatter'd like some vast caravan,
When, stretch'd at evening round the well,
They hear the thirsting tiger's yell.

Breathless she stands, with eyes cast down,
Shrinking beneath the fiery frown,
Which, fancy tells her, from that brow
Is flashing o'er her fiercely now:
And shuddering as she hears the tread
Of his retiring warrior band.—
Never was pause so full of dread;
Till Hafed with a trembling hand
Took hers, and, leaning o'er her, said,
" Hinda,"—that word was all he spoke,
And 't was enough—the shriek that broke
From her full bosom told the rest.—
Panting with terror, joy, surprise,
The maid but lifts her wondering eyes,
To hide them on her Gheber's breast!
'Tis he, 'tis he—the man of blood,
The fellest of the Fire-fiend's brood,
Hafed, the demon of the fight,
Whose voice unnerves, whose glances blight—
Is her own loved Gheber, mild
And glorious as when first he smiled
In her lone tower, and left such beams
Of his pure eye to light her dreams,
That she believed her bower had given
Rest to some wanderer from heaven!

Moments there are, and this was one,
Snatch'd like a minute's gleam of sun
Amid the black Simoom's eclipse—
Or, like those verdant spots that bloom
Around the crater's burning lips,
Sweetening the very edge of doom!
The past—the future—all that Fate
Can bring of dark or desperate
Around such hours, but makes them cast
Intenser radiance while they last!

Even he, this youth—though dimm'd and gone
Each star of Hope that cheer'd him on—

His glories lost—his cause betray'd—
Iran, his dear-loved country, made
A land of carcasses and slaves,
One dreary waste of chains and graves!—
Himself but lingering, dead at heart,
To see the last long struggling breath
Of Liberty's great soul depart,
Then lay him down and share her death—
Even he, so sunk in wretchedness,
With doom still darker gathering o'er him,
Yet, in this moment's pure caress,
In the mild eyes that shone before him,
Beaming that blest assurance, worth
All other transports known on earth,
That he was loved—well, warmly loved—
Oh! in this precious hour he proved
How deep, how thorough-felt the glow
Of rapture, kindling out of woe;—
How exquisite one single drop
Of bliss, thus sparkling to the top
Of misery's cup—how keenly quaff'd,
Though death must follow on the draught!

She, too, while gazing on those eyes
That sink into her soul so deep,
Forgets all fears, all miseries,
Or feels them like the wretch in sleep,
Whom fancy cheats into a smile,
Who dreams of joy, and sobs the while!
The mighty Ruins where they stood,
Upon the mount's high rocky verge,
Lay open towards the ocean flood,
Where lightly o'er the illumined surge
Many a fair bark that, all the day,
Had lurk'd in sheltering creek or bay
Now bounded on, and gave their sails,
Yet dripping, to the evening gales;
Like eagles, when the storm is done,
Spreading their wet wings in the sun.
The beauteous clouds, though daylight's Star
Had sunk behind the hills of Lar,
Were still with lingering glories bright—
As if, to grace the gorgeous West,
The Spirit of departing Light
That eve had left his sunny vest
Behind him, ere he wing'd his flight.
Never was scene so form'd for love!
Beneath them waves of crystal move
In silent swell—Heaven glows above,
And their pure hearts, to transport given,
Swell like the wave, and glow like Heaven.

But ah! too soon that dream is past—
Again, again her fear returns;
Night, dreadful night, is gathering fast,
More faintly the horizon burns,

(1 "The Arabians call the mandrake 'the Devil's candle,' on account of its shining appearance in the night."
—Richardson.

48

And every rosy tint that lay
On the smooth sea hath died away.
Hastily to the darkening skies
A glance she casts—then wildly cries
"*At night*, he said—and, look, 'tis near—
Fly, fly—if yet thou lovest me, fly—
Soon will his murderous band be here,
And I shall see thee bleed and die.—
Hush! heard'st thou not the tramp of men
Sounding from yonder fearful glen?—
Perhaps even now they climb the wood—
Fly, fly—though still the West is bright,
He'll come—oh! yes—he wants thy blood—
I know him—he'll not wait for night!"

In terrors even to agony
She clings around the wondering Chief,—
"Alas, poor wilder'd maid! to me
Thou owest this raving trance of grief.
Lost as I am, nought ever grew
Beneath my shade but perish'd too—
My doom is like the Dead Sea air,
And nothing lives that enters there!
Why were our barks together driven
Beneath this morning's furious heaven?
Why, when I saw the prize that chance
Had thrown into my desperate arms—
When, casting but a single glance
Upon thy pale and prostrate charms,
I vow'd (though watching viewless o'er
Thy safety through that hour's alarms)
To meet the unmanning sight no more—
Why have I broke that heart-wrung vow?
Why weakly, madly meet thee now?—
Start not—that noise is but the shock
Of torrents through yon valley hurl'd—
Dread nothing here—upon this rock
We stand above the jarring world—
Alike beyond its hope—its dread—
In gloomy safety, like the Dead!
Or, could even earth and hell unite
In league to storm this Sacred Height,
Fear nothing thou—myself, to-night,
And each o'erlooking star that dwells
Near God, will be thy sentinels;—
And, ere to-morrow's dawn shall glow,
Back to thy sire ——"
                    "To-morrow!—no—"
The maiden scream'd—"thou 'lt never see
To-morrow's sun—death, death will be
The night-cry through each reeking tower,
Unless we fly, aye, fly this hour!
Thou art betray'd—some wretch who knew
That dreadful glen's mysterious clew—
Nay, doubt not—by yon stars, 't is true—
Hath sold thee to my vengeful sire.
This morning, with that smile so dire

He wears in joy, he told me all,
And stamp'd in triumph through our hall,
As though thy heart already beat
Its last life-throb beneath his feet!
Good Heaven! how little dream'd I then
His victim was my own loved youth!—
Fly—send—let some one watch the glen—
By all my hopes of heaven 't is truth!"

Oh! colder than the wind that freezes
Founts, that but now in sunshine play'd,
Is that congealing pang which seizes
The trusting bosom, when betray'd.
He felt it—deeply felt—and stood
As if the tale had frozen his blood;
So mazed and motionless was he,
Like one whom sudden spells enchant,
Or some mute marble habitant
Of the still Halls of Ishmonie!(1)

But soon the painful chill was o'er,
And his great soul, herself once more,
Look'd from his brow in all the rays
Of her best, happiest, grandest days.
Never, in moment most elate,
Did that high spirit loftier rise;
While bright, serene, determinate,
His looks are lifted to the skies,
As if the signal lights of Fate
Were shining in those awful eyes!
'T is come—his hour of martyrdom
In Iran's sacred cause is come;
And, though his life hath pass'd away
Like lightning on a stormy day,
Yet shall his death-hour leave a track
Of glory, permanent and bright,
To which the brave of after-times,
The suffering brave, shall long look back
With proud regret—and by its light
Watch through the hours of slavery's night
For vengeance on the oppressor's crimes.
This rock, his monument aloft,
Shall speak the tale to many an age;
And hither bards and heroes oft
Shall come in secret pilgrimage,
And bring their warrior sons, and tell
The wondering boys where Hafed fell;
And swear them on those lone remains
Of their lost country's ancient fanes,
Never—while breath of life shall live
Within them—never to forgive
The accursed race, whose ruthless chain
Hath left on Iran's neck a stain
Blood, blood alone, can cleanse again!

Such are the swelling thoughts that now
Enthrone themselves on Hafed's brow;

(1) For an account of Ishmonie, the petrified city in Upper Egypt, where it is said there are many statues of men, women, etc., to be seen to this day, see *Perry's View of the Levant.*

And ne'er did Saint of Issa(1) gaze
On the red wreath, for martyrs twined,
More proudly than the youth surveys
That pile, which through the gloom behind,
Half lighted by the altar's fire,
Glimmers—his destined funeral pyre!
Heap'd by his own, his comrades' hands,
Of every wood of odorous breath,
There, by the Fire-God's shrine it stands,
Ready to fold in radiant death
The few still left of those who swore
To perish there, when hope was o'er—
The few, to whom that couch of flame,
Which rescues them from bonds and shame,
Is sweet and welcome as the bed
For their own infant Prophet spread,
When pitying Heaven to roses turn'd
The death-flames that beneath him burn'd!(2)

With watchfulness the maid attends
His rapid glance, where'er it bends—
Why shoot his eyes such awful beams?
What plans he now? what thinks or dreams?
Alas! why stands he musing here,
When every moment teems with fear?
"Hafed, my own beloved lord,"
She kneeling cries—"first, last adored!
If in that soul thou'st ever felt
Half what thy lips impassion'd swore,
Here, on my knees that never knelt
To any but their God before,
I pray thee, as thou lovest me, fly—
Now, now—ere yet their blades are nigh.
Oh haste—the bark that bore me hither
Can waft us o'er yon darkening sea
East—west—alas, I care not whither,
So thou art safe, and I with thee!
Go where we will, this hand in thine,
Those eyes before me smiling thus,
Through good and ill, through storm and shine,
The world's a world of love for us!
On some calm blessed shore we 'll dwell,
Where 't is no crime to love too well;—
Where thus to worship tenderly
An erring child of light like thee
Will not be sin—or, if it be,
Where we may weep our faults away,
Together kneeling, night and day,
Thou, for my sake, at Alla's shrine,
And I—at any God's, for thine!"

(1) Jesus.
(2) The Ghebers say that when Abraham, their great Prophet, was thrown into the fire by order of Nimrod, the flame turned instantly into " a bed of roses, where the child sweetly reposed." —*Tavernier.*
Of their other Prophet, Zoroaster, there is a story told in *Dion Prusæus*, Orat. 36, that the love of wisdom and virtue leading him to a solitary life upon a mountain,

Wildly these passionate words she spoke—
Then hung her head, and wept for shame,
Sobbing, as if a heart-string broke
With every deep-heaved sob that came.
While he, young, warm—oh! wonder not
If, for a moment, pride and fame,
His oath—his cause—that shrine of flame,
And Iran's self, are all forgot
For her whom at his feet he sees
Kneeling in speechless agonies.
No, blame him not, if Hope awhile
Dawn'd in his soul, and threw her smile
O'er hours to come—o'er days and nights,
Wing'd with those precious, pure delights
Which she, who bends all beauteous there,
Was born to kindle and to share.
A tear or two, which, as he bow'd
To raise the suppliant, trembling stole,
First warn'd him of this dangerous cloud
Of softness passing o'er his soul.
Starting, he brush'd the drops away,
Unworthy o'er that cheek to stray;—
Like one who, on the morn of fight,
Shakes from his sword the dews of night
That had but dimm'd, not stain'd its light.

Yet, though subdued the unnerving thrill,
Its warmth, its weakness linger'd still
So touching in each look and tone,
That the fond, fearing, hoping maid
Half counted on the flight she pray'd,
Half thought the hero's soul was grown
As soft, as yielding as her own,
And smiled and bless'd him, while he said—
" Yes—if there be some happier sphere,
Where fadeless truth like ours is dear—
If there be any land of rest
For those who love and ne'er forget,
Oh! comfort thee—for safe and blest
We 'll meet in that calm region yet!"
Scarce had she time to ask her heart
If good or ill these words impart,
When the roused youth impatient flew
To the tower-wall, where, high in view,
A ponderous sea-horn(3) hung, and blew
A signal, deep and dread as those
The storm-fiend at his rising blows.—
Full well his Chieftains, sworn and true
Through life and death, that signal knew;
For 't was the appointed warning-blast,
The alarm, to tell when hope was past,
And the tremendous death-die cast!

he found it one day all in a flame, shining with celestial fire, out of which he came without any harm, and instituted certain sacrifices to God, who, he declared, then appeared to him.— V. *Patrick on Exodus,* iii , 2.
(3) " The shell called Shankos, common to India, Africa, and the Mediterranean, and still used in many parts as a trumpet for blowing alarms or giving signals . it sends forth a deep and hollow sound."—*Pennant.*

And there, upon the mouldering tower,
Hath hung this sea-horn many an hour,
Ready to sound o'er land and sea
That dirge-note of the brave and free.

They came—his Chieftains at the call
Came slowly round, and with them all—
Alas! how few!—the worn remains
Of those who late o'er Kerman's plains
Went gaily prancing to the clash
Of Moorish zel and tymbalon,
Catching new hope from every flash
Of their long lances in the sun,
And, as their coursers charged the wind,
And the white ox-tails stream'd behind, (1)
Looking, as if the steeds they rode
Were wing'd, and every Chief a God!
How fallen, how alter'd now! how wan
Each scarr'd and faded visage shone,
As round the burning shrine they came;—
    How deadly was the glare it cast,
As mute they paused before the flame
    To light their torches as they pass'd!
'T was silence all—the youth hath plann'd
The duties of his soldier-band;
And each determined brow declares
His faithful Chieftains well know theirs.

But minutes speed—night gems the skies—
And oh, how soon, ye blessed eyes,
That look from heaven, ye may behold
Sights that will turn your star-fires cold!
Breathless with awe, impatience, hope,
The maiden sees the veteran group
Her litter silently prepare,
    And lay it at her trembling feet;—
And now the youth, with gentle care,
    Hath placed her in the shelter'd seat,
And press'd her hand—that lingering press
Of hands, that for the last time sever;
Of hearts, whose pulse of happiness,
    When that bold breaks, is dead for ever.
And yet to *her* this sad caress
Gives hope—so fondly hope can err!
'T was joy, she thought, joy's mute excess—
Their happy flight's dear harbinger;
'T was warmth—assurance—tenderness—
'T was any thing but leaving her.

"Haste, haste!" she cried, "the clouds grow dark,
But still, ere night, we'll reach the bark;
And by to-morrow's dawn—oh bliss!
    With thee upon the sun-bright deep,
Far off, I'll but remember this,
    As some dark vanish'd dream of sleep;
And thou——" but ah!—he answers not—
Good Heaven!—and does she go alone?
She now has reach'd that dismal spot,
    Where, some hours since, his voice's tone

Had come to soothe her fears and ills,
Sweet as the angel Israfil's, (2)
When every leaf on Eden's tree
Is trembling to his minstrelsy—
Yet now—oh, now, he is not nigh,—
    "Hafed! my Hafed!—if it be
Thy will, thy doom this night to die,
    Let me but stay to die with thee,
And I will bless thy loved name,
Till the last life-breath leave this frame.
Oh! let our lips, our cheeks be laid
But near each other while they fade;
Let us but mix our parting breaths,
And I can die ten thousand deaths!
You too, who hurry me away
So cruelly, one moment stay—
    Oh! stay—one moment is not much—
He yet may come—for *him* I pray—
Hafed! dear Hafed!—" all the way
In wild lamentings, that would touch
A heart of stone, she shriek'd his name
To the dark woods—no Hafed came:—
No—hapless pair—you've look'd your last:
Your hearts should both have broken then;
The dream is o'er—your doom is cast—
    You'll never meet on earth again!

Alas for him, who hears her cries!
    Still half-way down the steep he stands,
Watching with fix'd and feverish eyes
    The glimmer of those burning brands,
That down the rocks, with mournful ray,
Light all he loves on earth away!
Hopeless as they who, far at sea,
    By the cold moon have just consign'd
The corse of one, loved tenderly,
    To the bleak flood they leave behind;
And on the deck still lingering stay,
And long look back, with sad delay,
To watch the moonlight on the wave,
That ripples o'er that cheerless grave.

But see—he starts—what heard he then?
That dreadful shout!—across the glen
From the land-side it comes, and loud
Rings through the chasm; as if the crowd
Of fearful things that haunt that dell,
Its Gholes and Dives and shapes of hell,
Had all in one dread howl broke out,
So loud, so terrible that shout!
    "They come—the Moslems come!"—he cries,
His proud soul mounting to his eyes;—

(1) "The finest ornament for the horses is made of six
large flying tassels of long white hair, taken out of the
tails of wild oxen, that are to be found in some places of
the Indies."—*Thevenot.*

(2) "The angel Israfil, who has the most melodious
voice of all God's creatures."—*Sale.*

" Now, spirits of the Brave, who roam
Enfranchised through yon starry dome,
Rejoice—for souls of kindred fire
Are on the wing to join your choir!"
He said—and, light as bridegrooms bound
To their young loves, reclimb'd the steep
And gain'd the Shrine—his Chiefs stood round—
Their swords, as with instinctive leap,
Together, at that cry accurst,
Had from their sheaths, like sunbeams, burst.
And hark!—again—again—it rings ;
Near and more near its echoings
Peal through the chasm—oh! who that then
Had seen those listening warrior-men,
With their swords grasp'd, their eyes of flame
Turn'd on their Chief—could doubt the shame,
The indignant shame with which they thrill
To hear those shouts and yet stand still ?

He read their thoughts—they were his own—
  "What! while our arms can wield these blades,
Shall we die tamely? die alone?
  Without one victim to our shades,
One Moslem heart, where, buried deep,
The sabre from its toil may sleep?
No—God of Iran's burning skies!
Thou scorn'st the inglorious sacrifice.
No—though of all earth's hope bereft,
Life, swords, and vengeance still are left.
We'll make yon valley's reeking caves
Live in the awe-struck minds of men,
Till tyrants shudder, when their slaves
Tell of the Gheber's bloody glen.
Follow, brave hearts!—this pile remains
Our refuge still from life and chains ;
But his the best, the holiest bed,
Who sinks entomb'd in Moslem dead!"

Down the precipitous rocks they sprung,
While vigour, more than human, strung
Each arm and heart.—The exulting foe
Still through the dark defiles below,
Track'd by his torches' lurid fire,
  Wound slow, as through Golconda's vale (1)
The mighty serpent, in his ire,
  Glides on with glittering, deadly trail.
No torch the Ghebers need—so well
They know each mystery of the dell,
So oft have, in their wanderings,
Cross'd the wild race that round them dwell,
  The very tigers from their delves
Look out, and let them pass, as things
  Untamed and fearless like themselves !

There was a deep ravine, that lay
Yet darkling in the Moslem's way ;
Fit spot to make invaders rue
The many fallen before the few.
The torrents from that morning's sky
Had fill'd the narrow chasm breast-high

And, on each side, aloft and wild,
Huge cliffs and toppling crags were piled—
The guards with which young Freedom lines
The pathways to her mountain-shrines.
Here, at this pass, the scanty band
Of Iran's last avengers stand ;
Here wait, in silence like the dead,
And listen for the Moslem's tread
So anxiously, the carrion-bird
Above them flaps his wing unheard !

They come—that plunge into the water
Gives signal for the work of slaughter.
Now, Ghebers, now—if e'er your blades
  Had point or prowess, prove them now—
Woe to the file that foremost wades !
  They come—a falchion greets each brow,
And, as they tumble, trunk on trunk,
Beneath the gory waters sunk,
Still o'er their drowning bodies press
New victims, quick and numberless ;
Till scarce an arm in Hafed's hand,
  So fierce their toil, hath power to stir,
But listless from each crimson hand
  The sword hangs, clogg'd with massacre.
Never was horde of tyrants met
With bloodier welcome—never yet
To patriot vengeance hath the sword
More terrible libations pour'd !

All up the dreary long ravine,
By the red murky glimmer seen
Of half-quench'd brands, that o'er the flood
Lie scatter'd round and burn in blood,
What ruin glares! what carnage swims!
Heads, blazing turbans, quivering limbs,
Lost swords that, dropp'd from many a hand,
In that thick pool of slaughter stand ;—
Wretches who wading, half on fire
  From the toss'd brands that round them fly,
'Twixt flood and flame in shrieks expire ;—
  And some who, grasp'd by those that die,
Sink woundless with them, smother'd o'er
In their dead brethren's gushing gore!
But vainly hundreds, thousands bleed,
Still hundreds, thousands more succeed ;
Countless as towards some flame at night
The North's dark insects wing their flight,
And quench or perish in its light,
To this terrific spot they pour—
Till, bridged with Moslem bodies o'er,
It bears aloft their slippery tread,
And o'er the dying and the dead,
Tremendous causeway! on they pass,
Then, hapless Ghebers, then, alas,
What hope was left for you? for you,
Whose yet warm pile of sacrifice
Is smoking in their vengeful eyes ;—

(1) See Hoole upon the Story of Sinbad

Whose swords how keen, how fierce they
    knew,
And burn with shame to find how few.

Crush'd down by that vast multitude,
Some found their graves where first they stood;
While some with hardier struggle died,
And still fought on by Hafed's side,
Who, fronting to the foe, trod back
Towards the high towers his gory track;
And, as a lion swept away
    By sudden swell of Jordan's pride
From the wild covert where he lay, (1)
    Long battles with the o'erwhelming tide,
So fought he back with fierce delay,
And kept both foes and fate at bay.

But whither now? their track is lost,
    Their prey escaped—guide, torches gone—
By torrent-beds and labyrinths crost,
    The scatter'd crowd rush blindly on—
" Curse on those tardy lights that wind,"
They panting cry, " so far behind;
Oh for a bloodhound's precious scent,
To track the way the Gheber went!"
Vain wish—confusedly along
They rush, more desperate as more wrong:
Till, wilder'd by the far-off lights,
Yet glittering up those gloomy heights,
Their footing, mazed and lost, they miss,
And down the darkling precipice
Are dash'd into the deep abyss;
Or midway hang, impaled on rocks,
A banquet, yet alive, for flocks
Of ravening vultures—while the dell
Re-echoes with each horrible yell.

Those sounds—the last, to vengeance dear,
That e'er shall ring in Hafed's ear—
Now reach'd him, as aloft, alone,
Upon the steep way breathless thrown,
He lay beside his reeking blade,
    Resign'd, as if life's task were o'er,
Its last blood offering amply paid,
    And Iran's self could claim no more.
One only thought, one lingering beam
Now broke across his dizzy dream
Of pain and weariness—'t was she,
    His heart's pure planet, shining yet
Above the waste of memory,
    When all life's other lights were set.
And never to his mind before
Her image such enchantment wore.
It seem'd as if each thought that stain'd,
    Each fear that chill'd their loves, was past,
And not one cloud of earth remain'd
    Between him and her radiance cast;—

As if to charms, before so bright,
    New grace from other worlds was given,
And his soul saw her by the light
    Now breaking o'er itself from heaven!

A voice spoke near him—'t was the tone
Of a loved friend, the only one
Of all his warriors left with life
From that short night's tremendous strife.
" And must we then, my chief, die here?
Foes round us, and the Shrine so near!"
These words have roused the last remains
    Of life within him—" what! not yet
Beyond the reach of Moslem chains!"
    The thought could make even Death forget
His icy bondage—with a bound
He springs, all bleeding, from the ground,
And grasps his comrade's arm, now grown
Even feebler, heavier than his own,
And up the painful pathway leads,
Death gaining on each step he treads.
Speed them, thou God, who heard'st their vow
They mount—they bleed—oh save them now—
The crags are red they 've clamber'd o'er,
The rock-weed 's dripping with their gore;
Thy blade too, Hafed, false at length;
Now breaks beneath thy tottering strength!
Haste, haste—the voices of the foe
Come near and nearer from below—
One effort more—thank Heaven! 't is past,
They 've gain'd the topmost steep at last.
And now they touch the temple's walls,
Now Hafed sees the Fire divine—
When, lo!—his weak worn comrade falls
Dead on the threshold of the shrine.
" Alas, brave soul, too quickly fled!
    And must I leave thee withering here,
The sport of every ruffian's tread,
    The mark for every coward's spear?
No, by yon altar's sacred beams!"
He cries, and, with a strength that seems
Not of this world, uplifts the frame
Of the fallen Chief, and towards the flame
Bears him along;—with death-damp hand
    The corpse upon the pyre he lays,
Then lights the consecrated brand,
    And fires the pile, whose sudden blaze
Like lightning bursts o'er Oman's sea.
" Now, Freedom's God! I come to Thee,"
The youth exclaims, and with a smile
Of triumph vaulting on the pile,
In that last effort, ere the fires
Have harm'd one glorious limb, expires!

What shriek was that on Oman's tide?
    It came from yonder drifting bark,

<hr/>

(1) " In this thicket upon the banks of the Jordan several sorts of wild beasts are wont to harbour themselves, whose being washed out of the covert by the overflowings of the river gave occasion to that allusion of Jeremiah, *he shall come up like a lion from the swelling of Jordan*."— *Maundrell's Aleppo.*

That just hath caught upon her side
　The death-light—and again is dark.
It is the boat—ah, why delay'd?—
That bears the wretched Moslem maid;
Confided to the watchful care
Of a small veteran band, with whom
Their generous Chieftain would not share
　The secret of his final doom,
But hoped when Hinda, safe and free,
　Was render'd to her father's eyes,
Their pardon, full and prompt, would be
　The ransom of so dear a prize.—
Unconscious, thus, of Hafed's fate,
And proud to guard their beauteous freight,
Scarce had they clear'd the surfy waves
That foam around those frightful caves,
When the curst war-whoops, known so well,
Came echoing from the distant dell—
Sudden each oar, upheld and still,
　Hung dripping o'er the vessel's side,
And, driving at the current's will,
　They rock'd along the whispering tide;
While every eye, in mute dismay,
　Was toward that fatal mountain turn'd,
Where the dim altar's quivering ray
　As yet all lone and tranquil burn'd.

Oh! 't is not, Hinda, in the power
Of Fancy's most terrific touch
To paint thy pangs in that dread hour—
　Thy silent agony—'t was such
As those who feel could paint too well,
But none e'er felt and lived to tell!
'T was not alone the dreary state
Of a lorn spirit, crush'd by fate,
When, though no more remains to dread,
　The panic chill will not depart;—
When, though the inmate Hope be dead,
　Her ghost still haunts the mouldering heart;
No—pleasures, hopes, affections gone,
The wretch may bear, and yet live on,
Like things, within the cold rock found
Alive, when all 's congeal'd around.
But there 's a blank repose in this,
A calm stagnation, that were bliss
To the keen, burning, harrowing pain
Now felt through all thy breast and brain;—
That spasm of terror, mute, intense,
That breathless, agonised suspense,
From whose hot throb, whose deadly aching,
The heart hath no relief but breaking!

Calm is the wave—heaven's brilliant lights
　Reflected dance beneath the prow;—
Time was when, on such lovely nights,
　She who is there, so desolate now,
Could sit all cheerful, though alone,
　And ask no happier joy than seeing
That star-light o'er the waters thrown—

No joy but that, to make her blest,
　And the fresh, buoyant sense of Being,
Which bounds in youth's yet careless breast—
　Itself a star, not borrowing light,
But in its own glad essence bright.
How different now!—but, hark, again
The yell of havoc rings—brave men!
In vain, with beating hearts, ye stand
On the bark's edge—in vain each hand
Half draws the falchion from its sheath;
　All 's o'er—in rust your blades may lie:
He, at whose word they 've scatter'd death,
　Even now, this night, himself must die!
Well may ye look to yon dim tower,
And ask, and wondering guess what means
The battle-cry at this dead hour—
　Ah! she could tell you—she, who leans,
Unheeded there, pale, sunk, aghast,
With brow against the dew-cold mast;—
Too well she knows—her more than life,
Her soul's first idol and its last,
Lies bleeding in that murderous strife.

But see—what moves upon the height?—
Some signal!—'t is a torch's light.
　What bodes its solitary glare?
In gasping silence toward the Shrine
All eyes are turn'd—thine, Hinda, thine
　Fix their last fading life-beams there.
'T was but a moment—fierce and high
The death-pile blazed into the sky,
And far away, o'er rock and flood
　Its melancholy radiance sent;
While Hafed, like a vision stood
Reveal'd before the burning pyre,
Tall, shadowy, like a Spirit of Fire
　Shrined in its own grand element!
"'T is he!"—the shuddering maid exclaims—
　But, while she speaks, he 's seen no more;
High burst in air the funeral flames,
And Iran's hopes and hers are o'er!

One wild heart-broken shriek she gave;
　Then sprung, as if to reach that blaze,
Where still she fix'd her dying gaze,
And, gazing, sunk into the wave—
Deep, deep—where never care or pain
Shall reach her innocent heart again!

Farewell—farewell to thee, Araby's daughter!
　(Thus warbled a Peri beneath the dark sea,)
No pearl ever lay, under Oman's green waters,
　More pure in its shell than thy Spirit in thee.

Oh! fair as the sea-flower close to thee growing,
　How light was thy heart till Love's witchery came,
Like the wind of the south (1) o'er a summer lute
　　blowing,
And hush'd all its music, and wither'd its frame!

(1) " This wind (the Samoor) so softens the strings of

But long, upon Araby's green sunny highlands,
Shall maids and their loveis remember the doom
Of her, who lies sleeping among the Pearl Islands,
With nought but the sea-star (1) to light up her
    tomb

And still, when the merry date-season is burning,(2)
And calls to the palm-groves the young and the old,
The happiest there, from their pastime returning
At sunset, will weep when thy story is told.

The young village-maid when with flowers she
    dresses
Her dark flowing haii for some festival day,
Will think of thy fate till, neglecting her tresses,
She mournfully tui ns from the mirror away.

Nor shall Iran, beloved of her Hero! forget thee—
Though tyiants watch over her tears as they start,
Close, close by the side of that Hero she'll set thee,
Embalm'd in the innermost shrine of her heart.

Farewell—be it ours to embellish thy pillow
With everything beauteous that grows in the deep,
Each flower of the rock and each gem of the billow
Shall sweeten thy bed and illumine thy sleep.

Around thee shall glisten the loveliest amber
That ever the sorrowing sea-bird has wept; (3)
With many a shell, in whose hollow-wreathed
    chamber
We, Peris of Ocean, by moonlight have slept.

We'll dive where the gardens of coral lie darkling,
And plant all the rosiest stems at thy head;
We'll seek where the sands of the Casplan (4) are
    sparkling,
And gather their gold to strew over thy bed.

Farewell—farewell—until Pity's sweet fountain
Is lost in the hearts of the fair and the brave,
They'll weep for the Chieftain who died on that
    mountain,
They'll weep for the Maiden who sleeps in this
    wave.

THE singular placidity with which Fadladeen had
listened, during the latter part of this obnoxious

---

story, surprised the Princess and Feramorz exceedingly; and even inclined towards him the hearts of these unsuspicious young persons, who little knew the source of a complacency so marvellous. The tiuth was, he had been organising, for the last few days, a most notable plan of persecution against the poet, in consequence of some passages that had fallen from him on the second evening of recital—which appeared to this worthy Chamberlain to contain language and piinciples, for which nothing short of the summary criticism of the Chabuk (5) would be advisable. It was his intention, therefore, immediately on their arrival at Cashmere, to give information to the King of Bucharia of the very dangerous sentiments of his minstrel; and if, unfortunately, that monarch did not act with suitable vigour on the occasion, (that is, if he did not give the Chabuk to Feramorz, and a place to Fadladeen,) theie would be an end, he feared, of all legitimate government in Bucharia. He could not help, however, auguring better both for himself and the cause of potentates in general; and it was the pleasure aiising from these mingled anticipations that diffused such unusual satisfaction through his features, and made his eyes shine out, like poppies of the desert, over the wide and lifeless wilderness of that countenance.

Having decided upon the Poet's chastisement in this manner, he thought it but humanity to spare him the minor tortuies of criticism. Accordingly, when they assembled the following evening in the pavilion, and Lalla Rookh was expecting to see all the beauties of her bard melt away, one by one, in the acidity of criticism, like pearls in the cup of the Egyptian queen—he agreeably disappointed her, by meiely saying, with an ironical smile, that the merits of such a poem deserved to be tried at a much higher tribunal, and then suddenly passed off into a panegyric upon all Mussulman sovereigns, more particularly his august and Imperial master, Aurungzebe—the wisest and best of the descendants of Timur—who, among other great things he had done for mankind, had given to him, Fadladeen, the very profitable posts of Betel-carrier, and Taster of Sherbets to the Emperor, Chief Holder of the Girdle of Beautiful Forms, (6) and Grand Nazir, or Chamberlain of the Haram.

They were now not far from that Forbidden

---

lutes, that they can never be tuned while it lasts."—*Stephen's Persia.*

1) " One of the greatest curiosities found in the Persian Gulf is a fish which the English call Star-fish. It is circular, and at night very luminous, resembling the full moon surrounded by rays."—*Mirza Abu Taleb.*

(2) For a description of the merriment of the date-time, of their work, their dances, and their return home from the palm-groves at the end of Autumn with the fruits, see *Kempfer, Amœnitat. Exot.*

(3) Some naturalists have imagined that amber is a concretion of the tears of birds.—See *Trevoux, Chambers.*

(4) "The bay Kieselarke, which is otherwise cal'ed the Golden Bay, the sand whereof shines as fire."—*Struy.*

5) " The application of whips or rods."—*Dubois.*

(6) Kempfer mentions such an officer among the attendants of the King of Persia, and calls him " formæ corporis estimator." His business was, at stated periods, to measure the ladies of the Haram by a sort of regulation-girdle, whose limits it was not thought graceful to exceed. If any of them outgrew this standaid of shape, they were reduced by abstinence till they came within proper bounds.

River, (1) beyond which no pure Hindoo can pass; and were reposing for a time in the rich valley of Hussun Abdaul, which had always been a favourite resting-place of the Emperors in their annual migrations to Cashmere. Here often had the Light of the Faith, Jehanguire, been known to wander with his beloved and beautiful Nourmahal; and here would Lalla Rookh have been happy to remain for ever, giving up the throne of Bucharia and the world, for Feramorz and love in this sweet lonely valley. But the time was now fast approaching when she must see him no longer—or, what was still worse, behold him with eyes whose every look belonged to another; and there was a melancholy preciousness in these last moments, which made her heart cling to them as it would to life. During the latter part of the journey, indeed, she had sunk into a deep sadness, from which nothing but the presence of the young minstrel could make awake her. Like those lamps in tombs, which only light up when the air is admitted, it was only at his approach that her eyes became smiling and animated. But here, in this dear valley, every moment appeared an age of pleasure; she saw him all day, and was, therefore, all day happy—resembling, she often thought, that people of Zinge, (2) who attribute the unfading cheerfulness they enjoy to one genial star that rises nightly over their heads. (3)

The whole party, indeed, seemed in their liveliest mood during the few days they passed in this delightful solitude. The young attendants of the Princess, who were here allowed a much freer range than they could safely be indulged with in a less sequestered place, ran wild among the gardens and bounded through the meadows, lightly as young roes over the aromatic plains of Tibet. While Fadladeen, in addition to the spiritual comfort derived

by him from a pilgrimage to the tomb of the Saint from whom the valley is named, had also opportunities of indulging, in a small way, his taste for victims, by putting to death some hundreds of those unfortunate little lizards, (4) which all pious Mussulmans make it a point to kill;—taking for granted, that the manner in which the creature hangs its head is meant as a mimicry of the attitude in which the Faithful say their prayers.

About two miles from Hussun Abdaul were those Royal Gardens, (5) which had grown beautiful under the care of so many lovely eyes, and were beautiful still, though those eyes could see them no longer. This place, with its flowers and its holy silence, interrupted only by the dipping of the wings of birds in its marble basins, filled with the pure water of those hills, was to Lalla Rookh all that her heart could fancy of fragrance, coolness, and almost heavenly tranquillity. As the Prophet said of Damascus, "it was too delicious;" (6)—and here, in listening to the sweet voice of Feramorz, or reading in his eyes what yet he never dared to tell her, the most exquisite moments of her whole life were passed. One evening, when they had been talking of the Sultana Nourmahal, the Light of the Haram, (7) who had so often wandered among these flowers, and fed with her own hands, in those marble basins, the small shining fishes of which she was so fond, (8)— the youth, in order to delay the moment of separation, proposed to recite a short story, or rather rhapsody, of which this adored Sultana was the heroine. It related, he said, to the reconcilement of a sort of lovers' quarrel which took place between her and the Emperor during a Feast of Roses at Cashmere; and would remind the Princess of that difference between Haroun-al-Raschid and his fair mistress Marida, (9) which was so happily made up by the soft strains of

(1) The Attock.

"Akbar on his way ordered a fort to be built upon the Nilab, which he called Attock, which means in the Indian language Forbidden, for, by the superstition of the Hindoos, it was held unlawful to cross that river."—*Dow's Hindostan.*

(2) "The inhabitants of this country (Zinge) are never afflicted with sadness or melancholy; on this subject the Sheikh *Abu-al-kheir-Azhari* has the following distich —

'Who is the man without care or sorrow, tell that I may rub my hand to him.'

'(Behold) the Zingians, without care or sorrow, frolicksome with lipsiness and mirth.'

"The philosophers have discovered that the cause of this cheerfulness proceeds from the influence of the star Soheil, or Canopus, which rises over them every night'—*Extract from a Geographical Persian Manuscript called Heft Aklim, or the Seven Climates, translated by W. Ouseley, Esq.*

(3) The star Soheil, or Canopus.

(4) "The lizard Stellio The Arabs call it Hardun The Turks kill it, for they imagine that by declining the head it mimics them when they say their prayers."—*Hasselquist.*

(5) For these particulars respecting Hussun Abdaul I am indebted to the very interesting Introduction of Mr. Elphinstone's work upon Caubul.

(6 "As you enter at that Bazar, without the gate of Damascus, you see the Green Mosque, so called because it hath a steeple faced with green glazed bricks, which render it very resplendent, it is covered at top with a pavilion of the same stuff. The Turks say this mosque was made in that place, because Mahomet, being come so far, would not enter the town, saying it was too delicious."— *Thevenot.* This reminds one of the following pretty passage in Isaac Walton —"When I sat last on this primrose bank, and looked down these meadows, I thought of them as Charles the Emperor did of the city of Florence, 'that they were too pleasant to be looked on, but only on holidays.'"

(7 Nourmahal signifies Light of the Haram. She was afterwards called Nourjehan, or the Light of the World.

(8 See note (7), p. 372.

(9) "Haroun Al Raschid, cinquième Calife des Abassides s'étant un jour brouillé avec une de ses maîtresses nommée Maridah, qu'il aimoit cependant jusqu'à l'excès, et cette mesintelligence ayant déjà duré quelque temps, commença à s'ennuyer. Giafar Barmaki, son favori, qui s'en aperçut, commanda à Abbas Ben Ali af excellent poète

the musician, Moussali. As the story was chiefly to be told in song, and Feramorz had unluckily forgotten his own lute in the valley, he borrowed the vina of Lalla Rookh's little Persian slave, and thus began:—

THE LIGHT OF THE HARAM.

Who has not heard of the Vale of Cashmere,
  With its roses the brightest that earth ever gave, (1)
Its temples, and grottos, and fountains as clear
  As the love-lighted eyes that hang over their wave?

Oh! to see it at sunset—when warm o'er the Lake
  Its splendour at parting a summer eve throws,
Like a bride, full of blushes, when lingering to take
  A last look of her mirror at night ere she goes!—
When the shrines through the foliage are gleaming
    half shown,
And each hallows the hour by some rites of its own.
Here the music of prayer from a minaret swells,
  Here the Magian his urn, full of perfume, is swinging,
And here, at the altar, a zone of sweet bells
  Round the waist of some fair Indian dancer is ringing. (2)
Or to see it by moonlight—when mellowly shines
The light o'er its palaces, gardens, and shrines;
When the water-falls gleam, like a quick fall of stars,
And the nightingale's hymn from the Isle of Chenars
Is broken by laughs and light echoes of feet
From the cool shining walks where the young
    people meet.—
Or at morn, when the magic of daylight awakes
A new wonder each minute, as slowly it breaks,
Hills, cupolas, fountains, call'd forth every one
Out of darkness, as if but just born of the Sun.
When the Spirit of Fragrance is up with the day,
From his Haram of night-flowers stealing away;
And the wind, full of wantonness, woos like a lover
The young aspen-trees, (3) till they tremble all
    over.
When the East is as warm as the light of first hopes,
  And Day, with his banner of radiance unfurl'd,
Shines in through the mountainous portal (4) that
    opes,
  Sublime, from that Valley of Bliss to the world!

But never yet, by night or day,
In dew of Spring or Summer's ray,
Did the sweet Valley shine so gay
As now it shines—all love and light,
Visions by day and feasts by night!
A happier smile illumes each brow,
  With quicker spread each heart uncloses,
And all is ecstasy—for now
  The Valley holds its Feast of Roses, (5)
The joyous time, when pleasures pour
Profusely round, and, in their shower,
Hearts open, like the Season's Rose—
  The floweret of a hundred leaves, (6)
Expanding while the dew-fall flows,
  And every leaf its balm receives.

'Twas when the hour of evening came
Upon the Lake, serene and cool,
When Day had hid his sultry flame
  Behind the palms of Baramoule, 7
When maids began to lift their heads,
Refresh'd from their embroider'd beds,
Where they had slept the sun away,
And waked to moonlight and to play.
All were abroad—the busiest hive
On Bela's (8) hills is less alive,
When saffron-beds are full in flower,
Than look'd the Valley in that hour.
A thousand restless torches play'd
Through every grove and island shade;
A thousand sparkling lamps were set
On every dome and minaret;
And fields and pathways, far and near,
Were lighted by a blaze so clear,
That you could see, in wandering round,
The smallest rose-leaf on the ground.
Yet did the maids and matrons leave
Their veils at home, that brilliant eve,
And there were glancing eyes about,
And cheeks, that would not dare shine out
In open day, but thought they might
Look lovely then, because 't was night.
And all were free, and wandering,
  And all exclaim'd to all they met,
That never did the Summer bring
  So gay a Feast of Roses yet;

de ce temps-là, de composer quelques vers sur le sujet de cette brouillerie. Ce poëte exécuta l'ordre de Giafar, qui fit chanter ces vers par Moussali en presence du calife, et ce prince fut tellement touché de la tendresse des vers du poëte et de la douceur de la voix du musicien qu'il alla aussitôt trouver Maridah, et fit sa paix avec elle."—*D'Herbelot*.

(1 "The rose of Kashmire for its brilliancy and delicacy of odour has long been proverbial in the East."—*Forster*.

(2) "Tied round her waist the zone of bells, that sounded with ravishing melody."—*Song of Jayadeva*.

3) "The little isles in the Lake of Cachemire are set

with arbours and large-leaved aspen-trees, slender and tall."—*Bernier*.

(4) The Tuckt Suliman, the name bestowed by the Mahommetans on this hill, forms one side of a grand portal to the Lake."—*Forster*.

(5) "The Feast of Roses continues the whole time of their remaining in bloom."—*See Pietro de la Valle*.

6) "Gul sad berk, the Rose of a hundred leaves. I believe a particular species."—*Ouseley*.

(7 *Bernier*.

(8) A place mentioned in the Toozek Jehangeery, or Memoirs of Jehanguire, where there is an account of the beds of saffron-flowers about Cashmere.

The moon had never shed a light
  So clear as that which bless'd them there,
The roses ne'er shone half so bright,
  Nor they themselves look'd half so fair

And what a wilderness of flowers!
It seem'd as though from all the bowers
And fairest fields of all the year,
The mingled spoil were scatter'd here.
The Lake, too, like a garden breathes,
  With the rich buds that o'er it lie—
As if a shower of fairy wreaths
  Had fallen upon it from the sky!
And then the sounds of joy—the beat
Of tabors and of dancing feet;—
The minaret-crier's chaunt of glee
Sung from his lighted gallery, (1)
And answer'd by a ziraleet
From neighbouring Haram, wild and sweet,
The merry laughter, echoing
From gardens, where the silken swing (2
Wafts some delighted girl above
The top leaves of the orange-grove,
Or, from those infant groups at play
Among the tents (3) that line the way,
Flinging, unawed by slave or mother,
Handfuls of roses at each other.—
Then, the sounds from the Lake—the low whisper-
    ing in boats,
  As they shoot through the moonlight,—the dip-
    ping of oars,
And the wild airy warbling that every where floats,
  Through the groves, round the islands, as if all
    the shores,
Like those of Kathay, utter'd music, and gave
An answer in song to the kiss of each wave. (4)
But the gentlest of all are those sounds, full of feel-
    ing,
That soft from the lute of some lover are stealing—
Some lover, who knows all the heart-touching power
Of a lute and a sigh in this magical hour.
Oh! best of delights as it every where is
To be near the loved One—what a rapture is his
Who in moonlight and music thus sweetly may glide
O'er the Lake of Cashmere, with that One by his
    side!

If woman can make the worst wilderness dear,
Think, think what a Heaven she must make of
    Cashmere!

So felt the magnificent Son of Acbar, (5)
When from power and pomp and the trophies of war
He flew to that Valley, forgetting them all,
With the Light of the Haram, his young Nour-
    mahal.
When free and uncrown'd as the Conqueror roved
By the banks of that Lake, with his only beloved,
He saw, in the wreaths she would playfully snatch,
From the hedges, a glory his crown could not match
And preferr'd in his heart the least ringlet that curl'd
Down her exquisite neck to the throne of the world.

There's a beauty, for ever unchangingly bright,
Like the long sunny lapse of a summer-day's light,
Shining on, shining on, by no shadow made tender,
Till Love falls asleep in its sameness of splendour.
This *was* not the beauty—oh, nothing like this,
That to young Nourmahal gave such magic of bliss!
But that loveliness, ever in motion, which plays
Like the light upon Autumn's soft shadowy days,
Now here and now there, giving warmth as it flies
From the lip to the cheek, from the cheek to the eyes,
Now melting in mist and now breaking in gleams,
Like the glimpses a saint hath of Heaven in his
    dreams.
When pensive, it seem'd as if that very grace,
That charm of all others, was born with her face!
And when angry—for even in the tranquillest climes
Light breezes will ruffle the blossoms sometimes—
The short passing anger but seem'd to awaken
New beauty, like flowers that are sweetest when
    shaken.
If tenderness touch'd her, the dark of her eye
At once took a darker, a heavenlier dye,
From the depth of whose shadow, like holy revealings
From inner most shrines, came the light of her feelings
Then her mirth—oh! 'twas sportive as ever took
    wing
From the heart with a burst, like the wild-bird in
    Spring;
Illumed by a wit that would fascinate sages,
Yet playful as Peris just loosed from their cages. (6

1) " It is the custom among the women to employ the
Maazeen to chaunt from the gallery of the nearest mi-
naret, which on that occasion is illuminated, and the
women assembled at the house respond at intervals with
a ziraleet or joyous chorus   Russell.

(2 " The swing is a favourite pastime in the East, as
promoting a circulation of air, extremely refreshing in
those sultry climates." —Richardson.

" The swings are adorned with festoons This pastime
is accompanied with music of voices and of instruments,
hired by the masters of the swings " —Thevenot

(3) " At the keeping of the Feast of Roses we beheld an
infinite number of tents pitched, with such a crowd of men,
women, boys, and girls, with music, dances," etc Herbert.

(4) " An old commentator of the Chou-King says, the
ancients having remarked that a current of water made
some of the stones near its banks send forth a sound, they
detached some of them, and, being charmed with the de-
lightful sound they emitted, constructed King or musical
instruments of them." —Grosier.

This miraculous quality has been attributed also to the
shore of Attica. " Hujus littus, ait Capella, concentum
musicum illisis terræ undis reddere, quod propter tantam
eruditionis vim puto dictum."—Ludov. Vives in Augusti
de Civitat. Dei, lib. xviii, c 8.

(5) Jehanguire was the son of the Great Acbar.

(6) In the wars of the Dives with the Peris, whenever
the former took the latter prisoners, they shut them up

While her laugh, full of life, without any control
But the sweet one of gracefulness, rung from her soul
And where it most sparkled no glance could discover,
In lip, cheek, or eyes, for she brighten'd all over—
Like any fair lake that the breeze is upon,
When it breaks into dimples and laughs in the sun.
Such, such were the peerless enchantments, that gave
Nourmahal the proud Lord of the East for her slave ·
And though bright was his Haram—a living parterre
Of the flowers (1) of this planet—though treasures
                   were there,
For which Soliman's self might have given all the store
That the navy from Ophir e'er wing'd to his shore,
Yet dim before *her* were the smiles of them all,
And the Light of his Haram was young Nourmahal

But where is she now, this n ght of Jov,
When bliss is every heart's employ?—
When all around her is so bright,
    So like the visions of a trance,
    That one might think, who came by chance,
Into the vale this happy night,
He saw that City of Delight (2)
In Fairy-land, whose streets and towers
Are made of gems and light and flowers!
Where is the loved Sultana? where,
When mirth brings out the young and fair,
Does she, the fairest, hide her brow,
In melancholy stillness now?

Alas!—how light a cause may move
Dissension between hearts that love!
Hearts that the world in vain had tried,
And sorrow but more closely tied;
That stood the storm, when waves were rough,
Yet in a sunny hour fall off,
Like ships that have gone down at sea,
When heaven was all tranquillity!
A something, light as air—a look,
    A word unkind or wrongly taken—
Oh! love, that tempests never shook,
    A breath, a touch like this, hath shaken.
And ruder words will soon rush in
To spread the breach that words begin ;
And eyes forget the gentle ray
They wore in courtship's smiling day ;
And voices lose the tone that shed
A tenderness round all they said ;
Till fast declining, one by one,
The sweetnesses of love are gone,

And hearts, so lately mingled, seem
Like broken clouds—or like the stream,
That smiling left the mountain's brow
    As though its waters ne'er could sever,
Yet, ere it reach the plain below,
    Breaks into floods, that part for ever.

Oh, you, that have the charge of Love,
Keep him in rosy bondage bound,
As in the Fields of Bliss above
    He sits, with flowerets fetter'd round ;—(3)
Loose not a tie that round him clings,
Nor ever let him use his wings ;
For even an hour, a minute's flight
Will rob the plumes of half their light.
Like that celestial bird—whose nest
    If found beneath far Eastern skies—
Whose wings, though radiant when at rest,
    Lose all their glory when he flies !(4)

Some difference, of this dangerous kind—
By which, though light, the links that bind
The fondest hearts may soon be riven ;
Some shadow in Love's summer heaven,
Which, though a fleecy speck at first,
May yet in awful thunder burst ;—
Such cloud it is, that now hangs over
The heart of the Imperial Lover,
And far hath banish'd from his sight
His Nourmahal, his Haram's Light !
Hence is it, on this happy night,
When Pleasure through the fields and groves
Has let loose all her world of loves,
And every heart has found its own,
He wanders, joyless and alone,
And weary, as that bird of Thrace
Whose pinion knows no resting-place. (5)

In vain the loveliest cheeks and eyes
This Eden of the Earth supplies
    Come crowding round—the cheeks are
        pale,
The eyes are dim ;—though rich the spot
With every flower this earth has got,
    What is it to the nightingale,
If there his darling rose is not? (6)
In vain the Valley's smiling throng
Worship him, as he moves along ;
He heeds them not—one smile of hers
Is worth a world of worshippers.

in iron cages, and hung them on the highest trees. Here
they were visited by their companions, who brought them
the choicest odours."—*Richardson.*

(1 In the Malay language the same word signifies women
and flowers.   (2) The capital of Shadukiam.
(3) See the representation of the Eastern Cupid, pinion-
ed closely round with wreaths of flowers, in *Picart's Céré-
monies Religieuses.*
(4) "Among the birds of Tonquin is a species of gold-
finch, which sings so melodiously that it is called the

Celestial Bird. Its wings, when it is perched, appear
variegated with beautiful colours, but when it flies they
lose all their splendour."—*Grosier.*
5) "As these birds on the Bosphorus are never known
to rest, they are called by the French 'les âmes dam-
nées.' "—*Dallou ay.*
(6 "You may place a hundred handfuls of fragrant
herbs and flowers before the nightingale, yet he wishes
not, in his constant heart, for more than the sweet breath
of h s beloved rose."—*Jami*

They but the Star's adorers are,
She is the Heaven that lights the Star!

Hence is it, too, that Nourmahal,
    Amid the luxuries of this hour,
Far from the joyous festival,
    Sits in her own sequester'd bower,
With no one near, to soothe or aid,
But that inspired and wondrous maid,
Namouna, the Enchantress;—one,
O'er whom his race the golden sun
For unremember'd years has run,
Yet never saw her blooming brow
Younger or fairer than 'tis now.
Nay, rather—as the west wind's sigh
Freshens the flower it passes by—
Time's wing but seem'd, in stealing o'er
To leave her lovelier than before.
Yet on her smiles a sadness hung,
And when, as oft, she spoke or sung
Of other worlds, there came a light
From her dark eyes so strangely bright,
That all believed nor man nor earth
Were conscious of Namouna's birth!
All spells and talismans she knew,
    From the great Mantra, (1) which around
The Air's sublimer Spirits drew,
    To the gold gems (2) of Afric, bound
Upon the wandering Arab's arm,
To keep him from the Siltim's (3) harm.
And she had pledged her powerful art—
Pledged it with all the zeal and heart
Of one who knew, though high her sphere,
What 't was to lose a love so dear—
To find some spell that should recall
Her Selim's (4) smile to Nourmahal!

'T was midnight — through the lattice, wreathed
With woodbine, many a perfume breathed
From plants that wake when others sleep,
From timid jasmine buds, that keep
Their odour to themselves all day,
But, when the sun-light dies away,
Let the delicious secret out
To every breeze that roams about;—

When thus Namouna:—"'Tis the hour
That scatters spells on herb and flower,
And garlands might be gather'd now,
That, twined around the sleeper's brow,
Would make him dream of such delights,
Such miracles and dazzling sights,
As Genii of the Sun behold,
At evening, from their tents of gold
Upon the horizon—where they play
Till twilight comes, and, ray by ray,
Their sunny mansions melt away.
Now, too, a chaplet might be wreathed
Of buds o'er which the moon has breathed,
Which worn by her, whose love has stray'd,
    Might bring some Peri from the skies,
Some sprite whose very soul is made
    Of flowerets' breath and lovers' sighs,
And who might tell ——"
                            "For me, for me,"
Cried Nourmahal impatiently—
" Oh! twine that wreath for me to-night."
Then, rapidly, with foot as light
As the young musk-roe's, out she flew
To cull each shining leaf that grew
Beneath the moonlight's hallowing beams,
For this enchanted Wreath of Dreams.
Anemones and Seas of Gold, (5)
    And new-blown lilies of the river,
And those sweet flowerets, that unfold
    Their buds on Camadeva's quiver;— (6)
The tube-rose, with her silvery light,
    That in the Gardens of Malay
Is call'd the Mistress of the Night, (7)
So like a bride, scented and bright,
    She comes out when the sun 's away;—
Amaranths, such as crown the maids
That wander through Zamara's shades;— (8)
And the white moon-flower, as it shows,
On Serendib's high crags, to those
Who near the isle at evening sail,
Scenting her clove-trees in the gale;
In short, all flowerets and all plants,
    From the divine Amrita tree, (9)
That blesses heaven's inhabitants
    With fruits of immortality,
Down to the basil tuft, (10) that waves

1 " He is said to have found the great *Mantra*, spell or talisman, through which he ruled over the elements and spirits of all denominations."—*Wilford.*

2) " The gold jewels of Jinnie, called by the Arabs El Herrez, from the supposed charm they contain."*Jackson.*

(3) " A demon, supposed to haunt woods, etc., in a human shape."—*Richardson.*

(4) The name of Jehanguire before his accession to the throne.

(5) " Hemasagara, or the Sea of Gold, with flowers of the brightest gold colour."—*Sir W. Jones.*

(6) " This tree (the Nagacesara) is one of the most delightful on earth, and the delicious odour of its blossoms justly gives them a place in the quiver of Camadeva, or the God of Love."—*Id.*

(7 "The Malayans style the tube-rose (Polianthes tuberosa Sandal Malam, or the Mistress of the Night." *Pennant.*

(8) The people of the Batta country in Sumatra (of which Zamara is one of the ancient names), " when not engaged in war, lead an idle inactive life, passing the day in playing on a kind of flute, crowned with garlands of flowers, among which the globe-amaranthus, a native of the country, mostly prevails." —*Marsden.*

(9) The largest and richest sort (of the Jambu or roseapple) is called Amrita, or immortal, and the mythologists of Tibet apply the same word to a celestial tree, bearing ambrosial fruit."—*Sir W. Jones.*

(10) Sweet basil, called Rayhan in Persia, and generally found in churchyards.

" The women in Egypt go, at least two days in the week,

Its fragrant blossom over graves,
    And to the humble rosemary,
Whose sweets so thanklessly are shed
To scent the desert(1) and the dead:—
All in that garden bloom, and all
Are gather'd by young Nourmahal,
Who heaps her baskets with the flowers
    And leaves, till they can hold no more,
Then to Namouna flies, and showers
    Upon her lap the shining store.

With what delight the Enchantress views
So many buds, bathed with the dews
And beams of that bless'd hour!—her glance
    Spoke something past all mortal pleasures,
As, in a kind of holy trance,
    She hung above those fragrant treasures,
Bending to drink their balmy airs,
As if she mix'd her soul with theirs.
And 't was, indeed, the perfume shed
From flowers and scented flame, that fed
Her charmed life—for none had e'er
Beheld her taste of mortal fare,
Nor ever in aught earthly dip,
But the morn's dew, her roseate lip.
Fill'd with the cool inspiring smell,
The Enchantress now begins her spell,
Thus singing as she winds and weaves
In mystic form the glittering leaves:—

I know where the winged visions dwell
    That around the night-bed play;
I know each herb and floweret's bell,
    Where they hide their wings by day.
        Then hasten we, maid,
        To twine our braid,
To-morrow the dreams and flowers will fade.

The image of love, that nightly flies
    To visit the bashful maid,
Steals from the jasmine flower, that sighs
    Its soul, like her, in the shade.
The dream of a future, happier hour,
    That alights on misery's brow,

Springs out of the silvery almond-flower,
    That blooms on a leafless bough. 2)
        Then hasten we, maid,
        To twine our braid,
To-morrow the dreams and flowers will fade.

The visions, that oft to worldly eyes
    The glitter of mines unfold,
Inhabit the mountain-herb, (3) that dyes
    The tooth of the fawn like gold.
The phantom shapes—oh touch not them—
    That appal the murderer's sight,
Lurk in the fleshly mandrake's stem,
    That shrieks, when pluck'd at night!
        Then hasten we, maid,
        To twine our braid,
To-morrow the dreams and flowers will fade.

The dream of the injured patient mind,
    That smiles at the wrongs of men,
Is found in the bruised and wounded rind
    Of the cinnamon, sweetest then.
        Then hasten we, maid,
        To twine our braid,
To-morrow the dreams and flowers will fade.

No sooner was the flowery crown
Placed on her head, than sleep came down,
Gently as nights of Summer fall,
Upon the lids of Nourmahal;—
And, suddenly, a tuneful breeze,
As full of small rich harmonies
As ever wind, that o'er the tents
Of Azab (4) blew, was full of scents,
Steals on her ear, and floats and swells,
Like the first air of morning creeping
Into those wreathy Red-Sea shells,
    Where Love himself, of old, lay sleeping, 5
And now a Spirit form'd, 't would seem,
    Of music and of light—so fair,
So brilliantly his features beam,
    And such a sound is in the air
Of sweetness when he waves his wings—
Hovers around her, and thus sings.—

to pray and weep at the sepulchres of the dead, and the custom then is to throw upon the tombs a sort of herb, which the Arabs call *rihan*, and which is our sweet basil." —*Maillet*, Lett. 10.

1) "In the Great Desert are found many stalks of lavender and rosemary." —*Asiat. Res.*

(2) "The almond-tree, with white flowers, blossoms on the bare branches." —*Hasselquist.*

(3) An herb on Mount Libanus, which is said to communicate a yellow golden hue to the teeth of the goats and other animals that graze upon it. *Niebuhr* thinks this may be the herb which the Eastern alchymists look to as a means of making gold. "Most of those alchymical enthusiasts think themselves sure of success, if they could but find out the herb, which gilds the teeth and gives a yellow colour to the flesh of the sheep

that eat it. Even the oil of this plant must be of a golden colour. It is called *Haschischat ed dab.*"

Father Jerom Dandini, however, asserts that the teeth of the goats at Mount Libanus are of a *silver* colour, and adds, "this confirms me in that which I observed in Candia to wit, that the animals that live on Mount Ida eat a certain herb, which renders their teeth of a golden colour, which, according to my judgment, cannot otherwise proceed than from the mines which are under ground." —*Dandini, Voyage to Mount Libanus.*

(4) The myrrh country.

(5) "This idea of deities living in shells was not unknown to the Greeks, who represent the young Nerites, one of the Cupids, as living in shells on the shores of the Red Sea."—*Wilford.*

From Chindara's (1) warbling fount I come,
Call'd by that moonlight garland's spell,
From Chindara's fount, my fairy home,
Where in music, morn and night, I dwell.
Where lutes in the air are heard about,
And voices are singing the whole day long,
And every sigh the heart breathes out
Is turn'd, as it leaves the lips, to song!
  Hither I come
  From my fairy home,
And if there's a magic in Music's strain,
  I swear by the breath
  Of that moonlight wreath,
Thy Lover shall sigh at thy feet again.

For mine is the lay that lightly floats,
And mine are the murmuring dying notes,
That fall as soft as snow on the sea,
And melt in the heart as instantly :—
And the passionate strain that, deeply going,
Refines the bosom it trembles through,
As the musk-wind, over the water blowing,
Ruffles the wave, but sweetens it too.

Mine is the charm, whose mystic sway
The Spirits of past Delight obey ;—
Let but the tuneful talisman sound,
And they come, like Genii, hovering round.
And mine is the gentle song that bears
  From soul to soul, the wishes of love,
As a bird, that wafts through genial airs
  The cinnamon-seed from grove to grove. (2)

'T is I that mingle in one sweet measure
The past, the present, and future of pleasure; (3)
When Memory links the tone that is gone
  With the blissful tone that's still in the ear;
And Hope, from a heavenly note flies on
  To a note more heavenly still that is near.

The warrior's heart, when touch'd by me,
Can as downy soft and as yielding be
As his own white plume, that high amid death
Through the field has shone—yet moves with a
And, oh, how the eyes of Beauty glisten, [breath!
  When Music has reach'd her inward soul,
Like the silent stars, that wink and listen
  While Heaven's eternal melodies roll.
    So, hither I come
    From my fairy home,
  And if there's a magic in Music's strain
    I swear by the breath
    Of that moonlight wreath,
  Thy lover shall sigh at thy feet again.

'T is dawn—at least that earlier dawn,
Whose glimpses are again withdrawn, (4)
As if the morn had waked, and then
Shut close her lids of light again.
And Nourmahal is up, and trying
The wonders of her lute, whose strings—
Oh, bliss !—now murmur like the sighing
From that ambrosial Spirit's wings.
And then, her voice—'t is more than human—
Never, till now, had it been given
To lips of any mortal woman
To utter notes so fresh from heaven,
Sweet as the breath of angel sighs,
  When angel sighs are most divine.—
" Oh! let it last till night," she cries,
  " And he is more than ever mine."
And hourly she renews the lay,
So fearful lest its heavenly sweetness
Should, ere the evening, fade away—
  For things so heavenly have such fleetness!
But, far from fading, it but grows
Richer, diviner as it flows;
Till rapt she dwells on every string,
And pours again each sound along,

(1 " A fabulous fountain, where instruments are said
to be constantly playing." —Richardson.

(2) " The Pompadour pigeon is the species, which, by
carrying the fruit of the cinnamon to different places, is
a great disseminator of this valuable tree."—See Brown's
Illustr., Tab. 19.

(3 "Whenever our pleasure arises from a succession
of sounds, it is a perception of a complicated nature, made
up of a sensation of the present sound or note, and an
idea or remembrance of the foregoing, while their mix-
ture and concurrence produce such a mysterious delight,
as neither could have produced alone. And it is often
heightened by an anticipation of the succeeding notes.
Thus Sense, Memory, and Imagination, are conjunctively
employed." — Gerrard on Taste.

This is exactly the Epicurean theory of Pleasure, as
explained by Cicero —"Quocirca corpus gaudere tamdiu,
dum præsentem sentiret voluptatem : animum et præsen-
tem percipere pariter cum corpore et prospicere venien-
tem, nec præteritam præterfluere sinere."

Madame de Staël accounts upon the same principle for

the gratification we derive from rhyme. — "Elle est
l'image de l'espérance et du souvenir. Un son nous fait
desirer celui qui doit lui répondre, et quand le second
retentit il nous rappelle celui qui vient de nous échap-
per."

(4) "The Persians have two mornings, the Soobhi Kazim
and the Soobhi Sadig, the false and the real day-break.
They account for this phenomenon in a most whimsical
manner. They say that as the sun rises from behind the
Kohi Qaf (Mount Caucasus), it passes a hole perforated
through that mountain, and that darting its rays through
it, it is the cause of the Soobhi Kazim, or this temporary
appearance of day-break. As it ascends, the earth is
again veiled in darkness, until the sun rises above the
mountain, and brings with it the Soobhi Sadig, or real
morning."—Scott Waring. He thinks Milton may allude
to this, when he says—

  " Ere the blabbing Eastern scout,
  The nice morn on the Indian steep
  From her cabin d loop-hole peep

Like echo, lost and languishing,
In love with her own wondrous song.

That evening, (trusting that his soul
  Might be from haunting love released
By mirth, by music, and the bowl,
  The Imperial Selim held a feast
In his magnificent Shalimar:—(1)
In whose saloons, when the first star
Of evening o'er the waters trembled,
The Valley's loveliest all assembled;
All the bright creatures that, like dreams,
Glide through its foliage, and drink beams
Of beauty from its founts and streams;(2)
And all those wandering minstrel-maids,
Who leave—how can they leave?—the shades
Of that dear Valley, and are found
  Singing in gardens of the South(3)
Those songs that ne'er so sweetly sound
  As from a young Cashmerian's mouth.

There, too, the Haram's inmates smile;—
  Maids from the West, with sun-bright hair,
And from the Garden of the Nile,
  Delicate as the roses there;—(4)
Daughters of Love from Cyprus' rocks,
With Paphian diamonds in their locks;—(5)
Light Peri forms, such as there are
On the gold meads of Candahar;(6)
And they, before whose sleepy eyes,
  In their own bright Kathian bowers,
Sparkle such rainbow butterflies,
  That they might fancy the rich flowers,

That round them in the sun lay sighing,
Had been by magic all set flying. (7)

Every thing young, every thing fair
From East and West is blushing there,
Except—except—oh, Nourmahal!
Thou loveliest, dearest of them all,
The one, whose smile shone out alone,
Amidst a world the only one;
Whose light, among so many lights,
Was like that star on starry nights,
The seaman singles from the sky,
To steer his bark for ever by!
Thou wert not there—so Selim thought,
  And every thing seem'd drear without thee,
But, ah! thou wert, thou wert—and brought
  Thy charm of song all fresh about thee.
Mingling unnoticed with a band
Of lutanists from many a land,
And veil'd by such a mask as shades
The features of young Arab maids—(8)
A mask that leaves but one eye free,
To do its best in witchery—
  She roved, with beating heart, around,
  And waited, trembling, for the minute,
When she might try if still the sound
  Of her loved lute had magic in it.

The board was spread with fruits and wine;
With grapes of gold, like those that shine
On Casbin's hills;(9)— pomegranates full
  Of melting sweetness, and the pears,
And sunniest apples (10) that Caubul
  In all its thousand gardens (11) bears;—

(1) "In the centre of the plain, as it approaches the Lake, one of the Delhi Emperors, I believe Shah Jehan, constructed a spacious garden called the Shalimar, which is abundantly stored with fruit-trees and flowering shrubs. Some of the rivulets which intersect the plain are led into a canal at the back of the garden, and flowing through its centre, or occasionally thrown into a variety of waterworks, compose the chief beauty of the Shalimar. To decorate this spot the Mogul Princes of India have displayed an equal magnificence and taste; especially Jehan Ghee, who, with the enchanting Noor Mahl, made Kashmire his usual residence during the summer months. On arches thrown over the canal are erected, at equal distances, four or five suites of apartments, each consisting of a saloon, with four rooms at the angles, where the followers of the court attend, and the servants prepare sherbets, coffee, and the hookah. The frame of the doors of the principal saloon is composed of pieces of a stone of a black colour, streaked with yellow lines, and of a closer grain and higher polish than porphyry. They were taken, it is said, from a Hindoo temple, by one of the Mogul princes, and are esteemed of great value."—Forster.

(2 "The waters of Cachemir are the more renowned from its being supposed that the Cachemirians are indebted for their beauty to them."—Ali Yezdi.

(3) "From him I received the following little Gazzel, or Love Song, the notes of which he committed to paper from the voice of one of those singing girls of Cashmere,

who wander from that delightful valley over the various parts of India." — Persian Miscellanies.

(4) "The roses of the Jinan Nile, or Garden of the Nile (attached to the Emperor of Marocco's palace), are unequalled, and matrasses are made of their leaves for the men of rank to recline upon."—Jackson.

5) "On the side of a mountain near Paphos there is a cavern which produces the most beautiful rock-crystal. On account of its brilliancy it has been called the Paphian diamond."—Mariti.

(6) "There is a part of Candahar, called Peria, or Fairy Land." — Thevenot. · In some of those countries to the north of India vegetable gold is supposed to be produced.

(7) "These are the butterflies which are called in the Chinese language Flying Leaves. Some of them have such shining colours, and are so variegated, that they may be called flying flowers; and indeed they are always produced in the finest flower-gardens."—Dunn.

(8) "The Arabian women wear black masks with little clasps prettily ordered."— Carreri. Niebuhr mentions their showing but one eye in conversation.

(9) "The golden grapes of Casbin."—Descrip of Persia.
(10) "The fruits exported from Caubul are apples, pears, pomegranates," etc.—Elphinstone.

(11 "We sat down under a tree, listened to the birds, and talked with the son of our Mehmaundar about our country and Caubul, of which he gave an enchanting account . that city and its 100,000 gardens," etc.—Id.

Plantains, the golden and the green,
Malaya's nectar'd mangusteen; (1
Prunes of Bokara, and sweet nuts
  From the far groves of Samarcand,
And Basra dates, and apricots,
  Seed of the Sun, (2) from Iran's land;—
With rich conserve of Visna cherries, (3)
Of orange flowers, and of those berries
That, wild and fresh, the young gazelles
Feed on in Erac's rocky dells. (4)
All these in richest vases smile,
  In baskets of pure sandal-wood,
And urns of porcelain from that isle (5)
  Sunk underneath the Indian flood,
Whence oft the lucky diver brings
Vases to grace the halls of kings.
Wines, too, of every clime and hue,
Around their liquid lustre threw,
Amber Rosolli (6)—the bright dew
From vineyards of the Green-Sea gushing, (7)
And Shiraz wine, that richly ran
  As if that jewel, large and rare,
The ruby for which Kublai-Khan
Offer'd a city's wealth, (8) was blushing
  Melted within the goblets there!

And amply Selim quaffs of each,
And seems resolved the flood shall reach
His inward heart—shedding around
  A genial deluge, as they run,
That soon shall leave no spot undrown'd
  For Love to rest his wings upon.

He little knew how well the boy
  Can float upon a goblet's streams,
Lighting them with his smile of joy;—
  As bards have seen him in their dreams,
Down the blue Ganges laughing glide
  Upon a rosy lotus wreath, (9)
Catching new lustre from the tide
  That with his image shone beneath.

But what are cups, without the aid
  Of song to speed them as they flow?

And see—a lovely Georgian maid,
  With all the bloom, the freshen'd glow
Of her own country maidens' looks,
When warm they rise from Teflis' brooks; (10)
And with an eye, whose restless ray,
  Full, floating, dark—oh, he, who knows
His heart is weak, of Heaven should pray
  To guard him from such eyes as those!—
With a voluptuous wildness flings
Her snowy hand across the strings
Of a syrinda, (11) and thus sings —

Come hither, come hither—by night and by day,
  We linger in pleasures that never are gone;
Like the waves of the Summer, as one dies away,
  Another as sweet and as shining comes on.
And the love that is o'er, in expiring, gives birth
  To a new one as warm, as unequall'd in bliss;
And, oh! if there be an Elysium on earth,
    It is this, it is this. (12)

Here maidens are sighing, and fragrant their sigh
  As the flower of the Amra just oped by a bee; (13)
And precious their tears, as that rain from the sky (14)
  Which turns into pearls as it falls in the sea.
Oh! think what the kiss and the smile must be worth
  When the sigh and the tear are so perfect in bliss,
And own if there be an Elysium on earth,
    It is this, it is this.

Here sparkles the nectar that, hallow'd by love,
  Could draw down those angels of old from their
      sphere,
Who for wine of this earth (15) left the fountains above,
  And forgot heaven's stars for the eyes we have here.
And, bless'd with the odour our goblet gives forth,
  What Spirit the sweets of his Eden would miss?
For, oh! if there be an Elysium on earth,
    It is this, it is this.

  The Georgian's song was scarcely mute,
    When the same measure, sound for sound,
  Was caught up by another lute,
    And so divinely breathed around,

(1) "The mangusteen, the most delicate fruit in the world, the pride of the Malay islands."—*Marsden.*
(2) "A delicious kind of apricot, called by the Persians tokm-ek-shems, signifying sun's seed."—*Description of Persia.*
(3) "Sweetmeats, in a crystal cup, consisting of rose-leaves in conserve, with lemon of Visna cherry, orange flowers," etc. —*Russell.*
(4) "Antelopes cropping the fresh berries of Erac.' — *The Moallakat*, Poem of Tarafa
(5) "Mauri-ga-Sima, an island near Formosa, supposed to have been sunk in the sea for the crimes of its inhabitants. The vessels which the fishermen and divers bring up from it are sold at an immense price in China and Japan —See *Kempfer.*
(6) Persian Tales.   (7) The white wine of Kishma
(8) "The King of Zeilan is said to have the very finest ruby that was ever seen. Kublai-Khan sent and offered

the value of a city for it, but the King answered he would not give it for the treasure of the world." — *Marco Polo*
(9) The Indians feign that Cupid was first seen floating down the Ganges on the Nymphea Nelumbo.—See *Pennant*
(10) Teflis is celebrated for its natural warm baths.—See *Ebn Haukal.*
(11 "The Indian Syrinda, or guitar."—*Symes.*
(12 "Around the exterior of the Dewan Khass (a building of Shah Allum's in the cornice are the following lines, in letters of gold upon a ground of white marble — 'If there be a paradise upon earth, it is this, it is this.'"—*Franklin.*
(13) " Delightful are the flowers of the Amra trees on the mountain-tops, while the murmuring bees pursue their voluptuous toil."—*Song of Jayadeva.*
(14 "The Nisan, or drops of spring rain, which they believe produce pearls if they fall into shells."—*Richardson.*
(15 For an account of the share which wine had in the fall of the angels, see *Marit.*

50

That all stood hush'd and wondering,
  And turn'd and look'd into the air,
As if they thought to see the wing
Of Israfil, (1) the Angel, there;—
So powerfully on every soul
That new enchanted measure stole.
While now a voice, sweet as the note
  Of the charm'd lute, was heard to float
Along its chords, and so entwine
  Its sounds with theirs, that none knew whether
The voice or lute was most divine,
  So wondrously they went together —

There's a bliss beyond all that the minstrel has told,
  When two, that are link'd in one heavenly tie,
With heart never changing, and brow never cold,
  Love on through all ills, and love on till they die!
One hour of a passion so sacred is worth
  Whole ages of heartless and wandering bliss;
And, oh! if there be an Elysium on earth,
    It is this, it is this.

  'Twas not the air, 'twas not the words,
  But that deep magic in the chords
  And in the lips, that gave such power
  As Music knew not till that hour.
  At once a hundred voices said,
  " It is the mask'd Arabian maid!"
  While Selim, who had felt the strain
  Deepest of any, and had lain
  Some minutes rapt, as in a trance,
  After the fairy sounds were o'er,
  Too inly touch'd for utterance,
  Now motion'd with his hand for more —

Fly to the desert, fly with me,
Our Arab tents are rude for thee;
But, oh! the choice what heart can doubt,
Of tents with love, or thrones without?

Our rocks are rough, but smiling there
The acacia waves her yellow hair,
Lonely and sweet, nor loved the less
For flowering in a wilderness.

Our sands are bare, but down their slope
The silvery-footed antelope
As gracefully and gaily springs
As o'er the marble courts of kings.

Then come—thy Arab maid will be
The loved and lone acacia-tree,
The antelope, whose feet shall bless
With their light sound thy loneliness.

Oh! there are looks and tones that dart
An instant sunshine through the heart—
As if the soul that minute caught
Some treasure it through life had sought;

As if the very lips and eyes,
Predestined to have all our sighs,
And never be forgot again,
Sparkled and spoke before us then!

So came thy every glance and tone,
When first on me they breathed and shone,
New, as if brought from other spheres,
Yet welcome as if loved for years.

Then fly with me—if thou hast known
No other flame, nor falsely thrown
A gem away, that thou hadst sworn
Should ever in thy heart be worn.

Come, if the love thou hast for me
Is pure and fresh as mine for thee—
Fresh as the fountain under ground,
When first 'tis by the lapwing found. 2)

But if for me thou dost forsake
Some other maid, and rudely break
Her worshipp'd image from its base,
To give to me the ruin'd place—

Then, fare thee well—I'd rather make
My bower upon some icy lake
When thawing suns begin to shine,
Than trust to love so false as thine!

There was a pathos in this lay
  That, even without enchantment's art,
Would instantly have found its way
  Deep into Selim's burning heart;
But, breathing, as it did, a tone
To earthly lutes and lips unknown;
With every chord fresh from the touch
Of Music's Spirit—'twas too much!
Starting, he dash'd away the cup—
  Which, all the time of this sweet air,
His hand had held, untasted, up,
  As if 'twere fix'd by magic there—
And naming her, so long unnamed,
So long unseen, wildly exclaim'd,
" Oh Nourmahal! oh Nourmahal!
  Hadst thou but sung this witching strain,
I could forget—forgive thee all,
  And never leave those eyes again."

The mask is off—the charm is wrought—
And Selim to his heart has caught,
In blushes, more than ever bright,
His Nourmahal, his Haram's Light!
And well do vanish'd frowns enhance
The charm of every brighten'd glance,
And dearer seems each dawning smile
For having lost its light awhile:

1 The Angel of Music. See note (2), p. 380.
(2) The hudhud, or lapwing, is supposed to have the
power of discovering water under ground.

And, happier now for all her sighs,
　As on his arm her head reposes,
She whispers him, with laughing eyes,
　"Remember, love, the Feast of Roses!"

FADLADEEN, at the conclusion of this light rhapsody, took occasion to sum up his opinion of the young Cashmerian's poetry—of which, he trusted, they had that evening heard the last. Having recapitulated the epithets, "frivolous"—"inharmonious"—"nonsensical," he proceeded to say that, viewing it in the most favourable light, it resembled one of those Maldivian boats, to which the Princess had alluded in the relation of her dream (1)—a slight gilded thing, sent adrift without rudder or ballast, and with nothing but vapid sweets and faded flowers on board. The profusion, indeed, of flowers and birds, which this poet had ready on all occasions—not to mention dews, gems, etc.—was a most oppressive kind of opulence to his hearers; and had the unlucky effect of giving to his style all the glitter of the flower-garden without its method, and all the flutter of the aviary without its song. In addition to this, he chose his subjects badly, and was always most inspired by the worst parts of them. The charms of paganism, the merits of rebellion—these were the themes honoured with his particular enthusiasm; and, in the poem just recited, one of his most palatable passages was in praise of that beverage of the Unfaithful, wine;—"being, perhaps," said he, relaxing into a smile, as conscious of his own character in the Haram on this point, "one of those bards, whose fancy owes all its illumination to the grape, like that painted porcelain, (2) so curious and so rare, whose images are only visible when liquor is poured into it." Upon the whole, it was his opinion, from the specimens which they had heard, and which, he begged to say, were the most tiresome part of the journey, that—whatever other merits this well-dressed young gentleman might possess—poetry was by no means his proper avocation "and indeed," concluded the critic, "from his fondness for flowers and for birds, I would venture to suggest that a

(1 See p 37)

2) "The Chinese had formerly the art of painting on the sides of porcelain vessels fish and other animals, which were only perceptible when the vessel was full of some liquor. They call this species Kia-tsin, that is, *azure is put in press*, on account of the manner in which the azure is laid on."—"They are every now and then trying to recover the art of this magical painting, but to no purpose "—Dwin

(3) An eminent carver of idols, said in the Koran to be father to Abraham. "I have such a lovely idol as is not to be met with in the house of Azor "—Hafiz.

(4) Kachmire be Nazeer.—Forster.

(5 "The pardonable superstition of the sequestered inhabitants has multiplied the places of worship of Mahadeo, of Beschan, and of Brama. A l Cashmere is holy land, and miraculous fountains abound."—Major Rennel's Memoirs of a Map of Hindostan

florist or a bird-catcher is a much more suitable calling for him than a poet."

They had now begun to ascend those barren mountains, which separate Cashmere from the rest of India; and, as the heats were intolerable, and the time of their encampments limited to the few hours necessary for refreshment and repose, there was an end to all their delightful evenings, and Lalla Rookh saw no more of Feramorz. She now felt that her short dream of happiness was over, and that she had nothing but the recollection of its few blissful hours, like the one draught of sweet water that serves the camel across the wilderness, to be her heart's refreshment during the dreary waste of life that was before her. The blight that had fallen upon her spirits soon found its way to her cheek, and her ladies saw with regret—though not without some suspicion of the cause—that the beauty of their mistress, of which they were almost as proud as of their own, was fast vanishing away at the very moment of all when she had most need of it. What must the King of Bucharia feel, when, instead of the lively and beautiful Lalla Rookh, whom the poets of Delhi had described as more perfect than the divinest images in the house of Azor, 3) he should receive a pale and inanimate victim, upon whose cheek neither health nor pleasure bloomed, and from whose eyes Love had fled—to hide himself in her heart '

If any thing could have charmed away the melancholy of her spirits, it would have been the fresh airs and enchanting scenery of that Valley, which the Persians so justly called the Unequalled. (4) But neither the coolness of its atmosphere, so luxurious after toiling up those bare and burning mountains—neither the splendour of the minarets and pagodas, that shone out from the depth of its woods, nor the grottos, hermitages, and miraculous fountains, (5) which make every spot of that region holy ground—neither the countless waterfalls, that rush into the Valley from all those high and romantic mountains that encircle it, nor the fair city on the Lake, whose houses, roofed with flowers, (6) appeared at a distance like one vast and variegated

Jehanguire men ions "a fountain in Cashmere called Tirnagh, which signifies a snake, probably because some large snake had formerly been seen there."—"During the lifetime of my father, I went twice to this fountain, which is about twenty coss from the city of Cashmere. The vestiges of places of worship and sanctity are to be traced without number amongst the ruins and the caves which are interspersed in its neighbourhood."—Toozek Jehangeery.—V. Asiat. Misc, vol. u.

There is another account of Cashmere by Abul-Fazl, the author of the Ayin-Acbaree, "who," says Major Rennel, "appears to have caught some of the enthusiasm of the valley, by his description of the holy places in it."

(6) "On a standing roof of wood is laid a covering of fine earth, which shelters the building from the great quantity of snow that falls in the winter season This fence communicates an equal warmth in winter, as a refreshing coolness in the summer season, when the tops of the

parterre;—not all these wonders and glories of the most lovely country under the sun could steal her heart for a minute from those sad thoughts, which but darkened, and grew bitterer every step she advanced.

The gay pomps and processions that met her upon her entrance into the Valley, and the magnificence with which the roads all along were decorated, did honour to the taste and gallantry of the young King. It was night when they approached the city, and, for the last two miles, they had passed under arches, thrown from hedge to hedge, festooned with only those rarest roses from which the Attar Gul, more precious than gold, is distilled, and illuminated in rich and fanciful forms with lanterns of the triple-coloured tortoise-shell of Pegu.(1) Sometimes, from a dark wood by the side of the road, a display of fire-works would break out, so sudden and so brilliant, that a Brahmin might fancy he beheld that grove in whose purple shade the God of Battles was born, bursting into a flame at the moment of his birth; —while, at other times, a quick and playful irradia-tion continued to brighten all the fields and gardens by which they passed, forming a line of dancing lights along the horizon; like the meteors of the north, as they are seen by those hunters(2) who pursue the white and blue foxes on the confines of the Icy Sea.

These arches and fire-works delighted the Ladies of the Princess exceedingly; and, with their usual good logic, they deduced from his taste for illumina-tions, that the King of Bucharia would make the most exemplary husband imaginable. Nor, indeed, could Lalla Rookh herself help feeling the kindness and splendour with which the young bridegroom welcomed her;—but she also felt how painful is the gratitude, which kindness from those we cannot love excites; and that their best blandishments come over the heart with all that chilling and deadly sweet-ness, which we can fancy in the cold odoriferous wind (3) that is to blow over this earth in the last days.

The marriage was fixed for the morning after her arrival, when she was, for the first time, to be pre-sented to the monarch in that Imperial Palace beyond the lake, called the Shalimar. Though never before had a night of more wakeful and anxious thought been passed in the Happy Valley, yet, when she rose in the morning, and her Ladies came around her, to assist in the adjustment of the bridal ornaments, they thought they had never seen her look half so

beautiful. What she had lost of the bloom and radiancy of her charms was more than made up by that intellectual expression, that soul beaming forth from the eyes, which is worth all the rest of loveli-ness. When they had tinged her fingers with the Henna leaf, and placed upon her brow a small coronet of jewels, of the shape worn by the ancient Queens of Bucharia, they flung over her head the rose-coloured bridal veil, and she proceeded to the barge that was to convey her across the lake;—first kissing, with a mournful look, the little amulet of cornelian, which her father at parting had hung about her neck.

The morning was as fresh and fair as the maid on whose nuptials it rose, and the shining lake, all covered with boats, the minstrels playing upon the shores of the islands, and the crowded summer-houses on the green hills around, with shawls and banners waving from their roofs, presented such a picture of animated rejoicing, as only she, who was the object of it all, did not feel with transport. To Lalla Rookh alone it was a melancholy pageant, nor could she have even borne to look upon the scene, were it not for a hope that, among the crowds around, she might once more perhaps catch a glimpse of Fera-morz. So much was her imagination haunted by this thought, that there was scarcely an islet or boat she passed on the way, at which her heart did not flutter with the momentary fancy that he was there. Happy, in her eyes, the humblest slave upon whom the light of his dear looks fell!—In the barge imme-diately after the Princess sat Fadladeen, with his silken curtains thrown widely apart, that all might have the benefit of his august presence, and with his head full of the speech he was to deliver to the King, "concerning Feramorz, and literature, and the Cha-buk, as connected therewith."

They now had entered the canal which leads from the Lake to the splendid domes and saloons of the Shalimar, and went gliding on through the gardens that ascended from each bank, full of flowering shrubs that made the air all perfume; while from the middle of the canal rose jets of water, smooth and unbroken, to such a dazzling height, that they stood like tall pillars of diamond in the sunshine. After sailing under the arches of various saloons, they at length arrived at the last and most magnificent, where the monarch awaited the coming of his bride; and such was the agitation of her heart and frame, that it was with difficulty she could walk up the marble steps, which were covered with cloth of gold for her ascent from the barge. At the end of the hall stood two

---

houses, which are planted with a variety of flowers, ex-hibit at a distance the spacious view of a beautifully chec-quered parterre."—Forster.

1) "Two hundred slaves there are, who have no other office than to hunt the woods and marshes for triple-co-loured tortoises for the King's Vivary. Of the shells of these also lanterns are made."—Vincent le Blanc's Travels.

2) For a description of the Aurora Borealis as it ap-pears to these hunters, v Encyclopædia.

(3) This wind, which is to blow from Syria Damascena, is, according to the Mahometans, one of the signs of the Last Day's approach. Another of the signs is, "Great dis-tress in the world, so that a man when he passes by an-other's grave shall say, Would to God I were in his place."—Sale's Preliminary Discourse.

tl iones, as precious as the Cerulean Throne of Coolburga, (1) on one of which sat Aliris, the youthful King of Bucharia, and on the other was, in a few minutes, to be placed the most beautiful Princess in the world. Immediately upon the entrance of Lalla Rookh into the saloon, the monarch descended from his throne to meet her; but scarcely had he time to take her hand in his, when she screamed with surprise, and fainted at his feet. It was Feramorz himself that stood before her!—Feramorz was, himself, the Sovereign of Bucharia, who in this disguise had accompanied his young bride from Delhi, and, having won her love as an humble minstrel, now amply deserved to enjoy it as a King.

The consternation of Fadladeen at this discovery was, for the moment, almost pitiable. But change of opinion is a resource too convenient in courts for

this experienced courtier not to have learned to avail himself of it. His criticisms were all, of course, recanted instantly; he was seized with an admiration of the King's verses, as unbounded as, he begged him to believe, it was disinterested; and the following week saw him in possession of an additional place, swearing by all the Saints of Islam that never had there existed so great a poet as the Monarch Aliris, and, moreover, ready to prescribe his favourite regimen of the Chabuk for every man, woman, and child that dared to think otherwise.

Of the happiness of the King and Queen of Bucharia, after such a beginning, there can be but little doubt; and, among the lesser symptoms, it is recorded of Lalla Rookh, that, to the day of her death, in memory of their delightful journey, she never called the King by any other name than Feramorz.

THE FUDGE FAMILY IN PARIS.

Le leggi della maschera richiedono che una persona mascherata non sia salutata per nome da uno che la conosce malgrado il suo travestimento —*Castiglione.*

PREFACE.

THE station assigned to "The Fudge Family," in the following pages, immediately after "Lalla Rookh," agrees but too closely with the actual order in which these two works were originally written and published. The success, far exceeding my hopes and deserts, with which Lalla Rookh was immediately crowned, relieved me at once from the anxious feeling of responsibility under which, as my readers have seen, that enterprise had been commenced, and which continued for some time to haunt me amidst all the enchantments of my task. I was therefore in the true holiday mood, when a dear friend, with whom is associated the brightest and pleasantest hours of my past life, (2) kindly offered me a seat in his carriage for a short visit to Paris. This proposal I, of course, most gladly accepted; and in the autumn of the year 1817, found myself, for the first time, in that gay capital.

As the restoration of the Bourbon dynasty was still of too recent a date for any amalgamation to have yet taken place between the new and ancient order of things, all the most prominent features of both *régimes* were just then brought, in their fullest relief, into juxta-position; and, accordingly, the

result was such as to suggest to an unconcerned spectator quite as abundant matter for ridicule as for grave political consideration. It would be difficult, indeed, to convey to those who had not themselves seen the Paris of that period, any clear notion of the anomalous aspect, both social and political, which it then presented. It was as if, in the days succeeding the Deluge, a small coterie of antediluvians had been suddenly evoked from out of the deep to take the command of a new and freshly starting world.

To me, the abundant amusement and interest which such a scene could not but afford was a good deal heightened by my having, in my youthful days, been made acquainted with some of those personages who were now most interested in the future success of the Legitimate cause. The Comte d'Artois, or Monsieur, I had met in the year 1802-3, at Donington Park, the seat of the Earl of Moira, under whose princely roof I used often and long, in those days, to find a most hospitable home. A small party of distinguished French emigrants were already staying on a visit in the house when Monsieur and his suite arrived; and among those were the present King of France, and his two brothers, the Duc de Montpensier and the Comte de Beaujolais.

(1 "On Mahommed Shaw's return to Koolburga (the capital of Dekkan, he made a great festival, and mounted this throne with much pomp and magnificence, calling it Firozeh or Cerulean. I have heard some old persons, who saw the throne Firozeh in the reign of Sultan Mamood Bhamenee, describe it. They say that it was in length nine feet, and three in breadth, made of ebony, covered with plates of pure gold, and set with precious stones of immense value. Every prince of the house of

Bhamenee, who possessed this throne, made a point of adding to it some rich stones; so that when in the reign of Sultan Mamood it was taken to pieces, to remove some of the jewels to be set in vases and cups, the jewellers valued it at one crorore of oons (nearly four millions sterling). I learned also that it was called Firozeh from being partly enamelled of a sky-blue colour, which was in time totally concealed by the number of jewels." —*Ferishta.*

2) Mr. Rogers

Some doubt and uneasiness had, I remember, been felt by the two latter brothers, as to the reception they were likely to encounter from the new guest; and as, in those times, a cropped and unpowdered head was regarded generally as a symbol of Jacobinism, who, like many other young men, wore his hair in this fashion, thought it, on the present occasion, most prudent, in order to avoid all risk of offence, not only to put powder in his hair, but also to provide himself with an artificial queue. This measure of precaution, however, led to a slight incident after dinner, which, though not very royal or dignified, was at least creditable to the social good-humour of the future Charles X. On the departure of the ladies from the dining-room, we had hardly seated ourselves in the old-fashioned style, round the fire, when Monsieur, who had happened to place himself next to Beaujolais, caught a glimpse of the ascititious tail—which, having been rather carelessly put on, had a good deal straggled out of its place. With a sort of scream of jocular pleasure, as if delighted at the discovery, Monsieur seized the stray appendage, and bringing it round into full view, to the great amusement of the whole company, popped it into poor grinning Beaujolais' mouth.

On one of the evenings of this short visit of Monsieur, I remember Curran arriving unexpectedly, on his way to London; and, having come too late for dinner, he joined our party in the evening. As the foreign portion of the company was then quite new to him, I was able to be useful, by informing him of the names, rank, and other particulars of the party he found assembled, from Monsieur himself down to the old Duc de Lorge and the Baron de Rolle. When I had gone through the whole list, " Ah, poor fellows ! " he exclaimed, with a mixture of fun and pathos in his look, truly Irish, " Poor fellows, *all* dismounted cavalry ! "

On the last evening of Monsieur's stay, I was made to sing for him, among other songs, " Farewell, Bessy ! " one of my earliest attempts at musical composition. As soon as I had finished, he paid me the compliment of reading aloud the words as written under the music ; and most royal havoc did he make, as to this day I remember, of whatever little sense or metre they could boast.

Among my earlier poetic writings, more than one grateful memorial may be found of the happy days I passed in this hospitable mansion (1)—

Of all my sunny morns and moonlight nights
On Donington's green lawns and breezy heights.

But neither verse nor prose could do any justice to

the sort of impression I still retain of those long-vanished days. The library at Donington was (2) extensive and valuable, and through the privilege kindly granted to me of retiring thither for study, even when the family were absent, I frequently passed whole weeks alone in that fine library, indulging in all the first airy castle-building of authorship. The various projects, indeed, of future works that used then to pass in fruitless succession through my mind, can be compared only to the waves as described by the poet—

" And one no sooner touch'd the shore, and died,
Than a new follower rose."

With that library is also connected another of my earlier poems—the verses addressed to the Duke of Montpensier on his portrait of the Lady Adelaide Forbes ; (3) for it was there that this truly noble lady, then in the first dawn of her beauty, used to sit for that picture ; while, in another part of the library, the Duke of Orleans —engaged generally at that time with a volume of Clarendon—was by such studies unconsciously preparing himself for the high and arduous destiny, which not only the Good Genius of France, but his own sagacious and intrepid spirit, had marked out for him.

I need hardly say how totally different were all the circumstances under which Monsieur himself and some of his followers were again seen by me in the year 1817 ;—the same actors, indeed, but with an entirely new change of scenery and decorations. Among the variety of aspects presented by this change, the ridiculous certainly predominated ; nor could a satirist who, like Philoctetes, was smitten with a fancy for shooting at geese, (4) ask any better supply of such game than the high places, in France, at that period, both lay and ecclesiastical, afforded. As I was not versed, however, sufficiently in French politics to venture to meddle with them, even in sport, I found a more ready conductor of laughter —for which I was then much in the mood—in those groups of ridiculous English who were at that time swarming in all directions throughout Paris, and of all whose various forms of cockneyism and nonsense I endeavoured, in the personages of the Fudge Family, to collect the concentrated essence.

The result, as usual, fell very far short of what I had myself preconceived and intended. But, making its appearance at such a crisis, the work brought with it that best seasoning of all such *jeux d'esprit*, the *à-propos* of the moment; and, accordingly, in the race of successive editions, "Lalla Rookh" was for sometime kept pace with by Miss Biddy Fudge.

(1) See the Epistle addressed to Lady Charlotte Rawdon in " *Poems relating to America.*'

(2) In employing the past tense here, I do the present lord injustice, whose filial wish I know it is to keep all at Donington exactly as his noble father left it

(3) See the lines dated from Donington Park, commencing "To catch the thought, by painting's spell," etc.

(4) "Pinnigero, non armigero in corpore tela exerceantur " — the words put by Accius in the mouth of Philoctetes

ORIGINAL PREFACE.

In what manner the following Epistles came into my hands, it is not necessary for the public to know. It will be seen by Mr. Fudge's Second Letter, that he is one of those gentlemen whose *Secret Services* in Ireland, under the mild ministry of my Lord C——gh, have been so amply and gratefully remunerated. Like his friend and associate, Thomas Reynolds, Esq., he had retired upon the reward of his honest industry; but has lately been induced to appear again in active life, and superintend the training of that *Delatorian Cohort*, which Lord S—dm—th, in his wisdom and benevolence, has organised.

Whether Mr. Fudge, himself, has yet made any discoveries, does not appear from the following pages. But much may be expected from a person of his zeal and sagacity, and, indeed, to *him*, Lord S—dm—th, and the Greenland-bound ships, the eyes of all lovers of *discoveries* are now most anxiously directed.

I regret much that I have been obliged to omit Mr. Bob Fudge's Third Letter, concluding the adventures of his Day with the Dinner, Opera, etc., etc.; —but, in consequence of some remarks upon Marinette's thin drapery, which, it was thought, might give offence to certain well-meaning persons, the manuscript was sent back to Paris for his revision, and had not returned when the last sheet was put to press.

It will not, I hope, be thought presumptuous, if I take this opportunity of complaining of a very serious injustice I have suffered from the public. Dr. King wrote a treatise to prove that Bentley "was not the author of his own book," and a similar absurdity has been asserted of *me*, in almost all the best-informed literary circles. With the name of the real author staring them in the face, they have yet persisted in attributing my works to other people; and the fame of the Twopenny Post-Bag—such as it is—having hovered doubtfully over various persons, has at last settled upon the head of a certain little gentleman, who wears it, I understand, as complacently as if it actually belonged to him; without even the honesty of avowing, with his own favourite author, (he will excuse the pun,)

Ἐγὼ δ᾽ Ο ΜΩΡΟΣ αραις
Ἐδησαμην μετωπω.

I can only add, that if any lady or gentleman, curious in such matters, will take the trouble of calling at my lodgings, 245, Piccadilly, I shall have the honour of assuring them, *in proprid personā*, that I am—his, or her,

Very obedient and very humble Servant,
THOMAS BROWN, THE YOUNGER.

April 17, 1818.

(1) To commemorate the landing of Louis le Desire from England, the impression of his foot is marked out on

THE FUDGE FAMILY IN PARIS.

LETTER I.

FROM MISS BIDDY FUDGE TO MISS DOROTHY ——, OF
CLONKILTY, IN IRELAND.

Amiens.

DEAR Doll, while the tails of our horses are plaiting,
The trunks tying on, and Papa, at the door,
Into very bad French is, as usual, translating
His English resolve not to give a *sou* more,
I sit down to write you a line—only think —
A letter from France, with French pens and French ink,
How delightful! though, would you believe it, my dear?
I have seen nothing yet *very* wonderful here;
No adventure, no sentiment, far as we 've come,
But the corn-fields and trees quite as dull as at home,
And *but* for the post-boy, his boots and his queue,
I might *just* as well be at Clonkilty with you!
In vain, at Dessein's, did I take from my trunk
That divine fellow, Sterne, and fall reading " The
Monk;"
In vain did I think of his charming Dead Ass,
And remember the crust and the wallet—alas!
No monks can be had now for love or for money,
(All owing, Pa says, to that infidel Boney;)
And, though *one* little Neddy we saw in our drive
Out of classical Nampont, the beast was alive!

By the by, though, at Calais, Papa *had* a touch
Of romance on the pier, which affected me much.
At the sight of that spot, where our darling Dix-huit
Set the first of his own dear legitimate feet, (*1*)
(Modell'd ont so exactly, and—God bless the mark !
'T is a foot, Dolly, worthy so *Grand* a *Monarque*),
He exclaim'd, " Oh, mon Roi!" and, with tear-dropping eye,
Stood to gaze on the spot—while some Jacobin, nigh,
Mutter'd out with a shrug (what an insolent thing!)
" Ma foi, he be right—'t is de Englishman's King;
And dat *gros pied de cochon*—begar, me vil say
Dat de foot look mosh better, if turn'd toder way."
There 's the pillar, too—Lord! I had nearly forgot—
What a charming idea!—raised close to the spot,
The mode being now, (as you 've heard, I suppose,)
To build tombs over legs, (2) and raise pillars to toes.

This is all that 's occurr'd sentimental as yet;
Except, indeed, some little flower-nymphs we 've met,
Who disturb one's romance with pecuniary views,
Flinging flowers in your path, and then—bawling for
sous!
And some picturesque beggars, whose multitudes seem
To recall the good days of the *ancien régime*,
All as ragged and brisk, you 'll be happy to learn,
And as thin as they were in the time of dear Sterne.

the pier at Calais, and a pillar with an inscription raised opposite to the spot 2 Ci-git la jambe d', etc., etc.

Our party consists (in a neat Calais job)
Of Papa and myself, Mr. Connor and Bob.
You remember how sheepish Bob look'd at Kilrandy,
But, Lord! he's quite alter'd —they've made him a
　　Dandy;
A thing, you know, whisker'd, great-coated, and laced,
Like an hour-glass, exceedingly small in the waist
Quite a new sort of creatures, unknown yet to scholars,
With heads so immovably stuck in shirt-collars,
That seats like our music-stools soon must be found
　　them,
To twirl, when the creatures may wish to look round
　　them.
In short, dear, " a Dandy" describes what I mean,
And Bob's far the best of the *genus* I've seen:
An improving young man, fond of learning, ambi-
　　tious,
And goes now to Paris to study French dishes,
Whose names—think, how quick! he already knows,
　　pat,
A la braise, petits pâtés, and—what d' ye call that
They inflict on potatoes?—oh! *mattre-d'hôtel*—
I assure you. dear Dolly, he knows them as well
As if nothing else all his life he had eat,
Though a bit of them Bobby has never touch'd yet;
But just knows the names of French dishes and cooks,
As dear Pa knows the titles of authors and books.

As to Pa, what d' ye think?—mind, it's all *entre nous*,
But you know, love, I never keep secrets from you—
Why, he's writing a book—What! a tale? a romance?
No, ye Gods, would it were!—but his Travels in
　　France;
At the special desire (he let out t' other day)
Of his great friend and patron, my Lord C—stl—gh,
Who said, " My dear Fudge"——I forget the exact
　　words,
And, it 's strange, no one ever remembers my Lord's;
But 't was something to say that, as all must allow,
A good orthodox work is much wanting just now,
To expound to the world the new—thingummie—
　　science,
Found out by the—what 's-its-name—Holy Alliance,
And prove to mankind that their rights are but folly,
Their freedom a joke (which it *is*, you know, Dolly),
"There 's none," said his Lordship, " if *I* may be
　　judge,
Half so fit for this great undertaking as Fudge!"

The matter 's soon settled—Pa flies to *the Row*
(The *first* stage your tourists now usually go),
Settles all for his quarto—advertisements, praises—
Starts post from the door, with his tablets—French
　　phrases—
"Scott's Visit," of course—in short every thing *he* has
An author can want, except words and ideas:

(1) A celebrated mantua-maker in Paris.
(2 This excellent imitation of the noble Lord's style
shows how deeply Mr. Fudge must have studied his great
original Irish oratory, indeed, abounds with such startling

And, lo! the first thing, in the spring of the year,
Is Phil. Fudge at the front of a quarto, my dear!

But, bless me, my paper 's near out, so I 'd better
Draw fast to a close.—this exceeding long letter
You owe to a *déjeûner à la fourchette*,
Which Bobby *would* have, and is hard at it yet.—
What 's next.' oh, the tutor, the last of the party,
Young Connor—they say he 's so like Bonaparte,
His nose and his chin—which Papa rather dreads,
As the Bourbons, you know, are suppressing all heads
That resemble old Nap's, and who knows but their
　　honours
May think, in their fright, of suppressing poor
　　Connor's?
Au reste (as we say), the young lad 's well enough,
Only talks much of Athens, Rome, virtue, and stuff;
A third cousin of ours, by the way—poor as Job
(Through of royal descent by the side of Mamma),
And for charity made private tutor to Bob;—
Entre nous, too, a Papist—how liberal of Pa!

This is all, dear—forgive me for breaking off thus,
But Bob's *déjeûner* 's done, and Papa 's in a fuss.
　　　　　　　　　　　　　　　B. F.
P. S.
How provoking of Pa! he will not let me stop
Just to run in and rummage some milliner's shop;
And my *début* in Paris, I blush to think on it,
Must now, Doll, be made in a hideous low bonnet.
But Paris, dear Paris!—oh, *there* will be joy,
And romance, and high bonnets, and Madame Le
　　Roi! (1)
　　　　　　　—o**o—
LETTER II.

FROM PHIL. FUDGE, ESQ. TO THE LORD VISCOUNT
　　　　　C—ST—R—GH.　　　　*Paris*
At length, my Lord, I have the bliss
　　To date to you a line from this
　　"Demoralised" metropolis;
Where, by plebeians low and scurvy,
　　The throne was turn'd quite topsy-turvy,
And Kingship, tumbled from its seat,
　　" Stood prostrate" at the people's feet;
Where (still to use your Lordship's tropes)
　　The *level* of obedience *slopes*
Upward and downward, as the *stream*
　　Of *hydra* faction *kicks the beam!* (2)
Where the poor Palace changes masters
　　Quicker than a snake its skin,
And Louis is roll'd out on castors,
　　While Boney 's borne on shoulders in:—
But where, in every change, no doubt,
　　One special good your Lordship traces—
That 't is the *Kings* alone turn out,
　　The *Ministers* still keep their places.

peculiarities. Thus the eloquent Counsellor B———,
in describing some hypocritical pretender to charity, said,
"He put his hand in his breeches-pocket, like a crocodile,
and," etc, etc.

How oft, dear Viscount C——gh,
I've thought of thee upon the way,
As in my *job* (what place could be
More apt to wake a thought of thee.')—
Or, oftener far, when gravely sitting
Upon my dicky, (as is fitting
For him who writes a Tour, that he
May more of men and manners see,)
I've thought of thee and of thy glories,
Thou guest of Kings, and King of Tories!
Reflecting how thy fame has grown

And spread, beyond man's usual share,
At home, abroad, till thou art known,
Like Major Semple, every where!
And marvelling with what powers of breath
Your Lordship, having speech'd to death
Some hundreds of your fellow-men,
Next speech'd to Sovereigns' ears—and when
All Sovereigns else were dozed at last
Speech'd down the Sovereign (1) of Belfast.
Oh! 'mid the praises and the trophies
Thou gain'st from Morosophs and Sophis;
'Mid all the tributes to thy fame,
There's *one* thou shouldst be chiefly pleased at,
That Ireland gives her snuff thy name,
And C——gh's the thing now sneezed at!

But hold, my pen!—a truce to praising—
Though even your Lordship will allow
The theme's temptations are amazing;
But time and ink run short, and now,
(As *thou* wouldst say, my guide and teacher
In these gay metaphoric fringes,
I must *embark* into the *feature*
On which this letter chiefly *hinges;*—(2)
My Book, the Book that is to prove—
And *will*, (so help ye Sprites above—
That sit on clouds, as grave as judges,
Watching the labours of the Fudges!)
Will prove that all the world, at present,
Is in a state extremely pleasant;
That Europe—thanks to royal swords
And bayonets, and the Duke commanding—
Enjoys a peace which, like the Lord's,
Passeth all human understanding:
That France prefers her go-cart King
To such a coward scamp as Boney;
Though round, with each a leading-string,
There standeth many a Royal crony,

For fear the chubby tottering thing
Should fall, if left there *loney-poney;* —
That England, too, the more her debts,
The more she spends, the richer gets;
And that the Irish, grateful nation!
Remember when by *thee* reign'd over,
And bless thee for their flagellation,
As Heloisa did her lover!—(3
That Poland, left for Russia's lunch
Upon the side-board, snug reposes·
While Saxony's as pleased as Punch,
And Norway "on a bed of roses!"
That, as for some few million souls,
Transferr'd by contract, bless the clods!
If half were strangled—Spaniards, Poles,
And Frenchmen—'t would n't make much odds,
So Europe's goodly Royal ones
Sit easy on their sacred thrones;
So Ferdinand embroiders gaily, (4)
And Louis eats his *salmi*, (5) daily;
So time is left to Emperor Sandy
To be *half* Cæsar and *half* Dandy;
And G——ge the R—g—t (who'd forget
That doughtiest chieftain of the set?)
Hath wherewithal for trinkets new,
For dragons, after Chinese models,
And chambers where Duke Ho and Soo
Might come and nine times knock their
noddles —
All this my Quarto 'll prove—much more
Than Quarto ever proved before:—
In reasoning with the *Post* I 'll vie,
My facts the *Courier* shall supply,
My jokes V—ns—t, P—le my sense,
And thou, sweet Lord, my eloquence!

My Journal, penn'd by fits and starts,
On Biddy's back or Bobby's shoulder,
(My son, my Lord, a youth of parts,
Who longs to be a small place-holder,)
Is—though *I* say 't, that should n't say—
Extremely good; and, by the way,
One extract from it—*only* one—
To show its spirit, and I 've done.

"*Jul. thirty-first.*—Went, after snack,
To the Cathedral of St. Denny,
Sigh'd o'er the Kings of ages back,
And—gave the old concierge a penny.

(1) The title of chief magistrate of Belfast, before whom his Lordship with the "studium immate loquendi" attributed by Ovid to that chattering and rapacious class of birds, the pies) delivered sundry long and self-gratulatory orations, on his return from the Continent At one of these Irish dinners his brother, Lord S., proposed the health of "The best cavalry officer in Europe—the Regent "

(2) Verbatim from one of the noble Viscount's speeches —"And now, Sir, I must embark into the feature on which this question chiefly hinges."

3) See her letters.

4) It would be an edifying thing to write a history of the private amusements of sovereigns, tracing them down from the fly-sticking of Domitian, the mole-catching of Artabanus, the hog-mimicking of Parmenides, the horse-currying of Aretas, to the petticoat-embroidering of Ferdinand, and the patience-playing of the P —e R——t!

(5) Οψα τε, οια εδουσι διοτρεφεες βασιληες.
Ho mer, Odyss. 3

51

(*Mem.*—Must see *Rheims*, much famed, 't is said,
For making Kings and gingerbread.)
Was shown the tomb where lay, so stately,
A little Bourbon, buried lately,
Thrice high and puissant, we were told,
Though only twenty-four hours old!(1)
Hear this, thought I, ye Jacobins :
Ye Burdetts, tremble in your skins!
If Royalty, but aged a day,
Can boast such high and puissant sway,
What impious hand its power would fix,
Full fledged and wigg'd 2) at fifty-six'"
The argument 's quite new, you see,
And proves exactly Q. E. D.
So now, with duty to the R—g—t,
I am, dear Lord,

           Your most obedient,
                        P. F.

Hôtel Breteuil, Rue Rn li.

Neat lodging—either dear for me,
But Biddy said she thought 't would look
Genteeler thus to date my Book ;
And Biddy 's right—besides, it curries
Some favour with our friends at Murray's,
Who scorn what any man can say,
That dates from Rue St. Honore!(3)

        —⊶—

LETTER III.

FROM MR. BOB FUDGE TO RICHARD ——, ESQ.

Oh, Dick! you may talk of your writing and reading,
Your Logic and Greek, but there 's nothing like
   feeding ;
And *this* is the place for it, Dicky, you dog,
Of all places on earth—the head-quarters of Prog!
Talk of England—her famed Magna Charta, I swear, is
A humbug, a flam, to the Carte 4) at old Very's;
And as for your Juries—*who* would not set o'er 'em
A Jury of Tasters (5) with woodcocks before 'em ?
Give Cartwright his Parliaments, fresh every year ;
But those friends of *short Commons* would never do
   here ;

1) So described on the coffin "très-haute et puis-
sante Princesse, agee d'un jour "
2 There is a fulness and breadth in this portrait of
Royalty, which reminds us of what Pliny says, in speaking
of Trajan's great qualities —" nonne longe *lateque* Prin-
cipem ostentant ? "
3) See the *Quarterly Review* for May, 1816, where Mr
Hobhouse is accused of having written his book "in a
back street of the French capital."
(4) The Bill of Fare.—Very, a well-known restaurateur
(5) Mr. Bob alludes particularly, I presume, to the
famous Jury Dégustateur, which used to assemble at the
Hotel of M. Grimod de la Reynière, and of which this mo-
dern Archestratus has given an account in his *Almanach
des Gourmands,* cinquième année, p. 78.
(6) The fairy-land of cookery and *gourmandise ;* " Pays
ou le ciel offre les viandes toutes cuites, et ou, comme
on parle, les louettes tombent toutes rôties. Du Latin,
coquere."—*Duchat.*
7 The process by which the liver of the unfortunate

And, let Romilly speak as he will on the question,
No D gest of Law's like the laws of digestion '

By the by, Dick, *I* fatten—but *n'importe* for that,
'T is the mode—your Legitimates always get fat.
There 's the R—g—t, there 's Louis—and Boney
   tried too,
But, though somewhat imperial in paunch, 't wouldn't
   do :—
He improved, indeed, much in this point, when he wed,
But he ne'er grew right royally fat *in the head.*

Dick, Dick, what a place is this Paris!—but stay—
As my raptures may bore you, I 'll just sketch a day,
As we pass it, myself and some comrades I 've got,
All thorough-bred *Gnostics,* who know what is what.

After dreaming some hours of the land of Cocaigne, (6)
   That Elysium of all that is *friand* and nice,
Where for had they have *bon-bons,* and claret for rain,
   And the skaiters in winter show off on *cream-ice ;*
Where so ready all nature its cookery yields,
Macaroni au parmesan grows in the fields ;
Little birds fly about with the true pheasant taint,
And the geese are all born with a liver complaint!(7)
I rise—put on neck-cloth—stiff, t ght, as can be—
For a lad who *goes into the world,* Dick, like me,
Should have his neck tied up, you know—there's no
   doubt of it—
Almost as tight as *some* lads who *go out of it.*
With whiskers well oil'd, and with boots that "hold
   up
The mirror to nature"—so bright you could sup
Off the leather like china; with coat, too, that draws
On the tailor, who suffers, a martyr's applause!—
With head bridled up, like a four-in-hand leader,
And stays—devil 's in them—too tight for a feeder,
I strut to the old Café Hardy, which yet
Beats the field at a *déjeûner à la fourchette.*
There, Dick, what a breakfast!—oh, not like your
   ghost
Of a breakfast in England, your curst tea and toast; 8)

goose is enlarged, in order to produce that richest of all
dainties, the *foie gras,* of which such renowned *pâtés* are
made at Strasbourg and Toulouse, is thus described in the
Cours Gastronomique : — " On déplume l'estomac des
oies, on attache ensuite ces animaux aux chenets d une
cheminée, et on les nourrit devant le feu. La captivité
et la chaleur donnent à ces volatiles une maladie hepa-
tique, qui fait gonfler leur foie," etc., p. 206.
8 Is Mr. Bob aware that his contempt for *tea* renders
him liable to a charge of *atheism ?* Such, at least, is the
opinion cited in *Christian. Falster. Amœnitat. Philolog.*
— " Atheum interpretabatur hominem ad herbâ The
aversum " He would not, I think, have been so irreve-
rent to this beverage of scholars, if he had read *Peter
Petit's* Poem in praise of Tea, addressed to the learned
Huet — or the Epigraphe which *Pechlinus* wrote for an
altar he meant to dedicate to this herb—or the Anacreon-
tics of *Peter Francius,* in which he calls Tea

       Θεαν, Θεην, Θεαιναν.

But a side-board, you dog, where one's eye roves
about,
Like a Turk's in the Haram, and thence singles out
One's *pâté* of larks, just to tune up the throat,
One's small limbs of chickens, done *en papillote*,
One's erudite cutlets, drest all ways but plain,
Or one's kidneys—imagine, Dick—done with cham-
pagne!
Then, some glasses of *Beaune*, to dilute—or mayhap,
Chambertin, (1) which you know 's the pet tipple of
Nap,
And which Dad, by the by, that legitimate stickler,
Much scruples to taste, but *I'm* not so particular.—
Your coffee comes next, by prescription ; and then,
Dick, 's
The coffee's ne'er-failing and glorious appendix,
(If books had but such, my old Grecian, depend on 't,
I'd swallow even W—tk—n's, for sake of the end
on 't,)
A neat glass of *parfait-amour*, which one sips
Just as if bottled velvet (2) tipped over one's lips.
This repast being ended, and *paid for*—(how odd!
Till a man 's used to paying, there 's something so
queer in 't!)—
The sun now well out, and the girls all abroad,
And the world enough air'd for us, Nobs, to appear
in 't,
We lounge up the Boulevards, where—oh, Dick, the
phizzes,
The turn-outs, we meet—what a nation of quizzes!
Here toddles along some old figure of fun,
With a coat you might date Anno Domini 1 ;
A laced hat, worsted stockings, and—noble old soul!
A fine ribbon and cross in his best button-hole ;
Just such as our Pr——ce, who nor reason nor fun
dreads,
Inflicts, without even a court-martial, on hundreds. (3)
Here trips à *grisette*, with a fond roguish eye
(Rather eatable things these *grisettes* by the by) ;
And there an old *demoiselle*, almost as fond,
In a silk that has stood since the time of the Fronde.
There goes a French Dandy—ah, Dick! unlike some
ones
We 've seen about White's—the Mounseers are but
rum ones ;

The following passage from one of these Anacreontics
will, I have no doubt, be gratifying to all true Theists.

Θεοις, θεως τε πατρι,
Ἐν χρυσεοις σκυφοισι
Διδοι το νεκταρ Ἡβη.
Σε μοι διακονοιτο
Σκυφοις εν μυρρινοισι,
Τω καλλει πρεπουσαι
Καλαις χερεσσι χουροι.

Which may be thus translated :—

> Yes, let Hebe, ever young,
> High in heaven her nectar hold,
> And to Jove's immortal throng
> Pour the tide in cups of gold

Such hats!—fit for monkeys—I'd back Mrs. Draper
To cut neater weather-boards out of brown paper :
And coats—how I wish, if it would n't distress 'em,
They'd club for old Br—mm—l, from Calais, to dress
'em!
The collar sticks out from the neck such a space,
That you'd swear 't was the plan of this head-lop-
ping nation,
To leave there behind them a snug little place
For the head to drop into, on decapitation.
In short, what with mountebanks, counts, and fri-
seurs,
Some mummers by trade, and the rest amateurs—
What with captains in new jockey-boots and silk
breeches,
Old dustmen with swinging great opera-hats,
And shoeblacks reclining by statues in niches,
There never was seen such a race of Jack Sprats!

From the Boulevards — but hearken!—yes—as I'm
a sinner,
The clock is just striking the half-hour to dinner :
So *no* more at present—short time for adorning—
My day must be finish'd some other fine morning.
Now, hey for old Beauvilliers' (4) larder, my boy!
And, once *there*, if the Goddess of Beauty and Joy
Were to write "Come and kiss me, dear Bob!" I'd
not budge—
Not a step, Dick, as sure as my name is
R. FUDGE.

—◦♦◦—

LETTER IV.

FROM PHELIM CONNOR TO ——.

"RETURN!"—no, never, while the withering hand
Of bigot power is on that hapless land ;
While, for the faith my fathers held to God,
Even in the fields where free those fathers trod,
I am proscribed, and—like the spot left bare
In Israel's halls, to tell the proud and fair
Amidst their mirth, that Slavery had been there— 5)
On all I love, home, parents, friends, I trace
The mournful mark of bondage and disgrace!
No!—let *them* stay, who in their country's pangs
See nought but food for factions and harangues ;

> I'll not envy heaven s Princes,
> While, with snowy hands, for me,
> Kate the china tea-cup rinses,
> And pours out her best Bohea

(1 The favourite wine of Napoleon.
(2 *Velours en bouteille.*
(3 It was said by Wicquefort, more than a hundred
years ago, "Le roi d'Angleterre fait seul plus de cheva-
liers que tous les autres rois de la Chretiente ensemble."
—What would he say now ?
(4) A celebrated restaurateur.
5) "They used to leave a yard square of the wall of the
house unplastered, on which they write, in large letters,
either the fore-mentioned verse of the Psalmist ('If I
forget thee, O Jerusal'm,' etc or the words—'The me-
mory of the desolation '— *Leo of Modena.*

Who yearly kneel before their masters' doors,
And hawk their wrongs, as beggars do their sores:
Still let your '   *   *   *   * 1
   *   *   *   *   *

Still hope and suffer, all who can!—but I,
Who durst not hope, and cannot bear, must fly.

But whither?—everywhere the scourge pursues—
Turn where he will, the wretched wanderer views,
In the bright broken hopes of all his race,
Countless reflections of the Oppressor's face.
Every where gallant hearts, and spirits true,
Are served up victims to the vile and few;
While E—gl—d, every where—the general foe
Of Truth and Freedom, whereso'er they glow—
Is first, when tyrants strike, to aid the blow.

Oh, E—gl—d! could such poor revenge atone
For wrongs, that well might claim the deadliest one,
Were it a vengeance, sweet enough to sate
The wretch who flies from thy intolerant hate,
To hear his curses on such barbarous sway
Echo'd, where'er he bends his cheerless way; —
Could *this* content him, every lip he meets
Teems for his vengeance with such poisonous
      sweets;
Were *this* his luxury, never is thy name
Pronounced, but he doth banquet on thy shame;
Hears maledictions ring from every side
Upon that grasping power, that selfish pride,
Which vaunts its own, and scorns all rights be-
      side;
That low and desperate envy, which to blast
A neighbour's blessings, risks the few thou hast,—
That monster, Self, too gross to be conceal'd,
Which ever lurks behind thy proffer'd shield;—
That faithless craft, which, in thy hour of need,
Can court the slave, can swear he shall be freed,
Yet basely spurns him, when thy point is gain'd,
Back to his masters, ready gagg'd and chain'd!
Worthy associate of that band of Kings,
That royal ravening flock, whose vampire wings
O'er sleeping Europe treacherously brood,
And fan her into dreams of promised good,
Of hope, of freedom—but to drain her blood!
If *thus* to hear thee branded be a bliss
That Vengeance loves, there 's yet more sweet than
      this,
That 't was an Irish head, an Irish heart,
Made thee the fallen and tarnish'd thing thou art;
That, as the centaur (2) gave the infected vest
In which he died, to rack his conqueror's breast,
We sent thee C——gh:—as heaps of dead
Have slain their slayers by the pest they spread,

So hath our land breathed out, thy fame to dim,
Thy strength to waste, and rot thee, soul and limb,
Her worst infections all condensed in him!
   *   *   *   *   *

When will the world shake off such yokes? oh, when
Will that redeeming day shine out on men,
That shall behold them rise, erect and free
As Heaven and Nature meant mankind should be!
When Reason shall no longer blindly bow
To the vile pagod things, that o'er her brow,
Like him of Jaghernaut, drive trampling now;
Nor Conquest dare to desolate God's earth;
Nor drunken Victory, with a Nero's mirth,
Strike her lewd harp amidst a people's groans;—
But, built on love, the world's exalted thrones
Shall to the virtuous and the wise be given—
Those bright, those sole Legitimates of Heaven!

When will this be?—or, oh! is it, in truth,
But one of those sweet day-break dreams of youth,
In which the Soul, as round her morning springs,
'Twixt sleep and waking, sees such dazzling things;
And must the hope, as vain as it is bright,
Be all resign'd?—and are *they* only right,
Who say this world of thinking souls was made
To be by Kings partition'd, truck'd, and weigh'd
In scales that, ever since the world begun,
Have counted millions but as dust to one?
Are *they* the only wise, who laugh to scorn
The rights, the freedom to which man was born?
Who   *   *   *   *
   *   *   *   *   *

Who, proud to kiss each separate rod of power,
Bless, while he reigns, the minion of the hour;
Worship each would-be God that o'er them moves,
And take the thundering of his brass for Jove's!
If *this* be wisdom, then farewell, my books,
Farewell, ye shrines of old, ye classic brooks,
Which fed my soul with currents, pure and fair,
Of living Truth, that now must stagnate there!—
Instead of themes that touch the lyre with light,
Instead of Greece, and her immortal fight
For Liberty, which once awaked my strings,
Welcome the Grand Conspiracy of Kings,
The High Legitimates, the Holy Band,
Who, bolder even than He of Sparta's land,
Against whole millions, panting to be free,
Would guard the pass of right-line tyranny.
Instead of him, the Athenian bard, whose blade
Had stood the onset which his pen pourtray'd,
Welcome   *   *   *   *

And, 'stead of Aristides—woe the day
Such names should mingle!—welcome C——gh!

---

(1) I have thought it prudent to omit some parts of Mr.
Phelim Connor's letter. He is evidently an intemperate
young man, and has associated with his cousins, the
Fudges, to very little purpose.

(2)   Membra et Herculeos toros
      Urit lues Nessea. . . . .
      Ille, ille victor vincitur.
                        Senec. Hercul. Œt

Here break we off, at this unhallow'd name, i
Like priest of old, when words ill-omen'd came.
My next shall tell thee, bitterly shall tell,
Thoughts that   *   *   *
   *   *   *   *
Thoughts that—could patience hold—'t were wiser far
To leave still hid and burning where they are.

—————

LETTER V.

FROM MISS BIDDY FUDGE TO MISS DOROTHY ——.

WHAT a time since I wrote!—I'm a sad naughty girl—
For, though, like a tee-totum, I 'm all in a twirl,
Yet even (as you wittily say) a tee-totum
Between all its twirls gives a *letter* to note 'em.
But, Lord, such a place! and then, Dolly, my dresses,
My gowns, so divine!—there 's no language expresses,
Except just the *two* words "superbe," "magnifique,"
The trimmings of that which I had home last week!
It is call'd—I forget—*à la*—something which sounded
Like *alicampane*—but, in truth, I'm confounded
And bother'd, my dear, 't wixt that troublesome boy's
(Bob's) cookery language, and Madame le Roi's:
What with fillets of roses, and fillets of veal,
Things *garni* with lace, and things *garni* with eel,
One's hair and one's cutlets both *en papillote*,
And a thousand more things I shall ne'er have by rote,
I can scarce tell the difference, at least as to phrase,
Between beef à *la Psyché* and curls à *la braise.*—
But, in short, dear, I 'm trick'd out quite à la Française,
With my bonnet—so beautiful!—high up and poking,
Like things that are put to keep chimneys from
   smoking.

Where *shall* I begin with the endless delights
Of this Eden of milliners, monkeys, and sights—
This dear busy place, where there's nothing trans-
   acting
But dressing and dinnering, dancing and acting?
Imprimis, the Opera—mercy, my ears! [one,—
Brother Bobby's remark, t'other night, was a true
" This *must* be the music," said he, " of the *spears,*
  For I 'm curst if each note of it does n't run
    through one!"
Pa says (and you know, love, his Book's to make out
'T was the Jacobins brought every mischief about)

(1) The late Lord C. of Ireland had a curious theory
about names;—he held that every man with *three* names
was a Jacobin. His instances in Ireland were numerous;
—VIZ. Archibald Hamilton Rowan, Theobald Wolfe Tone,
James Napper Tandy, John Philpot Curran, etc , etc., and,
in England, he produced as examples Charles James Fox,
Richard Brinsley Sheridan, John Horne Tooke, Francis
Burdett Jones, etc., etc.

The Romans called a thief "homo trium literarum."

   Tun' trium literarum homo
  Me vituperas? Fur.*

     Plautus, Aulular., Act ii , Scene 4

* *Dissaldeus* supposes this word to be a *glossema* that
he thinks " Fur" has made his escape from the margin into the
text.

That this passion for roaring has come in of late,
Since the rabble all tried for a *voice* in the State.—
What a frightful idea, one's mind to o'erwhelm!
  What a chorus, dear Dolly, would soon be let
   loose of it,
If, when of age, every man in the realm
  Had a voice like old Lais, 2) and chose to make
   use of it!
No—never was known in this riotous sphere
Such a breach of the peace as their singing, my dear.
So bad too, you 'd swear that the God of both arts,
  Of Music and Physic, had taken a frolic
For setting a loud fit of asthma in parts,
  And composing a fine rumbling base to a cholic!

But, the dancing—*ah! parlez-moi*, Dolly, *de ça*—
There, *indeed*, is a treat that charms all but Papa.
Such beauty—such grace—oh ye sylphs of romance!
  Fly, fly to Titania, and ask her if *she* has
One light-footed nymph in her train, that can dance
  Like divine Bigottini and sweet Fanny Bias!
Fanny Bias in Flora—dear creature!—you 'd swear,
  When her delicate feet in the dance twinkle round,
That her steps are of light, that her home is the air,
  And she only *par complaisance* touches the ground.
And when Bigottini in Psyche dishevels
  Her black flowing hair, and by demons is driven,
Oh! who does not envy those rude little devils,
  That hold her and hug her, and keep her from
   heaven?
Then, the music—so softly its cadences die,
So divinely—oh, Dolly! between you and I,
It 's as well for my peace that there 's nobody nigh
To make love to me then—*you 've* a soul, and can
  judge
What a crisis 't would be for your friend Biddy
  Fudge!

The next place (which Bobby has near lost his
  heart in)
They call it the Playhouse—I think—of St. Mar-
  tin; 3)
Quite charming—and *very* religious—what folly
To say that the French are not pious, dear Dolly,
When here one beholds, so correctly and rightly,
The Testament turn'd into melo-drames nightly; (4)

(2) The oldest, most celebrated, and most noisy of the
singers at the French Opera.

(3) The Theatre de la Porte-St.-Martin, which was built
when the Opera House in the Palais-Royal was burned
down, in 1781.—A few days after this dreadful fire, which
lasted a week, and in which several persons perished,
the Parisian *élégantes* displayed flame-coloured dresses,
" couleur de feu d'Opéra "—*Dulaure Curiosités de Paris.*

4) "The Old Testament," says the theatrical Critic in
the *Gazette de France,* "is a mine of gold for the ma-
nagers of our small play-houses. A multitude crowd
round the Théâtre de la Gaiete every evening to see the
Passage of the Red Sea. '

In the play-bill of one of these sacred melo-dramas at
Vienna, we find " The Voice of G—d," by M. Schwartz.

And, doubtless, so fond they're of scriptural facts,
They will soon get the Pentateuch up in five acts.
Here Daniel, in pantomime, (1) bids bold defiance
To Nebuchadnezzar and all his stuff'd lions,
While pretty young Israelites dance round the
          Prophet,
In very thin clothing, and *but* little of it;—
Here Bégrand, (2) who shines in this scriptural path,
As the lovely Susanna, without even a relic
Of drapery round her, comes out of the bath
In a manner that, Bob says, is quite *Eve-angelic!*
But in short, dear, 't would take me a month to recite
All the exquisite places we're at, day and night;
And, besides, ere I finish, I think you'll be glad
Just to hear one delightful adventure I've had.

Last night, at the Beaujon, (3 a place where—I doubt
If its charms I can paint—there are cars, that set out
From a lighted pavilion, high up in the air,
And rattle you down, Doll—you hardly know where.
These vehicles, mind me, in which you go through
This delightfully dangerous journey, hold *two.*
Some cavalier asks, with humility, whether
You'll venture down *with* him—you smile—'t is a
          match;
In an instant you're seated, and down both together
Go thundering, as if you went post to old scratch! (4)
Well, it was but last night, as I stood and remark'd
On the looks and odd ways of the girls who em-
          bark'd,
The impatience of some for the perilous flight,
The forced giggle of others, 'twixt pleasure and
          fright—
That there came up—imagine, dear Doll, if you can—
A fine sallow, sublime, sort of Werter-faced man,
With mustachios that gave (what we read of so oft)
The dear Corsair expression, half savage, half soft,
As Hyænas in love may be fancied to look, or
A something between Abelard and old Blucher!
Up he came, Doll, to me, and, uncovering his head
(Rather bald, but so warlike!) in bad English said,
"Ah! my dear—if Ma'mselle vil be so very good—
Just for von littel course"—though I scarce under-
          stood
What he wish'd me to do, I said, thank him, I would.
Off we set—and, though 'faith, dear, I hardly knew
          whether
My head or my heels were the uppermost then,

(1) A piece very popular last year, called "Daniel, ou La
Fosse aux Lions." The following scene will give an idea
of the daring sublimity of these scriptural pantomimes.
"*Scene* 20.—La fournaise devient un berceau de nuages
azurés, au fond duquel est un grouppe de nuages plus lu-
mineux, et au milieu 'Jehovah' au centre d'un cercle de
rayons brillans, qui annonce la presence de l'Éternel."

(2) Madame Bégrand, a finely-formed woman, who acts in
"Susanna and the Elders,"—"L'Amour et la Folie," etc.

3) The Promenades Aériennes, or French Mountains.
—See a description of this singular and fantastic place of
amusement in a pamphlet, truly worthy of it, by "F. F.

For 't was like heaven and earth, Dolly, coming
          together—
Yet, spite of the danger, we dared it again.
And oh! as I gazed on the features and air
Of the man, who for me all this peril defied,
I could fancy almost he and I were a pair
Of unhappy young lovers, who thus, side by side,
Were taking, instead of rope, pistol, or dagger, a
Desperate dash down the falls of Niagara!

This achieved, through the gardens (5) we saunter'd
          about,
Saw the fire-works, exclaim'd "magnifique!" at
          each cracker,
And, when 't was all o'er the dear man saw us out
With the air, I *will* say, of a Prince, to our *fiacre.*

Now, hear me—this Stranger—it may be mere folly—
But *who* do you think we all think it is, Dolly?
Why, bless you, no less than the great King of
          Prussia,
Who's here now incog. (6)—he who made such a
          fuss, you
Remember, in London, with Blucher and Platoff,
When Sal was near kissing old Blucher's cravat off!
Pa says he's come here to look after his money,
(Not taking things now as he used under Boney,)
Which suits with our friend, for Bob saw him, he
          swore,
Looking sharp to the silver received at the door.
Besides, too, they say that his grief for his Queen
(Which was plain in this sweet fellow's face to be seen)
Requires such a stimulant dose as this car is,
Used three times a-day with young ladies in Paris.
Some Doctor, indeed, has declared that such grief
Should—unless 't would to utter despairing its
          folly push—
Fly to the Beaujon, and there seek relief
          By rattling, as Bob says, "like shot through a
          holly-bush."

I must now bid adieu;—only think, Dolly, think
If this *should* be the King—I have scarce slept a wink
With imagining how it will sound in the papers,
And how all the Misses my good luck will grudge,
When they read that Count Ruppin, to drive away
          vapours,
Has gone down the Beaujon with Miss Biddy Fudge.

Cotterel, Médecin, Docteur de la Faculté de Paris," etc., etc.

(4) According to Dr. Cotterel the cars go at the rate of
forty-eight miles an hour.

(5) In the Café attached to these gardens there are to be
(as Doctor Cotterel informs us) "douze nègres, très alertes,
qui contrasteront par l'ébène de leur peau avec le teint
de lis et de roses de nos belles. Les glaces et les sorbets,
servis par une main bien noire, fera davantage ressortir
l'albâtre des bras arrondis de celles-ci."—P. 22.

(6 His Majesty, who was at Paris under the travelling
name of Count Ruppin, is known to have gone down the
Beaujon very frequently

Nota Bene.—Papa's almost certain 'tis he—
For he knows the Legitimate cut, and could see,
In the way he went poising and managed to tower
So erect in the car, the true *Balance of Power.*

—ɔ❦ɕ—

LETTER VI.

FROM PHIL. FUDGE, ESQ., TO HIS BROTHER TIM
FUDGE, ESQ., BARRISTER AT LAW.

Yours of the 12th received just now—
Thanks for the hint, my trusty brother!
'Tis truly pleasing to see how
We Fudges stand by one another.
But never fear—I know my chap,
And he knows *me* too—*verbum sap.*
My Lord and I are kindred spirits,
Like in our ways as two young ferrets;
Both fashion'd, as that supple race is,
To twist into all sorts of places;—
Creatures lengthy, lean, and hungering,
Fond of blood and *burrow-*mongering.

As to my Book in 91,
    Call'd "Down with Kings, or, Who'd have
        thought it?"
Bless you, the Book's long dead and gone—
    Not even the Attorney-General bought it.
And, though some few seditious tricks
I play'd in 95 and 6,
As you remind me in your letter,
His Lordship likes me all the better,—
We proselytes, that come with news full,
Are, as he says, so vastly useful!

Reynolds and I—(you know Tom Reynolds—
Drinks his claret, keeps his chaise—
Lucky the dog that first unkennels
Traitors and Luddites now-a-days;
Or who can help to *bag* a few,
When S—d——th wants a death or two;)
Reynolds and I, and some few more,
All men, like us, of *information,*
Friends, whom his Lordship keeps in store,
As *under-*saviours of the nation—(1)
Have form'd a Club this season, where
His Lordship sometimes takes the chair,

(1 Lord C's tribute to the character of his friend, Mr.
Reynolds, will long be remembered with equal credit to
both.

(2) This interpretation of the fable of Midas's ears seems
the most probable of any, and is thus stated in Hoffmann
— "Hác allegoriâ significatum, Midam, utpote tyrannum,
sub auscultatores dimittere solitum, per quos, quæcum-
que per omnem regionem vel fierent, vel dicerentur,
cognosceret, nimirum illis utens aurium vice."

(3) Brossette, in a note on this line of Boileau,

" Midas, le roi Midas, a des oreilles d'âne,'

tells us, that "M. Perrault le médecin voulut faire à notre
auteur un crime d'etat de ce vers, comme d'une maligne
allusion au roi " I trust, however, that no one will

And gives us many a bright oration
In praise of our sublime vocation;
Tracing it up to great King Midas,
Who, though in fable typified as
A royal Ass, by grace divine
And right of ears, most asinine,
Was yet no more, in fact historical,
    Than an exceeding well-bred tyrant;
And these, his *ears,* but allegorical,
    Meaning Informers, kept at high rent—(2)
Gem'men, who touch'd the Treasury glisteners,
Like us, for being trusty listeners;
And picking up each tale and fragment,
For royal Midas's Green Bag meant.
" And wherefore," said this best of Peers,
" Should not the R—g—t too have ears,(3)
To reach as far, as long and wide as
Those of his moded, good King Midas?"
This speech was thought extremely good,
And (rare for him) was understood—
Instant we drank "The R—g—t's Ears,"
With three times three illustrious cheers,
    Which made the room resound like thunder—
"The R—g—t's Ears, and may he ne'er
From foolish shame, like Midas, wear
Old paltry *wigs* to keep them under!" (4)
This touch at our old friends, the Whigs,
Made us as merry all as grigs.
In short I'll thank you not to mention
    These things again), we get on gaily;
And, thanks to pension and Suspension,
    Our little Club increases daily.
Castles, and Oliver, and such,
Who don't as yet full salary touch,
Nor keep their chaise and pair, nor buy
Houses and lands, like Tom and I,
Of course don't rank with us, *salvators,* (5)
But merely serve the Club as waiters.
Like Knights, too, we've our *collar* days,
(For *us,* I own, an awkward phrase,)
When, in our new costume adorn'd—
The R—g—t's buff-and-blue coats *turn'd*—
We have the honour to give dinners
To the chief Rats in upper stations; (6)
Your W——ys, V——ns,—half-fledged sinners,
Who shame us by their imitations;

suspect the line in the text of any such indecorous allu-
sion.

(4 It was not under wigs, but tiaras, that King Midas
endeavoured to conceal these appendages :

Tempora purpureis tentat velare tiaris. —Ovid.

The Noble Giver of the toast, however, had evidently, with
his usual clearness, confounded King Midas, Mr. Liston,
and the P——e R—g—t together.

(5) Mr. Fudge and his friends ought to go by this name
—as the man who, some years since, saved the late R ght
Hon. George Rose from drowning, was ever after called
Salvator Rosa.

(6) This intimacy between the rats and Informers is just
as it should be— "verè dulce sodalitium."

Who turn, 'tis true—but what of that?
Give me the useful *peaching* Rat;
Not things as mute as Punch, when bought,
Whose wooden heads are all they've brought;
Who, false enough to shirk their friends,
    But too faint-hearted to betray,
Are, after all their twists and bends,
    But souls in Limbo, damn'd half way.
No, no, we nobler vermin are
A *genus* useful as we're rare;
'Midst all the things miraculous
    Of which your natural histories brag,
The rarest must be Rats like us,
    Who *let the cat out of the bag.*
Yet still these Tyros in the cause
Deserve, I own, no small applause;
And they're by us received and treated
With all due honours—only seated
In the inverse scale of their reward,
The merely *promised* next my Lord;
Small pensions then, and so on, down,
Rat after rat, they graduate
Through job, red ribbon, and silk gown,
To Chancellorship and Marquisate.
This serves to nurse the ratting spirit,
The less the bribe the more the merit.

Our music's good, you may be sure;
My Lord, you know, 's an amateur—(1)
Takes every part with perfect ease,
    Though to the Base by nature suited;
And, form'd for all, as best may please,
For whips and bolts, or chords and keys,
Turns from his victims to his glees,
    And has them both well *executed.* (2)
H——t——d, who, though no Rat himself,
    Delights in all such liberal arts,
Drinks largely to the House of Guelph,
    And superintends the *Corni* parts,
While C——nn—g, (3) who'd be *first* by choice,
Consents to take an *under* voice;
And Gr—v—s, (4) who well that signal knows,
Watches the *Volti Subitos.* (5)

In short, as I've already hinted,
    We take, of late, prodigiously;
But as our Club is somewhat stinted
    For *Gentlemen,* like Tom and me,

(1) His Lordship, during one of the busiest periods of
his Ministerial career, took lessons three times a-week
from a celebrated music-master, in glee-singing.
(2 How amply these two propensities of the Noble Lord
would have been gratified among that ancient people of
Etruria, who, as Aristotle tells us, used to whip their slaves
once a-year to the sound of flutes!
3 This Right Hon. Gentleman ought to give up his
present alliance with Lord C., if upon no other principle
than that which is inculcated in the following arrangement
between two Ladies of Fashion —

We'll take it kind if you'll provide
A few *Squireens* (6) from t'other side;—
Some of those loyal cunning elves
    (We often tell the tale with laughter),
Who used to hide the pikes themselves,
    Then hang the fools who found them after.
I doubt not you could find us, too,
Some Orange Parsons that might do;
Among the rest, we've heard of one,
The Reverend—something—Hamilton,
Who stuff'd a figure of himself
    Delicious thought!) and had it shot at,
To bring some Papists to the shelf,
    That couldn't otherwise be got at—
If *he'll* but join the Association,
We'll vote him in by acclamation.

And now, my brother, guide, and friend,
This somewhat tedious scrawl must end.
I've gone into this long detail,
    Because I saw your nerves were shaken
With anxious fears lest I should fail
    In this new, *loyal,* course I've taken.
But, bless your heart! you need not doubt—
We, Fudges, know what we're about.
Look round, and say if you can see
A much more thriving family,
There's Jack, the Doctor—night and day
Hundreds of patients so besiege him,
You'd swear that all the rich and gay
    Fell sick on purpose to oblige him.
And while they think, the precious ninnies,
He's counting o'er their pulse so steady,
The rogue but counts how many guineas
He's fobb'd, for that day's work, already.
I'll ne'er forget the old maid's alarm,
    When, feeling thus Miss Sukey Flirt, he
Said, as he dropp'd her shrivell'd arm,
    "Damn'd bad this morning—only thirty!'"

Your dowagers, too, every one,
So generous are, when they call *him* in,
That he might now retire upon
    The rheumatisms of three old women.
Then, whatsoe'er your ailments are,
    He can so learnedly explain ye 'em—
Your cold, of course, is a *catarrh,*
    Your headach is a *hemi-cranium —*

> Says Clarinda, "though tears it may cost,
>   It is time we should part, my dear Sue
> For *your* character's totally lost,
>   And *I* have not sufficient for *two* !'"

(4) The rapidity of this Noble Lord's transformation, at
the same instant, into a Lord of the Bed-chamber and an
opponent of the Catholic Claims, was truly miraculous
5) *Turn instantly* — a frequent direction in music
books.
(6) The Irish diminutive of *Squire*

His skill, too, in young ladies' lungs,
  The grace with which, most mild of
    men,
He begs them to put out their tongues,
  Then bids them—put them in again:
In short, there's nothing now like Jack!—
  Take all your doctors great and small,
Of present times and ages back,
  Dear Doctor Fudge is worth them all.

So much for physic—then, in law too,
  Counsellor Tim, to thee we bow;
Not one of us gives more éclat to
  The immortal name of Fudge than thou.
Not to expatiate on the art
  With which you play'd the patriot's part,
Till something good and snug should offer,—
  Like one, who, by the way he acts
The enlightening part of candle-snuffer,
  The manager's keen eye attracts,
And is promoted thence by him
  To strut in robes, like thee, my Tim!—
Who shall describe thy powers of face,
  Thy well-fee'd zeal in every case,
Or wrong or right—but ten times warmer
  (As suits thy calling) in the former—
Thy glorious lawyer-like delight
  In puzzling all that's clear and right,
Which, though conspicuous in thy youth,
  Improves so with a wig and band on,
That all thy pride's to waylay Truth,
  And leave her not a leg to stand on.
Thy patent, prime, morality—
  Thy cases, cited from the Bible—
Thy candour, when it falls to thee
  To help in trouncing for a libel;—
"God knows, I, from my soul, profess
  To hate all bigots and benighters!
God knows, I love, to even excess,
  The sacred Freedom of the Press,
My only aim's to—crush the writers."
  These are the virtues, Tim, that draw
The briefs into thy bag so fast;
  And these, oh Tim—if Law be Law—
Will raise thee to the Bench at last.

I blush to see this letter's length—
  But 't was my wish to prove to thee
How full of hope, and wealth, and strength,
  Are all our precious family.
And, should affairs go on as pleasant
  As, thank the Fates, they do at present—
Should we but still enjoy the sway
  Of S—dm—h and of C———gh.
I hope, ere long, to see the day

When England's wisest statesmen, judges,
Lawyers, peers, will all be—Fudges!

Good-bye—my paper 's out so nearly,
I've only room for   Yours sincerely.

————————

LETTER VII.

FROM PHELIM CONNOR TO ————.

BEFORE we sketch the Present—let us cast
A few, short, rapid glances to the Past.

When he, who had defied all Europe's strength,
Beneath his own weak rashness sunk at length;—
When, loosed, as if by magic, from a chain
That seem'd like Fate's, the world was free again,
And Europe saw, rejoicing in the sight,
The cause of Kings, for once, the cause of Right;—
Then was, indeed, an hour of joy to those
Who sigh'd for justice—liberty—repose,
And hoped the fall of one great vulture's nest
Would ring its warning round, and scare the rest.
All then was bright with promise;—Kings began
To own a sympathy with suffering Man,
And Man was grateful; Patriots of the South
Caught wisdom from a Cossack Emperor's mouth,
And heard, like accents thaw'd in Northern air,
Unwonted words of freedom burst forth there!

Who did not hope, in that triumphant time,
When monarchs, after years of spoil and crime,
Met round the shrine of Peace, and Heaven look'd on—
Who did not hope the lust of spoil was gone;
That that rapacious spirit, which had play'd
The game of Pilnitz o'er so oft, was laid;
And Europe's Rulers, conscious of the past,
Would blush, and deviate into right at last?
But no—the hearts, that nursed a hope so fair,
Had yet to learn what men on thrones can dare;
Had yet to know, of all earth's ravening things,
The only quite untameable are Kings!
Scarce had they met when, to its nature true,
The instinct of their race broke out anew;
Promises, treaties, charters, all were vain,
And "Rapine! rapine!" was the cry again.
How quick they carved their victims, and how well,
Let Saxony, let injured Genoa tell;—
Let all the human stock that, day by day,
Was, at that Royal slave-mart, truck'd away—
The million souls that, in the face of heaven,
Were split to fractions, (1) barter'd, sold, or given
To swell some despot Power, too huge before,
And weigh down Europe with one Mammoth more.
How safe the faith of Kings let France decide;—
Her charter broken, ere its ink had dried;—

---

(1) "Whilst the Congress was re-constructing Europe—not according to rights, natural affiances, language, habits, or laws, but by tables of finance, which divided and sub-divided her population into souls, demi-souls, and even

fractions, according to a scale of the direct duties or taxes, which could be levied by the acquiring state," etc. —Sketch of the Military and Political Power of Russia The words on the protocol are ames, demi-ames, etc.

Her Press enthiall'd—her Reason mock'd again
With all the monkery it had spurn'd in vain ;
Her crown d sgraced by one, who dared to own
He thank'd not France but England for his throne ,
Her triumphs cast into the shade by those
Who had grown old among her bitterest foes,
And now return'd, beneath her conquerors' shields,
Unblushing slaves ! to claim her heroes' fields ;
To tread down every trophy of her fame,
And curse that glory which to them was shame !—
Let these—let all the damning deeds, that then
Were dared through Europe, cry aloud to men,
With voice like that of crashing ice that rings
Round Alpine huts, the perfidy of Kings ;
And tell the world, when hawks shall harmless bear
The shrinking dove, when wolves shall learn to spare
The helpless victim for whose blood they lusted,
Then, and then only, monarchs may be trusted.

It could not last—these horrors could not last—
France would herself have risen, in might, to cast
The insulters off—and oh ! that then, as now,
Chain'd to some distant islet's rocky brow,
Napoleon ne'er had come to force, to blight,
Ere half matured, a cause so proudly bright , —
To palsy patriot arts with doubt and shame,
And write on Freedom's flag a despot's name ;—
To rush into the lists, unask'd, alone,
And make the stake of all the game of one !
Then would the world have seen again what power
A people can put forth in Freedom's hour ;
Then would the fire of France once more have
        blazed ;—
For every single sword, reluctant raised
In the stale cause of an oppressive throne,
Millions would then have leap'd forth in her own ;
And never, never had the unholy stain
Of Bourbon feet disgraced her shores again.

But fate decreed not so—the Imperial Bird,
That, in his neighbouring cage, unfear'd, unstirr'd,
Had seem'd to sleep with head beneath his wing,
Yet watch'd the moment for a daring spring ;—
Well might he watch, when deeds were done, that
        made
His own transgressions whiten in their shade ,
Well might he hope a world, thus trampled o'er
By clumsy tyrants, would be his once more ·—
Forth from his cage the eagle burst to light,
From steeple on to steeple (1) wing'd his flight,
With calm and easy grandeur, to that throne
From which a Royal craven just had flown ,
And resting there, as in his ærie, furl'd
Those wings, whose very rustling shook the world

What was your fury then, ye crown'd array,
Whose feast of spoil, whose plundering holiday
Was thus broke up, in all its greedy mirth,
By one bold chieftain's stamp on Gallic earth !
Fierce was the cry, and fulminant the ban—
"Assassinate, who will—enchain, who can,
The vile, the faithless, outlaw'd, low-born man !"
"Faithless !"—and this from you—from you, for-
        sooth,
Ye pious Kings, pure paragons of truth,
Whose honesty all knew, for all had tried ;
Whose true Swiss zeal had served on every side ;
Whose fame for breaking faith so long was known,
Well might ye claim the craft as all your own,
And lash your lordly tails, and fume to see
Such low-born apes of Royal perfidy !
Yes—yes—to you alone did it belong
To sin for ever, and yet ne'er do wrong.—
The frauds, the lies of Lords legitimate
Are but fine policy, deep strokes of state ;
But let some upstart dare to soar so high
In Kingly craft, and "outlaw" is the cry !
What, though long years of mutual treachery
Had peopled full your diplomatic shelves
With ghosts of treaties, murder'd 'mong yourselves ;
Though each by turns was knave and dupe—what
        then ?
A Holy League would set all straight again ;
Like Juno's virtue, which a dip or two
In some bless'd fountain made as good as new ! (2)
Most faithful Russia—faithful to whoe'er
Could plunder best, and give him amplest share ;
Who, even when vanquish'd, sure to gain his ends,
For want of foes to rob, made free with friends,(3)
And, deepening still by amiable gradations,
When foes were stript of all, then fleeced rela-
        tions ! (4)
Most mild and saintly Prussia—steep'd to the ears
In persecuted Poland's blood and tears,
And now, with all her harpy wings outspread
O'er sever'd Saxony's devoted head !
Pure Austria too—whose history nought repeats
But broken leagues and subsidized defeats ;
Whose faith, as Prince, extinguish'd Venice shows,
Whose faith, as man, a widow'd daughter knows !
And thou, oh England—who, though once as shy
As cloister'd maids, of shame or perfidy,
Art now broke in, and, thanks to C——gh,
In all that 's worst and falsest lead'st the way !

Such was the pure divan, whose pens and wits
The escape from Elba frighten'd into fits ;—
Such were the saints, who doom'd Napoleon's life,
In virtuous frenzy, to the assassin's knife.

---

(1) " L'aigle volera de clocher en clocher, jusqu'aux
tours de Notre-Dame." — Napoleon's Proclamation on
landing from Elba.

(2) Singulis annis in quodam Atticæ fonte lota virgini-
tatem recuperasse fingitur.

(3 At the Peace of Tilsit, where he abandoned his ally,
Prussia, to France, and received a portion of her terri-
tory.

(4) The seizure of Finland from his relative of Swe-
den.

Disgusting crew!—*who* would not gladly fly
To open, downright, bold-faced tyranny,
To honest guilt, that dares do all but lie,
From the false juggling craft of men like these,
Their canting crimes and varnish'd villanies ;—
These Holy Leaguers, who then loudest boast
Of faith and honour when they 've stain'd them most ;
From whose affection men should shrink as loath
As from their hate, for they 'll be fleeced by both ;
Who, even while plundering, forge Religion's name
To frank their spoil, and, without fear or shame,
Call down the Holy Trinity (1) to bless
Partition leagues, and deeds of devilishness !
But hold—enough—soon would this swell of rage
O'erflow the boundaries of my scanty page ;—
So, here I pause—farewell—another day,
Return we to those Lords of prayer and prey,
Whose loathsome cant, whose frauds by right divine
Deserve a lash—oh ! weightier far than mine !

—◦❈◦—

LETTER VIII.

FROM MR. BOB FUDGE TO RICHARD ——, ESQ.

DEAR Dick, while old Donaldson 's (2) mending my
    stays,   [days,
Which I *knew* would go smash with me one of these
And, at yesterday's dinner, when, full to the throttle,
We lads had begun our dessert with a bottle
Of neat old Constantia, on *my* leaning back
Just to order another, by Jove, i went crack !—
Or, as honest Tom said, in his nautical phrase,
  " D—n my eyes, Bob, in *doubling* the *Cape* you 've
    miss'd stays." (2)   [them,
So, of course, as no gentleman's seen out without
They 're now at the Schneider's (4)—and, while he's
    about them,
Here goes for a letter, post-haste, neck and crop.
Let us see—in my last I was—where did I stop?
Oh, I know—at the Boulevards, as motley a road as
Man ever would wish a day's lounging upon ;
With its cafés and gardens, hotels and pagodas,
  Its founts, and old Counts sipping beer in the sun :
With its houses of all architectures you please,
From the Grecian and Gothic, Dick, down by degrees
To the pure Hottentot, or the Brighton Chinese ;
Where in temples antique you may breakfast or
    dinner it,
Lunch at a mosque, and see Punch from a minaret.

1) The usual preamble of these flagitious compacts.
In the same spirit, Catherine, after the dreadful massacre
of Warsaw, ordered a solemn "thanksgiving to God in all
the churches, for the blessings conferred upon the Poles,"
and commanded that each of them should "swear fidelity
and loyalty to her, and to shed in her defence the last
drop of their blood, as they should answer for it to God,
and his terrible judgment, kissing the holy word and cross
of their Saviour !"

2) An English tailor at Paris.

(3 A ship is said to miss stays, when she does not obey
the helm in tacking.

(4 The dandy term for a tailor.

Then, Dick, the mixture of bonnets and bowers,
Of foliage and frippery, *fiacres* and flowers,
Green-grocers, green gardens—one hardly knows
    whether
'T is country or town, they 're so mess'd up together !
And there, if one loves the romantic, one sees
Jew clothes-men, like shepherds, reclined under trees ;
Or Quidnuncs, on Sunday, just fresh from the barber's,
Enjoying their news and *groseille* (5) in those ar-
    bours ,
While ga ly their wigs, like the tendrils, are curling,
And founts of red currant-juice 6 round them are
    purling.

Here, Dick, arm in arm as we chattering stray,
And receive a few civil " God-dems" by the way—
For, 't is odd, these mounseers — though we 've
    wasted our wealth
  And our strength, till we 've thrown ourselves into
    a phthisic,
To cram down their throats an old King for their
    health,
  As we whip little children to make them take
    physic ;—
Yet, spite of our good-natured money and slaughter,
They hate us, as Beelzebub hates holy-water !
But who the deuce cares, Dick, as long as they
    nourish us
Neatly as now, and good cookery flourishes—
Long as, by bayonets protected, we, Natties,
May have our full fling at their *salmis* and *pâtés?*
And, truly, I always declared 't would be pity
To burn to the ground such a choice-feeding city.
Had *Dad* but his way, he'd have long ago blown
The whole batch to old Nick—and the *people*, I own,
If for no other cause than their curst monkey looks,
Well deserve a blow-up—but then, damn it, their
    Cooks !
As to Marshals, and Statesmen, and all their whole
    lineage,
For aught that *I* care, you may knock them to spinage,
But think, Dick, their Cooks—what a loss to man-
    kind !   [behind !
What a void in the world would their art leave
Their chronometer spits—their intense salamanders—
Their ovens—their pots, that can soften old ganders,
All vanish'd for ever—their miracles o'er,
And the *Marmite Perpétuelle* (7) bubbling no more !

(5) Lemonade and *eau-de-groseille* are measured out
at every corner of every street, from fantastic vessels,
jingling with bells, to thirsty tradesmen or wearied mes-
sengers."—See Lady Morgan's lively description of the
streets of Paris, in her very amusing work upon France,
book vi

(6) These gay portable fountains, from which the gro-
seille water is administered, are among the most charac-
teristic ornaments of the streets of Paris.

7 "Cette merveilleuse marmite perpétuelle, sur le feu
depuis près d'un siècle, qui a donné le jour a plus de
300,000 chapons." —*Alman. des Gourmands*, quatrième
année, p. 152.

Forbid it, forbid it, ye Holy Allies!
　Take whatever ye fancy—take statues, take mo-
　　ney—
But leave them, oh leave them, their Perigueux pies,
　Their glorious goose-livers, and high - pickled
　　tunny! (1)　　　　　　　　　　　[us,
Though many, I own, are the evils they 've brought
　Though Royalty 's here on her very last legs,
Yet, who can help loving the land that has taught us
　Six hundred and eighty-five ways to dress eggs? (2)

You see, Dick, in spite of their cries of " God-dem,"
" Coquin Anglais," et cætera—how generous I am!
And now (to return, once again, to my " Day,"
Which will take us all night to get through in this
　way,)
From the Boulevards we saunter through many a
　street,
Crack jokes on the natives—mine, all very neat—
Leave the Signs of the Times to political fops,
And find *twice* as much fun in the Signs of the
　Shops ;—
Here, a Louis Dix-huit—*there* a Martinmas goose,
(Much in vogue since your eagles are gone out of
　　　　　　　　　　　　　　　　　[use)—
Henri Quatres in shoals, and of Gods a great many,
But Saints are the most on hard duty of any :—
St. Tony, who used all temptations to spurn,
Here hangs o'er a beer-shop, and tempts in his turn,
While *there* St. Venecia (3) sits hemming and frilling
　her
Holy *mouchoir* o'er the door of some milliner ;—
Saint Austin 's the " outward and visible sign
Of an inward" cheap dinner, and pint of small wine;
While St. Denis hangs out o'er some hatter of *ton*,
And possessing, good bishop, no head of his own, (4)
Takes an interest in Dandies, who've got—next to
　none!　　　　　　　　　　　　. [*fiches*—
Then we stare into shops—read the evening's *af*-
Or, if some, who're Lotharios in feeding, should wish

(1) Le thon marine, one of the most favourite and indi-
gestible *hors-d'œuvres*. This fish is taken chiefly in the
Golfe de Lyon. " La tête et le ventre sont les parties les
plus recherchees des gourmets."—*Cours Gastronomique.*

(2) The exact number mentioned by M. de la Reynière
— " On connoît en France 685 manières différentes d'ac-
commoder les œufs, sans compter celles que nos savants
imaginent chaque jour."

(3 Veronica, the Saint of the Holy Handkerchief, is also,
under the name of Venisse or Venecia, the tutelary saint
of milliners.

(4 St. Denis walked three miles after his head was cut
off. The *mot* of a woman of wit upon this legend is well
known :—" Je le crois bien, en pareil cas, il n'y a que le
premier pas qui coûte."

(5 Off the Boulevards Italiens.

(6) In the Palais Royal , successor, I believe, to the Fla-
mand, so long celebrated for the *moelleux* of his Gauffres

(7) Doctor Cotterel recommends, for this purpose, the
Beaujon or French Mountains, and calls them " une mé-
lecine aérienne, couleur de rose," but I own I prefer the
authority of Mr. Bob, who seems, from the following note

Just to flirt with a luncheon, (a devilish bad trick,
As it takes off the bloom of one's appetite, Dick,)
To the *Passage des*—what d'ye call't—*des Pano-
　ramas* (5)
We quicken our pace, and there heartily cram as
Seducing young *pâtés*, as ever could cozen
One out of one's appetite, down by the dozen.
We vary, of course—*petits pâtés* do *one* day,
The *next* we 've our lunch with the Gauffrier Hol-
　landais, (6)
That popular artist, who brings out, like Sc—tt,
His delightful productions so quick, hot and hot;
Not the worse for the exquisite comment that fol-
　lows—
Divine *maresquino*, which—Lord, how one swallows!

Once more, then, we saunter forth after our snack, or
Subscribe a few francs for the price of a *fiacre*,
And drive far away to the old Montagnes Russes,
Where we find a few twirls in the car of much use
To regenerate the hunger and thirst of us sinners,
Who 've lapsed into snacks—the perdition of dinners.
And here, Dick—in answer to one of your queries,
　About which we, Gourmands, have had much
　　discussion—
I 've tried all these mountains, Swiss, French, and
　Ruggieri's,
　And think, for *digestion*, (7) there 's none like the
　　Russian ;
So equal the motion—so gentle, though fleet—
　It, in short, such a light and salubrious scamper is,
That take whom you please—take old L—s D—x-
　h—t,
　And stuff him—ay, up to the neck—with stew'd
　　lampreys, (8)
So wholesome these Mounts, such a *solvent* I 've
　found them,
That, let me but rattle the Monarch well down them,
The fiend, Indigestion, would fly far away,
And the regicide lampreys (9) be foil'd of their prey!

found in his own hand-writing, to have studied all these
mountains very carefully ;—
　Memoranda—The Swiss little notice deserves,
　While the fall at Ruggieri's is death to weak nerves,
　And (whate'er Doctor Cotterel may write on the question)
　The turn at the Beaujon 's too sharp for digestion.
I doubt whether Mr. Bob is quite correct in accenting the
second syllable of Ruggieri

(8) A dish so indigestible, that a late novelist, at the end
of his book, could imagine no more summary mode of
getting rid of all his heroes and heroines than by a hearty
supper of stewed lampreys

(9) They killed Henry I. of England : — " a food says
Hume, gravely,) which always agreed better with his pa-
late than his constitution."
Lampreys, indeed, seem to have been always a favourite
dish with kings—whether from some congeniality between
them and that fish, I know not, but *Dio Cassius* tells us
that Pollio fattened his lampreys with human blood. St.
Louis of France was particularly fond of them.—See the
anecdote of Thomas Aquinas eating up his majesty's
lamprey, in a note upon *Rabelais*, liv. iii., chap. 2.

Such, Dick, are the classical sports that content us,
Till five o'clock brings on that hour so momentous,(1)
That epoch——but woa! my lad—here comes the
    Schneider,
And, curse him, has made the stays three inches
    wider—
Too wide by an inch and a half—what a Guy!
But, no matter—'t will all be set right by-and-by.
As we've Massinot's (2) eloquent *carte* to eat still up,
An inch and a half's but a trifle to fill up.

So—not to lose time, Dick—here goes for the task;
Au revoir, my old boy—of the Gods I but ask,
That my life, like "the Leap of the German,"(3)
    may be,
"Du lit à la table, d' la table au lit!"

R. F.

—◦ ◦ ◦—

LETTER IX.

FROM PHIL. FUDGE, ESQ. TO THE LORD VISCOUNT
C—ST——GH.

My Lord, the Instructions, brought to-day,
"I shall in all my best obey."
Your Lordship talks and writes so sensibly!
And—whatsoe'er some wags may say—
Oh! not at *all* incomprehensibly.

I feel the inquiries in your letter
    About my health and French most flattering,
Thank ye, my French, though somewhat better,
    Is, on the whole, but weak and smattering :—
Nothing, of course, that can compare
With his who made the Congress stare
(A certain Lord we need not name),
    Who even in French, would have his trope,
And talk of "*bâtir* un système
    "Sur *l'équilibre* de l'Europe!"
Sweet metaphor!—and then the Epistle,
Which bid the Saxon King go whistle—
That tender letter to "Mon Prince,"(4)
Which show'd alike thy French and sense;—
Oh no, my Lord—there's none can do
Or say *un-English* things like you;
And, if the schemes that fill thy breast
    Could but a vent congenial seek,
And use the tongue that suits them best,
    What charming Turkish wouldst thou speak!

1) Had Mr. Bob's *Dinner* Epistle been inserted, I was
prepared with an abundance of learned matter to illus-
trate it, for which, as, indeed for all my "scientia po-
pina,"* I am indebted to a friend in the Dublin Uni-
versity—whose reading formerly lay in the *magic* line;
but, in consequence of the Provost's enlightened alarm
at such studies, he has taken to the authors, "*de recibaria*"
instead, and has left *Bodin, Remigius, Agrippa* and his
little dog *Filiolus*, for *Apicius Nonius*, and that most
learned and savoury jesuit, *Bulengerus*.

2) A famous Restaurateur—now Dupont.

* Seneca

But as for *me*, a Frenchless grub,
    At Congress never born to stammer,
Nor learn like thee, my Lord, to snub
    Fall'n Monarchs, out of Chambaud's grammar—
Bless you, you do not, *cannot* know
How far a little French will go;
For all one's stock, one need but draw
    On some half-dozen words like these—
Comme ça—par-là—là-bas—ah ha!
They'll take you all through France with ease.

Your Lordship's praises of the scraps
    I sent you from my Journal lately,
(Enveloping a few laced caps
    For Lady C.), delight me greatly.
Her flattering speech—"What pretty things
    One finds in Mr. Fudge's pages!"
Is praise which (as some poet sings)
    Would pay one for the toils of ages.

Thus flatter'd, I presume to send
A few more extracts by a friend;
And I should hope they'll be no less
Approved of than my last MS.—
The former ones, I fear, were creased,
    As Biddy round the caps *would* pin them,
But these will come to hand, at least
    Unrumpled, for there 's—nothing in them.

*Extracts from Mr. Fudge's Journal, addressed to
Lord C.*

Aug. 10.

Went to the Mad-house—saw the man,(5)
    Who thinks, poor wretch, that, while the Fiend
Of Discord here full riot ran,
    He, like the rest, was guillotined;—
But that when, under Boney's reign,
    (A more discreet, though quite as strong one,)
The heads were all restored again,
    He, in the scramble, got a *wrong* one.
Accordingly, he still cries out
    This strange head fits him most unpleasantly;
And always runs, poor devil, about,
    Inquiring for his own incessantly!

While to his case a tear I dropt,
    And saunter'd home, thought I—ye Gods!

(3 An old French saying;—"Faire le saut de l'Allemand,
du lit à la table et de la table au lit."

(4) The celebrated letter to Prince Hardenburgh(written,
however, I believe, originally in English,) in which his
Lordship, professing to see "no moral or political objec-
tion" to the dismemberment of Saxony, denounced the
unfortunate King as "not only the most devoted, but the
most favoured of Bonaparte's vassals."

(5) This extraordinary madman is, I believe, in Bi-
cêtre. He imagines, exactly as Mr. Fudge states it, that,
when the heads of those who had been guillotined were
restored, he by mistake got some other person's instead
of his own.

How many heads might thus be swopp'd,
    And, after all, not make much odds!
For instance, there's V—s—t's head—
("Tam *carum*" (1) it may well be said)
If by some curious chance it came
    To settle on Bill Soames's (2) shoulders,
The effect would turn out much the same
    On all respectable cash-holders:
Except that while, in its *new* socket,
    The head was planning schemes to win
A *zig-zag* way into one's pocket,
    The hands would plunge *directly* in.

Good Viscount S—dm—h, too, instead
    Of his own grave respected head,
Might wear (for aught I see that bars)
    Old Lady Wilhelmina Frump's—
So while the hand sign'd *Circulars*,
    The head might lisp out "What is trumps?"—
The R—g—t's brains could we transfer
To some robust man-milliner,
The shop, the shears, the lace, and ribbon
Would go, I doubt not, quite as glib on;
And, *vice versâ*, take the pains
To give the P—ce the shopman's brains,
One only change from thence would flow,
Ribbons would not be wasted so.

'T was thus I ponder'd on, my Lord;
    And, even at night, when laid in bed,
I found myself, before I snored,
    Thus chopping, swopping head for head.
At length I thought, fantastic elf!
How such a change would suit *myself*.
'T wixt sleep and waking, one by one,
    With various pericraniums saddled,
At last I tried your Lordship's own,
    And then I grew completely addled—
Forgot all other heads, od rot 'em!
And slept, and dreamt that I was—Bottom.

Aug. 21
Walk'd out with daughter Bid—was shown
The House of Commons, and the Throne,
Whose velvet cushion's just the same (3)
Napoleon sat on—what a shame!
Oh! can we wonder, best of speechers,
    When Louis seated thus we see,

(1) Tam cari capitis.—*Horat.*

(2 A celebrated pickpocket.

3) The only change, if I recollect right, is the substitution of lilies for bees. This war upon the bees is, of course, universal; "exitium misère apibus," like the angry nymphs in Virgil :—but may not *new swarms* arise out of the *victims* of Legitimacy yet?

(4) I am afraid that Mr. Fudge alludes here to a very awkward accident, which is well known to have happened to poor L—s le D—s—é, some years since, at one of the R—g—t's Fêtes. He was sitting next our gracious Queen at the time.

That France's "fundamental features"
    Are much the same they used to be?
However—God preserve the Throne,
    And *cushion* too—and keep them free
From accidents, which *have* been known
    To happen even to Royalty!(4)

Aug. 28.
Read, at a stall (for oft one pops
On something at these stalls and shops,
That does to *quote*, and gives one's Book
A classical and knowing look.—
Indeed I've found, in Latin, lately,
A course of stalls improves me greatly)—
'T was thus I read, that, in the East,
    A monarch's *fat*'s a serious matter;
And once in every year, at least,
    He's weigh'd—to see if he gets fatter : (5)
Then, if a pound or two he be
Increased, there's quite a jubilee!(6)
Suppose, my Lord—and far from me
To treat such things with levity—
But just suppose the R—g—t's weight
Were made thus an affair of state;
And, every sessions, at the close—
    'Stead of a speech, which, all can see, is
Heavy and dull enough, God knows—
    We were to try how heavy *he* is.
Much would it glad all hearts to hear
    That, while the Nation's Revenue
Loses so many pounds a-year,
    The P——e, God bless him! *gains* a few.

With bales of muslin, chintzes, spices,
    I see the Easterns weigh their Kings;—
But, for the R—g—t, my advice is,
    We should throw in much *heavier* things:
For instance ——'s quarto volumes,
    Which, though not spices, serve to wrap them,
Dominie St—dd—t's Daily columns,
    "Prodigious!"—in, of course, we'd clap them—
Letters, that C—rtw—t's pen (7) indites,
    In which, with logical confusion,
The *Major* like a *Minor* writes,
    And never comes to a *Conclusion:*—
Lord S—m—rs' pamphlet—or his head—
(Ah, *that* were worth its weight in lead!)

(5) "The third day of the Feast the King causeth himself to be weighed with great care."—*F. Bernier's Voyage to Surat,* etc.

(6) "I remember," says Bernier, "that all the Omrahs expressed great joy that the King weighed two pounds more now than the year preceding."—Another author tells us that "Fatness, as well as a very large head, is considered, throughout India, as one of the most precious gifts of heaven. An enormous skull is absolutely revered, and the owner is looked up to as a superior being. To a *Prince* a jolter-head is invaluable."—*Oriental Field Sports.*

(7 Major Cartwright

Along with which we *in* may whip, sly,
The Speeches of Sir John C—x H—pp—sly,
That Baronet of many words,
Who loves so, in the House of Lords,
To whisper Bishops—and so nigh
Unto their wigs in whispering goes,
That you may always know him by
A patch of powder on his nose!—
If this wo'n't do, we in must cram
The " Reasons" of Lord B—ck—gh—m ;
(A book his Lordship means to write,
Entitled " Reasons for my Ratting :")
Or, should these prove too small and light,
His r——p 's a host—we 'll bundle *that* in '
And, *still* should all these masses fail
To stir the R—g—t's ponderous scale,
Why then, my Lord, in heaven's name,
Pitch in, without reserve or stint,
The whole of R—gl—y's beauteous Dame—
If *that* wo'n't raise him, devil 's in 't !

Aug. 31

Consulted Murphy's *Tacitus*
About those famous spies at Rome, (1)
Whom certain Whigs—to make a fuss—
Describe as much resembling us, (2)
Informing gentlemen, at home.
But, bless the fools, they *can't* be serious,
To say Lord S—dm—th 's like Tiberius!
What ! *he*, the Peer, that injures no man,
Like that severe blood-thirsty Roman !—
'T is true, the Tyrant lent an ear to
All sorts of spies—so doth the Peer, too.
'T is true my Lord's Elect tell fibs,
And deal in perjury—*ditto* Tib's.
'T is true the Tyrant screen'd and hid
His rogues from justice(3)—*ditto* Sid.
'T is true the Peer is grave and glib
At moral speeches—*ditto* Tib. (4)
'T is true, the feats the Tyrant did
Were in his dotage—*ditto* Sid.

So far, I own, the parallel
'Twixt Tib and Sid goes vastly well;
But there are points in Tib that strike
My humble mind as much more like
Yourself, my dearest Lord, or him,
Of the India Board—that soul of whim !

Like him, Tiberius loved his joke, (5)
On matters, too, where few can bear one;
E. g. a man, cut up, or broke
Upon the wheel—a devilish fair one!
Your common fractures, wounds, and fits,
Are nothing to such wholesale wits ;
But, let the sufferer gasp for life,
The joke is then worth any money ;
And if he writhe beneath a knife,
Oh dear, that 's something *quite* too funny.
In this respect, my Lord, you see
The Roman wag and ours agree :
Now as to *your* resemblance—mum—
This parallel we need not follow ; (6)
Though 't is, in Ireland, said by some
Your Lordship beats Tiberius hollow;
Whips, chains—but these are things too serious
For me to mention or discuss;
Whene'er your Lordship acts Tiberius,
Phil. Fudge's part is *Tacitus !*

Sept. 2.

Was thinking, had Lord S—dm—th got
Any good decent sort of Plot
Against the winter-time—if not,
Alas, alas, our ruin 's fated ;
All done up, and *spifflicated !*
Ministers and all their vassals,
Down from C—tl——gh to Castles—
Unless we can kick up a riot,
Ne'er can hope for peace or quiet !

What 's to be done?—Spa-Fields was clever ;
But even *that* brought gibes and mockings
Upon our heads—so, *mem.*—must never
Keep ammunition in old stockings ;
For fear some wag should in his curst head
Take it to say our force was *worsted*.
Mem. too—when Sid. an army raises,
It must not be " incog." like *Bayes's* :
Nor must the General be a hobbling
Professor of the art of cobbling ;
Lest men, who perpetrate such puns,
Should say, with Jacobinic grin,
He felt, from *soleing Wellingtons*, (7)
A *Wellington's* great *soul* within!
Nor must an old Apothecary
Go take the Tower, for lack of pence,

(1) The name of the first worthy who set up the trade of informer at Rome (to whom our Olivers and Castleses ought to erect a statue was Romanus Hispo,—" qui formam vitæ init, quam postea celebrem miseriæ temporum et audaciæ hominum fecerunt."—*Tacit. Annal.*, i. 74.

(2) They certainly possessed the same art of *instigating* their victims, which the Report of the Secret Committee attributes to Lord Sidmouth's agents — " *socius* (says Tacitus of one of them) libidinum et necessitatum, *quo pluribus indiciis inligaret*."

(3) " Neque tamen id Sereno noxæ fuit, *quem odium publicum tutiorem faciebat.* Nam ut quis districtior accusator *velut sacrosanctus erat*."—*Annal*, lib. iv., 36.—

Or, as it is translated by Mr. Fudge's friend, Murphy ·— " This daring accuser had the *curses of the people*, and the *protection* of the *Emperor. Informers*, in proportion as they rose in guilt, *became sacred characters*."

(4) Murphy even confers upon one of his speeches the epithet " constitutional." Mr. Fudge might have added to his parallel, that Tiberius was a *good private* character . egregium vitâ famâque *quoad privatus*."

(5 " *Ludibria serus* permiscere solitus "

(6) There is one point of resemblance between Tiberius and Lord C. which Mr. Fudge *might* have mentioned— " *suspensa semper et obscura verba*."

(7) Short boots, so called

With (what these wags would call, so merry,
Physical force and *phial*-ence!
No, no—our Plot, my Lord, must be
Next time contrived more skilfully.
John Bull, I grieve to say, is growing
So troublesomely sharp and knowing,
So wise—in short, so Jacobin—
'T is monstrous hard to *take him in.*

Sept 6

Heard of the fate of our Ambassador
　In China, and was sorely nettled;
But think, my Lord, we should not pass it o'er
　Till all this matter's fairly settled.
And here's the mode occurs to me:—
As none of our Nobility,
Though for their *own* most gracious King
(They would kiss hands, or—any thing,)
Can be persuaded to go through
This farce-like trick of the *Ko-tou;*
And as these Mandarins *woo'n't* bend,
　Without some mumming exhibition,
Suppose, my Lord, you were to send
　Grimaldi to them on a mission:
As *Legate,* Joe could play his part,
And if, in diplomatic art,
The "volto sciolto" (1) 's meritorious,
Let Joe but grin, he has it, glorious!

A *title* for him's easily made;
　And, by-the-by, one Christmas time,
If I remember right, he play'd
　Lord Morley in some pantomime;—(2)
As Earl of M—rl—y then gazette him,
If *t'other* Earl of M—rl—y'll let him.
(And why should not the world be blest
With *two* such stars, for East and West?)
Then, when before the Yellow Screen
He's brought—and, sure, the very essence
Of etiquette would be that scene
　Of Joe in the Celestial Presence!
He thus should say :—"Duke Ho and Soo,
I'll play what tricks you please for you,
If you'll, in turn, but do for me
A few small tricks you now shall see.
If I consult *your* Emperor's liking,
At least you'll do the same for *my* King."
He then should give them nine such grins,
As would astound even Mandarins ;
And throw such somersets before
　The picture of King George (God bless him!)
As, should Duke Ho but try them o'er,
　Would, by Confucius, *much* distress him!

(1 The *open countenance,* recommended by Lord Chesterfield.

(2) Mr. Fudge is a little mistaken here. It was *not* Grimaldi, but some very inferior performer, who played this part of "Lord Morley" in the pantomime—so much to the horror of the distinguished Earl of that name. The expostulatory letters of the Noble Earl to Mr H—rr—s, upon

I start this merely as a hint,
But think you'll find some wisdom in 't ;
And, should you follow up the job,
My son, my Lord (you *know* poor Bob ,
Would in the suite be glad to go
And help his Excellency, Joe;—
At least, like noble Amh—rst's son,
The lad will do to *practise* on. (2)

—◦◉◦—

LETTER X.

WELL, it *is n't* the King, after all, my dear creature!
　But *don't* you go laugh, now—there's nothing to
　　quiz in 't—
For grandeur of air and for grimness of feature,
He *might* be a King, Doll, though, hang him, he
At first, I felt hurt, for I wish'd it, I own,　[is n't.
If for no other cause but to vex Miss Malone—
(The great heiress, you know, of Shandangan, who's
　here,
Showing off with *such* airs, and a real Cashmere, (4)
While mine's but a paltry old rabbit-skin, dear ')
But Pa says, on deeply considering the thing,
" I am just as well pleased it should *not* be the King;
As I think for my Biddy, so *gentille* and *jolie,*
Whose charms may their price in an *honest* way fetch,
" That a Brandenburgh"—(what *is* a Brandenburgh,
　Dolly ?)—
Would be, after all, no such very great catch.
If the R—g—t indeed—" added he, looking sly—
(You remember that comical squint of his eye)
But I stopp'd him with " La, Pa, how *can* you say so,
When the R—g—t loves none but old women, you
　know!"
Which is fact, my dear Dolly—we, girls of eighteen,
And so slim—Lord, he'd think us not fit to be seen ;
And would like us much better as old—ay, as old
As that Countess of Desmond, of whom I've been told
That she lived to much more than a hundred and ten,
And was kill'd by a fall from a cherry-tree then !
What a frisky old girl! but—to come to my lover,
Who, though not a King, is a *hero* I'll swear—
You shall hear all that's happen'd, just briefly run
　over,
Since that happy night, when we whisk'd through
　the air !

Let me see—'t was on Saturday—yes, Dolly, yes—
From that evening I date the first dawn of my bliss;
When we both rattled off in that dear little carriage,
Whose journey, Bob says, is so like Love and
　Marriage,

this vulgar profanation of his spick-and-span new title,
will, I trust, some time or other, be given to the world.

(3) See Mr. Ellis's account of the Embassy.

4) See Lady Morgan's "France" for the anecdote, told
her by Madame de Genlis, of the young gentleman whose
love was cured by finding that his mistress wore a *shawl*
" *peau de lapin.*"

"Beginning gay, desperate, dashing, down-hilly,
And ending as dull as a six-inside Dilly!"(1)
Well, scarcely a wink did I sleep the night through;
And, next day, having scribbled my letter to you,
With a heart full of hope this sweet fellow to meet,
I set out with Papa, to see Louis Dix-huit
Make his bow to some half-dozen women and boys,
Who get up a small concert of shrill *Vive le Rois*—
And how vastly genteeler, my dear, even this is,
Than vulgar Pall-Mall's oratorio of hisses!
The gardens seem'd full—so, of course, we walk'd
   o'er 'em,
'Mong orange-trees, clipp'd into town-bred decorum,
And Daphnes, and vases, and many a statue
There staring, with not even a stitch on them, at you!
The ponds, too, we view'd—stood awhile on the brink
To contemplate the play of those pretty gold fishes—
"*Live bullion*," says merciless Bob, "which, I think,
"Would, if *coin'd*, with a little *mint* sauce, be
   delicious!"(2)

But *what*, Dolly, what, is the gay orange-grove,
Or gold fishes, to her that's in search of her love?
In vain did I wildly explore every chair
Where a thing *like* a man was—no lover sate there!
In vain my fond eyes did I eagerly cast
At the whiskers, mustachios, and wigs that went
   past,
To obtain, if I could, but a glance at that curl—
A glimpse of those whiskers, as sacred, my girl,
As the lock that, Pa says,(3) is to Mussulmen given,
For the angel to hold by that "lugs them to heaven!"
Alas, there went by me full many a quiz,
And mustachios in plenty, but nothing like his!
Disappointed, I found myself sighing out "well-a-
   day"—
Thought of the words of T—m M—re's Irish Melody,

Something about the "green spot of delight"(4)
  (Which, you know, Captain Macintosh sung to us
   one day):
Ah, Dolly, *my* "spot" was that Saturday night,
And its verdure, how fleeting, had wither'd by
   Sunday!
We dined at a tavern—La, what do I say?
If Bob was to know!—a *Restaurateur's*, dear;
Where your *properest* ladies go dine every day,
And drink Burgundy out of large tumblers, like beer.
Fine Bob for he's really grown *super-*fine)
Condescended, for once, to make one of the party;
Of course, though but three, we had dinner for nine,
And in spite of my grief, love, I own I eat hearty.
Indeed, Doll, I know not how 'tis, but, in grief,
I have always found eating a wondrous relief;
And Bob, who's in love, said he felt the same, *quite*—
"My sighs," said he, "ceased with the first glass
   I drank you;
The *lamb* made me tranquil, the *puffs* made me light,
And—now that all's o'er—why, I'm—pretty well,
   thank you!"
To *my* great annoyance, we sat rather late;
For Bobby and Pa had a furious debate
About singing and cookery—Bobby, of course,
Standing up for the latter Fine Art in full force;(5)
And Pa saying, "God only knows which is worst,
  "The French Singers or Cooks, but I wish us well
   over it—
What with old Lais and Véry, I'm curst
If *my* head or my stomach will ever recover it!"

'T was dark when we got to the Boulevards to stroll,
  And in vain did I look 'mong the street Macaronis,
When, sudden it struck me—last hope of my soul—
  That some angel might take the dear man to
   Tortoni's!(6)

(1) The cars, on the return, are dragged up slowly by a
chain.

(2) Mr. Bob need not be ashamed of his cookery jokes,
when he is kept in countenance by such men as *Cicero*,
St. Augustine, and that jovial bishop, *Venantius Fortuna-
tus*. The pun of the great orator upon the "jus Verri-
num," which he calls bad *hog-broth*, from a play upon
the Saint's puns upon the conversion of Lot's wife into
salt, are equally ingenious.—"In salem conversa homini-
bus fidelibus quoddam præstitit *condimentum*, quo *sapiant*
aliquid, unde illud caveatur exemplum." *De Civitat. Dei*,
lib. xvi., cap. 30.—The jokes of the pious favourite of Queen
Radagunda, the convivial Bishop *Venantius*, may be found
among his poems, in some lines against a cook who had
robbed him. The following is similar to *Cicero's* pun.—
   Plus *juscella* Coci quam mea *jura* valent.
See his poems, *Corpus Poetar. Latin.*, tom. ii , p. 1732.—
Of the same kind was *Montmaur's* joke, when a dish was
spilt over him—"summum jus, summa injuria ," and the
same celebrated parasite, in ordering a sole to be placed
before him, said,—
   Eligi cui dicas, tu mihi *sola* places
The reader may likewise see, among a good deal of
kitchen erudition, the learned *Lipsius's* jokes on cutting
up a capon in his *Saturnal. Sermon.*, lib. ii., cap. 2.

(3) For this scrap of knowledge "Pa" was, I suspect,
indebted to a note upon Volney's *Ruins*; a book which
usually forms part of a Jacobin's library, and with which
Mr. Fudge must have been well acquainted at the time
he wrote his "Down with Kings," etc. The note in Volney
is as follows :—"It is by this tuft of hair (on the head), worn
by the majority of Mussulmans, that the Angel of the Tomb
is to take the elect and carry them to Paradise."

(4) The young lady, whose memory is not very correct,
must allude, I think, to the following lines :—
   Oh that fairy form is ne'er forgot,
    Which First Love traced ;
   Still it lingering haunts the greenest spot
    On Memory's waste!

(5) Cookery has been dignified by the researches of a
Bacon, (see his *Natural History*, *Receipts*, etc.) and takes
its station as one of the Fine Arts in the following passage
of Mr. *Dugald Stewart* — "Agreeably to this view of the
subject, *sweet* may be said to be *intrinsically* pleasing,
and *butter* to be relatively pleasing , while both are, in
many cases, equally essential to those effects, which, in
the art of cookery, correspond to that *composite beauty*,
which it is the object of the painter and of the poet to
create."—*Philosophical Essays*.

(6 A fashionable *café glacier* on the Italian Boulevards.
   53

We enter'd—and, scaicely had Bob, with an air,
For a *grappe à la jardinière* call'd to the waiters,
When, oh Doll! I saw him—my hero was theie
    (For I knew his white small-clothes and brown
      leather gaiters),
A group of fair statues fiom Greece smiling o'ei
    him, (1)
And lots of red currant-juice sparkling before him !
Oh Dolly, these heroes—what creatures they aie ;
   In the *boudoir* the same as in fields full of slaughter !
As cool in the Beaujon's precipitous car,
   As when safe at Tortoni's, o'er iced currant watei !
He join'd us—imagine, dear creature, my ecstasy—
Join'd by the man I'd have broken ten necks to see!
Bob wish'd to treat him with Punch *à la glace*,
But the sweet fellow swoie, that my *beauté*, my *grâce*,
And my *je-ne-sais-quoi* then his whiskers he twirl'd
Were, to *him*, "on de top of all Ponch in de world."—
How pretty !—though oft as, of course, it must be
Both his French and his English are Greek, Doll, to me.
But, in short, I felt happy as ever fond heart did ;
And happier still, when 'twas fix'd, ere we parted,
That if the next day should be *pastoral* weather,
We all would set off, in French buggies, together,
To see *Montmorency*—that place which, you know,
Is so famous for cherries and Jean Jacques Rousseau.
His card then he gave us—the *name*, rather creased—
But 'twas Calicot—something—a Colonel, at least !
After which—sure there never was hero so civil—he
Saw us safe home to our door in *Rue Rivoli*,
Where his *last* words, as, at parting, he threw
A soft look o'er his shoulders, weie—"How do you
   do !" (2)

But, lord—there's Papa for the post—I'm so vext—
Montmorency must now, love, be kept for my next.
That dear Sunday night !—I was charmingly drest,
And—*so* providential !—was looking my best ;
Such a sweet muslin gown, with a flounce—and my
   frills,
You've no notion how rich—(though Pa has by the
   bills)   [near
And you'd smile had you seen, when we sat rather
Colonel Calicot eyeing the cambric, my dear.
Then the flowers in my bonnet—but, la, it's in vain—
So, good-by, my sweet Doll—I shall soon write again.
                           B. F.

Nota bene—our love to all neighbours about—
Your Papa in particulai—how is his gout?

P.S.—I've just open'd my letter to say,
In your next you must tell me, (now *do*, Dolly, pray,
For I hate to ask Bob, he's so ready to quiz,)
What sort of a thing, dear, a *Brandenburgh* is.

  (1 "You eat your ice at Tortoni's," says Mr. Scott,
"under a Grecian group."
  (2 Not an unusual mistake with foreigners.
  (3) See Ælian, lib. v., cap. 29,—who tells us that these
geese, from a consciousness of their own loquacity, al-

LETTER XI.

FROM PHELIM CONNOR TO ——.

YES, 'twas a cause, as noble and as great
As ever hero died to vindicate—
A Nation's right to speak a Nation's voice,
And own no power but of the Nation's choice !
Such was the grand, the glorious cause that now
Hung trembling on Napoleon's single brow ;
Such the sublime arbitrement, that pour'd,
In patiiot eyes, a light around his sword,
A hallowing light, which never, since the day
Of his young victories, had illumed its way !

Oh 'twas not then the time for tame debates,
Ye men of Gaul, when chains were at your gates ;
When he, who late had fled your Chieftain's eye,
As geese from eagles on Mount Taurus fly, (3)
Denounced against the land, that spurn'd his chain,
Myriads of swords to bind it fast again—
Myriads of fierce invading swords, to track
Through your best blood his path of vengeance back ;
When Europe's Kings, that never yet combined
But (like those uppers Stars, that when conjoin'd,
Shed war and pestilence,) to scourge mankind,
Gather'd around, with hosts from every shore,
Hating Napoleon much, but Freedom more,
And, in that coming strife, appall'd to see
The world yet left one chance for liberty !—
No, 'twas not *then* the time to weave a net
Of bondage round your Chief ; to curb and fret
Your veteran war-horse, pawing for the fight,
When every hope was in his speed and might—
To waste the hour of action in dispute,
And coolly plan how freedom's *boughs* should shoot,
When your Invader's axe was at the *root !*
No, sacred Liberty ! that God, who throws
Thy light around, like his own sunshine, knows
How well I love thee, and how deeply hate
All tyrants, upstart and legitimate—
Yet, in that hour, were France my native land,
I would have follow'd, with quick heart and hand,
Napoleon, Nero—ay, no matter whom—
To snatch my country from that damning doom,
That deadliest curse that on the conquer'd waits—
A conqueror's satrap, throned within her gates !

True, he was false—despotic—all you please—
Had trampled down man's holiest liberties—
Had, by a genius form'd for nobler things
Than lie within the grasp of *vulgar* Kings,
But raised the hopes of men—as eaglets fly
With tortoises aloft into the sky—
To dash them down again more shatteringly !
All this I own—but still (4   *   *

ways cross Mount Taurus with stones in their bills, to
prevent any unlucky cackle from betraying them to the
eagles—διατετονται σιωπωντες.
  (4 Somebody (Fontenelle, I believe,) has said, that if
he had his hand full of truths, he would open but one

LETTER XII.

At last, Dolly—thanks to a potent emetic,
Which Bobby and Pa, with grimace sympathetic,
Have swallow'd this morning, to balance the bliss
Of an eel *matelote* and a *bisque d'écrevisses*—
I 've a morning at home to myself, and sit down
To describe you our heavenly trip out of town.
How agog you must be for this letter, my dear!
Lady Jane, in the novel, less languish'd to hear
If that elegant cornet she met at Lord Neville's
Was actually dying with love or—blue devils.
But Love, Dolly, Love is the theme *I* pursue ;
With Blue Devils, thank heaven, I have nothing to
    do—
Except, indeed, dear Colonel Calicot spies
Any imps of that colour in *certain* blue eyes,
Which he stares at till *I*, Doll, at *his* do the same;
Then he simpers—I blush—and would often exclaim,
If I knew but the French for it, "Lord, Sir, for
    shame!"

Well, the morning was lovely—the trees in full
    dress
For the happy occasion—the sunshine *express*—
Had we order'd it, dear, of the best poet going,
It scarce could be furnish'd more golden and glowing.
Though late when we started, the scent of the air
Was like Gattie's rose-water—and, bright, here and
    there,
On the grass an odd dew-drop was glittering yet,
Like my aunt's diamond pin on her green tabbinet !
While the birds seem'd to warble as blest on the
    boughs
As if *each* a plumed Calicot had for her spouse;
And the grapes were all blushing and kissing in rows,
And—in short, need I tell you, wherever one goes
With the creature one loves, 't is all *couleur de rose*;
And, ah, I shall ne'er, lived I ever so long, see
A day such as that at divine Montmorency !

There was but *one* drawback—at first whon we
    started,
The Colonel and I were inhumanly parted ;
How cruel—young hearts of such moments to rob!
He went in Pa's buggy, and I went with Bob ;

And, I own, I felt spitefully happy to know
That Papa and his comrade agreed but *so-so*.
For the Colonel, it seems, is a stickler of Boney's—
Served *with* him of course—nay, I 'm sure they were
    cronies.
So martial his features ! dear Doll, you can trace
Ulm, Austerlitz, Lodi, as plain in his face
As you do on that pillar of glory and brass, (1
Which the poor Duc de B—ri must hate so to pass !
It appears, too, he made—as most foreigners do—
About English affairs an odd blunder or two.
For example—misled by the names, I dare say—
He confounded Jack Castles with Lord C——gh;
And—sure such a blunder no mortal hit ever on—
Fancied the *present* Lord C—md—n the *clever* one !

But politics ne'er were the sweet fellow's trade;
'T was for war and the ladies my Colonel was made.
And, oh, had you heard, as together we walk'd
Through that beautiful forest, how sweetly he talk'd;
And how perfectly well he appear'd, Doll, to know
All the life and adventures of Jean Jacques Rous-
    seau !—
" 'T was there," said he—not that his *words* I can
    state—
'T was a gibberish that Cupid alone could translate ;—
But "there," said he, (pointing where, small and
    remote,
The dear Hermitage rose,) "there his *Julie* he wrote—
Upon paper gilt-edged, (2) without blot or erasure;
Then sanded it over with silver and azure,
And—oh, what will genius and fancy not do?—
Tied the leaves up together with *nonpareille* blue!"
What a trait of Rousseau ! what a crowd of emotions
From sand and blue ribbons are conjured up here !
Alas, that a man of such exquisite (3) notions
    Should send his poor brats to the Foundling, my
    dear !

" 'T was here, too, perhaps," Colonel Calicot said—
As down the small garden he pensively led—
Though once I could see his sublime forehead wrinkle
With rage not to find there the loved periwinkle) (4)
" 'T was here he received from the fair D'Epinay
(Who call'd him so sweetly her *Bear*, (5) every day,)
That dear flannel petticoat, pull'd off to form
A waistcoat, to keep the enthusiast warm!" (6)

finger at a time , and the same sort of reserve I find to be
necessary with respect to Mr. Connor's very plain-spoken
letters. The remainder of this Epistle is so full of unsafe
matter-of-fact, that it must, for the present at least, be
withheld from the public.

(1) The column in the Place Vendôme.

(2) " Employant pour cela le plus beau papier dore, se-
chant l'ecriture avec de la poudre d'azur et d'argent, et
cousant mes cahiers avec de la nonpareille bleue."— *Les
Confessions*, part ii., liv 9.

3) This word, "exquisite," is evidently a favourite of
Miss Fudge's, and I understand she was not a litle angry

when her brother Bob committed a pun on the last two
syllables of it in the following couplet.—

    " I 'd fain praise your Poem—but tell me, how is it
        When *I* cry out " Exquisite," Echo cries " quiz it ? "

(4 The flower which Rousseau brought into such fa-
shion among the Parisians, by exclaiming one day, " Ah,
voilà de la pervenche !"

(5 "*Mon ours*, voilà votre asile—et vous, *mon ours*,
ne viendrez-vous pas aussi ?"—etc , etc.

(6 " Un jour qu'il geloit très fort, en ouvrant un paquet
qu elle m'envoyoit, je trouvai un petit jupon de flanelle
d'Angleterre, qu'elle me marquoit avoir porté, et dont

Such, Doll, were the sweet recollections we ponder'd,
As, full of romance, through that valley we wander'd.
The flannel (one's train of ideas, how odd it is!)
Led us to talk about other commodities,
Cambric, and silk, and—I ne'er shall forget,
For the sun was then hastening in pomp to its set,
And full on the Colonel's dark whiskers shone down,
When he ask'd me, with eagerness—who made my
    gown?
The question confused me—for, Doll, you must know,
And I *ought* to have told my best friend long ago,
That, by Pa's strict command, I no longer employ (1)
That enchanting *couturière*, Madame Le Roi;
But am forced now to have Victorine, who—deuce
    take her!—
It seems is, at present, the King's mantua-maker—
I mean *of his party*—and, though much the smartest,
Le Roi is condemn'd as a rank Bonapartist. (2)

Think, Doll, how confounded I look'd—so well know-
    ing
The Colonel's opinions—my cheeks were quite glow
    ing;
I stammer'd out something—nay, even half named
The *legitimate* sempstress, when, loud, he exclaim'd,
"Yes, yes, by the stitching 't is plain to be seen
It was made by that Bourbonite b——h, Victorine!"
What a word for a hero!—but heroes *will* err,
And I thought, dear, I 'd tell you things *just* as they
    were.
Besides, though the word on good manners intrench,
I assure you 't is not *half* so shocking in French.

But this cloud, though embarrassing, soon pass'd
    away,
And the bliss altogether, the dreams of that day,
The thoughts that arise, when such dear fellows woo
    us—
The *nothings* that then, love, are *every thing* to us—
That quick correspondence of glances and sighs,
And what Bob calls the "Twopenny-post of the
    Eyes"—
Ah, Doll! though I *know* you 've a heart, 't is in vain
To a heart so unpractised these things to explain.
They can only be felt, in their fulness divine,
By her who has wander'd, at evening's decline,
Through a valley like that, with a Colonel like mine!

But here I must finish—for Bob, my dear Dolly,
Whom physic, I find, always makes melancholy,
Is seized with a fancy for church-yard reflections;
And, full of all yesterday's rich recollections,

elle vouloit que je me fisse faire un gilet. Ce soin, plus
qu'amical, me parut si tendre, comme si elle se fût dé-
pouillée pour me vêtir, que, dans mon émotion, je baisai
vingt fois en pleurant le billet et le jupon."

1) Miss Biddy's notions of French pronunciation may
be perceived in the rhymes which she always selects for
" *Le Roi* "

(2) Le Roi, who was the *Couturière* of the Empress

Is just setting off for Montmartre—"for *there* is,"
Said he, looking solemn, "the tomb of the Vérys! (3)
Long, long have I wish'd, as a votary true,
O'er the grave of such talents to utter my moans;
And, to-day—as my stomach is not in good cue
For the *flesh* of the Verys—I 'll visit their *bones!*"
He insists upon *my* going with him—how teasing!
This letter, however, dear Dolly, shall he
Unseal'd in my drawer, that, if any thing pleasing
Occurs while I 'm out, I may tell you—good-bye.
                                                    B. F.

                                        Four o'clock.
Oh, Dolly, dear Dolly, I 'm ruin'd for ever—
I ne'er shall be happy again, Dolly, never!
To think of the wretch—what a victim was I!
'T is too much to endure—I shall die, I shall die,—
My brain 's in a fever—my pulses beat quick—
I shall die, or, at least, be exceedingly sick!
Oh, what do you think? after all my romancing,
My visions of glory, my sighing, my glancing,
This Colonel—I scarce can commit it to paper—
This Colonel 's no more than a vile linen-draper!!
'T is true as I live—I had coax'd brother Bob so,
(You 'll hardly make out what I 'm writing, I sob so,)
For some little gift on my birth-day—September
The thirtieth, dear, I 'm eighteen, you remember—
That Bob to a shop kindly order'd the coach,
(Ah, little I thought who the shopman would prove,)
To bespeak me a few of those *mouchoirs de poche*,
Which, in happier hours, I have sigh'd for, my love—
(The most beautiful things—two Napoleons the price—
And one's name in the corner embroider'd so nice!)
Well, with heart full of pleasure, I enter'd the shop,
But—ye Gods, what a phantom!—I thought I should
    drop—
There he stood, my dear Dolly—no room for a doubt—
There, behind the vile counter, these eyes saw him
    stand,
With a piece of French cambric, before him roll'd out,
And that horrid yard-measure upraised in his hand
Oh—Papa, all along, knew the secret, 't is clear—
'T was a *shopman* he meant by a "Brandenburgh,"
    dear!
The man, whom I fondly had fancied a King,
And, when *that* too delightful illusion was past,
As a hero had worshipp'd—vile treacherous thing—
To turn out but a low linen-draper at last!
My head swam around—the wretch smiled, I believe,
But his smiling, alas, could no longer deceive—
I fell back on Bob—my whole heart seem'd to wither—
And, pale as a ghost, I was carried back hither!

Maria Louisa, is at present, of course, out of fashion, and
is succeeded in her station by the Royalist mantua-maker,
Victorine.

(3 It is the *brother* of the present excellent Restaurateur
who lies entombed so magnificently in the Cimetière
Montmartre. The inscription on the column at the head
of the tomb concludes with the following words.—" Toute
sa vie fut consacrée aux *arts utiles*."

I only remember that Bob, as I caught him,
With cruel facetiousness said, " Curse the Kiddy!
A staunch Revolutionist always I 've thought him,
But now I find out he 's a *Counter* one, Biddy ! "

Only think, my dear creature, if this should be known
To that saucy satirical thing, Miss Malone!
What a story 't will be at Shandangan for ever! [men,
What laughs and what quizzing she 'll have with the
It will spread through the country—and never, oh
Can Biddy be seen at Kilrandy again! [never

Farewell—I shall do something desperate, I fear—
And, ah! if my fate ever reaches your ear,
One tear of compassion my Doll will not grudge
To her poor—broken-hearted—young friend,
BIDDY FUDGE.

Nota bene—I am sure you will hear, with delight,
That we 're going, all three, to see Brunet to-night.
A laugh will revive me—and kind Mr. Cox
(Do you know him?) has got us the Governor's
box.)

FABLES FOR THE HOLY ALLIANCE.

Tu Regibus alas
Eripe.   *Virgil., Georg.*, lib. iv.
—— Clip the wings
Of these high-flying, arbitrary Kings.—*Dryden's Translation.*

TO LORD BYRON.

DEAR LORD BYRON,

THOUGH this Volume should possess no other merit in your eyes than that of reminding you of the short time we passed together at Venice, when some of the trifles which it contains were written, you will, I am sure, receive the dedication of it with pleasure, and believe that I am,

My dear Lord, ever faithfully yours,

T. B.

————ᐁ◉€◦————

PREFACE.

THOUGH it was the wish of the Members of the Poco-curante Society (who have lately done me the honour of electing me their Secretary) that I should prefix my name to the following Miscellany, it is but fair to them and to myself to state, that, except in the "painful pre-eminence" of being employed to transcribe their lucubrations, my claim to such a distinction in the title-page is not greater than that of any other gentleman who has contributed his share to the contents of the volume.

I had originally intended to take this opportunity of giving some account of the origin and objects of our Institution, the names and characters of the different members, etc., etc.—but, as I am at present preparing for the press the First Volume of the "Transactions of the Poco-curante Society," I shall reserve for that occasion all further details upon the subject ; and content myself here with referring, for a general insight into our tenets, to a Song which will be found at the end of this work, and which is sung to us on the first day of every month, by one of our oldest members, to the tune of (as far as I can recollect, being no musician,) either "Nancy Dawson" or "He stole away the Bacon."

It may be as well also to state, for the information

of those critics, who attack with the hope of being answered, and of being, thereby, brought into notice, that it is the rule of this Society to return no other answer to such assailants, than is contained in the three words " Non curat Hippoclides," (meaning, in English, " Hippoclides does not care a fig,") which were spoken two thousand years ago by the first founder of Poco-curantism, and have ever since been adopted as the leading *dictum* of the sect.

THOMAS BROWN.

————ᐁ◉€◦————

FABLE I.

THE DISSOLUTION OF THE HOLY ALLIANCE.

A DREAM.

I 've had a dream that bodes no good
    Unto the Holy Brotherhood.
I may be wrong, but I confess—
    As far as it is right or lawful
For one, no conjurer, to guess—
    It seems to me extremely awful.

Methought, upon the Neva's flood
A beautiful Ice Palace stood,
A dome of frost-work, on the plan
Of that once built by Empress Anne, (1)
Which shone by moonlight—as the tale is—
Like an Aurora Borealis.

In this said Palace, furnish'd all
    And lighted as the best on land are,
I dreamt there was a splendid Ball,
    Given by the Emperor Alexander,
To entertain with all due zeal,
    Those holy gentlemen, who 've shown a
Regard so kind for Europe's weal,
    At Troppau, Laybach, and Verona.

(1) " It is well known that the Empress Anne built a palace of ice on the Neva, in 1740, which was fifty-two feet in length, and when illuminated had a surprising effect."— *Pinkerton.*

The thought was happy—and design'd
To hint how thus the human Mind
May, like the stream imprison'd there,
Be check'd and chill'd, till it can bear
The heaviest Kings, that ode or sonnet
E'er yet be-praised, to dance upon it.

And all were pleased, and cold and stately,
Shivering in grand illumination—
Admired the superstructure greatly,
Nor gave one thought to the foundation.
Much too the Czar himself exulted,
To all plebeian fears a stranger,
For, Madame Krudener, when consulted,
Had pledged her word there was no danger.
So, on he caper'd, fearless quite,
Thinking himself extremely clever,
And waltz'd away with all his might,
As if the Frost would last for ever.

Just fancy how a bard like me,
Who reverence monarchs, must have trem-
bled
To see that goodly company,
At such a ticklish sport assembled.

Nor were the fears, that thus astounded
My loyal soul, at all unfounded—
For, lo! ere long, those walls so massy
Were seized with an ill-omen'd dripping,
And o'er the floors, now growing glassy,
Their Holinesses took to slipping.
The Czar, half through a Polonaise,
Could scarce get on for downright stumbling;
And Prussia, though to slippery ways
Well used, was cursedly near tumbling.

Yet still 't was who could stamp the floor most,
Russia and Austria 'mong the foremost.—
And now, to an Italian air,
This precious brace would, hand in hand, go;
Now—while old Louis, from his chair,
Intreated them his toes to spare—
Call'd loudly out for a Fandango.

And a Fandango, 'faith, they had,
At which they all set to, like mad!
Never were Kings (though small the expense is
Of wit among their Excellencies)
So out of all their princely senses.
But, ah, that dance—that Spanish dance—
Scarce was the luckless strain begun,
When, glaring red, as 't were a glance
Shot from an angry Southern sun,
A light through all the chambers flamed,
Astonishing old Father Frost,
Who, bursting into tears, exclaim'd
    "A thaw, by Jove—we're lost, we're
    lost!

Run, France—a second *Waterloo*
Is come to drown you—*sauve qui peut!*"

Why, why will monarchs caper so
In palaces without foundations?
Instantly all was in a flow,
    Crowns, fiddles, sceptres, decorations—
Those Royal Arms, that look'd so nice,
Cut out in the resplendent ice—
Those Eagles, handsomely provided
    With double heads for double dealings—
How fast the globes and sceptres glided
    Out of their claws on all the ceilings!
Proud Prussia's double bird of prey
Tame as a spatch cock, slunk away;
While—just like France herself, when she
    Proclaims how great her naval skill is—
Poor Louis' drowning fleurs-de-lys
    Imagined themselves *water*-lilies.

And not alone rooms, ceilings, shelves,
    But—still more fatal execution—
The Great Legitimates themselves
    Seem'd in a state of dissolution.
The indignant Czar—when just about
    To issue a sublime Ukase,
    "Whereas all light must be kept out"—
    Dissolved to nothing in its blaze.
Next Prussia took his turn to melt,
And, while his lips illustrious felt
The influence of this southern air,
    Some word, like "Constitution"—long
Congeal'd in frosty silence there—
Came slowly thawing from his tongue.
While Louis, lapsing by degrees,
    And sighing out a faint adieu
To truffles, salmis, toasted cheese,
    And smoking *fondus*, quickly grew,
Himself, into a *fondu* too;—
Or like that goodly King they make
Of sugar for a Twelfth-night cake,
When, in some urchin's mouth, alas,
It melts into a shapeless mass!

In short, I scarce could count a minute,
Ere the bright dome, and all within it,
Kings, Fiddlers, Emperors, all were gone—
    And nothing now was seen or heard
But the bright river, rushing on,
    Happy as an enfranchised bird,
And prouder of that natural ray,
Shining along its chainless way—
More proudly happy thus to glide
    In simple grandeur to the sea,
Than when, in sparkling fetters tied,
'T was deck'd with all that kingly pride
    Could bring to light its slavery!

Such is my dream—and, I confess,
I tremble at its awfulness.

That Spanish Dance—that southern beam—
But I say nothing—there's my dream—
And Madame Krudener, the she-prophet,
May make just what she pleases of it.

—◦⊹◦—

FABLE II.

THE LOOKING-GLASSES.

PROEM.

WHERE Kings have been by mob-elections
Raised to the throne, 't is strange to see
What different and what odd perfections
Men have required in Royalty.
Some, liking monarchs large and plumpy,
Have chosen their Sovereigns by the weight;
Some wish'd them tall, some thought your dumpy
Dutch-built the true legitimate. (1)
The Easterns in a Prince, 't is said,
Prefer what 's call'd a jolter-head : (2)
The Egyptians were n't at all particular
So that their Kings had *not* red hair—
This fault not even the greatest stickler
For the blood-royal well could bear.

A thousand more such illustrations
Might be adduced from various nations,
But, 'mong the many tales they tell us,
Touching the acquired or natural right
Which some men have to rule their fellows,
There's one, which I shall here recite —

FABLE.

There was a land—to *name* the place
Is neither now my wish nor duty—
Where reign'd a certain Royal race,
By right of their superior beauty.

What was the cut legitimate
Of these great persons' chins and noses,
By right of which they ruled the state,
No history I have seen discloses.

But so it was—a settled case—
Some Act of Parliament, pass'd snugly,
Had voted *them* a beauteous race,
And all their faithful subjects ugly.

As rank, indeed, stood high or low,
Some change it made in visual organs;
Your Peers were decent—Knights, so so—
But all your *common* people, gorgons!

Of course, if any knave but hinted
That the King's nose was turn'd awry,
Or that the Queen (God bless her!) squinted—
The judges doom'd that knave to die.

But rarely things like this occurr'd,
The people to their King were duteous,

And took it, on his Royal word,
That they were frights, and he was beauteous.

The cause whereof, among all classes,
Was simply this—these island elves
Had never yet seen looking-glasses,
And, therefore, did not *know themselves.*

Sometimes, indeed, their neighbours' faces
Might strike them as more full of reason,
More fresh than those in certain places—
But, Lord, the very thought was treason!

Besides, howe'er we love our neighbour,
And take his face's part, 't is known
We ne'er so much in earnest labour,
As when the face attack'd 's our own.

So, on they went—the crowd believing—
(As crowds well govern'd always do)
Their rulers, too, themselves deceiving—
So old the joke, they thought 't was true.

But jokes, we know, if they too far go,
Must have an end—and so, one day,
Upon that coast there was a cargo
Of looking-glasses cast away.

'T was said, some Radicals, somewhere,
Had laid their wicked heads together,
And forced that ship to founder there—
While some believe it was the weather.

However this might be, the freight
Was landed without fees or duties;
And from that hour historians date
The downfall of the Race of Beauties.

The looking-glasses got about,
And grew so common through the land,
That scarce a tinker could walk out,
Without a mirror in his hand.

Comparing faces, morning, noon,
And night, their constant occupation—
By dint of looking-glasses, soon,
They grew a most reflecting nation.

In vain the Court, aware of errors,
In all the old establish'd mazards,
Prohibited the use of mirrors,
And tried to break them at all hazards:—

In vain—their laws might just as well
Have been waste paper on the shelves;
That fatal freight had broke the spell;
People had look'd—and knew themselves.

(1) The Goths had a law to choose always a short thick man for their King.—*Munster, Cosmog.*, lib. iii., p. 164.

(2) "In a Prince a jolter-head is invaluable." *Oriental Field Sports.*

If chance a Duke, of birth sublime,
　Presumed upon his ancient face,
(Some calf-head, ugly from all time,
　They popp'd a mirror to his Grace:

Just hinting, by that gentle sign,
　How little Nature holds it true,
That what is call'd an ancient line,
　Must be a line of Beauty too.

From Dukes' they pass'd to regal phizzes,
　Compared them proudly with their own,
And cried, "How *could* such monstrous quizzes
　In Beauty's name usurp the throne!"—

They then wrote essays, pamphlets, books,
　Upon Cosmetical Œconomy,
Which made the King try various looks,
　But none improved his physiognomy.

And satires at the Court were levell'd,
　And small lampoons, so full of slynesses,
That soon, in short, they quite be-devil'd
　Their Majesties and Royal Highnesses.

At length—but here I drop the veil,
　To spare some loyal folks' sensations;—
Besides, what follow'd is the tale
　Of all such late-enlighten'd nations;

Of all to whom old Time discloses
　A truth they should have sooner known—
That Kings have neither rights nor noses
　A whit diviner than their own.

—⊶✠⊷—

FABLE III.

THE TORCH OF LIBERTY.

I saw it all in Fancy's glass—
　Herself the fair, the wild magician,
Who bid this splendid day-dream pass,
　And named each gliding apparition.

'T was like a torch-race—such as they
　Of Greece perform'd, in ages gone,
When the fleet youths, in long array,
　Pass'd the bright torch triumphant on.

I saw the expectant nations stand,
　To catch the coming flame in turn;—
I saw, from ready hand to hand,
　The clear, though struggling, glory burn.

And, oh, their joy, as it came near,
　'T was, in itself, a joy to see;
While Fancy whisper'd in my ear,
　"That torch they pass is Liberty!"

And each, as she received the flame,
　Lighted her altar with its ray;

Then, smiling, to the next who came,
　Speeded it on its sparkling way.

From Albion first, whose ancient shrine
　Was furnish'd with the fire already,
Columbia caught the boon divine,
　And lit a flame, like Albion's, steady.

The splendid gift then Gallia took,
　And, like a wild Bacchante, raising
The brand aloft, its sparkles shook,
　As she would set the world a-blazing!

Thus kindling wild, so fierce and high
　Her altar blazed into the air,
That Albion, to that fire too nigh,
　Shrunk back, and shudder'd at its glare!(1)

Next, Spain, so new was light to her,
　Leap'd at the torch—but, ere the spark
That fell upon her shrine could stir,
　'T was quench'd—and all again was dark.

Yet, no—*not* quench'd—a treasure, worth
　So much to mortals, rarely dies:
Again her living light look'd forth,
　And shone, a beacon, in all eyes.

Who next received the flame? alas,
　Unworthy Naples—shame of shames,
That ever through such hands should pass
　That brightest of all earthly flames!

Scarce had her fingers touch'd the torch,
　When, frighted by the sparks it shed,
Nor waiting even to feel the scorch,
　She dropp'd it to the earth—and fled.

And fall'n it might have long remain'd;
　But Greece, who saw her moment now,
Caught up the prize, though prostrate, stain'd,
　And waved it round her beauteous brow.

And Fancy bade me mark where, o'er
　Her altar, as its flame ascended,
Fair laurell'd spirits seem'd to soar,
　Who thus in song their voices blended:

"Shine, shine for ever, glorious Flame,
　Divinest gifts of Gods to men!
From Greece thy earliest splendour came,
　To Greece thy ray returns again.

"Take, Freedom, take thy radiant round,
　When dimm'd, revive, when lost, return,
Till not a shrine through earth be found
　On which thy glories shall not burn!"

(1) This verse originally stood—
　　And, when she fired her altar, high
　　It flash'd into the reddening air
　　So fierce, that Albion, who stood nigh,
　　Shrunk, almost blinded by the glare —P. E

FABLE. IV.
THE FLY AND THE BULLOCK.
PROEM.

Of all that, to the sage's survey,
This world presents of topsy-turvy,
There's nought so much disturbs one's patience
As little minds in lofty stations.
'T is like that sort of painful wonder,
Which slender columns, labouring under
    Enormous arches, give beholders ;—
Or those poor Caryatides,
Condemn'd to smile and stand at ease,
    With a whole house upon their shoulders.

If, as in some few royal cases,
Small minds are *born* into such places—
If they are there, by Right Divine,
    Or any such sufficient reason,
Why—Heaven forbid we should repine !—
    To wish it otherwise were treason;
Nay, even to see it in a vision
Would be what lawyers call *misprision.*

Sir Robert Filmer saith—and he,
    Of course, knew all about the matter—
" Both men and beasts love Monarchy ; "
    Which proves how rational—the *latter.*
Sidney, we know, or wrong or right,
Entirely differ'd from the Knight:
Nay, hints a King may lose his head,
    By slipping awkwardly his bridle:—
But this is treasonous, ill-bred,
And (now-a-days, when Kings are led
    In patent snaffles) downright idle.

No, no—it is n't right-line Kings,
(Those sovereign lords in leading-strings
Who, from their birth, are Faith-Defenders,)
That move my wrath—'t is your pretenders,
Your mushroom rulers, sons of earth,
Who—not like t'others, bores by birth,
Establish'd *gratiâ Dei* blockheads,
Born with three kingdoms in their pockets—(1)
Yet, with a brass that nothing stops,
    Push up into the loftiest stations,
And, though too dull to manage shops,
    Presume, the dolts, to manage nations!

This class it is that moves my gall,
And stirs up bile, and spleen, and all.
While other senseless things appear
To know the limits of their sphere—
While not a cow on earth romances
So much as to conceit she dances—

(1) Some verbal changes have been made in the preced-
ing lines since their first publication —

> No, no—it is n't foolish Kings
> (Those fix'd inevitable things—
> Bores paramount, by right of birth)
> That move my wrath, but your pretenders,
> Your mushroom rulers, sons of earth,
> Who, not like t' others, *crown'd offenders*

While the most jumping frog we know of
Would scarce at Astley's hope to show off—
Your * * *s, your * * 's dare,
    Untrain'd as are their minds, to set them
To *any* business, *any* where,
    At *any* time that fools will let them.

But leave we here these upstart things—
My business is, just now, with Kings ;
To whom, and to their right-line glory,
I dedicate the following story.

FABLE.

The wise men of Egypt were secret as dummies ;
    And, even when they most condescended to teach,
They pack'd up their meaning, as they did their
        mummies,
    In so many wrappers, 'twas out of one's reach.

They were also, good people, much given to Kings—
    Fond of craft and of crocodiles, monkeys and
        mystery ;
But blue-bottle flies were their best-beloved things,(2)
    As will partly appear in this very short history.

A Scythian philosopher (nephew, they say,
    To that other great traveller, young Anacharsis,)
Stept into a temple at Memphis one day,
    To have a short peep at their mystical farces.

He saw (3) a brisk blue-bottle Fly on an altar,
    Made much of, and worshipp'd as something divine ,
While a large handsome Bullock, led there in a halter,
    Before it lay stabb'd at the foot of the shrine.

Surprised at such doings, he whisper'd his teacher—
    " If 't is n't impertinent, may I ask why
Should a Bullock, that useful and powerful creature,
    Be thus offer'd up to a blue-bottle Fly ? "

" No wonder"—said t' other—" you stare at the sight,
    But *we* as a Symbol of Monarchy view it—
That Fly on the shrine is Legitimate Right,
    And that Bullock, the People, that's sacrificed to it."

—◆◆◆◆◆◆—

FABLE V.
CHURCH AND STATE.
PROEM

" The moment any religion becomes national, or esta-
blished, its purity must certainly be lost, because it is
then impossible to keep it unconnected with men's in-
terest ; and, if connected, it must inevitably be perverted
by them."—*Soame Jenyns.*

Thus did Soame Jenyns—though a Tory,
    A Lord of Trade and the Plantations—
Feel how Religion's simple glory
    Is stain'd by State associations.

(Regular *gratia Dei* blockheads,
Born with three kingdoms in their pockets),
Nor leaving, on the scale of mind,
These royal Zeros far behind.—P. E.

(2) Changed from—

> Fond of monarchs and crocodiles, monkeys and mystery,
> Bats, hierophants, blue-bottle flies, and such things —P E.

(3) According to Ælian, it was in the island of Leucadia

54

When Catherine, ere she crush'd the Poles,
   Appeal'd to the benign Divinity;
Then cut them up in protocols,
Made fractions of their very souls—(1)
   All in the name of the bless'd Trinity:
Or when her grandson, Alexander,
That mighty Northern salamander, (2)
Whose icy touch, felt all about,
Puts every fire of Freedom out—
When he, too, winds up his Ukases
With God and the Panagia's praises—
When he, of royal Saints the type,
   In holy water dips the sponge,
With which, at one imperial wipe,
   He would all human rights expunge·
When Louis (whom as King, and eater,
Some name *Dix-huit,* and some *Des huîtres,*
Calls down "St. Louis' God" to witness
The right, humanity, and fitness
Of sending eighty thousand Solons,
   Sages, with muskets and laced coats,
To cram instruction, nolens volens,
   Down the poor struggling Spaniards' throats
I can't help thinking, (though to Kings
   I must, of course, like other men, bow,
That when a Christian monarch brings
Religion's name to gloss these things,
   Such blasphemy out-Benbows Benbow!(3)

Or—not so far for facts to roam,
Having a few much nearer home—
When we see Churchmen, who, if ask'd
"Must Ireland's slaves be tithed, and task'd,
And driven, like Negroes or Croats,
   That *you* may roll in wealth and bliss?"
Look from beneath their shovel hats
   With all due pomp, and answer "Yes!"
But then, if question'd, "Shall the brand
Intolerance flings throughout that land—
Shall the fierce strife now taught to grow
   Betwixt her palaces and hovels,
Be ever quench'd?"—from the same shovels
Look grandly forth and answer "No!"—
Alas, alas! have *these* a claim
To merciful Religion's name?
If more you seek, go see a bevy
Of bowing parsons at a levee—
(Choosing your time, when straw's before
Some apoplectic bishop's door,)
Then, if thou canst, with life, escape
That rush of lawn, that press of crape,

Just watch their reverences and graces,
   As on each smirking suitor frisks, (4)
And say, if those round shining faces
   To heaven or earth most turn their disks?

This, this it is—Religion, made,
'Twixt Church and State, a truck, a trade
This most ill-match'd, unholy Co.,
From whence the ills we witness flow;
The war of many creeds with one—
The extremes of *too* much faith, and none—(5)
Till, betwixt ancient trash and new,
'Twixt Cant and Blasphemy—the two
Rank ills with which this age is curst
We can no more tell *which* is worst,
Than erst could Egypt, when so rich
In various plagues, determine which
She thought most pestilent and vile,
Her frogs, like Benbow and Carlisle,
Croaking their native mud-notes loud,
Or her fat locusts, like a cloud
Of pluralists, obesely lowering,
At once benighting and devouring!—

This—this it is—and here I pray
   Those sapient wits of the Reviews,
Who make us poor dull authors say,
   Not what we mean, but what they choose;
Who to our most abundant shares
Of nonsense add still more of theirs,
And are to poets just such evils
   As caterpillars find those flies, (6)
Which, not content to sting like devils,
   Lay eggs upon their backs likewise—
To guard against such foul deposits
   Of other's meaning in my rhymes,
(A thing more needful here, because it's
   A subject ticklish in these times)—
I, here, to all such wits make known,
   Monthly and Weekly, Whig and Tory,
'T is *this* Religion—this alone—
   I aim at in the following story.—

FABLE.

When Royalty was young and bold,
   Ere, touch'd by Time, he had become—
If 't is n't civil to say *old,*
   At least, a *ci-devant jeune homme;*

One evening, on some wild pursuit,
   Driving along, he chanced to see
Religion, passing by on foot,
   And took him in his vis-à-vis.

---

they practised this ceremony—Συευ βουν ταις μυιαι..
—*De Animal,* lib. 11 , cap. 8

(1 *Ames, demi-ames,* etc.

(2) The salamander is supposed to have the power of
extinguishing fire by its natural coldness and moisture.

(3) A well-known publisher of irreligious books

(4) Formerly—
   Shouldering their way on at all risks —P E

(5) The following lines have been here omitted—
   The qualms, the fumes of sect and sceptic,
   And all that Reason, grown dyspeptic
   By swallowing forced or noxious creeds,
   From downright indigestion breeds.—P E.

6) "The greatest number of the ichneumon tribe are
seen settling upon the back of the caterpillar, and darting
at different intervals their stings into its body—at every
dart they depose an egg."—*Goldsmith.*

This said Religion was a Friar,
    The humblest and the best of men,
Who ne'er had notion or desire
    Of riding in a coach till then.

" I say"—quoth Royalty, who rather
    Enjoy'd a masquerading joke—
" I say, suppose, my good old father,
    You lend me, for a while, your cloak."

The Friar consented—little knew
    What tricks the youth had in his head,
Besides, was rather tempted too
    By a laced coat he got instead.

Away ran Royalty, slap-dash,
    Scampering like mad about the town;
Broke windows, shiver'd lamps to smash,
    And knock'd whole scores of watchmen down.

While nought could they, whose heads were broke,
    Learn of the "why" or the "wherefore,"
Except that 't was Religion's cloak
    The gentleman, who crack'd them, wore.

Meanwhile, the Friar, whose head was turn'd
    By the laced coat, grew frisky too;
Look'd big—his former habits spurn'd—
    And storm'd about, as great men do:

Dealt much in pompous oaths and curses—
    Said "d—mn you" often, or as bad—
Laid claim to other people's purses—
    In short, grew either knave or mad.

As work like this was unbefitting,
    And flesh and blood no longer bore it,
The Court of Common Sense, then sitting,
    Summon'd the culprits both before it.

Where, after hours in wrangling spent
    (As Courts must wrangle to decide well),
Religion to St. Luke's was sent,
    And Royalty pack'd off to Bridewell.

With this proviso—should they be
    Restored, in due time, to their senses,
They both must give security,
    In future, against such offences—

Religion ne'er to lend his cloak,
    Seeing what dreadful work it leads to;
And Royalty to crack his joke—
    But not to crack poor people's heads too.

(1) Andreas.
(2) Quand il étoit occupé d'aucune essoine, il envoyoit Novelle, sa fille, en son lieu, lire aux escholes en charge, et, afin que la biauté d'elle n'empêchât la pensée des oyants, elle avoit une petite courtine devant elle.—*Christ de Pise, Cité des Dames*, p. 11, cap. 36.

FABLE VI.
THE LITTLE GRAND LAMA.
PROEM

Novella, a young Bolognese,
    The daughter of a learn'd Law Doctor, 1)
Who had with all the subtleties
    Of old and modern jurists stock'd her,
Was so exceeding fair, 'tis said,
    And over hearts held such dominion,
That when her father, sick in bed,
    Or busy, sent her, in his stead,
        To lecture on the Code Justinian,
She had a curtain drawn before her,
    Lest, if her charms were seen, the students
Should let their young eyes wander o'er her,
    And quite forget their jurisprudence. 2)

Just so it is with Truth; when *seen*,
    Too dazzling far—'t is from behind
A light thin allegoric screen,
    She thus can safest teach mankind.

FABLE.

In Thibet once there reign'd, we 're told,
A little Lama, one year old—
Raised to the throne, that realm to bless,
Just when his little Holiness
Had cut—as near as can be reckon'd—
Some say his *first* tooth, some his *second*.
Chronologers and Nurses vary,
Which proves historians should be wary.
We only know the important truth,
His Majesty *had* cut a tooth. (3)
And much his subjects were enchanted—
As well all Lamas' subjects *may* be,
And would have given their heads, if wanted,
    To make tee-totums for the baby.
Throned as he was by Right Divine—
    (What Lawyers call *Jure Divino*,
Meaning a right to yours, and mine,
    And every body's goods and rhino,)
Of course, his faithful subjects' purses
    Were ready with their aids and succours;
Nothing was seen but pension'd Nurses,
    And the land groan'd with bibs and tuckers.
Oh! had there been a Hume or Bennet,
Then sitting in the Thibet Senate,
Ye Gods, what room for long debates
Upon the Nursery Estimates!
What cutting down of swaddling-clothes
    And pinafores, in nightly battles!
What calls for papers to expose
    The waste of sugar-plums and rattles!

(3) See Turner's Embassy to Thibet for an account of his interview with the Lama.— "Teshoo Lama he says) was at this time eighteen months old. Though he was unable to speak a word, he made the most expressive signs, and conducted himself with astonishing *dignity* and decorum."

But no—if Thibet *had* M. P.s,
They were far better bred than these ;
Nor gave the slightest opposition,
During the monarch's whole dentition.

But short this calm ;—for, just when he
Had reach'd the alarming age of three,
When Royal natures, and, no doubt,
Those of *all* noble beasts break out—
The Lama, who till then was quiet,
Show'd symptoms of a taste for riot ;
And, ripe for mischief, early, late,
Without regard for Church or State,
Made free with whosoe'er came nigh ;
   Tweak'd the Lord Chancellor by the nose,
Turn'd all the Judges' wigs awry,
   And trod on the old Generals' toes ;
Pelted the Bishops with hot buns,
   Rode cock-horse on the City maces,
And shot from little devilish guns
   Hard peas into his subjects' faces.
In short, such wicked pranks he play'd,
   And grew so mischievous, God bless him!
That his Chief Nurse—with even the aid
Of an Archbishop—was afraid,
   When in these moods, to comb or dress him.
Nay, even the persons most inclined
   Through thick and thin for Kings to stickle,
Thought him (if they'd but speak their mind,
   Which they did *not*) an odious pickle.

At length some patriot lords—a breed
   Of animals they've got in Thibet,
Extremely rare, and fit, indeed,
   For folks like Pidcock to exhibit—
Some patriot lords, who saw the length
To which things went, combined their strength,
And penn'd a manly, plain, and free
Remonstrance to the Nursery ;
Protesting warmly that they yielded
   To none, that ever went before 'em,
In loyalty to him who wielded
   The hereditary pap-spoon o'er 'em,
That, as for treason, 't was a thing
   That made them almost sick to think of—
That they and theirs stood by the King,
   Throughout his measles and his chin-cough,
When others, thinking him consumptive,
Had ratted to the Heir Presumptive !—
But, still—though much admiring King
(And chiefly those in leading-strings),
They saw, with shame and grief of soul,
   There was no longer now the wise
And constitutional control
   Of *birch* before their ruler's eyes ;
But that, of late, such pranks, and tricks,
   And freaks occurr'd the whole day long,
As all, but men with bishopricks,
   Allow'd, in even a King, were wrong.

Wherefore it was they humbly pray'd
   That honourable Nursery,
That such reforms be henceforth made,
   As all good men desired to see ;—
In other words (lest they might seem
Too tedious), as the gentlest scheme
For putting all such pranks to rest,
   And in its bud the mischief nipping—
They ventured humbly to suggest
   His Majesty should have a whipping !

When this was read, no Congreve rocket,
   Discharged into the Gallic trenches,
E'er equall'd the tremendous shock it
   Produced upon the Nursery benches.
The Bishops, who of course had votes,
By right of age and petticoats,
Were first and foremost in the fuss—
   "What, whip a Lama! suffer birch
To touch his sacred——infamous !
Deistical !—assailing thus
   The fundamentals of the Church !—
No—no—such patriot plans as these,
(So help them Heaven—and their Sees!)
They held to be rank blasphemies."

The alarm thus given, by these and other
   Grave ladies of the Nursery side,
Spread through the land, till, such a pother,
   Such party squabbles, far and wide,
Never in history's page had been
Recorded, as were then between
The Whippers and Non-whippers seen.
Till, things arriving at a state
   Which gave some fears of revolution,
The patriot lords' advice, though late,
   Was put at last in execution.
The Parliament of Thibet met—
   The little Lama, call'd before it,
Did, then and there, his whipping get,
And (as the Nursery Gazette
   Assures us) like a hero bore it.

And though, 'mong Thibet Tories, some
Lament that Royal Martyrdom
(Please to observe, the letter D
In this last word's pronounced like B),
Yet to the example of that Prince
   So much is Thibet's land a debtor,
That her long line of Lamas, since,
   Have all behaved themselves *much* better.

FABLE VII.
THE EXTINGUISHERS.
PROEM.

THOUGH soldiers are the true supports,
The natural allies of Courts,
Woe to the Monarch, who depends
Too *much* on his red-coated friends ;

For even soldiers sometimes *think*—
　Nay, Colonels have been known to *reason*—
And reasoners, whether clad in pink,
Or red, or blue, are on the brink
　(Nine cases out of ten) of treason.

Not many soldiers, I believe, are
　As fond of liberty as Mina ;
Else—woe to Kings, when Freedom's fever
　Once turns into a *Scarletina !*
For then—but hold—'t is best to veil
My meaning in the following tale :—

FABLE.

A Lord of Persia, rich and great,
　Just come into a large estate,
Was shock'd to find he had, for neighbours,
　Close to his gate, some rascal Ghebers.
Whose fires, beneath his very nose,
In heretic combustion rose.
But Lords of Persia can, no doubt,
　Do what they will—so, one fine morning,
He turn'd the rascal Ghebers out,
　First giving a few kicks for warning.
Then, thanking Heaven most piously,
　He knock'd their Temple to the ground,
Blessing himself for joy to see
　Such Pagan ruins strew'd around.
But much it vex'd my Lord to find,
　That, while all else obey'd his will,
The Fire these Ghebers left behind,
　Do what he would, kept burning still.
Fiercely he storm'd, as if his frown
Could scare the bright insurgent down ;
But, no—such fires are headstrong things,
And care not much for Lords or Kings.
Scarce could his Lordship well contrive
　The flashes in *one* place to smother,
Before—hey presto !—all alive,
　They sprung up freshly in another.

At length when, spite of prayers and damns,
　'T was found the sturdy flame defied him,
His stewards came, with low *salams*,
　Offering, by *contract*, to provide him
Some large Extinguishers, (a plan,
Much used, they said, at Ispahan,
Vienna, Petersburgh—in short,
Wherever Light's forbid at court,)
Machines no Lord should be without,
Which would, at once, put promptly out
All kinds of fires—from staring stark
Volcanos to the tiniest spark ;
Till all things slept as dull and dark
As, in a great Lord's neighbourhood,
'Twas right and fitting all things should.

Accordingly, some large supplies
　Of these Extinguishers were furnish'd
(All of the true Imperial size),
　And there, in rows, stood black and burnish'd,

Ready, where'er a gleam but shone
Of light or fire, to be clapp'd on.

But, ah, how lordly wisdom errs,
In trusting to extinguishers !
One day, when he had left all sure,
(At least, so thought he) dark, secure—
The flame, at all its exits, entries,
　Obstructed to his heart's content,
And black extinguishers, like sentries,
　Placed over every dangerous vent—
Ye Gods, imagine his amaze,
His wrath, his rage, when, on returning,
He found not only the old blaze,
　Brisk as before, crackling and burning—
Not only new young conflagrations,
　Popping up round in various stations—
But, still more awful, strange, and dire,
The Extinguishers themselves on fire !! (1)
They, they—those trusty blind machines
His Lordship had so long been praising,
As, under Providence, the means
　Of keeping down all lawless blazing,
Were now, themselves—alas, too true
The shameful fact—turn'd blazers too,
And, by a change as odd as cruel,
Instead of dampers, served for fuel

Thus, of his only hope bereft,　　　　[done ?"—
　" What," said the great man, " must be
All that, in scrapes like this, is left
　To great men is—to cut and run.
So run he did ; while to their grounds
　The banish'd Ghebers blest return'd :
And, though their Fire had broke its bounds,
　And all abroad now wildly burn'd,
Yet well could they, who loved the flame,
　Its wandering, its excess reclaim ;
And soon another fairer Dome
Arose to be its sacred home,
Where, cherish'd, guarded, not confined,
The living glory dwelt inshrined,
And, shedding lustre strong, but even,
Though born of earth, grew worthy heaven.

MORAL.

The moral hence my Muse infers
　Is, that such Lords are simple elves,
In trusting to Extinguishers,
　That are combustible themselves.

—◦▶◀◦—

FABLE VIII.

LOUIS FOURTEENTH'S WIG.

THE money raised—the army ready—
Drums beating, and the Royal Neddy

(1) The idea of this Fable was caught from one of those brilliant *mots*, which abound in the conversation of my friend, the author of the *Letters to Julia*—a product on which contains some of the happiest specimens of playful poetry that have appeared in this or any age.

Valiantly braying, in the van
To the old tune " *Eh, eh, Sire Ane !* " (1)
Nought wanting, but some *coup* dramatic,
To make French *sentiment* explode,
Bring in, at once, the *goût* fanatic,
And make the war " *la dernière mode* "—
Instantly, at the *Pav'llon Marsan*,
Is held an Ultra consultation—
What 's to be done, to help the farce on?
What stage-effect, what decoration,
To make this beauteous France forget,
In one grand glorious *pirouette*,
All she had sworn to but last week,
And, with a cry of " *Magnifique !* "
Rush forth to this, or *any* war,
Without inquiring once—what for ?"

After some plans proposed by each,
Lord Chateaubriand made a speech,
(Quoting, to show what men's rights are,
Or rather what men's rights *should be*,
From Hobbes, Lord Castlereagh, the Czar,
And other friends to Liberty,)
Wherein he—having first protested
'Gainst humouring the mob—suggested
(As the most high-bred plan he saw
For giving the new war *éclat*)
A grand Baptismal Melo-drame,
To be got up at Notre Dame,
In which the Duke (who, bless his Highness !
Had by his *hilt* acquired such fame,
'T was hoped that he as little shyness
Would show, when to *the point* he came,)
Should, for his deeds so lion-hearted,
Be christen'd *Hero*, ere he started ;
With power, by Royal Ordonnance,
To bear that name—at least in France.
Himself—the Viscount Chateaubriand—
(To help the affair with more *esprit* on)
Offering, for this baptismal rite,
Some of his own famed Jordan water—(2)
(Marie Louise not having quite
Used all that, for young Nap, he brought her,)
The baptism, in *this* case, to be
Applied to that extremity,
Which Bourbon heroes most expose ;
And which (as well all Europe knows)
Happens to be, in this Defender
Of the true Faith, extremely tender.(3)
Or if (the Viscount said) this scheme
Too rash and premature should seem—

If thus discounting heroes, *on* tick—
This glory, by anticipation,
Was too much in the *genre romantique*
For such a highly classic nation,
He begg'd to say, the Abyssinians
A practice had in their dominions,
Which, if at Paris got up well,
In full *costume*, would, sure to tell.
At all great epochs, good or ill,
They have, says Bruce (and Bruce ne'er budges
From the strict truth), a Grand Quadrille
In public danced by the twelve Judges— 4
And, he assures us, the grimaces,
The *entre-chats*, the airs and graces
Of dancers, so profound and stately,
Divert the Abyssinians greatly.

" Now (said the Viscount), there 's but few
Great Empires where this plan would do :
For instance, England ;—let them take
What pains they would—'t were vain to strive—
The twelve stiff Judges there would make,
The worst Quadrille-set now alive.
One must have seen them, ere one could
Imagine properly Judge Wood
Performing, in his wig, so gaily,
A *queue-de-chat* with Justice Bailey !
French Judges, though, are by no means
This sort of stiff be-wigg'd machines ;
And we, who 've seen them at *Saumur*
And *Poitiers* lately, may be sure
They 'd dance quadrilles, or any thing,
That would be pleasing to the King—
Nay, stand upon their heads, and more do,
To please the little Duke de Bordeaux ! "

After these several schemes there came
Some others—needless now to name,
Since that, which Monsieur plann'd, himself,
Soon doom'd all others to the shelf,
And was received *par acclamation*,
As truly worthy the *Grande Nation*.

It seems (as Monsieur told the story)
That Louis the Fourteenth, that glory,
That *Coryphée* of all crown'd pates—
That pink of the Legitimates—
Had, when, with many a pious prayer, he
Bequeath'd unto the Virgin Mary
His marriage deeds, and *cordon bleu*, (5)
Bequeathed to her his State Wig too—

---

1) They celebrated in the dark ages, at many churches, particularly at Rouen, what was called the Feast of the Ass. On this occasion the ass, finely drest, was brought before the altar, and they sung before him this elegant anthem, "Eh, eh, eh, Sire Ane, eh, eh, eh, Sire Ane."—*Warton's Essay on Pope.*

2) Brought from the river Jordan by M. Chateaubriand, and presented to the French Empress for the christening of young Napoleon

(3) See the Duke's celebrated letter to Madame, written

during his campaign in 1815, in which he says, "J'ai le postérieur légèrement endommagé."

(4) " On certain great occasions, the twelve Judges, who are generally between sixty and seventy years of age) sing the song and dance the figure-dance," etc.—Book v.

(5) " Louis XIV fit présent à la Vierge de son cordon bleu, que l'on conserve soigneusement, et lui envoya ensuite son contrat de mariage et le *Traité des Pyrénées* magnifiquement relié."—*Mémoires, Anecdotes pour servir*, etc.

(An offering which, at Court, 't is thought,
The Virgin values as she ought)—
That Wig, the wonder of all eyes,
The Cynosure of Gallia's skies,
To watch and tend whose curls adored,
  Re-build its towering roof, when flat,
And round its rumpled base, a Board
  Of sixty Barbers daily sat, (1)
With Subs, on State-Days, to assist,
Well pension'd from the Civil List :—
That wondrous Wig, array'd in which,
And form'd alike to awe or witch,
He beat all other heirs of crowns,
In taking mistresses and towns,
Requiring but a shot at *one*,
A smile at *t'other*, and 't was done'—

" That Wig (said Monsieur, while his brow
Rose proudly,) is existing now ;—
That grand Perruque, amid the fall
  Of every other Royal glory,
With curls erect survives them all,
  And tells in every hair their story.
Think, think, how welcome at this time
A relic, so beloved, sublime !
What worthier standard of the Cause
  Of Kingly Right can France demand ?
Or who among our ranks can pause
  To guard it, while a curl shall stand?
Behold, my friends—(while thus he cried,
A curtain, which conceal'd this pride
Of Princely Wigs was drawn aside)—

Behold that grand Perruque—how big
  With recollections for the world—
For France—for us—Great Louis' Wig,
  By Hippolyte (2 new frizz'd and curl'd—
New frizz'd! alas, 't is but too true,
Well may you start at that word *new*—
But such the sacrifice, my friends,
The Imperial Cossack recommends ,
Thinking such small concessions sage,
To meet the spirit of the age,
And do what best that spirit flatters,
In Wigs—if not in weightier matters.
Wherefore, to please the Czar, and show
That *we* too, much-wrong'd Bourbons, know
What liberalism in Monarchs is,
We have conceded the New Friz !
Thus arm'd, ye gallant Ultras, say,
Can men, can Frenchmen, fear the fray?
With this proud relic in our van,
  And d'Angoulême our worthy leader,
Let rebel Spain do all she can,
  Let recreant England arm and feed her—
Urged by that pupil of Hunt's school,
That Radical, Lord Liverpool—   ,
France can have nought to fear—far from it—
  When once astounded Europe sees
The Wig of Louis, like a Comet,
  Streaming above the Pyrenees,
All 's o'er with Spain—then on, my sons,
  On, my incomparable Duke,
And, shouting for the Holy Ones,
  Cry, *Vive la Guerre—et la Perruque !* "

RHYMES ON THE ROAD,

EXTRACTED FROM THE JOURNAL

OF

A TRAVELLING MEMBER OF THE POCO-CURANTE SOCIETY, 1819.

PREFACE.

THE series of trifles designated " Rhymes on the Road," were written partly as their title implies, and partly at a subsequent period from memorandums made on the spot. This will account for so many of those pieces being little better, I fear, than "prose fringed with rhymes." The journey to a part of which those Rhymes owed their existence was commenced in company with Lord John Russell in the Autumn of the year 1819. After a week or two passed at Paris, to enable Lord John to refer to Barillon's Letters for a new edition of his Life of Lord Russell then preparing, we set out together for the Simplon. At Milan, the agreeable society of the late Lord Kinnaird detained us for a few days ; and then my companion took the route to Genoa, while I proceeded on a visit to Lord Byron, at Venice.

It was during the journey thus briefly described, I addressed the well-known Remonstrance to my noble friend, (3) which has of late been frequently coupled with my prophetic verses (4) on the Duke of

(1) The learned author of *Recherches Historiques sur les Perruques* says that the Board consisted but of Forty —the same number as the Academy "Le plus beau temps des perruques fut celui ou Louis XIV commença a porter lui-même perruque ; . . . . On ignore l'epoque où se fit cette révolution ; mais on sait qu'elle engagea Louis le Grand à y donner ses soins paternels, en creant, en 1656, quarante charges de perruquiers, suivant la cour,

et en 1673 il forma un corps de deux cents perruquiers pour la ville de Paris "—P. 111.

(2 A celebrated *coiffeur* of the present day

(3) See the poem entitled "Remonstrance," commencing —
  " What ! thou, with thy genius, thy youth, and thy name," etc.

(4) See the Irish Melody, page 213.
  " While History's Muse the Memorial was keeping," etc.

Wellington, from the prescient spirit with which it so confidently looked forward to all that Lord John has since become in the eyes of the world.

Of my visit to Lord Byron—an event to me so memorable—I have already detailed all the most interesting particulars in my published Life of the poet; and shall here only cite, from that work, one passage, as having some reference to a picture mentioned in the following pages. "As we were conversing after dinner about the various collections of paintings I had seen that morning, on my saying that, fearful as I was of ever praising any picture, lest I should draw on myself the connoisseur's sneer, for my pains, I would yet, to him, venture to own that I had seen a picture at Milan, which——' The Hagar!' (1) he exclaimed, eagerly interrupting me; and it was, in fact, that very picture I was about to mention to him as having awakened in me, by the truth of its expression, more real emotion than any I had yet seen among the *chefs-d'œuvre* of Venice."

In the society I chiefly lived with, while at Rome, I considered myself singularly fortunate; though but a blind worshipper of those powers of Art of which my companions were all high-priests. Canova himself, Chantrey, Lawrence, Jackson, Turner, Eastlake—such were the men of whose presence and guidance I enjoyed the advantage in visiting all that unrivalled Rome can boast of beautiful and grand. That I derived from this course of initiation any thing more than a very humbling consciousness of my own ignorance and want of taste, in matters of art, I will not be so dishonest as to pretend. But to the stranger in Rome every step forms an epoch; and, in addition to all its own countless appeals to memory and imagination, the agreeable auspices under which I first visited all its memorable places could not but render every impression I received more vivid and permanent. Thus, with my recollection of the Sepulchre of St. Peter, and its ever-burning lamps, for which splendid spot Canova was then meditating a statue, (2) there is always connected in my mind the exclamation which I heard break from Chantrey, after gazing, for a few moments, in silence, upon that glorious site—"What a place to work for!"

In one of the poems (3) allusion is made to an evening not easily forgotten, when Chantrey and myself were taken by Canova to the Borghese Palace, for the purpose of showing us, by the light of a taper—his favourite mode of exhibiting that work —his beautiful statue of the Princess Borghese, called the Venere Vincitrice. In Chantrey's eagerness to point out some grace or effect that peculiarly struck him, he snatched the light out of Canova's hand; and to this circumstance the following passage

of the poem referred to was meant to allude:—

> When he, thy peer in art and fame,
> Hung o'er the marble with delight, (4)
> And, while his lingering hand would steal •
>   O'er every grace the taper's ray,
> Gave thee, with all the generous zeal
> Such master-spirits only feel,
>   That best of fame—a rival's praise.

One of the days that still linger most pleasantly in my memory, and which, I trust, neither Lady Calcott nor Mr. Eastlake have quite forgotten, was that of our visit together to the Palatine Mount, when as we sauntered about that picturesque spot, enjoying the varied views of Rome which it commands, they made me, for the first time, acquainted with Guidi's spirited Ode on the Arcadians, in which there is poetry enough to make amends for all the nonsense of his rhyming brethren. Truly and grandly does he exclaim—

> "Indomita e superba ancor è Roma
> Benchè si veggia col gran busto a terra,
>   *   *   *   *
> Son piene di splendor le sue ruine,
> E il gran cenere suo si mostra eterno."

With Canova, while sitting to Jackson for a portrait ordered by Chantrey, I had more than once some interesting conversation—or, rather, listened while he spoke—respecting the political state of Europe at that period, and those "bricconi," as he styled them, the sovereigns of the Holy Alliance, and, before I left Rome, he kindly presented to me a set of engravings from some of his finest statues, together with a copy of the beautifully-printed collection of Poems, which a Roman poet named Missirini had written in praise of his different "Marmi.'

When Lord John Russell and myself parted, at Milan, it was agreed between us that, after a short visit to Rome, and (if practicable within the allowed time) to Naples, I was to rejoin him at Genoa, and from thence accompany him to England. But the early period for which Parliament was summoned, that year, owing to the violent proceedings at Manchester, rendered it necessary for Lord John to hasten his return to England. I was, therefore, most fortunate, under such circumstances, in being permitted by my friends Chantrey and Jackson to join in their journey homeward; through which lucky arrangement, the same precious privilege I had enjoyed, at Rome, of hearing the opinions of such practised judges, on all the great works of art I saw in their company, was afterwards continued to me through the various collections we visited together, at Florence, Bologna, Modena, Parma, Milan, and Turin.

To some of those pictures and statues that most took my fancy, during my tour, allusions will be found in a few of the poems which immediately follow.

(1) Abraham dismissing Hagar, by Guercino.
2 A statue, I believe, of Pius VI.
(3) See the lines concluding Extract XV , commencing—
    "Wonderful artist! praise, like mine," etc

(4) A slight alteration here has rendered these verses more true to the actual fact than they were in their original form.

But the great pleasure I derived from these and many other such works arose far more from the poetical nature of their subjects than from any judgment I had learned to form of their real merit as works of art—a line of lore in which, notwithstanding my course of schooling, I remained, I fear, unenlightened to the last. For all that was lost upon me, however, in the halls of Art, I was more than consoled in the cheap picture-gallery of Nature; and a glorious sunset I witnessed in ascending the Simplon is still remembered by me with a depth and freshness of feeling which no one work of art I saw in the galleries of Italy has left behind.

ORIGINAL PREFACE.

THE greater part of the following Rhymes were written or composed in an old *calèche*, for the purpose of beguiling the *ennui* of solitary travelling; and as verses, made by a gentleman in his sleep, have been lately called "a *psychological* curiosity," it is to be hoped that verses, composed by a gentleman to keep himself awake, may be honoured with some appellation equally Greek.

RHYMES ON THE ROAD.

INTRODUCTORY RHYMES.

Different Attitudes in which Authors compose.—Bayes, Henry Stephens, Herodotus, etc —Writing in Bed—in the Fields —Plato and Sir Richard Blackmore —Fiddling with Gloves and Twigs —Madame de Staël.—Rhyming on the Road, in an old Calèche.

WHAT various attitudes, and ways,
    And tricks, we authors have in writing!
While some write sitting, some, like Bayes,
    Usually stand, while they 're inditing.
Poets there are, who wear the floor out,
    Measuring a line at every stride;
While some, like Henry Stephens, pour out
    Rhymes by the dozen, while they ride.(1)

Herodotus wrote most in bed;
    And Richerand, a French physician,
Declares the clock-work of the head
    Goes best in that reclined position.
If you consult Montaigne (2) and Pliny on
    The subject, 't is their joint opinion
That Thought its richest harvest yields
    Abroad, among the woods and fields;
That bards, who deal in small retail,
    At home may, at their counters, stop;

(1) Pleraque sua carmina equitans composuit — *Paravicin. Singular.*

(2) "Mes pensées dorment, si je les assis "—*Montaigne.* Animus eorum qui in aperto acre ambulant attollitur. *Pliny.*

(3 The only authority I know for imputing this practice to Plato and Herodotus, is a Latin poem by M. de Valois on his Bed, in which he says :—

But that the grove, the hill, the vale,
Are Poesy's true wholesale shop.
And, verily, I think they 're right—
    For, many a time, on summer eves,
Just at that closing hour of light,
    When, like an Eastern Prince, who leaves
For distant war his Haram bowers,
    The Sun bids farewell to the flowers,
Whose heads are sunk, whose tears are flowing
'Mid all the glory of his going !—
Even I have felt, beneath those beams,
    When wandering through the fields alone,
Thoughts, fancies, intellectual gleams,
    Which, far too bright to be my own,
Seem'd lent me by the Sunny Power,
That was abroad at that still hour.

If thus I 've felt, how must *they* feel,
    The few, whom genuine Genius warms;
Upon whose souls he stamps his seal,
    Graven with Beauty's countless forms;—
The few upon this earth, who seem
    Born to give truth to Plato's dream,
Since in their thoughts, as in a glass,
    Shadows of heavenly things appear,
Reflections of bright shapes that pass
    Through other worlds, above our sphere!

But this reminds me I digress ;—
    For Plato, too, produced, 't is said,
'As one, indeed, might almost guess,)
    His glorious visions all in bed. (3)
'T was in his carriage that sublime
    Sir Richard Blackmore used to rhyme;
    And (if the wits do n't do him wrong)
'Twixt death (4) and epics pass'd his time,
    Scribbling and killing all day long—
Like Phœbus in his car, at ease,
    Now warbling forth a lofty song,
Now murdering the young Niobes.

There was a hero 'mong the Danes,
    Who wrote, we 're told, 'mid all the pains
    And horrors of exenteration,
Nine charming odes, which, if you 'll look,
    You 'll find preserved, with a translation,
By Bartholinus in his book. (5
In short, 't were endless to recite
    The various modes in which men write.
Some wits are only in the mind,
    When beaus and belles are round them prating,

Lucifer Herodotum vidit Vesperque cubantem,
    Desedit totos haec Plato saepe dies

(4) Sir Richard Blackmore was a physic an, as well as a bad poet.

(5) Eâdem curâ nec minores inter cruciatus animam infelicem agenti fuit Asbiorno Prudæ Danico heroi, cum Bruso ipsum, intestina extrahens, immaniter torqueret, tunc enim novem carmina cecinit, etc. — *Bartholin., de Causis Contempt Mort.*

55

Some, when they dress for dinner, find
  Their muse and valet both in waiting,
And manage, at the self-same time,
  To adjust a neckcloth and a rhyme.

Some bards there are who cannot scribble
  Without a glove, to tear or nibble;
  Or a small twig to whisk about—
    As if the hidden founts of Fancy,
Like wells of old, were thus found out
  By mystic tricks of rhabdomancy.
Such was the little feathery wand, (1)
That, held for ever in the hand
Of her (2) who won and wore the crown
  Of female genius in this age,
Seem'd the conductor, that drew down
  Those words of lightning to her page.

As for myself—to come, at last,
  To the odd way in which I write—
Having employ'd these few months past
  Chiefly in travelling, day and night,
I've got into the easy mode,
  Of rhyming thus along the road—
Making a way-bill of my pages,
  Counting my stanzas by my stages—
'Twixt lays and re-lays no time lost—
In short, in two words, *writing post*. (3)

—◦◦◦—

EXTRACT I.   *Geneva*
View of the Lake of Geneva from the Jura. (4)—*Anxious
to reach it before the Sun went down.—Obliged to pro
ceed on Foot.—Alps.—Mont Blanc.—Effect of the Scene*

'T was late—the sun had almost shone
  His last and best, when I ran on,
Anxious to reach that splendid view,
  Before the day-beams quite withdrew;
And feeling as all feel, on first
    Approaching scenes, where they are told,
Such glories on their eyes will burst,
    As youthful bards in dreams behold.

'T was distant yet, and, as I ran,
  Full often was my wistful gaze
Turn'd to the sun, who now began
  To call in all his out-post rays,
And form a denser march of light,
  Such as beseems a hero's flight.
Oh, how I wish'd for Joshua's power,
  To stay the brightness of that hour!

(1 Made of paper, twisted up like a fan or feather.
(2) Madame de Staël
(3 The following lines formerly concluded these intro-
ductory rhymes —

  My verses, I suspect, not ill
  Resembling the crazed vehicle
  (An old *caleche* for which a villain
  Charged me some twenty Naps at Milan
  In which I wrote them—patch'd-up things
  On weak, but rather easy, springs,
  Jingling along, with little in 'em,
    And (where the road is not so rough,

But no—the sun still less became,
  Diminish'd to a speck—as splendid
And small as were those tongues of flame,
  That on the Apostles' heads descended!

'T was at this instant—while there glow'd
  This last, intensest, gleam of light—
Suddenly, through the opening road,
  The valley burst upon my sight!
That glorious valley, with its Lake,
  And Alps on Alps in clusters swelling,
Mighty, and pure, and fit to make
  The ramparts of a Godhead's dwelling.

I stood entranced—as Rabbins say
  This whole assembled gazing world
Will stand, upon that awful day,
  When the Ark's Light, aloft unfurl'd,
Among the opening clouds shall shine,
  Divinity's own radiant sign!
Mighty Mont Blanc, thou wert to me,
  That minute, with thy brow in heaven,
As sure a sign of Deity
  As e'er to mortal gaze was given.
Nor, ever, were I destined yet
  To live my life twice o'er again,
Can I the deep-felt awe forget,
  The dream, the trance that rapt me then!

'T was all that consciousness of power
And life, beyond this mortal hour;—
Those mountings of the soul within
  At thoughts of Heaven—as birds begin
By instinct in the cage to rise,
  When near their time for change of skies,—
That proud assurance of our claim
  To rank among the Sons of Light,
Mingled with shame—oh bitter shame!—
  At having risk'd that splendid right,
For aught that earth, through all its range
  Of glories, offers in exchange!
'T was all this, at that instant brought,
Like breaking sunshine, o'er my thought—
'T was all this, kindled to a glow
  Of sacred zeal, which, could it shine
Thus purely ever, man might grow,
  Even upon earth, a thing divine,
And be, once more, the creature made
To walk unstain'd the Elysian shade!

  Or deep, or lofty, as to spin 'em,
    Down precipices) safe enough —
  Too ready to take fire, I own,
  And *then*, too, nearest a break-down;
  But, for my comfort, hung so low,
  I have n't, in falling, far to go.—
  With all this, light, and swift, and airy,
    And carrying which is best of all)
  But little for the *Doganieri* *
    Of the Reviews to overhaul —P. E.

'4) Between Vattay and Gex.

          * Custom-house officers

No, never shall I lose the trace
Of what I 've felt in this bright place.
And, should my spirit's hope grow weak,
Should I, oh God, e'er doubt thy power,
This mighty scene again I 'll seek,
At the same calm and glowing hour,
And here, at the sublimest shrine
That Nature ever rear'd to Thee,
Rekindle all that hope divine,
And *feel* my immortality!

——⊶⊷⊷——

EXTRACT II.

Geneva.

Fate of Geneva in the year 1782
A FRAGMENT.

Yes—if there yet live some of those
Who, when this small Republic rose,
Quick as a startled hive of bees,
Against her leaguering enemies— (1)
When, as the Royal Satrap shook
His well-known fetters at her gates,
Even wives and mothers arm'd, and took
Their stations by their sons and mates;
And on these walls there stood—yet, no,
Shame to the traitors—*would* have stood
As firm a band as e'er let flow
At Freedom's base their sacred blood,
If those yet live who, on that night,
When all were watching, girt for fight,
Stole, like the creeping of a pest,
From rank to rank, from breast to breast,
Filling the weak, the old, with fears,
Turning the heroine's zeal to tears—
Betraying Honour to that brink,
Where, one step more, and he must sink—
And quenching hopes which, though the last,
Like meteors on a drowning mast,
Would yet have led to death more bright
Than life e'er look'd, in all its light!
Till soon, too soon, distrust, alarms
Throughout the embattled thousands ran,
And the high spirit, late in arms,
The zeal, that might have work'd such charms,
Fell, like a broken talisman—
Their gates, that they had sworn should be
The gates of Death, that very dawn,
Gave passage widely, bloodlessly,
To the proud foe—nor sword was drawn,
Nor even one martyr'd body cast
To stain their footsteps, as they pass'd;
But, of the many sworn at night,
To do or die, some fled the sight,
Some stood to look, with sullen frown,
While some, in impotent despair,

(1) In the year 1782, when the forces of Berne, Sardinia, and France laid siege to Geneva, and when, after a demonstration of heroism and self-devotion, which promised to rival the feats of their ancestors in 1602 against Savoy, the Genevans, either panic-struck or betrayed, to the surprise of all Europe, opened their gates to the besiegers,

Broke their bright armour and lay down,
Weeping upon the fragments there!—
If those, I say, who brought that shame,
That blast upon Geneva's name,
Be living still—though crime so dark
Shall hang up, fix'd and unforgiven,
In History's page—the eternal mark
For Scorn to pierce—so help me, Heaven,
I wish the traitorous slaves no worse,
No deeper, deadlier disaster,
From all earth's ills no fouler curse
Than to have ⁎ ⁎ ⁎ ⁎ ⁎ ⁎ ⁎ ⁎ ⁎ their master!

——⊶⊷⊷——

EXTRACT III.

Geneva.

Fancy and Truth.—Hippomenes and Atalanta —Mont Blanc.—Clouds.

Even here, in this region of wonders, I find
That light-footed Fancy leaves Truth far behind;
Or, at least, like Hippomenes, turns her astray
By the golden illusion he flings in her way. (2

What a glory it seem'd the first evening I gazed!
Mont Blanc, like a vision, then suddenly raised
On the wreck of the sunset—and all his array
Of high-towering Alps, touch'd still with a light
Far holier, purer, than that of the Day,
As if nearness to Heaven had made them so bright!
Then the dying, at last, of these splendours away
From peak after peak, till they left but a ray,
One roseate ray, that, too precious to fly,
O'er the Mighty of Mountains still glowingly hung,
Like the last sunny step of Astræa, when high
From the summit of earth to Elysium she sprung!
And those infinite Alps, stretching out from the sight
Till they mingled with Heaven, now shorn of their light,
Stood lofty, and lifeless, and pale in the sky,
Like the ghosts of a Giant Creation gone by!

That scene—I have view'd it this evening again,
By the same brilliant light that hung over it then—
The valley, the lake, in their tenderest charms—
Mont Blanc in his awfullest pomp—and the whole
A bright picture of Beauty, reclined in the arms
Of Sublimity, bridegroom elect of her soul!
But where are the mountains, that round me at first,
One dazzling horizon of miracles, burst?
Those Alps beyond Alps, without end swelling on
Like the waves of eternity—where are *they* gone?
Clouds—clouds—they were nothing but clouds,
after all!(3)
That chain of Mont Blancs, which my fancy flew o'er,

and submitted without a struggle to the extinction of their liberties.—See an account of this Revolution in Coxe's *Switzerland.*

(2) ———— nitidique cupidine pomi
Declinat cursus, aurumque volubile tollit.—*Ovid.*

(3) It is often very difficult to distinguish between

With a wonder that nought on this earth can recall,
Were but clouds of the evening, and now are no
more.

What a picture of Life's young illusions! Oh, Night,
Drop thy curtain, at once, and hide *all* from my sigh.

—⟶⊷⊶⟵—

EXTRACT IV.

Milan

The Picture Gallery.—Albano's Rape of Proserpine. Reflections. — Universal Salvation. — Abraham sending away Agar, by Guercino.—Genius.

WENT to the *Brera*—saw a Dance of Loves
By smooth Albano, 1) him, whose pencil teems
With Cupids, numerous as in summer groves
The leaflets are, or motes in summer beams.

'Tis for the theft of Enna's flower (2 from earth
These urchins celebrate their dance of mirth
Round the green tree, like fays upon a heath—
    Those, that are nearest, link'd in order bright,
    Cheek after cheek, like rose-buds in a wreath;
And those, more distant, showing from beneath
    The others' wings their little eyes of light.
While see, among the clouds, their eldest brother,
    But just flown up, tells with a smile of bliss
This prank of Pluto to his charmed mother,
    Who turns to greet the tidings with a kiss!

Well might the Loves rejoice—and well did they,
    Who wove these fables, picture, in their weaving,
That blessed truth, (which, in a darker day,
    Origen lost his saintship for believing,)—(3)
That Love, eternal Love, whose fadeless ray
    Nor time, nor death, nor sin can overcast,
Even to the depths of hell will find his way,
    And soothe, and heal, and triumph there at last!

————

Guercino's Agar—where the bond-maid hears
    From Abram's lips that he and she must part;
And looks at him with eyes all full of tears,
    That seem the very last drops from her heart.
Exquisite picture!—let me not be told
Of minor faults, of colouring tame and cold—
If thus to conjure up a face so fair, (4)
So full of sorrow; with the story there
Of all that woman suffers, when the stay
Her trusting heart hath lean'd on falls away—
If thus to touch the bosom's tenderest spring,
By calling into life such eyes as bring

Back to our sad remembrance some of those
We 've smiled and wept with, in their joys and woes,
Thus filling them with tears, like tears we 've known,
Till all the pictured grief becomes our own—
If *this* be deem'd the victory of Art—
    If thus, by pen or pencil, to lay bare
The deep, fresh, living fountains of the heart
    Before all eyes, be Genius—it is *there!*

⊷⊶⊷

EXTRACT V.

Padua

Fancy and Reality.—Rain-drops and Lakes.—Plan of a Story.—Where to place the Scene of it.—In some unknown Region.—Psalnanazar's Imposture with respect to the Island of Formosa.

THE more I 've view'd this world, the more I 've found,
That, fill'd as 'tis with scenes and creatures rare,
Fancy commands, within her own bright round,
    A world of scenes and creatures far more fair.
Nor is it that her power can call up there
    A single charm, that 's not from Nature won,
No more than rainbows, in their pride, can wear
    A single hue unborrow'd from the sun—
But 'tis the mental medium it shines through,
That lends to Beauty all its charm and hue;
As the same light, that o'er the level lake
    One dull monotony of lustre flings,
Will, entering in the rounded rain-drop, make
    Colours as gay as those on Peris' wings!
And such, I deem, the difference between real
Existing Beauty and that form ideal,
Which she assumes, when seen by poets' eyes,
Like sunshine in the drop—with all those dyes
Which Fancy's variegating prism supplies.

I have a story of two lovers, fill'd
    With all the pure romance, the blissful sadness,
And the sad doubtful bliss, that ever thrill'd [ness.
Two young and longing hearts in that sweet mad-
But where to choose the region of my vision
    In this wide vulgar world—what real spot
Can be found out sufficiently Elysian
    For two such perfect lovers, I know not.
Oh for some fair Formosa, such as he,
    The young Jew fabled of, in the Indian Sea,
By nothing but its name of Beauty known,
And which Queen Fancy might make all her own,
Her fairy kingdom—take its people, lands,
And tenements into her own bright hands,
And make, at least, one earthly corner fit
For Love to live in, pure and exquisite!

clouds and Alps, and on the evening when I first saw this magnificent scene, the clouds were so disposed along the whole horizon, as to deceive me into an idea of the stupendous extent of these mountains, which my subsequent observation was very far, of course, from confirming.

(1) This picture, the Agar of Guercino, and the Apostles of Guido (the two latter of which are now the chief ornaments of the Brera), were formerly in the Palazzo Zampieri at Bologna.

(2   ————that fair field
    Of Enna, where Proserpine, gathering flowers,
    Herself a fairer flower, by gloomy Dis was gather'd.

(3 The extension of the Divine Love ultimately even to the regions of the damned.

(4) It is probable that this fine head is a portrait, as we find it repeated in a picture by Guercino, which is in the possession of Signor Camuccini, the brother of the celebrated painter at Rome.

EXTRACT VI.

Venice

*The Fall of Venice not to be lamented.—Former Glory
Expedition against Constantinople. — Giustiniani*
*Republic —Characteristics of the old Government
Golden Book.—Brazen Mouths.— Spies.— Dungeons
Present Desolation.*

MOURN not for Venice—let her rest
    In ruin, 'mong those States unblest,
Beneath whose gilded hoofs of pride,
Where'er they trampled, Freedom died.
No—let us keep our tears for them,
    Where'er they pine, whose fall hath been
Not from a blood-stain'd diadem,
    Like that which deck'd this ocean-queen,
But from high daring in the cause
Of human Rights—the only good
And blessed strife, in which man draws
    His mighty sword on land or flood.

Mourn not for Venice ; though her fall
    Be awful, as if Ocean's wave
Swept o'er her, she deserves it all,
    And Justice triumphs o'er her grave.
Thus perish every King and State
    That run the guilty race she ran,
Strong but in ill, and only great
    By outrage against God and man!

True, her high spirit is at rest,
    And all those days of glory gone,
When the world's waters, east and west,
    Beneath her white-wing'd commerce shone ;

(1) Under the Doge Michaeli, in 1171.

2) " La famille entière des Justiniani, l'une des plus
illustres de Venise, voulut marcher tout entière dans
cette expédition ; elle fournit cent combattans, c'était
renouveler l'exemple d'une illustre famille de Rome, le
même malheur les attendait.—*Histoire de Venise, par
Daru.*

(3) The celebrated Fra Paolo. The collection of Maxims
which this bold monk drew up at the request of the Ve-
netian Government, for the guidance of the Secret Inqui-
sition of State, are so atrocious as to seem rather an over-
charged satire upon despotism, than a system of policy,
seriously inculcated, and but too readily and constantly
pursued.

The spirit, in which these maxims of Father Paul are
conceived, may be judged from the instructions which
he gives for the management of the Venetian colonies
and provinces. Of the former he says :—"Il faut les trai-
ter comme des animaux feroces, leur rogner les dents et
les griffes, les humilier souvent, surtout leur ôter les oc-
casions de s'aguerrir. Du pain et le bâton, voilà ce qu'il
leur faut, gardons l'humanité pour une meilleure occa-
sion."

For the treatment of the provinces he advises thus
" Tendre à dépouiller les villes de leurs privileges, faire
que les habitans s'appauvrissent, et que leurs biens soient
achetes par les Vénitiens. Ceux qui, dans les conseils
municipaux, se montreront ou plus audacieux ou plus

When, with her countless barks she went
    To meet the Orient Empire's might, (1)
And her Giustinianis sent
    Their hundred heroes to that fight. (2)

Vanish'd are all her pomps, 'tis true,
But mourn them not—for vanish'd, too,
    (Thanks to that Power, who, soon or late,
Hurls to the dust the guilty Great,)
Are all the outrage, falsehood, fraud,
    The chains, the rapine, and the blood
That fill'd each spot, at home, abroad,
    Where the Republic's standard stood.

Desolate Venice ! when I track
Thy haughty course through centuries back ;
Thy ruthless power, obey'd but curst—
    The stern machinery of thy State,
Which hatred would, like steam, have burst,
    Had stronger fear not chill'd even hate ;—
Thy perfidy, still worse than aught
Thy own unblushing Sarpi (3) taught ;—
Thy friendship, which, o'er all beneath
    Its shadow, rain'd down dews of death ;—(4)
Thy Oligarchy's Book of Gold,
    Closed against humble Virtue's name, (5)
But open'd wide for slaves who sold
    Their native land to thee and shame ;—(6)
Thy all-pervading host of spies,
    Watching o'er every glance and breath,
Till men look'd in each others' eyes,
    To read their chance of life or death ;—
Thy laws, that made a mart of blood,
    And legalized the assassin's knife ;—(7)

dévoués aux intérêts de la population, il faut les perdre ou
les gagner à quelque prix que ce soit : enfin, s'il se trouve
dans les provinces quelques chefs de parti, il faut les ex-
terminer sous un prétexte quelconque, mais en évitant
de recourir a la justice ordinaire. Que le poison fasse
l'office de bourreau, cela est moins odieux et beaucoup
plus profitable."

(4) Conduct of Venice towards her allies and depen-
dencies, particularly to unfortunate Padua—Fate of
Francesco Carrara, for which see *Daru,* vol. ii., p. 141.

(5) "A l'exception des trente citadins admis au grand
conseil pendant la guerre de Chiozzi, il n'est pas arrivé
une seule fois que les talens ou les services aient paru à
cette noblesse orgueilleuse des titres suffisans pour s'as-
seoir avec elle."—*Daru*

(6) Among those admitted to the honour of being in-
scribed in the *Libro d'Oro* were some families of Brescia,
Treviso, and other places, whose only claim to that dis-
tinction was the zeal with which they prostrated them-
selves and their country at the feet of the Republic.

(7) By the infamous statutes of the State Inquisition, *

* M. Daru has given an abstract of these Statutes, from a manu-
script in the Bibliothèque du Roi, and it is hardly credible that
such a system of treachery and cruelty should ever have been
established by any government, or submitted to, for an instant,
by any people. Among various precautions against the intrigues
of their own Nobles, we find the following — " Pour persuader
aux etrangers qu'il etait difficile et dangereux d'entretenir quel-

Thy sunless cells beneath the flood,
  And racks, and leads, (1) that burnt out life ;—

When I review all this, and see
The doom that now hath fallen on thee ;
Thy nobles, towering once so proud,
Themselves beneath the yoke now bow'd—
A yoke, by no one grace redeem'd,
Such as, of old, around thee beam'd,
But mean and base as e'er yet gall'd
Earth's tyrants, when, themselves, en-
    thrall'd—(2)
I feel the moral vengeance sweet,
And, smiling o'er the wreck, repeat
" Thus perish every King and State,
  That tread the steps which Venice trod,
Strong but in ill, and only great,
  By outrage against man and God !"

—◦◦◦◦—

EXTRACT VII.

                    Venice.

Lord Byron's Memoirs, written by himself.—Reflections
when about to read them.

LET me, a moment—ere with fear and hope
Of gloomy, glorious things, these leaves I ope—
As one, in fairy tale, to whom the key
Of some enchanter's secret halls is given,
Doubts, while he enters, slowly, tremblingly
If he shall meet with shapes from hell or heaven—
Let me, a moment, think what thousands live
O'er the wide earth this instant, who would give,
Gladly, whole sleepless nights to bend the brow
Over these precious leaves, as I do now.

not only was assassination recognized as a regular mode
of punishment, but this secret power over life was dele-
gated to their minions at a distance, with nearly as much
facility as a licence is given under the game laws of Eng-
land. The only restriction seems to have been the ne-
cessity of applying for a new certificate, after every indi-
vidual exercise of the power.

(1) "Les prisons des plombs ; c'est-à-dire, ces fournaises
ardentes qu'on avait distribuées en petites cellules sous
les terrasses qui couvrent le palais."

(2) The preceding lines originally read—

    When I review all this, and see
    What thou art sunk and crush'd to now—

que intrigue secrète avec les nobles Vénitiens, on imagina de faire
avertir mystérieusement le Nonce du Pape afin que les autres
ministres en fussent informés) que l'inquisition avait autorisé
les patriciens à poignarder quiconque essaierait de tenter leur
fidélité. Mais craignant que les ambassadeurs ne prissent for
difficilement à une délibération, qui en effet n'existait pas, l'In-
quisition voulait prouver qu'elle en était capable. Elle ordonna
des recherches pour découvrir s'il n'y avait pas dans Venise
quelque exilé au-dessus du commun, qui eût rompu son ban ;
ensuite un des patriciens qui étaient aux gages du tribunal reçut
la mission d'assassiner ce malheureux, et l'ordre de s'en vanter,
en disant qu'il s'était porté à cet acte, parce que ce banni était
l'agent d'un ministre étranger, et avait cherché à le corrompre."
"Remarquons," adds M. Daru, "que ceci n'est pas une simple
anecdote ; c'est une mission projetée, délibérée, écrite d'avance,
une règle de conduite tracée par des hommes graves à leurs suc-
cesseurs, et consignée dans des statuts."

How all who know—and where is he unknown ?
To what far region have his songs not flown,
Like Psaphon's birds, (3) speaking their master's
    name,
In every language, syllabled by Fame?—
How all, who've felt the various spells combined
Within the circle of that master-mind—
Like spells, derived from many a star, and met
Together in some wondrous amulet—
Would burn to know when first the Light awoke
In his young soul—and if the gleams that broke
From that Aurora of his genius raised
Most pain or bliss in those on whom they blazed ;
Would love to trace the unfolding of that power,
Which hath grown ampler, grander, every hour ;
And feel, in watching o'er his first advance,
  As did the Egyptian traveller, (4) when he stood
By the young Nile, and fathom'd with his lance
  The first small fountains of that mighty flood.

They, too, who, 'mid the scornful thoughts that dwell
  In his rich fancy, tinging all its streams—
As if the Star of Bitterness, which fell
  On earth of old, (5) had touch'd them with its
    beams—
Can track a spirit which, though driven to hate,
From Nature's hands came kind, affectionate ;
And which, even now, struck as it is with blight,
Comes out, at times in love's own native light ;—
How gladly all, who've watch'd these struggling rays
Of a bright ruin'd spirit through his lays,
Would here inquire, as from his own frank lips,
  What desolating grief, what wrongs had driven

    Each harpy maxim, hatch'd by thee,
      Return'd to roost on thy own brow—
    Thy Nobles, towering once aloft,
      Now sunk in chains in chains, that have
      Not even that borrow'd grace, which oft
      The master's fame sheds o'er the slave,
    But are as mean as e'er were given
    To stiff-neck'd Pride by angry Heaven.—P E

(3) Psaphon, in order to attract the attention of the
world, taught multitudes of birds to speak his name, and
then let them fly away in various directions ; whence the
proverb, "*Psaphonis aves.*"   4 Bruce.

(5) "And the name of the star is called Wormwood, and the
third part of the waters became wormwood."—*Rev.* viii.

The cases, in which assassination is ordered by these Statutes,
are as follow :—

"Un ouvrier de l'arsenal, un chef de ce qu'on appelle, parmi
les marins, le menstrance, passait-il au service d'une puissance
étrangère : il fallait le faire assassiner, surtout si c'était un homme
réputé brave et habile dans sa profession." *Art.* 3. *des Statuts.*)

"Avait-il commis quelque action qu'on ne jugeait pas à pro-
pos de punir juridiquement, on devait le faire empoisonner."
Art. 14

"Un artisan passait-il à l'étranger en y exportant quelque pro-
cédé de l'industrie nationale : c'était encore un crime capital, que
la loi inconnue ordonnait de punir par un assassinat." (*Art.* 26

The facility with which they got rid of their Duke of Bedfords,
Lord Fitzwilliams, etc., was admirable It was thus :—

"Le patricien qui se permettrait le moindre propos contre le
gouvernement était admonesté deux fois, et à la troisième *noyé
comme incorrigible*" *Art.* 30

That noble nature into cold eclipse;
  Like some fair orb that, once a sun in heaven,
And born, not only to surprise, but cheer
With warmth and lustre all within its sphere,
Is now so quench'd, that of its grandeur lasts
Nought, but the wide cold shadow which it casts!

Eventful volume! whatsoe'er the change
  Of scene and clime—the adventures, bold and
    strange—
The griefs—the frailties, but too frankly told—
The loves, the feuds, thy pages may unfold,
If Truth with half so prompt a hand unlocks
His virtues as his failings, we shall find
The record there of friendships, held like rocks,
  And enmities, like sun-touch'd snow, resign'd,
Of fealty, cherish'd without change or chill,
In those who served him, young, and serve him still,
Of generous aid, given with that noiseless art
Which wakes not pride, to many a wounded heart,
Of acts—but, no—*not* from himself must aught
Of the bright features of his life be sought.
While they, who court the world, like Milton's
    cloud, (1)
"Turn forth their silver lining" on the crowd,
This gifted Being wraps himself in night;
  And, keeping all that softens, and adorns,
And gilds his social nature hid from sight,
  Turns but its darkness on a world he scorns.

———◦◦◦◦———

EXTRACT VIII.

                  Venice.

*Female Beauty at Venice.—No longer what it was in the
Time of Titian.—His Mistress.—Various Forms in which
he has painted her.—Venus—Divine and profane Love
—La Fragilità d'Amore.—Paul Veronese.—His Women.
—Marriage of Cana.—Character of Italian Beauty.—
Raphael's Fornarina.—Modesty.*

Thy brave, thy learn'd, have past away;
Thy beautiful!—ah, where are they?
The forms, the faces, that once shone,
  Models of grace, in Titian's eye,
Where are they now? while flowers live on
  In ruin'd places, why, oh why
Must Beauty thus with Glory die?
That maid, whose lips would still have moved,
  Could art have breathed a spirit through them;
Whose varying charms her artist loved
  More fondly every time he drew them,

So oft beneath his touch they pass'd,
Each semblance fairer than the last);
Wearing each shape that Fancy's range
  Offers to Love—yet still the one
Fair idol, seen through every change,
  Like facets of some orient stone—
  In each the same bright image shown.
Sometimes a Venus, unarray'd
  But in her beauty (2)—sometimes deck'd
In costly raiment, as a maid
That kings might for a throne select. (3)
Now high and proud, like one who thought
The world should at her feet be brought;
Now, with a look reproachful, sad—(4)
Unwonted look from brow so glad;
And telling of a pain too deep
For tongue to speak or eyes to weep.
Sometimes, through allegory's veil,
  In double semblance seen to shine,
Telling a strange and mystic tale
  Of Love Profane and Love Divine—(5)
Akin in features, but in heart
As far as earth and heaven apart.
Or else (by quaint device to prove
The frailty of all worldly love)
Holding a globe of glass, as thin
  As air-blown bubbles, in her hand,
With a young Love confined therein,
  Whose wings seem waiting to expand—
And telling, by her anxious eyes,
That, if that frail orb breaks, he flies! (6)

Thou, too, with touch magnificent,
  Paul of Verona!—where are they,
The oriental forms, (7) that lent
  Thy canvass such a bright array?
Noble and gorgeous dames, whose dress
Seems part of their own loveliness;
Like the sun's drapery, which, at eve,
The floating clouds around him weave
Of light they from himself receive!
Where is there now the living face
  Like those that, in thy nuptial throng, (8)
By their superb voluptuous grace,
Make us forget the time, the place,
  The holy guests they smile among—
Till, in that feast of heaven-sent wine,
We see no miracles but thine.

---

(1)   "Did a sable cloud
    Turn forth her silver lining on the night?"
                           Comus

(2 In the Tribune at Florence.
(3 In the Palazzo Pitti.
(4) Alludes particularly to the portrait of her in the
Sciarra collection at Rome, where the look of mournful
reproach in those full shadowy eyes, as if she had been
unjustly accused of something wrong, is exquisite
  (5 The fine picture in the Palazzo Borghese, called (it
is not easy to say why) "Sacred and Profane Love," in

which the two figures, sitting on the edge of the fountain,
are evidently portraits of the same person.
  (6 This fanciful allegory is the subject of a picture by
Titian in the possession of the Marquis Cambian at Turin,
whose collection, though small, contains some beautiful
specimens of all the great masters.
  7) As Paul Veronese gave but little into the *beau ideal*,
his women may be regarded as pretty close imitations of
the living models which Venice afforded in his time.
  (8) The Marriage of Cana.

If e'er, except in Painting's dream,
  There bloom'd such beauty here, 'tis gone—
Gone, like the face that in the stream
  Of Ocean for an instant shone,
When Venus at that mirror gave
  A last look, ere she left the wave.
And though, among the crowded ways,
  We oft are startled by the blaze
Of eyes that pass, with fitful light,
  Like fire-flies on the wing at night, (1)
'T is not that nobler beauty, given
  To show how angels look in heaven.
Even in its shape most pure and fair,
  'T is beauty, with but half her zone—
All that can warm the Sense is there,
  But the Soul's deeper charm is flown :—
'T is Raphael's Fornarina—warm,
  Luxuriant, arch, but unrefined ;
A flower, round which the noontide swarm
  Of young Desires may buzz and wind,
But where true Love no treasure meets
  Worth hoarding in his hive of sweets.
Ah no—for this, and for the hue
  Upon the rounded cheek, which tells
How fresh, within the heart, this dew
  Of Love's unrifled sweetness dwells,
We must go back to our own Isles,
  Where Modesty, which here but gives
A rare and transient grace to smiles,
  In the heart's holy centre lives ;
And thence, as from her throne diffuses
  O'er thoughts and looks so bland a reign,
That not a thought or feeling loses
  Its freshness in that gentle chain.

————◦◦◦◦————

EXTRACT IX.
                          Venice.
The English to be met with every where.—Alps and
Threadneedle Street.—The Simplon and the Stocks.—
Rage for travelling.—Blue Stockings among the Waha-
bees.—Parasols and Pyramids.—Mrs. Hopkins and the
Wall of China.

AND is there then no earthly place,
  Where we can rest, in dream Elysian,
Without some curst round English face
  Popping up near, to break the vision ?
'Mid northern lakes, 'mid southern vines,
  Unholy cits we 're doom'd to meet ;
Nor highest Alps nor Appennines
  Are sacred from Threadneedle Street !

(1) "Certain it is (as Arthur Young truly and feelingly
says) one now and then meets with terrible eyes in Italy."
(2) It was pink *spencers*, I believe, that the imagination
of the French traveller conjured up.
(3) The first twelve lines of this translation, it will be
perceived, have been already given. See page 281.—P. E.
(4) Utque ferunt lætus convivia læta
     Et celebras lentis otia mista jocis,
   Aut cithara æstivum attenuas cantuque calorem,
   Hei mihi, quam dispar nunc mea vita tuæ !
   Nec mihi displiceant quæ sunt tibi grata, sed ipsa est
   Te sine, lux oculis pene inimica meis.

If up the Simplon's path we wind,
  Fancying we leave this world behind,
Such pleasant sounds salute one's ear
  As—"Baddish news from 'Change, my dear—
The Funds—(phew, curse this ugly hill)—
  Are lowering fast—(what, higher still?)—
And—(zooks, we 're mounting up to heaven !)—
  Will soon be down to sixty-seven."

Go where we may—rest where we will,
  Eternal London haunts us still.
The trash of Almack's or Fleet Ditch—
  And scarce a pin's head difference *which*—
Mixes, though even to Greece we run,
  With every rill from Helicon !
And, if this rage for travelling lasts,
  If Cockneys, of all sects and castes,
Old maidens, aldermen, and squires,
  Will leave their puddings and coal fires,
To gape at things in foreign lands
  No soul among them understands ;
If Blues desert their coteries,
  To show off 'mong the Wahabees,
If neither sex nor age controls,
  Nor fear of Mamelukes forbids
Young ladies, with pink parasols,
  To glide among the Pyramids—(2)
Why, then, farewell all hope to find
  A spot that 's free from London-kind !
Who knows, if to the West we roam,
  But we may find some *Blue* "at home"
Among the *Blacks* of Carolina—
  Or, flying to the Eastward, see
Some Mrs. Hopkins, taking tea
  And toast upon the Wall of China !

————◦◦◦————

EXTRACT X.
                          Mantua
  Verses of Hippolyta to her Husband. 3
THEY tell me thou 'rt the favour'd guest(4)
  Of every fair and brilliant throng ;
No wit, like thine, to wake the jest,
  No voice like thine, to breathe the song.
And none could guess, so gay thou art,
  That thou and I are far apart.
Alas, alas, how different flows,
  With thee and me, the time away :
Not that I wish thee sad, Heaven knows—
  Still, if thou canst, be light and gay ;

Non auro aut gemmâ caput exornare nitenti
Me juvat, aut Arabo spargere odore comas :
Non celebres ludos fastus spectare diebus.

Sola tuos vultus referens Raphaelis imago
Picta manu, curas allevat usque meas.
Huic ego delicias facio, arrideoque jocorque,
Alloquor et tanquam reddere verba queat.
Assensu nutuque mihi sæpe illa videtur
Dicere velle aliquid et tua verba loqui.
Agnoscit balboque patrem puer ore salutat.
Hoc solor longas decipioque dies.

I only know that without thee
The sun himself is dark for me.

Do I put on the jewels rare
Thou 'st always loved to see me wear?
Do I perfume the locks that thou
So oft hast braided o'er my brow,
    Thus deck'd, through festive crowds to run,
    And all the assembled world to see—
All but the one, the absent one,
    Worth more than present worlds to me!
No, nothing cheers this widow'd heart—
My only joy, from thee apart,
From thee thyself, is sitting hours
    And days, before thy pictured form—
That dream of thee, which Raphael's powers
    Have made with all but life-breath warm!
And as I smile to it, and say
The words I speak to thee in play,
I fancy from their silent frame,
Those eyes and lips give back the same;
And still I gaze, and still they keep
Smiling thus on me—till I weep!
Our little boy, too, knows it well,
    For there I lead him every day,
And teach his lisping lips to tell
    The name of one that 's far away.
Forgive me, love, but thus alone
My time is cheer'd, while thou art gone.

—◦♦◦—
EXTRACT XI.
Florence.

No—'t is not the region where Love 's to be found—
    They have bosoms that sigh, they have glances
        that rove,
They have language a Sappho's own lip might resound,
    When she warbled her best—but they 've nothing
        like Love.

Nor is 't that pure *sentiment* only they want,
    Which Heaven for the mild and the tranquil hath
        made—
Calm wedded affection, that home-rooted plant,
    Which sweetens seclusion, and smiles in the shade;

That feeling which, after long years have gone by,
    Remains, like a portrait we 've sat for in youth,
Where, even though the flush of the colours may fly,
    The features still live, in their first smiling truth;

That union where all that in Woman is kind,
    With all that in Man most ennoblingly towers,
Grow wreathed into one—like the column, combined
    Of the *strength* of the shaft and the capital's *flowers*.

Of this—bear ye witness, ye wives, every where,
    By the Arno, the Po, by all Italy's streams—
Of this—heart-wedded love, so delicious to share,
    Not a husband hath even one glimpse in his dreams.

But it *is* not this, only;—born full of the light
    Of a sun, from whose fount the luxuriant festoons
Of these beautiful valleys drink lustre so bright,
    That, beside him, our suns of the north are but
        moons—

We might fancy, at least, like their climate they
        burn'd;
    And that Love, though unused, in this region of
        spring,
To be thus to a tame Household Deity turn'd,
    Would yet be all soul, when abroad on the wing.

And there *may* be, there *are* those explosions of heart,
    Which burst, when the senses have first caught
        the flame;
Such fits of the blood as those climates impart,
    Where Love is a sun-stroke, that maddens the frame.

But that Passion which springs in the depth of the soul,
    Whose beginnings are virginly pure as the source
Of some small mountain rivulet, destined to roll
    As a torrent, ere long, losing peace in its course—

A course, to which Modesty's struggle but lends
    A more headlong descent, without chance of recall;
But which Modesty even to the last edge attends,
    And, then, throws a halo of tears round its fall!

This exquisite Passion—ay, exquisite, even
    'Mid the ruin its madness too often hath made,
As it keeps, even then, a bright trace of the heaven,
    That heaven of Virtue from which it has stray'd—

This entireness of love, which can only be found
    Where Woman, like something that 's holy,
        watch'd over,
And fenced, from her childhood, with purity round,
    Comes, body and soul, fresh as Spring, to a lover!

Where not an eye answers, where not a hand presses,
    Till spirit with spirit in sympathy move;
And the Senses, asleep in their sacred recesses,
    Can only be reach'd through the temple of Love!—

This perfection of Passion—how *can* it be found,
    Where the mystery nature hath hung round the tie
By which souls are together attracted and bound,
    Is laid open, for ever, to heart, ear, and eye,—

Where nought of that innocent doubt can exist,
    That ignorance, even than knowledge more bright,
Which circles the young, like the morn's sunny mist,
    And curtains them round in their own native light;

Where Experience leaves nothing for Love to reveal,
    Or for Fancy, in visions, to gleam o'er the thought;
But the truths which, alone, we would die to conceal
    From the maiden's young heart, are the *only* ones
        taught.

56

No, no, 't is not here, howsoever we sigh,
   Whether purely to Hymen's *one* planet we play,
Or adore, like Sabæans, each light of Love's sky,
   Here *is* not the region to fix or to stray.

For faithless in wedlock, in gallantry gross,
   Without honour to guard, or reserve to restrain,
What have they a husband can mourn as a loss?
   What have they a lover can prize as a gain?

--o)(o--

EXTRACT XII.   *Florence*

Music in Italy.—Disappointed by it.—Recollections of other Times and Friends.—Dalton.—Sir Stevenson.—His Daughter.—Musical Evenings together.

*   *   *   *   *

IF it *be* true that Music reigns,
      Supreme, in Italy's soft shades,
'T is like that Harmony, so famous,
   Among the spheres, which He of Samos
Declared had such transcendent merit,
That not a soul on earth could hear it;
For, far as I have come—from Lakes,
Whose sleep the Tramontana breaks,
Through Milan, and that land which gave
   The Hero of the rainbow vest—(1)
By Mincio's banks, and by that wave (2)
   Which made Verona's bard so blest—
Places, that (like the Attic shore,
   Which rung back music, when the sea
Struck on its marge) should be, all o'er,
   Thrilling alive with melody—
I 've heard no music—not a note
Of such sweet native airs as float
In my own land, among the throng,
And speak our nation's soul for song.

Nay, even in higher walks, where Art
Performs, as 't were, the gardener's part,
And richer, if not sweeter, makes
The flowers she from the wild-hedge takes—
Even there, no voice hath charm'd my ear,
   No taste hath won my perfect praise,
Like thine, dear friend(3)—long, truly dear—
   Thine and thy loved Olivia's lays.
She, always beautiful, and growing
   Still more so every note she sings—
Like an inspired young Sibyl, (4) glowing
   With her own bright imaginings!
And thou, most worthy to be tied
   In music to her, as in love,
Breathing that language by her side,
   All other language far above,
Eloquent Song—whose tones and words
In every heart find answering chords!

(1) Bergamo—the birth-place, it is said, of Harlequin.
(2 The Lago di Garda.
(3 Edward Tuite Dalton, the first husband of Sir John Stevenson's daughter, the late Marchioness of Headfort.
(4) Such as those of Domenichino in the Palazzo Borghese, at the Capitol, e.c.

How happy once the hours we past,
   Singing or listening all day long,
Till Time itself seem'd changed, at last,
   To music, and we lived in song!
Turning the leaves of Haydn o'er,
   As quick, beneath her master hand,
They open'd all their brilliant store,
   Like chambers, touch'd by fairy wand;
Or o'er the page of Mozart bending,
   Now by his airy warblings cheer'd,
Now in his mournful *Requiem* blending
   Voices, through which the heart was heard.

And still, to lead our evening choir,
   Was he invoked, thy loved-one's She—(5)
He, who, if aught of grace there be
   In the wild notes I write or sing,
First smoothed their links of harmony,
   And lent them charms they did not bring;—
He, of the gentlest, simplest heart,
   With whom, employ'd in his sweet art,
(That art, which gives this world of ours
   A notion how they speak in heaven,)
I 've pass'd more bright and charmed hours
   Than all earth's wisdom could have given.
Oh happy days, oh early friends,
   How Life, since then, hath lost its flowers!
But yet—though Time *some* foliage rends,
   The stem, the Friendship, still is ours;
And long may it endure, as green,
And fresh as it hath always been!

How I have wander'd from my theme!
   But where is he, that could return
To such cold subjects from a dream,
   Through which these best of feelings burn?—
Not all the works of Science, Art,
   Or Genius in this world are worth
One genuine sigh, that from the heart
   Friendship or Love draws freshly forth.

--o)(o--

EXTRACT XIII.

Rome.

Reflections on reading Du Cerceau's Account of the Conspiracy of Rienzi, in 1347. (6)—The Meeting of the Conspirators on the Night of the 19th May.—Their procession in the Morning to the Capitol.—Rienzi's Speech.

'T was a proud moment—even to hear the words
Of truth and Freedom 'mid these temples breathed,
And see, once more, the Forum shine with swords,
   In the Republic's sacred name unsheathed—
That glimpse, that vision of a brighter day
For his dear Rome, must to a Roman be,
Short as it was, worth ages past away
In the dull lapse of hopeless slavery.

(5) Sir John Stevenson.
(6) The "Conjuration de Nicolas Gabrini, dit de Rienzi," by the Jesuit Du Cerceau, is chiefly taken from the much more authentic work of Fortifiocca on the same subject. Rienzi was the son of a laundress.

'T was on a night of May, beneath that moon,
Which had, through many an age, seen Time untune
The strings of this Great Empire, till it fell
From his rude hands, a broken silent shell—
The sound of the church clock,(1) near Adrian's Tomb,
Summon'd the warriors, who had risen for Rome,
To meet unarm'd—with none to watch them there,
But God's own eye—and pass the night in prayer.
Holy beginning of a holy cause,
When heroes, girt for Freedom's combat, pause
Before high Heaven, and, humble in their might,
Call down its blessing on that coming fig it.
At dawn, in arms, went forth the patriot band;
And, as the breeze, fresh from the Tiber, fann'd
Their gilded gonfalons, all eyes could see
    The palm-tree there, the sword, the keys of
        Heaven— (2)
Types of the justice, peace, and liberty,   [riven
    That were to bless them, when their chains were
On to the Capitol the pageant moved,
    While many a Shade of other times, that still
Around that grave of grandeur sighing roved,
    Hung o'er their footsteps up the Sacred Hill,
And heard its mournful echoes, as the last
H gh-minded heirs of the Republic pass'd.
'I was then that thou, their Tribune, (3) (name, which
        brought
Dreams of lost glory to each patriot's thought,)
Didst, with a spirit Rome in vain shall seek
To wake up in her sons again, thus speak :—
" Romans, look round you—on this sacred place
There once stood shrines, and gods, and godlike men.
What see you now? what solitary trace
Is left of all that made Rome's glory then ?
The shrines are sunk, the Sacred Mount bereft
Even of its name—and nothing now remains
But the deep memory of that glory, left
To whet our pangs and aggravate our chains!
But *shall* this be?—our sun and sky the same—
Treading the very soil our fathers trod—
What withering curse hath fallen on soul and frame,
What visitation hath there come from God,

(1 It is not easy to discover what church is meant by
Du Cerceau here —" Il fit crier dans les rues de Rome,
a son de trompe, que chacun eût a se trouver, sans armes,
la nuit du lendemain, dix-neuvième, dans l'église du châ-
teau de Saint-Ange, au son de la cloche, afin de pourvoir
au Bon État."

2) " Les gentilshommes conjures portaient devant lui
trois étendards. Nicolas Guallato, surnommé *le bon di-
seur*, portait le premier, qui était de couleur rouge, et
plus grand que les autres. On y voyait des caractè-
res d'or avec une femme assise sur deux lions, tenant
d'une main le globe du monde, et de l'autre *une palme*,
pour représenter la ville de Rome. C'etait le gonfalon
de *la Liberté*. Le second, à fonds blanc, avec un Saint
Paul tenant de la droite *une épée* nue, et de la gauche,
la couronne de *Justice*, était porté par Étienne Magnacuc-
cia, notaire apostolique Dans le troisieme, Saint Pierre
avait en main *les clefs* de la Concorde et de la Paix
Tout ce insinuait le dessein de Rienzi, qui était de re-

To blast our strength, and rot us into slaves,
Here, on our great forefathers' glorious graves?
It cannot be—rise up, ye Mighty Dead—
    If we, the living, are too weak to crush
These tyrant priests, that o'er your empire tread,
Till all but Romans at Rome's tameness blush!

" Happy, Palmyra, in thy desert domes,
    Where only date-trees sigh and serpents hiss ,
And thou, whose pillars are but silent homes
    For the stork's brood, superb Persepolis!
Three happy both, that your extinguish'd race
Have left no embers—no half-living trace—
No slaves, to crawl around the once proud spot,
Till past renown in present shame's forgot.
While Rome, the Queen of all, whose very wrecks,
    If lone and lifeless through a desert hurl'd,
Would wear more true magnificence than decks
    The assembled thrones of all the existing world —
Rome, Rome alone, is haunted, stain'd and curst,
    Through every spot her princely Tiber laves,
By living human things—the deadliest, worst,
    This earth engenders—tyrants and their slaves !
And we—oh shame !—we, who have ponder'd o'er
    The patriot's lesson and the poet's lay, (4)
Have mounted up the streams of ancient lore,
    Tracking our country's glories all the way—
Even *we* have tamely, basely, kiss'd the ground
Before that Papal Power—that Ghost of Her,
The World's Imperial Mistress—sitting, crown'd
And ghastly, on her mouldering sepulchre ! (5)

" But this is past :—too long have lordly priests
    And priestly lords led us, with all our pride
Withering about us—like devoted beasts,
    Dragg'd to the shrine, with faded garlands tied.
'T is o'er—the dawn of our deliverance breaks!
Up from his sleep of centuries awakes
The Genius of the Old Republic, free
As first he stood, in chainless majesty,
And sends his voice through ages yet to come,
Proclaiming Rome, Rome, Rome, Eternal Rome!"

tablir la liberte, la justice et la paix "—*Du Cerceau*,
liv. ii

(3 Rienzi

4 The whole Canzone of Petrarch, beginning " Spirto
gentil," is supposed, by Volta re and others, to have been
addressed to Rienzi ; but there is much more evidence of
its having been written, as Cinguene asserts, to the young
Stephen Colonna, on his being created a Senator of Rome.
That Petrarch, however, was filled with high and patriotic
hopes by the first measures of this extraordinary man,
appears from one of his letters, quoted by Du Cerceau,
where he says,— " Pour tout dire, en un mot, j'atteste
non comme lecteur, mais comme temoin oculaire, qu'il
nous a ramené la justice, la paix, la bonne foi, la securité,
et tous les autres vestiges de l'âge d'or."

(5 This image is borrowed from Hobbes, whose words
are, as near as I can recollect —" For what is the Papacy,
but the Ghost of the old Roman Empire, sitting crowned
on the grave thereof ?"

EXTRACT XIV.

Rome.

Fragment of a Dream.—The great Painters supposed to be Magicians.—The Beginnings of the Art.—Gildings on the Glories and Draperies.—Improvements under Giotto, etc.—The first Dawn of the true Style in Masaccio.—Studied by all the great Artists who followed him.—Leonardo da Vinci, with whom commenced the Golden Age of Painting.—His Knowledge of Mathematics and of Music.—His female Heads all like each other.—Triangular Faces.—Portraits of Mona Lisa, etc.—Picture of Vanity and Modesty.—His chef-d'œuvre, the Last Supper.—Faded and almost effaced.

FILL'D with the wonders I had seen
　　In Rome's stupendous shrines and halls,
I felt the veil of sleep, serene,
　　Come o'er the memory of each scene,
As twilight o'er the landscape falls.
Nor was it slumber, sound and deep,
　　But such as suits a poet's rest—
That sort of thin transparent sleep,
　　Through which his day-dreams shine the best.

Methought upon a plain I stood,
　　Where certain wondrous men, 't was said,
With strange miraculous power endued,
　　Were coming, each in turn, to shed
His art's illusions o'er the sight,
And call up miracles of light.
The sky above this lonely place
　　Was of that cold uncertain hue
The canvass wears, ere, warm'd apace,
　　Its bright creation dawns to view.

But soon a glimmer from the east
　　Proclaim'd the first enchantments nigh ; (1)
And as the feeble light increased,
　　Strange figures moved across the sky.
With golden glories deck'd, and streaks
　　Of gold among their garments' dyes ; (2)
And life's resemblance tinged their cheeks,
　　But nought of life was in their eyes;—
Like the fresh-painted Dead one meets
Borne slow along Rome's mournful streets.

But soon these figures pass'd away,
　　And forms succeeded to their place,

(1) The paintings of those artists who were introduced into Venice and Florence from Greece.

(2) Margaritone of Orezzo, who was a pupil and imitator of the Greeks, is said to have invented this art of gilding the ornaments of pictures, a practice which, though it gave way to a purer taste at the beginning of the 16th century, was still occasionally used by many of the great masters ; as by Raphael in the ornaments of the Fornarina, and by Rubens in glories and flames.

(3) Cimabue, Giotto, etc.

(4) The Works of Masaccio.—For the character of this powerful and original genius, see Sir Joshua Reynolds's twelfth discourse. His celebrated frescos are in the church of St. Pietro del Carmine, at Florence.

With less of gold in their array,
　　But shining with more natural grace,
And all could see the charming wands
Had pass'd into more gifted hands. (3)

Among these visions there was one, (4)
Surpassing fair, on which the sun,
　　That instant risen, a beam let fall,
　　Which through the dusky twilight trembled,
And reach'd at length the spot where all
　　Those great magicians stood assembled.
And as they turn'd their heads, to view
　　The shining lustre, I could trace
The bright varieties it threw
　　On each uplifted studying face ; (5)
While many a voice with loud acclaim
Call'd forth " Masaccio," as the name
Of him, the Enchanter, who had raised
This miracle, on which all gazed.

'T was daylight now—the sun had risen,
　　From out the dungeon of old Night—
Like the Apostle, from his prison
　　Led by the Angel's hand of light ;
And, as the fetters, when that ray
Of glory reach'd them, dropp'd away, (6)
So fled the clouds at touch of day !
Just then, a bearded sage (7) came forth,
　　Who oft in thoughtful dream would stand,
To trace upon the dusky earth
　　Strange learned figures with his wand : (8)
And oft he took the silver lute (9)
　　His little page behind him bore,
And waked such music as, when mute,
　　Left in the soul a thirst for more !

Meanwhile, his potent spells went on,
　　And forms and faces, that from out
A depth of shadow mildly shone,
　　Were in the soft air seen about.
Though thick as midnight stars they beam'd,
Yet all like living sisters seem'd,
So close, in every point, resembling
　　Each other's beauties—from the eyes
Lucid as if through crystal trembling,
　　Yet soft as if suffused with sighs,

(5) All the great artists studied, and many of them borrowed from Masaccio. Several figures in the Cartoons of Raphael are taken, with but little alteration, from his frescos.

(6) "And a light shined in the prison. . . and his chains fell off from his hands."—*Acts.*

(7) Leonardo da Vinci.

(8) His treatise on Mechanics, Optics, etc., preserved in the Ambrosian library at Milan.

(9) "On dit que Léonard parut pour la première fois à la cour de Milan dans une espèce de concours ouvert entre les meilleurs joueurs de lyre d'Italie. Il se présenta avec une lyre de sa façon, construite en argent."—*Histoire de la Peinture en Italie.*

To the long fawn-like mouth, and chin,
  Lovelily tapering, less and less,
  Till, by this very charm's excess,
Like virtue on the verge of sin,
  It touch'd the bounds of ugliness.
Here look'd as when they lived the shades
Of some of Arno's dark-eyed maids—
Such maids as should alone live on,
In dreams thus, when their charms are gone :
Some Mona Lisa, on whose eyes
  A painter for whole years might gaze, (1
  Nor find in all his pallet's dyes,
  One that could even approach their blaze!

Here float two spirit shapes, (2) the one,
With her white fingers to the sun
Outspread, as if to ask his ray
Whether it e'er had chanced to play
On lilies half so fair as they!
This self-pleased nymph was Vanity—
And by her side another smiled,
  In form as beautiful as she,
But with that air, subdued and mild,
  That still reserve of purity,
Which is to beauty like the haze
  Of evening to some sunny view,
Softening such charms as it displays,
  And veiling others in that hue,
  Which fancy only can see through!
This phantom nymph, who could she be,
But the bright Spirit, Modesty?

Long did the learn'd enchanter stay
  To weave his spells, and still there pass'd,
As in the lantern's shifting play,
Group after group in close array,
  Each fairer, grander, than the last.
But the great triumph of his power
  Was yet to come :—gradual and slow,
(As all that is ordain'd to tower
  Among the works of man must grow,)
The sacred vision stole to view,
  In that half light, half shadow shown,
Which gives to even the gayest hue
  A sober'd melancholy tone.
It was a vision of that last (3)
Sorrowful night which Jesus pass'd
With his disciples, when he said
  Mournfully to them—"I shall be
Betray'd by one, who here hath fed
  This night at the same board with me."

And though the Saviour, in the dream,
Spoke not these words, we saw them beam
Legibly in his eyes (so well
The great magician work'd his spell),
And read, in every thoughtful line
Imprinted on that brow divine,
The meek, the tender nature, grieved,
Not anger'd, to be thus deceived—
Celestial love requited ill
For all its care, yet loving still —
Deep, deep regret that there should fall
  From man's deceit so foul a blight
Upon that parting hour—and all
  His Spirit must have felt that night,
Who, soon to die for human-kind,
  Thought only, 'mid his mortal pain,
How many a soul was left behind
  For whom he died that death in vain!

Such was the heavenly scene—alas
That scene so bright so soon should pass!
But pictured on the humid air,
Its tints, ere long, grew languid there ; (4
And storms came on, that, cold and rough,
  Scatter'd its gentlest glories all—
As when the baffling winds blow off
  The hues that hang o'er Terni's fall—
Till, one by one, the vision's beams
  Faded away, and soon it fled,
To join those other vanish'd dreams
  That now flit palely 'mong the dead—
The shadows of those shades that go
Around Oblivion's lake, below!

—◦◦◦—

EXTRACT XV.

Rome.

*Mary Magdalen.—Her Story.—Numerous Pictures of her.
—Correggio. — Guido. —Raphael, etc.— Canova's two
exquisite Statues.—The Sommariva Magdalen.— Chantrey's Admiration of Canova's Works.*

No wonder, Mary, that thy story
  Touches all hearts—for there we see
The soul's corruption, and its glory,
  Its death and life combined in thee.

From the first moment, when we find
  Thy spirit haunted by a swarm
Of dark desires—like demons shrined
  Unholily in that fair form—
Till when, by touch of Heaven set free,
  Thou camest, with those bright locks of gold

(1) He is said to have been four years employed upon the portrait of this fair Florentine, without being able, after all, to come up to his idea of her beauty.

(2 Vanity and Modesty, in the collection of Cardinal Fesch, at Rome. The composition of the four hands is rather awkward, but the picture, altogether, is very delightful. Lucien Bonaparte possesses a repetition of the subject.

(3) The Last Supper of Leonardo da Vinci, which is in the Refectory of the Convent delle Grazie at Milan. See

l'Histoire de la Peinture en Italie, liv. iii., chap. 45. The writer of that interesting work (to whom I take this opportunity of offering my acknowledgments for the copy he sent me a year since from Rome,) will see I have profited by some of his observations on this celebrated picture.

(4) Leonardo appears to have used a mixture of oil and varnish for this picture, which alone, without the various other causes of its ruin, would have prevented any long duration of its beauties. It is now almost entirely effaced.

(So oft the gaze of Bethany),
　And, covering in their precious fold
Thy Saviour's feet, didst shed such tears
　As paid, each drop, the sins of years!—
Thence on, through all thy course of love
　To Him, thy Heavenly Master—Him,
Whose bitter death-cup from above
　Had yet this cordial round the brim,
That woman's faith and love stood fast
　And fearless by Him to the last :—
Till, oh, blest boon for truth like thine !

Thou wert, of all, the chosen one,
　Before whose eyes that Face Divine,
When risen from the dead, first shone ;
　That thou might'st see how, like a cloud,
Had pass'd away its mortal shroud,
　And make that bright revealment known
To hearts, less trusting than thy own.
　All is affecting, cheering, grand ;
The kindliest record ever given,
　Even under God's own kindly hand,
　Of what Repentance wins from Heaven !

No wonder, Mary, that thy face,
　In all its touching light of tears,
Should meet us in each holy place,
　Where Man before his God appears,
Hopeless—were he not taught to see
　All hope in Him, who pardon'd thee !
No wonder that the painter's skill
　Should oft have triumph'd in the power
Of keeping thee all lovely still
　Even in thy sorrow's bitterest hour ;
That soft Correggio should diffuse
　His melting shadows round thy form ;
That Guido's pale unearthly hues
　Should, in pourtraying thee, grow warm ,
That all—from the ideal, grand,
　Inimitable Roman hand,
Down to the small enamelling touch
　Of smooth Carlino—should delight
In picturing her, who "loved so much,"
　And was, in spite of sin, so bright !

But, Mary, 'mong these bold essays
　Of Genius and of Art to raise
A semblance of those weeping eyes—
　A vision, worthy of the sphere
Thy faith has earn'd thee in the skies,
　And in the hearts of all men here—
None e'er hath match'd, in grief or grace,
　Canova's day-dream of thy face, (1)

(1) Changed from—
　　　Not one hath equall'd, hath come nigh
　　　　Canova's fancy,; oh, not one
　　　Hath made thee feel, and live, and die
　　　　In tears away, as *he* hath done,
　　　In those bright images, more bright, etc.—P. E.

(2) This statue is one of Canova's last works, and was
not yet in marble when I left Rome. The other, which
seems to prove, in contradiction to very high authority,

In those bright sculptured forms, more bright
　With true expression's breathing light,
Than ever yet, beneath the stroke
　Of chisel, into life awoke.
The one, (2) pourtraying what thou wert
　In thy first grief—while yet the flower
Of those young beauties was unhurt
　By sorrow's slow consuming power ;
And mingling earth's seductive grace
　With heaven's subliming thoughts so well,
We doubt, while gazing, in *which* place
　Such beauty was most form'd to dwell !—
The other, as thou look'dst when years
　Of fasting, penitence, and tears
Had worn thy frame ;—and ne'er did Art
　With half such speaking power express
The ruin which a breaking heart
　Spreads, by degrees, o'er loveliness.
Those wasting arms, that keep the trace,
　Even still, of all their youthful grace,
That loosen'd hair, of which thy brow
　Was once so proud—neglected now !—(3)
Those features, even in fading worth
　The freshest bloom to others given,
And those sunk eyes, now lost to earth,
　But, to the last, still full of heaven !

Wonderful artist ! praise, like mine—
　Though springing from a soul, that feels
Deep worship of those works divine,
　Where Genius all his light reveals—
How weak 'tis to the words that came
　From him, thy peer in art and fame, (4)
Whom I have known, by day, by night,
　Hang o'er thy marble with delight ;
And, while his lingering hand would steal
　O'er every grace the taper's rays, (5)
Give thee, with all the generous zeal
　Such master spirits only feel,
　That best of fame, a rival's praise !

—◦→←◦—

EXTRACT XVI.
Les Charmettes.

A Visit to the House where Rousseau lived with Madame
de Warens.—Their Ménage.—Its Grossness.—Claude
Anet.—Reverence with which the Spot is now visited.
—Absurdity of this blind Devotion to Fame.—Feelings
excited by the Beauty and Seclusion of the Scene.—
Disturbed by its Associations with Rousseau's History.
—Impostures of Men of Genius.—Their Power of mi-
micking all the best Feelings, Love, Independence, etc.

STRANGE power of Genius, that can throw
　Round all that 's vicious, weak, and low,

that expression, of the intensest kind, is fully within the
sphere of sculpture, was executed many years ago, and is
in the possession of the Count Sommariva at Paris.

(3) In the original copy—
　　　Those tresses, of thy charms the last
　　　　Whose pride forsook thee, wildly cast.—P. E

4) Chantrey.

(5) Canova always shows his fine statue, the Venere
Vincitrice by the light of a small candle.

Such magic lights, such rainbow dyes
As dazzle even the steadiest eyes. (1)

.   .   .   .   .

'T is worse than weak—'t is wrong, 't is shame,
This mean prostration before Fame;
This casting down, beneath the car
Of Idols, whatsoe'er they are,
Life's purest holiest decencies,
To be career'd o'er, as they please.
No—give triumphant Genius all
For which his loftiest wish can call.
If he be worshipp'd, let it be
For attributes, his noblest, first;
Not with that base idolatry,
    Which sanctifies his last and worst.

I may be cold—may want that glow
Of high romance, which bards should know;
That holy homage, which is felt
In treading where the great have dwelt;
This reverence, whatsoe'er it be,
    I fear, I feel, I have it *not*:—
For here, at this still hour, to me
    The charms of this delightful spot—
Its calm seclusion from the throng,
    From all the heart would fain forget—
This narrow valley, and the song
    Of its small murmuring rivulet—
The flitting, to and fro, of birds,
    Tranquil and tame as they were once
In Eden, ere the startling words
    Of Man disturb'd their orisons—
Those little shadowy paths, that wind
Up the hill-side, with fruit-trees lined,
And lighted only by the breaks
The gay wind in the foliage makes,
Or vistas, here and there, that ope
    Through weeping willows, like the snatches
Of far-off scenes of light, which Hope
    Even through the shade of sadness catches!—

(1) In the original edition we find the following lines,
but which no longer form part of the poem —

        About a century since, or near,
    A middle-aged Madame lived here,
    With character, even worse than most
    Such middle-aged Madames can boast
        Her footman was—to gloss it over
    With the most gentle term—her lover,
    Nor yet so jealous of the truth
        And charms of this impartial fair,
    As to deny a pauper youth,
        Who join d their snug *ménage* his share
    And there they lived, this precious three,
        With just as little sense or notion
    Of what the world calls decency,
        As hath the sea-calf in the ocean.
    And, doubtless, 'moong the grave, and good,
    And gentle of their neighbourhood,
    If known at all, they were but known
        As strange low people, low and bad—
    Madame, herself, to footmen proue,
        And her young pauper, all but mad

All this, which—could I once but lose
    The memory of those vulgar ties,
Whose grossness all the heavenhest hues
    Of Genius can no more disguise,
Than the sun's beams can do away
I he filth of fens o'er which they play—
This scene, which would have fill'd **my**
    heart
    With thoughts of all that happiest is ;—
Of Love, where self hath only part,
    As echoing back another's bliss—
Of solitude, secure and sweet,
Beneath whose shade the Virtues meet;
    Which, while it shelters, never chills
    Our sympathies with human woe,
But keeps them, like sequester'd rills,
    Purer and fresher in their flow ;—
Of happy days, that share their beams
    'Twixt quiet mirth and wise employ ;—
Of tranquil nights, that give, in dreams,
    The moonlight of the morning's joy!—
All this my heart could dwell on here,
But for those gross mementos near;
Those sullying truths, that cross the track
Of each sweet thought, and drive them back
Full into all the mire, and strife,
And vanities of that man's life,
Who, more than all that e'er have glow'd
    With Fancy's flame (and it was *his*,
In fullest warmth and radiance) show'd
    What an impostor Genius is;
How, with that strong mimetic art,
    Which forms its life and soul, it takes
All shapes of thought, all hues of heart,
    Nor feels, itself, one throb it wakes;
How like a gem its light may smile
    O'er the dark path, by mortals trod,
Itself as mean a worm, the while,
    As crawls at midnight o'er the sod;
What gentle words and thoughts may fall
From its false lip, what zeal to bless,

        Who could have thought this very spot
            Would, one day, be a sort of shrine,
        Where—all its grosser taunts forgot,
            Or gilt by Fancy till they shine—
        Pilgrims would meet, from many a shore,
        To trace each mouldering chamber o'er!
        Young bards to dream of virtuous fame,
        Young maids to lisp *De Warens'* name,
        And mellower spinsters—of an age
        Licensed to read *Jean Jacques's* page—
        To picture all those blissful hours
        He pass'd in these sequester'd bowers,
        With his dear Maman and his flowers!
        Spinsters, who—if, from glowing heart
            Or erring head, some living maid
        Had wander'd even the thousandth par
            Of what this worthy Maman stray'd—
        Would bridle up their virtuous chins
        In horror at her sin of sins,
        And—could their chaste eyes kill with flashes—
        I rown the fair culprit into ashes !—P. E

While home, friends, kindred, country, all,
Lie waste beneath its selfishness;
How, with the pencil hardly dry
From colouring up such scenes of love
And beauty, as make young hearts sigh,
And dream, and think through heaven they rove,
They, who can thus describe and move,
The very workers of these charms,
Nor seek, nor know a joy, above
Some Maman's or Theresa's arms!

How all, in short, that makes the boast
Of their false tongues, they want the most;
And, while with freedom on their lips,
Sounding their timbrels, to set free

This bright world, labouring in the eclipse
Of priestcraft, and of slavery—
They may, themselves, be slaves as low
As ever Lord or Patron made
To blossom in his smile, or grow,
Like stunted brushwood, in his shade.
Out on the craft!—I'd rather be
One of those hinds, that round me tread,
With just enough of sense to see
The noonday sun that's o'er his head,
Than thus, with high-built genius curst,
That hath no heart for its foundation,
Be all, at once, that's brightest, worst,
Sublimest, meanest in creation!

THE LOVES OF THE ANGELS. [1]

On my return from the interesting visit to Rome, of which some account has been given in the Preface to "Rhymes on the Road," I took up my abode in Paris, and, being joined there by my family, continued to reside in that capital, or its environs, till about the close of the year 1822. As no life, however sunny, is without its clouds, I could not escape, of course, my share of such passing shadows; and this long estrangement from our happy English home, towards which my family yearned even more fondly than myself, had been caused by difficulties of a pecuniary nature, and to a large amount, in which I had been involved by the conduct of the person who acted as my deputy in the small office I held at Bermuda.

That I should ever have come to be chosen for such an employment seems one of those freaks or anomalies of human destiny which baffle all ordinary speculation; and went far, indeed, to realise Beaumarchais' notion of the sort of standard by which, too frequently, qualification for place is regulated—"Il fallait un calculateur; ce fut un danseur qui l'obtint."

But however much, in this instance, I suffered from my want of schooling in matters of business, and more especially from my having neglected the ordinary precaution of requiring security from my deputy, I was more than consoled for all such embarrassment, were it even ten times as much, by the eager kindness with which friends pressed forward to help to release me from my difficulties. Could I venture to name the persons—and they were many —who thus volunteered their aid, it would be found they were all of them men whose characters enhanced such a service, and that, in all, the name and the act reflected honour upon each other.

I shall so far lift the veil in which such delicate generosity seeks to shroud itself, as to mention briefly the manner in which one of these kind friends—himself possessing but limited means— proposed to contribute to the object of releasing me from my embarrassments. After adverting, in his letter, to my misfortunes, and "the noble way," as he was pleased to say, "in which I bore them," he adds—"would it be very impertinent to say, that I have 500*l.* entirely at your disposal, to be paid when you like; and as much more that I could advance, upon any reasonable security, payable in seven years?" The writer concludes by apologising anxiously and delicately for "the liberty which he thus takes," assuring me that "he would not have made the offer if he did not feel that he would most readily accept the same assistance from me." I select this one instance from among the many which that trying event of my life enables me to adduce, both on account of the deliberate feeling of manly regard which it manifests, and also from other considerations which it would be out of place here to mention, but which rendered so genuine a mark of friendship from such a quarter peculiarly touching and welcome to me.

When such were the men who hastened to my aid in this emergency, I need hardly say, it was from no squeamish pride—for the pride would have been in receiving favours from such hands—that I came to the resolution of gratefully declining their offers, and endeavouring to work out my deliverance by my own efforts. With a credit still fresh in the market of literature, and with publishers ready as ever to risk their thousands on my name, I could not but feel that, however gratifying was the generous zeal of such friends, I should best show that I, in some

(1) The greater part of the Notes which, in former editions of the "Loves of the angels," served to explain or elucidate particular passages have been omitted in the last London one. In conformity with the plan of the present edition, they have been restored to the places they originally occupied. The reader will recognise them by the initial letters P. E. (Paris Editor), which have been appended.

degree, deserved their offers, by declining, under such circumstances, to accept them.

Meanwhile, an attachment had issued against me from the Court of Admiralty; and as a negotiation was about to be opened with the American claimants, for a reduction of their large demand upon me —supposed, at that time, to amount to six thousand pounds—it was deemed necessary that, pending the treaty, I should take up my abode in France.

To write for the means of daily subsistence, and even in most instances to "forestall the slow harvest of the brain," was for me, unluckily, no novel task. But I had now, in addition to these home calls upon the Muse, a new, painful, and, in its first aspect, overwhelming exigence to provide for; and, certainly, Paris, swarming throughout as it was, at that period, with rich, gay, and dissipated English, was, to a person of my social habits and multifarious acquaintance, the very worst possible place that could have been resorted to for even the semblance of a quiet or studious home. The only tranquil, and, therefore, to me, most precious portions of that period, were the two summers passed by my family and myself with our kind Spanish friends, the V * * * * * * * ls, at their beautiful place, La Butte Coaslin, on the road up to Bellevue. There, in a cottage belonging to M. V * * * * * * * l, and but a few steps from his house, we contrived to conjure up an apparition of Sloperton; (1) and I was able for some time to work with a feeling of comfort and home. I used frequently to pass the morning in rambling alone through the noble park of St. Cloud, with no apparatus for the work of authorship but my memorandum-book and pencils, forming sentences to run smooth, and moulding verses into shape. In the evenings I generally joined with Madame V * * * * * * * l in Italian duets, or, with far more pleasure, sate as listener, while she sung to the Spanish guitar those sweet songs of her own country to which few voices could do such justice.

One of the pleasant circumstances connected with our summer visits to La Butte was the near neighbourhood of our friend, Mr. Kenny, the lively dramatic writer, who was lodged picturesquely in the remains of the Palace of the King's Aunts, at Bellevue. I remember, on my first telling Kenny the particulars of my Bermuda mishap, his saying, after a pause of real feeling, "Well—it's lucky you're a poet;—a philosopher never could have borne it." Washington Irving also was, for a short time, our visitor; and still recollects, I trust, his reading to me some parts of his then forthcoming work, "Bracebridge Hall," as we sate together on the grass walk that leads to the Rocher, at La Butte.

Among the writings, then but in embryo, to which I looked forward for the means of my enfranchisement, one of the most important, as well as most likely to be productive, was my intended life of Sheridan. But I soon found that, at such a distance from all those living authorities from whom alone I could gain any interesting information respecting the private life of one who left behind him so little epistolary correspondence, it would be wholly impossible to proceed satisfactorily with this task. Accordingly I wrote to Mr. Murray and Mr. Wilkie, who were at that time the intended publishers of the work, to apprize them of this temporary obstacle to its progress.

Being thus baffled in the very first of the few resources I had looked to, I next thought of a Romance in verse, in the form of Letters, or Epistles; and with this view sketched out a story, on an Egyptian subject, differing not much from that which, some years after, formed the groundwork of the "Epicurean." After labouring, however, for some months, at this experiment, amidst interruption, dissipation, and distraction, which might well put all the Nine Muses to flight, I gave up the attempt in despair;— fully convinced of the truth of that warning conveyed in some early verses of my own, addressed to the Invisible Girl :—

> O hint to the bard, 'tis retirement alone
> Can hallow his harp or ennoble its tone
> Like you, with a veil of seclusion between,
> His song to the world let him utter unseen, etc. (2)

It was, indeed, to the secluded life I led during the years 1813—1816, in a lone cottage among the fields, in Derbyshire, that I owed the inspiration, whatever may have been its value, of some of the best and most popular portions of "Lalla Rookh." It was amidst the snows of two or three Derbyshire winters that I found myself enabled, by that concentration of thought which retirement alone gives, to call up around me some of the sunniest of those Eastern scenes, which have since been welcomed in India itself, as almost native to its clime.

Abortive, however, as had now been all my efforts to woo the shy spirit of Poesy, amidst such unquiet scenes, the course of reading I found time to pursue, on the subject of Egypt, was of no small service in storing my mind with the various knowledge respecting that country, which some years later I turned to account, in writing the story of the "Epicurean." The kind facilities, indeed, towards this object, which some of the most distinguished French scholars and artists afforded me, are still remembered by me with thankfulness. Besides my old acquaintance, Denon, whose drawings of Egypt, then of some value, I frequently consulted, I found Mons. Fourier and Mons. Langlès no less prompt in placing books at my disposal. With Humboldt, also, who was at that time in Paris, I had more than once some conversation on the subject of Egypt, and remember his expressing himself in no very laudatory

(1) " A little cot, with trees around,
And, like its master, very low."—*Pope*.

(2) See page 71, column 2.

terms respecting the labours of the French *savants* in that country.

I had now been foiled and frustrated in two of those literary projects on which I had counted most sanguinely in the calculation of my resources; and, though I had found sufficient time to furnish my musical publisher with the Eighth Number of the " Irish Melodies," and also a Number of the "National Airs," these works alone, I knew, would yield but an insufficient supply, compared with the demands so closely and threateningly hanging over me. In this difficulty I called to mind a subject — the Eastern allegory of the Loves of the Angels — on which I had, some years before, begun a prose story, but in which, as a theme for poetry, I had now been anticipated by Lord Byron, in one of the most sublime of his many poetical miracles, " Heaven and Earth." Knowing how soon I should be lost in the shadow into which so gigantic a precursor would cast me, I had endeavoured, by a speed of composition which must have astonished my habitually slow pen, to get the start of my noble friend in the time of publication, and thus give myself the sole chance I could perhaps expect, under such unequal rivalry, of attracting to my work the attention of the public. In this humble speculation, however, I failed; for both works, if I recollect right, made their appearance at the same time.

In the mean while, the negotiation which had been entered into with the American claimants, for a reduction of the amount of their demands upon me, had continued to " drag its slow length along;" nor was it till the month of September, 1822, that, by a letter from the Messrs. Longman, I received the welcome intelligence that the terms offered, as our ultimatum, to the opposite party, had been at last accepted, and that I might now with safety return to England. I lost no time, of course, in availing myself of so welcome a privilege; and as all that remains now to be told of this trying episode in my past life may be comprised in a small compass, I shall trust to the patience of my readers for tolerating the recital.

On arriving in England I learned, for the first time — having been, till then, kept very much in darkness on the subject — that, after a long and frequently interrupted course of negotiation, the amount of the claims of the American merchants had been reduced to the sum of one thousand guineas, and that towards the payment of this the uncle of my deputy — a rich London merchant — had been brought, with some difficulty, to contribute three hundred

(1) See note on Harut and Marut in a succeeding page.

(2) Hyde, *de Relig. Vet. Persarum*, p. 272.

(3) In the original edition, the " Loves of the Angels" was introduced to the reader by the following observations: —

This poem, somewhat different in form, and much more limited in extent, was originally designed as an episode for a work about which I have been, at intervals, employed

pounds. I was likewise informed, that a very dear and distinguished friend of mine, to whom, by his own desire, the state of the negotiation was, from time to time, reported, had, upon finding that there appeared, at last, some chance of an arrangement, and learning also the amount of the advance made by my deputy's relative, immediately deposited in the hands of a banker the remaining portion (750*l.*) of the required sum, to be there in readiness for the final settlement of the demand.

Though still adhering to my original purpose of owing to my own exertions alone the means of relief from these difficulties, I yet felt a pleasure in allowing this thoughtful deposit to be applied to the generous purpose for which it was destined ; and having employed in this manner the 750*l.*, I then transmitted to my kind friend — I need hardly say with what feelings of thankfulness — a cheque on my publishers for the amount.

Though this effort of the poet's purse was but, as usual, a new launch into the Future — a new anticipation of yet unborn means — the result showed, I am happy to say, that, in *this* instance at least, I had not counted on my bank " *in nubibus*" too sanguinely; for, on receiving my publishers' account, in the month of June following, I found 1000*l.* placed to my credit from the sale of the " Loves of the Angels," and 500*l.* from the " Fables of the Holy Alliance."

I must not omit to mention, that, among the resources at that time placed at my disposal, was one small and sacred sum, which had been set apart by its young possessor for some such beneficent purpose. This fund, amounting to about 300*l.*, arose from the proceeds of the sale of the first edition of a biographical work, then recently published, which will long be memorable, as well from its own merits and subject, as from the lustre that has been since shed back upon it from the public career of its noble author. To a gift from such hands might well have been applied the words of Ovid,

> —— acceptissima semper
> Munera sunt, auctor quæ pretiosa facit.

⁘⚬❄⚬⁘

PREFACE.

The Eastern story of the angels Harut and Marut, (1) and the Rabbinical fictions of the loves of Uzziel and Shamchazai, (2) are the only sources to which I need refer, for the origin of the notion on which this Romance is founded. (3) In addition to the fitness of the subject for poetry, it struck me during the last two years. Some months since, however, I found that my friend Lord Byron had, by an accidental coincidence, chosen the same subject for a drama; and as I could not but feel the disadvantage of coming after so formidable a rival, I thought it best to publish my humble sketch immediately, with such alterations and additions as I had time to make, and thus, by an earlier appearance in the literary horizon, give myself a chance of what as-also as capable of affording an allegorical medium, through which might be shadowed out (as I have endeavoured to do in the following stories) the fall of the Soul from its original purity (1)—the loss of light and happiness which it suffers, in pursuit of this world's perishable pleasures—and the punishments, both from conscience and Divine justice, with which impurity, pride, and presumptuous inquiry into the awful secrets of Heaven are sure to be visited. The beautiful story of Cupid and Psyche owes its chief charm to this sort of "veiled meaning," and it has been my wish (however I may have failed in the attempt) to communicate to the following pages the same *moral* interest.

Among the doctrines, or notions, derived by Plato from the East, one of the most natural and sublime is that which inculcates the pre-existence of the soul, and its gradual descent into this dark material world, from that region of spirit and light which it is supposed to have once inhabited, and to which after a long

lapse of purification and trial it will return. This belief, under various symbolical forms, may be traced through almost all the Oriental theologies. The Chaldeans represent the Soul as originally endowed with wings, which fall away when it sinks from its native element, and must be re-produced before it can hope to return. Some disciples of Zoroaster once inquired of him, " How the wings of the Soul might be made to grow again? "—"By sprinkling them," he replied, "with the Waters of Life."—"But where are those Waters to be found?" they asked.—" In the Garden of God," replied Zoroaster.

The mythology of the Persians has allegorised the same doctrine, in the history of those genii of light who strayed from their dwellings in the stars, and obscured their original nature by mixture with this material sphere; while the Egyptians, connecting it with the descent and ascent of the sun in the zodiac, considered Autumn as emblematic of the Soul's

---

 tronomers call an *Heliacal rising*, before the luminary in whose light I was to be lost, should appear.

As objections may be made, by persons whose opinions I respect, to the selection of a subject of this nature from the Scripture, I think it right to remark that, in point of fact, the subject is *not* scriptural— the notion upon which it is founded that of the love of angels for women) having originated in an erroneous translation by the LXX, of that verse in the sixth chapter of Genesis, upon which the sole authority for the fable rests. (a) The foundation of my story, therefore, has as little to do with Holy Writ as have the dreams of the later Platonists, or the reveries of the Jewish divines, and, in appropriating the notion thus to the uses of poetry, I have done no more than establish it in that region of fiction, to which the opinions of the most rational Fathers, and of all other Christian theologians, have long ago consigned it.—P. E.

(a) The error of these interpreters 'and, it is said, of the old Italic version also) was in making it οἱ Ἄγγελοι τοῦ Θεοῦ. " The *Angels* of God," instead of " the *Sons* "—a mistake which, assisted by the allegorising comments of Philo, and the rhapsodical fictions of the Book of Enoch," was more than sufficient to affect the imaginations of such half-Pagan writers as Clemens Alexandrinus, Tertullian, and Lactantius, who, chiefly, among the Fathers, have indulged themselves in fanciful reveries upon the subject. The greater number, however, have rejected the fiction with indignation. Chrysostom, in his twenty-second Homily upon Genesis, earnestly exposes its absurdity, " and Cyril accounts such a supposition as ἐγγὺς μωρίας, "bor-

dering on folly." "" According to these Fathers (and their opinion has been followed by all the theologians, down from St. Thomas to Caryl and Lightfoot §), the term "Sons of God," must be understood to mean the descendants of Seth, by Enos—a family peculiarly favoured by Heaven, because with them men first began to " call upon the name of the Lord ,"—while, by " the daughters of men," they suppose that the corrupt race of Cain is designated. The probability, however, is, that the words in question ought to have been translated "the sons of the nobles or great men," as we find them interpreted in the Targum of Onkelos(the most ancient and accurate of all the Chaldaic paraphrases), and as, it appears from Cyril, the version of Symmachus also rendered them. This translation of the passage removes all difficulty, and at once relieves the Sacred History of an extravagance which, however it may suit the imagination of the poet, is inconsistent with all our notions, both philosophical and religious.

1) The account which Macrobius gives of the downward journey of the Soul, through that gate of the zodiac which opens into the lower spheres, is a curious specimen of the wild fancies that passed for philosophy in ancient times.

In the system of Manes, the luminous or spiritual principle owes its corruption not to any evil tendency of its own, but to a violent inroad of the spirits of darkness, who, finding themselves in the neighbourhood of this pure light, and becoming passionately enamoured of its beauty, break the boundaries between them, and take forcible possession of it. o

---

' It is lamentable to think that this absurd production, of which we now know the whole from Dr Laurence s translation, should ever have been considered as an inspired or authentic work. See the Preliminary Dissertation, prefixed to the Translation.

"" One of the arguments of Chrysostom is, that Angels are no where else, in the Old Testament, called " Sons of God;"—but his commentator, Montfaucon, shows that he is mistaken, and that in the Book of Job they are so designated, c 1 , v 6.) both in the original Hebrew and the Vulgate, though not in the Septuagint, which alone, he says, Chrysostom read

""" Lib ii., *Glaphyrorum* —Philastrius, in his enumeration of heresies, classes this story of the Angels among the number, and says it deserves only to be ranked with those fictions about gods

and goddesses, to which the fancy of the Pagan poets gave birth : " Sicuti et Paganorum et Poetarum mendacia asserunt deos deasque transformatos nefanda conjugia commisisse." — *De Hæres* , Edit. Basil., p. 101.

§ Lightfoot says, "The sons of God, or the members of the Church, and the progeny of Seth, marrying carelessly and promiscuously with the daughters of men, or brood of Cain," etc. I find in Pole that, according to the Samaritan version, the phrase may be understood as meaning " the Sons of the *Judges*."—So variously may the Hebrew word, Elohim, be interpreted.

|| *In Somn. Scipionis*, cap. 12.

o See a Treatise, *De la Religion des Perses*, by the Abbé Foucher, *Mémoires de l'Académie*, tom xxxi., p 456.

decline towards darkness, and the re-appearance of Spring as its return to life and light.

Besides the chief spirits of the Mahometan heaven, such as Gabriel, the angel of Revelations, Israfil, by whom the last trumpet is to be sounded, and Azrael, the angel of death, there were also a number of subaltern intelligences, of which tradition has preserved the names, appointed to preside over the different stages, or ascents, into which the celestial world was supposed to be divided. (1) Thus Kelail governs the fifth heaven; while Sadiel, the presiding spirit of the third, is also employed in steadying the motions of the earth, which would be in a constant state of agitation, if this angel did not keep his foot planted upon its orb. (2)

Among other miraculous interpositions in favour of Mahomet, we find commemorated in the pages of the Koran the appearance of five thousand angels on his side at the battle of Bedr.

The ancient Persians supposed that Ormuzd appointed thirty angels to preside successively over the days of the month, and twelve greater ones to assume the government of the months themselves; among whom Bahman (to whom Ormuzd committed the custody of all animals except man,) was the greatest. Mihr, the angel of the seventh month, was also the spirit that watched over the affairs of friendship and love;—Chûr had the care of the disk of the sun ;—Mah was agent for the concerns of the moon ; —Isphandârmaz (whom Cazvin calls the Spirit of the Earth) was the tutelar genius of good and virtuous women, etc. etc. etc. For all this the reader may consult the 19th and 20th chapters of *Hyde de Relig. Vet. Persarum,* where the names and attributes of these daily and monthly angels are with much minuteness and erudition explained. It appears from the Zend-avesta, that the Persians had a certain office or prayer for every day of the month (addressed to the particular angel who presided over it), which they called the Sirouzé.

The Celestial Hierarchy of the Syrians, as described by Kircher, appears to be the most regularly graduated of any of these systems. In the sphere of the Moon they placed the angels, in that of Mercury the archangels, Venus and the Sun contained the Principalities and the Powers ;—and so on to the summit of the planetary system, where, in the sphere of Saturn, the Thrones had their station. Above this was the habitation of the Cherubim in the sphere of the fixed stars; and still higher, in the region of those stars which are so distant as to be imperceptible, the Seraphim, we are told, the most perfect of all celestial creatures, dwelt.

The Sabeans also (as D'Herbelot tells us) had their classes of angels, to whom they prayed as mediators or intercessors; and the Arabians worshipped *female* angels, whom they called Benab Hasche, or, Daughters of God.

THE LOVES OF THE ANGELS.

'T was when the world was in its prime,
    When the fresh stars had just begun
Their race of glory, and young Time
    Told his first birth-days by the sun;
When, in the light of Nature's dawn
    Rejoicing, men and angels met (3)
On the high hill and sunny lawn—
    Ere sorrow came, or Sin had drawn
'Twixt man and heaven her curtain yet!
When earth lay nearer to the skies
    Than in these days of crime and woe,
And mortals saw, without surprise,
    In the mid-air, angelic eyes
    Gazing upon this world below.

Alas, that Passion should profane,
    Even then the morning of the earth!
That, sadder still, the fatal stain
    Should fall on hearts of heavenly birth—
And that from Woman's love should fall
So dark a stain, most sad of all!

One evening, in that primal hour,
    On a hill's side, where hung the ray
Of sunset, brightening rill and bower,
    Three noble youths conversing lay;
And as they look'd from time to time,
    To the far sky, where Daylight furl'd
His radiant wing, their brows sublime
    Bespoke them of that distant world—
Spirits who once in brotherhood
Of faith and bliss, near Alla stood,
And o'er whose cheeks full oft had blown
The wind that breathes from Alla's throne, (4)
Creatures of light, such as *still* play,
    Like motes in sunshine, round the Lord,
And through their infinite array
    Transmit each moment, night and day,
    The echo of His luminous word!(5)

---

(1) "We adorned the lower heaven with lights, and placed therein a guard of angels."—*Koran,* chap. xli.

(2) See D'Herbelot, *passim.*

(3) The Mahometans believe, says D'Herbelot, that in that early period of the world, "les hommes n'eurent qu'une seule religion, et furent souvent visités des anges, qui leur donnoient la main."

(4 "To which will be joined the sound of the bells hanging on the trees, which will be put in motion by the wind proceeding from the Throne, so often as the Blessed wish for music."—See Sale's *Koran, Prelim. Dissert.*

(5) Dionysius (*De Cælest. Hierarch.*) is of opinion, that when Isaiah represents the Seraphim as crying out "one unto the other," his intention is to describe those communications of the divine thought and will, which are continually passing from the higher orders of the angels to the lower.—οἷα καὶ αὐτοὺς τοὺς θεοτάτους Σεραφιμ οἱ θεολόγοι φασὶν ἕτερον πρὸς τὸν ἕτερον κεκραγέναι,

Of Heaven they spoke, and still more oft,
Of the bright eyes that charm'd them thence;
Till, yi...ding gradual to the soft
And balmy evening's influence—
The silent breathing of the flowers—
The melting light that beam'd above,
As on their first, fond, erring hours—
Each told the story of his love,
The history of that hour unblest,
When, like a bird, from its high nest
Won down by fascinating eyes,
For Woman's smile he lost the skies.

The First who spoke was one, with look
The least celestial of the three—
A Spirit of light mould, that took
The prints of earth most yieldingly;
Who, even in heaven, was not of those
Nearest the Throne, (1) but held a place
Far off, among those shining rows
That circle out through endless space,
And o'er whose wings the light from Him
In Heaven's centre falls most dim.

Still fair and glorious, he but shone
Among those youths the unheavenliest one—
A creature, to whom light remain'd
From Eden still, but alter'd, stain'd,
And o'er whose brow not Love alone
A blight had, in his transit, cast,
But other, earthlier joys had gone,
And left their foot-prints as they pass'd.
Sighing, as back through ages flown,
Like a tomb-searcher, Memory ran,
Lifting each shroud that time had thrown
O'er buried hopes, he thus began :—

FIRST ANGEL'S STORY.

'T was in a land, that far away
Into the golden orient lies,
Where Nature knows not night's delay,
But springs to meet her bridegroom, Day,
Upon the threshold of the skies.
One morn, on earthly mission sent, (2)
And mid-way choosing where to light,

I saw, from the blue element—
Oh beautiful, but fatal sight!—
One of earth's fairest womankind,
Half veil'd from view, or rather shrined
In the clear crystal of a brook ;(3) .
Which, while it hid no single gleam
Of her young beauties, made them look
More spirit-like, as they might seem
Through the dim shadowing of a dream.

Pausing in wonder I look'd on,
While, playfully around her breaking
The waters, that like diamonds shone,
She moved in light of her own making.
At length, as from that airy height
I gently lower'd my breathless flight, (4)
The tremble of my wings all o'er
(For through each plume I felt the thrill)
Startled her, as she reach'd the shore
Of that small lake—her mirror still—
Above whose brink she stood, like snow
When rosy with a sunset glow.
Never shall I forget those eyes!—
The shame, the innocent surprise
Of that bright face, when in the air
Uplooking, she beheld me there.
It seem'd as if each thought, and look,
And motion, were that minute chain'd
Fast to the spot, such root she took,
And—like a sunflower by a brook,
With face upturn'd—so still remain'd!

In pity to the wondering maid,
Though loath from such a vision turning,
Downward I bent, beneath the shade
Of my spread wings, to hide the burning
Of glances, which—I well could feel—
For me, for her, too warmly shone ;
But, ere I could again unseal
My restless eyes, or even steal
One sidelong look, the maid was gone—
Hid from me in the forest leaves,
Sudden as when, in all her charms
Of full-blown light, some cloud receives
The Moon into his dusky arms.

σαφως ει τουτω, καθαπερ οιμαι, δηλουντες, ότι των
Θεολογικων γνωσεων οἱ πρωτοι τοις δευτεροις μεταδι-
δοασι—See also, in the Paraphrase of Pachymer upon
Dionysius, cap. 2, rather a striking passage, in which he
represents all living creatures as being, in a stronger or
fainter degree, " echoes of God."—P. E.

(1) The ancient Persians supposed that this Throne was
placed in the Sun, and that through the stars were distri-
buted the various classes of Angels that encircled it.
The Basilidians supposed that there were three hundred
and sixty-five orders of angels, "dont la perfection alloit
en decroissant, à mesure qu'ils s'éloignoient de la pre-
mière classe d'esprits placés dans le premier ciel."—See
Dupuis, Orig. des Cultes, tom. ii., p. 112.
, (2) It appears that, in most languages, the term employ-
ed for an angel means also a messenger. Firischteh, the

Persian word for angel, is derived (says D'Herbelot) from
the verb Firischtin, to send. The Hebrew term, too,
Melak, has the same signification.
(3 This is given upon the authority, or rather according
to the fancy, of some of the Fathers, who suppose that the
women of earth were first seen by the angels in this si-
tuation ; and St. Basil has even made it the serious foun-
dation of rather a rigorous rule for the toilet of his fair
disciples, adding, ἱκανον γαρ εστι παραγυμνουμενον
καλλος και υἱους Θεου προς ἡδονηνγοητευσαι, και ὡς αι-
θρωπους δια ταυτην αποθνησκοντας, Θνητους αποδειξαι
—De Vera Virginitat., tom. i., p. 747, edit. Paris. 1618.—
P. E.

(4) Formerly given—
    At length, as slowly I descended
    To view more near a sight so splendid.—P. E.

'T is not in words to tell the power,
The despotism that, from that hour,
Passion held o'er me. Day and night
     I sought around each neighbouring spot;
And in the chase of this sweet light,
     My task, and heaven, and all forgot—
All, but the one, sole, haunting dream
     Of her I saw in that bright stream.

Nor was it long, ere by her side
     I found myself, whole happy days,
Listening to words, whose music vied
     With our own Eden's seraph lays,
When seraph lays are warm'd by love,
But, wanting *that*, far, far above!—
And looking into eyes where, blue
And beautiful, like skies seen through
The sleeping wave, for me there shone
A heaven more worshipp'd than my own.
Oh what, while I could hear and see
Such words and looks, was heaven to me?
Though gross the air on earth I drew,
'T was blessed, while she breathed it too;
Though dark the flowers, though dim the sky,
Love lent them light, while she was nigh.
Throughout creation I but knew
Two separate worlds—the *one*, that small,
     Beloved, and consecrated spot
Where Lea *was*—the other, all
     The dull wide waste where she was *not!*

But vain my suit, my madness vain;
Though gladly, from her eyes to gain
     One earthly look, one stray desire,
I would have torn the wings that hung
     Furl'd at my back, and o'er the Fire
In Gehim's (1) pit their fragments flung ;—
     'T was hopeless all—pure and unmoved
          She stood, as lilies in the light
     Of the hot noon but look more white ;—
And though she loved me, deeply loved,
'T was not as man, as mortal—no,
Nothing of earth was in that glow—

She loved me but as one, of race
Angelic, from that radiant place
She saw so oft in dreams—that Heaven,
     To which her prayers at morn were sent,
And on whose light she gazed at even,
     Wishing for wings, that she might go
Out of this shadowy world below,
     To that free glorious element!

Well I remember by her side
Sitting at rosy even-tide,
When—turning to the star, whose head
Look'd out as from a bridal bed,
At that mute blushing hour—she sa'd,
" Oh! that it were my doom to be
     The Spirit of yon beauteous star, (2)
Dwelling up there in purity,
     Alone, as all such bright things are,—
My sole employ to pray and shine,
     To light my censer at the sun,
And cast its fire towards the shrine
     Of Him in heaven, the Eternal One!"

So innocent the maid, so free
     From mortal taint in soul and frame,
Whom 't was my crime—my destiny—
     To love, ay, burn for, with a flame
     To which earth's wildest fires are tame.
Had you but seen her look, when first
From my mad lips the avowal burst;
Not anger'd—no—the feeling came
From depths beyond mere anger's flame—
It was a sorrow, calm as deep,
A mournfulness that could not weep,
So fill'd her heart was to the brink,
So fix'd and frozen with grief, to think
That angel natures—that even I,
Whose love she clung to, as the tie
Between her spirit and the sky—
Should fall thus headlong from the height
Of all that heaven hath pure and bright! (3)

That very night—my heart had grown
     Impatient of its inward burning;

---

(1) The name given by the Mahometans to the infernal regions, over which, they say, the angel Tabhek presides.

By the seven gates of hell, mentioned in the Koran, the commentators understand seven different departments or wards, in which seven different sorts of sinners are to be punished. The first, called Gehennem, is for sinful Mussulmans; the second, Ladha, for Christian offenders; the third, Hothama, is appointed for Jews, and the fourth and fifth, called Sair and Sacar, are destined to receive the Sabæans and the worshippers of fire in the sixth, named Gehim, those pagans and idolaters who admit a plurality of gods are placed, while into the abyss of the seventh, called Derk Asfal, or the Deepest, the hypocritical canters of *all* religions are thrown.

(2) It is the opinion of Kircher, Ricciolus, etc. (and was, I believe, to a certain degree, that of Origen), that the stars are moved and directed by intelligences or angels who preside over them. Among other passages from

Scripture in support of this notion, they cite those words of the Book of Job, "When the morning stars sang together."—Upon which Kircher remarks, "Non de materialibus intelligitur." *Itin.* 1., *Isagog. Astronom.* See also Caryl's most wordy *Commentary* on the same text.—P. E.

(3) This couplet now replaces the following passage, which appeared in former editions :—

     Should fall thus headlong from the height
          Of such pure glory into sin—
     The sin of all most sure to blight—
     The sin, of all, that the soul's light
          Is soonest lost, extinguish'd in!
     That, though but frail and human, she
     Should, like the half-bird of the sea,
     Try with her wing sublimer air,
     While I, a creature born up there,
     Should meet her, in my fall from light,
     From heaven and peace, and turn her flight
     Downward again, with me to drink
     Of the salt tide of sin, and sink '—P. E.

The term, too, of my stay was flown,
And the bright Watchers near the throne, (1)
Already, if a meteor shone
Between them and this nether zone,
    Thought 't was their herald's wing returning.
Oft did the potent spell-word, given
    To Envoys hither from the skies,
To be pronounced, when back to heaven
    It is their time or wish to rise,
Come to my lips that fatal day;
    And once, too, was so nearly spoken,
That my spread plumage in the ray
And breeze of heaven began to play;—
    When my heart fail'd—the spell was broken—
The word unfinish'd died away,
And my check'd plumes, ready to soar,
Fell slack and lifeless as before.

How could I leave a world which she,
Or lost or won, made all to me? (2)
No matter where my wanderings were,
    So there she look'd, breathed, moved about—
Woe, ruin, death, more sweet with her,
    Than Paradise itself, without!

But, to return—that very day
A feast was held, where, full of mirth,
Came—crowding thick as flowers that play
In summer winds—the young and gay
    And beautiful of this bright earth.
And she was there, and 'mid the young
    And beautiful stood first, alone;

Though on her gentle brow still hung
    The shadow I that morn had thrown—
The first that ever shame or woe
Had cast upon its vernal snow.
My heart was madden'd;—in the flush
    Of the wild revel I gave way
To all that frantic mirth—that rush
    Of desperate gaiety, which they
Who never felt how pain's excess
Can break out thus, think happiness!
Sad mimicry of mirth and life,
    Whose flashes come but from the strife
Of inward passions—like the light
Struck out by clashing swords in fight.

Then, too, that juice of earth, (3) the bane
And blessing of man's heart and brain—
That draught of sorcery, which brings
Phantoms of fair forbidden things—
Whose drops, like those of rainbows, smile
    Upon the mists that circle man,
Brightening not only Earth, the while,
    But grasping Heaven, too, in their span!—
Then first the fatal wine-cup rain'd
    Its dews of darkness through my lips, (4)
Casting whate'er of light remain'd
    To my lost soul into eclipse;
And filling it with such wild dreams,
    Such fantasies and wrong desires,
As, in the absence of heaven's beams,
    Haunt us for ever—like wild-fires
    That walk this earth, when day retires.

---

(1) "The Watchers, the offspring of Heaven."—*Book of Enoch.* In *Daniel* also the angels are called watchers.— " And behold a watcher and an holy one came down from heaven." c. iv., v. 13.—P. E.

(2) The following lines are here omitted :—
    Beyond home—glory—every thing?
    How fly, while yet there was a chance,
    A hope—ay, even of perishing
    Utterly by that fatal glance?—P. E.

(3) For all that relates to the character and attributes of angels, the time of their creation, the extent of their knowledge, and the power which they possess, or can occasionally assume, of performing such human functions as eating, drinking, etc. etc., I shall refer those who are inquisitive upon the subject to the following works :— The Treatise upon the Celestial Hierarchy, written under the name of Dionysius the Areopagite, in which, among much that is heavy and trifling, there are some sublime notions concerning the agency of these spiritual creatures —The questions *de Cognitione Angelorum* of St. Thomas, where he examines most prolixly into such puzzling points as "whether angels illuminate each other," "whether

* The following may serve as specimens :—"Les anges ne savent point la langue chaldaïque; c'est pourquoi ils ne portent point à Dieu les oraisons de ceux qui prient dans cette langue Ils se trompent souvent, ils font des erreurs dangereuses, car l'Ange de la mort, qui est chargé de faire mourir un homme, en prend quelquefois un autre, ce qui cause de grands désordres . . . . . ils sont chargés de chanter devant Dieu le cantique, *Saint, Saint est le Dieu des armées*, mais ils ne remplissent cet office qu'une fois le jour, dans une semaine, dans un mois, dans un an, dans un siècle, ou dans l'éternité. L'ange qui luttoit contre Jacob le pressa de chanter le cantique ce jour-là, ce qu'il n'avoit encore jamais fait."

they speak to each other," etc. etc.—The *Thesaurus* of Cocceius, containing extracts from almost every theologian that has written on the subject—The 9th, 10th, and 11th chapters, sixth book, of *l'Histoire des Juifs*, where all the extraordinary reveries of the Rabbins * about angels and demons are enumerated—The Questions attributed to St. Athanasius—The treatise of Bonaventure upon the Wings of the Seraphim **—and, lastly, the ponderous folio of Suarez *de Angelis*, where the reader will find all that has ever been fancied or reasoned, upon a subject which only *such* writers could have contrived to render so dull.—P. E.

4) I have already mentioned that some of the circumstances of this story were suggested to me by the eastern legend of the two angels, Harut and Marut, as given by Marut, who says that the author of the *Taalim* founds upon it the Mahometan prohibition of wine. *** I have since found that Marut's version of the tale (which differs also from that of Dr. Prideaux, in his *Life of Mahomet*,) is taken from the French *Encyclopédie*, in which work, under the head "Arot et Marot," the reader will find it.

** This work (which, notwithstanding its title, is, probably, quite as dull as the rest) I have not, myself, been able to see, having searched for it in vain through the King's Library at Paris, though assisted by the seal and kindness of M Langlès and M. Vonprodt, whose liberal administration of that most liberal establishment entitles them — not only for the immediate effect of such conduct, but for the useful and civilising example it holds forth—to the most cordial gratitude of the whole literary world.

*** The *Bahardanush* tells the fable differently

Now hear the rest;—our banquet done,
I sought her in the accustom'd bower,
Where late we oft, when day was gone,
And the world hush'd, had met alone,
At the same silent moonlight hour. (1)
Her eyes, as usual, were upturn'd
To her loved star, whose lustre burn'd
Purer than ever on that night;
While she, in looking, grew more bright,
As though she borrow'd of its light. (2)

There was a virtue in that scene,
A spell of holiness around,
Which, had my burning brain not been
Thus madden'd, would have held me bound,
As though I trod celestial ground.
Even as it was, with soul all flame,
And lips that burn'd in their own sighs,
I stood to gaze, with awe and shame—
The memory of Eden came
Full o'er me when I saw those eyes;
And though too well each glance of mine
To the pale shrinking maiden proved
How far, alas, from aught divine,
Aught worthy of so pure a shrine,
Was the wild love with which I loved,
Yet must she, too, have seen—oh yes,
'T is soothing but to *think* she saw
The deep, true, soul-felt tenderness,
The homage of an Angel's awe
To her, a mortal, whom pure love
Then placed above him—far above—
And all that struggle to repress
A sinful spirit's mad excess,
Which work'd within me at that hour,
When, with a voice, where Passion shed
All the deep sadness of her power,
Her melancholy power—I said,
" Then be it so: if back to heaven
I must unloved, unpitied fly,
Without one blest memorial given
To soothe me in that lonely sky;
One look, like those the young and fond
Give when they 're parting—which would be,
Even in remembrance, far beyond
All heaven hath left of bliss for me!

" Oh, but to see that head recline
A minute on this trembling arm,

(1) Four lines of the text, with the accompanying note,
which appeared in former editions, are here omitted:—

    I found her—oh, so beautiful ! *
     Why, why have hapless angels eyes?

  * Tertullian imagines that the words of St. Paul, " woman ought
to have a veil on her head † *on account of the angels*," have an
evident reference to the fatal effects which the beauty of women
once produced upon these spiritual beings. See the strange pas-
sage of this Father *(de Virgin. Velandis* , beginning, " Si enim
propter angelos," etc., where his editor Pamelius endeavours to

    † Corinth., c. xi., v. 10, Dr. Macknight's Translation.

And those mild eyes look up to mine,
Without a dread, a thought of harm !
To meet, but once, the thrilling touch
Of lips too purely fond to fear me—
Or, if that boon be all too much,
Even thus to bring their fragrance near me!
Nay, shrink not so—a look—a word—
Give them but kindly and I fly;
Already, see, my plumes have stirr'd,
And tremble for their home on high.
Thus be our parting—cheek to cheek—
One minute's lapse will be forgiven,
And thou, the next, shalt hear me speak
The spell that plumes my wing for heaven!"

While thus I spoke, the fearful maid,
Of me, and of herself afraid,
Had shrinking stood, like flowers beneath
The scorching of the south-wind's breath :
But when I named—alas, too well,
I now recall, though wilder'd then—
Instantly, when I named the spell,
Her brow, her eyes uprose again,
And, with an eagerness, that spoke
The sudden light that o'er her broke,
" The spell, the spell!—oh, speak it now,
And I will bless thee !" she exclaim'd.
Unknowing what I did, inflamed,
And lost already, on her brow
I stamp'd one burning kiss, and named
The mystic word, till then ne'er told
To living creature of earth's mould!
Scarce was it said, when, quick as thought,
Her lips from mine, like echo, caught
The holy sound—her hands and eyes
Were instant lifted to the skies,
And thrice to heaven she spoke it out
With that triumphant look Faith wears,
When not a cloud of fear or doubt,
A vapour from this vale of tears,
Between her and her God appears!

That very moment her whole frame
All bright and glorified became,
And at her back I saw unclose
Two wings, magnificent as those
That sparkle around Alla's Throne,
Whose plumes, as buoyantly she rose
Above me, in the moon-beam shone

    Or why are there not flowers to cull,
     As fair as woman, in yon skies?—P. E.
(2) Changed from—
    As though that planet were an urn
    From which her eyes drank liquid light.—P. E.

save his morality, at the expense of his laimity, by substituting
the word " excussat" for " excusat." Such instances of indecorum,
however, are but too common throughout the Fathers, in proof
of which I need only refer to some passages in the same writer's
treatise, *De Anima*—to the Second and Third Books of the *Pæda-
gogus* of Clemens Alexandrinus, and to the instances which La
Mothe le Vayer has adduced from Chrysostom in his *Hexameron
Rustique, Journée Seconde.*

With a pure light, which—from its hue
Unknown upon this earth—I knew
Was light from Eden, glistening through!
Most holy vision! ne'er before
    Did aught so radiant—since the day
When Eblis, in his downfall, bore
    The third of the bright stars away—(1)
Rise, in earth's beauty, to repair
That loss of light and glory there! (2)

But did I tamely view her flight?
Did not I, too, proclaim out thrice
The powerful words that were, that night—
Oh even for heaven too much delight!—
    Again to bring us, eyes to eyes,
    And soul to soul, in Paradise?
I did—I spoke it o'er and o'er—
    I pray'd, I wept, but all in vain;
For me the spell had power no more.
    There seem'd around me some dark chain,
Wh'ch still, as I essay'd to soar,
    Baffled, alas, each wild endeavour:
Dead lay my wings, as they have lain
Since that sad hour, and will remain—
    So wills the offended God—for ever!

It was to yonder star I traced
Her journey up the illumined waste—
That isle in the blue firmament,
To which so oft her fancy went
    In wishes and in dreams before,
And which was now—such, Purity,
Thy blest reward—ordain'd to be
    Her home of light for evermore!
Once—or did I but fancy so?—
    Even in her flight to that fair sphere,
'Mid all her spirit's new-felt glow,
    A pitying look she turn'd below
On him who stood in darkness here;
Him whom, perhaps, if vain regret
Can dwell in heaven, she pities yet;
And oft, when looking to this dim
And distant world, remembers him.

But soon that passing dream was gone,
    Farther and farther off she shone,

Till lessen'd to a point, as small
    As are those specks that yonder burn—
Those vivid drops of light, that fall
    The last from Day's exhausted urn.
And when at length she merged, afar,
Into her own immortal star,
And when at length my straining sight
    Had caught her wing's last fading ray,
That minute from my soul the light
    Of heaven and love both pass'd away,
And I forgot my home, my birth,
    Profaned my spirit, sunk my brow,
And revell'd in gross joys of earth,
    Till I became—what I am now!

The Spirit bow'd his head in shame;
    A shame, that of itself would tell—
Were there not even those breaks of flame,
Celestial, through his clouded frame—
    How grand the height from which he fell!
That holy Shame, which ne'er forgets
    The unblench'd renown it used to wear;
Whose blush remains, when Virtue sets,
    To show her sunshine has been there.
Once only, while the tale he told,
Were his eyes lifted to behold
That happy stainless star, where she
Dwelt in her bower of purity!
One minute did he look, and then—
    As though he felt some deadly pain
From its sweet light through heart and brain—
Shrunk back, and never look'd again.

Who was the Second Spirit? he
    With the proud front and piercing glance—
Who seem'd, when viewing heaven's expanse,
As though his far-sent eye could see
On, on into the Immensity
Behind the veils of that blue sky,
Where Alla's grandest secrets lie?—
His wings, the while, though day was gone,
    Flashing with many a various hue
Of light they from themselves alone,
    Instinct with Eden's brightness, drew. (3)
'T was Rubi (4)—once among the prime
And flower of those bright creatures, named

(1) "And his tail drew the third part of the stars of
heaven, and did cast them to the earth." Rev., c. xii.,
v. 4.—"Docent sancti says Suarez supremum angelum
traxisse secum tertiam partem stellarum." Lib. 7,
cap. 7.—P. E.

(2) The idea of the Fathers was, that the vacancies oc-
casioned in the different orders of angels by the fall were
to be filled up from the human race. There is, however,
another opinion, backed by papal authority, that it was
only the tenth order of the Celestial Hierarchy that fell,
and that, therefore, the promotions which occasionally
take place from earth are intended for the completion
of that grade alone, or as it is explained by Salonius
(Dial. in Eccl.)—"Decem sunt ordines angelorum, sed
unus cecidit per superbiam, et idcirco boni angeli semper

laborant, ut de hominibus numerus adimpleatur, et pro-
veniat ad perfectum numerum, id est, denarium." Ac-
cording to some theologians, virgins alone are admitted
"ad collegium angelorum," but the author * of the "Spe-
culum Peregrinarum Quæstionum" rather questions this
exclusive privilege:— "Hoc non videtur verum, quia
multi, non virgines, ut Petrus et Magdalena, multis etiam
virginibus eminentiores sunt." Decad. 2, cap. 10.—P. E.
(3) An elision of five lines occurs here:—

        A breathing forth of beams at will,
            Of living beams, which, though no more
        They kept their early lustre, still
            Were such, when glittering out all o'er,
        As mortal eyelids wink'd before. — P. E.
(4 I might have chosen, perhaps, some better name,
        * F Bartholomæus Sibylla

58

Spirits of Knowledge, (1) who o'er Time
   And Space and Thought an empire claim'd,
Second alone to Him, whose light
Was, even to theirs, as day to night;
'Twixt whom and them was distance far
   And wide, as would the journey be
To reach from any island star
   The vague shores of Infinity!

'Twas Rubi, in whose mournful eye
Slept the dim light of days gone by;
Whose voice, though sweet, fell on the ear
Like echoes, in some silent place,
When first awaked for many a year;
   And when he smiled, if o'er his face
Smile ever shone, 't was like the grace
Of moonlight rainbows, fair, but wan,
The sunny life, the glory gone.
Even o'er his pride, though still the same,
A softening shade from sorrow came;
And though at times his spirit knew
   The kindlings of disdain and ire,
Short was the fitful glare they threw—
Like the last flashes, fierce but few,
   Seen through some noble pile on fire!

Such was the Angel who now broke
   The silence that had come o'er all,
When he, the Spirit that last spoke,
   Closed the sad history of his fall;
And, while a sacred lustre, flown
   For many a day, relumed his cheek—
Beautiful, as in days of old;
And not those eloquent lips alone,
   But every feature seem'd to speak—
Thus his eventful story told:—(2)

SECOND ANGEL'S STORY.

You both remember well the day,
   When unto Eden's new-made bowers,
Alla convoked the bright array
   Of his supreme angelic powers, (3)
To witness the one wonder yet,
   Beyond man, angel, star, or sun,

He must achieve, ere he could set
   His seal upon the world, as done—
To see that last perfection rise,
   That crowning of creation's birth,
When, 'mid the worship and surprise
   Of circling angels, Woman's eyes
First open'd upon heaven and earth;
And from their lids a thrill was sent,
That through each living spirit went
Like first light through the firmament!

Can you forget how gradual stole
The fresh-awaken'd breath of soul
Throughout her perfect form—which seem'd
To grow transparent, as there beam'd
That dawn of mind within, and caught
New loveliness from each new thought?
Slow as o'er summer seas we trace
   The progress of the noontide air,
Dimpling its bright and silent face
Each minute into some new grace,
   And varying heaven's reflections there—
Or, like the light of evening, stealing
   O'er some fair temple, which all day
Hath slept in shadow, slow revealing
   Its several beauties, ray by ray,
Till it shines out, a thing to bless,
All full of light and loveliness.

Can you forget her blush, when round
Through Eden's lone enchanted ground
She look'd, and saw the sea—the skies—
   And heard the rush of many a wing,
On high behests then vanishing;
And saw the last few angel eyes,
Still lingering—mine among the rest—
Reluctant leaving scenes so blest?
From that miraculous hour, the fate
Of this new glorious Being dwelt,
For ever, with a spell-like weight,
Upon my spirit—early, late,
   Whate'er I did, or dream'd, or felt,

---

but it is meant (like that of Zaraph in the following story to define the particular class of spirits to which the angel belonged. The author of the book of Enoch, who estimates at 200 the number of angels that descended upon Mount Hermon, for the purpose of making love to the women of earth, has favoured us with the names of their leader and chiefs — Samyaza, Urakabarameel, Akibeel, Tamiel, etc. etc. Josephus, too, mentions, among the religious rites of the Essenes, their swearing " to preserve the names of the angels,"—συντηρησειν τα των αγγελων ονοματα. Bell. Jud , lib. 2, cap. 8.—See upon this subject Van Dale, de Orig. et Progress. Idololat., cap. 9.—P. E.

(1) The Kerubim, as the Mussulmans call them, are often joined indiscriminately with the Asrafil or Seraphim, under one common name of Azazil, by which all spirits who approach near the throne of Alla are designated.
   The word cherub signifies knowledge — το γνος'ικον αυτων και 3εοπτικον, says Dionysius. Hence it is that Ezekiel, to express the abundance of their knowledge, represents them as "full of eyes."—P. E.
(2 These last four lines occupy the place of—
      And not those sky-tuned lips alone,
      But his eyes, brows, and tresses, roll'd
      Like sunset waves, all seem'd to speak—
      Thus his eventful story told.—F. E.
(3) The two preceding lines originally stood—
      He, whom all livings thing obey,
      Summon'd his chief angelic powers.
St. Augustin, upon Genesis, seems rather inclined to admit that the angels had some share ("aliquod ministerium") in the creation of Adam and Eve.—P. E.

The thought of what might yet befall
That matchless creature mix'd with all.—
Nor she alone, but her whole race
Through ages yet to come—whate'er
Of feminine, and fond, and fair,
Should spring from that pure mind and face,
All waked my soul's intensest care;
Their forms, souls, feelings, still to me
Creation's strangest mystery!

It was my doom—even from the first,
When witnessing the primal burst
Of Nature's wonders, I saw rise
Those bright creations in the skies—
Those worlds instinct with life and light,
Which Man, remote, but sees by night—(1
It was my doom still to be haunted
By some new wonder, some sublime
And matchless work, that, for the time,
Held all my soul, enchain'd, enchanted,
And left me not a thought, a dream,
A word, but on that only theme!

The wish to know—that endless thirst,
Which even by quenching is awaked,
And which becomes or blest or curst,
As is the fount whereat 't is slaked—
Still urged me onward, with desire
Insatiate, to explore, inquire—
Whate'er the wondrous things might be,
That waked each new idolatry—
Their cause, aim, source, whence-ever sprung—
Their inmost powers, as though for me
Existence on that knowledge hung.

Oh what a vision were the stars,
When first I saw them burn on high,
Rolling along, like living cars
Of light, for gods to journey by!(2)
They were my heart's first passion—days
And nights, unwearied, in their rays
Have I hung floating, till each sense
Seem'd full of their bright influence.
Innocent joy! alas, how much
Of misery had I shunn'd below,
Could I have still lived blest with such;
Nor, proud and restless, burn'd to know
The knowledge that brings guilt and woe.

(1) In the original—

It was my doom—even from the first,
When summon'd with my cherub peers,
To witness the young vernal burst
Of nature through those blooming spheres,
Those flowers of light, that sprung beneath
The first touch of the Eternal's breath —P. E.

(2) "C'est un fait indubitable que la plupart des anciens
philosophes, soit chaldéens, soit grecs, nous ont donné les
astres comme animés, et ont soutenu que les astres qui nous
éclairent n'étoient que, ou les chars, ou même les navires
des intelligences qui les conduisoient. Pour les *Chars*, cela
se lit partout; on n'a qu'ouvrir Pline, Saint Clement," etc.

Often—so much I loved to trace
The secrets of this starry race—
Have I at morn and evening run
Along the lines of radiance spun
Like webs, between them and the sun,
Untwisting all the tangled ties
Of light into their different dyes—
Then fleetly wing'd I off, in quest
Of those, the farthest, loneliest,
That watch, like waking sentinels, (3)
The void, beyond which Chaos dwells;
And there, with noiseless plume, pursued
Their track through that grand solitude,
Asking intently all and each
What soul within their radiance dwelt,
And wishing their sweet light were speech,
That they might tell me all they felt.

Nay, oft, so passionate my chase
Of these resplendent heirs of space,
Oft did I follow—lest a ray
Should 'scape me in the farthest night—
Some pilgrim Comet, on his way
To visit distant shrines of light,
And well remember how I sung
Exultingly, when on my sight
New worlds of stars, all fresh and young,
As if just born of darkness, sprung!

Such was my pure ambition then,
My sinless transport, night and morn;
Ere yet this newer world of men,
And that most fair of stars was born
Which I, in fatal hour saw rise
Among the flowers of Paradise!
Thenceforth my nature all was changed,
My heart, soul, senses turn'd below;
And he who but so lately ranged
Yon wonderful expanse, where glow
Worlds upon worlds—yet found his mind
Even in that luminous range confined—
Now blest the humblest meanest sod
Of the dark earth where Woman trod!
In vain my former idols glisten'd
From their far thrones; in vain these ears
To the once-thrilling music listen'd,
That hymn'd around my favourite spheres—
To earth, to earth each thought was given,
That in this half-lost soul had birth;

—*Mémoire historique sur le Sabiisme*, par M. Fourmont.
A belief that the stars are either spirits or the vehicles of
spirits, was common to all the religions and heresies, of the
East. Kircher has given the names and stations of the seven
archangels, who were by the Cabala of the Jews distributed
through the planets.

(3) According to the cosmogony of the ancient Persians,
there were four stars set as sentinels in the four quarters
of the heavens, to watch over the other fixed stars, and
superintend the planets in their course. The names of
these four sentinel stars are, according to the Boundesh,
Taschter, for the east. Satevis, for the west; Venand, for
the south; and Haftorang, for the north.

Like some high mount, whose head 's in heaven,
  While its whole shadow rests on earth!

Nor was it Love, even yet, that thrall'd
  My spirit in his burning ties;
And less, still less could it be call'd
  That grosser flame, round which Love flies
  Nearer and nearer, till he dies—
No, it was wonder, such as thrill'd
  At all God's works my dazzled sense;
The same rapt wonder, only fill'd
  With passion, more profound, intense—
A vehement but wandering fire,
Which, though nor love, nor yet desire—
Though through all womankind it took
  Its range, as lawless lightnings run,
Yet wanted but a touch, a look,
  To fix it burning upon One.

Then, too, the ever-restless zeal,
  The insatiate curiosity
To know how shapes, so fair, must feel—
To look, but once, beneath the seal
  Of so much loveliness, and see
What souls belong'd to such bright eyes—
  Whether, as sun-beams find their way
Into the gem that hidden lies,
  Those looks could inward turn their ray,
And make the soul as bright as they:
All this impell'd my anxious chase,
  And still the more I saw and knew
Of Woman's fond, weak, conquering race,
  The intenser still my wonder grew.

I had beheld their First, their Eve,
  Born in that splendid Paradise, (1)

Which sprung there solely to receive
  The first light of her waking eyes.
I had seen purest angels lean
  In worship o'er her from above;
And man—oh yes, had envying seen
  Proud man possess'd of all her love.

I saw their happiness, so brief,
  So exquisite—her error, too, (2)
That easy trust, that prompt belief
  In what the warm heart wishes true;
That faith in words, when kindly said,
By which the whole fond sex is led—
Mingled with—what I durst not blame,
  For 't is my own—that zeal to *know*,
Sad, fatal zeal, so sure of woe;
Which, though from heaven all pure it came,
Yet stain'd, misused, brought sin and shame
  On her, on me, on all below!

I had seen this; had seen man arm'd,
  As his soul is, with strength and sense,
By her first words to ruin charm'd;
  His vaunted reason's cold defence,
Like an ice-barrier in the ray
Of melting Summer, smiled away.
Nay, stranger yet, spite of all this—
  Though by her counsels taught to err,
  Though driven from Paradise for her,
(And *with* her—*that*, at least, was bliss,)
  Had I not heard him, ere he cross'd
  The threshold of that earthly heaven,
Which by her wildering smile he lost—
  So quickly was the wrong forgiven!—
Had I not heard him, as he press'd
The frail fond trembler to a breast

---

(1) Whether Eve was created *in* Paradise or not is a question that has been productive of much doubt and controversy among the theologians. With respect to Adam, it is agreed on all sides that *he* was created *outside*; and it is accordingly asked, with some warmth, by one of the commentators, why should woman, the ignobler creature of the two, be created *within?* * Others, on the contrary, consider this distinction as but a fair tribute to the superior beauty and purity of women, and some, in their zeal, even seem to think that, if the scene of her creation was not already Paradise, it became so, immediately upon that event, in compliment to her. Josephus is one of those who think that Eve was formed outside; Tertullian, too, among the Fathers—and, among the theologians, Rupertus, who, to do him justice, never misses an opportunity of putting on record his ill-will to the sex. Pererius, however (and his opinion seems to be considered the most orthodox), thinks it much more consistent with the order of the Mosaic narration, as well as with the sentiments of Basil and other Fathers, to conclude that Eve was created *in* Paradise.—P. E.

(2) The comparative extent of Eve's delinquency, and

* " Cur denique Evam, quæ Adamo ignobilior erat, formavit *intra Paradisum?* "
** Rupertus considers these *variantes* as intentional and prevaricatory, and as the first instance upon record of a wilful vitiation

the proportion which it bears to that of Adam, is another point which has exercised the tiresome ingenuity of the Commentators; and they seem generally to agree (with the exception always of Rupertus) that, as she was not yet created when the prohibition was issued, and therefore could not have heard it a conclusion remarkably confirmed by the inaccurate way in which she reports it to the serpent), ** her share in the crime of disobedience is considerably lighter than that of Adam. *** In corroboration of this view of the matter, Pererius remarks that it is to Adam alone the Deity addresses his reproaches for having eaten of the forbidden tree, because to Adam alone the order had been originally promulgated. So far, indeed, does the gallantry of another commentator, Hugh de St. Victor, carry him, that he looks upon the words "I will put enmity between thee and the woman" as a proof that the sex was from that moment enlisted into the service of Heaven, as the chief foe and obstacle which the Spirit of Evil would have to contend with in his inroads on this world —"si deinceps Eva inimica Diabolo, ergo fuit grata et amica Deo."—P. E.

of the works of God, for the purpose of suiting the corrupt views and propensities of human nature.—*De Trinitat.*, lib. iii., cap. 5.
*** Cajetanus, indeed, pronounces it to be "minimum peccatum."

Which she had doom'd to sin and strife,
Call her—even then—his Life! his Life! (1)
Yes, such the love-taught name, the first,
That ruin'd Man to Woman gave,
Even in his outcast hour, when curst
By her fond witchery, with that worst
And earliest boon of love, the grave!
She, who brought death into the world,
There stood before him, with the light
Of their lost Paradise still bright
Upon those sunny locks, that curl'd
Down her white shoulders to her feet—
So beautiful in form, so sweet
In heart and voice, as to redeem
The loss, the death of all things dear,
Except herself—and make it seem
Life, endless Life, while she was near!

Could I help wondering at a creature,
Thus circled round with spells so strong—
One to whose every thought, word, feature,
In joy and woe, through right and wrong,
Such sweet omnipotence heaven gave,
To bless or ruin, curse or save?

Nor did the marvel cease with her—
New Eves in all her daughters came,
As strong to charm, as weak to err,
As sure of man, through praise and blame,
Whate'er they brought him, pride or shame,
He still the unreasoning worshipper,
And they, throughout all time, the same
Enchantresses of soul and frame,
Into whose hands, from first to last,
This world with all its destinies,
Devotedly by heaven seems cast,
To save or ruin, as they please!
Oh, 't is not to be told how long,
How restlessly I sigh'd to find
Some one, from out that witching throng,
Some abstract of the form and mind

Of the whole matchless sex, from which,
In my own arms beheld, possest,
I might learn all the powers to witch,
To warn, and (if my fate unblest
Would have it) ruin, of the rest!
Into whose inward soul and sense
I might descend, as doth the bee
Into the flower's deep heart, and thence
Rifle, in all its purity,
The prime, the quintessence, the whole
Of wondrous Woman's frame and soul!

At length, my burning wish, my prayer—
(For such—oh what will tongues not dare,
When hearts go wrong?—this lip preferr'd)—
At length my ominous prayer was heard—
But whether heard in heaven or hell,
Listen—and thou wilt know too well.

There was a maid, of all who move
Like visions o'er this orb, most fit
To be a bright young angel's love,
Herself so bright, so exquisite!
The pride, too, of her step, as light
Along the unconscious earth she went,
Seem'd that of one, born with a right
To walk some heavenlier element,
And tread in places where her feet
A star at every step should meet.
'T was not alone that loveliness
By which the wilder'd sense is caught—
Of lips, whose very breath could bless;
Of playful blushes, that seem'd nought
But luminous escapes of thought;
Of eyes that, when by anger stirr'd,
Were fire itself, but, at a word
Of tenderness, all soft became,
As though they could, like the sun's bird,
Dissolve away in their own flame—
Of form, as pliant as the shoots
Of a young tree, in vernal flower;

---

(1) Chavah, or, as it is in Arabic, Havah (the name by which Adam called the woman after their transgression), means "Life."

Chavah in the Latin version, Eva) has the same signification as the Greek, Zoe.

Epiphanius, among others, is not a little surprised at the application of such a name to Eve, so immediately, too, after that awful denunciation of death, "dust thou art," etc. etc. * Some of the commentators think that it was meant as a sarcasm, and spoken by Adam, in the first bitterness of h s heart—in the same spirit of irony (says Pererius) as that of the Greeks in calling their Furies, Eumenides, or Gentle. ** But the Bishop of Chalon rejects this supposition :—"Explodendi sane qui id nominis ab Adamo per ironiam inditum uxori suæ putant: atque quod mortis causa esset, amaro joco vitam appellasse. ***

* Καὶ μετὰ τὸ ἀκροῦσαι, γῆ εἰ, καὶ εἰς γῆν ἀπελεύσῃ, μετὰ τὴν παράβασιν· καὶ ἦν θαυμαςοὶ ὅτι μετὰ τὴν παράβασιν ταύτην τὴν μεγάλην ἐσχεν ἐπωνυμιαν.—

With a similar feeling of spleen against women, some of these "distillateurs des Saintes Lettres" (as Bayle calls them), in rendering the text "I will make him a help meet for him," translate these last words "against or contrary to him" a meaning which, it appears, the original will bear), and represent them as prophetic of those contradictions and perplexities which men experience from women in this life.

It is rather strange that these two instances of perverse commentatorship should have escaped the researches of Bayle, in his curious article upon Eve. He would have found another subject of discussion, equally to his taste, in Gataker's whimsical dissertation upon Eve's knowledge of the τεχνη ὑφαςτικη, and upon the notion of Epiphanius that it was taught her in a special revelation from Heaven. —Miscellan., lib. ii., cap. 3, p. 200.—P. E.

Hares, 78, sec. 18, tom. 1, edit. Paris. 1622.
** Lib 6, p. 231.
*** Pontus Tyard de Recta Nominum Impositione, p 14.

Yet round and glowing as the fruits
   That drop from it in Summer's hour ;—
'T was not alone this loveliness
   That falls to loveliest women's share,
Though, even here, her form could spare
From its own beauty's rich excess
   Enough to make even *them* more fair—
But 't was the Mind, outshining clear
Through her whole frame—the soul, still near,
To light each charm, yet independent
   Of what it lighted, as the sun
That shines on flowers, would be resplendent
   Were there no flowers to shine upon—
'T was this, all this, in one combined—
The unnumber'd looks and arts that form
The glory of young womankind,
   Taken, in their perfection, warm,
   Ere time had chill'd a single charm,
And stamp'd with such a seal of Mind,
   As gave to beauties, that might be
   Too sensual else, too unrefined,
     The impress of Divinity!

'T was this—a union, which the hand
   Of Nature kept for her alone,
Of every thing most playful, bland,
Voluptuous, spiritual, grand,
   In angel-natures and her own—
Oh this it was that drew me nigh
One, who seem'd kin to heaven as I,
A bright twin-sister from on high—
One, in whose love, I felt, were given
   The mix'd delights of either sphere,
All that the spirit seeks in heaven,
   And all the senses burn for here.

Had we—but hold—hear every part
Of our sad tale—spite of the pain
Remembrance gives, when the fix'd dart
Is stirr'd thus in the wound again—
Hear every step, so full of bliss,
   And yet so ruinous, that led
Down to the last dark precipice,
   Where perish'd both—the fallen, the dead!

From the first hour she caught my sight,
I never left her—day and night
Hovering unseen around her way,
And 'mid her loneliest musings near,
I soon could track each thought that lay,
   Gleaming within her heart, as clear
   As pebbles within brooks appear ;
And there, among the countless things
That keep young hearts for ever glowing,
Vague wishes, fond imaginings,
   Love-dreams, as yet no object knowing—
Light winged hopes, that come when bid,
   And rainbow joys that end in weeping—
And passions, among pure thoughts hid,
   Like serpents under flowerets sleeping ;—

'Mong all these feelings—felt where'er
Young hearts are beating—I saw there
Proud thoughts, aspirings high—beyond
Whate'er yet dwelt in soul so fond—
Glimpses of glory, far away
   Into the bright vague future given ;
And fancies, free and grand, whose play
   Like that of eaglets, is near heaven!
With this, too—what a soul and heart
To fall beneath the tempter's art !—
A zeal for knowledge, such as ne'er
Enshrined itself in form so fair,
Since that first fatal hour, when Eve,
   With every fruit of Eden blest,
Save one alone—rather than leave
   That *one* unreach'd, lost all the rest.

It was in dreams that first I stole
   With gentle mastery o'er her mind—
In that rich twilight of the soul,
   When reason's beam, half hid behind
The clouds of sleep, obscurely gilds
Each shadowy shape the Fancy builds—
'T was then, by that soft light, I brought
   Vague glimmering visions to her view ;—
Catches of radiance, lost when caught,
Bright labyrinths, that led to nought,
   And vistas with no pathway through ;—
Dwellings of bliss that opening shone,
   Then closed, dissolved, and left no trace—
All that, in short, could tempt Hope on,
   But give her wing no resting-place ;
Myself the while, with brow, as yet,
Pure as the young moon's coronet,
Through every dream *still* in her sight,
   The enchanter of each mocking scene,
Who gave the hope, then brought the blight,
Who said, " Behold yon world of light,"
   Then sudden dropp'd a veil between !

At length, when I perceived each thought,
Waking or sleeping, fix'd on nought
   But these illusive scenes, and me—
The phantom, who thus came and went,
In half revealments, only meant
   To madden curiosity—
When by such various arts I found
   Her fancy to its utmost wound,
One night—'t was in a holy spot,
Which she for prayer had chosen—a grot
Of purest marble, built below
Her garden beds, through which a glow
From lamps invisible then stole,
   Brightly pervading all the place—
Like that mysterious light the soul,
   Itself unseen, sheds through the face ;
There, at her altar while she knelt,
And all that woman ever felt,
   When God and man both claim'd her sighs—
Every warm thought, that ever dwelt,

Like summer clouds, 'twixt earth and skies,
Too pure to fall, too gross to rise,
Spoke in her gestures, tones, and eyes—
Then, as the mystic light's soft ray
Grew softer still, as though its ray
Was breathed from her, I heard her say:—

" Oh, idol of my dreams! whate'er
Thy nature be—human, divine,
Or but half heavenly (1)—still too fair,
Too heavenly to be ever mine!

" Wonderful Spirit, who dost make
Slumber so lovely, that it seems
No longer life to live awake,
Since heaven itself descends in dreams,

" Why do I ever lose thee? why,
When on thy realms and thee I gaze
Still drops that veil, which I could die,
Oh gladly, but one hour to raise?

" Long ere such miracles as thou
And thine came o'er my thoughts, a thirst
For light was in this soul, which now
Thy looks have into passion nursed.

" There's nothing bright above, below,
In sky—earth—ocean, that this breast
Doth not intensely burn to know,
And thee, thee, thee, o'er all the rest!

" Then come, oh Spirit, from behind
The curtains of thy radiant home,
If thou wouldst be as angel shrined,
Or loved and clasp'd as mortal, come!

" Bring all thy dazzling wonders here,
That I may, waking, know and see;
Or waft me hence to thy own sphere,
Thy heaven or—ay, even that with thee!

" Demon or God, who hold'st the book
Of knowledge spread beneath thine eye,
Give me, with thee, but one bright look
Into its leaves, and let me die!

" By those ethereal wings, whose way
Lies through an element, so fraught
With living Mind, that, as they play,
Their every movement is a thought!

" By that bright wreathed hair, between
Whose sunny clusters the sweet wind
Of Paradise so late hath been,
And left its fragrant soul behind!

" By those impassion'd eyes, that melt
Their light into the inmost heart;
Like sunset in the waters, felt
As molten fire through every part—

" I do implore thee, oh most bright
And worshipp'd Spirit, shine but o'er
My waking wondering eyes this night,
This one blest night—I ask no more!"

Exhaustless, breathless, as she said
These burning words, her languid head
Upon the altar's steps she cast,
As if that brain-throb were its last—

Till, startled by the breathing, nigh,
Of lips that echo'd back her sigh,
Sudden her brow again she raised;
And there, just lighted on the shrine,
Beheld me—not as I had blazed
Around her, full of light divine,
In her late dreams, but soften'd down
Into more mortal grace;—my crown
Of flowers, too radiant for this world,
Left hanging on yon starry steep;
My wings shut up, like banners furl'd,
When Peace hath put their pomp to sleep;
Or like autumnal clouds, that keep
Their lightnings sheathed, rather than mar
The dawning hour of some young star;
And nothing left but what beseem'd
The accessible though glorious mate
Of mortal woman—whose eyes beam'd
Back upon hers, as passionate;
Whose ready heart brought flame for flame,
Whose sin, whose madness was the same;

(1) In an article upon the Fathers which appeared, some years since, in the *Edinburgh Review* (No xlvii.), and of which I have made some little use in these notes (having that claim over it—as " quiddam notum *propriumque* " — which Lucretius gives to the cow over the calf), there is the following remark — " The belief of an intercourse between angels and women, founded upon a false version of a text in Genesis, is one of those extravagant notions of St. Justin and other Fathers, which show how little they had yet purified themselves from the grossness of heathen mythology, and in how many respects their heaven was but Olympus, with other names. Yet we can hardly be angry with them for this one error, when we recollect that possibly to their enamoured angels we owe the fanciful world of sylphs and gnomes, and that at this moment we might have wanted Pope's most exquisite poem, if the version of the LXX. had translated the Book of Genesis correctly."

The following is one among many passages, which may be adduced from the Comte de Gabalis, in confirmation of this remark · — " Ces enfants du ciel engendrèrent les géants fameux, s'étant fait aimer aux filles des hommes, et les mauvais cabalistes Joseph et Philo (comme tous les Juifs sont ignorants '), et après eux tous les auteurs que j'ai nommés tout à l'heure, on dit que c'etoit des anges, et n'ont pas su que c'était les sylphes et les autres peuples des elemens, qui, sous le nom d'enfans d'Eloïm, sont distingués des enfans des hommes."—See *Entret.*II.—P. E.

And whose soul lost, in that one hour,
　For her and for her love—oh more
Of heaven's light than even the power
　Of heaven itself could now restore!

And yet, that hour!——

　　　　The spirit here
Stopp'd in his utterance, as if words
Gave way beneath the wild career
　Of his then rushing thoughts—like chords,
Midway in some enthusiast's song,
Breaking beneath a touch too strong;
While the clench'd hand upon the brow
Told how remembrance throbb'd there now!
But soon 'twas o'er—that casual blaze
From the sunk fire of other days—
That relic of a flame, whose burning
　Had been too fierce to be relumed,
Soon pass'd away, and the youth, turning
　To his bright listeners, thus resumed:—

Days, months elapsed, and though what most
　On earth I sigh'd for was mine, all—
Yet—was I happy? God, thou know'st,
　Howe'er they smile, and feign, and boast,
　What happiness is theirs, who fall!
'Twas bitterest anguish—made more keen
Even by the love, the bliss, between
Whose throbs it came, like gleams of hell
　In agonising cross-light given
Athwart the glimpses they who dwell
　In purgatory (1) catch of heaven!
The only feeling that to me
　Seem'd joy—or rather my sole rest
From aching misery—was to see
　My young, proud, blooming Lilis blest.
She, the fair fountain of all ill
　To my lost soul—whom yet its thirst
Fervidly panted after still,
　And found the charm fresh as at first—

To see *her* happy—to reflect
　Whatever beams still round me play'd
Of former pride, of glory wreck'd,
　On her, my Moon, whose light I made,
　And whose soul worshipp'd even my shade—
This was, I own, enjoyment—this
My sole last lingering glimpse of bliss.
And proud she was, fair creature!—proud,
　Beyond what even most queenly stirs
In woman's heart, nor would have bow'd
　That beautiful young brow of hers
To aught beneath the First above,
So high she deem'd her Cherub's love!(2)

Then, too, that passion, hourly growing
　Stronger and stronger—to which even
Her love, at times, gave way—of knowing
　Every thing strange in earth and heaven;
Not only all that, full reveal'd,
　The eternal Alla loves to show,
But all that He hath wisely seal'd
　In darkness, for man *not* to know—
Even this desire, alas, ill-starr'd
　And fatal as it was, I sought
To feed each minute, and unbarr'd
　Such realms of wonder on her thought,
As ne'er, till then, had let their light
Escape on any mortal's sight!
In the deep earth—beneath the sea—
　Through caves of fire—through wilds of air—
Wherever sleeping Mystery
　Had spread her curtain, we were there—
Love still beside us, as we went,
At home in each new element,
And sure of worship every where!

Then first was Nature taught to lay
　The wealth of all her kingdoms down
At woman's worshipp'd feet, and say,
　"Bright creature, this is all thine own!"
Then first were diamonds from the night (3)
Of earth's deep centre brought to light,

(1) Called by the Mussulmans Al Araf—a sort of wall or partition which, according to the 7th chapter of the Koran, separates hell from paradise, and where they who have not merits sufficient to gain them immediate admittance into heaven are supposed to stand for a certain period, alternately tantalised and tormented by the sights that are on either side presented to them.

Manes, who borrowed in many instances from the Platonists, placed his purgatories, or places of purification, in the Sun and Moon.—*Beausobre*, liv. iii., chap. 8.

'Nihil plus desiderare potuerint quæ angelos possidebant—magno scilicet nupserant." *Tertull. de Habitu Muheb.*, cap. 2.—P. E.

(3) "Quelques gnomes, désireux de devenir immortels, avoient voulu gagner les bonnes graces de nos filles, et leur avoient apporté des pierreries dont ils sont gardiens naturels : et ces auteurs ont cru, s'appuyant sur le livre d'Enoch mal entendu; que c'étoient des pièges que les anges amoureux," etc. etc.—*Comte de Gabalis.*

As the fiction of the loves of angels with women gave birth to the fanciful world of sylphs and gnomes, so we owe to it also the invention of those beautiful Genii and Peris, which embellish so much the mythology of the East; for in the fabulous histories of Caioumarath, of Thamurath, etc , these spiritual creatures are always represented as the descendants of Seth, and called the Bani Algiann, or children of Giann.

Tertullian traces all the chief luxuries of female attire, necklaces, armlets, rouge, and the black powder for the eye-lashes, to the researches of these fallen angels into the inmost recesses of nature, and the discoveries they were, in consequence, enabled to make, of all that could embellish the beauty of their earthly favourites. The passage is so remarkable that I shall give it entire — "Nam et illi qui ea constituerant, damnati in pœnam mortis deputantur illi scilicet angeli, qui ad filias hominum de cœlo ruerunt, ut hæc quoque ignominia accedat Nam cum et materias quasdam bene occultas et artes pleras-

And made to grace the conquering way
Of proud young beauty with their ray.
Then, too, the pearl from out its shell
Unsightly, in the sunless sea,
(As 't were a spirit, forced to dwell
In form unlovely) was set free,
And round the neck of woman threw
A light it lent and borrow'd too.
For never did this maid—whate'er
The ambition of the hour—forget
Her sex's pride in being fair;
Nor that adornment, tasteful, rare,
Which makes the mighty magnet, set
In Woman's form, (1) more mighty yet.
Nor was there aught within the range
Of my swift wing in sea or air,
Of beautiful, or grand, or strange,
That, quickly as her wish could change,
I did not seek, with such fond care,
That when I 've seen her look above
At some bright star admiringly,
I 've said, " Nay, look not there, my love, (2)
Alas, I *cannot* give it thee!"

But not alone the wonders found
Through Nature's realm—the unveil'd, material,
Visible glories, that abound,
Through all her vast enchanted ground—
But whatsoe'er unseen, ethereal,
Dwells far away from human sense,
Wrapp'd in its own intelligence—
The mystery of that Fountain-head,
From which all vital spirit runs,
All breath of Life, where'er 'tis spread
Through men or angels, flowers or suns—
The workings of the Almighty Mind,
When first o'er Chaos he design'd
The outlines of this world, and through
That depth of darkness—like the bow,

Call'd out of rain-clouds, hue by hue—(3)
Saw the grand gradual picture grow;—
The covenant with human kind
By Alla made (4)—the chains of Fate
He round himself and them hath twined,
Till his high task he consummate;—
Till good from evil, love from hate,
Shall be work'd out through sin and pain,
And Fate shall loose her iron chain,
And all be free, be bright again!

Such were the deep-drawn mysteries,
And some, even more obscure, profound,
And wildering to the mind than these,
Which—far as woman's thought could sound,
Or a fallen outlaw'd spirit reach—
She dared to learn, and I to teach.
Till—fill'd with such unearthly lore,
And mingling the pure light it brings
With much that fancy had, before,
Shed in false tinted glimmerings—
The enthusiast girl spoke out, as one
Inspired, among her own dark race,
Who from their ancient shrines would run,
Leaving their holy rites undone,
To gaze upon her holier face.
And, though but wild the things she spoke,
Yet, 'mid that play of error's smoke
Into fair shapes by fancy curl'd,
Some gleams of pure religion broke—
Glimpses, that have not yet awoke,
But startled the still dreaming world!
Oh, many a truth, remote, sublime,
Which Heaven would from the minds of men
Have kept conceal'd, till its own time,
Stole out in these revealments then—
Revealments dim, that have fore-run,
By ages, the great, Sealing One! (5)

---

que non bene revelatas, sæculo multo magis imperito prodidissent (siquidem et metallorum opera nudaverant, et herbarum ingenia traduxerant et incantationum vires provulgaverant, et omnem curiositatem usque ad stellarum interpretationem designaverant) proprie et quasi peculiariter fœm nis instrumentum istud muliebris gloriæ contulerunt · lumina lapillorum quibus monilia variantur, et circulos ex auro quibus brachia arctantur : et medicamenta ex fuco, quibus lanæ colorantur, et illum ipsum nigrum pulverem, quo oculorum exordia producuntur "— *De Habitu Mulieb.*, cap 2.— See him also *De Cultu Fœm.*, cap. 10.—P. E.

(1) The same figure, as applied to female attractions, occurs in a singular passage of St. Basil, of which the following is the conclusion —Δια την ειουσαι κατα τοι αρρενος αυτης φυσικην δυναςειαν, ως σιδηρος, φημι, πορρωθεν μαγιετις, τουτο προς εαυτον μαγγανευι. *De Vera Virginitat.*, tom 1., p. 727. It is but fair, however, to add, that Hermant, the biographer of Basil, has pronounced this most unsanctified treatise to be spurious.—P. E.

(2) I am aware that this happy saying of Lord Albemarle's

loses much of its grace and playfulness by being put into the mouth of any but a human lover.

3) According to Whitehurst's theory, the mention of rainbows by an antediluvian angel is an anachronism; as he says, " There was no rain before the flood, and consequently no rainbow, which accounts for the novelty of this sight after the Deluge."

4) For the terms of this compact, of which the angels were supposed to be witnesses, see the chapter of the Koran, entitled *Al-Araf*, and the article *Adam* in D'Herbelot.

(5) In acknowledging the authority of the great Prophets who had preceded him, Mahomet represented his own mission as the final "*Seal*," or consummation of them all.

It is the opinion of some of the Fathers, that the knowledge which the heathens possessed of the Providence of God, a future state, and other sublime doctrines of Christianity, was derived from the premature revelations of these fallen angels to the women of earth.

Clemens Alexandrinus is one of those who suppose that the knowledge of such sublime doctrines was derived from the disclosure of the angels. *Stromat.*, lib. v., p. 48. To the same source Cassianus and others trace all un-

Like that imperfect dawn, or light (1)
Escaping from the Zodiac's signs,
Which makes the doubtful east half bright,
Before the real morning shines!

Thus did some moons of bliss go by—
Of bliss to her, who saw but love
And knowledge throughout earth and sky;
To whose enamour'd soul and eye
I seem'd—as is the sun on high—
The light of all below, above,
The spirit of sea, and land, and air,
Whose influence felt every where,
Spread from its centre, her own heart,
Even to the world's extremest part;
While through that world her reinless mind
Had now career'd so fast and far,
That earth itself seem'd left behind,
And her proud fancy, unconfined,
Already saw Heaven's gates ajar!

Happy enthusiast! still, oh, still,
Spite of my own heart's mortal chill,
Spite of that double-fronted sorrow,
    Which looks at once before and back,
Beholds the yesterday, the morrow,
    And sees both comfortless, both black—
Spite of all this, I could have still
In her delight forgot all ill;
Or, if pain *would* not be forgot,
At least have borne and murmur'd not.
When thoughts of an offended Heaven,
Of sinfulness, which I—even I,
While down its steep most headlong driven—
Well knew could never be forgiven,
    Came o'er me with an agony
Beyond all reach of mortal woe—
A torture kept for those who know,
Know *every* thing, and—worst of all—
Know and love Virtue while they fall!
Even then, her presence had the power
    To soothe, to warm—nay, even to bless—
If ever bliss could graft its flower
    On stem so full of bitterness—
Even then her glorious smile to me
Brought warmth and radiance, if not balm;

pious and daring sciences, such as magic, alchemy, etc
"From the fallen angels (says Zozimus) came all that
miserable knowledge which is of no use to the soul."—
Παντα τα πονηρα και μηδεν ωφελουντα την ψυχην.—
Ap. Photium.

(1) The zodiacal light.

(2) Pococke, however, gives it as the opinion of the
Mahometan doctors, that all souls, not only of men and
of animals, living either on land or in the sea, but of the
angels also, must necessarily taste of death.

'3) To this part of the narration were formerly ap-
pended the following lines :—

  There seem'd a freshness in her breath,
  Beyond the reach, the power of death !

Like moonlight o'er a troubled sea,
Brightening the storm it cannot calm.

Oft, too, when that disheartening fear,
    Which all who love, beneath yon sky,
Feel, when they gaze on what is dear—
    The dreadful thought that it must die!
That desolating thought, which comes
Into men's happiest hours and homes;
Whose melancholy boding flings
Death's shadow o'er the brightest things,
Sicklies the infant's bloom, and spreads
The grave beneath young lovers' heads!
Tl is fear, so sad to all—to me
    Most full of sadness, from the thought
That I must still live on, (2) when she
    Would, like the snow that on the sea
Fell yesterday, in vain be sought;
That Heaven to me this final seal
    Of all earth's sorrow would deny,
And I eternally must feel
    The death-pang, without power to die!
Even this, her fond endearments—fond
As ever cherish'd the sweet bond
'Twixt heart and heart—could charm away;
Before her look no clouds would stay,
Or, if they did, their gloom was gone,
Their darkness put a glory on! (3)
But 't is not, 't is not for the wrong,
The guilty, to be happy long;
And she, too, now, had sunk within
The shadow of her tempter's sin.
Too deep for even Omnipotence
To snatch the fated victim thence! (4)

Listen, and, if a tear there be
Left in your hearts, weep it for me.

'T was on the evening of a day,
Which we in love had dreamt away;
In that same garden, where—the pride
Of seraph splendour laid aside,
And those wings furl'd, whose open light
For mortal gaze were else too bright—
I first had stood before her sight,
And found myself—oh, ecstasy,
    Which even in pain I ne'er forget—

And then, her voice—oh, who could doubt
  That 't would for ever thus breathe out
A music, like the harmony
Of the tuned orbs, too sweet to die!
While in her lip s awakening touch
There thrill'd a life ambrosial—such
As mantles in the fruit steep'd through
With Eden's most delicious dew—
Till I could almost think, though known
And loved as human, they had grown
By bliss, celestial as my own!—P. E.

(4) These two lines now occupy the place of—
  Shadow of death, whose withering frown
  Kills whatsoe'er it lights upon—
  Too deep for even *her* soul to shun
  The desolation it brings down!—P. E.

Worshipp'd as only God should be,
And loved as never man was yet!
In that same garden were we now,
Thoughtfully side by side reclining,
Her eyes turn'd upward, and her brow
With its own silent fancies shining.
It was an evening bright and still
As ever blush'd on wave or bower,
Smiling from heaven as if nought ill
Could happen in so sweet an hour.
Yet, I remember, both grew sad
In looking at that light—even she,
Of heart so fresh, and brow so glad,
Felt the still hour's solemnity,
And thought she saw in that repose,
The death-hour not alone of light,
But of this whole fair world—the close
Of all things beautiful and bright—
The last grand sunset, in whose ray
Nature herself died calm away!

At length, as though some livelier thought
Had suddenly her fancy caught, (1)
She turn'd upon me her dark eyes,
Dilated into that full shape
They took in joy, reproach, surprise,
As 't were to let more soul escape,
And, playfully as on my head
Her white hand rested, smiled and said:—

"I had, last night, a dream of thee,
Resembling those divine ones, given,
Like preludes to sweet minstrelsy,
Before thou camest, thyself, from heaven.

"The same rich wreath was on thy brow,
Dazzling as if of starlight made;
And these wings, lying darkly now,
Like meteors round thee flash'd and play'd.

"Thou stood'st, all bright, as in those dreams,
As if just wafted from above;
Mingling earth's warmth with heaven's beams,
A creature to adore and love. (2)

"Sudden I felt thee draw me near
To thy pure heart, where fondly placed,
I seem'd within the atmosphere
Of that exhaling light embraced;

"And felt, methought, the ethereal flame
Pass from thy purer soul to mine·
Till—oh, too blissful—I became,
Like thee, all spirit, all divine!

(1) In preceding editions—
At length, as if some thought awaking
Suddenly, sprung within her breast—
Like a young bird, when day-light breaking
Startles him from his dreamy nest.— P. E.

"Say, why did dream so blest come o'er me,
If, now I wake, 'tis faded, gone?
When will my Cherub shine before me
Thus radiant, as in heaven he shone?

"When shall I, waking, be allow'd
To gaze upon those perfect charms,
And clasp thee once, without a cloud,
A chill of earth, within these arms?

"Oh what a pride to say, this, this
Is my own Angel—all divine,
And pure, and dazzling as he is,
And fresh from heaven—he's mine! he's mine!

"Think'st thou, were Lilis in thy place,
A creature of yon lofty skies,
She would have hid one single grace,
One glory from her lover's eyes?

"No, no—then, if thou lovest like me,
Shine out, young Spirit, in the blaze
Of thy most proud divinity,
Nor think thou 'lt wound this mortal gaze.

"Too long and oft I've look'd upon
Those ardent eyes, intense even thus—
Too near the stars themselves have gone,
To fear aught grand or luminous.

"Then doubt me not—oh, who can say
But that this dream may yet come true,
And my blest spirit drink thy ray,
Till it becomes all heavenly too?

"Let me this once but feel the flame
Of those spread wings, the very pride
Will change my nature, and this frame
By the mere touch be deified!"

Thus spoke the maid, as one, not used
To be by earth or heaven refused—
As one, who knew her influence o'er
All creatures, whatsoe'er they were,
And, though to heaven she could not soar,
At least would bring down heaven to her.

Little did she, alas, or I—
Even I, whose soul, but half-way yet
Immerged in sin's obscurity,
Was as the earth whereon we lie,
O'er half whose disk the sun is set—
Little we foresee the fate,
The dreadful—how can it be told?

2 Changed from—
All bright as in those happy dreams
Thou stood'st, a creature to adore
No less than love, breathing out beams,
As flowers do fragrance, at each pore!'—P. E.

Such pain, such anguish to relate
  Is o'er again to feel, behold!
But, charged as 't is, my heart must speak
  Its sorrow out, or it will break!
Some dark misgivings *had*, I own,
  Pass'd for a moment through my breast—
Fears of some danger, vague, unknown,
  To one, or both—something unblest
  To happen from this proud request.
But soon these boding fancies fled;
  Nor saw I aught that could forbid
My full revealment, save the dread
  Of that first dazzle, when, unhid,
  Such light should burst upon a lid
Ne'er tried in heaven;—and even this glare
She might, by love's own nursing care,
Be, like young eagles, taught to bear.
For well I knew, the lustre shed
From cherub wings, when proudliest spread,
Was, in its nature, lambent, pure,
  And innocent as is the light
The glow-worm hangs out to allure
  Her mate to her green bower at night.
Oft had I, in the mid-air, swept
Through clouds in which the lightning slept,
As in its lair, ready to spring,
Yet waked it not—though from my wing
A thousand sparks fell glittering!
Oft too when round me from above
  The feather'd snow, in all its whiteness,
Fell, like the moultings of heaven's Dove—(2)
  So harmless, though so full of brightness,
Was my brow's wreath, that it would shake
From off its flowers each downy flake
As delicate, unmelted, fair,
And cool as they had lighted there.

Nay, even with Lilis—had I not
  Around her sleep all radiant beam'd,
Hung o'er her slumbers, nor forgot
  To kiss her eye-lids as she dream'd? (2)
And yet, at morn, from that repose,
  Had she not waked, unscathed and bright,

(1) The Dove, or pigeon which attended Mahomet as his Familiar, and was frequently seen to whisper into his ear, was, if I recollect right, one of that select number of animals including also the ant of Solomon, the dog of the Seven Sleepers, etc.) which were thought by the Prophet worthy of admission into Paradise.

"The Moslems have a tradition that Mahomet was saved (when he hid himself in a cave in Mount Shur by his pursuers finding the mouth of the cave covered by a spider's web, and a nest built by two pigeons at the entrance, with two eggs unbroken in it, which made them think no one could have entered it. In consequence of this, they say, Mahomet enjoined his followers to look upon pigeons as sacred, and never to kill a spider."—*Modern Universal History*, vol. i.

(2) These four lines have undergone some slight verbal changes :—

> Nay even with *Lilis*—had I not
> Around her sleep in splendour come—

As doth the pure unconscious rose,
  Though by the fire-fly kiss'd all night? (3)

Thus having—as, alas, deceived
By my sin's blindness, I believed—
No cause for dread, and those dark eyes
  Now fix'd upon me eagerly,
As though the unlocking of the skies
  Then waited but a sign from me—
How could I pause? how even let fall
  A word, a whisper, that could stir
In her proud heart a doubt, that all
  I brought from heaven belong'd to her?
Slow from her side I rose, while she
Arose, too, mutely, tremblingly,
But not with fear—all hope and pride,
  She waited for the awful boon,
Like priestesses, at eventide,
  Watching the rise of the full moon,
Whose light, when once its orb hath shone,
'T will madden them to look upon!

Of all my glories, the bright crown,
Which, when I last from heaven came down,
Was left behind me, in yon star
That shines from out those clouds afar—
Where, relic sad, 't is treasured yet,
The downfallen angel's coronet!—(4)
Of all my glories, this alone
Was wanting :—but the illumined brow,
The sun-bright locks, the eyes that now (5)
Had love's spell added to their own,
And pour'd a light till then unknown;—
  The unfolded wings, that, in their play,
Shed sparkles bright as Alla's throne;
All I could bring of heaven's array,
Of that rich panoply of charms
  A Cherub moves in, on the day
Of his best pomp, I now put on;
And, proud that in her eyes I shone
Thus glorious, glided to her arms;
Which still (though at a sight so splendid,
  Her dazzled brow had, instantly,

> Hung o'er each beauty, nor forgot
> To print my radiant lips on some?—P. E.

(3) The descriptive narration was formerly continued thus :—

> Even when the rays I scatter'd stole
> Intensest to her dreaming soul,
> No thrill disturb'd the insensate frame—
> So subtle, so refined that flame,
> Which, rapidly as lightnings melt
> The blade within the unharm'd sheath,
> Can, by the outward form unfelt,
> Reach and dissolve the soul beneath.—P. E.

(4) These four lines originally read—

> I left—see where those clouds afar
> Sail through the west—there hangs it yet,
> Shining remote, more like a star
> Than a fallen angel's coronet.—P. E.

(5) Changed from—

> The curls, like tendrils that had grown
> Out of the sun—the eyes, that now, etc.—P. E.

Sunk on her breast,) were wide extended
To clasp the form she durst not see!(1)

Great Heaven! how *could* thy vengeance light
So bitterly on one so bright?
How could the hand, that gave such charms,
Blast them again, in love's own arms?
Scarce had I touch'd her shrinking frame,
    When—oh most horrible!—I felt
That every spark of that pure flame—
    Pure, while among the stars I dwelt—
Was now, by my transgression, turn'd
Into gross earthly fire, which burn'd,
Burn'd all it touch'd, as fast as eye
    Could follow the fierce ravening flashes,
Till there—oh God, I still ask why
Such doom was hers?—I saw her lie
    Blackening within my arms to ashes!
That brow, a glory but to see—
Those lips whose touch was what the first
Fresh cup of immortality
Is to a new-made angel's thirst!
Those clasping arms, within whose round—
My heart's horizon—the whole bound
Of its hope, prospect, heaven was found!
Which even in this dread moment, fond
    As when they first were round me cast,
Loosed not in death the fatal bond,
    But burning held me to the last!(2)
All, all that, but that morn, had seem'd
As if Love's self there breathed and beam'd
Now, parch'd and black, before me lay,
Withering in agony away;
And mine, oh misery! mine the flame,
From which this desolation came;
I, the curst spirit, whose caress
Had blasted all that loveliness!

'T was maddening!—but now hear even worse—
Had death, death only, been the curse
I brought upon her—had the doom
But ended here, when her young bloom
Lay in the dust—and did the spirit
No part of that fell curse inherit,
'T were not so dreadful—but, come near—
Too shocking 'tis for earth to hear—
Just when her eyes, in fading, took
Their last, keen, agonised farewell,
And look'd in mine with—oh, that look!
    Great vengeful Power, whate'er the hell
Thou may'st to human souls assign,
The memory of that look is mine!—

In her last struggle, on my brow
    Her ashy lips a kiss impress'd
So withering!—I feel it now—
    'T was fire—but fire, even more unbless'd
Than was my own, and like that flame
The angels shudder but to name,
Hell's everlasting element!
    Deep, deep it pierced into my brain,
Maddening and torturing as it went;
    And here—mark here, the brand, the stain
It left upon my front—burnt in
By that last kiss of love and sin—
A brand, which all the pomp and pride
Of a fallen Spirit cannot hide!(3)

But is it thus, dread Providence—
    Can it, indeed, be thus, that she,
Who, (but for *one* proud fond offence,)
    Had honour'd heaven itself, should be
Now doom'd—I cannot speak it—no,
Merciful Alla! 'tis not so—
Never could lips divine have said
The fiat of a fate so dread.
And yet, that look—so deeply fraught
    With more than anguish, with despair—
That new fierce fire, resembling nought
    In heaven or earth—this scorch I bear!—
Oh—for the first time that these knees
Have bent before thee since my fall,
Great Power, if ever thy decrees
Thou couldst for prayer like mine recall,
Pardon that spirit, and on me,
    On me, who taught her pride to err,
Shed out each drop of agony
    Thy burning phial keeps for her!
See, too, where low beside me kneel
Two other outcasts, who, though gone
And lost themselves, yet dare to feel
And pray for that poor mortal one.
Alas, too well, too well they know
The pain, the penitence, the woe
That Passion brings upon the best,
The wisest, and the loveliest.—
Oh, who is to be saved, if such
Bright erring souls are not forgiven?
So loath they wander, and so much
Their very wanderings lean towards heaven!
Again, I cry, just Power, transfer
    That creature's sufferings all to me—
Mine, mine, the guilt, the torment be;
    To save one minute's pain to her,
Let mine last all eternity!"

(1) "Mohammed (says Sale), though a prophet, was not able to bear the sight of Gabriel, when he appeared in his proper form, much less would others be able to support it."

(2) The following lines no longer form part of the poem:
    That hair, from under whose dark veil,
    The snowy neck, like a white sail
    At moonlight seen 'twixt wave and wave,
    Shone out by gleams—that hair, to save
    But one of whose long glossy wreaths,
    I could have died ten thousand deaths!—P. E

(3) In former editions—
    A brand, which even the wreathed pride
    Of these bright curls, still forced aside
    By its foul contact, cannot hide!—P. E

He paused, and to the earth bent down
  His throbbing head ; while they, who felt
That agony as 't were their own,
  Those angel youths, beside him knelt,
And, in the night's still silence there,
While mournfully each wandering air
Play'd in those plumes, that never more
To their lost home in heaven must soar,
Breathed inwardly the voiceless prayer,
Unheard by all but Mercy's ear—
And which if Mercy did not hear,
Oh, God would not be what this bright
  And glorious universe of His,
This world of beauty, goodness, light,
  And endless love, proclaims He is !

Not long they knelt, when, from a wood
That crown'd that airy solitude,
They heard a low uncertain sound,
As from a lute that just had found
Some happy theme, and murmur'd round
The new-born fancy, with fond tone,
Scarce thinking aught so sweet its own! (1)
Till soon a voice, that match'd as well
  That gentle instrument, as suits
The sea-air to an ocean-shell,
  (So kin its spirit to the lute's,)
Tremblingly follow'd the soft strain,
Interpreting its joy, its pain,
  And lending the light wings of words
To many a thought, that else had lain
Unfledged and mute among the chords.

All started at the sound—but chief
  The third young Angel, in whose face
Though faded like the others, grief
  Had left a gentler, holier trace ;
As if, even yet, through pain and ill,
Hope had not fled him—as if still
  Her precious pearl, in sorrow's cup,
Unmelted at the bottom lay,
To shine again, when, all drunk up,
  The bitterness should pass away.
Chiefly did he, though in his eyes
There shone more pleasure than surprise,
Turn to the wood, from whence that sound
  Of solitary sweetness broke ;
Then, listening, look delighted round
  To his bright peers, while thus it spoke :—

" Come, pray with me, my seraph love,
  My angel-lord, come pray with me ;
In vain to-night my lip hath strove
  To send one holy prayer above—
The knee may bend, the lip may move,
  But pray I cannot, without thee !
I 've fed the altar in my bower
  With droppings from the incense tree ;
I 've shelter'd it from wind and shower,
  But dim it burns the livelong hour,

As if, like me, it had no power
  Of life or lustre, without thee !

" A boat at midnight sent alone
  To drift upon the moonless sea,
A lute, whose leading chord is gone,
A wounded bird, that hath but one
Imperfect wing to soar upon,
  Are like what I am, without thee !

" Then ne'er, my spirit-love, divide,
  In life or death, thyself from me ;
But when again, in sunny pride,
Thou walk'st through Eden, let me glide,
A prostrate shadow, by thy side—
  Oh happier thus than without thee ! "

The song had ceased, when from the wood
  Which, sweeping down that airy height,
Reach'd the lone spot whereon they stood—
  There suddenly shone out a light
From a clear lamp, which, as it blazed
Across the brow of one, who raised
  Its flame aloft (as if to throw
The light upon that group below),
Display'd two eyes, sparkling between
The dusky leaves, such as are seen
  By fancy only, in those faces,
That haunt a poet's walk at even,
Looking from out their leafy places
  Upon his dreams of love and heaven.
'T was but a moment—the blush brought
O'er all her features at the thought
  Of being seen thus, late, alone,
By any but the eyes she sought,
  Had scarcely for an instant shone
  Through the dark leaves, when she was gone—
Gone, like a meteor that o'erhead
Suddenly shines, and, ere we 've said,
" Behold, how beautiful ! "—'t is fled.

Yet, ere she went, the words, " I come,
  I come, my Nama," reach'd her ear,
  In that kind voice, familiar, dear,
Which tells of confidence, of home—
  Of habit, that hath drawn hearts near,
Till they grow one—of faith sincere,
And all that Love most loves to hear ;
A music breathing of the past,
  The present, and the time to be,
Where Hope and Memory, to the last,
  Lengthen out life's true harmony !

Nor long did he, whom call so kind
Summon'd away, remain behind ;

(1) A line has been here elided—
  The new-born fancy—with fond tone,
  Like that of ring-dove o'er her brood—
  Scarce thinking aught so sweet its own '—P. E.

Nor did there need much time to tell
What they—alas, more fall'n than he
From happiness and heaven—knew well,
His gentler love's short history!

Thus did it run—*not* as he told
The tale himself, but as 't is graved
Upon the tablets that, of old,
By Seth, (1) were from the deluge saved,(2)
All written over with sublime
And saddening legends of the unblest
But glorious Spirits of that time,
And this young Angel's 'mong the rest. (3)

THIRD ANGEL'S STORY.

AMONG the Spirits, of pure flame,
That in the eternal heavens abide—
Circles of light, that from the same
Unclouded centre sweeping wide,
Carry its beams on every side— (4)
Like spheres of air that waft around
The undulations of rich sound—
Till the far-circling radiance be
Diffused into infinity!
First and immediate near the Throne
Of Alla, (5) as if most his own,
The seraphs stand (6)—this burning sign
Traced on their banner, " Love Divine!"

Their rank, their honours, far above
Even those to high-brow'd Cherubs given,
Though knowing all;—so much doth Love
Transcend all Knowledge even in heaven!

'Mong these was Zaraph once—and none
E'er felt affection's holy fire,
Or yearn'd towards the Eternal One,
With half such longing, deep desire.
Love was to his impassion'd soul
Not, as with others, a mere part
Of its existence, but the whole—
The very life-breath of his heart!

Oft, when from Alla's lifted brow
A lustre came, too bright to bear,
And all the seraph ranks would bow,
To shade their dazzled sight, nor dare
To look upon the effulgence there—
This Spirit's eyes would court the blaze
(Such pride he in adoring took),
And rather lose, in that one gaze,
The power of looking, than *not* look!
Then too, when angel voices sung
The mercy of their God, and strung
Their harps to hail, with welcome sweet,
That moment, watch'd for by all eyes,

(1) Seth is a favourite personage among the Orientals, and acts a conspicuous part in many of their most extravagant romances. The Syrians pretended to have a Testament of this Patriarch in their possession, in which was explained the whole theology of angels, their different orders, etc., etc. The Curds, too (as Hyde mentions in his Appendix), have a book, which contains all the rites of their religion, and which they call Sohuph Sheit, or the Book of Seth.

In the same manner that Seth and Cham are supposed to have preserved these memorials of antediluvian knowledge, Xixuthrus is said in Chaldæan fable to have deposited in Siparis, the city of the Sun, those monuments of science which he had saved out of the waters of a deluge.—See Jablonski's learned remarks upon these columns or tablets of Seth, which he supposes to be the same with the pillars of Mercury, or the Ægyptian Thoth.—*Pantheon. Egypt*, lib. v., cap. 5.

2) The place in this line now occupied by Seth was, in former editions, filled up by *Cham*, and the passage illustrated by the following note :—

"The pillars of Seth are usually referred to as the depositories of antediluvian knowledge but they were inscribed with none but astronomical secrets. I have, therefore, preferred here the tablets of Cham, as being, at least, more miscellaneous in their information. The following account of them is given in Jablonski from Cassianus · — "Quantum enim antiquæ traditiones ferunt Cham filius Noæ, qui superstitionibus ac profanis fuerit artibus institutus, sciens nullum se posse superbis memorialem librum in arcam inferre, in quam erat ingressurus, sacrilegas artes ac profana commenta durissimis insculpsit lapidibus."—P. E.

3 Pachymer, in his Paraphrase on the Book *de Divinis Nominibus* of Dionysius, speaking of the incarnation of

Christ, says, that it was a mystery ineffable from all time, and "unknown even to the first and *oldest* angel,"—justifying this last phrase by the authority of St. John in the Revelation.—P. E.

(4 See the 13th chapter of Dionysius for his notions of the manner in which God's ray is communicated, first to the Intelligences near him, and then to those more remote, gradually losing its own brightness as it passes into a denser medium —προσβαλλουσα δε ταις παχυτεραις υλαις, αμυδροτεραν εχει της διαδοτικην επιφανειων.—P. E.

(5) The Mussulmans, says D'Herbelot, apply the general name, Mocarreboun, to all those Spirits "qui approchent le plus près le trône." Of this number are Mikaïl and Gebraïl.

6) The Seraphim, or Spirits of Divine Love. There appears to be, among writers on the East, as well as among the Orientals themselves, considerable indecision with regard to the respective claims of Seraphim and Cherubim to the highest rank in the celestial hierarchy. The derivation which Hyde assigns to the word *Cherub* seems to determine the precedence in favour of that order of spirits—Cherubim, *i. e.* Propinqui Angeli, qui sc. Deo proprius quam alii accedunt, nam *Charab*, est *i. q. Karab*, appropinquare." (P. 263) Al Beidawi, too, one of the commentators of the Koran, on that passage, "the angels, who bear the throne, and those who stand about it," chap. xl.) says, "These are the Cherubim, the highest order of angels." On the other hand, we have seen, in a preceding note, that the Syrians place the sphere in which the Seraphs dwell at the very summit of all the celestial systems; and *even*, among Mahometans, the word Azazil and Mocarreboun (which mean the spirits that stand nearest to the throne of Alla) are indiscriminately applied to both Seraphim and Cherubim.

When some repentant sinner's feet
  First touch'd the threshold of the skies,
Oh then how clearly did the voice
  Of Zaraph above all rejoice!
Love was in every buoyant tone—
  Such love, as only could belong
To the blest angels, and alone
  Could, even from angels, bring such song!

Alas, that it should e'er have been
  In heaven as 't is too often here,
Where nothing fond or bright is seen
  But it hath 'pain and peril near;
Where right and wrong so close resemble,
  That what we take for virtue's thrill
Is often the first downward tremble
  Of the heart's balance unto ill;
Where Love hath not a shrine so pure,
  So holy, but the serpent, Sin,
In moments, even the most secure,
  Beneath his altar may glide in!

So was it with that Angel—such
  The charm that sloped his fall along,
From good to ill, from loving much,
  Too easy lapse, to loving wrong.
Even so that amorous Spirit, bound
  By beauty's spell, where'er 't was found,
From the bright things above the moon
  Down to earth's beaming eyes descended,
Till love for the Creator soon
  In passion for the creature ended.

'T was first at twilight, on the shore
  Of the smooth sea, he heard the lute
And voice of her he loved steal o'er
  The silver waters that lay mute,
As loath, by even a breath, to stay
  The pilgrimage of that sweet lay;
Whose echoes still went on and on,
  Till lost among the light that shone
Far off, beyond the ocean's brim—
  There, where the rich cascade of day
Had o'er the horizon's golden rim,
  Into Elysium roll'd away!
Of God she sung, and of the mild
  Attendant Mercy, that beside
His awful throne for ever smiled,
  Ready, with her white hand, to guide
His bolts of vengeance to their prey—
  That she might quench them on the way!
Of Peace—of that Atoning Love,
Upon whose star, shining above
This twilight world of hope and fear,
  The weeping eyes of Faith are fix'd
So fond, that with their every tear
  The light of that love-star is mix'd!—
All this she sung, and such a soul
  Of piety was in that song,

That the charm'd Angel, as it stole
  Tenderly to his ear, along
Those lulling waters where he lay,
Watching the daylight's dying ray,
Thought 't was a voice from out the wave,
An echo, that some sea-nymph gave
To Eden's distant harmony,
Heard faint and sweet beneath the sea!

Quickly, however, to its source,
Tracking that music's melting course,
He saw upon the golden sand
Of the sea-shore a maiden stand,
Before whose feet the expiring waves
  Flung their last offering with a sigh—
As, in the East, exhausted slaves
  Lay down the far-brought gift and die—
And while her lute hung by her, hush'd,
  As if unequal to the tide
Of song that from her lips still gush'd,
  She raised, like one beatified,
Those eyes, whose light seem'd rather given
  To be adored than to adore—
Such eyes, as may have look'd *from* heaven,
  But ne'er were raised to it before!

Oh Love, Religion, Music (1)—all
  That's left of Eden upon earth—
The only blessings, since the fall
  Of our weak souls, that still recall
  A trace of their high glorious birth—
How kindred are the dreams you bring!
  How Love, though unto earth so prone,
Delights to take Religion's wing,
  When time or grief hath stain'd his own!
How near to Love's beguiling brink
  Too oft entranced Religion lies!
While Music, Music is the link
  They *both* still hold by to the skies,
The language of their native sphere,
Which they had else forgotten here.

How then could Zaraph fail to feel
  That moment's witcheries?—one, so fair,
Breathing out music, that might steal
  Heaven from itself, and rapt in prayer
  That seraphs might be proud to share!
Oh, he *did* feel it, all too well—
  With warmth, that far too dearly cost—
Nor knew he, when at last he fell,
To which attraction, to which spell,
  Love, Music, or Devotion, most
  His soul in that sweet hour was lost.

Sweet was the hour, though dearly won,
  And pure, as aught of earth could be,

(1 "Les Égyptiens disent que la Musique est *sœur de
la Religion.*"—*Voyages de Pythagore*, tom. 1, p. 422.

For then first did the glorious sun
　Before religion's altar see
Two hearts in wedlock's golden tie
　Self-pledged, in love to live and die. (1)
Blest union! by that Angel wove,
　And worthy from such hands to come;
Safe, sole asylum, in which Love,
　When fallen or exiled from above,
　In this dark world can find a home.

And, though the Spirit had transgress'd,
Had, from his stat on 'mong the blest
Won down by woman's smile, allow'd
　Terrestrial passion to breathe o'er
The mirror of his heart, and cloud
　God's image, there so bright before—
Yet never did that Power look down
　On error with a brow so mild;
Never did Justice wear a frown,
　Through which so gently Mercy smiled.
For humble was their love—with awe
　And trembling like some treasure kept,
That was not theirs by holy law—
Whose beauty with remorse they saw,
　And o'er whose preciousness they wept.
Humility that low, sweet root,
From which all heavenly virtues shoot,
Was in the hearts of both—but most
　In Nama's heart, by whom alone
Those charms, for which a heaven was lost,
　Seem'd all unvalued and unknown;
And when her Seraph's eyes she caught,
　And hid hers glowing on his breast,
Even bliss was humbled by the thought—
　"What claim have I to be so blest?"

Still less could maid, so meek, have nursed
Desire of knowledge—that vain thirst,
With which the sex hath all been cursed,
From luckless Eve to her who near
The Tabernacle stole to hear
The secrets of the angels: (2) no—
　To love as her own Seraph loved,
With Faith, the same through bliss and woe—
Faith that, were even its light removed,

Could, like the dial, fix'd remain,
And wait till it shone out again;—
With Patience that, though often bow'd
　By the rude storm, can rise anew,
And Hope that, even from Evil's cloud,
　Sees sunny Good half breaking through!
This deep replying Love, worth more
In heaven than all a Cherub's lore—
This Faith, more sure than aught beside,
Was the sole joy, ambit on, pride
Of her fond heart—the unreasoning scope
　Of a l its views, above, below—
So true she felt it that to hope,
　To trust, is happier than to know.

And thus in humbleness they trod,
Abash'd, but pure before their God;
Nor e'er did earth behold a sight
　So meekly beautiful as they,
When, with the altar's holy light
　Full on their brows, they knelt to pray,
Hand within hand, and side by side,
Two links of love, awhile untied
From the great chain above, but fast
Holding together to the last'—
Two fallen Splendors, (3) from that tree,
Which buds with such eternally, (4)
Shaken to earth, yet keeping all
Their light and freshness in the fall.

Their only punishment, (as wrong,
　However sweet, must bear its brand,)
Their only doom was this—that, long
　As the green earth and ocean stand,
They both shall wander here—the same,
Throughout all time, in heart and frame—
Still looking to that goal sublime,
　Whose light remote, but sure, they see;
Pilgrims of Love, whose way is Time,
　Whose home is in Eternity!
Subject, the while, to all the strife,
True Love encounters in this life—
The wishes, hopes, he breathes in vain;
　The chill, that turns his warmest sighs
　To earthly vapour, ere they rise;

(1) Four lines have been here elided, with the accompanying note—

　　Then first did woman's virgin brow
　　That hymeneal chaplet wear,
　　Which, when it dies, no second vow
　　Can bid a new one bloom out there

In the Cathol c church, when a widow is married, she is not, I believe, allowed to wear flowers on her head. The ancient Romans honoured with a "corona pudicitiæ," or crown of modesty, those who entered but once into the marriage state.—P. E.　　(2) Sara

(3 An allusion to the Sephiroths or Splendors of the Jewish Cabbala, represented as a tree, of which God is the crown or summit.

The Sephiroths are the higher orders of emanative being in the strange and incomprehensible system of the Jew-

ish Cabbala. They are called by various names, Pity, Beauty, etc. etc., and their influences are supposed to act through certain canals, which communicate with each other.

4 The reader may judge of the rationality of this Jewish system by the following explanation of part of the machinery —"Les canaux qui sortent de la Miséricorde et de la force, et qui vont aboutir à la Beauté, sont chargés d'un grand nombre d'anges. Il y en a trente-cinq sur le canal de la Miséricorde, qui recompensent et qui couronnent la vertu des saints,' etc. etc.—For a concise account of the Cabalistic Philosophy, see Enfield's very useful compendium of Brucker.

"On les représente quelquefois sous la figure d'un arbre . . . . l'Ensoph qu'on met au dessus de l'arbre Sephirotique ou des Splendeurs divins, est l'Infini."—L'Histoire des Juifs, liv. ix., 11.

The doubt he feeds on, and the pain
  That in his very sweetness lies :—
Still worse, the illusions that betray
  His footsteps to their shining brink;
That tempt him, on his desert way
  Through the bleak world, to bend and drink,
Where nothing meets his lips, alas—
But he again must sighing pass
On to that far-off home of peace,
In which alone his thirst will cease.

All this they bear, but, not the less,
Have moments rich in happiness—
Blest meetings, after many a day
Of widowhood past far away,
When the loved face again is seen
Close, close, with not a tear between—
Confidings frank, without control,
Pour'd mutually from soul to soul ;
As free from any fear or doubt
As is that light from chill or stain,
The sun into the stars sheds out,
  To be by them shed back again !—
That happy minglement of hearts,
  Where, changed as chemic compounds are,
Each with its own existence parts,
  To find a new one, happier far!
Such are their joys—and, crowning all,
  That blessed hope of the bright hour,
When, happy and no more to fall,
  Their spirits shall, with freshen'd power,
Rise up rewarded for their trust
In Him from whom all goodness springs,
And, shaking off earth's soiling dust
  From their emancipated wings,

Wander for ever through those skies
Of radiance, where Love never dies !

In what lone region of the earth
  These Pilgrims now may roam or dwell,
God, and the Angels, who look forth
  To watch their steps, alone can tell.
But should we, in our wanderings,
  Meet a young pair, whose beauty wants
But the adornment of bright wings,
  To look like heaven's inhabitants—
Who shine where'er they tread, and yet
  Are humble in their earthly lot,
As is the way-side v'olet,
  That shines unseen, and were it not
For its sweet breath would be forgot—
Whose hearts, in every thought, are one,
  Whose voices utter the same wills—
Answering, as Echo doth some tone
  Of fairy music 'mong the hills,
So like itself, we seek in vain
Which is the echo, which the strain—
Whose piety is love, whose love,
  Though close as 't were their souls' embrace,
Is not of earth, but from above—
Like two fair mirrors, face to face,
Whose light, from one to the other thrown,
Is heaven's reflection, not their own—
Should we e'er meet with aught so pure,
So perfect here, we may be sure
'T is Zaraph and his bride we see; (1)
And call young lovers round, to view
The pilgrim pair, as they pursue
Their pathway towards eternity.

THE FUDGES IN ENGLAND;
BEING A SEQUEL TO
"THE FUDGE FAMILY IN PARIS."

PREFACE. (2)

THE name of the country town, in England—a well-known fashionable watering-place—in which the events that gave rise to the following correspondence occurred, is, for obvious reasons, suppressed. The interest attached, however, to the facts and personages of the story, renders it independent of all time and place; and when it is recollected that the whole

(1) Changed from—
  There is but one such pair below ;
  And, as we bless them on their way
  Through the world's wilderness, may say,
  « There Zaraph and his Name go."—P. E.

(2) In the present edition Mr. Moore has prefaced these "Letters" by the following notice — "The only portion of the mass of trifles proceeding from my pen that first found its way to the public eye through any more responsible channel than a newspaper, was the Letters of the Fudge Family in England—a work which was sure,

train of romantic circumstances so fully unfolded in these Letters has passed during the short period which has now elapsed since the great Meetings in Exeter Hall, due credit will, it is hoped, be allowed to the Editor for the rapidity with which he has brought the details before the Public; while, at the same time, any errors that may have been the result of such haste will, he trusts, with equal consideration be pardoned.

from its very nature, to encounter the double risk of being thought dull as a mere sequel, and light and unsafe as touching on follies connected with the name of Religion. Into the question of the comparative dulness of any of my productions, it is not for me, of course, to enter; but to the charge of treating religious subjects irreverently, I shall content myself with replying in the words of Pascal, —'Il y a bien de la différence entre rire de la religion et rire de ceux qui la profanent par leurs opinions extravagantes.'"

LETTER I.

FROM PATRICK MAGAN, ESQ., TO THE REV. RICHARD
———, CURATE OF ———, IN IRELAND.

Who d' ye think we 've got here? — quite reform'd
　from the giddy
Fantastic young thing, that once made such a noise,
Why, the famous Miss Fudge—that delectable Biddy,
　Whom you and I saw once at Paris, when boys,
In the full blaze of bonnets, and ribands, and airs—
　Such a thing as no rainbow hath colours to paint,
Ere time had reduced her to wrinkles and prayers,
　And the Flirt found a decent retreat in the Saint.
Poor "Pa" hath popp'd off—gone, as charity judges,
To some choice Elysium reserved for the Fudges;
And Miss, with a fortune, besides expectations
From some much-revered and much-palsied relations,
Now wants but a husband, with requisites meet—
Age thirty, or thereabouts—stature six feet,
And warranted godly—to make all complete.
Nota bene—a Churchman would suit, if he 's *high*,
But Socinians or Catholics need not apply.

What say you, Dick? does n't this tempt your am-
　bition?
The whole wealth of Fudge, that renown'd man
　of pith,
All brought to the hammer, for Church competition,
　Sole encumbrance, Miss Fudge to be taken there-
　　with.
Think, my boy, for a Curate how glorious a catch!
　While instead of the thousands of souls you *now*
To save Biddy Fudge's is all you need do;　[watch,
And her purse will, meanwhile, be the saving of *you.*

You may ask, Dick, how comes it that I, a poor elf,
Wanting substance even more than your spiritual self,
Should thus generously lay my own claims on the
　shelf,　　　　　　　　　　　　　　　　[yet
When, God knows! there ne'er was young gentleman
So much lack'd an old spinster to rid him from debt,
Or had cogenter reasons than mine to assail her
With tender love-suit—at the suit of his tailor.

But thereby there hangs a soft secret, my friend,
Which thus to your reverend breast I commend:
Miss Fudge hath a niece—such a creature!—with eyes
Like those sparklers that peep out from summer-night
At astronomers-royal, and laugh with delight [skies
To see elderly gentlemen spying all night.
While her figure — oh, bring all the gracefullest
　things　　　　　　　　　　　　　　　[wings,
That are borne through the light air by feet or by

(1) That floor which a facetious garreteer called "le
premier en descendant du ciel.'

(2 See the *Dublin Evening Post,* of the 9th of this month
(July , for an account of a scene which lately took place at
a meeting of the Synod of Ulster, in which the performance
of the above-mentioned part by the personage in question
appears worthy of all his former reputation in that line.

Not a single new grace to that form could they teach,
　Which combines in itself the perfection of each;
While, rapid or slow, as her fairy feet fall,
The mute music of symmetry modulates all.

Ne'er, in short, was there creature more form'd to be-
　A gay youth like me, who of castles aërial [wilder
　(And *only* of such) am, God help me! a builder;
Still peopling each mansion with lodgers ethereal,
And now, to this nymph of the seraph-like eye,
Letting out, as you see, my first floor next the
　　　　　　　　　　　　　　　　　　　[sky. (1)
But, alas! nothing 's perfect on earth—even she,
　This divine little gipsy, does odd things sometimes;
Talks learning—looks wise (rather painful to see),
　Prints already 'n two county papers her rhymes;
And raves—the sweet, charming, absurd little dear!
About *Amulets, Bijous,* and *Keepsakes,* next year,
In a manner which plainly bad symptoms portends
Of that Annual *blue* fit, so distressing to friends;
A fit which, though lasting but one short edition,
Leaves the patient long after in sad inanition,

However, let 's hope for the best—and, meanwhile,
Be it mine still to bask in the niece's warm smile:
While you, if you 're wise, Dick, will play the gallant
　(Uphill work, I confess,) to her Saint of an Aunt.
Think, my boy, for a youngster like you, who 've a
　Not indeed of rupees, but of all other specie, [lack,
　What luck thus to find a kind witch at your back,
An old goose with gold eggs, from all debts to
　release ye!
Never mind, though the spinster be reverend and thin,
　What are all the Three Graces to her Three per Cents.'
While her acres!—oh Dick, it don't matter one pin
　How she touches the affections, so *you* touch the
　rents;　　　　　　　　　　　　　　　[him, he
And Love never looks half so pleased as when, bless
Sings to an old lady's purse "Open, Sesame."

By the way, I 've just heard, in my walks, a report,
　Which, if true, will insure for your visit some sport,
'T is rumour'd our Manager means to bespeak
The Church tumblers from Exeter Hall for next week;
And certainly ne'er did a queerer or rummer set
Throw, for the amusement of Christians, a summerset.
'T is fear'd their chief "Merriman," C—ke, cannot
　come,
Being called off, at present, to play Punch at home; (2)
And the loss of so practised a wag in divinity
Will grieve much all lovers of jokes on the Trinity;—
His pun on the name Unigenitus, lately　　[ly. (3)
Having pleased Robert Taylor, the *Reverend,* great-

(3) "All are punsters if they have wit to be so; and there-
fore when an Irishman has to commence with a Bull, you
will naturally pronounce it a *bull.* (A laugh.) Allow me
to bring before you the famous Bull that is called Uni-
genitus, referring to the only begotten Son of God."—
Report of the Rev Doctor's Speech, June 20, *in the Record
Newspaper*

'T will prove a sad drawback, if absent he be,
As a wag Presbyterian 's a thing quite to see;
And, 'mong the Five Points of the Calvinists, none
Ever yet reckon'd a point of wit one of 'em. [of 'em
But even though deprived of this comical elf,
We 've a host of *buffoni* in Murtagh himself,
Who of all the whole troop is chief mummer and mime,
As C—ke takes the *Ground* Tumbling, *he* the *Sub-
     lime;* (1)
And of him we 're quite certain, so, pray, come in time.

—◦❦◦—

LETTER II.

FROM MISS BIDDY FUDGE, TO MRS.
ELIZABETH ———.

Just in time for the post, dear, and monstrously busy,
   With godly concernments—and worldly ones, too,
Things carnal and spiritual mix'd, my dear Lizzy,
   In this little brain till, bewilder'd and dizzy,
'Twixt heaven and earth, I scarce know what I do.

First, I've been to see all the gay fashions from Town,
   Which our favourite Miss Gimp for the Spring has
      had down.
Sleeves *still* worn (which *I* think is wise), *à la folle*,
Charming hats, *pou de soie*—though the shape rather
   droll.
But you can't think how nicely the caps of *tulle* lace,
With the *mentonnières*, look on this poor sinful face;
And I mean, if the Lord in his mercy thinks right,
To wear one at Mrs. Fitz-wigram's to-night.
The silks are quite heavenly:—I 'm glad, too, to say,
Gimp herself grows more godly and good every day;
Hath had sweet experience—yea, even doth begin
To turn from the Gentiles, and put away sin—
And all since her last stock of goods was laid in.
What a blessing one's milliner, careless of pelf,
Should thus " walk in newness" as well as one's self!

So much for the blessings, the comforts of Spirit
I 've had since we met, and they 're more than I
   merit!—
Poor, sinful, weak creature in every respect, [Elect.
Though ordain'd (God knows why) to be one of the
But now for the picture's reverse.—You remember
That footman and cook-maid I hired last December;
He, a Baptist Particular—*she*, of some sect
Not particular, I fancy, in any respect;

(1) In the language of the play-bills, " Ground and Lofty
Tumbling."
(2) "Morning Manna, or British Verse-book, neatly done
up for the pocket," and chiefly intended to assist the mem-
bers of the British Verse Association, whose design is, we
are told, " to induce the inhabitants of Great Britain and
Ireland to commit one and the same verse of Scripture to
memory every morning. Already, it is known, several
thousand persons in Scotland, besides tens of thousands
in America and Africa, are *every morning learning the
same verse.*"
(3) *The Evangelical Magazine.*—A few specimens taken
at random from the wrapper of this highly-esteemed pe-

But desirous, poor thing, to be fed with the Word,
And "to wait," as she said, " on Miss Fudge and the
   Lord. "

Well, my dear, of all men, that Particular Baptist
At preaching a sermon. off hand, was the aptest;
And, long as he staid, do him justice, more rich in
Sweet savours of doctrine, there never was kitchen.
He preach'd in the parlour, he preach'd in the hall,
He preach'd to the chambermaids, scullions, and all.
   All heard with delight his reprovings of sin,
But above all, the cook-maid;—oh, ne'er would she
   tire—
Though, in learning to save sinful souls from the fire
   She would oft let the soles she was frying fall in.
(God forgive me for punning on points thus of piety—
A sad trick I've learn'd in Bob's heathen society.)
But ah! there remains still the worst of my tale;
Come, Ast'risks, and help me the sad truth to veil—
Conscious stars, that at even your own secret turn
   pale!
   .   .   .   .   .   .

In short, dear, this preaching and psalm-singing pair,
Chosen "vessels of mercy," as *I* thought they were,
Have together this last week eloped, making bold
To whip off as much goods as both vessels could hold—
Not forgetting some scores of sweet Tracts from my
   shelves,
Two Family Bibles as large as themselves,
And besides, from the drawer—I neglecting to lock
   it—
My neat " Morning Manna, done up for the pocket." (2)
Was there e'er known a case so distressing, dear Liz?
It has made me quite ill :—and the worst of it is,
When rogues are *all* pious, 'tis hard to detect
Which rogues are the reprobate, *which* the elect.
This man " had a *call*," he said—impudent mockery!
What call had he to *my* linen and crockery?

I 'm now, and have been for this week past, in chase
Of some godly young couple this pair to replace.
The inclosed two announcements have just met my
   eyes,
In that venerable Monthly where Saints advertise
For such temporal comforts as this world supplies; (3)
And the fruits of the Spirit are properly made
An essential in every craft, calling, and trade;

riodical will fully justify the character which Miss Fudge
has here given of it. "Wanted, in a pious pawnbroker's
family, an active lad as an apprentice." "Wanted, as
housemaid, a young female who has been brought to a
saving knowledge of the truth." "Wanted immediately,
a man of decided piety, to assist in the baking business."
"A gentleman who understands the Wine Trade is desirous
of entering into partnership, etc. etc. He is not desirous
of being connected with any one whose system of business
is not of the strictest integrity as in the sight of God, and
seeks connection only with a truly pious man, either
Churchman or Dissenter."

Where the attorney requires for his 'prentice some
youth
Who has "learn'd to fear God and to walk in the
truth;"
Where the sempstress, in search of employment,
declares,
That pay is no object, so she can have prayers;
And the Establish'd Wine Company proudly gives out
That the whole of the firm, Co. and all, are devout.

Happy London, one feels, as one reads o'er the pages,
Where Saints are so much more abundant than sages;
Where Parsons may soon be all laid on the shelf,
As each Cit can cite chapter and verse for himself,
And the *serious* frequenters of market and dock
All lay in religion as part of their stock. (1)
Who can tell to what lengths we may go on improving,
When thus through all London the Spirit keeps
moving,
And heaven 's so in vogue, that each shop adver*tise*-
ment
Is now not so much for the earth as the skies meant?

P. S.

Have mislaid the two paragraphs—can't stop to look,
But both describe charming—both Footman and
Cook.
She, "decidedly pious"—with pathos deplores
The increase of French cookery, and sin on our
shores;
And adds—(while for further accounts she refers
To a great Gospel preacher, a cousin of hers,)
That "though *some* make their Sabbaths mere
matter-of-fun days,
She asks but for tea and the Gospel, on Sundays."
The footman, too, full of the true saving knowledge,
Has late been to Cambridge—to Trinity College;
Served last a young gentleman, studying divinity,
But left—not approving the morals of Trinity.

P. S.

I inclose, too, according to promise, some scraps
Of my Journal—that Day-book I keep of my heart,
Where, at some little items, (partaking, perhaps,
More of earth than of heaven,) thy prudery may
start,
And suspect something tender, sly girl as thou art.
For the present, I 'm mute—but, whate'er may befall,
Recollect, dear, (in Hebrews, xiii., 4.) St. Paul
Hath himself declared, "marriage is honourable in
all."

(1 According to the late Mr. Irving, there is even a pe-
culiar form of theology got up expressly for the money-
market. "I know how far wide,' he says, "of the mark
my views of Christ's work in the flesh will be viewed by
those who are working with the stock-jobbing theology of
the religious world " "Let these preachers," he adds,
"(for I will not call them theologians), cry up, broker-
like, their article."—*Morning Watch.*—No. iii, 442, 443.
From the statement of another writer, in the same pub-
lication, it would appear that the stock-brokers have

EXTRACTS FROM MY DIARY.
Monday.

Tried a new châlé gown on—pretty.
No one to see me in it—pity!
Flew in a passion with Fritz, my maid;—
The Lord forgive me!—she look'd dismay'd;
But got her to sing the 100th Psalm,
While she curl'd my hair, which made me calm.
Nothing so soothes a Christian heart
As sacred music—heavenly art!

Tuesday

At two, a visit from Mr. Magan—
A remarkably handsome nice young man,
And, all Hibernian though he be,
As civilised, strange to say, as we!

I own this young man's spiritual state
Hath much engross'd my thoughts of late;
And I mean, as soon as my niece is gone,
To have some talk with him thereupon.
At present, I nought can do or say,
But that troublesome child is in the way:
Nor is there, I think, a doubt that he
Would also her absence much prefer,
As oft, while listening intent to me,
He 's forced, from politeness, to look at her.

Heigho!—what a blessing should Mr. Magan
Turn out, after all, a "renew'd" young man;
And to me should fall the task, on earth,
To assist at the dear youth's second birth.
Blest thought! and, ah, more blest the tie,
Were it heaven's high will, that he and I—
But I blush to write the nuptial word—
Should wed, as St. Paul says, "in the Lord;"
Not *this* world's wedlock—gross, gallant,
But pure—as when Amram married his aunt.

Our ages differ—but who would count
One's natural sinful life's amount,
Or look in the Register's vulgar page
For a regular twice-born Christian's age,
Who, blessed privilege! only then
Begins to live when he's born again.
And, counting in *this* way—let me see—
I myself but five years old shall be,
And dear Magan, when the event takes place,
An actual new-born child of grace—
Should Heaven in mercy so dispose—
A six-foot baby in *swaddling* clothes.

even set up a new Divinity of their own. "This shows,"
says the writer in question, "that the doctrine of the
union between Christ and his members is quite as essential
as that of substitution, by taking which latter alone the
Stock-Exchange Divinity has been produced."—No. x.,
p. 375.

Among the ancients, we know the money-market was
provided with more than one presiding Deity.— "Deæ
Pecuniæ (says an ancient author) commendabantur ut pe-
cuniosi essent."

Wednesday.

Finding myself, by some good fate,
With Mr. Magan left *tête-à-tête*,
Had just begun—having stirr'd the fire,
And drawn my chair near his—to inquire
What his notions were of Original Sin,
When that naughty Fanny again bounced in;
And all the sweet things I had got to say
Of the Flesh and the Devil were whisk'd away!

Much grieved to observe that Mr. Magan
Is actually pleased and amused with Fan!
What charms any sensible man can see
In a child so foolishly young as she—
But just eighteen, come next May-day,
With eyes, like herself, full of nought but play—
Is, I own, an exceeding puzzle to me.

—◦❊◦—

LETTER III.

FROM MISS FANNY FUDGE, TO HER COUSIN,
MISS KITTY ———.

STANZAS (INCLOSED)

TO MY SHADOW; OR, WHY?—WHAT?—HOW?

Dark comrade of my path! while earth and sky
Thus wed their charms, in bridal light array'd,
Why in this bright hour, walk'st thou ever nigh,
Blackening my footsteps with thy length of shade—
            Dark comrade, Why?

Thou mimic Shape that, 'mid these flowery scenes,
Glidest beside me o'er each sunny spot,
Saddening them as thou goest—say, what means
So dark an adjunct to so bright a lot—
            Grim goblin, What?

Still, as to pluck sweet flowers I bend my brow,
Thou bendest, too—then risest when I rise;—
Say, mute mysterious Thing! how is't that thou
Thus comest between me and those blessed skies—
            Dim shadow, How?

(ADDITIONAL STANZA, BY ANOTHER HAND.)

Thus said I to that Shape, far less in grudge
Than gloom of soul; while, as I eager cried,
Oh Why? What? How?—a Voice, that one might
To be some Irish echo's, faint replied,   [judge
            Oh fudge, fadge, fudge!

You have here, dearest Coz, my last lyric effusion;
And with it, that odious "additional stanza,"
Which Aunt *will* insist I must keep, as conclusion,
And which, you'll *at once* see, is Mr. Magan's;—a
Most cruel and dark-design'd extravaganza,
And part of that plot in which he and my Aunt are
To stifle the flights of my genius by banter.

Just so 't was with Byron's young eagle-eyed strain,
Just so did they taunt him;—but vain, critics, vain
All your efforts to saddle Wit's fire with a chain!

To blot out the splendour of Fancy's young stream,
Or crop, in its cradle, her newly-fledged beam!!!
Thou perceivest, dear, that, even while these lines I
            indite,
Thoughts burn, brilliant fancies break out, wrong or
            r'ght,
And I'm all over poet, in Criticism's spite!

That my Aunt, who deals only in Psalms, and regards
Messrs. Sternhold and Co. as the first of all bards—
That *she* should make light of my works I can't
            blame;
But that nice, handsome, odious Magan—what a
            shame!
Do you know, dear, that, high as on most points I
            rate him,
I'm really afraid—after all, I—*must* hate him.
He is *so* provoking—nought's safe from his tongue,
He spares no one authoress, ancient or young.
Where you Sappho herself, and in *Keepsake* or *Byou*
Once shown as contributor, Lord how he'd quiz you
He laughs at *all* Monthlies—I've actually seen
A sneer on his brow at the *Court Magazine!*—
While of Weeklies, poor things, there's but one he
            peruses,
And buys every book which that Weekly abuses.
But I care not how others such sarcasm may fear,
One spirit, at least, will not bend to his sneer;
And, though tried by the fire, my young genius shall
            burn as
Uninjured as crucified gold in the furnace!
(I suspect the word "crucified" must be made
            "crucible,"
Before this fine image of mine is producible.)

And now, dear—to tell you a secret which, pray
Only trust to such friends as with safety you may—
You know, and, indeed the whole county suspects
(Though the Editor often my best things rejects),
That the verses sign'd so ⟨⟩, which you now and
            then see
In our *County Gazette* (vide *last*) are by me.
But 't is dreadful to think what provoking mistakes
The vile country Press in one's prosody makes.
For you know, dear—I may, without vanity, hint—
Though an angel should write, still 't is *devils* must
            print;
And you can't think what havoc these demons
            sometimes
Choose to make of one's sense, and, what's worse,
            of one's rhymes.
But a week or two since, in my Ode upon Spring,
Which I *meant* to have made a most beautiful thing,
Where I talk'd of the "dewdrops from freshly-
            blown roses,"
The nasty things made it "from freshly-blown
            noses!"
And once when, to please my cross Aunt, I had tried
To commem'rate some saint of her *clique*, who'd
            just died,

Having said he " had taken up in heaven his position,"
They made it, he 'd " taken up to heaven his phy-
sician !"

This is very disheartening ;—but brighter days shine,
I rejoice, love, to say both for me and the Nine ;
For, what do you think ?—so delightful ! next year,
  Oh ! prepare, dearest girl, for the grand news
    prepare—
I 'm to write in the *Keepsake*—yes, Kitty, my dear,
  To write in the *Keepsake*, as sure as you 're
    there ! !
T' other night, at a Ball, 't was my fortunate chance
With a very nice elderly Dandy to dance,
Who, 't was plain from some hints which I now and
    then caught,
Was the author of *something*—one could n't tell
    what ;
But his satisfied manner left no room to doubt
It was something that Colburn had lately brought out.

We conversed of *belles-lettres* through all the
    quadrille—
Of poetry, dancing ; of prose, standing still ;
Talk'd of Intellect's march—whether right 't was or
    wrong—
And then settled the point in a bold *en avant*.
In the course of this talk 't was that, having just
    hinted
That *I* too had Poems which long'd to be printed,
He protested, kind man ! he had seen at first sight,
I was actually *born* in the *Keepsake* to write.
" In the Annals of England let some," he said,
    " shine,
But a place in her Annuals, Lady, be thine !
Even now future *Keepsakes* seem brightly to rise,
Through the vista of years, as I gaze on those eyes—
All letter'd and press'd, and of large-paper size !"
How un*like* that Magan, who my genius would
    smother,
And how we, true geniuses, find out each other !

This and much more he said, with that fine frenzied
    glance
One so rarely now sees, as we slid through the dance ;
Till between us 't was finally fix'd that, next year,
  In this exquisite task I my pen should engage ;
And, at parting, he stoop'd down and lisp'd in my ear
  These mystical words, which I could but *just* hear,
  " Terms for rhyme—if it 's *prime*—ten and six-
    pence per page."
Think, Kitty, my dear, if I heard his words right,
  What a mint of half-guineas this small head
    contains ;
If for nothing to write is itself a delight,
  Ye gods, what a bliss to be paid for one's strains !

(1) With regard to the exact time of this event, there
appears to be a difference only of about two or three years
among the respective calculators. M. Alphonse Nicole,
docteur en droit et avocat, merely doubts whether it is

Having dropp'd the dear fellow a curtsey profound,
  Off at once, to inquire all about him, I ran ;
And from what I could learn, do you know. dear,
    I 've found
  That he 's quite a new species of literary man ;
One whose task is—to what will not fashion accus-
    tom us ?—
To *edite* live authors, as if they were posthumous.
For instance—the plan, to be sure, is the oddest !—
If any young he or she author feels modest
In venturing abroad, this kind gentleman usher
Lends promptly a hand to the interesting blusher ;
Indites a smooth Preface, brings merit to light,
Which else might, by accident, shrink out of sight,
And, in short, renders readers and critics polite.
My Aunt says—though scarce on such points one can
    credit her—
He was Lady Jane Thingumbob's last novel's editor.
'T is certain the fashion 's but newly invented ;
  And, quick as the change of all things and all
    names is,
Who knows but, as authors, like girls, are *presented*,
We, girls, may be *edited* soon at James's ?

I must now close my letter—there 's Aunt, in full
    screech,
Wants to take me to hear some great Irvingite preach.
God forgive me, I 'm not much inclined, I must say,
To go and sit still to be preach'd at, to-day.
And, besides—'t will be all against dancing, no doubt,
Which my poor Aunt abhors, with such hatred devout,
That so far from presenting young nymphs with a
    head,
For their skill in the dance, as of Herod is said,
She 'd wish their own heads in the platter, instead.
There, again—coming, Ma'am !—I 'll write more, if
    I can,
Before the post goes,
                Your affectionate Fan.

                        Four o'clock.
Such a sermon !—though *not* about dancing, my dear ;
'T was only on the end of the world being near.
Eighteen Hundred and Forty 's the year that some state
As the time for that accident—some Forty-eight :(1)
And I own, of the two, I 'd prefer much the latter,
As then I shall be an old maid, and 't won't matter,
Once more, love, good-bye—I 've to make a new cap ;
But am now so dead tired with this horrid mishap
Of the end of the world, that I *must* take a nap.

———◦∙◦◦———
LETTER IV.
FROM PATRICK MAGAN, ESQ., TO THE REV.
RICHARD ———.

HE comes from Erin's speechful shore
Like fervid kettle, bubbling o'er

to be in 1846 or 1847. "A cette epoque," he says, " les
fidèles peuvent espérer de voir s'effectuer la purification
du sanctuaire."

With hot effusions—hot and weak ;
Sound, Humbug, all your hollowest drums,
He comes, of Erin's martyrdoms
    To Britain's well-fed Church to speak.

Puff him, ye Journals of the Lord, (1)
Twin prosers, *Watchman* and *Record!*
Journals reserved for realms of bliss,
Being much too good to sell in this.
Prepare, ye wealthier Saints, your dinners,
    Ye Spinsters, spread your tea and crumpets ,
And you, ye countless Tracts for Sinners,
    Blow all your little penny trumpets.
He comes, the reverend man, to·tell
    To all who still the Church's part take,
Tales of parsonic woe, that well
    Might make even grim Dissenter's heart ache :—
Of ten whole Bishops snatch'd away
For ever from the light of day ;
(With God knows, too, how many more,
For whom that doom is yet in store)—
Of Rectors cruelly compell'd
    From Bath and Cheltenham to haste home,
Because the tithes, by Pat withheld,
    Will *not* to Bath or Cheltenham come ;
Nor will the flocks consent to pay
Their parsons thus to stay away ;
Though, with *such* parsons, one may doubt
If 't is n't money well laid out ;—
Of all, in short, and each degree
Of that once happy Hierarchy,
    Which used to roll in wealth so pleasantly ;
But now, alas, is doom'd to see
    Its surplus brought to nonplus presently !

Such are the themes this man of pathos,
Priest of prose and Lord of bathos,
    Will preach and preach t' ye, till you 're dull
    again ;
Then, hail him, Saints, with joint acclaim,
Shout to the stars his tuneful name,
Which Murtagh *was*, ere known to fame,
    But now is *Mortimer* O'Mulligan !

All true, Dick, true as you 're alive—
I 've seen him, some hours since, arrive.
Murtagh is come, the great Itinerant—
    And Tuesday, in the market-place,
Intends to every saint and sinner in't,
    To state what *he* calls Ireland's Case ;
Meaning thereby the case of *his* shop—
Of curate, vicar, rector, bishop,
And all those other grades seraphic,
That make men's souls their special traffic,
Though caring not a pin *which* way
The erratic souls go, so they *pay*.—
Just as some roguish country nurse,
    Who takes a foundling babe to suckle,
First pops the payment in her purse,
    Then leaves poor dear to—suck its knuckle :

Even so these reverend rigmaroles
Pocket the money—starve the souls.
Murtagh, however, in his glory,
Will tell next week a different story ;
Will make out all these men of barter,
As each a saint, a downright martyr,
Brought to the *stake*—i. e. a *beef* one,
Of all their martyrdoms the chief one ;
Though try them even at this, they 'll bear it,
If tender and wash'd down with claret.
Meanwhile Miss Fudge, who loves all lions,
Your saintly, *next* to great and high 'uns—
(A Viscount, be he what he may,
Would cut a Saint out, any day,)
Has just announced a godly rout,
Where Murtagh 's to be first brought out,
And shown in his tame *week-day* state.—
" Prayers, half-past seven, tea at eight."
Even so the circular missive orders—
Pink cards, with cherubs round the borders.

Haste, Dick—you 're lost, if you lose time ;
    Spinsters at forty-five grow giddy,
And Murtagh, with his tropes sublime,
    Will surely carry off old Biddy,
Unless some spark at once propose,
And distance him by downright prose.
That sick rich squire, whose wealth and lands
All pass, they say, to Biddy's hands,
(The patron, Dick, of three fat rectories !)
Is dying of *angina pectoris ;*—
So that, unless you 're stirring soon,
    Murtagh, that priest of puff and pelf,
May come in for a honey-*moon*,
    And be the *man* of it, himself !

As for *me*, Dick—'t is whim, 't is folly,
But this young niece absorbs me wholly.
'T is true, the girl 's a vile verse-maker—
    Would rhyme all nature, if you 'd let her ;—
But even her oddities, plague take her,
    But make me love her all the better.
Too true it is, she 's bitten sadly
With this new rage for rhyming badly,
Which late hath seized all ranks and classes,
Down to that new Estate, " the masses ; "
    Till one pursuit all tastes combines—
One common rail-road o'er Parnassus,
    Where, sliding in whose tuneful grooves,
Call'd couplets, all creation moves,
    And the whole world runs mad *in lines.*
Add to all this—what 's even still worse,
As rhyme itself, though still a curse,
    Sounds better to a chinking purse—
Scarce sixpence hath my charmer got,
While I can muster just a groat ;
So that computing self and Venus,
Ten-pence would clear the amount between us.

(1   "Our anxious desire is to be found on the side of
the Lord."—*Record Newspaper*

However, things may yet prove better:—
Meantime, what awful length of letter!
And how, while heaping thus with gibes
The Pegasus of modern scribes,
My own small hobby of farrago
Hath beat the pace at which even *they* go!

—◦⊶◦—

LETTER V.

FROM LARRY O'BRANIGAN, IN ENGLAND, TO HIS WIFE
JUDY, AT MULLINAFAD.

DEAR Judy, I sind you this bit of a letther,
By mail-coach conveyance—for want of a betther—
To tell you what luck in this world I have had
Since I left the sweet cabin, at Mullinafad.
Och, Judy, that night!—when the pig which we
    meant
To dry-nurse in the parlour, to pay off the rent,
Julianna, the craythur—that name was the death
    of her—(1)
Gave us the shlip, and we saw the last breath of her!
And *there* were the childher, six innocent sowls,
For their nate little play-fellow tuning up howls;
While yourself, my dear Judy (though grievin's a
    folly ,
Stud over Julianna's remains, melancholy—
Cryin', half for the craythur, and half for the money,
"Arrah, why did ye die till we'd sowld you, my
    honey?"

But God's will be done!—and then, faith, sure
    enough,
As the pig was desaiced 't was high time to be off.
So we gother'd up all the poor duds we could catch,
Lock'd the owld cabin-door, put the kay in the thatch,
Then tuk leave of each other's sweet lips in the dark,
And set off, like the Christians turn'd out of the Ark:
The six childher with you, my dear Judy, ochone!
And poor I wid myself, left condolin' alone.

How I came to this England, o'er say and o'er lands,
And what cruel hard walkin' I've had on my hands,
Is, at this present writin', too tadious to speak,
So I'll mintion it all in a postscript next week :—
Only starved I was, surely, as thin as a lath,
Till I came to an up-and-down place they call Bath,
Where, as luck was, I managed to make a meal's
    meat,
By dhraggin' owld ladies all day through the street—
Which their docthors (who pocket, like fun, the
    pound starlins,)
Have brought into fashion to please the owld darlins.
Div'l a boy in all Bath, though *I* say it, could carry
The grannies up hill half so handy as Larry;
And the higher they lived, like owld crows in the air,
The more *I* was wanted to lug them up there.

But luck has two handles, dear Judy, they say,
And mine has *both* handles put on the wrong way.

(1) The Irish peasantry are very fond of giving fine
names to their p gs. I have heard of one instance in

For ponderin', one morn, on a drame I'd just had
Of yourself and the babbies, at Mullinafad,
Och, there came o'er my sinses so plasin' a flutther,
That I spilt an owld Countess right clane in the
    gutther,
Muff, feathers and all!—the discint was most awful,
And—what was still worse, faith—I knew 't was un-
    lawful:
For, though, with mere *women*, no very great evil,
T' upset an owld *Countess* in Bath is the divil!
So, liftin' the chair, with herself safe upon it,
(For nothing about her was kilt, but her bonnet,)
Without even mentionin' "By your lave, ma'am,"
I tuk to my heels, and—here, Judy, I am!

What's the name of this town I can't say very well,
But your heart sure will jump when you hear what
    befell
Your own beautiful Larry, the very first day,
(And a Sunday it was, shinin' out mighty gay,)
When his brogues to this city of luck found their way.
Bein' hungry, God help me, and happenin' to stop
Just to dine on the shmell of a pasthry-cook's shop,
I saw in the window a large printed paper,
And read there a name, och! that made my heart
    caper—
Though printed it was in some quare A B C,
That might bother a schoolmaster, let alone *me*.
By gor, you'd have laugh'd, Judy, could you 've but
    listen'd,
As, doubtin', I cried, "why, it *is!*—no, it *isn't;*
But it *was*, after all—for, by spellin' quite slow,
First I made out "Rev. Mortimer"—then a great
    "O;"
And, at last, by hard readin' and rackin' my skull
    again,
Out it came, nate as imported, "O'Mulligan!"

Up I jump'd, like a sky-lark, my jew'l, at that name—
Div'l a doubt on my mind, but it *must* be the same.
"Masther Murthagh, himself," says I, "all the
    world over!
My own fosther-brother—by jinks, I'm in clover.
Though *there*, in the play-bill, he figures so grand,
One wet-nurse it was brought us *both* up by hand,
And he'll not let me shtarve in the inemy's land!"

Well, to make a long hishtory short, niver doubt
But I managed, in no time, to find the lad out;
And the joy of the meetin' bethuxt him and me,
Such a pair of owld cumrogues—was charmin' to see.
Nor is Murthagh less plas'd with the evint than *I* am,
As he just then was wanting a Valley-de-sham;
And, for *dressin'* a gintleman, one way or t' other,
Your nate Irish lad is beyant every other.

But now, Judy, comes the quare part of the case;
And, in throth, it 's the only drawback on my place.

which a couple of young pigs were named, at their birth,
Abelard and Eloisa.

'T was Murthagh's ill luck to be cross'd, as you know,
With an awkward mishfortune some short time ago;
That's to say, he turn'd Protestant—*why*, I can't
 larn ;
But, of coorse, he knew best, an' it's not *my* consarn.
All I know is, we both were good Cath'lics, at nurse,
And myself am so still—nayther betther nor worse.
Well, our bargain was all right and tight in a jiffey,
And lads more contint never yet left the Liffey,
When Murthagh—or Morthimer, as he's *now*
 chrishen'd,
His *name* being convarted, at lalst, if *he* is n't—
Lookin' sly at me (faith, 't was divartin' to see)
" *Of coorse*, you're a Protestant, Larry," says he.
Upon which says myself, wid a wink just as shly,
" Is 't a Protestant?—oh yes, *I am*, sir," says I ;—
And there the chat ended, and div'l a more word
Controvarsial between us has since then occurr'd.
What Murthagh could mane, and, in troth, Judy
 dear,
What *I myself* meant, does n't seem mighty clear ;
But the thruth is, though still for the Owld Light a
 stickler,
I was just then too shtarv'd to be over partic'lar : —
And, God knows, between us, a comic'ler pair
Of twin Protestants could n't be seen *any* where.

Next Tuesday (as towld in the play-bills I mintion'd,
Address'd to the loyal and godly-intintion'd,)
His riverince, my master, comes forward to preach—
Myself does n't know whether sarmon or speech,
But it's all one to him, he's a dead hand at each ;
Like us, Paddys, in gin'ral, whose skill in orations
Quite bothers the blarney of all other nations.

But, whisht!—there's his Riverince, shoutin' out
 " Larry,"
And sorra a word more will this shmall paper carry,
So, here, Judy, ends my short bit of a letther,
Which, faix, I'd have made a much bigger and betther,
But div'l a one Post-office hole in this town
Fit to swallow a dacent sized-billy-dux down.
So good luck to the childer!—tell Molly, I love her ;
Kiss Oonagh's sweet mouth, and kiss Katty all over—
Not forgettin' the mark of the red-currant whiskey
She got at the fair when yourself was so frisky.
The heavens be your bed!—I will write, when I can
 again,
Yours to the world's end,
                              LARRY O'BRANIGAN.
                    ──◦◦◦◦──
                    LETTER VI.
              FROM MISS BIDDY FUDGE, TO MRS.
              ELIZABETH ———.

How I grieve you 're not with us !—pray come, if
 you can,
Ere we 're robb'd of this dear oratorical man,
Who combines in himself all the multiple glory
Of Orangeman, Saint, *quondam* Papist, and Tory ;—

(Choice mixture! like that from which, duly con-
 founded,
The best sort of *brass* was, in old times, com-
 pounded)—
The sly and the saintly, the worldly and godly,
All fused down in brogue so deliciously oddly!
In short, he's a *dear*—and *such* audiences draws,
Such loud peals of laughter and shouts of applause,
As *can't* but do good to the Protestant cause.

Poor dear Irish Church !—he to-day sketch'd a view
Of her history and prospects, to *me* at least new,
And which (if it *takes* as it ought) must arouse
The whole Christian world her just rights to espouse.
As to *reasoning*—you know, dear, that 's now of no use,
People still will their *facts* and dry *figures* produce,
As if saving the souls of a Protestant flock were
A thing to be managed " according to Cocker !"
In vain do we say, (when rude radicals hector
At paying some thousands a-year to a Rector,
In places where Protestants *never yet were*,)
" Who knows but young Protestants *may* be born
 there ?
And, granting such accident, think, what a shame,
If they did n't find Rector and Clerk when they came!
It is clear that, without such a staff on full pay,
These little Church embryos *must* go astray ;
And, while fools are computing what Parsons would
 cost,
Precious souls are meanwhile to the Establishment
 lost !"
In vain do we put the case sensibly thus ;—
They 'll still with their figures and facts make a fuss,
And ask " if, while all, choosing each his own road,
Journey on, as we can, towards the Heavenly Abode,
It is right that *seven* eighths of the travellers should
 pay
For *one* eighth that goes quite a different way ?"—
Just as if, foolish people, this wasn't, in reality,
A proof of the Church's extreme liberality,
That, though hating Popery in *other* respects,
She to Catholic *money* in no way objects ;
And so liberal her very best Saints, in this sense,
That they even go to heaven at the Catholic's expense.

But, though clear to *our* minds all these arguments be,
People cannot or *will* not their cogency see ;
And, I grieve to confess, did the poor Irish Church
Stand on reasoning alone, she 'd be left in the lurch.
It was therefore, dear Lizzy, with joy most sincere,
That I heard this nice Reverend O' *something* we've
 here,
Produce, from the depths of his knowledge and
 reading,
A view of that marvellous Church, far exceeding,
In novelty, force, and profoundness of thought,
All that Irving himself, in his glory, e'er taught.

Looking through the whole history, present and past,
Of the Irish Law Church, from the first to the *last* ;

Considering how strange its original birth—
Such a thing having *never* before been on earth—
How opposed to the instinct, the law, and the force
Of nature and reason has been its whole course ;
Through centuries encountering repugnance, resistance,
Scorn, hate, execration—yet still in existence!
Considering all this, the conclusion he draws
Is that Nature exempts this one Church from her laws—
That Reason, dumb-founder'd, gives up the dispute,
And before the portentous anomaly stands mute ;—
That, in short, 'tis a Miracle!—and, *once* begun,
And transmitted through ages, from father to son,
For the honour of miracles, *ought to go on.*

Never yet was conclusion so cogent and sound,
Or so fitted the Church's weak foes to confound.
For, observe, the more low all her merits they place,
The more they make out the miraculous case,
And the more all good Christians must deem it profane
To disturb such a prodigy's marvellous reign.

As for scriptural proofs, he quite placed beyond doubt
That the whole in the Apocalypse may be found out,
As clear and well-proved, he would venture to swear,
As any thing else has been *ever* found there :—
While the mode in which, bless the dear fellow, he deals
With that whole lot of vials and trumpets and seals,
And the ease with which vial on vial he strings,
Shows him quite a *first-rate* at all these sort of things.

So much for theology :—as for the affairs
Of this temporal world—the light drawing-room cares
And gay toils of the toilet, which, God knows, I seek,
From no love of such things, but in humbleness meek,
And to be, as the Apostle was, "weak with the weak,"
Thou wilt find quite enough (till I 'm somewhat less busy)
In the extracts inclosed, my dear news-loving Lizzy.

EXTRACTS FROM MY DIARY.

Thursday.

Last night, having nought more holy to do,
Wrote a letter to dear Sir Andrew Agnew,
About the "Do-nothing-on-Sunday-Club,"
Which we wish by some shorter name to dub:—
As the use of more vowels and consonants
Than a Christian, on Sunday, *really* wants,
Is a grievance that ought to be done away,
And the Alphabet left to rest, that day.

(1) The title given by the natives to such of their country-
men as become converts.
(2) Of such relapses we find innumerable instances in
the accounts of the Missionaries.

Sunday.

Sir Andrew's answer!—but, shocking to say,
Being frank'd unthinkingly yesterday,
To the horror of Agnews yet unborn,
It arrived on this blessed Sunday morn!!—
How shocking!—the postman's self cried "shame on 't,"
Seeing the immaculate Andrew's name on 't!!
What will the Club do?—meet, no doubt.
'T is a matter that touches the Class Devout,
And the friends of the Sabbath *must* speak out.

Tuesday.

Saw to-day, at the raffle—and saw it with pain—
That those stylish Fitz-wigrams begin to dress plain.
Even gay little Sophy smart trimmings renounces—
She, who long has stood by me through all sorts of flounces,
And show'd, by upholding the toilet's sweet rites,
That we, girls, may be Christians, without being frights.
This, I own, much alarms me ; for though one's religious,
And strict, and—all that, there 's no need to be hideous;
And why a nice bonnet should stand in the way
Of one's going to heaven, 't is n't easy to say.

Then, there 's Gimp, the poor thing—if her custom we drop,
Pray, what 's to become of her soul and her shop?
If by saints like ourselves no more orders are given,
She 'll lose all the interest she now takes in heaven;
And this nice little "fire-brand, pluck'd from the burning,"
May fall in again at the very next turning.

Wednesday.

Mem.—To write to the India-Mission Society ;
And send 20*l.*—heavy tax upon piety !

Of all Indian luxuries we now-a-days boast,
Making "Company's Christians" (1) perhaps costs the most.
And the worst of it is, that these converts full grown,
Having lived in *our* faith, mostly die in their *own*,(2)
Praying hard, at the last, to some god who, they say,
When incarnate on earth, used to steal curds and whey. (3)   [away.;
Think, how horrid, my dear !—so that all 's thrown
And (what is still worse) for the rum and the rice
They consumed, while believers, we saints pay the price.

Still 't is cheering to find that we *do* save a few—
The Report gives six Christians for Cunnangcadoo ;
Doorkotchum reckons seven, and four Trevandrum,
While but one and a half's left at Cooroopadum.

(3) The god Krishna, one of the incarnations of the god
Vishnu. "One day (says the Bhagavata Krishna's play-
fellows complained to Tasuda that he had pilfered and ate
their curds."

In this last-mention'd place 't is the barbers enslave
    'em,
For, once they turn Christians, no barber will shave
    'em. (1)

To atone for this rather small Heathen amount,
Some Papists, turn'd Christians, (2) are tack'd to the
    account.
And though, to catch Papists, one need n't go so far,
Such fish are worth hooking, wherever they are;
And *now*, when so great of such converts the lack is,
One Papist well caught is worth millions of Blackies.

                         Friday
Last night had a dream so odd and funny,
    I cannot resist recording it here.—
Methought that the Genius of Matrimony
    Before me stood, with a joyous leer,
Leading a husband in each hand,
    And both for *me*, which look'd rather queer;—
One I could perfectly understand,
    But why there were *two* was n't quite so clear.
'T was meant, however, I soon could see,
    To afford me a *choice*—a most excellent plan;
And—who should this brace of candidates be,
    But Messrs. O'Mulligan and Magan :—
A thing, I suppose, unheard of till then,
To dream, at once, of *two* Irishmen!—
That handsome Magan, too, with wings on his
    shoulders
    (For all this pass'd in the realms of the Blest,)
And quite a creature to dazzle beholders;
    While even O'Mulligan, feather'd and drest
As an elderly cherub, was looking his best.
Ah, Liz, you, who know me, scarce can doubt
As to *which* of the two I singled out.
But—awful to tell—when, all in dread
    Of losing so bright a vision's charms,

I grasp'd at Magan, his image fled,
Like a mist, away, and I found but the head
    Of O'Mulligan, wings and all, in my arms!
The Angel had flown to some nest divine,
And the elderly Cherub alone was mine!
Heigho !—It is certain that foolish Magan
Either can't or *wo'n't* see that he *might* be the man;
And, perhaps, dear—who knows?—if nought better
    befall
But—O'Mulligan *may* be the man, after all.

N. B.

Next week mean to have my first scriptural rout,
For the special discussion of matters devout;—
Like those *soirées*, at Powerscourt, (3) so justly re-
    nown'd,
For the zeal with which doctrine and negus went
    round;
Those theology-routs which the pious Lord R—d—n,
That pink of Christianity, first set the mode in;
Where, blessed down-pouring ! (4) from tea until nine,
The subjects lay all in the Prophecy line ;—
Then, supper—and then, if for topics hard driven,
From thence until bed-time to Satan was given;
While R—d—n, deep read in each topic and tome,
On all subjects (especially the last) was *at home*.

—◦•◦—

LETTER VII.

FROM MISS FANNY FUDGE, TO HER COUSIN,
MISS KITTY ———.

IRREGULAR ODE.

Bring me the slumbering souls of flowers,
    While yet, beneath some northern sky,
Ungilt by beams, ungemm'd by showers,
    They wait the breath of summer hours,
    To wake to light each diamond eye,
    And let loose every florid sigh !

---

(1) "Roteen wants shaving; but the barber here will not do it. He is run away lest he should be compelled. He says he will not shave Yesoo Kreest's people."—*Bapt. Mission Society*, vol. ii., p. 493.

(2) In the Reports of the Missionaries, the Roman Catholics are almost always classed along with the Heathen. "I have extended my labours, (says James Venning, in a Report for 1831,) to the Heathen, Mahomedans, and Roman Catholics." "The Heathen and Roman Catholics in this neighbourhood (says another missionary for the year 1832) are not indifferent, but withstand, rather than yield to, the force of truth."

(3) An account of these Powerscourt Conversazioni (under the direct presidency of Lord Roden,) as well as a list of the subjects discussed at the different meetings, may be found in the *Christian Herald*, for the month of December, 1832. The following is a specimen of the nature of the questions submitted to the company : —
"*Monday Evening, Six o'clock, September* 24, 1832.—
'An examination into the quotations given in the New Testament from the Old, with their connection and explanation, viz.' etc. etc.—*Wednesday.*— ' Should we expect a personal Antichrist? *and to whom will he be revealed?* ' etc. etc.— *Friday.*— ' What light does Scrip-

ture throw on present events, and their moral character? *What is next to be looked for or expected?*" etc.

The rapid progress made at these tea-parties in settling points of Scripture may be judged from a paragraph in the account given of one of their evenings by the *Christian Herald :* —

"On Daniel a good deal of light was thrown, and there was some, I think not so much, perhaps, upon the Revelations ; though particular parts of it were discussed with considerable accession of knowledge. There was some very interesting inquiry as to the quotation of the Old Testament in the New; particularly on the point, whether there was any ' accommodation,' or whether they were quoted according to the mind of the Spirit in the Old, this gave occasion to some very interesting development of Scripture. The progress of the Antichristian powers was very fully discussed."

(4) "About eight o'clock the Lord began to pour down his spirit copiously upon us—for they had all by this time assembled in my room for the purpose of prayer. This down-pouring continued till about ten o'clock."—Letter from Mary Campbell to the Rev. John Campbell, of Row, (dated Fernicary, April 4, 1830,) giving an account of her "miraculous cure."

Bring me the first-born ocean waves,
From out those deep primeval caves,
Where from the dawn of Time they've lain—
The Embryos of a future Main!—
Untaught as yet, young things, to speak
   The language of their *Parent Sea*
(Polyphlysbæan (1) named, in Greek),
Though soon, too soon, in bay and creek,
Round startled isle and wondering peak,
They'll thunder loud and long as He !

Bring me, from Hecla's iced abode,
   Young fires——

         I had got, dear, thus far in my *Ode,*
Intending to fill the whole page to the bottom,
But, having invoked such a lot of fine things,
Flowers, billows and thunderbolts, rainbows and
      wings,
Did n't know *what* to do with 'em, when I had got
      'em.
The truth is, my thoughts are too full, at this minute,
   Of past MSS. any new ones to try.
This very night's coach brings my destiny in it—
   Decides the great question, to live or to die !
And, whether I'm henceforth immortal or no,
   All depends on the answer of Simpkins and Co. !

You'll think, love, I rave, so 'tis best to let out
   The whole secret, at once—I have publish'd a
      Book !!!
Yes, an actual Book :—if the marvel you doubt,
   You have only in last Monday's *Courier* to look,
And you'll find "This day publish'd by Simpkins
   and Co.
A Romaunt,'in twelve Cantos, entitled 'Woe Woe!'
By Miss Fanny F——, known more commonly
   so ☞."
This I put that my friends may n't be left in the dark,
But may guess at my *writing* by knowing my *mark.*

How I managed, at last, this great deed to achieve,
Is itself a "Romaunt" which you'd scarce, dear,
   believe,
Nor can I just now, being all in a whirl,
Looking out for the Magnet, (2) explain it, dear girl.
Suffice it to say, that one half the expense
Of this leasehold of fame for long centuries hence—
(Though "God knows," as aunt says, my humble
   ambition
Aspires not beyond a small second edition)—
One half the whole cost of the paper and printing,
I've managed to scrape up, this year past, by stint-
   ing
My own little wants in gloves, ribands, and shoes,
Thus defrauding the toilet to fit out the Muse !

And who, my dear Kitty, would not do the same?
What's *eau de Cologne* to the sweet breath of fame ?

Yards of riband soon end—but the measures of
   rhyme,
Dipp'd in hues of the rainbow, stretch out through
   all time.
Gloves languish and fade away, pair after pair,
While couplets shine out, but the brighter for wear,
And the dancing-shoe's gloss in an evening is gone,
While light-footed lyrics through ages trip on.

The remaining expense, trouble, risk—and, alas !
My poor copyright too—into other hands pass ;
And my friend, the Head Devil of the *County
   Gazette*
(The only Mecænas I've ever had yet),
He who set up in type my first juvenile lays,
Is now set up by them for the rest of his days ;
And while Gods (as my "Heathen Mythology" says)
Live on nought but ambrosia, *his* lot how much
   sweeter
To live, lucky devil, on a young lady's metre !

As for *puffing*—that first of all literary boons,
And essential alike both to bards and balloons,
As, unless well supplied with inflation, 't is found
Neither bards nor balloons budge an inch from the
   ground ;—
In *this* respect, nought could more prosperous befall ;
As my friend (for no less this kind imp can I call)
Knows the whole world of critics—the *hypers* and all.
I suspect he himself, indeed, dabbles in rhyme,
Which, for imps diabolic, is not the first time ;
As I've heard uncle Bob say, 't was known among
   Gnostics,
That the Devil on Two Sticks was a devil at Acrostics.

But hark ! there's the Magnet just dash'd in from
   town—
How my heart, Kitty, beats ! I shall surely drop down.
That awful *Court Journal, Gazette, Athenæum,*
All full of my book—I shall sink when I see 'em.
And then the great point—whether Simpkins and
   Co.
Are actually pleased with their bargain or no !—

                           Five o'clock.
All's delightful—such praises !—I really fear
That this poor little head will turn giddy, my dear;
I've but time now to send you two exquisite scraps—
All the rest by the Magnet, on Monday, perhaps.

FROM THE "MORNING POST."
'T is known that a certain distinguish'd physician
Prescribes, for *dyspepsia,* a course of light read-
   ing ;
And Rhymes by young Ladies, the first, fresh edi-
   tion

(1) If you guess what this word means, 'tis more than
   I can ;
   I but give 't as I got it from Mr. Magan.—*F. F.*
(2) A day-coach of that name.

(Ere critics have injured their powers of nutrition),
  Arc, he thinks, for weak stomachs, the best sort
    of feeding.
Satires irritate—love-songs are found calorific;
But smooth female sonnets he deems a specific,
And, if taken at bed-time, a sure soporific.
Among works of this kind, the most pleasing we
    know,
Is a volume just publish'd by Simpkins and Co.,
Where all such ingredients—the flowery, the sweet,
And the gently narcotic—are mix'd *per* receipt,
With a hand so judicious, we've no hesitation
To say that—'bove all, for the young generation—
'T is an elegant, soothing, and safe preparation.

Nota bene—for readers, whose object's *to sleep*,
And who read, in their nightcaps, the publishers keep
Good fire-proof binding, which comes very cheap.

ANECDOTE—FROM THE "COURT JOURNAL."

T' other night, at the Countess of " * * "'s rout,
An amusing event was much whisper'd about.
It was said that Lord ——, at the Council, that day,
  Had, more than once, jump'd from his seat, like a
    rocket,
And flown to a corner, where—heedless, they say,
How the country's resources were squander'd away—
  He kept reading some papers he 'd brought in his
    pocket.
Some thought them despatches from Spain or the
    Turk,
  Others swore they brought word we had lost the
    Mauritius;
But it turn'd out 't was only Miss Fudge's new work,
  Which his Lordship devour'd with such zeal ex-
    peditious—
Messrs. Simpkins and Co., to avoid all delay,
Having sent it in sheets, that his Lordship might say,
He had distanced the whole reading world by a day!

———◦❖◦———

LETTER VIII.

FROM BOB FUDGE, ESQ., TO THE REV. MORTIMER
O'MULLIGAN.

Tuesday evening.

I MUCH regret, dear Reverend Sir,
  I could not come to * * * to meet you;
But this curst gout wo'n't let me stir—
  Even now I but by proxy greet you;
As this vile scrawl, whate'er its sense is,
Owes all to an amanuensis.
Most other scourges of disease
Reduce men to *extremities*—
But gout wo'n't leave one even *these*.

From all my sister writes, I see
That you and I will quite agree.
I'm a plain man, who speak the truth,
  And trust you'll think me not uncivil,

When I declare that, from my youth,
  I've wish'd your country at the devil:
Nor can I doubt, indeed, from all
  I've heard of your high patriot fame—
From every word your lips let fall—
  That you most truly wish the same.
It plagues one's life out—thirty years
Have I had dinning in my ears,
  "Ireland wants this, and that, and t' other,"
And, to this hour, one nothing hears
  But the same vile eternal bother.
While, of those countless things she wanted,
Thank God, but little has been granted,
And even that little, if we 're men
And Britons, we 'll have back again!

I really think that Catholic question
Was what brought on my indigestion;
And still each year, as Popery's curse
Has gather'd round us, I've got worse;
Till even my pint of port a-day
Can 't keep the Pope and bile away.
And whereas, till the Catholic bill,
I never wanted draught or pill,
The settling of that cursed question
Has quite *unsettled* my digestion.

Look what has happen'd since—the Elect
Of all the bores of every sect,
The chosen triers of men's patience,
From all the Three Denominations,
Let loose upon us;—even Quakers
Turn'd into speechers and law-makers,
Who 'll move no question, stiff-rump'd elves,
Till first the Spirit moves themselves;
And whose shrill Yeas and Nays, in chorus,
Conquering our Ays and Nos sonorous,
Will soon to death's own slumber snore us.
Then, too, those Jews!—I really sicken
  To think of such abomination;
Fellows, who wo'n't eat ham with chicken,
  To legislate for this great nation!—
Depend upon 't, when once they 've sway,
  With rich old Goldsmid at the head o' them!
The Excise laws will be done away,
  And *Circum*cise ones pass'd instead o' them!

In short, dear sir, look where one will,
Things all go on so devilish ill,
That, 'pon my soul, I rather fear
  Our reverend Rector may be right,
Who tells me the Millennium 's near;
  Nay, swears he knows the very year,
    And regulates his leases by 't;—
Meaning their terms should end, no doubt,
Before the world's own lease is out.
He thinks, too, that the whole thing 's ended
So much more soon than was intended,

THE FUDGES IN ENGLAND.

Purely to scourge those men of sin
Who brought the accurst Reform Bill in. (1)

However, let's not yet despair;
Though Toryism's eclipsed, at present,
And—like myself, in this old chair—
Sits in a state by no means pleasant;
Feet crippled—hands, in luckless hour,
Disabled of their grasping power;
And all that rampant glee, which revell'd
In this world's sweets, be-dull'd, bedevil'd—
Yet, though condemn'd to frisk no more,
   And both in Chair of Penance set,
There's something tells me, all's not o'er
   With Toryism or Bobby yet;
That though between us, I allow
We've not a leg to stand on now;
Though curst Reform and *colchicum*
Have made us both look deuced glum,
Yet still, in spite of Grote and Gout,
Again we'll shine triumphant out!

Yes—back again shall come, egad,
Our turn for sport, my reverend lad.
And then, O'Mulligan—oh then,
When mounted on our nags again,
You, on your high-flown Rosinante,
Bedizen'd out, like Show-Gallantee
(Glitter great from substance scanty);—
While I, Bob Fudge, Esquire, shall ride
Your faithful Sancho by your side;
Then—talk of tilts and tournaments!
Dam'me, we'll ——

 *   *   *   *   *

                   'Squire Fudge's clerk presents
To Reverend Sir his compliments;
Is grieved to say an accident
Has just occurr'd, which will prevent
The Squire—though now a little better—
From finishing this present letter.
Just when he'd got to "Dam'me, we'll ——"
His Honour, full of martial zeal,
Grasp'd at his crutch, but not being able
   To keep his balance or his hold,
Tumbled, both self and crutch, and roll'd
Like ball and bat, beneath the table.

All's safe—the table, chair, and crutch;—
Nothing, thank God, is broken much,
But the Squire's head, which, in the fall,
Got bump'd considerably—that's all.
At this no great alarm we feel,
As the Squire's head can bear a deal.

(1) This appears to have been the opinion also of an eloquent writer in the *Morning Watch.* "One great object of Christ's second Advent, as the Man and as the King of the Jews, is to *punish the Kings* who do not acknowledge that their authority is derived from him, and *who submit to receive it from that many-headed monster, the mob.*" No. x., p. 373.

(2) "I am of your Patriarchs, I, a branch of one of your

Wednesday morning.
Squire much the same—head rather light—
Raved about "Barbers' Wigs" all night.

Our housekeeper, old Mrs. Griggs,
Suspects that he meant "barbarous Whigs."

—— ◦◦◦ ——

LETTER IX.

FROM LARRY O'BRANIGAN, TO HIS WIFE JUDY.

As it was but last week that I sint you a letther,
   You'll wondher, dear Judy, what this is about;
And throth, it's a letther myself would like betther,
   Could I manage to lave the contints of it out;
For sure, if it makes even *me* onaisy,
Who takes things quiet, 't will dhrive *you* crazy.

Oh, Judy, that riverind Murthagh, bad scran to him!
That e'er I should come to 've been sarvant-man to
   him,
Or so far demane the O'Branigan blood,
And my Aunts, the Diluvians (whom not even the
   Flood
Was able to wash away clane from the earth) (2)
As to sarve one whose name, of mere yestherday's
   birth,
Can no more to a great O, *before* it, purtend
Than mine can to wear a great Q at its *end.*

But that's now all over—last night I gev warnin',
And, masth'r as he is, will discharge him this mornin'.
The thief of the world!—but it's no use balrag-
   gin';—(3)
All I know is, I'd rather be fifty times draggin'
Owld ladies up hill to the ind of my days,
Than with Murthagh to rowl in a chaise, at my aise,
And be forced to discind thro' the same dirty ways.
Arrah, sure, if I'd heerd where he'd last show'd
   his phiz,
I'd have known what a quare sort of monsther he is;
For, by gor, 't was at Exether Change, sure enough,
That himself and his other wild Irish show'd off;
And it's pity, so 't is, that they had n't got no man
Who knew the wild crathurs to act as their show-
   man—
Sayin', " Ladies and Gintlemen, plaze to take notice,
How shlim and how shleek this black animal's coat
   is;
All by raison, we're towld, that the nathur o' the
   baste
Is to change its coat *once* in its lifetime, *at laste;*
And such objiks, in *our* counthry, not bein' common
   ones,
Are *bought up,* as this was, by way of Fine Nomenons.
antediluvian families—fellows that the Flood could not wash away."—*Congreve, Love for Love.*

(3) To *balrag* is to abuse.—Mr. Lover makes it *ballyrag,* and he is high authority: but if I remember rightly, Curran in his national stories used to employ the word as above.—See Lover's most amusing and genuinely Irish work, the *Legends and Stories of Ireland.*

In regard of its *name*—why, in throth, I'm con-
    sarn'd
To differ on this point so much with the larn'd,
Who call it a '*Morthimer*,' whereas the craythur
Is plainly a '*Murthagh*,' by name and by nathur."

This is how I'd have towld them the rights of it all,
Had *I* been their showman at Exether Hall—
Not forgettin' that other great wondher of Airin
(Of th' owld bitther breed which they call Prosbe-
    tairin),
The famed Daddy C—ke—who, by gor, I'd have
    shown 'em
As proof how such bastes may be tamed, when you've
    thrown 'em
A good frindly sop of the rale *Raigin Donem*. (1)

But, throth, I've no laisure just now, Judy dear,
For any thing, barrin' our own doings here,
And the cursin' and dammin' and thund'rin', like
    mad,
We Papists, God help us, from Murthagh have had.
He says we're all murtherers—div'l a bit less—
And that even our priests, when we go to confess,
Give us lessons in murth'ring, and wish us success!

When ax'd how he daar'd, by tongue or by pen,
To belie, in this way, seven millions of men,
Faith, he said 't was all towld him by Docthor Den! (2)
"And who the div'l 's *he*?" was the question that flew
From Chrishtian to Chrishtian—but not a sowl knew.
While on went Murthagh, in iligant style,
Blasphaming us Cath'lies all the while,
As a pack of desaivers, parjurers, villians,
All the whole kit of the aforesaid millions— (3)
Yourself, dear Judy, as well as the rest,
And the·innocent craythur that's at your breast,
All rogues together, in word and deed,
Owld Den our insthructor and Sin our creed!

When ax'd for his proofs again and again,
Div'l an answer he'd give but Docthor Den.
Could n't he call into coort some livin' men?
"No, thank you"—he'd stick to Docthor Den—
An owld gintleman dead a century or two,
Who all about *us*, live Catholics, knew;
And of coorse was more handy, to call in a hurry,
Than Docthor Mac Hale or Docthor Murray!

(1) Larry evidently means the *Regium Donum* — a sum
contributed by the government annually to the support of
the Presbyterian churches in Ireland.
(2) Correctly, Dens—Larry not being very particular in
his nomenclature.
3) "The deeds of darkness which are reduced to horrid
practice over the drunken debauch of the midnight as-
sassin are debated, in principle, in the sober morning
religious conferences of the priests."—*Speech of the Rev.
Mr. M'Ghee.*—" The character of the Irish people *gene-
rally* is, that they are given to lying and to acts of theft."
—*Speech of the Rev. Robert Daly.*

But, throth, it's no case to be jockin' upon,
Though myself, from bad hab ts, is *makin'* it one.
Even *you*, had you witness'd his grand climacthenes,
Which actually threw one owld maid in hysterics—
Or, och! had you heerd such a purty remark as his,
That Papists are only *Humanity's carcasses*,
"*Risen*"—but, by dad, I'm afeard I can't give it ye—
"*Risen from the sepulchre of—inactivity;*
And, like owld corpses, dug up from antikity,
Wanderin' about in all sorts of inikity!!" — 4)
Even you, Judy, true as you are to the Owld Light,
Would have laugh'd, out and out, at this iligant flight
Of that figure of speech call'd the Blatherumskite.
As for me, though a funny thought now and then
    came to me,
Rage got the betther at last—and small blame to me!
So, slapping my thigh, "by the Powers of Delf,"
Says I bowldly "I'll make a noration myself."
And with that up I jumps—but, my darlint, the minit
I cock'd up my head, div'l a sinse remain'd in it.
Though *saited*, I could have got beautiful on,
When I tuck to my legs, faith, the gab was all gone.—
Which was odd, for us, Pats, who, whate'er we've
    a hand in,
At laste in our *legs* show a sthrong undeistandin'.

Howsumdever, determin'd the chaps should pursaive
What I thought of their doin's, before I tuk lave,
"In regard of all that," says I—there I stopp'd short—
Not a word more would come, though I shruggled
    hard for 't.
So, shnapping my fingers at what's call'd the Chair,
And the owld Lord (or Lady, I b'lieve) that sat there—
"In regard of all that," says I bowldly again—
"To owld Nick I pitch Murtimer—*and* Docthor
    Den;"—
Upon which the whole company cried out "Amen;"
And myself was in hopes 't was to what *I* had said,
But, by gor, no such thing—they were not so well
    bred:
For, 't was all to a prayer Murthagh just had read out,
By way of fit finish to job so devout;
That is—*afther* well damning one half the com-
    munity,
To pray God to keep all in pace an' in unity!

This is all I can shtuff in this letther, though plinty
Of news, faith, I've got to fill more—if 't was twinty.

(4) "But she (Popery) is no longer *the tenant of the
sepulchre of inactivity.* She has come from the burial-
place, walking forth a monster, as if the spirit of evil had
corrupted *the carcass of her departed humanity;* noxious
and noisome, an object of abhorrence and dismay to all
who are not *leagued with her in iniquity.*"—Report of the
Rev. Gentleman's Speech, June 20, in the *Record* News-
paper.
We may well ask, after reading this and other such re-
verend ravings, "Quis dubitat quin omne sit hoc rationis
egestas?"

But I'll add, on the *outside*, a line, should I need it,
(Writin' " Private" upon it, that no one may read it,)
To tell you how *Mortimer* (as the Saints chrishten
   him)
Bears the big shame of his sarvant's dismisshin' him.

(*Private Outside.*)

Just come from his riv'rence—the job is all done—
By the powers, I've discharged him as sure as a gun!
And now, Judy dear, what on earth I 'm to do
With myself and my appetite—both good as new—
Without even a single traneen in my pocket,
Let alone a good dacent pound starlin' to stock it—
Is a mysht'ry I lave to the One that's above,
Who takes care of us, dissolute sowls, when hard
   dhrove!

—————

LETTER X.

FROM THE REV. MORTIMER O'MULLIGAN, TO THE
REV. ———.

These few brief lines, my reverend friend,
By a safe private hand I send
(Fearing lest some low Catholic wag
Should pry into the Letter-bag),
To tell you, far as pen can reach,
How we, poor errant martyrs, fare;—
Martyrs, not quite to fire and rack,
As Saints were, some few ages back,
But, scarce less trying in its way—
To laughter wheresoe'er we stray;
To jokes, which Providence mysterious
Permits on men and things so serious,
Lowering the Church still more each minute,
And—injuring our preferment in it.
Just think, how worrying 't is, my friend,
To find, where'er our footsteps bend,
   Small jokes, like squibs, around us whizzing;
And bear the eternal torturing play
Of that great engine of our day,
   Unknown to the Inquisition—quizzing!

(1) "Among other amiable enactments against the Catholics at this period (1649), the price of five pounds was set on the head of a Romish priest—being exactly the same sum offered by the same legislators for the head of a wolf."
   Memoirs of Captain Rock, book 1., chap. 10.

2 The following lines and accompanying notes, which originally formed part of this satirical production, have been suppressed:—

   Wise state of things! when sons were bribed
    With their sires wealth ; and *one* profest
   Conformist, of a race proscribed,
    Had power to beggar all the rest ! *
   Then, then, indeed, good converts brought
   A price that set all shame at nought,
   Nay, made it glory to be bought.

 * By the laws now in force in this kingdom, a son, however undutiful and profligate, shall not merely, by the merit of conforming to the established religion, deprive the Roman Catholic father of the free and full possession of his estate, the power to mortgage, etc , etc , but shall himself have full liberty immediately to mortgage, or otherwise alienate, the reversion of that estate from his family for ever."—*Address presented by the Catholics in 1775.*

 ** Lord Kenyon — "A previous engagement renders it ne-

Your men of thumb-screws and of racks
Aim'd at the *body* their attacks;
But modern torturers, more refined,
Work *their* machinery on the *mind.*
Had St. Sebastian had the luck
   With me to be a godly rover,
Instead of arrows, he'd be stuck
   With stings of ridicule all over;
And poor St. Lawrence, who was kill'd
By being on a gridiron grill'd,
Had he but shared *my* errant lot,
Instead of grill on gridiron hot,
A *moral* roasting would have got.
Nor should I (trying as all this is)
   Much heed the suffering or the shame—
As like an actor, *used* to hisses,
I long have known no other fame,
But that (as I may own to *you,*
Though to the *world* it would not do,)
No hope appears of fortune's beams
Shining on *any* of my schemes ,
No chance of something more *per ann.*
As supplement to K—llym—n ;
No prospect that, by fierce abuse
Of Ireland, I shall e'er induce
The rulers of this thinking nation
To rid us of Emancipation ;
To forge anew the sever'd chain,
And bring back Penal Laws again.

Ah happy time ! when wolves and priests
Alike were hunted, as wild beasts;
And five pounds was the price *per* head,
For bagging *either,* live or dead ; (1)
Though oft, we 're told, *one* outlaw'd brother
Saved cost, by eating up *the other.* (2)
Finding thus all those schemes and hopes
I built upon my flowers and tropes
All scatter'd, one by one, away,
As flashy and unsound as they,

   Ah, how unlike the paltry pay
   We fetch in this degenerate day!
   A poor small rectory all our lot—
   If zealous, laugh'd at, and, if not,
   Scored off as " paid for," and forgot !
   Yes, all's now o'er—I see too plain
   Those good times ne'er can come again.
   Our very progress here betrays
   That we are fallen on thankless days
   So dull are thought our " yaras " devout,
   Not Kenyon's self can sit them out , '"
   Nor even that Saint, Lord Mandeville,
   Gulp down such endless length of pill.
   So that, at last—so dire our punch,
   When thus all decent chairmen flinch—
   We 're forced to take to Mr. F—nch !

cessary for me to depart at four o'clock ; — that hour has now arrived, and I must *leave* I would therefore suggest to the meeting that my noble friend Lord Mandeville do take the chair." The motion that Lord Mandeville should take the chair was agreed to ; but it appeared that the noble Viscount had left the platform a short time before. Lord Kenyon then said, " I am informed that my friend Lord Mandeville has left the platform , I will therefore move that Mr Finch do take the chair."—*Report of the Proceedings, June 20th, in the Record Newspaper*

The question comes—what 's to be done?
And there 's but one course left me—*one*.
Heroes, when tired of war's alarms,
Seek sweet repose in beauty's arms.
The weary Day-God's last retreat is
The breast of silvery-footed Thetis;
And mine, as mighty Love 's my judge,
Shall be the arms of rich Miss Fudge!

Start not, my friend—the tender scheme,
Wild and romantic though it seem,
Beyond a parson's fondest dream,
Yet shines, too, with those golden dyes,
So pleasing to a parson's eyes—
That only *gilding* which the Muse
Cannot around *her* sons diffuse;—
Which, whencesoever flows its bliss,
From wealthy Miss or benefice,
To Mortimer indifferent is,
So he can only make it *his*.
There is but one slight damp I see
Upon this scheme's felicity,
And that is the fair heroine's claim
That I shall take *her* family name.
To this (though it may look henpeck'd),
I can't quite decently object,
Having myself long chosen to shine
Conspicuous in the *alias* (1) line;
So that henceforth, by wife's decree,
For Biddy from this point won't budge)
Your old friend's new address must be
The *Rev. Mortimer O'Fudge*—
The "O" being kept that all may see
We 're *both* of ancient family.

Such, friend, nor need the fact amaze you,
My public life's calm Euthanasia.
Thus bid I long farewell to all
The freaks of Exeter's old Hall—

Then, too, they tell us, with what zeal
All England throbs to our appeal:
But, why if the interest so intense is
Why don't they pay the room's expenses? *
When Kenyon begg'd, in our behalf,
He raised—*not* money, but a laugh!
'T is true, they flock to us, as a show—
As men dug up (dead long ago),
A sort of strolling Corpse and Co.
(Like those old carcasses that lately
I set upon their legs so stately)
All Doctor Dens' contemporaries,
And quoting still his dead vagaries,
'Mong living thinking men, who stare
To see such resurrections there,
And bear a dead dull Doctor's thought
As witness of live feelings brought!
While even the Church, in whose defence
We 've drawn the oratoric blade,

* Several touching appeals have been made to the public on
this point, and Lord Kenyon, at the close of the second day's pro-
ceedings, said, "I hope the meeting will permit me to remind
them, that very considerable expense has been incurred by the
deputation and the committee. There will be a collection made
at the door, in order to defray those expenses, and I trust that
those who are able will contribute liberally." From the follow-

Freaks, in grimace, its apes exceeding,
And rivalling its bears in breeding.
Farewell, the platform fill'd with preachers—
The prayer given out, as grace, (2) by speechers,
Ere they cut up their fellow-creatures:—
Farewell to dead old Dens's volumes,
And, scarce less dead, old *Standard's* columns:—
From each and all I now retire,
My task, henceforth, as spouse and sire,
To bring up little filial Fudges,
To be M.P.s, and Peers, and Judges—
Parsons I 'd add too, if, alas!
There yet were hope the Church could pass
The gulf now oped for hers and her,
Or long survive what *Exeter*—
Both Hall and Bishop of that name—
Have done to sink her reverend fame.

Adieu, dear friend—you 'll oft hear *from* me,
Now I 'm no more a travelling drudge;
Meanwhile I sign (that you may judge
How well the surname will become me)
Yours truly,
                         MORTIMER O'FUDGE.

LETTER XI.

FROM PATRICK MAGAN, ESQ., TO THE REV.
RICHARD ———.

———, *Ireland.*
DEAR DICK—Just arrived at my own humble *gite*,
I inclose you, post-haste, the account, all complete,
Just arrived, *per* express, of our late noble feat.

[*Extract from the " County Gazette."*]
"This place is getting gay and full again.
*   *   *   *   *   *

Last week was married, ' in the Lord,'
The Reverend Mortimer O'Mulligan,
Preacher, in *Irish*, of the Word,

Dreads the uplifted eloquence
And shudders at such perilous aid—
" Foes I can brave," she shrinking cries,
" But save me from my dear Allies."—P. E.

(1) In the first edition of his Dictionary, Dr. Johnson
very significantly exemplified the meaning of the word
"alias" by the instance of Mallet, the poet, who had ex-
changed for this more refined name his original Scotch
patronymic, Malloch. "What *other* proofs he gave (says
Johnson) of disrespect to his native country, I know not;
but it was remarked of him that he was the only Scot whom
Scotchmen did not commend."—*Life of Mallet.*

(2 " I think I am acting in unison with the feelings of a
Meeting assembled for this *solemn* object, when I call on
the Rev. Doctor Holloway to open it by prayer."—*Speech
of Lord Kenyon.*

ing complaint, however, in the *Record* (July 9), it appears that
the noble Lord's appeal was unavailing : " We have to remark
that the contributions at the doors at the last meeting at Exeter
Hall by no means defrayed the expenses, which are somewhat
heavy *l40l* is charged for the room alone , and we may be ex-
cused for requesting our readers to exercise a little more libe-
rality at the approaching meeting on Saturday."

(He, who the Lord's force lately led on—
Exeter Hall his Armagh-geddon,) (1)
To Miss B. Fudge, of Pisgah Place,
One of the chosen, as 'heir of grace,'
And likewise heiress of Phil. Fudge,
Esquire, defunct, of Orange Lodge.

"Same evening, Miss F. Fudge, 't is hinted—
Niece of the above, (whose 'Sylvan Lyre,'
In our Gazette, last week, we printed,)
Eloped with Pat. Magan, Esquire.
The fugitives were track'd, some time,
After they'd left the Aunt's abode,
By scraps of paper, scrawl'd with rhyme,
Found strew'd along the Western road;—
Some of them, ci-devant curl-papers,
Others, half burnt in lighting tapers.
This clue, however, to their flight,
After some miles was seen no more;
And, from inquiries made last night,
We find they've reach'd the Irish shore."

Every word of it true, Dick—the escape from Aunt's
        thrall—
Western road—lyric fragments—curl-papers and all.
My sole stipulation, ere link'd at the shrine
(As some balance between Fanny's numbers and
        mine),
Was that, when we were one, she must give up the
        Nine;
Nay, devote to the Gods her whole stock of MS.
With a vow never more against prose to transgress.
This she did, like a heroine;—smack went to bits
The whole produce sublime of her dear little wits—
Sonnets, elegies, epigrams, odes, canzonets—
Some twisted up neatly, to form allumettes,

Some turn'd into papillotes, worthy to rise
And enwreathe Berenice's bright locks in the skies!
While the rest, honest Larry (who's now in my pay),
Begg'd, as "lover of po'thry," to read on the way.

Having thus of life's poetry dared to dispose,
How we now, Dick, shall manage to get through its
        prose,
With such slender materials for style, Heaven knows!
But—I'm call'd off abruptly—another Express!
What the deuce can it mean?—I'm alarm'd, I con-
        fess.

P. S.
Hurrah, Dick, hurrah, Dick, ten thousand hurrahs
I'm a happy rich dog to the end of my days.
There—read the good news—and while glad, for my
        sake,
That Wealth should thus follow in Love's shining
        wake,
Admire also the moral—that he, the sly elf,
Who has fudged all the world, should be now fudged
        himself!

EXTRACT FROM LETTER INCLOSED.
With pain the mournful news I write,
Miss Fudge's uncle died last night;
And, much to mine and friends' surprise,
By will doth all his wealth devise—
Lands, dwellings—rectories likewise—
To his "beloved grand-niece," Miss Fanny,
Leaving Miss Fudge herself, who many
Long years hath waited—not a penny!
Have notified the same to latter,
And wait instructions in the matter.
                For self and partners, etc., etc.

TOM CRIB'S MEMORIAL TO CONGRESS.

ΑΛΛ᾽ ουκ οιοι ΠΥΚΤΙΚΗΣ ΠΛΕΟΝ ΜΕΤΕΧΕΙΝ τους πλουσιους επιςημη τε και εμπειρια 'Η
ΠΟΛΕΜΙΚΗΣ; Εγω εφη.—Plato de Rep., lib 4.
"If any man doubt the significancy of the language, we refer him to the third volume of Reports, set forth by the
learned in the laws of Canting, and published in this tongue."—Ben Jonson.

PREFACE.

The Public have already been informed, through the medium of the daily prints, that, among the distinguished visitors to the Congress lately held at Aix-la-Chapelle, were Mr. Bob Gregson, Mr. George Cooper, and a few more illustrious brethren of the Fancy. It had been resolved at a Grand Meeting of the Pugilistic Fraternity, that, as all the milling Powers of Europe were about to assemble, personally or by deputy, at Aix-la-Chapelle, it was but right that The Fancy should have its representatives there as well as the rest, and these gentlemen were accordingly selected

(1) The rectory which the Rev. gentleman holds is situated in the county of Armagh!—a most remarkable coin-

for that high and honourable office. A description of this Meeting, of the speeches spoken, the resolutions, etc., etc., has been given in a letter written by one of the most eminent of the profession, which will be found in the Appendix, No. I. Mr. Crib's Memorial, which now for the first time meets the public eye, was drawn up for the purpose of being transmitted by these gentlemen to Congress; and, as it could not possibly be in better hands for the enforcement of every point connected with the subject, there is every reason to hope that it has made a suitable impression upon that body.

The favour into which this branch of Gymnastics,

cidence—and well worthy of the attention of certain expounders of the Apocalypse.

called Pugilism (from the Greek πυξ, as the author of *Boxiana* learnedly observes), has risen with the Public of late years, and the long season of tranquillity which we are now promised by the new Millennarians of the Holy League, encourage us to look forward with some degree of sanguineness to an order of things, like that which Plato and Tom Crib have described (the former in the motto prefixed to this work, and the latter in the interesting Memorial that follows), when the *Milling* shall succeed to the *Military* system, and The Fancy will be the sole arbitress of the trifling disputes of mankind. From a wish to throw every possible light on the history of an Art, which is destined ere long to have such influence upon the affairs of the world, I have, for some time past, been employed in a voluminous and elaborate work, entitled "A Parallel between Ancient and Modern Pugilism," which is now in a state of considerable forwardness, and which I hope to have ready for delivery to subscribers on the morning of the approaching fight between Randall and Martin. Had the elegant author of *Boxiana* extended his inquiries to the *ancient* state of the art, I should not have presumed to interfere with a historian so competent. But, as his researches into antiquity have gone no farther than the *one* valuable specimen of erudition which I have given above, I feel the less hesitation

——— novos decerpere flores,
Insignemque meo capiti petere inde coronam,
Unde prius nulli velarint tempora Musæ. (1)

Lucret., lib. 4, vol. 3.

The variety of studies necessary for such a task, and the multiplicity of references which it requires, as well to the living as the dead, can only be fully appreciated by him who has had the patience to perform it. Alternately studying in the Museum and the Fives Court—passing from the Academy of Plato to that of Mr. Jackson—now indulging in *Attic flashes* with Aristophanes, and now studying *Flash* in the *Attics* of *Cock Court* (2)—between so many and such various associations has my mind been divided during the task, that sometimes, in my bewilderment, I have confounded Ancients and Moderns together—mistaken the *Greek* of St. Giles's for that of Athens, and have even found myself tracing Bill Gibbons and his Bull in the "*taurum tibi, pulcher Apollo*," of Virgil.

(1) To wander through the Fancy's bowers,
To gather new unheard-of flowers,
And wreathe such garlands for my brow,
As Poet never wreathed till now!

(2 The residence of the Nonpareil, Jack Randall—where, the day after his last great victory, he held a levee, which was attended, of course, by all the leading characters of St. Giles's.

(3) *Idyl.* 22.   (4 *Argonaut.*, lib. 2.   (5) Lib. 4.

(6 Except one, βουτυπος οἴ, which is good, and which Fawkes, therefore, has omitted. The following couplet from his translation is, however, *fanciful* enough —

So from their batter'd cheeks loud echoes sprung,
Their dash'd teeth crackled and their jaw-bones rung.

My printer, too, has been affected with similar hallucinations. The *Mil. Glorios.* of Plautus he converted, the other day, into a *Glorious Mill*; and more than once, when I have referred to *Tom. prim.* or *Tom. quart.* he has substituted Tom Crib and Tom Oliver in their places. Notwithstanding all this, the work will be found, I trust, tolerably correct; and as an Analysis of its opening Chapters may not only gratify the impatience of the *Fanciful* World, but save my future reviewers some trouble, it is here given as succinctly as possible.

Chap. 1 contains some account of the ancient Inventors of pugilism, Epēus and Amycus.—The early exploit of the former, in *milling* his twin-brother, *in ventre matris*, and so getting before him into the world, as related by Eustathius on the authority of Lycophron.—Amycus, a Royal Amateur of the Fancy, who challenged to *the scratch* all strangers that landed on his shore.—The Combat between him and Pollux (who, to use the classic phrase, *served* him *out*), as described by Theocritus, (3) Apollonius Rhodius, (4) and Valerius Flaccus. (5)—Respective merits of these three descriptions.—Theocritus by far the best; and, altogether, perhaps, the most scientific account of a Boxing-match in all antiquity.—Apollonius ought to have done better, with such a model before him; but, evidently not *up to* the thing (whatever Scaliger may say), and his similes all *slum*. (6)—Valerius Flaccus, the first Latin Epic Poet after Virgil, has done ample justice to this *Set-to; feints, facers,* (7) and *ribbers,* all described most spiritedly.

Chap. 2 proves that the Pancratium of the ancients, as combining boxing and wrestling, was the branch of their Gymnastics that most resembled our modern Pugilism; *cross-buttocking* (or what the Greeks called ὑποσκελίζειν) being as indispensable an ingredient as *nobbing, flooring,* etc., etc.—Their ideas of a *stand-up fight* were very similar to our own, as appears from the το παιειν αλληλους ΟΡΘΟΣΤΑΔΗΝ of Lucan—περι Γυμνας.

Chap. 3 examines the ancient terms of the Fancy, as given by Pollux (*Onomast. ad. fin. lib.* 3.) and others; and compares them with the modern.—For example, αγχειν, to *throttle*—λυγιζειν, evidently the origin of our word to *lug*—αγκυρίζειν, to anchor a fellow (see Grose's *Greek* Dictionary, for the word

7) Emicat huc, dextramque parat, dextramque minatur
Tyndarides; redit huc oculis et pondere Bebryx
Sic ratus: ille autem celeri rapit ora sinistra.

Lib. 4, v. 290.

We have here a *feint* and a *facer* together. The manner in which Valerius Flaccus describes the multitude of *black*guards that usually assemble on such occasions is highly poetical and picturesque : he supposes them to be Shades from Tartarus.—

Et pater oranies cæsorum Tartaros umbras
Nube cava tandem ad meritæ spectacula pugnæ
Emittit; summis nigrescunt culmina montis.—V. 258.

anchor)—δρασσειν (perf. pass. δεδραγμαι), from which is derived to *drag*; and whence, also, a *flash* etymologist might contrive to derive δραμα, *drama*, Thespis having first performed in a *drag*. (1) This chapter will be found highly curious; and distinguished, I flatter myself, by much of that acuteness which enabled a late illustrious Professor to discover that our English "Son of a Gun" was nothing more than the Παις Γυνης (Dor.) of the Greeks.

Chap. 4 enumerates the many celebrated Boxers of antiquity.—Eryx (grandson of the Amycus already mentioned), whom Hercules is said to have *finished* in style.—Phrynon, the Athenian General, and Autolycus, of whom, Pausanias tell us, there was a statue in the Prytaneum—The celebrated Pugilist, who, at the very moment he was expiring, had game enough to make his adversary *give in;* which interesting circumstance forms the subject of one of the Pictures of Philostratus, *Icon., lib.* 2, *imag.* 6—and, above all, that renowned Son of the Fancy, Melancomas, the favourite of the Emperor Titus, in whose praise Dio Chrysostomus has left us two elaborate orations. (2) —The peculiarities of this boxer discussed—his power of standing with his arms extended for two whole days, without any rest (δυνατος ην, says Dio, και δυο ουρας εξης μελετι αποτετασως τας χειρας, και ουκ αν ειδεν ουδεις υπερτα αυτον η απαπαυσαμενον ωσπερ ειωθασι. *Orat.* 28 , by which means he wore out his adversary's *bottom*, and conquered without either *giving* or *taking*. This bloodless system of *milling*, which trusted for victory to patience alone, has afforded to the orator, Themistus, a happy illustration of the peaceful conquests which he attributes to the Emperor Valens. (3)

Chap. 5 notices some curious points of similarity between the ancient and modern Fancy.—Thus, Theocritus, in his Milling-match, calls Amycus "a *glutton*," which is well known to be the classical phrase at Moulsey-Hurst, for one who, like Amycus, takes a deal of *punishment* before he is *satisfied.*

Πως γαρ δη Διος υιος ΑΔΗΦΑΓΟΝ ανδρα καθειλεν.

In the same Idyl the poet describes the Bebrycian Lero ас πληγαις μεθυων, "drunk with blows," which is precisely the language of our Fancy bulletins; for

(1 The flash term for a *cart*.
(2 The following words, in which Dio so decidedly prefers the art of the Boxer to that of the soldier, would perhaps have been a still more significant motto to Mr. Crib's Memorial than that which I have chosen from Plato
Και καθοιου δε εγωγε τουτο της εν τοις πολεμοις αρετης προσοιων.
(3 Ην τις επι των προγονων των ημετερων πυκτης ανηρ, Μελαγκομας ονομα αυτω. . . . . . . ουτος ουδενα πωποτε τρωσας, ουδε ποταξας, μονη τη φασει και τη των χειρων αναρσει πακτας απεκλαιε τους ανττταλους. —Themist. *Orat.* περι Ειρηνης.
4) Kent's *Weekly Dispatch.*
(5 Yet, not unmindful of his art, he hies.
But turns his face, and combats as he flies.—*Leu it*

example, "Turner appeared as if drunk, and made a heavy lolloping hit," (4) etc., etc.—The resemblance in the *manner* of fighting still more striking and important. Thus we find Crib's favourite system of *milling on the retreat,* which he practised so successfully in his combats with Gregson and Molyneux, adopted by Alcidamus, the Spartan, in the battle between him and Capaneus, so minutely and vividly described by Statius, *Thebaid., lib.* 6.

. . . . . sed non, tamen, immemor artis,
Adversus fugit, et *fugiens tamen ictibus obstat.* (5)

And it will be only necessary to compare together two extracts from *Boxiana* and the Bard of Syracuse, to see how similar in their manœuvres have been the *millers* of all ages—"The Man of Colour, to prevent being *fibbed,* grasped tight hold of Carter's hand "(6) —(Account of the Fight between Robinson the Black and Carter), which, (translating λιλαιομενος, "the Lilly-white," (7) is almost word for word with the following:—

Ητοι ογε ρεξαι τι λιλαιομενος μεγα εργον
Σκαιη μεν σκαιην Πολυδευκεος ελλαβε χειρα.
Theocrit.

Chap. 6 proves, from the *jawing*-match and *Set-to* between Ulysses and the Beggar, in the 18th Book of the *Odyssey,* that the ancients (notwithstanding their δικαια μαχοντων, or Laws of Combatants, which, Artemidorus says in his chap. 33, περι Μονομαχ. extended to pugilism as well as other kinds of combats) did not properly understand *fair play;* as Ulysses is here obliged to require an oath from the standers-by, that they will not *deal* him a *sly knock,* while he is *cleaning out* the *mumper*—

Μη τις επ' Ιρω ηρα φερων εμε χειρι παχειη
Πληξη ατασθαλλων, τουτω δε με ιρι δαμασση.

Chap. 7 describes the Cestus, and shows that the Greeks, for mere exercise of *sparring,* made use of *muffles* or *gloves,* as we do, which they called σφαιραι. This appears particularly from a passage in Plato, *de Leg., lib.* 8, where, speaking of *training,* he says, it is only by frequent use of the gloves that a knowledge of *stopping* and *hitting* can be acquired. The whole passage is curious, as proving that the Divine Plato was not altogether a *novice* in the *Fancy lay.* (8)—

6) A manœuvre, commonly called *Tom Owen's stop.*
7) The *Flash* term for a negro, and also for a chimney-sweeper.
8 Another philosopher, Seneca, has shown himself equally *flash* on the subject, and, in his 13th Epistle, lays it down as an axiom, that no pugilist can be considered worth any thing, till he has had his *peepers taken measure of* for a *suit of mourning,* or, in common language, has received a pair of black eyes. The whole passage is edifying:— "Non potest athleta magnos spiritus ad certamen afferre, qui nunquam *sugillatus est.* Ille qui videt sanguinem suum, cujus dentes crepuerunt sub pugno, ille qui supplantatus adversarium toto tulit corpore, nec projecit animum projectus, qui quoties cecidit contumacior resurrexit, cum magna spe descendit ad pugnam."

Και ὡς εγγυτατα του ὁμοιου, αντι ἱμαιπτω, ΣΦΑΙΡΑΣ αν περιεδουμεθα, ὁπως αἱ ΠΛΗΓΑΙ τε και αἱ ΤΩΝ ΠΛΗΓΩΝ ΕΥΛΑΒΕΙΑΙ διεμελετωντο εις τι δυνατον ἱκανως.—These *muffles* were called by the Romans *sacculi*, as we find from Trebellius Pollio, who, in describing a triumph of Gallienus, mentions the " Pugiles *sacculis* non veritate pugilantes."

Chap. 8 adverts to the pugilistic exhibitions of the Spartan ladies, which Propertius has thus commemorated—

Pulverulentaque ad extremas stat fœmina metas,
Et patitur duro vulnera pancratio,
Nunc ligat ad cæsium gaudentia brachia loris, etc., etc.
Lib 3, el. 14.

and, to prove that the moderns are not behind-hand with the ancients in this respect, cites the following instance recorded in *Boxiana*:—" George Madox, in this battle, was seconded by his sister, Grace, who, upon its conclusion, tossed up her hat in defiance, and offered to fight any man present;"—also the memorable challenge, given in the same work (vol i., p. 300), which passed between Mrs. Elizabeth Wilkinson of Clerkenwell, and Miss Hannah Hyfield of Newgate-Market—another proof that the English may boast many a "dolce guerriera" as well as the Greeks.

Chap. 9 contains Accounts of all the celebrated *Set-tos* of antiquity, translated from the works of the different authors that have described them—viz. the famous Argonautic Battle, as detailed by the three poets mentioned in chap. 1—the Fight between Epēus and Euryalus, in the 2*d* Book of the *Iliad*, and between Ulysses and Irus in the 18th Book of the *Odyssey*—the Combat of Dares and Entellus in the 5th *Æneid*—of Capaneus and Alcidamus, already referred to, in Statius, and of Achelous and Hercules in the 9th Book of the *Metamorphoses;* though this last is rather a wrestling-bout than a *mill*, resembling that between Hercules(1) and Antæus in the 4th Book of Lucan. The reader who is anxious to know how I have succeeded in this part of my task will find, as a specimen, my translation from Virgil in the Appendix to the present work, No. 2.

Chap. 10 considers the various arguments for and against Pugilism, advanced by writers ancient and modern.—A strange instance of either ignorance or

wilful falsehood in Lucian, who, in his *Anacharsis*, has represented Solon as one of the warmest advocates for Pugilism, whereas we know from Diogenes Laertius that that legislator took every possible pains to discourage and suppress it.—Alexander the Great, too, tasteless enough to prohibit The Fancy (Plutarch *in Vit*.).—Galen in many parts of his works, but particularly in the *Hortat. ad. Art.* condemns the practice as enervating and pernicious. (2)—On the other side, the testimonies in its favour, numerous.—The greater number of Pindar's Nemean Odes written in praise of pugilistic champions; — and Isocrates, though he represents Alcibiades as despising the art, yet acknowledges that its professors were held in high estimation through Greece, and that those cities where victorious pugilists were born became illustrious from that circumstance; 3) just as Bristol has been rendered immortal by the production of such heroes as Tom Crib, Harry Harmer, Big Ben, Dutch Sam, etc., etc.—Ammianus Marcellinus tells us how much that religious and pugnacious Emperor, Constantius, delighted in the *Set-tos*, " pugilum (4) vicissim se concidentium perfusorumque sanguine. " —To these are added still more flattering testimonies ; such as that of Isidorus, who calls Pugilism "virtus," as if *par excellence;* (5) and the yet more enthusiastic tribute with which Eustathius reproaches the Pagans of having enrolled their boxers in the number of the Gods.—In short, the whole chapter is full of erudition and νους;—from *Ly*cophron (whose very name smacks of pugilism) down to *Boxiana* and the *Weekly Dispatch*, not an author on the subject is omitted.

So much for my "Parallel between Ancient and Modern Pugilism. " And now with respect to that peculiar language called *Flash*, or *St. Giles's Greek*, in which Mr. Crib's Memorial and the other articles in the present work are written, I beg to trouble the reader with a few observations. As this expressive language was originally invented, and is still used, like the cipher of the diplomatists, for purposes of secrecy, and as a means of eluding the vigilance of a certain class of persons called, *flashicè*, *Traps*, or, in common language, Bow-street Officers, it is subject, of course, to continual change, and is perpetually

---

(1) Though wrestling was evidently the favourite sport of Hercules, we find him, in the Alcestes, just returned from a *Bruising-match;* and it is a curious proof of the superior consideration in which these arts were held, that for the lighter exercises, he tells us, horses alone were the reward, while to conquerors in the higher games of pugilism and wrestling, whole herds of cattle with sometimes a young lady into the bargain) were given as prizes.

τοισι δ' αυ τα μειῖονα
Νικωσι, πυγμην και παλην, βουφορβια
Γυνη δ' επ' αυτοις ειπε τ'.—Eurip.

(2) It was remarked by the ancient physicians, that men who were in the habit of boxing and wrestling became remarkably lean and slender from the loins downward,

while the upper parts of their frame acquired prodigious size and strength. I could name some pugilists of the present day whose persons seem to warrant the truth of this observation.

(3) Τους τ αθλητας ζηλουμενους, και τας πολεις ονομαζας γεγνουενος των νικωντων. Isocrat. περι του Ζευγους. An oration written by Isocrates for the son of Alcibiades.

(4) Notwithstanding that the historian expressly says " pugilum," Lipsius is so anxious to press this circumstance into his Account of the Ancient Gladiators, that he insists such an effusion of *claret* could only have taken place in the gladiatorial combat. But Lipsius never was at Moulsey-Hurst. See his *Saturnal. Sermon.*, lib. i., cap. 2.

(5) *Origin.*, lib. xviii., c. 18.

either altering the meaning of old words, or adding new ones, according as the great object, secrecy, renders it prudent to have recourse to such innovations. In this respect, also, it resembles the cryptography of kings and ambassadors, who by a continual change of cipher contrive to baffle the inquisitiveness of the *enemy*. But, notwithstanding the Protean nature of the *Flash* or *Cant* language, the greater part of its vocabulary has remained unchanged for centuries, and many of the words used by the Canting Beggars in Beaumont and Fletcher, (1) and the Gipsies in Ben Jonson's Masque, (2) are still to be heard among the *Gnostics* of Dyot-street and Tothillfields. To *prig* is still to steal; (3) to *fib*, to beat; *lour*, money; *duds*, clothes; (4) *prancers*, horses; *bouzing-ken*, an ale-house; *cove*, a fellow; a *sow's baby*, a pig; etc., etc. There are also several instances of the same term, preserved with a totally different signification. Thus, to *mill*, which was originally "to rob," (5) is now "to beat or fight;" and the word *rum*, which in Ben Jonson's time, and even so late as Grose, meant *fine* and *good*, is now generally used for the very opposite qualities; as, "he's but a *rum* one," etc. Most of the Cant phrases in Head's *English Rogue*, which was published, I believe, in 1666, would be intelligible to a *Greek* of the present day; though it must be confessed that the Songs which both he and Dekker have given would puzzle even that "Graiæ gentis decus," Caleb Baldwin himself. For instance, one of the simplest begins—

Bing out, bien Morts, and toure and toure
Bing out, bien Morts and toure.
For all your duds are bing'd awast;
The bien Cove hath the loure.

To the cultivation, in our times, of the science of Pugilism, the *Flash* language is indebted for a considerable addition to its treasures. Indeed, so impossible is it to describe the operations of The Fancy without words of proportionate energy to do justice to the subject, that we find Pope and Cowper, in their translation of the *Set-to* in the *Iliad*, pressing words into the service which had seldom, I think, if ever, been enlisted into the ranks of poetry before. Thus Pope,

Secure this hand shall his whole frame confound,
Mash all his bones, and all his body pound.

(1) In their amusing comedy of "*The Beggar's Bush*."

(2 The Masque of the *Gipsies Metamorphosed*. — The Gipsy language, indeed, with the exception of such terms as relate to their own peculiar customs, differs but little from the regular Flash; as may be seen by consulting the Vocabulary subjoined to the Life of Bamfylde Moore Carew.

(3) See the third chapter, 1st book, of the History of Jonathan Wild, for an "undeniable testimony of the great antiquity of *Priggism*."

(4) An *angler* for *duds* is thus described by Dekker — "He carries a short staff in his hand, which is called a *filch*, having, in the *nab* or head of it, a *ferme* that is to say a hole), into which, upon any piece of service, when he goes a *filching*, he putteth a hooke of iron, with which hooke he angles at a window in the dead of night for shirts, smockes, or any other linen or woollen." — *English Flashes*.

Cowper, in the same manner, translates κοψε δε..... παρηιον, "*pash'd* him on the cheek;" and, in describing the wrestling-match, makes use of a term, now more properly applied to a peculiar kind of blow, (6) of wh'ch Mendoza is supposed to have been the inventor.

Then I is wiles
Forgat not he, but on the ham behind
Chopp'd him.

Before I conclude this Preface, which has already, I fear, extended to an unconscionable length, I cannot help expressing my regret at the selection which Mr. Crib has made of *one* of the combatants introduced into the imaginary *Set-to* that follows. That person has already been exhibited, perhaps, "*usque ad nauseam*," before the Public; and, without entering into the propriety of meddling with such a personage at all, it is certain that, as a mere matter of *taste*, he ought now to be let alone. All that can be alleged for Mr. Crib is—what Rabelais has said in defending the moral notions of another kind of cattle—he "knows no better." But for myself, in my editorial capacity, I take this opportunity of declaring, that, as far as *I* am concerned, the person in question shall henceforward be safe and inviolate; and, as the Covent Garden Managers said, when they withdrew their much-hiss'd elephant, *this is positively the last time of his appearing on the stage.*

TOM CRIB'S
MEMORIAL TO CONGRESS.

Most Holy, and High, and Legitimate *squad*,
First *Swells* (7) of the world, since *Bony's* in *quod*, (8)
Who have every thing now, as *Bill Gibbons* would say,
"Like the Bull in the china-shop, all your own way"—
Whatsoever employs your magnificent *nobs* (9)
Whether *diddling* your subjects, and *gutting* their *fobs* (10)
(While you *hum* the poor *spoonies* (11) with speeches so pretty,
'Bout Freedom, and Order, and—*all my eye, Betty*),

(5) "Can they *cant* or *mill?* are they masters in their art?"—Ben Jonson.—To *mill*, however, sometimes signified "to kill." Thus, to *mull a bleating cheat*, i. e. to kill a sheep.

(6) "A *chopper* is a blow, struck on the face with the back of the hand. Mendoza claims the honour of its invention, but unjustly; he certainly revived, and considerably improved it. It was practised long before our time. —Broughton occasionally used it, and Slack, it also appears, struck the *chopper* in giving the return in many of his battles."—*Boxiana*, vol. ii., p. 20.

(7) *Swell*, a great man.

(8) In prison. The *dab's* in *quod:* the rogue is in prison.

(9 Heads

(10) Taking out the contents. Thus, *gutting* a quart-pot (or *taking out the lining of it*), i. e. drinking it off.

(11) Simpletons, alias *Innocents*.

Whether praying, or dressing, or *dancing* the *hays*,
Or *lapping* your *congo* (1) at Lord C–stl–r—gh's
(While his Lordship, as usual, that very great *dab* (2)
At the flowers of rhetoric, is *flashing* his *gab*—(3)
Or holding State Dinners, to talk of the weather,
And cut up your mutton and Europe together!
Whatever your *gammon*, whatever your talk,
Oh deign, ye illustrious *Cocks of the Walk*,
To attend for a moment—and if the Fine Arts
Of *fibbing* (4) and *boring* (4) be dear to your hearts;
If to *level*, (4) to *punish*, (4) to *ruffian* (4) mankind,
And to *darken* their *daylights*, (5) be pleasures refined
(As they *must* be) for every Legitimate mind—
Oh listen to one, who, both able and willing
To spread through creation the mysteries of *milling*
(And, as to whose politics, search the world round,
Not a sturdier *Pit-tite* (6) e'er lived under ground),
Has thought of a plan, which—excuse his presumption,
He hereby submits to your Royal *rumgumption.* (7)

It being now settled that emperors and kings,
Like kites made of *foolscap*, are *high-flying* things,
To whose tails a few millions of subjects, or so,
Have been tied in a string, to be whisk'd to and fro,
Just wherever it suits the said *foolscap* to go—
This being all settled, and freedom all *gammon*, (8)
And nought but your Honours worth wasting a
d—n on;
While snug and secure you may now *run* your
rigs, (9)
Without fear that old Boney will *bother* your *gigs*—
As your Honours, too, bless you! though all of *a
trade*,
Yet agreeing like *new ones*, have lately been made
Special constables o'er us, for keeping the peace—
Let us hope now that wars and *rumbustions* will cease;
That soldiers and guns, like "the Devil and his
works,"
Will henceforward be left to Jews, Negers, and Turks;

(1) Drinking your tea.
(2) An adept.
(3) Showing off his talk.—Better expressed, perhaps, by
a late wit, who, upon being asked what was going on in
the House of Commons, answered, "only Lord C. *airing*
his *vocabulary*."
(4) All terms of the Fancy, and familiar to those who
read the Transactions of the Pugilistic Society.
(5) To close up their eyes—alias, to *sew up* their
sees.
6) Tom received his first education in a coal-pit; from
whence he has been honoured with the name of "the
black Diamond."
(7) *Gumption* or *Rumgumption*, comprehension, capacity.
(8) Nonsense or humbug.
(9) Play your tricks.
10) A soldier's fire-lock.
(11) Soldiers, from the colour of their clothes. "*To
boil one's lobster* means for a churchman to turn soldier,
—lobsters, which are of a bluish black, being made red

Till *Brown Bess* (10) shall soon, like Miss Tabitha
Fusty,
For want of a *spark to go off with*, grow rusty,
And *lobsters* (11) will lie such a drug upon hand,
That our *do-nothing* Captains must all get *ja-
pann'd !* (12)
My eyes, how delightful !—the rabble well *gagg'd*.
The *Swells* in *high feather*, and old Boney *lagg'd* !(13)

But though we must hope for such good times as
these,
Yet as something *may* happen to *kick up a breeze*—
Some quarrel reserved for your own *private pick-
ing*— [sticking
Some grudge, even now in your great gizzards
(God knows about what—about money mayhap,
Or the Papists, or Dutch, or that *kid*,(14) Master Nap)
And, seeing in case there should come such a *rumpus*,
As *some* mode of *settling the chat* we must compass,
With which the *tag-rag* (15) will have nothing to do—
What think you, great *Swells*, of a Royal Set-to? (16)
A *Ring* and fair *fist-work*, at Aix-la-Chapelle,
Or at old Moulsey-Hurst, if you likes it as well—
And that all may be *fair* as to *wind, weight*, and
science,
I'll answer to train the whole Holy Alliance !
Just think, please your Majesties, how you'd prefer it,
To *mills* such as Waterloo, where all the merit
To vulgar red-coated *rapscallions* must fall,
Who have no Right Divine to have merit at all !
How much more select your own quiet *Set-tos !*
And how vastly genteeler 't would sound in the news,
(*Kent's Weekly Dispatch*, that beats all others hollow
For *Fancy* transactions), in terms such as follow :—

ACCOUNT OF THE GRAND SET-TO BETWEEN LONG SANDY AND GEORGY THE PORPUS.

Last Tuesday, at Moulsey, the Balance of Power
Was settled by Twelve *Tightish* Rounds in an hour—
The *Buffers*,(17) both "Boys of the Holy Ground;" (18
Long Sandy, by name of the *Bear* much renown'd,

by boiling."—*Grose.* Butler's ingenious simile will occur
to the reader : —

　　When, like a lobster boil'd, the morn
　　From black to red began to turn.

(12) Ordained—i. e. become clergymen.
(13) Transported.
(14) Child.—Hence our useful word, kidnapper—to *nab
a kid* being to steal a child. Indeed, we need but recollect
the many excellent and necessary words to which Johnson
has affixed the stigma of "cant term," to be aware how
considerably the English language has been enriched by
the contributions of the Fish fraternity.
(15 The common people—the mobility.
(16) A boxing-match.　　(17 Boxers—Irish cant.
(18) The hitch in the metre here was rendered necessary
by the quotation, which is from a celebrated *Fancy Chant*,
ending, every verse, thus —
　　For we are the boys of the *Holy Ground*,
　　And we 'll dance upon nothing, and turn us round !
It is almost needless to add, that the *Holy Ground* or
Land is a well-known region of St. Giles's.

And Georgy the *Porpus*, *prime glutton* reckon'd—
Old *thingumnee* Pottso (1) was Long Sandy's second,
And Georgy's was *Pat* C—stl–r—gh—h, he who lives
At the sign of the *King's Arms a-kimbo*, and gives
His *small* beer about, with the air of a *chap*
Who bel eved it himself a prodigious *strong tap*.
This being the first true Legitimate *Match*
Since Tom took to *training* these *Swells* for the *scratch*,
Every *lover of life*, that had *rhino* to spare,
From sly little Moses to B—r—g, was there.
Never since the renown'd days of B roughton and Figg (2)
Was the *Fanciful World* in such very *prime twig*—(3)
And long before daylight, gigs, *rattlers*, (4 and *prads*, (5)
Were in motion for Moulsey, brimful of *the Lads*.
Jack Eld–n, O d Sid., and some more had come down,
On the evening before, and put up at *The Crown*—
Their old favourite sign, where themselves and their brothers
Get *grub*(6) at cheap rate, though it *fleeces* all others;
Nor matters it how we plebeians condemn,
As *The Crown*'s always sure of its *license* from them.

'T was diverting to see, as one *ogled* around,
How *Corinthians* (7) and *Commoners* mix'd on the ground.
Here M—ntr—se and an Israelite met face to face,
The Duke, a place-hunter—the Jew, from Duke's Place;
While Nicky V—ns—tt—t, not caring to roam,
Got among the *white-bag-men*, (8) and felt quite *at home*.
Here stood in a corner, well screen'd from the wea-[ther,
Old Sid. and the great Doctor Eady together,
Both famed *on the walls*—with a d—n, in addition,
Prefix'd to the name of the *former* Physician.
Here C—md—n, who never till now was suspected
Of *Fancy*, or aught that is therewith connected,
Got close to a *dealer in donkies*, who eyed him,
Jack Scroggins remark'd, "just as if he'd have *buy'd him;*"

1) Tom means, I presume, the celebrated diplomatist, Pozzo di Borgo —The Irish used to claim the dancer Didelot as their countryman, insisting that the O had slipped out of its right place, and that his real name was Mr. O'Diddle. On the same principle, they will, perhaps, assert their right to M. Pozzo.

(2) The chief founders of the modern school of pugilism.
(3) High spirits or condition
(4) Coaches. 5) Horses. (6 Victuals.
(7) Men of rank—vide *Boxiana*, *passim*.
(8 Pick-pockets. (9) A cart or waggon. (10) A watch.
(11) The ropes and stakes used at the prize-fights, being the property of the Pugilistic Club, are marked with the initials P C.
(12) For "Holy Alliance" (13 Hat.
(14) "The fine manly form of Humphries was seen to great advantage: he had on a pair of fine flannel drawers, white silk stockings, the clocks of which were spangled

While poor *Bogy* B—ck—gh—m well might look pale,
As there stood a great *Rat-catcher* close to his tail!
'Mongst the vehicles, too, which were many and va- rious,
From *natty barouche* down to *buggy precarious*,
We *twigg'd* more than one *queerish* sort of *turn–out;*
C—nn—g came in a *job*, and then canter'd about
On a showy, but hot and unsound, *bit of blood*
(For a *leader* once meant, but cast off, as not good),
Looking round to secure a *snug place* if he could :—
While Eld—n, long doubting between a *grey* nag
And a *white* one to mount, took his stand in a *drag*.(9)
At a quarter past ten, by Pat C—stl—r—gh's *tat-tler*, (10)
Cr b came on the ground in a four-in-hand *rattler*
(For Tom, since he took to these Holy Allies,
Is as *tip-top a beau* as all Bond-street supplies) ;
And, on seeing the Champion, loud cries of "Fight, fight,"
" Ring, ring," " Whip the Gemmen," were heard left and right.
But the *kids*, though impatient, were doom'd to delay,
As the old P. C. (11) ropes (which are *now* mark'd H. A.)(12)
Being hack'd in the service, it seems had given way ;
And, as rope is an article much *up* in price
Since the Bank took to hanging, the lads had to *splice*.

At length the two *Swells* having enter'd the Ring,
To the *tune the Cow died of*, call'd "God save the King,"
Each threw up his *castor* (13) mid general huzzas—
And, if *dressing* would do, never yet, since the days
When Humphries *stood up* to the Israelite's *thumps*,
In gold spangled stockings and *touch-me-not* pumps,(14)
Has there any thing equall'd the *fal-lals* and tricks
That bedizen'd old Georgy's *bang-up tog and kicks!*(15)
Having first shaken *daddles* (16) (to show, Jackson
It was "pro bono *Pimlico*"(17) chiefly they bled),
Both *peel'd*(18)—but, on laying his *Dandy belt* by,
Old Georgy *went floush*, and his *backers* look'd *shy;*

with gold, and pumps tied with riband." (Account of the First Battle between Humphries and Mendoza.) —The epistle which Humphries wrote to a friend, communicating the result of this fight, is worthy of a Lacedæmonian :— "Sir, I have *done* the Jew, and am in good health. Rich. Humphries."

(15) *Tog* and *kicks*, coat and breeches.—*Tog* is one of the cant words which Dekker cites, as " retaining a certain salt and tasting of some wit and learning," being derived from the Latin *toga*.
(16) Hands.
(17) Mr. Jackson's residence is in Pimlico.—This gentleman (as he well deserves to be called, from the correctness of his conduct and the peculiar urbanity of his manners forms that useful link between the amateurs and the professors of pugilism, which, when broken, it will be difficult, if not wholly impossible, to replace.
(18) Stripped.

For they saw, notwithstanding Crib's honest endeavour
To train down the *crummy*, (1) 'twas monstrous as ever!
Not so with Long Sandy—*prime meat* every inch—
Which, of course, made the *Gnostics* (2) on t' other side flinch ;
And Bob W—ls—n from Southwark, the *gamest* chap there,
Was now heard to *sing out*, "Ten to one on the Bear!"

First Round. Very cautious—the *Kiddies* both sparr'd
As if *shy* of the *scratch*—while the Porpus kept guard
O'er his beautiful *mug*, (3 as if fearing to hazard
One *damaging* touch n so dandy a *mazzard*.
Which 't other observing, *put in his One-Two* (4)
Between Georgy's left ribs, with a knuckle so true,
That had his heart lain *in the right place* no doubt
But the Bear's *double-knock* would have rummaged it out—
As it *was*, Master Georgy came *souse* with the whack,
And there sprawl'd, like a turtle turn'd *queer* on its back.

Second Round. Rather sprightly—the Bear, in *high gig*,
Took a fancy to *flirt* with the Porpus's wig ;
And had it been either a loose tie or *bob*,
He'd have *claw'd* it *clean* off, but 't was glued to his nob.
So he *tipp'd* him a *settler* they call "a Spoil-Dandy"
Full plump in the whisker.—*High betting on Sandy.*

Third Round. Somewhat slack—Georgy tried to *make play*,
But his own *victualling-office* (5) stood much in the way ;
While Sandy's long arms—long enough for a *douse*
All the way from Kamschatka to Johnny Groat's House—

(1) Fat. (2) Knowing ones. (3) Face.
(4) Two blows succeeding each other rapidly. Thus (speaking of Randall) "his one-two are put in with the sharpness of lightning."
(5) The stomach or paunch.
(6) Mouth. (7) Hot cross-buns.
(8) "Some have censured shifting as an unmanly custom."—*Boxiana.*
(9 Humbug or gammon.
(10) *Dead Men* are Bakers—so called from the loaves falsely charged to their master's customers The following is from an Account of the Battle fought by Nosworthy, the Baker, with Martin, the Jew.—
"First Round. Nosworthy, on the alert, planted a tremendous hit on Martin's mouth, which not only drawed forth a profusion of *claret*, but he went down.—Loud shouting from the *Dead Men.*
"Second Round. Nosworthy began to serve the Jew in

Kept *paddling* about the poor Porpus's *muns* (6)
Till they made him as *hot* and as *cross* as *Lent buns!* (7)

Fourth Round. Georgy's *backers* look'd blank at the lad,
When they saw what a *rum knack of shifting* (8) he had—
An old *trick of his youth*—but the Bear, *up to snuff*, (9)
Follow'd close on my gentleman, kneading his *crum*
As expertly as any *Dead Man* (10) about town,
All the way to the ropes—where, as Georgy went down,
Sandy *tipp'd* him a *dose* of that kind, that, when taken,
It is n't the *stuff*, but the *patient* that's *shaken*.

Fifth Round. Georgy tried for his *customer's* head—
(The part of Long Sandy that's *softest*, 't is said ;
And the chat is that Nap, when he had him in tow,
Found his *knowledge-box* (11) always the first thing to go)—
Neat *milling* this Round—what with *clouts* on the nob,
Home-hits in the *bread-basket,* (12) *clicks* in the gob, (13)
And *plumps* in the *daylights,* (14) a prettier treat
Between two *Johnny Raws* (15) 'tis not easy to meet.

Sixth Round. Georgy's friends in high flourish and hopes ;
Jack Eld—n, with others, came close to the ropes—
And when Georgy, one time, *got the head* of the Bear
Into Chancery, (16) Eld—n sung out, "*keep him there ;*"
But the *cull* broke away, as he would from *Lob's pound,* (17)
And, after a *rum* sort of *ruffianing* Round,
Like *cronies* they *hugg'd*, and came *smack* to the ground ;
Poor Sandy the undermost, smother'd and spread
Like a German tuck'd under his huge feather-bed! (18)

style, and his hits told most tremendously. The *Dead Men* now opened their mouths wide, and loudly offered six to four on the *Master of the Rolls.*
(11) The head. (12) The stomach. (13) The mouth
(14) The eyes. (15) Novices.
(16) Getting the head under the arm, for the purpose of *fibbing.*
17) A prison —See Dr. Grey's explanation of this phrase in his notes upon *Hudibras.*
(18) The Germans sleep between two beds and it is related that an Irish traveller, upon finding a feather-bed thus laid over him, took it into his head that the people slept in *strata*, one upon the other, and said to the attendant, "will you be good enough to tell the gentleman or lady that is to lie over me to make haste, as I want to go asleep!"

All pitied the *patient*, and loud exclamations,
" *My eyes !*" and " *my wig !*" spoke the general sen-
sations—
'T was thought Sandy's soul was squeezed out of his
corpus,
So heavy the crush.—*Two to one on the Porpus !*

Nota bene.—'T was curious to see all the pigeons
Sent off by Jews, Flashmen, and *other* religions,
To *office*, (1) with all due dispatch, through the air,
To the *Bulls* of the Alley the fate of the Bear
For in these *Fancy* times, 'tis your *hits* in the *muns*,
And your *choppers*, and *floorers*, that govern the
Funds —
And Consols, which had been all day *shy* enough,
When 'twas known in the Alley that *Old Blue and
Buff*
Had been down on the Bear, rose at once—*up to
snuff*. (2)

Seventh Round. Though *hot-press'd*, and as flat as
a crumpet,
Long Sandy show'd *game* again, scorning to *rump* it;
And, fixing his eye on the Porpus's *snout*, (3)
Which he knew that Adonis felt *peery* 4) about,
By a *feint*, truly elegant, tipp'd him a *punch* in
The critical place where he *cupboards* his luncheon,
Which knock'd all the rich Curaçoa into *cruds*,
And *doubled* him up, like a bag of old *duds !* 5)
There he lay almost *frummagem'd* (6 —every one said
'T was *all Dicky with* Georgy, his *mug* hung so dead:
And 't was only by calling " your wife, Sir, your wife !"
(As a man would cry " fire !") they could start him to
life.
Up he rose in a *funk*, (7) *lapp'd a toothful* of brandy,
And *to it* again.—*Any odds* upon Sandy.

Eighth Round. Sandy worked like a first-rate *de-
molisher :*
Bear as he is, yet his *lick* is no *polisher :*
And, take him at *ruffianing* work (though in common he
Hums about Peace and *all that*, like a *Domine*), (8)
Sandy's the boy, if once to it they fall,
That will *play up old gooseberry* soon with them all.
This round was but short—after humouring awhile,
He proceeded to *serve* an *ejectment*, in style,
Upon Georgy's front *grinders*, (9) which *damaged* his
smile

(1) To sign fy by letter
(2) This phrase, denoting *elevation* of various kinds, is
often rendered more emphatic by such adjuncts *as " up
to snuff and twopenny"*—"*up to snuff, and a punch above
it,*" etc., etc. (3) Nose.
(4) Suspicious 5) Clothes. (6) Choked. (7) Fright.
(8) A Parson.—Thus in that truly classical song, the
Christening of Little Joey,
When *Domine* had named the *Kid*,
Then bonne again they piled it
A *flash of lightning* was prepared
F r every one that liked it

So completely, that bets ran a hundred to ten
The Adonis would ne'er *flash his ivory* (10) again—
And 'twas pretty to see him *roll'd* round with the
shock,
Like a cask of fresh blubber in old Greenland Dock !

Ninth Round. One of Georgy's bright *ogles* (11) was
put
On the *bankruptcy list*, with its shop-windows *shut;*
While the *other* soon made quite as *tag-rag* a show,
All *rimm'd* round with *black*, like the *Courier* in
woe !
Much alarm was now seen 'mong the Israelite
Kids,
And B—r—g, the *devil's own boy* for the *quids*, (12)
Dispatch'd off a pigeon (the species, no doubt,
That they call B—r—g's *stock*-dove) with word ' to
sell out. "

From this to the finish 't was all *fiddle faddle*—
Poor Georgy, at last, could scarce hold up his *daddle*—
With *grinders* dislodged and with *peepers* both
poach'd, (13)
'T was not till the Tenth Round his *claret* (14) was
broach'd :
As the *cellarage* lay so deep down in the fat,
Like his old M——'s purse, 't was cursed hard to
get at.
But a *pelt* in the *smeller*, (15) (too pretty to shun,
If the lad even *could* set it going *like fun;*
And this being the first Royal *claret* let flow,
Since Tom *took* the Holy Alliance *in tow*,
The *uncorking* produced much sensation about,
As *bets* had been *flush* on the first *painted snout.*
Nota bene.—A note was wing'd off to the *Square*,
Just to hint of this awful phlebotomy there,—
Bob Gregson, whose wit at such things is exceed-
ing, (16)
Inclosing a large sprig of " *Love lies a bleeding !*"

In short, not to dwell on each *facer* and *fall*,
Poor Georgy was *done up in no time at all*,
And his *spunkiest* backers were forced to *sing
small.* 17)
In vain did they try to *fig up* the old lad,
'T was like using *persuaders* (18) upon a dead
prad; (19)
In vain *Bogy* (20) B—ck—gh—m fondly besought him,
To show like himself, if not *game*, at least *bottom ;*

(9) Teeth. (10) Show his teeth·
(11) Eyes. (12) Money.
13) French cant Les yeux *pochés au beurre noir.*—
See the *Dictionnaire Comique.*
(14) Blood.
(15) The nose.
(16 Some specimens of Mr. Gregson's lyrical talents are
given in the Appendix. No. 3.
(17) To be humbled or abashed.
(18) Spurs.
(19) Horse.
(20) For the meaning of this term, see *Grose.*

While M—il—y, that *very* great Count, stood deplor-
   ing   [*ing :* (1)
He had n't taught Georgy his new modes of *bor-*
All useless—no art can *transmogrify* truth—
It was plain the *conceit* was *mill'd out* of the youth.
In the Twelfth and Last Round Sandy fetch'd him a
   downer,
That left him all 's one as *cold meat* for the *Crown-
   er ;* (2)
On which the whole populace *flash'd* the *white grin
Like a basket of chips,* and poor Georgy *gave in :* (3)
While the fiddlers (old Potts having *tipp'd* them a
   bandy) (4)
Play'd "Green grow the *rushes,*" (5) in honour of
   Sandy !

Now, what say your Majesties ?—is n't this *prime ?*
Was there ever French bulletin half so sublime ?
Or could old Nap himself, in his glory, have *wish'd*
To *show up* a *fat Gemman* more handsomely *dish'd ?*
Oh, bless your great hearts, let them say what they
Nothing 's half so *genteel* as a *regular Mill ;*   [will,
And, for *settling of balances,* all I know is,
'T is the way Caleb Baldwin *prefers* settling *his.* (6)
As for *backers,* you 've lots of *Big-wigs* about Court,
That will *back* you—the *raff* being tired of that
   sport—
And if *quids* should be wanting to make the match
   good,
There 's B—r—g, the Prince of *Rag Rhino,* who stood
(T' other day, you know) bail for the *seedy* (7) Right
   Liners ;
Who knows but, if coax'd, he may *shell out* the
   shiners ? (8)
The *shiners !* Lord, Lord, what a *bounce* do I say !
As if we could hope to have *rags* done away !
Or see *any* thing *shining,* while Van. has the sway !

As to *training,* a Court 's but a *rum* sort of station
To choose for that sober and chaste operation ; (9)

(1) "The ponderosity of Crib, when in close quarters
with his opponent, evidently *bored* in upon him," etc.
(2) The Coroner.
(3) The *ancient* Greeks had a phrase of similar struc-
ture, ενδιδωμι, cedo.
(4) A *bandy* or *cripple,* a sixpence ; "that piece being
commonly much bent and distorted."—*Grose.*
(5) The well-known compliment paid to the Emperor
of all the *Russias* by some Irish musicians.
(6) A trifling instance of which is recorded in *Boxiana* .
— "A *fracas* occurred between Caleb Baldwin and the
keepers of the gate. The latter, not immediately recog-
nising the *veteran of the ring,* refused his vehicle admit-
tance without the usual *tip,* but Caleb, finding *arguifying
the topic* would not do, instead of paying them in the *new
coinage,* dealt out another sort of *currency* , and, although
destitute of the W. W. P., it had such an instantaneous
effect upon the *Johnny Raws,* that the gate flew open, and
Caleb rode through in triumph."
(7) Poor.   (8) Produce the guineas.
(9) The **extreme** rigour, in these respects, of the ancient

For, as old Ikey Pig (10) said of Courts, "by de
   Heavens,
Dey 're all, but the *Fives* Court, at *sixes* and *sevens.*"
What with *snoozing,* (11) high *grubbing,* (12) and
   guzzling like Cloe,
Your Majesties, pardon me, all get so *doughy,*
That take the whole *kit,* down from Sandy the Bear,
To him who makes *duds* for the Virgin to wear,
I'd chuse but Jack Scroggins, and feel disappointed
If Jack did n't *tell out* the whole Lord's Anointed !

But, barring these natural defects (which, I feel,
My remarking on thus may be thought *ungenteel*),
And allowing for delicate *fams,* (13) which have
   merely
Been handling the sceptre, and *that,* too, but *queerly,*
I'm not without hopes, and would *stand a tight bet,*
That I'll make something *game* of your Majesties
   yet.
So, say but the word—if you 're *up* to the freak,
Let us have a prime *match* of it, *Greek* against *Greek,*
And I'll put you on *beef-steaks* and *sweating* next
   week—
While, for teaching you every perfection that
   throws a
Renown upon *milling*—the tact of Mendoza—
The charm, by which Humphries (14) contrived to
   infuse
The *three Graces* themselves into all his *One-Twos*—
The *nobbers* of Johnson (15)—Big Ben's (16) *banging
   brain-blows*—
The *weaving* of Sam, (17) that turn'd faces to rain-
   bows—
Old Corcoran's *click,* (18) that laid *customers* flat—
Paddy Ryan *from Dublin's* (18) renown'd "coup de
   Pat ;"
And *my* own *improved* method of *tickling a rib,*
You may always command
                Your devoted,
                       TOM CRIB.

system of training, may be inferred from the instances
mentioned by Ælian. Not only pugilists, but even players
on the harp, were, during the time of their probation,
συ,ουσιας αμαθεις και απειροι. — *De Animal.,* lib. 6,
cap. 1.
(10) A Jew, so nick-named—one of the *Big ones.* He
was beaten by Crib, on Blackheath, in the year 1805.
(11) Sleeping.   (12) Feeding.
(13) *Fams* or *fambles,* hands.
(14) Humphries was called "The Gentleman Boxer."
He was (says the author of *Boxiana*) remarkably graceful,
and his attitudes were of the most elegant and impressive
nature.
(15) Tom Johnson, who, till his fight with Big Ben, was
hailed as the Champion of England.
(16) Ben Brain, *alias* Big Ben, wore the honours of the
Championship till his death.
(17) Dutch Sam, a hero of whom all the lovers of the
Fancy speak, as the Swedes do of Charles the Twelfth,
with tears in their eyes.
· (18) Celebrated Irish pugilists.

APPENDIX.

No. I.—*Account of a Grand Pugilistic Meeting, held at* Belcher's (*Castle Tavern, Holborn*), Tom Crib *in the Chair, to take into consideration the propriety of sending Representatives of the Fancy to Congress.—Extracted from a letter written by* Harry Harmer, *the* Hammerer,(1) *to* Ned Painter.

Ἀλλ᾽ οὐδεις το ΚΑΝ
Λειρει, ἑως αν
Τον ηχωδεα αχουση ΤΩΜ. (2)

LAST Friday night a *bang-up* set
Of *milling blades* at Belcher's met,
All high-bred Heroes of *the Ring*,
  Whose very *gammon* would delight one,
Who, nursed beneath *The Fancy's* wing,
  Show all her *feathers*—but the *white one.*

Brave Tom, the Champion, with an air,
Almost *Corinthian* (3) took the Chair ;
And kept the *Coves* (4) in quiet tune,
  By showing such a *fist* of *mutton*
As, on a Point of Order, soon
  Would *take the shine* from Speaker Sutton.
And all the lads look'd gay and bright,
  And *gin* and *genius* flash'd about ;
And whosoe'er grew unpolite,
  The well-bred Champion *served him out.*

As we'd been summon'd thus to quaff
  Our *Deady* (5) o'er some State Affairs,
Of course we mix'd not with the *raff*,
  But had the *Sunday room*, up stairs.
And when we well had *sluiced* our *gobs*, (6)
  Till all were in *prime twig* for *chatter*,
Tom rose, and to our learned *nobs*   .
  Propounded thus the important matter:—

" *Gemmen*," says he—Tom's words, you know,
Come like his *hitting*, strong but slow—
" Seeing as how those *Swells*, that made
Old Boney quit the *hammering* trade
(All prime ones in their own conceit),
Will shortly at the Congress meet—

(1) So called in his capacity of *Boxer* and *Coppersmith.*
(2) The passage in Pindar, from which the following lines of " Hark the merry Christ Church Bells," are evidently borrowed —
        The devil a man will leave his can
        Till he hears the *Mighty Tom.*
(3) i e. With the air, almost, of a man of rank and fashion. Indeed, according to Horace's notions of a *peerage*, *Tom's* claims to it are indisputable —
        —— Illum superare pugnis
        Nobilem.
(4) Fellows.
(5) Deady's gin, otherwise Deady's *brilliant stark naked.*
(6) Had drunk heartily.
(7) A public-house in Covent-Garden, memorable as one of the places where the Gentlemen Depredators of the night (the Holy League of the Road meet, early in the

(Some place that's like the Finish,(7) lads,
Where all your high pedestrian *pads*,
That have been *up* and *out* all night,
  Running their *rigs* among the *rattlers*, (8
At morning meet, and—*honour bright*—
  Agree to share the *blunt* and *tattlers!*—(9)
Seeing as how, I say, these *Swells*
Are soon to meet, by special summons,
To ch me together like ' *hell's bells*,'
  And laugh at all mankind as *rum ones*—
I see no reason, when such things
Are going on among these Kings,
Why *We*, who 're of the *Fancy* lay, (10)
As *dead hands* at a *mill* as they,
And quite as ready *after* it,
To share the spoil, and *grab the bit*, (11)
Should not be there to *join the chat*,
To see, at least, what *fun* they 're at,
And help their Majesties to find
New modes of *punishing* mankind.
What say you, lads? is any spark
Among you ready for a *lark* (12)
To this same Congress?—Caleb, Joe,
Bill, Bob, what say you?—yes or no ? "
Thus spoke the Champion, Prime of men,
  And loud and long we *cheer'd* his *prattle*
With shouts, that thunder'd through the *ken*,(13)
  And made Tom's *Sunday tea-things* rattle !

A pause ensued—till cries of " Gregson "
Brought Bob, the Poet, on his legs soon—
(*My eyes*, how prettily Bob writes !
  Talk of your *Camels, Hogs*, and *Crabs*, (14)
And twenty more such *Pidcock* frights—
  Bob's worth a hundred of these *dabs ;*
For a short *turn-up* (15) at a sonnet,
  A *round* of odes, or Pastoral *bout*,
All Lombard-street to *nine-pence* on it, (16)
  Bobby's the boy would *clean* them *out!*)
" *Gemmen*," says he—(Bob's eloquence
Lies much in C—nn—g's line, 't is said,
For, when Bob can't afford us *sense*,
  He *tips* us *poetry*, instead—)

morning, to share the spoil, and arrange other matters connected with their most Christian Alliance
(8) Robbing travellers in chaises, etc.
(9 The money and watches.
(10) Particular pursuit or enterprise. Thus, " he is on the *kid-lay*," *i. e.* stopping children with parcels and robbing them—the *kencrack-lay*, house-breaking, etc.
(11) To seize the money.
(12) A frolic, or party of pleasure.   (13) House.
(14 By this curious zoological assemblage (something like Berni's " porci, e poet , e piddochi") the writer means, I suppose, Messrs. Campbell, Crabbe, and Hogg.
(15) A *turn-up* is properly a casual and hasty *set-to.*
(16 More usually " Lombard-street to a China orange." There are several of these *fanciful* forms of betting— " Chelsea College to a sentry-box," " Pompey's Pillar to a stick of sealing-wax," etc., etc

" *Gemmen*, before I touch the matter,
On which I 'm here *had up* for *patter*, (1)
A few short words I first must spare,
To him the hero, that sits there,
Swigging Blue Ruin, (2) in that chair.
(*Hear—hear*)—His fame I need not tell,
  For *that*, my friends, all England 's loud with;
But this I 'll say, a civiler *Swell*
  I 'd never wish to *blow a cloud* (3) with ! "

At these brave words, we, every one,
Sung out " hear—hear"—and clapp'd *like fun*.
For knowing how, on Moulsey's plain,
  The Champion *fibb'd* the Poet's *nob*, (4)
This *buttering up*, (5) against the grain,
  We thought was *cursed* genteel in Bob.
And, here again, we may remark
  Bob's likeness to the Lisbon jobber—(6)
For, though all know that *flashy spark*
  From C—st—r—gh received a *nobber*,
That made him look like *sneaking Jerry*,
  And *laid him up* in *ordinary*, (7)
Yet now, such loving *pals* (8) are they,
  That Georgy, wiser as he 's older,
Instead of *facing* C—st—r—gh,
  Is proud to be his *bottle-holder !*

But to return to Bob's harangue,
'T was deuced fine—no *slum* or *slang*—
But such as you could *smoke* the bard in—
All full of *flowers*, like Common Garden,
With *lots of figures*, neat and bright,
Like Mother Salmon's—wax-work quite !

The next was Turner—*nobbing* Ned—
Who put his right leg forth (9) and said,
" Tom, I admire your notion much ;
  And *please the pigs*, if well and hearty,

I somehow thinks I 'll *have a touch*,
  Myself, at this said Congress party.
Though *no great shakes* at learned *chat*,
  If settling Europe be the *sport*,
They 'll find I 'm just the boy for that,
  As *tipping settlers* (10) is my *forte !* "

Then up rose Ward, the veteran Joe,
  And 'twixt his whiffs,(11) suggested briefly
That but a *few*, at first, should go,
  And those, the *light-weight Gemmen* chiefly ;
As if too many " *Big ones* went,
  They might alarm the Continent !! "

Joe added, then, that as 't was known
The R—g—t, bless his wig ! had shown
A taste for Art (like Joey's own) (12)
And meant, 'mong other sporting things,
To have the heads of all those Kings,
And conquerors, whom he loves so dearly,
Taken off—on canvas, merely ;
God forbid the *other* mode !—
He (Joe) would from his own abode
(*The Dragon* (13)—famed for *Fancy* works,
Drawings of Heroes, and of—*corks*)
Furnish such *Gemmen* of *the Fist*, (14)
As would complete the R—g—t's list.
" Thus, Champion Tom," said he, " would look
Right well, hung up beside *the Duke*—
Tom's noddle being (if its *frame*
Had but *the gilding*) much the same—
And, as a partner for *Old Blu*,
Bill Gibbons or *myself* would do."

Loud cheering at this speech of Joey's—
Who as the *Dilettanti* know, is
(With all his other learned parts)
Down as a hammer (15) to the Arts !

---

(1) Talk.   (2) Gin.
(3) To smoke a pipe. This phrase is highly poetical, and explains what Homer meant by the epithet νεφεληγερετης.
(4) In the year 1808, when Crib defeated Gregson.
(5) Praising or flattering.
(6) These parallels between great men are truly edifying.
(7) Sea-cant—a good deal of which has been introduced into the regular Flash, by such *classic* heroes as Scroggins, Crockey, etc.
(8) Friends.
(9) Ned's favourite Pro*legomena* in battle as well as in debate. As this position is said to render him "very hard to be got at," I would recommend poor Mr. V—ns-t-tart to try it as a last resource, in his next *set-to* with Mr. T—rn-y.
(10) A kind of blow, whose *sedative* nature is sufficiently explained by the name it bears.
(11) Joe being particularly fond of "that costly and gentleman-like smoke," as Dekker calls it. The talent which Joe possesses of uttering *Flash* while he *smokes*—"ex *fumo dare lucem*"—is very remarkable.
(12) Joe's taste for pictures has been thus commemorated by the great Historian of Pugilism—" If Joe Ward cannot boast of a splendid gallery of pictures formed of selections

from the great *foreign* masters, he can sport such a collection of *native* subjects as, in many instances, must be considered unique. Portraits of nearly all the pugilists (many of them in whole lengths and attitudes) are to be found, from the days of Figg and Broughton down to the present period, with likenesses of many distinguished amateurs, among whom are Captain Barclay, the classic Dr. Johnson, the Duke of Cumberland, etc. His parlour is decorated in a similar manner ; and his partiality for pictures has gone so far, that even the tap-room contains many excellent subjects "—*Boxiana*, vol. i., p. 431.
(13) The *Green Dragon*, King-street, near Swallow-street, "where (says the same author) any person may have an opportunity of verifying what has been asserted, in viewing Ward's Cabinet of the Fancy."
(14) Among the portraits is one of Bill Gibbons, by a pupil of the great Fuseli, which gave occasion to the following impromptu :—

  Though you *are* one of Fuseli's scholars,
    This question I 'll dare to propose—
  How the devil could you use *water*-colours,
    In painting Bill Gibbons's nose ?

(15) To be *down to* any thing is pretty much the same as being *up to* it, and "*down as a hammer*" is, of course, the *intensivum* of the phrase.

Old Bill, the Black(1)—you know him. Neddy—
(With *muq*, (2) whose hue the ebon shames,
Reflected in a pint of *Deady*,
Like a large Collier in the Thames
Though somewhat *cut*, (3) just begg'd to say
He hoped that *Swell*, Lord C—st—r—gh,
Would show the *Lily-Whites* (4) fair play;
" And not—as *once* he did "—says Bill,
" Among those Kings, so high and *squirish*,
Leave us poor Blacks, to fare as ill
As if we were but pigs, or Irish !"

Bill Gibbons, rising, wish'd to know
Whether 't was meant *his Bull* should go—
" As should their Majesties be dull,"
Says Bill, " there 's nothing like a Bull : (5)
And *blow me tight*,"—(Bill Gibbons ne'er
In all his days was known to swear,
Except light oaths to grace his speeches,
Like " *dash my wig*," or " *burn my breeches !* ")
" *Blow me—*"
—Just then, the Chair, (6) already
Grown rather *lively* with the *Deady*,

. 　 . 　 . 　 . 　 .

—◦H◦—

No. II.—*Account of the Milling-match between En-
tellus and Dares, translated from the Fifth Book
of the Æneid.* (7)

BY ONE OF THE FANCY.

WITH *daddles* (8) high upraised, and *nob* held back,
In awful prescience of the impending *thwack*,

(1) Richmond.　　(2) Face
(3 *Cut*, tipsy another remarkable instance of the si-
milarity that exists between the language of the Classics
and that of St. Giles's.—In Martial we find " Incaluit quo-
ties *saucia* vena *mero*." Ennius, too, has " *saucuunt* se
flore Liberi ," and Justin, " *hesterno mero saucu.*"
(4) *Lily-whites* (or *Snow-balls*), Negroes.
(5) Bill Gibbons has, I believe, been lately rivalled in
this peculiar Walk of the Fancy, by the superior merits of
Tom Oliver's *Game Bull.*
(6) From the respect which I bear *to all sorts* of digni-
taries, and my unwillingness to meddle with the " imputed
weaknesses of the great," I have been induced to suppress
the remainder of this detail.
(7) Virgil. Æ icid., lib. v., v. 426.

Los s tut in digitos extemp o arrectus uterque,
Brachiaque ad superas int rritus extulit auras.
Abduxere retro longe capita ardua ab ictu
Immiscentque manus manibus, pugnamque lacessunt
Ille, pedum melior motu, fretusque juventa
Hic, membris et mole valios , sed tarda trementi
Genua labant, vastos quatit æger anhelitus artus
Multa viri in quaquam inter se vulnera jaciant,
Multa cavo lateri ingeminant, et pectore vastos
Dant sonitus , circatque aures et tempora circum
Crebra manus duro crepitant sub vulnere malæ
Stat gravis Entellus, nisuque immotus eodem,
Corpore tela modo atque oculis vigilantibus exit
Ille, velut celsam oppugnat qui molibus urbem,
Aut montana sedet circum castella sub armis ,
Nunc hos, nunc illos aditus, omnemque pererrat
Arte locum, et variis assultibus irritus urget
Ostendit dextram insurgens Entellus, et a e
Extulit ille ictum venientem a vertice velox
Prævidit, celerique elapsus corpore cessi
Entellus vires in ventum effudit, et ul ro

Both *kiddies* 9) stood—and with prelusive *spar*,
And light manœuvr ng, kindled up the war !
The one, in bloom of youth—a *light weight blade*—
The other, vast, gigantic, as if made,
Express, by Nature for the *hammering* trade ;
But aged, (10) slow, with stiff limbs, tottering much,
And lungs that lack'd the *bellows-mender's* touch.

Yet, sprightly *to the Scratch* both *Buffers* came,
While *ribbers* rung from each resounding frame,
And divers *digs*, and many a ponderous *pelt*,
Were on their broad *bread-baskets* heard and felt.
With roving aim, but aim that rarely miss'd,
Round *lugs* and *ogles* (11) flew the frequent fist ;
While showers of *facers* told so deadly well,
That the crush'd jaw-bones crackled as they fell !
But firmly stood Entellus—and still bright,
Though bent by age, with all the Fancy's light,
Stopp'd with a skill, and *rallied* with a fire
The Immortal Fancy could alone inspire !
While Dares, *shifting* round, with looks of thought,
An opening to the *Cove's* huge carcase sought
(Like General Preston, in that awful hour,
When on *one* leg he hopp'd to—take the Tower !)
And here, and there, explored with active *fin*, (12)
And skilful *feint*, some guardless pass to win,
And prove a *boring* guest when once *let in.*

And now Entellus, with an eye that plann'd
Punishing deeds, high raised his heavy hand ;

Ipse gravis graviterque ad terram pondere vasto
Concidit ut quondam cava concidit, aut Erymantho,
Aut Ida in magna, radicibus eruta pinus.
Consurgunt studiis Teucri et Trinacria pubes :
It clamor cœlo · primusque accurrit Acestes
Æquevumque ab humo miserans attollit amicum.
At non tardatus casu, neque territus heros
Acrior ad pugnam redit, ac vim suscitat ira
Tum pudor incendit vires, et conscia vir us ;
Præcipitemque Daren ardens agit æquore toto,
Nunc dextra ingeminans ictus, nunc ille sinistra
Nec mora, nec requies quam multa grandine nimbi
Culminibus crepitant, sic densis ictibus heros
Creber utraque manu pulsat versatque Dareta.
Tum pater Æneas procedere longius iras,
Et sævire animis Entellum haud passus acerbis ;
Sed finem imposuit pugnæ, fessumque Dareta
Eripuit, mulcens dictis, ac talia fatur :
Infelix ! quæ tanta animum dementia cepit ?
Non vires alias, conversaque numina sentis ?
Cede Deo Dixitque, et prælia voce diremit.
Ast illum fidi æquales, genua ægra trahentem,
Jactantemque utroque caput, crassumque cruorem
Ore rejectantem, mixtosque in sanguine dentes,
Ducunt ad naves

(8) Hands.　　(9) Fellows, usually *young* fellows.
(10) Macrobius, in his explanation of the various pro-
perties of the number Seven, says, that the fifth Hebdomas
of man's life (the age of 35) is the completion of his strength ;
that therefore pugilists, if not successful, usually give
over their profession at that time.— " Inter pugiles de-
nique hæc consuetudo conservatur, ut quos jam corona-
vere victoriæ, nihil de se amplius in incrementis virtum
sperent, qui vero expertes hujus gloriæ usque illo man-
serunt, a professione discedant."— *In somn. Scip.*, lib. 1.

(11) Ears and Eyes　　(12) Arm.

But ere the *sledge* came down, young Dares spied
Its shadow o'er his brow, and slipp'd aside—
So nimbly sl pp'd, that the vain *nobber* pass'd
Through empty air; and he, so high, so vast,
Who dealt the stroke, came thundering to the
    ground '—
Not B—ck—gh—m himself, with bulk er sound, (1)
Uprooted from the field of Whiggish glories,
Fell *souse*, of late, among the astonish'd Tories ! (2)

Instant the *Ring* was broke, and shouts and yells
From Trojan *Flashmen* and Sicilian *Swells*
Fill'd the wide heaven—while touch'd with grief
    to see
His *pal*, (3) well-known through many a *lark* and
    spree,(4)
Thus *rumly floor'd*, the kind Acestes ran,
And pitying rai-ed from earth the *game* old man.
Uncow'd, undamaged to the *sport* he came,
His limbs all muscle, and his soul all flame.
The memory of his *milling* glories past,
The shame that aught but death should see him
    grass'd,
All fired the veteran's *pluck*—-with fury flush'd—
Full on his light-limb'd *customer* he rush'd—
And *hammering* right and left, with ponderous
    swing, (5)
Ruffian'd the reeling youngster round the *Ring*—
Nor rest, nor pause, nor breathing-time was given,
But, rapid as the rattling hail from heaven
Beats on the house-top, showers of Randall's *shot* (6)
Around the Trojan's *lugs* flew peppering hot !
Till now Æneas, fill'd with anxious dread,
Rush'd in between them, and with words well-
    bred,
Preserved alike the peace and Dares' head,
Both which the veteran much inclined to *break*—
Then kindly thus the *punish'd* youth bespake:

(1) As the uprooted trunk in the original is said to be
"cava," the epithet here ought, perhaps, to be "*hollower*
sound."

(2) I trust my conversion of the Erymanthian pine into
his L—ds—p will be thought happy and ingenious. It was
suggested, indeed, by the recollection that Erymanthus
was also famous for another sort of natural production,
very common in society at all periods, and which no one
but Hercules ever seems to have known how to manage
—though even *he* is described by Valerius Flaccus as
"Erymanthæi *sudantem pondere* monstri."

(3 Friend.   (4 Party of pleasure and frolic.
(5 This phrase is but too applicable to the *round hitting*
of the ancients, who, it appears by the engravings in Mer-
curialis *de art. Gymnast.*, knew as little of our *straight-
forward* mode as the uninitiated Irish of the present day.
I have, by the by, discovered some errors in Mercurialis,
as well as in two other modern authors upon Pugilism
(viz. Petrus Faber, in his *Agonisticon*, and that indefati-
gable classic antiquary, M. Burette, in his "*Mémoire pour
servir à l'Histoire du Pugilat des Anciens*,") which I shall
have the pleasure of pointing out in my forthcoming
"Parallel."

" Poor *Johnny Raw !* what madness could impel
So *rum* a *Flat* to face so *prime* a *Swell ?*
See'st thou not, boy, the Fancy, heavenly Maid,
Herself descends to this great *Hammerer's* aid,
And, singing *him* from all her *flash* adorers,
Shines in his *hits*, and thunders in his *floorers?*
Then, y eld thee, youth—nor such a *spooney* be,
To think mere man can *mill* a Deity ! "

Thus spoke the Chief—and now, the *scrimmage* o'er,
His faithful *pals* the *done-up* Dares bore
Back to his home, with tottering *gams*, sunk
    heart,
And *muns* and *noddle pink'd* in every part. (7)
While from his *gob* the guggling *claret* gush'd,
And lots of *grinders*, from their sockets crush'd,
Forth with the crimson tide in rattling fragments
    rush'd !

—⟶•◦•⟵—

No. III.—BOB GREGSON,

POET LAUREATE OF THE FANCY.

" For *hitting* and *getting away*, (says the elegant
Author of *Boxiana*,) Richmond is distinguished ; and
the brave Molineux keeps a strong hold in the circle
of boxers, as a pugilist of the first class; while the
Champion of England stands unrivalled for his
punishment, *game*, and *milling* on the *retreat!*—
but, notwithstanding the above variety of qualifica-
tions, it has been reserved for Bob Gregson, alone,
from his union of Pugilism and Poetry, to recount
the deeds of his Brethren of the Fist in heroic verse,
like the bards of old, sounding the praises of their
warlike champions." The same author also adds,
that, "although not possessing the terseness and
originality of Dryden, or the musical cadence and
correctness of Pope, yet still Bob has entered into

(6) A favourite blow of *the Nonpareil's*, so called.

7) There are two or three Epigrams in the Greek An-
thology, ridiculing the state of mutilation and disfi-
gurement to which the pugilists were reduced by their
combats. The following four lines are from an Epigram
by Lucilius, lib. 2.

Κοσκινον ἡ κεφαλη σου, Απολλοφανες, γεγενηται,
  'Η των σητοκοπων βυβλαριων τα κατω.
Οντως μυρμηκων τρυπηματα λοξα και ορθα,
  Γραμματα των λυρικων Λυδια και Φρυγια.

Literally, as follows — " Thy head, O Apollophanes, is
perforated like a sieve, or like the leaves of an old worm-
eaten book; and the numerous scars, both straight and
cross-ways, which have been left upon thy pate by the
cestus, very much resemble the score of a Lydian or
Phrygian piece of music." Periphrastically, thus —

  Your noddle, dear Jack, full of holes like a sieve,
    Is so figured, and dotted, and scratch d, I declare,
  By your *customers'* fists, one would almost believe
    They had *punch'd* a whole verse of " The Woodpecker" there!

It ought to be mentioned, that the word "*punching*" is
used both in boxing and music-engraving.

his peculiar subject with a characteristic energy and apposite spirit." Vol. i., p. 357.

This high praise of Mr. Gregson's talents is fully borne out by the specimen which his eulogist has given, *page* 358—a very spirited Chaunt or Nemean ode, entitled "British Lads and Black *Millers*."

The connection between poetical and pugnacious propensities seems to have been ingeniously adumbrated by the ancients, in the bow with which they armed Apollo:—

Φοιβω γαρ και ΤΟΞΟΝ ϵπιτρϵπϵται και ΑΟΙΔΗ.
Callimach Hymn in Apollin , v 44.

The same mythological bard informs us that, when Minerva bestowed the gift of inspiration upon Tiresias, she also made him a present of a large cudgel :—

Δωσω και ΜΕΓΑ ΒΑΚΤΡΟΝ :

another evident intimation of the congeniality supposed to exist between the exercises of the Imagination and those of The Fancy. To no one of the present day is the *double wreath* more justly due than to Mr. Bob Gregson. In addition to his numerous *original* productions, he has condescended to give imitations of some of our living poets—particularly of Lord Byron and Mr. Moore, and the amatory style of the latter gentleman has been caught with peculiar felicity, in the following lines, which were addressed, some years ago, to Miss Grace Maddox, a young Lady of pugilistic celebrity, of whom I have already made honourable mention in the Préface.

———◦◦◦◦———

LINES
TO MISS GRACE MADDOX, THE FAIR PUGILIST.
Written in imitation of the style of Moore.
BY BOB GREGSON, P. P.

Sweet Maid of *the Fancy !* whose *ogles,* (1) adorning
That beautiful cheek, ever budding like bowers,
Are bright as the gems that the first Jew(2) of
   morning
Hawks round Covent-Garden, 'mid cart-loads of
   flowers !

Oh Grace of the Graces! whose kiss to my lip
Is as sweet as the brandy and tea, rather thinnish,
That *Knights* of the *Rumpad*(3) so rurally sip,
   At the first blush of dawn, in the Tap of the
   Finish ! (4

Ah, never be false to me, fair as thou art,
   Nor belie all the many kind things thou hast sa d,

1 Eyes.
(2) By the trifling alteration of "dew" into "Jew," Mr Gregson has contrived to collect the three chief ingredients of Moore's poetry, viz., dews, gems, and flowers, into the short compass of these two lines.   (3 Highwaymen.
(4) See *Note*, page 501. Brandy and tea is the favourite beverage at the Finish.   5 Fetters.
(6) *Prisoner*—This being the only bird in the whole range of Ornithology which the author of *Lalla Rookh* has not pressed into his service, Mr. Gregson may consider himself very lucky in being able to lay hold of it.

The falsehood of *other* nymphs touches the *Heart,*
   But thy *fibbing,* my dear, plays the devil with the
   Head !

Yet, who would not prize, beyond honours and pelf,
   A maid to whom Beauty such treasures has
   granted,
That, ah! she not only has black eyes herself,
   But can furnish a friend with a pair, too, if wanted !

Lord St—w—rt's a hero as many suppose),
   And the Lady he woos is a rich and a rare one;
His *heart* is in *Chancery,* every one knows,
   And so would his *head* be, if thou wert his fair one.

Sweet Maid of the Fancy ! when love first came o'er
   me,
I felt rather *queerish,* I freely confess ;
But now I 've thy beauties each moment before me,
   The pleasure grows more, and the queerishness less.

Thus a new set of *darbies,*(5) when first they are
   worn,
Makes the *Jail-bird* (6) uneasy, though splendid
   their ray ;
But the links will lie lighter the longer they 're borne,
   And the comfort increase, as the *shine* fades away.

I had hoped that it would have been in my power to gratify the reader with several of Mr. Gregson's lyrical productions, but I have only been able to procure a copy of a Song or Chaunt, written by him for a Masquerade, or *Fancy Ball,* given lately at one of the most Fashionable Cock-and-Hen clubs in St. Giles's. Though most of the company were without characters, there were a few very lively and interesting maskers; among whom, we particularly noticed Bill Richmond, as the *Emperor of Hayti,* (7 attended by Sutton, as a sort of *black* Mr. V—ns—t—t ; and Ikey Pig made an excellent L—s D—xh—t. The beautiful Mrs. Crockey, (8) who keeps the Great *Rag Shop* in Bermondsey, went as the *Old Lady of Threadneedle Street.* She was observed to flirt a good deal with the black Mr. V—ns—t—t, but, to do her justice, she guarded her "Hesperidum mala" with all the vigilance of a dragoness. Jack Holmes,(9) the pugilistic *Coachman,* personated Lord C—st—r—gh, and sang in admirable style

Ya-hip, my Hearties' here am I
That drive the Constitution Fly.

(7) H s Majesty (in a Song which I regret I cannot give) professed his intentions

To take to *strong measures* like some of his kin—
To turn away *Count Lemonade,* and bring in
A more *spirited* ministry under *Duke* Gin !

(8) A relative of poor Crockey, who was *lagged* some time since.
(9) The same, I suppose, that *served* out Blake (alias *Tom Tough* some years ago, at Wilsden Green. The *Fancy* Gazette, on that occasion, remarked that poor Holmes's face was "rendered *perfectly unintelligible.*"

64

This Song (which was written for him by Mr. Gregson, and in which the language and sentiments of *Coachee* are transferred so ingeniously to the Noble person represented) is as follows :—

YA-HIP, MY HEARTIES!

Sung by Jack Holmes, the Coachman, at a late Masquerade in St. Giles's, in the Character of Lord C—st—r—gh.

I FIRST was hired to *peg* a *Hack*(1)
They call "The Erin," sometime back,
Where soon I learn'd to *patter flash*, (2)
To curb the *tits*(3) and *tip the lash*—
Which pleased the *Master of the Crown*
So much, he had me up to town,
And gave me *lots of quids* (4) a-year,
To *tool*(5) " The Constitution ' here.
  So, ya-hip, Hearties ! here am I
  That drive the Constitution Fly.

Some wonder how the Fly holds out,
So *rotten* 't is, within, without;
So loaded too, through thick and thin,
And with such *heavy creturs In.*

But, Lord, 't will last our time—or if
The wheels should, now and then, get stiff,
Oil of *Palm* 's (6) the thing that, flowing,
Sets the *naves* and *felloes* (7) going !
  So, ya-hip, Hearties ! etc.

Some wonder, too, the *tits* that pull
This *rum concern* along, so full,
Should never *back* or *bolt*, or kick
The load and driver to Old Nick.
But, never fear—the breed, though British,
Is now no longer *game* or skittish;
Except sometimes about their *corn*,
Tamer *Houyhnhnms* (8) ne'er were born.
  So, ya-hip, Hearties ! etc.

And then so sociably we ride !—
While some have *places*, snug, inside,
Some hoping to be there anon,
Through many a dirty road *hang on.*
And when we reach a filthy spot
(Plenty of which there are, God wot),
You 'd laugh to see with what an air
We *take* the spatter—each his share !
  So, ya-hip, Hearties! etc.

SATIRICAL AND HUMOROUS POEMS. [9]

PREFACE.

THE following trifles, having enjoyed, in their circulation through the newspapers, all the celebrity and length of life to which they were entitled, would have been suffered to pass quietly into oblivion without pretending to any further distinction, had they not already been published, in a collective form, both in London and Paris, and, in each case, been mixed up with a number of other productions, to which, whatever may be their merit, the author of the following pages has no claim. A natural desire to separate his own property, worthless as it is, from that of others, is, he begs to say, the chief motive of the present publication.

In one of those Notices, no less friendly than they

(1) To drive a hackney-coach. *Hack*, however, seems in this place to mean an old broken-down stage-coach.

2 To talk slang, parliamentary or otherwise.

3) Horses.   4) Money.

(5) A process carried on successfully under the Roman Emperors, as appears from what Tacitus says of the '*Instrumenta* Regni."—To *tool* is a technical phrase among the knights of the Whip, thus, that illustrious member of the Society, Richard Cypher, Esq., says : "I 've dash'd at every thing—*pegg'd* at a *jervy*—*tool'd* a mail-coach."

(6 Money.

(7) In Mr. Gregson's MS. these words are spelled "*knaves* and *fellows*," but I have printed them according to the proper wheelwright orthography.

(8) The extent of Mr. Gregson's learning will, no doubt, astonish the reader ; and it appears by the following lines

are able and spirited, which this Edition of my Poetical Works while going through the press has called forth from a leading political journal, I find, in reference to those delinquencies of mine in the way of satire, written during the last twenty or thirty years, the following suggestion : (10)—" It is now more than a quarter of a century since this bundle of political pasquinades set the British public in a roar; and, though the events to which they allude may be well known to every reader,

  'Cujus octavum trepidavit ætas
          Claudere lustrum,'

there are many persons, now forming a part of the literary public, who have come into existence since they happened, and who cannot be expected, even if they had the leisure and opportunity, to rummage

from a Panegyric written upon him, by one of the Fancy, that he is also a considerable adept in the Latin language :

  As to sciences—Bob knows a little of all :
    And, in Latin, to show that he 's no ignoramus,
  He wrote once an Ode on his friend, *Major Paul*,
    And the motto was, *Paulo majora canamus*'

(9) In consequence of the London edition of Mr. Moore's works having appeared in monthly parts, some irregularities in the arrangement of the lesser pieces have ensued, and hence a few poems under the title of "Satirical and Humorous" have already been given in this volume. The author has since collected a variety of pieces under the same head in parts 7, 8, and 9 of the London Edition, which for the sake of uniformity are now brought together in a connected form.—P. E.

(10) *The Times*, Jan. 6, 1841.

the files of our old newspapers for a history of the perishable facts on which Mr. Moore has so often rested the flying artillery of his wit. Many of those facts will be considered beneath the notice of the grave historian; and it is, therefore, incumbent on Mr. Moore—if he wishes his political squibs, imbued as they are with a wit and humour quite Aristophanic, to be relished, as they deserve to be relished, by our great grand-children—to preface them with a rapid summary of the events which gave them birth."

Without pausing here to say how gratifying it is to me to find my long course of Anti-Tory warfare thus tolerantly, and even generously, spoken of, and by so distinguished an organ of public opinion, I shall, as briefly as I can, advert to the writer's friendly suggestion, and then mention some of those reasons which have induced me not to adopt it. I was disposed, at first, to annex some such commentary to this series of squibs, but a little further consideration has led me to abandon this intention.

To that kind of satire which deals only with the lighter follies of social life, with the passing modes, whims, and scandal of the day, such illustrative comments become, after a short time, necessary. But the true preserving salt of political satire is its applicability to future times and generations, as well as to those which had first called it forth; its power of transmitting the scourge of ridicule through succeeding periods, with a lash still fresh for the back of the bigot and the oppressor, under whatever new shapes they may present themselves. I can hardly flatter myself with the persuasion that any one of the satirical pieces contained in this Volume is likely to possess this principle of vitality; but I feel quite certain that, *without* it, not all the notes and illustrations in which even the industry of Dutch commentatorship could embalm them would insure to these trifles a life much beyond the present hour.

Already, to many of them, that sort of relish—by far the least worthy source of their success—which the names of *living* victims lend to such sallies, has become, in the course of time, wanting. But, as far as the r appositeness to the passing political events of the day has yet been tried—and the dates of these satires range over a period of nearly thirty years—their ridicule, thanks to the undying nature of human absurdity, appears to have lost, as yet, but little of the original freshness of its first application. Nor is this owing to any peculiar felicity of aim, in the satire itself, but to the sameness, throughout that period, of all its original objects;—the unchangeable nature of that spirit of Monopoly by which, under all its various impersonations, commercial, religious, and pol t'cal, these sat'res had been first provoked. To refer but to one instance, the Corn Quest on—assuredly, the entire appositeness, at this very moment, of such versicles as the follow'ng, redounds far less to the credit of poesy than to the disgrace of legislation:—

How *can* you, my Lord, thus delight to torment all
The Peers of the realm about cheapening their corn,
When you know if one hasn't a very high rental,
'T is hardly worth while to be very high-born.

That, being by nature so little prone to spleen or bitterness, I should yet have frequented so much the thorny paths of satire, has always, to myself and those best acquainted with me, been a matter of some surprise. By supposing the imagination, however, to be, in such cases, the sole or chief prompter of the satire—which, in my own instance, I must say, it has generally been—an easy solution is found for the difficulty. The same readiness of fancy which, with but little help from reality, can deck out "the Cynthia of the minute" with all possible attractions, will likewise be able, when in the vein, to shower ridicule on a political adversary, without allowing a single feeling of real bitterness to mix itself with the operation. Even that sternest of all satirists, Dante, who, not content with the penal fire of the pen, kept an Inferno ever ready to receive the victims of his wrath—even Dante, on becoming acquainted with some of the persons whom he had thus doomed, not only revoked their awful sentence, but even honoured them with warm praise; (1) and probably, on a little further acquaintance, would have admitted them into his Paradiso. When thus loosely and shallowly even the sublime satire of Dante could strike its roots in his own heart and memory, it is easy to conceive how light and passing may be the feeling of hostility with which a partisan in the field of satire plies his laughing warfare; and how often it may happen that even the pride of hitting his mark hardly outlives the flight of the shaft.

I cannot dismiss from my hands these political trifles—

"This swarm of themes that settled on my pen,
Which I, like summer-flies, shake off again "—

without venturing to add that I have now to connect with them one mournful recollection—one loss from among the circle of those I have longest looked up to with affection and admiration—which I little thought, when I began this series of prefatory sketches, I should have to mourn before their close. I need hardly add, that, in thus alluding to a great light of the social and political world recently gone out, I mean the late Lord Holland.

It may be recollected, perhaps, that, in mentioning some particulars respecting an early squib of mine, —the Parody on the Prince Regent's Letter—I spoke of a dinner at which I was present, on the very day of the first publication of that Parody, when it was the subject of much conversation at table, and none of the party, except our host, had any suspicion that I was the author of it. 2) This host was Lord Hol-

(1) In his *Convito* he praises very warmly some persons whom he had before abused.—See Foscolo, *Discorso sul Testo di Dante.*

(2 See page 167, col. 1.

land; and as such a name could not but lend value to any anecdote connected with literature, I only forbore the pleasure of adding such an ornament to my page, from knowing that Lord Holland had long viewed with disapprobation and regret much of that conduct of the Whig party towards the Regent, in 1812-13, (1) of the history of which this squib, and the welcome reception it met with, forms an humble episode.

Lord Holland himself, in addition to his higher intellectual accomplishments, possessed in no ordinary degree the talent of writing easy and playful *vers de société;* and, among the instances I could give of the lightness of his hand at such trifles, there is one no less characteristic of his good-nature than his wit, as it accompanied a copy of the octavo edition of Bayle, 2) which, on hearing me rejoice one day that so agreeable an author had been at last made portable, he kindly ordered for me from Paris.

So late, indeed, as only a month or two before his lordship's death, he was employing himself, with all his usual cheerful eagerness, in translating some verses of Metastasio; and occasionally consulted both Mr. Rogers and myself as to different readings of some of the lines. In one of the letters which I received from him while thus occupied, I find the following postscript:—

> "'T is thus I turn the Italian's song,
> Nor deem I read his meaning wrong.
> But with rough English to combine
> The sweetness that's in every line,
> Asks for your Muse, and not for mine.
> *Sense only* will not quit the score,
> We must have that, and—little *More.*"

He then adds, "I send you, too, a melancholy Epigram of mine, of which I have seen many, alas, witness the truth:—

> "A minister's answer is always so kind '
> I starve, and he tells me he'll keep me in mind.
> *Half* his promise, God knows, would my spirits restore :
> Let him *keep* me—and, faith, I will ask for no more."

SATIRICAL AND HUMOROUS POEMS.

EPISTLE

FROM TOM CRIB TO BIG BEN, (3)
CONCERNING SOME FOUL PLAY IN A LATE TRANSACTION. (4)
" Ahi, mio Ben "—*Metastasio.* 5)

WHAT! Ben, my old hero, is this your renown?
Is *this* the new *go?*—kick a man when he's down!

1) This will be seen whenever those valuable papers come to be published, which Lord Holland left behind him, containing Memoirs of his own times, and of those immediately preceding them.

(2) In sixteen volumes, published at Paris, by Desoer.

(3) A nickname given, at this time, to the Pr—ce R—g—t.

(4) Written soon after Bonaparte's transportation to St. Helena.

(5) Tom, I suppose, was "assisted" to this motto by Mr.

When the foe has knock'd under, to tread on him then—
By the fist of my father, I blush for thee, Ben!
"Foul! foul!" all the lads of the Fancy exclaim—
Charley Shock is electrified—Belcher spits flame—
And Molyneux—ay, even Blacky (6 cries " shame!"

Time was when John Bull little difference spied
'Twixt the foe at his feet, and the friend at his side:
When he found (such his humour in fighting and eating)
His foe, like his beef-steak, the sweeter for beating.
But this comes, Master Ben, of your curst foreign notions,
Your trinkets, wigs, thingumbobs, gold lace, and lotions,
Your Noyaus, Curaçoas, and the Devil knows what—
(One swig of *Blue Ruin* (7) is worth the whole lot!
Your great and small *crosses*— (my eyes, what a brood!)
A *cross*-buttock from *me* would do some of them good!)
Which have spoilt you, till hardly a drop, my old porpoise,
Of pure English *claret* is left in your *corpus;*
And (as Jim says) the only one trick, good or bad,
Of the Fancy you 're up to, is *fibbing,* my lad.
Hence it comes—*Boxiana,* disgrace to thy page!—
Having floor'd, by good luck, the first *swell* of the age,
Having conquer'd the *prime one,* that *mill'd* us all round,
You kick'd him, old Ben, as he gasp'd on the ground!
Ay—just at the time to show spunk, if you'd got any—
Kick'd him, and jaw'd him, and *lagg'd* (8) him to Botany!
Oh, shade of the *Cheesemonger!* (9) you, who, alas,
Doubled up, by the dozen, those Mounseers in brass,
On that great day of *milling,* when blood lay in lakes,
When Kings held the bottle, and Europe the stakes,
Look down upon Ben—see him, *dunghill* all o'er,
Insult the fallen foe that can harm him no more!
Out, cowardly *spooney !*—again and again,
By the fist of my father, I blush for thee, Ben.
To *show the white feather* is many men's doom,
But, what of *one* feather?—Ben shows a *whole Plume.*

TO THE EDITOR OF THE MORNING CHRONICLE.

SIR—In order to explain the following Fragment, it is necessary to refer your readers to a late florid Jackson, who, it is well known, keeps the most learned company going.

(6) Names and nicknames of celebrated pugilists at that time.

(7) Gin.

(8) Transported.

(9) A Life Guardsman, one of *the Fancy,* who distinguished himself, and was killed in the memorable *set-to* at Waterloo.

description of the Pavilion at Brighton, in the apartments of which, we are told, "Fum, *The Chinese Bird of Royalty*," is a principal ornament.

I am, Sir, yours, etc.
MUM.

FUM AND HUM, THE TWO BIRDS OF ROYALTY.

ONE day the Chinese Bird of Royalty, Fum,
Thus accosted our own Bird of Royalty, Hum,
In that Palace or China-shop (Brighton, which is it?
Where Fum had just come to pay Hum a short
visit.—
Near akin are these Birds, though they differ in nat on
(The breed of the Hums is as old as creation);
Both full-craw'd Legitimates—both birds of prey,
Both cackling and ravenous creatures, half way
'Twixt the goose and the vulture, like Lord C—st—
r—gh.

While Fum deals in Mandarins, Bonzes, Bohea,
Peers, Bishops, and Punch, Hum, are sacred to thee!
So congenial their tastes, that, when Fum first did
light on
The floor of that grand China-warehouse at Brighton,
The lanterns, and dragons, and things round the
dome
Were so like what he left, "Gad," says Fum, "I'm
at home."—
And when, turning, he saw Bishop L——ge, "Zooks,
it is," [his phiz—
Quoth the Bird, "Yes—I know him—a Bonze, by
And that jolly old idol he kneels to so low
Can be none but our round-about godhead, fat Fo!"
It chanced at this moment, the Episcopal Prig
Was imploring the P——e to dispense with his wig,(1)
Which the Bird, overhearing, flew high o'er his head,
And some Tobit-like marks of his patronage shed,
Which so dimm'd the poor Dandy's idolatrous eye,
That, while Fum cried "Oh Fo!" all the court cried
"Oh fie!"

But, a truce to digression;—these Birds of a feather
Thus talk'd, t' other night, on State matters together;
(The P——e just in bed, or about to depart for 't,
His legs full of gout, and his arms full of H—rt—
f—d, [Chinese,
"I say, Hum," says Fum—Fum, of course, spoke
But, bless you, that's nothing—at Brighton one sees
Foreign lingoes and Bishops *translated* with ease—
"I say, Hum, how fares it with Royalty now?
Is it *up*? is it *prime*? is it *spooney*—or how?"
(The Bird had just taken a flash-man's degree
Under B—rr—m—re, Y——th, and young Master
L—e)
"As for us in Pekin"——here, a devil of a din
From the bed-chamber came, where that long Man-
darin,

(1) In consequence of an old promise, that he should
be allowed to wear his own hair, whenever he might be
elevated to a Bishopric by his R——l H——ss.
(2) Ovid is mistaken in saying that it was "At Paris"

C—st—r—gh (whom Fum calls the *Confucius* of
Prose),
Was rehearsing a speech upon Europe's repose
To the deep double bass of the fat Idol's nose.

(*Nota bene*—his Lordship and L—v—rp—l come,
In collateral lines, from the old Mother Hum,
C—st—r—gh a Hum-bug—L—v—rp—l a Hum-
drum.)
The Speech being finish'd, out rush'd C—st—r—gh,
Saddled Hum in a hurry, and, whip, spur, away,
Through the regions of air, like a Snip on his hobby,
Ne'er paused, till he lighted in St. Stephen's lobby.

* * * * *

—◦❀◦—

LINES

ON THE DEPARTURE OF LORDS C—ST—R—GH AND
ST—W—RT FOR THE CONTINENT.

At Paris (1) et Fratres, et qui rapuére sub illis
Vix tenuére manus (scis hoc, Menelaë) nefandas.
Ovid. Metam., lib. xiii., v. 202.

Go, Brothers in wisdom—go, bright pair of Peers,
And may Cupid and Fame fan you both with their
pinions!
The *One*, the best lover we have—*of his years*,
And the *other* Prime Statesman of Britain's domi-
[nions.

Go, Hero of Chancery, blest with the smile
Of the Misses that love and the monarchs that prize
Forget Mrs. Ang—lo T—yl—r a while, [thee;
And all tailors but him who so well *dandifies* thee.

Never mind how thy juniors in gallantry scoff,
Never heed how perverse affidavits may thwart
thee,
But show the young Misses thou'rt scholar enough
To translate "Amor Fortis," a love *about forty*!

And sure 'tis no wonder, when, fresh as young Mars,
From the battle you came, with the Orders you'd
earn'd in 't,
That sweet Lady Fanny should cry out "my *stars*!"
And forget that the *Moon*, too, was some way
concern'd in 't.

For not the great R—g—t himself has endured
(Though I've seen him with badges and orders all
shine,
Till he look'd like a house that was *over* insured)
A much heavier burden of glories than thine.

And 'tis plain, when a wealthy young lady so mad is,
Or *any* young ladies can so go astray,
As to marry old Dandies that might be their daddies,
The *stars* (3) are in fault, my Lord St—w—rt, not
they!

these rapacious transactions took place—we should read
"At Vienna."
(3) "When weak women go astray,
The stars are more in fault than they."

Thou, too, t' other brother, thou Tully of Tories,
   Thou *Malaprop* Cicero, over whose lips
Such a smooth rigmarole about "monarchs," and
     " glories,"
And "*mulledge*," (1) and "features," like syllabub
   slips.

Go, haste, at the Congress pursue thy vocation
   Of adding fresh sums to this National Debt of ours,
Leaguing with Kings, who, for mere recreation,
     Break promises, fast as your Lordship breaks
   metaphors.

Fare ye well, fare ye well, bright Pair of Peers,
   And may Cupid and Fame fan you both with their
   pinions!
The one, the best lover we have—*of his years*,
   And the other, Prime Statesman of Britain's do-
   minions.

—◦H◦—

TO THE SHIP

IN WHICH LORD C—ST—R—GH SAILED FOR THE
CONTINENT.

Imitated from Horace, lib. i., ode 3.

So may my Lady's prayers prevail, (2)
   And C—nn—g's too, and *lucid* Br—gge's,
And Eld—n beg a favouring gale
   From Eolus, that *older* Bags, (3)
To speed thee on thy destined way,
Oh ship, that bear'st our C—st—r—gh, (4)
Our gracious R—g—t's better half (5)
   And, *therefore*, quarter of a King—
(As Van, or any other calf,
   May find, without much figuring).

Waft, him, oh ye kindly breezes,
   Waft this Lord of place and pelf,
Any where his Lordship pleases,
   Though 't were to Old Nick himself!

Oh, what a face of brass was his, (6)
Who first at Congress show'd his phiz—

(1) It is thus the noble lord pronounces the word "know-
ledge"—deriving it, as far as his own share is concerned,
from the Latin, "nullus."

2)   Sic te Diva potens Cypri,
     Sic fratres Helenæ, lucida sidera,
     Ventorumque regat pater.

(3) See a description of the ασκοι, or *Bags* of Eolus, in
the *Odyssey*, lib. 10.

(4)   Navis, quæ tibi creditum
     Debes Virgilium.

(5   ——— Animæ dimidium meum.

(6)   Illi robur et æs triplex,
     Circa pectus erat, qui, etc.

(7)   ——— præcipitem Afr cum
     Decertantem Aquilonibus.

(8)   Nequicquam Deus abscidit
     Prudens oceano dissociabili
     Terras, si tamen impiæ
     Non tangenda *Rates* transiliunt vada.

To sign away the Rights of Man
   To Russian threats and Austrian juggle;
And leave the sinking African (7)
   To fall without one saving struggle—
'Mong ministers from North and South,
   To show his lack of shame and sense,
And hoist the S gn of "Bull and Mouth"
   For blunders and for eloquence!

In vain we wish our *Secs.* at home (8)
   To mind their papers, desks, and shelves,
If silly *Secs.* abroad *will* roam
   And make such noodles of themselves.

But such hath always been the case—
   For matchless impudence of face,
There's nothing like your Tory race! (9)
First, Pitt, (10) the chosen of England, taught her
A taste for famine, fire, and slaughter.
Then came the Doctor, (11) for our ease,
With E—d—ns, Ch—th—ms, H—wk—b—s,
And other deadly maladies.
When each, in turn, had run their rigs,
Necessity brought in the Whigs: (12)
And oh, I blush, I blush to say,
   When these in turn were put to flight, too,
Illustrious T—mp—e flew away
   With *lots of pens he had no right to!* (13)
In short, what *will* not mortal man do? (14)
   And now, that—strife and bloodshed past—
We 've done on earth what harm we can do,
   We gravely take to heaven at last, (15)
And think its favouring smile to purchase
Oh Lord, good Lord! by—building churches!

—◦H◦—

THE ANNUAL PILL.

Supposed to be sung by Old Prosy, the Jew, in the
character of Major C—rtw—ght.

Vill nobodies try my nice *Annual Pill*,
Dat's to purify every ting nashty avay?

This last line, we may suppose, alludes to some distin-
guished *Rats* that attended the voyager.

(9)   Audax omnia perpeti
     Gens ruit per vetitum nefas.

10   Audax Japeti genus
     Ignem fraude malâ gentibus intulit.

(11)   Post ———
     ——— macies, et nova febrium
     Terris incubit cohors.

(12)   ——— tarda necessitas
     Lethi corripuit gradum.

(13   Expertus *vacuum* Dædalus aëra
     Pennis non homini datis.

Th s alludes to the 1200*l.* worth of stationery, which his
Lordship is said to have ordered when on the point of
vacating his place.

(14)   Nil mortalibus arduum est.

(15)   Cœlum ipsum petimus stultitiâ.

Pless ma heart, pless ma heart, let ma say vat I vill,
Not a Chrishtian or Shentlean minds vat I say!
'T is so pretty a bolus!—just down let it go,
And, at vonce, such a *radical* shange you vill see,
Dat I 'd not be surptish'd, like de horse in de show,
If your heads all vere found vere your tailsh ought
    to be!
    Vill nobodies try my nice *Annual Pill*, etc.

'T will cure all Electors, and purge avay clear
Dat mighty bad itch ng dey 've got in deir hands—
'T will cure, too, all Statesmen, of dulness, ma tear,
Though the case vas as desperate as poor Mister
    Van's.
Dere is not ng at all vat dis Pill vill not reach—
Give the Sinecure Shentleman von little grain,
Pless ma heart, it vill act, like de salt on de leech,
And he 'll throw de pounds, shillings, and pence,
    up again!
    Vill nobodies try my nice *Annual Pill*, etc.

'T vould be tedious, ma tear, all its peauties to paint—
But, among oder tings *fundamentally* wrong,
It vill cure de *Proad Pottom*(1)—a common com-
    plaint
Among M. P.'s and veavers—from *sitting* too
    long. (2)
Should symptoms of *speeching* preak out on a dunce
(Vat is often de case), it vill stop de disease,
And pring avay all de long speeches at vonce,
Dat else vould, like tape-worms, come by degrees!

Vill nobodies try my nice *Annual Pill*,
Dat 's to purify every ting nashty avay?
Pless ma heart, pless ma heart, let me say vat I vill,
Not a Chrishtian or Shentleman minds vat I say!
    —◦◉◦—
TO SIR HUDSON LOWE.
    Effare causam nominis,
    Utrumne mores hoc tui
    Nomen dedere, an nomen hoc
    Secuta morum regula. —*Ausonius*
             1816.

Sir Hudson Lowe, Sir Hudson *Low*,
    (By name, and ah! by nature so)
As thou art fond of persecutions,
Perhaps thou 'st read, or heard repeated,
How Captain Gulliver was treated,
    When thrown among the Lilliputians.

They tied him down—these little men did—
And having valiantly ascended

Upon the mighty man's protuberance,
They did so strut!—upon my soul,
It must have been extremely droll
    To see their pigmy pride's exuberance!

And how the doughty mannikins
Amused themselves with sticking pins
And needles in the great man's breeches:
And how some very little things,
That pass'd for Lords, on scaffoldings
Got up, and worried h m with speeches.

Alas, alas! that it should happen
To mighty men to be caught napping!—
    Though different, too, these persecutions;
For Gulliver, *there*, took the nap,
While, *here*, the *Nap*, oh sad mishap,
    Is taken by the Lilliputians!
    —◦◉◦—
AMATORY COLLOQUY BETWEEN BANK
    AND GOVERNMENT.
                    1826.
        BANK.
Is all then forgotten? those amorous pranks [play'd;
    You and I, in our youth, my dear Government,
When you call'd me the fondest, the truest of Banks,
    And enjoy'd the endearing *advances* I made!

When left to ourselves, unmolested and free,
    To do all that a dashing young couple should do,
A law against *paying* was laid upon me,
    But none against *owing*, dear helpmate, on you.

And is it then vanish'd?—that "hour (as Othello
    So happily calls it) of Love and *Direction?*"(3)
And must we, like other fond doves, my dear fellow,
    Grow good in our old age, and cut the connection?
        GOVERNMENT.
Even so, my beloved Mrs. Bank, it must be;
    This paying with cash plays the devil with woo-
        ing: (4)
We 've both had our swing, but I plainly foresee
    There must soon be a stop to our *bill-*ing and cooing.

Propagation in reason—a small child or two—
    Even Reverend Malthus himself is a friend to;
The issue of some folks is moderate and few—
    But *ours*, my dear corporate Bank, there 's no
        end to!

So—hard though it be on a pair who 've already
    Disposed of so many pounds, shillings, and pence;

---

1) Meaning, I presume, *Coalition* Administrations.
(2) Whether sedentary habits have any thing to do with
this peculiar shape, I cannot determine, but that some
have supposed a sort of connection between them, appears
from the following remark, quoted in Kornmann's curious
book, *de Virginitatis Iure*—"Ratio perquam lepida est
apud Kirchner- in Legalo, cum natura illas partes, quæ ad
sessionem sunt destina æ, latiores in fœminis fecerit quam

in viris, innuens dom eas manere debere."—Cap. 40.—P.E.
(3)   ————"An hour
      Of love, of worldly matter and direction."
(4) It appears, however, that Ovid was a friend to the
resumption of payment in specie :—
    ————"finem, *specie* cœleste *resumpta*,
    Luctibus imposuit, venitque salut'er urbi."
                  Met., l xv, v. 743.

And, in spite of that pink of prosperity, Freddy, (1)
So lavish of cash and so sparing of sense—

The day is at hand, my Papyria (2) Venus,
   When—high as we once used to carry our capers—
Those soft *billets-doux* we 're now passing between us
   Will serve but to keep Mrs. Coutts in curl-papers

And when—if we *still* must continue our love,
   (After all that has pass'd)—our amour, it is clear
Like that which Miss Danae managed with Jove,
   Must all be transacted in *bullion*, my dear!

—◦◦◦—

DIALOGUE BETWEEN A SOVEREIGN AND A ONE POUND NOTE.

"O ego non felix, quam tu fugis, ut pavet acres
Agna lupos, capreæque leones."—*Hor.*

   SAID a Sovereign to a Note,
     In the pocket of my coat,
Where they met in a neat purse of leather,
    "How happens it, I prithee,
    That, though I 'm wedded *with* thee,
Fair Pound, we can never live together?

    "Like your sex, fond of *change*,
    With Silver you can range,
And of lots of young sixpences be mother;
    While with *me*—upon my word,
    Not my Lady and my Lord
Of W—stm—th see so little of each other!"

    The indignant Note replied
    (Lying crumpled by his side),
"Shame, shame, it is yourself that roam, Sir—
    One cannot look askance,
    But, whip! you 're off to France,
Leaving nothing but old rags at home, Sir.

    "Your scampering began
    From the moment Parson Van,
Poor man, made us *one* in Love's fetter;
    'For better or for worse'
    Is the usual marriage curse,
But ours is all 'worse' and no 'better.'

    "In vain are laws pass'd,
    There 's nothing holds you fast,
Though you know, sweet Sovereign, I adore you—
    At the smallest hint in life,
    You forsake your lawful wife,
As *other* Sovereigns did before you.

(1) Honourable Frederick R—b—ns—n.
(2 So called, to distinguish her from the "Aurea" or *Golden* Venus.
(3) See the proceedings of the Lords, Wednesday, March 1, 1826, when Lord King was severely reproved by several of the noble Peers for making so many speeches against the Corn Laws.
(4) This noble Earl said, that "when he heard the pe-

"I flirt with Silver, true—
   But what can ladies do,
When disown'd by their natural protectors?
   And as to falsehood, stuff
   I shall soon be *false* enough,
When I get among those wicked Bank Directors."

    The Sovereign, smiling on her,
    Now swore, upon his honour,
To be henceforth domestic and loyal;
    But, within an hour or two,
    Why—I sold him to a Jew,
And he 's now at No. 10, Palais Royal.

—◦◦◦—

AN EXPOSTULATION TO LORD KING.

"Quem das finem, Rex magne, laborum?"—*Virgil.*
1826.

How *can* you, my Lord, thus delight to torment all
   The Peers of the realm about cheapening their corn, (3)
When you know, if one has n't a very high rental,
   'Tis hardly worth while being very high-born?

Why bore them so rudely, each night of your life,
   On a question, my Lord, there 's so much to abhor in?
A question—like asking one, "How is your wife?"—
   At once so confounded *domestic* and *foreign.*

As to weavers, no matter how poorly they feast,
   But Peers, and such animals, fed up for show,
(Like the well-physick'd elephant lately deceased,)
   Take a wonderful quantum of cramming, you know.

You might see, my dear Baron, how bored and distrest
   Were their high noble hearts by your merciless tale,
When the force of the agony wrung even a jest
   From the frugal Scotch wit of my Lord L-d-d-le! (4

Bright Peer! to whom Nature and Berwickshire gave
   A humour, endow'd with effects so provoking,
That when the whole House looks unusually grave,
   You may always conclude that Lord L-d-d-le's
                      [joking!
And then, those unfortunate weavers of Perth—
   Not to know the vast difference Providence dooms
Between weavers of Perth and Peers of high birth,
   'Twixt those who have *heir*-looms, and those who 've but looms!

"To talk *now* of starving!"—as great Ath-l said— (5
   And the nobles all cheer'd, and the bishops all wonder'd,)

tition came from ladies' boot and shoemakers, he thought it must be against the 'corns' which they inflicted on the fair sex."

(5 The Duke of Athol said, that "at a former period, when these weavers were in great distress, the landed interest of Perth had supported 1500 of them. It was a poor return for these very men now to petition against the persons who had fed them."

"When, some years ago, he and others had fed
Of these same hungry devils about fifteen hundred!"

It follows from hence—and the Duke's very words
    Should be publish'd wherever poor rogues of this
        craft are—
That weavers, *once* rescued from starving by Lords
Are bound to be starved by said Lords ever after.

When Rome was uproarious, her knowing patricians
Made "Bread and the Circus" a cure for each *row;*
But not so the plan of *our* noble physicians,
    "No Bread and the Tread-mill" 's the regimen now.

So cease, my dear Baron of Ockham, your prose,
    As I shall my poetry—neither convinces;
And all we have spoken and written but shows,
    When you tread on a nobleman's *corn,* (1) how he
        winces!

—◦◦◦—

THE SINKING FUND CRIED.

"Now what, we ask, is become of this Sinking Fund—
these eight millions of surplus above expenditure, which
were to reduce the interest of the national debt by the
amount of four hundred thousand pounds annually?
Where, indeed, is the Sinking Fund itself?"—*The Times,*
Feb. 1.

TAKE your bell, take your bell,
    Good Crier, and tell
To the Bulls and the Bears, till their ears are stunn'd,
        That lost, or stolen,
        Or fallen through a hole in
The Treasury floor, is the Sinking Fund!

        O yes! O yes!
        Can any body guess
What the deuce has become of this Treasury wonder?
        It has Pitt's name on 't,
        All brass, in the front,
And R—b—ns—n's, scrawl'd with a goose-quill,
        under.

        Folks well knew what
        Would soon be its lot,
When Frederick and Jenky set hob-nobbing, (2)
        And said to each other,
        "Suppose, dear brother,
We make this funny old Fund worth robbing."

        We are come, alas!
        To a very pretty pass—
Eight Hundred Millions of score to pay,
        With but Five in the till,
        To discharge the bill,
And even that Five, too, whipp'd away!

(1) An improvement, we flatter ourselves, on Lord L.'s
joke.
(2) In 1824, when the Sinking Fund was raised by the
imposition of new taxes to the sum of five millions.
(3 A sort of "breakfast powder," composed of roasted

Stop thief! stop thief!
    From the Sub to the Chief,
These *Gemmen* of Finance are plundering cattle—
        Call the watch—call Brougham,
        Tell Joseph Hume,
That best of Charleys, to spring his rattle.

        Whoever will bring
        This aforesaid thing
To the well-known House of Robinson and Jenkin,
        Shall be paid, with thanks,
        In the notes of banks,
Whose Funds have all learn'd "the Art of Sinking."

        O yes! O yes!
        Can any body guess
What the devil has become of this Treasury wonder?
        Is has Pitt's name on 't,
        All brass, in the front,
And R—b—ns—n's, scrawl'd with a goose-quill,
        under.

—◦◦◦—

ODE TO THE GODDESS CERES.

BY SIR TH—M—S L—THBR—E.

"Legiferæ Cereri Phœboque."—*Virgil.*

DEAR Goddess of Corn, whom the ancients, we know,
    (Among other odd whims of those comical bodies,)
Adorn'd with somniferous poppies, to show
    Thou wert always a true Country-gentleman's
        goddess.

Behold, in his best shooting-jacket, before thee,
    An eloquent 'Squire, who most humbly beseeches,
Great Queen of Mark-lane (if the thing does n't bore
        thee),
    Thou 'lt read o'er the last of his *never*-last speeches.

Ah! Ceres, thou know'st not the slander and scorn
    Now heap'd upon England's Squirearchy, so
        boasted;
Improving on Hunt, (3) 'tis no longer the Corn,
    'T is the *growers* of Corn that are now, alas!
        roasted.

In speeches, in books, in all shapes they attack us—
    Reviewers, economists—fellows, no doubt,
That you, my dear Ceres, and Venus, and Bacchus,
    And Gods of high fashion, know little about.

There's B—nth—m, whose English is all his own'
        making—
    Who thinks just as little of settling a nation
As he would of smoking his pipe, or of taking
    (What he, himself calls) his "post-prandial vibra-
        tion." (4)

corn, was about this time introduced by Mr. Hunt, as a
substitute for coffee.
(4) The venerable Jeremy's phrase for his after-dinner
walk.

65

There are two Mr. M——lls, too, whom those that
    love reading,
Through all that 's unreadable, call very clever; —
And, whereas M——ll Senior makes war on *good*
    breeding,
M——ll Junior makes war on all *breeding* what-
    ever!

In short, my dear Goddess, Old England 's divided
    Between *ultra* blockheads and superfine sages;—
With *which* of these classes we, landlords, have sided
    Thou 'lt find in my Speech, if thou 'lt read a few
    pages.

For therein I 've proved, to my own satisfaction,
    And that of all 'Squires I 've the honour of meeting,
That 't is the most senseless and foul-mouth'd de-
    traction
    To say that poor people are fond of cheap eating.

On the contrary, such the "*chaste* notions"(1) of food
    That dwell in each pale manufacturer's heart,
They would scorn any law, be it ever so good,
    That would make thee, dear Goddess, less dear
    than thou art!

And, oh! for Monopoly what a blest day,
    When the Land and the Silk(2) shall in fond com-
    bination,
(Like *Sulky* and *Silky*, that pair in the play,(3)
    Cry out, with one voice, for High Rents and Star-
    vation!

Long life to the Minister!—no matter who,
    Or how dull he may be, if, with dignified spirit, he
Keeps the ports shut—and the people's mouths, too—
    We shall all have a long run of Freddy's prosperity.

And, as for myself, who 've, like Hannibal, sworn
    To hate the whole crew who would take our rents
    from us,
Had England but *One* to stand by thee, Dear Corn,
    That last, honest Uni-Corn(4) would be Sir
    Th—m—s!

—◦н◦—

A HYMN OF WELCOME AFTER THE RECESS.

"*Animas sapientiores fieri quiescendo.*"

AND now—cross-buns and pancakes o'er—.
Hail, Lords and Gentlemen, once more!

(1) A phrase in one of Sir T—m—s's last speeches.
(2) Great efforts were, at that time, making for the ex-
clusion of foreign silk.
(3) *Road to Ruin.*
(4) This is meant not so much for a pun, as in allusion
to the natural history of the Unicorn, which is supposed
to be something between the Bos and the Asinus, and, as
Rees's *Cyclopædia* assures us, has a particular liking for
every thing "chaste."
(5) An item of expense which Mr. Hume in vain endea-
voured to get rid of:—trumpeters, it appears, like the

Thrice hail and welcome, Houses Twain!
The short eclipse of April-Day
Having (God grant it!) pass'd away,
    Collective Wisdom, shine again!

Come, Ayes and Noes, through thick and thin—
With Paddy H—lmes for whipper-in—
    Whate'er the job, prepared to back it;
Come, voters of Supplies—bestowers
Of jackets upon trumpet-blowers,
    At eighty mortal pounds the jacket!(5)

Come—free, at length, from Joint-Stock cares—
Ye Senators of many Shares,
    Whose dreams of premium knew no boundary;
So fond of aught like *Company*,
That you would even have taken *tea*
    (Had you been ask'd) with Mr. Goundry.(6)

Come, matchless country gentlemen;
Come, wise Sir Thomas—wisest then
    When creeds and corn-laws are debated;
Come, rival even the Harlot Red,
And show how wholly into *bread*
    A 'Squire is *transubstantiated.*

Come, L—derd—e, and tell the world,
That—surely as thy scratch is curl'd,
    As never scratch was curl'd before—
Cheap eating does more harm than good,
And working-people, spoil'd by food,
    The less they eat, will work the more.

Come, G—lb—rn, with thy glib defence
(Which thou 'dst have made for Peter's Pence)
    Of Church-Rates, worthy of a halter;
Two pipes of port (*old* port, 't was said
By honest *Newport*) (7) bought and paid
    By Papists for the Orange Altar!(8)

Come, H—rt—n, with thy plan, so merry,
For peopling Canada from Kerry—
    Not so much rendering Ireland quiet,
As grafting on the dull Canadians
That liveliest of earth's contagions,
    The *bull-*pock of Hibernian riot!

Come all, in short, ye wondrous men
Of wit and wisdom, come again;

men of All-Souls, must be "*bene vestiti.*"
(6) The gentleman, lately before the public, who kept
his Joint-Stock Tea Company all to himself, singing "*Te*
solo adoro.*"
(7) Sir John Newport.
(8) This charge of two pipes of port for the sacramental
wine is a precious specimen of the sort of rates levied
upon their Catholic fellow-parishioners by the Irish Pro-
testants.
    "The thirst that from the soul doth rise
     Doth ask a drink divine"

Though short your absence, all deplore it—
Oh, come and show, whate'er men say,
That you can, *after* April-Day,
Be just as—sapient as *before* it.

—⇒ ⊶⊶ ∘—

MEMORABILIA OF LAST WEEK.

MONDAY, MARCH 13, 1826.

THE Budget—quite charming and witty—no hearing,
  For plaudits and laughs, the good things that
    were in it ;—
Great comfort to find, though the Speech is n't *cheer-*
    ing,
That all its gay auditors *were*, every minute.

What, *still* more prosperity!—mercy upon us,
  " This boy 'll be the death of me"—oft as, already,
Such smooth Budgeteers have genteelly undone us,
  For *Ruin made easy* there 's no one like Freddy.

TUESDAY.

Much grave apprehension express'd by the Peers,
  Lest —calling to life the old Peachums and
    Lockitts—
The large stock of gold we 're to have in three years
  Should all find its way into highwaymen's pock-
    ets!!(1)

   *   *   *   *

WEDNESDAY.

Little doing—for sacred, oh Wednesday, thou art
  To the seven-o'-clock joys of full many a table—
When *the Members* all meet, to make much of that
    part,
  With which they so rashly fell out, in the Fable.

It appear'd, though, to-night, that—as churchwar-
    dens, yearly,
Eat up a small baby—those cormorant sinners,
The Bankrupt-Commissioners *bolt* very nearly
  A moderate-sized bankrupt, *tout chaud*, for their
    dinners!(2)

Nota Bene—a rumour to-day, in the City,
  " Mr. R—b—ns—n just has resign'd "—what a pity !
The Bulls and the Bears all fell a sobbing,
  When they heard of the fate of poor Cock *Robin ;*
While thus, to the nursery tune, so pretty,
  A murmuring *Stock*-dove breathed her ditty:—

Alas, poor *Robin*, he crow'd as long
  And as sweet as a prosperous Cock could crow ;
But his *note* was *small*, and the *gold*-finch's song
  Was a pitch too high for Robin to go.
          Who 'll make his shroud ?

" I," said the Bank, " though he play'd me a prank,
  While I have a rag, poor *Rob* shall be roll'd in 't,
With many a pound I 'll paper him round,
  Like a plump rouleau—*without* the gold in 't."

   *   *   *   *

ALL IN THE FAMILY WAY.

A NEW PASTORAL BALLAD.

(SUNG IN THE CHARACTER OF BRITANNIA.)

" The Public Debt is due from ourselves to ourselves, and
resolves itself into a Family Account."—*Sir Robert Peel's
Letter.*

TUNE—*My banks are all furnish'd with bees.*

My banks are all furnish'd with rags,
  So thick, even Freddy can't thin 'em ;
I 've torn up my old money-bags,
  Having little or nought to put in 'em.
My tradesmen are smashing by dozens,
  But this is all nothing, they say ;
For bankrupts, since Adam, are cousins—
  So it 's all in the family way.

My Debt not a penny takes from me,
  As sages the matter explain ;
Bob owes it to Tom, and then Tommy
  Just owes it to Bob back again.
Since all have thus taken to *owing*,
  There 's nobody left that can *pay ;*
And this is the way to keep going—
  All quite in the family way.

My senators vote away millions,
  To put in Prosperity's budget ;
And though it were billions or trillions,
  The generous rogues would n't grudge it.
'T is all but a family *hop*,
  'T was Pitt began dancing the hay ;
Hands round !—why the deuce should we stop?
  'T is all in the family way.

My labourers used to eat mutton,
  As any great man of the State does ;
And now the poor devils are put on
  Small rations of tea and potatoes.
But cheer up, John, Sawney, and Paddy,
  The King is your father, they say ;
So, even if you starve for your Daddy,
  'T is all in the family way.

My rich manufacturers tumble,
  My poor ones have nothing to chew ;
And, even if themselves do not grumble,
  Their stomachs undoubtedly do.
But coolly to fast *en famille*,
  Is as good for the soul as to pray ;
And famine itself is genteel,
  When one starves in a family way.

I have found out a secret for Freddy,
  A secret for next Budget day ;

(1) " Another objection to a metallic currency was, that
it produced a greater number of highway robberies."
—*Debate in the Lords.*

(2) Mr. Abercromby's statement of the enormous tavern
bills of the Commissioners of Bankrupts.

Though, perhaps, he may know it already,
    As *he*, too, 's a sage in his way.
When next for the Treasury scene he
    Announces " the Devil to pay,"
Let him write on the bills, " *Nota bene*,
    'T is all in the family way."

BALLAD FOR THE CAMBRIDGE ELECTION.

" I authorised my Committee to take the step which they
    did, of proposing a fair comparison of strength, upon the
    understanding that *whichever of the two should prove to
    be the weakest* should give way to the other."—*Extract
    from Mr. W. J. B—kes's Letter to Mr. G—lb—n.*

B—KES is weak, and G—lb—n too,
    No one e'er the fact denied ;—
Which is "*weakest*" of the two,
    Cambridge can alone decide.
Choose between them, Cambridge, pray;
Which is weakest, Cambridge, say.

G—lb—n of the Pope afraid is,
    B—kes, as much afraid as he ;
Never yet did two old ladies
    On this point so well agree.
Choose between them, Cambridge, pray ;
Which is weakest, Cambridge, say.

Each a different mode pursues,
    Each the same conclusion reaches ;
B—kes is foolish in Reviews,
    G—lb—n, foolish in his speeches.
Choose between them, Cambridge, pray ;
Which is weakest, Cambridge, say.

Each a different foe doth damn,
    When his own affairs have gone ill ;
B—kes he damneth Buckingham,
    G—lb—n damneth Dan O'Connell.
Choose between them, Cambridge, pray ;
Which is weakest, Cambridge, say.

Once, we know, a horse's neigh
    Fix'd the election to a throne ;
So, whichever first shall *bray*,
    Choose him, Cambridge, for thy own.
Choose him, choose him by his bray,
Thus elect him, Cambridge, pray.

June, 1826.

MR. ROGER DODSWORTH.

1826.

TO THE EDITOR OF THE TIMES.

Sir—Having just heard of the wonderful resurrection of
Mr. Roger Dodsworth from under an *avalanche*, where
he had remained, *bien frappé*, it seems, for the last 166
years, I hasten to impart to you a few reflections on the
subject.—Yours, etc.—*Laudator Tcmporis Acti.*

WHAT a lucky turn-up!—just as Eld—n 's with-
        drawing,
To find thus a gentleman, frozen in the year

Sixteen hundred and sixty, who only wants thawing,
    To serve for *our* times quite as well as the Peer ;—

To bring thus to light, not the Wisdom alone
    Of our Ancestors, such as 't is found on our shelves,
But in perfect condition, full-wigg'd and full-grown,
    To shovel up one of those wise bucks themselves !

Oh thaw Mr. Dodsworth, and send him safe home—
    Let him learn nothing useful or new on the way ;
With his wisdom kept snug from the light let him
        come,
    And our Tories will hail him with " Hear ! " and
        " Hurra ! "

What a God-send to *them* !—a good obsolete man,
    Who has never of Locke or Voltaire been a reader ;—
Oh thaw Mr. Dodsworth as fast as you can,
    And the L—nsd—les and H—rtf—rds shall choose
        him for leader.

Yes, Sleeper of Ages, thou *shalt* be their chosen ;
    And deeply with thee will they sorrow, good men,
To think that all Europe has, since thou wert frozen,
    So alter'd thou hardly wilt know it again.

And Eld—n will weep o'er each sad innovation
    Such oceans of tears, thou wilt fancy that he
Has been also laid up in a long congelation,
    And is only now thawing, dear Roger, like thee.

COPY OF AN INTERCEPTED DESPATCH,

FROM HIS EXCELLENCY DON STREPITOSO DIABOLO, EN-
VOY EXTRAORDINARY TO HIS SATANIC MAJESTY.

St. James's Street, July 1, 1826.

GREAT Sir, having just had the good luck to catch
    An official young Demon preparing to go,
Ready booted and spurr'd, with a black-leg despatch
    From the Hell here, at Cr—ckf—rd's, to *our* Hell,
        below—

I write these few lines to your Highness Satanic,
    To say that, first having obey'd your directions,
And done all the mischief I could in " the Panic,"
    My next special care was to help the Elections.

Well knowing how dear were those times to thy soul,
    When every good Christian tormented his bro-
        ther,
And caused, in thy realm, such a saving of coal,
    From all coming down, ready grill'd by each other ;

Remembering, besides, how it pain'd thee to part
    With the Old Penal Code—that *chef-d'œuvre* of
        Law,
In which (though to own it too modest thou art)
    We could plainly perceive the fine touch of thy
        claw ;

I thought, as we ne'er can those good times revive,
(Though Eld—n, with help from your highness,
    would try,)
'T would still keep a taste for Hell's music alive,
    Could we get up a thundering No-Popery cry;—

That yell which, when chorus'd by laics and clerics,
    So like is to *ours*, in its spirit and tone,
That I often nigh laugh myself into hysterics,
    To think that Religion should make it her own.

So, having sent down for the original notes
    Of the chorus, as sung by your Majesty's choir,
With a few pints of lava, to gargle the throats
    Of myself and some others, who sing it " with
      fire," (1)

Thought I, " if the Marseillais Hymn could command
    Such audience, though yell'd by a *Sans-culotte*
      crew,
What wonders shall *we* do, who 've men in our band
    That not only wear breeches, but petticoats too."

Such *then* were my hopes ; but, with sorrow, your
    Highness,
I 'm forced to confess—be the cause what it will,
Whether fewness of voices, or hoarseness or shy-
    ness—
Our Beelzebub Chorus has gone off but ill.

The truth is, no placeman now knows his right key,
    The Treasury pitch-pipe of late is so various ;
And certain *base* voices, that look'd for a fee
    At the *York* music-meeting, now think it preca-
    rious.

Even some of our Reverends *might* have been
    warmer—
Though one or two capital roarers we 've had ;
Doctor wise (2) is, for instance, a charming performer,
    And *Huntingdon* Maberley's yell was not bad !

Altogether, however, the thing was not hearty ; —
    Even Eld—n allows we got on but so so ;
And when next we attempt a No-Popery party,
    We *must*, please your Highness, recruit *from below*.

But, hark, the young Black-leg is cracking his whip—
    Excuse me, Great Sir—there 's no time to be
    civil ;—
The next opportunity shan't be let slip,
    But, till then,
        I 'm in haste, your most dutiful,
                      DEVIL.

(1) *Con fuoco*—a music-book direction.
(2 This reverend gentleman distinguished himself at
the Reading election.
(3) "A measure of wheat for a penny, and three mea-
sures of barley for a penny."—*Rev.* vi.
(4) See the oration of this reverend gentleman, where
he describes the connubial joys of Paradise, and paints
the angels hovering round "each happy fair."
(5) When Whiston presented to Prince Eugene the Essay

THE MILLENNIUM.

SUGGESTED BY THE LATE WORK OF THE REVEREND
MR. IRV—NG " ON PROPHECY."
1826.

A MILLENNIUM at hand !—I 'm delighted to hear it—
    As matters, both public and private, now go,
With multitudes round us all starving, or near it,
    A good rich Millennium will come *à-propos*.

Only think, Master Fred, what delight to behold,
    Instead of thy bankrupt old City of Rags,
A bran-new Jerusalem, built all of gold,   [flags—
    Sound bullion throughout, from the roof to the

A City, where wine and cheap corn (3) shall abound—
    A celestial *Cocaigne*, on whose buttery shelves
We may swear the best things of this world will be
    found,
    As your Saints seldom fail to take care of them-
    selves !

Thanks, reverend expounder of raptures Elysian, (4)
    Divine Squintifobus, who, placed within reach
Of two opposite worlds, by a twist of your vision,
    Can cast, at the same time, a sly look at each ;—

Thanks, thanks for the hope thou affordest, that we-
    May, even in our own times, a jubilee share,
Which so long has been promised by prophets like thee,
    And so often postponed, we began to despair.

There was Whiston, (5) who learnedly took Prince
    Eugene
For the man who must bring the Millennium about ;
There 's Faber, whose pious productions have been
    All belied, ere his book's first edition was out ;—

There was Counsellor Dobbs, too, an Irish M.P.,
    Who discoursed on the subject with signal *éclat*,
And each day of his life sat expecting to see
    A Millennium break out in the town of Armagh ! (6)

There was also—but why should I burden my lay
    With your Brotherses, Southcotes, and names less
    deserving,
When all past Millenniums henceforth must give way
    To the last new Millennium of Orator Irv—ng.

Go on, mighty man—doom them all to the shelf—
    And when next thou with Prophecy troublest thy
    sconce,
Oh forget not, I pray thee, to prove that thyself
    Art the Beast (Chapter iv.) that sees nine ways at
    once.

in which he attempted to connect his victories over the
Turks with Revelation, the Prince is said to have replied,
that "he was not aware he had ever had the honour of
being known to St. John."
(6) Mr. Dobbs was a member of the Irish Parliament,
and, on all other subjects but the Millennium, a very sen-
sible person ; he chose Armagh as the scene of his Mil-
lennium, on account of the name Armageddon, mentioned
in Revelation.

THE THREE DOCTORS.

Doctoribus lætamur tribus.

1826.

Though many great Doctors there be,
  There are three that all Doctors out-top,
Doctor Eady, that famous M. D.,
  Doctor S—th—y, and dear Doctor Slop. (1)

The purger—the proser—the bard—
  All quacks in a different style;
Doctor S—th—y writes books by the yard,
  Doctor Eady writes puffs by the mile! (2)

Doctor Slop, in no merit outdone
  By his scribbling or physicking brother,
Can dose us with stuff like the one,
  Ay, and *dose* us with stuff like the other.

Doctor Eady good company keeps
  With " No Popery " scribes, on the walls;
Doctor S—th—y as gloriously sleeps
  With " No Popery " scribes, on the stalls.

Doctor Slop, upon subjects divine,
  Such Bedlamite slaver lets drop,
That, if Eady should take the *mad* line,
  He 'll be sure of a patient in Slop.

Seven millions of Papists, no less,
  Doctor S—th—y attacks like a Turk ; (3)
Doctor Eady, less bold. I confess,
  Attacks but his maid-of-all-work. (4)

Doctor S—th—y, for *his* grand attack,
  Both a laureate and pensioner is ;
While poor Doctor Eady, alack,
  Has been *had up* to Bow-street, for his !

And truly, the law does so blunder,
  That, though little blood has been spilt, he
May probably suffer, as under
  The *Chalking* Act, *known* to be guilty.

So much for the merits sublime
  (With whose catalogue ne'er should I stop)
Of the three greatest lights of our time,
  Doctor Eady, and S—th—y, and Slop!

(1) The editor of the *Morning Herald*, so nick-named.
(2) Alluding to the display of this doctor's name, in chalk, on all the walls round the metropolis.
(3) This seraphic doctor, in the preface to his last work (*Vindiciæ Ecclesiæ Anglicanæ*,) is pleased to anathematise not only all Catholics, but all advocates of Catholics :—"They have for their immediate allies (he says) every faction that is banded against the State, every demagogue, every irreligious and seditious journalist, every open and every insidious enemy to Monarchy and to Christianity."
(4) See the late accounts in the newspapers of the ap-

Should you ask me, to *which* of the three
  Great Doctors the preference should fall,
As a matter of course, I agree
  Doctor Eady must go to *the wall.*

But as S—th—y with laurels is crown'd,
  And Slop with a wig and a tail is,
Let Eady's bright temples be bound
  With a swingeing " Corona *Muralis!*" (5)

———o**o———

EPITAPH ON A TUFT-HUNTER.

Lament, lament, Sir Isaac Heard,
  Put mourning round thy page, Debrett,
For here lies one, who ne'er preferr'd
  A Viscount to a Marquis yet.

Beside him place the God of Wit,
  Before him Beauty's rosiest girls,
Apollo for a *star* he'd quit,
  And Love's own sister for an Earl's.

Did niggard fate no peers afford,
  He took, of course, to peers' relations ;
And, rather than not sport a Lord,
  Put up with even the last creations.

Even Irish names, could he but tag 'em
  With "Lord" and Duke," were sweet to call ;
And at a pinch, Lord Ballyraggum
  Was better than no Lord at all.

Heaven grant him now some noble nook,
  For, rest his soul ! he'd rather be
Genteelly damn'd beside a Duke,
  Then saved in vulgar company.

———o**o———

ODE TO A HAT.

———" altum
Ædificat caput."—*Juvenal.*

1826.

Hail, reverend Hat!—sublime 'mid all
  The minor felts that round thee grovel ;—
Thou, that the Gods " a Delta" call,
  While meaner mortals call thee " shovel."

When on thy shape (like pyramid,
  Cut horizontally in two) (6)
I raptured gaze, what dreams, unbid,
  Of stalls and mitres bless my view !

pearance of this gentleman at one of the Police-offices, in consequence of an alleged assault on his "maid-of-all-work."

(5. A crown granted as a reward among the Romans to persons who performed any extraordinary exploits upon *walls*, such as scaling them, battering them, etc.— No doubt, writing upon them, to the extent Dr. Eady does, would equally establish a claim to the honour.

(6) So described by a Reverend Historian of the Church : —"A Delta hat, like the horizontal section of a pyramid." *Grant's History of the English Church.*

SATIRICAL AND HUMOROUS POEMS. 519

That brim of brims, so sleekly good—
Not flapp'd, like dull Wesleyans', down,
But looking (as all churchmen's should)
Devoutly upward towards the *crown*.

Gods! when I gaze upon that brim,
So redolent of Church all over,
What swarms of Tithes, in vision dim—
Some pig-tail'd, some like cherubim,
With ducklings' wings—around it hover!
Tenths of all dead and living things,
That Nature into being brings,
From calves and corn to chitterlings.

Say, holy Hat, that hast, of cocks,
The very cock most orthodox,
To *which*, of all the well-fed throng
Of Zion, (1) joy'st thou to belong?
Thou 'rt *not* Sir Harcourt Lees's—no—
For hats grow like the heads that wear 'em ;
And hats, on heads like his, would grow
Particularly *harum-scarum*.
Who knows but thou may'st deck the pate
Of that famed Doctor Ad—mth—te,
(The reverend rat, whom we saw stand
On his hind-legs in Westmoreland,)
Who changed so quick from *blue* to *yellow*,
And would from *yellow* back to *blue*,
And back again, convenient fellow,
If 't were his interest so to do.

Or, haply, smartest of triangles,
Thou art the hat of Doctor Ow—n ;
The hat that, to his vestry wrangles,
That venerable priest doth go in—
And then, and there, amid the stare
Of all St. Olave's, takes the chair,
And quotes, with phiz right orthodox,
The example of his reverend brothers,
To prove that priests all fleece their flocks,
And *he* must fleece as well as others.

Blest Hat! (whoe'er thy lord may be)
Thus low I take off mine to thee,
The homage of a layman's *castor*,
To the spruce *delta* of his pastor.
Oh may'st thou be, as thou proceedest,
Still smarter cock'd, still brush'd the brighter,
Till, bowing all the way, thou leadest
Thy sleek possessor to a mitre!

——◦ ◦◦ ◦——

NEWS FOR COUNTRY COUSINS.

September, 1826.
DEAR COZ, as I know neither you nor Miss Draper,
When Parliament 's up, ever take in a paper,
But trust for your news to such stray odds and ends
As you chance to pick up from political friends—
Being one of this well-inform'd class, I sit down
To transmit you the last newest news that 's in town.

As to Greece and Lord Cochrane, things could n't
look better—
His Lordship (who promises now to fight faster)
Has just taken Rhodes, and despatch'd off a letter
To Daniel O'Connell, to make him Grand Master;
Engaging to change the old name if he can,
From the Knights of St. John to the Knights of St.
Dan;—
Or, if Dan should prefer (as a still better whim)
Being made the Colossus, 't is all one to him.

From Russia the last accounts are that the Czar—
Most generous and kind, as all sovereigns are,
And whose first princely act (as you know, I suppose)
Was to give away all his late brother's old clothes—(2)
Is now busy collecting, with brotherly care,
The late Emperor's nightcaps, and thinks of be-
stowing
One nightcap a-piece (if he has them to spare)
On all the distinguish'd old ladies now going.
(While I write, an arrival from Riga—the "Bro-
thers"—
Having nightcaps on board for Lord Eld—n and
others.)

Last advices from India—Sir Archy, 't is thought,
Was near catching a Tartar (the first ever caught
In N. Lat. 21.)—and his Highness Burmese,
Being very hard press'd to shell out the rupees,
And not having rhino sufficient, they say, meant
To pawn his august Golden Foot (3) for the payment.
(How lucky for monarchs, that thus, when they
choose,
Can establish a *running* account with the Jews!)
The security being what Rothschild calls "goot,"
A loan will be shortly, of course, set *on foot*;
The parties are Rothschild, A. Baring and Co.,
With three other great pawnbrokers: each takes a toe,
And engages (lest Gold-foot should give us *leg*-bail,
As he did once before) to pay down *on the nail*.

This is all for the present—what vile pens and paper!
Yours truly, dear Cousin—best love to Miss Draper.
——◦ ◦◦ ◦——
A VISION.
BY THE AUTHOR OF CHRISTABEL.
" UP!" said the Spirit, and, ere I could pray
One hasty orison, whirl'd me away
To a Limbo, lying—I wist not where—
Above or below, in earth or air;
For it glimmer'd o'er with a *doubtful* light,
One could n't say whether 't was day or night;
And 't was crost by many a mazy track,
One did n't know how to get on or back;

(1) Archbishop Magee affectionately calls the Church
Establishment of Ireland "the little Zion."
(2) A distribution was made of the Emperor Alexander's
military wardrobe by his successor.
(3) This potentate styles himself the Monarch of the
Golden Foot.

And I felt like a needle that's going astray
(With its *one* eye out) through a bundle of hay;
When the Spirit he grinn'd, and whisper'd me,
" Thou 'rt now in the Court of Chancery !"

Around me flitted unnumber'd swarms
Of shapeless, bodiless, tailless forms ;
(Like bottled-up babes, that grace the room
Of that worthy knight, Sir Everard Home)—
All of them things half-kill'd in rearing ;
Some were lame—some wanted *hearing ;*
Some had through half a century run,
Though they had n't a leg to stand upon.
Others, more merry, as just beginning,
Around on a *point of law* were spinning ;
Or balanced aloft, 'twixt *Bill* and *Answer,*
Lead at each end, like a tight-rope dancer.
Some were so *cross,* that nothing could please 'em ;—
Some gulp'd down *affidavits* to ease 'em ;—
All were in motion, yet never a one,
Let it *move* as it might, could ever move *on.*
" These," said the Spirit, " you plainly see,
Are what they call suits in Chancery !"

I heard a loud screaming of old and young,
Like a chorus by fifty Vellutis sung ;
Or an Irish Dump (" the words by Moore ")
At an amateur concert scream'd in score ;—
So harsh on my ear that walling fell
Of the wretches who in this Limbo dwell !
It seem'd like the dismal symphony
Of the shapes Æneas in hell did see ;
Or those frogs, whose legs a barbarous cook
Cut off, and left the frogs in the brook,
To cry all night, till life's last dregs,
" Give us our legs !—give us our legs !"
Touch'd with the sad and sorrowful scene,
I ask'd what all this yell might mean,
When the Spirit replied, with a grin of glee,
" 'T is the cry of the Suitors in Chancery !"

I look'd, and I saw a wizard rise, (1)
With a wig like a cloud before men's eyes.
In his aged hand he held a wand,
Wherewith he beckon'd his embryo band,
And they moved and moved, as he waved it o'er,
But they never got on one inch the more.
And still they kept limping to and fro,
Like Ariels round old Prospero—
Saying, " Dear Master, let us go,"
But still old Prospero answer'd " No."
And I heard, the while, that wizard elf
Muttering, muttering spells to himself,
While o'er as many old papers he turn'd,
As Hume e'er moved for, or Omar burn'd.
He talk'd of his virtue—" though some, less nice,
(He own'd with a sigh) preferr'd his *Vice* "—

(1) The Lord Chancellor Eld—n.
(2) To such important discussions as these the greater
part of Dr. Southey's *Vindiciæ Ecclesiæ Anglicanæ* is
devoted.

And he said, " I think"—" I doubt "—" I hope,"
Call'd God to witness, and damn'd the Pope ;
With many more sleights of tongue and hand
I could n't, for the soul of me, understand.
Amazed and posed, I was just about
To ask his name, when the screams without,
The merciless clack of the imps within,
And that conjuror's mutterings, made such a din,
That, startled, I woke—leap'd up in my bed—
Found the Spirit, the imps, and the conjuror fled,
And bless'd my stars, right pleased to see,
That I was n't, as yet, in Chancery.

—◦◦◦◦—

THE PETITION OF THE ORANGEMEN OF
IRELAND.
                                    1826.

To the people of England, the humble Petition
    Of Ireland's disconsolate Orangemen, showing—
That sad, very sad, is our present condition ;—
    Our jobbing all gone, and our noble selves going ;—

That, forming one seventh, within a few fractions,
    Of Ireland's seven millions of hot heads and hearts,
We hold it the basest of all base transactions
    To keep us from murdering the other six parts ;—

That, as to laws made for the good of the many,
    We humbly suggest there is nothing less true ;
As all human laws (and our own, more than any)
    Are made *by* and *for* a particular few ;—

That much it delights every true Orange brother,
    To see you, in England, such ardour evince,
In discussing *which* sect most tormented the other,
    And burn'd with most *gusto,* some hundred years
    since ;—

That we love to behold, while old England grows
    faint,
    Messrs. Southey and Butler nigh coming to blows,
To decide whether Dunstan, that strong-bodied Saint,
    Ever truly and really pull'd the Devil's nose ;

Whether t' other Saint, Dominic, burnt the Devil's
    paw—
    Whether Edwy intrigued with Elgiva's old mo-
    ther—(2)   [draw
And many such points, from which Southey can
    Conclusions most apt for our hating each other.

That 't is very well known this devout Irish nation
    Has now, for some ages, gone happily on,
Believing in two kinds of Substantiation,
    One party in *Trans* and the other in *Con* ; (3)

That we, your petitioning *Cons,* have, in right
    Of the said monosyllable, ravaged the lands,

(3) Consubstantiation—the true Reformed belief ; at
least, the belief of Luther, and, as Mosheim asserts of
Melancthon also.

And embezzled the goods, and annoy'd, day and
    night,   [*Trans;*—
Both the bodies and souls of the sticklers for

That we trust to Peel, Eldon, and other such sages,
  For keeping us still in the same state of mind;
Pretty much as the world used to be in those ages
  When still smaller syllables madden'd mankind;—

When the words *ex* and *per* (1) served as well, to
  annoy
One's neighbours and friends with, as *con* and *trans*
  now ;
And Christians, like S—th—y, who stickled for *oi*,
  Cut the throats of all Christians who stickled for
  ou. (2)

That, relying on England, whose kindness already
  So often has help'd us to play this game o'er,
We have got our red coats and our carabines ready,
  And wait but the word to show sport, as before.

That, as to the expense—the few millions, or so,
  Which for all such diversions John Bull has to pay—
'Tis, at least, a great comfort to John Bull to know,
  That to Orangemen's pockets 't will all find its way.
For which your petitioners ever will pray,
        etc., etc., etc., etc., etc.

—————

COTTON AND CORN.

A DIALOGUE.

SAID Cotton to Corn, t' other day,
  As they met and exchanged a salute:—
(Squire Corn in his carriage so gay,
  Poor Cotton, half famish'd, on foot):

"Great Squire, if it is n't uncivil
  To hint at starvation before you,
Look down on a poor hungry devil,
  And give him some bread, I implore you!"

Quoth Corn then, in answer to Cotton,
  Perceiving he meant to make *free*—
"Low fellow, you 've surely forgotten
  The distance between you and me!

"To expect that we, Peers of high birth,
  Should waste our illustrious acres,
For no other purpose on earth
  Than to fatten curst calico-makers!—

(1 When John of Ragusa went to Constantinople (at
the time this dispute between "ex" and "per" was going
on), he found the Turks, we are told, "laughing at the
Christians for being divided by two such insignificant
particles."

(2) The Arian controversy. — Before that time, says
Hooker, "in order to be a sound believing Christian, men
were not curious what syllables or particles of speech they
used."

(3) A great part of the income of Joanna Southcott arose

"That Bishops to bobbins should bend—
  Should stoop from their Bench's sublimity,
Great dealers in *lawn*, to befriend
  Such contemptible dealers in dimity!

"No—vile Manufacture! ne'er harbour
  A hope to be fed at our boards;—
Base offspring of Arkwright the barber,
  What claim canst *thou* have upon Lords?

"No—thanks to the taxes and debt,
  And the triumph of paper o'er guineas,
Our race of Lord Jemmys, as yet,
  May defy your whole rabble of *Jennys!*"

So saying—whip, crack, and away
  Went Corn in his chaise through the throng,
So headlong, I heard them all say,
  "Squire Corn would be *down* before long."

—⚬❈⚬—

THE CANONIZATION OF SAINT
B—TT—RW—RTH.

"A Christian of the best edition."—*Rabelais.*

CANONIZE him!—yea, verily, we 'll canonize him;
  Though Cant is his hobby, and meddling his bliss,
Though sages may pity, and wits may despise him,
  He 'll ne'er make a bit the worse Saint for all this.

Descend, all ye Spirits, that ever yet spread
  The dominion of Humbug o'er land and o'er sea,
Descend on our B—tt—rw—rth's biblical head,
  Thrice-Great, Bibliopolist, Saint, and M. P.

Come, shade of Joanna, come down from thy sphere,
  And bring little Shiloh—if 't is n't too far— [dear,
Such a sight will to B—tt—rw—rth's bosom be
  His conceptions and *thine* being much on a par.

Nor blush, Saint Joanna, once more to behold
  A world thou hast honour'd by cheating so many;
Thou 'lt find still among us one Personage old,
  Who also by tricks and the *Seals* (3) makes a
        [penny.
Thou, too, of the Shakers, divine Mother *Lee!* (4)
  Thy smiles to beatified B—tt—rw—rth deign;
Two "lights of the Gentiles" are thou, Anne, and he,
  One hallowing Fleet Street, and *t'other* Toad
    Lane! (5)
           [wood,
The Heathens, we know, made their Gods out of
  And Saints may be framed of as handy materials;—

from the Seals of the Lord's protection, which she sold to
her followers.

(4) Mrs. Anne Lee, the "chosen vessel" of the Shakers,
and "Mother of all the children of regeneration."

(5) Toad Lane, in Manchester, where Mother Lee was
born. In her "Address to Young Believers," she says,
that "it is a matter of no importance with them from
whence the means of their deliverance come, whether
from a stable in Bethlehem, or from Toad Lane, Man-
chester."

66

Old women and B—tt—rw—rths make just as good
    As any the Pope ever *book'd* as Ethereals,

Stand forth, Man of Bibles!—not Mahomet's pigeon,
    When, perch'd on the Koran, he dropp'd there,
        they say,
Strong marks of his faith, ever shed o'er religion
    Such glory as B—tt—rw—rth sheds every day.

Great Galen of souls, with what vigour he crams
    Down Erin's idolatrous throats, till they crack
        again,
Bolus on bolus, good man!— and then damns
    Both their stomachs and souls, if they dare cast
                [them back again.
How well might his shop—as a type representing
    The creed of himself and his sanctified clan—
On its counter exhibit "the Art of Tormenting,"
    Bound neatly, and Letter'd "Whole Duty of
                [Man!" (1)
Canonize him!—by Judas, we *will* canonize him,
    For Cant is his hobby, and twaddling his bliss;
And, though wise men may pity and wits may de-
        spise him,
    He 'll make but the better *shop*-saint for all this.

Call quickly together the whole tribe of Canters,
    Convoke all the *serious* Tag-rag of the nation;
Bring Shakers and Snufflers and Jumpers and Ranters,
    To witness their B—tt—rw—rth's Canonization!

Yea, humbly I 've ventured his merits to paint,
    Yea, feebly have tried all his gifts to portray;
And they form a sum-total for making a Saint,
    That the Devil's own Advocate could not gainsay.

Jump high, all ye Jumpers! ye Ranters, all roar!
    While B—tt—rw—rth's spirit, upraised from your
        eyes,
Like a kite made of foolscap, in glory shall soar,
    With a long tail of rubbish behind, to the skies!

—◦◦◦◦—

AN INCANTATION.

SUNG BY THE BUBBLE SPIRIT.

AIR—*Come with me, and we will go*
    Where the rocks of coral grow.

COME with me, and we will blow
Lots of bubbles as we go;
Bubbles, bright as ever Hope
Drew from fancy—or from soap;

Bright as e'er the South Sea sent
From its frothy element!
Come with me, and we will blow
Lots of bubbles, as we go.
Mix the lather, Johnny W—lks,
Thou, who rhymest so well to bilks, (2)
Mix the lather—who can be
Fitter for such task than thee,
Great M. P. for *Sudsbury!*
Now the frothy charm is ripe,
Puffing Peter, (3) bring thy Pipe—
Thou, whom ancient Coventry
Once so dearly loved, that she
Knew not which to her was sweeter,
Peeping Tom or Puffing Peter;—
Puff the bubbles high in air,
Puff thy best to keep them there.

Bravo, bravo, Peter M—re!
Now the rainbow humbugs (4) soar,
Glittering all with golden hues,
Such as haunt the dreams of Jews; –
Some, reflecting mines that lie
Under Chili's glowing sky;
Some, those virgin pearls that sleep
Cloister'd in the southern deep;
Others, as if lent a ray
From the streaming Milky Way,
Glistening o'er with curds and whey
From the cows of Alderney.
Now 's the moment—who shall first
Catch the bubbles, ere they burst?
Run, ye Squires, ye Viscounts, run,
Br—gd—n, T—ynh—m, P—lm—t—n;—
John W—lks junior runs beside ye!
Take the good the knaves provide ye!(5)
See, with upturn'd eyes and hands,
Where the *Shareman*, (6) Br—gd—n, stands,
Gaping for the froth to fall
Down his gullet—*lye* and all.
See!—
            But, hark, my time is out—
Now, like some great water-spout,
Scatter'd by the cannon's thunder,
Burst, ye bubbles, all asunder!

[*Here the stage darkens—a discordant crash is heard
from the orchestra—the broken bubbles descend in a
saponaceous but unclearly mist over the heads of the
Dramatis Personœ, and the scene drops, leaving the
bubble-hunters——all in the suds.*]

(1) The following lines have been suppressed :—
As to politics—*there*, too, so strong his digestion,
Having learn'd from the law-books, by which he 's surrounded,
To cull all that 's worst on all sides of the question,
    His black dose of politics thus is compounded—
The rinsing of any old Tory's dull noddle,
    Made radical-hot, and then mix'd with some grains
Of that gritty Scotch gabble, that virulent twaddle,
    Which Murray's New Series of Blackwood contains. – P. E.
(2) Strong indications of character may be sometimes
traced in the rhymes to names. Marvell thought so, when
he wrote

" Sir Edward Sutton,
The foolish Knight who rhymes to mutton."
(3) The Member, during a long period, for Coventry.
(4) An humble imitation of one of our modern poets,
who, in a poem against War, after describing the splendid
habiliments of the soldier, thus apostrophises him—" thou
rainbow ruffian !"
(5)   "Lovely Thais sits beside thee :
        Take the good the Gods provide thee."
(6) So called by a sort of Tuscan dulcification of the *eh*,
in the word " Chairman."

A DREAM OF TURTLE.

BY SIR W. CURTIS.

1826.

'T was evening time, in the twilight sweet
I sail'd along, when—whom should I meet
But a Turtle journeying o'er the sea,
" On the service of his Majesty." (1)

When spying him first through twilight dim,
I did n't know what to make of him;
But said to myself, as slow he plied
His fins and roll'd from side to side
Conceitedly o'er the watery path—
"'Tis my Lord of Stowell taking a bath,
And I hear him now, among the fishes,
Quoting Vatel and Burgersdicius!"
But, no—'t was, indeed, a Turtle, wide
And plump as ever these eyes descried;
A Turtle juicy as ever yet
Glued up the lips of a Baronet!
And much did it grieve my soul to see
That an animal of such dignity,
Like an absentee abroad should roam,
When he *ought* to stay and be ate at home.

But now "a change came o'er my dream,"
Like the magic lantern's shifting slider;
I look'd, and saw, by the evening beam,
On the back of that Turtle sat a rider—
A goodly man, with an eye so merry,
I knew 't was our Foreign Secretary, (2)
Who there, at his ease, did sit and smile,
Like Waterton on his crocodile; (3)
Cracking such jokes, at every motion,
As made the Turtle squeak with glee,
And own they gave him a lively notion
Of what his *forced*-meat balls would be.

So, on the Sec. in his glory went,
Over that briny element,
Waving his hand, as he took farewell,
With graceful air, and bidding me tell,
Inquiring friends that the Turtle and he
Were gone on a foreign embassy—
To soften the heart of a *Diplomate*,
Who is known to dote upon verdant fat,
And to let admiring Europe see,
That *calipash* and *calipee*
Are the English forms of Diplomacy.

(1) We are told that the passport of this grand diplomatic Turtle (sent by the Secretary for Foreign Affairs to a certain noble envoy) described him as " on his majesty's service."

— dapibus Supremi
Grata testudo Jovis.

(2) Mr. Canning.

(3) *Wanderings in South America.* " It was the first and last time (says Mr. Waterton) I was ever on a crocodile's back."

THE DONKY AND HIS PANNIERS.

A FABLE.

—— " fessus jam sudat asellus,
Parce illi; vestrum delicium est asinus."—*Virgil. Copa.*

A Donky, whose talent for burdens was wondrous,
So much that you 'd swear he rejoiced in a load,
One day had to jog under panniers so pond'rous,
That—down the poor Donky fell smack on the
road!

His owners and drivers stood round in amaze—
What! Neddy, the patient, the prosperous Neddy,
So easy to drive, through the dirtiest ways,
For every description of job-work so ready!

One driver (whom Ned might have "hail'd" as a
" brother ") (4)
Had just been proclaiming his Donky's renown
For vigour, for spirit, for one thing or other—
When, lo, 'mid his praises, the Donky came down!

But, how to upraise him?—*one* shouts t'other whistles,
While Jenky, the Conjurer, wisest of all,
Declared that an "over-production of thistles—(5)
(Here Ned gave a stare)—was the cause of his fall."

Another wise Solomon cries, as he passes—
" There, let him alone, and the fit will soon cease;
The beast has been fighting with other jack-asses,
And this is his mode of ! *transition to peace.'*"

Some look'd at his hoofs, and, with learned grimaces,
Pronounced that too long without shoes he had
gone—
" Let the blacksmith provide him a *sound metal basis*
(The wise-acres said), "and he 's sure to jog on." (6)

Meanwhile, the poor Neddy, in torture and fear,
Lay under his panniers, scarce able to groan;
And—what was still dolefuller—lending an ear
To advisers, whose ears were a match for his own.

At length, a plain rustic, whose wit went so far
As to see others' folly, roar'd out, as he pass'd—
" Quick—off with the panniers, all dolts as ye are,
Or your prosperous Neddy will soon kick his last!"
October, 1826.

(4) Alluding to an early poem of Mr. Coleridge's, addressed to an Ass, and beginning, "I hail thee, brother:"
(5) A certain country gentleman having said in the House, "that we must return at last to the food of our ancestors," somebody asked Mr. T. "what food the gentleman meant?"—"Thistles, I suppose," answered Mr. T.
(6) The following appeared in the original edition:—
But others, who gabbled a jargon half Gaelic,
Exclaim'd, " Hoot awa, mon, you 're a' gane astray "—
And declared that, whoe'er might prefer the *metallic*,
They 'd shoe their own donkies with *papier mache*."—P. E.

ODE TO THE SUBLIME PORTE.
1826.

GREAT Sultan, how wise are thy state compositions!
And oh, above all, I admire that Decree,
In which thou command'st, that all *she* politicians
Shall forthwith be strangled and cast in the sea.

'Tis my fortune to know a lean Benthamite spinster—
A maid, who her faith in old Jeremy puts;
Who talks, with a lisp, of "the last new West*minster*,"
And hopes you're delighted with "Mill upon Gluts;"

Who tells you how clever one Mr. Fun-blank is,
How charming his Articles 'gainst the Nobility;—
And assures you that even a gentleman's rank is,
In Jeremy's school, of no sort of *utility*.

To see her, ye Gods, a new Number perusing—
ART. 1. "On the *Needle's* variations," by Pl—e ;(1)
ART. 2. By her favorite Fun-blank(2)—"so amusing!
Dear man! he makes Poetry quite a *Law* case."

ART. 3. "Upon Fallacies," Jeremy's own—
(Chief Fallacy being his hope to find readers);—
ART. 4. "Upon Honesty," author unknown;—
ART. 5. (by the young Mr. M——) "Hints to
Breeders."

Oh, Sultan, oh, Sultan, though oft for the bag
And the bowstring, like thee, I am tempted to call—
Though drowning's too good for each blue-stocking
hag,
I would bag this *she* Benthamite first of them all!

And, lest she should ever again lift her head
From the watery bottom, her clack to renew—
As a clog, as a sinker, far better than lead,
I would hang round her neck her own darling
Review.

———oo———

CORN AND CATHOLICS.
Utrum horum
Dirius borum?—Incerti Auctoris.

WHAT! *still* those two infernal questions,
That with our meals, our slumbers mix—
That spoil our tempers and digestions—
Eternal Corn and Catholics!

Gods! were there ever two such bores?
Nothing else talk'd of night or morn—
Nothing *in* doors, or *out* of doors,
But endless Catholics and Corn!

(1) A celebrated political tailor.
(2) This pains-taking gentleman has been at the trouble
of counting, with the assistance of Cocker, the number of
metaphors in Moore's *Life of Sheridan*, and has found
them to amount, as nearly as possible, to 2235— and some
fractions.

(3) Author of the late Report on Foreign Corn.
(4) The Horn Gate, through which the ancients supposed

Never was such a brace of pests—
While Ministers, still worse than either,
Skill'd but in feathering their nests,
Plague us with both, and settle neither.

So addled in my cranium meet
Popery and Corn, that oft I doubt,
Whether, this year, 'twas bonded Wheat,
Or bonded Papists, they let out.

Here, landlords, *here*, polemics nail you,
Arm'd with all rubbish they can rake up;
Prices and *Texts* at once assail you—
From Daniel *these*, and *those* from Jacob. (3)

And when you sleep, with head still torn
Between the two, their shapes you mix,
Till sometimes Catholics seem Corn—
Then Corn again seems Catholics.

Now Dantzic wheat before you floats—
Now Jesuits from California—
Now Ceres, link'd with Titus *Oats*,
Comes dancing through the "Porta Cornea." (4)

Oft, too, the Corn grows animate,
And a whole crop of heads appears,
Like Papists, *bearding* Church and State—
Themselves, together *by the ears!* (5)

In short, these torments never cease;
And oft I wish myself transferr'd off
To some far lonely land of peace,
Where Corn or Papists ne'er were heard of.

Yes, waft me Parry, to the Pole;
For—if my fate is to be chosen
'Twixt bores and icebergs—on my soul,
I'd rather, of the two, be frozen!

———oo———

A CASE OF LIBEL.
"The greater the truth, the worse the libel."

A CERTAIN Sprite, who dwells below,
('Twere a libel, perhaps, to mention where,)
Came up *incog.*, some years ago,
To try, for a change, the London air.

So well he look'd, and dress'd, and talk'd,
And hid his tail and horns so handy,
You'd hardly have known him, as he walk'd,
From C——e, or any other Dandy.

all true dreams (such as those of the Popish Plot, etc.) to
pass.
(5) This humorous production has been curtailed of the
following verse :—

> While, leaders of the wheat, a row
> Of Poppies, gaudily declaiming,
> Like Counsellor O'Bric and Co.,
> Stand forth, somniferously flaming !—P. E.

(His horns, it seems, are made t' unscrew;
  So, he has but to take them out of the socket,
And—just as some fine husbands do—
  Conveniently clap them into his pocket.)

In short, he look'd extremely natty,
  And even contrived—to his own great wonder—
By dint of sundry scents from Gattie,
  To keep the sulphurous *hogo* under.

And so my gentleman hoof'd about,
  Unknown to all but a chosen few
At White's and Crockford's, where, no doubt,
  He had many *post-obits* falling due.

Alike a gamester and a wit,
  At night he was seen with Crockford's crew.
At morn with learned dames would sit—
  So pass'd his time 'twixt *black* and *blue*.

Some wish'd to make him an M. P.,
  But, finding W—lks was also one, he
Swore, in a rage, "he'd be d—d if he
  Would ever sit in one house with Johnny."

At length, as secrets travel fast,
  And devils, whether he or she,
Are sure to be found out at last,
  The affair got wind most rapidly.

The Press, the impartial Press, that snubs
  Alike a fiend's or an angel's capers—
Miss Paton's soon as Beelzebub's—
  Fired off a squib in the morning papers:

"We warn good men to keep aloof
  From a grim old Dandy, seen about,
With a fire-proof wig, and a cloven hoof
  Through a neat-cut Hoby smoking out."

Now—the Devil being a gentleman,
  Who piques himself on well-bred dealings—
You may guess, when o'er these lines he ran,
  How much they hurt and shock'd his feelings

Away he posts to a Man of Law,
  And 't would make you laugh could you have seen 'em,
As paw shook hand, and hand shook paw, ['em.
  And 't was "hail, good fellow, well met," between

Straight an indictment was preferr'd—
  And much the Devil enjoy'd the jest,
When, asking about the Bench, he heard
  That, of all the Judges, his own was *Best*. (1)

(1) A celebrated Judge, so named.

(2) This lady also favours us, in her Memoirs, with the address of those apothecaries who have, from time to time, given her pills that agreed with her; always desiring that the pills should be ordered "*comme pour elle*."

In vain Defendant proffer'd proof
  That Plaintiff's self was the Father of Evil—
Brought Hoby forth, to swear to the hoof,
  And Stultz to speak to the tail of the Devil.

The Jury (saints, all snug and rich,
  And readers of virtuous Sunday papers)
Found for the Plaintiff—on hearing which
  The Devil gave one of his loftiest capers.

For oh, 't was nuts to the Father of Lies
  (As this wily fiend is named in the Bible)
To find it settled by laws so wise,
  That the greater the truth, the worse the libel!

—o﹖o—

LITERARY ADVERTISEMENT.

WANTED—Authors of all-work, to job for the season,
  No matter which party, so faithful to neither;
Good hacks, who, if posed for a rhyme or a reason,
  Can manage, like ******, to do without either.

If in gaol, all the better for out-o'-door topics;
  Your gaol is for Travellers a charming retreat;
They can take a day's rule for a trip to the Tropics,
  And sail round the world, at their ease, in the Fleet.

For a Dramatist, too, the most useful of schools—
  He can study high life in the King's Bench community;
Aristotle could scarce keep him more *within rules*,
  And *of place* he, at least, must adhere to the *unity*.

Any lady or gentleman, come to an age
  To have good "Reminiscences" (three-score or higher),
Will meet with encouragement—so much, *per* page,
  And the spelling and grammar both found by the buyer.

No matter with *what* their remembrance is stock'd,
  So they'll only remember the *quantum* desired;—
Enough to fill handsomely Two Volumes, *oct.*,
  Price twenty-four shillings, is all that's required.

They may treat us, like Kelly, with old *jeu-d'esprits*,
  Like Dibdin, may tell of each farcical frolic;
Or kindly inform us, like Madame Genlis, (2)
  That gingerbread-cakes always give them the [colic. (3)
Wanted, also, a new stock of Pamphlets on Corn,
  By "Farmers" and "Landholders"—(worthies whose lands
Enclosed all in bow-pots, their attics adorn,
  Or, whose share of the soil may be seen on their hands).

(3) The following lines no longer form part of the poem:—

> Theres's nothing, at present, so popular growing
>   As your Autobiographers—fortunate elves,
> Who manage to know all the best people going,
>   Without having ever been heard of themselves.—P. R.

No-Popery Sermons, in ever so dull a vein,
 Sure of a market;—should they, too, who pen 'em,
Be renegade Papists, like Murtagh O'S—ll—v—n, (1)
 Something *extra* allow'd for the additional venom.

Funds, Physic, Corn, Poetry, Boxing, Romance,
 All excellent subjects for turning a penny;—
To write upon all is an author's sole chance
 For attaining, at last, the least knowledge of *any*.

Nine times out of ten, if his *title* is good,
 The material *within* of small consequence is;—
Let him only write fine, and, if not understood,
 Why—that's the concern of the reader, not his.

Nota Bene—an Essay, now printing, to show,
 That Horace (as clearly as words could express it)
Was for taxing the Fund-holders, ages ago,
 When he wrote thus—" Quodcunque *in Fund is*,
  assess it." (2)

—————

THE IRISH SLAVE. (3)

I HEARD, as I lay, a wailing sound,
 " He is dead—he is dead," the rumour flew;
And I raised my chain, and turn'd me round,
 And ask'd, through the dungeon-window, "Who?"

I saw my livid tormentors pass;
 Their grief 'twas bliss to hear and see!
For, never came joy to them, alas,
 That did n't bring deadly bane to me.

Eager I look'd through the mist of night,
 And ask'd, " What foe of my race hath died?
Is it he—that Doubter of law and right,
 Whom nothing but wrong could e'er decide—

" Who, long as he sees but wealth to win,
 Hath never yet felt a qualm or doubt
What suitors for justice he'd keep in,
 Or what suitors for freedom he'd shut out—

" Who, a clog for ever on Truth's advance,
 Hangs round her (like the Old Man of the Sea
Round Sinbad's neck), (4) nor leaves a chance
 Of shaking him off—is 't he? is 't he? "

Ghastly my grim tormentors smiled,
 And thrusting me back to my den of woe,
With a laughter even more fierce and wild
 Than their funeral howling, answer'd " No. "

But the cry still pierced my prison-gate,
 And again I ask'd, " What scourge is gone?
Is it he—that Chief, so coldly great,
 Whom Fame unwillingly shines upon—

(1) A gentleman, who distinguished himself by his evi-
dence before the Irish Committees.
(2) According to· the common reading, " quodcunque
infundis, acescit."

" Whose name is one of the ill-omen'd words
 They link with hate, on his native plains;
And why?—they lent him hearts and swords,
 And he, in return, gave scoffs and chains!

" Is it he? is it he? " I loud inquired,
 When, hark!—there sounded a Royal knell;
And I knew what spirit had just expired,
 And, slave as I was, my triumph fell.

He had pledged a hate unto me and mine,
 He had left to the future nor hope nor choice,
But seal'd that hate with a Name Divine,
 And he now was dead, and—I *couldn't* rejoice!

He had fann'd afresh the burning brands
 Of a bigotry waxing cold and dim;
He had arm'd anew my torturers' hands,
 And *them* did I curse—but sigh'd for him.

For *his* was the error of head, not heart;
 And—oh, how beyond the ambush'd foe,
Who to enmity adds the traitor's part,
 And carries a smile, with a curse below!

If ever a heart made bright amends
 For the fatal fault of an erring head—
Go, learn *his* fame from the lips of friends,
 In the orphan's tear be his glory read.

A Prince without pride, a man without guile,
 To the last unchanging, warm, sincere,
For Worth he had ever a hand and smile,
 And for Misery ever his purse and tear.

Touch'd to the heart by that solemn toll,
 I calmly sunk in my chains again;
While, still as I said " Heaven rest his soul!"
 My mates of the dungeon sigh'd " Amen!"
  January, 1827.

————

ODE TO FERDINAND.

1827.

QUIT, the sword, thou King of men,
Grasp the needle once again;
Making petticoats is far
Safer sport than making war;
Trimming is a better thing,
Than the *being* trimm'd, oh King!
Grasp the needle bright with which
Thou didst for the Virgin stitch
Garment such as ne'er before
Monarch stitch'd or Virgin wore.
Not for her, oh sempster nimble!
Do I now invoke thy thimble;
Not for her thy wanted aid is,
But for certain grave old ladies,

(3) Written on the death of the Duke of York.
(4) " You fell, said they, into the hands of the Old Man of
the Sea, and are the first who ever escaped strangling by
his malicious tricks."—*Story of Sinbad.*

Who now sit in England's cabinet,
Waiting to be clothed in tabinet,
Or whatever choice *étoffe* is
Fit for Dowagers in office.

First, thy care, oh King, devote
To Dame Eld—n's petticoat.
Make it of that silk, whose dye
Shifts for ever to the eye,
Just as if it hardly knew
Whether to be pink or blue.
Or—material fitter yet—
If thou couldst a remnant get
Of that stuff, with which of old,
Sage Penelope, we 're told,
Still by doing and undoing,
Kept her *suitors* always wooing—
That's the stuff which, I pronounce, is
Fittest for Dame Eld—n's flounces.

After this, we 'll try thy hand,
Mantua-making Ferdinand,
For old Goody W—stm—l—d ;
One who loves, like Mother Cole,
Church and State with all her soul ;
And has pass'd her life in frolics
Worthy of your Apostolics.
Choose, in dressing this old flirt,
Something that wo'n't show the dirt,
As from habit every minute
Goody W—stm—l—d is in it.

This is all I now shall ask,
Hie thee, monarch, to thy task ;
Finish Eld—n's frills and borders,
Then return for further orders.
Oh what progress for our sake,
Kings in millinery make !
Ribands, garters, and such things,
Are supplied by *other* Kings—
Ferdinand his rank denotes
By providing petticoats.

—◦●◦—

HAT VERSUS WIG.

1827.

" At the interment of the Duke of York, Lord Eld-n, in
order to guard against the effects of the damp, stood
upon his hat during the whole of the ceremony."
————metus omnes et inexorabile fatum
Subjecit pedibus, strepitumque Acherontis avari.

'Twixt Eld—n's Hat and Eld—n's Wig
There lately rose an altercation—
Each with its own importance big,
Disputing *which* most serves the nation.

Quoth Wig, with consequential air,
"Pooh! pooh! you surely can't design,

(1) " Love rules the court, the camp, the grove,
And men below and gods above,
For Love is Heaven and Heaven is Love."—*Scott.*
(2) " *Brim*—a naughty woman."—*Grose.*

My worthy beaver, to compare
Your station in the state with mine.

" Who meets the learned legal crew?
Who fronts the lordly Senate's pride?
The Wig, the Wig, my friend—while you
Hang dangling on some peg outside.

" Oh, 't is the Wig, that rules, like Love,
Senate and Court, with like *éclat*—
And wards below, and lords above,
For Law is Wig and Wig is Law !(1)

" Who tried the long, *Long* W—ll—sl—y suit,
Which tried one's patience, in return?
Not thou, oh Hat !—though, *couldst* thou do 't,
Of other *brims* (2) than thine thou'dst learn.

" 'T was mine our master's toil to share ;
When, like 'Truepenny,' in the play, (3)
He every minute, cried out ' Swear,'
And merrily to swear went they ;—(4)

" When, loath poor W—ll—sl—y to condemn, he
With nice discrimination weigh'd,
Whether 't was only ' Hell and Jemmy,'
Or ' Hell and Tommy' that he play'd.

" No, no, my worthy beaver, no—
Though cheapen'd at the cheapest hatter's,
And smart enough, as beavers go,
Thou ne'er wert made for public matters."

Here Wig concluded his oration,
Looking, as wigs do, wondrous wise ;
While thus, full cock'd for declamation,
The veteran Hat enraged replies :—

" Ha ! dost thou then so soon forget
What thou, what England owes to me?
Ungrateful Wig !—when will a debt,
So deep, so vast be owed to thee?

" Think of that night, that fearful night,
When, through the steaming vault below,
Our master dared, in gout's despite,
To venture his podagric toe !

" Who was it then, thou boaster, say,
When thou had'st to thy box sneak'd off,
Beneath his feet protecting lay,
And saved him from a mortal cough ?

" Think, if Catarrh had quench'd that sun,
How blank this world had been to thee !
Without that head to shine upon,
Oh Wig, where would thy glory be?

(3) " *Ghost* [beneath].—Swear !
" *Hamlet.*—Ha, ha ! say'st thou so? Art thou there,
Truepenny ' Come on."
(4) His demand for fresh affidavits was incessant.

" You, too, ye Britons—had this hope
  Of Church and State been ravish'd from ye,
Oh think, how Canning and the Pope
  Would then have play'd up ' Hell and Tommy!'

" At sea, there 's but a plank, they say,
  'Twixt seamen and annihilation ;
A Hat, that awful moment, lay
  'Twixt England and Emancipation!

" Oh!!! ——"

    At this " Oh!!!" *The Times'* Reporter
Was taken poorly and retired ;
Which made him cut Hat's rhetoric shorter,
  Than justice to the case required.

On his return, he found these shocks
  Of eloquence all ended quite ;
And Wig lay snoring in his box,
  And Hat was—hung up for the night.

—◦❀◦—

NEW CREATION OF PEERS.

BATCH THE FIRST.

"His 'prentice han'
He tried on man,
And then he made the lasses."

1827.

" AND now," quoth the Minister, (eased of his
    panics,
  And ripe for each pastime the Summer affords, }
" Having had our full swing at destroying mechanics,
  By way of *set-off*, let us make a few Lords.

" 'T is pleasant—while nothing but mercantile frac-
    tures,
  Some simple, some *compound*, is dinn'd in our
    ears—
To think that, though robb'd of all coarse manufac-
    tures,
  We still have our fine manufacture of Peers ;—

" Those *Gobelin* productions, which Kings take a
    pride
  In engrossing the whole fabrication and trade of ;
Choice tapestry things, very grand on *one* side,
  But showing, on t' other, what rags they are
    made of."

The plan being fix'd, raw material was sought,—
  No matter how middling, if Tory the creed be ;
And first, to begin with, Squire W———, 't was
    thought,
  For a Lord was as raw a material as need be.

Next came, with his *penchant* for painting and pelf,
  The tasteful Sir Charles, (1) so renown'd, far and
    near,
For purchasing pictures, and selling himself—
  And *both* (as the public well knows) very dear.

Beside him Sir John comes, with equal *éclat*, in ;—
  Stand forth, chosen pair, while for titles we mea-
    sure ye ;
Both connoisseur baronets, both fond of *drawing*,
  Sir John after nature, Sir Charles on the Trea-
    sury.

But, bless us!—behold a new candidate come—
  In his hand he upholds a prescription, new written ;
He poiseth a pill-box 'twixt finger and thumb,
  And he asketh a seat 'mong the Peers of Great
    Britain !

" Forbid it," cried Jenky, " ye Viscounts, ye Earls!—
  Oh Rank, how thy glories would fall disen-
    chanted,
If coronets glisten'd with pills 'stead of pearls,
  And the strawberry-leaves were by rhubarb sup-
    planted !

" No—ask it not, ask it not, dear Doctor H—lf—rd ;
  If nought but a Peerage can gladden thy life,
And young Master H—lf—rd as yet is too small
    for 't,
  Sweet Doctor, we 'll make a *she* Peer of thy wife.

" Next to bearing a coronet on our *own* brows,
  Is to bask in its light from the brows of another ;
And grandeur o'er thee shall reflect from thy spouse,
  As o'er V—y F—tz—d 't will shine through his
    mother." (2)

Thus ended the *First* Batch—and Jenky, much tired
  (It being no joke to make Lords by the heap),
Took a large dram of ether—the same that inspired
  His speech 'gainst the Papists—and prosed off to
    sleep.

—◦❀◦—

THE PERIWINKLES AND THE LOCUSTS.

A SALMAGUNDIAN HYMN.

" To Panurge was assigned the Lairdship of Salmagundi,
which was yearly worth 6,787,106,789 ryals, besides the
revenue of the *Locusts* and *Periwinkles*, amounting one
year with another to the value of 2,435,768," etc. etc.
—*Rabelais.*

"HURRA! hurra!" I heard them say,
  And they cheer'd and shouted all the way,
  As the Laird of Salmagundi went,
  To open in state his Parliament.

The Salmagundians once were rich,
  Or *thought* they were—no matter which—
  For, every year, the Revenue (3)
  From their Periwinkles larger grew ;

(1) Created Lord F—rnb—gh.
(2) Among the persons mentioned as likely to be raised
to the Peerage are the mother of Mr. V—y F—tz—d, etc.
  (3) Accented as in Swift's line—
    "Not so a nation's revenue are paid."

And their rulers, skill'd in all the trick
And legerdemain of arithmetic,
Knew how to place 1, 2, 3, 4,
 5, 6, 7, 8, and 9 and 10,
Such various ways, behind, before,
That they made a unit seem a score,
 And proved themselves most wealthy men!
So, on-they went, a prosperous crew,
 The people wise, the rulers clever—
And God help those, like me and you,
Who dared to doubt (as some now do)
That the Periwinkle Revenue
 Would thus go flourishing on for ever.

"Hurra! hurra!" I heard them say,
And they cheer'd and shouted all the way,
As the Great Panurge in glory went
To open his own dear Parliament.

But folks at length began to doubt
What all this conjuring was about;
For, every day, more deep in debt
They saw their wealthy rulers get :—
"Let's look (said they) the times through,
And see if what we're told be true
Of our Periwinkle Revenue."
But, lord! they found there was n't a tittle
Of truth in aught they heard before;
For they gain'd by Periwinkles little,
 And lost by Locusts ten times more!
These Locusts are a lordly breed
Some Salmagundians love to feed.
Of all the beasts that ever were born,
Your Locust most delights in *corn;*
And, though his body be but small,
To fatten him takes the devil and all !(1)
"Oh fie! oh fie!" was now the cry,
As they saw the gaudy show go by,
And the Laird of Salmagundi went
To open his Locust Parliament!

—◦※◦—

SPEECH ON THE UMBRELLA(2) QUESTION.
BY LORD ELD—N.
\os *inumbrellcs* video. (3)—*Ex Juvenil. Georgii Canningii.*
1827.
My Lords, I 'm accused of a trick that, God knows, is
 The last into which, at my age, I could fall—
Of leading this grave House of Peers, by their noses,
 Wherever I choose, princes, bishops, and all.

My Lords, on the question before us at present,
 No doubt I shall hear, "'T is that cursed old fellow,

(1) Lines now omitted in the poem :—
 Nor this the worst, for, direr still,
 Alack, alack, and a well-a-day !
 Their Periwinkles—once the stay
 And prop of the Salmagundian till—
 For want of feeding, all fell ill!
 And still, as they thinn'd and died away,
 The Locusts, ay, and the Locusts' Bill,
 Grew fatter and fatter every day !—P. E.
(2) A case which interested the public very much at this
period. A gentleman, of the name of Bell, having left his

That bugbear of all that is liberal and pleasant,
 Who wo'n't let the Lords give the man his um-
 [brella !"
God forbid that your Lordships should knuckle to me;
 I am ancient—but were I as old as King Priam,
Not much, I confess, to your credit 't would be,
 To mind such a twaddling old Trojan as I am.

I own, of our Protestant laws I am jealous,
 And, long as God spares me, will always maintain,
That, *once* having taken men's rights, or umbrellas,
 We ne'er should consent to restore them again.

What security have you, ye Bishops and Peers,
 If thus you give back Mr. Bell's parapluie,
That he mayn't, with its stick, come about all your
 ears, [be ?
 And then—*where* would your Protestant periwigs

No, heaven be my judge, were I dying to-day,
 Ere I dropp'd in the grave, like a medlar that's
 mellow,
"For God's sake"—at that awful moment I'd say—
 "For God's sake, *don't* give Mr. Bell his um-
 brella."

["This address," says a ministerial journal, "delivered
 with amazing emphasis and earnestness, occasioned
 an extraordinary sensation in the House. Nothing
 since the memorable address of the Duke of York has
 produced so remarkable an impression."]

—◦※◦—

A PASTORAL BALLAD.
BY JOHN BULL.
Dublin, March 12, 1827.—Friday, after the arrival of the
packet bringing the account of the defeat of the Catholic
Question, in the House of Commons, orders were sent
to the Pigeon House to forward 5,000,000 rounds of
musket-ball cartridge to the different garrisons round
the country.—*Freeman's Journal.*

I HAVE found out a gift for my Erin,
 A gift that will surely content her ;—
Sweet pledge of a love so endearing !
 Five millions of bullets I 've sent her.

She ask'd me for Freedom and Right,
 But ill she her wants understood;—
Ball cartridges, morning and night,
 Is a dose that will do her more good.

There is hardly a day of our lives
 But we read, in some amiable trials,
How husbands make love to their wives
 Through the medium of hemp and of phials.

umbrella behind him in the House of Lords, the door-
keepers(standing, no doubt, on the privileges of that noble
body) refused to restore it to him ; and the above speech,
which may be considered as a *pendant* to that of the
Learned Earl on the Catholic Question, arose out of the
transaction.
(3) From Mr. Canning's translation of Jekyl's—
 " i say, my good fellows,
 As you 're no umbrellas."

67

One thinks, with his mistress or mate
　A good halter is sure to agree—
That love-knot which, early and late,
　I have tried, my dear Erin, on thee.

While *another*, whom Hymen has bless'd
　With a wife that is not over placid,
Consigns the dear charmer to rest
　With a dose of the best Prussic acid.

Thus, Erin! my love do I show—
　Thus quiet thee, mate of my bed!
And, as poison and hemp are too slow,
　Do thy business with bullets instead.

Should thy faith in my medicine be shaken,
　Ask R—d—n, that mildest of saints;
He 'll tell thee, lead, inwardly taken,
　Alone can remove thy complaints;—

That, blest as thou art in thy lot,
　Nothing 's wanted to make it more pleasant
But being hang'd, tortured, and shot,
　Much oftener than thou art at present.

Even W—ll—t—n's self hath averr'd
　Thou art yet but half sabred and hung,
And I loved him the more when I heard
　Such tenderness fall from his tongue.

So take the five millions of pills,
　Dear partner, I herewith inclose;
'T is the cure that all quacks for thy ills,
　From Cromwell to Eld—n, propose.

And you, ye brave bullets that go,
　How I wish that, before you set out,
The *Devil* of the Freischutz could know
　The good work you are going about.

For he 'd charm ye, in spite of your lead,
　Into such supernatural wit,
That you 'd all of you know, as you sped,
　Where a bullet of sense *ought* to hit.

———◦H◦———

A LATE SCENE AT SWANAGE. (1)

Regnis *ex*-sul ademtis.—*Virg.*

1827.

To Swanage—that neat little town, in whose bay
　Fair Thetis shows off, in her best silver slippers—
Lord Bags (2) took his annual trip t' other day,
　To taste the sea breezes, and chat with the dip-
　　pers.

(1) A small bathing-place on the coast of Dorsetshire,
long a favourite summer resort of the ex-nobleman in
question, and, *till this season*, much frequented also by
gentlemen of the church.
(2) The Lord Chancellor Eld—n.

There—learn'd as he is in conundrums and laws—
　Quoth he to his dame (whom he oft plays the wag
　　on),
" Why are chancery suitors like bathers?"—"Because
　Their *suits* are *put off*, till—they have n't a rag on."

Thus on he went chatting—but, lo, while he chats,
　With a face full of wonder around him he looks;
For he misses his parsons, his dear shovel hats,
　Who used to flock round him at Swanage like rooks.

" How is this, Lady Bags?—to this region aquatic
　Last year they came swarming, to make me their
　　bow,
As thick as Burke's cloud o'er the vales of Carnatic,
　Deans, Rectors, D. D.'s—where the devil are they
　　　　　　　　　　　　　　　　[now?"
" My dearest Lord Bags!" saith his dame, "*can* you
　　doubt?
I am loath to remind you of things so unpleasant;
But *don't* you perceive, dear, the Church have found
　　out
That you 're one of the people call'd *Ex's*, at pre-
　sent?"

" Ah, true—you have hit it—I *am*, indeed, one
　Of those ill-fated *Ex's* (his Lordship replies),
And, with tears, I confess—God forgive me the pun—
　We X's have proved ourselves *not* to be Y's."

———◦H◦———

WO! WO! (3)

Wo, wo unto him who would check or disturb it—
　That beautiful Light, which is now on its way;
Which, beaming, at first, o'er the bogs of Belturbet,
　Now brightens sweet Ballinafad with its ray!

Oh F—rnh—m, Saint F—rnh—m, how much do we
　owe thee!
How form'd to all tastes are thy various employs!
The old, as a catcher of Catholics, know thee,
　The young, as an amateur scourger of boys.

Wo, wo to the man, who such doings would smo-
　　ther!—
On, Luther of Cavan! On, Saint of Kilgroggy!
With whip in one hand, and with Bible in t' other,
　Like Mungo's tormentor, both " preachee and
　　floggee."

Come, Saints from all quarters, and marshal his way;
　Come, L—rt—n, who, scorning profane erudition,
Popp'd Shakspeare, they say, in the river one day,
　Though 't was only old Bowdler's *Velluti* edition.

(3) Suggested by a speech of the Bishop of Ch—st—r on
the subject of the New Reformation in Ireland, in which his
Lordship denounced "Wo! wo! wo!" pretty abundantly on
all those who dared to interfere with its progress.

Come, R—den, who doubtest—so mild are thy
    views—
Whether Bibles or bullets are best for the nation ;
Who leavest to poor Paddy no medium to choose,
    'Twixt good old Rebellion and new Reformation.

What more from her Saints can Hibernia require?
    St. Bridget, of yore, like a dutiful daughter,
Supplied her, 't is said, with perpetual fire, (1)
    And Saints keep her now in eternal hot water.

Wo, wo to the man, who would check their career,
    Or stop the Millennium, that 's sure to await us,
When, bless'd with an orthodox crop every year,
    We shall learn to raise Protestants, fast as potatoes.

In kidnapping Papists, our rulers, we know,
    Had been trying their talent for many a day ;
Till F—rnh—m, when all had been tried, came to
    show,
    Like the German flea-catcher, " anoder goot way."

And nothing 's more simple than F—rnh—m's re-
    ceipt ;—
    " Catch your Catholic, first—soak him well in
      poteen—(2)
Add salary sauce, (3) and the thing is complete,
    You may serve up your Protestant, smoking and
        [clean."
" Wo, wo to the wag, who would laugh at such
    cookery !"
    Thus, from his perch, did I hear a black crow (4)
Caw angrily out, while the rest of the rookery
    Open'd their bills, and re-echo'd " Wo! wo !"

TOUT POUR LA TRIPE.

" If, in China or among the natives of India, we claimed
   civil advantages which were connected with religious
   usages, little as we might value those forms in our
   hearts, we should think common decency required us
   to abstain from treating them with offensive contumely;
   and, though unable to consider them sacred, we would
   not sneer at the name of Fot, or laugh at the imputed
   divinity of Fisthnou."—Courier, Tuesday, Jan. 16.
                              1827.

Come, take my advice, never trouble your cranium,
    When " civil advantages" are to be gain'd,
What god or what goddess may help to obtain
    you 'em,
    Hindoo or Chinese, so they 're only obtain'd.

In this world (let me hint in your organ auricular)
    All the good things to good hypocrites fall ;
And he, who in swallowing creeds is particular,
    Soon will have nothing to swallow at all.

(1) The inextinguishable fire of St. Bridget, at Kildare.
(2) Whiskey.
(3) " We understand that several applications have
   lately been made to the Protestant clergymen of this
   town (Wexford), by fellows inquiring ' What are they

Oh place me where Fo (or, as some call him, Fot)
    Is the god from whom " civil advantages " flow,
And you 'll find, if there 's any thing snug to be got,
    I shall soon be on excellent terms with old Fo.

Or were I where Vishnu, that four-handed god,
    Is the quadruple giver of pensions and places,
I own I should feel it unchristian and odd
    Not to find myself also in Vishnu's good graces.

For, among all the gods that humanely attend
    To our wants in this planet, the gods to my wishes
Are those that, like Vishnu and others, descend
    In the form, so attractive, of loaves and of fishes ! (5)

So, take my advice—for, if even the devil
    Should tempt men again as an idol to try him,
'T were best for us Tories, even then, to be civil,
    As nobody doubts we should get something by him.

ENIGMA.

Monstrum nulla virtute redemptum.

Come, riddle-me-ree, come, riddle-me-ree,
    And tell me what my name may be.
I am nearly one hundred and thirty years old,
    And therefore no chicken, as you may suppose ;—
Though a dwarf in my youth (as my nurses have
      told),
    I have, every year since, been outgrowing my
      clothes ;
Till, at last, such a corpulent giant I stand,
    That, if folks were to furnish me now with a suit,
It would take every morsel of scrip in the land
    But to measure my bulk from the head to the foot.
Hence, they who maintain me, grown sick of my
      stature,
    To cover me nothing but rags will supply ;
And the doctors declare that, in due course of na-
      ture,
    About the year 30 in rags I shall die.
Meanwhile, I stalk hungry and bloated around,
    An object of interest, most painful, to all ;
In the warehouse, the cottage, the palace I 'm found,
    Holding citizen, peasant, and king in my thrall.
    Then riddle-me-ree, oh riddle-me-ree,
    Come, tell me what my name may be.

When the lord of the counting-house bends o'er his
      book,
    Bright pictures of profit delighting to draw,
O'er his shoulders with large cipher eyeballs I look,
    And down drops the pen from his paralised paw !
When the Premier lies dreaming of dear Waterloo,
    And expects through another to caper and prank it,

giving a head for converts?' "—Wexford Post.
(4) Of the rook species—Corvus frugilegus, i. e. a great
   consumer of corn.
(5) Vishnu was (as Sir W. Jones calls him) " a pisciform
   god,"—his first Avatar being in the shape of a fish.

You'd laugh did you see, when I bellow out "Boo!"
  How he hides his brave Waterloo head in the
    blanket.
When mighty Belshazzar brims high in the hall
  His cup, full of gout, to the Gaul's overthrow,
Lo, "*Eight Hundred Millions*" I write on the wall,
  And the cup falls to earth and—the gout to his toe!
But the joy of my heart is when largely I cram
  My maw with the fruits of the Squirearchy's acres,
And, knowing who made me the thing that I am,
  Like the monster of Frankenstein, worry my
    makers.
      Then riddle-me-ree, come, riddle-me-ree,
      And tell, if thou know'st, who *I* may be.

DOG-DAY REFLECTIONS.

BY A DANDY KEPT IN TOWN.

"Vox clamantis in deserto."

1827.

SAID Malthus, one day, to a clown
  Lying stretch'd on the beach, in the sun—
"What's the number of souls in this town?"—
  "The number! Lord bless you, there's none.

"We have nothing but *dabs* in this place,
  Of *them* a great plenty there are;—
But the *soles*, please your reverence and grace,
  Are all t' other side of the bar."

And so 't is in London just now,
  Not a soul to be seen, up or down;—
Of *dabs* a great glut, I allow,
  But your *soles*, every one, out of town.

East or west, nothing wondrous or new;
  No courtship or scandal, worth knowing;
Mrs. B——, and a Mermaid (1) or two,
  Are the only loose fish that are going.

Ah, where is that dear house of Peers,
  That, some weeks ago, kept us merry?
Where, Eld—n, art thou, with thy tears?
  And thou, with thy sense, L—d—d—y?

Wise Marquis, how much the Lord Mayor,
  In the dog-days, with *thee* must be puzzled!—
It being his task to take care
  That such animals shan't go unmuzzled.

Thou, too, whose political toils
  Are so worthy a captain of horse—
Whose amendments (2) (like honest Sir Boyle's)
  Are "*amendments*, that make matters *worse;*" (3)

(1) One of the shows of London.
(2) More particularly his Grace's celebrated amendment
to the Corn Bill; for which, and the circumstances con-
nected with it, see *Annual Register* for A. D. 1827.
(3) From a speech of Sir Boyle Roche's, in the Irish
House of Commons.

Great Chieftain, who takest such pains
  To prove—what is granted, *nem. con.*—
With how moderate a portion of brains
  Some heroes contrive to get on.

And, thou, too, my R—d—sd—e, ah, where
  Is the peer, with a star at his button,
Whose *quarters* could ever compare
  With R—d—sd—e's five quarters of mutton? (4)

Why, why have ye taken your flight,
  Ye diverting and dignified crew?
How ill do three farces a-night,
  At the Haymarket, pay us for you!

For, what is Bombastes to thee,
  My Ell—nbro', when thou look'st big?
Or, where's the burletta can be
  Like L—d—rd—le's wit, and his wig?

I doubt if even Griffinhoof (5) could
  (Though Griffin 's a comical lad)
Invent any joke half so good
  As that precious one, "This is too bad!"

Then come again, come again, Spring!
  Oh haste thee, with Fun in thy train;
And—of all things the funniest—bring
  These exalted Grimaldis again!

THE "LIVING DOG" AND "THE DEAD LION."

1828.

NEXT week will be publish'd (as "Lives" are the
  rage)
  The whole Reminiscences, wondrous and strange,
Of a small puppy-dog, that lived once in the cage
  Of the late noble Lion at Exeter 'Change.

Though the dog is a dog of the kind they call "sad,"
  'T is a puppy that much to good breeding pretends;
And few dogs have such opportunities had
  Of knowing how Lions behave—among friends;

How that animal eats, how he snores, how he drinks,
  Is all noted down by this Boswell so small;
And 't is plain, from each sentence, the puppy-dog
    thinks,
  That the Lion was no such great things after all.

Though he roar'd pretty well—this the puppy allows—
  It was all, he says, borrow'd—all second-hand
    roar;
And he vastly prefers his own little bow-wows
  To the loftiest war-note the Lion could pour.

(4) The learning his Lordship displayed, on the subject
of the butcher's "fifth quarter" of mutton, will not speedi-
ly be forgotten.
(5) The *nom de guerre* under which Colman has written
some of his best farces.

'T is, indeed, as good fun as a *Cynic* could ask,
  To see how this cockney-bred setter of rabbits
Takes gravely the Lord of the Forest to task,
  And judges of lions by puppy-dog habits.

Nay, fed as he was (and this makes it a dark case)
  With sops every day from the Lion's own pan,
He lifts up his leg at the noble beast's carcass,
  And—does all a dog, so diminutive, can.

However, the book 's a good book, being rich in
  Examples and warnings to lions high-bred,
How they suffer small mongrelly curs in their kitchen,
  Who 'll feed on them living, and foul them when
    dead.
  Exeter 'Change.   T. PIDCOCK.

—◦◆◦—

ODE TO DON MIGUEL.

Et tu, *Brute !*
                                1828. (1)
WHAT ! Miguel, *not* patriotic? oh, fy !
  After so much good teaching 't is quite a *take-in,*
    Sir ;—
First school'd, as you were, under Metternich's eye,
  And then (as young misses say) "finish'd" at
    Windsor !(2)

I ne'er in my life knew a case that was harder ;—
  Such feasts as you had, when you made us a call !
Three courses each day from his Majesty's larder—
  And now, to turn absolute Don, after all !!

Some authors, like Bayes, to the style and the matter
  Of each thing they *write* suit the way that they
    dine,
Roast sirloin for Epic, broil'd devils for Satire,
  And hotchpotch and *trifle* for rhymes such as mine.

That Rulers should feed the same way, I 've no
    doubt ;—
  Great Despots on *bouilli* served up à *la Russe,*(3)
Your small German Princes on frogs and sour crout,
  And your Viceroy of Hanover always on *goose.*

Some Dons, too, have fancied (though this may be
    fable)
  A dish rather dear, if, in cooking, they blunder it ;—
Not content with the common *hot* meat *on* a table,
  They 're partial (eh, Mig?) to a dish of *cold under*
    it !(4)

No wonder a Don of such appetites foun l
  Even Windsor's collations plebeianly plain ;

(1) At the commencement of this year. the designs of
Don Miguel and his partisans against the constitution es-
tablished by his brother had begun more openly to de-
clare themselves.
  (2) Don Miguel had paid a visit to the English court at
the close of the year 1827.
  (3) Dressed with a pint of the strongest spirits—a fa-

Where the dishes most *high* that my Lady sends
    round
  Are her *Maintenon* cutlets and soup à *la Reine.*

Alas ! that a youth with such charming beginnings,
  Should sink, all at once, to so sad a conclusion,
And, what is still worse, throw the losings and win-
    nings
  Of worthies on 'Change into so much confusion !

The Bulls, in hysterics—the Bears just as bad—
  The few men who *have,* and the many who've *not*
    tick,
All shock'd to find out that that promising lad,
  Prince Metternich's pupil, is—*not* patriotic !

—◦◆◦—

THOUGHTS ON THE PRESENT GOVERNMENT OF IRELAND.

                                1828.
OFT have I seen, in gay, equestrian pride,
Some well-rouged youth round Astley's Circus ride
Two stately steeds—standing, with graceful straddle,
Like him of Rhodes, with foot on either saddle,
While to soft tunes—some jigs, and some *andantes*—
He steers around his light-paced Rosinantes.

So rides along, with canter smooth and pleasant,
That horseman bold, Lord Anglesea, at present ;—
Papist and *Protestant* the coursers twain,
That lend their necks to his impartial rein,
And round the ring—each honour'd, as they go,
With equal pressure from his gracious toe—
To the old medley tune, half " Patrick's Day"
And half "Boyne Water," take their cantering way,
While Peel, the showman in the middle, cracks
His long-lash'd whip, to cheer the doubtful backs.
Ah, ticklish trial of equestrian art !
How blest, if neither steed would bolt or start ;—
If *Protestant's* old restive tricks were gone,
And *Papist's* winkers could be still kept on !
But no, false hopes—not even the great Ducrow
'Twixt two such steeds could 'scape an overthrow :
If *solar* hacks play'd Phaëton a trick,
What hope, alas, from hackneys *lunatic?*

If once my Lord his graceful balance loses,
Or fails to keep each foot where each horse chooses ;
If Peel but gives one *extra* touch of whip
To *Papist's* tail or *Protestant's* ear-tip—
That instant ends their glorious horsemanship !
Off bolt the sever'd steeds, for mischief free,
And down, between them, plumps Lord Anglesea !

vourite dish of the Great Frederick of Prussia, and which
he persevered in eating even on his death-bed, much to
the horror of his physician, Zimmerman.
  (4) This quiet case of murder, with all its particulars—
the hiding the body under the dinner-table, etc., etc —
is, no doubt, well known to the reader.

THE LIMBO OF LOST REPUTATIONS.

A DREAM.

"Ciò che si perde qui, là si raguna."—*Ariosto.*

"——a valley, where he sees
Things that on earth were lost."—*Milton.*

1828.

Know'st thou not him (1) the poet sings,
  Who flew to the moon's serene domain,
And saw that valley, where all the things
  That vanish on earth are found again—
The hopes of youth, the resolves of age,
The vow of the lover, the dream of the sage,
  The golden visions of mining cits,
  The promises great men strew about them;
And, pack'd in compass small, the wits
  Of monarchs, who rule as well without them!—
Like him, but diving with wing profound,
I have been to a Limbo under ground,
Where characters lost on earth, (and *cried*,
In vain, like H—rr—s's, far and wide,)
In heaps, like yesterday's orts, are thrown,
And there, so worthless and fly-blown,
That even the imps would not purloin them,
Lie, till their worthy owners join them.

Curious it was to see this mass
  Of lost and torn-up reputations ;—
Some of them female wares, alas,
  Mislaid at *innocent* assignations ;
Some, that had sigh'd their last amen
  From the canting lips of saints that would be ;
And some once own'd by " the best of men,"
  Who had proved—no better than they should be.
'Mong others, a poet's fame I spied,
  Once shining fair, now soak'd and black—
"No wonder " (an imp at my elbow cried),
  " For I pick'd it out of a butt of sack!"

Just then a yell was heard o'er head,
  Like a chimney-sweeper's lofty summons ;
And lo! a devil right downward sped,
  Bringing, within his claws so red,
Two statesmen's characters, found, he said,
  Last night, on the floor of the House of Commons;
The which, with black official grin,
He now to the Chief Imp handed in ;—
Both these articles much the worse
  For their journey down, as you may suppose ;
But *one* so devilish rank—"Odd's curse ! "
  Said the Lord Chief Imp, and held his nose.

" Ho, ho!" quoth he, "I know full well
From whom these two stray matters fell ; "—
Then, casting away, with loathful shrug,
The uncleaner waif (as he would a drug
The invisible's own dark hand had mix'd),
His gaze on the other (2) firm he fix'd,
And trying, though mischief laugh'd in his eye,
To be moral, because of the *young* imps by,

" What a pity!" he cried—" so fresh its gloss,
So long preserved—'t is a public loss !
This comes of a man, the careless blockhead,
Keeping his character in his pocket ;
And there—without considering whether
There's room for that and his gains together—
Cramming, and cramming, and cramming away,
Till—out slips character some fine day!

" However "—and here he view'd it round—
" This article still may pass for sound.
Some flaws, soon patch'd, some stains are all
The harm it has had in its luckless fall.
Here, Puck !"—and he call'd to one of his train--
" The owner may have this back again.
Though damaged for ever, if used with skill,
It may serve, perhaps, to *trade on* still ;
Though the gem can never, as once, be set,
It will do for a Tory Cabinet. "

HOW TO WRITE BY PROXY.

Qui facit per alium facit per se.

'Mong our neighbours, the French, in the good olden
        time
  When Nobility flourish'd, great Barons and Dukes
Often set up for authors in prose and in rhyme,
  But ne'er took the trouble to write their own books.

Poor devils were found to do this for their betters ;—
  And, one day, a Bishop, addressing a *Blue*,
Said, "Ma'am, have you read my new Pastoral
        Letters?"
  To which the *Blue* answer'd—" No, Bishop ; have
        you?"

The same is now done by *our* privileged class ;
  And, to show you how simple the process it needs,
If a great Major-General (3) wishes to pass
  For an author of History, thus he proceeds :—

First, scribbling his own stock of notions as well
  As he can, with a *goose*-quill that claims him as *kin*,
He settles his neckcloth—takes snuff—rings the bell,
  And yawningly orders a Subaltern in.

The Subaltern comes—sees his General seated,
  In all the self-glory of authorship swelling ;—
" There, look," saith his Lordship, " my work is
        completed—
  It wants nothing now, but the grammar and
        spelling."

Well used to a *breach*, the brave Subaltern dreads
  Awkward breaches of syntax a hundred times more;
And, though often condemn'd to see breaking of
        heads,
  He had ne'er seen such breaking of Priscian's be-
        fore.

(1) Astolpho.   (2) H—k—n.
(3) Or Lieutenant-General, as it may happen to be.

However, the job's sure to *pay*—that's enough—
So, to it he sets with his tinkering hammer,
Convinced that there never was job half so tough
As the mending a great Major-General's grammar.

But, lo, a fresh puzzlement starts up to view—
New toil for the Sub.—for the Lord new expense:
'T is discover'd that mending his *grammar* wo'n't do,
As the Subaltern also must find him in *sense!*

At last—even this is achieved by his aid;
Friend Subaltern pockets the cash and—the story;
Drums beat—the new Grand March of Intellect's
play'd—
And off struts my Lord, the Historian, in glory!

—◦◦◦◦—

IMITATION OF THE INFERNO OF DANTE.

" Così quel fiato gli spiriti mali
Di quà, di là, di giù, di su gli mena."—*Inferno*, canto 5.

I TURN'D my steps, and lo, a shadowy throng
Of ghosts came fluttering towards me—blown along,
Like cockchafers in high autumnal storms,
By many a fitful gust that through their forms
Whistled, as on they came, with wheezy puff,
And puff'd as—though they'd never puff enough.

" Whence and what are ye?" pitying I inquired
Of these poor ghosts, who, tatter'd, tost, and tired
With such eternal puffing, scarce could stand
On their lean legs while answering my demand.
" We once were authors"—thus the Sprite, who led
This tag-rag regiment of spectres, said—
" Authors of every sex, male, female, neuter,
Who, early snit with love of praise and—*pewter*, (1)
On C—lb—n's shelves first saw the light of day,
In ——'s (2) puffs exhaled our lives away—
Like summer windmills, doom'd to dusty peace,
When the brisk gales, that lent them motion, cease.
Ah, little knew we then what ills await
Much-lauded scribblers in their after-state;
Bepuff'd on earth—how loudly Str—t can tell—
And, dire reward, now doubly puff'd in hell!"

Touch'd with compassion for this ghastly crew,
Whose ribs, even now, the hollow wind sung through
In mournful prose—such prose as Rosa's (3) ghost
Still, at the accustom'd hour of eggs and toast,
Sighs through the columns of the *M—rn—g P—t*—
Pensive I turn'd to weep, when he, who stood
Foremost of all that flatulential brood,
Singling a *she*-ghost from the party, said,
" Allow me to present Miss X. Y. Z., (4)
One of our *letter'd* nymphs—excuse the pun—
Who gain'd a name on earth by—having none;

(1) The *classical* term for money.
(2) The reader may fill up this gap with any one of the
dissyllabic publishers of London that occurs to him.
(3) Rosa Matilda, who was for many years the writer of
the political articles in the *Post*, and whose spirit still
seems to preside—" Regnat Rosa"—over its pages.

And whose initials would immortal be,
Had she but learn'd those plain ones, A. B. C.

" Yon smirking ghost, like mummy dry and neat,
Wrapp'd in his own dead rhymes—fit winding-
sheet—
Still marvels much that not a soul should care
One single pin to know who wrote *May Fair*;—
While this young gentleman," (here forth he drew
A dandy spectre, puff'd quite through and through,
As though his ribs were an Æolian lyre
For the whole Row's soft *trade*-winds to inspire,)
" This modest genius breathed one wish alone,
To have his volume read, himself unknown;
But different far the course his glory took,
All knew the author, and—none read the book.

" Behold, in yonder ancient figure of fun,
Who rides the blast, Sir J—n—h B—rr—t—n;—
In tricks to raise the wind his life was spent,
And now the wind returns the compliment.
This lady here, the Earl of ——'s sister,
Is a dead novelist; and this is Mister—
Beg pardon—*Honourable* Mister L—st—r,
A gentleman who, some weeks since, came over
In a smart puff (wind S. S. E.) to Dover.
Yonder behind us limps young Vivian Grey,
Whose life, poor youth, was ·long since blown
away—
Like a torn paper kite, on which the wind
No further purchase for a puff can find."

"And thou, thyself"—here, anxious, I exclaim'd—
" Tell us, good ghost, how thou, thyself, art named."
" Me, Sir!" he blushing cried—"Ah, there's the rub,
Know, then—a waiter once at Brooks's Club,
A waiter still I might have long remain'd,
And long the club-room's jokes and glasses drain'd;
But, ah, in luckless hour, this last December,
I wrote a book, (5) and Colburn dubb'd me 'Mem-
ber'—
'Member of Brooks's!'—oh Promethean puff,
To what wilt thou exalt even kitchen-stuff!
With crumbs of gossip, caught from dining wits,
And half-heard jokes, bequeath'd, like half-chew'd
bits,   [bits,
To be, each night, the waiter's perquisites;
With such ingredients, served up oft before,
But with fresh fudge and fiction garnish'd o'er,
I managed, for some weeks, to dose the town,
Till fresh reserves of nonsense ran me down;
And, ready still even waiters' souls to damn,
The Devil but rang his bell, and—here I am;—
Yes—' Coming *up*, Sir,' once my favourite cry,
Exchanged for ' Coming *down*, Sir,' here am I!"

(4) *Not* the charming L. E. L., and still less, Mrs. F. H.,
whose poetry is among the most beautiful of the present
day.
(5) *History of the Clubs of London*, announced as by
" a Member of Brooks's."

Scarce had the Spectre's lips these words let drop,
When, lo, a.breeze—such as from ——'s shop
Blows in the vernal hour when puffs prevail,
And speeds the *sheets* and swells the lagging *sale*—
Took the poor waiter rudely in the poop,
And, whirling him and all his grisly group
Of literary ghosts—Miss X. Y. Z.—
The nameless author, better known than read—
Sir Jo.—the Honourable Mr. L—st—r,
And, last, not least, Lord Nobody's twin-sister—
Blew them, ye gods, with all their prose and rhymes
And sins about them, far into those climes
"Where Peter pitch'd his waistcoat" (1) in old times,
Leaving me much in doubt, as on I prest,
With my great master, through this realm unblest,
Whether Old Nick or C—lb—n puffs the best.

—◦◦◦—

LAMENT FOR THE LOSS OF LORD B—TH—ST'S TAIL. (2)

ALL *in* again—unlook'd for bliss !
Yet, ah, *one* adjunct still we miss ;—
One tender tie, attach'd so long
To the same head through right and wrong.
Why, B—th—st, why didst thou cut off
    That memorable tail of thine?
Why—as if *one* was not enough—
    Thy pig-tie with thy place resign,
And thus at once, both *cut* and *run* ?
Alas, my Lord, 't was not well done,
'T was not indeed—though sad at heart,
From office and its sweets to part,
Yet hopes of coming in again,
Sweet Tory hopes ! beguiled our pain ;
But thus to miss that tail of thine,
Through long, long years our rallying sign—
As if the State and all its powers
By tenancy *in tail* were ours—
To see it thus by scissors fall,
This was "the unkindest *cut* of all !"
It seem'd as though the ascendant day
Of Toryism had pass'd away,
And, proving Samson's story true,
She lost her vigour with her *queue.*

Parties are much like fish, 't is said—
The tail directs them, not the head ;
Then, how could *any* party fail
That steer'd its course by B—th—st's tail?
Not Murat's plume through Wagram's fight,
    E'er shed such guiding glories from it,
As erst, in all true Tories' sight,
    Blazed from our old Colonial comet!
If you, my Lord, a Bashaw were,
    (As W—ll—gt—n will be anon,)

(1) A *Dantesque* allusion to the old saying, "Nine miles beyond H—ll, where Peter pitched his waistcoat."
(2) The noble Lord, it is well known, cut off this much-respected appendage, on his retirement from office some months since.

Thou might'st have had a tail to spare ;
    But no, alas, thou hadst but one,
And *that*—like Troy, or Babylon,
A tale of other times—is gone !

Yet—weep ye not, ye Tories true—
    Fate has not yet of all bereft us;
Though thus deprived of B—th—st's *queue,*
We 've El—nb—h's *curls* still left us ;—
Sweet curls, from which young Love, so vicious,
His shots, as from nine-pounders, issues ;
Grand, glorious curls, which, in debate,
Surcharged with all a nation's fate,
His Lordship shakes as Homer's God did,(3)
    And oft in thundering talk comes near him ;—
Except that there, the *speaker* nodded,
    And here, 't is only those who hear him.
Long, long, ye ringlets, on the soil
    Of that fat cranium may ye flourish,
With plenty of Macassar oil,
    Through many a year your growth to nourish !
And, ah, should Time too soon unsheath
    His barbarous shears such locks to sever,
Still dear to Tories even in death,
    Their last loved relics we 'll bequeath,
A *hair*-loom to our sons for ever!

—◦◦◦—

THE CHERRIES.

A PARABLE. (4)

1828.

SEE those cherries, how they cover
    Yonder sunny garden wall ;—
Had they not that network over,
    Thieving birds would eat them all.

So, to guard our posts and pensions,
    Ancient sages wove a net,
Through whose holes, of small dimensions,
    Only *certain* knaves can get.

Shall we then this network widen?
    Shall we stretch these sacred holes,
Through which, even already, slide in
    Lots of small dissenting souls?

"God forbid!" old *Testy* crieth ;
    "God forbid!" so echo I ;
Every ravenous bird that flieth
    Then would at our cherries fly.

Ope but half an inch or so,
    And, behold, what bevies break in ;—
Here, some curst old Popish crow
    Pops his long and lickerish beak in ;

(3) "Shakes his ambrosial curls, and gives the nod."
                    Pope's Homer.
(4) Written during the late discussion on the Test and Corporation Acts.

Here, sly Arians flock unnumber'd,
  And Socinians, slim and spare,
Who, with small belief encumber'd,
  Slip in easy any where ;—

Methodists, of birds the aptest,
  Where there 's *pecking* going on ;
And that water-fowl, the Baptist—
  All would share our fruits anon ;—

Every bird, of every city,
  That, for years, with ceaseless din,
Hath reversed the starling's ditty,
  Singing out, "I can't get *in*."

"God forbid !" old *Testy* snivels ;
  "God forbid !" I echo too ;
Rather may ten thousand d—v—ls
  Seize the whole voracious crew !

If less costly fruit wo'n't suit 'em,
  Hips and haws and such like berries,
Curse the cormorants ! stone 'em, shoot 'em,
  Any thing—to save our cherries.

—◦₦◦—

STANZAS WRITTEN IN ANTICIPATION OF DEFEAT.(1)

1828.

Go seek for some abler defenders of wrong,
  If we *must* run the gauntlet through blood and
    expense;
Or, Goths as ye are, in your multitude strong,
  Be content with success, and pretend not to sense.

If the words of the wise and the generous are vain,
  If Truth by the bowstring *must* yield up her breath,
Let Mutes do the office—and spare her the pain
  Of an I—gl—s or T—nd—l to talk her to death.

Chain, persecute, plunder—do all that you will—
  But save us, at least, the old womanly lore
Of a F—st—r, who, dully prophetic of ill,
  Is, at once, the *two* instruments, *augur* (2) and
    bore.

Bring legions of Squires—if they 'll only be mute—
  And array their thick heads against reason and
    right,
Like the Roman of old, of historic repute, (3)
  Who with droves of dumb animals carried the fight;

Pour out, from each corner and hole of the Court,
  Your Bedchamber lordlings, your salaried slaves,
Who, ripe for all job-work, no matter what sort,
  Have their consciences tack'd to their patents and
    staves.

(1) During the discussion of the Catholic question in the House of Commons last session.
(2) This rhyme is more for the ear than the eye, as the carpenter's tool is spelt *auger*.

Catch all the small fry who, as Juvenal sings,
  Are the Treasury's creatures, wherever they
    swim ;(4)
With all the base time-serving *toadies* of Kings,
  Who, if Punch were the monarch, would worship
    even him ;

And while, on the *one* side, each name of renown
  That illumines and blesses our age is combined ;
While the Foxes, the Pitts, and the Cannings look
    down,
  And drop o'er the cause their rich mantles of Mind ;

Let bold Paddy H—lmes show his troops on the other,
  And, counting of noses the quantum desired,
Let Paddy but say, like the Gracchi's famed mother,
  "Come forward, my *jewels*"—'t is all that 's re-
    quired.

And thus let your farce be enacted hereafter—
  Thus honestly persecute, outlaw, and chain ;
But spare even your victims the torture of laughter,
  And never, oh never, try *reasoning* again !

—◦₦◦—

ODE TO THE WOODS AND FORESTS.

BY ONE OF THE BOARD.

1828.

Let other bards to groves repair,
  Where linnets strain their tuneful throats,
Mine be the Woods and Forests, where
  The Treasury pours its sweeter *notes*.

No whispering winds have charms for me,
  Nor zephyr's balmy sighs I ask ;
To raise the wind for Royalty
  Be all our Sylvan zephyr's task !

And, 'stead of crystal brooks and floods,
  And all such vulgar irrigation,
Let Gallic rhino through our Woods
  Divert its "course of liquid-ation."

Ah, surely, Virgil knew full well
  What Woods and Forests *ought* to be,
When, sly, he introduced in hell
  His guinea-plant, his bullion-tree :—(5)

Nor see I why, some future day,
  When short of cash, we should not send
Our H—rr—s down—he knows the way—
  To see if Woods in hell will *lend*.

Long may ye flourish, sylvan haunts,
  Beneath whose "*branches* of expense"
Our gracious K——g gets all he wants—
  Except a little taste and sense.

(3) Fabius, who sent droves of bullocks against the enemy.
(4) Res Fisci est, ubicumque natal.—*Juvenal*.
(5) Called by Virgil, botanically, "*species auri frondentis*."

68

Long, in your golden shade reclined,
  Like him of fair Armida's bowers,
May W—ll—n some *wood*-nymph find,
  To cheer his dozenth lustrum's hours;

To rest from toil the Great Untaught,
  And sooth the pangs his warlike brain
Must suffer, when, unused to thought,
  It tries to think, and—tries in vain.

Oh long may Woods and Forests be
  Preserved, in all their teeming graces,
To shelter Tory bards, like me,
  Who take delight in Sylvan *places!* (1)

—o••o—

STANZAS FROM THE BANKS OF THE SHANNON. (2)

1828.

"Take back the virgin page."—Moore's Irish Melodies.

No longer, dear V—sey, feel hurt and uneasy
  At hearing it said by thy Treasury brother,
That thou art a sheet of blank paper, my V—sey,
  And he, the dear innocent placeman, another. (3)

For, lo, what a service we, Irish, have done thee;—
  Thou now art a sheet of blank paper no more;
By St. Patrick, we've scrawl'd such a lesson upon thee
  As never was scrawl'd upon foolscap before.

Come—on with your spectacles, noble Lord Duke,
  (Or O'Connell has *green* ones he haply would lend you,)
Read V—sey all o'er (as you *can't* read a book),
  And improve by the lesson we bog-trotters send you;

A lesson, in large *Roman* characters traced,
  Whose awful impressions from you and your kin
Of blank-sheeted statesmen will ne'er be effaced—
  Unless, 'stead of *paper*, you're mere *asses' skin.*

Shall I help you to construe it? ay, by the Gods,
  Could I risk a translation, you *should* have a rare one;
But pen against sabre is desperate odds,
  And you, my Lord Duke (as you *hinted* once), wear one.

Again and again I say, read V—sey o'er;—
  You will find him worth all the old scrolls of papyrus,
That Egypt e'er fill'd with nonsensical lore,
  Or the learned Champollion e'er wrote of, to tire us.

(1) Tu facis, ut *silvas*, ut amem loca——*Ovid.*

(2) These verses were suggested by the result of the Clare election, in the year 1828, when the Right Honourable W. Vesey Fitzgerald was rejected, and Mr. O'Connell returned.

(3. Some expressions to this purport, in a published

All blank as he was, we've return'd him on hand,
  Scribbled o'er with a warning to Princes and Dukes,
Whose plain simple drift if they *wo'n't* understand,
  Though caress'd at St. James's, they're fit for St. Luke's.

Talk of leaves of the Sibyls!—more meaning convey'd is
  In one single leaf such as now we have spell'd on,
Than e'er hath been utter'd by all the old ladies
  That ever yet spoke, from the Sibyl to Eld—n.

—o••o—

"IF" AND "PERHAPS." (4)

Oh tidings of freedom! oh accents of hope!
  Waft, waft them, ye zephyrs, to Erin's blue sea,
And refresh with their sounds every son of the Pope,
  From Dingle-a-cooch to far Donaghadee.

"*If* mutely the slave will endure and obey,
  Nor clanking his fetters, nor breathing his pains,
His masters, *perhaps*, at some far distant day,
  May *think* (tender tyrants!) of loosening his chains."

Wise "*If*" and "*perhaps!*"—precious salve for our wounds,
  If he, who would rule thus o'er manacled mutes,
Could check the free spring-tide of Mind, that resounds,
  Even now, at his feet, like the sea at Canute's.

But, no, 'tis in vain—the grand impulse is given—
  Man knows his high Charter, and knowing will claim;
And if ruin *must* follow where fetters are riven,
  Be theirs, who have forged them, the guilt and the shame.

"*If* the slave will be silent!"—vain Soldier, beware—
  There *is* a dead silence the wrong'd may assume,
When the feeling, sent back from the lips in despair,
  But clings round the heart with a deadlier gloom;—

When the blush, that long burn'd on the suppliant's cheek,
  Gives place to the avenger's pale resolute hue;
And the tongue, that once threaten'd, disdaining to *speak,*
  Consigns to the arm the high office—to *do.*

If men, in that silence, should think of the hour,
  When proudly their fathers in panoply stood,
Presenting, alike, a bold front-work of power
  To the despot on land and the foe on the flood:—

letter of one of these gentlemen, had then produced a good deal of amusement.

(4) Written after hearing a celebrated speech in the House of Lords, June 10, 1828, when the motion in favour of Catholic Emancipation, brought forward by the Marquis of Lansdowne, was rejected by the House of Lords.

That hour, when a Voice had come forth from the
    west,
  To the slave bringing hopes, to the tyrant alarms;
And a lesson, long look'd for, was taught the opprest,
  That kings are as dust before freemen in arms!

If, awfuller still, the mute slave should recall
  That dream of his boyhood, when Freedom's sweet
    day
At length seem'd to break through a long night of
    thrall,
  And Union and Hope went abroad in its ray;—

If Fancy should tell him, that Day-spring of Good,
  Though swiftly its light died away from his chain,
Though darkly it set in a nation's best blood,
  Now wants but invoking to shine out again;—

If—if, I say—breathings like these should come o'er
  The chords of remembrance, and thrill, as they come,
Then, *perhaps*—ay, *perhaps*—but I dare not say
    more;
  Thou hast will'd that thy slaves should be mute—
    I am dumb.

—◦◦◦—

WRITE ON, WRITE ON.

A BALLAD.

AIR—*" Sleep on, sleep on, my Kathleen dear."*
Salvete, fratres Asini.—*St. Francis.*

WRITE on, write on, ye Barons dear,
  Ye Dukes, write hard and fast;
The good we've sought for many a year
  Your quills will bring at last.
One letter more, N—wc—stle, pen,
  To match Lord K—ny—n's *two,*
And more than Ireland's host of men
  One brace of Peers will do.
            Write on, write on, etc.

Sure, never, since the precious use
  Of pen and ink began,
Did letters, writ by fools, produce
  Such signal good to man.
While intellect, 'mong high and low,
  Is marching *on,* they say,
Give *me* the Dukes and Lords, who go,
  Like crabs, the *other* way.
            Write on, write on, etc.

Even now I feel the coming light—
  Even now, could Folly lure
My Lord M—ntc—sh—l, too, to write,
  Emancipation 's sure.

(1) A rev. prebendary of Hereford, in an Essay on the
Revenues of the Church of England, assigns the origin of
Tithes to "some unrecorded revelation made to Adam."
  (2) "The tenth calf is due to the parson of common
right; and if there are seven he shall have one."—*Rees's
Cyclopœdia,* art. "*Tithes.*"

By geese (we read in history),
  Old Rome was saved from ill;
And now, to *quills* of geese, we see
  Old Rome indebted still.
            Write on, write on, etc.

Write, write, ye Peers, nor stoop to style,
  Nor beat for sense about—
Things, little worth a Noble's while,
  You 're better far without.
Oh ne'er, since asses spoke of yore,
  Such miracles were done;
For, write but four such letters more,
  And Freedom's cause is won!

—◦◦◦—

SONG OF THE DEPARTING SPIRIT OF TITHE.

" The parting Genius is with sighing sent."—*Milton.*

IT is o'er, it is o'er, my reign is o'er;
I hear a Voice, from shore to shore,
From Dunfanaghy to Baltimore,
And it saith, in sad parsonic tone,
" Great Tithe and Small are dead and gone!"

Even now, I behold your vanishing wings,
Ye Tenths of all conceivable things,
Which Adam first, as Doctors deem,
Saw, in a sort of night-mare dream, (1)
After the feast of fruit abhorr'd—
First indigestion on record!—
Ye decimate ducks, ye chosen chicks,
Ye pigs which, though ye be Catholics,
Or of Calvin's most select depraved,
In the Church must have your bacon saved;—
Ye fields, where Labour counts his sheaves,
And, whatsoever *himself* believes,
Must bow to the Establish'd *Church* belief,
That the tenth is always a *Protestant* sheaf;—
Ye calves, of which the man of Heaven
Takes *Irish* tithe, one calf in seven; (2)
Ye tenths of rape, hemp, barley, flax,
Eggs, (3) timber, milk, fish, and bees' wax;
All things, in short, since earth's creation,
Doom'd by the Church's dispensation,
To suffer eternal decimation—
Leaving the whole *lay*-world, since then,
Reduced to nine parts out of ten;
Or—as we calculate thefts and arsons—
Just *ten per cent.* the worse for Parsons!

Alas, and is all this wise device
For the saving of souls thus gone in a trice?—
The whole put down, in the simplest way,
By the souls resolving *not* to pay!

(3) Chaucer's Plowman complains of the parish rectors,
that

> " For the tithing of a duck,
>   Or an apple, or an aye (egg),
> They make him swear upon a boke;
>   Thus they foulen Christ's fay."

And even the Papists, thankless race,
Who have had so much the easiest case—
To *pay for* our sermons doom'd, 'tis true,
But not condemn'd to *hear them*, too—
(Our holy business being, 't is known,
With the ears of their barley, not their own,)
Even they object to let us pillage,
By right divine, their tenth of tillage,
And, horror of horrors, even decline
To find us in sacramental wine! (1)

It is o'er, It is o'er, my reign is o'er,
Ah, never shall rosy Rector more,
Like the shepherds of Israel, idly eat,
And make of his flock " a prey and meat."(2)
No more shall be his the pastoral sport
Of suing his flock in the Bishop's Court,
Through various steps, Citation, Libel—
Scriptures all, but *not* the Bible;
Working the Law's whole apparatus,
To get at a few pre-doom'd potatoes,
And summoning all the powers of wig,
To settle the fraction of a pig!
Till, parson and all committed deep
In the case of " Shepherds *versus* Sheep,"
The Law usurps the Gospel's place,
And, on Sundays, meeting face to face,
While Plaintiff fills the preacher's station,
Defendants form the congregation.

So lives he, Mammon's priest, not Heaven's,
For *tenths* thus all at *sixes* and *sevens*,
Seeking what parsons love no less
Than tragic poets—a good *distress*.
Instead of studying St. Augustin,
Gregory Nyss., or old St. Justin
(Books fit only to hoard dust in),
His reverence stints his evening readings
To learn'd Reports of Tithe Proceedings,
Sipping, the while, that port so ruddy,
Which forms his only *ancient* study;—
Port so old, you'd swear its tartar
Was of the age of Justin Martyr,
And had he sipp'd of such, no doubt
His martyrdom would have been—to gout.

Is all then lost?—alas, too true—
Ye tenths beloved, adieu, adieu !
My reign is o'er, my reign is o'er—
Like old Thumb's ghost, " I can no more."
—o◆◆o—
THE EUTHANASIA OF VAN.
" We are told that the bigots are growing old and fast
wearing out. If it be so, why not let us die in peace ?"
—*Lord Bexley's Letter to the Freeholders of Kent.*

Stop, Intellect, in mercy stop,
    Ye curst improvements cease ;

(1) Among the specimens laid before Parliament of the
sort of Church-rates levied upon Catholics in Ireland, was
a charge of two pipes of port for sacramental wine.
(2) Ezekiel, xxxiv., 10.— " Neither shall the shepherds

And let poor Nick V—ns—tt—t drop
    Into his grave in peace.

Hide, Knowledge, hide thy rising sun,
    Young Freedom, veil thy head ;
Let nothing good be thought or done,
    Till Nick V—ns—tt—t 's dead !

Take pity on a dotard's fears,
    Who much doth light detest ;
And let his last few drivelling years
    Be dark as were the rest.

You, too, ye fleeting one-pound notes,
    Speed not so fast away—
Ye rags, on which old Nicky gloats,
    A few months longer stay.(3)

Together soon, or much I err,
    You *both* from life may go—
The notes unto the scavenger,
    And Nick—to Nick below.

Ye Liberals, whate'er your plan,
    Be all reforms suspended ;
In compliment to dear old Van,
    Let nothing bad be mended.

Ye Papists, whom oppression wrings,
    Your cry politely cease,
And fret your hearts to fiddle-strings
    That Van may die in peace.

So shall he win a fame sublime
    By few old rag-men gain'd ;
Since all shall own, in Nicky's time,
    Nor sense nor justice reign'd.

So shall his name through ages pass,
    And dolts ungotten yet
Date from " the days of Nicholas,"
    With fond and sad regret—

And, sighing, say, " Alas, had he
    Been spared from Pluto's bowers,
The blessed reign of Bigotry
    And rags might still be ours !"
—o◆◆o—
TO THE REVEREND ——.
ON THE SIXTEEN REQUISITIONISTS OF NOTTINGHAM.
1828.
What, you, too, my * * ' * * *, in hashes so knowing,
Of sauces and soups Aristarchus profest !
Are you, too, my savoury Brunswicker, going
To make an old fool of yourself with the rest ?

Far better to stick to your kitchen receipts ;
And—if you want *something* to tease—for variety,
feed themselves any more ; for I will deliver my flock
from their mouth, that they may not be meat for them."
(3) Perituræ parcere chartæ.

Go study how Ude, in his *Cookery*, treats
Live eels when he fits them for polish'd society.

Just snuggling them in, 'twixt the bars of the fire,
He leaves them to wriggle and writhe on the
   coals, (1)
In a manner that H—rn—r himself would admire,
   And wish, 'stead of *eels*, they were Catholic souls.

Ude tells us, the fish little suffering feels;
   While Papists, of late, have more sensitive grown;
So, take my advice, try your hand at live eels,
   And, for *once*, let the other poor devils alone.

I have even a still better receipt for your cook—
   How to make a goose die of confirm'd *hepatitis;*(2)
And, if you'll for once *fellow*-feelings o'erlook,
   A well-tortured goose a most capital sight is.

First, catch him, alive—make a good steady fire—
   Set your victim before it, both legs being tied,
(As, if left to himself he *might* wish to retire,)
   And place a large bowl of rich cream by his side.

There roasting by inches, dry, fever'd, and faint,
   Having drunk all the cream, you socivilly laid, off,
He dies of as charming a liver complaint
   As ever sleek parson could wish a pie made of.

Besides, only think, my dear one of Sixteen,
   What an emblem this bird, for the epicure's use
    meant,
Presents of the mode in which Ireland has been
   Made a tid-bit of yours and your brethren's amuse-
    ment:

Tied down to the stake, while her limbs, as they
    quiver,
   A slow fire of tyranny wastes by degrees—
No wonder disease should have swell'd up her liver,
   No wonder you, Gourmands, should love her
    disease.

—◦◦◦—

IRISH ANTIQUITIES.

ACCORDING to some learn'd opinions
   The Irish once were Carthaginians;
But, trusting to more late descriptions,
   I'd rather say they were Egyptians.
My reason's this:—the Priests of Isis,
   When forth they march'd in long array,
Employ'd 'mong other grave devices,
   A Sacred Ass to lead the way; (3)

(1 The only way, Monsieur Ude assures us, to get rid
of the oil so objectionable in this fish.

2 A liver complaint. The process by which the livers
of geese are enlarged for the famous *Patés de foie d'oie.*

(3) To this practice the ancient adage alludes, "Asinus
portans mysteria."

(4) See the anecdote, which the Duchess of Marlborough
relates in her *Memoirs,* of this polite hero appropriating

And still the antiquarian traces
   'Mong Irish Lords this Pagan plan,
For still, in all religious cases,
   They put Lord R—d—n in the van.

—◦◦◦—

A CURIOUS FACT.

THE present Lord K—ny—n (the peer who writes
   letters,
For which the waste-paper folks much are his debtors)
Hath one little oddity, well worth reciting,
Which puzzleth observers, even more than his writing
Whenever Lord K—ny—n doth chance to behold
A cold Apple-pie—mind, the pie *must* be cold—
His Lordship looks solemn (few people know why),
And he makes a low bow to the said apple-pie.
This idolatrous act, in so "vital" a Peer,
Is, by most serious Protestants, thought rather
   queer—
Pie-worship, they hold, coming under the head
(Vide *Crustium,* chap. iv.) of the Worship of Bread.
Some think 't is a tribute, as author, he owes
For the service that pie-crust has done to his prose;—
The only good things in his pages, they swear,
Being those that the pastry-cook sometimes puts there.
Others say, 't is a homage, through pie-crust con-
   vey'd,
To our Glorious Deliverer's much-honour'd shade;
As that Protestant Hero (or Saint if you please)
Was as fond of cold pie as he was of green peas, (4)
And 't is only in loyal remembrance of that,
My Lord K—ny—n to apple-pie takes off his hat.
While others account for this kind salutation
By what Tony Lumpkin calls "concatenation , —
A certain good-will that, from sympathy's ties,
'Twixt old *Apple*-women and *Orange*-men lies.

But, 't is needless to add, these are all vague surmises,
For thus, we're assured, the whole matter arises:
Lord K—y—n's respected old father (like many
Respected old fathers) was fond of a penny;
And loved so to save, (5) that there's not the least
   question—
His death was brought on by a bad indigestion,
From cold apple-pie-crust his Lordship *would* stuff in,
At breakfast, to save the expense of hot muffin.
Hence it is, and hence only, that cold apple-pies
Are beheld by his Heir with such reverent eyes—
Just as honest King Stephen his beaver might doff
To the fishes that carried his kind uncle off—
And while *filial* piety urges so many on,
'T is pure *Apple*-pie-ety moves my Lord K—ny—n.

to himself one day, at dinner, a whole dish of green peas—
—the first of the season—while the poor Princess Anne,
who was then in a longing condition, sat by, vainly en-
treating, with her eyes, for a share.

(5) The same prudent propensity characterises his de-
scendant, who (as is well known), not to go to the expense
of a diphthong on his father's monument, had the inscrip-
tion spelled, economically, thus :—"*Mors Janua vita.*"

NEW-FASHIONED ECHOES.

Sir—Most of your readers are, no doubt, acquainted with the anecdote told of a certain, not over-wise, judge, who, when in the act of delivering a charge in some country court-house, was interrupted by the braying of an ass at the door. "What noise is that?" asked the angry judge. "Only an extraordinary *echo* there is in court, my Lord," answered one of the counsel. As there are a number of such "extraordinary echoes" abroad just now, you will not, perhaps, be unwilling, Mr. Editor, to receive the following few lines suggested by them.   Yours, etc.   S.

Huc coeamus (1) ait: nullique libentius unquam
Responsura sono, Cocamus, retulit echo.—*Ovid.*

THERE are echoes, we know, of all sorts,
    From the echo that "dies in the dale,"
To the "airy-tongued babbler," that sports
    Up the tide of the torrent her "tale."

There are echoes that bore us, like Blues,
    With the latest smart *mot* they have heard;
There are echoes, extremely like shrews,
    Letting nobody have the last word.

In the bogs of old Paddy-land, too,
    Certain "talented" echoes (2) there dwell,
Who on being ask'd, "How do you do?"
    Politely reply, "Pretty well."

But why should I talk any more
    Of such old-fashion'd echoes as these,
When Britain has new ones in store,
    That transcend them by many degrees?

For of all repercussions of sound,
    Concerning which bards make a pother,
There's none like that happy rebound
    When one blockhead echoes another;—

When K—ny—n commences the bray,
    And the Borough-Duke follows his track;
And loudly from Dublin's sweet bay,
    R—thd—ne brays, with interest, back;—

And while, of *most* echoes the sound
    On our ear by reflection doth fall,
These Brunswickers (3) pass the bray round,
    Without any reflection at all.

Oh Scott, were I gifted like you,
    Who can name all the echoes there are
From Benvoirlich to bold Ben-venue,
    From Benledi to wild Uamvar;

I might track, through each hard Irish name,
    The rebounds of this asinine strain,
Till from Neddy to Neddy, it came
    To the *chief* Neddy, K—ny—n, again;

Might tell how it roar'd in R—thd—ne,
    How from D—ws—n it died off genteelly—

How hollow it rung from the crown
    Of the fat-pated Marquis of E—y;

How, on hearing my Lord of G——e,
    Thistle-eaters, the stoutest, gave way,
Outdone, in their own special line,
    By the forty-ass power of his bray!

But, no—for so humble a bard
    'Tis a subject too trying to touch on;
Such noblemen's names are too hard,
    And their noddles too soft, to dwell much on.

Oh Echo, sweet nymph of the hill,
    Of the dell, and the deep-sounding shelves;
If, in spite of Narcissus, you still
    Take to fools who are charm'd with themselves,

Who knows but, some morning retiring,
    To walk by the Trent's wooded side,
You may meet with N—we—stle, admiring
    His own lengthen'd ears in the tide!

Or, on into Cambria straying,
    Find K—ny—n, that double-tongued elf,
In his love of *ass*-cendency, braying
    A Brunswick duet with himself!

—————

INCANTATION.

FROM THE NEW TRAGEDY OF THE "BRUNSWICKERS."
1828.

SCENE—*Penenden Plain. In the middle, a caldron boiling.
    Thunder.—Enter three Brunswickers.*
    1st Bruns.—THRICE hath scribbling K—ny—n
    scrawl'd,
    2d Bruns.—Once hath fool N—we—stle bawl'd,
    3d Bruns.—It—xl—y snores:—'t is time, 't is time.
    1st Bruns.—Round about the caldron go;
In the poisonous nonsense throw.
Bigot spite, that long hath grown,
Like a toad within a stone,
Sweltering in the heart of Sc—tt,
Boil we in the Brunswick pot.
    All.—Dribble, dribble, nonsense dribble,
Eld—n, talk, and K—ny—n, scribble.
    2d Bruns.—Slaver from N—we—stle's quill
In the noisome mess distil,
Brimming high our Brunswick broth
Both with venom and with froth.
Mix the brains (though apt to hash ill,
Being scant) of Lord M—ntc—shel,
With that malty stuff which Ch—nd—s
Drivels as no other man does.
Catch (*i. e.* catch if you can)
One idea, spick and span,

(1) "Let us form Clubs."
(2) Commonly called "Paddy Blake's Echoes."
(3) Anti-Catholic associations, under the title of Brunswick Clubs, were at this time becoming numerous both in England and Ireland.

From my Lord of S—l—sb—y—
One idea, though it be
Smaller than the " happy flea,"
Which his sire, in sonnet terse,
Wedded to immortal verse.(1)
Though to rob the son is sin,
Put his *one* idea in;
And to keep it company,
Let that conjuror W—nch—ls—a
Drop but *half* another there,
If he have so much to spare.
Dreams of murders and of arsons,
Hatch'd in heads of Irish parsons,
Bring from every hole and corner,
Where ferocious priests, like ll—rn—r,
Purely for religious good,
Cry aloud for Papists' blood,
Blood for W—lls, and such old women,
At their ease to wade and swim in.
  All.—Dribble, dribble, nonsense dribble,
B—xl—y, talk, and K—ny—n, scribble.
  3d Bruns.—Now the charm begin to brew ;
Sisters, sisters, add thereto
Scraps of L—thbr—dge's old speeches,
Mix'd with leather from his breeches.
Rinsings of old B—xl—y's brains,
Thicken'd (if you 'll take the pains)
With that pulp which rags create,
In their middle *nympha* state,
Ere, like insects frail and sunny,
Forth they wing abroad as money.
There the Hell-broth we 've enchanted—
Now but *one* thing more is wanted.
Squeeze o'er all that Orange juice,
C—— keeps cork'd for use,
Which, to work the better spell, is
Colour'd deep with blood of ——,
Blood, of powers far more various,
Even than that of Januarius,
Since so great a charm hangs o'er it,
England's parsons bow before it!
  All.—Dribble, dribble, nonsense dribble,
B—xl—y, talk, and K—ny—n, scribble.
  2d Bruns.—Cool it now with ——'s blood,
So the charm is firm and good.   [*Exeunt.*

—◦H◦—

HOW TO MAKE A GOOD POLITICIAN.

WHENE'ER you 're in doubt, said a Sage I once knew,
'Twixt two lines of conduct *which* course to pursue,
Ask a woman's advice, and, whate'er she advise,
Do the very reverse, and you 're sure to be wise.

Of the same use as guides are the Brunswicker
    throng;   [wrong,
In their thoughts, words, and deeds, so instinctively

(1) Alluding to a well-known lyric composition of the
late Marquis, which, with a slight alteration, might be ad-
dressed either to a flea or a fly. For instance :—
   "Oh, happy, happy, happy fly,
    If I were you, or you were I."

That, whatever they counsel, act, talk, or indite,
Take the opposite course, and you 're sure to be right.

So golden this rule, that, had nature denied you
The use of that finger-post, Reason, to guide you—
Were you even more doltish than any given man is,
More soft than N—wc—stle, more twaddling than
    Van is,
I 'd stake my repute, on the following conditions,
To make you the soundest of sound politicians.

Place yourself near the skirts of some high-flying
    Tory—
Some Brunswicker parson, of port-drinking glory—
Watch well how he dines, during any great Ques-
    tion—
What makes him feed gaily, what spoils his diges-
    tion—
And always feel sure that *his* joy o'er a stew
Portends a clear case of dyspepsia to *you.*
Read him backwards, like Hebrew—whatever he
    wishes,
Or praises, note down as absurd, or pernicious.
Like the folks of a weather-house, shifting about,
When he 's *out,* be an *In*—when he 's *in,* be an *Out.*
Keep him always reversed in your thoughts, night
    and day,
Like an Irish barometer turn'd the wrong way :—
If he 's *up,* you may swear that foul weather is nigh ;
If he 's *down,* you may look for a bit of blue sky.
Never mind what debaters or journalists say,
Only ask what *he* thinks, and then think t' other way.
Does he hate the Small-note Bill ? then firmly rely
The Small-note Bill 's a blessing, though *you* don't
    know why.
Is Brougham his aversion ? then Harry 's your man.
Does he quake at O'Connell ? take doubly to Dan.
Is he all for the Turks ? then, at once, take the whole
Russian Empire (Czar, Cossacks, and all) to your
    soul.
In short, whatsoever he talks, thinks, or is,
Be your thoughts, words, and essence the contrast of
    his.
Nay, as Siamese ladies—at least, the polite ones—
All paint their teeth black, 'cause the devil has white
    ones—
If even, by the chances of time or of tide,
Your Tory, for once, should have sense on his side,
Even *then* stand aloof—for, be sure that Old Nick,
When a Tory talks sensibly, means you some trick.

Such my recipe is—and, in one single verse,
I shall now, in conclusion, its substance rehearse.
Be all that a Brunswicker *is* not, nor *could* be,
And then—you 'll be all that an honest man should be.

Or,

    "Oh, happy, happy, happy flea,
    If I were you, or you were me ;
    But since, alas ! that cannot be,
    I must remain Lord S———y."

EPISTLE OF CONDOLENCE,

FROM A SLAVE-LORD TO A COTTON-LORD.

ALAS! my dear friend, what a state of affairs!
  How unjustly we both are despoil'd of our rights!
Not a pound of black flesh shall I leave to my heirs,
  Nor must *you* any more work to death little whites.

Both forced to submit to that general controller
  Of King, Lords, and cotton-mills, Public Opinion,
No more shall *you* beat with a big billy-roller,
  Nor *I* with the cart-whip assert my dominion.

Whereas, were we suffer'd to do as we please
    With our Blacks and our Whites, as of yore we
    were let,
We might range them alternate, like harpsichord
    keys,
  And between us thump out a good piebald duet.

But this fun is all over;—farewell to the zest
  Which Slavery now lends to each tea-cup we sip;
Which makes still the cruellest coffee the best,
  And that sugar the sweetest which smacks of the
    whip.

Farewell, too, the Factory's white picaninnies—
    Small living machines, which, if flogg'd to their
    tasks,
Mix so well with their namesakes, the "Billies" and
    "Jennies,"
  That *which* have got souls in 'em nobody asks;—

Little Maids of the Mill, who, themselves but ill-fed,
  Are obliged, 'mong their other benevolent cares,
To "keep feeding the scribblers" (1)—and better,
    't is said,
  Than old Blackwood or Fraser have ever fed theirs.

All this is now o'er, and so dismal *my* loss is,
  So hard 't is to part from the smack of the thong,
That I mean (from pure love for the old whipping
    process)
  To take to whipt syllabub all my life long.

—◦➤◦—

THE GHOST OF MILTIADES.

Ab quoties dubius *Scriptis* exarsit amator!—*Ovid.*

THE Ghost of Miltiades came at night,
  And he stood by the bed of the Benthamite,
And he said, in a voice that thrill'd the frame,
  "If ever the sound of Marathon's name
Hath fired thy blood or flush'd thy brow,
  Lover of Liberty, rouse thee now!"

The Benthamite, yawning, left his bed—
  Away to the Stock Exchange he sped,
And he found the Scrip of Greece so high,
  That it fired his blood, it flush'd his eye,
And oh, 't was a sight for the Ghost to see,
  For never was Greek more Greek than he!

And still as the premium higher went,
  His ecstasy rose—so much *per cent.*
(As we see in a glass, that tells the weather,
  The heat and the *silver* rise together,)
And Liberty sung from the patriot's lip,
  While a voice from his pocket whisper'd "Scrip!"
The Ghost of Miltiades came again;—
  He smiled, as the pale moon smiles through rain,
For his soul was glad at that patriot strain;
  (And, poor dear ghost—how little he knew
The jobs and the tricks of the Philhellene crew!)
  "Blessings and thanks!" was all he said,
Then, melting away, like a night-dream, fled!

The Benthamite hears—amazed that ghosts
  Could be such fools—and away he posts,
A patriot still? Ah no, ah no—
  Goddess of Freedom, thy Scrip is low,
And, warm and fond as thy lovers are,
  Thou triest their passion, when under *par.*
The Benthamite's ardour fast decays,
  By turns he weeps, and swears, and prays,
And wishes the d—l had Crescent and Cross,
  Ere *he* had been forced to sell at a loss.
They quote him the Stock of various nations,
  But, spite of his classic associations,
Lord, how he loathes the Greek *quotations!*

"Who'll buy my Scrip? Who'll buy my Scrip?"
  Is now the theme of the patriot's lip,
As he runs to tell how hard his lot is
  To Messrs. Orlando and Luriottis,
And says, "Oh Greece, for Liberty's sake,
  Do buy my Scrip, and I vow to break
Those dark unholy *bonds* of thine—
  If you'll only consent to buy up *mine!*"
The Ghost of Miltiades came once more;—
  His brow, like the night, was lowering o'er,
And he said, with a look that flash'd dismay,
  "Of Liberty's foes the worst are they,
Who turn to a trade her cause divine,
  And gamble for gold on Freedom's shrine!"
Thus saying, the Ghost, as he took his flight,
  Gave a Parthian kick to the Benthamite,
Which sent him, whimpering, off to Jerry—
  And vanish'd away to the Stygian ferry!

—◦➤◦—

ALARMING INTELLIGENCE—REVOLUTION IN THE DICTIONARY—ONE *GALT* AT THE HEAD OF IT.

GOD preserve us!—there's nothing now safe from
    assault;—
Thrones toppling around, churches brought to the
    hammer;
And accounts have just reach'd us that one Mr. *Galt*
  Has declared open war against English and
    Grammar!

(1) One of the operations in cotton-mills usually per-
formed by children.

He had long been suspected of some such design,
  And, the better his wicked intents to arrive at,
Had lately among C—lb—n's troops of *the line*
  (The penny-a-line men) enlisted as private.

There school'd, with a rabble of words at command,
  Scotch, English, and slang, in promiscuous alliance,
He, at length, against Syntax has taken his stand,
  And sets all the Nine Parts of Speech at defiance.

Next advices, no doubt, further facts will afford ;
  In the mean time the danger most imminent
    grows,
He has taken the Life of one eminent Lord,
  And whom he 'll *next* murder the Lord only knows.

             Wednesday evening.
Since our last, matters, luckily, look more serene ;
  Though the rebel, 't is stated, to aid his defection,
Has seized a great Powder—no, Puff Magazine,
  And the explosions are dreadful in every direction.

What his meaning exactly is, nobody knows,
  As he talks (in a strain of intense botheration)
Of lyrical "ichor," (1) " gelatinous " prose, (2)
  And a mixture call'd " amber immortalization."(3)

Now, he raves of a bard he once happen'd to meet,
  Seated high " among rattlings," and churning a
    sonnet ; (4)
Now, talks of a mystery, wrapp'd in a sheet,
  With a halo (by way of a nightcap) upon it! (5)

We shudder in tracing these terrible lines ;
  Something bad they must mean, though we can't
    make it out;
For whate'er may be guess'd of Galt's secret de-
    signs,
  That they 're all *Anti*-English no Christian can
    doubt.

      —◦••◦—

RESOLUTIONS

PASSED AT A LATE MEETING OF
REVERENDS AND RIGHT REVERENDS.

RESOLVED—to stick to every particle
  Of every Creed and every Article ;

(1) "That dark diseased ichor which coloured his effu-
sions."—*Galt's Life of Byron.*

(2) " That gelatinous character of their effusions."—
Ibid.

(3) " The poetical embalmment, or, rather, amber im-
mortalization."—*Ibid.*

(4) "Sitting amidst the shrouds and rattlings, churning
an inarticulate melody."—*Ibid.*

(5) "He was a mystery in a winding-sheet, crowned
with a halo."—*Ibid.*

(6) One of the questions propounded to the Puritans
in 1573 was—"Whether the Book of Service was good and
godly, every tittle grounded on the Holy Scripture ?" On
which an honest Dissenter remarks— "Surely they had a

Reforming nought, or great or little,
We 'll stanchly stand by every tittle," (6)
And scorn the swallow of that soul
Which cannot boldly bolt the whole.

Resolved, that, though St. Athanasius
In damning souls is rather spacious—
Though wide and far his curses fall,
Our Church " hath stomach for them all ;"
And those who 're not content with such
May e'en be d—d ten times as much.

Resolved—such liberal souls are we—
Though hating Nonconformity,
We yet believe the cash no worse is
That comes from Nonconformist purses.
Indifferent *whence* the money reaches
The pockets of our reverend breeches,
To us the Jumper's jingling penny
Chinks with a tone as sweet as any ;
And even our old friends Yea and Nay
May through the nose for ever pray,
If *also* through the nose they 'll pay.

Resolved, that Hooper, (7) Latimer, (8)
And Cranmer, (9) all extremely err,
In taking such a low-bred view
Of what Lords Spiritual ought to do :—
All owing to the fact, poor men,
That Mother Church was modest then,
Nor knew what golden eggs her goose,
The Public, would in time produce.
One Pisgah peep at modern Durham
To far more lordly thoughts would stir 'em.

Resolved, that when we, Spiritual Lords,
Whose income just enough affords
To keep our Spiritual Lordships cozy,
Are told, by Antiquarians prosy,
How ancient Bishops cut up theirs,
Giving the poor the largest shares—
Our answer is, in one short word,
We think it pious, but absurd.
Those good men made the world their debtor,
But we, the Church reform'd, know better ;
And, taking all that all can pay,
Balance the account the other way.

wonderful opinion of their Service Book that there was
not a *tittle* amiss in it.

(7) "They," the Bishops, "know that the primitive
Church had no such Bishops. If the fourth part of the bi-
shopric remained unto the Bishop, it were sufficient."—*On
the Commandments,* p. 72.

(8) " Since the Prelates were made Lords and Nobles,
the plough standeth, there is no work done, the people
starve."—*Lat. Serm.*

(9) " Of whom have come all these glorious titles, styles,
and pomps into the Church. But I would that I, and all
my brethren, the Bishops, would leave all our styles, and
write the styles of our offices," etc.—*Life of Cranmer, by
Strype, Appendix.*

69

Resolved, our thanks profoundly due are
To last month's Quarterly Reviewer,
Who proves (by arguments so clear
One sees how much he holds *per* year)
That England's Church, though out of date,
Must still be left to lie in state,
As dead, as rotten, and as grand as
The mummy of King Osymandyas,
All pickled snug—the brains drawn out—(1)
With costly cerements swathed about—
And " Touch me not," those words terrific,
Scrawl'd o'er her in good hieroglyphic.

—◦◉◦—

SIR ANDREW'S DREAM.

" Nec tu sperne piis venientia somnia portis :
   Cum pia venerunt somnia, pondus habent."
            Propert. lib. iv., eleg. 7.

As snug, on a Sunday eve, of late,
In his easy chair Sir Andrew sate,
Being much too pious, as every one knows,
To do aught, of a Sunday eve, but doze,
He dreamt a dream, dear holy man,
And I 'll tell you his dream as well as I can.
He found himself, to his great amaze,
In Charles the First's high Tory days,
And just at the time that gravest of Courts
Had publish'd its Book of Sunday Sports.—(2)
Sunday Sports! what a thing for the ear
Of Andrew, even in sleep, to hear!—
It chanced to be, too, a Sabbath day,
When the people from church were coming away ;
And Andrew with horror heard this song,
As the smiling sinners flock'd along :—
" Long life to the Bishops, hurrah! hurrah!
For a week of work and a Sunday of play
Make the poor man's life run merry away."

" The Bishops!" quoth Andrew, " Popish, I guess,"
And he grinn'd with conscious holiness.
But the song went on, and, to brim the cup
Of poor Andy's grief, the fiddles struck up!

" Come, take out the lasses—let 's have a dance—
For the Bishops allow us to skip our fill,
Well knowing that no one 's the more in advance
On the road to heaven, for standing still.

" Oh, it never was meant that grim grimaces
Should sour the cream of a creed of love ;
Or that fellows with long disastrous faces
Alone should sit among cherubs above.
     Then hurrah for the Bishops, etc.

(1) Part of the process of embalmment.

(2) *The Book of Sports* drawn up by Bishop Moreton was
first put forth in the reign of James I., 1618, and afterwards
republished, at the advice of Laud, by Charles I., 1633,
with an injunction that it should be " made public by
order from the Bishops." We find it therein declared,
that " for his good people's recreation, his Majesty's plea-

" For Sunday fun we never can fail,
     When the Church herself each sport points out;—
There 's May-games, archery, Whitsun-ale,
     And a May-pole high to dance about.
Or, should we be for a pole hard driven,
     Some lengthy saint, of aspect fell,
With his pockets on earth, and his nose in heaven,
     Will do for a May-pole just as well.
Then hurrah for the Bishops, hurrah! hurrah!
A week of work and a Sabbath of play
Make the poor man's life run merry away."

To Andy, who does n't much deal in history,
This Sunday scene was a downright mystery ;
And God knows where might have ended the joke,
But, in trying to stop the fiddles, he woke.
And the odd thing is (as the rumour goes)
That since that dream—which, one would suppose,
Should have made his godly stomach rise,
Even more than ever, 'gainst Sunday pies—
He has view'd things quite with different eyes ;
Is beginning to take, on matters divine,
Like Charles and his Bishops, the *sporting* line—
Is all for Christians jigging in pairs,
As an interlude 'twixt Sunday prayers ;—
Nay, talks of getting Archbishop H—l—y
To bring in a Bill, enacting duly,
That all good Protestants, from this date,
May, freely and lawfully, recreate,
Of a Sunday eve, their spirits moody,
With Jack in the Straw, or Punch and Judy.

—◦◉◦—

A BLUE LOVE-SONG.

TO MISS — —.

AIR—" *Come, live with me and be my love.*"

Come wed with me, and we will write,
My Blue of Blues, from morn till night.
Chased from our classic souls shall be
All thoughts of vulgar progeny ;
And thou shalt walk through smiling rows
Of chubby duodecimos ;
While I, to match thy products nearly,
Shall lie-in of a quarto yearly.
'Tis true, even books entail some trouble ;
But *live* productions give one double.
Correcting children is *such* bother—
While printers' devils correct the other.
Just think, my own Malthusian dear,
How much more decent 't is to hear
From male or female—as it may be—
" How is your book?" than " How's your baby?"

sure was, that after the end of divine service they should
not be disturbed, letted, or discouraged from any lawful
recreations, such as dancing, either of men or women,
archery for men, leaping, vaulting, or any such harmless
recreations, not having of May-games, Whitsun-ales, or
Morris-dances, or setting up of May-poles, or other sports
therewith used," etc.

And, whereas physic and wet nurses
Do much exhaust paternal purses,
Our books, if rickety, may go
And be well dry-nursed in *the Row;*
And, when God wills to take them hence,
Are buried at *the Row's* expense.

Besides, (as 't is well proved by thee,
In thy own Works, vol. 93,)
The march, just now, of population
So much outstrips all moderation,
That even prolific herring-shoals
Keep pace not with our erring souls. (1)
Oh far more proper and well-bred
To stick to writing books instead;
And show the world how two Blue lovers
Can coalesce, like two book-covers,
(Sheep-skin, or calf, or such wise leather,)
Letter'd at back, and stitch'd together,
Formally as first the binder fix'd 'em,
With nought but—literature betwixt 'em.

—————

SUNDAY ETHICS.

A SCOTCH ODE.

Puir profligate Londoners, having heard tell
That the De'il's got amang ye, and fearing 't is true,
We ha' sent ye a mon wha's a match for his spell,
A chiel o' our ain, that the Deevil himsel
Will be glad to keep clear of, one Andrew Agnew.

So, at least, ye may reckon, for ane day entire
In ilka lang week ye'll be tranquil eneugh,
As Auld Nick, do him justice, abhors a Scotch squire,
An' would sooner gae roast by his ain kitchen fire
Than pass a hale Sunday wi' Andrew Agnew.

For, bless the gude mon, gin he had his ain way,
He'd na let a cat on the Sabbath say "mew;"
Nae birdie maun whistle, nae lambie maun play,
An' Phœbus himsel could na travel that day,
As he'd find a new Joshua in Andie Agnew.

Only hear, in your Senate, how awfu' he cries,
"Wae, wae to a' sinners who boil an' who stew!
Wae, wae to a' eaters o' Sabbath-baked pies,
For as surely again shall the crust thereof rise
In judgment against ye," saith Andrew Agnew!

Ye may think, from a' this, that our Andie's the lad
To ca' o'er the coals your nobeelity, too;
That their drives, o' a Sunday, wi' flunkies, (2) a' clad
Like shawmen, behind 'em, would mak the mon
    mad—
But he's nae sic a noodle, our Andie Agnew.

(1) See *Ella of Garveloch.*—Garveloch being a place
where there was a large herring-fishery, but where, as
we are told by the author, " the people increased much
faster than the produce."

If Lairds an' fine Ladies, on Sunday, think right
To gang to the Deevil—as maist o' em do—
To stop them our Andie would think na polite;
And 't is odds (if the chiel could get ony thing by 't)
But he'd follow 'em, booing, (3) would Andrew
    Agnew.

—————

AWFUL EVENT.

Yes, W—nch—ls—a (I tremble while I pen it),
W—nch—ls—a's Earl hath *cut* the British Senate—
Hath said to England's Peers, in accent gruff,
" *That* for ye all" [snapping his fingers], and exit,
    in a huff!

Disastrous news!—like that, of old, which spread
From shore to shore, " our mighty Pan is dead,"
O'er the cross benches (cross from *being* crost)
Sounds the loud wail, " Our W—nch—ls—a is lost!"

Which of ye, Lords, that heard him, can forget
The deep impression of that awful threat,
"I quit your house!!"—'midst all that histories tell,
I know but *one* event that's parallel :—

It chanced at Drury Lane, one Easter night,
When the gay gods, too blest to be polite,
Gods at their ease, like those of learn'd Lucretius,
Laugh'd, whistled, groan'd, uproariously facetious—
A well-dress'd member of the middle gallery,
Whose " ears polite" disdain'd such low canaillerie,
Rose in his place—so grand, you'd almost swear
Lord W—nch—ls—a himself stood towering there—
And like that Lord of dignity and *nous,*
Said, "Silence, fellows, or—I'll leave the house!!"

How brook'd the gods this speech? Ah well-a-day,
That speech so fine should be so thrown away!
In vain did this mid-gallery grandee
Assert his own two-shilling dignity—
In vain he menaced to withdraw the ray
Of his own full-price countenance away—
Fun against Dignity is fearful odds,
And as the Lords laugh *now,* so giggled *then* the gods!

—————

THE NUMBERING OF THE CLERGY.

PARODY ON SIR CHARLES HAN. WILLIAMS'S FAMOUS ODE,

"COME, CLOE, AND GIVE ME SWEET KISSES."

" We want more Churches and more Clergymen."
        Bishop of London's late Charge.

" Rectorum numerum, terris pereuntibus, augent."
        Claudian in Eutrop.

Come, give us more Livings and Rectors,
    For, richer no realm ever gave;

(2) Servants in livery.
(3) For the "gude effects and uteelity of booing," see
the *Man of the World.*

But why, ye unchristian objectors,
　Do ye ask us how many we crave? (1)

Oh, there can't be too many rich Livings
　For souls of the Pluralist kind,
Who, despising old Cocker's misgivings,
　To numbers can ne'er be confined. (2)

Count the cormorants hovering about, (3)
　At the time their fish season sets in,
When these models of keen diners-out
　Are preparing their beaks to begin.

Count the rooks that, in clerical dresses,
　Flock round when the harvest's in play,
And, not minding the farmer's distresses,
　Like devils in grain peck away.

Go, number the locusts in heaven, (4)
　On their way to some titheable shore;
And when so many Parsons you've given,
　We still shall be craving for more.

Then, unless ye the Church would submerge, ye
　Must leave us in peace to augment,
For the wretch who could number the Clergy,
　With few will be ever content. (5)

———◦••◦———

A SAD CASE.

" If it be the undergraduate season at which this *rabies
religiosa* is to be so fearful, what security has Mr. G—l—
b—n against it at this moment, when his son is actually
exposed to the full venom of an association with Dis-
senters?"—*The Times*, March 25.

How sad a case !—just think of it—
If G—lb—n junior should be bit
By some insane Dissenter, roaming
Through Granta's halls at large and foaming,
And with that aspect, *ultra* crabbed,
Which marks Dissenters when they're rabid!
God only knows what mischiefs might
Result from this one single bite,
Or how the venom, once suck'd in,
Might spread and rage through kith and kin.
Mad folks, of all denominations,
First turn upon their own relations :
So that one G—lb—n, fairly bit,
Might end in maddening the whole kit,
Till, ah, ye gods, we'd have to rue
Our G—lb—n senior bitten too ;

(1) 　Come, Cloe, and give me sweet kisses,
　　　　For sweeter sure never girl gave ;
　　　But why, in the midst of my blisses,
　　　　Do you ask me how many I'd have ?
(2) 　For whilst I love thee above measure,
　　　　To numbers I'll ne'er be confined.
(3) 　Count the bees that on Hybla are playing,
　　　　Count the flowers that enamel its fields,
　　　Count the flocks, etc.

The Hychurchphobia in those veins,
Where Tory blood now redly reigns ;—
And that dear man, who now perceives
Salvation only in lawn sleeves,
Might, tainted by such coarse infection,
Run mad in the opposite direction,
And think, poor man, 'tis only given
To linsey-woolsey to reach Heaven !

Just fancy what a shock 't would be
Our G—lb—n in his fits to see,
Tearing into a thousand particles
His once-loved Nine and Thirty Articles ;
(Those Articles his friend, the Duke, (6)
For Gospel, t'other night, mistook ;)
Cursing cathedrals, deans, and singers—
Wishing the ropes might hang the ringers—
Pelting the church with blasphemies,
Even worse than Parson B—v—rl—y's ;—
And ripe for severing Church and State,
Like any creedless reprobate,
Or like that class of Methodists
Prince Waterloo styles " Atheists !"

But 'tis too much—the Muse turns pale,
And o'er the picture drops a veil,
Praying, God save the G—lb—ns all
From mad Dissenters, great and small!

———◦••◦———

A DREAM OF HINDOSTAN.

—— *risum teneatis, amici.*

" THE longer one lives, the more one learns,"
　Said I, as off to sleep I went,
Bemused with thinking of Tithe concerns,
And reading a book, by the Bishop of Ferns, (7)
　On the Irish Church Establishment.
But, lo, in sleep not long I lay,
　When Fancy her usual tricks began,
And I found myself bewitch'd away
　To a goodly city in Hindostan—
A city, where he, who dares to dine
　On aught but rice, is deem'd a sinner ;
Where sheep and kine are held divine,
　And, accordingly—never drest for dinner.

" But how is this ?" I wondering cried—
As I walk'd that city, fair and wide,
And saw, in every marble street,
A row of beautiful butchers' shops—
" What means, for men who don't eat meat,
　This grand display of loins and chops?"

(4) 　Go, number the stars in the heaven,
　　　　Count how many sands on the shore ;
　　　When so many kisses you've given,
　　　　I still shall be craving for more.
(5) 　But the wretch who can number his kisses,
　　　　With few will be ever content,
(6) The Duke of Wellington, who styled them " the Ar-
ticles of Christianity."
(7) An indefatigable scribbler of anti-Catholic pamphlets.

In vain I ask'd—'t was plain to see
That nobody dared to answer me.

So, on, from street to street I strode;
And you can't conceive how vastly odd
The butchers look'd—a roseate crew,
Inshrined in *stalls*, with nought to do;
While some on a *bench*, half dozing, sat,
And the Sacred Cows were not more fat.

Still posed to think what all this scene
Of sinecure trade was *meant* to mean,
" And, pray," ask'd I—" by whom is paid
The expense of this strange masquerade?"—
" The expense!—oh, that's of course defray'd
(Said one of these well-fed Hecatombers)
By yonder rascally rice-consumers."
" What? *they*, who must n't eat meat!"—
                              " No matter—
(And, while he spoke, his cheeks grew fatter,)
The rogues may munch their *Paddy* crop,
But the rogues must still support *our* shop.
And, depend upon it, the way to treat
Heretical stomachs that thus dissent,
Is to burden all that wo'n't eat meat,
    With a costly *Meat Establishment*."

On hearing these words so gravely said,
    With a volley of laughter loud I shook;
And my slumber fled, and my dream was sped,
And I found I was lying snug in bed,
    With my nose in the Bishop of Ferns's book?

——o♦♦o——

THE BRUNSWICK CLUB.

A letter having been addressed to a very distinguished
personage, requesting him to become the Patron of this
Orange Club, a polite answer was forthwith returned,
of which we have been fortunate enough to obtain a copy.

Brimstone-hall, September 1, 1828.

Private.—Lord Belzebub presents
To the Brunswick Club his compliments,
And much regrets to say that he
Cannot, at present, their Patron be.
In stating this, Lord Belzebub
Assures, on his honour, the Brunswick Club,
That 't is n't from any lukewarm lack
Of zeal or fire he thus holds back—
As even Lord *Coal* (1) himself is not
For the Orange party more red-hot:
But the truth is, till their Club affords
A somewhat decenter show of Lords,
And on its list of members gets
A few less rubbishy Baronets,
Lord Belzebub must beg to be
Excused from keeping such company.

Who the devil, he humbly begs to know,
Are Lord Gl—nd—ne, and Lord D—nlo?
Or who, with a grain of sense, would go
To sit and be bored by Lord M—yo?

What living creature—*except his nurse*—
For Lord M—ntc—sh—l cares a curse,
Or thinks 't would matter if Lord M—sk—rry
Were t' other side of the Stygian ferry?
Breathes there a man in Dublin town,
Who'd give but half of half-a-crown
To save from drowning my Lord R—thd—ne,
Or who would n't also gladly hustle in
Lords R—d—n, B—nd—n, C—le, and J—c—l—n?
In short, though, from his tenderest years,
Accustom'd to all sorts of Peers,
Lord Belzebub much questions whether
He ever yet saw, mix'd together,
As 't were in one capacious tub,
Such a mess of noble silly-bub
As the twenty Peers of the Brunswick Club.

'T is therefore impossible that Lord B.
Could stoop to such society,
Thinking, he owns (though no great prig),
For one in his station 't were *infra dig.*
But he begs to propose, in the interim
(Till they find some properer Peers for him),
His Highness of C—mb—d, as *Sub*,
To take his place at the Brunswick Club—
Begging, meanwhile, himself to dub
Their obedient servant,   BELZEBUB.

It luckily happens, the R—y—l Duke
Resembles so much, in air and look,
The head of the Belzebub family,
That few can any difference see;
Which makes him, of course, the better suit
To serve as Lord B.'s substitute.

——o♦♦o——

PROPOSALS FOR A GYNÆCOCRACY.

ADDRESSED TO A LATE RADICAL MEETING.
——" Quas ipsa decus sibi dia Camilla
Delegit pacisque bonas bellique ministras."—*Virgil.*

As Whig Reform has had its range,
    And none of us are yet content,
Suppose, my friends, by way of change,
    We try a *Female Parliament;*
And since, of late, with *he* M. P.'s
We've fared so badly, take to she's—
Petticoat patriots, flounced John Russells,
Burdetts in *blonde*, and Broughams in *bustles*.
The plan is startling, I confess—
But 'tis but an affair of dress;
Nor see I much there is to choose
    'Twixt Ladies (so they're thorough-bred ones)
In ribands of all sorts of hues,
    Or Lords in only blue or red ones.

At least, the fiddlers will be winners,
    Whatever other trade advances;
As then, instead of Cabinet dinners,
    We'll have, at Almack's, Cabinet dances;

(1) Usually written "Cole."

Nor let this world's important questions
Depend on Ministers' digestions.

If Ude's receipts have done things ill,
  To Weippert's band they may go better ;
There's Lady * *, in one quadrille,
  Would settle Europe, if you 'd let her :
And who the deuce or asks, or cares,
  When Whigs or Tories have undone 'em,
Whether they 've *danced* through State affairs,
  Or simply, dully, *dined* upon 'em ?

Hurrah then for the Petticoats!
  To them we pledge our free-born votes ;
We 'll have all *she*, and only *she*—
  Pert blues shall act as " best debaters,"
Old dowagers our Bishops be,
  And termagants our Agitators.

If Vestris, to oblige the nation,
  Her own Olympus will abandon,
And help to prop the Administration,
  It *'can't'* have better legs to stand on.
The famed Macaulay (Miss) shall show,
  Each evening, forth in learn'd oration ;
Shall move ('midst general cries of " Oh !")
  For full returns of population :
And, finally, to crown the whole,
  The Princess Olive, (1) Royal soul,
Shall from her bower in Banco Regis,
Descend, to bless her faithful lieges,
And, 'mid our Unions' loyal chorus,
Reign jollily for ever o'er us.

—*◦◦◦*—

TO THE EDITOR OF THE * * *.

Sir—Having heard some rumours respecting the strange
and awful visitation under which Lord H—nl—y has for
some time past been suffering, in consequence of his de-
clared hostility to " anthems, solos, duets," (2) etc., I took
the liberty of making inquiries at his Lordship's house this
morning, and lose no time in transmitting to you such
particulars as I could collect. It is said that the screams
of his Lordship, under the operation of this nightly concert,
(which is, no doubt, some trick of the Radicals,) may be
heard all over the neighbourhood. The female who per-
sonates St. Cecilia is supposed to be the same that, last
year, appeared in the character of Isis, at the Rotunda.
How the cherubs are managed, I have not yet ascertained.
                               Yours, etc.—P. P.

LORD H—NL—Y AND ST. CECILIA.

——*in Metii descendat Judicis aures.—Horat.*

As snug in his bed Lord H—nl—y lay,
  Revolving much his own renown,
And hoping to add thereto a ray,
  By putting duets and anthems down,

---

(1) A personage, so styling herself, who attained con-
siderable notoriety at that period.

(2) In a work, on Church Reform, published by his
Lordship in 1832.

(3) "Asseyez-vous, mes enfans."—"Il n'y a pas de quoi,
mon Seigneur."

Sudden a strain of choral sounds
  Mellifluous o'er his senses stole ;
Whereat the Reformer mutter'd, " Zounds ! "
  For he loathed sweet music with all his soul.

Then, starting up, he saw a sight
  That well might shock so learn'd a snorer—
Saint Cecilia, robed in light,
  With a portable organ slung before her.

And round were Cherubs, on rainbow wings,
  Who, his Lordship fear'd, might tire of flitting,
So begg'd they 'd sit—but ah! poor things,
  They 'd, none of them, got the means of sitting. (3)

" Having heard," said the Saint, " you 're fond of
    hymns,
  And indeed, that musical snore betray'd you,
Myself, and my choir of cherubims,
  Are come, for a while, to serenade you."

In vain did the horrified H—nl—y say
  " 'T was all a mistake "—" she was misdirected ;"
And point to a concert, over the way,
  Where fiddlers and angels were expected.

In vain—the Saint could see in his looks
  (She civilly said) much tuneful lore ;
So, at once, all open'd their music-books,
  And herself and her Cherubs set off at score.

All night duets, terzets, quartets,
  Nay, long quintets most dire to hear ;
Ay, and old motets, and canzonets,
  And glees, in sets, kept boring his ear.

He tried to sleep—but it would n't do ;
  So loud they squall'd, he *must* attend to 'em ;
Though Cherubs' songs, to his cost he knew,
  Were like themselves, and had no end to 'em.

Oh judgment dire on judges bold,
  Who meddle with music's sacred strains !
Judge Midas tried the same of old,
  And was punish'd, like H—nl—y, for his pains.

But worse on the modern judge, alas !
  Is the sentence launch'd from Apollo's throne ;
For Midas was given the ears of an ass,
  While H—nl—y is doom'd to keep his own !

—*◦◦◦*—

ADVERTISEMENT. (4)

1830.

Missing or lost, last Sunday night,
  A Waterloo coin, whereon was traced

---

(4) Written at that memorable crisis when a distin-
guished Duke, then Prime Minister, acting under the in-
spirations of Sir Cl—d—s H—nt—r and other City worthies,
advised his Majesty to give up his announced intention of
dining with the Lord Mayor.

The inscription, "Courage!" in letters bright,
　Though a little by rust of years defaced.

The metal thereof is rough and hard,
　And ('tis thought of late) mix'd up with brass ;
But it bears the stamp of Fame's award,
　And through all Posterity's hands will pass.

How it was lost, God only knows,
　But certain *City* thieves, they say,
Broke in on the owner's evening doze,
　And filch'd this "gift of gods" away

One ne'er could, of course, the Cits suspect,
　If we had n't, that evening, chanced to see,
At the robb'd man's door, a *Mare* elect,
　With an ass to keep her company.

Whosoe'er of this lost treasure knows,
　Is begg'd to state all facts about it,
As the owner can't well face his foes,
　Nor even his friends, just now, without it.

And if Sir Clod will bring it back,
　Like a trusty Baronet, wise and able,
He shall have a ride on the whitest hack (1)
　That's left in old King George's stable.

—◦◦◦—

MISSING.

Carlton Terrace, 1832.

WHEREAS, Lord ****** de *******
Left his home last Saturday,
And, though inquired for, round and round,
　Through certain purlieus, can't be found ;
And whereas, none can solve our queries
As to where this virtuous Peer is,
Notice is hereby given, that all
May forthwith to inquiring fall,
As, once the thing's well set about,
No doubt but we shall hunt him out.

His Lordship's mind, of late, they say,
Hath been in an uneasy way.
Himself and colleagues not being let
To climb into the Cabinet,
To settle England's state affairs,
Hath much, it seems, *unsettled* theirs ;
And chief to this stray Plenipo
Hath been a most distressing blow.

Already—certain to receive a
Well-paid mission to the Neva,

And be the bearer of kind words
To tyrant Nick from Tory Lords—
To fit himself for free discussion,
His Lordship had been learning Russian ;
And all so natural to him were
The accents of the Northern bear,
That, while his tones were in your ear, you
Might swear you were in sweet Siberia.
And still, poor Peer, to old and young,
He goes on raving in that tongue ;
Tells you how much you would enjoy a
Trip to Dalnodoubrowskoya ; (2)
Talks of such places, by the score, on
As Oulisfflirmchinagoboron, (3)
And swears (for he at nothing sticks)
That Russia swarms with Raskol-niks, (4)
Though *one* such Nick, God knows, must be
A more than ample quantity.

Such are the marks by which to know
This stray'd or stolen Plenipo ;
And whosoever brings or sends
The unhappy statesman to his friends,
On Carlton Terrace, shall have thanks,
And—any paper but the Bank's.

P. S.—Some think, the disappearance
Of this our diplomatic Peer hence
Is for the purpose of reviewing,
In person, what dear Mig is doing,
So as to 'scape all tell-tale letters
'Bout B—s—d, and such abettors,—
The only "wretches" for whose aid (5)
Letters seem not to have been made.

—◦◦◦—

THE DANCE OF BISHOPS;

OR, THE EPISCOPAL QUADRILLE. (6)

A DREAM.

1833.

"Solemn dances were, on great festivals and celebrations,
admitted among the primitive Christians, in which even
the Bishops and dignified Clergy were performers.
Scaliger says, that the first Bishops were called *Præ-
sules*, (7) for no other reason than that they led off these
dances."—*Cyclopædia*, art. *Dances*.

I've had such a dream—a frightful dream—
Though funny, mayhap, to wags 't will seem,
By all who regard the Church, like us,
'T will be thought exceedingly ominous!

As reading in bed I lay last night—
Which (being insured) is my delight—

(1) Among other remarkable attributes by which Sir
Cl—d—s distinguished himself, the dazzling whiteness of
his favourite steed was not the least conspicuous.

(2) In the Government of Perm.

(3) Territory belonging to the mines of Kolivano-Koss-
kressense.

(4) The name of a religious sect in Russia. "Il existe
en Russie plusieurs sectes ; la plus nombreuse est celle

des Roskol-niks, ou vrai-croyants."—*Gamba, Voyage dans
la Russie Méridionale.*

(5) "Heaven first taught letters for some wretch's aid."
　　　　　　　　　　　　　　　　　　　　　Pope.

(6) Written on the passing of the memorable Bill, in the
year 1833, for the abolition of ten Irish Bishoprics.

(7) Literally, First Dancers.

I happen'd to doze off just as I got to
The singular fact which forms my motto.
Only think, thought I, as I dozed away,
Of a party of Churchmen dancing the hay!
Clerks, curates, and rectors, capering all,
With a neat-legg'd Bishop to open the ball!
Scarce had my eyelids time to close,
When the scene I had fancied before me rose—
An Episcopal Hop, on a scale so grand
As my dazzled eyes could hardly stand.
For Britain and Erin clubb'd their Sees
To make it a Dance of Dignities,
And I saw—oh brightest of Church events!
A quadrille of the two Establishments,
Bishop to Bishop *vis-à-vis,*
Footing away prodigiously.

There was Bristol capering up to Derry,
And Cork with London making merry ;
While huge Llandaff, with a See, so so,
Was to dear old Dublin pointing his toe.
There was Chester, hatch'd by woman's smile,
Performing a *chaine des dames* in style ;
While he who, whene'er the Lords' House dozes,
Can waken them up by citing Moses, (1)
The portly Tuam, was all in a hurry
To set, *en avant,* to Canterbury.

Meantime, while pamphlets stuff'd his pockets,
(All out of date, like spent sky-rockets,)
Our Exeter stood forth to caper,
As high on the floor as he doth on paper—
Much like a dapper Dancing Dervise,
Who pirouettes his whole church-service—
Performing, 'midst those reverend souls,
Such *entrechats,* such *cabrioles,*
Such *balonnés,* (2) such—rigmaroles,
Now high, now low, now this, now that,
That none could guess what the devil he'd be at ;
Though, watching his various steps, some thought
That a step in the Church was all he sought.

But alas, alas! while thus so gay,
These reverend dancers frisk'd away,
Nor Paul himself (not the saint, but he
Of the Opera-house) could brisker be,
There gather'd a gloom around their glee—
A shadow, which came and went so fast,
That ere one could say " 'Tis there," 'twas past—
And, lo, when the scene again was clear'd,
Ten of the dancers had disappear'd !
Ten able-bodied quadrillers swept
From the hallow'd floor where late they stept,
While twelve was all that footed it still,
On the Irish side of that grand Quadrille !

Nor this the worst :—still danced they on,
But the pomp was sadden'd, the smile was gone ;
And again, from time to time, the same
Ill-omen'd darkness round them came—
While still, as the light broke out anew,
Their ranks look'd less by a dozen or two ;
Till ah! at last there were only found
Just Bishops enough for a four-hands-round ;
And when I awoke, impatient getting,
I left the last holy pair *poussetting !*

N. B.—As ladies in years, it seems,
Have the happiest knack at solving dreams,
I shall leave to my ancient feminine friends
Of the *Standard* to say what *this* portends.

DICK * * * *

A CHARACTER.

Of various scraps and fragments built,
Borrow'd alike from fools and wits,
Dick's mind was like a patchwork quilt,
Made up of new, old, motley bits—
Where, if the *Co.* call'd in their shares,
If petticoats their quota got,
And gowns were all refunded theirs,
The quilt would look but shy, God wot.

And thus he still, new plagiaries seeking,
Reversed ventriloquism's trick,
For, 'stead of Dick through others speaking,
'Twas others we heard speak through Dick.
A Tory now, all bounds exceeding,
Now best of Whigs, now worst of rats ;
One day, with Malthus, foe to breeding,
The next, with Sadler, all for brats.

Poor Dick!—and how else could it be?
With notions all at random caught,
A sort of mental fricassee,
Made up of legs and wings of thought—
The leavings of the last Debate, or
A dinner, yesterday, of wits,
Where Dick sate by and, like a waiter,
Had the scraps for perquisites.

A CORRECTED REPORT OF SOME LATE SPEECHES.

"Then I heard one saint speaking, and another saint said unto that saint."
1834.

St. S—NCL—R rose and declared in sooth,
That he would n't give sixpence to Maynooth.

---

(1) " And what does Moses say ?" —One of the ejaculations with which this eminent prelate enlivened his famous speech on the Catholic question.
(2) A description of the method of executing this step may be useful to future performers in the same line : —"Ce pas est composé de deux mouvemens differens, savoir, plier, et sauter sur *un* pied, et se rejeter sur *l'autre.*"— Dictionnaire de Danse, art. *Contre-temps.*

He had hated priests the whole of his life,
For a priest was a man who had no wife, (1)
And, having no wife, the Church was his mother,
The Church was his father, sister, and brother.
This being the case, he was sorry to say,
That a gulf 'twixt Papist and Protestant lay, (2)
So deep and wide, scarce possible was it
To say even " how d' ye do?" across it:
And though your Liberals, nimble as fleas,
Could clear such gulfs with perfect ease,
'T was a jump that nought on earth could make
Your proper heavy-built Christian take.
No, no—if a Dance of Sects *must* be,
He would set to the Baptist willingly, (3)
At the Independent deign to smirk,
And rigadoon with old Mother Kirk ;
Nay even, for once, if needs must be,
He 'd take hands round with all the three;
But, as to a jig with Popery, no—
To the Harlot ne'er would he point his toe.

St. M—nd—v—le was the next that rose—
A Saint who round, as pedlar, goes,
With his pack of piety and prose,
Heavy and hot enough, God knows—
And he said that Papists were much inclined
To extirpate all of Protestant kind,
Which he could n't, in truth, so much condemn,
Having rather a wish to extirpate *them;*
That is—to guard against mistake—
To extirpate them for their doctrine's sake;
A distinction Churchmen always make—
Insomuch that, when they 've prime control,
Though sometimes roasting heretics whole,
They but cook the body for sake of the soul.

Next jump'd St. J—hnst—n jollily forth,
The spiritual Dogberry of the North, (4)
A right " wise fellow, and, what 's more,
An officer,"(5) like his type of yore ;
And he ask'd, if we grant such toleration,
Pray, what 's the use of our Reformation ? (6)
What is the use of our Church and State?
Our Bishops, Articles, Tithe, and Rate ?
And, still as he yell'd out " what 's the use ? "
Old Echoes, from their cells recluse,
Where they 'd for centuries slept, broke loose,
Yelling responsive, " *What's the use?*"

(1) " He objected to the maintenance and education of
a clergy *bound by the particular vows of celibacy, which,
as it were, gave them the church as their only family,
making it fill the places of father and mother and bro-
ther.*"—Debate on the Grant to Maynooth College, *The
Times,* April 19.
(2) " It had always appeared to him that *between the Ca-
tholic and Protestant a great gulf* intervened, which ren-
dered it impossible," etc.
(3) " The Baptist might acceptably extend the offices of
religion to the Presbyterian and the Independent, or the

MORAL POSITIONS,

A DREAM.

" His Lordship said that it took a long time for a moral
position to find its way across the Atlantic. He was
very sorry that its voyage had been so long," etc.—
Speech of Lord Dudley and Ward on Colonial Slavery,
March 8.

T'OTHER night, after hearing Lord Dudley's oration
   (A treat that comes once a-year as May-day does)
I dreamt that I saw—what a strange operation !
   A " moral position " shipp'd off for Barbadoes.

The whole Bench of Bishops stood by in grave atti-
      tudes,
   Packing the article tidy and neat—
As their Reverences know, that in southerly latitudes
   " Moral positions " don't keep very sweet.

There was B—th—st arranging the custom-house
      pass ;
   And, to guard the frail package from tousing and
      routing,
There stood my Lord Eld—n, endorsing it " Glass,"
   Though, as to which side should lie uppermost,
      doubting.

The freight was, however, stow'd safe in the hold ;
   The winds were polite, and the moon look'd ro-
      mantic,
While off in the good ship " The Truth " we were
      roll'd,
   With our ethical cargo, across the Atlantic.

Long, dolefully long, seem'd the voyage we made;
   For " The Truth," at all times but a very slow
      sailer,
By friends, near as much as by foes, is delay'd,
   And few come aboard her, though so many hail
      her.

At length, safe arrived, I went through " tare and
      tret,"
   Deliver'd my goods in the primest condition,
And next morning read, in the *Bridgetown Gazette,*
   " Just arrived by ' The Truth,' a new moral po-
      sition.

member of the Church of England to any of the other
three ; but the Catholic," etc.
(4) " Could he then, holding as he did a spiritual office in
the Church of Scotland, (cries of hear, and laughter,) with
any consistency give his consent to a grant of money ?" etc.
(5) " I am a wise fellow, and, which is more, an officer."
Much Ado about Nothing.
(6) " What, he asked, was the use of the Reformation ?
What was the use of the Articles of England, or of the
Church of Scotland ?" etc.

70

"The Captain "—here, startled to find myself named
   As " the Captain "—(a thing which, I own it with
     pain,
I through life have avoided,) I woke—look'd
     ashamed,
Found I *was n't* a captain, and dozed off again.

THE MAD TORY AND THE COMET.

FOUNDED ON A LATE DISTRESSING INCIDENT.

1832-3.

" Mutantem regna cometem."—*Lucan.* (1)

" Though all the pet mischiefs we count upon fail,
   Though cholera, hurricanes, Wellington leave us,
We 've still in reserve, mighty Comet, thy tail ;—
   Last hope of the Tories, wilt thou too deceive us ?

" No—'t is coming, 'tis coming, the avenger is nigh ;
   Heed, heed not, ye placemen, how Herapath
     flatters ;
One whisk from that tail, as it passes us by,
   Will settle, at once, all political matters ;—

" The East-India Question, the Bank, the Five
     Powers,
   (Now turn'd into two) with their rigmarole Pro-
     tocols ; (2)
Ha ! ha! ye gods, how this new friend of ours
   Will knock, right and left, all diplomacy's what-
     d' ye-calls !

" Yes, rather than Whigs at our downfall should
     mock,
   Meet planets, and suns, in one general hustle !
While, happy in vengeance, we welcome the shock
   That shall jerk from their places Grey, Althorp,
     and Russell."

Thus spoke a mad Lord, as, with telescope raised,
   His wild Tory eye on the heavens he set ;
And, though nothing destructive appear'd as he
     gazed,
   Much hoped that there *would*, before Parliament
     met.

And still, as odd shapes seem'd to flit through his glass,
   " Ha ! there it is now," the poor maniac cries ;
While his fancy with forms but too monstrous, alas !
   From his own Tory zodiac, peoples the skies :—

" Now I spy a big body, good heavens, how big !
   Whether Bucky (3) or Taurus I cannot well say ;—
And, yonder, there 's Eld—n's old Chancery-wig,
   In its dusty aphelion fast fading away.

(1) Eclipses and comets have been always looked to as
great changers of administrations. Thus Milton, speaking
of the former :—

      " With fear of change
       Perplexing monarchs."

And in Statius we find,

      " Mutant quæ sceptra cometæ."

" I see, 'mong those fatuous meteors behind,
   L—nd—nd—ry, *in vacuo*, flaring about ;—
While that dim double star, of the nebulous kind,
   Is the Gemini, R—den and L—rt—n, no doubt.

" Ah, El—b'r—h ! 'faith, I first thought 't was the
     Comet ;
So like that in Milton, it made me quite pale ;
The head with the same ' horrid hair' (4) coming
     from it,
   And plenty of vapour, but—where is the tail ?"

Just then, up aloft jump'd the gazer elated—
   For, lo, his bright glass a phenomenon show'd,
Which he took to be C—nb—rl—d, *upwards* trans-
     lated,
   Instead of his natural course, *t' other* road !

But too awful that sight for a spirit so shaken—
   Down dropp'd the poor Tory in fits and grimaces,
Then off to the Bedlam in Charles Street was taken,
   And is now one of Halford's most favourite cases.

FROM THE HON. HENRY ——,

TO LADY EMMA ——.

Paris, March 30, 1832.

You bid me explain, my dear angry Ma'amselle,
How I came thus to bolt without saying farewell ;
And the truth is—as truth you *will* have, my sweet
     railer—
   There are two worthy persons I always feel loath
To take leave of at starting—my mistress and
     tailor—
   As somehow one always has *scenes* with them
     both ;
The Snip in ill-humour, the Syren in tears,
   She calling on Heaven, and he on the attorney—
Till sometimes, in short, 'twixt his duns and his
     dears,
   A young gentleman risks being stopp'd in his
     journey.

But, to come to the point—though you think, I dare
     say,
That 't is debt or the cholera drives me away,
'Pon honour you 're wrong ;—such a mere bagatelle
   As a pestilence, nobody, now-a-days, fears ;
And the fact is, my love, I 'm thus bolting, pell-mell,
   To get out of the way of those horrid new Peers ;(5)
This deluge of coronets, frightful to think of,
   Which England is now, for her sins, on the brink of ;
This coinage of *nobles*—coin'd, all of 'em, badly,
   And sure to bring Counts to a *discount* most sadly,

(2) See, for some of these Protocols, the *Annual Register*,
for the year 1832.

(3) The D—e of B—ck—m.

(4)   " And from his horrid hair
      Shakes pestilence and war."

(5) A new creation of Peers was generally expected at
this time.

Only think, to have Lords overrunning the nation,
As plenty as frogs in a Dutch inundation;
No shelter from Barons, from Earls no protection,
And tadpole young Lords, too, in every direction—
Things created in haste, just to make a Court list of,
Two legs and a coronet all they consist of!
The prospect's quite frightful, and what Sir George
    R—se
(My particular friend) says is perfectly true,
That, so dire the alternative, nobody knows,
    'Twixt the Peers and the Pestilence, what he's to
    do;
And Sir George even doubts—could he choose his
    disorder—
'Twixt coffin and coronet, *which* he would order.
This being the case, why, I thought, my dear Emma,
'T were best to fight shy of so cursed a dilemma;
And though I confess myself somewhat a villain,
To 've left *idol mio* without an *addio,*
Console your sweet heart, and, a week hence, from
    Milan
I'll send you—some news of Bellini's last trio.

N.B.—Have just pack'd up my travelling set-out,
Things a tourist in Italy *can't* go without—
Viz. a pair of *gants gras,* from old Houbigant's shop,
Good for hands that the air of Mont Cenis might chap.
Small presents for ladies—and nothing so wheedles
The creatures abroad as your golden-eyed needles.
A neat pocket Horace, by which folks are cozen'd
To think one knows Latin, when—one, perhaps,
    does n't;
With some little book about heathen mythology,
Just large enough to refresh one's theology;
Nothing on earth being half such a bore as
Not knowing the difference 'twixt Virgins and Floras.
Once more, love, farewell, best regards to the girls,
And mind you beware of damp feet and new Earls.
                   HENRY.

—◦◦◦—

TRIUMPH OF BIGOTRY.

"COLLEGE.—We announced, in our last that Lefroy and
Shaw were returned. They were chaired yesterday;
the students of the College determined, it would seem,
to imitate the mob in all things, harnessing themselves
to the car, and the Masters of Arts bearing Orange flags
and bludgeons before, beside, and behind the car."—
Dublin Evening Post, Dec. 20, 1832.

    AY, yoke ye to the bigot's car,
      Ye chosen of Alma Mater's scions;—
    Fleet chargers drew the God of War,
      Great Cybele was drawn by lions,
    And Sylvan Pan, as Poets dream,
    Drove four young panthers in his team.

(1) See the lives of these two poets for the circumstances
under which they left Dublin College.
(2) In the year 1799, the Board of Trinity College,
Dublin, thought proper, as a mode of expressing their dis-
approbation of Mr. Grattan's public conduct, to order his

Thus classical L—fr—y, for once, is,
    Thus, studious of a like turn-out—
He harnesses young sucking dunces,
    To draw him, as their Chief, about,
And let the world a picture see
Of Dulness yoked to Bigotry;
Showing us how young College hacks
Can pace with bigots at their backs,
As though the cubs were *born* to draw
Such luggage as L.—fr—y and Sh—w.

Oh, shade of Goldsmith, shade of Swift,
    Bright spirits whom in days of yore,
This Queen of Dulness sent adrift,
    As aliens to her foggy shore :—(1)
Shade of our glorious Grattan, too,
    Whose very name her shame recalls;
Whose effigy her bigot crew
Reversed upon their monkish walls—(2)
Bear witness (lest the world should doubt)
    To your mute mother's dull renown,
Then famous but for wit turn'd *out,*
    And Eloquence *turn'd upside down;*
But now ordain'd new wreaths to win,
    Beyond all fame of former days,
By breaking thus young donkies in
    To draw M.P.s, amid the brays
Alike of donkies and M.A.s :—
Defying Oxford to surpass 'em
In this new "Gradus ad Parnassum."

—◦◦◦—

TRANSLATION FROM THE GULL LANGUAGE.

BY DR. BOWRING.

Scripta manet.
                           1533.

'T WAS graved on the Stone of Destiny, (3)
In letters four, and letters three;
And ne'er did the King of the Gulls go by
But those awful letters scared his eye;
For he knew that a Prophet Voice had said,
"As long as those words by man were read,
The ancient race of the Gulls should ne'er
One hour of peace or plenty share."
But years on years successive flew,
And the letters still more legible grew—
At top, a T, an H, an E,
And underneath, D. E. B. T.

Some thought them Hebrew—such as Jews,
More skill'd in Scrip than Scripture, use;
While some surmised 't was an ancient way
Of keeping accounts, (well known in the day
Of the famed Didlerius Jeremias,
Who had thereto a wonderful bias,)

portrait, in the Great Hall of the University, to be turned
upside down, and in this position it remained for some
time.
(3) Liafail, or the Stone of Destiny—for which see West-
minster Abbey

And proved in books most learn'dly boring,
'T was call'd the Pon*tick* way of scoring.

Howe'er this be, there never were yet
Seven letters of the alphabet,
That, 'twixt them, form'd so grim a spell,
Or scared a Land of Gulls so well,
As did this awful riddle-me-ree
Of T. H. E.   D. E. B. T.

 .   .   .   .   .   .

Hark!—it is struggling Freedom's cry;
" Help, help, ye nations, or I die:
'T is Freedom's fight, and, on the field
Where I expire, *your* doom is seal'd.
The Gull-King hears the awakening call,
He hath summon'd his Peers and Patriots all,
And he asks, " Ye noble Gulls, shall we
Stand basely by at the fall of the Free,
Nor utter a curse, nor deal a blow ? "
And they answer, with voice of thunder, " No!"

Out fly their flashing swords in the air!—
But—why do they rest suspended there?
What sudden blight, what baleful charm,
Hath chill'd each eye, and check'd each arm?
Alas ! some withering hand hath thrown
The veil from off that fatal stone,
And pointing now, with sapless finger,
Showeth where dark those letters linger—
Letters four, and letters three,
T. H. E.   D. E. B. T.

At sight thereof each lifted brand
Powerless falls from every hand;
In vain the Patriot knits his brow—
Even talk, his staple, fails him now.
In vain the King like a hero treads,
His Lords of the Treasury shake their heads;
And to all his talk of " brave and free,"
No answer getteth His Majesty
But " T. H. E.   D. E. B. T."

In short, the whole Gull nation feels   .
They 're fairly spell-bound, neck and heels ;
And so, in the face of the laughing world,
Must e'en sit down, with banners furl'd,
Adjourning all their dreams sublime
Of glory and war to—some other time.

———◦⊹◦———

NOTIONS ON REFORM.

BY A MODERN REFORMER.

Of all the misfortunes as yet brought to pass
  By this comet-like Bill, with its long tail of speeches,

(1) It will be recollected that the learned gentleman
himself boasted, one night, in the House of Commons, of
having sat in the very chair which this allegorical lady had
occupied.
(2) Lucan's description of the effects of the tripod on the

The saddest and worst is the schism which, alas!
  It has caused between W—th—r—l's waistcoat
    and breeches.

Some symptoms of this Anti-Union propensity
  Had often broken out in that quarter before;
But the breach, since the Bill, has attain'd such im-
    mensity,
  Daniel himself could have scarce wish'd it more.

Oh ! haste to repair it, ye friends of good order,
  Ye Atw—ds and W—nns, ere the moment is past;
Who can doubt that we tread upon Anarchy's border,
  When the ties that should hold men are loosening
    so fast?

Make W—th—r—l yield to " some sort of Reform"
  (As we all must, God help us! with very wry
    faces);
And loud as he likes let him bluster and storm
  About Corporate Rights, so he 'll only wear braces.
                                                    [session,
Should those he now sports have been long in pos-
  And, like his own borough, the worse for the wear,
Advise him, at least, as a prudent concession
  To Intellect's progress, to buy a new pair.

Oh ! who that e'er saw him, when vocal he stands,
  With a look something midway 'twixt Filch's and
    Lockit's,
While still, to inspire him, his deeply thrust hands
  Keep jingling the rhino in both breeches-pockets—

Who that ever has listen'd, through groan and
    through cough,
  To the speeches inspired by this music of pence—
But must grieve that there 's any thing like *falling off*
  In that great nether source of his wit and his sense ?

Who that knows how he look'd when with grace
    debonair,
  He began first to court—rather late in the season—
Or when, less fastidious, he sat in the chair
  Of his old friend, the Nottingham Goddess of Rea-
    son ; (1)

That Goddess, whose borough-like virtue attracted
  All mongers in *both* wares to proffer their love;
Whose chair like the stool of the Pythoness acted,
  As W—th—r—l's rants ever since go to prove ; (2)

Who, in short, would not grieve, if a man of his graces
  Should go on rejecting, unwarn'd by the past,
The " moderate Reform " of a new pair of braces,
  Till, some day—he 'll all fall to pieces at last.

appearance and voice of the sitter, shows that the symp-
toms are, at least, very similar :—

  Spumea tunc primum rabies vesana per ora
  Effluit. . . . .
     tunc mœstus vastis ululatus in antris.

TORY PLEDGES.

I PLEDGE myself through thick and thin,
To labour still, with zeal devout,
To get the Outs, poor devils, in,
And turn the Ins, the wretches, out.

I pledge myself, though much bereft
Of ways and means of ruling ill,
To make the most of what are left,
And stick to all that 's rotten still.

Though gone the days of place and pelf,
And drones no more take all the honey,
I pledge myself to cram myself
With all I can of public money.

To quarter on that social purse
My nephews, nieces, sisters, brothers,
Nor, so *we* prosper, care a curse
How much 't is at the expense of others.

I pledge myself, whenever Right
And Might on any point divide,
Not to ask which is black or white,
But take, at once, the strongest side.

For instance, in all Tithe discussions,
I 'm *for* the Reverend encroachers :—
I loathe the Poles, applaud the Russians—
Am *for* the Squires, *against* the Poachers.

Betwixt the Corn-Lords and the Poor
I 've not the slightest hesitation—
The People *must* be starved, t' insure
The Land its due remuneration.

I pledge myself to be no more
With Ireland's wrongs beprosed or shamm'd—
I vote her grievances a *bore*,
So she may suffer and be d—d !

Or if she kick, let it console us,
We still have plenty of red coats
To cram the Church, that general bolus,
Down any given amount of throats.

I dearly love the Frankfort Diet—
Think newspapers the worst of crimes ;
And would, to give some chance of quiet,
Hang all the writers of The Times ;

Break all their correspondents' bones,
All-authors of "Reply," "Rejoinder,"
From the Anti-Tory, Colonel J—es,
To the Anti-Suttee, Mr. P—ynd—r.

Such are the Pledges I propose ;
And though I can't now offer gold,
There 's many a way of buying those
Who 've but the taste for being sold.

So here 's, with three times three hurrahs,
A toast, of which you 'll not complain—
"Long life to jobbing ; may the days
Of Peculation shine again !"

———

ST. JEROME ON EARTH.

FIRST VISIT.

1832.

As St. Jerome, who died some ages ago,
Was sitting, one day, in the shades below,
"I 've heard much of English bishops," quoth he,
"And shall now take a trip to earth, to see
How far they agree, in their lives and ways,
With our good old bishops of ancient days."

He had learn'd—but learn'd without misgivings—
Their love for good living, and eke good livings ;
Not knowing (as ne'er having taken degrees)
That good *living* means claret and fricassees,
While its plural means simply—pluralities.
"From all I hear," said the innocent man,
"They are quite on the good old primitive plan.
For wealth and pomp they little can care,
As they all say ' *No* ' to the Episcopal chair ;
And their vestal virtue it well denotes
That they all, good men, wear petticoats."

Thus saying, post-haste to earth he hurries,
And knocks at the Archbishop of Canterbury's.
The door was oped by a lackey in lace,
Saying, "What 's your business with his Grace ?"
"His Grace !" quoth Jerome—for posed was he,
Not knowing what *sort* this Grace could be ;
Whether Grace *preventing,* Grace *particular,*
Grace of that breed called *Quinquarticular—*(1)
In short, he rummaged his holy mind,
The exact description of Grace to find,
Which thus could represented be
By a footman in full livery.
At last, out loud in a laugh he broke,
(For dearly the good saint loved his joke) (2)
And said—surveying, as sly he spoke,
The costly palace from roof to base—
"Well, it is n't, at least, a *saving* Grace !"
"Umph !" said the lackey, a man of few words,
"The Archbishop is gone to the House of Lords."
"To the house of the Lord, you mean, my son,
For, in *my* time, at least, there was but one ;
Unless such many-*fold* priests as these
Seek, even in their Lord, pluralities !"(3)
"No time for gab," quoth the man in lace :
Then, slamming the door in St. Jerome's face,

---

(1) So called from the proceedings of the Synod of Dort.
(2) Witness his well-known pun on the name of Vigilantius, whom he calls facetiously Dormitantius.

(3) The suspicion attached to some of the early Fathers of being Arians in their doctrine would appear to derive some confirmation from this passage.

With a curse to the single knockers all,
Went to finish his port in the servants' hall,
And propose a toast (humanely meant
To include even curates in its extent)
"To all as serves the Establishment!"

—◦◦◦—

ST. JEROME ON EARTH.

SECOND VISIT.

"This much I dare say, that, since *lording* and loitering
hath come up, preaching hath come down, contrary to
the Apostles' times. For they preached and *lorded*
not : and now they *lord* and preach not. . . . . . Ever
since the Prelates were made Lords and Nobles, the
plough standeth; there is no work done, the people
starve."—*Latimer, Sermon of the Plough.*

"ONCE more," said Jerome, "I 'll run up and see
How the Church goes on "—and off set he.
Just then the packet-boat, which trades
Betwixt our planet and the shades,
Had arrived below, with a freight so queer,
"My eyes!" said Jerome, "what have we here?"—
For he saw, when nearer he explored,
They 'd a cargo of Bishops' wigs aboard.
"They are ghosts of wigs," said Charon, "all,
Once worn by nobs Episcopal. (1)
For folks on earth, who 've got a store
Of cast-off things they 'll want no more,
Oft send them down, as gifts, you know,
To a certain Gentleman here below.

"A sign of the times, I plainly see,"
Said the Saint to himself as, pondering, he
Sail'd off in the death-boat gallantly.

Arrived on earth, quoth he, "No more
I 'll affect a body, as before;
For I think I 'd best, in the company
Of spiritual Lords, a spirit be,
And glide, unseen, from See to See."
But oh! to tell what scenes he saw—
It was more than Rabelais' pen could draw.
For instance, he found Ex—t—r,
Soul, body, inkstand, all in a stir—
For love of God? for sake of King?
For good of people?—no such thing;
But to get for himself, by some new trick,
A shove to a better bishoprick.

He found that pious soul, Van M—ld—t,
Much with his money-bags bewilder'd ;
Snubbing the Clerks of the Diocess, (2)
Because the rogues showed restlessness
At having too little cash to touch,
While he so Christianly bears too much.

---

(1) The wig, so long an essential part of the dress of an
English bishop, was now being dispensed with.
(2) See the Bishop's Letter to Clergy of his Diocese.
(3) 1 John, v. 7. A text which, though long given up
by all the rest of the orthodox world, is still pertinaciously
adhered to by this Right Reverend scholar.

He found old Sarum's wits as gone
As his own beloved text in John—(3)
Text he hath prosed so long upon,
That 't is thought when ask'd, at the gate of heaven,
His name, he 'll answer "John, v. 7."

"But enough of Bishops I 've had to-day,"
Said the weary Saint—"I must away.
Though I own I should like, before I go,
To see for once (as I 'm ask'd below
If really such odd sights exist)
A regular six-fold Pluralist."
Just then he heard a general cry—
"There 's Doctor Hodgson galloping by!"
"Ay, that 's the man," says the Saint, "to follow,"
And off he sets, with a loud view-hollo,
At Hodgson's heels, to catch, if he can,
A glimpse of this singular plural man.
But—talk of Sir Boyle Roche 's bird! (4)
To compare him with Hodgson is absurd.
"Which way, sir, pray, is the doctor gone?"—
"He is now at his living at Hillingdon."
"No, no—you 're out, by many a mile,
He 's away at his Deanery, in Carlisle."—
"Pardon me, sir ; but I understand
He 's gone to his living in Cumberland."—
"God bless me, no—he can't be there ;
You must try St. George's, Hanover Square."

Thus all in vain the Saint inquired,
From living to living, mock'd and tired ;—
'T was Hodgson here, 't was Hodgson there,
'T was Hodgson nowhere, everywhere ;
Till, fairly beat, the Saint gave o'er,
And flitted away to the Stygian shore,
To astonish the natives under ground
With the comical things he on earth had found.

—◦◦◦—

THOUGHTS ON TAR-BARRELS.

(VIDE DESCRIPTION OF A LATE FÊTE.) (5)

1832.

WHAT a pleasing contrivance! how aptly devised
'Twixt tar and magnolias to puzzle one's noses!
And how the tar-barrels must all be surprised
To find themselves seated like "Love among
[roses !"
What a pity we can't, by precautions like these,
Clear the air of that other still viler infection;
That radical pest, that old whiggish disease,
Of which cases, true-blue, are in every direction.

Stead of barrels, let 's light up an Auto da Fé
Of a few good combustible Lords of "the Club,"

---

(4) It was a saying of the well-known Sir Boyle, that "a
man could not be in two places at once, unless he was a
bird."
(5) The M—s of H—tf—d's Fête. — From dread of
cholera his Lordship had ordered tar-barrels to be burned
in every direction.

They would fume, in a trice, the Whig cholera away,
And there's B—cky would burn like a barrel of
bub.

How R—d—n would blaze! and what rubbish throw
out!
A volcano of nonsense, in active display;
While V—ne, as a butt, amidst laughter, would spout
The hot nothings he's full of, all night and all day.

And then, for a finish, there's C—mb—d's Duke—
Good Lord, how his chin-tuft would crackle in air!
Unless (as is shrewdly surmised from his look)
He's already bespoke for combustion elsewhere.

—◦◦◦◦—

THE CONSULTATION. (1)

"When they *do* agree, their unanimity is wonderful."—
The Critic.
1833.

*Scene discovers Dr. Whig and Dr. Tory in consultation.
Patient on the floor between them.*

Dr. Whig.—This wild Irish patient *does* pester me
so,
That what to do with him, I'm curst if I know.
I've *promised* him anodynes ——
Dr. Tory.   Anodynes!—Stuff.
Tie him down—gag him well—he'll be tranquil
enough.
That's *my* mode of practice.
Dr. Whig.   True, quite in *your* line,
But unluckily not much, till lately, in *mine.*
'Tis so painful ——
Dr. Tory.—Pooh, nonsense—ask Ude how he
feels,
When, for Epicure feasts, he prepares his live eels,
By flinging them in, 'twixt the bars of the fire,
And letting them wriggle on there till they tire.
He, too, says "'tis painful"—"quite makes his
heart bleed"—
But "your eels are a vile oleaginous breed."—
He would fain use them gently, but Cookery says
"No,"
And—in short—eels were *born* to be treated just
so. (2)
'Tis the same with these Irish—who're odder fish
still—
Your tender Whig heart shrinks from using them ill;
I, myself, in my youth, ere I came to get wise,
Used, at some operations, to blush to the eyes;—
But, in fact, my dear brother—if I may make bold
To style you, as Peachum did Lockit, of old—

(1) These verses, as well as some others, that follow,
("Paddy's Metamorphosis,") were extorted from me by
that lamentable measure of the Whig ministry, the Irish
Coercion Act.
(2) This eminent artist, in the second edition of the work
wherein e propounds this mode of purifying his eels,
professes himself much concerned at the charge of inhu-
manity brought against his practice; but still begs leave

We, Doctors, *must* act with the firmness of Ude,
And, indifferent like him—so the fish is *but* stew'd—
Must torture live Pats for the general good.
            [*Here patient groans and kicks a little.*
Dr. Whig.—But what, if one's patient's so devil-
ish perverse,
That he *wo'n't* be thus tortured?
Dr. Tory   Coerce, sir, coerce.
You're a juvenile performer, but once you begin,
You can't think how fast you may train your hand
in :
And *(smiling)* who knows but old Tory may take to
the shelf,
With the comforting thought that, in place and in
pelf,
He's succeeded by one just as—bad as himself?
Dr. Whig (looking flattered).—Why, to tell you
the truth, I've a small matter here,
Which you help'd me to make for my patient last
year—
            [*Goes to a cupboard and brings out a
            strait-waistcoat and gag.*
And such rest I've enjoy'd from his raving, since
then,
That I've made up my mind he shall wear it again.
Dr. Tory (embracing him).—Oh, charming!—
My dear Doctor Whig, you're a treasure.
Next to torturing, *myself,* to help *you* is a pleasure.
            [*Assisting Dr. Whig.*
Give me leave—I've some practice in these mad
machines ;
There—tighter—the gag in the mouth, by all means.
Delightful!—all's snug—not a squeak need you
fear—
You may now put your anodynes off till next year.
            [*Scene closes.*

—◦◦◦◦—

TO THE REV. CH—RL—S OV—RT—N,
CURATE OF ROMALDKIRK,
AUTHOR OF THE POETICAL PORTRAITURE OF THE
CHURCH. (3)
1833.

SWEET singer of Romaldkirk, thou who art reckon'd,
By critics Episcopal, David the Second, (4)
If thus, as a Curate, so lofty your flight,
Only think, in a Rectory, how you *would* write!
Once fairly inspired by the "Tithe-crown'd Apollo,"
(Who beats, I confess it, our *lay* Phœbus hollow,
Having gotten, besides the old *Nine's* inspiration,
The *Tenth* of all eatable things in creation,)
There's nothing, in fact, that a poet like you,
So be-*nined* and be-*tenth'd,* could n't easily do.

respectfully to repeat that it *is* the only proper mode of
preparing eels for the table.
(3) See *Edinburgh Review,* No. 117.
(4) "Your Lordship," says Mr. Ov—rt—n, in the Dedi-
cation of his Poem to the Bishop of Chester, "has kindly
expressed your persuasion that my 'Muse will always be
a Muse of sacred song, and that it *will be tuned as David's*
was.' "

Round the lips of the sweet-tongued Athenian (1)
they say,
While yet but a babe in his cradle he lay,
Wild honey-bees swarm'd, as a presage to tell [fell.
Of the sweet-flowing words that thence afterwards
Just so round our Ov—rt—n's cradle, no doubt,
Tenth' ducklings and chicks were seen flitting about;
Goose embryos, waiting their doom'd decimation,
Came, shadowing forth his adult destination,
And small sucking tithe-pigs, in musical droves,
Announced the Church poet whom Chester approves.

O Horace! when thou, in thy vision of yore,
Didst dream that a snowy-white plumage came o'er
Thy etherealised limbs, stealing downily on,
Till, by Fancy's strong spell, thou wert turn'd to a
swan, (2)
Little thought'st thou such fate could a poet befall,
Without any effort of fancy, at all ;   [find
Little thought'st thou the world would in Ov—rt—n
A bird, ready-made, somewhat different in kind,
But as perfect as Michaelmas' self could produce,
By gods yclept *anser*, by mortals a *goose !*

—◦◆◦—

SCENE

FROM A PLAY, ACTED AT OXFORD, CALLED "MATRICULATION." (3)

1834.

[Boy discovered at a table, with the Thirty-Nine Articles
before him.—Enter the Rt. Rev. Doctor Ph—llp—ts.]

Doctor. P.—There, my lad, lie the Articles—*(Boy
begins to count them)* just thirty-nine—
No occasion to count—you 've now only to sign.
At Cambridge, where folks are less High-Church
than we,
The whole Nine-and-Thirty are lump'd into Three.
Let 's run o'er the items ;—there 's Justification,
Predestination, and Supererogation—
Not forgetting Salvation and Creed Athanasian,
Till we reach, at last, Queen Bess's Ratification.
That 's sufficient—now, sign—having read quite
enough,
You " believe in the full and true meaning thereof ?"
                        (Boy stares.)
Oh, a mere form of words, to make things smooth
and brief—
A commodious and short make-believe of belief,
Which our Church has drawn up, in a form thus
articular,
To keep out, in general, all who 're particular.
But what 's the boy doing ? what ! reading all through,
And my luncheon fast cooling !—this never will do.

(1. Sophocles.
(2)   ——album mutor in alitem
    Superne : nascunturque læves
    Per digitos, humerosque plumæ.
(3) " It appears that when a youth of fifteen goes to be
matriculated at Oxford, and is required first to subscribe

Boy (poring over the Articles).—Here are points
which—pray, Doctor, what 's " Grace of Con-
gruity ?"
Doctor P. (sharply).—You 'll find out, young sir,
when you 've more ingenuity.
At present, by signing, you pledge yourself merely,
Whate'er it may be, to believe it sincerely.
Both in *dining* and *signing* we take the same plan—
First, swallow all down, then digest—as we can.
Boy (still reading).—I 've to gulp, I see, St. Atha-
nasius's Creed,
Which, I 'm told, is a very tough morsel, indeed ;
As he damns ——
Doctor P. (aside).—Ay, and so would *I,* willingly,
too,
All confounded particular young boobies, like you.
This comes of Reforming !—all 's o'er with our land,
When people wo'n't stand what they can't *under-
stand ;*
Nor perceive that our ever-revered Thirty-Nine
Were made, not for men to *believe,* but to *sign.*
                  [Exit Dr. P. in a passion.

—◦◆◦—

LATE TITHE CASE.

"Sic vos non vobis."

1833.

" The Vicar of B—mh—m desires me to state that, in
consequence of the passing of a recent Act of Parliament
he is compelled to adopt measures which may by some be
considered harsh or precipitate ; but, *in duty to what he
owes to his successors,* he feels bound to preserve the
rights of the vicarage."—*Letter from Mr. S. Powell,*
August 6.

No, *not* for yourselves, ye reverend men,
Do you take one pig in every ten,
But for Holy Church's future heirs,
Who 've an abstract right to that pig as theirs ;—
The law supposing that such heirs male—
Are already seized of the pig, in tail.
No, *not* for himself hath B—mh—m's priest
His " well-beloved " of their pennies fleeced :
But it is that, before his prescient eyes,
All future Vicars of B—mh—m rise,
With their embryo daughters, nephews, nieces,
And 't is for *them* the poor he fleeces.
He heareth their voices, ages hence,
Saying "Take the pig "—" oh take the pence ;"
The cries of little Vicarial dears,
The unborn B—mh—mites, reach his ears ;
And, did he resist that soft appeal,
He would *not* like a true-born Vicar feel.

Thou, too, L—ndy of L —ck—ngt—n !
A Rector true, if e'er there was one,

Thirty-Nine Articles of Religious Belief, this only means
that he engages himself afterwards to understand what
is now above his comprehension ; that he expresses no
assent at all to what he signs ; and that he is (or, *ought to
be)* at full liberty, when he has studied the subject, to with-
draw his provisional assent."—*Edinburgh Review,* No. 120.

Who, for sake of the L—ndies of coming ages,
Gripest the tenths of labourers' wages. (1)
'T is true, in the pockets of *thy* small-clothes
The claim'd "obvention" (2) of four-pence goes;
But its abstract spirit, unconfined,
Spreads to all future Rector-kind,
Warning them all to their rights to wake,
And rather to face the block, the stake,
Than give up their darling right to *take*.

One grain of musk, it is said, perfumes
(So subtle its spirit) a thousand rooms,
And a single four-pence, pocketed well,
Through a thousand rectors' lives will tell.
Then still continue, ye reverend souls,
And still as your rich Pactolus rolls,
Grasp every penny on every side,
From every wretch, to swell its tide:
Remembering still what the Law lays down,
In that pure poetic style of its own,
"If the parson *in esse* submits to loss, he
Inflicts the same on the parson *in posse*."

—◦◦◦—

FOOLS' PARADISE.

DREAM THE FIRST.

I HAVE been, like Puck, I have been in a trice,
To a realm they call Fools' Paradise,
Lying N. N. E. of the Land of Sense,
And seldom bless'd with a glimmer thence.
But they want it not in this happy place,
Where a light of its own gilds every face;
Or, if some wear a shadowy brow,
'T is the *wish* to look wise—not knowing *how*.
Self-glory glistens o'er all that's there,
The trees, the flowers have a jaunty air;
The well-bred wind in a whisper blows,
The snow, if it snows, is *couleur de rose*,
The falling founts in a titter fall,
And the sun looks simpering down on all.

Oh, 't is n't in tongue or pen to trace
The scenes I saw in that joyous place.
There were Lords and Ladies sitting together,
In converse sweet, "What charming weather!—
You'll all rejoice to hear, I'm sure,
Lord Charles has got a good sinecure;
And the Premier says, my youngest brother
(Him in the Guards) shall have another.
Is n't this very, *very* gallant!—
As for my poor old virgin aunt,
Who has lost her all, poor thing, at whist,
We must quarter *her* on the Pension List."
Thus smoothly time in that Eden roll'd;
It seem'd like an Age of *real* gold,
Where all who liked might have a slice,
So rich was that Fools' Paradise.

But the sport at which most time they spent
Was a puppet-show, call'd Parliament,
Perform'd by wooden Ciceros,
As large as life, who rose to prose,
While, hid behind them, lords and squires,
Who own'd the puppets, pull'd the wires;
And thought it the very best device
Of that most prosperous Paradise,
To make the vulgar pay through the nose
For them and their wooden Ciceros.

And many more such things I saw
In this Eden of Church, and State, and Law;
Nor e'er were known such pleasant folk
As those who had the *best* of the joke.
There were Irish Rectors, such as resort
To Cheltenham yearly to drink—port,
And bumper, "Long may the Church endure,
May her cure of souls be a sinecure,
And a score of Parsons to every soul
A moderate allowance on the whole."
There were Heads of Colleges, lying about,
From which the sense had all run out,
Even to the lowest classic lees,
Till nothing was left but *quantities;*
Which made them heads most fit to be
Stuck up on a University,
Which yearly hatches, in its schools,
Such flights of young Elysian fools.

Thus all went on, so snug and nice,
In this happiest possible Paradise.
But plain it was to see, alas!
That a downfall soon must come to pass.
For grief is a lot the good and wise
Do n't quite so much monopolise,
But that ("lapt in Elysium" as they are)
Even blessed fools must have their share.
And so it happen'd:—but what befell,
In Dream the Second I mean to tell.

—◦◦◦—

THE RECTOR AND HIS CURATE;

OR, ONE POUND TWO.

"I trust we shall part. as we met, in peace and charity.
My last payment to you paid your salary up to the 1st
of this month. Since that, I owe you for one month,
which, being a long month, of thirty-one days, amounts,
as near as I can calculate, to six pounds eight shillings.
My steward returns you as a debtor to the amount of
seven pounds ten shillings for con-acre ground, which
leaves some trifling balance in my favour."—*Letter of
Dismissal from the Rev. Marcus Beresford to his Curate,
the Rev. T. A. Lyons.*

THE account is balanced—the bill drawn out—
The debit and credit all right, no doubt—

<hr/>

(1) Fourteen agricultural labourers (one of whom received six guineas for yearly wages, one eight, one nine, another ten guineas, and the best paid of the whole 18*l.* annually) were, in the autumn of 1832, served with demands

of tithe at the rate of 4*d.* in the 1*l.*, on behalf of the Rev. F. L—dy, Rector of ——, etc. — *Times*, August, 1833.

(2) One of the various general terms under which oblations, tithes, etc., are comprised.

The Rector rolling in wealth and state,
Owes to his Curate six pound eight;
The Curate, that *least* well-fed of men,
Owes to his Rector seven pound ten,
Which maketh the balance clearly due,
From Curate to Rector, one pound two.

Ah balance, on earth unfair, uneven!
But sure to be all set right in heaven,
Where bills like these will be check'd, some day,
And the balance settled the other way:
Where Lyons the curate's hard-wrung sum
Will back to his shade with interest come;
And Marcus, the rector, deep may rue
This tot, in his favour, of one pound two.

—◦••◦—

PADDY'S METAMORPHOSIS.(1)
1833.

ABOUT fifty years since, in the days of our daddies,
  That plan was commenced which the wise now
    applaud,
Of shipping off Ireland's most turbulent Paddies,
  As good raw material for *settlers*, abroad.

Some West-India island, whose name I forget,
  Was the region then chosen for this scheme so
    romantic;
And such the success the first colony met,
  That a second, soon after, set sail o'er the Atlantic.

Behold them now safe at the long-look'd for shore,
  Sailing in between banks that the Shannon might
    greet,
And thinking of friends whom, but two years before,
  They had sorrow'd to lose, but would soon again
    [meet.

And, hark! from the shore a glad welcome there
    came—   [boy?"
  "Arrah, Paddy from Cork, is it you, my sweet
While Pat stood astounded, to hear his own name
  Thus hail'd by black devils, who caper'd for joy!

Can it possibly be?—half amazement—half doubt,
  Pat listens again—rubs his eyes and looks steady;
Then heaves a deep sigh, and in horror yells out,
  "Good Lord! only think—black and curly al-
    [ready!"
Deceived by that well-mimick'd brogue in his ears,
  Pat read his own doom in these wool-headed figures,
And thought, what a climate, in less than two years,
  To turn a whole cargo of Pats into niggers!

MORAL.

'T is thus—but alas! by a ·arvel more true
  Than is told in this rival of Ovid's best stories—
Your Whigs, when in office a short year or two,
  By a *lusus naturæ*, all turn into Tories.

And thus, when I hear them "strong measures" ad-
    vise,   [steady,
  Ere the seats that they sit on have time to get

I say, while I listen, with tears in my eyes,
  "Good Lord! only think—black and curly al-
    ready!"

—◦••◦—

COCKER, ON CHURCH REFORM.
FOUNDED UPON SOME LATE CALCULATIONS.
1833.

FINE figures of speech let your orators follow,
Old Cocker has figures that beat them all hollow.
Though famed for his rules Aristotle may be,
In but *half* of this Sage any merit I see,
For, as honest Joe Hume says, the "*tottle*" (2) for me!

For instance, while others discuss and debate,
It is thus about Bishops *I* ratiocinate.

In England, where, spite of the infidel's 'aughter,
'T is certain our souls are look'd *very* well after,
Two Bishops can well (if judiciously sunder'd)
Of parishes manage two thousand two hundred—
Said number of parishes, under said teachers,
Containing three millions of Protestant creatures—
So that each of said Bishops full ably controls
One million and five hundred thousands of souls.
And now comes old Cocker. In Ireland we 're told,
Half a million includes the whole Protestant fold;
If, therefore, for *three* million souls, 't is conceded
Two proper-sized Bishops are all that is needed,
'T is plain, for the Irish *half* million who want 'em,
One third of *one* Bishop is just the right quantum.
And thus, by old Cocker's sublime Rule of Three,
The Irish Church question 's resolved to a T;
Keeping always that excellent maxim in view,
That, in saving men's souls, we must save money too.

Nay, if—as St. Roden complains is the case—
The half million of *soul* is decreasing apace,
The demand, too, for *bishop* will also fall off,
Till the *tithe* of one, taken in kind, be enough.
But, as fractions imply that we 'd have to dissect,
And to cutting up Bishops I strongly object, [spare,
We 've a small fractious prelate whom well we could
Who has just the same decimal worth, to a hair;
And, not to leave Ireland too much in the lurch,
We 'll let her have Ex—t—r, *sole*,(3) as her Church.

—◦••◦—

LES HOMMES AUTOMATES.
1834.

"We are persuaded that this our artificial man will not
only walk and speak, and perform most of the outward
functions of animal life, but (being wound up once a-
week) will perhaps reason as well as most of your
country parsons." — *Memoirs of Martinus Scriblerus*,
chap. xii.

IT being an object now to meet
With Parsons that do n't want to eat,

(1) I have already referred to this squib, as being one
of those wrung from me by the Irish Coercion Act of my
friends, the Whigs.
(2) The *total*—so pronounced by this industrious senator.
(3) Corporation sole.

Fit men to fill those Irish rectories,
Which soon will have but scant refectories,
It has been suggested—lest that Church
Should, all at once, be left in the lurch,
For want of reverend men endued
With this gift of ne'er requiring food—
To try, by way of experiment, whether
There could n't be made, of wood and leather, (1)
(Howe'er the notion may sound chimerical,)
Jointed figures, not *lay*, (2) but clerical,
Which, wound up carefully once a-week,
Might just like parsons look and speak,
Nay even, if requisite, reason too,
As well as most Irish parsons do.

The experiment having succeeded quite,
(Whereat those Lords must much delight,
Who 've shown, by stopping the Church's food,
They think it is n't for her spiritual good
To be served by parsons of flesh and blood,)
The Patentees of this new invention
Beg leave respectfully to mention,
They now are enabled to produce
An ample supply, for present use,
Of these reverend pieces of machinery,
Ready for vicarage, rectory, deanery,
Or any such-like post of skill
That wood and leather are fit to fill.

N.B.—In places addicted to arson,
We can't recommend a wooden parson:
But, if the Church any such appoints,
They 'd better, at least, have iron joints.
In parts, not much by Protestants haunted,
A figure to *look at* 's all that 's wanted—
A block in black, to eat and sleep,
Which (now that the eating 's o'er) comes cheap.

P.S.—Should the Lords, by way of a treat,
Permit the clergy again to eat,
The Church will, of course, no longer need
Imitation-parsons that never feed;
And these *wood* creatures of ours will sell
For secular purposes just as well—
Our Beresfords, turn'd to bludgeons stout,
May, 'stead of beating their own about,
Be knocking the brains of Papists out;
While our smooth O'Sullivans, by all means,
Should transmigrate into *turning* machines.

—→ ❦ ◦—

HOW TO MAKE ONE'S SELF A PEER.
ACCORDING TO THE NEWEST RECEIPT, AS DISCLOSED
IN A LATE HERALDIC WORK. (3)
1834.

Choose some title that 's dormant—the Peerage hath
Lord Baron of Shamdos sounds nobly as any. [many

(1) The materials of which those Nuremberg Savans
mentioned by Scriblerus, constructed their artificial man.
(2) The wooden models used by painters are, it is well
known, called "lay figures."

Next, catch a dead cousin of said defunct Peer,
And marry him, off hand, in some given year,
To the daughter of somebody—no matter who—
Fig, the grocer himself, if you 're hard run, will do;
For, the Medici *pills* still in heraldry tell,
And why should n't *lollypops* quarter as well?
Thus, having your couple, and one a lord's cousin,
Young materials for peers may be had by the dozen;
And 't is hard if, inventing each small mother's son
                of 'em.   [of 'em.
You can't somehow manage to prove *yourself* one
Should registers, deeds, and such matters refractory,
Stand in the way of this lord-manufactory,
I 've merely to hint, as a secret auricular,
One *grand* rule of enterprise—*do n't* be particular.
A man who once takes such a jump at nobility
Must *not* mince the matter, like folks of nibility, (4)
But clear thick and thin with true lordly agility.

'T is true, to a would-be descendant from Kings,
Parish-registers sometimes are troublesome things;
As oft, when the vision is near brought about,
Some goblin, in shape of a grocer, grins out;
Or some barber, perhaps, with my Lord mingles
                bloods,
And one's patent of peerage is left in the suds.

But there *are* ways—when folks are resolved to be
                Lords—
Of expurging even troublesome parish records.
What think ye of scissors? depend on 't no heir
Of a Shamdos should go unsupplied with a pair,
As, whate'er *else* the learn'd in such lore may invent,
Your scissors does wonders in proving descent.
Yes, poets may sing of those terrible shears   [peers,
With which Atropos snips off both bumpkins and
But they 're nought to that weapon which shines in
                the hands
Of some would-be Patrician, when proudly he stands
O'er the careless churchwarden's baptismal array,
And sweeps at each cut generations away.
By some babe of old times is his peerage resisted?
One snip—and the urchin hath *never* existed!
Does some marriage, in days near the Flood, interfere
With his one sublime object of being a Peer?
Quick the shears at once nullify bridegroom and
        bride—
No such people have ever lived, married, or died!

Such the newest receipt for those high-minded elves,
Who 're a fancy for making great lords of themselves.
Follow this, young aspirer, who pant'st for a peerage,
Take S—m for thy model and B—z for thy steerage,
Do all and much worse than old Nicholas Flam does,
And—*who* knows but you 'll be Lord Baron of
        Shamdos?

(3) The claim to the barony of Chandos (if I recollect
right) advanced by the late Sir Eg—r—t—n Br—d—s.
(4) "This we call pure nihility, or mere nothing."—
Watts's Logic.

THE DUKE IS THE LAD.

AIR—"A master I have, and I am his man,
Galloping dreary dun."

Castle of Andalusia.

THE Duke is the lad to frighten a lass,
  Galloping dreary duke;
The Duke is the lad to frighten a lass,
  He's an ogre to meet, and the d—l to pass,
    With his charger prancing,
    Grim eye glancing,
    Chin, like a Mufti,
    Grizzled and tufty,
  Galloping dreary Duke.

Ye misses, beware of the neighbourhood
  Of this galloping dreary Duke;
Avoid him, all who see no good
In being run o'er by a Prince of the Blood.
    For, surely, no nymph is
    Fond of a grim phiz,
    And of the married,
    Whole crowds have miscarried
  At sight of this dreary Duke.

—————

EPISTLE

FROM ERASMUS ON EARTH TO CICERO IN THE SHADES.

Southampton.

As 't is now, my dear Tully, some weeks since I started
By rail-road, for earth, having vow'd, ere we parted,
To drop you a line, by the Dead-Letter post,
Just to say how I thrive, in my new line of ghost,
And how deucedly odd this live world all appears,
To a man who's been dead now for three hundred
    years,
I take up my pen, and, with news of this earth,
Hope to waken, by turns, both your spleen and your
    mirth.

In my way to these shores, taking Italy first,
Lest the change from Elysium too sudden should
    burst,
I forgot not to visit those haunts where, of yore,
You took lessons from Pætus in cookery's lore, (1)
Turn'd aside from the calls of the rostrum and Muse,
To discuss the rich merits of *rôtis* and stews,
And preferr'd to all honours of triumph or trophy,
A supper on prawns with that rogue, little Sophy. (2)

Having dwelt on such classical musings awhile,
I set off, by a steam-boat, for this happy isle,
(A conveyance *you* ne'er, I think, sail'd by, my Tully,
And therefore, *per* next, I'll describe it more fully,)
Having heard, on the way, what distresses me greatly,
That England's o'er-run by *idolaters* lately,

(1) See his Letters to Friends, lib. ix., epist. 19, 20, etc.
(2) Ingentium squillarum cum Sophia Septimæ.—Lib.ix.,
epist. 10.
(3) Tithes were paid to the Pythian Apollo.
(4) See Dr. Wiseman's able letter to Mr. Poynder.

Stark staring adorers of wood and of stone,
Who will let neither stick, stock, or statue alone.
Such the sad news I heard from a tall man in black,
Who from sports continental was hurrying back,
To look after his tithes ;—seeing, doubtless, 't would
    follow,
That, just as, of old, your great idol, Apollo,
Devour'd all the Tenths, (3) so the idols in question,
These wood and stone gods, may have equal digestion,
And the idolatrous crew, whom this Rector despises,
May eat up the tithe-pig which *he* idolises.

London.

'T is all but too true—grim Idolatry reigns,
In full pomp, over England's lost cities and plains!
On arriving just now, as my first thought and care
Was, as usual, to seek out some near House of Prayer,
Some calm holy spot, fit for Christians to 'pray on,
I was shown to—what think you?—a downright
    Pantheon!
A grand pillar'd temple, with niches and halls, (4)
Full of idols and gods, which they nickname St.
    Paul's ;—
Though 't is clearly the place where the Idolatrous
    crew,
Whom the Rector complain'd of, their dark rites
    pursue;
And, 'mong all the "strange gods" Abraham's father
    carved out, (5)
That he ever carved *stranger* than these I much doubt.

Were it even, my dear Tully, your Hebes and
    Graces,
And such pretty things, that usurp'd the Saints' places,
I shouldn't much mind—for, in this classic dome,
Such folks from Olympus would feel quite at home.
But the gods they've got here!—such a queer om-
    nium gatherum
Of misbegot things, that no poet would father 'em ;—
Britannias, in light summer-wear for the skies—
Old Thames, turn'd to stone, to his no small surprise—
Father Nile, too—a portrait, (in spite of what's said,
That no mortal e'er yet got a glimpse of his *head*,)(6)
And a Ganges, which India would think somewhat
    fat for 't,
Unless 't was some full-grown Director had sat for 't ;—
Not to mention the *et cæteras* of Genii and Sphinxes,
Fame, Victory, and other such semi-clad minxes ;—
Sea Captains (7)—the idols here most idolised ;
And of whom some, alas, might too well be comprised
Among ready-made Saints, as they died *cannon-*
    ized ;—
With a multitude more of odd cockneyfied deities,
Shrined in such pomp that quite shocking to see it
    'tis ;

(5) Joshua, xxiv., 2.
(6)   ——"Nec contigit ulli
        Hoc vidisse caput."—*Claudian.*
(7) Captains Mosse, Riou, etc., etc.

Nor know I what better the Rector could do
Than to shrine there his own beloved quadruped too;
As most surely a tithe-pig, whate'er the world thinks, is
A much fitter beast for a church than a Sphinx is.

But I'm call'd off to dinner—grace just has been said,
And my host waits for nobody, living or dead.

————⊙◉⊙————

SKETCH OF THE FIRST ACT OF A NEW ROMANTIC DRAMA.

" AND now," quoth the goddess, in accents jocose,
" Having got good materials, I'll brew such a dose
Of Double X mischief as, mortals shall say,
They 've not known its equal for many a long day."
Here she wink'd to her subaltern imps to be steady,
And all wagg'd their fire-tipp'd tails and stood ready.

" So, now for the ingredients:—first, hand me that bishop;"
Whereon, a whole bevy of imps run to fish up,
From out a large reservoir, wherein they pen 'em,
The blackest of all its black dabblers in venom;
And wrapping him up (lest the virus should ooze,
And one "drop of the immortal"(1) Right Rev. (2) they might lose)
In the sheets of his own speeches, charges, reviews,
Pop him into the caldron, while loudly a burst
From the by-standers welcomes ingredient the first!

" Now fetch the Ex-Chancellor," mutter'd the dame—
" He who's call'd after Harry the Older, by name."
The Ex-Chancellor !" echo'd her imps, the whole crew of 'em—
Why talk of one Ex, when your Mischief has two of 'em ?"
" True, true," said the hag, looking arch at her elves,
" And a double-Ex dose they compose, in themselves."
This joke, the sly meaning of which was seen lucidly,
Set all the devils a laughing most deucedly.
So, in went the pair, and (what none thought surprising)
Show'd talents for sinking as great as for rising ;
While not a grim phiz in that realm but was lighted
With joy to see spirits so twin-like united—
Or (plainly to speak) two such birds of a feather,
In one mess of venom thus spitted together.
Here a flashy imp rose—some connection, no doubt,
Of the young lord in question—and, scowling about,
" Hoped his fiery friend, St—n!—y, would not be left out;
As no schoolboy unwhipp'd, the whole world must agree,
Loved mischief, *pure* mischief, more dearly than he."

(1) " To lose no drop of the immortal man."
(2) The present Bishop of Ex—t—r.

But, no—the wise hag would n't hear of the whipster ;
Not merely because, as a shrew, he eclipsed her,
And nature had given him, to keep him still young,
Much tongue in his head and no head in his tongue ;
But because she well knew that, for change ever ready,
He 'd not even to mischief keep properly steady ;
That soon even the *wrong* side would cease to delight,
And, for want of a change, he must swerve to the *right* ;
While, on *each*, so at random his missiles he threw,
That the side he attack'd was most safe, of the two.—
This ingredient was therefore put by on the shelf,
There to bubble, a bitter hot mess, by itself.
"And now," quoth the hag, as her caldron she eyed,
And the tidbits so friendlily rankling inside,
"There wants but some seasoning ;—so, come, ere I stew 'em,
By way of a relish, we 'll throw in ' X John Tuam.'
In cooking up mischief, there 's no flesh or fish
Like your meddling High Priest, to add zest to the dish."
Thus saying, she pops in the Irish Grand Lama—
Which great event ends the First Act of the Drama.

————→◉◉←————

ANIMAL MAGNETISM.

THOUGH famed was Mesmer, in his day,
Not less so, in ours, is Dupotet,
To say nothing of all the wonders done
By that wizard, Dr. Elliotson,
When, standing as if the gods to invoke, he
Up waves his arm, and—down drops Okey !(3)

Though strange these things, to mind and sense,
If you wish still stranger things to see—
If you wish to know the power immense
Of the true magnetic influence,
Just go to her Majesty's Treasury,
And learn the wonders working there—
And I'll be hang'd if you don't stare!
Talk of your animal magnetists,
And that wave of the hand no soul resists,
Not all its witcheries can compete
With the friendly beckon towards Downing Street,
Which a Premier gives to one who wishes
To taste of the Treasury loaves and fishes.
It actually lifts the lucky elf,
Thus acted upon, *above* himself ;—
He jumps to a state of *clairvoyance*,
And is placeman, statesman, all at once!

These effects, observe (with which I begin),
Take place when the patient 's motion'd *in* ;
Far different, of course, the mode of affection,
When the wave of the hand 's in the *out* direction ;

(3) The name of the heroine of the performances at the North London Hospital.

The effects being then extremely unpleasant,
As is seen in the case of Lord B——m, at present;
In whom this sort of manipulation
Has lately produced such inflammation,
Attended with constant irritation,
That, in short—not to mince his situation—
It has work'd in the man a transformation
That puzzles all human calculation!

Ever since the fatal day which saw
That "pass" (1) perform'd on this Lord of Law—
A pass potential, none can doubt,
As it sent Harry B——m to the right about—
The condition in which the patient has been
Is a thing quite awful to be seen.
Not that a casual eye could scan
　　This wondrous change by outward survey;
It being, in fact, the *interior* man
　　That 's turn'd completely topsy-turvy:—
Like a case that lately, in reading o'er 'em,
I found in the *Acta Eruditorum*,
Of a man in whose inside, when disclosed,
The whole order of things was found transposed; (2)
By a *lusus naturæ*, strange to see,
The liver placed where the heart should be,
And the *spleen* (like B——m's, since laid on the shelf)
As diseased and as much *out of place* as himself.

In short, 'tis a case for consultation,
If e'er there was one, in this thinking nation;
And therefore I humbly beg to propose,
That those *savans* who mean, as the rumour goes,
To sit on Miss Okey's wonderful case,
Should also Lord Harry's case embrace;
And inform us, in *both* these patients' states,
Which *ism* it is that predominates,
Whether magnetism and somnambulism,
Or, simply and solely, mountebankism.

　　　　　—◦◆◦—
　　THE SONG OF THE BOX.

LET History boast of her Romans and Spartans,
　　And tell how they stood against tyranny's shocks;
They were all, I confess, in *my* eye, Betty Martins,
　　Compared to George Gr——te and his wonderful Box.

Ask, where Liberty now has her seat?—Oh, it is n't
　　By Delaware's banks or on Switzerland's rocks;—
Like an imp in some conjuror's bottle imprison'd,
　　She 's slily shut up in Gr——te's wonderful Box.
　　　　　　　　　　　　　　　　[minions,
How snug!—'stead of floating through ether's do-
Blown *this* way and *that,* by the "*populi vox,*"

(1) The technical term for the movements of the mag-
netiser's hand.
(2) Omnes fere internas corporis partes inverso ordine
sitas.—*Act. Erudit.,* 1690.
(3) "And all Arabia breathes from yonder box."—*Pope's
Rape of the Lock.*
(4) *Groot,* or *Grote,* latinised into Grotius.
(5) For the particulars of this escape of Grotius from

To fold thus in silence her sinecure pinions,
　　And go fast asleep in Gr——te's wonderful Box.

Time was, when free speech was the life-breath of
　　freedom—
　　So thought once the Seldens, the Hampdens, the
　　　　Lockes;
But mute be *our* troops, when to ambush we lead
　　'em,
　　For "Mum" is the word with us Knights of the
　　　　Box.

Pure, exquisite Box! no corruption can soil it;
　　There 's Otto of Rose in each breath it unlocks;
While Gr——te is the "Betty," that serves at the toilet,
　　And breathes all Arabia around from his Box. (3)

'T is a singular fact, that the famed Hugo Grotius (4)
　　(A namesake of Gr——te's—being both of Dutch
　　　　stocks),
Like Gr——te, too, a genius profound as precocious,
　　Was also, like him, much renown'd for a Box;—

An immortal old clothes-box, in which the great
　　Grotius
When suffering, in prison, for views heterodox,
　　Was pack'd up incog. spite of gaolers ferocious, (5)
And sent to his wife, (6) carriage-free, in a Box!

But the fame of old Hugo now rests on the shelf,
　　Since a rival hath risen that all parallel mocks;—
That Grotius ingloriously saved but himself, [Box!
　　While *ours* saves the whole British realm by a

And oh when, at last, even this greatest of Gr——tes
　　Must bend to the Power that at every door
　　　　knocks, (7)
May he drop in the urn like his own "silent votes,"
　　And the tomb of his rest be a large Ballot-Box."

While long at his shrine, both from county and city,
　　Shall pilgrims triennially gather in flocks,
And sing, while they whimper, the appropriate ditty,
　　"Oh breathe not his *name,* let it sleep—in the
　　　　Box."

　　　　　—◦◆◦—
　　ANNOUNCEMENT OF A NEW THALABA.

　　ADDRESSED TO ROBERT SOUTHEY, ESQ.

WHEN erst, my Southéy, thy tuneful tongue
The terrible tale of Thalaba sung—
Of him, the Destroyer, doom'd to rout
That grim divan of conjurors out,

the Castle of Louvenstein, by means of a box (only three
feet and a half long, it is said in which books used to be
occasionally sent to him and foul linen returned, see any
of the Biographical Dictionaries.
(6) This is not quite according to the facts of the case;
his wife having been the contriver of the stratagem, and
remained in the prison herself to give him time for escape.
(7) Pallida Mors æquo pulsat pede, etc.—*Horat.*

Whose dwelling dark, as legends say,
Beneath the roots of the ocean lay,
(Fit place for deep ones, such as they,)
How little thou knew'st, dear Dr. Southey,
Although bright genius all allow thee,
That, some years thence, thy wondering eyes
Should see a second Thalaba rise—
As ripe for ruinous rigs as thine,
Though his havoc lie in a different line,
And should find this new improved Destroyer
Beneath the wig of a Yankee lawyer;
A sort of an "alien," *alias* man,
Whose country or party guess who can,
Being Cockney half, half Jonathan;
And his life, to make the thing completer,
Being all in the genuine Thalaba metre,
Loose and irregular as thy feet are;—
First, into Whig Pindarics rambling,
Then in low Tory doggrel scrambling;
Now *love* his theme, now *Church* his glory
(At once both Tory and ama-tory),
Now in the Old Bailey-*lay* meandering,
Now in soft *couplet* style philandering;
And, lastly, in lame Alexandrine,
Dragging his wounded length along, (1)
When scourged by Holland's silken thong.

In short, dear Bob, Destroyer the Second
May fairly a match for the First be reckon'd;
Save that *your* Thalaba's talent lay
In sweeping old conjurors clean away,
While ours at aldermen deals his blows,
(Who no great conjurors are, God knows,)
Lays Corporations, by wholesale, level,
Sends Acts of Parliament to the devil,
Bullies the whole Milesian race—
Seven millions of Paddies, face to face;
And, seizing that magic wand, himself,
Which erst thy conjurors left on the shelf,
Transforms the boys of the Boyne and Liffey
All into *foreigners*, in a jiffey—
Aliens, outcasts, every soul of 'em,
Born but for whips and chains, the whole of 'em!

Never, in short, did parallel
Betwixt two heroes *gee* so well;
And, among the points in which they fit,
There's one, dear Bob, I can't omit.

(1) "A needless Alexandrine ends the song   [along.'
    That, *like a wounded snake*, drags its slow length
(2) "Vain are the spells, the Destroyer
    Treads the Domdaniel floor."
                    Thalaba, a Metrical Romance.
(3) "You will increase the enmity with which they are
regarded by their associates in heresy, thus tying these
foxes by the tails, that their faces may tend in opposite
directions."—*Bob's Bull*, read at Exeter Hall, July 14.
(4) "An ingenious device of my learned friend."—*Bob's
Letter to Standard.*

That hacking hectoring blade of thine
Dealt much in the *Domdaniel* line; (2)
And 'tis but rendering justice due,
To say that ours and his Tory crew
Damn Daniel most devoutly too.

—⊶⊷—

LETTER

FROM LARRY O'BRANIGAN TO THE REV.
MURTAGH O'MULLIGAN.

ARRAH, where were *you*, Murthagh, that beautiful
    day?—
  Or, how came it your riverence was laid on the
    shelf,
  When that poor craythur, Bobby—as *you* were
    away—
  Had to make *twice* as big a Tom-fool of *himself*.

Throth, it was n't at all civil to lave in the lurch
  A boy so desarving your tindh'rest affection;—
Two such iligant Siamase twins of the Church,
  As Bob and yourself, ne'er should cut the con-
    nection.

If thus in two different directions you pull,
  'Faith, they'll swear that yourself and your ri-
    verend brother
Are like those quare foxes, in Gregory's Bull,
  Whose tails were join'd *one* way, while they look'd
    another! (3)

Och blessed be he, whosomdever he be,
  That help'd soft Magee to that Bull of a Letther!
Not even my own self, though I sometimes make free
  At such bull-manufacture, could make him a
    betther.

To be sure, when a lad takes to *forgin'*, this way,
  'Tis a thrick he's much timpted to carry on gaily;
Till, at last, his "injanious devices," (4) some day,
  Show him up, not at Exether Hall, but the Ould
    Bailey.

That parsons should forge thus appears mighty odd,
  And (as if somethin' "odd" in their *names*, too,
    must be,)
One forger, of ould, was a riverend Dod,
  While a riverend Todd's now his match, to a T. (5)

(5) Had I consulted only my own wishes, I should not have
allowed this hasty attack on Dr. Todd to have made its ap-
pearance in this Collection; being now fully convinced
that the charge brought against that reverend gentleman
of intending to pass off as genuine his famous mock Papal
Letter was altogether unfounded. Finding it to be the
wish, however, of my reverend friend—as I am now glad
to be permitted to call him— that both the wrong and the
reparation, the Ode and the Palinode, should be thus
placed in juxtaposition, I have thought it but due to him
to comply with his request.

But, no matther *who* did it—all blessins betide him,
  For dishin' up Bob, in a manner so nate;
And there wanted but *you*, Murthagh 'vourneen,
    beside him,   [plate.
  To make the whole grand dish of *bull*-calf com-

THE BOY STATESMAN.

BY A TORY.

" That boy will be the death of me."—*Matthews at Home.*

Ah, Tories dear, our ruin is near,
  With St—nl—y to help us, we can't but fall;
Already a warning voice I hear,
Like the late Charles Matthews' croak in my ear,
  "That boy—that boy'll be the death of you all."

He will, God help us!—not even Scriblerius
  In the " Art of Sinking" his match could be ;
And our case is growing exceeding serious,
  For, all being in the same boat as he,
  If down my Lord goes, down go we,
    Lord Baron St—nl—y and Company,
As deep in Oblivion's swamp below
As such " Masters Shallow " well could go;
And where we shall all both low and high,
Embalm'd in mud, as forgotten lie
As already doth Gr—h—m of Netherby !
But that boy, that boy !—there's a tale I know,
Which in talking of him comes *à-propos.*
Sir Thomas More had an only son,
And a foolish lad was that only one.
  And Sir Thomas said, one day, to his wife,
  " My dear, I can't but wish you joy,
For you pray'd for a boy, and you now have a boy
  Who 'll continue a boy to the end of his life."

Even such is our own distressing lot,
  With the ever-young statesman we have got ;—
Nay even still worse ; for Master More
Was n't more a youth than he 'd been before,
While *ours* such power of boyhood shows,
That, the older he gets, the more juvenile he grows,
And, at what extreme old age he 'll close
His schoolboy course, heaven only knows.
Some century hence, should he reach so far,
  And ourselves to witness it Heaven condemn,
We shall find him a sort of *cub* Old Parr,
  A whipper-snapper Methusalem ;
Nay, even should he make still longer stay of it,
The boy 'll want *judgment,* even to the day of it !
Meanwhile, 'tis a serious, sad infliction ;
  And, day and night, with awe I recall
The late Mr. Matthews' solemn prediction,
  "That boy'll be the death, the death of you all."

MUSINGS OF AN UNREFORMED PEER.

Of all the odd plans of this monstrously queer age,
The oddest is that of reforming the peerage ;—

(1) The *Casa Santa,* supposed to have been carried by
angels through the air from Galilee to Italy.

Just as if we, great dons, with a title and star,
Did not get on exceedingly well as we are,
And perform all the functions of noodles, by birth,
As completely as any born noodles on earth.

How *acres* descend, is in law-books display'd,
But we as *wiseacres* descend, ready made;
And, by right of our rank in Debrett's nomenclature,
Are, all of us, born legislators by nature ;—
Like ducklings, to water instinctively taking,
So we, with like quackery, take to law-making ;
And God forbid any reform should come o'er us,
To make us more wise than our sires were before us.

The Egyptians of old the same policy knew—
If your sire was a cook, you must be a cook too :
Thus making, from father to son, a good trade of it,
Poisoners *by right* (so no more could be said of it),
The cooks, like our lordships, a pretty mess made of
  it ;
While, famed for *conservative* stomachs, the Egyp-
  tians
Without a wry face bolted all the prescriptions.

It is true, we 've among us some peers of the past,
Who keep pace with the present most awfully fast—
Fruits, that ripen beneath the new light now arising
With speed that to *us,* old conserves, is surprising,
Conserves, in whom—potted, for grandmamma
  uses—
'T would puzzle a sunbeam to find any juices.
'T is true, too, I fear, midst the general movement,
Even *our* House, God help it, is doom'd to improve-
  ment,
And all its live furniture, nobly descended,
But sadly worn out, must be sent to be mended.
With *moveables* 'mong us, like Br——m and like
  D—rh—m,
No wonder even *fixtures* should learn to bestir 'em ;
And distant, ye gods, be that terrible day,
When—as playful Old Nick, for his pastime, they say,
Flies off with old houses, sometimes in a storm—
So *ours* may be whipt off, some night by Reform
And, as up, like Loretto's famed house,(1) through
  the air,
Not angels, but devils, our lordships shall bear,
Grim radical phizzes, unused to the sky,
Shall flit round like cherubs, to wish us " good by,"
While, perch'd up on clouds, little Imps of plebeians,
Small Grotes and O'Connells, shall sing Io Pæans.

RIVAL TOPICS. (2)

AN EXTRAVAGANZA.

Oh W—ll—ngt—n and Stephenson,
  Oh morn and evening papers,

(2) The date of this squib must have been, I think,
about 1828-9.

Times, Herald, Courier, Globe, and *Sun,*
When will ye cease our ears to stun
    With these two heroes' capers?
Still "Stephenson" and " W—ll—ngt--n,
    The everlasting two !—
Still doom'd, from rise to set of sun,
To hear what mischief one has done,
    And t' other means to do :—
What bills the Banker pass'd to friends,
    But never meant to pay ;
What Bills the other wight intends,
    As honest, in their way ;—
Bills, payable at distant sight,
    Beyond the Grecian kalends,
When all good deeds will come to light,
When W—ll—ngt--n will do what 's right,
    And Rowland pay his balance.

To catch the banker all have sought,
    But still the rogue unhurt is ;
While t' other juggler—who'd have thought?
Though slippery long, has just been caught
    By old Archbishop Curtis ;—
And, such the power of papal crook,
    The crosier scarce had quiver'd
About his ears, when, lo, the Duke
    Was of a Bull deliver'd !

Sir Richard Birnie doth decide
    That Rowland " must be mad,"
In private coach, with crest, to ride,
    When chaises could be had.
And t' other hero, all agree,
    St. Luke's will soon arrive at,
If thus he shows off publicly,
    When he might pass in private.

Oh W—ll—gnt—n, oh Stephenson,
    Ye ever-boring pair,
Where'er I sit, or stand, or run,
    Ye haunt me every where.
Though Job had patience tough enough,
    Such duplicates would try it;
Till one 's turn'd out and t' other off,
    We shan't have peace or quiet.
But small 's the chance that Law affords—
    Such folks are daily let off ;
And, 'twixt the Old Bailey and the Lords,
    They both, I fear, will get off.

—o⁑o—

THE REVEREND PAMPHLETEER.

A ROMANTIC BALLAD.

On, have you heard what hap'd of late?
    If not, come lend an ear,
While sad I state the piteous fate
    Of the Reverend Pamphleteer.

All praised his skilful jockeyship,
    Loud rung the Tory cheer,

While away, away, with spur and whip,
    Went the Reverend Pamphleteer.

The nag he rode—how *could* it err?
    'T was the same that took, last year,
That wonderful jump to Exeter
    With the Reverend Pamphleteer.

Set a beggar on horseback, wise men say,
    The course he will take is clear ;
And in *that* direction lay the way
    Of the Reverend Pamphleteer.

" Stop, stop," said Truth, but vain her cry—
    Left far behind in the rear,
She heard but the usual gay " Good-by"
    From her faithless Pamphleteer.

You may talk of the jumps of Homer's gods,
    When cantering o'er our sphere—
I 'd back for a *bounce,* 'gainst any odds,
    This Reverend Pampleteer.

But ah, what tumbles a jockey hath !
    In the midst of his career,
A file of the *Times* lay right in the path
    Of the headlong Pamphleteer !

Whether he tripp'd or shy'd thereat,
    Doth not so clear appear :
But down he came, as his sermons flat—
    This Reverend Pamphleteer !

Lord King himself could scarce desire
    To see a spiritual Peer
Fall much more dead, in the dirt and mire,
    Than did this Pamphleteer.

Yet pitying parsons, many a day,
    Shall visit his silent bier,
And, thinking the while of Stanhope, say
    " Poor dear old Pamphleteer !

" He has finish'd, at last, his busy span,
    And now *lies coolly* here—
As often he did in life, good man,
    Good Reverend Pamphleteer !"

—o⊛o—

A RECENT DIALOGUE.

1825.

A BISHOP and a bold dragoon,
    Both heroes in their way,
Did thus, of late, one afternoon,
    Unto each other say :—
" Dear bishop," quoth the brave hussar,
    " As nobody denies
That you a wise logician are,
    And I am—otherwise ;
'T is fit that in this question, we
    Stick each to his own art—

That *yours* should be the sophistry,
   And *mine* the *fighting* part.
My creed I need not tell you, is
   Like that of W——n,
To whom no harlot comes amiss,
   Save her of Babylon ;(1)
And when we 're at a loss for words,
   If laughing reasoners flout us,
For lack of sense we 'll draw our swords—
   The sole thing sharp about us."
" Dear bold dragoon," the bishop said,
   " 'T is true for war thou art meant ;
And reasoning—bless that dandy head!—
   Is not in thy department.
So leave the argument to me—
   And, when my holy labour
Hath lit the fires of bigotry,
   Thou 'lt poke them with thy sabre.
From pulpit and from sentry-box,
   We 'll make our joint attacks,
I at the head of my *Cassocks*,
   And you, of your *Cossacks*.
So here 's your health, my brave hussar,
   My exquisite old fighter—
Success to bigotry and war,
   The musket and the mitre!"
Thus pray'd the minister of heaven—
   While Y—k, just entering then,
Snored out (as if some *Clerk* had given
   His nose the cue) " Amen."
                        T. B.

—◦∞◦—

THE WELLINGTON SPA.

" And drink oblivion to our woes."—*Anna Matilda.*
                             1829.

TALK no more of your Cheltenham and Harrowgate
     springs,
'T is from *Lethe* we now our potations must draw ;
Your *Lethe* 's a cure for—all possible things,
   And the doctors have named it the Wellington Spa.

Other physical waters but cure you in part;
   One cobbles your gout—t' *other* mends your di-
     gestion—
Some settle your stomach, but *this*—bless your
     heart !—
It will settle, for ever, your Catholic Question.

Unlike, too, the potions in fashion at present,
   This Wellington nostrum, restoring by stealth,
So purges the memory of all that 's unpleasant,
   That patients *forget* themselves into rude health.

For instance, the inventor—his having once said
   "He should think himself mad, if, at *any one's* call,

(1) Cui nulla meretrix displicuit præter Babylonicam.
(2) The only parallel I know to this sort of oblivion is
to be found in a line of the late Mr. R. P. Knight—
     "The pleasing memory of things forgot."

He became what he is "—is so purged from his head,
   That he now does n't think he 's a madman at all.

Of course, for your memories of very long standing—
   Old chronic diseases, that date back, undaunted,
To Brian Boroo and Fitz-Stephens' first landing—
   A devil of a dose of the *Lethe* is wanted.

But even Irish patients can hardly regret
   An oblivion, so much in their own native style,
So conveniently plann'd, that, whate'er they forget,
   They may go on remembering it still, all the
     while ! (2)

—◦∞◦—

A CHARACTER.
                             1834.

HALF Whig, half Tory, like those midway things,
'Twixt bird and beast, that by mistake have wings;
A mongrel Statesman, 'twixt two factions nurst,
Who, of the faults of each, combines the worst—
The Tory's loftiness, the Whigling's sneer,
The leveller's rashness, and the bigot's fear;
The thirst for meddling, restless still to show
How Freedom's clock, repair'd by Whigs, will go ;
The alarm when others, more sincere than they,
Advance the hands to the true time of day.

By Mother Church, high-fed and haughty dame,
The boy was dandled, in his dawn of fame;
Listening, she smiled, and bless'd the flippant tongue
On which the fate of unborn tithe-pigs hung.
Ah, who shall paint the grandam's grim dismay,
When loose Reform enticed her boy away;
When shock'd she heard him ape the rabble's tone,
And, in Old Sarum's fate, foredoom her own !
Groaning she cried, while tears roll'd down her cheeks,
   " Poor glib-tongued youth, he means not what he
     speaks.
Like oil at top, these Whig professions flow,
But, pure as lymph, runs Toryism below.
Alas, that tongue should start thus, in the race,
Ere mind can reach and regulate its pace !—
For, once outstripp'd by tongue, poor lagging mind,
At every step, still further limps behind,
But, bless the boy !—whate'er his wandering be,
Still turns his heart to Toryism and me.
Like those odd shapes, portray'd in Dante's lay, (3)
With heads fix'd on, the wrong and backward way,
His feet and eyes pursue a diverse track,
While *those* march onward, *these* look fondly back."
And well she knew him—well foresaw the day,
Which now hath come, when, snatch'd from Whigs
     away,
The self-same changeling drops the mask he wore,
And rests, restored, in granny's arms once more.

(3)   " Che dalle reni era tornato 'l volto,
       E indietro venir li convenia,
      Perché 'l veder dinanzi era lor tolto."

But whither now, mixt brood of modern light
And ancient darkness, can'st thou bend thy flight?
Tried by both factions, and to neither true,
Fear'd by the *old* school, laugh'd at by the *new;*
For *this* too feeble, and for *that* too rash,
This wanting more of fire, *that* less of flash,
Lone shalt thou stand, in isolation cold,
Betwixt two worlds, the new one and the old,
A small and "vex'd Bermoothes," which the eye
Of venturous seaman sees—and passes by.

—◦◦◦—

A GHOST STORY.

To the Air of "Unfortunate Miss Bailey."
1835.

Not long in bed had L—ndh—rst lain,
When, as his lamp burn'd dimly,
The ghosts of corporate bodies slain, (1)
Stood by his bed-side grimly.
Dead aldermen who once could feast,
But now themselves are fed on,
And skeletons of mayors deceased,
This doleful chorus led on :—
    " Oh Lord L—ndh—rst,
Unmerciful Lord L—ndh—rst,
    Corpses we,
    All burk'd by thee,
Unmerciful Lord L—ndh—rst!"

" Avaunt, ye frights!" his Lordship cried,
    " Ye look most glum and whitely."
" Ah, L—ndh—rst dear!" the frights replied,
    " You 've used us unpolitely.
And now, ungrateful man! to drive
    Dead bodies from your door so,
Who quite corrupt enough, alive,
    You 've made, by death, still more so.
        Oh, Ex-Chancellor,
    Destructive Ex-Chancellor,
        See thy work,
        Thou second Burke,
    Destructive Ex-Chancellor !"

Bold L—ndh—rst then, whom nought could keep
    Awake, or surely *that* would,
Cried "Curse you all "—fell fast asleep—
    And dreamt of "Small *v.* Attwood."
While, shock'd, the bodies flew down stairs,
    But, courteous in their panic,
Precedence gave to ghosts of mayors,
    And corpses aldermanic,
        Crying, "Oh, Lord L—ndh—rst,
    That terrible Lord L—ndh—rst,
        Not Old Scratch
        Himself could match
    That terrible Lord L—ndh—rst."

THOUGHTS ON THE LATE DESTRUCTIVE PROPOSITIONS OF THE TORIES. (2)

BY A COMMON-COUNCILMAN.
1835.

I sat me down in my easy chair,
    To read, as usual, the morning papers;
But—who shall describe my look of despair,
    When I came to Lefroy's "destructive" capers!
That *he*—that, of all live men, Lefroy
Should join in the cry "Destroy, destroy!"
Who, even when a babe, as I've heard said,
On Orange conserve was chiefly fed,
And never, till now, a movement made
That was n't most manfully retrograde!
Only think—to sweep from the light of day
Mayors, maces, criers, and wigs away;
To annihilate—never to rise again—
A whole generation of aldermen,
Nor leave them even the accustom'd tolls,
To keep together their bodies and souls!—
At a time, too, when snug posts and places
Are falling away from us, one by one,
Crash—crash—like the mummy-cases
    Belzoni, in Egypt, sat upon,
Wherein lay pickled, in state sublime,
Conservatives of the ancient time;—
To choose such a moment to overset
The few snug nuisances left us yet;
To add to the ruin that round us reigns,
By knocking out mayors' and town-clerks' brains;
By dooming all corporate bodies to fall,
Till they leave, at last, no bodies at all—
Nought but the ghosts of by-gone glory,
Wrecks of a world that once was Tory!—
Where pensive criers, like owls unblest,
    Robb'd of their roosts, shall still hoot o'er them;
Nor *mayors* shall know where to seek a *nest*,
    Till Gully Knight shall *find* one for them;—
Till mayors and kings, with none to rue 'em,
    Shall perish all in one common plague;
And the *sovereigns* of Belfast and Tuam
    Must join their brother, Charles Dix, at Prague.

Thus mused I, in my chair, alone,
    (As above described) till dozy grown,
And nodding assent to my own opinions,
I found myself borne to sleep's dominions,
Where, lo, before my dreaming eyes,
A new House of Commons appear'd to rise,
Whose living contents, to fancy's survey,
Seem'd to me all turn'd topsy-turvy—
A jumble of polypi—nobody knew
Which was the head or which the queue.
Here, Inglis, turn'd to a sans-culotte,
Was dancing the hays with Hume and Grote;

(1) Referring to the line taken by Lord L—ndh—rst, on the question of Municipal Reform,
(2) These verses were written in reference to the Bill brought in at this time, for the reform of Corporations, and the sweeping amendments proposed by Lord Lyndhurst and other Tory Peers, to obstruct the measure.

There, ripe for riot, Recorder Shaw
Was learning from Roebuck " Ça-ira;"
While Stanley and Graham, as *poissarde* wenches,
Scream'd "*à-bas!*" from the Tory benches;
And Peel and O'Connell, cheek by jowl,
Were dancing an Irish carmagnole.

The Lord preserve us!—if dreams come true,
What *is* this hapless realm to do?

ANTICIPATED MEETING OF THE BRITISH ASSOCIATION IN THE YEAR 2836.

1836.

AFTER some observations from Dr. M'Grig
On that fossile reliquium call'd Petrified Wig,
Or *Perruquolithus*— a specimen rare
Of those wigs, made for antediluvian wear,
Which, it seems, stood the Flood without turning a
hair—
Mr. Tomkins rose up, and requested attention
To facts no less wondrous which *he* had to mention.

Some large fossil creatures had lately been found,
Of a species no longer now seen above ground,
But the same (as to Tomkins most clearly appears)
With those animals, lost now for hundreds of years,
Which our ancestors used to call " Bishops" and
"Peers,"
But which Tomkins more erudite names has bestow'd
on,
Having call'd the Peer fossil the *Aristocratodon*, (1)
And, finding much food under t' other one's thorax,
Has christen'd that creature the Episcopus Vorax.

Lest the *savantes* and dandies should think this all
fable,
Mr. Tomkins most kindly produced, on the table,
A sample of each of these species of creatures,
Both tolerably human, in structure and features,
Except that the Episcopus seems, Lord deliver us!
To 've been carnivorous as well as granivorous;
And Tomkins, on searching its stomach, found there
Large lumps, such as no modern stomach could bear,
Of a substance call'd Tithe, upon which, as 'tis said,
The whole Genus Clericum formerly fed;
And which having lately himself decompounded,
Just to see what 't was made of, he actually found it
Composed of all possible cookable things
That e'er tripp'd upon trotters or soar'd upon wings—
All products of earth, both gramineous, herbaceous,
Hordeaceous, fabaceous, and eke farinaceous,
All clubbing their quotas, to glut the œsophagus
Of this ever greedy and grasping Tithophagus. (2)
"Admire," exclaim'd Tomkins, "the kind dispensation
By Providence shed on this much-favour'd nation,

(1) A term formed on the model of the Mastodon, etc.
(2) The zoological term for a tithe-eater.
(3) The man found by Scheuchzer, and supposed by him

In sweeping so ravenous a race from the earth,
That might else have occasion'd a general dearth—
And thus burying 'em, deep as even Joe Hume would
sink 'em,
With the Ichthyosaurus and Palæorynchum,
And other queer *ci-devant* things, under ground—
Not forgetting that fossilised youth, (3) so renown'd,
Who lived just to witness the Deluge—was gratified
Much by the sight, and has since been found *stratified!*"

This picturesque touch—quite in Tomkins's way—
Call'd forth from the *savantes* a general hurrah;
While inquiries among them went rapidly round,
As to where this young stratified man could be found.

The "learn'd Theban's" discourse next as livelily
flow'd on,
To sketch t' other wonder, the *Aristocratodon*—
An animal, differing from most human creatures
Not *so* much in speech, inward structure, or features,
As in having a certain excrescence, T. said,
Which in form of a coronet grew from its head,
And devolved to its heirs, when the creature was
dead;   [mitted,
Nor matter'd it, while this heir-loom was trans-
How unfit were the *heads*, so the coronet fitted.

He then mention'd a strange zoological fact,
Whose announcement appear'd much applause to
attract.
In France, said the learned professor, this race
Had so noxious become, in some centuries' space,
From their numbers and strength, that the land was
o'errun with 'em,
Every one's question being, "What's to be done
with 'em?"
When, lo! certain knowing ones *sarans*, mayhap,
Who, like Buckland's deep followers, understood
trap, (4)
Slily hinted that nought upon earth was so good
For *Aristocratodons*, when rampant and rude,
As to stop, or curtail, their allowance of food.
This expedient was tried, and a proof it affords
Of the effect that short commons will have upon lords;
For this whole race of bipeds, one fine summer's
morn,
Shed their coronets, just as a deer sheds his horn,
And the moment these gewgaws fell off, they became
Quite a new sort of creature — so harmless and
tame,
That zoologists might, for the first time, maintain 'em
To be near akin to the *genus humanum*,
And the experiment, tried so successfully then,
Should be kept in remembrance, when wanted again.

*   *   *   *   *

to have witnessed the Deluge ("homo diluvii testis,") but
who turned out, I am sorry to say, to be only a great lizard.
(4) Particularly the formation called *Transition* Trap.

LEAVE ME ALONE.

A PASTORAL BALLAD.

" We are ever standing on the defensive. All that we
say to them is, ' *leave us alone.*' The Established
Church is part and parcel of the constitution of this
country. You are bound to conform to this constitu-
tion. We ask of you nothing more;—*let us alone.*"
—Letter in *The Times*, Nov. 1838.

Come, list to my pastoral tones,
  In clover my shepherds I keep;
My stalls are well furnish'd with drones,
  Whose preaching invites one to sleep.
At my *spirit* let infidels scoff,
  So they leave but the *substance* my own ;
For, in sooth, I 'm extremely well off,
  If the world will but let me alone.

Dissenters are grumblers, we know ;—
  Though excellent men, in their way,
They never like things to be *so*,
  Let things be however they may.
But dissenting 's a trick I detest ;
  And, besides, 't is an axiom well known,
The creed that 's best paid is the best,
  If the *unpaid* would let it alone.

To me, I own, very surprising
  Your Newmans and Puseys all seem,
Who start first with rationalising,
  Then jump to the other extreme.
Far better, 'twixt nonsense and sense,
  A nice *half*-way concern, like our own,
Where piety 's mix'd up with pence,
  And the latter are *ne'er* left alone.

Of all our tormentors, the Press Is
  The one that most tears us to bits ;
And now, Mrs. Woolfrey's "excesses"
  Have thrown all its imps into fits.
The devils have been at us, for weeks,
  And there 's no saying when they 'll have done;—
Oh dear, how I wish Mr. Breeks
  Had left Mrs. Woolfrey alone !

If any need pray for the dead,
  'T is those to whom post-obits fall;
Since wisely hath Solomon said,
  'T is "money that answereth all."
But ours be the patrons who *live* ;
  For, once in their glebe they are thrown,
The dead have no living to give,
  And therefore we leave them alone.

(1) Mirari se, se augur augurem aspiciens sibi tempe-
raret a risu.
(2) So spelled in those ancient versicles which John,
we understand, frequently chants :—
  "Had every one Suum,
  You would n't have Tuum,

Though in morals we may not excel,
  Such perfection is rare to be had ;
A good life is, of course, very well,
  But good living is also—not bad.
And when, to feed earth-worms, I go,
  Let this epitaph stare from my stone,
" Here lies the Right Rev. so and so;
  Pass, stranger, and—leave him alone."

—◦※◦—

EPISTLE FROM HENRY OF EX—T—R TO JOHN OF TUAM.

Dear John, as I know, like our brother of London,
You 've sipp'd of all knowledge, both sacred and
    mundane,
No doubt, in some ancient Joe Miller, you 've read
What Cato, that cunning old Roman, once said—
That he ne'er saw two reverend soothsayers meet,
Let it be where it might, in the shrine or the street,
Without wondering the rogues, 'mid their solemn
    grimaces,
Did n't burst out a laughing in each other's faces. (1)
What Cato then meant, though 't is so long ago,
Even we in the present times pretty well know;
Having soothsayers also, who—sooth to say, John—
Are no better in some points than those of days gone,
And a pair of whom, meeting (between you and me),
Might laugh in their sleeves, too—all lawn though
    they be.

But this, by the way—my intention being chiefly
In this, my first letter, to hint to you briefly,
That, seeing how fond you of *Tuum* (2) must be,
While *Meum* 's at all times the main point with me,
We scarce could do better than form an alliance,
To set these sad Anti-Church times at defiance :
You, John, recollect, being still to embark,
With no share in the firm but your title (3) and *mark;*
Or even should you feel in your grandeur inclined
To call yourself Pope, why, I should n't much mind;
While *my* church as usual holds fast by your Tuum,
And every one else's, to make it all Suum.

Thus allied, I 've no doubt we shall nicely agree,
As no twins can be liker, in most points, than we ;
Both, specimens choice of that mix'd sort of beast,
(See Rev. xiii., 1.) a political priest;
Both mettlesome *chargers*, both brisk pamphleteers,
Ripe and ready for all that sets men by the ears ;
And I, at least one, who would scorn to stick longer
By any given cause than I found it the stronger,
And who, smooth in my turnings, as if on a swivel,
When the tone ecclesiastic wo'n't do, try the *civil*.

  But I should have Meum,
  And sing Te Deum."
(3) For his keeping the title be may quote classical au-
thority, as Horace expressly says, "Poteris servare Tuam.'
—*De Art. Poet.*, v., 329.—*Chronicle.*

In short (not to bore you, even *jure divino*)
We've the same cause in common, John—all but the
 rhino;
And that vulgar surplus, whate'er it may be,
As you're not used to cash, John, you'd best leave
 to me.
And so, without form—as the postman wo'n't tarry—
I'm, dear Jack of Tuam,
                                    Yours,
                                        EXETER HARRY.

—◦◦◦—

SONG OF OLD PUCK.

"And those things do best please me,
 That befall preposterously."
                Puck Junior, Midsummer Night's Dream.

WHO wants old Puck? for here am I,
A mongrel imp, 'twixt earth and sky,
Ready alike to crawl or fly;
Now in the mud, now in the air,
And, so 'tis for mischief, reckless where.

As to my knowledge, there 's no end to 't,
For, where I have n't it, I pretend to 't;
And, 'stead of taking a learn'd degree
At some dull university,
Puck found it handier to commence
With a certain share of impudence,
Which passes one off as learn'd and clever.
Beyond all other degrees whatever;
And enables a man of lively sconce
To be Master of *all* the Arts at once.
No matter what the science may be—
Ethics, Physics, Theology,
Mathematics, Hydrostatics,
Aerostatics or Pneumatics—
Whatever it be, I take my luck,
'Tis all the same to ancient Puck;
Whose head's so full of all sorts of wares,
That a brother imp, old Smugden, swears
If I had but of *law* a little smattering,
I'd then be *perfect* (1)—which is flattering.

My skill as a linguist all must know
Who met me abroad some months ago;
(And heard me *abroad* exceedingly, too,
In the moods and tenses of *parlex-vous*)
When, as old Chambaud's shade stood mute,
I spoke such French to the Institute
As puzzled those learned Thebans much,
To know if 't was Sanscrit or High Dutch,
And *might* have pass'd with the unobserving
As one of the unknown tongues of Irving.
As to my talent for ubiquity,
There's nothing like it in all antiquity.

(1) Verbatim, as said. This tribute is only equalled by
that of Talleyrand to his medical friend, Dr. ——: "Il se
connaît en tout; et même un peu en médecine."
(2) Song in *The Padlock.*

Like Mungo (my peculiar care)
"I'm here, I'm dere, I'm ebery where."(2)
If any one's wanted to take the chair,
Upon any subject, any where,
Just look around, and—Puck is there!
When slaughter's at hand, your bird of prey
Is never known to be out of the way;
And wherever mischief's to be got,
There's Puck *instanter*, on the spot.

Only find me in negus and applause,
And I'm your man for *any* cause.
If *wrong* the cause, the more my delight;
But I don 't object to it, even when *right*,
If I only can vex some old friend by 't;
There's D—rh—m, for instance;—to worry *him*
Fills up my cup of bliss to the brim!

(NOTE BY THE EDITOR.)

Those who are anxious to run a muck
Can't do better than join with Puck.
They'll find him *bon diable*- spite of his phiz—
And, in fact, his great ambition is,
While playing old Puck in first-rate style,
To be *thought* Robin Good-fellow all the while.

—◦◦◦—

POLICE REPORTS.
CASE OF IMPOSTURE.

AMONG other stray flashmen, disposed of, this week,
 Was a youngster, named St—nl—y, genteelly con-
 nected,
Who has lately been passing off coins, as antique,
 Which have proved to be *sham* ones, though long
 unsuspected.

The ancients, our readers need hardly be told,
 Had a coin they call'd "Talents," for wholesale
 demands; (3)
And 't was some of said coinage this youth was so
 bold
 As to fancy he 'd got, God knows how, in his hands.

People took him, however, like fools, at his word;
 And these talents (all prized at his own valuation,)
Were bid for, with eagerness even more absurd
 Than has often distinguish'd this great thinking
 nation.

Talk of wonders one now and then sees advertised,
 "Black swans"—"Queen Anne farthings"—or
 even "a child's caul"—
Much and justly as all these rare objects are prized,
 "St—nl—y's talents" outdid them—swans, far-
 things, and all!

(3) For an account of the coin called Talents by the an-
cients, see Budæus de Asse, and the other writers de Re
Nummaria.

At length, some mistrust of this coin got abroad;
　Even quondam believers began much to doubt of it;
Some rung it, some rubb'd it, suspecting a fraud—
　And the hard rubs it got rather took the shine out
　　of it.

Others, wishing to break the poor prodigy's fall,
　Said 't was known well to all who had studied the
　　matter,
That the Greeks had not only *great* talents but
　small, (1)
　And those found on the youngster were clearly *the
　　latter.*

While others, who view'd the grave farce with a grin—
　Seeing counterfeits pass thus for coinage so massy,
By way of a hint to the dolts taken in,
　Appropriately quoted Budæus de *Asse.*

In short, the whole sham by degrees was found out,
　And this coin, which they chose by such fine
　　names to call,
Proved a mere lacker'd article—showy, no doubt,
　But, ye gods, not the true Attic Talent at all.

As the impostor was still young enough to repent,
　And, besides, had some claims to a grandee con-
　　nection,
Their Worships—considerate for once—only sent
　The young Thimblerig off to the House of Cor-
　　rection.

—◦❀◦—

REFLECTIONS,

**ADDRESSED TO THE AUTHOR OF THE ARTICLE OF
THE CHURCH IN THE LAST NUMBER OF THE
" QUARTERLY REVIEW."**

I'm quite of your mind ;—though these Pats cry aloud
　That they 've got " too much Church," 'tis all
　　nonsense and stuff ;
For Church is like Love, of which Figaro vow'd
　That even *too much* of it 's not quite enough. (2)

Ay, dose them with parsons, 't will cure all their
　ills ;—
　Copy Morison's mode when from pill-box undaunt-
　　ed he
Pours through the patient his black-coated pills,
　Nor cares what their quality, so there's but quan-
　　tity.

I verily think, 't would be worth England's while
　To consider, for Paddy's own benefit, whether
'T would not be as well to give up the green isle
　To the care, wear, and tear of the Church altoge-
　　ther.

The Irish are well used to treatment so pleasant ;
　The harlot Church gave them to Henry Planta-
　　genet, (3)

And now, if King William would make them a pre-
　sent
　To t'other chaste lady—ye Saints, just imagine it !

Chief Secs., Lord-Lieutenants, Commanders-in-chief,
　Might then all be cull'd from the episcopal benches ;
While colonels in black would afford some relief
　From the hue that reminds one of the old scarlet
　　wench's.

Think how fierce at a *charge* (being practised therein)
　The Right Reverend Brigadier Ph—ll—tts would
　　slash on !
How General Bl—mf—d, through thick and through
　thin,
　To the end of the chapter (or chapters) would dash
　　on !

For in one point alone do the amply-fed race
　Of bishops to beggars similitude bear—
That, set them on horseback, in full steeple chase,
　And they 'll ride, if not pull'd up in time—you
　　know where.

But, bless you, in Ireland, that matters not much,
　Where affairs have for centuries gone the same
　　way ;
And a good stanch Conservative's system is such
　That he 'd back even Beelzebub's long-founded
　　sway.

I am therefore, dear Quarterly, quite of your mind ;—
　Church, Church, in all shapes, into Erin let 's pour ;
And the more she rejecteth our medicine so kind,
　The more let 's repeat it—" Black dose, as before."

Let Coercion, that peace-maker, go hand in hand
　With demure-eyed Conversion, fit sister and bro-
　　ther ;
And covering with prisons and churches the land,
　All that won't *go to one,* we 'll put *into* the other.

For the sole leading maxim of us who 're inclined
　To rule over Ireland, not well, but religiously,
Is to treat her like ladies, who 've just been confined,
　(Or who *ought* to be so,) and to *church* her pro-
　　digiously.

—◦❀◦—

NEW GRAND EXHIBITION OF MODELS

OF THE

TWO HOUSES OF PARLIAMENT.

Come, step in, gentlefolks, here ye may view
　An exact and natural representation

(1) The Talentum Magnum and the Talentum Atticum
appear to have been the same coin.
(2) " En fait d'amour, trop même n'est pas assez."—
Barbier de Seville.
(3) Grant of Ireland to Henry II. by Pope Adrian.

(Like Siburn's *Model of Waterloo*) (1)
Of the Lords and Commons of this here nation.

There they are—all cut out in cork—
  The "Collective Wisdom" wondrous to see;
My eyes! when all them heads are at work,
  What a vastly weighty consarn it must be.

As for the "wisdom"—*that* may come anon ;
  Though, to say truth, we sometimes see
(And I find the phenomenon no uncommon 'un)
  A man who 's M. P. with a head that 's M. T.

Our Lords are *rather* too small, 'tis true ;
  But they do well enough for Cabinet shelves ;
And, besides—*what's* a man with creeturs to do
  That make such *werry* small figures themselves?

There—don't touch those lords, my pretty dears—
    (*Aside.*)
  Curse the children!—this comes of reforming a
    nation :
Those meddling young brats have so damaged my
    peers,
  I must lay in more cork for a new creation.

Them yonder 's our bishops—"to whom much is
    given,"
  And who 're ready to take as much more as you
    please :
The seers of old times saw visions of heaven,
  But these holy seers see nothing but Sees.

Like old Atlas (2) (the chap, in Cheapside,there below,)
  'T is for so much *per cent.* they take heaven on
    their shoulders ;
And joy 'tis to know that old High Church and Co.,
  Though not capital priests, are such capital-holders,

There 's one on 'em, Ph——llp——ts, who now is away,
  As we 're having him fill'd with bumbustible stuff,
Small crackers and squibs, for a great gala-day,
  When we annually fire his Right Reverence off.

'T would do your heart good, ma'am, then to be by,
  When, bursting with gunpowder, 'stead of with
    bile,
Crack, crack, goes the bishop, while dowagers cry,
  "How like the dear man, both in matter and style!"

Should you want a few Peers and M. P.s, to bestow,
  As presents to friends, we can recommend
    these :—(3)
Our nobles are come down to nine-pence, you know,
  And we charge but a penny a-piece for M. P.s.

Those of *bottle*-corks made take most with the trade,
  (At least, 'mong such as my *Irish* writ summons),

Of old *whiskey* corks our O'Connells are made,
  But those we make Shaws and Lefroys of, are *rum
    'uns.*
So, step in, gentlefolks, etc., etc.
           Da Capo.

ANNOUNCEMENT
OF
A NEW GRAND ACCELERATION COMPANY FOR THE PROMOTION OF THE SPEED OF LITERATURE.

Loud complaints being made, in these quick-reading
    times,
Of too slack a supply, both of prose works and
    rhymes,
A new Company, form'd on the keep-moving plan,
First proposed by the great firm of Catch-'em-who-can,
Beg to say they 've now ready, in full wind and speed,
Some fast-going authors, of quite a new breed—
Such as not he who *runs* but who *gallops* may read—
And who, if well curried and fed, they 've no doubt,
Will beat even Bentley's swift stud out and out.
It is true, in these days, such a drug is renown,
We 've "Immortals" as rife as M.P.s about town ;
And not a Blue's rout but can off-hand supply
Some invalid bard who 's insured " not to die."
Still, let England but once try *our* authors, she 'll find
How fast they 'll leave even these Immortals behind ;
And how truly the toils of Alcides were light,
Compared with *his* toil who can read all they write.

In fact, there 's no saying, so gainful the trade,
How fast immortalities now may be made ;
Since Helicon never will want an "Undying One,"
As long as the public continues a Buying One ;
And the company hope yet to witness the hour,
When, by strongly applying the mare-motive (4)
    power,
A three-decker novel, 'midst oceans of praise,
May be written, launch'd, read, and—forgot, in three
           [days!
In addition to all this stupendous celerity,
Which—to the no small relief of posterity—
Pays off at sight the whole debit of fame,
Nor troubles futurity even with a name
(A project that wo'n't as much tickle Tom Tegg as *us,*
Since 't will rob *him* of his second-priced Pegasus) ;
We, the Company—still more to show how immense
Is the power o'er the mind of pounds, shillings, and
    pence ;
And that not even Phœbus himself, in our day,
Could get up a *lay* without first an *out-lay*—
Beg to add, as our literature soon may compare,
In its quick make and vent, with our Birmingham
    ware,

(1) One of the most interesting and curious of all the
  exhibitions of the day.
(2) The sign of the Insurance Office in Cheapside.
(3) Producing a bag full of lords and gentlemen.
(4) "'T is money makes the mare to go."

And it does n't at all matter in either of these lines,
How *sham* is the article, so it but *shines*—
We keep authors ready, all perch'd, pen in hand,
To write off, in any given style, at command.
No matter what bard, be he living or dead, (1)
Ask a work from his pen, and 't is done soon as said:
There being, on the establishment, six Walter Scotts,
One capital Wordsworth, and Southeys in lots ;—
Three choice Mrs. Nortons, all singing like syrens,
While most of our pallid young clerks are Lord Byrons.
Then we've ***'s and ***'s for whom there's small
    call),
And ***'s and ***'s (for whom no call at all).

In short, whosoe'er the last " Lion " may be,
We've a Bottom who'll copy his roar (2) to a T,
And so well, that not one of the buyers who've got'em
Can tell which is lion, and which only Bottom.

N. B.—The company, since they set up in this line,
Have moved their concern, and are now at the sign
Of the Muse's Velocipede, *Fleet* Street, where all
Who wish well to the scheme are invited to call.

———o**o———

SOME ACCOUNT OF THE LATE DINNER TO DAN.

FROM tongue to tongue the rumour flew;
All ask'd, aghast, " Is 't true? is 't true? "
    But none knew whether 't was fact or fable:
And still the unholy rumour ran,
From Tory woman to Tory man,
    Though none to come at the truth was able—
Till, lo, at last, the fact came out,
The horrible fact, beyond all doubt,
    That Dan had dined at the Viceroy's table ;
Had flesh'd his Popish knife and fork
In the heart of the Establish'd mutton and pork!

Who can forget the deep sensation
That news produced in this orthodox nation ?
Deans, rectors, curates, all agreed,
If Dan was allow'd at the Castle to feed,
'T was clearly *all* up with the Protestant creed !
There had n't, indeed, such an apparition
Been heard of, in Dublin, since that day
When, during the first grand exhibition
    Of Don Giovanni, that naughty play,
There appear'd, as if raised by necromancers,
An *extra* devil among the dancers !
Yes—every one saw, with fearful thrill,
That a devil too much had join'd the quadrille; (3)
And sulphur was smelt, and the lamps let fall
A grim green light o'er the ghastly ball,
And the poor *sham* devils did n't like it at all ;
For they knew from whence the intruder had come,
Though he left, *that* night, his tail at home.

This fact, we see, is a parallel case
To the dinner that, some weeks since, took place.

With the difference slight of fiend and man,
    It shows what a nest of Popish sinners
That city must be, where the devil and Dan
    May thus drop in, at quadrilles and dinners!

But, mark the end of these foul proceedings,
These demon hops and Popish feedings.
Some comfort 't will be—to those, at least,
    Who've studied this awful dinner question—
To know that Dan, on the night of that feast,
    Was seized with a dreadful indigestion ;
That envoys were sent, post-haste, to his priest.
To come and absolve the suffering sinner,
For eating so much at a heretic dinner ;
And some good people were even afraid
That Peel's old confectioner—still at the trade—
Had poison'd the Papist with *orangeade.*

———o**o———

NEW HOSPITAL FOR SICK LITERATI.

WITH all humility we beg
To inform the public, that Tom Tegg—
Known for his spunky speculations,
In buying up dead reputations,
And, by a mode of galvanising
Which, all must own, is quite surprising,
Making dead authors move again,
As though they still were living men ;—
All this, too, managed in a trice,
By those two magic words, "Half Price,"
Which brings the charm so quick about,
That worn-out poets, left without
A second *foot* whereon to stand,
Are made to *go* at second *hand,*—
'T will please the public, we repeat,
To learn that Tegg, who works this feat,
And, therefore, knows what care it needs
To keep alive Fame's invalids,
Has oped an Hospital, in town,
For cases of knock'd-up renown—
Falls, fractures, dangerous Epic *fits*
(By some call'd *Cantos*), stabs from wits ;
And, of all wounds for which they're nurst,
Dead cuts from publishers, the worst ;—
All these, and other such fatalities,
That happen to frail immortalities,
By Tegg are so expertly treated,
That oft-times, when the cure's completed,
The patient 's made robust enough
To stand a few more rounds of *puff*,
Till, like the ghosts of Dante's lay,
He 's puff'd into thin air away !

As titled poets (being phenomenons)
Don't like to mix with low and common 'uns,

(1) We have lodgings apart, for our posthumous people,
  As we find that, if left with the live ones, they keep ill.
(2. " *Bottom* : Let me play the lion ; I will roar you as
 I were any nightingale."
(3) History of the Irish Stage.

Tegg's Hospital has separate wards,
Express for literary lords,
Where *prose*-peers of immoderate length,
Are nursed, when they 've outgrown their
    strength,
And poets, whom their friends despair of,
Are—put to bed and taken care of.

Tegg begs to contradict a story,
Now current both with Whig and Tory,
That Doctor W—rb—t—n, M. P.,
Well known for his antipathy,
His deadly hate, good man, to all
The race of poets, great and small—
So much that he 's been heard to own,
He would most willingly cut down
The holiest groves on Pindus' mount,
To turn the timber to account !—
The story actually goes, that he
Prescribes at Tegg's Infirmary ;
And oft, not only stints for spite,
The patients in their copyright,
But that, on being call'd in lately
To two sick poets, suffering greatly,
This vaticidal Doctor sent them
So strong a dose of Jeremy Bentham,
That one of the poor bards but cried,
" Oh, Jerry ! Jerry ! " and then died ;
While t' other, though less stuff was given,
Is on his road, 't is fear'd, to heaven !

Of this event, howe'er unpleasant,
Tegg means to say no more at present—
Intending shortly to prepare
A statement of the whole affair,
With full accounts, at the same time,
Of some late cases (prose and rhyme)
Subscribed with every author's name,
That 's now on the Sick List of Fame.

RELIGION AND TRADE.

" Sir Robert Peel believed it was necessary to originate
    all respecting religion and trade in a Committee of the
    House."—*Church Extension,* May 22, 1830.

SAY, who was the wag, indecorously witty,
    Who first, in a statute, this libel convey'd ;
And thus slily referr'd to the self-same committee,
    As matters congenial, Religion and Trade ?

Oh surely, my Ph—llp—ts, 't was thou did'st the
        deed ;
    For none but thyself, or some pluralist brother,
Accustom'd to mix up the craft with the creed,
    Could bring such a pair thus to twin with each
        other.

And yet, when one thinks of times present and gone,
    One is forced to confess, on maturer reflection,

That 'tis n't in the eyes of committees alone
    That the shrine and the shop seem to have some
        connection.

Not to mention those monarchs of Asia's fair land,
    Whose civil list all is in " good-money " paid ;
And where the whole people, by royal command,
    Buy their gods at the government mart, ready
        made ;—(1)

There was also (as mention'd, in rhyme and in prose,
        is)
    Gold heap'd, throughout Egypt, on every shrine,
To make rings for right reverend crocodiles' noses—
    Just such as, my Ph—llp—ts, would look well in
        thine.

But one need n't fly off, in this erudite mood ;
    And 't is clear, without going to regions so sunny,
That priests love to do the *least* possible good,
    For the largest *most* possible quantum of money.

" Ofthim," saith the text, " unto whom much is given,
    Of him much, in turn, will be also required :"—
" By *me*," quoth the sleek and obese man of
        heaven—
    " Give as much as you will—more will still be
        desired."

More money ! more churches !—oh Nimrod, hadst
        thou
    'Stead of *Tower*-extension, some shorter way
        gone—
Hadst thou known by what methods we mount to
        heaven *now*,
    And tried *Church*-extension, the feat had been
        done!

MUSINGS,

SUGGESTED BY THE LATE PROMOTION OF MRS.
NETHERCOAT.

"The widow Nethercoat is appointed gaoler of Loughrea,
    in the room of her deceased husband."—*Limerick
    Chronicle.*

WHETHER as queens or subjects, in these days,
    Women seem form'd to grace alike each station ;—
As Captain Flaherty gallantly says,
    " You, ladies, are the lords of the creation ! "

Thus o'er my mind did prescient visions float
    Of all that matchless woman yet may be ;
When, hark, in rumours less and less remote,
    Came the glad news o'er Erin's ambient sea,
The important news—that Mrs. Nethercoat
    Had been appointed gaoler of Loughrea :

(1) The Birmans may not buy the sacred marble in mass,
but must purchase figures of the deity already made.—
Symes.

Yes, mark it, History—Nethercoat is dead,
And Mrs. N. now rules his realm instead;
Hers the high task to wield the uplocking keys,
To rivet rogues and reign o'er Rapparees!

Thus, while your blusterers of the Tory school
Find Ireland's sanest sons so hard to rule,
One meek-eyed matron, in Whig doctrines nurst,
Is all that's ask'd to curb the maddest, worst!

Show me the man that dares, with blushless brow,
Prate about Erin's rage and riot now ;—
Now, when her temperance forms her sole excess;
   When long-loved whiskey, fading from her sight,
"Small by degrees, and beautifully less,"
   Will soon, like other *spirits,* vanish quite;
When of red coats the number's grown so small,
   That soon, to cheer the warlike parson's eyes,
No glimpse of scarlet will be seen at all,
   Save that which she of Babylon supplies ;—
Or, at the most, a corporal's guard will be
   Of Ireland's *red* defence the sole remains ;
While of its goals bright woman keeps the key
   And captive Paddies languish in her chains !

Long may such lot be Erin's, long be mine
Oh yes—if even this world, though bright it shine,
   In Wisdom's eyes a prison-house must be,
At least let woman's hand our fetters twine,
   And blithe I'll sing, more joyous than if free,
The Nethercoats, the Nethercoats for me !

—o**c—

INTENDED TRIBUTE

TO THE AUTHOR OF AN ARTICLE IN THE LAST NUMBER
OF THE "QUARTERLY REVIEW," ENTITLED
"ROMANISM IN IRELAND."

It glads us much to be able to say,
That a meeting is fix'd, for some early day,
Of all such dowagers—*he* or *she*—
(No matter the sex, so they dowagers be,)
Whose opinions, concerning Church and State,
From about the time of the Curfew date—
Staunch sticklers still for days by-gone,
And admiring *them* for their rust alone—
To whom if we would a leader give,
Worthy their tastes conservative,
We need but some mummy-statesman raise,
Who was pickled and potted in Ptolemy's days ;
For *that*'s the man, if waked from his shelf,
To conserve and swaddle this world, like himself.

(1) See Congreve's *Love for Love.*
(2) *Beaux Stratagem.*
(3) The writer of the article has groped about, with much success, in what he calls "the dark recesses of Dr. Dens's disquisitions."—*Quarterly Review.*
(4 "Pray, may we ask, has there been any rebellious movement of Popery in Ireland, since the planting of the Ulster colonies, in which something of the kind was not

Such, we're happy to state, are the old *he*-dames
Who've met in committee, and given their names
(In good hieroglyphics), with kind intent
To pay some handsome compliment
To their sister-author, the nameless he,
Who wrote, in the last new *Quarterly,*
That charming assault upon Popery ;
An article justly prized by them,
As a perfect antediluvian gem—
The work, as Sir Sampson Legend would say,
Of some "fellow the Flood could n't wash away."(1)

The fund being raised, there remain'd but to see
What the dowager-author's gift was to be.
And here, I must say, the Sisters Blue
Show'd delicate taste and judgment too.
For, finding the poor man suffering greatly
From the awful stuff he has thrown up lately—
So much so, indeed, to the alarm of all,
As to bring on a fit of what doctors call
The Antipapistico-monomania
(I'm sorry with such a long word to detain ye),
They've acted the part of a kind physician,
By suiting their gift to the patient's condition;
And, as soon as 'tis ready for presentation,
We shall publish the facts, for the gratification
Of this highly-favour'd and Protestant nation.

Meanwhile, to the great alarm of his neighbours,
He still continues his *Quarterly* labours;
And often has strong No-Popery fits,
Which frighten his old nurse out of her wits.
Sometimes he screams, like Scrub in the play, (2)
"Thieves ! Jesuits ! Popery !" night and day ;
Takes the Printer's Devil for Doctor Dens, (3)
And shies at him heaps of High-church pens ; (4)
Which the Devil (himself a touchy Dissenter)
Feels all in his hide, like arrows, enter.   [gist's,
'Stead of swallowing wholesome stuff from the drug-
He *will* keep raving of "Irish Thuggists;" (5)
Tells us they all go murdering, for fun,
From rise of morn till set of sun,
Pop, pop, as fast as a minute-gun ! (6)
If ask'd, how comes it the gown and cassock are
Safe and fat, 'mid this general massacre—
How haps it that Pat's own population
But swarms the more for this trucidation—
He refers you, for all such memoranda,
To the "*archives of the Propaganda !*" (7)
This is all we've got, for the present, to say—
But shall take up the subject some future day.

visible among the Presbyterians of the North ?"—*Quarterly Review.*
(5) "Lord Lorton, for instance, who, for clearing his estate of a village of Irish Thuggists," etc., etc.—*Ibid.*
(6) "Observe how murder after murder is committed, like minute-guns."—*Ibid.*
(7) "Might not the archives of the Propaganda possibly supply the key?"

GRAND DINNER OF TYPE AND CO.

A POOR POET'S DREAM. (1)

As I sate in my study, lone and still,
Thinking of Sergeant Talfourd's Bill,
And the speech, by Lawyer Sugden made,
In spirit congenial, for " the Trade,"
Sudden I sunk to sleep, and, lo,
  Upon Fancy's reinless night-mare flitting,
I found myself, in a second or so,
  At the table of Messrs. Type and Co.

With a goodly group of diners sitting ;—
All in the printing and publishing line,
Drest, I thought, extremely fine,
And sipping, like lords, their rosy wine ;
While I, in a state near inanition,
  With coat that had n't much nap to spare
(Having just gone into its second edition),
  Was the only wretch of an author there.

But think, how great was my surprise,
When I saw, in casting round my eyes,
That the dishes, sent up by Type's she-cooks,
Bore all, in appearance, the shape of books ;
Large folios—God knows where they got 'em,
In these *small* times—at top and bottom ;
And quartos (such as the Press provides
For no one to read them) down the sides.
Then flash'd a horrible thought on my brain,
And I said to myself, " 'T is all too plain,
Like those, well known in school quotations,
Who ate up for dinner their own relations,
I see now, before me, smoking here,
The bodies and bones of my brethren dear—
Bright sons of the lyric and epic Muse,
All cut up in cutlets, or hash'd in stews ;
Their *works*, a light through ages to go—
Themselves, eaten up by Type and Co. !"

While thus I moralised, on they went,
Finding the fare most excellent ;
And all so kindly, brother to brother,
Helping the tidbits to each other ;
" A slice of Southey let me send you "—
"This cut of Campbell I recommend you "—
" And here, my friends, is a treat indeed,
The immortal Wordsworth fricasseed !"

Thus having, the cormorants, fed some time,
Upon joints of poetry—all of the prime—
With also (as Type in a whisper averr'd it)
"Cold prose on the sideboard, for such as preferr'd
  it "—
They rested awhile, to recruit their force,
Then pounced, like kites, on the second course,

(1) Written during the late agitation of the question of
Copyright.

(2) "For a certain man named Demetrius, a silversmith,
which made shrines for Diana, brought no small gain unto

Which was singing-birds merely—Moore and
  others—
Who all went the way of their larger brothers ;
And, numerous now though such songsters be,
'T was really quite distressing to see
A whole dishful of Toms—Moore, Dibdin, Bayly—
Bolted by Type and Co. so gaily !

Nor was this the worst—I shudder to think
What a scene was disclosed when they came to drink.
The warriors of Odin, as every one knows,
Used to drink out of skulls of slaughter'd foes :
And Type's old port, to my horror I found,
Was in skulls of bards sent merrily round.
And still as each well-fill'd cranium came,
A health was pledged to its owner's name ;
While Type said slily, 'midst general laughter,
" We eat them up first, them drink to them after."

There was *no* standing this — incensed I broke
From my bonds of sleep, and indignant woke,
Exclaiming, " Oh shades of other times,
Whose voices still sound, like deathless chimes,
Could you e'er have foretold a day would be,
When a dreamer of dreams should live to see
A party of sleek and honest John Bulls
Hobnobbing each other in poets' skulls !"

·>·)·<·

CHURCH EXTENSION.

TO THE EDITOR OF THE MORNING CHRONICLE.

SIR—A well-known classical traveller, while employed in
exploring, some time since, the supposed site of the
Temple of Diana of Ephesus, was so fortunate, in the
course of his researches, as to light upon a very ancient
bark manuscript, which has turned out, on examina-
tion, to be part of an old Ephesian newspaper : — a
newspaper published, as you will see, so far back as
the time when Demetrius, the great Shrine-Extender, (2)
flourished.   I am, Sir, yours, etc.

EPHESIAN GAZETTE.

Second edition.

IMPORTANT event for the rich and religious !
  Great Meeting of Silversmiths held in Queen
    Square ;—
Church Extension their object—the excitement
    prodigious ;—
Demetrius, head man of the craft, takes the chair!

Third edition.

The Chairman still up, when our devil came away ;
  Having prefaced his speech with the usual state
    prayer,
That the Three-headed Dian (3) would kindly, this
    day,
Take the Silversmiths' Company under her care.

the craftsmen ; whom he called together with the workmen
of like occupation, and said, Sirs, ye know that by this
craft we have our wealth."—*Acts*, xix.

(3) Tria Virginis ora Dianæ.

Being ask'd by some low unestablish'd divines,
" When your churches are up, where are flocks to
be got?"
He manfully answer'd, "Let *us* build the shrines, (1)
And we care not if flocks are found for them or
not."

He then added—to show that the Silversmiths' Guild
Were above all confined and intolerant views—
" Only *pay* through the nose to the altars we build,
You may *pray* through the nose to what altars
you choose."

This tolerance, rare from a shrine-dealer's lip
(Though a tolerance mix'd with due taste for the
till)—
So much charm'd all the holders of scriptural scrip
That their shouts of "Hear!" "Hear!" are re-
echoing still.

                Fourth edition.
Great stir in the Shrine Market! altars to Phœbus
Are going dog-cheap—may be had for a rebus.
Old Dian's, as usual, outsell all the rest;—
But Venus's also are much in request.

—◦●●◦—

LATEST ACCOUNTS FROM OLYMPUS.

As news from Olympus has grown rather rare,
Since bards in their cruises have ceased to *touch*
there,
We extract for our readers the intelligence given
In our latest accounts from that *ci-devant* heaven—
That realm of the By-gones, where still sit, in state,
Old god-heads and nod-heads, now long out of date.

Jove himself, it appears, since his love-days are o'er,
Seems to find Immortality rather a bore;
Though he still asks for news of earth's capers and
. crimes,
And reads daily his old fellow-Thunderer, the *Times.*
He and Vulcan, it seems, by their wives still hen-
peck'd are,
And kept on a stinted allowance of nectar.

Old Phœbus, poor lad, has given up inspiration,
And pack'd off to earth on a *puff*-speculation.
The fact is, he found his old shrines had grown dim,
Since bards look'd to Bentley and Colburn, not him.
So, he sold off his stud of ambrosia-fed nags,
Came incog. down to earth, and now writes for the
Mags;
Taking care that his work not a gleam hath to
linger in 't,   [finger in 't.
From which men could guess that the god had a

There are other small facts, well deserving attention,
Of which our Olympic despatches make mention.
Poor Bacchus is still very ill, they allege,
Having never recover'd the Temperance Pledge.

" What, the Irish!" he cried—"those I look'd to
the most!
If they give up the *spirit,* I give up the ghost:"
While Momus, who used of the gods to make fun,
Is turn'd Socialist now, and declares there are none!

But these changes, though curious, are all a mere
farce
Compared to the new " casus belli " of Mars,
Who, for years, has been suffering the horrors of
quiet,
Uncheer'd by one glimmer of bloodshed or riot!
In vain from the clouds his belligerent brow
Did he pop forth, in hopes that somewhere or some-
how,
Like Pat at a fair, he might " coax up a row :"
But the joke would n't take—the whole world had
got wiser;
Men liked not to take a Great Gun for adviser ;
And, still less, to march in fine clothes to be shot,
Without very well knowing for whom or for what.
The French, who of slaughter had had their full
swing,
Were content with a shot, now and then, at their
King ;
While, in England, good fighting 's a pastime so hard
to gain,
Nobody's left to fight *with,* but Lord C—rd—g—n.

'T is needless to say, then, how monstrously happy
Old Mars has been made by what 's now on the *tapis;*
How much it delights him to see the French rally,
In Liberty's name, around Mehemet Ali;
Well knowing that Satan himself could not find
A confection of mischief much more to his mind
Than the old Bonnet Rouge and the Bashaw com-
bined.
Right well, too, he knows, that there ne'er were
attackers,
Whatever their cause, that they did n't find backers;
While any slight care for Humanity's woes
May be soothed by that " Art Diplomatique," which
shows
How to come, in the most approved method, to
blows.

This is all, for to-day—whether Mars is much vext
At his friend Thiers's exit, we'll know by our next.

—◦●●◦—

THE TRIUMPHS OF FARCE.

OUR earth, as it rolls through the regions of space,
Wears always two faces, the dark and the sunny;
And poor human life runs the same sort of race,
Being sad, on one side—on the other side, funny.

(1 The "shrines" are supposed to have been small
churches, or chapels, adjoining to the great temples;—
" ædiculæ, in quibus statuæ reponebantur."—*Erasm.*

Thus oft we, at eve, to the Haymarket hie,
    To weep o'er the woes of Macready ;—but scarce
Hath the tear-drop of Tragedy pass'd from the eye,
    When, lo, we 're all laughing in fits at the Farce.

And still let us laugh—preach the world as it may—
    Where the cream of the joke is, the swarm will
        soon follow ;
Heroics are very grand things, in their way,
    But the laugh at the long run will carry it hollow.

For instance, what sermon on human affairs
    Could equal the scene that took place t'other day
'Twixt Romeo and Louis Philippe, on the stairs—
    The Sublime and Ridiculous meeting half-way!

Yes, Jocus! gay god, whom the Gentiles supplied,
    And whose worship not even among Christians
        declines,
In our senate thou 'st languish'd since Sheridan died,
    But Sydney still keeps thee alive in our shrines.

Rare Sydney ! thrice honour'd the stall where he sits,
    And be his every honour he deigneth to climb at!
Had England a hierarchy form'd all of wits,
    Who but Sydney would England proclaim as its
        primate?

And long may he flourish, frank, merry, and brave—
    A Horace to hear, and a Paschal to read ; (1)
While he *laughs* all is safe, but, when Sydney grows
        grave,
    We shall then think the Church is in danger in-
        deed.

Meanwhile it much glads us to find he 's preparing
    To teach *other* bishops to "seek the right way ;(2)
And means shortly to treat the whole Bench to an
        airing,
    Just such as he gave to Charles James t'other day.

For our parts, though gravity 's good for the soul,
    Such a fancy have we for the side that there 's fun
        on,
We 'd rather with Sydney south-west take a "stroll,"
    Than *coach* it north-east with his Lordship of
        Lunnun.

—o H o—

THOUGHTS ON PATRONS, PUFFS, AND
OTHER MATTERS.

IN AN EPISTLE FROM T. M. TO S. R.

WHAT, *thou,* my friend ! a man of rhymes,
    And, better still, a man of guineas,
To talk of "patrons," in these times,
    When authors thrive, like spinning-jennies,

(1) Some parts of the *Provinciales* may be said to be of
the highest order of *jeux d'esprit*, or squibs.
(2) " This stroll in the metropolis is extremely well con-
trived for your Lordhip's speech ; but suppose, my dear

And Arkwright's twist and Bulwer's page
    Alike may laugh at patronage!

No, no—those times are past away,
    When, doom'd in upper floors to star it,
The bard inscribed to lords his lay—
    Himself, the while, my Lord Mountgarret.
No more he begs, with air dependent,
    His "little bark may sail attendant"
    Under some lordly skipper's steerage;
But launch'd triumphant in the Row,
Or ta'en by Murray's self in tow,
    Cuts both *Star Chamber* and the peerage.

Patrons, indeed ! when scarce a sail
Is whisk'd from England by the gale,
But bears on board some authors, shipp'd
For foreign shores, all well equipp'd
With proper book-making machinery,
To sketch the morals, manners, scenery,
Of all such lands as they shall see,
Or not see, as the case may be :—
It being enjoin'd on all who go
To study first Miss M ········,
And learn from her the method true
To *do* one's books—and readers, too.
For so this nymph of *nous* and nerve
Teaches mankind "How to Observe;"
And, lest mankind at all should swerve,
Teaches them also " *What* to Observe."

No, no, my friend—it can't be blink'd --
The Patron is a race extinct;
As dead as any Megatherion
That ever Buckland built a theory on.
Instead of bartering, in this age,
Our praise for pence and patronage,
We, authors, now, more prosperous elves,
Have learn'd to patronise ourselves;
And since all-potent Puffing 's made,
The life of song, the soul of trade,
More frugal of our praises grown,
We puff no merits but our own.

Unlike those feeble gales of praise
Which critics blew in former days,
Our modern puffs are of a kind
That truly, really *raise the wind;*
And since they 've fairly set in blowing,
We find them the best *trade*-winds going.
'Stead of frequenting paths so slippy
As her old haunts near Aganippe,
The Muse, now, taking to the till,
Has open'd shop on Ludgate Hill
(Far handier than the Hill of Pindus,
As seen from bard's back attic windows);

Lord, that instead of going E. and N. E. you had turned
about," etc., etc.—*Sydney Smith's Last Letter to the Bi-
shop of London.*

And swallowing there without cessation
Large draughts (*at sight*) of inspiration,
Touches the *notes* for each new theme,
While still fresh " *change* comes o'er her dream."

What Steam is on the deep—and more—
Is the vast power of Puff on shore;
Which jumps to glory's future tenses
Before the present even commences;
And makes " immortal" and "divine" of us
Before the world has read one line of us.

In old times, when the God of Song
Drove his own two-horse team along,
Carrying inside a bard or two,
Book'd for posterity "all through;"—
Their luggage, a few close-pack'd rhymes,
(Like yours, my friend,) for after-times—
So slow the pull to Fame's abode,
That folks oft slept upon the road;—
And Homer's self, sometimes, they say,
Took to his nightcap on the way.(1)
Ye Gods! how different is the story
With our new gallopping sons of glory,
Who, scorning all such slack and slow time,
Dash to posterity in *no* time!
Raise but one general blast of Puff
To start your author—that's enough.
In vain the critics, set to watch him,
Try at the starting-post to catch him;
He's off—the puffers carry it hollow—
The critics, if they please, may follow.
Ere *they*'ve laid down their first positions,
He's fairly blown through six editions!
In vain doth Edinburgh dispense
Her blue and yellow pestilence
(That plague so awful in my time
To young and touchy sons of rhyme)—
The Quarterly, at three months' date,
To catch the Unread One, comes too late;
And nonsense, litter'd in a hurry,
Becomes "immortal," spite of Murray.

But, bless me!—while I thus keep fooling,
I hear a voice cry, " Dinner's cooling."
That postman, too, (who truth to tell,
'Mong men of letters bears the bell,)
Keeps ringing, ringing, so infernally
That I *must* stop—
                                Yours sempiternally.

—○⦂○—

THOUGHTS ON MISCHIEF.

BY LORD ST—NL—Y.

(HIS FIRST ATTEMPT IN VERSE.)

" Evil, be thou my good."—*Milton.*

How various are the inspirations
Of different men, in different nations!
As genius prompts to good or evil,
Some call the Muse, some raise the devil.

Old Socrates, that pink of sages,
Kept a pet demon, on board wages,
To go about with him incog.,
And sometimes give his wits a jog.
So L—nd—st, in *our* day, we know,
Keeps fresh relays of imps below,
To forward, from that nameless spot,
His inspirations, hot and hot.

But, neat as are old L—nd—st's doings—
Beyond even Hecate's "hell-broth" brewings—
Had I, Lord Stanley, but my will,
I'd show you mischief prettier still;
Mischief, combining boyhood's tricks
With age's sourest politics;
The urchin's freaks, the veteran's gall,
Both duly mix'd, and matchless all;
A compound nought in history reaches
But Machiavel, when first in breeches!

Yes, Mischief, Goddess multiform,
Whene'er thou, witch-like ridest the storm,
Let Stanley ride cock-horse behind thee—
No livelier lackey could they find thee.
And, Goddess, as I'm well aware,
So mischief's *done*, you care not *where*,
I own, 't will most *my* fancy tickle
In Paddyland to play the Pickle;
Having got credit for inventing
A new brisk method of tormenting—
A way they call the Stanley fashion,
Which puts all Ireland in a passion;
So neat it hits the mixture due
Of injury and insult too;
So legibly it bears upon 't
The stamp of Stanley's brazen front.

Ireland, we're told, means land of *Ire;*
And *why* she's so none need inquire,
Who see her millions, martial, manly,
Spat upon thus by me, Lord St—nl—y.
Already in the breeze I scent
The whiff of coming devilment;
Of strife, to me more stirring far
Than the Opium or the Sulphur war,
Or any such drug ferments are.
Yes—sweeter to this Tory soul
Than all such pests, from pole to pole,
Is the rich "swelter'd venom" got
By stirring Ireland's " charmed pot;" (2)
And, thanks to practice on that land,
I stir it with a master-hand.

Again thou'lt see, when forth hath gone
The War-Church-cry, " On, Stanley on!"

(1) Quandoque bonus dormitat Homerus.—*Horat.*
(2)   " Swelter'd venom, sleeping got,
            Boil thou first i' the charmed pot."

How Caravats and Shanavests
Shall swarm from out their mountain nests,
With all their merry moonlight brothers)
To whom the Church (step-dame to others)
Hath been the best of nursing mothers.
Again o'er Erin's rich domain
Shall Rockites and right reverends reign ;
And both, exempt from vulgar toil,
Between them share that titheful soil ;
Puzzling ambition *which* to climb at,
The post of Captain, or of Primate.

And so, long life to Church and Co.—
Hurrah for mischief!—here we go.

—❦❦❦—

EPISTLE FROM CAPTAIN ROCK TO
LORD L—NDH—T.

Dear L—ndh—t—you 'll pardon my making thus
free—
But form is all fudge 'twixt such " comrogues " as
we,
Who, whate'er the smooth views we, in public, may
drive at,
Have both the same praiseworthy object in private—
Namely, never to let the old regions of riot,
Where Rock hath long reign'd, have one instant of
quiet,
But keep Ireland still in that liquid we 've taught her
To love more than meat, drink, or clothing—*hot
water.*

All the difference betwixt you and me, as I take it,
Is simply, that *you* make the law and *I* break it ;
And never, of big-wigs and small, were there two
Play'd so well into each other's hands as we do ;
Insomuch that the laws you and yours manufacture
Seem all made express for the Rock-boys to fracture.
Not Birmingham's self—to her shame be it spoken—
E'er made things more neatly contrived to be broken ;
And hence, I confess, in this island religious,
The breakage of laws—and of heads *is* prodigious.

And long may it thrive, my Ex-Bigwig, say I—
Though, of late, much I fear'd all our fun was gone by ;
As, except when some tithe-hunting parson show'd
sport,
Some rector—a cool hand at pistols and port,
Who " keeps dry " his *powder*, but never *himself*—
One who, leaving his Bible to rust on the shelf,
Sends his pious texts home, in the shape of ball-
cartridges,
Shooting his " dearly beloved," like partridges ;—
Except when some hero of this sort turn'd out,
Or the Exchequer sent, flaming, its tithe-writs (1)
about—
A contrivance more neat, I may say, without flattery,
Than e'er yet was thought of for bloodshed and battery ;
So neat, that even *I* might be proud, I allow,
To have hit off so rich a receipt for a *row* ;—

Except for such rigs turning up, now and then,
I was actually growing the dullest of men ;
And, had this blank fit been allow'd to increase,
Might have snored myself down to a Justice of Peace.
Like you, Reformation in Church and in State
Is the thing of all things I most cordially hate.
If once these curst Ministers do as they like,
All 's o'er, my good Lord, with your wig and my pike,
And one may be hung up on t' other, henceforth,
Just to show what *such* Captains and Chancellors
were worth.

But we must not despair—even already Hope sees
You 're about, my bold Baron, to kick up a breeze
Of the true baffling sort, such as suits me and you,
Who have box'd the whole compass of party right
through,
And care not one farthing, as all the world knows,
So we *but* raise the wind, from what quarter it blows.
Forgive me, dear Lord, that thus rudely I dare
My own small resources with thine to compare :
Not even Jerry Diddler, in " raising the wind," durst
Compete, for one instant, with thee, my dear L—nd-
h—t.

But, hark, there 's a shot!—some parsonic practi-
tioner?
No—merely a bran-new Rebellion Commissioner ;
The Courts having now, with true law erudition,
Put even Rebellion itself " in commission."
As seldom, in *this* way, I 'm any man's debtor,
I 'll just *pay my shot*, and then fold up this letter.
In the mean time, hurrah for the Tories and Rocks !
Hurrah for the parsons who fleece well their flocks !
Hurrah for all mischief in all ranks and spheres,
And, above all, hurrah for that dear House of Peers !

—❦❦❦—

CAPTAIN ROCK IN LONDON.

LETTER FROM THE CAPTAIN TO TERRY ALT, ESQ. (2)

Here I am, at head-quarters, dear Terry, once more,
Deep in Tory designs, as I 've oft been before :—
For, bless them! if 'twas n't for this wrong-headed
crew,
You and I, Terry Alt, would scarce know what to do ;
So ready they 're always, when dull we are growing,
To set our old concert of discord a-going,
While L—ndh—t's the lad, with his Tory-Whig face,
To play, in such concert, the true *double-base*.
I had fear'd this old prop of my realm was beginning
To tire of his course of political sinning,
And, like Mother Cole, when her heyday was past,
Meant, by way of a change, to try virtue at last.
But I wrong'd the old boy, who as staunchly derides
All reform in himself as in most things besides ;
And, by using *two* faces through life, all allow,
Has acquired face sufficient for *any* thing now.

(1) Exchequer tithe processes, served under a com-
mission of rebellion.—*Chronicle.*
(2) The subordinate officer or lieutenant of Captain Rock.

In short, he's all right; and, if mankind's old foe,
My "Lord Harry" himself—who's the leader, we know,
Of another red-hot Opposition, below— [spares
If that "Lord," in his well-known discernment, but
Me and L—ndh—t, to look after Ireland's affairs,
We shall soon such a region of devilment make it,
That Old Nick himself for his own may mistake it.

Even already—long life to such Big-wigs, say I,
For, as long as they flourish, we Rocks cannot die—
He has served our right riotous cause by a speech
Whose perfection of mischief he only could reach;
As it shows off both *his* and *my* merits alike,
Both the swell of the wig, and the point of the pike;
Mixes up, with a skill which one can't but admire,
The lawyer's cool craft with the incendiary's fire,
And enlists, in the gravest, most plausible manner,
Seven millions of souls under Rockery's banner!

Oh, Terry, my man, let this speech *never* die;
Through the regions of Rockland, like flame, let it fly
Let each syllable dark the Law-Oracle utter'd
By all Tipperary's wild echoes be mutter'd,
Till nought shall be heard, over hill, dale, or flood,
But "*You're aliens in language, in creed, and in
    blood;*"
While voices, from sweet Connemara afar,
Shall answer, like true *Irish* echoes, "We are!"
And, though false be the cry, and though sense must
    abhor it,
Still the echoes may quote *Law* authority for it,
And nought L—ndh—t cares for my spread of
    dominion
So he, in the end, touches cash "for the *opinion.*"
But I've no time for more, my dear Terry, just now,
Being busy in helping these Lords through their *row.*
They're bad hands at mob-work, but, once they
    begin,
They'll have plenty of practice to break them well in.

MISCELLANEOUS POEMS.

PREFACE.

A FEW words may be here devoted to a subject with which two of the poems contained in the following pages are closely connected. (1) In my Preface to the *Odes of Anacreon* I briefly noticed the taste for Private Theatrical Performances which prevailed during the latter half of the last century among the higher ranks in Ireland. This taste continued for nearly twenty years to survive the epoch of the Union, and in the performances of the Private Theatre of Kilkenny gave forth its last, as well as, perhaps, brightest flashes. The life and soul of this institution was our manager, the late Mr. Richard Power, a gentleman who could boast a larger circle of attached friends, and through a life more free from shadow or alloy, than any individual it has ever been my lot to know. No livelier proof, indeed, could be required of the sort of feeling entertained towards him than was once shown in the reception given to the two following homely lines which occurred in a Prologue I wrote to be spoken by Mr. Corry in the character of Vapid.

'T is said our worthy manager intends
To help my night, and *he*, you know, has friends. (2)

These few simple words I wrote with the assured conviction that they would produce more effect from the homefelt truism they contained than could be effected by the most laboured burst of eloquence; and the result was just what I had anticipated, for the house rung, for a considerable time, with the heartiest plaudits.

The chief comic, or rather farcical, force of the company lay in my friend Mr. Corry, and, "longo intervallo," myself; and though, as usual, with low

comedians, we were much looked down upon by the lofty lords of the buskin, many was the sly joke we used to indulge together, at the expense of our heroic brethren. Some waggish critic, indeed, is said to have declared that of all the personages of our theatre he most admired the prompter—"because he was least seen and best heard." But this joke was, of course, a mere good-humoured slander. There were two, at least, of our dramatic corps, Sir Wrixon Becher and Mr. Rothe, whose powers, as tragic actors, few amateurs have ever equalled; and Mr. Corry—perhaps alone of all our company—would have been sure of winning laurels on the public stage.

As to my own share in these representations, the following list of my most successful characters will show how remote from the line of the Heroic was the small orbit through which I ranged; my chief parts having been Sam, in *Raising the Wind*, Robin Roughhead, Mungo, Sadi, in the *Mountaineers*, Spado, and Peeping Tom. In the part of Spado there occur several allusions to that gay rogue's shortness of stature which never failed to be welcomed by my auditors with laughter and cheers; and the words "Even Sanguino allows I am a clever little fellow" was always a signal for this sort of friendly explosion. One of the songs, indeed, written by O'Keefe for the character of Spado so much abounds with points thus personally applicable, that many supposed, with no great compliment either to my poetry or my modesty, that the song had been writ-

(1) "Occasional Epilogue, spoken by Mr. Corry," and "Extract from a Prologue, written and spoken by the Author."

(2) "Occasional Epilogue."

ten, expressly for the occasion, by myself. The following is the verse to which I allude, and for the poetry of which I was thus made responsible:—

> "Though born to be little's my fate,
>   Yet so was the great Alexander;
> And, when I walk under a gate,
>   I've no need to stoop like a gander.
> I'm no lanky long hoddy-doddy,
>   Whose paper-kite sails in the sky;
> Though wanting two feet, in my body,
>   In soul, *I* am thirty feet high."

Some further account of the Kilkenny Theatre, as well as of the history of Private Theatricals in general, will be found in an article I wrote on the subject for the *Edinburgh Review*, vol. xlvi., No. 92, p. 368.

MISCELLANEOUS POEMS.

LINES ON THE DEATH OF MR. P—RC—V—L.

In the dirge we sung o'er him no censure was heard,
    Unembitter'd and free did the tear-drop descend;
We forgot, in that hour, how the statesman had err'd,
    And wept for the husband, the father, and friend.

Oh, proud was the meed his integrity won,
    And generous indeed were the tears that we shed,
When, in grief, we forgot all the ill he had done,
    And, though wrong'd by him, living, bewail'd him, when dead.

Even now, if one harsher emotion intrude,
    'Tis to wish he had chosen some lowlier state,
Had known what he was—and, content to be *good*,
    Had ne'er, for our ruin, aspired to be *great*.

So, left through their own little orbit to move,
    His years might have roll'd inoffensive away;
His children might still have been bless'd with his love,
    And England would ne'er have been cursed with his sway.

LINES ON THE DEATH OF SH—R—D—N.

Principibus placuisse viris!—*Horat.*

Yes, grief will have way—but the fast falling tear
    Shall be mingled with deep execrations on those,
Who could bask in that Spirit's meridian career,
    And yet leave it thus lonely and dark at its close:—

Whose vanity flew round him, only while fed
    By the odour his fame in its summer-time gave;—
Whose vanity now, with quick scent for the dead,
    Like the Ghole of the East, comes to feed at his grave.

Oh! it sickens the heart to see bosoms so hollow,
    And spirits so mean in the great and high-born;
To think what a long line of titles may follow
    The relics of him who died—friendless and lorn!

How proud they can press to the funeral array
    Of one, whom they shunn'd in his sickness and sorrow:—
How bailiffs may seize his last blanket, to-day,
    Whose pall shall be held up by nobles to-morrow!

And Thou, too, whose life, a sick epicure's dream,
    Incoherent and gross, even grosser had pass'd
Were it not for that cordial and soul-giving beam,
    Which his friendship and wit o'er thy nothingness cast:—

No, not for the wealth of the land, that supplies thee
    With millions to heap upon Foppery's shrine—
No, not for the riches of all who despise thee,
    Though this would make Europe's whole opulence mine—

Would I suffer what—even in the heart that thou hast—
    All mean as it is—must have consciously burn'd,
When the pittance, which shame had wrung from thee at last,
    And which found all his wants at an end, was return'd! (1)

"Was *this* then the fate"—future ages will say,
    When *some* names shall live but in history's curse;
When Truth will be heard, and these Lords of a day
    Be forgotten as fools, or remember'd as worse;—

"Was this then the fate of that high-gifted man,
    The pride of the palace, the bower, and the hall,
The orator—dramatist—minstrel—who ran
    Through each mode of the lyre, and was master of all;—

"Whose mind was an essence, compounded with art
    From the finest and best of all other men's powers;—
Who ruled, like a wizard, the world of the heart,
    And could call up its sunshine, or bring down its showers;—

"Whose humour, as gay as the fire-fly's light,
    Play'd round every subject, and shone as it play'd;—
Whose wit, in the combat, as gentle as bright,
    Ne'er carried a heart-stain away on its blade;—

"Whose eloquence—brightening whatever it tried,
    Whether reason or fancy, the gay or the grave—
Was as rapid, as deep, and as brilliant a tide,
    As ever bore Freedom aloft on its wave!"

(1) The sum was two hundred pounds—*offered* when Sh—r—d—n could no longer take any sustenance, and declined for him, by his friends.

Yes—such was the man, and so wretched his fate;—
And thus, sooner or later, shall all have to grieve,
Who waste their morn's dew in the beams of the Great,
And expect 't will return to refresh them at eve.

In the woods of the North there are insects that prey
On the brain of the elk till his very last sigh: (1)
Oh, Genius! thy patrons, more cruel than they,
First feed on thy brains, and then leave thee to die!

—◦⋅◦—

A MELOLOGUE UPON NATIONAL MUSIC.

THESE verses were written for a Benefit at the Dublin Theatre, and were spoken by Miss Smith, with a degree of success, which they owed solely to her admirable manner of reciting them. I wrote them in haste; and it very rarely happens that poetry, which has cost but little labour to the writer, is productive of any great pleasure to the reader. Under this impression, I certainly should not have published them if they had not found their way into some of the newspapers, with such an addition of errors to their own original stock, that I thought it but fair to limit their responsibility to those faults alone which really belong to them.

With respect to the title which I have invented for this Poem, I feel even more than the scruples of the Emperor Tiberius, when he humbly asked pardon of the Roman Senate for using "the outlandish term, *monopoly*." But the truth is, having written the Poem with the sole view of serving a Benefit, I thought that an unintelligible word of this kind would not be without its attraction for the multitude, with whom, "If 'tis not sense, at least 'tis Greek." To some of my readers, however, it may not be superfluous to say, that by "Melologue," I mean that mixture of recitation and music, which is frequently adopted in the performance of Collins's Ode on the Passions, and of which the most striking example I can remember is the prophetic speech of Joad in the *Athalie* of Racine.　T. M.

A short Strain of Music from the Orchestra.

THERE breathes a language, known and felt
　Far as the pure air spreads its living zone;
Wherever rage can rouse, or pity melt,
　That language of the soul is felt and known.
　　From those meridian plains,
　　Where oft, of old, on some high tower,
The soft Peruvian pour'd his midnight strains,
And call'd his distant love with such sweet power,
　That, when she heard the lonely lay,
　Not worlds could keep her from his arms away,(2)

(1) Naturalists have observed that, upon dissecting an elk, there was found in its head some *large* flies, with its brain almost eaten away by them.—*History of Poland.*
(2) "A certain Spaniard, one night late, met an Indian woman in the streets of Cozco, and would have taken her to his home, but she cried out, 'For God's sake, Sir, let me

To the bleak climes of polar night,
　Where blithe, beneath a sunless sky,
The Lapland lover bids his rein-deer fly,
And sings along the lengthening waste of snow,
　Gaily as if the blessed light
　Of vernal Phœbus burn'd upon his brow;
　　Oh Music! thy celestial claim
　　Is still resistless, still the same;
　　And, faithful as the mighty sea
To the pale star that o'er its realm presides,
　　The spell-bound tides
Of human passion rise and fall for thee!

Greek Air.

List! 'tis a Grecian maid that sings,
　While, from Ilissus' silvery springs,
She draws the cool lymph in her graceful urn;
And by her side, in Music's charm dissolving,
Some patriot youth, the glorious past revolving,
　Dreams of bright days that never can return;
　　When Athens nursed her olive bough,
　　With hands by tyrant power unchain'd;
　　And braided for the muse's brow
　　A wreath by tyrant touch unstain'd:
When heroes trod each classic field
　Where coward feet now faintly falter;
　When every arm was Freedom's shield,
　And every heart was Freedom's altar!

Flourish of Trumpets.

Hark, 'tis the sound that charms
　The war-steed's wakening ears!—
Oh! many a mother folds her arms
Round her boy-soldier when that call she hears;
　And, though her fond heart sink with fears,
　Is proud to feel his young pulse bound
　With valour's fever at the sound.
See, from his native hills afar
The rude Helvetian flies to war;
Careless for what, for whom he fights,
For slave or despot, wrongs or rights;
　　A conqueror of—a hero never—
Yet lavish of his life-blood still,
As if 't were like his mountain rill,
　And gush'd for ever!

Yes, Music, here, even here,
　Amid his thoughtless, vague career,
Thy soul-felt charm asserts its wondrous power.—
　There 's a wild air which oft, among the rocks
Of his own loved land, at evening hour,
　Is heard, when shepherds homeward pipe their flocks,

go; for that pipe, which you hear in yonder tower, calls me with great passion, and I cannot refuse the summons: for love constrains me to go, that I may be his wife, and he my husband.'"—*Garcilasso de la Vega*, in Sir Paul Rycaut's translation.

Whose every note hath power to thrill his mind
 With tenderest thoughts ; to bring around his
  knees
The rosy children whom he left behind,
 And fill each little angel eye
With speaking tears, that ask him why
He wander'd from his hut for scenes like these.
Vain, vain is then the trumpet's brazen roar ;
 Sweet notes of home, of love, are all he hears ;
And the stern eyes, that look'd for blood before,
 Now melting, mournful, lose themselves in tears.

Swiss Air—"Ranz des Vaches."

But, wake the trumpet's blast again,
 And rouse the ranks of warrior-men !
Oh War, when Truth thy arm employs,
And Freedom's spirit guides the labouring storm,
'T is then thy vengeance takes a hallow'd form,
 And, like Heaven's lightning, sacredly destroys.
Nor, Music, through thy breathing sphere,
Lives there a sound more grateful to the ear
 Of Him who made all harmony,
 Than the bless'd sound of fetters breaking,
 And the first hymn that man, awaking
From Slavery's slumber, breathes to Liberty.

Spanish Chorus.

Hark ! from Spain, indignant Spain,
Bursts the bold enthusiast strain,
Like morning's music on the air ;
And seems, in every note, to swear
By Saragossa's ruin'd streets,
 By brave Gerona's deathful story,
That, while *one* Spaniard's life-blood beats,
 That blood shall stain the conqueror's glory.

Spanish Air—"Ya Desperto."

But ah ! if vain the patriot's zeal,
If neither valour's force nor wisdom's light
Can break or melt that blood-cemented seal,
Which shuts so close the book of Europe's right—
 What song shall then in sadness tell
 Of broken pride, of prospects shaded,
 Of buried hopes, remember'd well,
 Of ardour quench'd, and honour faded ?
What muse shall mourn the breathless brave,
 In sweetest dirge at Memory's shrine?
What harp shall sigh o'er Freedom's grave ?
 Oh, Erin, Thine !

—◦)◦◦—

SONGS

FROM M. P.; OR, THE BLUE STOCKING.

YOUNG LOVE LIVED ONCE IN A HUMBLE SHED.

YOUNG Love lived once in a humble shed,
 Where roses breathing,
 And woodbines wreathing
Around the lattice their tendrils spread,
As wild and sweet as the life he led.

His garden flourish'd,
 For young Hope nourish'd
The infant buds with beams and showers ;
But lips, though blooming, must still be fed,
And not even Love can live on flowers.

Alas ! that Poverty's evil eye
 Should e'er come hither,
 Such sweets to wither !
The flowers laid down their heads to die,
And Hope fell sick as the witch drew nigh.
 She came one morning,
 Ere Love had warning,
And raised the latch, where the young god lay ;
"Oh ho !" said Love —" is it you? good by ;"
So he oped the window, and flew away !

———

THIS IS LOVE.

To sigh, yet feel no pain,
 To weep, yet scarce know why :
To sport an hour with Beauty's chain,
 Then throw it idly by.
To kneel at many a shrine,
 Yet lay the heart on none ;
To think all other charms divine,
 But those we just have won.
This is love, faithless love,
Such as kindleth hearts that rove.

To keep one sacred flame,
 Through life unchill'd, unmoved,
To love, in wintry age, the same
 As first in youth we loved ;
To feel that we adore,
 Even to such fond excess,
That though the heart would break, with *more*,
 It could not live with *less*.
This is love, faithful love,
Such as saints might feel above.

———

SPIRIT OF JOY.

SPIRIT of Joy, thy altar lies
 In youthful hearts that hope like mine ;
And 'tis the light of laughing eyes,
 That leads us to thy fairy shrine.
There if we find the sigh, the tear,
 They are not those to Sorrow known ;
But breath so soft, and drops so clear,
 That Bliss may claim them for her own.
Then give me, give me, while I weep,
 The sanguine hope that brightens woe,
And teaches even our tears to keep
 The tinge of pleasure as they flow.

The child who sees the dew of night
 Upon the spangled hedge at morn,
Attempts to catch the drops of light,
 But wounds his finger with the thorn.
Thus oft the brightest joys we seek,
 Are lost when touch'd and turn to pain ;

The flush they kindled leaves the cheek,
The tears they waken long remain.
        But give me, give me, etc., etc.

WHEN LEILA TOUCH'D THE LUTE.

WHEN Leila touch'd the lute,
  Not *then* alone 't was felt,
But, when the sounds were mute,
  In memory still they dwelt.
Sweet lute! in nightly slumbers
Still we heard thy morning numbers.

Ah, how could she, who stole
  Such breath from simple wire,
Be led, in pride of soul,
  To string with gold her lyre?
Sweet lute! thy chords she breaketh;
Golden now the strings she waketh!

But where are all the tales
  Her lute so sweetly told?
In lofty themes she fails,
  And soft ones suit not gold.
Rich lute! we see thee glisten,
But, alas! no more we listen!

BOAT GLEE.

THE song that lightens our languid way
    When brows are glowing,
    And faint with rowing,
Is like the spell of Hope's airy lay,
To whose sound through life we stray.
The beams that flash on the oar awhile,
As we row along through waves so clear,
Illume its spray, like the fleeting smile
  That shines o'er Sorrow's tear.

Nothing is lost on him who sees
  With an eye that Feeling gave;—
For him there 's a story in every breeze,
  And a picture in every wave.
Then sing to lighten the languid way;—
    When brows are glowing,
    And faint with rowing:
'T is like the spell of Hope's airy lay,
To whose sound through life we stray.

OH THINK, WHEN A HERO IS SIGHING.

OH think, when a hero is sighing,
  What danger in such an adorer!
What woman could dream of denying
  The hand that lays laurels before her.
No heart is so guarded around,
  But the smile of a victor would take it;
No bosom can slumber so sound,
  But the trumpet of Glory will wake it.

Love sometimes is given to sleeping,
  And woe to the heart that allows him;

For soon neither smiling nor weeping
  Will e'er from such slumber arouse him.
But though he were sleeping so fast,
  That the life almost seem'd to forsake him,
Even then, one soul-thrilling blast
  From the trumpet of Glory would wake him.

CUPID'S LOTTERY.

A LOTTERY, a Lottery,
In Cupid's Court there used to be;
    Two roguish eyes
    The highest prize,
In Cupid's scheming Lottery;
    And kisses, too,
    As good as new,
Which were not very hard to win,
    For he who won
    The eyes of fun
Was sure to have the kisses in.
      A Lottery, a Lottery, etc.

This Lottery, this Lottery,
In Cupid's Court went merrily,
    And Cupid play'd
    A Jewish trade
In this his scheming Lottery;
    For hearts, we 're told,
    In *shares* he sold
To many a fond believing drone,
    And cut the hearts
    So well in parts,
That each believed the whole his own.

Chor.—A Lottery, a Lottery,
  In Cupid's Court there used to be;
    Two roguish eyes
    The highest prize
  In Cupid's scheming Lottery.

LIBERTY. (1)

THOUGH sacred the tie that our country entwineth,
  And dear to the heart her remembrance remains,
Yet dark are the ties where no liberty shineth,
  And sad the remembrance that slavery stains.
Oh Liberty, born in the cot of the peasant,
  But dying of languor in luxury's dome,
Our vision when absent—our glory when present—
  Where thou art, O Liberty! there is my home.

Farewell to the land where in childhood I wander'd!
  In vain is she mighty, in vain is she brave;
Unbless'd is the blood that for tyrants is squander'd,
  And Fame has no wreaths for the brow of the slave.
But hail to thee, Albion! who meet'st the commotion
  Of Europe, as calm as thy cliffs meet the foam;
With no bonds but the law, and no slave but the ocean,
  Hail temple of Liberty! thou art my home.

(1) Sung in the character of a Frenchman.

OCCASIONAL EPILOGUE,

SPOKEN BY MR. CORRY, IN THE CHARACTER OF VAPID,
AFTER THE PLAY OF THE DRAMATIST, AT THE KIL-
KENNY THEATRE.

(Entering as if to announce the Play.)

LADIES and Gentlemen, on Monday night,
For the ninth time—oh accents of delight
To the poor author's ear, when *three times three*
With a full bumper crowns his Comedy!
When, long by money, and the muse, forsaken,
He finds at length his jokes and boxes taken,
And sees his play-bill circulate—alas,
The only bill on which his name will pass!
Thus, Vapid, thus shall Thespian scrolls of fame
Through box and gallery waft your well-known name,
While critic eyes the happy cast shall con,
And learned ladies spell your *Dram. Person.*

'Tis said our worthy Manager (1) intends
To help my night, and *he,* you know, has friends.
Friends, did I say? for fixing friends, or *parts.*
Engaging actors, or engaging hearts,
There's nothing like him! wits, at his request,
Are turn'd to fools, and dull dogs learn to jest ;
Soldiers, for him, good " trembling cowards " make,
And beaux, turn'd clowns, look ugly for his sake ;
For him even lawyers talk without a fee,
For him (oh friendship!) *I* act tragedy !
In short, like Orpheus, his persuasive tricks
Make boars amusing, and put life in *sticks.*

With *such* a manager we can't but please,
Though London sent us all her loud O. P.s, (2)
Let them come on, like snakes, all hiss and rattle,
Arm'd with a thousand fans, we'd give them battle ;
You, on our side, R. P. (3) upon our banners,
Soon should we teach the saucy O. P.'s manners :
And show that, here—howe'er John Bull may
       doubt—
In all *our* plays, the Riot-Act's cut out ;
And, while we skim the cream of many a jest,
Your well-timed thunder never sours its zest.

Oh gently thus, when three short weeks are past,
At Shakspeare's altar (4) shall we breathe our last ;
And, ere this long-loved dome to ruin nods,
Die all, die nobly, die like demigods !

EXTRACT

FROM A PROLOGUE WRITTEN AND SPOKEN BY THE
AUTHOR, AT THE OPENING OF THE KILKENNY
THEATRE, OCTOBER, 1809.

YET, even here, though Fiction rules the hour,
There shine some genuine smiles, beyond her power ;

(1) The late Mr. Richard Power.
(2) The brief appellation by which those persons were
distinguished who, at the opening of the new theatre of
Covent Garden, clamoured for the continuance of the old
prices of admission.

And there are tears, too—tears that Memory sheds
Even o'er the feast that mimic fancy spreads,
When her heart misses *one* lamented guest, (5)
Whose eye so long threw light o'er all the rest!
There, there, indeed, the Muse forgets her task,
And drooping weeps behind Thalia's mask.

Forgive this gloom—forgive this joyless strain,
Too sad to welcome pleasure's smiling train,
But, meeting thus, our hearts will part the lighter,
As mist at dawn but makes the setting brighter ;
Gay Epilogue will shine where Prologue fails—
As glow-worms keep their splendour for their tails.

I know not why—but time, methinks, hath pass'd
More fleet than usual since we parted last.
It seems but like a dream of yester-night,
Whose charm still hangs, with fond delaying light ;
And, ere the memory lose one glowing hue
Of former joy, we come to kindle new.
Thus ever may the flying moments haste
With trackless foot along life's vulgar waste,
But deeply print and lingeringly move,
When thus they reach the sunny spots we love.
Oh yes, whatever be our gay career,
Let this be still the solstice of the year,
Where Pleasure's sun shall at its height remain,
And slowly sink to level life again.

THE SYLPH'S BALL.

A SYLPH, as bright as ever sported
    Her figure through the fields of air,
By an old swarthy Gnome was courted,
    And, strange to say, he won the fair.

The annals of the oldest witch
    A pair so sorted could not show,
But how refuse?—the Gnome was rich,
    The Rothschild of the world below ;

And Sylphs, like other pretty creatures,
    Are told, betimes, they must consider
Love as an auctioneer of features,
    Who knocks them down to the best bidder.

Home she was taken to his Mine—
    A palace, paved with diamonds all—
And, proud as Lady Gnome to shine,
    Sent our her tickets for a ball.

The *lower* world, of course, was there,
    And all the best ; but of the *upper*
The sprinkling was but shy and rare—
    A few old Sylphids, who loved supper.

(3) The initials of our manager's name.
(4) This alludes to a scenic representation then preparing
for the last night of the performances.
(5) The late Mr. John Lyster, one of the oldest members
and best actors of the Kilkenny Theatrical Society.

As none yet knew the wondrous Lamp
  Of Davy, that renown'd Aladdin,
And the Gnome's halls exhaled a damp,
  Which accidents from fire were bad in;

The chambers were supplied with light
  By many strange but safe devices;
Large fire-flies, such as shine at night
  Among the Orient's flowers and spices;—

Musical flint-mills—swiftly play'd
  By elfin hands—that, flashing round,
Like certain fire-eyed minstrel maids,
  Gave out, at once, both light and sound.

Bologna stones, that drink the sun;
  And water from that Indian sea,
Whose waves at night like wild-fire run—
  Cork'd up in crystal carefully.

Glow-worms, that round the tiny dishes,
  Like little light-houses, were set up;
And pretty phosphorescent fishes,
  That by their own gay light were eat up.

'Mong the few guests from Ether, came
  That wicked Sylph, whom Love we call—
My Lady knew him but by name,
  My Lord, her husband, not at all.

Some prudent Gnomes, 'tis said, apprised
  That he was coming, and no doubt,
Alarm'd about his torch, advised
  He should, by all means, be kept out.

But others disapproved this plan,
  And, by his flame though somewhat frighted,
Thought Love too much a gentleman,
  In such a dangerous place to light it.

However *there* he was—and dancing
  With the fair Sylph, light as a feather;
They look'd like two fresh sunbeams, glancing,
  At daybreak, down to earth together.

And all had gone off safe and well,
  But for that plaguy torch, whose light,
Though not *yet* kindled—who could tell
  How soon, how devilishly, it *might*?

And so it chanced—which, in those dark
  And fireless halls was quite amazing;
Did we not know how small a spark
  Can set the torch of Love a-blazing.

Whether it came (when close entangled
  In the gay waltz) from her bright eyes,
Or from the *lucciole*, that spangled
  Her locks of jet—is all surmise;

But certain 'tis the ethereal girl
  Did drop a spark, at some odd turning,
Which, by the waltz's windy whirl
  Was fann'd up into actual burning.

Oh for that Lamp's metallic gauze,
  That curtain of protecting wire,
Which Davy delicately draws
  Around illicit, dangerous fire!—

The wall he sets 'twixt Flame and Air,
  (Like that, which barr'd young Thisbe's bliss,)
Through whose small holes this dangerous pair
  May see each other, but not kiss. (1)

At first the torch look'd rather bluely—
  A sign, they say, that no good boded—
Then quick the gas became unruly,
  And, crack! the ball-room all exploded.

Sylphs, gnomes, and fiddlers mix'd together,
  With all their aunts, sons, cousins, nieces,
Like butterflies in stormy weather,
  Were blown—legs, wings, and tails—to pieces!

While, 'mid these victims of the torch,
  The Sylph, alas, too, bore her part—
Found lying, with a livid scorch
  As if from lightning, o'er her heart!

. . . .

" Well done"—a laughing Goblin said—
  Escaping from this gaseous strife—
"'Tis not the *first* time Love has made
  A *blow-up* in connubial life!"

——◦••◦——

REMONSTRANCE,

AFTER A CONVERSATION WITH LORD JOHN RUSSELL,
IN WHICH HE HAD INTIMATED SOME IDEA OF GIV-
ING UP ALL POLITICAL PURSUITS.

What! *thou*, with thy genius, thy youth, and thy
    name—
  Thou, born of a Russell—whose instinct to run
The accustom'd career of thy sires is the same
  As the eaglet's to soar with his eyes on the sun!

Whose nobility comes to thee, stamp'd with a seal,
  Far, far more ennobling than monarch e'er set;
With the blood of thy race, offer'd up for the weal
  Of a nation, that swears by that martyrdom yet!

Shalt *thou* be faint-hearted and turn from the strife,
  From the mighty arena, where all that is grand,
And devoted, and pure, and adorning in life,
  'Tis for high-thoughted spirits like thine to com-
    mand?

1)   —— Partique dedère
        Oscula quisque suæ, non pervenientia contrà.—*Ovid.*

Oh no, never dream it—while good men despair
  Between tyrants and traitors, and timid men bow,
Never think, for an instant, thy country can spare
  Such a light from her darkening horizon as thou.

With a spirit, as meek as the gentlest of those
  Who in life's sunny valley lie shelter'd and warm;
Yet bold and heroic as ever yet rose
    To the top cliffs of Fortune, and breasted her
      storm;

With an ardour for liberty, fresh as, in youth,
  It first kindles the bard and gives life to his lyre;
Yet mellow'd, e'en now, by that mildness of truth,
  Which tempers, but chills not, the patriot fire;

With an eloquence—not like those rills from a
    height,
  Which sparkle, and foam, and in vapour are o'er;
But a current, that works out its way into light
    Through the filtering recesses of thought and of
      lore.

Thus gifted, thou never canst sleep in the shade;
  If the stirrings of Genius, the music of Fame,
And the charms of thy cause have not power to
    persuade,   [Name.
  Yet think how to Freedom thou'rt pledged by thy

Like the boughs of that laurel, by Delphi's decree,
  Set apart for the Fane and its service divine,
So the branches that spring from the old Russell
    tree
Are by Liberty *claim'd* for the use of her Shrine.

MY BIRTH-DAY.

"My birth-day"—what a different sound
  That word had in my youthful ears!
And how, each time the day comes round,
  Less and less white its mark appears!

When first our scanty years are told,
  It seems like pastime to grow old;
And, as Youth counts the shining links,
  That Time around him binds so fast,
Pleased with the task, he little thinks
  How hard that chain will press at last.

Vain was the man, and false as vain,
  Who said (1)—"were he ordain'd to run
His long career of life again,
  He would do all that he *had* done."—
Ah, 'tis not thus the voice, that dwells
  In sober birth-days, speaks to me;
Far otherwise—of time it tells,
  Lavish'd unwisely, carelessly;
Of counsel mock'd; of talents, made
  Haply for high and pure designs,

But oft, like Israel's incense, laid
  Upon unholy earthly shrines;
Of nursing many a wrong desire;
  Of wandering after Love too far,
And taking every meteor fire,
  That cross'd my pathway, for his star;—
All this it tells, and, could I trace
  The imperfect picture o'er again,
With power to add, retouch, efface
  The lights and shades, the joy and pain,
How little of the past would stay!
  How quickly all should melt away
All—but that Freedom of the Mind,
  Which hath been more than wealth to me;
Those friendships, in my boyhood twined,
  And kept till now unchangingly;
And that dear home, that saving ark,
  Where Love's true light at last I've found,
Cheering within, when all grows dark,
  And comfortless, and stormy round!

FANCY.

The more I've view'd this world, the more I've
    found,
That, fill'd as 't is with scenes and creatures rare,
Fancy commands, within her own bright round,
  A world of scenes and creatures far more fair.
Nor is it that her power can call up there
  A single charm, that's not from Nature won—
No more than rainbows, in their pride, can wear
  A single tint unborrow'd from the sun;
But 'tis the mental medium it shines through,
  That lends to Beauty all its charm and hue;
As the same light, that o'er the level lake
  One dull monotony of lustre flings,
Will, entering in the rounded rain-drop, make
  Colours as gay as those on angels' wings!

TRANSLATIONS FROM CATULLUS.

Carm. 70.
Dicebas quondam, etc.

TO LESBIA.

Thou told'st me, in our days of love,
  That I had all that heart of thine;
That, even to share the couch of Jove,
  Thou would'st not, Lesbia, part from mine.

How purely wert thou worshipp'd then!
  Not with the vague and vulgar fires
Which Beauty wakes in soulless men—
  But loved, as children by their sires.

That flattering dream, alas, is o'er;—
  I know thee now—and though these eyes
Doat on thee wildly as before,
  Yet, even in doating, I despise.

(1) *Fontenelle.*—"Si je recommençais ma carrière, je
ferais tout ce que j'ai fait."

Yes, sorceress—mad as it may seem—
With all thy craft, such spells adorn thee,
That passion even outlives esteem,
And I, at once, adore—and scorn thee.

Carm II.

Pauca nunciate meæ puellæ.

. . . .

COMRADES and friends! with whom, where'er
The fates have will'd, through life I 've roved,
Now speed ye home, and with you bear
These bitter words to her I 've loved.

Tell her from fool to fool to run,
Where'er her vain caprice may call;
Of all her dupes not loving one,
But ruining and maddening all.

Bid her forget—what now is past—
Our once dear love, whose ruin lies
Like a fair flower, the meadow's last,
Which feels the ploughshare's edge, and dies!

Carm. 29.

*Peninsularum Sirmio, insularumque
Ocelle.*

SWEET Sirmio! thou, the very eye
Of all peninsulas and isles,
That in our lakes of silver lie,
Or sleep, enwreathed by Neptune's smiles—

How gladly back to thee I fly!
Still doubting, asking—*can* it be
That I have left Bithynia's sky,
And gaze in safety upon thee?

Oh! what is happier than to find
Our hearts at ease, our perils past;
When, anxious long, the lighten'd mind
Lays down its load of care at last:

When, tired with toil o'er land and deep,
Again we tread the welcome floor
Of our own home, and sink to sleep
On the long-wish'd-for bed once more. (1)

This, this it is, that pays alone
The ills of all life's former track :
Shine out, my beautiful, my own
Sweet Sirmio, greet thy master back.

And thou, fair Lake, whose water quaffs
The light of heaven, like Lydia's sea,
Rejoice, rejoice—let all that laughs
Abroad, at home, laugh out for me!

(1) O quid solutis est beatius curis,
    Cum mens onus reponit, ac peregrino
    Labore fessi venimus larem ad nostrum,
    Desideratoque acquiescimus lecto.

TIBULLUS TO SULPICIA.

Nulla tuum nobis subducet femina lectum, etc., etc.
                                    Lib. iv., Carm. 13.

" NEVER shall woman's smile have power
    To win me from those gentle charms!"—
Thus swore I, in that happy hour,
    When Love first gave thee to my arms.

And still alone thou charm'st my sight—
    Still, though our city proudly shine
With forms and faces, fair and bright,
    I see none fair or bright but thine.

Would thou wert fair for only me,
    And couldst no heart but mine allure!
To all mén else unpleasing be,
    So shall I feel my prize secure. (2)

Oh, love like mine ne'er wants the zest
    Of others' envy, others' praise;
But, in its silence safely blest,
    Broods o'er a bliss it ne'er betrays.

Charm of my life! by whose sweet power
    All cares are hush'd, all ills subdued—
My light, in even the darkest hour,
    My crowd, in deepest solitude! (3)

No, not though Heaven itself sent down
    Some maid of more than heavenly charms,
With bliss undreamt thy bard to crown,
    Would he for her forsake those arms!

INVITATION TO DINNER,
ADDRESSED TO LORD LANSDOWNE.
                                    September, 1818.

SOME think we bards have nothing real;
    That poets live among the stars so,
Their very dinners are ideal—
    (And, Heaven knows, too oft they *are* so)—
For instance, that we have, instead
    Of vulgar chops, and stews and hashes,
First course—a Phœnix at the head,
    Done in its own celestial ashes;
At foot, a cygnet, which kept singing
All the time its neck was wringing.
Side dishes, thus—Minerva's owl,
Or any such like learned fowl:
Doves, such as Heaven's poulterer gets,
When Cupid shoots his mother's pets.
Larks, stew'd in Morning's roseate breath,
    Or roasted by a sunbeam's splendour;
And nightingales, berhymed to death—
    Like young pigs whipp'd to make them tender.

(2) Displiceas aliis, sic ego tutus ero.
(3) Tu mihi curarum requies, tu nocte vel atrâ
    Lumen, et in solis tu mihi turba locis.

Such fare may suit those bards, who 're able
To banquet at Duke Humphrey's table;
But as for me, who 've long been taught
   To eat and drink like other people;
And can put up with mutton, bought
   Where Bromham (1) rears its ancient steeple—
If Lansdowne will consent to share
My humble feast, though rude the fare,
Yet, season'd by that salt he brings
From Attica's salinest springs,
'T will turn to dainties;—while the cup,
Beneath his influence brightening up,
Like that of Baucis, touch'd by Jove,
Will sparkle fit for gods above!

—◦◦◦◦◦—

VERSES TO THE POET CRABBE'S INKSTAND. (2)

WRITTEN MAY, 1832.

ALL, as he left it!—even the pen,
   So lately at that mind's command,
Carelessly lying as if then
   Just fallen from his gifted hand.

Have we then lost him? scarce an hour,
   A little hour, seems to have past,
Since Life and Inspiration's power
   Around that relic breathed their last.

Ah, powerless now—like talisman,
   Found in some vanish'd wizard's halls,
Whose mighty charm with him began,
   Whose charm with him extinguish'd falls.

Yet though, alas! the gifts that shone
   Around that pen's exploring track,
Be now, with its great master, gone,
   Nor living hand can call them back;

Who does not feel, while thus his eyes
   Rest on the enchanter's broken wand,
Each earth-born spell it work'd arise
   Before him in succession grand?—

Grand, from the Truth that reigns o'er all;
   The unshrinking Truth, that lets her light
Through Life's low, dark, interior fall,
   Opening the whole, severely bright:

Yet softening as she frowns along,
   O'er scenes which angels weep to see—
Where Truth herself half veils the Wrong,
   In pity of the Misery.

(1) A picturesque village in sight of my cottage, and from which it is separated but by a small verdant valley.

(2) Soon after Mr. Crabbe's death, the sons of that gentleman did me the honour of presenting to me the inkstand, pencil, etc., which their distinguished father had long been in the habit of using.

True bard!—and simple, as the race
   Of true-born poets ever are,
When, stooping from their starry place,
   They 're children, near, though gods, afar.

How freshly doth my mind recall,
   'Mong the few days I 've known with thee,
One that, most buoyantly of all,
   Floats in the wake of memory; (3)

When he, the poet, doubly graced,
   In life, as in his perfect strain,
With that pure mellowing power of Taste,
   Without which Fancy shines in vain;

Who in his page will leave behind,
   Pregnant with genius though it be,
But half the treasures of a mind,
   Where Sense o'er all holds mastery;

Friend of long years! of friendship tried
   Through many a bright and dark event;
In doubts, my judge—in taste, my guide—
   In all, my stay and ornament!

He, too, was of our feast that day,
   And all were guests of one, whose hand
Hath shed a new and deathless ray
   Around the lyre of this great land;

In whose sea-odes—as in those shells
   Where Ocean's voice of majesty
Seems still to sound—immortal dwells
   Old Albion's Spirit of the Sea.

Such was our host; and though since then,
   Slight clouds have risen 'twixt him and me,
Who would not grasp such hand again,
   Stretch'd forth again in amity?

Who can, in this short life, afford
   To let such mists a moment stay,
When thus one frank atoning word,
   Like sunshine, melts them all away?

Bright was our board that day—though *one*
   Unworthy brother there had place;
As 'mong the horses of the Sun,
   One was, they say, of earthly race.

Yet, *next* to Genius is the power
   Of feeling where true Genius lies;
And there was light around that hour
   Such as, in memory, never dies;

(3) The lines that follow allude to a day passed in company with Mr. Crabbe, many years since, when a party, consisting only of Mr. Rogers, Mr. Crabbe, and the author of these verses, had the pleasure of dining with Mr. Thomas Campbell, at his house at Sydenham.

Light which comes o'er me, as I gaze,
Thou Relic of the Dead, on thee,
Like all such dreams of vanish'd days,
Brightly, indeed—but mournfully!

TO CAROLINE, VISCOUNTESS VALLETORT.

WRITTEN AT LACOCK ABBEY, JANUARY, 1832.

When I would sing thy beauty's light,
Such various forms, and all so bright,
I 've seen thee from thy childhood wear,
I know not which to call most fair,
Nor 'mong the countless charms that spring
For ever round thee, *which* to sing.

When I would paint thee, as thou *art*,
Then all thou *wert* comes o'er my heart—
The graceful child, in beauty's dawn,
Within the nursery's shade withdrawn,
Or peeping out—like a young moon
Upon a world 't will brighten soon.
Then next, in girlhood's blushing hour,
As from thy own loved Abbey-tower
I 've seen thee look, all radiant, down,
With smiles that to the hoary frown
Of centuries round thee lent a ray,
Chasing even Age's gloom away;—
Or, in the world's resplendent throng,
As I have mark'd thee glide along,
Among the crowds of fair and great
A spirit, pure and separate,
To which even Admiration's eye
Was fearful to approach too nigh;—
A creature circled by a spell
Within which nothing wrong could dwell;
And fresh and clear as from the source,
Holding through life her limpid course,
Like Arethusa through the sea,
Stealing in fountain purity.

Now, too, another change of light!
As noble bride, still meekly bright,
Thou bring'st thy Lord a dower above
All earthly price, pure woman's love;
And show'st what lustre Rank receives,
When with his proud Corinthian leaves
Her rose thus high-bred Beauty weaves.

Wonder not if, where all 's so fair,
To choose were more than bard can dare;
Wonder not if, while every scene
I 've watch'd thee through so bright hath been,
The enamour'd Muse should, in her quest
Of beauty, know not where to rest,
But, dazzled, at thy feet thus fall,
Hailing thee beautiful in all!

A SPECULATION.

Of all speculations the market holds forth,
The best that I know, for a lover of pelf,
Is to buy Marcus up, at the price he is worth,
And then sell him at that which he sets on himself.

TO MY MOTHER.

WRITTEN IN A POCKET-BOOK, 1822.

They tell us of an Indian tree,
Which, howsoe'er the sun and sky
May tempt its boughs to wander free,
And shoot, and blossom, wide and high,
Far better loves to bend its arms
Downward again to that dear earth,
From which the life, that fills and warms
Its grateful being, first had birth.

'T is thus, though woo'd by flattering friends,
And fed with fame (if fame it be)
This heart, my own dear mother, bends,
With love's true instinct, back to thee!

LOVE AND HYMEN.

Love had a fever—ne'er could close
His little eyes till day was breaking;
And wild and strange enough, Heaven knows,
The things he raved about while waking.

To let him pine so were a sin—
One, to whom all the world 's a debtor;—
So Doctor Hymen was call'd in,
And Love that night slept rather better.

Next day the case gave further hope yet,
Though still some ugly fever latent;—
"Dose, as before "—a gentle opiate,
For which old Hymen has a patent.

After a month of daily call,
So fast the dose went on restoring,
That Love, who first ne'er slept at all,
Now took, the rogue! to downright snoring.

LINES

ON THE ENTRY OF THE AUSTRIANS INTO NAPLES, 1821.

Carbone notati.

Ay—down to the dust with them, slaves as they are,
From this hour, let the blood in their dastardly
veins,
That shrunk at the first touch of Liberty's war,
Be wasted for tyrants, or stagnate in chains.

On, on like a cloud, through their beautiful vales,
Ye locusts of tyranny, blasting them o'er—
Fill, fill up their wide sunny waters, ye sails
From each slave-mart of Europe, and shadow their
[shore!

Let their fate be a mock-word—let men of all lands
Laugh out, with a scorn that shall ring to the poles,
When each sword, that the cowards let fall from
their hands,
Shall be forged into fetters to enter their souls.

And deep, and more deep, as the iron is driven,
  Base slaves! let the whet of their agony be,
To think—as the Doom'd often think of that heaven
  They had once within reach—that they *might* have
                       [been free.
Oh shame! when there was not a bosom, whose heat
  Ever rose 'bove the *zero* of C——h's heart,
That did not, like echo, your war-hymn repeat,
  And send all its prayers with your Liberty's start;

When the world stood in hope—when a spirit, that
    breathed
The fresh air of the olden time, whisper'd about;
And the swords of all Italy, half-way unsheathed,
  But waited one conquering cry, to flash out!

When around you the shades of your Mighty in fame,
  Filicajas and Petrarchs, seem'd bursting to view,
And their words, and their warnings, like tongues
    of bright flame
Over Freedom's apostles, fell kindling on you!

Oh shame! that, in such a proud moment of life,
  Worth the history of ages, when, had you but
    hurl'd
One bolt at your tyrant invader, that strife
  Between freemen and tyrants had spread through
    the world—

That then—oh! disgrace upon manhood—even then,
  You should falter, should cling to your pitiful
    breath;
Cower down into beasts, when you might have stood
    men,
And prefer the slave's life of prostration to death.

It is strange, it is dreadful:—shout, Tyranny, shout
  Through your dungeons and palaces, "Freedom is
    o'er;"—
If there lingers one spark of her light, tread it out,
  And return to your empire of darkness once more.

For if *such* are the braggarts that claim to be free,
  Come, Despot of Russia, thy feet let me kiss;
Far nobler to live the brute bondman of thee,
  Than to sully even chains by a struggle like this!

—◦◦◦—

SCEPTICISM.

Ere Psyche drank the cup, that shed
  Immortal Life into her soul,
Some evil spirit pour'd, 't is said,
  One drop of Doubt into the bowl—

Which, mingling darkly with the stream,
  To Psyche's lips— she knew not why—
Made even that blessed nectar seem
  As though its sweetness soon would die.

Oft, in the very arms of Love,
  A chill came o'er her heart—a fear

That Death might, even yet, remove
  Her spirit from that happy sphere.

"Those sunny ringlets," she exclaim'd,
  Twining them round her snowy fingers;
"That forehead, where a light, unnamed,
  Unknown on earth, for ever lingers;

"Those lips, through which I feel the breath
  Of Heaven itself, whene'er they sever—
Say, are they mine, beyond all death,
  My own, hereafter, and for ever?

"Smile not—I know that starry brow,
  Those ringlets, and bright lips of thine,
Will always shine, as they do now—
  But shall *I* live to *see* them shine?"

In vain did Love say, "Turn thine eyes
  On all that sparkles round thee here—
Thou 'rt now in heaven, where nothing dies,
  And in these arms—what *canst* thou fear?"

In vain—the fatal drop, that stole
  Into that cup's immortal treasure,
Had lodged its bitter near her soul,
  And gave a tinge to every pleasure.

And, though there ne'er was transport given
  Like Psyche's with that radiant boy,
Hers is the only face in heaven,
  That wears a cloud amid its joy.

—◦◦◦—

A JOKE VERSIFIED.

"Come, come," said Tom's father, "at your time
  of life,   [rake—
There 's no longer excuse for thus playing the
It is time you should think, boy, of taking a wife"—
"Why, so it is, father—whose wife shall I take?"

—◦◦◦—

ON THE DEATH OF A FRIEND.

Pure as the mantle which, o'er him who stood
  By *Jordan's* stream, descended from the sky,
Is that remembrance, which the wise and good
  Leave in the hearts that love them, when they die.
So pure, so precious shall the memory be,
  Bequeathed, in dying, to our souls by thee—
So shall the love we bore thee, cherish'd warm
  Within our souls through grief, and pain, and strife,
Be, like *Elisha's* cruise, a holy charm,
  Wherewith to "heal the waters" of this life!

—◦◦◦—

TO JAMES CORRY, ESQ.

ON HIS MAKING ME A PRESENT OF A WINE-STRAINER.
                      Brighton, June, 1825.

This life, dear Corry, who can doubt?—
  Resembles much friend Ewart's (1) wine;

(1) A wine-merchant.

When *first* the rosy drops come out,
How beautiful, how clear they shine!

And thus awhile they keep their tint,
So free from even a shade with some,
That they would smile, did you but hint,
That darker drops would *ever* come.

But soon the ruby tide runs short,
Each minute makes the sad truth plainer,
Till life, like old and crusty port,
When near its close, requires a strainer.

This friendship can alone confer,
Alone can teach the drops to pass,
If not as bright as *once* they were,
At least unclouded, through the glass.

Nor, Corry, could a boon be mine,
Of which this heart were fonder, vainer,
Than thus, if life grow like old wine,
To have *thy* friendship for its strainer.

—o**o—

FRAGMENT OF A CHARACTER.

Here lies Factotum Ned at last ;
Long as he breathed the vital air,
Nothing throughout all Europe pass'd,
In which Ned had n't some small share.

Whoe'er was *in*, whoe'er was *out*,
Whatever statesmen did or said,
If not exactly brought about,
'T was all, at least, contrived by Ned.

With *Nap*, if Russia went to war,
'T was owing, under Providence,
To certain hints Ned gave the Czar—
(Vide his pamphlet—price, sixpence,)

If France was beat at Waterloo—
As all but Frenchmen think she was—
To Ned, as Wellington well knew,
Was owing half that day's applause.

Then for his news—no envoy's bag
E'er pass'd so many secrets through it;
Scarcely a telegraph could wag
Its wooden finger, but Ned knew it.

Such tales he had of foreign plots,
With foreign names, one's ear to buzz in !
From Russia, *chefs* and *ofs* in lots,
From Poland, *owskis* by the dozen.

When George, alarm'd for England's creed,
Turn'd out the last Whig ministry,
And men ask'd—who advised the deed?
Ned modestly confess'd 't was he.

For though, by some unlucky miss,
He had not downright *seen* the King,

He sent such hints through Viscount *This*,
To Marquis *That*, as clench'd the thing.

The same it was in science, arts,
The Drama, Books, MS. and printed—
Kean learn'd from Ned his cleverest parts,
And Scott's last work by him was hinted.

Childe Harold in the proofs he read,
And, here and there, infused some soul in 't —
Nay, Davy's Lamp, till seen by Ned,
Had—odd enough—an awkward hole in 't.

'T was thus, all-doing and all-knowing,
Wit, statesman, boxer, chemist, singer,
Whatever was the best pie going,
In *that* Ned—trust him—had his finger.

. * . * . * .

—o**o—

IMITATION.

FROM THE FRENCH.

With women and apples both Paris and Adam
Made mischief enough in their day :
God be praised that the fate of mankind, my dear
    Madam
Depends not on *us*, the same way.
For, weak as I am with temptation to grapple,
  The world would have doubly to rue thee;
Like Adam, I 'd gladly take *from* thee the apple,
Like Paris, at once give it *to* thee.

—o**o—

WHAT SHALL I SING THEE?

TO ——.

What shall I sing thee? Shall I tell
Of that bright hour, remember'd well
As though it shone but yesterday,
When, loitering idly in the ray
Of a spring sun, I heard, o'er-head,
My name as by some spirit said,
And, looking up, saw two bright eyes
  Above me from a casement shine,
Dazzling my mind with such surprise
  As they, who sail beyond the Line,
Feel when new stars above them rise ;—
And it was thine, the voice that spoke,
  Like Ariel's, in the mid-air then ;
And thine the eye, whose lustre broke—
  Never to be forgot again !

What shall I sing thee? Shall I weave
A song of that sweet summer-eve,
(Summer, of which the sunniest part
Was that we, each, had in the heart,)
When thou and I, and one like thee,
  In life and beauty, to the sound
Of our own breathless minstrelsy,
  Danced till the sunlight faded round,

Ourselves the whole ideal Ball,
Lights, music, company, and all!
Oh, 't is not in the languid strain
  Of lute like mine, whose day is past,
To call up even a dream again
  Of the fresh light those moments cast.

———◦◦◦———

COUNTRY DANCE AND QUADRILLE.

ONE night the nymph call'd *Country Dance—*
  (Whom folks, of late, have used so ill,
Preferring a coquette from France,
  That mincing thing, *Mamselle Quadrille —*

Having been chased from London down
  To that most humble haunt of all
She used to grace—a Country Town—
  Went smiling to the New-Year's Ball.

"Here, here, at least," she cried though driven
  From London's gay and shining tracks—
Though, like a Peri cast from heaven,
  I 've lost, for ever lost, Almack's—

"Though not a London Miss alive
  Would now for her acquaintance own me;
And spinsters, even, of forty-five,
  Upon their honours ne'er have known me;

"Here, here, at least, I triumph still,
  And—spite of some few dandy Lancers,
Who vainly try to preach Quadrille—
  See nought but *true–blue* Country Dancers.

"Here still I reign, and fresh in charms,
  My throne, like Magna Charta, raise
'Mong sturdy free-born legs and arms,
  That scorn the threaten'd *Chaine Anglaise.*"

'T was thus she said, as 'mid the din
  Of footmen, and the town sedan,
She lighted at the King's Head Inn,
  And up the stairs triumphant ran.

The Squires and their Squiresses all,
  With young Squirinas, just *come out,*
And my Lord's daughters from the Hall,
  (Quadrillers, in their hearts, no doubt—

All these, as light she tripp'd up stairs,
  Were in the cloak-room seen assembling—
When, hark! some new outlandish airs,
  From the First Fiddle, set her trembling.

She stops—she listens—*can* it be?
  Alas, in vain her ears would 'scape it—
It *is* "Di tanti palpiti,"
  As plain as English bow can scrape it.

"Courage!" however—in she goes,
  With her best sweeping country grace;
When, ah too true, her worst of foes,
  Quadrille, there meets her, face to face.

Oh for the lyre, or violin,
  Or kit of that gay Muse, Terpsichore,
To sing the rage these nymphs were in,
  Their looks and language, airs and trickery.

There stood Quadrille, with cat-like face
  (The beau-ideal of French beauty),
A band-box thing, all art and lace
  Down from her nose-tip to her shoe-tie.

Her flounces, fresh from *Victorine—*
  From *Hippolyte,* her rouge and hair—
Her poetry, from *Lamartine—*
  Her morals, from—the Lord knows where.

And, when she danced—so slidingly,
  So near the ground she plied her art,
You 'd swear her mother-earth and she
  Had made a compact ne'er to part.

Her face too, all the while, sedate,
  No signs of life or motion showing,
Like a bright *pendule's* dial-plate—
  So still, you 'd hardly think 't was *going.*

Full fronting her stood *Country Dance*
  A fresh, frank nymph, whom you would know
For English, at a single glance—
  English all o'er, from top to toe.

A little *gauche,* 'tis fair to own,
  And rather given to skips and bounces;
Endangering thereby many a gown,
  And playing, oft, the devil with flounces.

Unlike *Mamselle—*who would prefer
  (As morally a lesser ill)
A thousand flaws of character,
  To one vile rumple of a frill.

No rouge did she of Albion wear;
  Let her but run that two-heat race
She calls a *Set,* not Dian e'er
  Came rosier from the woodland chase.

Such was the nymph, whose soul had in 't
  Such anger now—whose eyes of blue
(Eyes of that bright victorious tint,
  Which English maids call "*Waterloo*")—

Like summer lightnings, in the dusk
  Of a warm evening, flashing broke,

While—to the tune of "Money Musk," (1)
    Which struck up now—she proudly spoke—

" Heard you that strain—that joyous strain?
    'T was such as England loved to hear,
Ere thou, and all thy frippery train,
    Corrupted both her foot and ear—

" Ere Waltz, that rake from foreign lands,
    Presumed, in sight of all beholders,
To lay his rude licentious hands
    On virtuous English backs and shoulders—

" Ere times and morals both grew bad,
    And, yet unfleeced by funding blockheads,
Happy John Bull not only had,
    But danced to, ' Money in both pockets.'

" Alas, the change!—Oh, L—d—y,
    Where is the land could 'scape disasters,
With such a Foreign Secretary,
    Aided by Foreign Dancing Masters?

" Woe to ye, men of ships and shops!
    Rulers of day-books and of waves!
Quadrilled, on one side, into fops,
    And drill'd, on t' other, into slaves!

" Ye, too, ye lovely victims, seen,
    Like pigeons, truss'd for exhibition,
With elbows, à la crapaudine,
    And feet, in—God knows what position;

" Hemm'd in by watchful chaperons,
    Inspectors of your airs and graces,
Who intercept all whisper'd tones,
    And read your telegraphic faces;

" Unable with the youth adored,
    In that grim cordon of Mammas,
To interchange one tender word,
    Though whisper'd but in queue-de-chats.

" Ah did you know how blest we ranged,
    Ere vile Quadrille usurp'd the fiddle—
What looks in setting were exchanged,
    What tender words in down the middle;

" How many a couple, like the wind,
    Which nothing in its course controls,
Left time and chaperons far behind,
    And gave a loose to legs and souls;

" How matrimony throve—ere stopp'd
    By this cold, silent, foot-coquetting—
How charmingly one's partner popp'd
    The important question in pousette-ing.

" While now, alas—no sly advances—
    No marriage hints—all goes on badly—

'Twixt Parson Malthus and French Dances,
    We, girls, are at a discount sadly.

" Sir William Scott (now Baron Stowell)
    Declares not half so much is made
By Licenses—and he must know well—
    Since vile Quadrilling spoil'd the trade."

She ceased—tears fell from every Miss—
    She now had touch'd the true pathetic:—
One such authentic fact as this
    Is worth whole volumes theoretic.

Instant the cry was " Country Dance!"
    And the maid saw, with brightening face,
The Steward of the night advance,
    And lead her to her birthright place.

The fiddles, which awhile had ceased,
    Now tuned again their summons sweet,
And, for one happy night, at least,
    Old England's triumph was complete.

—◦◦◦—
GAZEL.

HASTE, Maaml, the Spring is nigh;
    Already, in the unopen'd flowers
That sleep around us, Fancy's eye
    Can see the blush of future bowers;
And joy it brings to thee and me,
My own beloved Maami!

The streamlet frozen on its way,
    To feed the marble Founts of Kings,
Now loosen'd by the vernal ray,
    Upon its path exulting springs—
As doth this bounding heart to thee,
My ever blissful Maami!

Such bright hours were not made to stay;
    Enough if they a while remain,
Like Irem's bowers, that fade away,
    From time to time, and come again.
And life shall all one Irem be
For us, my gentle Maami.

O haste, for this impatient heart,
    Is like the rose in Yemen's vale,
That rends its inmost leaves apart
    With passion for the nightingale;
So languishes this soul for thee,
My bright and blushing Maami!

—◦◦◦—
LINES ON THE DEATH
OF JOSEPH ATKINSON, ESQ. OF DUBLIN.

IF ever life was prosperously cast,
    If ever life was like the lengthen'd flow
Of some sweet music, sweetness to the last,
    'T was his who, mourn'd by many, sleeps below.

(1) An old English Country Dance.

The sunny temper, bright where all is strife;
  The simple heart above all worldly wiles;
Light wit that plays along the calm of life,
  And stirs its languid surface into smiles;

Pure charity, that comes not in a shower,
  Sudden and loud, oppressing what it feeds,
But, like the dew, with gradual silent power,
  Felt in the bloom it leaves along the meads:

The happy grateful spirit, that improves
  And brightens every gift by fortune given;
That, wander where it will with those it loves,
  Makes every place a home, and home a heaven:

All these were his.— Oh, thou who read'st this stone,
  When for thyself, thy children, to the sky
Thou humbly prayest, ask this boon alone,
  That ye like him may live, like him may die!

—◦◦◦◦—

GENIUS AND CRITICISM.

Scripsit quidem fata, sed sequitur.— *Seneca.*

Of old, the Sultan Genius reign'd,
  As Nature meant, supreme, alone;
With mind uncheck'd, and hands unchain'd,
  His views, his conquests were his own.

But power like his, that digs its grave
  With its own sceptre, could not last;
So Genius' self became the slave
  Of laws that Genius' self had pass'd.

As Jove, who forged the chain of Fate,
  Was, ever after, doom'd to wear it;
His nods, his struggles all too late—
  "*Qui semel jussit, semper paret.*"

To check young Genius' proud career,
  The slaves, who now his throne invaded,
Made Criticism his prime Vizir,
  And from that hour his glories faded.

Tied down in Legislation's school,
  Afraid of even his own ambition,
His very victories were by rule,
  And he was great but by permission.

His most heroic deeds—the same,
  That dazzled, when spontaneous actions—
Now, done by law, seem'd cold and tame,
  And shorn of all their first attractions.

If he but stirr'd to take the air,
  Instant, the Vizir's council sat—
"Good Lord, your Highness can't go there—
  Bless me, your Highness can't do that."

If, loving pomp, he chose to buy
  Rich jewels for his diadem,

"The taste was bad, the price was high—
  A flower were simpler than a gem."

To please them if he took to flowers—
  "What trifling, what unmeaning things!
Fit for a woman's toilet hours,
  But not at all the style for Kings."

If, fond of his domestic sphere,
  He play'd no more the rambling comet—
"A dull good sort of man, 'twas clear,
  But, as for great or brave, far from it."

Did he then look o'er distant oceans,
  For realms more worthy to enthrone him?—
"Saint Aristotle, what wild notions!
  Serve a '*ne exeat regno*' on him."

At length, their last and worst to do,
  They round him placed a guard of watchmen,
Reviewers, knaves in brown, or blue
  Turn'd up with yellow—chiefly Scotchmen;

To dog his footsteps all about,
  Like those in Longwood's prison grounds,
Who at Napoleon's heels rode out,
  For fear the Conqueror should break bounds.

Oh for some Champion of his power,
  Some *Ultra* spirit, to set free,
As erst in Shakspeare's sovereign hour,
  The thunders of his Royalty!—

To vindicate his ancient line,
  The first, the true, the only one,
Of Right eternal and divine,
  That rules beneath the blessed sun.(1)

—◦◦◦◦—

TO LADY J⋆ R⋆⋆Y,
ON BEING ASKED TO WRITE SOMETHING IN HER ALBUM.

Written at Middleton.

Oh albums, albums, how I dread
  Your everlasting scrap and scrawl!
How often wish that from the dead,
  Old Omar would pop forth his head,
And make a bonfire of you all!

So might I 'scape the spinster band,
  The blushless blues, who, day and night
Like duns in doorways, take their stand,
To waylay bards, with book in hand,
  Crying for ever, "Write, sir, write!"

(1) The following quatrain, which formerly concluded
this playful production, has been suppressed: —
  To crush the rebels, that would cloud
    His triumphs with restraint or blame,
  And, honouring even his faults, aloud
    Re-echo "*Vive le Roi! quand même*——" —P. E.

So might I shun the shame and pain,
That o'er me at this instant come,
When Beauty, seeking Wit in vain,
Knocks at the portal of my brain,
And gets, for answer, "Not at home!"

TO THE SAME,

ON LOOKING THROUGH HER ALBUM.

No wonder bards, both high and low,
From Byron down to ' * r * * and me,
Should seek the fame, which all bestow
On him whose task is praising thee.

Let but the theme be J * r * * y's eyes,
At once all errors are forgiven ;
As even old Sternhold still we prize,
Because, though dull, he sings of heaven.

TO LADY HOLLAND,

ON NAPOLEON'S LEGACY OF A SNUFF-BOX.

Gift of the Hero, on his dying day,
To her, whose pity watch'd, for ever nigh;
Oh! could he see the proud, the happy ray,
This relic lights up on her generous eye,
Sighing, he'd feel how easy 'tis to pay
A Friendship all his kingdoms could not buy.

Paris, July, 1821.

EPILOGUE,

WRITTEN FOR LADY DACRE'S TRAGEDY OF " INA."

Last night, as lonely o'er my fire I sat,
Thinking of cues, starts, exits, and—all that,
And wondering much what little knavish sprite
Had put it first in women's heads to write—
Sudden I saw—as in some witching dream—
A bright-blue glory round my book-case beam,
From whose quick-opening folds of azure light
Out flew a tiny form, as small and bright
As Puck the Fairy, when he pops his head,
Some sunny morning, from a violet bed.
"Bless me!" I starting cried, "what imp are you?"—
"A small he-devil, Ma'am—my name *Bas Bleu*—
A bookish sprite, much given to routs and reading;
'Tis I who teach your spinsters of good breeding,
The reigning taste in chemistry and caps,
The last new bounds of tuckers and of maps,
And, when the waltz has twirl'd her giddy brain,
With metaphysics twirl it back again!"

I view'd him, as he spoke—his hose were blue,
His wings—the covers of the last Review—
Cerulean, border'd with a jaundice hue,
And tinsell'd gaily o'er, for evening wear,
Till the next quarter brings a new-fledged pair.

"Inspired by me—(pursued this waggish Fairy)—
That best of wives and Sapphos, Lady Mary,
Votary alike of Crispin and the Muse,
Makes her own splay-foot epigrams and shoes.
For me the eyes of young Camilla shine,
And mingle Love's blue brilliances with mine;
For me she sits apart, from coxcombs shrinking,
Looks wise—the pretty soul!—and *thinks* she's thinking.
By my advice Miss Indigo attends
Lectures on Memory, and assures her friends,
''Pon honour !—(*mimics*)—nothing can surpass the plan
Of that professor—(*trying to recollect*)—psha! that memory-man—
That—what's his name?—him I attended lately—
'Pon honour, he improved *my* memory greatly.'"

Here, curtseying low, I ask'd the blue-legg'd sprite
What share he had in this our play to-night.
"Nay, there—(he cried)—there I am guiltless quite—
What! choose a heroine from that Gothic time,
When no one waltz'd, and none but monks could rhyme ;
When lovely woman, all unschool'd and wild,
Blush'd without art, and without culture smiled—
Simple as flowers, while yet unclass'd they shone,
Ere Science call'd their brilliant world her own,
Ranged the wild rosy things in learned orders,
And fill'd with Greek the garden's blushing borders!—
No, no—your gentle Inas will not do—
To-morrow evening, when the lights burn blue,
I'll come—(*pointing downwards*)—you understand
—till then adieu!"

And *has* the sprite been here? No—jests apart—
Howe'er man rules in science and in art,
The sphere of woman's glories is the heart.
And, if our Muse have sketch'd with pencil true
The wife—the mother—firm, yet gentle too—
Whose soul, wrapp'd up in ties itself hath spun,
Trembles, if touch'd in the remotest one;
Who loves—yet dares even Love himself disown,
When Honour's broken shaft supports his throne:
If such our Ina, she may scorn the evils,
Dire as they are, of Critics and—Blue Devils.

THE DAY-DREAM. (1)

They both were hush'd, the voice, the chords—
I heard but once that witching lay;
And few the notes, and few the words,
My spell-bound memory brought away;

Traces, remember'd here and there,
Like echoes of some broken strain ;
Links of a sweetness lost in air,
That nothing now could join again.

(1) In these stanzas I have done little more than relate a fact in verse; and the lady, whose singing gave rise to this curious instance of the power of memory in sleep, is Mrs. Robert Arkwright.

Even these, too, ere the morning, fled ;
And, though the charm still linger'd on,
That o'er each sense her song had shed,
The song itself was faded, gone ;—

Gone, like the thoughts that once were ours,
On summer days, ere youth had set ;
Thoughts bright, we know, as summer flowers,
Though *what* they were we now forget.

In vain, with hints from other strains,
I woo'd this truant air to come—
As birds are taught, on eastern plains,
To lure their wilder kindred home.

In vain :—the song that Sappho gave,
In dying, to the mournful sea,
Not muter slept beneath the wave
Than this within my memory.

At length, one morning, as I lay
In that half-waking mood, when dreams
Unwillingly at last give way
To the full truth of daylight's beams,

A face—the very face, methought,
From which had breathed, as from a shrine
Of song and soul, the notes I sought—
Came with its music close to mine ;

And sung the long-lost measure o'er—
Each note and word, with every tone
And look, that lent it life before—
All perfect, all again my own !

Like parted souls, when 'mid the Blest
They meet again, each widow'd sound
Through memory's realm had wing'd in quest
Of its sweet mate, till all were found.

Nor even in waking did the clue,
Thus strangely caught, escape again ;
For never lark its matins knew
So well as now I knew this strain.

And oft, when memory's wondrous spell
Is talk'd of in our tranquil bower,
I sing this lady's song, and tell
The vision of that morning hour.

—◦♦◦—

SONG.

WHERE is the heart that would not give
Years of drowsy days and nights,
One little hour, like this, to live—
Full to the brim, of life's delights?
Look, look around,
This fairy ground,

With love-lights glittering o'er;
While cups that shine
With freight divine
Go coasting round its shore.

Hope is the dupe of future hours,
Memory lives in those gone by ;
Neither can see the moment's flowers,
Springing up fresh beneath the eye.
Wouldst thou, or thou,
Forego what 's *now*,
For all that Hope may say ?
No—Joy's reply,
From every eye,
Is, " Live we while we may."

—◦♦◦—

SONG OF THE POCO-CURANTE SOCIETY.

Haud curat Hippoclides.—Erasm. Adag.

To those we love we 've drank to-night ;
But now attend, and stare not,
While I the ampler list recite
Of those for whom—*We care not.*

For royal men, howe'er they frown,
If on their fronts they bear not
That noblest gem that decks a crown,
The People's Love—*We care not.*

For slavish men, who bend beneath
A despot yoke, yet dare not
Pronounce the will, whose very breath
Would rend its links—*We care not.*

For priestly men, who covet sway
And wealth, though they declare not ;
Who point, like finger-posts, the way
They never go—*We care not.*

For martial men, who on their sword,
Howe'er it conquers, wear not
The pledges of a soldier's word,
Redeem'd and pure—*We care not.*

For legal men, who plead for wrong,
And though to lies they swear not,
Are hardly better than the throng
Of those who do—*We care not.*

For courtly men, who feed upon
The land, like grubs, and spare not
The smallest leaf, where they can sun
Their crawling limbs—*We care not.*

For wealthy men, who keep their mines
In darkness hid, and share not
The paltry ore with him who pines
In honest want—*We care not.*

For prudent men, who hold the power
Of Love aloof, and bare not
Their hearts in any guardless hour
To Beauty's shaft—*We care not.* (1)

For all, in short, on land or sea,
In camp or court, who *are* not,
Who never *were*, or o'er *will* be
Good men and true—*We care not.*

———◦●◦———

ANNE BOLEYN.

TRANSLATION FROM THE METRICAL "HISTOIRE
D'ANNE BOLEYN."

"S'elle estoit belle et de taille élégante,
Estoit des yeulx encor plus attirante,
Lesquelz sçavoit bien conduyre à propos
En les tenant quelquefoys en repos;
Aucunefoys envoyant en message
Porter du coeur le secret tesmoignage."

Much as her form seduced the sight,
   Her eyes could even more surely woo;
And when, and how to shoot their light
   Into men's hearts full well she knew.
For sometimes, in repose she hid
   Their rays beneath a downcast lid;
And then again, with wakening air,
   Would send their sunny glances out,
Like heralds of delight, to bear
   Her heart's sweet messages about.

———◦●◦———

THE DREAM OF THE TWO SISTERS.

FROM DANTE.

Nell' ora, credo, che dell' oriente
   Prima raggiò nel monte Citerea,
   Che di fuoco d' amor par sempre ardente,
Giovane e bella in sogno mi parea
   Donna vedere andar per una landa
   Cogliendo fiori, e cantando dicea:
Sappia qualunque 'l mio nome dimanda,
   Ch' io mi son Lia, e vo movendo 'ntorno
   Le belle mani a farmi una ghirlanda.
Per piacermi allo specchio qui m' adorno:
   Ma mia suora Rachel mai non si smaga
   Dal suo ammiraglio, e siede tutto giorno.
Ell' è de' suo, begli occhi veder vaga,
   Com' io dell' adornarmi con le mani;
   Lei lo vedere, e me l'ovrare appaga.
                    Dante, Purg., canto xxvii

'T WAS eve's soft hour, and bright, above,
   The star of Beauty beam'd,
While lull'd by light so full of love,
   In slumber thus I dream'd—
Methought, at that sweet hour,
   A nymph came o'er the lea,
Who, gathering many a flower,
   Thus said and sung to me:—
" Should any ask what Leila loves,
   Say thou, To wreathe her hair
With flowerets cull'd from glens and groves,
   Is Leila's only care.

While thus in quest of flowerets rare,
   O'er hill and dale I roam,
My sister, Rachel, far more fair,
   Sits lone and mute at home.
Before her glass untiring,
   With thoughts that never stray,
Her own bright eyes admiring,
   She sits the live-long day.
While I!—oh, seldom even a look
   Of self salutes my eye;—
My only glass, the limpid brook,
   That shines and passes by."

———◦●◦———

SOVEREIGN WOMAN.

A BALLAD.

The dance was o'er, yet still in dreams,
   That fairy scene went on;
Like clouds still flush'd with daylight gleams
   Though day itself is gone.
And gracefully to music's sound,
   The same bright nymphs went gliding round;
While thou, the Queen of all, wert there—
The Fairest still, where all were fair.

The dream then changed—in halls of state,
   I saw thee high enthroned;
While, ranged around, the wise, the great
   In thee their mistress own'd:
And still the same, thy gentle sway
O'er willing subjects won its way—
Till all confess'd the Right Divine
To rule o'er man was only thine!

But, lo, the scene now changed again—
   And borne on plumed steed,
I saw thee o'er the battle-plain
   Our land's defenders lead:
And stronger in thy beauty's charms,
Than man, with countless hosts in arms,
Thy voice, like music, cheer'd the Free,
Thy very smile was victory!

Nor reign such queens on thrones alone—
   In cot and court the same,
Wherever woman's smile is known,
   Victoria's still her name.
For though she almost blush to reign,
Though Love's own flowerets wreathe the chain,
Disguise our bondage as we will,
'T is woman, woman, rules us still.

———◦●◦———

COME, PLAY ME THAT SIMPLE AIR AGAIN.

A BALLAD.

Come, play me that simple air again,
   I used so to love, in life's young day,

(1) Lines omitted in the present edition :—
      For secret men who, round the bowl
      In friendship's circle, tear not
      The cloudy curtain from their soul,
      But draw it close—*We care not.*—P. E.

And bring, if thou canst, the dreams that
    then
Were waken'd by that sweet lay.
The tender gloom its strain
    Shed o'er the heart and brow,
Grief's shadow, without its pain—
    Say where, where is it now?
But play me the well-known air once more,
    For thoughts of youth still haunt its
      strain,
Like dreams of some far fairy shore
    We never shall see again.

Sweet air, how every note brings back
    Some sunny hope, some day-dream bright,
That shining o'er life's early track,
    Fill'd even its tears with light.
The new-found life that came
    With love's first echo'd vow;
The fear, the bliss, the shame—
    Ah—where, where are they now?
But, still the same loved notes prolong,
    For sweet 't were thus, to that old lay,
In dreams of youth and love and song,
    To breathe life's hour away.

SONGS AND PIECES

WHICH HAVE BEEN OMITTED IN THE NEW LONDON EDITION.

CEASE, OH! CEASE TO TEMPT.

Cease, oh! cease to tempt
    My tender heart to love!
It never, never can
    So wild a flame approve.
All its joys and pains
    To others I resign;
But be the vacant heart,
    The careless bosom mine.
Then cease, oh! cease to tempt
    My tender heart to love!
It never, never can
    So wild a flame approve.

Say, oh! say no more
    That lovers' pains are sweet!
I never, never can
    Believe the fond deceit.
Weeping day and night,
    Consuming life in sighs—
This is the lover's lot,
    And this I ne'er could prize.
Then say, oh! say no more
    That lovers' pains are sweet!
I never, never can
    Believe the fond deceit.

FANNY WAS IN THE GROVE.

Fanny was in the grove,
    And Lubin, her boy, was nigh;
Her eye was warm with love,
    And her soul was warm as her eye.
Oh! oh! if Lubin now would sue,
Oh! oh! what could Fanny do?

Fanny was made for bliss,
    But she was young and shy;
And when he had stolen a kiss,
    She blush'd, and said with a sigh—
"Oh! oh! Lubin, ah! tell me true,
Oh! oh! what are you going to do?"

They wander'd beneath the shade,
    Her eye was dimm'd with a tear,
For ah! the poor little maid
    Was thrilling with love and fear.
Oh! oh! if Lubin would but sue,
Oh! oh! what could Fanny do!

Sweetly along the grove
    The birds sang all the while,
And Fanny now said to her love,
    With a frown that was half a smile—
"Oh! oh! why did Lubin sue?
Oh! oh! why did Lubin sue?"

HOLY BE THE PILGRIM'S SLEEP.

Holy be the Pilgrim's sleep,
    From the dreams of terror free;
And may all, who wake to weep,
    Rest to-night as sweet as he!
Hark! hark! did I hear a vesper swell!
No, no, 't is my loved Pilgrim's prayer:
No, no, 't was but the convent bell,
    That tolls upon the midnight air.
Holy be the Pilgrim's sleep!
Now, now again, the voice I hear,
    Some holy man is wandering here.

O Pilgrim! where hast thou been roaming?
Dark is the way, and midnight 's coming.
Stranger I 've been o'er moor and mountain,
To tell my beads at Agnes' fountain.
And, Pilgrim, say, where art thou going?
Dark is the way, the winds are blowing.
Weary with wandering, weak, I falter,
To breathe my vows at Agnes' altar.
Strew, then, oh! strew his bed of rushes;
Here he shall rest till morning blushes.

Peace to them whose days are done,
    Death their eyelids closing;
Hark! the burial-rite 's begun—
    'T is time for our reposing.

Here, then, my Pilgrim's course is o'er:
'T is my master! 'tis my master! Welcome here
    once more;
Come to our shed—all toil is over;
Pilgrim no more, but knight and lover.

I CAN NO LONGER STIFLE.

I can no longer stifle
How much I long to rifle
    That litle part
    They call the heart
Of you, you lovely trifle!
You can no longer doubt it,
So let me be about it;
    Or on my word,
    And by the Lord,
I 'll try to do without it.

This pretty thing 's as light, Sir,
As any paper kite, Sir;
    And here and there,
    And God knows where,
She takes her wheeling flight, Sir.
Us lovers, to amuse us,
Unto her tail she nooses;
    There, hung like bobs
    Of straw, or nobs,
She whisks us where she chooses.

JOYS THAT PASS AWAY.

Joys that pass away like this
    Alas! are purchased dear,
If every beam of bliss
    Is follow'd by a tear.
Fare thee well! oh, fare thee well!
Soon, too soon, thou 'st broke the spell,
    Oh! I ne'er can love again
    The girl whose faithless art
Could break so dear a chain,
    And with it break my heart.

Once, when truth was in those eyes,
    How beautiful they shone!
But now that lustre flies,
    For truth, alas! is gone.
Fare thee well! oh, fare thee well!
How I loved my hate shall tell.
    Oh! how lorn, how lost would prove
    Thy wretched victim's fate,
If, when deceived in love,
    He could not fly to hate!

LITTLE MARY'S EYE.

Little Mary's eye
    Is roguish, and all that, Sir;
But her little tongue
    Is quite too full of chat, Sir,

Since her eye can speak
    Enough to tell her blisses,
If she stir her tongue,
    Why—stop her mouth with kisses!
Oh! the little girls,
    Wily, warm, and winning;
When angels tempt us to it,
    Who can keep from sinning?

Nanny's beaming eye
    Looks as warm as any;
But her cheek was pale—
    Well-a-day, poor Nanny!
Nanny, in the field,
    She pluck'd a little posy,
And Nanny's pallid cheek
    Soon grew sleek and rosy.
    Oh! the little girls, etc.

Sue, the pretty nun,
    Prays with warm emotion;
Sweetly rolls her eye
    In love or in devotion.
If her pious heart
    Softens to relieve you,
She gently shares the crime,
    With "Oh, may God forgive you!"
Oh! the little girls,
    Wily, warm, and winning;
When angels tempt us to it,
    Who can keep from sinning?

LOVE, MY MARY, DWELLS WITH THEE.

Love, my Mary, dwells with thee;
On thy cheek his bed I see.
No—that cheek is pale with care;
Love can find no roses there.
'T is not on the cheek of rose
Love can find the best repose:
In my heart his home thou 'lt see;
There he lives, and lives for thee.

Love, my Mary, ne'er can roam,
While he makes that eye his home.
No—the eye with sorrow dim
Ne'er can be a home for him.
Yet 't is not in beaming eyes
Love for ever warmest lies:
In my heart his home thou 'lt see;
There he lives and lives for thee.

NOW LET THE WARRIOR.

Now let the warrior plume his steed,
    And wave his sword afar;
For the men of the East this day shall bleed,
    And the sun shall blush with war.
Victory sits on the Christians' helm
    To guide her holy band:
The Knight of the Cross this day shall whelm
    The men of the Pagan land.

Oh! bless'd who in the battle dies!
God will enshrine him in the skies!
Now let the warrior plume his steed,
And wave his sword afar;
For the men of the East this day shall bleed,
And the sun shall blush with war.

—⁓◦◦◦⁓—

OH, LADY FAIR!

On, Lady fair! where art thou roaming?
The sun has sunk, the night is coming.
Stranger, I go o'er moor and mountain,
To tell my beads at Agnes' fountain.
And who is the man, with his white locks flowing?
Oh, Lady fair! where is he going?
A wandering Pilgrim, weak, I falter,
To tell my beads at Agnes' altar.
Chill falls the rain, night winds are blowing,
Dreary and dark 's the way we 're going.

Fair Lady! rest till morning blushes—
I 'll strew for thee a bed of rushes.
Oh, stranger! when my beads I 'm counting,
I 'll bless thy name at Agnes' fountain.
Then, Pilgrim, turn, and rest thy sorrow;
Thou 'lt go to Agnes' shrine to-morrow.
Good stranger, when my beads I 'm telling,
My saint shall bless thy leafy dwelling.
Strew, then, oh! strew our bed o rushes;
Here we must rest till morning blushes.

—⁓◦◦◦⁓—

OH! SEE THOSE CHERRIES.

On! see those cherries—though once so glowing,
They 've lain too long on the sun-bright wall;
And mark, already their bloom is going;
Too soon they 'll wither, too soon they 'll fall.
Once caught by their blushes, the light bird flew round,
Oft on their ruby lips leaving love's wound;
But now he passes them, ah! too knowing
To taste wither'd cherries, when fresh may be found.

Old Time thus fleetly his course is running;
If bards were not moral, how maids would go wrong!
And thus thy beauties, now sunn'd and sunning,
Would wither if left on the rose-tree too long.
Then love while thou 'rt lovely—e'en I should be glad
So sweetly to save thee from ruin so sad;
But, oh! delay not—we bards are too cunning
To sigh for old beauties when young may be had.

—⁓◦◦◦⁓—

POH, DERMOT! GO ALONG WITH YOUR GOSTER.

Pon, Dermot! go along with your goster,
You might as well pray at a jig,

Or teach an old cow pater-noster,
Or whistle Moll Roe to a pig!
Arrah, child! do you think I 'm a blockhead,
And not the right son of my mother,
To put nothing at all in one pocket,
And not half so much in the other?
    Poh, Dermot! etc.

Any thing else I can do for you,
Keadh mille faltha, and welcome,
Put up an ave or two for you,
Fear'd that you 'd ever to hell come.
If you confess you 're a rogue,
I will turn a deaf ear, and not care for 't;
Bid you put pease in your brogue,
But just tip you a hint to go barefoot.
    Then get along with, etc.

If you 've the whiskey in play,
To oblige you, I 'll come take a smack of it;
Stay with you all night and day,
Ay, and twenty-four hours at the back of it.
Oh! whiskey 's a papist, God save it!
The beads are upon it completely;
But I think before ever we 'd leave it,
We 'd make it a heretic neatly.
    Then get along with, etc.

If you 're afeard of a Banshee,
Or Leprochauns are not so civil, dear,
Let Father Luke show his paunch, he
Will frighten them all to the devil, dear.
It's I that can hunt them like ferrets,
And lay them without any fear, gra;
But for whiskey, and that sort of spirits,
Why them—I would rather lay here, (1) gra.
    Then get along with, etc.

—⁓◦◦◦⁓—

SEND THE BOWL ROUND MERRILY.

Send the bowl round merrily,
    Laughing, singing, drinking;
Toast it, toast it cheerily—
    Here 's to the devil with thinking!
Oh! for the round of pleasure,
    With sweetly-smiling lasses—
Glasses o'erflowing their measure,
    With hearts as full as our glasses.
Send the bowl round merrily,
    Laughing, singing, drinking;
Toast it, toast it cheerily—
    Here 's to the devil with thinking!

Once I met with a funny lass,
    Oh, I loved her dearly!
Left for her my bonny glass—
    Faith! I died for her—nearly.
But she proved damn'd uncivil,
    And thought to peck like a hen, sir;

(1) Putting his hand on his paunch.

So I pitch'd the jade to the devil,
    And took to my glass again, Sir.
        Then send the bowl, etc.

Now I 'm turn'd a rover,
    In love with every petticoat;
No matter whom it may cover,
    Or whether it 's Jenny's or Betty's coat;
And if the girls can put up
    With any good thing in pieces,
My heart I will certainly cut up,
    And share it with all young misses.
        Then send the bowl, etc.

A bumper round to the pretty ones!
    Here 's to the girl with the blue eyes!
Here 's to her with the jetty ones,
    Where the languishing dew lies!
Could all such hours as this is
    Be summ'd in one little measure,
I 'd live a short life of blisses,
    And die in a surfeit of pleasure!
        Then send the bowl, etc.

THE PROBABILITY.

My heart is united to Cloe's for ever,
No time shall the link of their tenderness sever;
And if Love be the parent of joy and of pleasure,
Sure Cloe and I shall be blest beyond measure.

Come tell me, my girl, what 's the sweetest of blisses?
"I 'll show you," she cries, and she gives me a sweet
        kisses;
Ah! Clo'! if that languishing eye 's not a traitor,
It tells me you know of a bliss that is greater.

"Indeed and I do not;"—then softly she blushes,
And her bosom the warm tint of modesty flushes—
"I 'm sure if I knew it, I 'd certainly show it;
But, Damon, now Damon dear, may be you know it?"

THE TABLET OF LOVE.

You bid me be happy, and bid me adieu—
Can happiness live when absent from you?
Will sleep on my eyelids e'er sweetly alight,
When greeted no more by a tender good night?
Oh, never! for deep is the record enshrined!
Thy look and thy voice will survive in my mind:
Though age may the treasures of memory remove,
Unfading shall flourish the Tablet of Love.

Through life's winding valley—in anguish, in rest;
Exalted in joy, or by sorrow depress'd—
From its place in the mirror that lies on my heart,
Thine image shall never one moment depart.
When time, life, and all that poor mortals hold dear,
Like visions, like dreams, shall at last disappear;
Though raised among seraphs to realms above,
Unfading shall flourish the Tablet of Love.

WHEN IN LANGUOR SLEEPS THE HEART.

When in languor sleeps the heart
Love can wake it with his dart;
When the mind is dull and dark,
Love can light it with his spark.

Come, oh! come then, let us haste,
All the bliss of love to taste;
Let us love both night and day,
Let us love our lives away!

And for hearts from loving free
(If, indeed, such hearts there be),
May they ne'er the rapture prove
Of the smile from lips we love.

WILL YOU COME TO THE BOWER?

Will you come to the bower I have shaded for you?
Our bed shall be roses all spangled with dew.
    Will you, will you, will you, will you
        Come to the bower?

There, under the bower, on roses you 'll lie,
With a blush on your cheek, but a smile in your eye.
    Will you, will you, will you, will you
        Smile, my beloved?

But the roses we press shall not rival your lip,
Nor the dew be so sweet as the kisses we 'll sip.
    Will you, will you, will you, will you
        Kiss me, my love?

And oh! for the joys that are sweeter than dew
From languishing roses, or kisses from you.
    Will you, will you, will you, will you,
        Won't you, my love?

THE RABBINICAL ORIGIN OF WOMEN.

They tell us that Woman was made of a rib
    Just pick'd from a corner so snug in the side;
But the Rabbins swear to you this is a fib,
    And 't was not so at all that the sex was supplied.
        Derry down, down, down derry down.

For old Adam was fashion'd, the first of his kind,
    With a tail like a monkey, full yard and a span;
And when Nature cut off this appendage behind,
    Why—then woman was made of the tail of the
        Man.
        Derry down, down, down derry down.

If such is the tie between women and men,
    The ninny who weds is a pitiful elf;
For he takes to his tail, like an idiot, again,
    And makes a most damnable ape of himself!
        Derry down, down, down derry down.

Yet, if we may judge as the fashions prevail,
  Every husband remembers the original plan,
And, knowing his wife is no more than his tail,
  Why—he leaves her behind him as much as he can.
    Derry down, down, down derry down.

—○◊◌—

FAREWELL, BESSY!

SWEETEST love! I 'll not forget thee,
  Time shall only teach my heart
Fonder, warmer, to regret thee,
  Lovely, gentle, as thou art.
      Farewell, Bessy!
      We may meet again.

Yes, oh yes! again we meet, love,
  And repose our hearts at last;
Oh! sure 't will then be sweet, love,
  Calm to think on sorrows past.
      Farewell, Bessy!
      We may meet again.

Yet I feel my heart is breaking
  When I think I stray from thee,
Round the world that quiet seeking,
  Which I fear is not for me.
      Farewell, Bessy!
      We may meet again.

Calm to peace thy lover's bosom—
  Can it, dearest! must it be?
Thou within an hour shalt lose him,
  He for ever loses thee!
      Farewell, Bessy!
      Yet oh! not for ever.

—○◊◌—

SONG.

I 'VE roam'd through many a weary round,
  I 've wander'd east and west;
Pleasure in every clime I 've found,
  But sought in vain for rest.

While glory sighs for other spheres,
  I feel that one 's too wide,
And think the home which love endears
  Worth all the world beside.

The needle thus too rudely moved,
  Wanders unconscious where;
Till having found the place it loved,
  It trembling settles there.

—○◊◌—

EPITAPH ON A WELL-KNOWN POET.

BENEATH these poppies buried deep,
  The bones of Bob the Bard lie hid;
Peace to his manes; and may he sleep
  As soundly as his readers did!

Through every sort of verse meandering,
  Bob went, without a hitch or fall,
Through Epic, Sapphic, Alexandrine
  To verse that was no verse at all;

Till fiction having done enough
  To make a bard at least absurd,
And give his readers *quantum suff.*,
  He took to praising George the Third:

And then, in virtue of his crown,
  Doomed us, poor Whigs, at once to slaughter;
Like Donellan, of bad renown,
  Poisoning us all with laurel-water.

And yet at times some awkward qualms he
  Felt about leaving honour's track;
And though he got a butt of Malmsey,
  It could not save him from a sack.

Death, weary of so dull a writer,
  Put to his works a *finis* thus.
Oh! may the earth on him lie lighter
  Than did his quartos upon us!

○◊◌

EPITAPH ON A LAWYER.

HERE lies a lawyer—one whose mind
(Like that of all the lawyer kind)
Resembled, though so grave and stately,
The pupil of a cat's eye greatly;
Which for the mousing deeds, transacted
In holes and corners, is well fitted,
But which in sunshine grows contracted,
As if 't would—*rather* not admit it;
As if, in short, a man would quite
Throw time away who tried to let in a
Decent portion of God's light
On lawyer's mind or pussy's retina.

Hence, when he took to politics,
  As a refreshing change of evil,
Unfit with grand affairs to mix
His little Nisi-Prius tricks,
  Like imps at bo-peep, play'd the devil;
And proved that when a small law wit
  Of statesmanship attempts the trial,
'T is like a player on the kit
  Put all at once to a bass viol.

Nay, even when honest (which he could
  Be, now and then), still quibbling daily,
He served his country as he would
  A client thief at the Old Bailey.

But—do him justice—short and rare
  His wish through honest paths to roam;
Born with a taste for the unfair,
  Where falsehood call'd he still was there,
And when least honest, most at home.

Thus shuffling, bullying, lying, creeping,
He work'd his way up near the throne,
And, long before he took the keeping
Of the king's conscience, lost his own.

ILLUSTRATION OF A BORE.

If ever you 've seen a gay party
Relieved from the pressure of Ned—
How instantly joyous and hearty
They 've grown when the damper was fled—
You may guess what a gay piece of work,
What delight to champagne it must be,
To get rid of its bore of a cork,
And come sparkling to you, love, and me!

FROM THE FRENCH.

Of all the men one meets about,
There 's none like Jack—he 's every where:
At church—park—auction—dinner—rout—
Go when and where you will, he 's there.
Try the West End, he 's at your back—
Meets you, like Eurus, in the East—
You 're call'd upon for " How do, Jack?"
One hundred times a-day at least.
A friend of his one evening said,
As home he took his pensive way,
"Upon my soul, I fear Jack's dead—
I 've seen him but three times to-day!"

ROMANCE.

I HAVE a story of two lovers, fill'd
With all the pure romance, the blissful sadness,
And the sad doubtful bliss, that ever thrill'd
Two young and longing hearts in that sweet mad-
But where to chuse the *locale* of my vision　[ness;
In this wide vulgar world—what real spot
Can be found out, sufficiently elysian
For two such perfect lovers, I know not.
Oh, for some fair Formosa, such as he,
The young Jew, (1) fabled of, in the Indian Sea,
By nothing but its name of Beauty known,
And which Queen Fancy might make all her own,
Her fairy kingdom—take its people, lands,
And tenements into her own bright hands,
And make, at least, one earthly corner fit
For Love to live in—pure and exquisite!

ON ———.

LIKE a snuffers, this loving old dame,
By a destiny grievous enough,
Though so oft she has snapp'd at the flame,
Hath never caught more than the snuff.

THE WITCH'S SABBATH.

A FRAGMENT.

" AY, write their names on my darkest page, "
Said Bigotry, opening wide her book—

That book, in whose leaves, now black with age,
None but the worm and Copley look:

" Write, write them down—as witches, of yore,
The name of each imp of darkness knew,
And nightly call'd their bead-roll o'er,
I 'll know the name of my servants too!"

She spoke—and, behold ! a scribe was near,
Who straightway taking a pen of flame
From behind his ancient ass-like ear,
Wrote down, as she bid, each minion's name.

And never, oh ! never—not even then
In her youthful days of murderous tricks—
Was Bigotry half so pleased as when
She counted Two Hundred and Seventy-six !

With joy, I wist, each name she kiss'd,
Though even in joy a sigh heaved she,
When out of that list one name she miss'd,
Her own dear Wilks, of Sudbury.

" 'T is well, 'tis well—so far our spell
Is a match for even my darkest days ;—
Now, draw me a circle round, and tell
What Sprite of them all I first shall raise."

The circle is drawn.—She squats within,
And " Arise," she cries, some " imp of flame,
Who will do my bidding, through thick and thin !"—
She spoke but the word, and Duigenan came!

His torch was ready—his eyes were wild—
Away to his northern hills he flew,
And 't was rare to see how the beldam smiled,
As she track'd his flight by the glare he threw;

As she saw, by her gift of second-sight,
The mingling flash of the pike and sword,
And the burning cottage's crimson light
On the baleful Orange banner pour'd !

But, see—what spell doth she now prepare?
What strange zigzaggeries round her draw,
As she mutters, backward, many a prayer?—
'Tis to call to her aid some imp of law ;

Some dusky Gnome, who shivers at light ;
Who, bred in the dark, his life hath pass'd,
In playing, for hire, with Wrong and Right,
Till he knows not one from t' other, at last ;

Who kept by his masters under cork
Like bottled-up imps, is but brought out
To help in any unholy work
The wise state-conjurors are about ;—

(1) Psalmanazar.

Who, ready at hand for dingy deeds,
  Not only is bottled, convenient sprite!
But labell'd and priced, and only needs
  A seal on his cork to fix him quite.

"Up!" said the hag, with visage stern,
  "My master imp, who art learn'd in all
The wise and good would most unlearn:"
  She said—and Copley came, at her call;

Came (while the beldam cried "All hail!")
  In a shape she loves the best of any—
A Rat,(1) who was n't "without a tale,"
  As he told of a cock and a "bull" (2) full many.

And much he squeak'd of queens and kings,
  Of James the first, and James the latter,
And "bloody Queen Mary," and lots of things
  Which, he own'd, had nothing to do with the
    matter.

Thus, one by one, did the Witch call up
  The legion of imps that fill'd that roll;
And to each she pledged her venomous cup,
  While each one pledged to her his soul:

Till, hark! in the midst of all their rites,
  While (counting two hundred and seventy-seven,
The hag included) this band of sprites
  Were playing their tricks before high heaven,
There came a loud crash!   *   *   *
     *   *   *

EXTEMPORE.

TO ——, TO WHOSE INTERFERENCE I CHIEFLY OWE THE
VERY LIBERAL PRICE GIVEN FOR "LALLA ROOKH."

WHEN they shall tell, in future times,
Of thousands given for idle rhymes
Like these—the pastime of an hour,
They 'll wonder at the lavish taste
That could, like tulip-fanciers, waste
A little fortune on a flower!

Yet wilt not thou, whose friendship set
  Such value on the bard's renown—
Yet wilt not thou, my friend, regret
  The golden shower thy spell brought down.
For thou dost love the free-born muse,
Whose flight no curbing chain pursues;
And thou dost think the song that shrines
That image—so adored by thee,
And spirits like thee—Liberty,
Of price beyond all India's mines!

A VOICE FROM MARATHON.

O FOR a voice, as loud as that of Fame,
  To breathe the word—Arise!
From Pindus to Taygetus to proclaim—
  Let every Greek arise!

Ye who have hearts to strike a *single* blow,
  Hear my despairing cries!
Ye who have hands to immolate *one* foe,
  Arise! arise! arise!

From the dim fields of Asphodel beneath,
  Upborne by cloudy sighs
Of those who love their country still in death —
  Even I—even I—arise!

These are not hands for earthly wringing—these!—
  Blood should not blind these eyes! ..
Yet here I stand, untomb'd Miltiades,
  Weeping—arise! arise!

Hear ye the groans that heave this burial-field?—
  Old Græcia's saviour-band
Cry from the dust —"Fight on! nor *dare* to yield!
  Save *ye* our father-land!

"Blunt with your bosom the barbaric spear!
  Break it within your breast;
Then come, brave Greek! and join your brothers here
  In our immortal rest!"

Shall modern Datis, swoln with Syrian pride,
  Cover the land with slaves! —
Ay—let them *cover* it, both far and wide —
  Cover it with their *graves!*

Much has been done—but more remains to do—
  Ye have fought long and well!
The trump that, on the Ægean, glory blew,
  Seem'd with a storm to swell!

Asia's grim tyrant shudder'd at the sound,
  He leap'd upon his throne!
Murmur'd his horse-tail'd chieftainry around —
  "*Another Marathon!*"

Dodona, 'mid her fanes and forests hoar
  Heard it with solemn glee:
And old Parnassus, with a lofty roar,
  Told it from sea to sea!

High-bosom'd Greece, through her unnumber'd vales,
  Broke forth in glorious song!
Her classic streams that plough the headlong dales
  Thunder'd the notes along!

But there 's a bloodier wreath to gain, oh friends!
  Now rise, or ever fall!
If ye fight now no fiercer than the fiends,
  Better not fight at all!

(1) "And like a rat without a tail."—*Macbeth.*
(2) The "Bull" part of the story belongs more properly
to Mr. Peel.

The feverish war-drum mingles with the fife
  In dismal symphony,
And Moslem strikes at liberty and life—
  For both, strike harder ye!

Hark! how Cithæron with his earthquake voice
  Calls to the utmost shores!
While Pluto bars, against the riving noise,
  His adamantine doors!

Athené, tiptoe on her crumbling dome,
  Cries—" Youth, ye must be men!"
And Echo shouts within her rocky tomb—
  " Greeks, become Greeks again!"

The stone first brought, his living tomb to close,
  Pausanias' mother piled:
Matrons of Greece! will ye do less for foes
  Than she did for her child?

Let boyhood strike!—let every rank and age
  Do each what each *can* do!
Let him whose arm is mighty as his rage
  Strike deep—strike home—strike *through!*

Be wise, be firm, be cautious, yet be bold!
  Be brother-true! be One!
I teach but what the Phrygian taught of old—
  Divide, and be undone!

Hallow'd in life, in death itself, is he
  Who for his country dies;
A light, a star, to all futurity—
  Arise ye, then! arise!

O countrymen! O countrymen! once more—
  By earth—and seas—and skies—
By Heaven—by sacred Hades—I implore—
  Arise! arise! arise!

THE TWO BONDSMEN.

When Joseph, a bondsman in Egypt, of old,
  Shunn'd the wanton embraces of Potiphar's dame,
She offer'd him jewels, she offer'd him gold,
  But more than all riches he valued his fame.
Oh Joseph! thou bondsman of Greece, can it be
  That the actions of namesakes so little agree?
Greek Scrip is a Potiphar's lady to thee;
  When with 13 per cent. she embellish'd her charms,
Didst thou fly, honest Joseph? Yes—into her arms.
  Oh Joseph! dear Joseph! bethink thee in time,
And take a friend's counsel, though tender'd in
  rhyme.
Refund, " honest " Joseph: how great were the
  shame,
If, when posteriority (1) sits on thy name,

(1) Remote posterity—a favourite word of the Attorney-General's.
(2) Really the Hon. Member for Montrose should take a

They should sternly decree, 'twixt your namesake
  and you,
That he was the Christian, and thou wert the Jew.

CROCKFORDIANA.

EPIGRAMS.

Mala vicini pecoris contagia lædunt.

1.

What can those workmen be about?
  Do, Crockford, let the secret out,
    Why thus your houses fall.—
Quoth he, " Since folks are not in town,
  I find it better to *pull down,*
    Than *have no pull at all.*"

2.

See, passenger, at Crockford's high behest,
Red coats by *black-legs* ousted from their nest—
The arts of peace o'ermatching reckless war,
And gallant *Rouge* undone by wily *Noir.*

3.

Impar congressus ——.

Fate gave the word—the King of dice and cards
In an *unguarded* moment took the Guards;
Contrived his neighbours in a trice to drub,
And did the trick by—*turning up a Club.*

4.

Nullum simile est idem.

'T is strange how some will differ—some advance
That the Guards' Club-House was pull'd down by
  chance;
While some, with juster notions in their *mazard,*
Stoutly maintain the deed was done by *hazard.*

LINES WRITTEN IN ST. STEPHEN'S CHAPEL, AFTER THE DISSOLUTION.

BY A MEMBER OF THE UPPER BENCHES.

The King's speech toll'd the Commons' knell,
  The House is clear'd, the chair vacated,
And gloom and loneliness now dwell
  Where Britain's wise men congregated.

The gallery is dark and lone,
  No longer throng'd with curious folk,
Happy to pay their good half-crown
  To hear bad speeches badly spoke.

The Treasury seats no placemen show,
  Clear'd is each Opposition bench;
And even never-ending Joe
  No longer cries—" Retrench! retrench!" (2)

Fred. Robinson no more his skill
  Employs in weaving speeches fair,
The Country gentlemen to fill
  With promises as thin as air.

little breath; his objections are most unfair; and what is
worse, they are *never-ending.*"—See the Chancellor of the
Exchequer's speech in reply to Mr. Hume, Feb. 23, 1826.

Dick Martin now no plan proposes
  To aid the brute part of the nation,
While Members cough and blow their noses,
  To drown his most humane oration.

Good Mr. Brogden, where art thou,
  Most worthy—Chairman of Committees?
To strip one laurel from thy brow
  Would surely be a thousand pities,

'T was a good joke, forsooth, to think
  Thou shouldst give up thy honest winnings,
And thereby own that thou didst wink,
  Pure soul! at other people's sinnings. (1)

Where 's Holmes, Corruption's ready hack,
  Who life and credit both consumes
In whipping in the Treasury pack,
  And jobbing in committee-rooms ? (2)

I look around—no well-known face
  Along the benches meets my eye—
No Member "rises in his place,"
  For all have other fish to fry.

Not one is left of King and sages,
  Who lately sat debating here ;

The crowded hustings now engages
  Their every hope and every fear.

Electors, rally to the poll,
  And Lord John Russell never heed :
Let gold alone your choice control—
  "The best man 's he who best can *bleed*." (3)

But if, too timid, you delay,
  (By Bribery Statute held in awe),
Fear not—there is a ready way
  To serve yourselves and cheat the law.

In times like these, when things are high,
  And candidates must be well fed,
Your cabbages they 'll freely buy,
  Kind souls! at two pounds ten a-head. (4)

Thus may we hope for many a law,
  And many a measure most discreet,
When—pure as even the last we saw—
  Britain's new Parliament shall meet.

Then haste ye, Candidates, and strive
  An M. P. to your names to tack,
And—after July twenty-five (5)
  Collective wisdom—welcome back !

ALCIPHRON.

A FRAGMENT.

PREFACE.

How little akin to romance or poesy were some of the circumstances under which the following poem was first projected by me, the reader may have seen from a preceding preface; (6) and the following rough outline, which I have found among my papers, dated Paris, July 25, 1820, will show both my first general conception, or fore-shadowing of the story, and likewise the extent to which I thought right, in afterwards working out this design, in the tale of the *Epicurean*, to reject or modify some of its details.

"Began my Egyptian Poem, and wrote about thirteen or fourteen lines of it. The story to be told in letters from a young Epicurean philosopher, who, in the second century of the Christian era, goes to Egypt for the purpose of discovering the elixir of immortality, which is supposed to be one of the secrets of the Egyptian priests. During a Festival on the Nile, he meets with a beautiful maiden, the daughter of one of the priests lately dead. She enters the catacombs, and disappears. He hovers around the spot, and at last finds the well and secret passages, etc., by which those who are initiated enter. He sees this maiden in one of those theatrical spectacles which formed a part of the subterranean Elysium of the Pyramids—finds opportunities of conversing with her—their intercourse in this mysterious region described. They are discovered; and he is thrown into those subterranean prisons, where they who violate the rules of initiation are confined. He is liberated from thence by the young maiden, and taking flight together, they reach some beautiful region, where they linger, for a time, delighted, and she is near becoming a victim to his arts. But, taking alarm, she flies, and seeks refuge with a Chris-

---

(1) Mr. Brogden said "he certainly should not refund the money, *because, by so doing, he should convict himself.*"—See the Report of a Meeting of the Proprietors of the Arigna Mining Company.

(2) The barefaced system of voting at private bill committees, without having heard an iota of evidence for or against, forms a distinguished feature in the history of the late parliament.

(3) A maxim which has been pretty well acted on in the present elections.

(4) "During the election at Sudbury, four cabbages sold for 10*l.* and a plate of gooseberries fetched 25*l.*, the sellers where these articles were so scarce being voters."—See the *Times* of Friday, June 20.

(5) The day on which the writs were returnable.

(6) See page 449, col. 2.

tian monk, in the Thebaid, to whom her mother, who was secretly a Christian, had consigned her in dying. The struggles of her love with her religion. A persecution of the Christians takes place, and she is seized (chiefly through the unintentional means of her lover), and suffers martyrdom. The scene of her martyrdom described, in a letter from the Solitary of the Thebaid, and the attempt made by the young philosopher to rescue her. He is carried off from thence to the cell of the Solitary. His letters from that retreat, after he has become a Christian, devoting his thoughts entirely to repentance and the recollection of the beloved saint who had gone before him.—If I do n't make something out of all this, the deuce is in 't."

According to this plan, the events of the story were to be told in Letters, or Epistolary Poems, addressed by the philosopher to a young Athenian friend. The great difficulty, however, of managing, in rhyme, the minor details of a story, so as to be clear without growing prosaic, and, still more, the diffuse length to which I saw narration in verse would extend, deterred me from following this plan any further; and I then commenced the tale of the Epicurean.

Of the Poems written for my first experiment, a few specimens, the best I could select, were introduced into the prose story; but the remainder I had thrown aside, and nearly forgotten even their existence, when a circumstance somewhat characteristic, perhaps, of that trading spirit, which has now converted Parnassus itself into a market, again called my attention to them. The late Mr. Macrone, to whose general talents and enterprise in business all who knew him will bear ready testimony, had long been anxious that I should undertake for him some new Poem or Story, affording such subjects for illustration as might call into play the fanciful pencil of Mr. Turner. Other tasks and ties, however, had rendered my compliance with this wish impracticable; and he was about to give up all thoughts of attaining his object, when on learning from me accidentally that the Epicurean was still my own property, he proposed to purchase of me the use of the copyright for a single illustrated edition.

The terms proffered by him being most liberal, I readily acceded to the proposed arrangement; but, on further consideration, there arose some difficulty in the way of our treaty—the work itself being found insufficient for a volume of such dimensions as would yield any hope of defraying the cost of the numerous illustrations then intended for it. Some modification, therefore, of our terms was thought necessary; and then first was the notion suggested to me of bringing forth from among my papers the original sketch, or opening of the story (Alciphron), and adding these fragments, as a sort of make-weight, in the mutual adjustment of our terms.

That I had myself regarded the first experiment

as a failure, was sufficiently shown by my relinquishment of it. But, as the Epicurean had then passed through several editions, and had been translated into most of the languages of Europe, it was thought that an insight into the anxious process by which such success had been attained might, as an encouragement, at least, to the humble merit of pains-taking, be deemed of some little use.

——◦❦❀❧◦——

ALCIPHRON.

LETTER I.

FROM ALCIPHRON AT ALEXANDRIA TO CLEON AT ATHENS.

WELL may you wonder at my flight
   From those fair Gardens, in whose bowers
Lingers whate'er of wise and bright,
   Of Beauty's smile or Wisdom's light,
   Is left to grace this world of ours.
Well may my comrades, as they roam,
   On such sweet eves as this, inquire
Why I have left that happy home
   Where all is found that all desire,
   And Time hath wings that never tire;
Where bliss, in all the countless shapes
   That Fancy's self to bliss hath given,
Comes clustering round, like road-side grapes
   That woo the traveller's lip, at even ;
Where Wisdom flings not joy away—
   As Pallas in the stream, they say,
Once flung her flute—but smiling owns
That woman's lips can send forth tones
Worth all the music of those spheres
So many dream of but none hears;
Where Virtue's-self puts on so well
   Her sister Pleasure's smile that, loath
From either nymph apart to dwell,
   We finish by embracing both.

Yes, such the place of bliss, I own,
From all whose charms I just have flown ;
And even while thus to thee I write,
   And by the Nile's dark flood recline,
Fondly in thought, I wing my flight
Back to those groves and gardens bright,
And often think, by this sweet light,
   How lovelily they all must shine ;
Can see that graceful temple throw
   Down the green slope its lengthen'd shade,
While, on the marble steps below,
   There sits some fair Athenian maid,
Over some favourite volume bending ;
   And, by her side, a youthful sage
Holds back the ringlets that, descending,
   Would else o'ershadow all the page.
But hence such thoughts !—nor let me grieve
O'er scenes of joy that I but leave,
As the bird quits awhile its nest
To come again with livelier zest.

And now to tell thee—what I fear
Thou 'lt gravely smile at—*why* I 'm here.
Though through my life's short sunny dream,
  I 've floated without pain or care,
Like a light leaf, down pleasure's stream,
  Caught in each sparkling eddy there;
Though never Mirth awaked a strain
That my heart echo'd not again;
Yet have I felt, when even most gay,
  Sad thoughts—I knew not whence or why—
Suddenly o'er my spirit fly,
Like clouds, that ere we 've time to say
  " How bright the sky is ! " shade the sky.
Sometimes so vague, so undefined
Were these strange darkenings of mind—
While nought but joy around me beam'd
  So causelessly they 've come and flown,
That not of life or earth they seem'd,
  But shadows from some world unknown.
More oft, however, 't was the thought
  How soon that scene, with all its play
Of life and gladness, must decay—
Those lips I press'd, the hands I caught—
Myself—the crowd that mirth had brought
  Around me—swept like weeds away!

This thought it was that came to shed
  O'er rapture's hour its worst alloys ;
And, close as shade with sunshine, wed
  Its sadness with my happiest joys.
Oh, but for this disheartening voice
  Stealing amid our mirth, to say
That all, in which we most rejoice,
  Ere night may be the earth-worm's prey—
But for this bitter—only this—
Full as the world is brimm'd with bliss,
And capable as feels my soul
  Of draining to its dregs the whole,
I should turn earth to heaven, and be,
  If bliss made Gods, a Deity !

Thou know'st that night—the very last
That 'mong my Garden friends I pass'd—
When the school held its feast of mirth
  To celebrate our founder's birth ;
And all that He in dreams but saw
  When he set Pleasure on the throne
Of this bright world, and wrote her law
  In human hearts, was felt and known—
Not in unreal dreams, but true,
Substantial joy as pulse e'er knew—
By hearts and bosoms, that each felt
Itself the realm where Pleasure dwelt.

That night, when all our mirth was o'er,
  The minstrels silent, and the feet
Of the young maidens heard no more—
  So stilly was the time, so sweet,
And such a calm came o'er that scene,
  Where life and revel late had been—

Lone as the quiet of some bay
From which the sea hath ebb'd away—
That still I linger'd, lost in thought,
  Gazing upon the stars of night,
Sad and intent, as if I sought
  Some mournful secret in their light ;
And ask'd them, 'mid that silence, why
Man, glorious man, alone must die,
While they, less wonderful than he,
Shine on through all eternity.

That night—thou haply may'st forget
  Its loveliness— but 't was a night
To make earth's meanest slave regret
  Leaving a world so soft and bright.
On one side, in the dark blue sky,
Lonely and radiant, was the eye
Of Jove himself while, on the other,
  'Mong stars that came out one by one,
The young moon— like the Roman mother
  Among her living jewels   shone.
" Oh that from yonder orbs," I thought,
  " Pure and eternal as they are,
There could to earth some power be brought,
Some charm with their own essence fraught,
  To make man deathless as a star,
And open to his vast desires
  A course as boundless and sublime
As that which waits those comet-fires,
  That burn and roam throughout all time ! "

While thoughts like these absorb'd my mind,
  That weariness which earthly bliss,
However sweet, still leaves behind,
  As if to show how earthly 't is,
Came lulling o'er me, and I laid
  My limbs at that fair statue's base
That miracle, which Art hath made
  Of all the choice of Nature's grace
To which so oft I 've knelt, and sworn
  That could a living mind like her
Unto this wondering world be born,
  I would myself turn worshipper.

Sleep came then o'er me—and I seem'd
  To be transported far away
To a blank desert plain, where gleam'd
  One single melancholy ray,
Throughout that darkness dimly shed
  From a small taper in the hand
Of one, who, pale as are the dead,
  Before me took his spectral stand,
And said, while awfully a smile
  Came o'er the wanness of his cheek
" Go, and, beside the sacred Nile,
  You 'll find the Eternal Life you seek."

Soon as he spoke these words, the hue
Of death o'er all his features grew

Like the pale morning, when o'er night
She gains the victory, full of light;
While the small torch he held became
A glory in his hand, whose flame
Brighten'd the desert suddenly,
Even to the far horizon's line—
Along whose level I could see
Gardens and groves, that seem'd to shine,
As if then o'er them freshly play'd
A vernal rainbow's rich cascade;
And music floated every where,
Circling, as 't were itself the air,
And spirits, on whose wings the hue
Of heaven still linger'd, round me flew,
Till from all sides such splendours broke,
That, with the excess of light, I woke!

Such was my dream;—and, I confess,
Though none of all our creedless school
E'er conn'd, believed, or reverenced less
The fables of the priest-led fool,
Who tells us of a soul, a mind,
Separate and pure, within us shrined,
Which is to live—ah, hope too bright!—
For ever in yon fields of light;
Who fondly thinks the guardian eyes
Of Gods are on him—as if, blest
And blooming in their own blue skies,
The eternal Gods were not too wise
To let weak man disturb their rest!—
Though thinking of such creeds as thou
And all our Garden sages think,
Yet is there something, I allow,
In dreams like this—a sort of link
With worlds unseen, which, from the hour
I first could lisp my thoughts till now,
Hath master'd me with spell-like power.
And who can tell, as we 're combined
Of various atoms—some refined,
Like those that scintillate and play
In the fix'd stars—some gross as they
That frown in clouds or sleep in clay—
Who can be sure, but 't is the best
And brightest atoms of our frame,
Those most akin to stellar flame,
That shine out thus, when we 're at rest;—
Even as the stars themselves, whose light
Comes out but in the silent night.
Or is it that there lurks, indeed,
Some truth in Man's prevailing creed,
And that our Guardians, from on high,
Come, in that pause from toil and sin,
To put the senses' curtain by,
And on the wakeful soul look in!

Vain thought!—but yet, howe'er it be,
Dreams, more than once, have proved to me
Oracles truer far than Oak,
Or Dove, or Tripod ever spoke.

And 't was the words—thou 'lt hear and smile—
The words that phantom seem'd to speak—
"Go, and beside the sacred Nile
You 'll find the Eternal Life you seek"—
That, haunting me by night, by day,·
At length, as with the unseen hand
Of Fate itself, urged me away
From Athens to this Holy Land;
Where, 'mong the secrets, still untaught,
The mysteries that, as yet, nor sun
Nor eye hath reach'd—oh, blessed thought!
May sleep this everlasting one.

Farewell—when to our Garden friends
Thou talk'st of the wild dream that sends
The gayest of their school thus far,
Wandering beneath Canopus' star,
Tell them that, wander where he will,
Or, howsoe'er they now condemn
His vague and vain pursuit, he still
Is worthy of the School and them;—
Still, all their own—nor e'er forgets,
Even while his heart and soul pursue
The Eternal Light which never sets,
The many meteor joys that do,
But seeks them, hails them with delight
Where'er they meet his longing sight.
And if his life must wane away,
Like other lives, at least the day,
The hour it lasts, shall, like a fire
With incense fed, in sweets expire.

————◦◦◦————

LETTER II.

FROM THE SAME TO THE SAME.
Memphis.

'T is true, alas—the mysteries and the lore
I came to study on this wondrous shore,
Are all forgotten in the new delights,
The strange wild joys that fill my days and nights.
Instead of dark dull oracles that speak
From subterranean temples, those *I* seek
Come from the breathing shrines where Beauty lives,
And Love, her priest, the soft responses gives.
Instead of honouring Isis in those rites
At Coptos held, I hail her, when she lights
Her first young crescent on the holy stream—
When wandering youths and maidens watch her beam
And number o'er the nights she hath to run,
Ere she again embrace her bridegroom sun.
While o'er some mystic leaf, that dimly lends
A clue into past times, the student bends,
And by its glimmering guidance learns to tread
Back through the shadowy knowledge of the dead—
The only skill, alas, *I* yet can claim
Lies in deciphering some new loved-one's name—
Some gentle missive, hinting time and place,
In language soft as Memphian reed can trace.
And where—oh where 's the heart that could with- [stand
The unnumber'd witcheries of this sun-born land,

Where first young Pleasure's banner was unfurl'd,
And Love hath temples ancient as the world!
Where mystery, like the veil by Beauty worn,
Hides but to win, and shades but to adorn;
Where that luxurious melancholy, born
Of passion and of genius, sheds a gloom
Making joy holy;—where the bower and tomb
Stand side by side, and Pleasure learns from Death
The instant value of each moment's breath.

Couldst thou but see how like a poet's dream
This lovely land now looks!—the glorious stream,
That late, between its banks, was seen to glide
'Mong shrines and marble cities, on each side
Glittering like jewels strung along a chain,
Hath now sent forth its waters, and o'er plain
And valley, like a giant from his bed
Rising with outstretch'd limbs, hath grandly spread,
While far as sight can reach, beneath as clear
And blue a heaven as ever bless'd our sphere,
Gardens, and pillar'd streets, and porphyry domes,
And high-built temples, fit to be the homes
Of mighty Gods, and pyramids, whose hour
Outlasts all time, above the waters tower!

Then, too, the scenes of pomp and joy, that make
One theatre of this vast peopled lake,
Where all that Love, Religion, Commerce gives
Of life and motion, ever moves and lives.
Here, up the steps of temples from the wave
Ascending, in procession slow and grave,
Priests in white garments go, with sacred wands
And silver cymbals gleaming in their hands;
While there, rich barks—fresh from those sunny
Far off, beyond the sounding cataracts—   [tracks
Glide, with their precious lading to the sea,
Plumes of bright birds, rhinoceros ivory,
Gems from the Isle of Meroe, and those grains
Of gold, wash'd down by Abyssinian rains.
Here, where the waters wind into a bay
Shadowy and cool, some pilgrims, on their way
To Saïs or Bubastus, among beds
Of lotus flowers, that close above their heads,
Push their light barks, and there, as in a bower,
Sing, talk, or sleep away the sultry hour;
Oft dipping in the Nile, when faint with heat,
That leaf, from which its waters drink most sweet.—
While haply, not far off, beneath a bank
Of blossoming acacias, many a prank
Is play'd in the cool current by a train
Of laughing nymphs, lovely as she, (1) whose chain
Around two conquerors of the world was cast,
But, for a third too feeble, broke at last.

For oh, believe not them, who dare to brand,
As poor in charms, the women of this land.
Though darken'd by that sun, whose spirit flows
Through every vein, and tinges as it goes,
'T is but the embrowning of the fruit that tells
How rich within the soul of ripeness dwells—

The hue their own dark sanctuaries wear,
Announcing heaven in half-caught glimpses there·
And never yet did tell-tale looks set free
The secret of young hearts more tenderly.
Such eyes!—long, shadowy, with that languid fall
Of the fringed lids, which may be seen in all
Who live beneath the sun's too ardent rays—
Lending such looks as, on their marriage days,
Young maids cast down before a bridegroom's gaze!
Then for their grace—mark but the nymph-like
                                                shapes
Of the young village girls, when carrying grapes
From green Anthylla, or light urns of flowers —
Not our own Sculpture, in her happiest hours,
E'er imaged forth, even at the touch of him (2)
Whose touch was life, more luxury of limb!
Then, canst thou wonder if, 'mid scenes like these,
I should forget all graver mysteries,
All lore but love's, all secrets but that best
In heaven or earth, the art of being blest!
Yet are there times—though brief, I own, their stay,
Like summer clouds that shine themselves away—
Moments of gloom, when even these pleasures pall
Upon my saddening heart, and I recall
That Garden dream—that promise of a power,
Oh, were there such!—to lengthen out life's hour,
On, on, as through a vista, far away
Opening before us into endless day!
And chiefly o'er my spirit did this thought
Come on that evening—bright as ever brought
Light's golden farewell to the world—when first
The eternal pyramids of Memphis burst
Awfully on my sight—standing sublime
'Twixt earth and heaven, the watch-towers of Time,
From whose lone summit, when his reign hath past
From earth for ever, he will look his last!

There hung a calm and solemn sunshine round
Those mighty monuments, a hushing sound
In the still air that circled them, which stole
Like music of past times into my soul.
I thought what myriads of the wise and brave
And beautiful had sunk into the grave,
Since earth first saw these wonders—and I said
"Are things eternal only for the Dead?
Hath Man no loftier hope than this, which dooms
His only lasting trophies to be tombs?
But 't is not so—earth, heaven, all nature shows
He may become immortal—may unclose
The wings within him wrapt, and proudly rise
Redeem'd from earth, a creature of the skies!

"And who can say, among the written spells
From Hermes' hand, that, in these shrines and cells
Have, from the Flood, lain hid, there may not be
Some secret clue to immortality,
Some amulet, whose spell can keep life's fire
Awake within us, never to expire?

(1) Cleopatra.   (2) Apelles.

T is known that, on the Emerald Table, (1) hid
For ages in yon loftiest pyramid,
The Thrice-Great (2) did himself, engrave, of old,
The chemic mystery that gives endless gold.
And why may not this mightier secret dwell
Within the same dark chambers? who can tell
But that those kings, who, by the written skill
Of the Emerald Table, call'd forth gold at will,
And quarries upon quarries heap'd and hurl'd
To build them domes that might outstand the
      world—
Who knows but that the heavenlier art, which
      shares
The life of gods with man, was also theirs—
That they themselves, triumphant o'er the power
Of fate and death, are living at this hour;
And these, the giant homes they still possess,
Not tombs, but everlasting palaces,
Within whose depths, hid from the world above,
Even now they wander, with the few they love,
Through subterranean gardens, by a light
Unknown on earth, which hath nor dawn nor
      night!
Else, why those deathless structures? why the grand
And hidden halls, that undermine this land?
Why else hath none of earth e'er dared to go
Through the dark windings of that realm below,
Nor aught from heaven itself, except the God
Of Silence, through those endless labyrinths trod?"

Thus did I dream—wild wandering dreams, I own,
But such as haunt me ever, if alone,
Or in that pause 'twixt joy and joy I be,
Like a ship hush'd between two waves at sea.
Then do these spirit whisperings, like the sound
Of the Dark Future, come appalling round;
Nor can I break the trance that holds me then,
Till high o'er Pleasure's surge I mount again!
Even now for new adventure, new delight,
My heart is on the wing;—this very night,
The Temple on that island, half-way o'er
From Memphis' gardens to the eastern shore,
Sends up its annual rite (3) to her, whose beams
Bring the sweet time of night-flowers and dreams;
The nymph, who dips her urn in silent lakes,
And turns to silvery dew each drop it takes;—
Oh, not our Dian of the North, who chains
In vestal ice the current of young veins,
But she who haunts the gay Bubastian (4) grove,
And owns she sees, from her bright heaven above,
Nothing on earth to match that heaven but Love.
Think, then, what bliss will be abroad to-night!—
Besides those sparkling nymphs, who meet the sight
Day after day, familiar as the sun,
Coy buds of beauty, yet unbreathed upon,
And all the hidden loveliness, that lies—
Shut up, as are the beams of sleeping eyes,
Within these twilight shrines—to-night shall be
Let loose, like birds, for this festivity!

And mark, 'tis nigh; already the sun bids
His evening farewell to the Pyramids,
As he hath done, age after age, till they
Alone on earth seem ancient as his ray;
While their great shadows, stretching from the light,
Look like the first colossal steps of Night,
Stretching across the valley, to invade
The distant hills of porphyry with their shade.
Around, as signals of the setting beam,
Gay gilded flags on every house-top gleam :
While, hark!—from all the temples a rich swell
Of music to the Moon—farewell—farewell.

LETTER III.

FROM THE SAME TO THE SAME.

Memphis.

THERE is some star—or it may be
    That moon we saw so near last night—
Which comes athwart my destiny
    For ever, with misleading light.
If for a moment, pure and wise
    And calm I feel, there quick doth fall
A spark from some disturbing eyes,
    That through my heart, soul, being, flies,
    And makes a wildfire of it all.
I've seen—oh, Cleon, that this earth
Should e'er have given such beauty birth !—
That man—but, hold—hear all that pass'd
Since yester-night, from first to last.

The rising of the Moon, calm, slow,
    And beautiful, as if she came
Fresh from the Elysian bowers below,
    Was, with a loud and sweet acclaim,
Welcomed from every breezy height,
Where crowds stood waiting for her light.
And well might they who view'd the scene
    Then lit up all around them say,
That never yet had Nature been
    Caught sleeping in a lovelier ray,
Or rivall'd her own noon-tide face,
With purer show of moonlight grace.
Memphis—still grand, though not the same
Unrivall'd Memphis, that could seize
From ancient Thebes the crown of Fame,
    And wear it bright through centuries—
Now, in the moonshine, that came down
Like a last smile upon that crown,
Memphis, still grand, among her lakes,
    Her pyramids and shrines of fire,
Rose, like a vision, that half breaks
On one who, dreaming still, awakes
    To music from some midnight choir :

(1) See Notes on the *Epicurean.*
(2) The Hermes Trismegistus.
(3) The great Festival of the Moon.
(4) Bubastis, or Isis, was the Diana of the Egyptian my-
thology.

78

While to the west—where gradual sinks
  In the red sands, from Lybia roll'd,
Some mighty column, or fair sphynx
  That stood in kingly courts, of old—
It seem'd as, 'mid the pomps that shone
Thus gaily round him, Time look'd on,
Waiting till all, now bright and blest,
Should sink beneath him like the rest.

No sooner had the setting sun
Proclaim'd the festal rite begun,
And, 'mid their idol's fullest beams,
  The Egyptian world was all afloat,
Than I, who live upon these streams,
  Like a young Nile-bird, turn'd my boat
To the fair island, on whose shores,
Through leafy palms and sycamores,
Already shone the moving lights
Of pilgrims, hastening to the rites.
While, far around, like ruby sparks
Upon the water, lighted barks,
Of every form and kind—from those
  That down Syene's cataract shoots,
To the grand gilded barge, that rows
  To tambour's beat and breath of flutes,
And wears at night, in words of flame,
On the rich prow, its master's name—
All were alive, and made this sea
  Of cities busy as a hill
Of summer ants, caught suddenly
  In the o'erflowing of a rill.

Landed upon the isle, I soon
Through marble alleys and small groves
Of that mysterious palm she loves,
Reach'd the fair Temple of the Moon ;
And there—as slowly through the last
Dim-lighted vestibule I pass'd—
Between the porphyry pillars, twined
  With palm and ivy, I could see
A band of youthful maidens wind,
  In measured walk, half dancingly,
Round a small shrine, on which was placed
That bird, (1) whose plumes of black and white
Wear in their hue, by Nature traced,
A type of the moon's shadow'd light.

In drapery, like woven snow,
These nymphs were clad ; and each, below
The rounded bosom, loosely wore
  A dark blue zone, or bandelet,
With little silver stars all o'er,
  As are the skies at midnight, set.
While in their tresses, braided through,
Sparkled that flower of Egypt's lakes,
The silvery lotus, in whose hue
  As much delight the young Moon takes,
  As doth the Day-God to behold
The lofty bean-flower's buds of gold.

And, as they gracefully went round
  The worshipp'd bird, some to the beat
Of castanets, some to the sound
  Of the shrill sistrum timed their feet ;
While others, at each step they took,
A tinkling chain of silver shook.

They seem'd all fair—but there was one
On whom the light had not yet shone,
Or shone but partly—so downcast
She held her brow, as slow she pass'd.
And yet, to me, there seem'd to dwell
  A charm about that unseen face—
A something, in the shade that fell
  Over that brow's imagined grace,
Which won me more than all the best
Outshining beauties of the rest.
And her alone my eyes could see,
Enchain'd by this sweet mystery ;
And her alone I watch'd, as round
She glided o'er that marble ground,
Stirring not more the unconscious air
Than if a Spirit were moving there.
Till suddenly, wide open flew
The Temple's folding gates, and threw
A splendour from within, a flood
Of glory where these maidens stood.
While, with that light—as if the same
Rich source gave birth to both—there came
A swell of harmony, as grand
As e'er was born of voice and hand,
Filling the gorgeous aisles around
With luxury of light and sound.

Then was it, by the flash that blazed
Full o'er her features—oh 't was then,
As startlingly her eyes she raised,
  But quick let fall their lids again,
I saw—not Psyche's self, when first
Upon the threshold of the skies
She paused, while heaven's glory burst
  Newly upon her downcast eyes,
Could look more beautiful or blush
  With holier shame than did this maid,
Whom now I saw, in all that gush
Of splendour from the aisles, display'd.
Never—though well thou know'st how much
  I 've felt the sway of Beauty's star—
Never did her bright influence touch
  My soul into its depths so far ;
And had that vision linger'd there
  One minute more, I should have flown,
Forgetful who I was and where,
  And, at her feet in worship thrown,
Proffer'd my soul through life her own.

But, scarcely had that burst of light
And music broke on ear and sight,

(1) The Ibis.

Than up the aisle the bird took wing,
  As if on heavenly mission sent,
While after him, with graceful spring,
  Like some unearthly creatures, meant
  To live in that mix'd element
Of light and song, the young maids went;
And she, who in my heart had thrown
A spark to burn for life, was flown.

In vain I tried to follow;—bands
  Of reverend chanters fill'd the aisle:
Where'er I sought to pass, their wands
  Motion'd me back, while many a file
Of sacred nymphs—but ah, not they
Whom my eyes look'd for—throng'd the way.
Perplex'd, impatient, 'mid this crowd
Of faces, lights—the o'erwhelming cloud
Of incense round me, and my blood
Full of its new-born fire—I stood,
Nor moved, nor breathed, but when I caught
  A glimpse of some blue spangled zone,
Or wreath of lotus, which, I thought,
  Like those she wore at distance shone.

But no, 'twas vain—hour after hour,
  Till my heart's throbbing turn'd to pain,
And my strain'd eyesight lost its power,
  I sought her thus, but all in vain.
At length, hot—wilder'd—in despair,
I rush'd into the cool night-air,
And hurrying (though with many a look
Back to the busy Temple) took
My way along the moonlight shore,
And sprung into my boat once more.

There is a Lake, that to the north
Of Memphis stretches grandly forth,
Upon whose silent shore the Dead
Have a proud City of their own, (1)
With shrines and pyramids o'erspread—
Where many an ancient kingly head
  Slumbers, immortalised in stone;
And where, through marble grots beneath,
  The lifeless, ranged like sacred things,
Nor wanting aught of life but breath,
  Lie in their painted coverings,
And on each new successive race,
  That visit their dim haunts below,
Look with the same unwithering face,
  They wore three thousand years ago.
There, Silence, thoughtful God, who loves
The neighbourhood of death, in groves
Of asphodel lies hid, and weaves
His hushing spell among the leaves—
Nor ever noise disturbs the air,
  Save the low, humming, mournful sound
Of priests, within their shrines, at prayer
For the fresh Dead entomb'd around.

'Twas toward this place of death—in mood
  Made up of thoughts, half bright, half dark—
I now across the shining flood
  Unconscious turn'd my light-wing'd bark.
The form of that young maid, in all
  Its beauty, was before me still;
And oft I thought, if thus to call
  Her image to my mind at will,
If but the memory of that one
Bright look of hers, for ever gone,
Was to my heart worth all the rest
Of woman-kind, beheld, possest—
What would it be, if wholly mine,
Within these arms, as in a shrine,
Hallow'd by Love, I saw her shine—
An idol, worshipp'd by the light
Of her own beauties, day and night—
If 'twas a blessing but to see
And lose again, what would this be?

In thoughts like these—but often crost
By darker threads—my mind was lost,
Till, near that City of the Dead,
Waked from my trance, I saw o'erhead—
As if by some enchanter bid
  Suddenly from the wave to rise—
Pyramid over pyramid
  Tower in succession to the skies;
While one, aspiring, as if soon
  'Twould touch the heavens, rose o'er all,
And, on its summit, the white moon
  Rested, as on a pedestal!

The silence of the lonely tombs
  And temples round, where nought was heard
But the high palm-tree's tufted plumes,
  Shaken, at times, by breeze or bird,
Form'd a deep contrast to the scene
Of revel, where I late had been;
To those gay sounds that still came o'er,
Faintly, from many a distant shore,
And the unnumber'd lights, that shone
Far o'er the flood, from Memphis on
To the Moon's Isle and Babylon.

My oars were lifted, and my boat
  Lay rock'd upon the rippling stream;
While my vague thoughts, alike afloat,
  Drifted through many an idle dream,
With all of which, wild and unfix'd
As was their aim, that vision mix'd,
That bright nymph of the Temple—now,
  With the same innocence of brow
She wore within the lighted fane—
Now kindling, through each pulse and vein,
  With passion of such deep-felt fire
As Gods might glory to inspire;—

(1 Necropolis, or the City of the Dead, to the north of
Memphis.

And now—oh Darkness of the tomb,
  That must eclipse even light like hers!
Cold, dead, and blackening 'mid the gloom
  Of those eternal sepulchres.

Scarce had I turn'd my eyes away
  From that dark death-place, at the thought,
When by the sound of dashing spray
  From a light oar my ear was caught,
While past me, through the moonlight, sail'd
  A little gilded bark, that bore
Two female figures, closely veil'd
  And mantled, towards that funeral shore.
They landed—and the boat again
Put off across the watery plain.

Shall I confess—to thee I may—
  That never yet hath come the chance
Of a new music, a new ray
  From woman's voice, from woman's glance,
Which—let it find me how it might,
  In joy or grief—I did not bless,
And wander after, as a light
  Leading to undreamt happiness.
And chiefly now, when hopes so vain
Were stirring in my heart and brain,
When Fancy had allured my soul
  Into a chase, as vague and far
As would be his, who fix'd his goal
  In the horizon, or some star—
Any bewilderment, that brought
More near to earth my high-flown thought—
The faintest glimpse of joy, less pure,
Less high and heavenly, but more sure,
Came welcome—and was then to me
What the first flowery isle must be
To vagrant birds, blown out to sea.

Quick to the shore I urged my bark,
  And by the bursts of moonlight, shed
Between the lofty tombs, could mark
  Those figures, as with hasty tread
They glided on—till in the shade
  Of a small pyramid, which through
Some boughs of palm its peak display'd,
  They vanish'd instant from my view.

I hurried to the spot—no trace
Of life was in that lonely place;
And, had the creed I hold by taught
Of other worlds, I might have thought
Some mocking spirits had from thence
Come in this guise to cheat my sense.

At length, exploring darkly round
The Pyramid's smooth sides, I found
An iron portal—opening high
  'Twixt peak and base—and, with a prayer
To the bliss-loving Moon, whose eye
  Alone beheld me, sprung in there.

Downward the narrow stairway led
Through many a duct obscure and dread,
  A labyrinth for mystery made,
With wanderings onward, backward, round,
And gathering still, where'er it wound,
  But deeper density of shade.

Scarce had I ask'd myself, "Can aught
  That man delights in sojourn here?"—
When, suddenly, far off, I caught
  A glimpse of light, remote, but clear—
Whose welcome glimmer seem'd to pour
  From some alcove or cell, that ended
The long, steep, marble corridor,
  Through which I now, all hope, descended.
Never did Spartan to his bride
With warier foot at midnight glide.
It seem'd as echo's self were dead
In this dark place, so mute my tread.
Reaching, at length, that light, I saw—
  Oh listen to the scene, now raised
Before my eyes—then guess the awe,
  The still rapt awe with which I gazed.
'T was a small chapel, lined around
With the fair spangling marble, found
In many a ruin'd shrine that stands
Half seen above the Lybian sands.
The walls were richly sculptured o'er,
And character'd with that dark lore
Of times before the Flood, whose key
Was lost in the "Universal Sea."—
While on the roof was pictured bright
  The Theban beetle, as he shines,
  When the Nile's mighty flow declines,
And forth the creature springs to light,
With life regenerate in his wings:—
Emblem of vain imaginings!
Of a new world, when this is gone,
In which the spirit still lives on!

Direct beneath this type, reclined
  On a black granite altar, lay
A female form, in crystal shrined,
  And looking fresh as if the ray
  Of soul had fled but yesterday.
While in relief, of silvery hue,
  Graved on the altar's front were seen
A branch of lotus, broken in two,
  As that fair creature's life had been,
And a small bird that from its spray
Was winging, like her soul, away.

But brief the glimpse I now could spare
  To the wild mystic wonders round;
For there was yet one wonder there,
  That held me as by witchery bound.
The lamp, that through the chamber shed
Its vivid beam, was at the head
Of her who on that altar slept;
  And near it stood, when first I came—

Bending her brow, as if she kept
　Sad watch upon its silent flame—
A female form, as yet so placed
　Between the lamp's strong glow and me,
That I but saw, in outline traced,
　The shadow of her symmetry.
Yet did my heart—I scarce knew why—
Even at that shadow'd shape beat high.
Nor was it long, ere full in sight
The figure turn'd; and by the light
That touch'd her features, as she bent
Over the crystal monument,
I saw 't was she—the same—the same—
　That lately stood before me, brightening
The holy spot, where she but came
　And went again like summer lightning!

Upon the crystal, o'er the breast
Of her who took that silent rest,
There was a cross of silver lying—
　Another type of that blest home,
Which hope, and pride, and fear of dying
　Build for us in a world to come :—
This silver cross the maiden raised
To her pure lips :—then, having gazed
Some minutes on that tranquil face,
Sleeping in all death's mournful grace,
Upward she turn'd her brow serene,
　As if, intent on heaven, those eyes
Saw then nor roof nor cloud between
　Their own pure orbits and the skies,
And, though her lips no motion made,
　And that fix'd look was all her speech,
I saw that the rapt spirit pray'd
　Deeper within than words could reach.

Strange power of Innocence, to turn
　To its own hue whate'er comes near,
And make even vagrant Passion burn
　With purer warmth within its sphere!
She who, but one short hour before,
　Had come, like sudden wild-fire, o'er
My heart and brain—whom gladly, even
　From that bright Temple, in the face
Of those proud ministers of heaven,
　I would have borne, in wild embrace,
And risk'd all punishment, divine
And human, but to make her mine;
She, she was now before me, thrown
By fate itself into my arms—
There standing, beautiful, alone,
　With nought to guard her, but her charms.
Yet did I, then—did even a breath
　From my parch'd lips, too parch'd to move,
Disturb a scene where thus, beneath
　Earth's silent covering, Youth and Death
Held converse through undying love?
No—smile and taunt me as thou wilt—
　Though but to gaze thus was delight,

Yet seem'd it like a wrong, a guilt,
　To win by stealth so pure a sight:
And rather than a look profane
　Should then have met those thoughtful eyes,
Or voice, or whisper broke the chain
　That link'd her spirit with the skies,
I would have gladly, in that place,
From which I watch'd her heavenward face,
Let my heart break, without one beat
That could disturb a prayer so sweet.
Gently, as if on every tread,
　My life, my more than life, depended,
Back through the corridor that led
　To this blest scene I now ascended,
And with slow seeking, and some pain,
And many a winding tried in vain,
Emerged to upper air again.

The sun had freshly risen, and down
　The marble hills of Araby,
Scatter'd, as from a conqueror's crown,
　His beams into that living sea.
There seem'd a glory in his light,
　Newly put on—as if for pride
Of the high homage paid this night
　To his own Isis, his young bride,
Now fading feminine away
In her proud Lord's superior ray.

My mind's first impulse was to fly
　At once from this entangling net—
New scenes to range, new loves to try,
Or, in mirth, wine, and luxury
　Of every sense, that night forget.
But vain the effort—spell-bound still,
I linger'd, without power or will
　To turn my eyes from that dark door,
Which now enclosed her 'mong the dead;
Oft fancying, through the boughs, that o'er
The sunny pile their flickering shed,
'T was her light form again I saw
　Starting to earth—still pure and bright,
But wakening, as I hoped, less awe,
　Thus seen by morning's natural light,
Than in that strange dim cell at night.

But no, alas!—she ne'er return'd :
　Nor yet—though still I watch—nor yet,
Though the red sun for hours hath burn'd,
　And now, in his 'mid course, hath met
The peak of that eternal pile
　He pauses still at noon to bless,
Standing beneath his downward smile,
　Like a great Spirit, shadowless!—
Nor yet she comes—while here, alone,
　Sauntering through this death-peopled place,
Where no heart beats except my own,
Or 'neath a palm-tree's shelter thrown,
　By turns I watch, and rest, and trace

These lines, that are to waft to thee
My last night's wondrous history.

Dost thou remember, in that Isle
  Of our own Sea, where thou and I
Linger'd so long, so happy a while,
  Till all the summer flowers went by—
How gay it was, when sunset brought
  To the cool Well our favourite maids—
Some we had won, and some we sought—
  To dance within the fragrant shades,
And, till the stars went down attune
Their Fountain Hymns(1) to the young moon?

That time, too—oh, 't is like a dream—
  When from Scamander's holy tide
I sprung as Genius of the Stream,
  And bore away that blooming bride,
Who thither came, to yield her charms
  (As Phrygian maids are wont, ere wed)
Into the cold Scamander's arms,
  But met and welcomed mine, instead—
Wondering, as on my neck she fell,
How river-gods could love so well!
Who would have thought that he, who roved
  Like the first bees of Summer then,
Rifling each sweet, nor ever loved
  But the free hearts that loved again,
Readily as the reed replies
To the least breath that round it sighs—
Is the same dreamer who, last night,
Stood awed and breathless at the sight
Of one Egyptian girl; and now
Wanders among these tombs, with brow
Pale, watchful, sad, as though he just,
Himself, had risen from out their dust!

Yet so it is—and the same thirst
  For something high and pure, above
This withering world, which, from the first,
  Made me drink deep of woman's love—
As the one joy, to heaven most near
Of all our hearts can meet with here—
Still burns me up, still keeps awake
A fever nought but death can slake.

Farewell ; whatever may befall—
Or bright, or dark—thou 'lt know it all.

——◦••◦——
LETTER IV.
FROM THE SAME TO THE SAME.
Wonders on wonders; sights that lie
  Where never sun gave floweret birth ;
Bright marvels, hid from the upper sky,
And mysteries that are born and die
  Deep in the very heart of earth !—
All that the ancient Orpheus, led
  By courage that Love only gives,
Dared for a matchless idol, dead,
  I 've seen and dared for one who lives.

Again the moon was up, and found
The echoes of my feet still round
The monuments of this lone place;
  Or saw me, if awhile my lid
Yielded to sleep, stretch'd at the base
  Of that now precious Pyramid,
In slumber that the gentlest stir,
The stillest air-like step of her,
Whom e'en in sleep I watch'd, could chase.
And then, such various forms she seem'd
To wear before me, as I dream'd!—
Now, like Neitha, on her throne
At Sais, all reveal'd she shone,
With that dread veil thrown off her brow,
Which mortal never raised till now; (2)
Then, quickly changed, methought 't was she
  Of whom the Memphian boatman tells
Such wondrous tales—fair Rhodope,
  The subterranean nymph, that dwells
'Mid sunless gems and glories hid,
The Lady of the Pyramid !

At length, from one of these short dreams
  Starting—as if the subtile beams,
Then playing o'er my brow, had brought
Some sudden light into my thought—
Down for my boat-lamp to the shore,
  Where still it palely burn'd, I went ;
Resolved that night to try once more
  The mystery of this monument.

Thus arm'd, I scarce had reach'd the gate,
  When a loud screaming—like the cry
Of some wild creature to its mate—
  Came startling from the palm-grove nigh ;—
Or, whether haply 't was the creak
Of those Lethæan portals, (3) said
To give thus out a mournful shriek,
  When oped at midnight for the dead.
Whate'er it was, the sound came o'er
  My heart like ice, as through the door
Of the small Pyramid I went,
And down the same abrupt descent,
And through long windings, as before,
Reach'd the steep marble corridor.
Trembling I stole along—the light
  In the lone chapel still burn'd on ;
But she, for whom my soul and sight
  Look'd with a thirst so keen, was gone—
By some invisible path had fled
Into that gloom, leaving the Dead
To its own solitary rest,
Of all lone things the loneliest.

(1) These Songs of the Well, as they were called by the
ancients, are still common in the Greek isles.
(2) See, for the veil of Neitha, the inscription upon her
temple, as given by Plutarch, de Is. et Osir.
(3) The brazen portals at Memphis, mentioned by Zoega,
called the Gates of Oblivion.

As still the cross, which she had kist,
　Was lying on the crystal shrine,
I took it up, nor could resist
　(Though the dead eyes, I thought, met mine)
Kissing it too, while, half ashamed
Of that mute presence, I exclaim'd,
" Oh Life to Come, if in thy sphere
　Love, Woman's love, our heaven could be,
Who would not e'en forego it here,
　To taste it there eternally?"
Hopeless, yet with unwilling pace,
Leaving the spot, I turn'd to trace
My pathway back, when, to the right,
I could perceive, by my lamp's light,
That the long corridor which, view'd
　Through distance dim, had seem'd to end
Abruptly here, still on pursued
　Its sinuous course, with snake-like bend,
Mocking the eye as down it wound
Still deeper through that dark profound.

Again my hopes were raised, and, fast
　As the dim lamp-light would allow,
Along that new-found path I pass'd,
　Through countless turns ; descending now
By narrow ducts, now up again,
'Mid columns, in whose date the chain
Of time is lost ; and thence along
Cold halls, in which a sapless throng
Of Dead stood up, with glassy eye
Meeting my gaze, as I went by.—
Till, lost among these winding ways,
　Coil'd round and round, like serpents' folds,
I thought myself in that dim maze
　Down under Mœris' Lake, which holds
The hidden wealth of the Twelve Kings,
Safe from all human visitings.

At length the path closed suddenly ;
　And, by my lamp, whose glimmering fell
Now faint and fainter, I could see
　Nought but the mouth of a huge well,
Gaping athwart my onward track—
A reservoir of darkness, black
As witches' cauldrons are, when fill'd
With moon-drugs, in the eclipse distill'd.
Leaning to look if foot might pass
Down through that chasm, I saw, beneath,
　As far as vision could explore,
The jetty sides all smooth as glass,
　Looking as if just varnish'd o'er
With that dark pitch the Sea of Death
　Throws out upon its slimy shore.

Doubting awhile, yet loath to leave
　Aught unexplored, the chasm I tried
With nearer search ; and could perceive
　An iron step that from the side

Stood dimly out ; while, lower still,
Another ranged, less visible,
But aptly placed, as if to aid
The adventurous foot, that dared the shade.
Though hardly I could deem that e'er
Weak woman's foot had ventured there,
Yet, urged along by the wild heat
That can do all things but retreat,
I placed my lamp—which for such task
Was aptly shaped, like cap or casque
To fit the brow—firm on my head,
　And down into the darkness went ;
Still finding for my cautious tread
　New foot-hold in that deep descent,
Which seem'd as though 't would thus descend
In depth and darkness without end.
At length, this step-way ceased ; in vain
I sought some hold, that would sustain
My down-stretch'd foot—the polish'd side,
Slippery and hard, all help denied :
Till, as I bow'd my lamp around,
　To let its now faint glimmer fall
On every side, with joy I found
　Just near me, in the shining wall,
A window (which had 'scaped my view
In that half shadow) and sprung through.
'T was downward still, but far less rude—
　By stairs that through the live rock wound
In narrow spiral round and round,
Whose giddy sweep my foot pursued
Till, lo, before a gate I stood,
Which oped, I saw, into the same
Deep well, from whence but now I came.
The doors were iron, yet gave way
Lightly before me, as the spray
Of a young lime-tree, that receives
Some wandering bird among its leaves.
But, soon as I had pass'd, the din,
　The o'erwhelming din, with which again
They clash'd their folds, and closed me in,
　Was such as seldom sky or main,
Or heaving earth, or all, when met
　In angriest strife, e'er equall'd yet.
It seem'd as if the ponderous sound
Was by a thousand echoes hurl'd
From one to the other, through the round
　Of this great subterranean world,
Till, far as from the catacombs
Of Alexandria to the Tombs
In ancient Thebes's Valley of Kings,
Rung its tremendous thunderings.
Yet could not e'en this rude surprise,
　Which well might move far bolder men,
One instant turn my charmed eyes
　From the blest scene that hail'd them then.
As I had rightly deem'd, the place
Where now I stood was the well's base,
The bottom of the chasm ; and bright
　Before me, through the massy bars

Of a huge gate, there came a light
  Soft, warm, and welcome, as the stars
Of his own South are to the sight
Of one who, from his sunny home,
To the chill North had dared to roam.

And oh the scene, now opening through
  Those bars that all but sight denied !—
A long fair alley, far as view
  Could reach away, along whose side
Went, lessening to the end, a row
  Of rich arcades, that, from between
Their glistening pillars, sent a glow
  Of countless lamps, burning unseen,
And that still air, as from a spring
  Of hidden light, illumining.
While—soon as the wild echoes roused
From their deep haunts again were housed—
I heard a strain of holy song
  Breathing from out the bright arcades
Into that silence—where, among
  The high sweet voices of young maids,
Which, like the small and heaven-ward spire
  Of Christian temples, crown'd the choir,
I fancied, (such the fancy's sway)
  Though never yet my ear had caught
Sound from her lips—yet, in that lay
  So worthy of her looks, methought
That maiden's voice I heard, o'er all
  Most high and heavenly,—to my ear
Sounding distinctly, like the call
  Of a far spirit from its sphere.

But vain the call—that stubborn gate,
  Like destiny, all force defied.
Anxious I look'd around—and, straight,
  An opening to the left descried,
Which, though like hell's own mouth it seem'd,
Yet led, as by its course I deem'd,
Parallel with those lighted ways,
That 'cross the alley pour'd their blaze.
Eager I stoop'd, this path to tread,
When, suddenly, the wall o'er-head
Grew with a fitful lustre bright,
Which, settling gradual on the sight
Into clear characters of light,
These words on its dark ground I read :—

  "You, who would try
      This terrible track,
  To live, or to die,
      But ne'er to look back ;

  "You, who aspire
      To be purified there
  By the terrors of Fire
      And Water and Air ;

  "If danger and pain
      And death you despise—

On—for again
  Into light you may rise—

  "Rise into light
      With that Secret Divine
  Now shrouded from sight
      By the Veils of the Shrine!

  But if————"

          The words here dimm'd away,
Till, lost in darkness, vague and dread,
Their very silence seem'd to say
Awfuller things than words e'er said.

"Am I then in the path," I cried,
  "To the Great Mystery? shall I see,
And touch—perhaps, e'en draw aside
Those venerable veils, which hide
  The secret of Eternity !"
This thought at once revived the zeal,
  The thirst for Egypt's hidden lore,
Which I had almost ceased to feel,
  In the new dreams that won me o'er.
For now—oh happiness !—it seem'd
As if both hopes before me beam'd—
As if that spirit-nymph, whose tread
  I traced down hither from above,
To more than one sweet treasure led—
Lighting me to the fountain-head
  Of Knowledge by the star of Love.

Instant I enter'd—though the ray
  Of my spent lamp was near its last—
And quick through many a channel-way
E'en ruder than the former, pass'd ;
Till, just as sunk the farewell spark,
I spied before me, through the dark,
A paly fire, that moment raised,
Which still as I approach'd it blazed
With stronger light—till, as I came
More near, I saw my pathway led
Between two hedges of live flame—
Trees all on fire, whose branches shed
A glow that, without noise or smoke,
  Yet strong as from a furnace, broke ;
While o'er the glaring ground between,
Where my sole onward path was seen,
Hot iron bars, red as with ire,
  Transversely lay—such as, they tell,
Compose that trellis-work of fire,
  Through which the doom'd look out in hell.

To linger there was to be lost—
  More and still more the burning trees
Closed o'er the path ; and as I crost—
  With tremour both in heart and knees—
Fixing my foot where'er a space
'Twixt the red bars gave resting-place,

Above me, each quick burning tree,
Tamarind, Balm of Araby,
And Egypt's Thorn, combined to spread
A roof of fire above my head.
Yet safe—or with but harmless scorch—
I trod the flaming ordeal through;
And promptly seizing, as a torch
   To light me on to dangers new,
A fallen bough that kindling lay
Across the path, pursued my way.

Nor went I far before the sound
   Of downward torrents struck my ear;
And, by my torch's gleam, I found
That the dark space which yawn'd around
   Was a wide cavern, far and near
Fill'd with dark waters, that went by
Turbid and quick, as if from high
They late had dash'd down furiously;
Or, awfuller, had yet that doom
Before them, in the untried gloom.
No pass appear'd on either side;
   And though my torch too feebly shone
To show what scowl'd beyond the tide,
   I saw but _one_ way left me—on!
So, plunging in, with my right hand
   The current's rush I scarce withstood,
While, in my left, the failing brand
   Shook its last glimmer o'er the flood.
'T was a long struggle—oft I thought
That, in that whirl of waters caught,
I must have gone, too weak for strife,
   Down, headlong, at the cataract's will—
Sad fate for one, with heart and life
   And all youth's sunshine round him still!
But, ere my torch was wholly spent,
   I saw—outstretching from the shade
Into those waters, as if meant
   To lend the drowning struggler aid—
A slender double balustrade,
With snow-white steps between, ascending
   From the grim surface of the stream,
Far up as eye could reach, and ending
   In darkness there, like a lost dream.
That glimpse—for 't was no longer—gave
   New spirit to my strength; and now,
With both arms combating the wave,
   I rush'd on blindly, till my brow
Struck on that railway's lowest stair;
   When, gathering courage from despair,
I made one bold and fearful bound,
And on the step firm footing found.

But short that hope—for, as I flew
Breathlessly up, the stairway grew
Tremulous under me, while each
Frail step, ere scarce my foot could reach
The frailer yet I next must trust,
Crumbled behind me into dust;

Leaving me, as it crush'd beneath,
   Like shipwreck'd wretch who, in dismay,
Sees but one plank 'twixt him and death,
   And shuddering feels that one give way!
And still I upward went—with nought
   Beneath me but that depth of shade,
And the dark flood, from whence I caught
   Each sound the falling fragments made.
Was it not fearful?—still more frail
   At every step crash'd the light stair,
While, as I mounted, even the rail
That up into that murky air
Was my sole guide, began to fail!—
When, stretching forth an anxious hand.
Just as, beneath my tottering stand,
Steps, railway, all, together went,
   I touch'd a massy iron ring,
That there—by what kind genius sent
I know not—in the darkness hung:
   And grasping it, as drowners cling,
To the last hold, so firm I clung
And through the void suspended swung.

Sudden, as if that mighty ring
   Were link'd with all the winds in heaven,
And, like the touching of a spring,
   My eager grasp had instant given
Loose to all blasts that ever spread
The shore or sea with wrecks and dead—
Around me, gusts, gales, whirlwinds rang
Tumultuous, and I seem'd to hang
   Amidst an elemental war,
   In which wing'd tempests—of all kinds
And strengths that winter's stormy star
   Lights through the Temple of the winds
In our own Athens—battled round,
Deafening me with chaotic sound.
Nor this the worst—for, holding still
   With hands unmoved, though shrinking oft,
I found myself at the wild will
   Of countless whirlwinds, caught aloft,
And round and round, with fearful swing,
Swept, like a stone-shot in a sling!
Till breathless, mazed, I had begun—
   So ceaselessly I thus was whirl'd—
To think my limbs were chain'd upon
   That wheel of the Infernal World,
To turn which, day and night, are blowing
   Hot withering winds that never slumber;
And whose sad rounds, still going, going,
   Eternity alone can number!
And yet, even then—while worse than Fear
Hath ever dreamt seem'd hovering near,
Had voice but ask'd me, "is not this
   A price too dear for aught below?"
I should have said "for knowledge, yes—
   But for bright glorious Woman—no."
At last, that whirl, when all my strength
   Had nearly fled, came to an end;

And, through that viewless void, at length,
  I felt the still-grasp'd ring descend
Rapidly with me, till my feet—
Oh, ne'er was touch of land so sweet
To the long sea-worn exile—found
A resting-place on the firm ground.
At the same instant o'er me broke
  A glimmer through that gloom so chill—
Like day-light, when beneath the yoke
Of tyrant darkness struggling still—
And by the imperfect gleam it shed,
I saw before me a rude bed,
Where poppies, strew'd upon a heap
Of wither'd lotus, woo'd to sleep.
Blessing that couch—as I would bless,
  Ay, even the absent tiger's lair,
For rest in such stark weariness—
I crawl'd to it, and sunk down there.

How long I slept, or by what means
  Was wafted thence, I cannot say;
But when I woke—oh the bright scenes,
  The glories that around me lay—
If ever yet a vision shone
On waking mortal, this was one!
But how describe it? vain, as yet,
  While the first dazzle dims my eyes,
All vain the attempt—I must forget
  The flush, the newness, the surprise,
The vague bewilderment, that whelms,
Even now, my every sense and thought,
Ere I can paint these sunless realms,
  And their hid glories, as I ought ;
While thou, if even but half I tell,
Wilt that but half believe—farewell !
—◦✦◦—
LETTER V.
FROM ORCUS, HIGH PRIEST OF MEMPHIS, TO
DECIUS, THE PRÆTORIAN PREFECT.
REJOICE, my friend, rejoice :—the youthful Chief
Of that light Sect which mocks at all belief,
And, gay and godless, makes the present hour
Its only heaven, is now within our power.
Smooth, impious school !—not all the weapons aim'd
At priestly creeds, since first a creed was framed,
E'er struck so deep as that sly dart they wield,
The Bacchant's pointed spear in laughing flowers
    conceal'd.
And oh, 't were victory to this heart, as sweet
As any thou canst boast—even when the feet
Of thy proud war-steed wade through Christian
    blood,
To wrap this scoffer in Faith's blinding hood,
And bring him, tamed and prostrate, to implore
The vilest gods even Egypt's saints adore.
What !—do these sages think, to them alone
The key of this world's happiness is known?
That none but they, who make such proud parade
Of Pleasure's smiling favours, win the maid,

Or that Religion keeps no secret place,
No niche, in her dark fanes, for Love to grace?
Fools !—did they know how keen the zest that 's
    given
To earthly joy, when season'd well with heaven ;
How Piety's grave mask improves the hue
Of Pleasure's laughing features, half seen through,
And how the Priest, set aptly within reach
Of two rich worlds, traffics for bliss with each,
Would they not, Decius—thou, whom the ancient
    tie
'Twixt Sword and Altar makes our best ally—
Would they not change their creed, their craft, for
    ours ?
Leave the gross daylight joys that, in their bowers,
Languish with too much sun, like o'er-blown
    flowers,
For the veil'd loves, the blisses undisplay'd
That slily lurk within the Temple's shade?
And, 'stead of haunting the trim Garden's school—
Where cold Philosophy usurps a rule,
Like the pale moon's, o'er passion's heaving tide,
Till Pleasure's self is chill'd by Wisdom's pride—
Be taught by us, quit shadows for the true
Substantial joys we sager Priests pursue,
Who, far too wise to theorise on bliss,
Or pleasure's substance for its shade to miss,
Preach other worlds, but live for only this :—
Thanks to the well-paid Mystery round us flung,
Which, like its type, the golden cloud that hung
O'er Jupiter's love-couch its shade benign,
Round human frailty wraps a veil divine.

Still less should they presume, weak wits, that
    they
Alone despise the craft of us who pray ;—
Still less their creedless vanity deceive
With the fond thought, that we who pray believe.
Believe !—Apis forbid—forbid it, all
Ye monster Gods, before whose shrines we fall—
Deities, framed in jest, as if to try
How far gross Man can vulgarise the sky ;
How far the same low fancy that combines
Into a drove of brutes yon zodiac's signs,
And turns that Heaven itself into a place
Of sainted sin and deified disgrace,
Can bring Olympus even to shame more deep,
Stock it with things that earth itself holds cheap,
Fish, flesh, and fowl, the kitchen's sacred brood,
Which Egypt keeps for worship, not for food—
All, worthy idols of a Faith that sees
In dogs, cats, owls, and apes, divinities !

Believe !—oh, Decius, thou, who feel'st no care
For things divine, beyond the soldier's share,
Who takes on trust the faith for which he bleeds,
A good fierce God to swear by, all he needs—
Little canst thou, whose creed around thee hangs
Loose as thy summer war-cloak, guess the pangs

Of loathing and self-scorn with which a heart,
Stubborn as mine is, acts the zealot's part—
The deep and dire disgust with which I wade
Through the foul juggling of this holy trade—
This mud profound of mystery, where the feet,
At every step, sink deeper in deceit.
Oh! many a time, when, 'mid the Temple's blaze,
O'er prostrate fools the sacred cist I raise,
Did I not keep still proudly in my mind
The power this priestcraft gives me o'er mankind—
A lever, of more might, in skilful hand,
To move this world, than Archimede e'er plann'd—
I should, in vengeance of the shame I feel
At my own mockery, crush the slaves that kneel
Besotted round; and—like that kindred breed
Of reverend well-drest crocodiles they feed,
At famed Arsinoë(1)—make my keepers bless,
With their last throb, my sharp-fang'd Holiness.

Say, *is* it to be borne, that scoffers, vain
Of their own freedom from the altar's chain,
Should mock thus all that thou thy blood hast sold,
And I my truth, pride, freedom, to uphold?
It must not be :—think'st thou that Christian sect,
Whose followers, quick as broken waves, erect
Their crests anew and swell into a tide,
That threats to sweep away our shrines of pride—
Think'st thou, with all their wondrous spells, even
        they
Would triumph thus, had not the constant play
Of Wit's resistless archery clear'd their way?—
That mocking spirit, worst of all the foes,
Our solemn fraud, our mystic mummery knows,
Whose wounding flash thus ever 'mong the signs
Of a fast-falling creed, prelusive shines,
Threatening such change as do the awful freaks
Of summer lightning, ere the tempest breaks.

But, to my point—a youth of this vain school,
But one whom Doubt itself hath fail'd to cool
Down to that freezing point where Priests despair
Of any spark from the altar catching there—
Hath, some nights since—it was, methinks, the night
That follow'd the full Moon's great annual rite—
Through the dark winding ducts, that downward
        stray
To these earth-hidden temples, track'd his way,
Just at that hour when, round the Shrine and me,
The choir of blooming nymphs thou long'st to see
Sing their last night-hymn in the Sanctuary.
The clangour of the marvellous Gate, that stands
At the Well's lowest depth—which none but hands
Of new untaught adventurers, from above,
Who know not the safe path, e'er dare to move—
Gave signal that a foot profane was nigh :—
'T was the Greek youth, who, by that morning's sky,
Had been observed, curiously wandering round
The mighty fanes of our sepulchral ground.

Instant, the Initiate's Trials were prepared—
The Fire, Air, Water; all that Orpheus dared,
That Plato, that the bright-hair'd Samian(2) pass'd,
With trembling hope, to come to—*what*, at last?
Go, ask the dupes of Priestcraft; question him
Who, 'mid terrific sounds and spectres dim,
Walks at Eleusis; ask of those, who brave
The dazzling miracles of Mithra's Cave,
With its seven starry gates; ask all who keep
Those terrible night-mysteries where they weep
And howl sad dirges to the answering breeze,
O'er their dead Gods, their mortal Deities—
Amphibious hybrid things, that died as men,
Drown'd, hang'd, empaled, to rise, as gods, again;—
Ask *them* what mighty secret lurks below
This seven-fold mystery—can they tell thee? No;
Gravely they keep that only secret, well
And fairly kept—that they have none to tell;
And, duped themselves, console their humbled
        pride
By duping thenceforth all mankind beside.

And such the advance in fraud since Orpheus' time—
That earliest master of our craft sublime—
So many minor Mysteries, imps of fraud,
From the great Orphic Egg have wing'd abroad
That, still to uphold our Temple's ancient boast,
And seem most holy, we must cheat the most;
Work the best miracles, wrap nonsense round
In pomp and darkness, till it seems profound;
Play on the hopes, the terrors of mankind,
With changeful skill; and make the human mind
Like our own Sanctuary, where no ray,
But by the Priest's permission, wins its way—
Where through the gloom as wave our wizard rods
Monsters, at will, are conjured into Gods;
While Reason, like a grave-faced mummy, stands,
With her arms swathed in hieroglyphic bands.
But chiefly in that skill with which we use
Man's wildest passions for Religion's views,
Yoking them to her car like fiery steeds,
Lies the main art in which our craft succeeds.
And oh be blest, ye men of yore, whose toil
Hath, for our use, scoop'd out from Egypt's soil
This hidden Paradise, this mine of fanes,
Gardens, and palaces, where Pleasure reigns
In a rich sunless empire of her own,
With all earth's luxuries lighting up her throne;—
A realm for mystery made, which undermines
The Nile itself, and, 'neath the Twelve Great
        Shrines
That keep Initiation's holy rite,
Spreads its long labyrinths of unearthly light,
A light that knows no change—its brooks that run
Too deep for day, its gardens without sun,

(1) For the trinkets with which the sacred Crocodiles
were ornamented, see the *Epicurean*, chap. x.
(2) Pythagoras.

Where soul and sense, by turns, are charm'd, sur-
    prised,
And all that bard or prophet e'er devised
For man's Elysium priests have realised.

Here, at this moment—all his trials past,
And heart and nerve unshrinking to the last—
Our new Initiate roves—as yet left free
To wander through this realm of mystery ;
Feeding on such illusions as prepare
The soul, like mist o'er waterfalls, to wear
All shapes and hues, at Fancy's varying will,
Through every shifting aspect vapour still ;—
Vague glimpses of the Future, vistas shown,
By scenic skill, into that world unknown,
Which saints and sinners claim alike their own ;
And all those other witching wildering arts,
Illusions, terrors, that make human hearts,

Ay, e'en the wisest and the hardiest, quail
To *any* goblin throned behind a veil.

Yes—such the spells shall haunt his eye, his ear,
Mix with his night-dreams, form his atmosphere ;
Till, if our Sage be not tamed down, at length,
His wit, his wisdom, shorn of all their strength,
Like Phrygian priests, in honour of the shrine—
If he become not absolutely mine,
Body and soul, and, like the tame decoy
Which wary hunters of wild doves employ,
Draw converts also, lure his brother wits
To the dark cage where his own spirit flits,
And give us, if not saints, good hypocrites—
If I effect not this, then be it said
The ancient spirit of our craft hath fled,
Gone with that serpent-god the Cross hath chased
To hiss its soul out in the Theban waste.

INDEX.

—o†♦o—

Abbott, Hon. Charles, 167 *n.* Ballad dedicated to, 186.
Abdalla, King of the Lesser Bucharia, 321, etc. *See* Lalla Rookh.
Abdallah, 174. His Gazel, 174.
Abdul Fazil, 395 *n.*
A beam of tranquillity smiled in the west, 121.
A broken cake, with honey sweet (Ode LXX. Anacreon), 46.
Adamthwaite, Dr., 519.
Ægean Sea, the 313, 315.
Agnew, Sir Andrew, 483, 546, 547, *et passim.*
Ah! where are they who heard, in former hours, 299.
Albano, his 'Rape of Proserpine.' 436.
Albemarle, Lord, anecdote of, 465 *n.*
Album, the, 75, 600.
Alciphron, a Fragment of ' The Epicurean,' as originally commenced in verse, 612. Epistle 1. From Alciphron at Alexandria to Cleon at Athens, 613. II. From Alciphron to Cleon, 615. III. Alciphron to Cleon, 617. IV. From Alciphron to Cleon, 622. V. From Orcus, high priest of Memphis, to Decius, the Prætorian praefect, 626.
Alexander, Emperor of Russia, 421, 426, 430, 496.
Alexander, Right Hon. H., 176.
Aliris, King, 321, 384. His nuptials with Lalla Rookh, 397.
All that's bright must fade, 239.
Alla, name of God in Mahometan countries, 325. (*See* Lalla Rookh, 452, 464. The throne of Alla, 456, 471.
Almighty God! when round thy shrine, 257.
Alone in crowds to wander on, 228.
Alps, Song of the, 291.
America, Poems relating to :—Preface, 112. Dedication to Francis Earl of Moira, 115. Original Preface, 116. The Poems, 117 to 142. Omitted in London Edition, 142 to 148.
Amherst, Lord, 416.
Amra tree, 395 *n.*
Amrita, the Immortal tree, 287.
Amystis, the, a single draught of wine, 24 *n.*
Anacreon, Odes of, 5.
, *The Odes are given in this Index in the order of the initial letter of each Ode.*
Anacreon. Biographical and Critical Remarks, 7. Epigram imputed to Anacreon, 33 *n.* Additional lyrics attributed to Anacreon, 47. Panegyrics in the Anthologia on Anacreon, 48.
Anacreontics, modern, 56,63, 65, 66, 181, 183.
And doth not a meeting likethis make amends, 225.
And hast thou mark'd the pensive shade, 91.
And now with all thy pencil's truth. (Ode XVII. Anacreon), 20.
Angels and archangels of the celestial

hierarchy of the primæval Syrians, 452, 468.
Angels, the Fallen, 393, 469.
Angerianus, Latin verses of, translated, 15 *n.*, 22 *n.*,
Anglesea, Marquis of, lord-lieutenant, 533.
Animal Magnetism, 565.
Anne Boleyn, 603.
Annual Pill, the, 510.
Antelope of Erac, 393.
Anthology, the Greek, 22 *n.*, 26 *n.*, 32 *n.*, 33 *n.*, 34 *n.*, 36 *n.*—Translations of some Epigrams of, 48 to 50. Songs from the Greek, 291.
Antipater, epigram of, 50.
Antique, a Study from the, 129.
Antiquity, a dream of, 125.
Apelles, 616.
Apollo, the High-Priest of, to a virgin of Delphi, 80.
Apricots, the 'Seed of the Sun,' 393.
Arab, the tyrant, Al Hassan, (*see* Lalla Rookh, the Story of The Fire-worshippers', 360, *et seq.*
Arab, Maid, the, 361, 364, 392, 394.
Arabia, 361, 362.
Arabian shepherd, his camel, 302 *n.*
Ararat, Mount, 362.
Archangels, 452, 459 *n.*
Argument, an, 107.
Ariadne, dance so named, 303.
Ariel, 125, 567.
Aristippus, to a Lamp given by Lais, 66.
Arm'd with byacinthine rod (Ode XXXI. Anacreon), 28.
Around the tomb, O bard divine! (Anthologia), 48.
Arranmore! loved Arranmore! 230.
Array thee, love, 311.
Art, 301.
As a beam o'er the face of the waters may glow, 197.
As by his Lemnian forge's flame (Ode XXVII. Anacreon), 26.
As by the shore, at break of day, 297.
As down in the sunless retreats, 256.
Ask not if still I love, 288.
As late I sought the spangled bowers (Ode VI. Anacreon , 14.
As o'er her loom the Lesbian maid, 295.
As once a Grecian maiden wove, 301.
Aspasia, 88.
Aspen-tree, the, 386.
As slow our ship, 216.
As vanquished Erin wept, 225.
Athens, the mother of art, 301.
Athol, Duke of, 512.
Atkinson, Joseph, Dedication to, 52. Epistle to, 85. Epistle from Bermuda to, 129. Tribute to his memory, 599.
At length thy golden hours have wing'd their flight (Anthologia), 50.
At night when all is still around, 148.
At the mid hour of night, 209.
Attar Gul, or (vulgarly) Otto of Roses, 396.
Augustin, St., to his Sister, 257.
Aurora Borealis, 396.

Aurungzebe, Mogul Emperor, of Delhi, 321, 384.
Austrians, their entry into Naples, 595.
Autumn and Spring, 252.
Avenging and bright fall the swift sword of Erin, 207
Awake, arise, thy light is come, 259.
Awake to life, my sleeping shell (Ode I.V. Anacreon , 42.
Away, away, ye men of rules (Ode LII. Anacreon), 37.
Away with this pouting and sadness! 106. ·
Awful event, 547.
A while I bloom'd, a happy flower (Ode LXXIII. Anacreon), 46.
Azim, 325. *See* Lalla Rookh.
Azor, idols of, 395.
Azrael, the angel of death, 452.
Azure of the Chinese painting of porcelain, 395 *n.*

Babylon, 362.
Ball and Gala described, 315. Allusion to Almack's, 598. *See* Waltz, 314, *et passim.* The Romaika, 296.
Ballads, legendary, 265.
Ballads, miscellaneous, 271 to 287.
Ballads, occasional, *passim.*
Bank, coquetry of the, with Government, 511.
Bankes, Mr. W. J., 516.
Bank-note, 512.
Bard, the Wandering, 228.
Bards, of, 12, 202, 248, 279, 285, *et passim.*
Baring, Sir —, 497, 499, 500.
Barrington, Sir Jonah, 535.
Bathurst, Lord, Lament for the Loss of his Tail, 536.
Battle, after the, 203.
Battle, before the, 203.
Battle eve, song of the, 228.
Battle, the parting before the, 270.
Beaujolais, Count de, 397.
Beautiful East Indian, on a, 147.
Beauty and Song, 285.
Beauty, of, 214, 226, 228, 229, 239, 249, 250, 307, 313, 322, etc., etc.
Beckford, To Miss Susan (now Duchess of Hamilton), 96.
Bee, the, 208, 247.
Behold the sun, how bright, 258.
Behold, the young, the rosy Spring (Ode XLVI. Anacreon), 35.
Belcher's, Pugilistic Meeting at, 501.
Believe me, if all those endearing young charms, 201.
Bell, the silver, 218.
Benab Hasche, or daughters of God, 452.
Benbow, 426.
Benshee, or Banshe, superstition of the, 199.
Bentham, Jeremy, 513, 524, 578.
Beresford, Rev. Marcus, 561.
Bermuda, Farewell to, 127. Some account of that island, 129 *n.*
Berri, Duc de, 419.
Best, Judge, 525.
Bicêtre, Story of, 413.
Big Ben, epistle from Tom Crib to, 508.

Bigotry, Triumph of, 555.
Birch, Alderman, 149, 154.
Bird, let loose in eastern skies, the, 254.
Birthday, my, 592.
Birthday, the, 84, 114.
Bishops, the dance of, a dream, 551.
Blackmore, Sir Richard, 433.
Blomfield, Dr. (Bishop of London), 575.
Blue Love Song, a, 546.
Blue Stocking, the, 588.
Boat glee, 589.
Bohlen, Professor Von, his translation into German of the 'Little Man and Little Soul,' 168.
Bolingbroke, 148.
Bonaparte. See Napoleon.
'Book, the,' 167, 170, 177.
Bore, illustration of a, 609.
Bordeaux, Duc de, 430.
Boston Frigate, to the ;—On leaving Halifax for England, 141.
Bowl, the, 197, 200, 209, 215, 217, 224, 228, 230, 247, 248, 250, 269, 307, 308.
Box, the song of the, 566.
Boy of the Alps, the, 279.
Boy sitting on the lotus flower, 229.
Boy statesman, the, 568.
Boy with a watch, to a, 53.
Boyle Farm, the seat of Lord Henry Fitzgerald, Summer Fête at, 308, et seq.
Boyne, river, 225.
Bride of the Vale, the, 255.
Brien the Brave, 195.
Bright be thy dreams, 244.
Brighton, the Pavilion at, 509.
Bring hither, bring thy lute, 315.
Bring me the slumbering souls of flowers, 484.
Bring the bright garlands hither, 250.
Brogden, Mr., 612.
Brougham, Lord, 543, 565, 566, 568, 574, 585.
Bruce, James, Esq., his journey, 438.
Brummel, Beau, 175, 181, 403.
Brunswick Club, the, 549.
Brunswickers,' Incantation from the Tragedy of ' The, 542.
Brydges, Sir Egerton, 563.
Bucharia, Abdalla, king of, (in Lalla Rookh), 321, 384, 395, 396, etc.
Buckingham, Duke of, 415, 497, 499, 504, 516, 559.
Buds of roses, virgin flowers (Ode XLIV. Anacreon), 34.
Bull, John, 599, a pastoral ballad by, 529.
Bunting, Mr., 189, 264, 321 n.
Burdett, Sir Francis, 164, 171, 570.
Burke, Hon. Edmund, 154 n.
Burns, Robert, 232, 263.
But who shall see the glorious day, 257.
Butterflies denominated flying leaves in China, 392.
Butterworth, Saint, Canonization of, 521.
Byron, Lord, his love of music, 262. Is visited by Mr. Moore at Venice, 431. Dedication to him of Mr. Moore's Fables for the Holy Alliance, 421. On his auto-biography, iii., His ' Heaven and Earth,' 450.
By that lake whose gloomy shore, 206.

Cage, the Love, 246.
Call the Loves around, 316.
Calm as, beneath its mother's eyes, 304.
Calm be thy sleep as infants'slumbers, 282.
Cambridge Election, Ballad for the, 516.

Camden, Lord, 156 n., 158, 172, 181, 419, 497.
Canadian Boat song, 114, 138.
Candahar, 392.
Can I again that form caress, 106.
Canning, Mr., 154 to 157, 172, 186, 188, 408, 523.
Canonization of the Saint, 521.
Canova, 432, 448.
Cant or Flash language, 491.
Capilupus, epitaph on a drunkard by, translated, 23 n. Epigram by, translated, 37 n.
Cara, to, 76.
Cardigan, Lord, 581.
Care, 215.
Carlisle, Lord, 426.
Carr, Sir John, 175.
Cartwright, Major, 171, 402, 414, 510.
Case, a sad, 548.
Cashmere, nuptials of Lalla Rookh at, 322. 'Cashmere, the vale of,' sung by Feramorz, 386. The lake of, and islets, 386 n. Mountain portal to the lake, 386 n. Roses of, 386 n. The unequalled valley, 395. Superstitions of, 395 n. A holy land, 395 n. The fountain Tirnagh, 395 n. ' Though sunny the lake of cool Cashmere,' 351.
Castalia, the fountain, 256 n.
Castlereagh, Lord, satirised, in Corruption and Intolerance, 148 to 160. The Sceptic, 162 to 166. Intercepted Letters, 171. Satirical Poems, 179 to 188. Ya-hip, my hearties, 506. The Fudge Family, 400. His theory about names, 405 n. His departure for the Continent, 509, 510.
Catalogue, the, 82.
Catherine, Empress of Russia, 426.
Catholic Question, the, 537, 538.
Catholics, the Roman, 488, 524.
Catullus, Translations from, 592. Ode by, translated, 17 n. Imitation of, 83.
Caubul, or Caboul, gardens of, 392.
Cease, oh! cease to tempt, 604.
Cecilia, Saint, 550.
Celebrated Letter, parody of a, 180.
Cephalus and Procris, 266.
Ceres, Ode to the Goddess, by Sir Thomas Lethbridge, 513.
Chabuk, the, 396, 397.
Chaldæans, astronomical notions of the ancient, 459 n.
Chancery, a Vision of, 519.
Chandos, Lord, 542.
Chantrey, Sir Francis, 432. His admiration of Canova, 445.
Character, a, 570.
Charity, Angel of, 258.
Charles X, king of France, 397, 398, 571.
Charlotte, Princess, Letter from, to Lady Barbara Ashley, 170.
Chateaubriand, Viscount, 430.
Chatsworth, the Derbyshire ducal mansion of, 193.
Cherries, a conserve in the East, 393.
Cherries, the, 536.
Cherubim, 471.
Chester, Bishop of, 530.
Child's song; I have a garden of my own, 283.
China, butterfly of, 392.
Chindara's warbling fount, 391
Chinese, peculiar porcelain painting of the, 395.
Chinese Bird of Royalty, the, or ' Fum,' 509.
Christ, the Saviour, 256, 258, 259, 260.
Church and State, 425.

Church extension, 580.
Church, Songs of the, 573.
Circassian slaves, the, 312.
Clare, Lord, 156 n., 191, 193 n.
Clarke, Mrs., 171.
Cleopatra, 616.
Clergy, the numbering of the, a Parody, 547.
Cloe and Susan, 246.
Cloe, to, imitated from Martial, 91.
Cloris and Fanny, 58.
Cloud, a summer, 462.
Coates, Romeo, Esq., 176, 582.
Cobbett, Mr. William, 164.
Cochrane, Lord, 519.
Cocker on Church Reform, 562.
Colburn, Mr., 535, 545.
Cole, Lord, 519.
College Exercises, Fragments of, 52.
Come, chase that starting tear away, 243.
Come fill round a bumper, 269.
Come hither, come hither, by night and by day, 393.
Come not, O Lord, in the dread robe of splendour, 256.
Come o'er the sea, maiden, with me, 212.
Come, play me that simple air again, 603.
Come, pray with me, my seraph love, 470.
Come, rest in this bosom, my own stricken deer, 214.
Come, send round the wine, 200.
Come, take my advice, 531.
Come, take the harp; 'tis vain to muse, 98.
Come, ye disconsolate, where'er you languish, 259.
Comet, poetically described, 459. The Mad Tory and the, 554.
Common Sense and Genius, 242.
Condolence, Epistle of;—From a Slave Lord to a Cotton-Lord, 544.
Connor, Phelim, his patriotic Poetical Letters, 403, 409, 418.
Consultation, the, 559.
Cookery, art of domestic; to the Rev. —, 540.
Coolburga, or Koolburga, city of the Deccan, 397.
Cork, Dowager Countess of, 167. Letter from, 173.
Corn Question, the, 507, 513, 524.
Correggio, 446.
Correspondence between a Lady and Gentleman respecting Law, 185.
Corruption, an Epistle, by an Irishman, 150.
Corry, Mr., his merit as an amateur comedian, 590. To James Corry, Esq., on the present of a wine-strainer, 596.
Cotton and Corn, a dialogue, 521.
Count me, on the summer trees (Ode XIV. Anacreon), 17.
Country Dance and Quadrille, 598.
Court Journal, the, 486.
Cousins, Country, News for, 519.
Coutts, Mrs. (afterwards Duchess o St. Alban's), 512.
Crabbe, the Poet, Verses on the Inkstand of, 594.
Crib, Tom, his Memorial to Congress, 491 to 506. Epistle from, to Big Ben, 508.
Critias of Athens, his verses on Anacreon, 50 n.
Criticism, the genius of, 600.
Crockfordiana, 611.
Cross, the, an emblem of future life in Egyptian hieroglyphics, 621.

Crowe, Rev. William, his poetic vein, 264.
Crystal Hunters, the, 244.
Cumberland, Duke of, 183 to 186, 549, 554, 559, 564.
Cupid and Psyche, 265.
Cupid arm'd, 286.
Cupid once upon a bed (Ode xxxv. Anacreon), 30.
Cupid, whose lamp has lent the ray (Anacreontic), 47.
Cupid, poetical allusions to, 47, 95, 101, 239, 277. See Love, 289, 292.
Cupid, Sale of, by Meleager, 291.
Cupid's Lottery, 589.
Curious Fact, a, 511.
Curran, John Philpot, his pleasantry, 398.
Curran, Miss, 190.
Curtis, Sir William, 523.

Dacre, Lady, Epilogue to her Tragedy of Ina, 601.
Damascus, the Green Mosque at, 385 n.
Dan, some account of the late dinner to, 577.
Dandies, 309, 314.
Danes, the, 200 n., 228, 230. The Scandinavian poetry, 433.
Dante, his Inferno, imitation of, 535. The Dream, 603. His contrition of mind, 507.
David, the harp of, 259.
Davidson, Lucretia, 194.
Davy, Sir Humphrey, his lamp, 591.
Dawn is breaking o'er us, 287.
Day, 253, 311.
Day-dream, the, 601.
Deadman's Isle:—Romance, 141.
Dear Fanny, 273.
Dear! in pity do not speak, 108.
Dear? Yes, though mine no more, 288.
Death and the dead, allusions to, 255, 258, 469.
Debt, National, 555.
Decius, Prætorian prefect, Orcus, high priest of Memphis, to, 626.
Delatorian Cohort, the, 399, etc.
Delhi, visit of Abdalla to Aurungzebe at, 321. Splendours of the court and city, 322. Mogul emperors of, 392 n.
Delphi, transport of laurel to, 67. The shrine, 285. To a virgin of, 30.
Deluge, tablets saved by Seth from the, 471.
Den, Doctor, 488, 490.
Denon, Baron, 449.
Derbyshire, Mr. Moore's residence in, 440.
Desmond's Song, and tradition relating to that chieftain, 226.
Destiny, the Island of, 229.
Devil among the Scholars, the, 101.
Dewan Khass, built by Shah Allum, its inscription, 393 n.
Dialogue, a recent, 569.
Diary of a Politician, extracts from the, 182.
Dick ———, a character, 552.
Dictionary, Revolution in the, headed by Mr. Galt, 544.
Did not, 55.
Die when you will, you need not wear, 83.
Dionysius, epigram by, translated, 24n.
Dissolution of the Holy Alliance, a Dream, 421.
Doctors, the Three, 518.
Dodsworth, Mr. Roger (anno 1826), 516.
Donegal, Marchioness of, Letter to, 191. Poetical Epistle from Bermu-

da to her Ladyship, 120. Dedication to, 194.
Donky and his Panniers, 523.
Do not say that life is waning, 248.
Dost thou remember, 240.
Dove, the, 257.
Dove of Mahomet, the, 468, 522.
Drama, Sketch of the First Act of a new Romantic, 565.
Dream of Hindostan, a, 548.
Dream of Home, the, 281.
Dream of the Two Sisters, from Dante, 603.
Dreams of those days, the, 231.
Dream of Turtle, by Sir W. Curtis, 523.
Dream, Sir Andrew's, 546.
Dream, the Limbo, etc., 534.
Dreaming for ever, vainly dreaming, 200.
Dreams, poetical mention of, 59, 61, 244, 247, 249, 564.
Drinking Songs, etc., 196, 200, 209, 224, 228, 230, 247, 248.
Drink of this cup, 220.
Drink to her who long, 201.
Druids, and Druidical superstitions, 229, 230.
Drummond, 165.
Dudley and Ward, Lord, 553.
Duigenan, Doctor, Letter from, to Sir J. Nichol, 172. See also 157, 169, 177, 192, 609.
Duke is the lad to frighten a lass, the, 564.
Durham, Lord, 568, 574.

East Indian, the, 272.
East, poetical romances of the (Lalla Rookh), 323, 395.
Eblis, the evil spirit, 329, 457.
Echo, 221, 240, 266, 315, 327, 474.
Echoes, New-fashioned, 542.
Eden, some of the poets' allusions to, 230, 231, 357, 453, 458.
Edinburgh Review, article by Mr. Moore in the, 463 n.
Egerton, Lord Francis, 309 n.
Egypt's dark sea, 256. The desolation of, 257.
Eldon, Lord Chancellor, conservative tears of, 516, 532. Nightcap of, 519. A wizard, 520. His hat and wig, 527. His Lordship on the Umbrella Question, 529. His conscientious conservatism (after Horace, Ode xxii. lib. i.) 184. His wig, 183, 554. See also 167 n., 170, 171, 177, 181, 182, 185, 187, 497, 498, 510, 517, 521, 530, 553.
Ellenborough, Lord, 171, 187, 532, 536, 554.
Elliotson, Dr., 565.
Eloquence, 586.
Ely, Marquis of, 542.
Emmett, Robert, 189. His eloquence, 189. His enthusiasm, 190. His offence, 192.
Emmett, Thomas Addis, 190.
Enigma, 531.
Entellus and Dares, translated from the Æneid, 503.
Epicure's dream, 586.
Epicurus, 99 n., 531.
Epigrams by Mr. Moore, 83, 105, 182, 183, 596.
Epigrams of the Anthologia in praise of Anacreon, 48.
Epilogue, occasional, spoken by Mr. Corry in the character of Vapid, after the play of the Dramatist, at the Kilkenny theatre, 590. To the tragedy of Ina, 601.

Erasmus on earth, to Cicero in the shades; an Epistle, 564.
Erin, oh Erin, 201.
Erin! the tear and the smile in thine eyes, 196.
Erin, poetical allusions to, 214, 225, 228, 230, 231.
Erin, some political allusions to, 529. See Ireland, et passim.
Essex, the late Earl of, 308.
Eternal life, ancient belief of an, 621.
Eve, the second angel describes her, 460. Alluded to by the third Angel, 473.
Eveleen's bower, 200
Evenings in Greece. First Evening, 293. Second Evening, 300.
Exeter, Henry of, to John of Tuam, 573. See Philpotts
Exeter Hall, the Reverends of, 487.
Exquisites, 309, 314.
Exile, the, 282.
Extinguishers, the, 428.
Eyes, black and blue, 273.

Fables for the Holy Alliance, 421.
Fadladeen, great Nazir of the Haram (in Lalla Rookh), his vanity, 384, et seq. His criticisms, 349, 357, 395.
Fairest! put on awhile, 224.
Fairy boat, the, 305.
Faith, 258, 261.
Fallen is thy throne, oh Israel! 254.
Family-way, All in the; a pastoral, 515.
Fancy, 592.
Fancy, prismatic dyes of, 436
Fancy, various allusions to, 96, 119, 313.
Fancy Fair, the, 282.
Fanny, dearest! 70.
Fanny was in the grove, 604.
Fare, the triumphs of, 581.
Fare thee well, thou lovely one, 240.
Fare thee well, perfidious maid (Ode LXXII. Anacreon), 46.
Farewell, Bessy! 568.
Farewell!—but whenever you welcome the hour, 211.
Farewell, Theresa, 247.
Fate gave the word, 611.
Fear not that, while around thee, 252.
Feramorz and the Princess, 324, 333, 351, 360, 384. His song, 359. Dénouement of the fiction of his disguise, 397.
Ferdinand VII., Ode to King, 526.
Fête, the, at Boyle Farm, 308. See Summer Fête.
Fill, me, boy, as deep a draught (Ode LXII. Anacreon), 44.
Fill the bumper fair, 215.
Fin M'Cumhal, the Finians, and Fingal, 230.
Fionnuala, the Song of, 200.
Fire-fly, to the, 131.
Fire-flies, 120, 231, 468, 586.
Fire-worship of Persia and the East, 360. The persecuted Ghebers, etc. Story, 'The Fire-worshippers,' 360. See Lalla Rookh.
Fitzgerald, the late Lord Henry, 309.
Fitzgerald, Lord Edward, 175, 193.
Fitzgerald, Mr. Vesey, 528, 538.
Fleetly o'er the moonlight snows, 290.
Flow on, thou shining river, 238.
Flowers, the language of, 287.
Fly and the Bullock, the, 425.
Fly from the world, O Bessy! to me, 70.
Fly not thus, my brow of snow (Ode LI. Anacreon , 37.
Fly not yet, 'tis just the hour, 196.

Fly swift, my light gazelle, 287.
Fly to the desert, fly with me, 394.
Flying fish, to the, 118.
Follies, the book of;—an album, 69.
Foublanque, A., Esq., 524.
Fontenelle, M., consistency of, 592.
Fool's Paradise; Dream the First, 561.
For thee alone I brave the boundless deep, 279.
Forbes, Lady Adelaide, portrait of, 93, 398.
Forbes, to Lord; from the city of Washington, 131.
Forget not the field where they perished, 218.
Formosa, island of, 436.
Fortune-Teller, the, 220
Fox, Right Hon. Charles James, 150, 156, 159 n., 160, 184.
Fragment, a, 82, 92, 111.
Fragment of a Character. 597.
Freedom, 273, 275, 313.
Friend, on the death of a, 596, 599.
Friends, on leaving some, 97.
Friendship, a temple to, 238.
Friendship and Love, 252.
From dread Leucadia's frowning sleep (Anacreontic), 48.
From the land beyond the sea, 139.
From this hour the pledge is given, 231.
Fruit, varieties of eastern, 392.
Fudge Family in Paris, the, 397.
Fudges, the, in England; being a Sequel to the ' Fudge Family in Paris.' 474.
Fudge, Phil., Esq., his political conduct and penchant, 400 to 420. His Poetical Letter to Lord C—st—r—gh, 400. To Tim. Fudge, Esq., 407. To Viscount C—st—r—gh, 413. His Journal, addressed to Lord C., 413.
Fudge, Mr. Bob., his Letters to Richard——, Esq., 402, 411. To the Rev. Mortimer O'Mulligan, 486.
Fudge, Miss Biddy, her Poetical Letters from Paris to Miss Dorothy ——, of Clonkilty in Ireland, 399, 405, 416, 419. See also 476, 482.
Fudge, Miss Fanny's Epistles, 478, 484. Her uncle's bequest, 491.
Fum and Hum, the two Birds of Roy alty, 509.

Gaily sounds the castanet, 243.
Galt, Mr., and the Dictionary, 544.
Galaxy, or Milky Way, 101.
Ganges, blue current of the, 393.
Garden, festival of the, 614. Dream of the, 614.
Gazel and Maami, 599.
Gazel, by Abdallah, 174.
Gazelle, the, 248.
Genius, poetical allusions to, 242.
Genius and Criticism, 600.
Genlis, Mme. de, 525.
Gentle youth! whose looks assume (in preceding editions, Ode LXVIII. Anacreon), 45 n.
George III., King, 180 et passim.
George IV. (Prince Regent, and King), Dedication to, of Odes of Anacreon, 5. See the Twopenny Post Bag, 166 to 179. Satirical and Humorous Poems, 179 to 188. The Prince's Day, 205. Memorial to Congress, 495 to 500. Preface, 507. Bird of Royalty, 509.
Georgian Maid, the, 393.
Geramb. Baron, and mustachios, 182.
Gheber, the, 364, et seq.
Ghost Story, a, 571.

Gifford, Mr., 158, 183.
Give me the harp of epic song (Ode II. Anacreon), 13.
Glees, set of, 269.
Gnomes, doctrine of, 464.
Go, let me weep, there's bliss in tears, 256.
Go now, and dream, 247.
Go then, if she whose shade thou art, 92.
Go, then! 'tis vain to hover, 244.
Go where glory waits thee, 195.
Godwin, Mr., 188.
Gondolas and gondoliers, 240, 245, 247, 313.
Goulburn, Mr., 514, 548.
Government, financial, 511.
Grammont, Count de, 104.
Grattan, on the death of, 222. See also 160, 172.
Grecian girl's dream of the Blessed Islands; to her lover, 88.
Grecian Maiden, the—Song, 301.
Grecian Youth, the, 307, et seq.
Greece, isles of, 293, 313. Zean maids, 293, et seq. Allusions to Greece in Lalla Rookh, 325, et seq. Evenings in Greece:—First Evening, 293, 295. Second Evening, 300.
Greek Ode, prefixed to the Translation of Anacreon, 6. Corrections of this Ode by an eminent Scholar, 6
Greeks, The group that late in garb of, 315.
Greyson, Bob, Poet Laureate to the Fancy, 504.
Grenada, the young muleteers of, 272.
Grote, Mr. George, 568, 571,
Guercino, his 'Hagar,' 432, 436.
Guess, guess;—the lady of my love, 289.
Guidi, sonnet by, with a translation, 23 n. Ode by Guidi on the Arcadians, 432.
Guido, 446.
Guitar of India, the Syrinda, 395.
Gull language, translation from the, 555.
Gulliver, Captain Lemuel, 511.
Gun, The Evening, 270.
Gynæcocracy, proposals for a, 549.

Hafez, the poet, 350.
Halcyon hangs o'er ocean, the, 284.
Halford, Sir Henry, 528.
Hall, Capt. Basil, 112.
Hamilton, Rev. —, 408.
Hampden, 152.
Haram, Jehanghir's, 385. The Light of the Haram, 386.
Hark! I hear a spirit sing, 253.
Hark! the vesper hymn is stealing, 241.
Hark! 'tis the breeze of twilight calling, 260.
Harmony, the genius of, 77.
Haroun-al-Raschid, the Caliph, 385.
Harp, certain of the poetical allusions to that instrument, 99, 216, 222, 227, 229, 241, 259.
Harp of my country! in darkness I found thee, 216.
Harp, the origin of the, 205.
Harp, Farewell to the, 194.
Harp that once through Tara's halls, 196.
Harut and Marut, the Angels, 455 n.
Harrowby, Lord, 170.
Has sorrow thy young days shaded, 212.
Hassan, Al, the Prophet Chief of Arabia, 362. See Story of the Fire-worshippers.

Haste thee, nymph, whose well-aimed spear (Ode LXIV. Anacreon), 44.
Hastings, Marquis of (Earl Moira), 166. Visit to his mansion at Donington, 139, 397. His library, 398. Dedication to Francis, Earl of Moira, 115.
Hat, Ode to a, 518.
Hat versus Wig, 517.
Have you not seen the timid tear, 54
Hawkesbury, Lord, 149 to 157.
He who instructs the youthful crew (Ode LVI. Anacreon), 40.
Headfort, Marchioness of, Dedication to. 238.
Headfort, Marquis of, 171 n., 172, 183, 188.
Hear me but once, while o'er the grave, 243.
Heard, Sir Isaac, and the Peerage, 518.
Heart and lute, my, 278.
Heart to rest, no, leave my, 249.
Heathcote, to Lady:—on a ring found at Tunbridge Wells, 104.
Hebe, the fall of:—a dithyrambic ode, 93.
Henley, Lord, and St. Cecilia, 550.
Henry to Lady Emma, 554.
Her last words at parting, how can I forget? 280.
Hercules to his daughter, song of, 280.
Here at thy tomb, 291.
Here is one leaf reserved for me, 75.
Here, take my heart, 271.
Here recline you, gentle maid (Ode XIX. Anacreon), 22.
Here sleeps Anacreon, in this ivied shade (Anthologia), 49.
Here sleeps the Bard, 248.
Here, while the moonlight dim, 299.
Here's the bower she loved so much, 274.
Hero and Leander, 265.
Herries, Mr., 537.
Hertford, Marchioness of, 182, 184, 185, 509.
Hertford, Marquis of, 177, 182, 408, 516.
Hewley, Dr., 546.
High-born Ladye, the, 268.
Hinda, the Arabian maid. See the Story of the Fire-worshippers, 360.
Hippesley, Sir John Cox, 415.
Hither, gentle Muse of mine (Ode LXXVI. Anacreon), 47.
Holkham, 164.
Holland, Lord, regret for the death of, 507. Translations by, 508.
Holland, to Lady, on a legacy by Napoleon, 601.
Holmes, Mr., 514, 537, 612.
Holy Alliance, Fables for the, 421.
Holy be the pilgrim's sleep, 604.
Homeward march, the, 281.
Hooker, Bishop, on οἱ and οὑ, 521.
Hope comes again, to this heart long a stranger, 250.
Hope, poetical allusions to, 241, 248, 262, 292, 588.
Horace, free translations of some Odes of:—Come, Yarmouth, my boy, never trouble your brains (Ode XI. lib. 2', 183. The man who keeps a conscience pure (Ode XXII. lib. 1), 182. I hate thee, oh Mob, as my Lady hates delf (Ode I lib. 3), 188. Boy, tell the cook that I hate all nick-nackeries (Ode XXXVIII. lib. 1), 188. Parody of ' Donec gratus eram tibi,' or Horace's return to Lydia, 314. On an assessment of revenue, 526.

Horn, the, 249.
Horner, Bishop, 541, 543.
Horton, Mr. Wilmot, 514.
How am I to punish thee (Odex. Anacreon), 15.
How can I sing of fragrant sighs, 144.
How dear to me the hour, 198.
How happy once, though wing'd with sighs, 277.
How heavenly was the poet's doom, 68.
How I love the festive boy (Ode xxxix. Anacreon), 32.
How lightly mounts the Muse's wing, 261.
How shall I woo? 252.
How sweetly does the moonbeam smile, 363.
Hudson, Edward, recollections of him and of his musical taste, 189, 191, 193.
Humboldt, Baron, 448.
Hume, David, History of England by, 165.
Hume, Joseph, Esq., 513, 514 n., 544, 562, 572, 611.
Hume, to Thomas, Esq., M.D.; written at Washington, 134.
Humorous and Satirical Poems, 179 to 188 ; 506 to 585.
Hunt, Henry, Esq., 172, 431. His spurious coffee, 513.
Hunt, Leigh, Esq., 532.
Hunter boy, the, 243, 249.
Hush, hush !—a glee, 269.
Hush, sweet lute, 290.
Hussun Abdaul, valley of, 385. Royal gardens near, 385.
Hymen, poetical allusions to, 245.
Hymn of a Virgin of Delphi, at the Tomb of her Mother, 63.
Hyperborean, 94 n. Song of a Hyperborean, 285.

I can no longer stifle, 605.
I care not for the idle state (Ode viii. Anacreon), 15.
I dreamt that in the Paphian groves, 60.
I had, last night, a dream of thee, 467.
I have a story of two lovers, 609.
I fear that love disturbs my rest (Anacreontic), 48.
I found her not—the chamber seem'd, 79.
I knew by the smoke that so gracefully curl'd, 138.
I know that Heaven hath sent me here, (Ode xi. Anacreon), 32.
I know that none can smile like thee, 147.
I know thou lovest a brimming measure (Anacreontic), 47.
I love but thee, 277.
I ne'er on that lip for a minute have gazed, 147.
I often wish that thou wert dead, 148.
I often wish this languid lyre (Ode xxiv. Anacreon), 24.
I pray thee, by the gods above! (Ode ix. Anacreon), 15.
I pray you, let us roam no more, 124.
I saw, from yonder silent cave, 298.
I saw from the beach, when the morning was shining, 216.
I saw the morn rise clear, 274.
I saw the smiling bard of pleasure (Ode i. Anacreon), 12.
I saw thy form in youthful prime, 206.
I stole along the flowery bank, 128.
I thought this heart enkindled lay, 62.
I 've a secret to tell thee, 229.
I 've press'd her bosom oft and oft, 148.

I've roam'd through many a weary round, 608.
I will, I will, the conflict's past (Ode xiii. Anacreon), 16.
I wish I was by that dim lake, 226.
I would tell her I love her, 251.
I'd mourn the hopes that leave me, 212.
I 'll ask the sylph who round thee flies, 65.
Ianthe, 309. Before her glass, 310.
Idols in the house of Azor, 395. Of King Crack, 182. Of Jaghernaut, 323.
If hoarded gold possess'd the power (Ode xxxvi. Anacreon), 31.
If, in the dream that hovers, 105.
If in loving, singing, night and day, 250.
If I swear by that eye, you'll allow, 53.
If I were yonder wave, my dear, 127.
If thou 'lt be mine, 218.
If thou wouldst have me sing and play, 282.
If to see thee be to love thee, 317.
Ill omens :—Young Kitty, etc., 203.
Imagination, etc., 313.
Imitation from the French, 597. See also Anthologia, Horace, etc.
Impromptus, 62, 97, 106, 108, 188, 336.
In myrtle wreaths my votive sword, 293.
In the morning of life, 215.
In wedlock a species of lottery lies, 62.
Ina, by Lady Dacre, 601.
Incantation, an, 522.
Inconstancy, 61.
India, poetical allusions to, 322, et seq.; 384, 392, 393, et seq.
Indian boat, the, 268.
Indian maid, the young, 281.
Indian tree, the, 595.
Inglis, Sir Robert, 537, 571.
Inkstand, the poet's, 594.
Innisfail, song of, 229.
Innisfallen, isle of, 223.
Insurrection of the Papers ; a Dream, 179.
Intercepted Despatch, Diabolo's, 516.
Intercepted Letters of the Twopenny Post-bag : Preface, 166. Dedication to S. Woolriche, Esq., 168. Original Preface, 168. Preface to Fourteenth Edition, 169. The Letters, 170 to 176. Appendix, 177.
Intolerance, a Satire: Account of 'Corruption' and 'Intolerance,' Preface, 148, and Original Preface, 149. The Satire, 157. Appendix, 160.
Invisible Girl, the, 71.
Invitation to dinner; addressed to Lord Lansdowne, 593.
Iran, Land of, 393. See Lalla Rookh, passim.
Ireland, and her national music, 189.
Ireland; certain traditions and romances respecting, 195, 200, 206, 207, 208, 210, 221, 225, 226, 228, 229, 230.
Ireland, politics and political sensibility of the kingdom of (see the Fudge Family), 399 to 421, and 475. The penal code, 516. The outbreak of 1798, 191. Romanism in, 579. Thoughts on the present government of (1828), 553.
Irish antiquities, 541.
Irish bed of roses, an, 188 n.
Irishman, Satires, etc., addressed to an Englishman, by an, 150.
Irish Melodies, Preface, 189. Dedication to the Marchioness Dowager of Donegal, 194. Original Preface,

195. The Melodies, 195. Advertisement to the first and second Nos., 232; to the third No., 232. Letter on Irish music, 233. Advertisements to the fourth, fifth, sixth and seventh Nos., 236, 237. Dedication to the Marchioness of Headfort, 238. See National Airs, 238, et seq.
Irish patronymics, 487, 488, 490.
Irish Peasant to his Mistress, 204.
Irish Slave, the, 526.
Irving, Rev. Edward, 517, 574.
Irving, Mr. Washington, 225 n., 449.
Is it not sweet to think, hereafter, 264.
Is not thy mind a gentle mind? 55.
Israfil, the angel, 394, 452.
It is not the tear at this moment shed, 204.

Jackson, Mr., 432.
J'Troy Mrs., Dedication to, 269.
Jeffrey, Francis Lord, allusion to his house at Craig Crook, Edinburgh, 263.'
Jehan Gheer, or Jehanquire, Emperor of Delhi and Hindostan, 385. His palace, 392 n. Romance, 387 n. His early name of Selim, 389. His bride, 394.
Jerome's love (St.), 254. St. Jerome's first visit on earth, 557. His second visit, 558.
Jerusalem, the holy city of, 254.
Jessica, young, 277.
Jessy on a bank was sleeping, 107.
Joan, Pope, Epistle of, 177.
Johnson, Dr. Samuel, on Nailet, 490 n.
Johnston, Mr., 553.
Joke versaified, a, 596.
Jones, Colonel, 557.
Journal, fragments of a, 144.
Joy alone be remembered now, 277.
Joys of youth, how fleeting ! 243.
Joys that pass away, 605.
Juan, Don, 184.
Jubal's shell, alluded to, 311.
Judgment Day, and a supposed wind from Syria Damascena to announce it, 396 n.
Judgment, the day of, 258.
Julia, to, in allusion to some illiberal criticisms, 56. Mock me no more with Love's beguiling dream, 56. Though Fate, my girl, may bid us part, 57. On her Birth-day, 58. To Julia, weeping, 58. Inconstancy, 61. Elegiac Stanzas, supposed to be written by Julia, on the death of her brother, 62. I saw the peasant's hand unkind, 63. Sympathy, 64. Well, Julia, if to love and live, 105. Sweet is the dream, divinely sweet, 106.
Juvenile Poems, 51 to 111. Preface by 'the Editor of Little's Poems,' 51. Dedication to Joseph Atkinson, Esq., 52.

Kathleen, 207.
Keder Khan of Turkistan, 322.
Keep those eyes still purely mine, 250.
Kenmare, Earl of, 223 n.
Kenyon, Lord, 539, 541, 542.
Kevin, Saint, tradition of, 207.
Khorassan, the Veiled Prophet of, 324.
Kilkenny amateur actors, talent of the, 585, 590. Extract from a Prologue, 591.
Killarney, lakes and traditions of, 221, 223.
King Crack and his idols, 182.

King, Lord, an Exposiulation to, 512.
Kishma, wine of, 393 n.
Kiss, Julia's, 110.
Kiss, the, 82, 107, 122.
Kublai Khan, 393.

Lackington, Messrs., 167. Letter from, 175.
Lahore, description of the city of, and the midland districts of India, 358.
Lake of the Dismal Swamp, 120.
Lalla Rookh, an Eastern Romance: Preface furnishing the history of this poem, 318. Representation of it as a dramatic pageant at the Château Royal, Berlin, in 1822, when the emperor and empress of Russia personated Aliris and Lalla Rookh, 321. 'The Veiled Prophet of Khorassan,' 324. The criticisms by Fadladeen on this story, 349. Paradise and the Peri, 351. Fadladeen renews his criticism, 357. The Fire-worshippers, 360. The Light of the Haram, 386. Design of this poetic undertaking related, 449.
Lambert, Daniel, 179.
Lansdowne, Lord, dedication to, 1. Invitation to dinner, addressed to, 593.
Lauderdale, Lord, 512, 514, 532.
Lawrence, Dr., friend of Edmund Burke, 5. His letter to Dr. Hume respecting the version of Anacreon by Mr. Moore, 5.
Lawyer, epitaph on a, 608
Lay his sword by his side, 230.
Leaf and the Fountain, a ballad, 266.
Learning, 88.
Lebanon, Mount, 260.
Leckie, G. F., Esq., 170.
Lefroy, Sergeant, 555, 571, 576.
Legacy, the, 199.
Legendary Ballads, 262 to 269.
Legend of Puck the fairy, 285.
Leila's lute, 589.
Leonardo da Vinci's ' Mona Lisa,' 315. His ' Last Supper,' 444.
Les hommes automates, 562.
Lesbia, to, 592.
Lesbia hath a beaming eye, 206.
Let Erin remember the days of old, 200.
Lethbridge, Sir Thomas, 513, 543.
Let joy alone be remember'd now, 277.
Let me resign this wretched breath, (Anacreontic), 47.
Let's take this world as some wide scene, 280.
Let us drain the nectar'd bowl (Ode xxxviii. Anacreon), 32.
Let us, with the clustering vine, 4.
Levee and couchee, the, 316.
Libel, a Case of, 524.
Liberty, 201, 215, 230, 231, 248, 293, 297, 589, et seq.
Liberty, the Torch of, 424.
Life is waning, do not say that, 248.
Life is all chequer'd with pleasures and woes, 208.
Life for me hath joy, etc., 278.
Life without freedom, 273.
Light sounds the harp when the combat is over, 69.
Like a snuffers, this loving old dame, 609.
Like morning, when her early breeze, 258.
Like one who doom'd o'er distant seas, 251.
Like some wanton filly sporting (Ode lxv. Anacreon), 44.
Like the bright lamp that shone in Kildare's holy fane, 201.
Lilis, 467, 468.

Limbo of lost reputations, 534.
Lion, dead, and the living dog, 532.
Lister, Hon. Mr., 535.
Listen to the Muse's lyre (Ode iii. Anacreon), 13.
Literary advertisement, to Authors, 525.
Literati, sick, 577.
Literature, speed of, 576.
Little Grand Lama, the, 427.
Little Man and Little Soul, a ballad, 168. 'There was a little man, and he had a little soul,' 186.
Little Mary's eye, 605.
Little, Thomas, Esq., his Poems, 51. Omitted in London Edition, 105.
Liverpool, Lord, 173, 180, 183, 431, 509.
Lizard (Stellio), account of the. 385 n.
Londonderry, Marquis of, 505, 509, 532, 534, 554, 559, 599.
Longepierre, epigrams quoted by, translated, 22 n., 26 n., 28 n., 30 n., 32 n., 33 n., 34 n., 36 n.
Longman, Messrs., ii., 318, 450.
Lonsdale, Lord, 516.
Looking-glasses, the, 423.
Lord, who shall bear that day, 258.
Lorton, Lord, 530, 554, 579 n.
Loss of a letter for Nea, on the, 146.
Lotus-tree, 393.
Lotus-branch, and the bird taking flight, mythos of the, 620.
Lotus-flower, 95. An emblem of beauty, 362 n.
Louis Philippe, King, 397, 582. Account of, when at Donington Park, 398.
Louis the Fourteenth's Wig, 429.
Louis XVIII., 399, 400, 401, 412, 417, 422, 426, 505.
Love, a few allusions to, 44, 46, 127, 130, 203, 208, 210, 228, 227, 240, 241, 244, 245, 247, 248, 251, 261, 275, 276, 292, 295, 301, 312, 317, 454, 460, 464, 472, 588, 596.
Love alone, 253.
Love, all-defying Love, 362.
Love and Hope, 241.
Love and Hymen, 595.
Love and Learning, 88.
Love and Marriage, 65.
Love and Reason, 87.
Love and the Novice, 208.
Love and the Sun-dial, 274.
Love and Time, 274.
Love and the Vine, 308.
Love came by, 267.
Love resting his wings, 393.
Love a sentinel: Glee—Hush, Hush, 269.
Love, one summer eve, was straying, 305.
Love is a hunter-boy, 243.
Love-knots, who'll buy my, 245.
Love, mythological hymn to, 92.
Love, my Mary, dwells with thee, 605.
Love wandering through the golden maze, 275.
Love, unbind thee, 288.
Love, who ruled as admiral o'er, 289.
Love thee?—so well, so tenderly, 275.
Love thee, dearest? 278.
Love but thee, I, 277.
Love's day, 276.
Love's light summer cloud, 274.
Love's victory, 280.
Love's young dream, 205.
Lover, the, 253, 266 n., 299, 311, 362, 454, 472.
Lover, the Persian, 174.
Lover, the Russian, 290.
Loves of the Angels : Preface, 448. Preface to the poem, 450. The poem, 452. First Angel's Story, 453. Se-

cond Angel's Story, 458. Third Angel's Story, 471.
Loves, the Sale of, 60.
Loves, the two, 284.
Lowe, Sir Hudson, to, 511.
Lusitanian war-song, 276.
Lute, the, 392, 589.
Lying, 66.
Lyndhurst, Lord, 571, 583, 584, 609.
Lyre, the poet's, 251.
Lyre, the tell-tale, 86.

Machiavelian policy, condemned, 437.
Madox, Miss, Lines to, 505.
Magan, Patrick, Esq., his Epistles to a Curate in Ireland. 475, 479, 490.
Magic Mirror, the, 267.
Magnet, woman a, 465.
Mahomet, religion of (see Lalla Rookh), 326, et seq.
Mahomet, the Seal of preceding prophecy, 465. The familiar dove of, 468, 521.
Mahometans, belief of the, 452, 454 n., 466, 471. The paradise, 456. The chief angels, 452, 453, 457, 458, 471.
Mahommed Shaw, feast and throne of, 397 n.
Maiden, the sleeping, 249.
Maidens of Zea, 299, et passim.
Maid, to a sleeping, 107.
Malthus, allusions to, 511, 532, 552, 599.
Mandeville, 553.
March : nor heed those arms that hold her, 307.
Marlborough, Duk of, 150.
Marliceau, Miss, 582.
Martyrs, the, 261.
Marvell, Andrew, 155, 522 n.
Mary, 206.
Mary, star of the sea, 300.
Mary, I believed thee true, 84.
Mathews, Mr. Charles, 568.
Matriculation, scene from a play acted at Oxford, called, 580.
Mauri-ga-Sima, or the sunken island, 393 n.
May-moon, the young, 210.
Mehemet Ali, 581.
Meleager:—Here at thy tomb these tears Ished, 291. Various imitations from, 69, 291, 293.
Melodies, Irish, 195. Succeeded by the National Airs, 238, et seq.
Memorabilia of last week (March 13, 1826), 515.
Memorial to Congress, Tom Crib's:— Preface, 491. Parallel between Ancient and Modern Pugilism, 492. Flash or Cant Language, 494. The Memorial, 495. Account of the Grand Set-to between Long Sandy and Georgy the Porpoise, 496. Appendix, No. I. Pugilistic Meeting at Belcher's, 501. No. II. Entellus and Dares, translated from the Æneid, 503. No. III. Bob Gregson, Poet-laureate of the Fancy, 504. Lines to Miss Madox, the fair Pugilist, 505. Ya-hip, my Hearties, 506.
Memory, poetical allusions to, 240, 453, 470.
Memphis, on the Nile, 616.
Menage, Anacreontics in Greek by, translated, 17 n., 27 n., 30 n.
Merou, city of Khorassan, 324.
Merrily every bosom boundeth, 275.
Methinks the pictured bull we see (Ode liv. Anacreon), 38.
Metternich, Prince, 533.
Miguel, Don, Ode to, 533.
Milesius and the Milesians, 229.

Millennium, the,—and the Rev. Mr. Irving, 517. The year of a, 486.
Milling, 492.
Miltiades, the Ghost of, 544.
Minaret, chants from an illuminated, 387 n.
Mind not though daylight, 283.
Minerva or Pallas, and Love, 305.
Minerva's thimble, 277.
Ministers, the new costume of the, 185. The Sale of the Tools, 187.
Ministers, wreaths for the, 183.
Minstrel Boy, the, 210.
Miriam's Song, 256.
Miscellaneous Poems, 585.
Mischief, thoughts on, by Lord St-nl-y, his first attempt, 583.
Missing, Lord de ***, 551.
Mix me, child, a cup divine (Anacreontic), 48.
M'Mahon, Col., Letter from, to G. F. Leckie, Esq., 170. See also, 172, 182.
Mœris, lake of, 623.
Mohawk River, lines written at the Cohos or Falls of the, 135.
Moira, Lord. See Hastings.
Mokanna, the prophet-chief of Khorassan, 324, 325, et seq.
Monarch Love, resistless boy (Ode LXXIV. Anacreon), 46.
Monopoly, present spirit of, 514.
Mont-Blanc, sublime prospect of, 434, 435.
Montaigne quoted, 433.
Montpensier, Duke of, to the, 93.
Montrose, Duke of, 497.
Moon, poetical mention of the, 298, 299, 301, 306, et passim.
Moon, that high in heaven art shining, 290.
Moore, Thomas, born May 28, 1780, i. His parentage, i. His early days and education, i. His schoolmaster, Mr. White, i. His first attempts at poetry in 1790, 2. His first political satire, in 1794, 3. His acquaintance with Edward Hudson and Robert Emmett in 1797, 189. Becomes a member of the Debating and Historical Societies, 189. Publishes a Letter in ' The Press,' 191. His examination before the Vice-Chancellor and Dr. Duigenan, 192. His acquittal, 193. Leaves Ireland for London in 1799, 5. His youthful appearance at that time, i. Publishes his Translation of the ' Odes of Anacreon' in 1800, i., and ' Little's Poems' in 1801, ii. His journey to Bermuda in 1803, i., 112. Visits New York, Philadelphia, and the Falls of Niagara, 113. His first notation of the Canadian Boat Song, 114. His impressions on America, 116. Publishes his ' Odes and Epistles' in 1806, ii., 116. His ' Corruption,' ' Intolerance,' and ' The Sceptic' in 1808, ii., 148. His visits to Carlton House, 166. Publishes his ' Intercepted Letters,' ii., 168. Marries Miss Dyke, iii. Challenges Lord Byron, and amicable settlement of the difference, iv. His visit to Chatsworth, 193. Visits Sir Walter Scott at Abbotsford, and Lord Jeffrey at Edinburgh, 263. Present at the Fête at Boyle Farm, 308. Publishes ' Lalla Rookh' in 1817, ii., 318. Visits Paris in 1817, and writes ' The Fudge Family,' ii., 397. Returns to Ireland in 1818, and a public dinner given to him, ii. His journey to Italy with Lord John Russell in 1819, 431. Visits Lord

Byron at Venice, 432. His recollections of Rome, 432. His pecuniary embarrassments, and second abode in Paris till 1822, 448. Dinner given to him by the British Residents in Paris, ii. Publishes ' The Loves of the Angels' in 1823, ii., 450. His transactions with Messrs. Longman respecting Lord Byron's Memoirs, iii. Conflicting opinions on the subject, iv. Catalogue of his Works, ii., iii. Remarks on the merits and defects of his poetical style, and panegyric by Lord Byron, v.
Moore, Mrs., 191. To my mother, 595.
Moore, Mr. Peter, 522.
Moore, to Miss, from Norfolk, in Virginia, 118.
Moral positions, a dream, 553.
Morality, an epistle, 85.
More, Sir Thomas, 568.
Morgan, George, Esq. (of Norfolk, Virginia), epistle to, from Bermuda, 122.
Morgan, Lady, 411 n., 416 n.
Morning, 216, 258.
Morning, an ode upon, 110.
Morning Herald, the, 518.
Morning Post, the, 485.
Morris, Capt., his song. ' My Muse, too, when her wings are dry,' 264.
Moschus, his first Idyl, quoted, 23 n.
Moses, 259.
Mountain Sprite, the, 225.
Mountcashel, Lord, 539, 542, 549.
' Mum' to the editor of the Morning Chronicle, 508.
Murray, Mr., his contemplated Mail-coach edition of Rokeby, 173.
Muse, the, 316.
Musgrave, Lord, 158, 163, 164.
Music and Melodies, an account of some of our modern poets who had a taste for, and a knowledge of, 262, 263, 264.
Music, the Prefatory Letter on Irish, 233.
Music, on :—Songs, 204, 287.
Music, poetical allusions to, 227, 231, 248, 249, 474.
Music, a Melologue upon National, 587.
Music of the spheres, 459.
Musical Box, the:—Rose and the Poet, 286.
Musical Shells, 77 n.
My gentle harp, 216.
My harp has one unchanging theme, 241.
My Mopsa is little, 292.

Nama, 470, 473.
Namouna, the enchantress, 389. Calls down sleep on Nourmahal, 390.
Naples, lines on the entry of the Austrians into, in 1821, 595
Napoleon, the Emperor, 156, 158, 163, 400 to 419. Consigned to the rock of St. Helena, 508, 511. Allusions to his fallen fortunes, 181, 183, 567, 601.
Natal Genius, the, a Dream: to ——, the morning of her birthday, 61.
National Airs, 238.
National Music, a Melologue upon, 587.
Nature's Labels, a fragment, 57.
Naugerius, epigram by, translated, 14 n.
Nay, do not weep, my Fanny dear, 88.
Nay, look not there, my love, 465.
Nay, tell me not, dear, 207.
Nay, tempt me not to love again, 211.
Nea, Odes to :—written at Bermuda, 124.

Necropolis, and lake near Memphis, 619.
Ne'er ask the hour, what is it to us? 219.
Ne'er talk of Wisdom's gloomy schools, 248.
Nethercoat, Mrs., 578.
Nets and Cages, 246.
Never mind how the pedagogue proses, 60.
Newcastle, Duke of, 539, 542, 543.
Niagara, Falls of, 113.
Nichol, Sir John, 172.
Nicholas, Emperor of Russia, 551.
Night-dance, the, 229.
Night-thought, a, 82.
Nightingales, song of, 277, 282, 285, 386.
Nights of Music, 273.
Nights, such as Eden's calm recall, 315.
Nile, the Garden of the, 392. Sources of the river, 438.
No—leave my heart to rest, 249.
No life is like the mountaineer's, 303.
No, not more welcome the fairy numbers, 213.
Noble and illustrious authors, 539, 542.
Nonsense, 83.
Nora Creina, 206.
Norton, Hon. Mrs., Dedication to, 309. Not from thee the wound should come, 288.
Nourjehan, ' the Light of the World,' 385 n.
Nourmahal, the Light of the Harem, 387. 388. Her spells, 389, 390. Her sleep, 390. She is regretted by Selim, 392. Her disguise, 392, 394. The Georgian maid's song, 393. Succeeded by that of Nourmahal herself, 393. Her reconciliation with Selim, 394.
Now let the warrior, 605.
Now Neptune's month our sky deforms, (Ode LXVIII. Anacreon), 46.
Now the star of day is high (Ode XVIII. Anacreon), 21.
Nymph of a fair but erring line, 352.

O'Branigan, Larry, to his wife Judy, 481, 487. To Murtagh O'Mulligan, 567.
O'Connell, Mr., 516, 519, 538, 543, 576, 577.
O'Connor, Arthur, Esq., 190.
O'Donohue's Mistress, 221.
O'Keefe's song for the character of Spado, 585.
O'Mulligan, Mortimer, his epistle (see ' Fudge Family in England '), 489.
O'Ruark, Prince of Breffni, the song of, 210.
Oblivion, the fabled gates of, 622.
Observe when mother earth is dry (Ode XXI. Anacreon), 23.
Of all the men one meets about, 609.
Oft, in the stilly night, 240.
Oft, when the watching stars grow pale, 247.
Oh ! breathe not his name, 196.
Oh ! banquet not in those shining bowers, 224.
Oh ! blame not the bard, if he fly to the bowers, 202.
Oh ! but to see that head recline, 456.
Oh ! call it by some better name, 271.
Oh ! come to me when daylight sets, 240.
Oh ' could we do with this world of ours ! 231.
Oh ! days of youth and joy, 245.
Oh, do not look so bright and blest, 286.
Oh! doubt me not,—the season, 211.

Oh fair! oh purest! be thou the dove, 257.
Oh for the swords of former time! 219.
Oh, guard our affection, 249.
Oh! had we some bright little isle of our own, 211.
Oh! hint to the bard, 'tis retirement alone, 449.
Oh! idol of my dreams! 463.
Oh, Lady fair! 606.
Oh! Love, Religion, Music, all, 472.
Oh, Memory, how coldly, 298.
Oh, no! not even when first we loved, 242.
Oh! nothing in life can sadden us, 110.
Oh, say! thou best and brightest, 251.
Oh! see those cherries, 606.
Oh, soon return, 275.
Oh, stranger! if Anacreon's shell (Anthologia), 49.
Oh! teach me to love thee, 258.
Oh! the sight entrancing, 222.
Oh! the shamrock, 208.
Oh! think not my spirits are always as light, 196.
Oh, think, when a hero is sighing, 589.
Oh, thou! of all creation blest (Ode xxxiv. Anacreon), 29.
Oh! thou who dry'st the mourner's tear, 255.
Oh, tidings of freedom! Oh, accents of hope, 538.
Oh! where art thou dreaming? 316.
Oh! where 's the slave so lowly, 214.
Oh, woman, if through sinful wile, 83.
Oh, ye dead! 224.
Olden time, The Song of the, 279.
Olympus, latest accounts from, 581.
On one of those sweet nights that oft, 315.
Once in each revolving year (Ode xxv. Anacreon), 25.
One bumper at parting, 209.
One day the Muses twined the bands, (Ode xx. Anacreon), 22.
Oppression, memory and record of, 248.
Orangemen of Ireland, their Petition, 520.
Orcus, High Priest, to the Prefect Decius, 626.
Ormuzd of the ancient Persians, and his angels, 452.
Ossian, allusions to, 230, 232.
Ossian, fragments in imitation of, 191.
O'Sullivan, Rev. M., 526, 563, 567.
Our first young love, 273.
Our home is on the sea, boy, 313.
Overton, Rev. Charles, Lines to, 559.
Owen, Dr., 519.

Paddy's Metamorphosis, 562.
Paine, Mr. Thomas, 164.
Painting, 120, 289, 301, 440.
Palestine and the river Jordan, 356.
Palmerston, Lord, 522.
Paradise and the Peri, 351. Criticisms of Fadladeen on this romance, 357.
Paradise of Mahomet, 456, 457.
Parallel, the, 220.
Parliament, the recess of, a hymn, 161. Occasional Address, for the opening of the New Theatre of St. Stephen (Nov. 24, 1812), 186. Satirical notice of some members of the House of Lords, 539 to 547, 551, etc. Report of Speeches relative to Maynooth college, 552. Exhibition of models of the two houses of, 515.
Passion, 261, 271, 289.
Patrick's Purgatory, and mystic lake in Donegal, 226 n.
Patrons and Puffs, etc., 582.

Paul the Silentiary, 122 n., 292.
Paul Veronese, 439.
Peace and glory, 86.
Peace be around thee, 242.
Peace to the slumberers! 245.
Peace! Peace to him that's gone, 278.
Pearls, 126, 248, 465. Mythos as to their production, 383 n.
Pearls, Irish, 224.
Peel, Sir Robert, 401, 521, 533, 578.
Peer, how to make oneself a, 563.
Peers, batch the first, 528.
Perceval, Right Hon. Spencer, 151 n., 154 n., 157, 159, 167 n., 180, 181. On the death of, 586.
Perfumes for the hair and beard, 15 n.
Peri, Paradise and the, 351.
Peris, and fairies, 392, 436. See Lalla Rookh, etc.
Perry, Mr., 167, 318.
Periwinkles and Locusts, 528.
Persia and the Persians, 174. See Lalla Rookh, 327 to 395, et passim. Superstitious notions of this eastern people, 452, 453 n.
Philadelphia and the Schuylkill river, 133.
Phillis, to, 84.
Philodemus:—'My Mopsa is little,' 292.
Philosophy, a vision of, 98. See the classical notes to this poem, 98.
Philosophy: Poems relative to, treating of Philosophers, ancient and modern, 66, 208, 459. Aristotle, Pythagoras, Democritus, Plato, and Epicurus, 99 n. Pyrrho, 161. Aristippus, 66. Zeno, 85. Maupertuis, 68 n.
Philostratus, a thought of, imitated by Ben Jonson, 12 n.
Philpotts, Dr. (Bishop of Exeter), 552, 558, 560, 562, 565, 569, 573, 575, 576, 578.
Pictures, Italian galleries of, 432.
Pigeons, carrier, 254.
Pilgrim, Man a, 260.
Pilgrim, the, 302. Still thus when twilight gleam'd, 267.
Pitt, Mr., 156, 515.
Planets, the, 459 n.
Plato, Epigram of, 24 n. He wrote abed, 433.
Platonic philosophy, and followers of Plato, 99, et seq.
Pleasure contrasted with Pain, 247.
Plumassier, to a (Anacreontic), 181.
Poco-Curante Society, the, 431. (See Rhymes on the Road.) Song of, 602.
Poems, omitted in London Edition; 105 to 111 ; 142 to 148 ; 447; 494 to 506 ; 604 to 612.
Poesy, 228, 231.
Poet, epitaph on a well-known, 608.
Poet's dream, dinner of Type and Co., 580.
Poh, Dermot! go along with your goster, 606.
Pole, Hon. Long Wellesley, 527.
Police Reports, case of imposture, 574.
Political allusions, by the author of these volumes : 148 to 165. The Two-penny Post-Bag, 166 to 179. Satirical Poems, 179 to 188. The Fudge Family, 397 to 421, and 475 to 490. Memorial to Congress, 491 to 506. Satirical Poems, 508 to 585. For the poet's allusions to the affairs of North America and of France, see 116.
Politician, how to make a good, 543.
Politics, Irish, allusions to, 189. See 508 to 585, et passim.
Polycrates of Samos, 8.

Poor broken flower, 272.
Poor wounded heart, 271.
Porcelain and china, 393, 395.
Porte, ode to the Sublime, 524.
Power, Mr. Richard, 585.
Poynder, Mr., 557.
Pozzo di Borgo, 497.
Prayer of Mahometans, 356.
Press the grape, and let it pour, 56.
'Press, the,' newspaper, 190.
Prince's day, the, 205.
Probability, the, 607.
Prologue, spoken at the opening of the Kilkenny Theatre, October, 1809, 590.
Proxy, how to write by, 534.
Psaphon, his birds taught to pronounce his name, 438.
Psyche, 79, 92, 596.
Puck, song of Old, 574.
Pugilism, ancient and modern, 492.
Puir prodigate Londoners, 547.
Purgatory, 464.
Put off the vestal veil, nor, oh! 75.
Pye, Mr. (Poet Laureate), 150, 154, 175.
Pyramids of Memphis, 617.

Quadrilles, 598. Episcopal, 551.
Quakers, 486.
Quarterly Review, the, 546, 579. Reflections addressed to the Author of the article of 'the Church' in the, 575.
Quick! we have but a second, 224.

Rabbinical origin of women, 102 n., 607.
Raise the buckler, poise the lance, 297.
Raphael, his Fornarina, 440.
Rathdowne, Lord, 549.
Rawdon, to the Lady Charlotte, from the banks of the St. Lawrence, 139.
Romance of the Indian Spirit, 139.
Reason, 87, 211, 239, 273, 291.
Reason, and Folly, and Beauty, 239.
Red Fox, the, 190.
Redbreast, the, in December, 239.
Redesdale, Lord, 159, 532.
Rector and his curate, the, 561.
Reflection, a, at sea, 58.
Reform, notions on, 556.
Religion, 565. The 'Sacred Songs,' 253. Religion and trade, 578. Religion in the East, Brahma, etc., 325. (See Lalla Rookh.)
Religious emblems and types, 257. 'Intolerance' satirised, 157, et seq. On Toleration, 174, et passim.
Remember him thou leavest behind, 53.
Remember the glories of Brien the brave, 195.
Remember the time in La Mancha's shades, 275.
Remember thee! 217.
Remonstrance ; addressed to Lord John Russell, after a conversation in which he had intimated some idea of giving up all political pursuits, 591.
Resemblance, the ; Yes, if 't were any common love, 70.
Reuben and Rose, 54,
Revenue, decimating—and decimal arithmetic, 528. .
Reverend Pamphleteer, the, 569.
Reverends and Right Reverends, resolutions passed at a meeting of, 53.
Reynolds, Mr. Thomas, 399, 407.
Rhodope, the Lady of the Pyramid, 622.

Rhymes on the Road, extracted from the Journal of a Travelling Member of the Poco-Curante Society, in 1819, 431 to 448.
Rich and rare were the gems she wore, 197.
Rich in bliss, I proudly scorn (Ode LXVII. Anacreon), 45.
Richmond, Duke of, 150 n.
Rienzi, 443.
Ring, the;—The happy day at length arrived, 72.
Ring, the;—No, Lady! Lady! keep the ring, 71.
Rings and Seals, 96.
Ripen'd by the solar beam (Ode LVIII. Anacreon), 42.
Rival Topics — an Extravaganza, 568.
Robinson, Hon. Frederick, 512, 513, 515, 517.
Roche, Sir Boyle, his blunders, 532.
Rock, Captain, his Epistle to Lord Lyndhurst, 584. His Letter to Terry Alt, Esq., 584.
Roden, Lord, 531, 541, 549, 554, 559, 562.
Rogers, Mr., accompanied by the author to Paris, 397. Dedication to, 321.
Rokeby, allusions to, 173, 175.
Romaika, the, danced in Zea, 296, et seq.
Romaldkirk, to the Curate of, 559. 'Romanism in Ireland;' see the Quarterly Review, 579.
Rome, artists at, 432. The Palatine Mount, 432.
Rondeau;—'Good night! good night,' 68.
Rosa, to, 64, 69, 84.
Rosa, to, written during illness, 59.
Rose, Mr. George, 154, 180, 181, 188, 407, 555.
Rose, the Alpine, 244.
Rose, the, and summer bee, 247.
Rose of the Desert! 278.
Rose and Nightingale, 285.
Rose, the young, 277.
Rose-tree, the pretty, 272.
Rose in nettles hid, the;—Conundrum, 104.
Roses, the Feast of, 322, 386, 387 n., 395. Of the Garden of the Nile, 392. Attar Gul, 396.
Roses, political, 188 n.
Rothesay, Lord Stuart de, 551.
Round the world goes, by day and night, 286.
Rousseau, 418, 419, 447 n.
Row gently here, 245.
Rubi, the second Angel, 457. His Story, 458.
Ruby, magnificent, 393.
Russell, Lord John, 431, 432. Remonstrance on his intended retirement from politics, 591.
Russian Lover, the;—Fleetly o'er the moonlit snows, 290.

Sacred Songs, 253. Dedication to Edward Tuite Dalton, Esq., 253.
Sail on, sail on, thou fearless bark, 219.
Sailor boy, 'tis day, 293.
Salisbury, Earl of, 543.
Salmagundi, 528.
Saunazaro, his Gallicio nell' Arcadia, quoted, 14 n.
Sappho, lyre of, 315. Legends of Leucadia, 295.
Sarpi, Fra Paolo, 437.
Satirical and Humorous Poems, 179 to 188; 508 to 585.

Say, what shall be our sport to-day, 244.
Say, what shall we dance, 270.
Sceptic, the; a philosophical Satire, 161. The Preface on Ancient Philosophy, and the Pyrrhonists, 161. The Satire, 162.
Scepticism, 596.
Scott, Sir Walter, his musical taste, 263. Interesting scene at the Edinburgh theatre, 263. Anecdote told by, to the Prince Regent. The Regent's remark, 166. His 'Rokeby,' 175.
Scriptures, the Holy, 257, 259.
Sculptor, wouldst thou glad my soul (Ode V. Anacreon), 13.
Sea, the Old Man of the, 526. A Reflection at, 58.
See, passenger, at Crockford's high behest, 611.
See the dawn from heaven, 246.
See the young, the rosy Spring (Ode XLVI. Anacreon), 35.
See you, beneath yon cloud so dark, 141.
Selim and Nourmahal, 389.
Send the bowl round merrily, 606.
Senses, the, 142.
Sephiroths or Splendors of the Cabala, 475 n.
Seraphim, 471.
Seth, traditions relative to the patriarch, 471.
Shakspeare, 165.
Shalimar Palace, the, 292, 396.
Shall the Harp then be silent, 222.
Shamrock, the, 208.
Shannon, Stanzas from the banks of the, 538.
Shaw, Mr., 555, 572, 576.
She is far from the land where her young hero sleeps, 207.
She never look'd so kind before, 63.
Sheridan, Rt. Hon. Richard Brinsley, 163, 172, 181. Lines on the Death of, 586. His character described, 586. Intended Life of, 449.
Sheridan, Mrs., air composed by, 253.
She sung of Love, 227.
She has beauty, but still you must keep your heart cool, 273.
Shield, the, 58.
Shine out, stars, 272.
Ship a-hoy!—Song, 269.
Ships and wrecks, 117, 122, 123, 216, 249, 251, 260.
Ships, the Meeting of the, 269.
Shiraz wine, 393.
Should those fond hopes, 239.
Shrine, the, 56.
Sidmouth, Lord, 170, 399, 407, 409, 414, 415, 497.
Silence, emblem of, 229, 619.
Silence is in our festal halls, 231.
Silence, chain of, 216 n.
Silent, oh Moyle, be the roar of thy water, 200.
Simonides, epitaphs on Anacreon by, 49 n.
Sin, 452, 467.
Since first thy word, 260.
Sinclair, Sir John, 552.
Sing, sweet harp, 227.
Sing, sing, music was given, 227.
Sinking Fund cried, 513.
Sinners, 261.
Sirmio, peninsula of, 593.
Slumber, oh slumber! if sleeping thou makest, 249.
Slumber, poetical allusions to, 240.
Smile, one dear, 276.

Smith, Rev. Sidney, 582.
Smoothly flowing through verdant vales, 313.
Snake, the, 64.
Snow Spirit, the;—No, ne'er did the wave in its elements sleep, 128.
So warmly we met, 239.
So! Rosa turns her back on me, 108.
Soliman, throne of, was called the star of the Genii, 325 n.
Some mortals there may be, so wise or so fine, 512.
Somers, Lord, 414.
Song of the olden time, 279.
Songs, some of the occasional; interwoven in Mr. Moore's poems;—Juvenile Poems, 53 to 111; Irish Melodies, 195 to 231; National Airs, 238 to 253; Evenings in Greece, 293 to 308; Miscellaneous Poems, 599 to 610.
Songs from the Greek Anthology, 291 to 293.
Songs from 'M. P.,' or the Blue Stocking,' 588, 589.
Songs, Sacred, 252 to 262.
Songs. Unpublished, etc., 288 to 291.
Sound the loud timbrel o'er Egypt's dark sea, 256.
Southcote, Joanna, 521.
Southey, Robert, Esq., 518, 521. Announcement of a new Thalaba, 566.
Sovereign, a golden, 512.
Sovereign woman, a ballad, 603.
Speculation, a 595.
Speeches, a Corrected Report of some late, 552.
Spencer, Hon. W. R., lines addressed to him from Buffalo and Lake Erie, in North America, 137.
Spirit of Joy, thy altar lies, 588.
Spirit of Love, whose locks unroll'd (Ode LXXV. Anacreon), 47.
Spirit of the Woods, the Evil;— ong, 136.
Spirit, the Indian (or North American), 139.
Spring and Autumn, 246, 252.
Squinting poetess, on a, 83.
St. Lawrence, river, 138, 139; the gulf of, 141.
St. Senanus and the Lady, 198.
Stael, Mme. de, 434.
Stanley, Lord, 565, 568, 574, 583.
Stanzas, elegiac, 107.
Stars, some of the poet's allusions to the, 198, 247, 255, 300, 302, 304, 459, 465.
Steele, Mr., 154.
Steersman's Song, the, 131.
Stephenson, Rowland, 568.
Stephens, Henry, wrote on horseback, 433.
Stevenson, Sir John, poetical tribute to, 231, 232. See also, 255 to 261.
Still, like dew in silence falling, 293.
Still thou fliest, and still I woo thee, 289.
Still when daylight o'er the wave, 283.
Stoddart, Dr., 518, 521, 566.
Storm at Sea; Lines written in a, 123.
Storm, love in a, 107.
Stranger, the heart-wounded, 268.
Strangford, to Lord; written on board the Phaeton frigate, off the Azores, 117.
Strew me a fragrant bed of leaves, Ode XXXII. Anacreon), 28.
Sublime was the warning that Liberty spoke, 201.
Sugden, Sir Edward, 574, 580.
Sulpicia, Tibullus to, 593.
Summer Fête, the, 309.

Summer webs that float and shine, 283.
Sunday Ethics, a Scotch ode, 547.
Supper, an invitation to, 109.
Surprise, the, 65.
Swans, the Muse's, 316.
Sweetest love! I'll not forget thee, 111.
Sweet Innisfallen, fare thee well, 223.
Sweet is your kiss, my Lais dear, 122.
Sweet lady, look not thus again, 57.
Sweet seducer! blandly smiling, 105.
Sweet spirit! if thy airy sleep, 61.
Swings, an Eastern pastime and exercise, 387.
Sword, the warrior's, 219, 228, 230.
Sylph's Ball, the, 590.
Sylphs and Gnomes, 464 n.
Syra, holy fount of, 299.

Tablet of love, the, 607.
Take back the sigh, 87.
Take back the virgin page, 198.
Take hence the bowl, 247.
Talfourd, Sergeant, 580.
Talleyrand, Prince, 574 n.
Tar-barrels, thoughts on, 558.
Tara, the halls of, 196.
Taylor, Rev. Robert, 475.
Tear, the, 64, 196, 204.
Tears, poetical allusions to, 243, 247, 255, 256, 261, 272, 291.
Teflis, or Tiflis, brooks of, 393.
Tegg, Mr. Thomas, 577.
Tell her, oh, tell her, 273.
Tell me, gentle youth, I pray thee (Ode xi. Anacreon), 16.
Tell me not of joys above, 359.
Tell me, why, my sweetest dove (Ode xv. Anacreon), 18.
Temple, the, at Jerusalem, 257, 259.
Teynham, Lord, 522.
Thalaba, announcement of a new, to Mr. Southey, 566.
That wrinkle, when first I espied it, 55.
The bird, let loose in Eastern skies, 254.
The garland I send thee, 252.
The harp that once through Tara's halls, 196.
The King's speech toll'd the Commons' knell, 611.
The meeting of the waters, 198.
The more I view'd this world, 592.
The Phrygian rock, that braves the storm (Ode xxii. Anacreon), 23.
The sky is bright, the breeze is fair, 293.
The song that lightens our languid way, 589.
The time I've lost in wooing, 214.
The turf shall be my fragrant shrine, 255.
The two bondsmen, 611.
The wine-cup is circling, 230.
The women tell me every day (Ode vii. Anacreon), 14.
The world had just begun to steal, 60.
The world was hush'd, 284.
The wreath you wove, 59.
Thee, thee, only thee, 222.
Then, fare thee well, 242.
Then first from Love, 289.
Theocritus, in praise of Anacreon, 49 n.
Theodosius, Anecdote of, 161.
There are sounds of mirth, 229.
There comes a time, 241.
There is a bleak desert, 260.
There's not a look, a word of thine, 129.
There's something strange:—Buffo Song, 288.
There was a vase of odour lay, 143.
They know not my heart, 226.
They may rail at this life, 219.

They met but once in youth's sweet hour, 283.
They say that love had once a book, 75.
They tell how Atys, wild with love (Ode xii. Anacreon), 16.
They tell us of an Indian tree, 595.
They tell me thou 'rt the favour'd guest, 281.
They wove the lotus band to deck (Ode lxix. Anacreon), 46.
Thiers, Mons., 581.
Think on that look whose melting ray, 82.
This life is all chequer'd with pleasures and woes, 208.
This tribute's from a wretched elf, 69.
Those evening bells! 239.
Thou art, O God, the life and light! 253.
Thou art not dead; Song, 304.
Thou lovest no more, 250.
Thou, whose soft and rosy hues (Ode xvi. Anacreon), 19.
Thou bid'st me sing the lay I sung to thee, 286.
Though humble the banquet, 227.
Though lightly sounds the song, 291.
Though sacred the tie that our country entwineth, 589.
Though sorrow long has worn my heart, 62.
Though the last glimpse of Erin, 197.
Though 'tis all but a dream at the best, 247.
Through grief and through danger, 204.
Thus have I charm'd with visionary lay, 440.
Thy harp may sing of Troy's alarms (Ode xxvi. Anacreon), 26.
Thy song has taught my heart to feel, 84.
Tibullus to Sulpicia, 593.
Tighe, to Mrs. Henry, on reading her Psyche, 79.
Time, a poet's allusions to the hand of, 206, 209, 242, 245, 249, 250, 474.
Timmol, Fanny of, 109.
'T is all for thee, 278.
'T is gone, and for ever, the light we saw breaking, 214.
'T is strange how some will differ, 611.
'T is sweet to think that where'er we rove, 203.
'T is the vine! 'tis the vine!' said the cup-loving boy, 308.
'T is true, my fading years decline (Ode xlvii. Anacreon), 35.
'T is time, I feel, to leave thee now, 97.
'T is the last rose of summer, 210.
Tithe Case, late, 560.
Tithe, Song of the Departing Spirit of, 539.
Titian, his Mistress, 439.
To all that breathe the air of heaven (Ode xxiv. Anacreon), 25.
To be the theme of every hour, 76.
To-day, dearest! is ours, 271.
To ladies' eyes around, 218.
To Love and Bacchus ever young, 9 n.
To Love, the soft and blooming child, (Ode lxiii. Anacreon), 44.
To my Shadow, 478.
To see thee every day that came, 101.
To sigh, yet feel no pain, 588.
To thee, the queen of nymphs divine (Ode lxvi. Anacreon), 45.
To weave a garland for the rose, 291.
Too plain, alas, my doom is spoken, 250.
Torch of Liberty, the, 424.
Tories, destructive propositions of the, 571.

Tortoise-shell of Pegu, triple-coloured, 396.
Tory, Mad, and the Comet, 554.
Tory Pledges, 557.
Tory, Doctor, and Dr. Whig, 559.
Translations:— From Catullus, 592, 593. From Tibullus, 593. Dante imitated, 535. See Horace, Anthology, etc.
Trinity College, Dublin, an examination political, 191.
Tripe, tout pour la, 531.
Truth, 215, 258, 287.
Truth characterized, 248, 260.
Tuam, Archbishop of, 565, 573.
Tuckt Suliman, mountain, 386 n.
Tuft-hunter, epitaph on a, 518.
'T was in a mocking dream of night (Ode xxx. Anacreon), 28.
'T was night, and many a circling bowl (Ode xxxvii. Anacreon), 31.
'T was noon of night, when round the pole (Ode xxxiii. Anacreon), 29.
'T was one of those dreams, 223.
'T was when the world was in its prime, 452.
'T was but for a moment, and yet in that time, 141.
Twin'st thou with lofty wreath thy brow, 292.
Twopenny Post-Bag, by Thomas Brown the Younger: The Preface, 166. Dedication to Stephen Woolriche, Esq., 168. The Intercepted Letters:—From the Princess Charlotte of Wales to Lady Barbara Ashley, Letter I., 170. From Colonel M'Mahon to G. F. Leckie, Esq., Letter II., 170. Its Postscript, 171. From the Regent to Lord Yarmouth, Letter III., 171. From the Rt. Hon. Patrick Duigenan to the Rt. Hon. Sir John Nichol, Letter IV., 172. Enclosing an 'Unanswerable Argument against the Papists,' 173. From the Countess Dowager of Cork, Letter V., 173. Its Postscript, 173. From Abdallah, in London, to Mohassan, in Ispahan, Letter VI., 174. From Lackington and Co. to ——, Esq., Letter VII., 175. From Colonel Thomas to —— Skeffington, Esq., Letter VIII., 175. Appendix to these Epistles, 177.
Tyrolese Song of Liberty:—Merrily every bosom boundeth, 275.
Tyrrwhit, Sir Thomas, 172.

Unbind thee, Love, 288.
Unpublished Songs, etc., 288 to 291.
Up and march! the timbrels sound, 302.
Up with the sparkling brimmer, 307.

Valletort, to Caroline Viscountess, written at Lacock Abbey in the year 1832, 595.
Valley, the Unequalled, 395.
Van, the Euthanasia of, 540.
Vansittart (Lord Bexley), 167 n., 170, 176, 177, 186, 188, 401, 414, 497, 500, 502, 505, 512, 540, 542.
Variety, 53.
Venice, former glory of, 437. Wars of, against the Turks, 437. Her tyrannical oligarchy, 437. Tortures, 438. Her fall a retribution, 438.
Venus, poetical allusions to the goddess, 227.
Venus, the planet, 123, 219, 603.
Venus Anadyomene, 440.
Venus Papyria, 512.
Vestris, Mme., 550.
Virgin of Delphi, the, 63.
Virtue, 118, 125.

Vishnu, 531.
Vision, a, by the author of Christabel, 519.
Voice from Marathon, a, 610.
Voice, the, 265.
Voiture's Kiss, rendered by Mrs. —, 68.
Vulcan! hear your glorious task (Ode IV. Anacreon), 13.

Waithman, Alderman, 180.
Wake thee, my dear—thy dreaming, 279.
Wake up, sweet melody! 282.
Walcott, Dr., 164.
Wales, Princess Charlotte of, 170, et seq.
Walton, Isaac, 385 n.
Waltz Duet, 314.
Waltzing, 599.
Warburton, Mr., 578.
Ward, Mr., 150.
Warens, Mme. de, 447 n.
Warning, a, 97.
War against Babylon! 262.
War's high-sounding harp, 261.
Warrior, the Dying, 267.
Washington, city of, and the American rivers, etc., 131, 134, et seq.
Watchman, the; a Glee, 270.
Waterloo coin, Advertisement of a, missing or lost, 550.
We care not; Song, 602.
We may roam through this world, 199.
We read the flying courser's name (Ode XXVII. Anacreon), 26.
Weep, Children of Israel! 259.
Weep not for those whom the veil of the tomb, 255.
Weep on! weep on! your hour is past, 206.
Weeping for thee, my love, through the long day, 296.
Welcome, sweet bird, through the sunny air winging, 306.
Well! peace to thy heart, though another's it be, 127.
Well, the Holy, alleged miraculous appearance of the moon night and day in the, 344.
Wellesley, Lord, 164.
Wellington Spa, the, 570.
Wellington, Field Marshal the Duke of, 193. Reinforcements for him, 187. His Grace and the Ministers, 188, 554. See also 180, 415, 530, 531, 536, 538, 568, 570, 597.
Were not the sinful Mary's tears, 256.
Western, Lord, 528.
Westmoreland, Lord, 180, 527.
Wetherell, Sir Charles, 556.
What can those workmen be about? 611.
What's my thought like? 183.
What shall I sing thee? 597.
What the bee is to the floweret, 208.
When abroad in the world, 250.
When Bacchus, Jove's immortal boy (Ode XLIX. Anacreon), 36.
When, casting many a look behind, 57.
When cold in the earth lies the friend thou hast loved, 217.
When Cupid sees how thickly now (Ode LXXVIII. Anacreon), 47.
When evening shades are falling, 300.
When first that smile, 545.
When first I met thee warm and young, 193, 213.
When Gold, as fleet as zephyr's pinion (Ode LVIII. Anacreon), 41.
When he who adores thee has left but the name, 196.
When I behold the festive train (Ode LIII. Anacreon), 38.

When in languor sleeps the heart, 607.
When I loved you, I can't but allow, 56.
When Love is kind, 252.
When Love, rock'd by his mother, 227.
When Love, who ruled, 289.
When next you see the black-eyed Caty, 147.
When night brings the hour, 251.
When Love was a child, 244.
When my thirsty soul I steep (Ode XLVIII. Anacreon), 35.
When Spring adorns the dewy scene (Ode XLI. Anacreon), 33.
When o'er the silent seas alone, 209.
When the Balaika, 296.
When the first summer bee, 247.
When the heart's feeling, 107.
When the wine-cup is smiling before us, 248.
When they shall tell in future times, 610.
When thou shalt wander, 245.
When the sad word 'Adieu,' 292.
When thou art nigh, it seems, 285.
When on the lip the sigh delays, 271.
When through life unblest we rove, 204.
When through the Piazzetta, 246.
When Time, who steals our years away, 54.
When wearied wretches sink to sleep, 65.
When wine I quaff, before my eyes (Ode I. Anacreon), 36.
Whene'er I see those smiling eyes, 218.
When to sad music silent you listen, 287.
When twilight dews are falling soft, 277.
When midst the gay I meet, 276.
Where is the heart that would not give, 602.
Where is the nymph, whose azure eye, 111.
Where are the visions, 249.
Where is your dwelling, ye sainted? 261.
Where shall we bury our shame? 248.
Whig, Dr., and Dr. Tory, their consultation, 559.
Whigs and Tories, 152.
While history's muse, 213.
While gazing on the moon's light, 202.
While our rosy fillets shed (Ode XLIII. Anacreon), 33.
While we invoke the wreathed spring (Ode LV. Anacreon), 38.
Whitbread, Samuel, Esq., 181.
Whitelock, General, 150.
Who comes so gracefully, 305.
Who is the maid my spirit seeks? 254.
Who'll buy my love-knots? 245.
Who'll buy? 'tis Folly's shop, 316.
Whose was the artist hand that spread (Ode LVII. Anacreon), 40.
Why does azure deck the sky? 68.
Why does she so long delay? 292.
Why, the world are all thinking about it, 105.
Wilks, Mr. John 'ex-member for Sudbury), 522, 525, 609.
Will you come to the bower? 607.
William III., 150, 152, 154, 157.
Wilson, Sir Robert, 493.
Winchelsea, Lord, 543, 547.
Wind thy horn, my hunter boy, 249.
Wine-cup is circling, the, 230.
Wine, praise of, in Lalla Rookh, 393, 395. See also other poems and songs, 197, 200, 209, 215, 224, 228, 230, 247, 248, 250, 307, 306.
Wisdom, 208, 214.
Wit, 308. The quiver of, 208.
Witch's sabbath, 609.

With all my soul, then, let us part, 62.
With moonlight beaming, 284.
With twenty chords my lyre is hung (Ode LXXI. Anacreon), 46.
Within this goblet, rich and deep (Ode XLV. Anacreon), 34.
With woman's form, 142.
Wo! wo unto him! 530.
Woman, 133, 229, 301, 305, 452, 458, 460, 461, 464, 603.
Woman;— Away, away—you're all the same, 97.
Wonder, the, 66.
Woods and Forests, Ode to the (political), 537.
Woodpecker, the : — I knew by the smoke that so gracefully curl'd, 138.
Woolriche, Stephen, Esq., Dedication to, 168
Word awaked my heart, thy, 260.
World is all a fleeting show, this, 255.
World, the fashionable, 310.
World, when abroad in the, 250.
Would that I were a tuneful lyre (Ode LXXVII. Anacreon), 47.
Wreath and the Chain, the, 91.
Wreath the bowl, 217.
Write on, write on, ye Barons dear, 539.

Ya-hip, my Hearties, 506.
Yarmouth, Lord, Letter to, (from George Prince Regent, 171. See also 167 n., 176, 180 to 186, 509.
Years have pass'd, old friend, since we, 290.
Yemen, and the rest of Arabia, alluded to, 361, et seq.
Yes, be the glorious revel mine (Ode XLII. Anacreon), 33.
Yes, I think I once heard of an amorous youth, 106.
Yes, Heaven can witness how I strove, 108.
Yes—loving is a painful thrill (Ode XXIX. Anacreon), 27.
Yes, sad one of Zion, if closely resembling, 220.
Yes, yes, when the bloom of Love's boyhood is o'er, 276.
York, Duke of, 180, 526, 529.
You read it in these spell-bound eyes, 125.
You bid me explain, my dear angry Ma'amselle, 554.
You remember Ellen, our hamlet's pride, 211.
You, who would try, 624.
Young Love, 252, 266.
Young Love lived once in an humble shed, 588.
Youth, poetical allusions to, 243, 245, 343.
Youth's endearing charms are fled (Ode LXI. Anacreon), 43.
Youth and Age, 266.

Zaraph, 471, 472. His bride, 474.
Zea, or Ceus, island of the Archipelago: —Scene of the First Evening in Greece, 293, et seq.
Zeilan, king of, his ruby, 393 n.
Zelica, see 'The Veiled Prophet of Khorassan,' 326, et seq.
Zinge, and the Zingians, 385.
Zion, 254, 257.
Zodiac, the, 466.
Zone of bells of an Indian dancing girl, 386.

Printed in Great Britain by
Amazon.co.uk, Ltd.,
Marston Gate.